GUINNESS BOOK OF RECORDS

EDITION
24

Editor and Compiler
NORRIS McWHIRTER
Sports Editor
STAN GREENBERG

EDITION 24

Standard Book Number ISBN: 0 900424 80 X
Standard Book Number ISBN: 0 900424 81 8
(Australian Edition)
Standard Book Number ISBN: 0 900424 82 6
(Canadian Edition)
Standard Book Number ISBN: 0 900424 84 2
(New Zealand Edition)
Copyright © 1977 Guinness Superlatives Ltd
and Norris & Ross McWhirter
World Copyright Reserved
Twenty Fourth Edition

OVERSEAS AND FOREIGN LANGUAGE EDITIONS

Language		Title	Latest Publication	Address
American	(Casebound)	Guinness Book of World Records	1977	Sterling Publishing Co. Inc., New York City, N.Y., U.S.A.
American	(Paperback)	Guinness Book of World Records	1977	Bantam Books Inc., New York City, N.Y., U.S.A.
Czech	(Casebound)	Guinnessova Kniha Rekordů	1975	Olympia, Prague, Czechoslovakia
Danish	(Casebound)	Guinness Rekord bog Først og Størst Sidst og Midst	1975	Politikens Forlag, Copenhagen, Denmark
Dutch	(Casebound)	Guinness Groot Record Boek	1977	Uitgeberij Luitingh BV., Laren, Netherlands
Finnish	(Casebound)	Guinness Suuri Ennätys Kirja	1976	Sanoma Osakeyhtio, Helsinki, Finland
French	(Casebound)	Le Livre des Records	1977	Éditions Denoël, Paris
German	(Paperback)	Guinness Lexikon Der Superlative	1977	Bertelsmann Lexikon-Verlag, Gütersloh, West Germany
Hebrew	(Casebound)	Guinness Sēfēr Ha'siim	1977	The Israel Map & Publishing Company, Jerusalem, Israel
Icelandic	(Casebound)	Heimsmetabok Guinness	1977	Bokautgafan Örn og Örlygur h.f., Reykjavik, Iceland
Italian	(Paperback)	Il Guinness dei Primati	1977	Arnoldo Mondadori Editore, Milan, Italy
Japanese	(Paperback)	Guinness Korega Sekai Ichi	1976	Kodan Sha Limited, Tokyo, Japan
Norwegian	(Casebound)	Guinness Rekordboken Først og Størst Sist og Minst	1976	Chr. Schibsteds Forlag, Oslo, Norway
Portuguese	(Casebound)	Guinness Livro dos Recordes	1974	Editora Abril, São Paulo, Brazil
Serbo-Croat		Contracted for publication		Prosvjeta, Zagreb, Yugoslavia
Slovenian	(Casebound)	Guinnessova Knjiga Rekordov	1977	Mladinska Knjiga, Ljubljana, Yugoslavia
Spanish (American)	(Paperback)	Enciclopedia Guinness de Superlativos Mundiales	1977	Editors Press Service Inc., New York City, N.Y., U.S.A.
Spanish (European)	(Casebound)	El Libro Guinness de los Records	1977	Editorial Minon, Valladolid, Spain
Swedish	(Casebound)	Guinness Rekord bok Först och Störst	1977	Bokforlaget Forum AB., Stockholm, Sweden

Note

Back numbers are not available from the publishers but may be obtainable through the second hand book trade. Orders for current editions published overseas will willingly be passed on to the publishers concerned.

Made and produced in Great Britain by
REDWOOD BURN LIMITED   Trowbridge & Esher
. . . . . .

GUINNESS SUPERLATIVES LIMITED
2 CECIL COURT, LONDON ROAD, ENFIELD, MIDDLESEX

OVERSEAS DISTRIBUTORS AND AGENTS

AUSTRALIA Collins Leutenegger Pty. Ltd. in Brisbane and Sydney; Collins Forlib Pty. Ltd. in Burwood, Victoria; Marley, W.A. and Forest Ville, S.A.
CANADA Saunders of Toronto Ltd., 850 York Mills Rd., Don Mills, Ontario
CHANNEL ISLANDS L.S.T., 9 Patriotic Street, St. Helier, Jersey
CARRIBEAN Wm. Collins Sons & Co. Ltd., P.O. Box 881, Kingston, Jamaica and P.O. Box 582, Port of Spain, Trinidad.
EUROPEAN D. Richard Bowen, Post Box 30037, S-200 61, Malmö 30, Sweden
INDIA Allied Publishers Private Ltd., 15 Graham Road, Ballard Estate, Bombay
LATIN AMERICA Eti Feeny, c/o Wm. Collins Sons & Co. Ltd., 14 St. James's Place, London, S.W.1.
MALTA Agius & Agius Ltd., 42a South Street, Valletta
MIDDLE EAST Nigel M. Ealand, Ealand Enterprises, Agios Vlasios, Platanidia, Volos, Greece
NEW ZEALAND Whitcoulls, Private Bag, Christchurch
SOUTH AFRICA P. B. Mayer, 902 Norwich House, Heerengracht, Cape Town
SOUTH EAST ASIA Times Distributors, Rivery Valley Rd., Singapore 9

FOREWORD by the Rt. Hon the Earl of Iveagh

When we first brought out this book, twenty two years ago, we did so in the hope of providing a means for peaceful settling of arguments about record performances in this record-breaking world in which we live. We realise, of course, that much joy lies in the argument, but how exasperating it can be if there is no final means of finding the answer.

In the event, we have found that the interest aroused by this book has exceeded our wildest expectations. In this edition we were obliged to revise the entry that records that the global sales of this book, now available in 16 languages, have surpassed the 30,000,000 mark.

Whether the discussion concerns the highest that any man has jumped over his own height, the greatest weight lifted by a woman, the nationality of the first woman to climb Everest, or—an old bone of contention—the longest time to become a Saint, I can but quote the words used in introducing the first edition, "How much heat these innocent questions can raise: Guinness, in producing this book, hopes that it may assist in resolving many such disputes, and may, we hope, turn heat into light".

Iveagh

Joint Chairman
Arthur Guinness, Son & Co., Ltd.   October 1977

PREFACE

This 24th Edition has been not only completely revised but re-illustrated throughout.

Due to the significant fluctuations in comparative foreign exchange rates, currency conversions have been converted at the rate ruling at the time of the event or record. To indicate this the word "*then*" has been inserted before the relevant conversion.

There has been in recent years a marked increase in efforts to establish records for sheer endurance in many activities. In the very nature of record breaking the duration of such 'marathons' will tend to be pushed to greater and greater extremes and it should be stressed that marathon attempts are not without possible dangers. Organizers of marathon events would be well counselled to seek medical advice before and surveillance during marathons which involve extended periods with little or no sleep. (See below for notes on rest periods).

If there are discrepancies between entries in one edition and another, it may be generally assumed that the *later* entry is the product of the more up to date research.

Finally the editorial office, which is concerned with maintaining and improving the quality of each succeeding edition, is unable to perform also the function of a free general information bureau for quiz competitions and the like, by telephone or by correspondence.

Norris McWhirter

Editor and compiler

October 1977
Guinness Superlatives Limited, 2 Cecil Court, London Road, Enfield, Middlesex

Artwork by Don Roberts

Layout by David Roberts *(no kin)*

Notes on acceptability of Records.

We are likely to publish only those records which improve upon previous records or which are newly significant in having become the subject of widespread and preferably international competitiveness.

It should be stressed that unique occurrences and interesting peculiarities are not in themselves necessarily records. Records in our sense essentially have to be both measureable and comparable. Records which are *qualified* in some way, for example, by age, day of the week, county, etc cannot be accommodated in a reference work so general as *The Guinness Book of Records*.

Claimants should send independent corroboration in the form of local or national newspaper cuttings, radio or TV coverage reports and signed authentication by independent adult witnesses or representatives of organisations of standing in their community. Signed log books should show there has been unremitting surveillance in the case of endurance events. Five minutes rest intervals (optional but aggregable) are *permitted* after each completed hour in marathon events except for those few "non-stop" categories in which minimal intervals may be taken only for purposes other than for resting. The rest break allowance does not apply to those games where more than the required number of players/teams take part on a rotating basis. In such attempts play must be continuous.

If an activity is one controlled by a recognised world or national governing body that body should be consulted and involved in ratifying it.

The publishers do *not* normally supply personnel to invigilate record attempts but reserve the right to do so.

CONTENTS

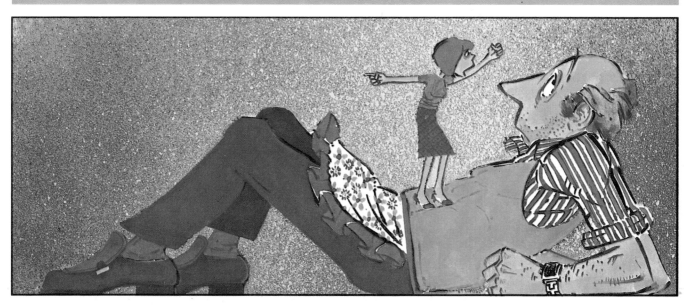

1. THE HUMAN BEING

1. DIMENSIONS

TALLEST GIANTS

The height of human giants is a subject on which accurate information is frequently obscured by exaggeration and commercial dishonesty. The only admissible evidence on the true height of giants is that collected in the last 100 years under impartial medical supervision. Some medical papers have, however, themselves perpetuated fanciful, as opposed to measured heights.

The assertion that Goliath of Gath (*c.* 1060 B.C.) stood 6 cubits and a span (9 ft 6½ in *290 cm*) suggests a confusion of units or some over-zealous exaggeration by the Hebrew chroniclers. The Jewish historian Flavius Josephus (born A.D. 37 or 38, died *post* A.D. 93) and some of the manuscripts of the Septuagint (the earliest Greek translation of the Old Testament) attribute to Goliath the quite credible height of 4 Greek cubits and a span (6 ft 10 in *208 cm*).

Extreme mediaeval data, taken from bone measurements, invariably refer to specimens of extinct whale, giant cave bear, mastodon, woolly rhinoceros or other prehistoric non-human remains.

Circus giants and others who are exhibited are normally under contract not to be measured and are, almost traditionally, billed by their promoters at heights up to 18 in *45 cm* in excess of their true heights. There are many notable examples of this, and 23 instances were listed in the *Guinness Book of Records* (14th edition). The acromegalic giant Eddie Carmel (b. Tel Aviv, Israel, 1938), formerly "The Tallest Man on Earth" of Ringling Bros. and Barnum & Bailey's Circus (1961–68) was allegedly 9 ft 0⅝ in *275 cm* tall (weighing 38 st. 3 lb. *242 kg*), but photographic evidence suggests that his true height was about 7 ft 6⅝ in *229,6 cm*. He died in New York City on 14 Aug. 1972 when his standing height due to severe kyphoscoliosis, was *c.* 7 ft *212 cm*.

An extreme case of exaggeration concerned Siah Khān ibn Kashmir Khān (b. 1913) of Bushehr (Bushire), Iran. Prof. D. H. Fuchs showed photographs of him at a meeting of the Society of Physicians in Vienna, Austria, in January 1935, claiming that he was 320 cm *10 ft 6 in* tall. Later, when Siah Khān entered the Imperial Hospital in Teheran for an operation, it was revealed that his actual height was a full metre less at 220 cm *7 ft 2.6 in*.

A model of the World's tallest human of all-time, Robert Wadlow, 8 ft 11.1 in *2,72 m* with Britain's tallest living man, Christopher Greener 7 ft 5¼ in *2,26 m*, alongside Norris McWhirter and Roy Castle. (*BBC Television*)

World

Modern opinion is that the tallest recorded man of whom there is irrefutable evidence was Robert Pershing Wadlow, born at 6.30 a.m. on 22 Feb. 1918 in Alton, Illinois, U.S.A.

Weighing 8½ lb. *3,85 kg* at birth, his abnormal growth began almost immediately. His height progressed as follows:

Age in Years	Height		Weight in lb.	kg	Age in Years	Height		Weight in lb.	kg
5	5'4"	*163 cm*	105	*48*	15	7'8"	*234 cm*	355	*161*
8	6'0"	*183 cm*	169	*77*	16	7'10½"	*240 cm*	374	*170*
9	6'2½"	*189 cm*	180	*82*	17	8'0½"	*245 cm*	315¹	*143*
10	6'5"	*196 cm*	210	*95*	18	8'3½"	*253 cm*	—	
11	6'7"	*200 cm*	—		19	8'5½"	*258 cm*	480	*218*
12	6'10½"	*210 cm*	—		20	8'6¾"	*261 cm*	—	
13	7'1¾"	*218 cm*	255	*116*	21	8'8¼"	*265 cm*	491	*223*
14	7'5"	*226 cm*	301	*137*	22.4²	8'11"	*272 cm*	439	*199*

¹ *Following severe influenza and infection of the foot.*
² *Wadlow was still growing during his terminal illness.*

Dr. C. M. Charles, Associate Professor of Anatomy at Washington University's School of Medicine in St. Louis, Missouri, measured Robert Wadlow at 272 cm *8 ft 11.1 in* in St. Louis on 27 June 1940. Wadlow died 18 days later, at 1.30 a.m. on 15 July 1940, in Manistee, Michigan, as a result of cellulitis (inflammation of cellular tissue) of the feet aggravated by a poorly fitted brace.

He was buried in Oakwood Cemetery, Alton, Illinois in a coffin measuring 10 ft 9 in *328 cm* in length, 32 in *81 cm* wide and 30 in *76 cm* deep. His greatest recorded weight was 35 st. 1 lb. *222,71 kg*, on his 21st birthday. He weighed 31 st. 5 lb. *199 kg* at the time of his death. His shoes were size 37AA (18½ in *47 cm* long) and his hands measured 12¾ in *32,5 cm* from the wrist to the tip of the middle finger (c.f. the depth of this page at 11¼ in *28,6 cm*).

His arm span was 9 ft 5¾ in *2,88 m* and his daily consumption attained 8,000 calories. At the age of 9 he was able to carry his father, the Mayor of Alton, up the stairs of the family home.

The only other men for whom heights of 8 ft *244 cm* or more have been reliably reported are the eight listed below. In six cases, gigantism was followed by acromegaly, a disorder which causes an enlargement of the nose, lips, tongue, lower jaw, hands and feet, due to renewed activity by an already swollen pituitary gland, which is located at the base of the brain.

John F. Carroll (1932–69) of Buffalo, New York State, U.S.A. (¹) 8 ft 7¾ in *263,5 cm*.

John William Rogan (1871–1905), a Negro of Gallatin, Tennessee, U.S.A. (²) 8 ft 6 in *259,1 cm*.

Don Koehler (b. 1925–*fl.* 1977) of Denton, Montana, U.S.A. (³) 8 ft 2 in *248,9 cm*, now lives in Chicago.

Bernard Coyne (1897–1921) of Anthon, Iowa U.S.A. (⁴) 8 ft 2 in *248,9 cm*

Vainö Myllyrinne (1909–63) of Helsinki, Finland (⁵) 8 ft 1.2 in *247 cm*.

Patrick Cotter O'Brien (1760–1806) of Kinsale, County Cork, Ireland (⁶) 8 ft 1 in *246 cm*.

"Constantine" (1872–1902) of Reutlingen, West Germany (⁷) 8 ft 0.8 in *245,8 cm*.

Sulaimān 'Alī Nashnush (1943–*fl.* 1976) of Tripoli, Libya (⁸) 8 ft 0.4 in *245 cm*.

(¹) *Severe kypho-scoliosis (two dimensional spinal curvature). The figure represenst his height with assumed normal spinal curvature, calculated from a standing height of 8 ft 0 in 244 cm, measured on 14 Oct. 1959. His standing height was 7 ft 8¼ in 234 cm shortly before his death.*
(²) *Measured in a sitting position. Unable to stand owing to ankylosis (stiffening of the joints through the formation of adhesions) of the knees and hips.*
(³) *Same spinal curvature. Present standing height c. 7 ft 10 in 238,4 cm. He has a twin sister who is 5 ft 9 in 175 cm tall. His father was 6 ft 2 in 1,87 m and his mother 5 ft 10 in 1,77 m.*
(⁴) *Eunuchoidal giant (Daddy-long legs syndrome). Rejected by Army in 1918 when 7 ft 9 in 236 cm.*
(⁵) *Stood 7 ft 3½ in 222 cm at the age of 21 years. Experienced a second phase of growth in his late thirties and may have stood 8 ft 3 in 251 cm at one time.*
(⁶) *Revised height based on skeletal remeasurement in 1975.*
(⁷) *Eunuchoidal. Height estimated, as both legs were amputated after they turned gangrenous. He claimed a height of 8 ft 6 in 259 cm.*
(⁸) *Operation in Rome to correct abnormal growth was successful in 1960.*

A table of the tallest giants of all-time in the 31 countries with men taller than 7 ft 4 in *223,5 cm* was listed in the 15th edition of the *Guinness Book of Records* (1968) at page 9.

A height of 8 ft 6 in *259 cm* has been claimed for another circus giant, Gabriel Estevão Monjane (b. 1944) of Monjacaze, Mozambique, but this measurement has not been confirmed. He stood 7 ft 6 in *228,2 cm* at the age of 17, and 7 ft 10 in *238,4 cm* in Dec. 1965. He has not been anthropometrically assessed since, but he could still be growing.

England

The tallest Englishman ever recorded was William Bradley (1788–1820), born in Market Weighton, Humberside. He stood 7 ft 9 in *236 cm*. John Middleton (1578–1623), the famous Childe of Hale, from near Liverpool, was credited with a height of 9 ft 3 in *282 cm* but a life-size impression of his right hand (length 11½ in *29,2 cm* c.f. Wadlow's 12¾ in *32,4 cm*) painted on a panel in Brasenose College, Oxford indicates his true stature was nearer 7 ft 8 in *233,3 cm*. James Toller (1795–1819) of St. Neots, Cambridgeshire was alleged to be 8 ft 6 in *259 cm* but was actually 7 ft 6 in *229 cm*. Albert Brough (1871–1919), a publican of Nottingham, reached a height of 7 ft 7½ in *232 cm*. Frederick Kempster (1889–1918) of Bayswater, London, was reported to have measured 8 ft 4½ in *255 cm* at the time of his death, but photographic evidence suggests that his height was 7 ft 8½ in *235 cm*. He measured 234 cm *7 ft 8.1 in* in 1913. Henry Daglish, who stood 7 ft 7 in *231 cm*. died in Upper Stratton, Wiltshire, on 16 March 1951, aged 25. The much-publicized Edward (Ted) Evans (1924–58) of Englefield Green, Surrey, was reputed to be 9 ft 3 in *282 cm* but actually stood 7 ft 8½ in *235 cm*. The tallest fully mobile man now living in Great Britain is Christopher Paul Greener (b. New Brighton, Merseyside, 21 Nov. 1943) of Hayes, Kent, who measures 7 ft 5¼ in *226,6 cm*. Terence Keenan (b. 1942) of Rock Ferry, Merseyside measures 7 ft 6 in *229 cm*, but is unable to stand erect owing to a leg condition. His abnormal growth began at the age of 17 when he was only 5 ft 4 in *163 cm* tall.

Scotland

The tallest Scotsman, and the tallest recorded "true" (non-pathological) giant, was Angus Macaskill (1825–63), born on the island of Berneray, in the Sound of Harris, in the Western Isles. He stood 7 ft 9 in *236 cm* and died in St. Anns', on Cape Breton Island, Nova Scotia, Canada. Lambert Quételet (1796–1874), a Belgian anthropometrist, considered that a Scotsman named MacQuail, known as "the Scotch Giant", stood 8 ft 3 in *251 cm*. He served in the famous regiment of giants of Frederick William I (1688–1740), King of Prussia. His skeleton, now in the Staatliche Museum zu Berlin, East Germany, measures 220 cm *7 ft 2.6 in*. Sam McDonald (1762–1802) of Lairg in Sutherland, was reputed to be 8 ft *244 cm* tall but actually stood 6 ft 10 in *208 cm*. The tallest Scotsman now living is George Gracie (b. 1938) of Forth, Strathclyde. He stands 7 ft 3 in *221 cm* and weighs 28 st. *178 kg*. His brother Hugh (b. 1941) is 7 ft 0½ in *215 cm*.

Wales

The tallest Welshman on record was William Evans (1599–1634) of Monmouthshire, who was porter to King James I. He stood 7 ft 6 in *228,2 cm*.

Ireland

The tallest Irishman was Patrick Cotter O'Brien (1760–1806), born in Kinsale, County Cork. He died at Hotwells, Clifton, Avon. (See Table above) The tallest Irishman now living is believed to be Jim Cully (b. 1926) of Tipperary, a former boxer and wrestler. He stands 7 ft 2 in *218 cm*.

TALLEST GIANTESSES

World *All-time*

Giantesses are rarer than giants but their heights are still spectacular. The tallest woman in medical history was the acromegalic giantess Jane ('Ginny') Bunford, born on 26 July 1895 at Bartley Green, Northfield, West Midlands. Her abnormal growth started at the age of 11 following a head injury, and on her 13th birthday she measured 6 ft 6 in *198 cm*. Shortly before her death on 1 April 1922 she stood 7 ft 7 in *231 cm* tall, but she had a severe curvature of the spine and would have measured about 7 ft 11 in *241 cm* with assumed normal curvature. Her skeleton, now preserved in the Anatomical Museum in the Medical School at Birmingham University, has a mounted height of 7 ft 4 in *223,5 cm*. It was announced on 10 Feb. 1972 that the skeleton of a mediaeval giantess measuring 8 ft 3 in *251 cm* had been found in the Laga mountains near Abruzzi, Italy by archaeologists but this was a hoax. Anna Hanen Swan (1846–88) of Nova Scotia, Canada, was billed at 8 ft 1 in *246 cm* but actually measured 7 ft 5½ in *227 cm*. In London on 17 June 1871 she married Martin van Buren Bates (1845–1919) of Whitesburg, Letcher County, Kentucky, U.S.A., who stood 7 ft 2½ in *220 cm*. Ella Ewing (b. Mar. 1872) of Gorin, Missouri, U.S.A., was billed at 8 ft 2 in *249 cm* and reputedly measured 6 ft 9 in *206 cm* at the age of 10 (*cf.* 6 ft 5 in *196 cm* for Robert Wadlow at this age). She measured 7 ft 4½ in *225 cm* at the age of 23 and may have attained 7 ft 6 in *229 cm* before her death in January 1913.

Living

The tallest living woman is Sandy Allen (b. 18 June 1955, Chicago). She now lives in Shelbyville, Indiana, U.S.A. In September 1974 she was measured to be 7 ft 5 ⁵⁄₁₆ in *226,74 cm* in height and is still growing. A 6½ lb. *2,910 kg* baby, her abnormal growth began soon after birth. She now weighs 30 st. 1 lb. *191 kg* and takes a 16EEE size shoe (U.S.); size 14½ (U.K.) or 50PP (Continental).

SHORTEST DWARFS

The strictures which apply to giants apply equally to dwarfs, except that exaggeration gives way to understatement. In the same way as 9 ft *274 cm* may be regarded as the limit towards which the tallest giants tend, so 23 in *58 cm* must be regarded as the limit towards which the shortest mature dwarfs tend (*cf.* the average length of new-born babies is 18–20 in *46–50 cm*). In the case of child dwarfs their *ages* are often enhanced by their agents or managers.

There are many forms of dwarfism. Ateleiotic dwarfs, known as midgets, who suffer from growth hormone deficiency, are usually well proportioned. Such dwarfs tended to be even shorter when human stature was generally shorter due to lower nutritional standards.

World *All-time*

The shortest mature human of whom there is independent evidence was Pauline Musters ('Princess Pauline'), a Dutch midget. She was born at Ossendrecht, on 26 Feb. 1876 and measured 30 cm *12 in* at birth. At the age of 9 she was 55 cm *21.65 in* tall and weighed only 1,5 kg *3 lb. 5 oz.* She died, at the age of 19, of pneumonia, with meningitis, her heart weakened from alcoholic excesses, on 1 March 1895 in New York City, N.Y., U.S.A. Although she was billed at 48 cm *19 in* she was found to be 59 cm *23.2 in* tall. A *post mortem* examination showed her to be exactly 61 cm *24 in* (her body was slightly elongated after death). Her mature weight varied from 3,4 kg to 4 kg *7½ lb.* to *9 lb.* and her "vital statistics" were 47-48-43 cm *18½-19-17 in*, which suggests she was overweight.

The Italian girl Caroline Crachami, born in Palermo, Sicily, in 1815, was only 20.2 in *51,3 cm* tall when she died in London in 1824, aged 9. At birth she measured 7 in *18 cm* long and weighed 1 lb. *450 g*. Her skeleton, measuring 19.8 in *50,3 cm*, is now part of the Hunterian collection in the Museum of the Royal College of Surgeons, London.

Male All-time

The shortest recorded adult male dwarf was Calvin Phillips, born on 14 Jan. 1791 in Bridgewater, Massachusetts, U.S.A. He weighed 2 lb. *907 g* at birth and stopped growing at the age of 5. When he was 19 he measured 26½ in *67 cm* tall and weighed 12 lb. *5,4 kg* with his clothes on. He died two years later, in April 1812, from progeria, a rare disorder characterised by dwarfism and premature senility.

The most famous midget in history was Charles Sherwood Stratton, *alias* "General Tom Thumb", born on 11 Jan. 1838. When he got into the clutches of the circus proprietor Mr. Barnum his birth date was changed to 11 Jan. 1832 so that when billed at 30½ in *77 cm* at the age of 18 he was in fact 12. He died of apoplexy on 15 July 1883 aged 45 (not 51) and was 3 ft 4 in *102 cm*.

The three Eris circus acrobats from Turkey. Süleyman (left) is a possible contender as the World's shortest man at 2 ft 6 in *76,5 cm*.

Another celebrated midget was Józef ('Count') Boruwalaski (b. November 1739) of Poland. He measured only 8 in *20 cm* long at birth, growing to 14 in *36 cm* at the age of one year. He stood 17 in *43 cm* at 6 years, 21 in *53 cm* at 10, 25 in *64 cm* at 15, 35 in *89 cm* at 25 and 39 in *99 cm* at 30. He died near Durham, England, on 5 Sept. 1837, aged 97.

William E. Jackson, *alias* "Major Mite", born on 2 Oct. 1864 in Dunedin, New Zealand, measured 9 in *23 cm* long and weighed 12 oz. *340 g* at birth. In November 1880 he stood 21 in *53 cm* and weighed 9 lb. *4 kg*. He died in New York City, N.Y., U.S.A., on 9 Dec. 1900, when he measured 27 in *70 cm*.

Living

The world's shortest living mature human reported is Nruturam (b. 28 May 1929) a rachitic dwarf in Naydwar, India, who measures 28 in *71 cm*. The circus acrobatic dancer Süleyman Eris (b. 24 Jan. 1955 in Turkey) was medically measured on 3 Mar. 1977 to be 76,5 cm *30.1 in* and weighed 11,4 kg *25 lb. 2 oz.* He and his brother (83,5 cm) and sister (96,5 cm) are primordial dwarfs.

United Kingdom

The shortest mature human ever recorded in Britain was Miss Joyce Carpenter (b. 21 Dec. 1929), a rachitic dwarf of Charford, Hereford and Worcester, who stood 29 in *74 cm* tall and weighed 30 lb. *13,60 kg*. She died on 7 Aug. 1973 aged 43. Hopkins Hopkins (1737–54) of Llantrisant, Mid Glamorgan was 31 in *79 cm*. Hopkins, who died from progeria (see above) weighed 19 lb. *8,62 kg* at the age of 7 and 13 lb. *6 kg* at the time of his death. There are an estimated 2,000 people of severely restricted growth i.e. under 4 ft 8 in *142 cm* living in Britain today.

The famous "Sir" Geoffrey Hudson (b. 1619) of Oakham, Leicestershire, was reputedly 18 in *46 cm* tall at the age of 30, but this extreme measurement is not borne out in portraits which show he was then about 3 ft 6 in *107 cm*. At the time of his death in London in 1682 he measured 3 ft 9 in *114 cm*.

Ireland

The shortest recorded Irish adult dwarf was Mrs. Catherine Kelly (b. in August 1756), known as "the Irish fairy", who stood 34 in *86 cm* tall and weighed 22 lb. *10 kg*. She died in Norwich, Norfolk, on 15 Oct. 1785. David Jones (b. 28 March 1903) of Lisburn, County Antrim, Northern Ireland, reputedly measured 26 in *66 cm* at the time of his death on

1 April 1970 aged 66. But as he weighed 4 st. *25 kg*, his height was probably nearer 36 in *91 cm*.

Most variable stature

Adam Rainer, born in Graz, Austria, in 1899, measured 118 cm *3 ft 10.45 in* at the age of 21. But then he suddenly started growing upwards at a rapid rate, and by 1931 he had reached 218 cm *7 ft 1¾ in*. He became so weak as a result that he was bed-ridden for the rest of his life. He died on 4 March 1950 aged 51.

TRIBES

Tallest

The tallest major tribe in the world is the Tutsi (also Watussi), Nilotic herdsmen of Rwanda and Burundi, Central Africa whose young adult males average 180 cm *5 ft 10¾ in*. The Tehuelches of Patagonia, long regarded as of gigantic stature (*i.e.* 7 to 8 ft *213 to 244 cm*), have in fact an average height (males) of 5 ft 10 in *178 cm*. A tribe with an average height of more than 6 ft *183 cm* was discovered in the inland region of Passis Manua of New Britain in December 1956. In December 1967 the inhabitants of Barbuda, Leeward Islands were reported to have an average height of 6 ft *183 cm*. The Montenegrins of Yugoslavia, with a male average of 5 ft 10 in *178 cm* (in the town of Trebinje the average height is 6 ft *183 cm*), compares with the men of Sutherland, at 5 ft 9½ in *176,5 cm*. In 1912 the average height of the men living in Balmaclellan, Kirkcudbrightshire was reported to be 5 ft 10.4 in *179 cm*.

Shortest

The smallest pygmies are the Mbuti, with an average height of 4 ft 6 in *137 cm* for men and 4 ft 5 in *135 cm* for women, with some groups averaging only 4 ft 4 in *132 cm* for men and 4 ft 1 in *124 cm* for women. They live in the forests near the river Ituri in the Congo (Kinshasa), Africa.

WEIGHT

Heaviest Men *World*

The greatest weight ever attributed to a human has been 84 st. 11 lb. (1,187 lb.) *538 kg* in the case of Francis John Lang (b. 1934) *alias* Michael Walker of Clinton, Iowa, U.S.A. He could not be admitted for treatment for inflammation of the gall bladder to the Veteran's Administration Hospital, Houston, Texas U.S.A. because of the impossibility of getting him through the doors. He was treated in a caravan in the car park and discharged on 5 Jan. 1972 unweighed but estimated to be between 900 and 1,000 lb. *408–453 kg*. The more precise weight above was claimed for him, while suffering from drug-induced bulimia, in the summer of 1971 when he was working with the Christian Farms of Killeen, Texas. There is, however, no independent corroboration for this precise upper weight quoted, although photographic evidence suggests the weight was possibly reliable.

The highest undisputed weight for a human remains 76 st. 5 lb. (1,069 lb.) *485 kg* for Robert Earl Hughes (b. 1926) buried in a coffin the size of a piano crate in Benville Cemetery, Illinois, U.S.A. on 10 July 1958.

Great Britain

The heaviest recorded man in Great Britain was William Campbell, who was born in Glasgow in 1856 and died on 16 June 1878, when a publican at High Bridge, Newcastle upon Tyne, Tyne and Wear. He was 6 ft 3 in *191 cm* tall and weighed 53 st. 8 lb. *340 kg* with an 85-in *216 cm* waist and a 96-in *244 cm* chest. His coffin weighed 1,500 lb. *680 kg*. He was "a man of considerable intelligence and humour". The only other British man with a recorded weight of more than 50 st. *317,5 kg* was the celebrated Daniel Lambert (1770–1809) of Leicester. He stood 5 ft 11 in *180 cm* tall, weighed 52 st. 11 lb. *335 kg* shortly before his death and had a girth of more than 92 in *234 cm*.

The highest weight attained by any man living in Britain today was that of Eric Keeling (born 1933) of Islington, Greater London who scaled 47 st. *299 kg* in mid-1971. An 11 lb. *5 kg* baby he weighed 18 st. *114,5 kg* at the age of 13. By November 1973 he had reduced by dieting (600 calories per day) to 33 st. *210 kg*. He is 6 ft 5 in *195,5 cm* tall.

George McAree (b. 24 Dec. 1923) of Newham, Greater London, is the heaviest man in Britain. In February 1977 he scaled 37 st. 10 lb. *240 kg*. He is 5 ft 10½ in *179 cm* tall and has vital statistics of 76½-72-82½ in *194-183-210 cm*.

Ireland

The heaviest Irishman is reputed to have been Roger Byrne, who was buried in Rosenallis, County Laoighis (Leix), on 14 March 1804. He died in his 54th year and his coffin and its contents weighed 52 st. *330 kg*. Another Irish heavyweight was Lovelace Love (1731–66), born in Brook Hill, County Mayo. He weighed "upward of 40 st. *254 kg*" at the time of his death.

Heaviest Women *World*

The heaviest woman ever recorded was the late Mrs. Percy Pearl Washington, 46 who died in a hospital in Milwaukee, on 9 Oct. 1972. The hospital scales registered only up to 800 lb. (57 st. 2 lb.) *362,8 kg* but she was believed to weigh about 880 lb. (62 st. 12 lb.) *399,1 kg*. The previous feminine weight record had been set 84 years earlier at 850 lb. (60 st. 10 lb.) *386 kg* although a wholly unsubstantiated report exists of a woman Mrs. Ida Maitland (1898–1932) of Springfield, Mississippi, U.S.A., who reputedly weighed 65 st. 1 lb. (911 lb.) *413,2 kg*.

A more reliable and better documented case was that of Mrs. Flora Mae Jackson (*née* King), a 5 ft 9 in *175 cm* negress born in 1930 at Shuqualak, Mississippi, U.S.A. She weighed 10 lb. *4,5 kg* at birth, 19 st. 1 lb. (267 lb.) *121 kg* at the age of 11, 44 st. 5 lb. (621 lb.) *282 kg* at 25 and 60 st. (840 lb.) *381 kg* shortly before her death in Meridian, Mississippi, on 9 Dec. 1965. She was known in show business as "Baby Flo". Mrs. Frances Voges (b. 1920) of Tampa, Florida claimed in Oct. 1976 to weigh 826 lb. (59 st.) *374,6 kg*. She stands 5 ft 1 in *155 cm* and measures 88½ in *225 cm* around the hips. She eats what she wants on the grounds that a few pounds makes no worthwhile difference.

The only other men for whom weights of more than 55 stone (770 lb.) *350 kg* have been reliably reported are the nine listed below:

	Stone	lb.	kg		Stone	lb.	kg
Mills Darden (1798–1857) U.S.A. (7 ft 6 in *2,29 m*)	72	12	463	David Maguire (1904–*fl.* 1935) U.S.A. (5 ft 10 in *1,78 m*)	57	12	367
John Hanson Craig (1856–94) U.S.A. (6 ft 5 in *1,95 m*)[1]	64	11	411	William J. Cobb (b. 1926) U.S.A. (6 ft 0 in *1,83 m*)[3]	57	4	364
Arthur Knorr (1914–60) U.S.A. (6 ft 1 in *1,85 m*)[2]	64	4	408	Unnamed Patient (b. 1936) Richmond, Virginia, U.S.A. Aug. 1973	57	2¼	363
Toubi (b. 1946) Cameroon	61	3½	389	Smith Poti (1900–1942) South Africa (5 ft 6 in *1,67 m*)	55	10	355
T. A. Valenzuela (1895–1937) Mexico (5 ft 11 in *1,80 m*)	60	10	386				

[1] Won $1,000 in a "Bonny Baby" contest in New York City in 1858.
[2] Gained 300 lb. 136 kg in the last 6 months of his life.
[3] Reduced to 16 st. 8 lb. 105 kg by July 1965.

Great Britain and Ireland
The heaviest recorded woman in Great Britain was Nellie Ensall (*née* Lambert) (b. 3 April 1894) of Leicester and later Birmingham who weighed 40 st. 3 lb. *255 kg* at the age of 19. She stood 5 ft 3 in *160 cm* tall, with a waist of 88 in *224 cm* and a 26 in *66 cm* upper arm. She claimed to be a great-great-granddaughter of Daniel Lambert (see above). The heaviest weight of a woman living in Britain today was that of Miss Jean Renwick (b. 1939) of Brixton, London, who weighed 40 st. 2 lb. *254 kg* (height 5 ft 3½ in *161 cm*) in January 1972 before she joined the Weight Watchers. By February 1977 she had reduced to 22 st. 2 lb. *141 kg*.

Heaviest twins
The heaviest twins in the world are the wrestlers Billy and Benny McCrary *alias* McGuire (b. 1948) of Hendersonville, North Carolina, U.S.A., who in March 1970 weighed 47 st. 2 lb. (660 lb.) *299 kg* and 45 st. 10 lb. (640 lb.) *290 kg*. As professional tag wrestlers they have been billed at weights up to 770 lb. (55 st.) *349 kg*. Their present weight is around 720 lb. (51½ st.) *326,58 kg*. After a 6 week strict slimming course in a hospital, they emerged weighing 5 lb. *2,26 kg* more.

Lightest World
The lightest adult human on record was Lucia Zarate (b. San Carlos, Mexico 2 Jan. 1863, d. October 1889), an emaciated Mexican ateleiotic dwarf of 26½ in *67 cm*, who weighed 2,125 kg *4.7 lb.* at the age of 17. She "fattened up" to 13 lb. *5 kg 90* by her 20th birthday. At birth she weighed 2½ lb. *1,1 kg*. The lightest adult ever recorded in the United Kingdom was Hopkins Hopkins (Shortest dwarfs, see p. 9).

The thinnest recorded adults of normal height are those suffering from Simmonds' Disease (Hypophyseal cachexia). Losses up to 65 per cent of the original body-weight have been recorded in females, with a "low" of 3 st. 3 lb. *20 kg* in the case of Emma Shaller (b. St. Louis, Missouri 8 July 1868, d. 4 Oct. 1890), who stood 5 ft 2 in *1,57 m*. Edward C. Hagner (1892–1962), *alias* Eddie Masher (U.S.A.) is alleged to have weighed only 3 st. 6 lb. *22 kg* at a height of 5 ft 7 in *170 cm*. He was also known as "the Skeleton Dude". In August 1825 the biceps measurement of Claude-Ambroise Seurat (b. 10 April 1797, d. 6 April 1826) of Troyes, France was 4 in *10 cm* and the distance between his back and his chest was less than 3 in *8 cm*. According to one report he stood 5 ft 7½ in *171 cm* and weighed 5 st. 8 lb. *35 kg*, but in another account was described as 5 ft 4 in *163 cm* and only 2 st. 8 lb. *16 kg*. It was recorded that the American exhibitionist Rosa Lee Plemons (b. 1873) weighed 27 lb. *12 kg* at the age of 18. In cases of anorexia nervosa, weights of under 5 st. *32 kg* have also been reported.

Lightest Great Britain
Robert Thorn (b. 1842) of March, Cambridgeshire weighed 49 lb. *22 kg* at the age of 32. He was 4 ft 6 in *137 cm* tall and had a 27 in *68 cm* chest (expanded) and 4½ in *11 cm* biceps.

A centenarian dwarf reputedly with a stature of 3 ft 4 in *101,6 cm* and weighing 48 lb. *21,7 kg* died in Matlock, Derbyshire on 5 Aug. 1874.

Slimming
The greatest recorded slimming feat was that of William J. Cobb (b. 1926), *alias* "Happy Humphrey", a professional wrestler of Macon, Georgia, U.S.A. It was reported in July 1965 that he had reduced from 57 st. 4 lb. *364 kg* to 16 st. 8 lb. *105 kg*, a loss of 40 st. 10 lb. *259 kg* in 3 years. His waist measurement declined from 101 in to 44 in *257 cm* to *112 cm*. In October 1973 it was reported that "Happy" was back to his normal weight of 46½ st. or 650 lb. *295 kg*.

The U.S. circus fat lady Mrs. Celesta Geyer (b. 1901), *alias* Dolly Dimples, reduced from 553 lb. *251 kg* to 152 lb. *69 kg* in 1950–51, a loss of 401 lb. *182 kg* in 14 months. Her vital statistics diminished *pari passu* from 79-84-84 in *200-213-213 cm* to a *svelte* 34-28-36 in *86-71-91 cm*. Her book "How I lost 400 lbs." was not a best-seller because of the difficulty of would-be readers identifying themselves with the dressmaking problems of losing more than 28 st. *178 kg* when

4 ft 11 in *150 cm* tall. In December 1967 she was reportedly down to 7 st. 12 lb. *50 kg*. The speed record for slimming was established by Paul M. Kimelman, 21, of Pittsburgh, Pennsylvania, U.S.A., who from 25 Dec. 1966 to August 1967 went on a crash diet of 300 to 600 calories per day to reduce from 487 lb. (34 st. 11 lb.) *215,9 kg* to 130 lb. (9 st. 4 lb.) *59 kg*—a total loss of 357 lb. (25 st. 7 lb.) *156,9 kg*. He has now stabilised at 175 lb. (12 st. 7 lb.) *79 kg*. On 4–8 February 1951 Mrs. Gertrude Levandowski (b. 1893) of Burnips, Michigan, U.S.A. successfully underwent a series of operations to reduce her weight from 44 st. *280 kg* to 22 st. *140 kg*.

Claude Halls (b. 1937) of Sible Hedingham, Essex reduced from 33 st. 6¾ lb. *212,6 kg* to 12 st. 10 lb. *80,7 kg*—a loss of 20 st. 10¾ lb. *131,8 kg*—in the 14 months January 1974 to March 1975. In the first 7 days with Weight Watchers he lost 5 st. 7 lb. *35 kg*.

The feminine Weight Watchers champion in Britain was Mrs. Dolly Wager (b. 1933) of Charlton, London, who, between Sept. 1971 and 22 May 1973 reduced from 31 st. 7 lb. *197 kg* to 11 st. 7 lb. *69,8 kg* so losing 20 st. 7 lb. *130 kg*.

Weight gaining
A probable record for gaining weight was set by Arthur Knorr (b. 17 May 1914), who died on 7 July 1960, aged 46, in Reseda, California, U.S.A. He gained 21 st. 6 lb. *136 kg* in the last 6 months of his life and weighed 64 st. 4 lb. *408 kg* when he died. Miss Doris James of San Francisco, California, U.S.A. is alleged to have gained 23 st. 3 lb. *147 kg* in the 12 months before her death in August 1965, aged 38, at a weight of 48 st. 3 lb. *306 kg*. She was only 5 ft 2 in *157 cm* tall.

Greatest Differential
The greatest weight differential recorded for a married couple is 65 st. 12 lb. *419 kg* in the case of Mills Darden (72 st. 12 lb. *463 kg*—see p. 10) and his wife Mary (7 st. *44,5 kg*). Despite her diminutiveness, however, Mrs. Darden bore her husband three children before her death in 1837.

---

2. ORIGINS

EARLIEST MAN

SCALE OF TIME
If the age of the Earth-Moon system (latest estimate at least 4,700 million years) is likened to a single year, Handy Man appeared on the scene at about 8.35 p.m. on 31 December, Britain's earliest known inhabitants arrived at about 11.32 p.m., the Christian era began about 13 sec before midnight and the life span of a 113-year-old woman (page 14) would be about three-quarters of a second. Present calculations indicate that the Sun's increased heat, as it becomes a "red giant", will make life insupportable on Earth in about 10,000 million years. Meanwhile there may well be colder epicycles. The period of 1,000 million years is sometimes referred to as an aeon.

Man (*Homo sapiens*) is a species in the sub-family Homininae of the family Hominidae of the super-family Hominoidea of the sub-order Simiae (or Anthropoidea) of the order Primates of the infra-class Eutheria of the sub-class Theria of the class Mammalia of the sub-phylum Vertebrata (Craniata) of the phylum Chordata of the sub-kingdom Metazoa of the animal kingdom.

Earliest *Primate*
The earliest known primates appeared in the Palaeocene period of about 80,000,000 years ago. The sub-order of higher primates, called Simiae (or Anthropoidea) evolved from the catarrhine or old-world sect more than 40,000,000 years later in the Lower Oligocene period. During the Middle and Upper Oligocene the super-family Hominoidea emerged. This contains three accepted families, *viz* Hominidae (bipedal, ground-dwelling man or near man), Pongidae (brachiating forest apes) and Oreopithecidae. The earliest known hominoid (man-like) fossil found is the *Oligopithecus savagei* found in El Faiyûm, Egypt and dated to *c* 33 million years ago.

Earliest *Hominid* (*Near Man*)
The characteristics of the Hominidae, such as a large brain, very fully distinguish them from any of the other Hominoidae. Evidence published in August 1969 indicated that *Ramapithecus*, discovered by G. E. Lewis at Siwalik Hill, northern India in 1934 can be dated from *c* 14 million years ago.

origins of man

THE CRADLE OF THE HUMAN RACE

Though the earliest evidence of hominids (near man) was found in northern India in 1934, the earliest evidence of Homo (true man) comes from East Africa in the post-war period.

Three of the principal sites are Lothagem near Lake Turkana (formerly Lake Rudolf) in Kenya and the Olduvai Gorge and Laelolil in Tanzania. The oldest dated of these remains of the genus Homo were found by Dr. Mary Leakey in the summer of 1975 and dated back to between 3,350,000 and 3,750,000 years ago. Hand bones believed to belong to *Homo erectus*, the forerunner of

Homo sapiens have been found in Ethiopia and dated to 3,500,000 years ago. Further finds will be necessary to close the gap in the period 4 to 8 million years before the present to trace the process of the evolution of near man into true man.

Illustration by Eddie Botchway   © Guinness Superlatives Ltd. 1977

Earliest *Genus* Homo (*True Man*)

The greatest age attributed to fossils of the genus *Homo* is for the remains of 8 adults and 3 children discovered in the summer of 1975 at Laetolil, Tanzania by Dr. Mary Leakey and dated by the University of California, Berkeley to between 3,350,000 and 3,750,000 B.C. An arm bone fragment from Kanapoi has been tentatively regarded as from *Homo* and has been dated *c* 4 million years ago.

Earliest *Homo sapiens*

The earliest recorded remains of the species *Homo sapiens*, variously dated from 300,000 to 450,000 years ago in the Middle Pleistocene, were discovered on 24 Aug. 1965 by Dr. László Vértes in a limestone quarry at Vértasszöllös, about 30 miles west of Budapest, Hungary. The remains, designated *Homo sapiens palaeo-hungaricus*, comprised an almost complete occipital bone, part of a skull with an estimated cranial capacity of nearly 1 400 cm³ *85 in³*.

Earliest man in the Americas date from at least 50,000 B.C. and "more probably 100,000 B.C." according to the late Dr. Leakey after the examination of some hearth stones found in the Mojave Desert, California and announced in October 1970. The earliest human relic is a skull found in the area of Los Angeles, California dated in December 1970 to be from 22,000 B.C.

Great Britain

The earliest firm evidence able to be established for human occupation in Great Britain dates from the time of the Hoxnian interglacial (200,000–250,000 B.C.) named from the Hoxne site in Suffolk, where hand axes were found in 1797. The earliest part of this period between the earlier Anglian and the later Wolstonian glaciations was characterized by Clactonian assemblages of chopping and pebble tools known only from the sites of Clacton-on-Sea, Essex, the lower deposits in the Barnfield Pit, Swanscombe, Kent in August 1969 and Barnham St. Gregory, Suffolk. Two seemingly pre-Hoxnian sites, dating possibly from a warmer interstadial of the Anglian glaciation (250,000–350,000 B.C.) are at Fordwich, Kent and Kent's Cavern, Torquay, Devon. The oldest human remains ever found in Britain are pieces of a brain case from a specimen of *Homo sapiens fossilis*, believed to be a woman, recovered in June 1935 and March 1936 by Dr. Alvan T. Marston from the Boyn Hill terrace in the Barnfield Pit, near Swanscombe, northern Kent, This find is attributed to Acheulian man, type *III* or *IV*, dating from the warm Hoxnian interglacial period (see above).

(Below) Parts of a skull of *Homo sapiens fossilis*, which constitute the oldest human remains yet found in Britain, recovered from Swanscombe, Kent.

3. LONGEVITY

No single subject is more obscured by vanity, deceit, falsehood and deliberate fraud than the extremes of human longevity. Extreme claims are generally made on behalf of the very aged rather than by them.

Many hundreds of claims throughout history have been made for persons living well into their second century and some, insulting to the intelligence, for people living even into their third. Centenarians surviving beyond their 110th year are in fact of the extremest rarity and the present absolute proven limit of human longevity does not yet admit of anyone living to celebrate a 114th birthday.

Longevity

It is highly significant that in Sweden, where alone proper and thorough official investigations follow the death of every allegedly very aged citizen, none has been found to have surpassed 110 years. The most reliably pedigreed large group of people in the world, the British peerage, has, after ten centuries, produced only two centenarian peers, but only one reached his 101st birthday. However, this is possibly not unconnected with the extreme draughtiness of many of their residences and the amount of lead in their game.

Scientific research into extreme old age reveals that the correlation between the claimed density of centenarians in a country and its regional illiteracy is 0.83 ± 0.03. In late life, very old people often tend to advance their ages at the rate of about 17 years per decade. This was nicely corroborated by a cross analysis of the 1901 and 1911 censuses of England and Wales. Early claims must necessarily be without the elementary corroboration of birth dates. England was among the earliest of all countries to introduce compulsory local registers (Sept. 1538) and official birth registration (1 July 1837) which was made fully compulsory only in 1874. Even in the United States, where in 1971 there were reputed to be 12,642 centenarians, 45 per cent of births occurring between 1890 and 1920 were unregistered.

Several celebrated super-centenarians are believed to have been double lives (father and son, brothers with the same names or successive bearers of a title). The most famous example is Christian Jakobsen Drackenberg allegedly born in Stavanger, Norway on 18 Nov. 1626 and died in Aarhus, Denmark aged seemingly 145 years 326 days on 9 Oct. 1772. A number of instances have been commercially sponsored, while a fourth category of recent claims are those made for political ends, such as the 100 citizens of the Russian Soviet Federative Socialist Republic (population about 132,000,000 at mid-1967) claimed in March 1960 to be between 120 and 156. From data on documented centenarians, actuaries have shown that only one 115-year life can be expected in 2,100

Mrs. Mito Umeta, the oldest ever Japanese, who died on 31 May 1975 aged 112 years 65 days.

million lives (*cf.* world population was estimated to be 4,025 million at mid-1975).

The height of credulity was reached on 5 May 1933, when a newsagency solemnly filed a story from China with a Peking date-line that Li Chung-yun, the "oldest man on Earth", born in 1680, had just died aged 256 years (*sic*). Recently the most extreme case of longevity claimed in the U.S.S.R. has been 168 years for Shirali "Baba" Mislimov of Barzavu, Azerbaijan, who died on 2 Sept. 1973 and was reputedly born on 26 Mar. 1805. No interview of this man has ever been permitted to any Western journalist or scientist. He was said

AUTHENTICATED NATIONAL LONGEVITY RECORDS

	Years	Days		Born		Died	
United States[1]	113	214	Delina Filkins (*née* Ecker)	4 May	1815	4 Dec.	1928
Canada[2]	113	124	Pierre Joubert	15 July	1701	16 Nov.	1814
Japan[3]	112	65	Mito Umeta (Mrs.)	27 Mar.	1863	31 May	1975
United Kingdom[4]	112	39	Alice Stevenson	10 July	1861	18 Aug.	1973
Morocco	>112		El Hadj Mohammed el Mokri (Grand Vizier)		1844	16 Sept.	1957
Ireland	111	327	The Hon. Katherine Plunket	22 Nov.	1820	14 Oct.	1932
South Africa[5]	111	151	Johanna Booyson	17 Jan.	1857	16 June	1968
Czechoslovakia	111	+	Marie Bernatkova	22 Oct.	1857	*fl.*Oct.	1968
Channel Islands	110	321	Margaret Ann Neve (*née* Harvey)	18 May	1792	4 April	1903
Northern Ireland	110	234	Elizabeth Watkins (Mrs.)	10 Mar.	1863	31 Oct.	1973
Yugoslavia	110	150+	Demitrius Philipovitch	9 Mar.	1818	*fl.*Aug.	1928
Australia[6]	110	39	Ada Sharp (Mrs.)	6 April	1861	15 May	1971
U.S.S.R.[7]	110	+	Khasako Dzugayev	7 Aug.	1860	*fl.*Aug.	1970
Netherlands	110	5	Baks Karnebeek (Mrs.)	2 Oct.	1849	7 Oct.	1959
France	109	309	Marie Philoméne Flassayer	13 June	1844	18 April	1954
Italy	109	179	Rosalia Spoto	25 Aug.	1847	20 Feb.	1957
Scotland	109	14	Rachel MacArthur (Mrs.)	26 Nov.	1827	10 Dec.	1936
Norway	109	+	Marie Olsen (Mrs.)	1 May	1850	*fl.*May	1959
Tasmania (State of)	109	+	Mary Ann Crow (Mrs.)	2 Feb.	1836		1945
Germany[8]	108	128	Luise Schwarz	27 Sept.	1849	2 Feb.	1958
Portugal[9]	108	+	Maria Luisa Jorge	7 June	1859	*fl.*July	1067
Finland	107	221	Amalia Wallenius (Mrs.)	6 Aug.	1867	24 Mar.	1975
Sweden	107	74	Anna Johansson	21 Nov.	1865	23 Feb.	1973
Belgium	106	267	Marie-Joseph Purnode (Mrs.)	17 April	1843	9 Nov.	1949
Austria	106	231	Anna Migschitz	3 Feb.	1850	1 Nov.	1956
Spain[10]	106	14	Jose Palido	15 Mar.	1866	29 Mar.	1972
Malaysia	106	+	Hassan Bin Yusoff	14 Aug.	1865	*fl.*Jan.	1972
Isle of Man	105	221	John Kneen	12 Nov.	1852	9 June	1958

[1] The U.S. Veteran Administration was in march 1974 paying pensions to 272 women attested to be widows of veterans of the Civil War (1860–65), the last soldier having died 15 years earlier in 1959. The oldest of these is Angela Felicia Virginia Davalos (Mrs. Harry Harrison Moran), who filed a claim dated 1928 with a baptismal certificate showing 17 May 1856 in Morelia, Mexico as her date and place of birth.

[2] Mrs. Ellen Carroll died in North River, Newfoundland, Canada on 8 December 1943, reputedly aged 115 years 49 days.

[3] A man named Nakamura of Kamaishi, northern Japan, was reported to have died on 4 May 1969 aged 116 years 329 days.

[4] London-born Miss Isabella Shepheard was allegedly 115 years old when she died at St. Asaph, Clwyd, North Wales, on 20 Nov. 1948, but her actual age was believed to have been 109 years 90 days. Charles Alfred Nunez Arnold died in Liverpool on 15 Sept. 1941 reputedly aged 112 years 66 days based on a baptismal claim (London, 10 Nov. 1829).

[5] Mrs. Susan Johanna Deporter of Port Elizabeth, South Africa, was reputedly 114 years old when she died on 4 August 1954. Mrs. Sarah Lawrence, Cape Town, South Africa was reputedly 112 on 3 June 1968.

[6] Reginald Beck of Sydney, New South Wales, Australia was allegedly 111 years old when he died on 13 April 1928.

[7] There are allegedly 21,700 centenarians in U.S.S.R. (c.f. 7,000 in U.S.A.). Of these 21,000 are ascribed to the Georgian S.S.R. i.e. one in every 232. In July 1962 it was reported that 128, mostly male, were in the one village of Medini.

[8] Friedrich Sadowski of Heidalberg reputedly celebrated his 111th birthday on 31 October 1936. Franz Joseph Eder d. Spitzburg 3 May 1911 allegedly aged 116.

[9] Senhora Jesuina da Conceicao of Lisbon was reputedly 113 years when she died on 10 June 1965.

[10] Juana Ortega Villarin, Madrid, Spain, was allegedly 112 in February 1962. Ana Maria Parraga of Murcia was reportedly 107 in Nov. 1969.

to have celebrated the 100th birthday of his third wife Hartun, in 1966, and that of one of his grandchildren in August 1973. It was reported in 1954 that in the Abkhasian Republic of Georgia, U.S.S.R., 2.58 per cent of the population was aged over 90—25 times the proportion in the U.S.A.

Dr. Zhores A. Medvedev, the expelled Soviet gerontologist, in Washington D.C., on 30 Apr. 1974 referring to U.S.S.R. claims stated "The whole phenomenon looks like a falsification" adding "He (Stalin) liked the idea that (other) Georgians lived to be a 100 or more". "Local officials tried hard to find more and more cases for Stalin". He points out (a) the *average* life span in the regions claiming the highest incidence of centenarians is lower than the U.S.S.R. average and (b) the number of centenarians claimed in the Caucasus has declined rapidly from 8,000 in 1950 to 4,500 in 1970. Dr. I. M. Spector, of the Institute of Traumatology, Kazan, U.S.S.R. quoted the maximum life-span of man in Apr. 1974 as "110–115 years".

The Andean valley of Vilcabamba in Ecuador became the source of reports of extreme longevity after the 1971 census in which 9 of the 819 inhabitants were returned at ages of more than 100, of whom 3 were listed as over 120. The two oldest claims were for Miguel Carpio Mendreta or Mendieta and José David Toledo, who were reputedly 122 and 140. Dr. David Davies of University College, London supports the claim of Francisco Camacho of Sacapalka as his best candidate for the title of the world's oldest living man with a baptismal registration on 19 Apr. 1847.

Charlie Smith of Bartow, Florida, U.S.A. obtained a Social Security card in 1955 when claiming to be born on 4 July 1842 in Liberia. The U.S. Department of Health, Education and Welfare state that they are "unable to disclose the type of evidence used" to determine Mr. Smith's age because such disclosure "would infringe on the confidentiality of the individual's record". The *essential* data on the ages entered for him in any of the 10 censuses from 1860 to 1950 remains undisclosed. He has a son born in 1902 and celebrated what he reckoned to be his 133rd birthday on 4 July 1975.

George Fruits, a War of Independence veteran, reputedly born in Baltimore, Maryland on 2 Feb. 1762 died on 6 Aug. 1876 at Alamo, Indiana aged 114 years.

Oldest authentic centenarian *World*
The greatest authenticated age to which a human has ever lived is 113 years 214 days in the case of Mrs. Delina Filkins *née* Ecker who was born at Stark, Herkimer County, New York on 4 May 1815 and died at Richfield Springs, New York on 4 Dec. 1928. She never wore spectacles. The national records listed in the accompanying table can be taken as authentic (see p. 13).

In the face of the above data the claim published in the April 1961 issue of the Soviet Union's *Vestnik Statistiki* ('Statistical Herald') that there were 224 male and 368 female Soviet citizens aged in excess of 120 recorded at the census of 15 Jan. 1959, indicates a reliance on hearsay rather than evidence. Official Soviet insistence on the unrivalled longevity of the country's citizenry is curious in view of the fact that the 592 persons in their unique "over 120" category must have spent at least the first 78 years of their prolonged lives under Tsarism. It has recently been suggested that the extreme ages claimed by some men in Georgia, U.S.S.R., are the result of attempts to avoid military service when they were younger, by assuming the identities of older men.

Oldest authentic centenarian *Great Britain*
The United Kingdom has an estimated population of 2,900 (2,360 women and 540 men) centenarians. The number of centenarians reported in Britain was only 140 in 1951, but 520 in 1961 and 2,430 in the 1971 census. Miss Alice Stevenson (1861–1973) (see above) is the only U.K. citizen with birth and death certificates more than 112 years apart. In April 1706 a John Bailes was buried at All Saints Church, Northampton, having apparently been baptized on 20 Aug. 1592. If the same person, he would have been 113 years 8 months. The oldest living centenarian known in Britain is

Mrs. Sarah Ellen Morgan (*née* Parkinson) born in Manchester on 23 Jan. 1867, now living in Sevenoaks, Kent, having celebrated her 110th birthday.

Oldest Triplets
The longest lived triplets on record were Faith, Hope and Charity Caughlin born at Marlboro, Massachusetts, U.S.A. on 27 Mar. 1868. The first to die was Mrs. (Ellen) Hope Daniels aged 93 on 2 Mar. 1962.

Oldest Twins *World*
The chances of identical twins both reaching 100 are said to be one in 700 million. The oldest recorded twins were Gulbrand and Bernt Morterud, born at Nord Odal, Norway, on 20 Dec. 1858. Bernt died on 1 Aug. 1960 in Chicago, Illinois, U.S.A. aged 101 and his brother died at Nord Odal on 12 Jan, 1964, aged 105. Twin sisters, Mrs. Vassilka Dermendjhieva and Mrs. Vassila Yapourdjieva of Sofia, Bulgaria allegedly celebrated their joint 104th birthday on 27 Sept. 1966.

Great Britain
The oldest twins on record in Great Britain have been the Bean twins Robert, of Birkenhead, Merseyside and Mary (now Mrs. Simpson) of Etton, Cambridgeshire who celebrated their 100th birthday on 19 Oct. 1973.

Most reigns
The greatest number of reigns during which any English subject could have lived is ten. A person born on the day (11 April) that Henry VI was deposed in 1471 had to live to only the comparatively modest age of 87 years 7 months and 6 days to see the accession of Elizabeth I on 17 Nov. 1558. Such a person could have been Thomas Carn of London, born 1471 and died 28 Jan. 1578 in his 107th year.

---

4. REPRODUCTIVITY

MOTHERHOOD
Most children *World*
The greatest number of children produced by a mother in an independently attested case is 69 by the first wife of Fyodor Vassilet, a peasant of the Moscow Jurisdiction, Russia, who, in 27 confinements, gave birth to 16 pairs of twins, 7 sets of triplets and 4 sets of quadruplets. Most of the children attained their majority. Mme. Vassilet (1816–72) became so renowned that she was presented at the court of Tsar Alexander II.

Currently the highest reported figure is a 32nd child born to Raimundo Carnauba, and his wife Madalena of Ceilandia, Brazil. She was married at 13 and has had 24 sons and 8 daughters. The mother in May 1972 said "They have given us a lot of work and worry but they are worth it", and the father "I don't know why people make such a fuss", The above figures are tentative since no two published interviews with this family seem to produce entirely consistent data.

Great Britain
The British record is probably held by Mrs. Elizabeth Greenhille (d. 1681) of Abbot's Langley, Hertfordshire. It is alleged that she gave birth to 39 children (32 daughters and 7 sons), all of whom attained their majority. She was married at 16, had a world record 38 confinements and died reputedly aged 64. Her last son Thomas (d. *c.* 1740) became surgeon to the 10th Duke of Norfolk and was the author of the "Art of Embalming" (1705). According to an inscription on a gravestone in Conway Church cemetery, Gwynedd, North Wales, Nicholas Hookes (d. 27 March 1637) was the 41st child of his mother Alice Hookes, but further details are lacking. It was reported in December 1634 that the wife of a Scottish weaver living in Newcastle upon Tyne had borne her husband 62 children. It has not been possible to corroborate or refute this report. The highest recent reported figure is 24 children born to Mrs. Emily Jane Lucas (b. 1881) of Tonbridge, Kent who died in July 1967.

Great Britain's champion mothers of today are believed to be Mrs. Margaret McNaught (b. 1923), of Balsall Heath, Birmingham (12 boys and 10 girls, all single births) and Mrs. Mabel Constable (b. 1920), of Long Itchington, Warwickshire who also has had 22 children including a set of triplets and two sets of twins.

Oldest mother *World*
Medical literature contains extreme but unauthenticated cases of septuagenarian mothers, such as Mrs. Ellen Ellis, aged 72, of Four Crosses, Clwyd, who allegedly produced a still-born 13th child on 15 May 1776 in her 46th year of marriage. Many cases are cover-ups for illegitimate grandchildren. The oldest recorded mother of whom there is certain evidence is Mrs. Ruth Alice Kistler (*née* Taylor), formerly Mrs. Shepard, of Portland, Oregon, U.S.A. She was born at Wakefield, Massachusetts, on 11 June 1899 and gave birth to a daughter, Suzan, at Glendale, near Los Angeles, California, on 18 Oct. 1956, when her age was 57 years 129 days. The incidence of quinquagenarian births varies widely with the highest purported rate being in Albania (with nearly 5,500 per million) compared with 2 per million in England & Wales.

Great Britain
The oldest British mother reliably recorded is Mrs. Winifred Wilson (*née* Stanley) of Eccles, Greater Manchester. She was born in Wolverhampton on 11 Nov. 1881 or 1882 and had her tenth child, a daughter Shirley, on Nov. 14 1936, when aged 54 or 55 years and 3 days. She died aged 91 or 92 in January 1974. At Southampton on 10 Feb. 1916, Mrs. Elizabeth Pearce gave birth to a son when aged 54 years 40 days.

Ireland
The oldest Irish mother recorded was Mrs. Mary Higgins of Cork, County Cork (b. 7 Jan. 1876) who gave birth to a daughter, Patricia, on 17 March 1931 when aged 55 years 69 days.

Descendants
In polygamous countries, the number of a person's descendants can become incalculable. The last Sharifian Emperor of Morocco, Moulay Ismail (1672–1727), known as "The Bloodthirsty", was reputed to have fathered a total of 548 sons and 340 daughters.

Capt. Wilson Kettle (b. 1860) of Grand Bay, Port aux Basques, Newfoundland, Canada, died on 25 Jan. 1963, aged 102, leaving 11 children by two wives, 65 grandchildren, 201 great-grandchildren and 305 great-great-grandchildren, a total of 582 living descendants. Mrs. Johanna Booyson (see page 14), of Belfast, Transvaal, was estimated to have 600 living descendants in South Africa in January 1968.

Mrs. Sarah Crawshaw (d. 25 Dec. 1844) left 397 descendants according to her gravestone in Stones Church, Ripponden, Halifax, West Yorkshire.

Multiple great-grandparents
Theoretically a great-great-great-great-grandparent is a possibility, though in practice countries in which young mothers are common, generally have a low expectation of life. At least eight cases of great-great-great-grandparents have been reported in the last 20 years. That with the longest span has been of Mrs. Margaret Hafel Sawyer of Bettendorf, Iowa, U.S.A. (b. 28 Dec. 1874), who was 101 years 8 months old when her great-granddaughter became a grandmother with the birth of Jennifer Grothus on 12 Aug. 1976.

MULTIPLE BIRTHS
Lightest Twins
The lightest recorded birthweight for a pair of surviving twins has been 2 lb. 3 oz. *992 g* in the case of Mary 16 oz. *453 g* and Margaret 19 oz. *538 g* born to Mrs. Florence Stimson, Queens Road, Old Fletton, Peterborough, England, delivered by Dr. Macaulay on 16 Aug. 1931. Margaret is now Mrs. M. J. Hurst.

"Siamese" Twins
Conjoined twins derived the name "Siamese" from the celebrated Chang and Eng Bunker (known in Thailand as Chan and In) born at Maklong, on 11 May 1811. They were joined by a cartilaginous band at the chest and married in April 1843 the Misses Sarah and Adelaide Yates and fathered ten and twelve children respectively. They died within three hours of each other on 17 Jan. 1874, aged 62. There is no genealogical evidence for the existence of the much-publicized Chalkhurst twins, Mary and Aliza, of Biddenden, Kent, allegedly born in *c.* 1550 (not 1100). The earliest certain record is one of 26 Apr. 1618 from Long Melford, Suffolk, England when conjoined twins were born to Mrs. Rose Shearhead. The earliest successful separation of Siamese twins was performed on Prisna and Napit Atkinson (b. May 1953 in Thailand) by Dr. Dragstedt at the University of Chicago on 29 March 1955.

MULTIPLE BIRTHS		
	World	**United Kingdom**
Highest number reported at single birth	10 (decaplets) (2 male, 8 female) Bacacay, Brazil 22 Apr. 1946 (also report from Spain, 1924 and China 12 May 1936)	
Highest number medically recorded	9 (nonuplets) (5 male, 4 female) to Mrs. Geraldine Broderick at Royal Hospital, Sydney, Australia on 13 June 1971. 2 males stillborn. Richard (12 oz. *340 g*) survived 6 days 9 (all also died) to patient at University of Pennsylvania, Philadelphia 29 May 1972	6 (sextuplets) (2 male, 4 female) to Mrs. Sheila Ann Thorns (*née* Manning) at New Birmingham Maternity Hospital on 2 Oct. 1968. Three survive 6 (1 male, 5 female) to Mrs. Rosemary Letts (*née* Egerton) at University College Hospital, Greater London on 15 Dec. 1969. One boy and 4 girls survive
Highest number surviving	6 out of 6 (3 males, 3 females) to Mrs. Susan Jane Rosen-kowitz (*née* Scoones) (b. Colombo, Sri Lanka, 28 Oct. 1947) at Mowbray, Cape Town, South Africa on 11 Jan. 1974 In order of birth they were: David, Nicolette, Jason, Emma, Grant and Elizabeth. They totalled 24 lb. 1 oz. *10,915 kg.*	5 out of 6 (as above) and also 5 out of 5 (5 females) to Mrs. Irene Mary Hanson (*née* Brown) at Queen Charlotte's Hospital London on 13 Nov. 1969 and 5 out of 5 (1 male, 4 females) to Mrs. James Bostock of Armadale, Lothian, Scotland (no use of fertility drugs) on 14 Apr. 1972
Quintuplets *World*	**Heaviest** 25 lb. *11,350 kg* Mrs. Lui Saulien, Chekiang, China 7 June 1953 25 lb. *11,350 kg* Mrs. Kamalammal Pondicherry, India, 30 Dec. 1956	**Most Sets** No recorded case of more than a single set
Quadruplets *World*	21 lb. 9 oz. *9,760 kg* Mrs. David Bergquist, University of Minnesota Hospital, Minneapolis U.S.A., 7 Sept. 1975 (4 girls)	4 Mde. Fyodor Vassilet, Moscow Jurisdiction, Russia (d. 1872)
Triplets *World* *U.K.*	26 lb. 6 oz. *11,960 kg* (unconfirmed) Iranian case (2 male, 1 female) 18 Mar. 1968 22 lb. 8 oz. *10,205 kg* Mrs. Elizabeth Parker, Stepping Hill Hospital, Stockport, Greater Manchester 21 Feb. 1972	15 Maddalena Granata (1839–*fl.* 1886)
Twins *World*	35 lb. 8 oz. *16,100 kg* (liveborn) Warren's case (2 males) reported in *The Lancet* from Derbyshire, England on 6 Dec. 1884 27 lb. 12 oz. *12,590 kg* (surviving) Mrs. J. P. Haskin, Fort Smith, Arkansas, U.S.A. 20 Feb. 1924	16 Mde. Vassilet (see above). *Note also* Mrs. Barbara Zulu of Barbeton, South Africa bore 3 sets of girls and 3 mixed sets in 7 years (1967–73) 15 Mrs. Mary Jonas of Chester (d. 4 Dec. 1899)—all sets were boy and girl

The rarest form of conjoined twins is Dicephales tetrabrachius dipus (two heads, four arms and two legs) of which only one example is known to exist today—in Russia. In a Brazilian case two girls, Juraci and Nadir Climerio de Oliveira, were born in Santo Amaro da Purificação, Bahia on 2 June 1957 and lived permanently at the Climerio de Oliveira Maternity Hospital in Salvador, sharing one intestinal and renal system until they died in 1974. The Russian pair Masha and Dasha were born on 4 Jan. 1950.

Fastest Triplet Birth

The fastest recorded natural birth of triplets has been 3 minutes in the case of Mrs. John R. Tyler of Houston, Texas, (Linda, Carol and Brenda) on 29 July 1952, and Mrs. Edward G. Wohl of Cleveland, Ohio, U.S.A. (Colleen, Bonnie and Allen) on 26 May 1958.

Quindecaplets

It was announced by Dr. Gennaro Montanino of Rome that he had removed the foetuses of 10 girls and 5 boys from the womb of a 35-year-old housewife on 22 July 1971. A fertility drug was responsible for this unique and unsurpassed instance of quindecaplets.

Longest pregnancy

Claims up to 413 days have been widely reported but accurate data are bedevilled by the increasing use of oral contraceptive pills which is a cause of amenorrhoea. Some women on becoming pregnant erroneously add some preceding periodless months to their pregnancy. In the pre-pill era English law has accepted pregnancies with extremes of 174 days (*Clark* v. *Clark*, 1939) and 349 days (*Hadlum* v. *Hadlum*, 1949).

BABIES

Heaviest *World*

The heaviest normal new-born child recorded in modern times was a boy weighing 11 kg *24 lb. 4 oz.*, born on 3 June 1961 to Mrs. Saadat Cor of Cegham, Southern Turkey. A report from Dezful, S.W. Iran, that Mrs. Massoumeh Valizadeh or Valli-Ullah 32, had given birth to a 12 kg *26 lb. 6½ oz.* boy on 7 Feb. 1972, was later officially stated to be incorrect. There is also an unconfirmed report of a woman giving birth to a 27 lb. *12,25 kg* baby in Essonnes, a suburb of Corbeil, central France, in June 1929. A deformed baby weighing 29¼ lb. *13,28 kg* was born in May 1939 in a hospital at Effingham, Illinois, U.S.A., but only lived for 2 hours.

Heaviest *United Kingdom*

The greatest recorded live birth weight in the United Kingdom is 21 lb. *9,53 kg* for a child born on Christmas Day, 1852. It was reported in a letter to the *British Medical Journal* (1 Feb. 1879) from a doctor in Torpoint, Cornwall. The only other reported birth weight in excess of 20 lb. *9,07 kg* is 20 lb. 2 oz. *9,13 kg* for a boy born to a 33-year-old schoolmistress in Crewe, Cheshire, on 12 Nov. 1884 with a 14½ in *36,8 cm* chest. A baby of 33 lb. *14,97 kg* was reportedly born to a Mrs. Lambert of Wandsworth Road, London *c.* 1930 but its measurements indicate a weight of about 17 lb. *7,7 kg*.

Most Bouncing Baby

The most bouncing baby on record was probably James Weir (1819–1821) who, according to his headstone in Cambushnethan, Old Parish Cemetery, Wishaw, Strathclyde, Scotland was 8 st. or 112 lb. *50,8 kg* at 13 months, 3 ft 4 in *1,01 m* in height and 39 in *99 cm* in girth.

Therese Parentean, who died in Rouyn, Quebec, Canada on 11 May 1936 aged 9 years, weighed 24 st. 4 lb. *154 kg*.

Lightest

The lowest birth weight for a surviving infant, of which there is definite evidence, is 10 oz. *283 g* in the case of Marion Chapman, born on 5 June 1938 in South Shields, Tyne and Wear. She was 12¼ in *31 cm* long. By her first birthday her weight had increased to 13 lb. 14 oz. *6 kg 290*. She was born unattended and was nursed by Dr. D. A. Shearer, who fed her hourly through a fountain pen filler. Her weight on her 21st birthday was 7 st. 8 lb. *48 kg 080*. The smallest viable baby reported from the United States has been Jacqueline

Benson born at Palatine, Illinois, on 20 Feb. 1936, weighing 12 oz. *340 g*.

Donna Marie daughter of Andrew and Lorraine McCamon born in Burnley General Hospital, Lancashire in June 1975 measured 12 in *30,4 cm* in length.

A weight of 8 oz. *227 g* was reported on 20 March 1938 for a baby born prematurely to Mrs. John Womack, after she had been knocked down by a lorry in East St. Louis, Illinois, U.S.A. The baby was taken alive to St. Mary's Hospital, but further information is lacking. On 23 Feb. 1952 it was reported that a 6 oz. *170 g* baby only 6½ in *17 cm* long lived for 12 hours in a hospital in Indianapolis, Indiana, U.S.A. A twin was still-born.

Coincident Birthdates

The only verified example of a family producing five single children with coincident birthdays is that of Catherine (1952); Carol (1953); Charles (1956); Claudia (1961) and Cecilia (1966), born to Ralph and Carolyn Cummins of Clintwood, Virginia, U.S.A., all on 20 February. The random odds against five single siblings sharing a birthdate are one in 17,797,577,730—almost 4 times the world's population.

Most Proximate Births

Mrs. John A. Baldwin, formerly of Nashville, Tennessee, gave birth to a daughter, Janice, on 26 Jan. 1952 and a second daughter Janet (3 months premature) on 14 Oct. 1952, 261 days later.

Janice and Janet Baldwin of Tennessee, who were born within 8½ months of each other in 1952.

5. PHYSIOLOGY AND ANATOMY

A U.S. scientific publication in 1975 set the value of the raw materials in a 150 lb. 68 kg human body at $5.60. It may be a commentary on world inflation that a 1936 figure was 98 U.S. cents, then 4s 10d. (24p). Hydrogen (63%) and oxygen (25.5%) constitute the commonest of the 24 elements in the human body. In 1972 four more trace elements were added—fluorine, silicon, tin and vanadium. The "essentially" of nickel has not yet been finally pronounced upon.

BONES

Longest

Excluding a variable number of sesamoids, there are 206 bones in the human body. The thigh bone or *femur* is the longest. It constitutes usually 27½ per cent of a person's stature, and may be expected to be 19¾ in *50 cm* long in a 6-ft *183 cm*-tall man. The longest recorded bone was the femur of the German giant Constantine, who died in Mons, Belgium, on 30 March 1902, aged 30 (see page 8). It measured 76 cm *29,9 in.* The femur of Robert Wadlow, the tallest man ever recorded, measured approximately 29½ in *75 cm.*

Smallest

The *stapes* or stirrup bone, one of the three auditory ossicles in the middle ear, is the smallest human bone, measuring from 2,6 to 3,4 mm *0.10 to 0.17 in.* in length and weighing from 2,0 to 4,3 mg *0.03 to 0.065 gr.*

MUSCLES

Largest

Muscles normally account for 40 per cent of the body weight and the bulkiest of the 639 muscles in the human body is the *gluteus maximus* or buttock muscle, which extends the thigh.

Smallest

The smallest muscle is the *stapedius*, which controls the *stapes* (see above,), an auditory ossicle in the middle ear, and which is less than 1/20th of an inch *0,127 cm* long.

Smallest waists

Queen Catherine de Medici (1519–89) decreed a waist measurement of 13 in *33 cm* for ladies of the French Court. This was at a time when females were more diminutive. The smallest recorded waist among women of normal stature in the 20th century is a reputed 13 in *33 cm* in the case of the French actress Mlle. Polaire (1881–1939) and Mrs. Ethel Granger (b. 12 April 1905) of Peterborough who reduced from a natural 22 in *56 cm* over the period 1929–1939.

Largest chest measurements

The largest chest measurements are among endomorphs (those with a tendency towards globularity). In the extreme case of Hughes (see page 10) this was reportedly 124 in *315 cm*, but in the light of his known height and weight a figure of 104 in *264 cm* would be more supportable. George McAree (see Britain's heaviest man) has a chest measurement of 76½ in *194 cm*. Among muscular subjects (mesomorphs) of normal height *expanded* chest measurements above 56 in *142 cm* are extremely rare. Louis Cyr (1865–1912), the famous French-Canadian strongman, had a chest measurement of 59 in *150 cm* at his best weight of 300 lb. *136 kg*, and former wrestler Shirley Crabtree (b. 1930) of Halifax, Yorkshire measured 58½ in *148,5 cm* (bodyweight 296 lb. *134,5 kg*) in 1962. Arnold Schwarzennegger (b. 1948) of Graz, Austria, former Mr. Universe and "the most perfectly developed man in the history of the world", has a chest measurement of 58 in *147 cm* at a bodyweight of 252 lb. *115 kg*. He also boasts a 22 in *56 cm* upper arm.

Longest necks

The maximum measured extension of the neck by the successive fitting of copper coils, as practised by the Padaung or Karen people of Burma, is 15¾ in *40 cm*.

BRAIN AND BRAIN POWER

Largest

The brain has 10×10^{10} nerve cells or neurons interconnected by dendrites or filaments and 10×10^{11} glia. Some of the brain's chemical reactions require only one millionth of a second. After the age of 18 the brain loses some 10^3 cells per day. The brain of an average adult male (*i.e.* 30–59 years) weighs 1 410 g *3 lb. 1.73 oz.* falling to 1 030 g *2 lb. 4.31 oz.* The heaviest brain ever recorded has been that of a 50 year old white male weighing 4 lb. 8.29 oz. *2 049 g* reported by Dr. Thomas F. Hegert, Chief Medical Examiner for District 9, State of Florida on 23 Oct. 1975. The brain of Oliver Cromwell (1599–1658) reputedly weighed 2 222 g *4 lb. 14.8 oz.*, but the size of his head in portraits does not support this

extreme figure. The brain of Lord Byron, who died in Greece in 1824 aged 36, reportedly weighed *6* Neopolitan pounds (1 924 g or *4 lb. 3.86 oz.*,) but this also included a certain amount of blood. In January 1891 the *Edinburgh Medical Journal* reported the case of a 75-year-old man in the Royal Edinburgh Asylum whose brain weighed 1 829 g *4 lb. 0.5 oz.*

Smallest

The non-atrophied brain of a female weighing only 1 096 g *2 lb. 4.6 oz.* without the membrane was reported from King's College Hospital Medical School, London in 1976.

Brains in extreme cases of microcephaly may weigh as little as 300 g *10,6 oz.* (*cf.* 20 oz. *567 g* for the adult male gorilla, and 16–20 oz. *454–567 g* for other anthropoid apes).

Highest I.Q.

On the Terman index for Intelligence Quotients, 150 represents "genius" level. The indices are sometimes held to be immeasurable above a level of 200 but a figure of 210 has been attributed to Kim Ung-Yong of Seoul, South Korea (b. 7 March 1963). He composed poetry and spoke four languages (Korean, English, German and Japanese), and performed integral calculus at the age of 4 years 8 months on television in Tokyo on "The World Surprise Show" on 2 Nov. 1967. Both his parents, Dr. and Mrs. Kim Soo Sun, are University professors and were both born at 11 a.m. on 23 May 1934. Research into past geniuses at Stanford University, California, U.S.A., has produced a figure of "over 200" for John Stuart Mill (United Kingdom) (1806–73), who began to learn ancient Greek at the age of three. A similar rating has also been attributed to Emanuel Swedenborg (1688–1772) and Johann Wolfgang von Goethe (1749–1832). More than 20 per cent of the 22,000 members of the International Mensa society have an I.Q. of 161 or above on the Cattell index which is equivalent to 142 on the Terman index.

Human Computer

The fastest time that anyone has been attested by purely mental process to extract a 73rd root from a 500 digit number is 2 min 43 sec by Willem Klein (Netherlands) in a demonstration at C.E.R.N., Switzerland on 27 Aug. 1976.

Human memory

Mehmed Ali Halici of Ankara, Turkey on 14 Oct. 1967 recited 6,666 verses of the Koran from memory in six hours. The recitation was followed by six Koran scholars. Rare instances of eidetic memory—the ability to re-project and hence "visually" recall material—are known to science.

Adding Numbers

Mr. R. H. Frost, 45, added 100 randomly selected digits in a test at York University, England in 32.57 seconds on 14 June 1976.

The greatest number of places of π

The greatest number of places to which Pi (ratio of circles' circumference to diameter) has been memorised is 5,050 by Michael John Poultney M.A. (Oxon) (b. 15 Dec. 1950) at Billingham Sixth Form College, Cleveland, England on 22 Mar. 1977. Note: The *approximation* of π at 22/7 recurs after its sixth decimal place and can, of course, be recited *ad nauseam*. It deviates from the true value after only the second decimal place.

HANDS AND HAIR

Touch sensitivity

The extreme sensitivity of the fingers is such that a vibration with a movement of 0.02 of a micron can be detected. On 12 Jan. 1963 the Soviet newspaper *Izvestiya* reported the case of a totally blindfolded girl. Rosa Kulgeshova, who was able to identify colours by touch alone. Later reports in 1970 completely refuted this claim.

Most fingers

In 1938 the extreme case of a baby girl with 14 fingers and 12 toes was reported from St. George's Hospital, Hyde Park, Greater London.

The longest ever moustache in Britain, that of Mr. John Roy, which has reached a maximum of 68½ in *174 cm*. (*R. J. Collorick*)

Longest finger nails

The longest finger nail ever reported is one of 23 in *58,4 cm* grown by Romesh Sharma of Delhi after 11 years, measured on 15 June 1976. The aggregate record for fingernails on one hand is 70½ in *179,07 cm* on the left hand (thumb 15 in) of Murari Aditya of Calcutta on 28 Feb. 1977 after 15 years.

Longest hair

The longest recorded hair was that of Swami Pandarasannadhi, the head of the Thiruvadu Thurai monastery in India. His hair was reported in 1949 to be 26 ft *7,93 m* in length, and being matted he was doubtless suffering from the disease Plica caudiformis. The hair of Jane Bunford (see p. 8–9) which she wore in two plaits, reached down to her ankles, indicating a length in excess of 8 ft *2,43 m*.

Longest beard

The longest beard preserved was that of Hans N. Langseth (b. 1846 in Norway) which measured 17½ ft *5,33 m* at the time of his death in 1927 after 15 years residence in the United States. The beard was presented to the Smithsonian Institution, Washington, D.C. in 1967. Richard Latter (b. Pembury, Kent, 1831) of Tunbridge Wells, Kent, who died in 1914 aged 83, reputedly had a beard 16 ft *4,87 m* long but contemporary independent corroboration is lacking and photographic evidence indicates this figure was exaggerated. The beard of the bearded lady Janice Deveree (b. Bracken Co., Kentucky, U.S.A., 1842) was measured at 14 in *36 cm* in 1884.

Longest moustache

The longest moustache on record is that of Masuriya Din (b. 1908), a Brahmin of the Partabgarh district in Uttar Pradesh, India. It grew to an extended span of 8 ft 6 in *2,59 m* between 1949 and 1962, and costs £13 per annum in upkeep. The longest moustache in Great Britain is that of Mr. John Roy (b. 14 Jan. 1910), licensee of the "Cock Inn" at Beazely End, near Braintree, Essex. It attained a peak span of 68½ in *174 cm* between 1939 and when measured on the BBC-TV *Nationwide* programme on 2 Apr. 1976.

DENTITION

Earliest

The first deciduous or milk teeth normally appear in infants at five to eight months, these being the mandibular and maxillary first incisors. There are many records of children born with teeth, the most distinguished example being Prince Louis Dieudonné, later Louis XIV of France, who was born with two teeth on 5 Sept. 1638. Molars usually appear at 24 months, but in Pindborg's case published in Denmark in 1970 a 6 week premature baby was documented with 8 natal teeth of which 4 were in the molar region.

Most

Cases of the growth in late life of a third set of teeth have been recorded several times. A reference to an extreme case in France of a fourth dentition, known as Lison's case was published in 1896. A triple row of teeth was noted in 1680 by Albertus Hellwigius.

Most dedicated dentist

Brother Giovanni Battista Orsenigo of the Ospedale Fatebenefratelli, Rome, Italy, a religious dentist, conserved all the teeth he extracted in three enormous cases during the time he exercised his profession from 1868 to 1904. In 1903 the number was counted and found to be 2,000,744 teeth.

OPTICS

Smallest visible object

The resolving power of the human eye is 0.0003 of a radian or an arc of one minute (1/60th of a degree), which corresponds to 100 microns at 10 in. A micron is a thousandth of a millimetre, hence 100 microns is 0.003937, or less than four thousandths, of an inch. The human eye can, however, detect a bright light source shining through an aperture only 3 to 4 microns across. In Oct. 1972 the University of Stuttgart, West Germany reported that their student Frl. Veronica Seider (b. 1953) possessed a visual acuity 20 times better than average. She could identify people at a distance of more than a mile *1,6 km*.

Colour sensitivity

The unaided human eye, under the best possible viewing conditions, comparing large areas of colour, in good illumination, using both eyes, can distinguish 10,000,000 different colour surfaces. The most accurate photo-electric spectrophotometers possess a precision probably only 40 per cent as good as this.

Colour blindness

About 7.5% of men and 0.1% of women are colour blind. The most extreme form, monochromatic vision, is very rare. The highest recorded rate of red-green colour blindness is in Czechoslovakia and the lowest rate among Fijians and Brazilian Indians.

VOICE

Highest and lowest

The highest and lowest recorded notes attained by the human voice before this century were a C in *alt-altissimo* (c^{iv}) by Lucrezia Agujari (1743–83), noted by the Austrian composer Wolfgang Amadeus Mozart (1756–91) in Parma, northern Italy, in 1770, and an A$_1$ (55 cycles per sec) by Kasper Foster (1617–73). Madeleine Marie Robin (1918–1960) the French operatic coloratura could produce and sustain the B♭ above high C in the Lucia mad scene in *Lucia di Lammermoor*. Since 1950 singers have achieved high and low notes far beyond the hitherto accepted extremes. However, notes at the bass and treble extremities of the register tend to lack harmonics and are of little musical value. Frl. Marita Gunther, trained by Alfred Wolfsohn, has covered the range of the piano from the lowest note, A_{11}, to c^v. Of this range of 7¼ octaves, six octaves are considered to be of musical value. Mr. Roy Hart, also trained by Wolfsohn, has reached notes below the range of the piano. The highest note being sung by a tenor is g in *alt-altissimo* by Louis Lavelle, coached by Mr. S. Pleeth, in *Lovely Mary Donelly*. The lowest note put into song is a D_{11} by the singer Tom King, of King's Langley, Hertfordshire. The highest note called for in singing was an f^{iv}♯, which occurred twice in Zervinetta's Recitative and Aria in the first (1912) version of the opera *Ariadne auf Naxos* by Richard Georg Strauss (1864–1949). It was transposed down a tone in 1916.

Greatest range
The normal intelligible outdoor range of the male human voice in still air is 200 yd *180 m*. The *silbo*, the whistled language of the Spanish-speaking Canary Island of La Gomera, is intelligible across the valleys, under ideal conditions, at five miles *8 km*. There is a recorded case, under freak acoustic conditions, of the human voice being detectable at a distance of 10½ miles *17 km* across still water at night. It was said that Mills Darden (see page 10) could be heard 6 miles *9 km* away when he shouted at the top of his voice.

At the "World" Shouting Competition at Scarborough, North Yorkshire on 17 Feb. 1973 the title was won by Skipper Kenny Leader with 111 decibels at 2½ metres *8 ft 1¼ in*. A feminine record of 110 dBA was set by Mrs. Grace Hall at Pathfinder Village, Exeter, Devon on 19 Nov. 1976.

Lowest detectable sound
The intensity of noise or sound is measured in terms of pressure. The pressure of the quietest sound that can be detected by a person of normal hearing at the most sensitive frequency of c. 2,750 Hz is 2×10^{-5} pascal. One tenth of the logarithm to this standard provides a unit termed a decibel. Prolonged noise above 150 decibels will cause immediate permanent deafness while 200 decibels could be fatal. A noise of 30 decibels is negligible.

Highest detectable pitch
The upper limit of hearing by the human ear has long been regarded as 20,000 Hz (cycles per sec), although children with asthma can often detect a sound of 30,000 cycles per sec. It was announced in February 1964 that experiments in the U.S.S.R. had conclusively proved that oscillations as high as 200,000 cycles per sec can be heard if the oscillator is pressed against the skull.

Fastest talker
Few people are able to speak *articulately* at a sustained speed above 300 words per min. The fastest broadcaster has been regarded as Gerry Wilmot (b. Victoria B.C., Canada 6 Oct. 1914) the ice hockey commentator in the post World War II period. Raymond Glendenning (1907–1974), the B.B.C. horseracing commentator, once spoke 176 words in 30 sec. while commentating on a greyhound race. In public life the highest speed recorded is a 327 words per min burst in a speech made in December 1961 by John Fitzgerald Kennedy (1917–63), then President of the United States. Tapes of attempts to recite Hamlet's 262 word Soliloquy in under 24 secs (655 w.p.m.) have proved unintelligible. A computer-based speech synthesis system is reported to be under development in the United States.

BLOOD
Blood groups
The preponderance of one blood group varies greatly from one locality to another. On a world basis Group O is the most common (46 per cent), but in some areas, for example Norway, Group A predominates.

The full description of the commonest sub-group in Britain is O MsNs, P+, Rr, Lu(a−), K−, Le(a−b+), Fy(a+b+), Jk(a+b+), which occurs in one in every 270 people.

The rarest blood group on the ABO system, one of 14 systems, is AB, which occurs in less than three per cent of persons in the British Isles. The rarest type in the world is a type of Bombay blood (sub-type A-h) found so far only in a Czechoslovak nurse in 1961 and in a brother (Rh positive) and sister (Rh negative) named Jalbert in Massachusetts, U.S.A. reported in February 1968. The American male has started a blood bank for himself.

Richest Natural Resources
Joe Thomas of Detroit, Michigan, U.S.A. was reported in August 1970 to have the highest known count of Anti-Lewis B, the rare blood antibody. A U.S. biological supply firm pays him $1,500 per quart *1,13 l*—an income of $12,000 (£5,000) per annum. The Internal Revenue regard this income as a taxable liquid asset.

Champion blood donor
Ed 'Spike' Howard (1877–1946), the professional strongman of Philadelphia, U.S.A. donated a lifetime total of 1,056 U.S. pints or *499,66 litres*. A 50-year-old haemophiliac Warren C. Jyrich required 2,400 donor units *1 080 litres* of blood when undergoing open heart surgery at the Michael Reese Hospital, Chicago, U.S.A. in December 1970.

Largest vein
The largest vein in the human body is a cardiac vein, known as the *vena cava*, which returns most of the blood from the body below the level of the heart.

Most alcoholic subject
It was recorded that a hard drinker named Vanhorn (1750–1811), born in London, averaged more than four bottles of ruby port per day for the 23 years from 1788 to his death aged 61 in 1811. The total of his "empties" was put at 35,688.

The youngest recorded death from alcoholic poisoning was that of a 4 year old boy, Joseph Sweet, in Wolverhampton, England in 1827 reported in the Stafford Assizes case *R. v. Martin*.

The United Kingdom's legal limit for motorists is 80 mg of alcohol per 100 ml of blood. The hitherto recorded highest figure in medical literature of 640 mg per 100 ml was submerged when the late Michael Thomas Mallaney of Muxton, Salop, was found by a pathologist to have a level of 656 mg on 26 Mar. 1976 after trying to hitch a lift on the road.

BODY TEMPERATURE
Highest body temperature
In Kalow's case (*Lancet*, 31 Oct. 1970) a woman following halothane anaesthesia ran a temperature of 112° F *44,4° C*. She recovered after a procainamide infusion. Marathon runners in hot weather attain 105.8° F *41° C*.

A temperature of 115° F *46,1° C* was recorded in the case of Christopher Legge in the Hospital for Tropical Diseases, London, on 9 Feb. 1934. A subsequent examination of the thermometer disclosed a flaw in the bulb, but it is regarded as certain that the patient sustained a temperature of more than 110° F *43,3° C*.

Lowest body temperature
There are two recorded cases of patients surviving body temperatures as low as 60.8° F *16,0° C* Dorothy Mae Stevens, (1929–74) was found in an alley in Chicago, Illinois on 1 Feb. 1951 and Vickie Mary Davis aged 2 years 1 month in an unheated house in Marshall-town, Iowa on 21 Jan. 1956 both with this temperature.

ILLNESS AND DISEASE
Commonest disease
The commonest non-contagious disease in the world is dental caries or tooth decay. In Great Britain 13 per cent of people have lost all their teeth before they are 21 years old. During their lifetime few completely escape its effects. Infestation with pinworm (*Enterobius vermicularis*) approaches 100 per cent in some areas of the world.

The commonest contagious disease in the world is coryza (acute nasopharyngitis) or the common cold. Only 2,690,000

Dennis Atkin, who has lived in an "iron lung" since October 1949.

working days were reportedly lost as a result of this illness in Great Britain between mid 1974 and mid 1975, since absences of less than three days are not reported. The greatest reported loss of working time in Britain is from bronchitis, which accounted for 29,460,000, or 9.50 per cent, of the total of 309,840,000 working days lost in the same period.

The most resistant recorded case to being infected at the Medical Research Council Common Cold Unit, Salisbury, Wiltshire is J. Brophy, who has had one mild reaction in 24 visits.

Rarest disease
Medical literature periodically records hitherto undescribed diseases. A disease as yet undescribed but predicted is podocytoma of the kidney—a tumour of the epithelial cells lining the glomerulus of the kidney.

Of once common diseases, rabies (hydrophobia) was unreported in Britain from 1922 until a field case reported in Kent in 1969 due to a dog imported from India despite 6 months quarantine. Kuru, or laughing sickness, afflicts only the Fore tribe of eastern New Guinea and is 100 per cent fatal. It is transmitted by the cannibalistic practice of eating human brains. The rarest fatal diseases in England and Wales have been those from which the last deaths (all males) were all recorded more than 40 years ago—yellow fever (1930), cholera nostras (1928) and bubonic plague (1926).

Most and least infectious disease
The most infectious of all diseases is the pneumonic form of plague, which also has a mortality rate of about 99.99 per cent. Leprosy transmitted by *Mycobacterium leprae* is the least infectious and most bacilliferous of communicable diseases.

Highest morbidity
Rabies in humans has been regarded as uniformly fatal when associated with the hydrophobia symptom. A 25-year-old woman Candida de Sousa Barbosa of Rio de Janeiro, Brazil, was believed to be the first ever survivor of the disease in November 1968, though some sources give priority to Matthew Winkler, 6, in 1970.

Most notorious carrier
The most notorious of all typhoid carriers has been Mary Mallon, known as Typhoid Mary, of New York City, N.Y., U.S.A. She was the source of the 1903 outbreak, with 1,300 cases. Because of her refusal to leave employment, often under assumed names, involving the handling of food, she was placed under permanent detention from 1915 until her death in 1938.

Earliest slipped disc
The earliest description of a prolapsed intervertebral cartilage was by George S. Middleton and John H. Teacher of Glasgow, Scotland, in 1911.

MEDICAL EXTREMES
Heart stoppage
The longest recorded heart stoppage is a minimum of 3 hours 32 minutes in the case of Miss Jean Jawbone, 20, who was revived by a team of 17 in Winnipeg Medical Centre, Manitoba, Canada on 19 Jan. 1977.

The longest recorded interval in a *post mortem* birth was one of at least 80 minutes in Magnolia, Mississippi, U.S.A. Dr. Robert E. Drake found Fanella Anderson, aged 25, dead in her home at 11.40 p.m. on 15 Oct. 1966 and he delivered her of a son weighing 6 lb. 4 oz. *2 kg 830* by Caesarean operation in the Beacham Memorial Hospital on 16 Oct. 1966.

Pulse Rates
A normal adult pulse rate is 70–72 beats per minute at rest for males and 78–82 for females. Rates increase to 200 or more during violent exercise and drop to as low as 12 in the extreme case of Dorothy Mae Stevens (see Lowest temperature above).

Longest coma
The longest recorded coma is that being undergone of Elaine Esposito (b. 3 Dec. 1934) of Tarpon Springs, Florida, U.S.A. She has never stirred since an appendicectomy on 6 Aug. 1941, when she was six, in Chicago, Illinois, U.S.A. On 6 Apr. 1977 her coma surpassed 35 years 8 months.

Longest Dream
Dreaming sleep is characterized by rapid eye movements known as REM. The longest recorded period of REM is one of 2 hours 23 minutes on 15 Feb. 1967 at the department of Psychology, University of Illinois, Chicago on Bill Carskadon, who had had his previous sleep interrupted.

Largest stone
The largest stone or vesical calculus reported in medical literature was one of 13 lb. 14 oz. *6 294 g* removed from an 80-year-old woman by Dr. Humphrey Arthure at Charing Cross Hospital, London, on 29 Dec. 1952.

Longest in iron lung
The longest recorded survival by an "iron lung" patient is 31 years by Lee Hale (b. 1912) of Crockett, Virginia, U.S.A. The longest survival in an "iron lung" in Britain is since 5 Oct. 1949 by Mr. Dennis Atkin in Lodge Moor Hospital, Sheffield, South Yorkshire. Paul Bates of Horsham, West Sussex entered his 24th year on a mechanical positive pressure respirator on 13 Aug. 1976. He has received an estimated 175,670,000 respirations into his lungs *via* his trachea up to 1 May 1977.

Fastest reflexes
The results of experiments carried out in 1943 have shown that the fastest messages transmitted by the nervous system travel at 265 m.p.h. *426 km/h*. With advancing age impulses are carried 15 per cent more slowly.

Hiccoughing
The longest recorded attack of hiccoughs was that afflicting Charles Osborne (b. 1894) of Anthon, Iowa, U.S.A., from 1922 to date. He contracted it when slaughtering a hog. His first wife left him and he is unable to keep in his false teeth. The infirmary at Newcastle upon Tyne is recorded to have admitted a young man from Long Witton, Northumberland on 25 March 1769 suffering from hiccoughs which could be heard at a range of more than a mile.

Sneezing
The most chronic sneezing fit ever recorded was that of June Clark, aged 17, of Miami, Florida, U.S.A. She started sneezing on 4 Jan. 1966, while recovering from a kidney ailment in the James M. Jackson Memorial Hospital, Miami. The sneezing was stopped by electric "aversion" treatment administered by Dr. Malcolm Rushmer on 8 June 1966, after 155 days. The highest speed at which expelled particles have been measured to travel is 103.6 m.p.h. *167 km/h*.

Snoring *Loudest*
Research at the Ear, Nose and Throat Department of St. Mary's Hospital, London, published in November 1968, shows that a rasping snore can attain a loudness of 69 decibels (*cf.* 70–90 for a pneumatic drill).

Yawning
In Lee's case, reported in 1888, a fifteen-year-old female patient yawned continuously for a period of five weeks.

Sleeplessness
Researches indicate that on the Circadian cycle for the majority peak efficiency is attained between 8 p.m. and 9 p.m. and the low point comes at 4 a.m. The longest recorded period for which a person has voluntarily gone without sleep is 449 hr (14 days 13 hours) by Mrs. Maureen Weston of Peterborough, Cambridgeshire in a rocking chair marathon on 14 Apr.–2 May 1977. Though she tended to hallucinate toward the end of this surely ill-advised test, she surprisingly suffered no lasting ill-effects.

Motionlessness
The longest that anyone has voluntarily remained motionless is 5 hr 40 min by William A. Fuqua of Corpus Christi, Texas, U.S.A., a former "freeze model" in Dillard's store astride a bicycle on a stand from 1 p.m.–6.40 p.m. on 19 Dec. 1975. The longest recorded case of involuntarily being made to stand to attention was when Staff Sgt. Samuel B. Moody U.S.A.F. was so punished in Narumi prison camp, Nagoya, Japan for 53 hours in spring of 1945. He survived to write *Reprieve from Hell*.

Swallowing
The worst reported case of compulsive swallowing was an insane female Mrs. H. aged 42, who complained of a "slight abdominal pain". She proved to have 2,533 objects, including 947 bent pins, in her stomach. These were removed by Drs. Chalk and Foucar in June 1927 at the Ontario Hospital, Canada. The heaviest object extracted from a human stomach has been a 5 lb. 3 oz. *2,530 kg* ball of hair in Swain's case from a 20 year female in the South Devon and East Cornwall Hospital, England on 30 Mar. 1895.

Sword
The longest length of sword able to be "swallowed" by a practised exponent, after a heavy meal, is 27 in *69 cm*. Perhaps the greatest exponent is Alex Linton, born on 25 Oct. 1904 in Boyle, County Roscommon, Ireland. Sandra Dee Reed (Lady Sandra) of Florida has swallowed five 30 in *152,4 cm* blades to two thirds of their length simultaneously.

Fasting
Most humans experience considerable discomfort after an abstinance from food for even 12 hr but this often passes off after 24–48 hr. Records claimed without unremitting medical surveillance are of little value. The longest period for which anyone has gone without solid food is 382 days by Angus Barbieri (b. 1940) of Tayport, Fife, who lived on tea, coffee, water, soda water and vitamins in Maryfield Hospital, Dundee, Angus, from June 1965 to July 1966. His weight declined from 33 st. 10 lb. *214,1 kg* to 12 st. 10 lb. *80 kg 740*. Sister Therese Neumann survived 35 years on the "bread" of the Holy Eucharist wafer at Mass each morning at Konnersreuth, Germany.

Hunger strike
The longest recorded hunger strike was one of 94 days by John and Peter Crowley, Thomas Donovan, Michael Burke, Michael O'Reilly, Christopher Upton, John Power, Joseph Kenny and Seán Hennessy in Cork Prison, Ireland, from 11 Aug. to 12 Nov. 1920. These nine survivors from 12 prisoners owed their lives to expert medical attention and an appeal by Arthur Griffith. The longest recorded hunger strike in a British gaol is 385 days from 28 June 1972 to 18 July 1973 by Denis Galer Goodwin in Wakefield Prison, West Yorkshire protesting his innocence of a rape charge. He was fed by tube orally.

The longest recorded case of survival without food *and* water is 252 hours (10½ days) by Sorin Crainic, 19, entombed under a collapsed block of flats by the earthquake in Bucharest, Romania from 4 to 15 March 1977.

Most voracious fire eater
Peter De-Valle (born Peter Ashton, 29 Apr. 1950) blew a flame from his mouth to a distance of 19 ft 8 in *6 m* in the Rugby Cattle Market on 28 Oct. 1975 in a test filmed for A.T.V. Fire eating is a highly dangerous activity.

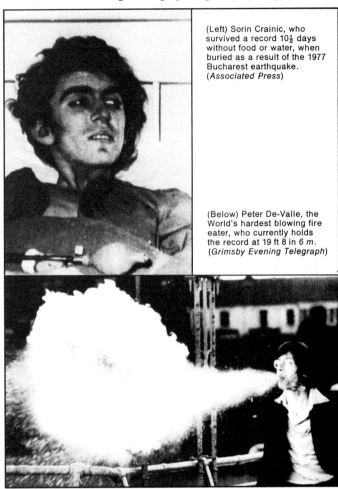

(Left) Sorin Crainic, who survived a record 10½ days without food or water, when buried as a result of the 1977 Bucharest earthquake. (*Associated Press*)

(Below) Peter De-Valle, the World's hardest blowing fire eater, who currently holds the record at 19 ft 8 in *6 m*. (*Grimsby Evening Telegraph*)

Human salamanders
The highest dry-air temperature endured by naked men in the U.S. Air Force experiments in 1960 was 400° F *204,4° C* and for heavily clothed men 500° F *260° C*. Steaks require only 325° F *162,8° C*. Temperatures of 140° C *284° F* have been found quite bearable in *Sauna* baths.

The highest temperature recorded by pyrometer for the coals in any fire walk was 1,494° F *812° C* for a walk by "Komar" (Vernon E. Craig) of Wooster, Ohio at the International Festival of Yoga and Esoteric Sciences, Maidenhead, England on 14 Aug. 1976.

Underwater
The world record for voluntarily staying underwater is 13 min 42.5 sec by Robert Foster, aged 32, an electronics technician of Richmond, California, who stayed under 10 ft *3,05 m* of water in the swimming pool of the Bermuda Palms Motel at San Rafael, California, U.S.A., on 15 March 1959. He hyperventilated with oxygen for 30 min before his descent. The longest unprepared record is 6 min 29.8 sec. by Georges Pouliquin in Paris on 3 Nov. 1912. It must be stressed that record-breaking of this kind is *extremely* dangerous.

g forces
The acceleration g, due to gravity, is 32 ft 1.05 in per sec per sec *978,02 cm/sec²* at sea-level at the Equator. A *sustained* acceleration of 31 g was withstood for 5 sec by R. Flanagan Gray, 39, at the Johnsville U.S. Naval Air Development Center in Warminster, Pennsylvania, on 5 Dec. 1958. This makes the bodyweight of a 13 st. 3 lb. *83 kg 910* man seem

like 2.54 tons *2 585 kg*. The highest value endured in a dry capsule is 25 g. The highest g value endured on a water-braked rocket sled is 82.6 g for 0.04 of a sec by Eli L. Beeding Jr. at Holloman Air Force Base, New Mexico, U.S.A., on 16 May 1958. He was put in hospital for 3 days. A man who fell off a 185 ft *56,39 m* cliff (before 1963) has survived a *momentary* g of 209 in decelerating from 68 mp.h. *109 km/h* to stationary in 0.015 of a sec.

The land divers of Penecost Island, New Hebrides dive from Platforms 70 ft *21,3 m* high with liana vines attached to their ankles. The jerk can transmit a momentary g force in excess of 100.

Electric Shock *Highest voltage*
Excluding lightning bolts, the highest reported voltage electric shock survived was one of 230,000 volts by Brian Latasa, 17 on the tower of an ultra-high voltage power line in Griffiith Park, Los Angeles on 9 Nov. 1967.

Isolation
The longest recorded period for which any volunteer has been able to withstand total deprivation of all sensory stimulation (sight, hearing and touch) is 92 hr, recorded in 1962 at Lancaster Moor Hospital, Lancashire.

The farthest that any human has been isolated from all other humans has been the lone pilots of lunar command modules when antipodal to their Apollo missions, two lunar explorers 2,200 miles *3 540 km* distant.

Pill-taking
The highest recorded total of pills swallowed by a patient is 280,131 between 9 June 1967 to 29 Nov. 1976 by C. H. A. Kilner (b. 1926) of Malawi, following a successful pancreatectomy.

Most tattoos
Vivian "Sailor Joe" Simmons, a Canadian tattoo artist, had 4,831 tattoos on his body. He died in Toronto on 22 Dec. 1965 aged 77. Britain's most tattooed man is George Bone (b. 10 Nov. 1946) of Ealing, Greater London whose last few gaps have been blocked in by the Aldershot tattoo artist Bill Skuse. Britain's most decorated woman is Mrs. Rusty Skuse *née* Field (b. 1944) of Aldershot, Hampshire, who after 12 years under the needle of Mr. Skuse, came within 15 per cent of totality. He stated he always had designs on her.

OPERATIONS
Longest
The most protracted operations are those involving brain surgery. Such an operation lasting 31 hours was performed on Victor Zazueta, 19, of El Centro at San Diego Hospital, California by Drs. John F. Alksne and Randall Smith on 17–18 Jan. 1972.

Most major
On 20 August 1975 Mr. Charles Hill (b. 1914) of Sydney, New South Wales, Australia underwent his 87th major operation. Most of the surgery has been abdominal.

Oldest subject
The greatest recorded age at which a person has been subjected to an operation is 111 years 105 days in the case of James Henry Brett, Jr. (b. 25 July 1849, d. 10 Feb. 1961) of Houston, Texas, U.S.A. He underwent a hip operation on 7 Nov. 1960. The oldest age established in Britain was the case of Miss Mary Wright (b. 28 Feb. 1862) who died during a thigh operation at Boston, Lincolnshire on 22 April 1971 aged 109 years 53 days.

Youngest subject
Babies are now increasingly operated on within minutes of birth so there is no specific record for the youngest subject.

Earliest Heart Transplant
The first human heart transplant operation was performed on Louis Washkansky, aged 55, at the Groote Schuur Hospital Cape Town, South Africa, between 1.00 a.m. and 6 a.m., on 3 Dec. 1967, by a team of 30 headed by Prof. Christiaan Neethling Barnard (b. Beaufort West, South Africa, 8 Oct. 1922). The donor was Miss Denise Ann Darvall, aged 25. Washkansky died on 21 Dec. 1967.

Longest surviving
The longest surviving heart transplantee has been Mrs. Betty Anick of Milwaukee, Wisconsin, U.S.A., who received the heart of a 30 year old man on 21 Dec. 1968. She died in Florida on 22 Mar. 1977—8 years and 152 days later. Britain's longest-surviving heart transplant patient has been Mr. Charles Hendrick who died in Guy's Hospital of a lung infection on 31 Aug. 1969, 107 days after his operation.

Earliest appendicectomy
The earliest recorded successful appendix operation was performed in 1736 by Claudius Amyand (1680–1740). He was Serjeant Surgeon to King George II (reigned 1727–60).

Earliest anaesthesia
The earliest recorded operation under general anaesthesia was for the removal of a cyst from the neck of James Venable by Dr. Crawford Williamson Long (1815–78), using diethyl ether $(C_2H_5)_2O)$, in Jefferson, Georgia, U.S.A., on 30 March 1842. The earliest amputation under an anaesthetic in Great Britain was by Dr. William Scott and Dr. James McLauchlan at the Dumfries and Galloway Infirmary, Scotland on 19 Dec. 1846.

Laryngectomy
On 24 July 1924 John I. Poole of Plymouth, Devon after diagnosis of carcinoma then aged 33 underwent total laryngectomy in Edinburgh. In July 1976 he entered his 53rd year as a "neck-breather".

Fastest amputation
The shortest time recorded for a leg amputation in the pre-anaesthetic era was 13 to 15 seconds by Napoleon's chief surgeon Dominique Larrey.

Surgical instruments
The largest surgical instruments are robot retractors used in abdominal surgery introduced by Abbey Surgical Instruments of Chingford, Essex in 1968 and weighing 11 lb. *5 kg*. Some bronchoscopic forceps measure 60 cm *23½ in* in length. The smallest are Elliot's eye trephine, which has a blade 0.078 in *0.20 cm* in diameter and "straight" stapes picks with a needle type tip or blade of 0,3 mm *0.013 in* long.

PSYCHIC FORCES
Extra-sensory perception
The highest consistent performer in tests to detect powers of extra-sensory perception is Pavel Stêpánek (Czechoslovakia) known in parapsychological circles as "P.S.". His performance on nominating hidden white or green cards from May 1967 to March 1968 departed from a chance probability yielding a Chi^2 value corresponding to $P < 10^{-50}$ or odds of more than 100 octillion to one against the achievement being one of chance. One of the two appointed referees recommended that the results should not be published. The highest published scores in any E.S.P. test were those of a 26-year-old female tested by Prof. Bernard F. Reiss of Hunter College, New York in 1936. In 74 runs of 25 guesses each she scored one with 25 all correct, two with 24 and an average of 18.24 instead of the random 5.00. Such a result would depart from chance probability by a factor $>10^{700}$. This produced the comment from some that there might be a defect in the theory of probability.

Most durable ghosts
Ghosts are not immortal and, according to the *Gazetteer of British Ghosts*, seem to deteriorate after 400 years. The most outstanding exception to their normal "half-life" would be the ghosts of Roman soldiers thrice reported still marching through the cellars of the Treasurer's House, York Minster after nearly 19 centuries. The book's author, Peter Underwood, states that Britain has more reported ghosts per square mile than any other country with Borley Rectory near Long Melford, Suffolk the site of unrivalled activity between 1863 and its destruction by fire in 1939.

2. THE ANIMAL AND PLANT KINGDOMS

ANIMAL KINGDOM
GENERAL RECORDS

Note—Guinness Superlatives Ltd. has published a specialist volume entitled *The Guinness Book of Animal Facts and Feats* (2nd Edition) (price £6.50). This work treats the dimensions and performances of the Classes of the Animal Kingdom in greater detail, giving also the sources and authorities for much of the material in this chapter.

Largest and heaviest

The largest and heaviest animal in the world, and probably the biggest creature which has *ever* existed, is the Blue or Sulphur-bottom whale (*Balaenoptera musculus*), also called Sibbald's rorqual. The largest specimen ever recorded was a female landed at the Cia Argentina de Pesca, South Georgia some time in the period 1904–1920 which measured 107 Norwegian fot 33.58 m *110 ft 2½ in* in length. Another female measuring 96¾ ft *29,48 m* brought into the shore station at Prince Olaf, South Georgia in *c.* 1931 was calculated to have weighted 163.7 tons *166 tonnes*, exclusive of blood and other body fluids, judging by the number of cookers that were filled by the animal's blubber, meat and bones and internal organs. The total weight of this whale was believed to have been 174 tons *177 tonnes*.

On the principle that the weight should vary as the cube of linear dimensions, a 100 ft *30,48 m* Blue whale in good condition should weigh about 160 tons *163 tonnes*, but in the case of pregnant females the weight could be as much as 190–200 tons *193–203 tonnes*—equivalent to 35 adult bull African elephants.

Tallest

The tallest living animal is the Giraffe (*Giraffa camelopardalis*), which is now found only in the dry savannah and semi-desert areas of Africa south of the Sahara. The tallest ever recorded was a Masai bull (*G. camelopardalis tippelskirchi*) named "George", received at Chester Zoo, England on 8 Jan. 1959 from Kenya. His head almost touched the roof of the 20 ft *6,09 m* high Giraffe House when he was 9 years old. George died on 22 July 1969. Less credible heights of up to 23 ft *7 m* have been claimed for bulls shot in the field.

The first giraffe ever seen in England was a two year-old cow of the Nubian race (*G.c. camelopardalis*) presented to George IV (1762–1830) by Mohammed Ali, Pasha of Egypt. The 9 ft 2 in *2,79 m* tall animal arrived in London *via* Malta in August 1827. It was kept at Windsor for 26 months, grew another 18 in *45 cm* and died in October 1829.

Longest

The longest animal ever recorded is the "Boot-lace worm" (*Lineus longissimus*). In 1864 a specimen measuring more than 180 ft *54 m* was washed ashore at St. Andrews, Fifeshire, Scotland. It is arguable that the tentacular span of the giant jellyfish *Cyanaea arctica* is 245 ft *75 m*.

Rarest

The best claimants to the title of the world's rarest land animal are those species which are known only from a single (type) specimen. One of these is the tenrec *Dasogale fontoynonti*, which is known only from a specimen collected in eastern Madagascar (Malagasy) and now preserved in the Museum d'Histoire Naturelle, Paris.

Commonest

It has been estimated that man shares the earth with about 3,000,000,000,000,000,000,000,000,000,000,000 (3,000 quintillion or 3×10^{33}) other living things. Of these, more than 75 per cent are bacteria, namely 2,200 quintillion or 2.2×10^{33}.

Fastest

The fastest reliably measured speed of any animal is 106.25 m.p.h. *171 km/h* for the Spine-tailed swift (*Chaetura caudacuta*) reported from the U.S.S.R. in 1942. In 1934 ground speeds ranging from 171.8 to 219.5 m.p.h. *276,5–353,3 km/h* were recorded by stop-watch for spine-tailed swifts over a 2-mile *3 km* course in the Cachar Hills of north-eastern India, but scientific tests have since revealed that this species of bird cannot be seen at a distance of 1 mile *1,6 km*, even with a standard binocular. This bird is the fastest moving living creature and has a blood temperature of 112.5° F *44,7° C*. Speeds even higher than a "free fall" maximum of 185 m.p.h. *297 km/h* have been ascribed to the Peregrine falcon (*Falco peregrinus*) in a stoop, but in recent experiments in which miniature air speedometers were fitted, the maximum recorded diving speed was 82 m.p.h. *132 km/h*.

Longest lived

Few non-bacterial creatures live longer than humans. It would appear that tortoises are the longest lived such animals. The greatest authentic age recorded for a tortoise is 152-plus years for a male Marion's tortoise (*Testudo sumeirii*) brought from the Seychelles to Mauritius in 1766 by the Chevalier de Fresne, who presented it to the Port Louis army garrison. This specimen (it went blind in 1908) was accidentally killed in 1918. When the famous Royal Tongan tortoise "Tu'malilia" (believed to be a specimen of *Testudo radiata*) died on 19 May 1966 it was reputed to be over 200 years old, having been presented to the then King of Tonga by Captain James Cook (1728–79) on 22 Oct. 1773, but this record may well have been compiled from two (or more) overlapping residents.

The bacteria *Thermoactinomyces vulgaris* has been found alive in cores of mud taken from the bottom of Windermere, Cumbria, England which have been dated to 1,500 yrs before the present.

Heaviest brain

The Sperm whale (*Physeter catodon*) has the heaviest brain of any living animal. The brain of a 49 ft *14,93 m* bull processed in the Japanese factory ship *Nissin Maru No. 1* in the Antarctic on 11 Dec. 1949 weighed 9,2 kg *20.24 lb.* compared with 6,9 kg *15.38 lb.* for a 90 ft *27 m* Blue whale. The heaviest brain recorded for an elephant was an exceptional 16.5 lb. *7,5 kg* in the case of a 1.94 ton *1957 kg* Asiatic cow. The brain of the adult bull African elephant is normally 9¼–12 lb. *4,2–5,4 kg*.

Largest eye

The giant squid *Architeuthis sp.* has the largest eye of any living animal. The ocular diameter may exceed 38 cm *15 in* compared to 10–12 cm *3.93 to 4.71 in* for the largest Blue whales.

Largest egg

The largest egg of any living animal is that of the Whale shark (*Rhiniodon typus*). One egg case measuring 12 in by 5.5 in by 3.5 in *30 × 14 × 9 cm* was picked up by the shrimp trawler "Doris" on 29 June 1953 at a depth of 31 fathoms (186 ft *56,6 m*) in the Gulf of Mexico 130 miles *209 km* south of Port Isabel, Texas, U.S.A. The egg contained a perfect embryo of a Whale shark 13.78 in *35 cm* long.

Longest gestation

The viviparous Alpine black salamander (*Salamandra atra*) has a gestation period of up to 38 months at altitudes above 1 400 m *4,600 ft* in the Swiss Alps, but this drops to 24–26 months at lower altitudes.

Fastest and slowest growth

The fastest growth in the Animal Kingdom is that of the Blue whale calf (see p. 23). A barely visible ovum weighing a fraction of a milligramme (0.000035 of an oz.) grows to a weight of *c.* 26 tons *26 tonnes* in 22¾ months, made up of 10¾ months gestation and the first 12 months of life. This is equivalent to an increase of 30,000 million-fold. The slowest growth in the Animal Kingdom is that of the deep-sea clam *Tindaria callistiformis* of the North Atlantic, which takes an estimated 100 years to reach a length of 8 mm *0.31 in*.

Greatest size difference between sexes

The largest female deep-sea angler fish of the species *Ceratias holboelki* on record weighed half a million times as much as the smallest known parasitic male. It has been suggested that this fish would make an appropriate emblem for the Women's Lib. Movement.

Highest G Force

The highest g force encountered in nature is the 400 g endured by the 12 mm *0.47 in* long click beetle *Athous haemorrhoidalis* (a common British species) when jack-knifing into the air to a height of 30 cm *11¾ in* to escape predators. According to Dr. Glyn Evans of Manchester University the parts of the click beetle farthest from its central pivot travel at an even greater acceleration, the brain being subjected to a peak deceleration at the end of the movement of 2000 g.

Blood temperatures

The highest mammalian blood temperature is that of the Domestic goat (*Capra hircus*) with an average of 103.8° F *39,9° C*, and a normal range of from 101.7° to 105.3° F *38,7° to 40,7° C*. The lowest mammalian blood temperature is that of the Spiny anteater (*Tachyglossus aculeatus*), a monotreme found in Australia and New Guinea, with a normal range of 72° to 87° F *22,2° to 24,4° C*. The blood temperature of the Golden hamster (*Mesocricetus auratus*) sometimes falls as low

as 38.3° F *3,5° C* during hibernation, and an extreme figure of 29.6° F *1,4° C* has been reported for a myotis bat (family Vespertilionidae) during a deep sleep.

Most valuable furs

The highest-priced animal pelts are those of the Sea otter (*Enhydra lutris*), also known as the Kamchatka beaver, which fetched up to $2,700 (then £675) before their 55-year-long protection started in 1912. The protection ended in 1967, and at the first legal auction of sea otter pelts at Seattle, Washington, U.S.A. on 31 January 1968 Neiman-Marcus, the famous Dallas department store, paid $9,200 (then £3,832) for four pelts from Alaska. In May 1970 a Kojah (a mink–sable cross) coat costing $125,000 £52,083 was sold by Neiman-Marcus to Welsh actor Richard Burton for his wife, Elizabeth Taylor.

Heaviest ambergris

The heaviest piece of ambergris (a fatty deposit in the intestine of the Sperm whale) on record was a 1,003 lb. *455 kg* lump recovered from a Sperm whale (*Physeter catodon*) taken in Australian waters on 3 Dec. 1912 by a Norwegian whaling fleet. It was later sold in London for £23,000.

Most valuable

The most valuable animals in cash terms are thoroughbred racehorses. *What a Pleasure* (see Chapter XII, Horseracing) was sold in 1976 for $8,000,000 (*then £3,900,000*). The most valuable zoo exhibit is the Giant Panda (*Ailuropoda melanoleuca*) for which $250,000 (£104,160) was offered by the San Diego Zoological Gardens for a fertile pair in 1971. The most valuable marine exhibit is the Killer Whale (*Orcinus orca*). In September 1975 the 6,500 lb *2 948 kg* female "Newtka" was flown from Dallas, Texas, U.S.A. to Niagara Falls insured for £71,400.

1. MAMMALS (*Mammalia*)

Largest and heaviest *World*

For details of the Blue whale (*Balaenoptera musculus*) see page 23. Further information: the tongue and heart of a 27,6 m *90 ft 8 in* long female Blue whale taken by the Slava whaling fleet in the Antarctic on 17 March 1947 weighed 4.22 tons *4,29 tonnes* and 1,540 lb. *698,5 kg* respectively.

Largest and heaviest *British waters*

The largest Blue whale ever recorded in British waters was probably an 88 ft *26,8 m* specimen killed near the Bunaveneader station in Harris in the Western Isles, Scotland in 1904. In Sept. 1750 a Blue whale allegedly measuring 101 ft *30,75 m* in length ran aground in the River Humber estuary. Another specimen stranded on the west coast of Lewis, Western Isles, Scotland in *c.* 1870 was credited with a length of 105 ft *32 m* but the carcase was cut up by the local people before the length could be verified. In both cases the length was probably exaggerated or taken along the curve of the body instead of in a straight line from the tip of the snout to the notch in the flukes. Four Blue whales have been stranded on British coasts since 1913. The last occurrence (*c.* 60 ft *18 m*) was at Wick, Highland, Scotland on 15 Oct. 1923.

Blue whales inhabit the colder seas and migrate to warmer waters in the winter for breeding. Observations made in the Antarctic in 1947–48 showed that a Blue whale can maintain a speed of 20 knots (23 m.p.h. *37 km/h*) for ten minutes when frightened. It has been calculated that a 90 ft *27 m* Blue whale travelling at 20 knots *37 km/h* would develop 520 h.p. *527 c.v.* Newborn calves measure 6,5 to 8,6 m *21 ft 3½ in to 28 ft 6 in* in length and weigh up to 3,000 kg *2.95 tons*.

It has been estimated that there were between 17,500 and 19,000 Blue whales living throughout the oceans in 1977. The species has been protected *de jure* since 1967.

Non member countries of the International Whaling Commission, *e.g.* Chile and Peru, are not bound by this agreement.

Deepest dive

The greatest *recorded* depth to which a whale has dived is 620 fathoms (3,720 ft *1 134 m*) by a 47 ft *14,32 m* bull Sperm whale (*Physeter catodon*) found with its jaw entangled with a submarine cable running between Santa Elena, Ecuador and Chorillos, Peru, on 14 Oct. 1955. At this depth the whale withstood a pressure of 1,680 lb/in² *118 kg.f/cm²* of body surface. On 25 August 1969 a Sperm whale was killed 100 miles *160 km* south of Durban after it had surfaced from a dive lasting 1 hr 52 min, and inside its stomach were found two small sharks which had been swallowed about an hour earlier. These were later identified as *Scymnodon sp.*, a species found only on the sea floor. At this point from land the depth of water is in excess of 1,646 fathoms (10,476 ft *3 193 m*) for a radius of 30–40 miles *48–64 km*, which now suggests that the Sperm whale sometimes may descend to a depth of over 10,000 ft *3 000 m* when seeking food.

Largest on land *World*

The largest living land animal is the African bush elephant (*Loxodonta africana africana*). The average adult bull stands 10 ft 6 in *3,20 m* at the shoulder and weighs 5.6 tons *5,7 tonnes*. The largest specimen ever recorded was a bull shot 48 miles *77 km* north-west of Macusso, Angola on 13 Nov. 1955. Lying on its side this elephant measured 13 ft 2 in *4,01 m* in a projected line from the highest point of the shoulder to the base of the forefoot, indicating that its standing height must have been about 12 ft 6 in *3,8 m*. Other measurements included an over-all length of 33 ft 2 in *10,10 m* (tip of extended trunk to tip of extended tail) and a maximum bodily girth of 19 ft 8 in *5,99 m*. The weight was estimated at 24,000 lb. (10.7 tons *10,9 tonnes*). On 6 March 1959 the mounted specimen was put on display in the rotunda of the U.S. National Museum in Washington, D.C., U.S.A. (see also Shooting, Chapter 12).

Largest on land *Britain*

The largest wild mammal in the British Isles is the Red deer (*Cervus elephus*). A full-grown stag stands 3 ft 8 in *1,11 m* at the shoulder and weighs 230–250 lb. *104–113 kg*. The heaviest ever recorded was probably a stag killed on Islay, Strathclyde in 1940, which weighed 456 lb. *207 kg*. This was clean without the liver, which would have accounted for another 6–8 lb. *2,7–3,6 kg*. The heaviest park Red deer on record was a stag weighing 476 lb. *215,9 kg* (height at shoulder 4 ft 6 in *1,37 m*) killed at Woburn, Bedfordshire in 1836. The wild pony (*Equus caballus*) may weigh up to 700 lb. *320 kg* but now lives under semi-feral conditions.

Tallest

The tallest mammal is the Giraffe (*Giraffa camelopardalis*). For details see page 23.

Smallest *Land*

The smallest recorded land mammal is the rare Kitti's hog-nosed bat (*Craseonycteris thonglongyai*) or Bumblebee bat, which is restricted to two caves near the forestry station at Ban Sai Yoke on the Kwae Noi River, Kanchanaburi, Thailand. Mature specimens (both sexes) have a wing span of *c* 160 mm *6.29 in* and weigh 1.75–2 g *0.062–0.071 oz*. The smallest mammal found in the British Isles is the European pygmy shrew (*Sorex minutus*). Mature specimens have a head and body length of 43–64 mm *1.69–2.5 in*, a tail length of 31–46 mm *1.22–1.81 in* and weigh between 2,4 and 6,1 g *0.084 and 0.213 oz*.

Smallest *Marine*

The smallest totally marine mammal is probably Heaviside's dolphin (*Cephalorhynchus heavisidei*) of the South Atlantic. Adult specimens have an average length of 4 ft *1,22 m* and weigh up to 90 lb. *41 kg*. The sea otter (*Enhydra lutris*) weighing 25–38,5 kg *55–81.4 lb.* sometimes comes ashore during storms.

Rarest

The rarest placental mammal in the world is now the fully protected Javan rhinoceros (*Rhinoceros sondaicus*). In May 1973 there were only 44 in the Udjung-Kulon (also called Oedjoeng Kuelon) Reserve of 117 miles² *300 km²* at the tip of western Java, Indonesia, but there may also be a few left in

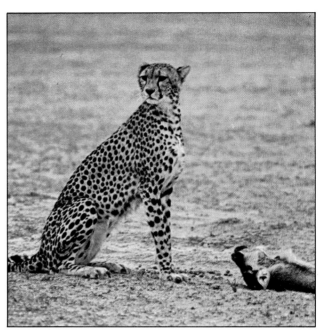

The Cheetah (*Acinonyx jubatus*), the fastest of all land animals over a short distance, seated alongside his prey, a Wildebeest calf. (*Aquila Photographics: W. S. Paton*)

the Tenasserim area on the Thai-Burmese border. Among sub-species, the Javan tiger (*Panthera tigris sondaica*) was probably reduced to 4 or 5 specimens by 1976. The Arabian oryx (*Oryx leucoryx*) has not been reported in the wild since 3 were killed and 4 captured in South Oman in 1972.

According to a report published jointly by the Nature Conservancy Council and the Society for the Promotion of Nature Conservancy in April 1977, the total British population of the Common otter (*Lutra lutra*) was now less than 300, compared to 14,000 before the Second World War. It thus appears to be rarer than the Pine marten (*Martes martes*).

Fastest *World*

The fastest of all land animals over a short distance (*i.e.* up to 600 yds *549 m*) is the Cheetah or Hunting Leopard (*Acinonyx jubatus*) of the open plains of East Africa, Iran, Turkmenia and Afghanistan, with a probable maximum speed of 60–63 m.p.h. *96–101 km/h* over suitably level ground. Speeds of 71, 84 and even 90 m.p.h. *114, 135 and 145 km/h* have been claimed for this animal, but these figures must be considered exaggerated. Tests in London in 1937 showed that on an oval greyhound track over 345 yds *316 m* a female cheetah's average speed over three runs was 43.4 m.p.h. *69,8 km/h* (*cf.* 43.26 m.p.h. *69,6 km/h* for the fastest racehorse), but this specimen was not running flat out. The fastest land animal over a sustained distance (*i.e.* 1,000 yds *914 m* or more) is the Pronghorn antelope (*Antilocapra americana*) of the western United States. Specimens have been observed to travel at 35 m.p.h. for 4 miles *56 km/h for 6 km*, at 42 m.p.h. for 1 mile *67 km/h for 1,6 km* and 55 m.p.h. for half a mile *88,5 km/h for 0,8 km*. On 14 Aug. 1936 at Spanish Lake, in Lake County, Oregon a hard-pressed buck was timed by a car speedometer at 61 m.p.h. *98 km/h* over 200 yds *183 m*.

Fastest *Britain*

The fastest British land mammal over a sustained distance is the Roe deer (*Capreolus capreolus*), which can cruise at 25–30 m.p.h. *40–48 km/h* for more than 20 miles *32 km*, with occasional bursts of up to 40 m.p.h. *64 km/h*. On 19 Oct. 1970 a frightened runaway Red deer (*Cervus elephus*) registered a speed of 42 m.p.h. *67,5 km/h* on a police radar trap as it charged through a street in Stalybridge, Greater Manchester.

Slowest

The slowest moving land mammal is the Ai or Three-toed sloth (*Bradypus tridactylus*) of tropical America. The usual ground speed is 6 to 8 ft *c. 2,10 m* a minute (0.068 to 0.098 m.p.h. *0,109–0,158 km/h*), but one mother sloth, speeded up by the calls of her infant, was observed to cover 14 ft *4 m* in one minute (0.155 m.p.h. *0,249 km/h*). In the trees this speed may be increased to 2 ft *0,61 m* a sec (1.36 m.p.h. *2,19 km/h*) (*cf*. these figures with the 0.03 m.p.h. *0,05 km/h* of the common garden snail and the 0.17 m.p.h. *0,27 km/h* of the giant tortoise).

Longest lived
No other mammal can match the extreme proven 113 years attained by Man (*Homo sapiens*) (see page 14). It is probable that the closest approach is among Blue and Fin whales (*Balaenoptera physalus*) the annual growth layers in the ear plugs of which indicate an age of 90–100 years. A bull Killer whale (*Orcinus orca*) with distinctive physical characteristics known as "Old Tom" was seen every winter from 1843 to 1930 in Twofold Bay, Eden, New South Wales, Australia.

The longest-living land mammal, excluding Man, is the Asiatic elephant (*Elephas maximus*). The greatest age that has been verified with certainty is 70 years in the case of a bull timber elephant 'Kyaw Thee' (Tusker 1342), who died in the Taunggyi Forest division, southern Shan States, Burma in 1965. The age of 78 years, attributed to '*Modoc*', the circus cow elephant, when she died at Lion Country Safari, Irvine, South California on 17 July 1975, is probably reliable.

Highest living
The highest living wild mammal in the world is probably the Yak (*Bos grunniens*), of Tibet and the Szechwanese Alps, China, which occasionally climbs to an altitude of 20,000 ft *6,100 m* when foraging. The Bharal (*Pseudois nayaur*) and the Pika or Mouse hare (*Ochotona thibetana*) may also reach this height in the Himalayas. In 1890 the tracks of an elephant were found at 15,000 ft *4 750 m* on Kilimanjaro, Tanzania.

Largest herds
The largest herds on record were those of the Springbok (*Antidorcas marsupialis*) during migration across the plains of the western parts of southern Africa in the 19th century. In 1849 John (later Sir John) Fraser observed a *trekbokken* that took three days to pass through the settlement of Beaufort West, Cape Province. Another herd seen moving near Nels Poortje, Cape Province in 1888 was estimated to contain 100,000,000 head. A herd estimated to be 15 miles *24 km* wide and more than 100 miles *160 km* long was reported from Karree Kloof, Orange River, South Africa in July 1896.

Longest and shortest gestation periods
The longest of all mammalian gestation periods is that of the Asiatic elephant (*Elephas maximus*), with an average of 609 days or just over 20 months and a maximum of 760 days—more than two and a half times that of a human. The gestation period of the American opossum (*Didelphis marsupialis*), also called the Virginian opossum, is normally 12 to 13 days but may be as short as eight days.

The gestation periods of the rare Water opossum or Yapok (*Chironectes minimus*) of Central and northern South America (average 12–13 days) and the Eastern native cat (*Dasyurus viverrinus*) of Australia (average 12 days) may also be as short as 8 days.

Largest litter
The greatest recorded number of young born to a *wild* mammal at a single birth is 32 (not all of which survived) in the case of the Common tenrec (*Centetes ecaudatus*) found in Madagascar and the Comoro Islands. The average litter size is 12–16. In March 1961 a litter of 32 was also reported for a House mouse (*Mus musculus*) at the Roswell Park Memorial Institute in Buffalo, N.Y., U.S.A. (average litter size 13–21) (see also Chapter 9 Agriculture, prolificacy records—pigs).

Youngest breeder
The Streaked tenrec (*Hemicentetes semispinosus*) of Madagascar is weaned after only 5 days, and females are capable of breeding 3–4 weeks after birth.

CARNIVORES
Largest Land *World*
The largest living terrestrial carnivore is the Kodiak bear (*Ursus arctos middendorffi*), which is found on Kodiak Island and the adjacent Afognak and Shuyak islands in the Gulf of Alaska, U.S.A. The average adult male has a nose to tail length of 8 ft *2,4 m* (tail about 4 in *10 cm*), stands 52 in *132 cm* at the shoulder and weighs between 1,050 and 1,175 lb. *476–533 kg*. In 1894 a weight of 1,656 lb. *751 kg* was recorded for a male shot at English Bay, Kodiak Island, whose *stretched* skin measured 13 ft 6 in *4,11 m* from the tip of the nose to the root of the tail. This weight was exceeded by a male in the Cheyenne Mountain Zoological Park, Colorado Springs, Colorado, U.S.A. which scaled 1,670 lb. *757 kg* at the time of its death on 22 Sept. 1955.

Weights in excess of 1,600 lb. *725 kg* have also been reported for the Polar bear (*Ursus maritimus*), but the average adult male weighs 850–900 lb. *386–408 kg* and measures 7¾ ft *2,4 m* nose to tail. In 1960 a polar bear allegedly weighing 2,210 lb. *1 002 kg* before skinning was shot at the polar entrance to Kotzebue Sound, north-west Alaska. In April 1962 the 11 ft 1½ in *3,39 m* tall over-mounted specimen was put on display at the Seattle World Fair, Washington, U.S.A.

Largest Land *Britain*
The largest land carnivore found in Britain is the badger (*Meles meles*). The average adult boar measures 3 ft *90 cm* including a 4 in *10 cm* tail and weighs 27 lb. *12,3 kg* in the early spring and 23 lb. *14,5 kg* at the end of the summer when it is in "grease". Weights up to 43 lb. *19,54 kg* have been reliably reported for boars and exceptionally may even exceed 50 lb. *22,72 kg*.

Largest Marine
The largest toothed mammal ever recorded is the Sperm whale (*Physeter catodon*), also called the cachalot. The average adult bull measures 47 ft *14,30 m* in length and weighs about 33 tons *33,5 tonnes*. The largest accurately measured specimen on record was a 67 ft 11 in *20,7 m* bull captured off the Kurile Islands, North-West Pacific, by a U.S.S.R. whaling fleet in the summer of 1950. Twelve cachalots have been stranded on British coasts since 1913. The largest, a bull measuring 61 ft 5 in *19 m* was washed ashore at Birchington, Kent on 18 Oct. 1914. Another bull estimated at 65 ft *19,8 m* but badly decomposed was stranded at Ferryloughan, Co. Galway, Ireland on 2 Jan. 1952.

Smallest
The smallest living carnivore is the Least weasel (*Mustela rixosa*), also called the Dwarf weasel, which is circumpolar in distribution. Four races are recognised, the smallest of which is *M.r.pygmaea* of Siberia. Mature specimens have an overall length of 177–207 mm *6.96–8.14 in* and weigh between 35 and 70 g *1¼ to 2½ oz*.

Largest feline
The largest member of the cat family (Felidae) is the long-furred Siberian tiger (*Pantheria tigris altaica*), also called the Amur or Manchurian tiger. Adult males average 10 ft 4 in *3,15 m* in length (nose to tip of extended tail), stand 39–42 in *99–107 cm* at the shoulder and weigh about 585 lb. *265 kg*. In November 1967 an outsize Indian tiger (*Panthera tigris tigris*) shot in northern Uttar Pradesh by David J. Hasinger of Philadelphia, U.S.A. weighed 857 lb. *388,7 kg* and measured 10 ft 7 in *3,22 m* between pegs or 11 ft 1 in *3,37 m* over the curves. It is now on display in the Smithsonian Institution, Washington, D.C.

The average adult African lion (*Pantheria leo*) measures 9 ft *2,7 m* overall, stands 36–38 in *91–97 cm* at the shoulder and weighs 400–410 lb. *181–185 kg*. The heaviest wild specimen on record was one weighing 690 lb. *313 kg* shot by Mr. Lennox Anderson just outside Hectorspruit in the eastern Transvaal, South Africa in 1936. In July 1970 a weight of 826 lb. *375 kg* was reported for a black-maned lion named "Simba" (b. Dublin Zoo, 1959) at Colchester Zoo, Essex. He died on 16 Jan. 1973 at Knaresborough Zoo, North Yorkshire, where his stuffed body is displayed.

Smallest feline

The smallest member of the cat family is the Rusty-spotted cat (*Felis rubiginosa*) of southern India and Ceylon. The average adult male has an overall length of 25–28 in *64–71 cm* (tail 9–10 in *23–25 cm*) and weighs about 3 lb. *1,350 kg.*

PINNIPEDS (Seals, Sea-lions and Walruses)

Largest *World*

The largest of the 32 known species of pinniped is the Southern elephant seal (*Mirounga leonina*), which inhabits the sub-Antarctic islands. Adult bulls average 16½ ft *5 m* in length (tip of inflated snout to the extremities of the outstretched tail flippers), 12 ft *3,7 m* in maximum bodily girth and weigh about 5,000 lb. (2.18 tons *2 268 kg*). The largest accurately measured specimen on record was a bull killed in Possession Bay, South Georgia on 28 February 1913 which measured 21 ft 4 in *6,50 m* after flensing (original length about 22½ ft *6,85 m*) and probably weighed at least 4 tons/*tonnes*. There are old records of bulls measuring 25–30 ft *7,62–9,14 m* and even 35 ft *10,66 m* but these figures must be considered exaggerated.

Largest *British*

The largest pinniped among British fauna is the Grey seal (*Halichoerus grypsus*), also called the Atlantic seal, which is found mainly on the western coasts of Britain. Adult bulls have been recorded up to 9 ft 6 in *2,90 m* in length and 700 lb. *318 kg* in weight.

Smallest

The smallest pinnipeds are the Baikal seal (*Pusa sibirica*) of Lake Baikal, U.S.S.R. and the Ringed Seal (*Pusa hispida*) of the Arctic. Adult specimens measure up to 5 ft 6 in *1,67 m* and weigh up to 280 lb. *127 kg.*

Rarest

The Caribbean or West Indian monk seal (*Monachus tropicalis*) has not been recorded since 1962 when a single specimen was sighted on the beach of Isla Mujeres off the Yucatan Peninsula, Mexico, and the species is now believed to be on the verge of extinction.

Fastest and deepest

The highest speed recorded for a pinniped is 25 m.p.h. *40 km/h* for a Californian sea lion (*Zalophys californianus*). The deepest diving pinniped is the Weddell seal (*Leptonychotes weddelli*), which is found along the Antarctic mainland and neighbouring islands. In March 1966 a large bull with a depth-gauge attached to it recorded a dive of 600 m *1,968 ft* in McMurdo Sound. At this depth the seal withstood a pressure of 875 lb./in² *6 033 k Pa* of body area.

Longest lived

A female Grey seal (*Halichoerus grypus*) shot at Shunni Wick in the Shetland Islands on 23 April 1969 was believed to be "at least 46 years old" based on a count of dental annuli.

BATS

Largest *World*

The only flying mammals are bats (order Chiroptera), of which there are about 1,000 living species. That with the greatest wing span is the Kalong (*Pteropus vampyrus*), a fruit bat found in Malaysia and Indonesia. It has a wing span of up to 170 cm *5 ft 7 in* and weighs up to 900 g *31.7 oz.*

Largest *Britain*

The largest bat found in Britain is the very rare Large mouse-eared bat (*Myotis myotis*). Mature specimens have a wing span of 355–450 mm *13.97–17.71 in* and weigh up to 45 g *1.58 oz.*

Smallest *World*

For details of Kitti's hog-nosed bat see p. 25.

Smallest *Britain*

The smallest native British bat is the Pipistrelle (*Pipistrellus pipistrellus*). Mature specimens have a wing span of 200–230 mm *7.87–9.05 in* and weigh between 5,5 and 7,5 g *0.19–0.26 oz.*

Rarest *Britain*

The rarest native British bat is Bechstein's bat (*Myotis bechsteini*), which is confined to a small area in southern England, with the New Forest as the main centre of population. There have been about a dozen records since 1900. In January 1965 fifteen specimens of the Grey long-eared bat (*Plecotus austriacus*) were discovered in the roof of the Nature Conservancy's Research Station at Furzebrook, Dorset. Up to then this species, which is found all over Europe, had only been recorded once in Britain (Hampshire, 1875).

Fastest

Because of the great practical difficulties few data on bat speeds have been published. The greatest speed attributed to a bat is 32 m.p.h. *51 km/h* in the case of a Free-tailed or Guano bat (*Tadarida mexicana*). This speed is closely matched by the Noctule bat (*Nyctalus noctula*) and the Long-winged bat (*Miniopterus schreibersi*), both of which have been timed at 31 m.p.h. *50 km/h.*

Longest lived

The greatest age reliably reported for a bat is "at least 24 years" for a female Little brown bat (*Myotis lucifugus*) found on 30 April 1960 in a cave on Mount Aeolis, East Dorset, Vermont, U.S.A. It had been banded at a summer colony in Mashpee, Massachusetts on 22 June 1937. There is an unconfirmed French report of a 26–27 year old Greater horseshoe bat (*Rhinolophus ferrumequinum*).

Highest detectable pitch

Because of their ultrasonic echolocation bats have most acute hearing of any terrestrial animal. Vampire bats (*Desmodontidae*) and fruit bats (*Pteropodidae*) can hear frequencies as high as 150 k Hz (*cf.* 20 k Hz for the adult human limit but 153 k Hz for the Bottle-nosed dolphin (*Tursiopis truncatus*)).

PRIMATES

Largest

The largest living primate is the Eastern lowland gorilla (*Gorilla gorilla grauei*) which inhabits the lowlands of the eastern part of Zaïre (formerly Democratic Republic of the Congo) and south-western Uganda. The average adult bull stands 5 ft 9 in *1,75 m* tall (including crest) and measures 58 to 60 in *147–152 cm* round the chest and weighs about 360 lb. *163 kg.* The greatest height (top of crest to heel) recorded for a gorilla is 6 ft 2 in *1,88 m* for a bull of the Mountain race (*Gorilla g. beringei*) shot in the eastern Congo in *c.* 1921.

The heaviest gorilla ever kept in captivity was an Eastern lowland bull named "Mbongo", who died in San Diego Zoological Gardens, California, U.S.A. on 15 March 1942. During an attempt to weigh him shortly before his death the platform scales "fluctuated from 645 pounds to nearly 670 (*293–304 kg*)". This specimen measured 5 ft 7½ in *1,71 m* in height and 69 in *175 cm* around the chest. The heaviest gorilla living in captivity today is the Western lowland (*Gorilla g. gorilla*) bull "Sampson" (b. 1949) of Milwaukee County Zoological Park, Wisconsin, U.S.A. He has weighed as much as 658 lb. *299 kg* but now fluctuates between 585 and 605 lb. *266–275 kg.*

Smallest

The smallest known primate is the rare Feather-tailed tree shrew (*Ptiolcercus lowii*) of Malaysia, Adult specimens have a total length of 230–330 mm *9–13 in* (head and body 100–140 mm *3.93–5.51 in.*, tail 130–190 mm *5.1–7.5 in*) and weigh 35–50 g *1.23–1.76 oz.* The mouse lemur (*Microcebus murinus*) of Madagascar is approximately the same length (274–300 mm *10.8–11.8 in*) but heavier, adults weighing 45–80 grammes, *1.58–2.82 oz.*

Rarest

The rarest primate is the Hairy-eared mouse lemur (*Cheirogaleus trichotis*) of Madagascar which, until fairly recently, was known only from the type specimen and two skins. In 1966, however, a live example was found on the east coast near Mananara.

The orangutans Guas (right) and Guarina, the oldest ever non-human primates. (*Courtesy: Zoological Society of Philadelphia*)

Longest lived

The greatest irrefutable age reported for a primate (excluding humans) is 57 years in the case of the orangutan Guas received by the Philadelphia Zoo, U.S.A. on 1 May 1931 aged at least 10 and died on 9 Feb. 1977.

Strength

In 1924 "Boma", a 165 lb. *74,80 kg* male chimpanzee at Bronx Zoo, New York, N.Y., U.S.A. recorded a right-handed pull (feet braced) of 847 lb. *384 kg* on a dynamometer (*cf.* 210 lb. *95 kg* for a man of the same weight). On another occasion an adult female chimpanzee named "Suzette" (estimated weight 135 lb. *61 kg*) at the same zoo registered a right-handed pull of 1,260 lb. *572 kg* while in a rage. A record from the U.S.A. of a 100 lb. *45 kg* chimpanzee achieving a two-handed dead lift of 600 lb. *272 kg* with ease suggests that a male gorilla could with training raise 1,800 lb. *816 kg !*

MONKEYS

Largest

The only species of monkey reliably credited with a weight of more than 100 lb. *45 kg* is the Mandrill (*Mandrillus sphinx*) of equatorial West Africa. The greatest reliable weight recorded is 119 lb. *54 kg* but an unconfirmed weight of 130 lb. *59 kg* has been reported.

Smallest

The smallest known monkey is the Pygmy marmoset (*Cebuella pygmaea*) of Ecuador, northern Peru and western Brazil. Mature specimens have a maximum total length of 304 mm *12 in* half of which is tail, and weigh from 49 to 80 g *1.7 to 2.81 oz.* which means it rivals the mouse lemur for the title of the smallest living primate (see page 31).

Longest lived

The greatest reliable age reported for a monkey is 47 years for a male White-faced capuchin (*Cebus capucinus*) named "Jerry", who died at Mesker Park Zoo, Evansville, Indiana, U.S.A. on 12 April 1976. He was received in May 1929 at an estimated age of one year.

The oldest ever monkey, Jerry, a White-faced capuchin, who attained the age of 47 years.

RODENTS

Largest

The world's largest rodent is the Capybara (*Hydrochoerus hydrochaeris*), also called the Carpincho or Water Hog, which is found in tropical South America. Mature specimens have a head and body length of 3¼ to 4½ ft *0,99–1,4 m* and weigh up to 174 lb *79 kg*. Britain's largest rodent is now the Coypu (*Myocastor coypus*), also known as the Nutria, which was introduced from Argentina by East Anglian fur-breeders in 1927. In 1937 four escaped from a nutria-farm near Ipswich, Suffolk. Adult males measure 30–36 in *76–91 cm* in length (including short tail) and weigh up to 28 lb. *13 kg* in the wild state (40 lb. *18 kg* in captivity).

Smallest

The smallest rodent is probably the Old World harvest mouse (*Micromys minutus*), of which the British form measures up to 135 mm *5.3 in* in total length and weighs between 4,2 and 10,2 g *0.15 to 0.36 of an oz*. In June 1965 it was announced that an even smaller rodent had been discovered in the Asian part of the U.S.S.R. (probably a more diminutive form of *M. minutus*), but further information is lacking.

Rarest

The rarest rodent in the world is believed to be the James Island rice rat (*Oryzomys swarthi*), also called Swarth's rice rat. Four specimens were collected on this island in the Galapagos group in 1906, and it was not heard of again until January 1966 when the skull of a recently dead animal was found.

Longest lived

The greatest reliable age reported for a rodent is 22 years 10 months for a female Bushtailed porcupine (*Atherurus africanus*), which died in Philadelphia Zoological Garden, Pennsylvania, U.S.A. on 6 May 1933. It was received as a young adult on 5 July 1910.

Fastest Breeder

The female Meadow vole (*Microtus agrestis*) found in Britain, can reproduce from the age of 25 days and have up to 17 litters of 6 to 8 young in a year.

INSECTIVORES

Largest

The largest insectivore is the Moon rat (*Echinosorex gymnurus*), also known as Raffles' gymnure, which is found in Burma, Thailand, Malaysia, Sumatra and Borneo. Mature specimens have a head and body length of 265–445 mm *10.43–17.52 in*, a tail measuring 200–210 mm *7.87–8.26 in* and weigh up to 1 400 g *3.08 lb*. Although Anteaters (family Myrmecophagidae) feed on termites and other soft-bodied insects they are not insectivores, but belong to the order Edentata, which means "without teeth".

Smallest

The smallest insectivore is Savi's white-toothed pygmy shrew (*Suncus etruscus*), also called the Etruscan shrew, which is found along the coast of the northern Mediterranean and southwards to Cape Province, South Africa. Mature specimens have a head and body length of 36–52 mm *1.32–2.04 in*, a tail length of 24–29 mm *0.94–1.14 in* and weigh between 1,5 and 2,5 g *0.052 and 0.09 oz*.

Longest lived

The greatest reliable age recorded for an insectivore is 10½ years for a Hedgehog tenrec (*Setifer setosus*), which died in London Zoo in 1971. There is an unconfirmed record of a Hedgehog (*Erinaceus europaeus*) living for 14 years.

ANTELOPES

Largest

The largest of all antelopes is the rare Derby eland (*Taurotragus derbianus*), also called the Giant eland, of West and north-central Africa, which may surpass 2,000 lb. *907 kg*. The Common eland (*T. oryx*) of East and South Africa has the same shoulder height of up to 5 ft 10 in *1,78 m* but is not quite so massive, although there is one record of a 5 ft 5 in *1,65 m* bull shot in Nyasaland (now Malawi) in *c.* 1937 which weighed 2,078 lb. *943 kg*.

Smallest

The smallest known antelope is the Royal antelope (*Neotragus pygmaeus*) of West Africa. Mature specimens measure 10–12 in *25–31 cm* at the shoulder and weigh only 7–8 lb. *3–3,6 kg* which is the size of a large Brown hare (*Lepus europaeus*). The slender Swayne's dik-dik (*Madoqua swaynei*) of Somalia, East Africa weighs only 5–6 lb. *2–2,7 kg* when adult, but this species stands about 13 in *33 cm* at the shoulder.

Rarest

The rarest antelope is probably Jentink's duiker (*Cephalophus jentinki*), also known as the Black-headed duiker, which is found only in a restricted area of tropical West Africa. The only example in captivity is "Alpha" a doe born on 1 Dec. 1971, in the Gladys Porter Zoo, Brownsville, Texas, U.S.A.

DEER

Largest

The largest deer is the Alaskan moose (*Alces alces gigas*). A bull standing 7 ft 8 in *2,3 m* at the withers and weighing an estimated 1,800 lb. *816 kg* was shot on the Yukon River in the Yukon Territory, Canada in Sept. 1897. Unconfirmed measurements up to 8½ ft *2,59 m* at the withers and estimated weights up to 2,600 lb. *1 180 kg* have been claimed. The record antler span is 78½ in *199 cm*.

Smallest

The smallest true deer (family Cervidae) is the Pudu (*Pudu mephistophiles*) of Ecuador the male of which stands 13–15 in *33–38 cm* at the shoulder and weighs 18–20 lb. *8–9 kg*. The smallest known ruminant is the Lesser Malayan chevrotain or Mouse deer (*Tragulus javanicus*) of south-eastern Asia. Adult specimens measure 8–10 in *20–25 cm* at the shoulder and weigh 6–7 lb. *2,7–3,2 kg*.

Rarest

The rarest deer in the world is Fea's muntjac (*Muntiacus feae*), which is known only from two specimens collected on the borders of Tennasserim, Lower Burma and Thailand.

Oldest

The greatest reliable age recorded for a deer is 26 years 6 months 2 days for a Red deer (*Cervus elephus*) which died in the National Zoological Park, Washington, D.C., U.S.A. on 24 March 1941.

MARSUPIALS

Largest

The largest of all marsupials is the Red kangaroo (*Macropus rufus*) of southern and eastern Australia. Adult males or "boomers" stand 6–7 ft *1,83–2,13 m* tall, weigh 150–175 lb. *68–79 kg* and measure up to 8 ft 11 in *2,71 m* in a straight line from the nose to the tip of the extended tail. The Great grey kangaroo (*Macropus giganteus*) of eastern Australia and Tasmania is almost equally as large, and there is an authentic record of a boomer measuring 8 ft 8 in *2,64 m* from nose to tail (9 ft 7 in *2,92 m* along the curve of the body) and weighing 200 lb. *90,7 kg*. The skin of this specimen is preserved in the Australian Museum, Sydney, New South Wales.

Smallest

The smallest known marsupial is the rare Kimberley planigale or flat-skulled marsupial mouse (*Planigale subtilissima*), which is found only in the Kimberley district of Western Australia. Adult males have a head and body length of 44,5 mm *1.75 in*, a tail length of 51 mm *2 in* and weigh about 4 g *0.141 oz*. Females are smaller than males.

Rarest

The rarest marsupial is probably the Thylacine (*Thylacinus cynocephalus*), also known as the "Tasmanian tiger" or the "Tasmanian wolf", the largest of the carnivorous marsupials, which—if not already extinct—is now confined to the remoter parts of south-western Tasmania. The last Thylacine held in captivity died in Hobart Zoo, Tasmania in 1934.

Longest Lived

The greatest reliable age recorded for a marsupial is 19 years 7 months for a South Australian wallaroo (*Macropus robustus*

A portrait of the Top Show Dog of all time—Chik T'Sun. (See page 32)

erubescens), which died in New York Zoological Park (Bronx Zoo) in 1968.

Highest and longest jumps

The greatest measured height cleared by a hunted kangaroo is 10 ft 6 in *3,20 m* over a pile of timber. During the course of a chase in January 1951 a female Red kangaroo (*Macropus rufus*) made a series of bounds which included one of 42 ft *12,80 m*. There is also an unconfirmed report of a Great grey kangaroo (*M. canguru*) jumping nearly 13,5 m *44 ft 8½ in* on the flat.

TUSKS

Longest

The longest recorded elephant tusks (excluding prehistoric examples) are a pair from the eastern Congo (Zaire) preserved in the National Collection of Heads and Horns kept by the New York Zoological Society in Bronx Park, New York City, N.Y., U.S.A. The right tusk measures 11 ft 5½ in *3,49 m* along the outside curve and the left 11 ft *3,35 m*. Their combined weight is 293 lb. *133 kg*. A single tusk of 11 ft 6 in *3,50 m* has been reported, but further details are lacking.

Heaviest

The greatest weight ever recorded for an elephant tusk is 117 kg. *258 lb.* for a specimen collected in Benin (formerly Dahomey), West Africa and exhibited at the Paris Exposition in 1900.

HORNS

Longest

The longest recorded animal horn was one measuring 81¼ in *206 cm* on the outside curve, with a circumference of 18¼ in *46 cm*, found on a specimen of domestic Ankole cattle (*Bos taurus*) near Lake Ngami, Botswana (formerly Bechuanaland). The largest head (horns measured from tip to tip across the forehead) is one of 13 ft 11 in *4,24 m* for a specimen of wild buffalo (*Bubalus bubalus*) shot in India in 1955. The maximum recorded for a Texas Longhorn steer is 9 ft 9 in *2,97 m* from tip to tip.

Longest *Rhinoceros*

The longest recorded anterior horn for a rhinoceros is one of 62¼ in *158 cm* found on a female southern race White rhinoceros (*Ceratotheriam simum simum*) shot in South Africa in *c.* 1848. The interior horn measured 22¼ in *57 cm*. There is also an unconfirmed record of an anterior horn measuring 81 in *206 cm*.

HORSES AND PONIES

The worlds' horse population is estimated to be 75,000,000.

Largest

The heaviest horse ever recorded was a 19.2-hand (6 ft 6 in *1,98 m*) pure-bred Belgian stallion named "Brooklyn Supreme" (foaled 12 April 1928) owned by Ralph Fogleman of Callender, Iowa, U.S.A. which weighed 3,200 lb. 1.42 tons *1,44 tonnes* shortly before his death on 6 Sept. 1948 aged 20. In April 1973 the Belgian mare "Wilma du Bos" (foaled 15 July 1966), owned by Mrs. Virgie Arden of Reno, Nevada, U.S.A. was reported to weigh slightly in excess of 3,200 lb. *1 451 kg.* when in foal and being shipped from Antwerp. The normal weight of this 18.2 hand *1,88 m* mare is about 2,400 lb *1 088 kg*. The heaviest horse ever recorded in Britain was probably the 17.2 hand (5 ft 10 in *1,78 m*) Shire stallion "Honest Tom" foaled in Littleport, Cambridgeshire in 1884, who weighed 2,912 lb. *1 325 kg* in *c.* 1890.

Tallest

The tallest horse documented was the Percheron-Shire cross "Firpon" (foaled 1959), owned by Julio Falabella which stood 21.1 hands (7 ft 1 in *2,16 m*) and weighed 2.976 lb. *1 350 kg*. He died on the Recco de Roca Ranch near Buenos Aires,

Little Pumpkin, a 3½ hand *35,5 cm* Falabella foal from the Mini-Horse Farm, Inman, South Carolina, U.S.A.

Argentina on 14 Mar. 1972. A height of 21.1 hands was also claimed for the Clydesdale gelding "Big Jim" (foaled 1950) bred by Lyall M. Anderson of West Broomley, Montrose, Scotland. He died in St. Louis, Missouri in 1957. A claim for 21.2 hands (7 ft 2 in *2,18 m*) was made in 1908 for a horse named "Morocco" weighing 2,835 lb. *1 286 kg* in Allentown, Pennsylvania, U.S.A. The tallest living horse bred in Britain today is the Shire stallion "Ladbrook Invader" (foaled 17 Apr. 1968), owned by Mr. Arthur Lewis of Tamworth, Staffordshire. He stands 19.1½ hands (6 ft 5½ in *1,97 m*) and weighs about 22 cwt. (2,464 lb. *1 120 kg*). He was shipped to the U.S.A. in 1976. "Wandle Henry Cooper" (foaled 1965) owned by Young & Co Brewery Ltd, Wandsworth, Greater London, stands 18.2½ hands (6 ft 2½ in *1,89 m*) and weighs c. 20 cwt *1 018 kg*.

Smallest

The smallest breed of horse (sic) is the Falabella of Argentina which was developed over a period of 45 years by crossing and recrossing a small group of undersized English Thoroughbreds with Shetland ponies. Adult specimens stand 15–30 in *38–74 cm* at the shoulder and weigh 40–80 lb. *18–36 kg*. The smallest breed of pony is the Shetland pony, which usually measures 8–10 hands (32–40 in *81–102 cm*) and weighs 275–385 lb. *125–175 kg*.

Oldest

The greatest reliable age recorded for a horse is 62 years in the case of "Old Billy" (foaled 1760), believed to be a cross between a Cleveland and Eastern blood, who was bred by Mr. Edward Robinson of Wild Grave Farm in Woolston, Lancashire. In 1762 or 1763 he was sold to the Mersey and Irwell Navigation Company and remained with them in a working capacity (i.e. marshalling and towing barges) until 1819 when he was retired to a farm at Latchford, near Warrington, where he died on 27 November, 1822. The skull of this horse is preserved in the Manchester Museum, and his

stuffed head is now on display in the Bedford Museum. The greatest reliable age recorded for a pony is 54 years for a stallion owned by a farmer in Central France which was still alive in 1919.

Strongest *draught*

The greatest load hauled by a pair of Clydesdale draught horses (combined weight 3,500 lb. *1 587 kg*) was 50 pine logs comprising 36,055 board-feet of timber (128½ tons *131 tonnes*) on a sledge litter 275 yds *251 m* across snow at the Nester Estate, Ewen, Ontanagon County, Michigan, U.S.A. on 26 Feb. 1893.

DOGS

Largest

The heaviest breed of domestic dog (*Canis familiaris*) is the St. Bernard. The heaviest recorded example was "Schwarzwald Hof Duke", owned by Dr. A. M. Bruner of Oconomowoc, Wisconsin, U.S.A. He was whelped on 8 Oct. 1964 and weighed 21 st. 1 lb. *133,8 kg* on 2 May 1969, dying three months later aged 4 years 10 months. The largest St. Bernard ever weighed in Britain was "Burton Black Magician", also called "Shane" (1969–1976), owned by Mrs. Sheila Bangs of Animal Mayday of Mitcham, Surrey. In Oct. 1973 he scaled a peak 19 st. 0 lb. 4¾ oz. *120,79 kg*.

Tallest

The tallest breeds of dog are the Irish wolfhound and the Great Dane, both of which can exceed 39 in *99 cm* at the shoulder. In the case of the Irish wolfhound the extreme recorded example was "Broadbridge Michael" (whelped in 1920), owned by Mrs. Mary Beynon of Sutton-at-Hone, Kent. He stood 39½ in *100,3 cm* at the age of two years. The Great Dane "Brynbank Apollo", also called "Dominic" (whelped in 1970), owned by Mrs. Iris Bates of Harlow, Essex, measures 39¼ in *99,7 cm*.

Smallest

The world's smallest fully grown dog is a Chihuahua of 10 oz. *283 g* owned by Rodney M. Sprott of Clemson, South Carolina, U.S.A. The same weight was reported in April 1971 for an adult bitch Yorkshire Terrier (Britain's smallest breed) "Sylvia", owned by Mrs. Connie Hutchins of Walthamstow, Greater London.

Oldest

Authentic records of dogs living over 20 years are extremely rare, but even 34 years has been accepted by one authority. The greatest reliable age recorded for a dog is 29 years 5 months for a Queensland "heeler" named "Bluey", owned by Mr. Les Hall of Rochester, Victoria, Australia. The dog was obtained as a puppy in 1910 and worked among cattle and sheep for nearly 20 years. He was put to sleep on 14 November 1939. The British record is 27 years 10 months for a Welsh sheepdog cross called "Toots", who was whelped in January 1948 and died on 4 November 1975 in the care of her life-time owner Barry Tuckey at Glebe Farm, Stockton, Warwickshire.

Strongest

The greatest load ever shifted by a dog was 6,000 lb. *2 721 kg* of lead ingots pulled by a 177½ lb. *81 kg* St. Bernard named "Worldtop's Kashwitna V Thor" at Bothell, Washington, U.S.A. on 9 August 1974. The dog, owned by Francis and Arloa B. Good of Palmer, Alaska, pulled the weight on a four-wheeled carrier across a cement surface for a distance of 15 ft *4,57 m* in less than 20 seconds. The record time for the annual 1,049 mile *1 680 km* dog sled race from Anchorage to Nome, Alaska is 14 days 14 hrs 43 min by "Emitt Peters" in the 1975 race.

Rarest

The rarest breed of dog is the *Shar-pei* or Chinese Fighting Dog, which, due to restriction on trading and ownership, is extinct in China. Only 60 specimens were known to exist in May 1977, all of them in North America. The rarest breed recognised by the Kennel Club is the Portuguese Water dog (*Caes de Agua*). There were no more than 145 known to be living anywhere in March 1977.

Fastest

The fastest breed of dog (excluding the greyhound or possibly the whippet) is the Saluki, also called the Arabian gazelle hound or Persian greyhound. Speeds up to 43 m.p.h. *69 km/h* have been claimed, but tests in the Netherlands have shown that it is not as fast as the present-day greyhound which has attained a measured speed of 41.7 m.p.h. *67,1 km/h* on a track.

Largest litter

The largest recorded litter of puppies is one of 23 thrown on 19 June 1944 by "Lena", a foxhound bitch owned by Commander W. N. Ely of Ambler, Pennsylvania, U.S.A. On 6–7th February 1975 "Careless Ann", a St. Bernard bitch, owned by Robert and Alice Rodden of Lebanon, Missouri, U.S.A. also produced a litter of 23, 14 of which survived. The British record is held by "Settrina Baroness Medina", a Red Setter bitch owned by Mgr. M. J. Buckley, Director of the Wood Hall Centre, Wetherby, West Yorkshire, who gave birth to 22 puppies, 15 of which survived, on 10 January 1974. All 17 puppies born in Feb. 1977 to "Trudi", an Irish setter owned by Mr. Alan Jenkins of Wolverhampton, survived.

Most prolific

The greatest sire of all time was the champion greyhound "Low Pressure", nicknamed "Timmy", whelped in September 1957 and owned by Mrs. Bruna Amhurst of Regent's Park, London. From December 1961 until his death on 27 November 1969 he fathered 2,414 registered puppies, with at least 600 others unregistered.

Most expensive

In January 1977 a "contract" worth $10,000 £5,880 was put out on the life of a very successful drug-sniffing police dog named "Sergeant Blitz" by the underworld in Savannah, Georgia, U.S.A. Shortly afterwards an 8 ft *2,43 m* high concrete wall was built round the dog's kennel as a precautionary measure.

"Top dog"

The greatest altitude attained by a mammal is 1,050 miles *1 690 km* by the Samoyed husky bitch fired as a passenger in Sputnik II on 3 Nov. 1957. The dog was variously named "Kudryavka" (feminine form of "Curly"). "Limonchik" (dimunitive of lemon), "Malyshka", "Zhuchka" or by the Russian breed name for husky, "Laika".

Most Pampered

A leading New York dog delicatessen catering for the topmost of the city's 470,000 dogs provide private dining rooms for pets riding up in chauffeured limousines. The menu includes Maryland lump crab-meat at $3.50 per 4 oz. *113 g* and shrimps at 65 cents a pair. One "client" with 75 coats has a red satin-lined pearl encrusted cloak and rhinestone-trimmed sunglasses. The Alsatian "Viking Baron von Heppeplatz" was left property worth £130,000 in the will of his master Herr Georg Ritt who died in Munich, West Germany in August 1971.

Highest and longest jump

The canine "high jump" record is held by an Alsatian named "Crumstone Danko" owned by the De Beers mining company, who scaled an 11 ft 3 in *3,43 m* high wall without a springboard in Pretoria, South Africa in May 1942. He was also credited with 16½ ft *5,03 m* off a springboard. The British record is 10 ft 6 in *3,20 m* by the Lancashire Police dog "Lancon Sultan VI", handled by P.C. John Evans at Hutton, near Preston, Lancashire on 8 Aug. 1973. The longest recorded canine long jump was one of 30 ft *9,14 m* by a greyhound named "Bang" made in jumping a gate in coursing a hare at Brecon Lodge, Gloucestershire in 1849.

Greatest escape

On 19 April 1975 a four-year-old mongrel named "Sue" owned by Mrs. Gloria Spaul of Deal, Kent, fell 300 ft *91 m* from the cliffs at Leathercote Point near St. Margaret's Bay—and escaped with two bloodshot eyes! The dog has suffered no ill-effects since the accident.

Ratting

The greatest ratter of all time was Mr. James Searle's bull terrier bitch "Jenny Lind", who killed 500 rats in 1 hr 30 min at "The Beehive", Old Crosshall Street, Liverpool on 12 July 1853. Another bull terrier named "Jacko", owned by Mr. Jemmy Shaw, was credited with killing 1,000 rats in 1 hr 40 min, but the feat was performed over a period of ten weeks in batches of 100 at a time. The last 100 were accounted for in 5 min 28 sec in London on 1 May 1862.

Tracking

The greatest tracking feat on record was performed by a Doberman Pinscher named "Sauer", trained by Detective-Sergeant Herbert Kruger. In 1925 he tracked a stock-thief 100 miles *160 km* across the Great Karroo, South Africa by scent alone. In 1923 a collie dog named "Bobbie", lost by his owners while they were on holiday in Wolcott, Indiana, U.S.A., turned up at the family home in Silverton, Oregon six months later, after covering a distance of some 2,000 miles *3 200 km*. The dog, later identified by householders who had looked after him along the route, had apparently travelled back through the states of Illinois, Iowa, Nebraska and Colorado, before crossing the Rocky Mountains in the depths of winter and then continuing through Wyoming and Idaho.

Top Show Dog

The record number of "Best in Show" awards won by any dog in all breed shows is 127 compiled by International Champion Chik T'Sun of Caversham, owned by Mr. & Mrs. Charles C. Venable of Marietta, Georgia, in North America from January 1957 to February 1960.

Top Trainer

The most successful dog trainer in the world—and the fastest—is Mrs. Barbara Woodhouse of Rickmansworth, Hertfordshire who has trained 16,323 dogs to a high standard from

1951 to 1 Apr. 1977. Her record for a single day is 80 dogs (Denver, Colorado, U.S.A., June 1973).

Police Dogs
The world's top police dog is "Trep" of Miami, Florida U.S.A. with $63 million (*then £36 million*) worth of narcotics sniffed out. Demonstrating at a school with 10 hidden packets, Trep once found 11.

Greatest Dog Funeral
The greatest dog funeral on record was for the mongrel dog "Lazaras" belonging to the eccentric Emperor Norton I of the United States, Protector of Mexico, held in San Francisco, California in 1862 which was attended by an estimated 10,000 people.

CATS
Heaviest
The heaviest domestic cat (*Felis catus*) on record was a ginger and white tom named "Spice", owned by Mrs. Loren C. Caddell of Ridgefield, Connecticut, U.S.A. who scaled 43 lb. *19,54 kg* on 26 June 1974. He reduced to 35 lb. *15,9 kg* but died on 17 Jan. 1977. The British record is held by a Mrs. Phyllis Dacey of Billericay, Essex, whose 7 year old tabby "Tiger" weighed 42½ lb. *19,27 kg* in April 1977. The average weight for an adult cat is 11 lb. *5 kg.*

Oldest
Cats are generally longer-lived than dogs. Information on this subject is often obscured by two or more cats bearing the same nickname in succession. The oldest cat ever recorded was probably the tabby "Puss", owned by Mrs. T. Holway of Clayhidon, Devon who celebrated his 36th birthday on 28 November 1939 and died the next day. A more recent and better-documented case was that of the female tabby "Ma", owned by Mrs. Alice St. George Moore of Drewsteignton, Devon. She was put to sleep on 5 Nov. 1957 aged 34. In January 1972 an unconfirmed age of 32 years was reported for a female cat named "Snow" owned by Mrs. Bridget Whidett of Islington, Greater London.

Rarest breed
The rarest of the 72 recognised breeds of cat in Britain is the Red self Persian or Long-haired red self.

Largest kindle
The largest live litter ever recorded was one of 14 kittens born in December 1974 to the Persian cat "Bluebell", owned by Mrs. Elenore Dawson of Wellington, South Africa. On 14 Apr. 1976 a black cat named "Clementine", owned by Marc and Natalie Albanese of East Aurora, New York, U.S.A. gave birth to a litter of 15 kittens, 11 of which survived. In July 1970 a litter of 19 kittens (four incompletely formed) was reportedly born by Caesarean section to "Tarawood Antigone", a brown Burmese owned by Mrs. Valerie Gane of Church Westcote, Kingham, Oxfordshire, but this claim has never been fully substantiated.

Most prolific
A cat named "Dusty", aged 17, living in Bonham, Texas, U.S.A., gave birth to her 420th kitten on 12 June 1952. A 21-year-old cat "Tippy" living in Kingston-upon-Hull, Humberside gave birth to her 343rd kitten in June 1933.

Richest and most valuable
Dr. William Grier of San Diego, California, U.S.A. died in June 1963 leaving his entire estate of $415,000 (then £148,000) to his two 15-year-old cats "Hellcat" and "Brownie". When the cats died in 1965 the money went to the George Washington University in Washington, D.C. In 1967 Miss Elspeth Sellar of Grafham, Surrey turned down an offer of 2,000 guineas (£2,100) from an American breeder for her champion copper-eyed white Persian tom "Coylum Marcus" (b. 28 March 1965).

Ratting and mousing
The greatest ratter on record was probably the female tabby named "Minnie" who during the six year period 1927 to 1933 killed 12,480 rats at the White City Stadium, London. The greatest mouser on record was a tabby named "Mickey", owned by Shepherd & Sons Ltd. of Burscough, Lancashire who killed more than 2,000 mice during 23 years with the firm. He died in November 1968.

Cat population
The largest cat population is that of the U.S.A. with 23,000,000. Of Britain's cat population of 4,200,000, an estimated 100,000 are "employed" by the Civil Service.

GUINEA PIGS
Oldest
The greatest recorded age for a domestic guinea pig (*Cavia porcellus*) is 10 years attained in June 1975 by a pet owned by Mr. R. Lockyer of Crayford, Kent, England. This is triple the average life-span.

RABBITS
Largest
The largest breed of domestic rabbit (*Oryctolagus cuniculus*) is the Flemish giant, which has an average toe to toe length of 36 in *91 cm* when fully extended and weighs 12–14 lb. *5,4–6,3 kg.* The heaviest recorded specimen was a male named "Floppy" who weighed 25 lb. *11,3 kg* shortly before his death in June 1963 aged eight .In May 1971 a weight of 25 lb. *11,3 kg* was also reported for a four-year-old Norfolk Star named "Chewer", owned by Mr. Edward Williams of Attleborough, Norfolk. The heaviest recorded wild rabbit is one of 6 lb. 12 oz. *3,06 kg* shot by Mr. Monty Forest in the Swinford Estate, Burford, Oxfordshire in February 1976.

Oldest
The greatest reliable age recorded for a domestic rabbit is 18 years for a doe which was still alive in 1947. A buck rabbit named "Blackie" owned by Mrs. H. H. Chivers of Brixham, Devon died on 13 March 1971 aged 16 years 3 months.

Most prolific
The most prolific domestic breed is the Norfolk Star. Females produce 9 to 10 litters a year, each containing about 10 young (*cf.* five litters and three to seven young for the wild rabbit). "Chewer" (see above) fathered over 40,000 offspring in the period 1968–73 before being retired from stud.

HARES
Largest
In November 1956 a Brown hare (*Lepus europaeus*) weighing 15 lb. 1 oz. *6,83 kg* was shot near Welford, Northamptonshire.

---

2. BIRDS (*Aves*)

Largest *Ratite*
The largest living bird is the North African ostrich (*Struthio camelus camelus*), which is found in reduced numbers south of the Atlas Mountains from Upper Senegal and Niger across to the Sudan and central Ethiopia. Male examples of this flightless or ratite sub-species have been recorded up to 9 ft *2,74 m* in height and 345 lb. *156,5 kg* in weight.

Largest *Carinate*
The heaviest flying bird or carinate is the Kori bustard or Paauw (*Otis kori*) of East and South Africa. Weights up to 40 lb. *18 kg* have been reliably reported for cock birds shot in South Africa. The Mute swan (*Cygnus olor*), which is resident in Britain, can also reach 40 lb. *18 kg* on occasion, and there is a record from Poland of a cob weighing 22,5 kg *49.5 lb.* which was probably too heavy to fly. The heaviest bird of prey is the Andean condor (*Vultur gryphus*), adult males averaging 20–25 lb. *9,09–11,30 kg.* An unconfirmed weight of 31 lb. *14,090 kg* has been claimed for a California condor (*Gymnogyps californianus*) (average weight 20 lb. *9 kg*) now preserved in the California Academy of Sciences, Los Angeles.

Largest wing span

The Wandering albatross (*Diomedea exulans*) of the southern oceans has the largest wing span of any living bird, adult males averaging 10 ft 4 in *3,15 m* with wings tightly stretched. The largest recorded specimen was a male measuring 11 ft 10 in *3,60 m* caught by banders in Western Australia in *c.* 1957, but some unmeasured birds may reach or possibly just exceed 13 ft *3,96 m*. The only other bird reliably credited with a wingspread in excess of 11 ft *3,35 m* is the vulture-like Marabou or Adjutant stork (*Leptoptilus crumeniferus*) of Africa and South-East Asia. In the 1930's an extreme measurement of 13 ft 4 in *4,06 m* was reported for a specimen shot in Central Africa, but this species rarely exceeds 9 ft. *2,43 m*.

Smallest *World*

The smallest bird in the world is Helena's hummingbird (*Mellisuga helenae*) of Cuba and the Isle of Pines. An average adult male measures 58 mm *2.28 in* in total length—bill 15 mm *0.59 in*, head and body 15 mm *0.59 in* and tail 28 mm *1.10 in*—and weighs about 2 g *0.07 oz.*, which means it is lighter than a Sphinx moth (0.08 oz. *2,2 g*). The smallest bird of prey is the 1¼ oz. *35 g* Bornean falconet (*Microhierax latifrons*) which is sparrow-sized.

Smallest *Great Britain*

The smallest regularly-breeding British bird is the Goldcrest (*Regulus regulus*), also known as the Golden crested wren or Kinglet. Adult specimens measure 90 mm *3.5 in* in total length and weigh between 3,8 and 4,5 g *0.108* and *0.127 oz.*

Most abundant *Wild*

The most abundant species of wild bird is the Red-billed quelea (*Quelea quelea*) of the drier parts of Africa south of the Sahara with a population estimated at 10,000,000,000 of which a tenth are destroyed each year by pest control units.

Most abundant *Domestic*

The most abundant species of domesticated bird is the Chicken, the domesticated form of the wild Red jungle fowl (*Gallus gallus*) of south-east Asia. In 1974 there were believed to be about 4,000,000,000 in the world, or about one chicken for every member of the human race. The fowl stock in Britain was estimated at 130,000,000 in 1972, producing 270,000,000 chicks annually. The most abundant sea bird is Wilson's petrel (*Oceanites oceanicus*). No population estimates have been published, but the number runs into hundreds—possibly thousands—of millions. The top-breeding British sea-bird is the Guillemot (*Uria aalge*) with an estimated 577,000 breeding pairs in 1973.

Most abundant *Great Britain*

The commonest wild breeding land bird in Great Britain is, according to a survey published in 1977, the wren (*Troglodytes troglodytes*) with a population of 10,000,000 pairs in early spring. It was estimated in 1967 that 250,000 pigeon fanciers owned an average of 40 racing pigeons per loft, making a population of *c.* 10,000,000 in Great Britain. At the start of the shooting season there may in some years be 2 million reared pheasants (*Phasianus colchicus*) in addition to *c.* 8 million wild birds.

Rarest *World*

Because of the practical difficulties involved in assessing bird populations in the wild, it is virtually impossible to establish the identity of the world's rarest living bird. One of the strongest contenders, however, must be the Kauai O-o (*Moho braccatus*) of Kauai, Hawaiian Islands, of which only a single pair survived in 1976. The world's rarest raptor (bird of prey) is the Mauritius kestrel (*Falco punctatus*). In March 1977 the total population was thirteen.

Rarest *Great Britain*

According to the British Ornithologists Union there are 28 species of birds which have been recorded only once in the British Isles—18 of them since the end of the Second World War in 1945. That which has not recurred for the longest period is the Black-capped petrel (*Pterodroma hasitata*), also known as the "Diablotin". A specimen was caught alive on a heath at Southacre, near Swaffham, Norfolk in March or April 1850. The most tenuously established British bird is the Snowy owl (*Nyctea scandiaca*), with one pair breeding recurringly on Fetlar, Shetland Islands. Another pair introduced into the Highland Wildlife Park, near Aviemore, Scotland reared two chicks in 1975.

Fastest flying

The fastest flying bird is the Spine-tailed swift (*Chaetura caudacuta*). For details see page 23.

The bird which presents the hunter with the greatest difficulty is the Red-breasted merganser (*Mergus serrator*). On 29 May 1960 a specimen flushed from the Kukpuk River, Cape Thompson, northern Alaska, U.S.A. by a light aircraft recorded an air speed of 80 m.p.h. *128 km/h* in level flight for nearly 13 secs before turning aside.

Fastest and slowest wing beat

The fastest recorded wing beat of any bird is that of the hummingbird (*Heliactin cornuta*) of tropical South America with a rate of ninety beats a second. This rate is probably exceeded by the Bee hummingbirds (*Mellisuga helenae*) and (*Acestrura bombus*) but no figures have yet been published. Large vultures (family Vulturidae) and albatrosses (Diomedeidae) can soar for hours without beating their wings, but sometimes exhibit a flapping rate as low as one beat per sec.

Longest lived

The greatest irrefutable age reported for any bird is 72+ years in the case of a male Andean condor (*Vultur gryphus* named "Kuzya", which died in Moskovskii Zoologicheskii Park, Moscow, U.S.S.R. in 1964. This bird had been received as an adult in 1892. The British record is 68+ years in the case of a female European eagle-owl (*Bubo bubo*) which was still alive in 1899. Other records which are regarded as *probably* reliable include 73 years (1818–91) for a Greater sulphur-crested cockatoo (*Cacatua galerita*); 72 years (1797–1869) for an African grey parrot (*Psittacus erithacus*); 70 years (1770–1840) for a Mute swan (*Cygnus olor*) and 69 years for a Raven (*Corvus corax*). In 1972 a Southern Ostrich (*Sturthio camelus australis*) aged 62 years and 3 months was killed in the Ostrich Abattoir at Oudtshoorn, Cape Province, South Africa.

"Jimmy", a red and green Amazon parrot owned by Mrs. Bella Ludford of Liverpool, England was allegedly hatched in captivity on 3 Dec. 1870 and lived 104 years in his original brass cage dying on 5 Jan. 1975.

Eggs *Largest*

The largest egg produced by any living bird is that of the Ostrich (*Struthio camelus*). The average example measures 6 to 8 in *15–20 cm* in length, 4 to 6 in *10–15 cm* in diameter and weighs 3.63 to 3.88 lb. *1,65–1,78 kg* (equal to the volume of two dozen hen's eggs). It requires about 40 min for boiling. The shell though $\frac{1}{16}$ in *1,5 mm* thick can support the weight of a 20 st. *127 kg* man. The largest egg laid by any bird on the British list is that of the Mute swan (*Cygnus olor*), which measures from 4.3 to 4.9 in *109–124 mm* in length and between 2.8 and 3.1 in *71–78,5 mm* in diameter. The weight is 12–13 oz. *340–368 g*.

Eggs *Smallest*

The smallest egg laid by any bird is that of Helena's hummingbird *Mellisuga helenae*, the world's smallest bird (see page 34). A specimen collected at Boyate, Santiago de Cuba on 8 May 1906 and later presented to the U.S. National Museum, Washington, D.C., U.S.A. measures 11,4 mm *0.45 in* in length, 8 mm *0.32 in* in diameter and weighs 0,5 g *0.176 oz.* The smallest egg laid by a bird on the British list is that of the Goldcrest (*Regulus regulus*), which measures 12,2–14,5 mm *0.48–0.57 in* in length and between 9,4 and 9,9 mm *0.37* and *0.39 in* in diameter. Eggs emitted from the oviduct before maturity, known as "sports", are not reckoned to be of significance in discussion of relative sizes.

Incubation *Longest and shortest*

The longest normal incubation period is that of the Wandering albatross (*Diomedea exulans*), with a normal range of 75 days to 82 days. There is a case of an egg of the Mallee fowl

(*Leipoa ocellata*) of Australia taking 90 days to hatch against its normal incubation of 62 days. The shortest incubation period is the 10 days of the Great spotted woodpecker (*Dendrocopus major*) and the Black-billed cuckoo (*Coccyzus erythropthalmus*). The idlest of cock birds include humming-birds (family Trochilidae), Eider duck (*Somateria mollissima*) and Golden pheasant (*Chrysolophus pictus*) among whom the hen bird does 100 per cent of the incubation, whereas the female Common kiwi (*Apteryx australis*) leaves this entirely to the male for 75 to 80 days.

Longest flights

The greatest distance covered by a ringed bird during migration is 12,000 miles *19 300 km* by an Arctic tern (*Sterna paradisaea*), which was banded as a nestling on 5 July 1955 in the Kandalaksha Sanctuary on the White Sea coast and was captured alive by a fisherman 8 miles *13 km* south of Fremantle, Western Australia on 16 May 1956.

Highest flying

The celebrated example of a skein of 17 Egyptian geese (*Alopochen aegptiacus*) photographed by an astronomer at Dehra Dun, northern India on 17 Sept. 1919 as they crossed the sun at an estimated height of between 11 and 12 miles (58,080–63,360 ft *17 700–19 310 m*), has been discredited by experts.

The highest acceptable altitude recorded for a bird is 8 200 m *26,900 ft* for a small number of Alpine choughs (*Pyrrhocorax graculus*) which followed the British Everest expedition of 1924 to Camp V. On 23 May 1960 a Steppe eagle (*Aquila nipalensis*) and two other raptors were found dead at nearly 26,000 ft *7 924 m* on the South Col. On three separate occasions in 1959 a radar station in Norfolk picked up flocks of small passerine night migrants flying in from Scandinavia at heights up to 21,000 ft *6 400 m*. They were probably Warblers (*Sylviidae*), Chats (*Turdidae*) and Flycatchers (*Muscicapidae*).

Most airborne

The most aerial of all birds is the Sooty tern (*Sterna fuscata*) which, after leaving the nesting grounds, remains continuously aloft for three or four years before returning to the breeding grounds. The most aerial land bird is the Common swift (*Apus apus*) which remains "airborne" for at least 9 months of the year.

Fastest swimmer

The fastest swimming bird is the Gentoo penguin (*Pygoscelis papua*). In January 1913 a small group were timed at 10 m/sec *22.3 m.p.h.* under water near the Bay of Isles, South Georgia. This is a respectable flying speed for some birds. The deepest diving bird is the Emperor penguin (*Aptenodytes forsteri*) of the Antarctic which can reach a depth of 265 m *870 ft* and remain submerged for up to 18 minutes.

Most acute vision

Tests have shown that under favourable conditions the Long-eared owl (*Asio otus*) and the Barn owl (*Tyto alba*) can swoop on targets from a distance of 6 ft *1,83 m* or more in an illumination of only 0.00000073 of a ft candle (equivalent to the light from a standard candle at a distance of 1,170 ft *356 m*). This acuity is 50–100 times as great as that of human night vision. In good light and against a contrasting background a Golden eagle (*Aquila chrysaetos*) can detect an 18 in *46 cm* long hare at a range of 2,150 yds *1 966 m* (possibly even 2 miles *3,2 km*).

Feathers *Longest*

The longest feathers grown by any bird are those of the cock Long-tailed fowl or Onagadori (a strain of *Gallus gallus*) which have been bred in south-western Japan since the mid 17th century. In 1973 a tail covert measuring 10,60 m *34 ft 9½ in* was reported by Masasha Kubota of Kochi, Shikoku. The tail feathers of the flying Reeve's pheasant (*Syrmaticus reevesi*) of north and west China can exceed 8 ft *2,43 m*.

Feathers *Most*

In a series of "feather counts" on various species of bird a Whistling swan (*Cygnus columbianus*) was found to have

wing spans of birds

Wandering albatross.   Wing span 11 ft 10 in *3,6 m* (record)

Marabou stork.
Wing span 11 ft 6 in
3,5 m (average)

Mute swan.   Wing span
8 ft *2,43 m* (average)

Golden Eagle (immature).
Wing span 7 ft 6 in *2,28 m*
(average)

Rook.   Wing span 2 ft 10 in *85 cm*
(average)

Anglo-French Jaguar Mrk 1.
Wing span 28 ft 6 ins *8,6 m*

Illustration by Pat Gibbon © Guinness Superlatives Ltd. 1977

Smallest British bird/egg

Actual size

Britain's smallest regularly-breeding bird, the Goldcrest, measuring only 3½ inches *90 mm* in overall length. It takes 8 or 9 to weigh an ounce *35 grammes*. Its egg sometimes measures less than ½ inch *12,5 mm* in length.

See p. 34.

25,216 feathers. A ruby-throated hummingbird (*Archilochus colubris*) had only 940, although hummingbirds have more feathers per area of body surface than any other living bird.

Earliest and latest cuckoo

It is unlikely that the Cuckoo (*Cuculus canorus*) has ever been *heard and seen* in Britain earlier than 2 March, on which date one was observed under acceptable conditions by Mr. William A. Haynes of Trinder Road, Wantage, Oxfordshire in 1972. The two latest dates are 16 Dec. 1912 at Anstey's Cove, Torquay, Devon and 26 Dec. 1897 or 1898 in Cheshire.

Champion Bird Spotter

The world's leading bird-spotter is G. Stuart Keith (G.B.), who works in the American Museum of Natural History, New York. Since April 1947 his score is 5,280 species, including the Mauritius kestrel, of the 8,650 known species of avifauna.

Nests, *Largest*

The largest bird's nest on record is one 9½ ft *2,9 m* wide and 20 ft *6 m* deep built by Bald eagles (*Halliaetus leucocephalus*) near St. Petersburg, Florida, U.S.A. reported in 1963 and estimated to weigh more than 2 tons/*tonnes*. The incubation mounds built by Scrubfowl (family Megapodidae) have however been measured up to 50 ft *15,25 m* in diameter and 20 ft *6 m* in height.

DOMESTICATED BIRDS

Chicken *Heaviest*

The heaviest breed of chicken is one called the White Sully developed by Mr. Grant Sullens of West Point, California, U.S.A. over a period of seven years. One monstrous rooster named "Weirdo" reportedly weighed 22 lb. *10 kg* in January 1973, and was so ferocious that he had already killed two cats and crippled a dog which came too close. The heaviest British breed is the Dorking, with roosters weighing up to 14 lb. *6,36 kg*. The record flight by a chicken is 267 ft 11 in *81,38 m* by "Mrs Cluck" at the annual contest at Luckenbach, Texas, U.S.A. on 8 June 1975.

Turkey *Heaviest*

The greatest *live* weight recorded for a Turkey (*Meleagris gallopavo*) is 75 lb. *34 kg 015* reported in December 1973 for a "holiday" turkey reared by Signe Olsen, Salt Lake City, Utah, U.S.A. The British record for a dressed bird is 71 lb. 12 oz. *32,54 kg* for a stag reared by J. P. Wood & Sons of Craven Arms, Salop in conjunction with Dale Turkeys Ltd of Ludlow, Salop. It won the British Heavyweight title on 3 Dec. 1975. Turkeys were introduced into Britain *via* Spain from Mexico in 1549.

Most Expensive

The record price for a turkey at auction (auctioneer Bernard Cribbins) has been £1,000 for the 71 lb. 4 oz. *32,31 kg* Mr. Chukie by Mr. Leslie Grindle of Sidcup at The Waldorf Hotel, London on 10 Dec. 1976.

Longest lived

The longest lived domesticated bird (excluding the Ostrich) is the domestic goose (*Anser anser domesticus*) which normally lives about 25 years. In Dec. 1976 the death was reported of a gander aged 49 years 8 months. He was hatched out in April 1927. The longest lived small cagebird is the Canary (*Serinus canaria*). The oldest example on record was a 34 year old cock bird named "Joey" owned by Mrs. K. Ross of Hull. The bird was purchased in Calabar, Nigeria in 1941 and died on 8 April 1975. In April 1976 a Budgerigar (*Melopsittacus undulatus*) named "Charlie" owned by Miss J. Dinsey of Stonebridge, London celebrated his 28th birthday. In Dec. 1976 a Linnet (*Carduelis cannabina*), owned by Miss K. Porter, died in Nottingham aged 28 years 3½ months.

Most talkative

The world's most talkative bird is a male African grey parrot (*Psittacus erythacus*) named "Prudle", owned by Mrs. Lyn Logue of Golders Green, London, which won the "Best talking parrot-like bird" title at the National Cage and Aviary Bird Show held in London each December for 12 consecutive years (1965–1976). Prudle, who has a vocabulary of nearly 1,000 words, was taken from a nest in a tree about to be felled at Jinja, Uganda in 1958.

3. REPTILES (*Reptilia*)

(Crocodiles, snakes, turtles, tortoises and lizards.)

Largest and heaviest

The largest reptile in the world is the Estuarine or Salt-water crocodile (*Crocodylus porosus*) of south-east Asia, northern Australia, New Guinea, the Philippines and the Solomon Islands. Adult bulls average 12–14 ft *3,7–4,3 m* in length and scale about 1,100 lb. *499 kg*. In 1823 a notorious man-eater 27 ft *8,23 m* in length and weighing an estimated 2 tons/*tonnes* was shot at Jala Jala on Luzon Island in the Philippines after terrorising the neighbourhood for many years. Its skull, the largest on record if we exclude fossil remains, is now preserved in the Museum of Comparative Zoology at Harvard University, Cambridge, Massachusetts, U.S.A. Another outsized example with a reputed length of 33 ft *10,05 m* and a maximum bodily girth of 13 ft 8 in *4,16 m* was shot in the Bay of Bengal in 1840, but the dimensions of its skull (preserved in the British Museum of Natural History, London) suggest that it must have come from a crocodile measuring about 24 ft *7,31 m*. In July 1957 a length of 28 ft 4 in *8,63 m* was reported for an Estuarine crocodile shot by Mrs. Kris Pawlowski on MacArthur Bank, in the Norman River, north-western Queensland, Australia. Only photographic evidence existed.

Smallest

The smallest known species of reptile is believed to be *Sphaerodactylus parthenopiom*, a tiny gecko found only on the island of Virgin Gorda, one of the British Virgin Islands, in the West Indies. It is known only from 15 specimens, including some gravid females found between 10 and 16 Aug. 1964. The three largest females measured 18 mm *0.71 in* from snout to vent, with a tail of approximately the same length. It is possible that another gecko, *Sphaerodactylus elasmorhynchus*, may be even smaller. The only known specimen was an apparently mature female with a snout-vent length of 17 mm *0.67 in* and a tail the same measurement found on 15 March 1966 among the roots of a tree in the western part of the Massif de la Hotte in Haiti. A species of dwarf chameleon, *Evoluticauda tuberculata* found in Madagascar, and known only from a single specimen, has a snout-vent length of 18 mm *0.71 in* and a tail length of 14 mm *0.55 in*. Chameleons, however, are more bulky than geckos, and it is not yet known if this specimen was fully grown.

The smallest reptile found in Britain is the Viviparous or Common lizard (*Lacerta vivipara*). Adult specimens have an overall length of 108–178 mm *4.25–7 in*.

Fastest

The highest speed measured for any reptile on land is 18 m.p.h. *29 km/h* for a Six-lined racerunner (*Cnemidophorus sexlineatus*) pursued by a car near McCormick, South Carolina, U.S.A. in 1941. The highest speed claimed for any reptile in water is 22 m.p.h. *35 km/h* by a frightened Pacific leatherback turtle (see below).

Lizards *Largest*

The largest of all lizards is the Komodo monitor or Ora (*Varanus komodoensis*), a dragonlike reptile found on the Indonesian islands of Komodo, Rintja, Padar and Flores. Adult males average 8 ft *2,43 m* in length and weigh 175–200 lb. *79–91 kg*. Lengths up to 23 ft *7 m* (*sic*) have been quoted for this species, but the largest specimen to be accurately measured was a male presented to an American zoologist in 1928 by the Sultan of Bima which taped 3,05 m *10 ft 0.8 in*

In 1937 this animal was put on display in St. Louis Zoological Gardens, Missouri, U.S.A. for a short period. It then measured 10 ft 2 in *3,10 m* in length and weighed 365 lb. *166 kg*. A specimen of the slender Salvadori dragon (*Varanus salvadori*) of New Guinea has been reliably claimed to be 15 ft 7 in *4,75 m* long.

Lizards *Oldest*

The greatest age recorded for a lizard is more than 54 years for a male Slow worm (*Anguis fragilis*) kept in the Zoological Museum in Copenhagen, Denmark from 1892 until 1946.

Chelonians *Largest*

The largest of all chelonians is the Pacific leatherback turtle (*Dermochelys coriacea schlegelii*). The average adult measures 6–7 ft *1,83–2,13 m* in overall length (length of carapace 4–5 ft *122–152 cm*) and weighs between 660 and 800 lb. *299–363 kg*. The greatest weight reliably recorded is 1,908 lb. *865 kg* for a specimen captured off Monterey, California, U.S.A. on 29 Aug. 1961 measuring 8 ft 4 in *2,54 m* overall. The largest chelonian found in British waters is the Atlantic leatherback turtle (*Dermochelys coriacea coriacea*). One weighing 997 lb. *425 kg* and measuring more than 7 ft *2,13 m* in length was caught by a French fishing trawler in the English Channel on 8 May 1958.

The largest living tortoise is *Geochelone* (*Testudo*) *gigantea* of the Indian Ocean islands of Aldabra, Mauritius, Réunion and Seychelles (introduced 1874). Adult males sometimes exceed 350 lb. *158 kg* in weight and a specimen weighing 900 lb. *408 kg* was allegedly collected in Aldabra in 1847.

Chelonians *Longest lived*

Tortoises are the longest lived of all vertebrates. (See Animal Kingdom Records above). Other reliable records over 100 years include a Common box tortoise (*Testudo carolina*) of 138 years and a European pond-tortoise (*Emys orbicularis*) of 120+ years. The greatest proven age of a continuously observed tortoise is 116+ years for a Mediterranean spur-thighed tortoise (*Testudo graeca*) which died in Paignton Zoo, Devon in 1957.

Chelonians *Slowest moving*

Tests on a giant tortoise (*Geochelone gigantea*) in Mauritius show that even when hungry and enticed by a cabbage it cannot cover more than 5 yds *4,57 m* in a min (0.17 m.p.h. *0,27 km/h*) on land. Over longer distances its speed is greatly reduced.

SNAKES

Longest *World*

The longest (and the heaviest) of all snakes is the Anaconda (*Eunectes murinus*) of tropical South America. The largest anaconda on record was probably a specimen shot on the upper Orinoco River, eastern Colombia in 1944 which later recovered and escaped. It had been provisionally measured at 37½ ft *11,43 m*. Another anaconda killed on the lower Rio Guaviare, in south-eastern Colombia in November 1956 reportedly measured 10,25 m *33 ft 7½ in*. but nothing of this snake was preserved. In 1912 a Reticulated python (*Python reticulatus*) measuring 10 m *32 ft 9½ in* was killed near a mining camp on the north coast of Celebes in the Malay Archipelago. An African rock python (*Python sebae*) measuring 9,81 m *32 ft 2¼ in* was killed in the grounds of a school at Bingerville, Ivory Coast in 1932.

Longest *In Captivity*

The longest snake ever kept in a zoo was probably "Colossus", a female Reticulated python (*Python reticulatus*), who died of reptilian tuberculosis on 15 April 1963 in the Highland Park Zoological Gardens, Pittsburgh, Pennsylvania, U.S.A. She measured 28 ft 6 in *8,68 m* on 15 Nov. 1956 and was probably at least 29 ft *8,84 m* at the time of her death. Her maximum girth before a feed was measured at 36 in *91 cm* on 2 March 1955 and she weighed 22 st. 12 lb. *145 kg* on 12 June 1957. A long-standing reward of $5,000 (now £2,940) offered by the New York Zoological Society in Bronx Park, New York City, U.S.A. for a living specimen of any snake measuring more than 30 ft *9,14 m* has never been collected.

The longest snake living in captivity anywhere in the world today is probably a female Reticulated python named "Cassius" owned by Mr. Adrian Nyoka managing director of Knaresborough Zoo, North Yorkshire, which measures c. 27½ ft *8,38 m* and scales 240 lb. *109 kg*. It was collected in Malaysia in 1972 since when it has grown 18 in *45 cm*. A 9 metre (*29 ft 6¼ in*) specimen has been reported in the Keban Binatang, Djakarta, Indonesia but is unconfirmed.

Longest *British*

The longest snake found in Britain is the Grass snake (*Natrix natrix*), which is found throughout southern England, parts of Wales and in Dumfries and Galloway, Scotland. Adult males average 660 mm *26 in* in length and adult females 760 mm *29.92 in*. The longest accurately measured specimen was probably a female killed in South Wales in 1887 which measured 1 775 mm *5 ft 10 in*.

Shortest

The shortest known snake is the Thread snake *Leptotyphlops bilineata*, which is found on the islands of Martinique, Barbados and St. Lucia in the West Indies. It has a maximum recorded length of 11,9 cm *4.7 in*. The shortest venomous snake is the Striped dwarf garter snake (*Elaps dorsalis*) of South Africa, adults average 6 in *152 mm* in length.

Heaviest

The heaviest snake is the Anaconda (*Eunectes murinus*). The specimen shot in eastern Colombia in 1944 (see above) probably weighed nearly 1,000 lb. *454 kg*. The heaviest venomous snake is the Eastern diamond-back rattlesnake (*Crotalus adamanteus*) of the south-eastern United States. One specimen measuring 7 ft 9 in *2,36 m* in length weighed 34 lb. *15 kg*. Less reliable lengths up to 8 ft 9 in *2,66 m* and weights up to 40 lb. *18 kg* have been reported. A 15 ft 7 in *4,75 m* King cobra (*Ophiophagus hannah*) captured alive on Singapore Island and presented to Raffles Museum weighed 26½ lb. *12 kg*.

Venomous *Longest and Shortest*

The longest venomous snake in the world is the King cobra (*Ophiophagus hannah*), also called the Hamadryad, of southeast Asia and the Philippines. A specimen collected near Port Dickson in the state of Negri Sembilan, Malaya in April 1937 grew to 18 ft 9 in *5,71 m* in London Zoo. It was destroyed at the outbreak of war in 1939.

Oldest

The greatest irrefutable age recorded for a snake is 40 years 3 months for a male Common boa (*Boa constrictor constrictor*), named "Popeye", at Philadelphia Zoological Gardens, Philadelphia, Pennsylvania, U.S.A. which died on 17 Apr. 1977. He was purchased from a London dealer in December 1936.

Fastest moving

The fastest moving land snake is probably the slender Black mamba (*Dendroaspis polylepis*). On 23 April 1906 an angry Black mamba was timed at a speed of 7 m.p.h. *11 km/h* over a measured distance of 47 yds *43 m* near Mbuyuni on the Serengeti Plains, Kenya. Stories that Black mambas can overtake galloping horses (maximum speed 43.26 m.p.h. *69,62 km/h*) are wild exaggerations, though a speed of 15 m.p.h. *24 km/h* may be possible for short bursts over level ground. The British grass snake (*Natrix natrix*) has a maximum speed of 4.2 m.p.h. *6,8 km/h*.

Most venomous

The world's most venomous snake is now believed to be the sea snake (*Hydrophis belcheri*) which has a venom one hundred times as lethal as that of the Australian taipan (*Oxyuranus scutellatus*). The snake abounds round Ashmore Reef in the Timor Sea, off North West Australia. The most venomous land snake is probably the peninsular tiger snake (*Notechis ater niger*) found on Kangaroo Island and in the Sir Joseph Banks Group in Spencers Gulf, South Australia which grows to a length of 4 to 5 ft *1,22–1,52 m*. The average venom yield is sufficient to kill 300 sheep. It is estimated that between 30,000 and 40,000 people (excluding Chinese and Russians) die from snakebite each year, 75 per cent of them in densely populated India. Burma has the highest mortality rate with 15.4 deaths per 100,000 population per annum.

The head of the Gaboon viper (*Bitis gabonica*) displaying the World's longest snake fangs.

Most venomous *Britain*

The only venomous snake in Britain is the Adder (*Vipera berus*). Since 1890 ten people have died after being bitten by this snake, including six children. The most recently recorded death was on 1 July 1975 when a 5 year old was bitten at Callandar, Central, Scotland and died 44 hours later. The longest specimen recorded was one of 38 in *96,5 cm* killed on Walberswick Common, Suffolk on 7 July 1971.

Longest fangs

The longest fangs of any snake are those of the Gaboon viper (*Bitis gabonica*) of tropical Africa. In a 6 ft *1,83 m* long specimen they measured 50 mm *1.96 in*. On 12 Feb. 1963 a Gaboon viper bit itself to death in the Philadelphia Zoological Gardens, Philadelphia, Pennsylvania, U.S.A. Keepers found the dead snake with its fangs deeply embedded in its own back.

4. AMPHIBIANS (*Amphibia*)

Largest *World*

The largest species of amphibian is the Chinese giant salamander (*Megalobatrachus davidianus*), which lives in the cold mountain streams and marshy areas of north-eastern, central and southern China. The average adult measures 1 m *39 in* in total length and weighs 11–13 kg *24.2 to 28.6 lb*. One huge individual collected in Kweichow (Guizhou) Province in southern China in the early 1920s measured 5 ft *1,52 m* in total length and weighed nearly 100 lb. *45 kg*. The Japanese giant salamander (*Megalobatrachus japonicus*) is slightly smaller, but one captive specimen weighed 40 kg *88 lb*. when alive and 45 kg *100 lb*. after death, the body having absorbed water from the aquarium.

Largest *Britain*

The longest British amphibian is the Warty or Great crested newt (*Triturus cristatus*). One specimen collected at Hampton, Greater London measured 162 mm *6,37 in* in total length, and another one collected at Dunbar, Lothian, Scotland weighed 10,6 g *0.37 oz*.

Smallest *World*

The smallest species of amphibian is believed to be the arrow-poison frog (*Sminthillus limbatus*), found only in Cuba. Adult specimens have a snout-vent length of 8,5–12,4 mm *0.44–0.48 in*.

Smallest *Britain*

The smallest amphibian found in Britain is the Palmate newt (*Triturus helveticus*). Adult specimens measure 7,5–9,2 cm *2.95–3.62 in* in total length and weigh up to 2,39 g *0.083 oz.* The Natterjack or Running toad (*Bufo calamita*) has a maximum snout-vent length of only 8 cm *3.14 in.* but it is a bulkier animal.

Longest lived
The greatest authentic age recorded for an amphibian is about 55 years for a male Japanese giant salamander (*Megalobatrachus japonicus*) which died in the aquarium at Amsterdam Zoological Gardens on 3 June 1881. It was brought to Holland in 1829, at which time it was estimated to be three years old.

Highest and lowest
The greatest altitude at which an amphibian has been found is 8 000 m *26,246 ft* for a Common toad (*Bufo vulgaris*) collected in the Himalayas. This species has also been found at a depth of 340 m *1,115 ft* in a coal mine.

Most poisonous
The most active known poison is the batrachotoxin derived from the skin secretions of the Kokoi (*Phyllobates latinasus*), an arrow-poison frog found in north-western Colombia, South America. Only about 1/100,000th of a gramme *0.0000004 oz.* is sufficient to kill a man.

Newt *Largest World*
The largest newt in the world is the Pleurodele or Ribbed newt (*Pleurodeles waltl*), which is found in Morocco and on the Iberian Peninsula. Specimens measuring up to 40 cm *15.74 in* in total length and weighing over 1 lb. *450 g* have been reliably reported.

Newt *Smallest World*
The smallest newt in the world is believed to be the Striped newt (*Notophthalmus perstriatus*) of the south-eastern United States. Adult specimens average 51 mm *2.01 in* in total length.

Frog *Largest World*
The largest known frog is the rare Goliath frog (*Rana goliath*) of Cameroun and Spanish Guinea, West Africa. A female weighing 3 306 g *7 lb. 4.5 oz.* was caught in the rapids of the River Mbia, Spanish Guinea on 23 Aug. 1960. It had a snout-vent length of 34 cm *13.38 in* and measured 81,5 cm *32.08 in* overall with legs extended. In December 1960 another giant frog known locally as "agak" or "carn-pnag" and said to measure 12–15 in *30–38 cm* snout to vent and weigh over 6 lb. *2,7 kg* was reportedly discovered in central New Guinea, but further information is lacking. In 1969 a new species of giant frog was discovered in Sumatra.

Frog *Largest Britain*
The largest frog found in Britain is the *introduced* Marsh frog (*Rana r. ridibunda*). Adult males have been measured up to 96 mm *3.77 in* snout to vent, and adult females up to 133 mm *5.25 in*, the weight ranging from 60 to 95 g *1.7 oz.* to *3 oz.*

Longest jump
The record for three consecutive leaps is 32 ft 3 in *9,83 m* by a 2 in *5 cm* long South African sharp-nosed frog (*Rana oxyrhyncha*) named "Leaping Lena" (later discovered to be a male) on Green Point Racetrack, Cape Town on 18 Jan. 1954. At the annual Calaveras County Jumping Frog Jubilee at Angels Camp, California, U.S.A. in 1975 "Ex Lax" made a *single* leap of 17 ft 6¾ in *5,35 m* for its owner Bill Moniz.

Tree frog *Largest*
The largest species of tree frog is *Hyla vasta*, found only on the island of Hispaniola (Haiti and the Dominican Republic) in the West Indies. The average snout-vent length is about 9 cm *3.54 in* but a female collected from the San Juan River, Dominican Republic, in March 1928 measured 14,3 cm *5.63 in.*

Tree frog *Smallest*
The smallest tree frog in the world is the Least tree frog (*Hyla ocularis*), found in the south-eastern United States. It has a maximum snout-vent length of 15,8 mm *0.62 in.*

The largest British amphibian, the Warty or Great Crested newt (*Triturus cristatus*). (See page 38). (*Heather Angel*)

Toad *Largest World*
The most massive toad in the world is probably the Marine toad (*Bufo marinus*) of tropical South America. An enormous female collected on 24 Nov. 1965 at Miraflores Vaupes, Colombia and later exhibited in the Reptile House at Bronx Zoo, New York City, U.S.A. had a snout vent length of 23,8 cm *9.37 in* and weighed 1 302 g *2 lb. 11¼ oz.* at the time of its death in 1967.

Toad *Largest Britain*
The largest toad and heaviest amphibian found in Britain is the Common toad (*Bufo bufo*). Females of up to 102 mm *3.94 in* in length and 114 g *3.2 oz.* have been recorded.

Toad *Smallest World*
The smallest toad in the world is the sub-species *Bufo taitanus beiranus*, first discovered in *c.* 1906 near Beira, Mozambique, East Africa. Adult specimens have a maximum recorded snout-vent length of 24 mm *0.94 in.*

Salamander *Smallest*
The smallest species of salamander is the Pygmy salamander (*Desmognathus wrighti*), which is found only in Tennessee, North Carolina and Virginia, U.S.A. Adult specimens measure from 37 to 50,8 mm *1.45 to 2.0 in* in total length.

---

5. FISHES (*Pisces, Bradyodonti, Selachii, Marsipoli*)

Largest Marine *World*
The largest fish in the world is the rare plankton-feeding Whale shark (*Rhiniodon typus*), which is found in the warmer areas of the Atlantic, Pacific and Indian Oceans. It is not, however, the largest marine animal, since it is smaller than the larger species of whales (mammals). In 1919 a Whale shark measuring 10 *wa* (= 60 ft 9 in, *18,5 m*) in length and weighing an estimated 42.4 tons *43 tonnes* was trapped in a bamboo stake-trap at Koh Chik, in the Gulf of Siam. The largest carnivorous fish (excluding plankton eaters) is the comparatively rare Great white shark (*Carcharodon charcharias*), also called the "Maneater", which ranges from the

tropics to temperate zone waters. In June 1930 a specimen measuring 37 ft *11,27 m* in length was reportedly trapped in a herring weir at White Head Island, New Brunswick, Canada but may have been a wrongly identified Basking shark (see below). In May 1948 a great white shark measuring 21 ft *6,40 m* in length was captured after a fierce battle by fishermen off Havana, Cuba. It weighed 7,302 lb. *3 312 kg*. The longest of the bony or "true" fishes (Pisces) is the Russian sturgeon (*Acipenser huso*), also called the Beluga, which is found in the temperate areas of the Adriatic, Black and Caspian Seas but enters large rivers like the Volga and the Danube for spawning. Lengths up to 8 m *26 ft 3 in* have been reliably reported, and a gravid female taken in the estuary of the Volga in 1827 weighed 1 474,2 kg *1.44 tons*. The heaviest bony fish in the world is the Ocean sunfish (*Mola mola*), which is found in all tropical, sub-tropical and temperate waters. On 18 Sept. 1908 a huge specimen was accidentally struck by the S.S. *Fiona* off Bird Island about 40 miles *65 km* from Sydney, New South Wales, Australia and towed to Port Jackson. It measured 14 ft *4,26 m* between the anal and dorsal fins and weighed 2.24 tons *2,28 tonnes*.

Britain

The largest fish ever recorded in the waters of the British Isles was a 36 ft 6 in *11,12 m* Basking shark (*Cetorhinus maximus*) washed ashore at Brighton, East Sussex in 1806. It weighed an estimated 8 tons/tonnes. The largest bony fish found in British waters is the Ocean sunfish (*Mola mola*). A specimen weighing 800 lb. *363 kg* stranded near Montrose, Scotland on 14 Dec. 1960 and was sent to the Marine Research Institute in Aberdeen.

Largest Freshwater *World*

The largest fish which spends its whole life in fresh or brackish water is the rare Pa beuk or Pla buk (*Pangasianodon gigas*), a giant catfish, which is found in the deep waters of the Mekong River of Laos and Thailand. Adult males average 8 ft *2,43 m* in length and weigh about 360 lb. *163 kg*. This size was exceeded by the European catfish or Wels (*Silurus glanis*) in earlier times (in the 19th century lengths up to 15 ft *4,57 m* and weights up to 720 lb. *336,3 kg* were reported for Russian specimens), but today anything over 6 ft *1,83 m* and 200 lb. *91 kg* is considered large. The Arapaima (*Arapaima glanis*), also called the Pirarucu, found in the Amazon and other South American rivers and often claimed to be the largest freshwater fish, averages 6½ ft *2 m* and 150 lb. *68 kg*. The largest "authentically recorded" measured 8 ft 1½ in *2,48 m* in length and weighed 325 lb. *147 kg*. It was caught in the Rio Negro, Brazil in 1836.

Largest Freshwater *Britain*

The largest fish ever caught in a British river was a Common sturgeon (*Acipenser sturio*) weighing 507½ lb. *230 kg* measuring 9 ft *2,74 m* which was accidentally netted in the Severn at Lydney, Gloucestershire on 1 June 1937. Larger specimens have been taken at sea—notably one weighing 700 lb. *317 kg* and 10 ft 5 in *3,18 m* long netted by the trawler *Ben Urie* off Orkney and landed at Aberdeen on 18 Oct. 1956.

Smallest *Marine*

The smallest recorded marine fishes are the Marshall Islands goby (*Eviota zonura*) measuring 12 to 16 mm *0.47 to 0.63 in* and *Schindleria praematurus* from Samoa, measuring 12 to 19 mm *0.47 to 0.74 in*, both in the Pacific Ocean. Mature specimens of the latter fish, which was not described until 1940, have been known to weigh only 2 mg, equivalent to 17,750 to the oz—the lightest of all vertebrates and the smallest catch possible for any fisherman. The smallest British marine fish is the goby (*Lebutus orca*), which grows to a length of 39 mm *1.53 in*. It has been recorded off south west Cornwall and in the Irish Sea. The smallest known shark is the Long-faced dwarf shark (*Squaliolus laticaudus*) of the western Pacific. Adult specimens measure about 110 mm *4.33 in* in length.

Smallest *Freshwater*

The shortest known fish, and the shortest of all vertebrates, is the Dwarf pygmy goby (*Pandaka pygmaea*), a colourless and nearly transparent fish found in the streams and lakes of Luzon in the Philippines. Adult males measure only 7,5 to 9,9 mm *0.28 to 0.38 in* in length and weigh 4 to 5 mg *0.00014 to 0.00017 oz*.

Fastest

The Sailfish (*Istiophorus platypterus*) is generally considered to be the fastest species of fish, although the practical difficulties of measurement make data extremely difficult to secure. A figure of 68.1 m.p.h. *109,7 km/h* (100 yds *91 m* in 3 sec) has been cited for one off Florida, U.S.A. The swordfish (*Xiphias gladius*) has also been credited with very high speeds, but the evidence is based mainly on bills that have been found deeply embedded in ships' timbers. A speed of 50 knots (57.6 m.p.h. *92,7 km/h*) has been calculated from a penetration of 22 in *56 cm* by a bill into a piece of timber, but 30 to 35 knots (35 to 40 m.p.h. *56–64 km/h* is the most conceded by some experts. Speeds in excess of 35 knots (40 m.p.h. *64 km/h*) have also been attributed to the Marlin (*Tetrapturus sp.*), the Wahoo (*Acanthocybium solandri*), the Great blue shark (*Prionace glauca*) and the Bonefish (*Albula vulpes*), and the Bluefin tuna (*Thunnus thynnus*) has been scientifically clocked at 43.4 m.p.h. *69,8 km/h* in a 20 sec dash. The Four-winged flying fish (*Cypselurus heterururs*) may also exceed 40 m.p.h. *64 km/h* during its rapid rush to the surface before take-off (the average speed in the air is about 35 m.p.h. *56 km/h*). Record flights of 90 sec, 36 ft *11 m* in altitude and 1 110 m *3,640 ft* length have been recorded in the tropical Atlantic.

The largest fish ever caught in British waters, a Common sturgeon (*Acipenser sturio*), weighing 700 lb. *317 kg*.

Longest lived

Aquaria are of too recent origin to be able to establish with certainty which species of fish can fairly be regarded as the longest lived. A Lake Sturgeon 6 ft 9 in *2,05 m* long and weighing 215 lb. *97 kg* caught in the Lake of the Woods Kenora, Ontario, Canada on 15 July 1953 was believed (but not by all authorities) to be 154 years old based on a growth ring. In July 1974 a growth ring count of 228 years was reported for a female Koi fish, a form of fancy carp, named "Hanako" living in a pond in Higashi Shirakawa, Gifu Prefecture, Japan, but the greatest authoritatively accepted age for this species is "more than 50 years". The coelacanth (*Latimeria chalumnae*) identified by Margaret Courtenay-Latimer and J. L. B. Smith in 1938 having been landed in East London, South Africa from the Mozambique Channel was thought to have been extinct for 70 million years. By the end of 1975 84 others had been discovered in Comoran waters.

Oldest goldfish

While goldfish (*Carassius auratus*) have been reported to live for over 40 years in China, the British record is probably 29 years 10 months 21 days for a specimen which lived in an aquarium at Woolwich, Greater London and died on 11 Apr. 1883.

Shortest lived

The shortest-lived fishes are probably certain species of the sub-order Cyprinodontei (killifish) found in Africa and South America which normally live about eight months in the wild state.

Deepest

The greatest depth from which a fish has been recovered is 8 300 m *27,230 ft* in the Puerto Rico Trench (27,488 ft *8 366 m*) in the Atlantic by Dr. Gilbert L. Voss of the U.S. research vessel *John Elliott* who took a 6½ in *16,5 cm* long *Bassogigas profundissimus* in April 1970. It was only the fifth such brotulid ever caught. Dr. Jacques Piccard and Lieutenant Don Walsh, U.S. Navy, reported they saw a sole-like fish about 1 ft *33 cm* long (tentatively identified as *Chascanopsetta lugubris*) from the bathyscaphe *Trieste* at a depth of 35,802 ft *10 912 m* in the Challenger Deep (Marianas Trench) in the western Pacific on 24 Jan. 1960. This sighting, however, has been questioned by some authorities, who still regard the brotulids of the genus *Bassogigas* as the deepest-living vertebrates.

Most and least eggs

The Ocean sunfish (*Mola mola*) produces up to 300,000,000 eggs, each of them measuring about 0.05 in *1,3 mm* in diameter. The egg yield of the tooth carp *Jordanella floridae* of Florida, U.S.A. is only *c.* 20 over a period of several days.

Most venomous

The most venomous fish in the world are the Stonefish (family Synanceidae) of the tropical waters of the Indo-Pacific. Direct contact with the spines of their fins, which contain a strong neurotoxic poison, often proves fatal.

Most electric

The most powerful electric fish is the Electric eel (*Electrophorus electricus*), which is found in the rivers of Brazil, Columbia, Venezuela and Peru. An average sized specimen can discharge 400 volts at 1 ampere, but measurements up to 650 volts have been recorded.

River Thames

The first salmon caught in the Thames since June 1833 was taken at West Thurrock Power Station, Essex in November 1974 and weighed 8 lb. 4½ oz. *3,757 kg*.

6. STARFISHES (*Asteroidea*)

Largest

The largest of the 1,600 known species of starfish in terms of total diameter is the very fragile brisingid *Midgardia xandaros*. A specimen collected by the Texas A & M University research

vessel *Alaminos* in the southern part of the Gulf of Mexico in the late summer of 1968, measured 1 380 mm *54.33 in* tip to tip, but the diameter of its disc was only 26 mm *1.02 in*. Its dry weight was 70 g *2.46 oz*. The most massive species of starfish is probably the five-armed *Evasterias echinosoma* of the North Pacific. One specimen collected by a Russian expedition in the flooded crater of a volcano in Broughton Bay, Semushir, one of the Kurile Islands in June 1970 measured 960 mm *37.79 in* in total diameter and weighed more than 5 kg *11 lb*. The largest starfish found in British waters is the Spiny starfish (*Marthasterias glacialis*), which has been measured up to 350 mm *13.78 in* in major radius or 665 mm *26.18 in* arm tip to arm tip.

Smallest

The smallest known starfish is *Marginaster capreenis*, found deep in the Mediterranean, which is not known to exceed 20 mm *0.78 in* in diameter. The smallest starfish found in British waters is the Cushion starfish (*Asterina gibbosa*) which measures up to *c.* 60 mm *2.36 in* in diameter but is usually *c.* 25 mm *1 in* across.

Deepest

The greatest depth from which a starfish has been recovered is 7 584 m *24,881 ft* for a specimen of *Porcellanaster ivanovi* collected by the U.S.S.R. research ship *Vityaz* in the Marianas Trench, in the West Pacific *c.* 1962.

7. ARACHNIDS (*Arachnida*)

SPIDERS (order Araneae)

Largest *World*

The world's largest known spider is the bird-eating spider *Theraphosa leblondi* of northern South America. A male specimen with a leg span of 10 in *25 cm* when fully extended and a body length of 3½ in *8,9 cm* was collected at Montague la Gabrielle, French Guiana in April 1925. It weighed nearly 2 oz. *56 g*. The heaviest spider ever recorded was a female "tarantula" of the long haired species *Lasiodora klugi* collected at Manaos, Brazil in 1945. It measured 9½ in *241 mm* across the legs and weighed almost 3 oz. *85 g*.

Largest *Britain*

Of the 617 known British species of spider covering an estimated population of over 500,000,000,000,000,000, the Cardinal spider (*Tegenaria parietina*) has the greatest leg span. In 1974 one spanning 5.3 in *13,4 cm* was trapped in a house in Wokingham, Berkshire but later escaped. This spider is found only in southern England. The well-known "Daddy Longlegs" spider (*Pholcus phalangoides*) rarely exceeds 3 in *75 mm* in leg span, but one outsized specimen collected in England measured 6 in *15,2 cm* across. The heaviest spider found in Britain is the orb weaver (*Araneus quadratus*) (formerly called *Araneus reaumuri*). A female, not of extreme size, collected in October 1943 weighed 1,174 g *0.041 oz*. and measured 15 mm *0.58 in* in body length.

Smallest *World*

The smallest known spider is *Patu marplesi* (family Symphytognathidae) of Western Samoa. The type specimen (male) found in moss at *c.* 2,000 ft *610 m* altitude near Malolelei, Upolu in January 1956 measure 0,43 mm *0.016 in* overall—or half the size of this full stop . The smallest spider found in Britain is the money spider *Glyphesis cottonae*, which is confined to a swamp near Beaulieu Road Station, New Forest, Hampshire and Thurley Heath, Surrey. Adult specimens of both sexes have a body length of 1 mm *0.039 in*.

Rarest

The most elusive of all spiders are the primitive atypical tarantulas of the genus *Liphistius*, which are found in South-east Asia. The most elusive spider in Britain is the handsome crimson and black Lace web eresus spider (*Eresus niger*), found in Hampshire, Dorset and Cornwall, which is known only from eight specimens (seven males and one female). In the early 1950's one was reportedly seen at Sandown on the Isle of Wight, but it escaped.

Fastest

The highest speed recorded for a spider on a level surface is 1.73 ft/sec *53 cm/sec* (1.17 m.p.h. *1,88 km/h*) in the case of a specimen of *Tegenaria atrica*. This is 33 times her body length per sec compared with the human record of $5\frac{1}{2}$ times.

Longest lived

The longest lived of all spiders are the primitive *Mygalomorphae* (tarantulas and allied species). One mature female tarantula collected at Mazatland, Mexico in 1935 and estimated to be 12 years old at the time, was kept in a laboratory for 16 years, making a total of 28 years. The longest-lived British spider is probably the purse web spider (*Atypus affinis*). One specimen was kept in a greenhouse for nine years.

Largest webs

The largest webs are the aerial ones spun by the tropical orb weavers of the genus *Nephila*, which have been measured up to 18 ft $9\frac{3}{4}$ in *573 cm* in circumference. The smallest webs are spun by spiders like *Glyphesis cottonae*, etc. which are about the size of a postage stamp.

Most venomous

The most venomous spider in the world is probably *Latrodectus mactans* of the Americas, which is better known as the "Black widow" in the United States. Females of this species (the much smaller males are harmless) have a bite capable of killing a human being, but deaths are rare. The Funnel web spider (*Atrax robustus*) of Australia, the Jockey spider (*Latrodectus hasseltii*) of Australia and New Zealand, the Button spider (*Latrodectus indistinctus*) of South Africa, the Podadora (*Glyptocranium gasteracanthoides*) of Argentina and the Brown recluse spider (*Loxosceles reclusa*) of the central and southern United States have also been credited with fatalities.

8. CRUSTACEANS (*Crustacea*)

(Crabs, lobsters, shrimps, prawns, crayfish, barnacles, water fleas, fish lice, woodlice, sandhoppers, krill, etc.)

Largest *World*

The largest of all crustaceans (although not the heaviest) is the giant spider crab (*Macrocheira kaempferi*), also called the stilt crab, which is found in deep waters off the south-eastern coast of Japan. Mature specimens usually have a 12–14 in *30–35 cm* wide body and a claw-span of 8–9 ft *2,43–2,74* m but unconfirmed measurements up to 19 ft *5,79 m* have been reported. A specimen with a claw span of 12 ft $1\frac{1}{2}$ in *3,69 m* weighed 14 lb. *6 kg*. The heaviest crab is the *Pseudocarcinus gigas* found in the Bass Strait, Australia, which weighs up to 30 lb. *13,6 kg*.

The largest species of lobster, and the heaviest of all crustaceans, is the American or North Atlantic lobster (*Homarus americanus*). One weighing 42 lb. 7 oz. *19,05 kg* and measuring 3 ft *91 cm* from the end of the tail-fan to the tip of the claw was caught by the smack *Hustler* in a deep-sea trawl off the Virginia Capes, Virginia, U.S.A. in 1934 and is now on display in the Museum of Science, Boston, Massachusetts. Another specimen allegedly weighing 48 lb. *21,77 kg* was caught off Chatham, New England, U.S.A. in 1949.

Largest *Britain*

The largest crustacean found in British waters is the Common or European lobster (*Homarus vulgarus*), which averages 2–3 lb. *900–1 360 g*. In June 1931 an outsized specimen weighing $20\frac{1}{2}$ lb. *5,80 kg* and measuring 4 ft $1\frac{1}{2}$ in *1,26 m* in total length, was caught in a caisson during the construction of No. 3 jetty at Fowey, Cornwall. Its crushing claw weighed 2 lb. 10 oz. *1,188 g* after the meat had been removed. The largest crab found in British waters is the Edible or Great crab (*Cancer pagurus*). In 1895 a crab measuring 11 in *279 mm* across the shell and weighing 14 lb. *6,35 kg* was caught off the coast of Cornwall.

Smallest

The smallest known crustaceans are water fleas of the genus *Alonella*, which may measure less than 0,25 mm *0.0098 in* in length. They are found in British waters. The smallest known lobster is the Cape lobster (*Homarus capensis*) of South Africa which measures 10–12 cm *3.9–4.7 in* in total length. The smallest crabs in the world are the aptly named pea crabs (family Pinnotheridae). Some species have a shell diameter of only 0.25 in *6,3 mm*, including *Pinnotheres pisum* which is found in British waters.

Longest lived

The longest lived of all crustaceans is the American lobster (*Homarus americanus*). Very large specimens may be as much as 50 years old.

Vertical Distribution

The greatest depth from which a crustacean has been recovered is 9 790 m *32,119 ft* for an amphipod (order Amphipoda) collected by the Galathea Deep Sea Expedition in the Philippine Trench in 1951. The marine crab *Ethusina abyssicola* has been taken at a depth of 14,000 ft *4 265 m*. Amphiopods have also been collected in the Ecuadorean Andes at a height of 13,300 ft *4 053 m*.

9. INSECTS (*Insecta*)

Heaviest *World*

The heaviest insect in the world is the Goliath beetle (*Goliathus goliathus*) of equatorial Africa. One specimen measured 120 mm *4.72 in* in length (tip of frontal horn to end of abdomen) and weighed 100 g *3.52 oz*.

Heaviest *Britain*

The heaviest beetle found in Britain is the Stag beetle (*Lucanus cervus*) which is widely distributed over southern England. The largest specimen on record was a male collected at Sheerness, Kent, in 1871 and now preserved in the British Museum (Natural History), London, which measures 87.4 mm *3.04 in* in length (body plus mandibles) and probably weighed over 6 000 mg *0.21 oz.* when alive.

Longest

The longest insect in the world is the tropical stick-insect *Pharnacia serratipes*, females of which have been measured up

One of the largest moths in the World, the Atlas moth, (*Attacus atlas*), with a wing span of up to 280 mm *11.02 in*. (See page 43).

to 330 mm *12.99 in* in body length. The longest known beetle (excluding antenae) is the Hercules beetle (*Dynastes hercules*) of Central and South America, which has been measured up to 180 mm *7.08 in* but only half of this length is accounted for by the "prong" from the thorax. The longhorn beetle *Batocera wallacei* of New Guinea has been measured up to 267 mm *10.5 in*, but 190 mm *7.5 in* of this was antenna.

Smallest *World*

The smallest insects recorded so far are the "Hairy-winged" beetles of the family Trichopterygidae and the "battledore-wing fairy flies" (parasitic wasps) of the family Mymaridae. They measure only 0,2 mm *0.008 in* in length, and the fairy flies have a wing span of only 1 mm *0.04 in*. This makes them smaller than some of the protozoa (single-celled animals). The male bloodsucking banded louse *Enderleinellus zonatus*, ungorged, and the parasitic wasp (*Caraphractus cinctus*) may each weigh as little as 0,005 mg, or *5,670,000 to an oz*. The eggs of the latter each weigh 0,0002 mg, or *141,750,000 to an oz*.

Commonest

The most numerous of all insects are the Springtails (Order Collembola), which have a very wide geographical range. It has been calculated that the top 9 in *288 mm* of soil in one acre of grassland contain 230,000,000 springtails or more than 5,000 per square foot *465/m²*.

Fastest flying

Experiments have proved that the widely publicised claim by an American entomologist in 1926 that the Deer bot-fly (*Cephenemyia pratti*) could attain a speed of 818 m.p.h. *1 316 km/h* (sic) was wildly exaggerated. If true it would have generated a supersonic 'pop'! Acceptable modern experiments have now established that the highest maintainable airspeed of any insect, including the Deer bot-fly, is 24 m.p.h. *39 km/h*, rising to a maximum of 36 m.p.h. *58 km/h* for short bursts. A relay of bees (maximum speed 11 m.p.h. *18 km/h*) would use only a gallon of nectar in cruising 4,000,000 miles *6,5 million km* at an average speed of 7 m.p.h. *11 km/h*.

Longest lived

The longest-lived insects are queen termites (*Isoptera*), which have been known to lay eggs for up to 50 years.

Loudest

The loudest of all insects is the male cicada (family Cicadidae). At 7,400 pulses/min its tymbal organs produce a noise (officially described by the United States Department of Agriculture as "Tsh-ee-EEEE-e-ou") detectable more than a quarter of a mile *400 m* distant. The only British species is the very rare Mountain cicada (*Cicadetta montana*), which is confined to the New Forest area in Hampshire.

Southernmost

The farthest south at which any insect has been found is 77° S (900 miles *1 450 km* from the South Pole) in the case of a springtail (order Collembola).

Largest locust swarm

The greatest swarm of Desert locusts (*Schistocerea gregaria*) ever recorded was one covering an estimated 2,000 miles² *5 180 km²* observed crossing the Red Sea in 1889. Such a swarm must have contained about 250,000,000,000 insects weighing about 500,000 tons *508 000 tonnes*.

Fastest wing beat

The fastest wing beat of any insect under natural conditions is 62,760 a min by a tiny midge of the genus *Forcipomyia*. In experiments with truncated wings at a temperature of 37° C *98.6° F* the rate increased to 133,080 beats/min. The muscular contraction-expansion cycle in 0.00045 or 1/2,218th of a sec, further represents the fastest muscle movement ever measured.

Slowest wing beat

The slowest wing beat of any insect is 300 a min by the swallowtail butterfly (*Papilio machaon*). Most butterflies beat their wings at a rate of 460 to 636 a min.

Hive record

The greatest reported amount of wild honey ever extracted from a single hive is 404 lb. *183,2 kg* recorded by Ormond R. Aebi of Santa Cruz, California on 29 Aug. 1974.

Bush-cricket *Largest*

The bush-cricket with the largest wing span is the New Guinean grasshopper *Siliquofera grandis* with female examples measuring more than 10 in *254 mm*. *Pseudophyllanax imperialis*, found on the island of New Caledonia in the south-western Pacific has antennae measuring up to 8 in *203 mm*. The largest bush-cricket found in Britain is *Tettigonia viridissima*, which normally has a body length of 1¼ in *31,8 mm*. In August 1953 a female measuring 77 mm *3.03 in* in body length (including ovipositor) was caught in a sand pit at Grays, Essex and later presented to London Zoological Gardens. The largest of the 14 true grasshoppers found in Britain is *Mecostethus grossus*, females of which measure up to 39 mm *1.53 in* in body length.

Dragonflies *Largest*

The largest dragonfly in the world is *Tetracanthagyna plagiata* of north-eastern Borneo. which is known only from a single specimen preserved in the British Museum of Natural History, London. This dragonfly has a wing span of 194 mm *7.63 in* and an overall length of 108 mm *4.25 in*. The largest dragonfly found in Britain is the Golden-ringed dragonfly (*Cordulegaster boltoni*), which has been measured up to 84 mm *3.3 in* in overall length and may have a wing span of more than 100 mm *3.93 in*. The smallest British dragonfly is the Scarce ischnura (*Ischnura pumilio*), which has a wing span of 33 mm *1.3 in*.

Flea *Largest*

The largest known flea is *Hystrichopsylla schefferi schefferi*, which was described from a single specimen taken from the nest of a Mountain beaver (*Aplodontia rufa*) at Puyallup, Washington, U.S.A. in 1913. Females measure up to 8 mm *0,31 in* in length which is the diameter of a pencil. The largest flea (61 species) found in Britain is the Mole and Vole flea (*H. talpae*), females of which have been measured up to 6 mm *0.23 in*.

Flea *Longest jump*

The champion jumper among fleas is the common flea (*Pulex irritans*). In one American experiment carried out in 1910 a specimen allowed to leap at will performed a long jump of 13 in *330 mm* and a high jump of 7¾ in *197 mm*. In jumping 130 times its own height a flea subjects itself to a force of 200 g. Siphonapterologists recognise 1,830 varieties.

Smallest and largest tick

The smallest known tick is a male *Ixodes soricis* from a British Columbian shrew, and the largest an engorged female, *Amblyomma varium* from a Venezuelan sloth.

BUTTERFLIES AND MOTHS (order Lepidoptera)

Largest *World*

The largest known butterfly is the Queen Alexandra birdwing (*Ornithoptera alexandrae*) of New Guinea. Females may have a wing span exceeding 280 mm *11.02 in* and weigh over 5 g *0.176 oz*. The largest moth in the world is the Hercules moth (*Coscinoscera hercules*) of tropical Australia and New Guinea. Females measure up to 10½ in *266 mm* across the outspread wings and have a wing area of up to 40.8 in² *263,2 cm²*. In 1948 an unconfirmed measurement of 360 mm *14.17 in* was reported for a female captured near the post office at the coastal town of Innisfail, Queensland, Australia. The rare Owlet moth (*Thysania agrippina*) of Brazil has been measured up to 30 cm *11.81 in* in wing span, and the Atlas moth (*Attacus atlas*) of south-east Asia up to 28 cm *11.02 in*, but both these species are less bulky than *C. hercules*.

Largest *Britain*

The largest (but not the heaviest) of the 21,000 species of insect found in Britain is the very rare Death's head hawk moth (*Acherontia atropos*), females of which have a body length of 60 mm *2.36 in*, a wing span of up to 133 mm *5.25 in* and weigh about 1,6 g *0.056 oz.* The largest butterfly found in Britain is the Monarch butterfly (*Danaus plexippus*), also called the Milkweek or Black-veined brown butterfly, a rare vagrant which breeds in the southern United States and Central America. It has a wing span of up to 5 in *127 mm* and weighs about 1 g *0.04 oz.* The largest *native* butterfly is the Swallowtail (*Papilo machaon*), females of which have a wing span of 70–100 mm *2.75–3.93 in.* This species is now confined to a small area of the Norfolk Broads.

Smallest *World and Britain*
The smallest of the 140,000 known species of Lepidoptera are the moth *Johanssonia acetosae* (*Stainton*) found in Britain, and *Stigmella ridiculosa* from the Canary Islands, which have a wing span of *c.* 2 mm *0.08 in* with a similar body length. The world's smallest known butterfly is the Dwarf blue (*Brephidium barberae*) of South Africa. It has a wing span of 14 mm *0.55 in.* The smallest butterfly found in Britain is the Small blue (*Cupido minimus*), which has a wing span of 19–25 mm *0.75–1.0 in.*

Rarest
The rarest of all butterflies (and the most valuable) is the giant birdwing *Troides allottei*, which is found only on Bougainville in the Solomon Islands. A specimen was sold for £750 at an auction in Paris on 24 Oct. 1966. The rarest British butterfly is the Large blue (*Maculinea arion*), which is now confined to 3 or 4 localities in north Cornwall. The total population is now so small (estimated at only 35–70 in 1975) that the British Butterfly Conservation Society believe that it would only need poor weather conditions during the flight season for this species to become extinct in Britain. Britain's rarest moth is the Tree-lichen Beauty (*Briophila algae*), one specimen of which was captured in Greater Manchester in July 1858.

Most acute sense of smell
The most acute sense of smell exhibited in nature is that of the male Emperor moth (*Eudia pavonia*) which, according to German experiments in 1961, can detect the sex attractant of the virgin female at the almost unbelievable range of 11 km *6.8 miles* upwind. This scent has been identified as one of the higher alcohols ($C_{16}H_{29}OH$), of which the female carries less than 0,0001 mg.

10. CENTIPEDES (*Chilopoda*)

Longest
The longest known species of centipede is a large variant of the widely distributed *Scolopendra morsitans*, found on the Andaman Islands, Bay of Bengal. Specimens have been measured up to 13 in *330 mm* in length and 1½ in *38 mm* in breadth. The longest centipede found in Britain is *Haplophilus subterraneus*, which measures up to 70 mm *2.75 in* in length and 1,4 mm *0.05 in* across the body, but on 1 Nov. 1973 Mr. Ian Howgate claims to have seen a thin amber-coloured specimen in St. Albans, Herts, measuring at least 4½ in *114 mm.*

Shortest
The shortest recorded centipede is an unidentified species which measures only 5 mm *0.19 in* The shortest centipede found in Britain is *Lithobius dubosequi*, which measures up to 9,5 mm *0.374 in* in length and 1,1 mm *0.043 in* across the body.

Most legs
The centipede with the greatest number of legs is *Himantarum gabrielis* of southern Europe which has 171–177 pairs when adult.

Fastest
The fastest centipede is probably *Scutigera coleoptrata* of southern Europe which can travel at a rate of 50 cm *19.68 in* a sec or 1.1 m.p.h. *1,8 km/h.*

11. MILLIPEDES (*Diplopoda*)

Longest
The longest known species of millipede are *Graphidostreptus gigas* of Africa and *Scaphistostreptus seychellarum* of the Seychelles in the Indian Ocean, both of which have been measured up to 280 mm *11.02 in* in length and 20 mm *0.78 in* in diameter. The longest millipede found in Britain is *Cylindroiulus londinensis* which measures up to 50 mm *1.96 in.*

Shortest
The shortest millipede in the world is the British species *Polyxenus lagurus*, which measures 2,1–4,0 mm *0.082–0.15 in* in length.

Most legs
The greatest number of legs reported for a millipede is 355 pairs (710 legs) for an unidentified South African species.

12. SEGMENTED WORMS (*Annelida or Annulata*)

Longest
The longest known species of giant earthworm is *Microchaetus rappi* (= *M. microchaetus*) of South Africa. An average-sized specimen measures 136 cm *4 ft 6 in* in length (65 cm *25½ in* when contracted), but much larger examples have been reliably reported. In *c.* 1937 a giant earthworm measuring 22 ft *6,70 m* in length when naturally extended and 20 mm *0.78 in* diameter was collected in the Transvaal, and in November 1967 another specimen measuring 11 ft *3,35 m* in length and 21 ft *6,40 m* when naturally extended was found reaching over the national road (width 6 m *19 ft 8½ in*) near Debe Nek, eastern Cape Province. The longest segmented worm found in Britain is the King rag worm (*Nereis virens*). On 19 Oct. 1975 a specimen of 38 in *965 mm* was collected by Mr. James Sawyer in Hauxley Bay, Northumberland.

Shortest
The shortest known segmented worm is *Chaetogaster annandalei*, which measures less than 0,5 mm *0.019 in* in length.

13. MOLLUSCS (*Mollusca*)

(Squids, octopuses, shellfish, snails, etc.)

Largest squid
The heaviest of all invertebrate animals is the Atlantic giant squid (*Architeuthis sp.*). The largest specimen ever recorded was one measuring 55 ft *16,75 m* in total length (head and body 20 ft *6,09 m* tentacles 35 ft *10,66 m*) captured on 2 Nov. 1878 after it had run aground in Thimble Tickle Bay, Newfoundland, Canada. It weighed an estimated 2 tons/*tonnes*. In October 1887 a giant squid (*Architeuchis longimanus*) measuring 57 ft *17,37 m* in total length was washed up in Lyall Bay, New Zealand, but 49 ft *14,93 m* of this was tentacle. The largest squid ever recorded in British waters was one found at the head of Whalefirth Voe, Shetland on 2 Oct. 1959 which measured 24 ft *7,31 m* in total length.

Largest octopus
In Nov. 1896 the remains of an unknown marine animal weighing an estimated 6–7 tons/*tonnes* were found on a beach near St. Augustine, Florida, U.S.A. Tissue samples were later sent to the U.S. National Museum in Washington, D.C., and in 1970 they were *positively* identified as belonging to a giant form of octopus. It is estimated that this creature had a tentacular span of 200 ft *60,9 m.* The largest octopus found in British waters is the Common octopus (*Octopus vulgaris*), which has been measured up to 7 ft *2,13 m* in radial spread and may weigh more than 10 lb. *4,5 kg.*

above: The largest known species of land snail, the African giant snail (*Achatina sp.*). (See page 46). (*Keystone Press*)

above: The largest live octopus ever captured, the 53,8 kg *118 lbs. 10 oz.* Common Pacific octopus (*P. apollyon*) with its captor, Donald E. Hagen. (See page 44.)

below: The rare "Lion's Mane" jellyfish (*Cyanea capillata*), sometimes known as the Common Sea blubber, the largest jellyfish found in British waters. (See page 47). (*Heather Angel*)

Most ancient mollusc

The longest existing living creature is *Neopilina galatheae*, a deep-sea worm-snail which had been believed extinct for about 320,000,000 years. In 1952, however, specimens were found at a depth of 11,400 ft *3 470 m* off Costa Rica by the Danish research vessel *Galathea*. Fossils found in New York State, U.S.A., Newfoundland, Canada, and Sweden show that this mollusc was also living about 500,000,000 years ago.

45

Longest lived mollusc

The longest lived mollusc is probably the deep-sea clam *Tindaria callistiformis*, which lives an estimated 100 years. The Giant clam (*Tridacna derasa*) lives about 30 years.

SHELLS

Largest

The largest of all existing bivalve shells is the marine Giant clam (*Tridacna derasa*), which is found on the Indo-Pacific coral reefs. A specimen measuring 43 in *109,2 cm* by 29 in *73,6 cm* and weighing 579½ lb. *262,9 kg* (over a quarter of a ton) was collected from the Great Barrier Reef in 1917, and is now preserved in the American Museum of Natural History, New York City, N.Y., U.S.A. Another lighter specimen was measured to be 137 cm *53.9 in* overall. The largest bivalve shell found in British waters is the Fan mussel (*Pinna fragilis*). One specimen found at Tor Bay, Devon measured 37 cm *14.56 in* in length and 20 cm *7.87 in* in breadth at the hind end.

Smallest

The smallest bivalve shell found in British waters is the coin-shell *Neolepton sykesi*, which has an average length of 1,2 mm *0.047 in*. This species is only known from a few examples collected off Guernsey, Channel Islands and West Ireland. The smallest British shell is the univalve *Ammonicera rota*, which measures 0,5 mm *0.02 in* in diameter.

Rarest

The most highly prized of all molluscan shells in the hands of conchologists is the 3 in *7,5 cm* long White-tooth cowrie (*Cypraea leucodon*), which is found in the deep waters off the Philippines. Only three examples are known, including one in the British Museum of Natural History, London. The highest price ever paid for a sea shell is £1,350 in a sale at Sotheby's, London, on 4 March 1971 for one of the four known examples of *Conus bengalensis*. The 4 in *10 cm* long shell was trawled by fishermen in the Andaman Sea, South East Asia in December 1970.

SNAILS

Largest

The largest known species of snail is the Sea hare *Tethys californicus*, which is found in coastal waters off California, U.S.A. The average weight is 7 to 8 lb. *3,15–3,60 kg* but one specimen scaled 15 lb. 13 oz. *7,172 kg*. The largest known land snail is the African giant snail (*Achatina sp.*). In June 1976 a huge specimen measuring 13½ in *343 mm* from snout to tail, weighing 1 lb. 7 oz. *650 g* was found by Christopher Hudson of Hove, East Sussex in Sierra Leone. The largest land snail found in Britain is the Roman or Edible snail (*Helix pomatia*), which measures up to 4 in *10 cm* in overall length and weighs up to 3 oz. *85 g*. The smallest British land snail is *Punctum pygmaeum*, which has a shell measuring 0.023–0.035 of an inch *0,6–0,9 mm* by 0.047–0.059 of an inch *1,2–1,5 mm*.

Speed

The fastest-moving species of land snail is probably the common garden snail (*Helix aspersa*). According to tests carried out in the United States of America absolute top speed for *Helix aspersa* is 0.0313 m.p.h. *0,05 km/h* (or 55 yds *50,3 m* per hr.) while some species are at full stretch at 0.00036 m.p.h. *0,0005 km/h* (or 23 in *58 cm* per hr). The snail-racing equivalent of a 4 minute mile is 24 inches in 3 minutes or the 7,920 minute or 5½ day mile.

14. RIBBON WORMS (*Nemertina or Rhynchopods*)

Longest

The longest of the 550 recorded species of ribbon worms, also called nemertines (or nemerteans), is the "Boot-lace worm" (*Lineus longissimus*), which is found in the shallow waters of the North Sea. A specimen washed ashore at St. Andrews, Fife, Scotland in 1864 after a severe storm measured more than 180 ft *55 m* in length, making it easily the longest recorded worm of any variety.

15. JELLYFISHES (*Scyphozoa or Scyphomedusia*)

Largest and smallest

The largest jellyfish is *Cyanea arctica*. For details see page 23.

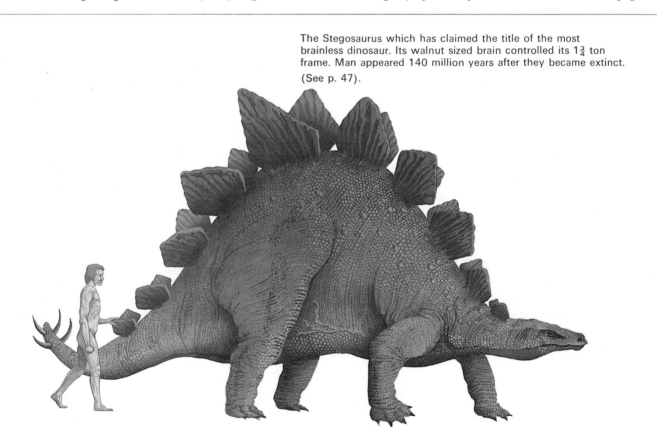

The Stegosaurus which has claimed the title of the most brainless dinosaur. Its walnut sized brain controlled its 1¾ ton frame. Man appeared 140 million years after they became extinct. (See p. 47).

The largest coelenterate found in British waters is the rare "Lion's mane" jellyfish (*Cyanea capillata*), which is also known as the Common sea blubber. One specimen measured at St. Andrew's Marine Laboratory, Fife, Scotland had a bell diameter of 91 cm *35.8 in* and tentacles stretching over 13,7 m *45 ft*. Some true jellyfishes have a bell diameter of less than 20 mm *0.78 in*.

Most venomous

The most venomous coelenterates are the box jellies of the genera *Chiropsalmus* and *Chironex* of the Indo-Pacific region. which carry a neuro-toxic venom similar in strength to that found in the Asiatic cobra. These jellyfish have caused the deaths of at least 60 people off the coast of Queensland, Australia in the past 25 years. Victims die within 1–3 min. A most effective defence is women's panty hose, outsize versions of which are now worn by Queensland life-savers at surf carnivals.

16. SPONGES (*Parazoa, Porifera or Spongida*)

Largest

The largest known sponge is the barrel-shaped Loggerhead sponge (*Spheciospongia vesparium*) of the West Indies and the waters off Florida, U.S.A. Single individuals measure up to 3 ft 6 in *105 cm* in height and 3 ft *91 cm* in diameter. Neptune's cup or goblet (*Poterion patera*) of Indonesia grows to 4 ft *120 cm* in height, but it is a less bulky animal. In 1909 a Wool sponge (*Hippospongia canaliculatta*) measuring 6 ft *183 cm* in circumference was collected off the Bahama Islands. When first taken from the water it weighed between 80 and 90 lb. *36 and 41 kg* but after it had been dried and relieved of all excrescences it scaled 12 lb. *5,44 kg* (this sponge is now preserved in the U.S. National Museum, Washington, D.C., U.S.A.).

Smallest

The smallest known sponge is the widely distributed *Leucosolenia blanca*, which measures 3 mm *0.11 in* in height when fully grown.

Deepest

Sponges have been recovered from depths of up to 18,500 ft *5 637 m*.

17. EXTINCT ANIMALS

Longest *World*

The first dinosaur to be scientifically described was *Megalosaurus* ("large lizard"), a 20 ft *6,09 m* long bipedal theropod, in 1824. A lower jaw and other bones of this animal had been found before 1818 in a slate quarry at Stonesfield, near Woodstock, Oxfordshire, It stalked across what is now southern England about 130,000,000 years ago. The word "dinosaur" ("fearfully great lizard") was not used for such reptiles until 1841. The longest recorded dinosaur was *Diplodocus* ("double-beam"), an attenuated sauropod which ranged over western North America about 150,000,000 years ago. A composite skeleton of three individuals excavated near Split Mountain, Utah between 1909 and 1922 and mounted in the Carnegie Museum of the Natural Sciences in Pittsburgh, Pennsylvania, measures 87½ ft *26,67 m* in total length (neck 22 ft *6,70 m* body 15 ft *4,57 m*, tail 50 ft 6 in *15,40 m*—nearly the length of three London double-decker buses—and 11 ft 9 in *3,6 m* at the pelvis (the highest point on the body). This animal weighed a computed 10,56 tonnes *10.4 tons* in life.

Longest *Britain*

In 1975 an amateur fossil-hunter working on the cliff-face near Brighstone, Isle of Wight, uncovered an unusual 228 mm *9 in* long bone which was later identified as the haemal arch (a bone running beneath the vertebrae of the tail) of a Diplodocus-type sauropod.

Heaviest

The heaviest of all prehistoric animals, and the heaviest land vertebrate of all time, was probably *Brachiosaurus* ("arm lizard") which lived from 135 to 165,000,000 years ago. Its remains have been found in East Africa (Rhodesia and Tanzania), U.S.A. (Colorado, Oklahoma and Utah) and Europe. A complete skeleton excavated near Tendaguru Hill, southern Tanganyika (Tanzania) in 1909 and now mounted in the Museum für Naturkunde, East Berlin, Germany, measures 74 ft 6 in *22,68 m* in total length and 21 ft *6,40 m* at the shoulder. This reptile weighed a computed 78,26 tonnes *77 tons* in life, but isolated bones have since been discovered in East Africa which indicate that some specimens may have weighed as much as 100 tons *102 tonnes* and measured over 90 ft *27 m* in total length.

In the summer of 1972 the remains of another enormous sauropod, new to science, were discovered in a flood-plain bonejam in Colorado, U.S.A. by an expedition from Brigham Young University, Provo, Utah. Excavations are still continuing, but a study of the incomplete series of cervical vertebrae indicate that this dinosaur must have had a neck length of approximately 39 ft *11,88 m* (compare 22 ft *6,70 m* for *diplodocus*) and measured over 100 ft *30,48 m* in total length when alive.

Largest predator

It is now known that some carnosaurs were even larger than the 6¾ ton/*tonnes* 47 ft *14,32 m* *Tyrannosaurus*. In 1930 the British Museum Expedition to East Africa dug up the pelvic bones and part of the vertebrae of another huge carnosaur at Tendaguru Hill which must have measured about 54 ft *16,45 m* in total length when alive. During the summers of 1963–65 a Polish-Mongolian expedition discovered the remains of a carnosaur in the Gobi Desert which had 8 ft 6 in *2,59 m* long forelimbs! It is not yet known, however, whether the rest of this dinosaur was built on the same colossal scale.

Most brainless

Stegosaurus ("plated reptile"), which measured up to 30 ft *9 m* in total length and weighed 1¾ ton/*tonnes*, had a walnut-sized brain weighing only 2½ oz. *70 g*, which represented 0.004 of one per cent of its body weight (*cf*. 0.074 of one per cent for an elephant and 1.88 per cent for a human). It roamed widely across the Northern Hemisphere about 150,000,000 years ago.

Largest dinosaur eggs

The largest known dinosaur eggs are those of *Hypselosaurus priscus*, a 30 ft *9,14 m* long sauropod which lived about 80,000,000 years ago. Some specimens found in the valley of the Durance near Aix-en-Provence southern France in October 1961 would have had, uncrushed, a length of 12 in *300 mm* and a diameter of 10 in *255 mm*.

Largest flying creature

The largest flying creature was a winged reptile (not yet named) of the order Pterosauria which glided over what is now the state of Texas, U.S.A. about 70,000,000 years ago. Partial remains (four wings, a neck, hind legs and mandibles) of three specimens discovered in Big Bend National Park, West Texas recently indicate that this pterosaur must have had a wing span of at least 11 m *36.08 ft* and that the maximum expanse may have been as great as 21 m *68.89 ft* (*cf*. 27 ft *8,23 m* for *Pteranodon ingens*.)

Largest marine reptile

The largest marine reptile ever recorded was *Kronosaurus queenslandicus*, a short-necked pliosaur which swam in the seas around what is now Australia about 100,000,000 years ago. It measured up to 55 ft *16,76 m* in length and had an 11½ ft *3,60 m* long skull. *Stretosaurus macromerus*, another short-necked pliosaur, was also of comparable size. A mandible found in Cumnor, Oxfordshire must have belonged to a reptile measuring at least 50 ft *15,23 m* in length.

Largest crocodile

The largest known crocodile was *Deinosuchus riograndensis*, which lived in the lakes and swamps of what is now the state of Texas, U.S.A. about 75,000,000 years ago. Fragmentary

The almost complete skeleton of the largest prehistoric marine turtle, *Archelon ischyros*, with an estimated live weight of 6,000 lbs. *2 721,5 kg*, now preserved at the Peabody Museum of Natural History, Connecticut, U.S.A.

remains discovered in Big Bend National Park, West Texas, indicate it must have measured at least 50 ft *15,24 m* in total length. The less bulky gavial *Rhamphosuchus*, which lived in what is now northern India about 7,000,000 years ago, also reached a length of 50 ft *15,24 m*.

Largest chelonians

The largest prehistoric marine turtle was probably *Archelon ischyros*, which lived in the shallow seas over what are now the states of South Dakota and Kansas, U.S.A. about 80,000,000 years ago. An almost complete skeleton with a carapace (shell) measuring 6 ft 6 in *1,98 m* in length was discovered in August 1895 near the south fork of the Cheyenne River in Custer County, South Dakota. The skeleton, which has an overall length of 11 ft 4 in *3,45 m* (20 ft *6,09 m* across the outstretched flippers) is now preserved in the Peabody Museum of Natural History at Yale University, New Haven, Connecticut, U.S.A. This specimen is estimated to have weighed 6,000 lb. (*2,720 kg*) when it was alive, In 1914 the fossil remains of another giant marine turtle (*Cratochelone berneyi*) which must have measured at least 12 ft *3,65 m* in overall length when alive were discovered at Sylvania Station, 20 miles *32 km* west of Hughenden, Queensland, Australia.

Largest tortoise

The largest prehistoric tortoise was probably *Colossochelys atlas*, which lived in what is now northern India between 7 and 12,000,000 years ago. The fossil remains of a specimen with a carapace 5 ft 5 in *165 cm* long (7 ft 4 in *2,23 m* over the curve) and 2 ft 11 in *89 cm* high were discovered near Chandigarh in the Siwalik Hills in 1923. This animal had a nose to tail length of 8 ft *2,43 m* and is computed to have weighed 2,100 lb. *952 kg* when it was alive. Recently fossil remains of a similarly sized tortoise were reported from Texas, U.S.A.

Longest snake

The longest prehistoric snake was the python-like *Gigantophis garstini*, which inhabited what is now Egypt about 50,000,000 years ago. Parts of a spinal column and a small piece of jaw discovered at El Faiyum indicate a length of *c*. 33 ft *10,05 m*, which is comparable with the longest constrictors living today.

Largest amphibian

The largest amphibian ever recorded was the alligator-like *Eogyrinus* which lived between 280,000,000 and 345,000,000 years ago. It measured nearly 15 ft *4,57 m* in length.

Largest fish

No prehistoric fish larger than living species has yet been discovered. The claim that the Great shark (*Carcharodon megalodon*), which abounded in Miocene seas some 15 million years ago, measured 80 ft *24 m* in length, based on ratios from fossil teeth has now been shown to be in error. The modern estimate is that this shark did not exceed 43 ft *13,1m*.

Largest insect

The largest prehistoric insect was the dragonfly *Meganeura monyi*, which lived between 280,000,000 and 325,000,000 years ago. Fossil remains (*i.e.* impressions of wings) discovered at Commentry, central France, indicate that it had a wing span reaching up to 70 cm *27.5 in*.

Most southerly

The most southerly creature yet found is a freshwater salamander-like amphibian *Labyrinthodont*, represented by a 2½ in *63,5 mm* piece of jawbone found near Beardmore Glacier Antarctica, 325 miles *532 km* from the South Pole, dating from the early Jurassic of 200,000,000 years ago. This discovery was made in December 1967.

Largest bird

The largest prehistoric bird was the Elephant bird (*Aepyornis maximus*), also known as the "Roc bird", which lived in southern Madagascar. It was a flightless bird standing 9–10 ft *2,74–3,04 m* in height and weighing nearly 1,000 lb. *453 kg*. Aepyornis also had the largest eggs of any known animal. One example preserved in the British Museum (Natural History), London measures 33¾ in *86 cm* round the long axis with a circumference of 28½ in *72 cm* giving a capacity of 2.35 gal *10,68 litres*—seven times that of an ostrich egg. A more cylindrical egg preserved in the Academie des Sciences, Paris, France measures 12⅞ by 15⅜ in *32,7–39 cm* and probably weighed about 27 lb. *12 kg* with its contents. This bird may have survived until *c*. 1660. In 1974 the fossilised remains of a huge emu-like bird were discovered near Alice Springs, central Australia. The bird, which lived about

	EARLIEST OF THEIR TYPES		
Type	Scientific name and year of discovery	Location	Estimated years before present
Ape	Aegyptopitherus zeuxis (1966)	El Faiyûm, Egypt	28,000,000
Primate	tarsier-like	Indonesia	70,000,000
	lemur	Madagascar	70,000,000
Social insect	Sphecomyrma freyi (1967)	New Jersey, U.S.A.	100,000,000
Bird	Archaeopteryx lithographica (1861)	Bavaria, W. Germany	140,000,000
Mammal	shrew-like (1966)	Thaba-ea-Litau, Lesotho	190,000,000
Reptiles	Hylonomus, Archerpeton, Protoclepsybrops Romericus	all in Nova Scotia	290,000,000
Amphibian	Ichthyostega (first quadruped)	Greenland	350,000,000
Spider	Palaeostenzia crassipes	Tayside, Scotland	370,000,000
Insect	Rhyniella procursor	Tayside, Scotland	370,000,000
Vertebrates	Agnathans (Jawless fish)	near Leningrad, U.S.S.R.	480,000,000
Mollusc	Neopilina galatheae (1952)	off Costa Rica	500,000,000
Crustacean	Karagassiema (12 legged)	Sayan Mts., U.S.S.R.	c. 650,000,000
Metazoans	Bore hole tracks	Zambia	1,050,000,000

10,000,000 years ago, stood more than 10 ft *3,04 m* tall and may have been even heavier than Aepyornis maximus. The flightless moa *Dinornis giganteus* of North Island, New Zealand was even taller, attaining a height of over 13 ft *3,96 m* but it only weighed about 500 lb. *227 kg.*

The largest prehistoric bird actually to fly was probably the condor-like *Teratornis incredibilis* which lived in what is now North America about 100,000,000 years ago. Fossil remains discovered in Smith Creek Cave, Nevada in 1952 indicate it had a wing span of 5 m *16 ft 4¾ in* and weighed nearly 50 lb. *22,5 kg.* A wing span measurement of 5 m *16 ft 4¼ in* has also been reported for another flying bird named *Ornithodesmus latidens*, which flew over what is now Hampshire and the Isle of Wight about 90,000,000 years ago. Another gigantic flying bird named *Osteodontornis orri*, which lived in what is now the state of California, U.S.A. about 20,000,000 years ago, had a wing span of 16 ft *4,87 m* and was probably even heavier. It was related to the pelicans and storks. The albatross-like *Gigantornis eaglesomei*, which flew over what is now Nigeria between 34,000,000 and 58,000,000 years ago, has been credited with a wing span of 20 ft *6,09 m* on the evidence of a single fossilised breastbone.

Largest mammal
The largest prehistoric land mammal ever recorded, was *Baluchitherium* (= *Indricotherium, Paraceratherium, Aceratherium, Thaumastotherium, Aralotherium* and *Benaratherium*), a long necked hornless rhinoceros which lived in Europe and central western Asia between 20,000,000 and 40,000,000 years ago. It stood up to 17 ft 9 in *5,41 m* to the top of the shoulder hump, (27 ft *8,23 m* to the crown of the raised head), measured 35–37 ft *10,66–11,27 m* in length and probably weighed nearly 20 tons/*tonnes*. The bones of this gigantic browser were first discovered in 1907–1908 in the Bugti Hills in east Baluchistan, Pakistan. The largest known prehistoric marine mammal was Basilosaurus (= Zeuglodon) of 50,000,000 years ago. A specimen from Alabama measured 70 ft *21,33 m* and weighed an estimated 27 tonnes.

Largest mammoth
The largest extinct elephant was *Paraelephas trogontherii* which roamed both central Europe and North America a million years ago. A fragmentary skeleton found in Mosbach, West Germany indicates a shoulder height of 4,5 m *14 ft 9 in.*

Tusks *Longest*
The longest tusks of any prehistoric animal were those of the straight-tusked elephant *Hesperoloxodon antiquus germanicus*, which lived in what is now northern Germany about 2,000,000 years ago. The average length in adult bulls was 5 m *16 ft 4¾ in.* A single tusk of a woolly mammoth (*Mammonteus primigenius*) preserved in the Franzens Museum at Brno, Czechoslovakia measures 5,02 m *16 ft 5½ in* along the outside curve. In *c.* August 1933, a single tusk of an Imperial mammoth (*Archidiskodon imperator*) measuring 16+ ft *4,87+ m* (anterior end missing) was unearthed near Post, Gorza County, Texas, U.S.A. In 1934 this tusk was presented to the American Museum of Natural History in New York City, N.Y., U.S.A.

Tusks *Heaviest*
The heaviest fossil tusk on record is one weighing 330 lb. *149,7 kg* with a maximum circumference of 35 in *89 cm* now preserved in the Museo Civico di Storia Naturale, Milan, Italy. The specimen (in two pieces) measures 11 ft 9 in *3,58 m* in length. The heaviest recorded mammoth tusks are a pair in the University of Nebraska Museum, Lincoln, Nebraska, U.S.A. which have a combined weight of 498 lb. *226 kg* and measure 13 ft 9 in *4,21 m* and 13 ft 7 in *4,14 m* respectively. They were found near Campbell, Nebraska in April 1915.

Antlers *Greatest Span*
The prehistoric Giant deer (*Megaceros giganteus*), which lived in northern Europe and northern Asia as recently as 50,000 B.C., had the longest horns of any known animal. One specimen recovered from an Irish bog had greatly palmated antlers measuring 14 ft *4,3 m* across.

KINGDOM PROTISTA

PROTISTA
Protista were first discovered in 1676 by Anton van Leeuwenhoek of Delft (1632–1723), a Dutch microscopist. Among Protista are characteristics common to both plants and animals. The more plant-like are termed Protophyta (protophytes), including unicellular algae, and the more animal-like are placed in the phylum Protozoa (protozoans), including amoeba and flagellates.

Largest
The largest protozoans which are known to have existed were the now extinct Nummulites, which each had a diameter of 0.95 in *24,1 mm.* The largest existing protozoan is *Pelomyxa palustris*, which may attain a length of up to 0.6 of an in *15,2 mm.*

Smallest
The smallest of all protophytes is *Micromonas pusilla*, with a diameter of less than 2 microns or micrometres (2×10^{-6}m) or *0.00008 of an in.*

Fastest moving
The protozoan *Monas stigmatica* has been measured to move a distance equivalent to 40 times its own length in a second. No human can cover even seven times his own length in a second.

Fastest reproduction
The protozoan *Glaucoma*, which reproduces by binary fission, divides as frequently as every three hours. Thus in the course of a day it could become a "six greats grandparent" and the progenitor of 510 descendants.

FUNGUS
Largest
The largest recorded specimen of the giant puff ball (*Lycoperdon gigantea*) was one 62 in *157 cm* in diameter and 18 in

45,5 cm high found at Mellor, Derbyshire in 1971. A flatter specimen 64 in *162,5 cm* in diameter was recorded in New York State, U.S.A. in 1877.

The largest officially recorded tree fungus was a specimen of *Oxyporus (Fomes) nobilissimus*, measuring 56 in *142 cm* by 37 in *94 cm* and weighing at least 300 lb. *136 kg* found by J. Hisey in Washington State, U.S.A., in 1946. The largest recorded in the United Kingdom is an ash fungus (*Fomes fraxineus*) measuring 50 in by 15 in *127 cm* by *38 cm* wide, found by the forester A. D. C. LeSueur on a tree at Waddesdon, Buckinghamshire, in 1954.

Most poisonous toadstool

The yellowish-olive death cap (*Amanita phalloides*) is regarded as the world's most poisonous fungus. It is found in England. From six to fifteen hours after tasting, the effects are vomiting, delirium, collapse and death. Among its victims was Cardinal Giulio de' Medici, Pope Clement VII (b. 1478) on 25 Sept. 1534.

The Registrar General's Report states that between 1920 and 1950 there were 39 fatalities from fungus poisoning in the United Kingdom. As the poisonous types are mostly *Amanita* varieties, it is reasonable to assume that the deaths were predominantly due to *Amanita phalloides*. The most recent fatality was probably in 1960.

Aeroflora

Fungi are classified in the subkingdom Protophyta of the Kingdom Protista. The highest total fungal spore count was 161,037 per m^3 near Cardiff on 21 July 1971. A plant tree pollen count of 2,160 per m^3 was recorded near London on 9 May 1971. The lowest counts of airborne allergens are nil. The highest recorded grass pollen count in Britain was one of 2,824 per m^3 recorded at Aberystwyth on 29 June 1961.

KINGDOM PROCARYOTA

BACTERIA

Largest

The largest of the bacteria is the sulphur bacterium *Beggiatoa mirabilis*, which is from 16 to 45 microns in width and which may form filaments several millimetres long.

Smallest Free-Living Entity

The smallest of all free-living organisms are pleuro-pneumonia-like organisms (P.P.L.O.) of the *Mycoplasma*. One of these, *Mycoplasma laidlawii*, first discovered in sewage in 1936, has a diameter during its early existence of only 100 millimicrons, or 0.000004 of an in. Examples of the strain known as H.39 have a maximum diameter of 300 millimicrons and weigh an estimated 1.0×10^{-16} of a gramme. Thus a 174 ton *177 tonnes* Blue whale would weigh 1.77×10^{23} or 177,000 trillion times as much.

Highest

In April 1967 the U.S. National Aeronautics and Space Administration reported that bacteria had been recently discovered at an altitude of 135,000 ft (25.56 miles) *41 100 m.*

Longest lived

The oldest deposits from which living bacteria are claimed to have been extracted are salt layers near Irkutsk, U.S.S.R., dating from about 600,000,000 years ago. The discovery was not accepted internationally. The U.S. Dry Valley Drilling Project in Antarctica claimed resuscitated rod-shaped bacteria from caves up to a million years old.

Toughest

The bacterium *Micrococus radiodurans* can withstand atomic radiation of 6.5 million röntgens or 10,000 times that fatal to the average man.

VIRUSES

Largest

The largest true viruses are the brick-shaped pox viruses (*e.g.* smallpox, vaccina, orf etc.) measuring *c.* 250 × 300 millimicrons (mμ) or 0.0003 of a mm.

Smallest

Of more than 1,000 identified viruses, the smallest is the sheep scrapie virus with a diameter of 14 nanometers or 14 millionths of a millimetre.

PLANT KINGDOM (*Plantae*)

Guinness Superlatives Ltd. has published a specialist volume entitled the *Guinness Book of Plant Facts and Feats* in which further details of Plant records may be found (Price £5.95).

PLANTS

Earliest life *World and United Kingdom*

If one accepts the definition of life as the ability of an organism to make replicas of itself by taking as building materials the simpler molecules in the medium around it, life probably appeared on Earth *c.* 3,355 million years ago. This date for the earliest spheroid photosynthesising micro-organisms (7–10 mμ in diameter) from the Lower Onverwacht strata of the South Africa-Swaziland border was announced in January 1973. The oldest known living life-form was announced in December 1970 by Drs. Sanford and Barbara Siegel of Harvard University, U.S.A., to be a microscopic organism, similar in form to an orange slice, first collected near Harlech, Gwynedd, Wales in 1964. It has been named *Kakabekia barghoorniana* and has existed from 2,000 million years ago.

Rarest

Plants thought to be extinct are rediscovered each year and there are thus many plants of which specimens are known in but a single locality. The rose purple Alpine coltsfoot (*Homogyne alpina*), recorded by Don prior to 1814 in the mountains of Colva, Tayside, Scotland, was not again confirmed until 1951. The only known location of the adder's-tongue spearwort (*Ranunculus ophioglossifolius*) in the British Isles is the Badgeworth Nature Reserve, Gloucestershire. *Pennantia baylisiana*, a tree found in 1945 on Three Kings Island, off New Zealand, only exists as a female and cannot fruit.

Northernmost

The yellow poppy (*Papaver radicatum*) and the Arctic willow (*Salix arctica*) survive, the latter in an extremely stunted form, on the northernmost land (83° N).

Southernmost

The most southerly plant life recorded is seven species of lichen found in 1933–34 by the second expedition of Rear-Admiral Richard E. Byrd, U.S. Navy, in latitude 86° 03′ S. in the Queen Maud Mountains, Antarctica. The southernmost recorded flowering plant is the carnation (*Colobanthus crassifolius*), which was found in latitude 67° 15′ S. on Jenny Island, Margaret Bay, Graham Land (Palmer Peninsula), Antarctica.

Highest

The greatest altitude at which any flowering plant has been found is 20,130 ft *6 135 m* in the Himalaya for *Stellaria decumbens*.

Roots

The greatest reported depth to which roots have penetrated is a calculated 400 ft *120 m* in the case of a wild fig tree at Echo Caves, near Ohrigstad, East Transvaal, South Africa.

A single winter rye plant (*Secale cereale*) has been shown to produce 387 miles *622,8 km* of roots in 1.83 cubic feet *0,051 m³* of earth.

Worst weeds

The most intransigent weed is the mat-forming water weed *Salvinia auriculata*, found in Africa. It was detected on the filling of Kariba Lake in May 1959 and within 11 months had choked an area of 77 miles² *199 km²* rising by 1963 to 387 miles² *1 002 km²*. The world's worst land weeds are regarded as purple nut sedge, Bermuda grass, barnyard grass, junglerice, goose grass, Johnson grass, Guinea grass, cogon grass and lantana. The most damaging and widespread cereal weeds in Britain are the wild oats *Avena fatua* and *A. ludoviciana*. Their seeds can withstand temperatures of 240° F *115,6° C* for 15 minutes and remain viable.

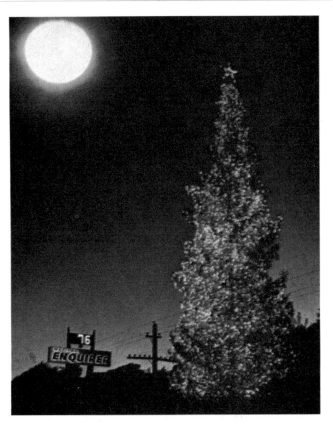

above: The tree in Britain with the greatest girth, a Sweet Chestnut (*Castanea sativa*) with a bole 43 ft 9 ins *13,33 m* in circumference. (See page 53). (*Guinness Superlatives Limited*)

right: The World's tallest cut Christmas tree, the 106 ft *32,3 m* Douglas Fir (*Pseudotsuga taxifolia*) erected at Lantana, Florida, U.S.A. (See page 53). (*National Enquirer*)

below right: Two specimens of the largest fungus, the giant puff ball (*Lycoperdon gigantea*), which have been known to measure 64 in *162,5 cm* in diameter. (See page 50). (*Heather Angel*)

Most spreading plant

The greatest area covered by a single clonal growth is that of the wild box huckleberry (*Gaylussacia brachyera*), a mat-forming evergreen shrub first reported in 1796. A colony covering 8 acres *3,2 hectares* was discovered in 1845 near New Bloomfield, Pennsylvania. Another colony, covering about 100 acres, was "discovered" on 18 July 1920 near the Juniata River, Pennsylvania. It has been estimated that this colony began 13,000 years ago.

Largest aspidistra

The aspidistra (*Aspidistra elatior*) was introduced to Britain as a parlour palm from Japan and China in 1822. The biggest aspidistra in the world is one 49¾ in *126 cm* tall and grown by George Munns at Perth University, Western Australia and measured in January 1972.

Earliest flower

The oldest fossil of a flowering plant with palm-like imprints was found in Colorado, U.S.A., in 1953 and dated about 65,000,000 years old.

Largest cactus

The largest of all cacti is the saguaro (*Cereus giganteus* or *Carnegiea gigantea*), found in Arizona, south eastern California, U.S.A. and Sonora, Mexico. The green fluted column is surmounted by candelabra-like branches rising to a height of 52 ft 5¾ in *16,00 m* in the case of a specimen measured on the boundary of the Saguaro National Monument, Arizona. They have waxy white blooms which are followed by edible crimson fruit. A cardon cactus in Baja California, Mexico was reputed to reach a height of 58 ft *17,67 m* and a weight of 9 tons/*tonnes*.

Tallest hedge *World*

The world's tallest hedge is the Meikleour beech hedge in Perthshire, Scotland. It was planted in 1746 and has now attained a trimmed height of 85 ft *26 m*. It is 600 yds *550 m* long. Some of its trees now exceed 100 ft *30,48 m*.

Tallest hedge *Yew*

The tallest yew hedge in the world is in Earl Bathurst's Park, Cirencester, Gloucestershire. It was planted in 1720, runs for 170 yds *155 m* reaches 36 ft *11 m*, is 15 ft *4,57 m* thick at its base and takes 20 man-days to trim.

Tallest hedge *Box*

The tallest box hedge is 35 ft *10,7 m* in height at Birr Castle, Offaly, Ireland dating from the 18th century.

Mosses

The smallest of mosses is the pygmy moss (*Ephemerum*) and the longest is the brook moss (*Fontinalis*), which forms streamers up to 3 ft *91 cm* long in flowing water.

Longest seaweed

Claims made that seaweed off Tierra del Fuego, South America, grows to 600 ft *182,5 m* and even to 1,000 ft *305 m* in length have gained currency. More recent and more reliable records indicate that the longest species of seaweed is the Pacific giant kelp (*Macrocystis pyrifera*), which does not exceed 196 ft *60 m* in length. It can grow 45 cm *17¾ in* in a day. The longest of the 700 species of seaweed recognised around the coasts of Britain is the brown seaweed *Chorda filum* which grows up to a length of 20 ft *6,10 m*. The largest British seaweed is *Saccorhiza polyschides*, single plants of which may weigh 2 cwt./*100 kg*.

RECORD DIMENSIONS AND WEIGHTS FOR FRUIT, VEGETABLES AND FLOWERS GROWN IN THE UNITED KINGDOM

Most data subsequent to 1958 comes from the annual *Garden News* Giant Vegetable and Fruit Contest and the Super Sunflower Contest.

Apple	3 lb. 1 oz.	1,375 kg	V. Loveridge	Ross-on-Wye, Hereford and Worcester	1965
Artichoke	8 lb.	3,625 kg	A. R. Lawson	Tollerton, North Yorkshire	1964
Beetroot	24 lb.	10,875 kg	R. G. Arthur	Longlevens, Gloucestershire	1971
Broad Bean	23⅜ in	59,3 cm	T. Currie	Jedburgh, Borders	1963
Broccoli	28 lb. 14¾ oz.	13,100 kg	J. T. Cooke	Funtington, West Sussex	1964
Brussels Sprout[1]	16 lb. 1 oz.	7,285 kg	E. E. Jenkins	Shipston-on-Stour, Warwickshire	1974
Cabbage[2]	96 lb. 0 z.	43,525 kg	C. Bowcock	Willaston, Merseyside	1973
Carrot[3]	7 lb. 5 oz.	3,300 kg	R. Clarkson	Freckleton, Lancashire	1970
Cauliflower	52 lb. 11½ oz.	23,900 kg	J. T. Cooke	Funtington, West Sussex	1966
Celery	35 lb. 0 oz.	15,875 kg	C. Bowcock	Willaston, Merseyside	1973
Cucumber[4]	11 lb. 6 oz. (indoor)	5,155 kg	C. Bowcock	Willaston, Merseyside	1973
	8 lb. 4 oz. (outdoor)	3,740 kg	C. Bowcock	Willaston, Merseyside	1973
Dahlia	9 ft tall	2,74 m	J. Crennan	Abbey Wood, London S.E.	1975
Dwarf Bean	17½ in	43,4 cm	C. Bowcock	Willaston, Merseyside	1973
Gourd	196 lb.	88,900 kg	J. Leathes	Herringfleet Hall, Suffolk	1846
Grapefruit*	3 lb. 8 oz.	1,585 kg	A. J. Frost	Willington, Bedfordshire	1977
Kale	12 ft tall	3,65 m	B. T. Newton	Mullion, Cornwall	1950
Leek	9 lb. 5½ oz.	4,235 kg	C. Bowcock	Willaston, Merseyside	1973
Lemon[5]	2 lb. 13 oz. (girth 23 in 58,4 cm)	1,275 kg	Dr. M. E. Nobbs	Shyrehill, Buckfast, S. Devon	1976
Lettuce	25 lb. 0 oz.	11,335 kg	C. Bowcock	Willaston, Merseyside	1974
Lupin*	6 ft 0½ in	1,84 m	J. Lawlor	New Maldon, Surrey	1971
Mangold	54½ lb.	24,720 kg	P. F. Scott	Sutton, Humberside	1971
Marrow[6]	60 lb.	27,200 kg	A. V. Bishop	Snailwell, Cambridgeshire	1963
Mushroom[7]	54 in circum.	1,37 m	—	Hasketon, Suffolk	1957
Onion	6 lb. 1¼ oz.	2,755 kg	A. N. Rowntree	Ammandford, Dyfed	1975
Parsnip[8]	10 lb. 0 oz.	4,525 kg	C. Bowcock	Willaston, Merseyside	1973
Pea Pod	10⅛ in	25,7 cm	T. Currie	Jedburgh, Borders	1964
Pear	2 lb. 10½ oz.	1,200 kg	Mrs. K. Loines	Hythe, Hampshire	1973
Potato[9]	7 lb. 1 oz.	3,200 kg	J. H. East	Spalding, Lincolnshire	1963
Pumpkin[10]	204 lb. 8 oz.	92,750 kg	F. H. Smith	Coventry, West Midlands	1970
Radish[11]	16 lb. 8 oz.	7,475 kg	E. E. Allen	Heston, Hounslow, Greater London	1966
Red Cabbage	33 lb. 2 oz.	15,025 kg	A. Bratton	Ryton, Salop	1963
Rhubarb	5 ft 1¾ in 4 lb. 3¾ oz.	155,2 cm 1,920 kg	A. C. Setterfield	Englefield, Berkshire	1974
Runner Bean	39 in long	99 cm	Mrs. E. Huxley	Churton, Cheshire	1976
Savoy	38 lb. 8 oz.	17,450 kg	W. H. Neil	Retford Nottinghamshire	1966
Shallot*	1 lb. 10 oz.	725 kg	C. Bowcock	Willaston, Merseyside	1973
Strawberry	7¼ oz.	205 kg	E. Oxley	Walton-on-the-Naze, Essex	1972
Sugar Beet[12]	21 lb.	9,525 kg	L. Hawcroft	Home-on-Spalding Moor, Humberside	1971
Sunflower	23 ft 6½ in tall	7,17 m	F. Kelland	Exeter, Devon	1976
Swede[13]	35 lb.	15,875 kg	J. G. Lang	Hilton of Carslogie, Fife	1976
Tomato[14]	4 lb. 4 oz.	1,925 kg	C. Roberts	Eastbourne, East Sussex	1974
Tomato Plant	20 ft tall, 34 lb. fruit	6,09 m 15,400 kg	—	Southport, Merseyside	1957
Tomato Truss	20 lb. 4 oz.	9,175 kg	C. Bowcock	Willaston, Merseyside	1973
Turnip[15]	35 lb. 4 oz.	15,975 kg	C. W. Butler	Nafferton, Humberside	1972

[1] *A Brussels Sprout plant measuring 10 ft 8 in 3,25 m was grown by G. Mobbs of Leavesden, Hertfordshire in May 1976. A claim for 16 lb. 1 oz. 7,285 kg has been made by E. E. Jenkins of Shipston-on-Stour, Warwickshire.*

[2] *The Swalwell, County Durham Red Cabbage of 1865 grown by William Collingwood (d. 8 Oct. 1867) reputedly weighed 123 lb. 55,7 kg and was 259 in 6,57 m in circumference*

[3] *One of 7 lb. 7 oz. 3,35 kg (15 in 38 m long) reported grown by Police Sgt. Alfred Garwood of Blidworth, Nottinghamshire in November 1970. A specimen of 11 lb. 4,79 kg was grown by Bob McEwan of Beeac, Victoria, Australia in Sept. 1967.*

[4] *A 12 lb. 11 oz. 5,75 kg example was reported from Ross Thomas of Wellington, N.S.W., on 28 June 1969.*

[5] *A lemon with a 28¾ in 73 cm girth was reported by Mrs. D. Knutzen of Whittier, California U.S.A. in Jan. 1977.*

[6] *A 96 lb. 43,525 kg marrow has been reported from Suffolk. A 63½ lb. 28,000 kg specimen grown by J. C. Lewis of Blackwood, Gwent, won a contest in 1937.*

[7] *Same size reported by J. Coombes at Mark, Somerset on 28 July 1965. In Sept. 1968 one weighing 18 lb. 10 oz. 8,425 kg was reported from Whidbey*

Is., Washington, U.S.A. A mushroom with an estimated circumference of 75 in 190 cm was reported by the Lulualaba river, Zaire in 1920.

[8] *60 in 152 cm long: M. Zaninovich of Wanneroo, Western Australia.*

[9] *One weighing 18 lb. 4 oz. 8,275 kg reported dug up by Thomas Siddal in his garden in Chester on 17 Feb. 1795. A yield of 2,963 lb. 1,344 kg from 6 uncut sets in 1974 by Colin Bowcock (see above). Six tubers weighing 54 lb. 8 oz. 24,72 kg by Alan Nunn of Rhodes, Greater Manchester were reported on 18 Sept. 1949.*

[10] *A pumpkin of 451 lb. 204,5 kg 125 in 3,17 m in girth was grown by Bob Ford at Coatesville, Pennsylvania, U.S.A. in 1976.*

[11] *A China rose radish of 25 lb. 11,34 kg 25½ in 64,5 cm long was grown by Glen Tucker of Stanbury, South Australia in Aug. 1974.*

[12] *One weighing 35 lb. 15,87 kg was grown by Fritz Kuhn of Imperial Valley, California in 1973.*

[13] *One weighing 39 lb. 8 oz. 17,9 kg claimed by E. R. Reay of Gaitsgill Hall, Dalston, Cumbria, 1940 (unratified).*

[14] *Grace's Gardens reported a 6 lb. 8 oz. 2,94 kg tomato grown by Clarence Dailey of Monona, Iowa.*

[15] *A 73 lb. 33,1 kg turnip was reported in December 1768.*

* *Not in official contest.*

Largest vines

The largest recorded grape vine was one planted in 1842 at Carpinteria, California, U.S.A. By 1900 it was yielding more than 9 tons/*tonnes* of grapes in some years, and averaging 7 tons/*tonnes* per year. It died in 1920. Britain's largest vine (1898–1964) was at Kippen, Stirling with a girth, measured in 1956, of 5 ft *1,52 m*. England's largest vine is the Great Vine, planted in 1768 at Hampton Court, Greater London. Its girth is 38 in *96,5 cm* with branches up to 110 ft *33,5 m* long and an average yield of 1,200 lb. *545 kg.*

Most Northerly

A vineyard at Sabile, Latvia, U.S.S.R. is just north of Lat. 57° N. The most northerly vineyard in Britain is that at Renishaw Hall, Derbyshire with 2,600 vines. It lies in Lat. 53° 18′ N.

TREES AND WOOD
Most massive tree

The most massive living thing on Earth is the biggest known California big tree (*Sequoiadendron giganteum*) named the "General Sherman", standing 272 ft 4 in *83 m* tall, in the Sequoia National Park, California, U.S.A. It has a true girth of 79.1 ft *24,11 m* (at 5 ft *1,52 m* above the ground). The "General Sherman" has been estimated to contain the equivalent of 600,120 board feet of timber, sufficient to make 5,000,000,000 matches. The foliage is blue-green, and the red-brown tan bark may be up to 24 in *61 cm* thick in parts. In 1968 the official published figure for its estimated weight was "2,145 tons" (1,915 long tons *2 030 tonnes*).

The seed of a "big tree" weighs only 1/6,000th of an oz. *4,7 mg.* Its growth at maturity may therefore represent an increase in weight of over 250,000 million fold.

Tallest *World*

The world's tallest known species of tree is the coast redwood (*Sequoia sempervirens*), now found growing indigenously only near the coast of California from just across the Oregon border south to Monterey.

The tallest example is now believed to be the Howard Libbey Tree in Redwood Creek Grove, Humboldt County, California announced at 367.8 ft *112,10 m* in 1964 but discovered to have an apparently dead top and re-estimated at 366.2 ft *111,60 m* in 1970. It has a girth of 44 ft *13,41 m*. The nearby tree announced to a Senate Committee by Dr. Rudolf W. Becking on 18 June 1966 to be 385 ft *117,34 m*, proved on re-measurement to be no more than 311.3 ft *94,88 m* tall. The tallest non-sequoia is a Douglas fir at Quinault Lake Park trail, Washington, U.S.A. of *c*. 310 ft *94,5 m*.

Tallest *All-time*

The identity of the tallest tree of all-time has never been satisfactorily resolved. Although there have been claims as high as 525 ft *160 m* (subsequently reduced in May 1889 on re-measurement to 220 ft *67 m*), the now accepted view is that maximum height recorded by a qualified surveyor was

the 375 ft *114,3 m* Cornthwaite Tree (*Eucalyptus regnans*, formerly *E. amygdalina*) in Thorpdale, Gippsland, Victoria in 1880. Claims for a Douglas fir (*Pseudotsuga taxifolia*) of 417 ft *127,10 m* with a 77 ft *23,47 m* circumference felled by George Carey in 1895 in British Columbia have been obscured, though not necessarily invalidated by a falsified photograph. The tallest specimen now known is *c*. 310 ft *94,5 m* (see above). A coast redwood of 367 ft 8 in *112,06 m* felled in 1873 near Guerneville, California, U.S.A., was thus almost precisely the same height as the Howard Libbey Tree as originally measured.

Tallest *Great Britain*

The tallest tree in Great Britain is a Grand fir (*Abies grandis*) at Strone, Cairndow, Strathclyde, now 188 ft *57 m* tall. The tallest in England is a Wellingtonia (*Sequoiadendron giganteum*) measured at 165 ft *50,29 m* in February 1970 at Endsleigh, Devon. The tallest measured in Northern Ireland is a Giant Sequoia (*Sequoiadendron giganteum*, measured in 1976 to be 158 ft *48 m* tall at Caledon Castle, County Armagh.

Tallest *Ireland*

The tallest tree in Ireland is a Sitka spruce (*Picea sitchensis*) 166 ft *50,59 m* tall at Curraghmore, Waterford, measured in March 1974.

Tallest Christmas Tree

The world's tallest cut Christmas tree was a 106 ft *32,3 m* Douglas fir (*Pseudotsuga taxifolia*) erected at Lantana, Florida, U.S.A. on 6 Dec. 1976 and decorated with 13,000 coloured lights and 6,900 other decorations. The tallest Christmas tree erected in Britain was the 85 ft 3¼ in *25,98 m* long spruce from Norway erected for the Canterbury Cathedral appeal on the South Bank, London on 20 Nov. 1975.

Greatest girth *World*

The Santa Maria del Tule Tree, in the state of Oaxaca, in Mexico is a Montezuma cypress (*Taxodium mucronatum*) with a girth of 112–113 ft *34,1–34,4 m* (1949) at a height of 5 ft *1,52 m* above the ground. A figure of 167 ft *51 m* in circumference was reported for the pollarded European chestnut (*Castanea sativa*) known as the "Tree of the 100 Horse" ("Castagno di Cento Cavalli") on Mount Etna, Sicily, Italy in 1972.

Greatest girth *Britain*

The tree of greatest girth in Britain is a Sweet Chestnut (*Castanea sativa*) at Canford, Dorset, with a bole 43 ft 9 in *13,33m* in circumference. The largest-girthed living British oak is one at Bowthorpe Farm near Bourne, south Lincolnshire, measured in Sept. 1973 to be 39 ft 1 in *11,91 m*. The largest "maiden" (*i.e.* not pollarded) oak is the Majesty Oak at Fredville Park, near Nonington, Kent, with a girth of (1973) 38 ft 1 in *11,60 m*.

Oldest tree *World*

The oldest recorded tree was a bristlecone pine (*Pinus longaeva*) designated WPN–114, which grew at 10,750 ft *3 275 m*

TALLEST TREES IN UNITED KINGDOM AND IRELAND—By species							
		ft	m			ft	m
Alder (Italian)	Westonbirt, Gloucester	92	28	Lime	Duncombe Park, North Yorks.	150	45
Alder (Common)	Sandling Park, Kent	85	25	Metasequoia	Wisley, Surrey	66	20
Ash	Chiswick Ho., Greater London	118	36	Monkey Puzzle	Bicton House, Devon	90	27,5
Beech	Whitfield Ho., Hereford & Wor.	135	41	Oak (Common)	Fountains Abbey, North Yorks.	120	36
Beech (Copper)	Longleat, Wiltshire	112	34	Oak (Sessile)	Whitfield Ho., Hereford & Worcs.	140	42
Birch (Silver)	Woburn Sands, Bedfordshire	97	29	Oak (Red)	Cowdray Park, West Sussex	115	35
Cedar (of Lebanon)	Petworth House, West Sussex	132	40	Pear	Borde Hill, West Sussex	64	19
Chestnut (Horse)	Petworth House, West Sussex	125	38	Pine (Corsican)	Stanage Park, Powys	144	43
Chestnut (Sweet)	Godinton Park, Kent	118	35	Plane	Bryanston, Dorset	145	44
Cypress (Lawson)	Endsleigh, Devon	133	40	Poplar (Black Italian)	Fairlawne, Kent	150	46
Cypress (Monterey)	Tregothnan, Cornwall	120	36	Poplar (Lombardy)	Marble Hill, Twickenham, G. London	118	35
Douglas Fir	Powis Castle, Powys	181	55	Redwood (Coast)	Undisclosed site, north Devon	138	42
Elm (Wych)	Rossie Priory, nr. Dundee	128	39	Silver Fir	Benmore, Strathclyde	158	48
Elm (Jersey)	Wilton, Wiltshire	122	37	Spruce (Sitka)	Murthly, Tayside	174	53
Eucalyptus (Blue Gum)	Glengariff, Co. Cork	140	42	Sycamore	Drumlanrig Castle, Dumfries & Gal.	112	34
Grand Fir	Strone, Cairndow, Strathclyde	188	57	Tulip-tree	Taplow House, Buckinghamshire	120	36
Ginkgo	Linton Park (Maidstone), Kent	93	28	Walnut	Mottisfont Abbey, Hampshire	74	22
Hemlock (Western)	Benmore, Strathclyde	152	46	Walnut, (Black)	Garendon Hall, Leicestershire	98	30
Holly	Staverton Thicks, Suffolk	74	22	Wellingtonia	Endsleigh, Devon	165	50
Hornbeam	Hutton-in-the-Forest, Cumbria	98	29	Willow (weeping)	Trinity College, Cambridge	76	23
Larch (European)	Hascombe, Surrey	146	44,5	Yew	Midhurst, West Sussex	85	25
Larch (Japanese)	Blair Castle, Tayside	121	36				

above sea-level on the north-east face of the Wheeler Ridge on the Sierra Nevada, California, U.S.A. During studies in 1963 and 1964 it was found to be about 4,900 years old but was cut down with a chain saw. The oldest known *living* tree is the bristlecone pine named *Methuselah* at 10,000 ft *3 050 m* in the California side of the White Mountains confirmed as 4,600 years old. In March 1974 it was reported that this tree had produced 48 live seedlings. Dendrochronologists estimate the *potential* life-span of a bristlecone pine at nearly 5,500 years, but that of a "Big Tree" at perhaps 6,000 years. A report in March 1976 stated that some enormous specimens of Japanese cedar (*Cryptomeria japonica*) had been dated by carbon-14 to 5,200 B.C.

Oldest tree *Great Britain*

Of all British trees that with the longest life is the yew (*Taxus baccata*), for which a maximum age well in excess of 1,000 years is usually conceded. The oldest known is the Fortingall Yew near Aberfeldy, Tayside, part of which still grows. In 1777 this tree was over 50 ft *15,24 m* in girth and it cannot be much less than 1,500 years old today.

Earliest species

The earliest species of tree still surviving is the maiden-hair tree (*Ginkgo biloba*) of Chekiang, China, which first appeared about 160,000,000 years ago, during the Jurassic era. It was "re-discovered" by Kaempfer (Netherlands) in 1690 and reached England *c.* 1754. It has been grown in Japan since *c.* 1100 where it was known as *ginkyō* ("silver apricot") and is now known as *icho*.

Fastest growing

Discounting bamboo, which is not botanically classified as a tree, but as a woody grass, the fastest rate of growth recorded is 35 ft 3 in *10,74 m* in 13 months by an *Albizzia falcataria* planted on 17 June 1974 in Sabah, Malaysia. The youngest recorded age for a tree to reach 100 ft *30,48 m* is 7 years for *Eucalyptus regnans* in Rhodesia.

Slowest growing

The speed of growth of trees depends largely upon conditions, although some species, such as box and yew, are always slow-growing. The extreme is represented by a specimen of Sitka spruce which required 98 years to grow to 11 in *28 cm* tall with a diameter of less than 1 in *2,5 cm* on the Arctic tree-line. The growing of miniature trees or *bonsai* is an oriental cult mentioned as early as *c.* 1320.

Remotest

The tree remotest from any other tree is believed to be one at an oasis in the Ténéré Desert, Niger Republic. In Feb. 1960 it survived being rammed by a lorry driven by a Frenchman. There were no other trees within 50 km *31 miles*. The tree was transplanted and it is now in the Museum at Niamey, Niger.

Most expensive

The highest price ever paid for a tree is $51,000 (then £18,214) for a single Starkspur Golden Delicious apple tree from near Yakuma, Washington, U.S.A., bought by a nursery in Missouri in 1959.

Largest forest *World*

The largest afforested areas in the world are the vast coniferous forests of the northern U.S.S.R., lying mainly between latitude 55° N, and the Arctic Circle. The total wooded area amount to 2,700,000,000 acres *1 100 million ha* (25 per cent of the world's forests), of which 38 per cent is Siberian larch. The U.S.S.R. is 34 per cent afforested.

Largest forest *Great Britain*

The largest forest in England is Kielder Forest (72,336 acres *29 273 ha*), in Northumberland. The largest forest in Wales is the Coed Morgannwg (Forest of Glamorgan) (42,555 acres *17 221 ha*). Scotland's most extensive forest is the Glen Trool Forest (51,376 acres *20 791 ha*) in Kirkcudbrightshire. The United Kingdom is 7 per cent afforested.

Wood *Heaviest*

The heaviest of all woods is black ironwood (*Olea laurifolia*), also called South African ironwood, with a specific gravity of up to 1.49, and weighing up to 93 lb./ft³ *1 490 kg/m³*. The heaviest British wood is boxwood (*Buxus sempervirens*) with an extreme of 64 lb./ft³ *1 025 kg/m³*.

Wood *Lightest*

The lightest wood is *Aeschynomene hispida*, found in Cuba, which has a specific gravity of 0.044 and a weight of only 2¾ lb./ft³ *44 kg/m³*. The wood of the balsa tree (*Ochroma pyramidale*) is of very variable density—between 2½ and 24 lb./ft³ *40 and 384 kg/m³*. The density of cork is 15 lb./ft³ *240 kg/m³*.

Bamboo *Tallest*

The tallest recorded bamboo was a Thorny bamboo culm (*Bambusa arundinacea*) felled at Pattazhi, Travancore, Southern India, in November 1904 measuring 121½ ft *37,03 m*.

Bamboo *Fastest growing*

Some species of the 45 genera of bamboo have attained growth rates of up to 36 in *91 cm* per day (0.00002 m.p.h. *0,00003 km/h*), on their way to reaching a height of 100 ft *30 m* in less than three months.

BLOOMS AND FLOWERS

Largest bloom *World*

The mottled orange-brown and white parasitic stinking corpse lily (*Rafflesia arnoldii*) has the largest of all blooms. These attach themselves to the cissus vines of the jungle in south-east Asia and measure up to 3 ft *91 cm* across and ¾ of an in *1,9 cm* thick, and attain a weight of 15 lb. *7 kg*.

The largest known inflorescence is that of *Puya raimondii*, a rare Bolivian plant with an erect panicle (diameter 8 ft *2,4 m*) which emerges to a height of 35 ft *10,7 m*. Each of these bears up to 8,000 white blooms (see also Slowest-flowering plant, below). The flower-spike of an agave was in 1974 measured to be 52 ft *15,8 m* long in Berkeley, California.

The world's largest blossoming plant is the giant Chinese wisteria at Sierra Madre, California, U.S.A. It was planted in 1892 and now has branches 500 ft *152 m* long. It covers nearly an acre, weighs 225 tons *228 tonnes* and has an estimated 1,500,000 blossoms during its blossoming period of five weeks, when up to 30,000 people pay admission to visit it. In November 1974 a Passion plant, fed by a hormone by Dennis and Patti Carlson, was reported to have grown to a length of 600 ft *182 m* at Blaine, Minnesota, U.S.A.

Largest bloom *Great Britain*

The largest bloom of any indigenous British flowering plant is that of the wild white water lily (*Nymphaea alba*), which measures 6 in *15 cm* across. Other species bear much larger inflorescences.

Smallest flowering plant

The smallest of all flowering plants are duckweeds, seen on the surface of ponds. Of these the rootless *Wolffia punctata* has fronds only 1/50th to 1/35th of an in *0,5 to 0,7 mm* long. Another species, *Wolffia arrhiza*, occurs in Great Britain but rarely, if ever, flowers there. The smallest plant regularly flowering in Britain is the chaffweed (*Cetunculus minimus*), a single seed of which weighs 0.00003 of a gramme.

Slowest flowering plant

The slowest flowering of all plants is the rare *Puyu raimondii*, the largest of all herbs, discovered in Bolivia in 1870. The panicle emerges after about 150 years of the plant's life. It then dies. (See also above under Largest blooms.) Some agaves, erroneously called Century plants, first flower after 40 years.

Largest wreath

The largest wreath ever constructed was the wreath constructed by the Teleflower conference at Rotorua, New Zealand on 27 Feb. 1975. It weighed 1,008 lb. *457 kg* and measured 25 ft 6 in *7,77 m* in diameter.

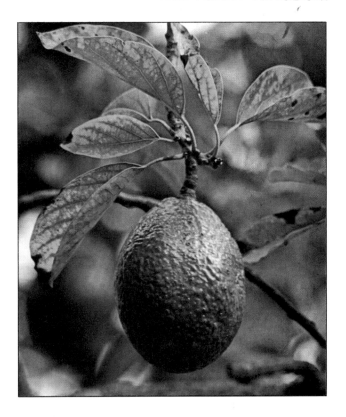

above: The largest wreath, weighing 1,008 lbs. *457 kg,* constructed by the Teleflower conference at Rotorua, New Zealand in 1975. (See page 54). (*Starlite Studios, N.Z.*)

right: The fruit with the highest calorific value, the Avocado Pear (*Persea americana*). (*Heather Angel*)

Longest daisy chain

The longest daisy chain on record is one of 3,234 ft *985 m* made of 18,000 daisies by the members of the Deanery Players, Harrogate, North Yorkshire, England in 8½ hours on 12 July 1975.

Tallest Hollyhock

The tallest reported hollyhock (*Althaea rosea*) is one of 18 ft 9½ in *5,72 m* grown by Loren and Gregory Sisley of Seattle, Washington, U.S.A. measured on 1 Nov. 1976.

Orchid *Largest*

The largest of all orchids is *Grammatophyllum speciosum*, native to Malaysia. Specimens have been recorded up to 25 ft *7,62 m* in height. The largest orchid flower is that of *Phragmipedium caudatum*, found in tropical areas of America, Its petals are up to 18 in *46 cm* long, giving it a maximum outstretched diameter of 3 ft *91 cm*. The flower is, however, much less bulky than that of the stinking corpse lily.

Orchid *Tallest*

The tallest free standing orchid is the *Grammatophyllum speciosum* (see above). *Galeola foliata* may attain 49 ft *15 m* on decaying rainforest trees in Queensland, Australia.

Orchid *Smallest*

The smallest orchid is *Bulbophyllum minutissimum*, found in Australia. Claims have also been made for *Notylia norae* found in Venezuela. The smallest orchid flowers are borne by *Stelis graminea* being less than 1 mm *0.04 in* long.

Orchid *Highest priced*

The highest price ever paid for an orchid is 1,150 guineas (£1,207.50), paid by Baron Schröder to Sanders of St. Albans for an *Odontoglossum crispum* (variety *pittianum*) at an auction by Protheroe & Morris of Bow Lane, London, on 22 March 1906. A Cymbidium orchid called Rosanna Pinkie was sold in the United States for $4,500 (then £1,600) in 1952.

Largest rhododendron

The largest species of rhododendron is the scarlet *Rhododendron arboreum*, examples of which reach a height of 60 ft *18,25 m* at Mangalbaré, Nepal. The cross-section of the trunk of a *Rhododendron giganteum*, reputedly 90 ft *27,43 m* high from Yunnan, China is preserved at Inverewe Garden, Highland. The largest in the United Kingdom is one 25 ft *7,60 m* tall and 272 ft *82,90 m* in circumference at Government House, Hillsborough, Co. Down. A specimen 35 ft *10,65 m* high and 3 ft 3 in in circumference has been measured at Tregothan, Truro, Cornwall.

Largest rose tree

A "Lady Banks" rose tree at Tombstone, Arizona, U.S.A., has a trunk 40 in *101 cm* thick, stands 9 ft *2,74 m* high and covers an area of 5,380 ft² *499 m²* supported by 68 posts and several thousand feet of piping. This enables 150 people to be seated under the arbour. The cutting came from Scotland in 1884.

FRUIT
Most and least nutritive

An analysis of the 38 commonly eaten raw (as opposed to dried) fruits shows that the one with the highest calorific value is avocado (*Persea americana*), with 741 calories per edible lb. or *163 cals per 100 gr*. That with the lowest value is cucumber with 73 calories per lb. *16 cals per 100 gr*. Avocados probably originated in Central and South America and contain also vitamins A, C, and E and 2.2 per cent protein.

Melon

A watermelon weighing 197 lb. *89,3 kg* was reported by Grace's Garden in 1975. The grower was Ed Weeks of Tarboro, North Carolina.

Pineapple *Largest*

A pineapple weighing 16 lb. 8 oz. *7,485 kg* was reported from a Dole Co. plantation in Mindanao, Philippine Islands in 1967.

FERNS
Largest

The largest of all the more than 6,000 species of fern is the tree fern (*Alsophila excelsa*) of Norfolk Island, in the South Pacific, which attains a height of up to 60 ft *18,28 m*.

Smallest

The world's smallest ferns are *Hecistopteris pumila*, found in Central America, and *Azolla caroliniana*, which is native to the United States.

GRASSES
Commonest and Fastest Growing

The world's commonest grass is *Cynodon ductylon* or Bermuda grass. The "Callie" hybrid, selected in 1966, grows as much as 6 in *15,2 cm* a day and stolons reach 18 ft *5,5 m* in length. The tallest of the 160 grasses found in Great Britain

55

is the common reed (*Phragmites communis*), which reaches a height of 9 ft 9 in *2,97 m*.

Shortest

The shortest grass native to Great Britain is the very rare sand bent (*Mibora minima*) from Anglesey, Gwynedd which has a maximum growing height of under 6 in *15 cm*.

LEAVES

Largest *World*

The largest leaves of any plant belong to the raffia palm (*Raphia raffia*) of the Mascarene Islands, in the Indian Ocean and the Amazonian bamboo palm (*R. toedigera*) of South America, whose leaf blades may measure up to 65 ft *19,81 m* in length with petioles up to 13 ft *3,96 m*.

The largest undivided leaf is that of *Alocasia macrorrhiza*, found in Sabah, East Malaysia. One found in 1966 was 9 ft 11 in *3,02 m* long and 6 ft 3½ in *1,92 m* wide, with a unilateral area of 34.2 ft² *3,17 m²*.

Largest *Great Britain*

The largest leaves to be found in outdoor plants in Great Britain are those of *Gunnera manicata* from Brazil with leaves 6 to 10 ft *1,82–3,04 m* across on prickly stems 5 to 8 ft *1,52–2,43 m* long.

Fourteen-leafed clover

A fourteen-leafed white clover (*Trifolium repens*) was found by Randy Farland near Sioux Falls, South Dakota, U.S.A. on 16 June 1975.

SEEDS

Largest

The largest seed in the world is that of the double coconut or Coco de Mer (*Lodoicea seychellarum*), the single-seeded fruit of which may weigh 40 lb. *18 kg*. This grows only in the Seychelles, in the Indian Ocean.

Smallest

The smallest seeds are those of *Epiphytic* orchids, at 35,000,000 to the oz. (*cf.* grass pollens at up to 6,000,000,000 grains/oz.). A single plant of the American ragweed can generate 8,000,000,000 pollen grains in five hours.

Most viable

The most protracted claim for the viability of seeds are those of the Arctic lupin (*Lupinus arcticus*) found in frozen silt at Miller Creek in the Yukon, Canada in July 1954. They were germinated in 1966 and were dated by the radio carbon method of associated material to at least 8,000 B.C. and more probably to 13,000 B.C.

Most Conquering Conker

The highest recorded battle honours for an untreated conker (fruit of the Common horse-chestnut or *Aesculus hippocastanum*) is a "five thousander plus", which won the BBC Conker Conquest in 1954. A professor of botany has however opined that this heroic specimen might well have been a "ringer", probably an ivory or tagua nut (*Phytelephas macrocarpa*).

PARKS, ZOOS, OCEANARIA AND AQUARIA

PARKS

Largest *World*

The world's largest park is the Wood Buffalo National Park in Alberta, Canada (established 1922), which has an area of 11,172,000 acres (17,560 miles² [*45 480 km²*]).

Largest *Britain*

The largest National Park in Great Britain is the Lake District National Park which has an area of 866 miles² *2 240 km²*. The largest private park in the United Kingdom is Woburn Park (3,000 acres *1 200 ha*), near Woburn Abbey, the seat of the Dukes of Bedford. The largest common in the

United Kingdom is Llansantffraed Cwmdauddwr (28,819 acres *11 662 ha*) in Powys, Wales.

ZOOS

Largest game reserve

It has been estimated that throughout the world there are some 500 zoos with an estimated annual attendance of 330,000,000. The largest zoological preserve in the world has been the Etosha Reserve, Namibia established in 1907 with an area which grew to 38,427 miles² *99 525 km²*.

Largest collection

The largest collection in any zoo is that in the Zoological Gardens of West Berlin, Germany. At 1 Jan. 1977 the zoo had a total of 12,253 specimens from 2,480 species. This total included 1,203 mammals (258 species), 2,838 birds (966 species), 606 reptiles (291 species), 368 amphibians (84 species), 2,141 fishes (642 species) and 5,097 invertebrates (239 species)

Oldest

The earliest known collection of animals was that set up by Shulgi, a 3rd dynasty ruler of Ur in 2094–2047 B.C. at Puzarish in south-east Iraq. The oldest known zoo is that at Schönbrunn, Vienna, Austria, built in 1752 by the Holy Roman Emperor Franz I for his wife Maria Theresa. The oldest privately owned zoo in the world is that of the Zoological Society of London, founded in 1826. Its collection, housed partly in Regent's Park, London (36 acres *14,5 ha*) and partly at Whipsnade Park, Bedfordshire (541 acres *219 ha*), (opened 22 May 1931) is the most comprehensive in the United Kingdom. The stocktaking on 1 Jan. 1977 accounted for a total of 10,910 specimens. These comprised 2,050 mammals, 2,223 birds, 608 reptiles and amphibians, an estimated total of 3,091 fish and an estimated total of 2,938 invertebrates. Locusts, ants and bees are excluded from these figures. The record annual attendances are 3,031,571 in 1950 for Regent's Park and 756,758 in 1961 for Whipsnade.

OCEANARIA

Earliest and largest

The world's first oceanarium is Marineland of Florida, opened in 1938 at a site 18 miles *29 km* south of St. Augustine, Florida, U.S.A. Up to 5,800,000 gal *26,3 million litres* of sea-water are pumped daily through two major tanks, one rectangular (100 ft *30,48 m* long by 40 ft *12,19*) wide by 18 ft *5,48 m* deep) containing 375,000 gal *1,7 million litres* and one circular (233 ft *71 m* in circumference and 12 ft *3,65 m* deep) containing 330,000 gal *1,5 million litres*. The tanks are seascaped, including coral reefs and even a shipwreck. The salt water tank at the Marineland of the Pacific Palos Verdes Peninsula, California, U.S.A. is 251½ ft *76,65 m* in circumference and 22 ft *6,7 m* deep, with a capacity of 530,000 gal *2,4 million litres*. The total capacity of this whole oceanarium is 1,830,000 gal *8,3 million litres*.

AQUARIA

Largest aquarium

The world's largest aquarium, as opposed to fish farm, is the John G. Shedd Aquarium on 12th Street and Grant Park, Chicago, Illinois, U.S.A. completed in November 1929 at a cost of $3,250,000 (then £668,725). The total capacity of its display tanks is 375,000 gal *1,7 million litres* with reservoir tanks holding 1,665,000 gal *7,5 million litres*. Exhibited are 7,500 specimens from 350 species. Salt water is brought in road and rail tankers from Key West, Florida, and a tanker barge from the Gulf of Mexico. The record attendances are 78,658 in a day on 21 May 1931, and 4,689,730 visitors in the single year of 1931.

The largest marine mammal ever held in captivity was a female Pacific grey whale (*Eschrichtius gibbosus*), named "Gigi", who was captured in Scammon's lagoon, Baja California, Mexico, on 13 March 1971 and then transferred to the Sea World Aquarium in Mission Bay, San Diego, California, U.S.A. She measured 18 ft 2 in *5,53 m* in length on arrival, and weighed 4,300 lb. *1 950 kg*. She was released at sea off the San Diego coast on 13 March 1972, after she had grown to an unmanageable 27 ft *8,23 m* and 14,000 lb. *6 350 kg*.

3. THE NATURAL WORLD

THE EARTH

The Earth is not a true sphere, but flattened at the poles and hence an ellipsoid. The polar diameter of the Earth (7,899.809 miles *12 713,510 km*) is 26.576 miles *42,770 km* less than the equatorial diameter (7,926.385 miles *17 756,280 km*). The Earth also has a slight elipticity of the equator since its long axis (about longitude 37° W) is 174 yds *159 m* greater than the short axis. The greatest departures from the reference ellipsoid are a protuberance of 244 ft *74 m* in the area of Papua/New Guinea and a depression of 354 ft *108 m* south of Sri Lanka, in the Indian Ocean.

The greatest circumference of the Earth, at the equator, is 24,901.47 miles *40 075,03 km*, compared with 24,859.75 miles *40 007,89 km* at the meridian. The area of the surface is estimated to be 196,937,600 miles² *510 066 100 km²*. The period of axial rotation, *i.e.* the true sidereal day, is 23 hrs 56 min 4.0996 sec, mean time.

The mass of the Earth is 5,882,000,000,000,000,000,000,000 tons *5 976 × 10¹⁸ tonnes* and its density is 5.517 times that of water. The volume is an estimated 259,875,620,000 miles³ *1 083 208 840 000 km³*. The Earth picks up cosmic dust but estimates vary widely with 30,000 tons/*tonnes* a year being the upper limit. Modern theory is that the Earth has an outer shell or lithosphere about 25 miles *40 km* thick, then an outer and inner rock layer or mantle extending 1,800 miles *2 900 km* deep, beneath which there is an iron-nickel core at an estimated temperature of 3 700° C *6,700° F*, and at a pressure of 22,000 tons/*tonnes* per in² or 3,400 kb. If the iron-nickel core theory is correct, iron must be by far the most abundant element in the Earth.

1. NATURAL PHENOMENA

EARTHQUAKES

(Note: Seismologists record all dates with the year first, based not on local time but on Greenwich Mean Time)

Greatest *World*

It is estimated that each year there are some 500,000 detectable seismic or micro-seismic disturbances of which 100,000 can be felt and 1,000 cause damage.

Using the comparative scale of Mantle Wave magnitudes (defined in 1968), the world's largest earthquake since 1930

has been the cataclysmic Alaska, U.S.A., or Prince William Sound earthquake (epicentre Lat. 61° 10′ N., Long. 147° 48′ W.) of 1964 March 28 with a magnitude of 8.9. The Kamchatka, U.S.S.R., earthquake (epicentre Lat. 52° 45′ N., Long. 159° 30′ E.) of 1952 Nov. 4 and the shocks around Lebu, south of Concepción, Chile on 1960 May 22 are both now assessed at a magnitude of 8.8. Formerly the largest earthquake during this period had been regarded as the submarine shock (epicentre Lat. 39° 30′ N., Long, 144° 30′ E.) about 100 miles off the Sanriku coast of north-eastern Honshū, Japan of 1933 March 2 estimated at 8.9 on the Gutenberg-Richter scale (1956). It is possible that the earthquake in Lisbon, Portugal, of 1755 Nov 1 would have been accorded a magnitude of between 8¾ and 9 if seismographs, invented in 1853, had been available to record traces. The first of the three shocks was at 9.40 a.m. and lasted for between 6 and 7 min. Lakes in Norway were disturbed. The energy of an earthquake of magnitude 8.9 is about 5.6 × 10²⁴ ergs, which is equivalent to 10,000 megatons—an explosion 100 times greater than the largest nuclear device ever detonated.

Worst death roll *World*

The greatest loss of life occurred in the earthquake (*ti chen*) in the Shensi, Shansi and Honan provinces of China, of 1556 Feb. 2, (new style) (Jan 23 o.s.) when an estimated 830,000 people were killed. The highest death roll in modern times has been in the Tangshan 'quake (Mag. 8.2) in Eastern China on 1976 July 26. An interim figure published on 4 Jan. 1977 revealed 655,237 killed and 79,000 seriously injured. The greatest material damage was in the 'quake on the Kwanto plain, Japan, of 1923 Sept. 1 (Mag. 8.2, epicentre in Lat. 35° 15′ N., Long. 139° 30′ E.). In Sagami Bay the sea-bottom in one area sank 400 m *1,310 ft*. The official total of persons killed and missing in the *Shinsai* or great 'quake and the resultant fires was 142,807. In Tōkyō and Yokohama 575,000 dwellings were destroyed. The cost of the damage was estimated at £1,000 million (now more than £4,000 million).

Worst death roll *Great Britain*

The East Anglian or Colchester earthquake of 1884 April 22 (9.18 a.m.) (epicentres Lat. 51° 48′ N., Long. 0° 53′ E., and Lat. 51° 51′ N., Long 0° 55′ E.) caused damage estimated at £10,000 to 1,200 buildings, and the death of at least 4 people. Langenhoe Church was wrecked. Windows and doors were rattled over an area of 53,000 miles² *137 250 km²* and the shock was felt in Exeter and Ostend, Belgium. The most marked since 1884 and the worst since instruments have been in use (*i.e.* since 1927) occurred in the Midlands at 3.43 p.m. on 1957 Feb. 11, showing a strength of between five and six

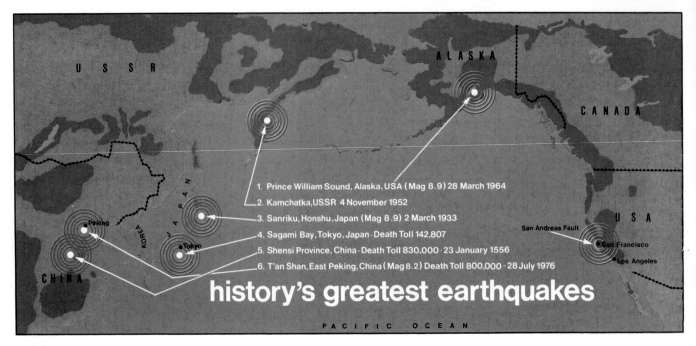

1. Prince William Sound, Alaska, USA (Mag 8.9) 28 March 1964

2. Kamchatka, USSR 4 November 1952

3. Sanriku, Honshu, Japan (Mag 8.9) 2 March 1933

4. Sagami Bay, Tokyo, Japan - Death Toll 142,807

5. Shensi Province, China - Death Toll 830,000 · 23 January 1556

6. T'an Shan, East Peking, China (Mag 8.2) Death Toll 800,000 · 28 July 1976

history's greatest earthquakes

PACIFIC OCEAN

on the Davison scale. The strongest Scottish tremor occurred at Inverness at 10.45 p.m. on 1816 Aug. 13, and was felt over an area of 50,000 miles² *130 000 km²*. The strongest Welsh tremor occurred in Swansea at 9.45 a.m. on 1906 June 27 (epicentre Lat. 51° 38′ N., Long 4° W.). It was felt over an area of 37,800 miles² *97 900 km²*.

Worst death roll *Ireland*
No earthquake with its epicentre in Ireland has ever been instrumentally measured, though the effects of remoter shocks have been felt. However, there was a shock in 1734 August which damaged 100 dwellings and five churches.

VOLCANOES
The total number of known active volcanoes in the world is 455 with an estimated 80 more that are submarine. The greatest active concentration is in Indonesia, where 77 of its 167 volcanoes have erupted within historic times. The name volcano derives from the now dormant Vulcano Island (from the God of fire Vulcanus) in the Aeolian group in the Mediterranean.

Greatest eruption
The total volume of matter discharged in the eruption of Tambora, a volcano on the island of Sumbawa, in Indonesia, 5–7 April 1815, has been estimated at 36.4 miles³ *151,7 km³*. The energy of this eruption was 8.4×10^{26} ergs. The volcano lost about 4,100 ft *1 250 m* in height and a crater seven miles *11 km* in diameter was formed. This compares with a probable 15 miles³ *62,5 km³* ejected by Santorini and 4.3 miles³ *18 km³* ejected by Krakatoa (see below). The internal pressure causing the Tambora eruption has been estimated at 46,500,000 lb./in² or more than 20,750 tons/in² *3 270 000 kg/cm²*.

Greatest explosion
The greatest volcanic explosion in historic times was the eruption in *c.* 1470 B.C. of Thíra (Santorini), a volcanic island in the Aegean Sea. It is highly probable that this explosion destroyed the centres of the Minoan civilization in Crete, about 80 miles *130 km* away, with a *tsunami* 165 ft *50 m* high.

The greatest explosion since Santorini occurred at *c.* 10 a.m. (local time), or 3.00 a.m. G.M.T., on 27 Aug. 1883, with an eruption of Krakatoa, an island (then 18 miles² *47 km²*) in the Sunda Strait, between Sumatra and Java, in Indonesia. A total of 163 villages were wiped out, and 36,380 people killed by the wave it caused. Rocks were thrown 34 miles *55 km* high and dust fell 3,313 miles *5 330 km* away 10 days later. The explosion was recorded four hours later on the island of Rodrigues, 2,968 miles *4 776 km* away, as "the roar of heavy

guns" and was heard over 1/13th part of the surface of the globe. This explosion has been estimated to have had about 26 times the power of the greatest H-bomb test detonation but was still only a fifth part of the Santorini cataclysm.

Highest *Extinct*
The highest extinct volcano in the world is Cerro Aconcagua (22,834 ft *6 960 m*) on the Argentine side of the Andes. It was first climbed on 14 Jan. 1897 and was the highest summit climbed anywhere until 12 June 1907.

Highest *Dormant*
The highest dormant volcano is Volcán Llullaillaco (22,057 ft *6 723 m*), on the frontier between Chile and Argentina.

Highest *Active*
The highest volcano regarded as active is Volcán Antofalla (6 450 m *21,162 ft*), in Argentina, though a more definite claim is made for Volcán Guayatiri or Guallatiri (19,882 ft *6 060 m*), in Chile, which erupted in 1959.

Northernmost and southernmost
The northernmost volcano is Beeren Berg (7,470 ft *2 276 m*) on the island of Jan Mayen (71° 05′ N.) in the Greenland Sea. It erupted on 20 Sept. 1970 and the island's 39 inhabitants (all male) had to be evacuated. It was possibly discovered by Henry Hudson in 1607 or 1608, but definitely visited by Jan Jacobsz May (Netherlands) in 1614. It was annexed by Norway on 8 May 1929. The Ostenso seamount (5,825 ft *1 775 m*) 346 miles *556 km* from the North Pole in Lat. 85° 10′ N., Long 133° W was volcanic. The most southerly known active volcano is Mount Erebus (12,450 ft *3 795 m*) on Ross Island (77° 35′ S.), in Antarctica. It was discovered on 28 Jan. 1841 by the expedition of Captain (later Rear-Admiral Sir) James Clark Ross, R.N. (1800–1862), and first climbed at 10 a.m. on 10 March 1908 by a British party of five, led by Professor (later Lieut.-Col. Sir) Tannatt William Edgeworth David (1858–1934).

Largest crater
The world's largest *caldera* or volcano crater is that of Mount Aso (5,223 ft *1 590 m*) in Kyūshū, Japan, which measures 17 miles *27 km* north to south, 10 miles *16 km* east to west and 71 miles *114 km* in circumference. The longest lava flow in historic times, known as *pahoehoe* (twisted cord-like solidifications), is that from the eruption of Laki in south east Iceland which flowed 65–70 km *40.5–43.5 miles*. The largest known pre-historic flow is the Roza basalt flow in North America *c.* 15 million years ago, which had an unsurpassed length (480 km *300 miles*), area (40 000 km² *15,400 miles²*) and volume (1 250 km³ *300 miles³*).

58

GEYSERS

Tallest World

The Waimangu geyser, in New Zealand, erupted to a height in excess of 1,500 ft *457 m* in 1904, but has not been active since it erupted violently in 1917. Currently the world's tallest active geyser is the U.S. National Parks' Service Steamboat Geyser, which from 1962–1969 erupted with intervals ranging from 5 days to 10 months to a height of 250–380 ft *76–115 m*. The most frequently erupting geyser is the nearby "Old Faithful", whose 90–180 ft *27–54,8 m* spire rarely varies more than 21 minutes either side of its 66 min. average. The *Geysir* ("gusher") near Mount Hekla in south-central Iceland, from which all others have been named, spurts, on occasions, to 180 ft *55 m*.

---

2. STRUCTURE AND DIMENSIONS

OCEANS

Largest

The area of the Earth covered by sea is estimated to be 139,670,000 miles² *361 740 000 km²* or 70.92 per cent of the total surface. The mean depth of the hydrosphere was once estimated to be 12,450 ft *3 795 m*, but recent surveys suggest a lower estimate, of 11,660 ft *3 554 m*. The total weight of the water is estimated to be 1.3×10^{18} tons, or 0.022 per cent of the Earth's total weight. The volume of the oceans is estimated to be 308,400,000 miles³ *1 285 600 000 km³* compared with only 8,400,000 miles³ *35 000 000 km³* of fresh water.

The largest ocean in the world is the Pacific. Excluding adjacent seas, it represents 45.8 per cent of the world's oceans and is about 63,800,000 miles² *165 250 000 km²* in area. The shortest navigable trans-Pacific distance from Guayaquil, Ecuador to Bangkok, Thailand is 10,905 miles *17 550 km*.

Deepest *World*

The deepest part of the ocean was first discovered in 1951 by H.M. Survey Ship *Challenger* in the Marianas Trench in the Pacific Ocean. The depth was measured by sounding and by echo-sounder and published as 5,960 fathoms (35,760 ft *10 900 m*). Subsequent visits to the Challenger Deep have resulted in claims by echo-sounder only, culminating in one of 6,033 fathoms (36,198 ft *11 033 m*) or 6.85 miles by the U.S.S.R.'s research ship *Vityaz* in March 1959. On 23 Jan. 1960 the U.S. Navy bathyscaphe *Trieste* descended to 35,820 ft *10 917 m*. A metal object, say a pound ball of steel, dropped into water above this trench would take nearly 63 min to fall to the sea-bed 6.85 miles *11,03 km* below. The average depth of the Pacific Ocean is 14,000 ft *4 267 m*.

Deepest *British waters*

The deepest point in the territorial waters of the United Kingdom is an area 6 cables (*1 100 m*) off the island of Raasay, Highland, in the Inner Sound at Lat. 57° 30′ 33″ N., Long. 5° 57′ 27″ W. A depth of 1,038 ft (173 fathoms, *316 m*) was found in Dec. 1959 by H.M.S. *Yarnton* (Lt.-Cdr. A. C. F. David, R. N.).

Largest sea

The largest of the world's seas is the South China Sea, with an area of 1,148,500 miles² *2 974 600 km²*. The Malayan Sea comprising the waters between the Indian Ocean and the South Pacific, south of the Chinese mainland covering 3,144,000 miles² *8 142 900 km²* is not now an entity accepted by the International Hydrographic Bureau.

Largest gulf

The largest gulf in the world is the Gulf of Mexico, with an area of 580,000 miles² *1 500 000 km²* and a shoreline of 3,100 miles *4 990 km* from Cape Sable, Florida, U.S.A., to Cabo Catoche, Mexico.

Largest bay

The largest bay in the world is Hudson Bay, northern Canada, with a shoreline of 7,623 miles *12 268 km* and with an area of 317,500 miles² *822 300 km²*. Great Britain's largest

bay is Cardigan Bay which has a 140 mile *225 km* long shoreline and measures 72 miles *116 km* across from the Lleyn Peninsula, Gwynedd to St. David's Head, Dyfed in Wales.

Longest fjords and sea lochs *World*

The world's longest fjord is the Nordvest Fjord arm of the Scoresby Sund in eastern Greenland, which extends inland 195 miles *313 km* from the sea. The longest of Norwegian fjords is the Sogne Fjord, which extends 183 km *113.7 miles* inland from Sygnefest to the head of the Lusterfjord arm at Skjolden. It averages barely 4,75 km *3 miles* in width and has a deepest point of 1 245 m *4,085 ft*. If measured from Huglo along the Bømlafjord to the head of the Sørfjord arm at Odda, the Hardangerfjorden can also be said to extend 183 km *113.7 miles*. The longest Danish fjord is the Limfjorden (100 miles *160 km* long).

Longest fjords and sea lochs *Great Britain*

Scotland's longest sea loch is Loch Fyne, which extends 42 miles *67,5 km* inland into Strathclyde (formerly Argyllshire).

Highest seamount

The highest known submarine mountain, or seamount is one discovered in 1953 near the Tonga Trench, between Samoa and New Zealand. It rises 28,500 ft *8 690 m* from the sea bed, with its summit 1,200 ft *365 m* below the surface.

Remotest spot from land

The world's most distant point from land is a spot in the South Pacific, approximately 48° 30′ S., 125° 30′ W., which is about 1,660 miles *2 670 km* from the nearest points of land, namely Pitcairn Island, Ducie Island and Cape Dart, Antarctica. Centred on this spot, therefore, is a circle of water with an area of about 8,657,000 miles² *22 421 500 km²* —about 7,000 miles² *18 000 km²* larger than the U.S.S.R., the world's largest country (see Chapter 10).

Most southerly

The most southerly part of the oceans is 85° 34′ S., 154° W., at the snout of the Robert Scott Glacier, 305 miles *490 km* from the South Pole.

Longest voyage

The longest possible great circle sea voyage is one of 19,860 miles *31 960 km* from a point 150 miles *240 km* west of Karachi, Pakistan to a point 200 miles *320 km* north of Uka' Kamchatka *via* the Mozambique Channel, Drake Passage and Bering Sea.

Sea temperature

The temperature of the water at the surface of the sea varies from −2° C *28.5° F* in the White Sea to 35,6° C *96° F* in the shallow areas of the Persian Gulf in summer. A freak geothermal temperature of 56° C *132.8° F* was recorded in February 1965 by the survey ship *Atlantis II* near the bottom of Discovery Deep (7,200 ft *2 195 m*) in the Red Sea. Ice-focused solar rays have been known to heat lake water to nearly 80° F *26,8° C*. The normal Red Sea temperature is 22° C *71.6° F*.

STRAITS

Longest

The longest straits in the world are the Tartarskiy Proliv or Tartar Straits between Sakhalin Island and the U.S.S.R. mainland running from the Sea of Japan to Sakhalinsky Zaliv. This distance is 800 km *497 miles*—thus marginally longer than the Malacca Straits.

Broadest

The broadest named straits in the world are the Davis Straits between Greenland and Baffin Island with a minimum width of 210 miles *338 km*. The Drake Passage between the Diego Ramirez Islands, Chile and the South Shetland Islands is 710 miles *1 140 km* across.

Narrowest

The narrowest navigable straits are those between the Aegean island of Euboea and the mainland of Greece. The gap is only 45 yds *40 m* wide at Khalkis. The Seil Sound, Strathclyde,

Scotland, narrows to a point only 20 ft *6 m* wide where a bridge joins the island of Seil to the mainland and is thus said to span the Atlantic.

WAVES

Highest
The highest officially recorded sea wave was measured by Lt. Frederic Margraff U.S.N. from the U.S.S. *Ramapo* proceeding from Manila, Philippines, to San Diego, California, U.S.A., on the night of 6–7 Feb. 1933, during a 68-knot (78.3 m.p.h. *126 km/h*) hurricane. The wave was computed to be 112 ft *34 m* from trough to crest. A stereo photograph of a wave calculated to be 24,9 m *81.7 ft* high was taken from the U.S.S.R.'s diesel-electric vessel *Ob'* in the South Pacific Ocean, about 600 km *370 miles* south of Macquarie Island, on 2 April 1956. The highest instrumentally measured wave was one 77 ft *23,5 m* high, recorded by the British ship *Weather Advisor* on station Juliett, in the North Atlantic at noon on 17 March 1968. Its length was 1,150 ft *350 m* and its period was 15 sec. It has been calculated on the statistics of the Stationary Random Theory that one wave in more than 300,000 may exceed the average by a factor of 4.

On 9 July 1958 a landslip caused a wave to wash 1,740 ft *530 m* high along the fjord-like Lituya Bay, Alaska, U.S.A.

Highest seismic wave
The highest recorded *tsunami* (often wrongly called a tidal wave) was one of 220 ft *67 m* which appeared off Valdez, south-west Alaska, after the great Prince William Sound earthquake of 28 March 1964. *Tsunami* (a Japanese word which is singular and plural) have been observed to travel at 490 m.p.h. *790 km/h*. Between 479 B.C. and 1967 there were 286 instances of devastating *tsunami*.

CURRENTS

Greatest
The greatest current in the oceans of the world is the Antarctic Circumpolar Current or West Wind Drift Current which was measured in 1969 in the Drake Passage between South America and Antarctica to be flowing at a rate of 9,500 million ft³ *270 000 000 m³* per sec—nearly treble that of the Gulf Stream. Its width ranges from 185 to 1,240 miles *300 to 2 000 km* and has a surface flow rate of ¾ of a knot *1,4 km/h*.

Strongest
The world's strongest currents are the Saltstraumen in the Satlfjord, near Bodø, Norway, which reach 15.6 knots (18.0 m.p.h. *29 km/h*). The flow rate through the 500 ft *150 m* wide channel surpasses 500,000 cu secs *14 250 m³/sec*. The fastest current in British territorial waters is 10.7 knots *19,8 km/h* in the Pentland Firth between the Orkney Islands and Highland, Scotland's northernmost mainland region.

GREATEST TIDES
Extreme tides are due to lunar and solar gravitational forces affected by their perigee, perihelion and conjunctions. Barometric and wind effects can superimpose an added "surge" element. Coastal and sea-floor configurations can accentuate these forces.

World
The greatest tides in the world occur in the Bay of Fundy, which divides the peninsula of Nova Scotia, Canada, from the United States' north-easternmost state of Maine and the Canadian province of New Brunswick. Burncoat Head in the Minas Basin, Nova Scotia, has the greatest mean spring range with 47.5 ft *14,50 m* and an extreme range of 53.5 ft *16,30 m*.

Great Britain
The place with the greatest mean spring range in Great Britain is Beachley, on the Severn, with a range of 40.7 ft *12,40 m*, compared with the British Isles' average of 15 ft *4,57 m*. Prior to 1933 tides as high as 28.9 ft *8,80 m* above and 22.3 ft *6,80 m* below datum (total range 51.2 ft *15,60 m*) were recorded at Avonmouth though an extreme range of 52.2 ft *15,90 m* for Beachley was officially accepted. In 1883 a freak tide of greater range was reported from Chepstow, Gwent.

Ireland
The greatest mean spring tidal range in Ireland is 17.3 ft *5,27 m* at Mellon, Limerick, on the banks of the River Shannon.

ICEBERGS

Largest
The largest iceberg on record was an Antarctic tabular 'berg of over 12,000 miles² *31 000 km²* (208 miles *335 km* long and 60 miles *97 km* wide and thus larger than Belgium) sighted 150 miles *240 km* west of Scott Island, in the South Pacific Ocean, by the U.S.S. *Glacier* on 12 Nov. 1956. The 200 ft *61 m* thick Arctic ice island T.1 (140 miles² *360 km²*) (discovered in 1946) was plotted for 17 years.

Most southerly Arctic
The most southerly Arctic iceberg was sighted in the Atlantic in 30° 50′ N., 45° 06′ W., on 2 June 1934. The tallest on record was one calved off north-west Greenland with 550 ft *167,6 m* above the surface. The southernmost iceberg reported in British home waters was one sighted 60 miles *96 km* from Smith's Knoll, on the Dogger Bank, in the North Sea.

Most northerly Antarctic
The most northerly Antarctic iceberg was a remnant sighted in the Atlantic by the ship *Dochra* in Latitude 26° 30′ S., Longitude 25° 40′ W., on 30 April 1894.

LAND
There is satisfactory evidence that at one time the Earth's land surface comprised a single primeval continent of 80 million miles² *2 × 10⁸ km²*, now termed Pangaea, and that this split about 190,000,000 years ago, during the Jurassic period, into two super-continents, termed Laurasia (Eurasia, Greenland and Northern America) in the north and Gondwanaland (Africa, Arabia, India, South America, Oceania and Antarctica) and named after Gondwana, India, which itself split 120 million years ago. The South Pole was apparently in the area of the Sahara as recently as the Ordovician period of *c.* 450 million years ago.

ROCKS
The age of the Earth is generally considered to be within the range of 4600 ± 100 million years, by analogy with directly measured ages of meteorites and of the moon. However, no rocks of this great age have yet been found on the Earth since geological processes have presumably destroyed the earliest record.

Oldest *World*
The greatest reported age for any scientifically dated rock is 3,800 ± 100 million years for granite gneiss rock found near Granite Falls in the Minnesota river valley, U.S.A. as measured by the lead-isotope and rubidium-uranium methods by the U.S. Geological Survey and announced on 26 Jan. 1975. These metamorphic samples compare with the Amitsoq gneiss from Godthaab, Greenland unreservedly accepted to be between 3700 and 3750 million years.

Oldest *Great Britain*
A considerable proportion of the Lewisian Complex of north west Highland, Scotland and of the Outer Hebrides has been proved to be 2800–2900 million years old by measurements using the rubidium-strontium and uranium-lead methods.

Largest
The largest exposed rocky outcrop is the 1,237 ft *377 m* high Mount Augustus (3,627 ft *1 105 m* above sea-level), discovered on 3 June 1858, 200 miles *320 km* east of Carnarvon, Western Australia. It is an upfaulted monoclinal gritty conglomerate 5 miles *8 km* long and 2 miles *3 km* across and thus twice the size of the celebrated monolithic arkose Ayer's Rock (1,100 ft *335 m*), 250 miles *400 km* south-west of Alice Springs, in Northern Territory, Australia.

CONTINENTS

Largest
Only 29.08 per cent, or an estimated 57,270,000 miles² *148 328 000 km²* of the Earth's surface is land, with a mean

height of 2,480 ft *756 m* above sea-level. The Eurasian land mass is the largest, with an area (including islands) of 21,053,000 miles² *54 527 000 km²*.

Smallest

The smallest is the Australian mainland, with an area of about 2,940,000 miles² *7 614 500 km²*, which, together with Tasmania, New Zealand, New Guinea and the Pacific Islands, is described sometimes as Oceania. The total area of Oceania is about 3,450,000 miles² *8 935 000 km²* including West Irian (formerly West New Guinea), which is politically in Asia.

Land remotest from the sea *World*

There is an as yet unpinpointed spot in the Dzoosotoyn Elisen (desert), northern Sinkiang, China, that is more than 1,500 miles *2 400 km* from the open sea in any direction. The nearest large town to this point is Wulumuchi (Urumchi) to its south.

Land remotest from the sea *Great Britain*

The point furthest from the sea in Great Britain is a point near Meriden, West Midlands, England, which is 72½ miles *117 km* equidistant from the Severn Bridge, the Dee and Mersey estuaries and the Welland estuary in the Wash. The equivalent point in Scotland is in the Forest of Atholl, north west Tayside 40½ miles *65 km* equidistant from the head of Loch Leven, Inverness Firth and the Firth of Tay.

Peninsula

The world's largest peninsula is Arabia, with an area of about 1,250,000 miles² *3 250 000 km²*.

ISLANDS

Largest *World*

Discounting Australia, which is usually regarded as a continental land mass, the largest island in the world is Greenland (part of the Kingdom of Denmark), with an area of about 840,000 miles² *2 175 000 km²*. There is evidence that Greenland is in fact several islands overlayed by an icecap without which it would have an area of 650,000 miles² *1 680 000 km²*.

Largest *Great Britain*

The mainland of Great Britain (Scotland, England and Wales) is the eighth largest in the world, with an area of 84,186 miles² *218 041 km²*. It stretches 603½ miles *971 km* from Dunnet Head in the north to Lizard Point in the south and 287½ miles *463 km* across from Porthaflod, Dyfed to Lowestoft, Suffolk. The island of Ireland (32,594 miles² *84 418 km²*) is the 20th largest in the world.

Details of the 1,040 British Islands will appear in the forthcoming **Guinness Book of British Islands** *due in 1978.*

Freshwater

The largest island surrounded by fresh water is the Ilha de Marajó (15,500 miles² *40 000 km²*), in the mouth of the River Amazon, Brazil. The world's largest inland island (*i.e.* land surrounded by rivers) is Ilha do Bananal, Brazil. The largest island in a lake is Manitoulin Island (1,068 miles² *2 766 km²*) in the Canadian (Ontario) section of Lake Huron. This island itself has on it a lake of 41.09 miles² *106,42 km²* called Manitou Lake, in which there are several islands. The largest lake island in Great Britain is Inchmurrin in Loch Lomond, Strathclyde/Central, Scotland with an area of 284 acres *115 ha*.

Remotest *World Uninhabited*

The remotest island in the world is Bouvet Øya (formerly Liverpool Island), discovered in the South Atlantic by J. B. C. Bouvet de Lozier on 1 Jan. 1739, and first landed on by Capt. George Norris on 16 Dec. 1825. Its position is 54° 26′ S., 3° 24′ E. This uninhabited Norwegian dependency is about 1,050 miles *1 700 km* from the nearest land—the uninhabited Queen Maud Land coast of eastern Antarctica.

Remotest *World Inhabited*

The remotest inhabited island in the world is Tristan da

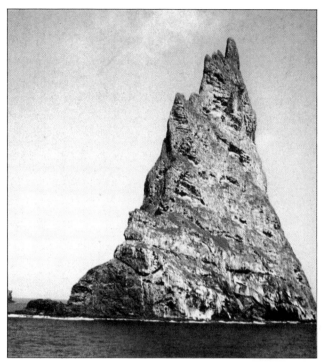

Ball's Pyramid, the World's highest rock pinnacle in the S.W. Pacific, measuring 1,843 ft *561 m* high. (*Dr. Edmund Potter*)

Cunha, discovered in the South Atlantic by Tristao da Cunha, a Portugese admiral, in March 1506. It has an area of 38 miles² *98 km²* (habitable area 12 miles² *31 km²*) and was annexed by the United Kingdom on 14 Aug. 1816. After evacuation in 1961 (due to volcanic activity), 198 islanders returned in Nov. 1963. The nearest inhabited land is the island of St. Helena, 1,320 miles *2 120 km* to the north-east. The nearest continent, Africa is 1,700 miles *2 735 km* away.

Remotest *Great Britain*

The remotest of the British islets is Rockall 191 miles *307 km* west of St. Kilda, allocated to the County of Inverness (now Highland) in 1971. This 70 ft *21 m* high rock measuring 83 ft *25 m* across was not formally annexed until 18 Sept. 1955. The remotest British island which has ever been inhabited is North Rona which is 44 miles *70,8 km* from the next nearest land at Cape Wrath and the Butt of Lewis. It was evacuated *c.* 1844. Muckle Flugga, off Unst, in the Shetlands, is the northern-most inhabited with a population of 3 (1971) and is in a latitude north of southern Greenland. Just to the north of it is Out Stack.

Highest Rock Pinnacle

The world's highest rock pinnacle is Ball's Pyramid near Lord Howe Is, Pacific which is 1,843 ft *561 m* high, but has a base axis of only 200 m *218 yds*. It was not scaled until 1965.

Northernmost land

The most northerly land is Kaffeklubben Øyen (Coffee Club Island) off the north-east of Greenland, 440 miles *708 km* from the North Pole, discovered by Dr. Lange Koch in 1921 but determined only in June 1969 to be in Latitude 83° 40′ 6″.

Southernmost land

The South Pole, unlike the North Pole, is on land. The Amundsen-Scott South Polar station was built there at an altitude of 9,370 ft *2 855 m* in 1957. It is drifting bodily with the ice cap 27–30 ft *8–9 m* per annum in the direction 43° W and was replaced by a new structure in 1975.

Greatest archipelago

The world's greatest archipelago is the 3,500 mile *5 600 km* long crescent of more than 13,000 islands which forms Indonesia.

Largest atoll

The largest atoll in the world is Kwajalein in the Marshall Islands, in the central Pacific Ocean. Its slender 176 mile *283 km* long coral reef encloses a lagoon of 1,100 miles² *2 850 km²*. The atoll with the largest land area is Christmas Island, in the Line Islands, in the central Pacific Ocean. It has an area of 184 miles² *477 km²*. Its two principal settlements, London and Paris, are 4 miles *6 km* apart.

Longest reef

The longest reef is the Great Barrier Reef off Queensland, north-eastern Australia, which is 1,260 statute miles *2 027 km* in length. Between 1959 and 1971 a large section between Cooktown and Townsville was destroyed by the proliferation of the Crown of Thorns starfish (*Acanthaster planci*).

DEPRESSIONS

Deepest *World*

The deepest depression so far discovered is beneath the Hollick-Kenyon Plateau in Marie Byrd Land, Antarctica, where, at a point 5,900 ft *1 800 m* above sea-level, the ice depth is 14,000 ft *4 267 m*, hence indicating a bed rock depression 8,100 ft *2 468 m* below sea-level. The greatest submarine depression is a large area of the floor of the north west Pacific which has an average depth of 15,000 ft *4 570 m*.

The deepest exposed depression on land is the shore surrounding the Dead Sea, 1,291 ft *393 m* below sea-level. The deepest point on the bed of this lake is 2,600 ft *792 m* below the Mediterranean. The deepest part of the bed of Lake Baykal in Siberia, U.S.S.R., is 4,872 ft *1 484 m* below sea-level.

Deepest *Great Britain*

The lowest lying area in Great Britain is in the Holme Fen area of the Great Ouse, in Cambridgeshire, at 9 ft *2,75 m* below sea-level. The deepest depression in England is the bed of part of Windermere, 94 ft *28,65 m* below sea-level, and in Scotland the bed of Loch Morar, Highland 987 ft *300,8 m* below sea-level.

Largest

The largest exposed depression in the world is the Caspian Sea basin in the Azerbaydzhani, Russian, Kazakh and Turkmen Republics of the U.S.S.R. and northern Iran (Persia). It is more than 200,000 miles² *518 000 km²* of which 143,550 miles² *371 800 km²* is lake area. The preponderant land area of the depression is the Prikaspiyskaya Nizmennost', lying around the northern third of the lake and stretching inland for a distance of up to 280 miles *450 km*.

CAVES

Longest

The most extensive cave system in the world is that under the Mammoth Cave National Park, Kentucky, U.S.A. first discovered in 1799. On 9 Sept. 1972 an exploration group led by Dr. John P. Wilcox completed a connection, pioneered by Mrs. Patricia Crowther on 30 Aug., between the Flint Ridge Cave system and the Mammoth Cave system so making a combined system with a total mapped passageway length of 181.44 miles *292 km*. The longest cave system in Great Britain is Ogof Ffynnon Ddu, Powys, in which 23.92 miles *38,5 km* of passages have so far been surveyed.

above: Gouffre de la Pierre Saint-Martin, in the Pyrenees, the World's deepest cave, with a vertical dimension of 4,370 ft *1 332 m* (*Dr. A. C. Waltham*)

DEEPEST CAVES BY COUNTRIES			
Depth		These depths are subject to continuous revisions	
Ft	m		
4,370	*1 332*	Gouffre de la Pierre Saint-Martin, Pyrenees	France-Spain
4,258	*1 298*	Gouffre Jean Bernard	France
3,543	*1 080*	Kievskaya	U.S.S.R.
3,182	*970*	Sumidero de Cellagua, Cantabria	Spain
3,025	*922*	Grotta di Monte Cucco, Apennines	Italy
2,884	*879*	Platteneckeishöhle	Austria
2,713	*827*	Hölloch, Muotathal, Schwyz	Switzerland
2,569	*783*	Jaskini Snieznej Tatras	Poland
2,493	*760*	Sótano de San Agustín	Mexico
2,464	*751*	Ghar Parau, Zagros Mountains	Iran
2,296	*700*	Kef Toghobeït	Morocco
2,296	*700*	Poloska Jama	Yugoslavia
1,010	*308*	Ogof Ffynnon Ddu	Wales
643	*196*	Giant's Hole, Oxlow Caverns, Derbyshire	England
459	*140*	Carrowmore Cavern	Ireland

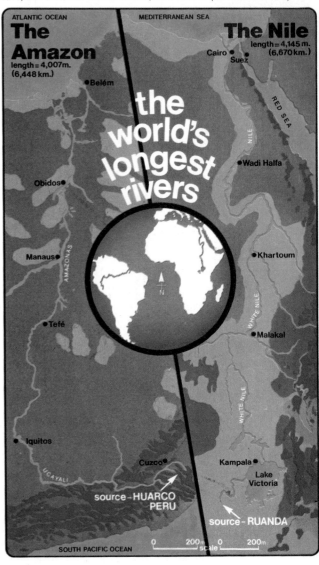

Longest stalactite

The longest known stalactite in the world is a wall-supported column extending 195 ft *59 m* from roof to floor in the Cueva de Nerja, near Málaga, Spain. The rather low tensile strength of calcite (calcium carbonate) precludes very long free-hanging stalactites, but one of 38 ft *11,60 m* exists in the Poll an Ionain cave in County Clare, Ireland.

Tallest stalagmite

The tallest known stalagmite in the world is La Grande Stalagmite in the Aven Armand cave, Lozère, France, which has attained a height of 98 ft *29 m* from the cave floor. It was found in September 1897.

MOUNTAINS

Highest *World*

An eastern Himalayan peak of 29,028 ft *8 848 m* above sea-level on the Tibet-Nepal border (in an area first designated Chu-mu-lang-ma on a map of 1717) was discovered to be the world's highest mountain in 1852 by the Survey Department of the Government of India, from theodolite readings taken in 1849 and 1850. In 1860 its height was computed to be 29,002 ft *8 840 m*. On 25 July 1973 the Chinese announced a height of 8 848,1 m or *29,029 ft 3 in*. In practice the altitude can only be justified as 29,028 ft ± 25 feet or a mean *8 848 m*. The 5½ mile *8,85 km* high peak was named Mount Everest after Sir George Everest, C.B. (1790–1866), formerly Surveyor-General of India. After a total loss of 11 lives since the first reconnaissance in 1921, Everest was finally conquered at 11.30 a.m. on 29 May 1953. (For details of ascents, see under Mountaineering in Chapter 12.) The mountain whose summit is farthest from the Earth's centre is the Andean peak of Chimborazo (20,561 ft *6 267 m*), 98 miles *158 km* south of the equator in Equador, South America. Its summit is 7,057 ft *2 150 m* further from the Earth's centre than the summit of Mt. Everest. The highest mountain on the equator is Volcán Cayambe (19,285 ft *5 878 m*), Ecuador, in Long. 77° 58′ W.

Highest *Insular*

The highest insular mountain in the world is the unsurveyed Ngga Pulu formerly Mount Sukarno, formerly Carstensz Pyramide in Irian Jaya, Indonesia, once Netherlands New Guinea, according to cross-checked altimeter estimates, it is 16,500 ft *5 030 m* high.

Highest *U.K. and Ireland*

A list of the highest points in the 72 geographical divisions of the United Kingdom and the 26 counties of the Republic of Ireland were listed on pages 63 of the 23rd (1977) Edition.

The highest mountain in the United Kingdom is Ben Nevis (4,406 ft *1 343 m* excluding the 12 ft *3,65 m* cairn), 4¼ miles *6,85 km* south-east of Fort William, Highland, Scotland. It was climbed before 1720 but was not discovered to be higher than Ben Macdhui (4,300 ft *1 310 m*) until 1870. In 1834 Ben Macdhui and Ben Nevis (Gaelic, Beinn Nibheis) were respectively quoted as 4,570 ft *1 393 m* and 4,370 ft *1 332 m*.

There is some evidence that, before being ground down by the ice-cap, mountains in the Loch Bà area of the Isle of Mull, Strathclyde were 15,000 ft *4 575 m* above sea-level.

Highest *Peaks over 3,000 ft*

There are 577 peaks and tops over 3,000 ft *915 m* in the whole British Isles and 165 peaks and 136 tops in Scotland higher than England's highest point, Scafell Pike. The highest mountain off the mainland is Sgùrr Alasdair (3,309 ft *1 008 m*) on Skye named after Alexander (in Gaelic Alasdair) Nicolson, who made the first ascent in 1873.

Highest unclimbed

Excluding the subsidiary peaks Kangchenjunga South and Middle peak and Lhotse II, the highest unclimbed separate mountain is now only the 30th highest Batura Muztagh I (Hunza Kunji I) (25,542 ft *7 785 m*) in the Karakoram.

Largest

The world's tallest mountain measured from its submarine base (3,280 fathoms *6 000 m*) in the Hawaiian Trough to peak is Mauna Kea (Mountain White) on the island of Hawaii, with a combined height of 33,476 ft *10 203 m* of which 13,796 ft *4 205 m* are above sea-level. Another mountain whose dimensions, but not height, exceed those of Mount Everest is the volcanic Hawaiian peak of Mauna Loa (Mountain Long) at 13,680 ft *4 170 m*. The axes of its elliptical base, 16,322 ft *4 975 m* below sea-level, have been estimated at 74 miles *119 km* and 53 miles *85 km*. It should be noted that Cerro Aconcagua (22,834 ft *6 960 m*) is more than 38,800 ft *11 826 m* above the 16,000 ft *4 875 m* deep Pacific abyssal plain or 42,834 ft *13 055 m* above the Peru-Chile Trench which is 180 miles *290 km* distant in the South Pacific.

Greatest ranges

The world's greatest land mountain range is the Himalaya-Karakoram, which contains 96 of the world's 109 peaks of over 24,000 ft *7 315 m*. The greatest of all mountain ranges is, however, the submarine Indian/East Pacific Oceans Cordillera extending 19,200 miles *30 720 km* from the Gulf of Aden to the Gulf of California by way of the seabed between Australia and Antarctica with an average height of 8,000 ft *2 430 m* above the base ocean depth.

Longest Lines of Sight

In Alaska Mt. McKinley (20,320 ft *6 193 m*) has been sighted from Mt. Sanford (16,237 ft *4 949 m*) from a distance of 230 miles *370 km*.

Greatest plateau

The most extensive high plateau in the world is the Tibetan Plateau in Central Asia. The average altitude is 16,000 ft *4 875 m* and the area is 77,000 miles² *200 000 km²*.

Sheerest Wall

The 3,200 ft *975 m* wide northwest face of Half Dome, Yosemite, California, U.S.A. is 2,200 ft *670 m* high but nowhere departs more than 7 degrees from the vertical. It was first climbed (Class VI) in 5 days in July 1957 by Royal Robbins, Jerry Gallwas and Mike Sherrick.

Highest halites

Along the northern shores of the Gulf of Mexico for 725 miles *1 160 km* there exist 330 subterranean "mountains" of salt, some of which rise more than 60,000 ft *18 300 m* from bed rock and appear as the low salt domes first discovered in 1862.

RIVERS

The river systems of the world are estimated to contain 55,000 miles³ *230 000 km³* of fresh water.

Longest *World*

The two longest rivers in the world are the Amazon (*Amazonas*), flowing into the South Atlantic, and the Nile (*Bahr-el-Nil*) flowing into the Mediterranean. Which is the longer is more a matter of definition than simple measurement.

The true source of the Amazon was discovered in 1953 to be a stream named Huarco, rising near the summit of Cerro Huagra (17,188 ft *5 238 m*) in Peru. This stream progressively becomes the Toro then the Santiago then the Apurimac, which in turn is known as the Ene and then the Tambo before its confluence with the Amazon prime tributary the Ucayali. The length of the Amazon from this source to the South Atlantic *via* the Canal do Norte was measured in 1969 to be 4,007 miles *6 448 km* (usually quoted to the rounded off figure of 4,000 miles *6 437 km*).

If, however, a vessel navigating down the river turns to the south of Ilha de Marajó through the straits of Breves and Boiuci into the Pará, the total length of the water-course becomes 4,195 miles 6 750 km. The Pará is not however a tributary of the Amazon, being hydrologically part of the basin of the Tocantins.

The length of the Nile watercourse, as surveyed by M. Devroey (Belgium) before the loss of a few miles of meanders due to the formation of Lake Nasser, behind the Aswan High Dam, was 4,145 miles *6 670 km*. This course is the hydrologically acceptable one from the source in Ruanda of the Luvironza branch of the Kagera feeder of the Victoria Nyanza *via* the White Nile (*Bahr-el-Jebel*) to the delta.

Longest *Ireland*

The longest river in Ireland is the Shannon, which is longer than any river in Great Britain. It rises 258 ft *78,6 m* above sea-level, in County Cavan, and flows through a series of loughs to Limerick. It is 240 miles *386 km* long, including the 56 mile *90 km* long estuary to Loop Head. The basin area is 6,060 miles^2 *15 695 km^2*.

Longest *Great Britain*

The longest river in Great Britain is the Severn, which empties into the Bristol Channel and is 220 miles *354 km* long. Its basin extends over 4,409 miles^2 *11 419 km^2*. It rises in North-eastern Powys and flows through Salop, Hereford and Worcester, Gloucestershire and Avon. The longest river *wholly* in England is the Thames, which is 215 miles, *346 km* long to the Nore. Its remotest source is at Seven Springs, Gloucestershire, whence the River Churn joins the other head waters. The source of the Thames proper is Trewsbury Mead, Coate, Cirencester, Gloucestershire. The basin measures, 3,841 miles^2 *9 948 km^2*. The longest river wholly in Wales is the Towy, with a length of 64 miles *102 km*. It rises in Dyfed and flows out into Carmarthen Bay. The longest river in Scotland is the Tay, with Dundee, Tayside, on the shore of the estuary. It is 117 miles *188 km* long from the source of its remotest head-stream, the River Tummel, Tayside and has the greatest volume of any river in Great Britain, with a flow of up to 49,000 cusecs *1 387 m^3* per sec. Its basin extends over 1,961 miles^2 *5 078 km^2*.

Shortest river

The strongest claimant to the title of the world's shortest river is the D River, Lincoln City, Oregon, U.S.A., which connects Devil's Lake to the Pacific Ocean and is 440 ft *134 m* long at low tide.

Largest basin and longest tributary

The largest river basin in the world is that drained by the Amazon (4,007 miles *6 448 km*). It covers about 2,720,000 miles^2 *7 045 000 km^2*. It has about 15,000 tributaries and subtributaries, of which four are more than 1,000 miles *1 609 km* long. These include the Madeira, the longest of all tributaries, with a length of 2,100 miles *3 380 km*, which is surpassed by only 14 rivers in the whole world.

Longest sub-tributary

The longest sub-tributary is the Pilcomayo (1,000 miles *1 609 km* long) in South America. It is a tributary of the Paraguay (1,500 miles *2 415 km* long), which is itself a tributary of the Paraná (2,500 miles *4 025 km*).

Longest estuary

The world's longest estuary is that of the Ob', in the northern U.S.S.R., at 450 miles *725 km*.

Largest delta

The world's largest delta is that created by the Ganga (Ganges) and Brahmaputra in Bangla Desh (formerly East Pakistan) and West Bengal, India. It covers an area of 30,000 miles^2 *75 000 km^2*.

Greatest flow

The greatest flow of any river in the world is that of the Amazon, which discharges an average of 4,200,000 cusecs *120 000 m^3/sec* into the Atlantic Ocean, rising to more than 7,000,000 cusecs *200 000 m^3/sec* in full flood. The lowest 900 miles *1 450 km* of the Amazon average 300 ft *90 m* in depth.

Submarine river

In 1952 a submarine river 250 miles *400 km* wide, known as the Cromwell current, was discovered flowing eastward 300 ft

90 m below the surface of the Pacific for 3,500 miles *5 625 km* along the equator. Its volume is 1,000 times that of the Mississippi.

Subterranean river

In August 1958 a crypto-river was tracked by radio isotopes flowing under the Nile with 6 times its mean annual flow or 500,000 million m^3 *20 million million ft^3*.

Largest swamp

The world's largest tract of swamp is in the basin of the Pripet or Pripyat River—a tributary of the Dnieper in the U.S.S.R. These swamps cover an estimated area of 18,125 miles^2 *46 950 km^2*.

RIVER BORES
World

The bore on the Ch'ient'ang'kian (Hang-chou-fe) in eastern China is the most remarkable in the world. At Spring tides the wave attains a height of up to 25 ft *7,5 m* and a speed of 13 knots *24 km/h*. It is heard advancing at a range of 14 miles *22 km*. The bore on the Hooghly branch of the Ganges travels for 70 miles *110 km* at more than 15 knots *27 km/h*. The annual downstream flood wave on the Mekong sometimes reaches a height of 46 ft *14 m*. The greatest volume of any tidal bore is that of the Canal do Norte (10 miles *16 km* wide) in the mouth of the Amazon.

Great Britain

The most notable river bore in the United Kingdom is that on the Severn, which attained a measured height of 9¼ ft *2,8 m* on 15 Oct. 1966 downstream of Stone-bench, and a speed of 13 m.p.h. *20 km/h*. It travels as far up as Severn Stoke, Hereford & Worcester.

Fastest rapids

The fastest rapids which have ever been navigated are the Lava Falls on the River Colorado, U.S.A. At times of flood these attain a speed of 30 m.p.h. *48 km/h* (26 knots) with waves boiling up to 12 ft *3,65 m*.

WATERFALLS
Highest

The highest waterfall in the world is the Salto Angel in Venezuela, on a branch of the River Carrao, an upper tributary of the Caroni with a total drop of 3,212 ft *979 m*—the longest single drop is 2,648 ft *807 m*. It was re-discovered by a United States pilot named James (Jimmy) Angel (died 8 Dec. 1956), who crashed nearby on 9 Oct. 1937. The falls, known by the Indians as Cherun-Meru, were first reported by Ernesto Sanchez La Cruz in 1910.

Highest *United Kingdom*

The tallest waterfall in the United Kingdom is Eas a'Chùal Aluinn, from Glas Bheinn (2,541 ft *774 m*), Highland, Scotland, with a drop of 658 ft *200 m*. England's highest fall above ground is Caldron (or Cauldron) Snout, on the Tees, with a fall of 200 ft *60 m* in 450 ft *135 m* of cataracts, but no sheer leap. It is at the junction of Durham, Cumbria and North Yorkshire. The cascade in the Gaping Gill Cave descends 365 ft *111 m*. The highest Welsh waterfall is the Pistyll Rhaiadr (240 ft *73 m*), on the River Rhaiadr, on the Clwyd-Powys border.

Highest *Ireland*

The highest falls in Ireland are the Powerscourt Falls (350 ft *106 m*), on the River Dargle, County Wicklow.

Greatest

On the basis of the average annual flow, the greatest waterfall in the world is the Guairá (374 ft *114 m* high), known also as the Salto dos Sete Quedas, on the Alto Paraná River between Brazil and Paraguay, Although attaining an average height of only 110 ft *33,5 cm*, its estimated annual average flow over the lip (5,300 yds *4 850 m* wide) is 470,000 cusecs *13 300 m^3/sec*. The amount of water this represents can be imagined by supposing that it was pouring into the dome of St. Paul's Cathedral—it would fill it completely in three-fifths of a sec. It has a peak flow of 1,750,000 cusecs *50 000*

m^3/sec. The seven cataracts of the Stanley Falls in the Congo (Kinshasa) have an average annual flow of 600,000 cusecs *17 000 m^3/sec*.

It has been calculated that, when some 5,500,000 years ago the Mediterranean basins began to be filled from the Atlantic through the Straits of Gibraltar, a waterfall 26 times greater than the Guairá and perhaps 800 m *2,625 ft* high was formed.

Widest
The widest waterfalls in the world are the Khône Falls (50 to 70 ft *15–21m* high) in Laos, with a width of 6.7 miles *10,8 km* and a flood flow of 1,500,000 cusecs *42 500 m^3/sec*.

LAKES AND INLAND SEAS
Largest *World*
The largest inland sea or lake in the world is the Kaspiskoye More (Caspian Sea) in the southern U.S.S.R. and Iran (Persia). It is 760 miles *1 225 km* long and its total area is 143,550 miles² *371 800 km²*. Of the total area some 55,280 miles² *143 200 km²* (38.6%) is in Iran, where it is named the Darya-ye-Khazar. Its maximum depth is 980 m *3,215 ft* and its surface is 92 ft *28 m* below sea-level. Its estimated volume is 21,500 miles³ *89 600 km³* of saline water. Since 1930 it has diminished 15,000 miles² *39 000 km²* in area with a fall of 62 ft *18,90 m* while the shore line has retreated more than 10 miles *16 km* in some places. The U.S.S.R. Government plan to reverse the flow of the upper Pechora River from flowing north to the Barents Sea by blasting a 70 mile *112 km* long canal with nuclear explosives into the south-flowing Kolva river so that *via* the Kama and Volga rivers the Caspian will be replenished.

Freshwater Lake *World*
The freshwater lake with the greatest surface area is Lake Superior, one of the Great Lakes of North America. The total area is 31,800 miles² *82 350 km²*, of which 20,700 miles² *53 600 km²* are in Minnesota, Wisconsin and Michigan, U.S.A. and 11,100 miles² *27 750 km²* in Ontario, Canada. It is 600 ft *182 m* above sea-level. The freshwater lake with the greatest volume is Baykal (see Deepest lake, below) with an estimated volume of 5,750 miles³ *24 000 km³*.

Freshwater lake *United Kingdom*
The largest lake in the United Kingdom is Lough Neagh (48 ft *14,60 m* above sea-level) in Northern Ireland. It is 18 miles *28,9 km* long and 11 miles *17,7 km* wide and has an area of 147.39 miles² *381,73 km²*. Its extreme depth is 102 ft *31 m*.

Freshwater lake *Great Britain*
The largest lake in Great Britain, and the largest inland loch in Scotland is Loch Lomond (23 ft *7,0 m* above sea-level), which is 22.64 miles *36,44 km* long and has a surface area of 27.45 miles² *70,04 km²*. It is situated in the regions of Strathclyde and Central and its greatest depth is 623 ft *190 m*. The lake with the greatest volume is however Loch Ness with 263,162,000,000 ft³ *7 451 920 000 m³*. The longest lake is Loch Ness which measures 24.23 miles *38,99 km*. The three arms of the Y-shaped Loch Awe aggregate however, 25.47 miles *40,99 km*. The largest lake in England is Windermere, in the county of Cumbria. It is 10½ miles *17 km* long and has a surface area of 5.69 miles² *14,74 km²*. Its greatest depth is 219 ft *66,75 m* in the northern half. The largest *natural* lake in Wales is Llyn Tegid, with an area of 1.69 miles² *4,38 km²*, although it should be noted that the largest lake in Wales is that formed by the reservoir at Lake Vyrnwy, where the total surface area is 1,120 acres *453,25 ha*.

Freshwater lake *Republic of Ireland*
The largest lough in the Republic of Ireland is Lough Corrib in the counties of Mayo and Galway. It measures 27 miles *43,5 km* in length and is 7 miles *11,25 km* across at its widest point with a total surface area of 41,616 acres (65.0 miles² *168 km²*).

Largest Lagoon
The largest lagoon in the world is Lagoa dos Patos in southernmost Brazil. It is 158 miles *254 km* long and extends over 4,110 miles² *10 645 km²*.

Deepest *World*
The deepest lake in the world is Ozero (Lake) Baykal in central Siberia, U.S.S.R. It is 385 miles *620 km* long and between 20 and 46 miles *32–74 km* wide. In 1957 the lake's Olkhon Crevice was measured to be 1 940 m *6,365 ft* deep and hence 1 485 m *4,872 ft* below sea-level.

Deepest *Great Britain*
The deepest lake in Great Britain is the 10.30 mile *16,57 km* long Loch Morar, in Highland. Its surface is 30 ft *9 m* above sea-level and its extreme depth 1,017 ft *310 m*. England's deepest lake is Wast Water (258 ft *78 m*), in Cumbria. The lake with the greatest mean depth is Loch Ness with *c.* 450 ft *137 m*.

Highest *World*
The highest steam-navigated lake in the world is Lago Titicaca (maximum depth 1,214 ft *370 m*), with an area of about 3,200 miles² *8 285 km²* (1,850 miles² *4 790 km²* in Peru, 1,350 miles² *3 495 km²* in Bolivia), in South America. It is 130 miles *209 km* long and is situated at 12,506 ft *3 811 m* above sea-level. There is an unnamed glacial lake near Everest at 19,300 ft *5 880 m*. Tibet's largest lake Na-mu Hu of 722 miles² *1 956 km²* is at 15,060 ft *4 578 m*.

Highest *United Kingdom*
The highest lake in the United Kingdom is the 1.9 acre *0,76 ha* Lochan Buidhe at 3,600 ft *1 097 m* above sea-level in the Cairngorm Mountains, Scotland. England's highest is Broad Crag Tarn (2,746 ft *837 m* above sea-level) on Scafell Pike, Cumbria and the highest named freshwater in Wales is The Frogs Pool, a tarn near the summit of Carnedd Llywelyn, Gwynedd at *c.* 2,725 ft *830 m*.

Lake in a lake
The largest lake in a lake is Manitou Lake (41.09 miles² *106,42 km²*) on the world's largest lake island Manitoulin Island (1,068 miles² *2 766 km²*) in the Canadian part of Lake Huron.

Underground Lake
Reputedly the world's largest underground lake is the Lost Sea 300 ft *91 m* subterranean in the Craighead Caverns, Sweetwater, Tennessee, U.S.A. measuring 4½ acres *1,8 ha* and discovered in 1905.

Desert *Largest*
Nearly an eighth of the world's land surface is arid with a rainfall of less than 25 cm (*9.8 in*) per annum. The Sahara Desert in N. Africa is the largest in the world. At its greatest length it is 3,200 miles *5 150 km* from east to west. From north to south it is between 800 and 1,400 miles *1 275 and 2 250 km*. The area covered by the desert is about 3,250,000 miles² *8 400 000 km²*. The land level varies from 436 ft *132 m* below sea-level in the Qattâra Depression, Egypt to the mountain Emi Koussi (11,204 ft *3 415 m*) in Chad. The diurnal temperature range in the western Sahara may be more than 80° F or *45° C*.

Sand dunes
The world's highest measured sand dunes are those in the Saharan sand sea of Isaouane-N-Tiferine of east central Algeria in Lat. 26° 42′ N., Long 6° 43′ E. They have a wavelength of near 3 miles *5 km* and attain a height of 1,410 ft *430 m*.

Gorge *Largest*
The largest land gorge in the world is the Grand Canyon on the Colorado River in north-central Arizona, U.S.A. It extends from Marble Gorge to the Grand Wash Cliffs, over a distance of 217 miles *349 km*. It varies in width from 4 to 13 miles *6 to 20 km* and is up to 7,000 ft *2 133 m* deep. The submarine Labrador Basin canyon is *c.* 2,150 miles *3 440 km* long.

Gorge *Deepest*
The deepest canyon in low relief territory is Hell's Canyon, dividing Oregon and Idaho, U.S.A. It plunges 7,900 ft *2 400 m* from the Devil Mountain down to the Snake River. A stretch of the Kali River in central Nepal flows 18,000 ft

5 485 m below its flanking summits of the Dhaulagiri and Annapurna groups. The deepest submarine canyon yet discovered is one 25 miles *40 km* south of Esperance, Western Australia, which is 6,000 ft *1 800 m* deep and 20 miles *32 km* wide.

Sea Cliffs *Highest*

The highest sea cliffs yet pinpointed anywhere in the world are those on the north coast of east Molokai, Hawaii near Umilehi Point, which descend 3,300 ft *1 005 m* to the sea at an average gradient of >55°. The highest cliffs in North West Europe are those on the north coast of Achill Island, in County Mayo, Ireland, which are 2,192 ft *668 m* sheer above the sea at Croaghan. The highest cliffs in the United Kingdom are the 1,300 ft *396 m* Conachair cliffs on St. Kilda, Western Isles (1,379 ft *425 m*). The highest sheer sea cliffs on the mainland of Great Britain are at Clo Mor, 3 miles *4,8 km* south east of Cape Wrath, Highland, Scotland which drop 921 ft *280,7 m*. England's highest cliffs are Holdstone Hill which descends 1,131 ft *344 m* in a ½ mile *800 m* and Great Hangman Hill, near Coombe Martin, also in North Devon, which descends from 1,029 ft *313 m* to the sea in less than ¼ mile *400 m*, the last 700 ft *213 m* of which is sheer.

Natural Arch *Longest*

The longest natural arch in the world is the Landscape Arch in the Arches and Canyonlands National Parks, Natural Bridges National Monument, Moab, Utah, U.S.A. This natural sandstone arch spans 291 ft *88 m* and is set about 100 ft *30 m* above the canyon floor. In one place erosion has narrowed its section to 6 ft *1,82 m*. Larger, however, is the Rainbow Bridge, Utah discovered on 14 Aug. 1909 with a span of 278 ft *84,7 m* but more than 22 ft *6,7 m* wide.

Natural Bridge *Highest*

The highest natural arch is the sandstone arch 25 miles *40 km* WNW of K'ashih, Sinkiang, China, estimated in 1947 to be nearly 1,000 ft *312 m* tall with a span of about 150 ft *45 m*.

Longest glaciers

It is estimated that 6,020,000 miles² *15 600 000 km²*, or about 10.4 per cent of the Earth's land surface, is permanently glaciated. The world's longest known glacier is the Lambert Glacier, discovered by an Australian aircraft crew in Australian Antarctic Territory in 1956–57. It is up to 40 miles *64 km* wide and, with its upper section, known as the Mellor Glacier, it measures at least 250 miles *402 km* in length. With the Fisher Glacier limb, the Lambert forms a continuous ice passage about 320 miles *514 km* long. The longest Himalayan glacier is the Siachen (47 miles *75,6 km*) in the Karakoram range, though the Hispar and Biafo combine to form an ice passage 76 miles *122 km* long.

Greatest avalanches

The greatest avalanches, though rarely observed, occur in the Himalaya but no estimates of their volume had been published. It was estimated that 3,500,000 m³ *120 000 000 ft³* of snow fell in an avalanche in the Italian Alps in 1885. (See also Disasters, end of Chapter 10.)

3. WEATHER

The meteorological records given below necessarily relate largely to the last 125 to 145 years, since data before that time are both sparse and unreliable. Reliable registering thermometers were introduced as recently as *c.* 1820.

Palaeo-entomological evidence is that there was a southern European climate in England *c.* 90,000 B.C., while in *c.* 6,000 B.C. the mean summer temperature reached 67° F *19,4° C*, or 6 deg F *3,3 deg C* higher than the present. The earliest authentic British weather records relate to the period 26–30 Aug. 55 B.C. The earliest reliably known hot summer was in A.D. 664 during our driest ever century and the earliest known severe winter was that of A.D. 763–4. In 1683–84 there was frost in London from November to April. Frosts were recorded during August in the period 1668–89.

Progressive extremes

The world's extremes of temperature have been noted progressively thus:

PROGRESSIVE LIST OF WORLD'S EXTREME HIGH TEMPERATURES			
127.4° F	53,0° C	Ouargla, Algeria	27 Aug. 1884
130° F	54,4° C	Amos, California, U.S.A.	17 Aug. 1885
130° F	54,4° C	Mammoth Tank, California, U.S.A.	17 Aug. 1885
134° F	56,7° C	Death Valley, California, U.S.A.	10 July 1913
136.4° F	58,0° C	Al'Aziziyah (el-Azizia), Libya*	13 Sept. 1922

* Obtained by the U.S. National Geographical Society but not officially recognized by the Libyan Ministry of Communications.

A reading of 140° F 60° C at Delta, Mexico, in August 1953 is not now accepted because of over-exposure to roof radiation. The official Mexican record of 136.4° F 58,0° C at San Luis, Sonora on 11 Aug. 1933 is not internationally accepted.

A freak heat flash reported from Coimbra, Portugal, in September 1933 said to have caused the temperature to rise to 70° C 158° F for 120 seconds is apocryphal.

PROGRESSIVE LIST OF WORLD'S EXTREME LOW TEMPERATURES			
—73° F	—58,3° C	Floeberg Bay, Ellesmere Is., Canada	1852
—90.4° F	—68° C	Verkhoyansk, Siberia, U.S.S.R.	3 Jan. 1885
—90.4° F	—68° C	Verkhoyansk, Siberia U.S.S.R.	5 & 7 Feb. 1892
—90.4° F	—68° C	Oymyakon, Siberia, U.S.S.R.	6 Feb. 1933
—100.4° F	—73,5° C	South Pole, Antarctica	11 May 1957
—102.1° F	—74,5° C	South Pole, Antarctica	17 Sept. 1957
—109.1° F	—78,34° C	Sovietskaya, Antarctica	2 May 1958
—113.3° F	—80,7° C	Vostok, Antarctica	15 June 1958
—114.1° F	—81,2° C	Sovietskaya, Antarctica	19 June 1958
—117.4° F	—83,0° C	Sovietskaya, Antarctica	25 June 1958
—122.4° F	—85,7° C	Vostok, Antarctica	7–8 Aug. 1958
—124.1° F	—86,7° C	Sovietskaya, Antarctica	9 Aug. 1958
—125.3° F	—87,4° C	Vostok, Antarctica	25 Aug. 1958
—126.9° F	—88,3° C	Vostok, Antarctica	24 Aug. 1960

Most equable temperature

The location with the most equable recorded temperature over a short period is Garapan, on Saipan, in the Mariana Islands, Pacific Ocean. During the nine years from 1927 to 1935, inclusive, the lowest temperature recorded was 19,6° C *67.3° F* on 30 Jan. 1934 and the highest was 31,4° C *88.5° F* on 9 Sept. 1931, giving an extreme range of 11,8 deg C *21.2 deg F*. Between 1911 and 1966 the Brazilian off-shore island of Fernando de Noronha had a minimum temperature of 18,6° C *65.5° F* on 17 Nov. 1913 and a maximum of 32,0° C *89.6° F* on 2 March 1965, an extreme range of 13,4 deg C *24.1 deg F*.

Greatest temperature ranges

The great recorded temperature ranges in the world are around the Siberian "cold pole" in the eastern U.S.S.R. Verkhoyansk (67° 33′ N., 133° 23′ E.) has ranged 192 deg F *106,7 deg C* from —94° F *—70° C* (unofficial) to 98° F *36,7° C*.

The greatest temperature variation recorded in a day is 100 deg F *55,5 deg C* (a fall from 44° F *6,7° C* to —56° F *—48,8° C*) at Browning, Montana, U.S.A., on 23–24 Jan. 1916. The most freakish rise was 49 deg F *27,2 deg C* in 2 min at Spearfish, South Dakota, from —4° F *—20° C* at 7.30 a.m. to 45° F *7,2° C* at 7.32 a.m. on 22 Jan. 1943. The British record is 50.9 deg F *28,3 deg C* (34° F *1,1° C* to 84.9° F *29° C*) in 9 hrs at Rickmansworth, Hertfordshire, on 29 Aug. 1936.

Longest freeze

The longest recorded unremitting freeze (maximum temperature 32° F *0° C* and below) in the British Isles was one of 34 days at Moor House, Cumbria, from 23 Dec. 1962 to 25 Jan. 1963. This was almost certainly exceeded at the neighbouring Great Dun Fell, where the screen temperature never rose above freezing during the whole of January 1963. Less rigorous early data includes a frost from 5 Dec. 1607 to 14 Feb. 1608 and a 91 day frost on Dartmoor, Devon in 1854–55. No temperature lower than 34° F *1° C* has ever been recorded on Bishop Rock, Isle of Scilly.

Upper atmosphere

The lowest temperature ever recorded in the atmosphere is —143° C *—225.4° F* at an altitude of about 50 to 60 miles

80,5–96,5 km, during noctilucent cloud research above Kronogård, Sweden, from 27 July to 7 Aug. 1963. A jet stream moving at 408 m.p.h. *656 km/h* at 154,200 ft *47 000 m* (29.2 miles *46 km*) was recorded by Skua rocket above South Uist, Outer Hebrides, Scotland on 13 Dec. 1967.

Deepest permafrost
The greatest recorded depth of permafrost is 1,5 km *4,920 ft* reported in April 1968 in the basin of the River Lena, Siberia, U.S.S.R.

Most recent White Christmas and Frost Fair
London has experienced seven "White" Christmas Days since 1900. These have been 1906, 1917 (slight), 1923 (slight), 1927, 1938, 1956 (slight) and 1970. These were more frequent in the 19th century and even more so before the change of the calendar, which, by removing 3–13 Sept. brought forward all dates subsequent to 2 Sept. 1752 by 11 days. The last of the nine recorded Frost Fairs held on the Thames since 1564/65 was in Dec. 1813 to 26 Jan. 1814.

Most intense rainfall
Difficulties attend rainfall readings for very short periods but the figure of 1.23 in *3,12 cm* in 1 min at Unionville, Maryland, U.S.A., at 3.23 p.m. on 4 July 1956, is regarded as the most intense recorded in modern times. The cloudburst of "near 2 ft [*609 mm*] in less than a quarter of half an hour" at Oxford on the afternoon of 31 May (Old Style) 1682 is regarded as unacademically recorded. The most intense rainfall in Britain recorded to modern standards has been 2.0 in *5,08 cm* in 12 min at Wisbech, Cambridgeshire on 28 June 1970.

Falsest St. Swithin's Days
The legend that the weather on St. Swithin's Day, celebrated on 15 July (Old and New Style) since A.D. 912, determines the rainfall for the next 40 days is one which has long persisted. There was a brilliant 13½ hrs sunshine in London on 15 July 1924, but 30 of the next 40 days were wet. On 15 July 1913 there was a 15 hour downpour, yet it rained on only 9 of the subsequent 40 days in London.

Best and worst British summers
According to Prof. Gordon Manley's survey over the period 1728 to 1976 the best (i.e. driest and hottest) British summer was that of 1976 and the worst (i.e. wettest and coldest) that of 1879. Temperatures of 90° F or more (>*32,2° C*) were recorded on 13 consecutive days (25 June–7 July 1976).

Humidity and discomfort
Human comfort or discomfort depends not merely on temperature but on the combination of temperature, humidity, radiation and wind-speed. The United States Weather Bureau uses a Temperature-Humidity Index, which equals two-fifths of the sum of the dry and wet bulb thermometer readings plus 15. A THI of 98.2 has been twice recorded in Death Valley, California—on 27 July 1966 (119° F and 31%) and on 12 Aug. 1970 (117° F and 37%).

Largest Mirage
The largest mirage on record was that sighted in the Arctic at 83° N 103° W by Donald B. MacMillan in 1913. This type of mirage known as the Fata Morgana appeared as the same "Hills, valleys, snow-capped peaks extending through at least 120 degrees of the horizon" that Peary had named Crocker Land 6 years earlier.

Lightning
The visible length of lightning strokes varies greatly. In mountainous regions, when clouds are very low, the flash may be less than 300 ft *91 m* long. In flat country with very high clouds, a cloud-to-earth flash sometimes measures 4 miles *6 km* though in extreme cases such flashes have been measured at 20 miles *32 km*. The intensely bright central core of the lightning channel is extremely narrow. Some authorities suggest that its diameter is as little as half an inch *1,27 cm*. This core is surrounded by a "corona envelope" (glow discharge) which may measure 10 to 20 ft *3–6 m* in diameter.

The speed of a lightning discharge varies from 100 to 1,000 miles/sec *160,9 to 1 609 km/sec* for the downward leader track, and reaches up to 87,000 miles/sec *140 012 km/sec* (nearly half the speed of light) for the powerful return stroke. In Britain there is an average of 6 strikes/mile[2] per annum or 3,7 per km[2] and an average of 4,200 per annum over Greater London alone. Every few million strokes there is a giant discharge, in which the cloud-to-earth and the return lightning strokes flash from the top of the thunder clouds. In these "positive giants" energy of up to 3,000 million joules $(3 \times 10^{16}$ ergs) is sometimes recorded. The temperature reaches about 30,000° C, which is more than five times greater than that of the surface of the Sun.

Highest waterspout
The highest waterspout of which there is a reliable record was one observed on 16 May 1898 off Eden, New South Wales, Australia. A theodolite reading from the shore gave its height as 5,014 ft *1 528 m.* It was about 10 ft *3 m* in diameter. A waterspout moved around Torbay, Devon on 17 Sept. 1969 which was according to press estimates 1,000 ft *300 m* in height.

Cloud extremes
The highest standard cloud form is cirrus, averaging 27,000 ft *8 250 m* and above, but the rare nacreous or mother-of-pearl formation sometimes reaches nearly 80,000 ft *24 000 m.* The lowest is stratus, below 3,500 ft *1 066 m.* The cloud form with the greatest vertical range is cumulo-nimbus, which has been observed to reach a height of nearly 68,000 ft *20 000 m* in the tropics.

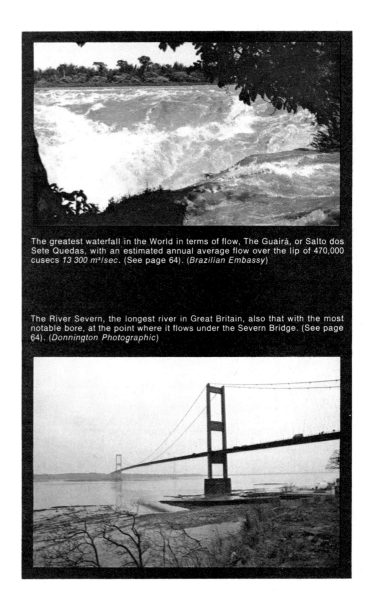

The greatest waterfall in the World in terms of flow, The Guairá, or Salto dos Sete Quedas, with an estimated annual average flow over the lip of 470,000 cusecs *13 300 m³/sec.* (See page 64). (*Brazilian Embassy*)

The River Severn, the longest river in Great Britain, also that with the most notable bore, at the point where it flows under the Severn Bridge. (See page 64). (*Donnington Photographic*)

WEATHER RECORDS

Polus Nedostupnosti, Antarctica, the coldest place in the World, with an annual mean temperature of —72° F —57,8° C. (*Novosti Press Agency*)

	World Records	United Kingdom & Ireland
Highest Shade Temperature:	136.4° F 57,7° C Al'Aziziyah, Libya, 13.9.1922	100.5° F 38° C, Tonbridge, Kent, 22.7.1868[1]
Lowest Screen Temperature:	—126.9° F —88,3° C Vostok, Antarctica, 24.8.1960[2]	—17° F —27,2° C, Braemar, Grampian, Scotland, 11.2.1895[3]
Greatest Rainfall (24 hours):	73.62 in 1 870 mm, Cilaos, La Reunion, Indian Ocean, 15–16.3.1952[4]	11.00 in 279 mm, Martinstown, Dorset, 18–19.7.1955
(Month):	366.14 in 9 299 mm, Cherrapunji, Meghalaya, India, July 1861	56.54 in 1 436 mm, Llyn Llydau, Snowdon, Gwynedd, October 1909
(12 months):	1,041.78 in 26 461 mm, Cherrapunji, Meghalaya, 1.8.1860–31.7.1861	257.0 in 6 527 mm, Sprinkling Tarn, Cumbria, in 1954[5]
Greatest Snowfall[6] (12 months):	1,224.5 in 31 102 mm, Paradise, Mt. Rainer, Washington, U.S.A. 19.2.1971 to 18.2.1972	60 in 1 524 mm, Upper Teesdale and Denbighshire Hills, Clwyd, Wales, 1947
Maximum Sunshine:[7]	97%+ (over 4,300 hours), eastern Sahara, annual average	78.3% (382 hours) Pendennis Castle, Falmouth, Cornwall, June 1925
Minimum Sunshine:	Nil at North Pole—for winter stretches of 186 days	Nil in a month at Westminster, London, in December, 1890[8]
Barometric Pressure (Highest)	1,083.8 mb. (32.00 in), Agata, Siberia, U.S.S.R. (alt. 862 ft 262 m), 31.12.1968	1,054.7 mb. (31.15 in), Aberdeen, 31.1.1902
(Lowest):[9]	877 mb. (25.90 in), about 600 miles 965 km north-west of Guam, Pacific Ocean, 24.9.1958	925.5 mb. (27.33 in), Ochtertyre, near Crieff, Tayside, 26.1.1884
Highest Surface Wind-speed:[10]	231 m.p.h. 371 km/h, Mt. Washington (6,288 ft 1 916 m), New Hampshire, U.S.A., 12.4.1934	144 m.p.h. 231 km/h (125 knots), Coire Cas ski lift (3,525 ft 1 074 m), Cairn Gorm, Highland, 6.3.1967[11]
Thunder-Days (Year):[12]	322 days, Bogor (formerly Buitenzorg), Java, Indonesia (average, 1916–19)	38 days, Stonyhurst, Lancashire, 1912 and Huddersfield, West Yorkshire, 1967
Hottest Place (Annual mean):[13]	Dallol, Ethiopia, 94° F 34,4° C (1960–66)	Penzance, Cornwall, and Isles of Scilly, both 52.7° F 11,5° C, average 1931–60
Coldest Place (Annual mean):	Polus Nedostupnosti, Pole of Cold (78° S., 96° E.), Antarctica, —72° F —57,8° C	Braemar, Grampian, 43.7° F 6,5° C, average 1931–60
Wettest Place (Annual mean):	Mt. Wai-'ale'ale (5,148 ft 1 569 m), Kauai, Hawaii, 451 in 11 455 mm (average 1920–72)	Styhead Tarn (1,600 ft 487 m), Cumbria, 172.9 in 4 391 mm
Driest Place (Annual mean):	Nil—In the Desierto de Atacama, near Calama, Chile	Great Wakering, Essex, 19.2 in 487 mm (1916–50)[14]
Longest Drought:	c. 400 years to 1971, Desierto de Atacama, Chile	73 days, Mile End, Greater London, 4.3 to 15.5.1893[15]
Most Rainy Days (Year):	Mt. Wai-'ale-'ale up to 350 per annum	Ballynahinch, Galway, 309 days in 1923
Heaviest Hailstones[16]	1.67 lb. 750 g (7½ in 19 cm diameter, 17½ in 44,45 cm circumference), Coffeyville, Kansas, U.S.A., 3.9.1970	5 oz. 141 g, Horsham, West Sussex, 5.9.1958
Longest Sea Level Fogs (Visibility less than 1,000 yds 914,4 m):	Fogs persist for weeks on the Grand Banks, Newfoundland, Canada, and the average is more than 120 days per year[17]	London, 26.11 to 1.12.1948 (4 days 18 hours). London, 5.12 to 9.12.1952 (4 days 18 hours)
Windiest Place:	The Commonwealth Bay, George V Coast, Antarctica, where gales reach 200 m.p.h. 320 km/h	Tiree, Strathclyde (89 ft 27 m); annual average 17.4 m.p.h. 28 km/h

[1] The Shade temperature in London on 8 July 1808 may have reached this figure. The highest temperature recorded in Great Britain in an orthodox Stevenson screen is 98.0° F 36,6° C at Ponders End, Enfield, Greater London on 9 Aug. 1911

[2] Vostok is 11,500 ft 3 505 m above sea-level. The coldest permanently inhabited place is the Siberian village of Oymyakon (63° 16' N., 143° 15' E.), in the U.S.S.R. where the temperature reached —96° F —71,1° C in 1964.

[3] The —23° F —30,5° C at Blackadder, Borders, on 4 Dec. 1879, and the — 20° F —28,9° C at Grantown-on-Spey on 24 Feb. 1955, were not standard exposures. The —11° F —23,9° C reported from Buxton Derbyshire on 11 Feb. 1895 was not standard. The lowest official temperature in England is —6° F —21,1° C at Bodiam, West Sussex on 20 Jan. 1940, at Ambleside, Cumbria on 21 Jan. 1940 and at Hough-all, Durham on 5 Jan. 1941 and 4 March 1947.

[4] This is equal to 7,435 tons 7 554 tonnes of rain per acre. Elevation 1 200 m 3,937 ft.

[5] The record for Ireland is 145.4 in 3 921 mm near Derriana Lough, County Kerry in 1948.

[6] The record for a single snow storm is 175.4 in 4 455 mm at Thompson Pass, Alaska, on 26—31 Dec. 1955, and for 24 hr, 76 in 1 870 mm at Silver Lake, Colorado. U.S.A. on 14–15 April 1921. The greatest depth of snow on the ground was 25 ft 5 in 7,74 m at Paradise on 17 Apr. 1972. London's earliest recorded snow was on 25 Sept. 1885, and the latest on 27 May 1821. Less reliable reports suggest snow on 12 Sept. 1658 (Old Style) and on 12 June 1791.

[7] St. Petersburg, Florida, U.S.A., recorded 768 consecutive sunny days from 9 Feb. 1967 to 17 March 1969.

[8] The south-eastern end of the village of Lochranza, Isle of Arran, Strathclyde is in shadow of mountains from 18 Nov. to 8 Feb. each winter.

[9] The U.S.S. Repose, a hospital ship, recorded 25.55 inches 856 mb. in the eye of a typhoon in 25° 35' N 128° 20' E off Okinawa on 16 Sept. 1945.

[10] The highest speed yet measured in a tornado is 280 m.p.h. 450 km/h at Wichita Falls, Texas, U.S.A., on 2 April 1958.

[11] The figure of 177.2 m.p.h. 285.2 km/h at R.A.F. Saxa Vord, Unst, in the Shetlands Scotland, on 16 Feb. 1962, was not recorded with standard equipment. There were gales of great severity on 15 Jan. 1362 and 26 Nov. 1703.

[12] Between Lat. 35° N. and 35° S. there are some 3,200 thunderstorms each 12 night-time hrs, some of which can be heard at a range of 18 miles 29 km.

[13] In Death Valley, California, U.S.A., maximum temperatures of over 120° F 48,9° C were recorded on 43 consecutive days—6 July to 17 Aug. 1917. At Marble Bar, Western Australia (maximum 121° F 49,4° C) 160 consecutive days with maximum temperatures of over 100° F 37,8° C were recorded—31 Oct. 1923 to 7 April 1924 at Wyndham, Western Australia, the temperature reached 90° F 32,2° C or more on 333 days in 1946.

[14] The lowest rainfall recorded in a single year was 9.29 in 23,6 cm at one station in Margate, Kent in 1921.

[15] The longest drought in Scotland was one of 38 days at Port William, Dumfries & Galloway on 3 Apr. to 10 May 1938.

[16] Much heavier hailstones are sometimes reported. These are usually not single but coalesced stones. An ice block of 1 to 2 kg 35–70 oz. was reputed at Withington, Manchester on 2 Apr. 1973.

[17] Lower visibilities occur at higher altitudes. Ben Nevis is reputedly in cloud 300 days per year.

4. THE UNIVERSE AND SPACE

LIGHT-YEAR—that distance travelled by light (speed 186,282.397 miles/sec *299 792,458 km s⁻¹ or 670,616,629.4 m.p.h. 1 079 258 848,8 km h⁻¹ in vacuo*) in one tropical year (365.24219878 mean solar days at January 0,12 hours Ephemeris time in A.D. 1900) and is 5,878,499,814,000 miles *9 460 528 405 000 km*. The unit was first used in March 1888.

MAGNITUDE—a measure of stellar brightness such that the light of a star of any magnitude bears a ratio of 2.511886 to that of a star of the next magnitude. Thus a fifth magnitude star is 2.511886 times as bright, while one of the first magnitude is exactly 100 (or 2.511886⁵) times as bright, as a sixth magnitude star. In the case of such exceptionally bright bodies as Sirius, Venus, the Moon (magnitude—11.2) or the Sun (magnitude—26.7), the magnitude is expressed as a minus quantity.

PROPER MOTION—that component of a star's motion in space which, at right angles to the line of sight, constitutes an apparent change of position of the star in the celestial sphere.

The universe is the entirety of space, matter and anti-matter. An appreciation of its magnitude is best grasped by working outward from the Earth, through the Solar System and our own Milky Way Galaxy, to the remotest extra-galactic nebulae.

METEOROIDS
Meteor shower

Meteoroids are mostly of cometary origin. A meteor is the light phenomenon caused by the entry of a meteoroid into the Earth's atmosphere. The greatest meteor "shower" on record occurred on the night of 16–17 Nov. 1966, when the Leonid meteors (which recur every $33\frac{1}{4}$ years) were visible between western North America and eastern U.S.S.R. It was calculated that meteors passed over Arizona, U.S.A., at a rate of 2,300 per min for a period of 20 min from 5 a.m. on 17 Nov. 1966.

METEORITES
Largest *World*

When a meteoroid penetrates to the Earth's surface, the remnant is described as a meteorite. This occurs about 150 times per year over the whole land surface of the Earth. Although the chances of being struck are deemed negligible, the most anxious time of day for meteorophobes is 3 p.m. The largest known meteorite is one found in 1920 at Hoba West, near Grootfontein in south west Africa. This is a block 9 ft *2,75 m* long by 8 ft *2,43 m* broad, estimated to be 132,000 lb. (59 tons/*tonnes*). The largest meteorite exhibited by any museum is the "Tent" meteorite, weighing 68,085 lb. (30.4 tons *30 882 kg*) found in 1897 near Cape York, on the west coast of Greenland, by the expedition of Commander (later Rear-Admiral) Robert Edwin Peary (1856–1920). It was known to the Eskimos as the Abnighito and is now exhibited in the Hayden Planetarium in New York City, N.Y., U.S.A. The largest piece of stony meteorite recovered is a piece of 1770 kg *3,902 lb.* part of a shower which struck Kirin,

China on 8 Mar. 1976. The oldest dated meteorites are from the Allende fall in Chihuahua, Mexico on 8 Feb. 1969. A piece of this has been dated to 4,610 million years—thus is several 100 million years older than the oldest dated rock on Earth.

There was a mysterious explosion of about 35 megatons in Latitude 60° 55′ N., Longitude 101° 57′ E., in the basin of the Podkamennaya Tunguska river, 40 miles north of Vanavar, in Siberia, U.S.S.R., at 00 hrs 17 min 11 sec U.T. on 30 June 1908. The energy of this explosion was about 10²⁴ ergs and the cause has been variously attributed to a meteorite (1927), a comet (1930), a nuclear explosion (1961) and to anti-matter (1965). This devastated an area of about 1,500 miles² *3 885 km²* and the shock was felt as far as 1 000 km (more than *600 miles*) away.

Largest *United Kingdom and Ireland*

The heaviest of the 22 meteorites known to have fallen on the British Isles since 1623 was one weighing at least 102 lb. *46,25 kg* (largest piece 17 lb. 6 oz. *7,88 kg*), which fell at 4.12 p.m. on 24 Dec. 1965 at Barwell, Leicestershire. Scotland's largest recorded meteorite fell in Strathmore, Tayside

The site in Kirin, China, where the world's heaviest stony meteorite penetrated the earth to a depth of 6,5 m *21 ft* on 8 Mar. 1976. (*Chinese Academy of Sciences*)

on 3 Dec. 1917. It weighed 22¼ lb. *10,09 kg* and was the largest of four stones totalling 29 lb. 6 oz. *13,324 kg*. The largest recorded meteorite to fall in Ireland was the Limerick Stone of 65 lb. *29,5 kg* part of a shower weighing more than 106 lb. *48 kg* which fell near Adare County Limerick, on 10 Sept. 1813. The larger of the two recorded meteorites to land in Wales was one weighing 28 oz. *794 g* of which a piece weighing 25½ oz. *723 g* went through the roof of the Prince Llewellyn Hotel in Beddgelert, Gwynedd, shortly before 3.15 a.m. on 21 Sept. 1949.

Largest craters

A crater 150 miles *241 km* and ½ mile *805 m* deep has been postulated in Wilkes Land, Antarctica since 1962. It would be caused by a 13,000 million ton meteorite striking at 44,000 m.p.h. *70 811 km/h* U.S.S.R. scientists reported in Dec. 1970 an astrobleme with a 60 mile *95 km* diameter and a maximum depth of 1,300 ft *400 m* in the basin of the River Popigai. There is a possible crater-like formation 275 miles *442,5 km* in diameter on the eastern shore of the Hudson Bay, Canada, where the Nastapoka Islands are just off the coast.

The largest proven crater is the Coon Butte or Barringer crater, discovered in 1891 near Canyon Diablo, Winslow, northern Arizona, U.S.A. It is 4,150 ft *1 265 m* in diameter and now about 575 ft *175 m* deep, with a parapet rising 130 to 155 ft *40–48 m* above the surrounding plain. It has been estimated that an iron-nickel mass with a diameter of 200 to 260 ft *61–79 m* and weighing about 2,000,000 tons/*tonnes* gouged this crater in *c.* 25,000 B.C. with an impact force equivalent to an explosion of 30,000,000 short tons *27,2 million tonnes* of trinitrotoluene or T.N.T. ($C_7H_5O_6N_3$).

Evidence was published in 1963 discounting a meteoric origin for the crypto-volcanic Vredefort Ring (diameter 26 miles *41,8 km*), to the south-west of Johannesburg, South Africa, but this has now been re-asserted. The New Quebec (formerly the Chubb) "Crater", first sighted on 20 June 1943 in northern Ungava, Canada, is 1,325 ft *404 m* deep and measures 6.8 miles *10,9 km* round its rim.

Fireball *Brightest*

The brightest fireball ever photographically recorded was one over Sumava, Czechoslovakia on 4 Dec. 1974 with a momentary magnitude of −22 or 10,000 times brighter than a full Moon.

Tektites

The largest tektite of which details have been published has been of 3,2 kg *7.04 lb.* found *c.* 1932 at Muong Nong, Saravane Province, Laos and now in the Paris Museum.

AURORAE
Most frequent

Polar lights, known as Aurora Borealis or Northern Lights in the northern hemisphere and Aurora Australis in the southern hemisphere, are caused by electrical solar discharges in the upper atmosphere and occur most frequently in high latitudes. Aurorae are visible at some time on *every* clear dark night in the polar areas within 20 degrees of the magnetic poles. The extreme height of aurorae has been measured at 1,000 km *620 miles,* while the lowest may descend to 45 miles *72,5 km*. Reliable figures exist only from 1952 since when the record high and low number of nights of auroral displays in Shetland (geomagnetic Lat. 63°) has been 203 (1957) and 58 (1965). The most recent great display in north-west Europe was that of 4–5 Sept. 1958.

Lowest Latitudes

Extreme cases of displays in very low latitudes are Cuzco, Peru (2 Aug. 1744); Honolulu, Hawaii (1 Sept. 1859) and questionably Singapore (25 Sept. 1909).

Noctilucent Clouds

Regular observations in Western Europe date only from 1964 since when the record high and low number of nights on which these phenomena (at heights of *c.* 52 miles *85 km*) have been observed have been 41 (1974) and 15 (1970).

THE MOON

The Earth's closest neighbour in space and only natural satellite is the Moon, at a mean distance of 238,855 statute miles *384 400 km* centre to centre or 233,812 miles *376 284 km* surface to surface. Its closest approach (perigee) and most extreme distance away (apogee) measured surface to surface are 216,420 and 247,667 miles *348 294 and 398 581 km* respectively or 221,463 and 252,710 miles *356 410/406 697 km* measured centre to centre. It has a diameter of 2,159.6 miles *3 475,6 km* and has a mass of 7.23×10^{19} tons *$7,35 \times 10^{19}$ tonnes* with a mean density of 3.34. The average orbital speed is 2,287 m.p.h. *3 680 km/h*.

The first direct hit on the Moon was achieved at 2 min 24 sec after midnight (Moscow time) on 14 Sept. 1959, by the Soviet space probe *Lunik II* near the *Mare Serenitatis*. The first photographic images of the hidden side were collected by the U.S.S.R.'s *Lunik III* from 6.30 a.m. on 7 Oct. 1959, from a range of up to 43,750 miles *70 400 km* and transmitted to the Earth from a distance of 470 000 km *292,000 miles*. The first "soft" landing was made by the U.S.S.R.'s *Luna IX*, in the area of the Ocean of Storms on 3 Feb. 1966.

"Blue Moon"

Owing to sulphur particles in the upper atmosphere from a forest fire covering 250,000 acres *100 000 ha* between Mile 103 and Mile 119 on the Alaska Highway in northern British Columbia, Canada, the Moon took on a bluish colour, as seen from Great Britain, on the night of 26 Sept. 1950. The Moon also appeared blue after the Krakatoa eruption of 27 Aug. 1883 (see page 58) and on other occasions.

Crater *Largest*

Only 59 per cent of the Moon's surface is directly visible from the Earth because it is in "captured rotation", *i.e.* the period of rotation is equal to the period of orbit. The largest wholly visible crater is the walled plain Bailly, towards the Moon's South Pole, which is 183 miles *295 km* across, with walls rising to 14,000 ft *4 250 m*. The Orientale Basin, partly on the averted side, measures more than 600 miles *965 km* in diameter.

Crater *Deepest*

The deepest crater is the Newton crater, with a floor estimated to be between 23,000 and 29,000 ft *7 000–8 850 m* below its rim and 14,000 ft *2 250 m* below the level of the plain outside. The brightest directly visible spot on the Moon is *Aristarchus*.

Highest mountains

In the absence of a sea level, lunar altitudes are measured relative to a reference sphere of radius 1 738,000 km or *1,079.943 miles*. Thus the greatest elevation attained by any of the 12 U.S. astronauts has been 7 830 m *25,688 ft* on the Descartes Highlands by Capt. John Walter Young U.S.N. and Major Charles M. Duke Jr. on 27 Apr. 1972.

Temperature extremes

When the Sun is overhead the temperature on the lunar equator reaches 243° F *117,2° C* (31 deg F *17,2 deg C* above the boiling point of water). By sunset the temperature is 58° F *14,4° C* but after nightfall it sinks to −261° F *−162,7° C*.

Moon samples

The age attributed to the oldest of the moon material brought back to Earth by the *Apollo* programme crews has been soil dated to 4,720 million years.

THE SUN
Distance extremes

The Earth's 66,620 m.p.h. *107 220 km/h* orbit of 584,017,800 miles *939 885 500 km* around the Sun is elliptical, hence our distance from the Sun varies. The orbital speed varies between 65,520 m.p.h. *105 450 km/h* (minimum) and 67,750 m.p.h. *109 030 km/h*. The average distance of the Sun is 1.000 000 230 astronomical units or 92,955,829 miles *149 597 906 km*.

The closest approach (perihelion) is 91,402,000 miles *147 097 000 km* and the farthest departure (aphelion) is 94,510,000 miles *152 099 000 km*. The Solar System is revolving around the centre of the Milky Way once in each 225,000,000 years, at a speed of 481,000 m.p.h. *774 000 km/h* and has a velocity of 42,500 m.p.h. *68 400 km/h* relative to stars in our immediate region such as Vega, towards which it is moving.

Temperature and dimensions

The Sun has an internal temperature of about 20 000 000 K., a core pressure of 500,000,000 tons/in^2 and uses up 4,000,000 tons/*tonnes* of hydrogen per sec. thus providing a luminosity of 3×10^{27} candlepower, with an intensity of 1,500,000 candles/in^2 *1 530 000 candelas*. The Sun has the stellar classification of a "yellow dwarf" and, although its density is only 1.409 times that of water, its mass is 332,946 times as much as that of the Earth. It has a mean diameter of 864,940 miles *1 391 980 km*. The Sun with a mass of 1.958×10^{27} tons *1,989 $\times 10^{27}$ tonnes* represents more than 99 per cent of the total mass of the Solar System.

Sun-spots *Largest*

To be visible to the *protected* naked eye, a Sun-spot must cover about one two-thousandth part of the Sun's disc and thus have an area of about 500,000,000 miles^2 *1 300 million km^2*. The largest recorded Sun-spot occurred in the Sun's southern hemisphere on 8 April 1947. Its area was about 7,000 million miles^2 *18 000 million km^2* with an extreme longitude of 187,000 miles *300 000 km* and an extreme latitude of 90,000 miles *145 000 km*. Sun-spots appear darker because they are more than 1 500 deg C cooler than the rest of the Sun's surface temperature of 5 660° C. The largest observed solar prominence was one measuring 70,000 miles *112 500 km* across its base and protruding 300,000 miles *480 000 km*, observed on 4 June 1936.

Most frequent

In October 1957 a smoothed Sun-spot count showed 263, the highest recorded index since records started in 1755 (*cf.* previous record of 239 in May 1778). In 1943 one Sun-spot lasted for 200 days from June to December.

ECLIPSES
Earliest recorded

The earliest extrapolated eclipses that have been identified are 1361 B.C. (lunar) and Oct. 2137 B.C. (solar). For the Middle East only, lunar eclipses have been extrapolated to 3450 B.C. and solar ones to 4200 B.C. No centre of the path of totality for a solar eclipse crossed London for the 575 years from 20 March 1140 to 3 May 1715. The next will be on 14 June 2051. The most recent occasion when a line of totality of a solar eclipse crossed Great Britain was on 29 June 1927 for 24.5 sec at 6.23 a.m. at West Hartlepool, Cleveland and the next instance will clip the Cornish coast on the morning of 11 Aug. 1999 and again in 23 Sept. 2090. On 30 June 1954 a total eclipse was witnessed in Unst, Shetland Islands but the centre of the path of totality was to the north of territorial waters.

Longest duration

The maximum *possible* duration of an eclipse of the Sun is 7 min 31 sec. The longest actually *measured* was on 20 June 1955 (7 min 8 sec), seen from the Philippines. One of 7 min 29 sec should occur in mid Atlantic on 16 July 2186, which will then be the longest for 1,469 years. The longest possible in the British Isles is 5½ min. That of 15 June 885 lasted nearly 5 min, as will that of 22 July 2381 also in northern England. An annular eclipse may last for 12 min 24 sec. The longest totality of any lunar eclipse is 104 min. This has occurred many times.

Most and least frequent

The highest number of eclipses possible in a year is seven, as in 1935, when there were five solar and two lunar eclipses; or four solar and three lunar eclipses, as will occur in 1982. The lowest possible number in a year is two, both of which must be solar, as in 1944 and 1969.

COMETS
Earliest recorded

The earliest records of comets date from the 7th century B.C. The speeds of the estimated 2,000,000 comets vary from 700 m.p.h. *1 125 km/h* in outer space to 1,250,000 m.p.h. *2 000 000 km/h* when near the Sun. The successive appearances of Halley's Comet have been traced back to 466 B.C. It was first depicted in the Nuremburg Chronicle of A.D. 684. The first prediction of its return by Edmund Halley (1656–1742) proved true on Christmas Day 1758, 16 years after his

death. Its next appearance should be at 9.9 (*viz.* at 9.30 p.m. on the 9th) February 1986, 75.81 years after the last, which was on 19 April 1910.

Closest approach

On 1 July 1770, Lexell's Comet, travelling at a speed of 23.9 miles/sec *38,5 km/sec* (relative to the Sun), came within 1,500,000 miles *2 400 000 km* of the Earth. However, the Earth is believed to have passed through the tail of Halley's Comet, most recently on 19 May 1910.

Largest

Comets are so tenuous that it has been estimated that even the head of one rarely contains solid matter much more than *c.* 1 km *0.6 miles* in diameter. In the tail 10,000 miles^3 contain less than a cubic inch of solid matter (or *2 500 km^3 contains less than 1 cm^3*). These tails, as in the case of the Great Comet of 1843, may trail for 200,000,000 miles *320 million km*. The head of Holmes Comet of 1892 once measured 1,500,000 miles *2 400 000 km* in diameter.

Comet Bennett which appeared in January 1970 was found to be enveloped in a hydrogen cloud measuring some 8,000,000 miles *12 750 000 km* in length.

Shortest period

Of all the recorded periodic comets (these are members of the Solar System), the one which most frequently returns is Encke's Comet, first identified in 1786. Its period of 1,206 days (3.3 years) is the shortest established. Not one of its 48 returns (up to May 1967) has been missed by astronomers. Now increasingly faint, it is expected to "die" by Feb. 1994. The most frequently observed comets are Schwassmann-Wachmann I, Kopff and Oterma which can be observed every year between Mars and Jupiter.

Longest period

At the other extreme is the comet 1910 a, whose path was not accurately determined. It is not expected to return for perhaps 4,000,000 years.

PLANETS
Largest

Planets (including the Earth) are bodies within the Solar System and which revolve round the Sun in definite orbits. Jupiter, with an equatorial diameter of 88,780 miles *142 880 km* and a polar diameter of 82,980 miles *133 540 km* is the largest of the nine major planets, with a mass 317.83 times, and a volume 1,318 times that of the Earth. It also has the shortest period of rotation resulting in a Jovian day of only 9 hrs 50 min 30.003 sec in the equatorial zone.

Smallest

Of the nine major planets, Mercury is the smallest with a diameter of 3,031 $\pm$ 1 mile *4 878 $\pm$ 2 km* and a mass of 0.055274 Earth masses or 325.0 trillion tons *330,2 $\times 10^{18}$ tonnes*. Mercury, which orbits the Sun at an average distance of 35,983,100 miles *57 909 200 km* has a period of revolution of 87.9686 days, so giving the highest average speed in orbit of 107,030 m.p.h. *172 248 km/h*.

Hottest

For Venus a surface temperature of *c.* 475° C *890° F* has been estimated from measurements made from the U.S.S.R. *Venera 7* and *Venera 8* probes. The planet with a surface temperature closest to Earth's average figure of 59° F *15° C* is Mars with a value of 55° F *12,8 °C* for the sub-solar point at a mean solar distances of 141,636,000 miles *227 940 000 km*.

Coldest

The coldest planet is, not unnaturally, that which is the remotest from the Sun, namely Pluto, which has an estimated surface temperature of −360° F *−220° C* (100 deg F *53 deg C* above absolute zero). Its mean distance from the Sun is 3,674,488,000 miles *5 913 514 000 km* and its period of revolution is 248.54 years. Its diameter is about 3,400 miles (*c.* 5 450 km) and has a mass about one twentieth of that of the Earth. Pluto was first recorded by Clyde William Tombaugh (b. 4 Feb. 1906) at Lowell Observatory, Flagstaff, Arizona, U.S.A., on 18 Feb. 1930 from photographs taken on 23 and 29 January. Because of its orbital eccentricity Pluto will move closer to the Sun than Neptune between 21 Jan. 1979 and 14 Mar. 1999.

Nearest
The fellow planet closest to the Earth is Venus, which is, at times, about 25,700,000 miles *41 360 000 km* inside the Earth's orbit, compared with Mars's closest approach of 34,600,000 miles *55 680 000 km* outside the Earth's orbit. Mars, known since 1965 to be cratered, has temperatures ranging from 85° F *29,4° C* to −190° F *−123° C*.

Surface features
Mariner 9 photographs have revealed a canyon in the Tithonias Lacus region of Mars which is 62 miles *100 km* wider and 4,000 ft *1 220 m* deeper than the 13 mile *21 km* wide 5,500 ft *1 675 m* deep Grand Canyon on Earth. The largest volcanic structure on Mars is Alba Patera with a diameter of 1 600 km *995 miles* and a height of 4–8 km *13,000–26,000 ft*. By far the highest and most spectacular is Olympus Mons (formerly Nix Olympica) in the Tharsis region with a diameter of 500–600 km *310–370 miles* and a height of 26 ± 3 km *75,450–95,150 ft.* above the surrounding plain.

Brightest and faintest
Viewed from the Earth, by far the brightest of the five planets visible to the naked eye (Uranus at magnitude 5.7 is only marginally visible) is Venus, with a maximum magnitude of −4.4. The faintest is Pluto, with a magnitude of 15.0. In April 1972 the existence of a tenth or trans-Plutonian planet more than 6,000 million miles *9 650 million km* from the Sun with 3 times the mass of Saturn was suggested but refuted in the same year.

Densest and least dense
Earth is the densest planet with an average figure of 5.515 times that of water, whilst Saturn has an average density only about one eighth of this value or 0.705 times that of water.

Conjunctions
The most dramatic recorded conjunction (coming together) of the other seven principal members of the Solar System (Sun, Moon, Mercury, Venus, Mars, Jupiter and Saturn) occurred on 5 Feb. 1962, when 16° covered all seven during an eclipse in the Pacific area. It is possible that the seven-fold conjunction of September 1186 spanned only 12°. The next notable conjunction will take place on 5 May 2000.

SATELLITES
Most
Of the nine major planets, all but Venus, Mercury and Pluto have satellites. The planet with the most is Jupiter, with four large and ten small moons. Jupiter's 14th moon (J-XIV) was first identified by Charles Kowal (U.S.) in October 1975. The Earth is the only planet with a single satellite. The distance from their parent planets varies from the 5,827 miles *9 378 km* of *Phobos* from the centre of Mars to the 14,730,000 miles *23 705 000 km* of Jupiter's outer satellite Sinope (Jupiter IX). The Solar System has (excluding Saturn's unproven 10th and 11th moons) a total of 34 satellites.

Largest and smallest
The largest satellite is the sixth moon of Saturn, *Titan*, with a diameter of 3,440 miles *5 530 km* and a possible atmospheric thickness of 90 miles *150 km*. The heaviest satellite is the third moon of Jupiter, *Ganymede*, which is 2.02 times heavier than our own Moon, but it is possible that the large satellite of Neptune, *Triton*, is both larger than *Titan* and heavier than *Ganymede*. The smallest satellite is the latest discovered, Jupiter XIV (see above) with a diameter of only 4 miles *6 km*.

Largest asteroids
In the belt which lies between Mars and Jupiter, there are some 45,000 (only 3,100 charted) minor planets or asteroids which are, for the most part, too small to yield to diameter measurement. The largest and first discovered (by Piazzi at Palermo, Sicily on 1 Jan. 1801) of these is *Ceres*, with a diameter of 593 miles *955 km*. The only one visible to the naked eye is *Vesta* (diameter 313 miles *503 km*) discovered on 29 March 1807 by Dr. Heinrich Wilhelm Olbers (1758–

1840), a German amateur astronomer. The closest measured approach to the Earth by an asteroid was 485,000 miles *780 000 km* in the case of *Hermes* on 30 Oct. 1937. It was announced in Dec. 1971 that the orbit of *Toro* (disc. 1964), though centred on the Sun, is also in resonance with the Earth-Moon system. Its nearest approach to Earth is 9,600,000 miles *15 450 000 km*. Helin or 1976AA has an orbit time of 347 days.

STARS
Largest and most massive
Of those measured, the star with the greatest diameter is believed to be the cold giant star IRS5 in the Perseus spiral arm of the Milky Way with a diameter larger than that of the entire Solar System of 9,200 million miles *15 000 million km*. This was announced in January 1973. The *Alpha Herculis* aggregation, consisting of a main star and a double star companion, is enveloped in a cold gas. This system, visible to the naked eye, has a diameter of 170,000 million miles *275 000 million km*. The fainter component of Plaskett's star discovered by J. S. Plaskett from the Dominion Astrophysical Observatory, Victoria, British Columbia, Canada c. 1920 is the most massive star known with a mass c. 55 times that of the Sun.

Smallest
The smallest known star is LP 327–186, a "white dwarf" with a diameter only half that of the Moon, 100 light-years distant and detected in May 1962 from Minneapolis, Minnesota, U.S.A. The claim that LP 768–500 is even smaller at <1,000 miles *<1 600 km* is not widely accepted. Some pulsars or neutron stars may however have diameters of only 10–20 miles *16–32 km*.

Oldest
The Sun is estimated to be about 7,500 million years old but our galaxy is estimated to be between 10,000 million and 12,000 million years old.

Brightest
Sirius A (*Alpha Canis Majoris*), also known as the Dog Star, is apparently the brightest star of the 5,776 stars visible in the heavens, with an apparent magnitude of −1.46. It is in the constellation *Canis Major* and is visible in the winter months of the northern hemisphere, being due south at midnight on the last day of the year. Sirius A is 8.65 light-years away and has a luminosity 23 times as much as that of the Sun. It has a diameter of 1,500,000 miles *2,4 million km* and a mass of 4,580,000,000,000,000,000,000,000,000 tons *4,65 × 10²⁷ tonnes*.

Farthest
The Solar System, with its Sun, nine principal planets, 34 satellites, asteroids and comets, was discovered in 1921 to be about 27,000 light-years from the centre of the lens-shaped Milky Way galaxy (diameter 100,000 light-years) of about 100,000 million stars. The most distant star in our galaxy is therefore about 75,000 light-years distant.

Nearest
Excepting the special case of our own Sun (*q.v.* above) the nearest star is the very faint *Proxima Centauri*, which is 4.28 light-years (25,200,000,000,000 miles *40,5 × 10¹² km*) away. The nearest star visible to the naked eye is the southern hemisphere star *Alpha Centauri*, or *Rigel Kentaurus* (4.38 light-years), with a magnitude of −0.29. By A.D. 11,800 the nearest star will be Barnard's Star (see below under Stellar Planets) at a distance of 3.75 light years.

Most and least luminous
If all stars could be viewed at the same distance, the most luminous would be the apparently faint variable *S. Doradûs*, in the Greater Magellanic Cloud (*Nebecula Major*), which can be 300,000 to 500,000 times brighter than the Sun, and has an absolute magnitude of −8.9. The faintest star detected visually is a very red star, known as LP 425-140, 23.5 light years distant with about one millionth of the Sun's brightness.

Coolest
A 16th magnitude star with a surface temperature of only about 425° C *800° F* was detected in *Cygnus* in 1965.

Brightest super-nova

Super-novae, or temporary "stars" which flare and then fade, occur perhaps five times in 1,000 years in our galaxy. The brightest "star" ever seen by historic man is believed to be the super-nova close to *Zeta Tauri*, visible by day for 23 days from 4 July 1054. The remains, known as the "Crab" Nebula, now appear to have a diameter of about 3×10^{13} miles *$4,8 \times 10^{13}$ km* and are still expanding at a rate of 800 miles/sec *1 275 km/sec* so indicating a diameter of 1.3×10^{14} miles *$2,1 \times 10^{14}$ km* now. It is about 4,100 light-years away indicating that the explosion actually occurred in about 3000 B.C.

Constellations

The largest of the 89 constellations is *Hydra* (the Sea Serpent), which covers 1,302,844 deg^2 or 6.3 per cent of the hemisphere and contains at least 68 stars visible to the naked eye (to 5.5 mag.). The constellation *Centaurus* (Centaur), ranking ninth in area embraces however at least 94 such stars. The smallest constellation is *Crux Australis* (Southern Cross) with an area of 68.477 deg^2 compared with the 41,252.96 deg^2 of the whole sky.

Stellar planets

Planetary companions, with a mass of less than 7 per cent of their parent star, have been reported for 61 *Cygni* (1942), *Lalande* 21185 (1960) *Krüger 60, Ci 2354, BD + 20° 2465* and one of the two components of 70 *Ophiuchi*. A planet of 6 times the mass of Jupiter 750 million miles *1 200 million km*, from *Epsilon Eridani* (see below) was reported by Peter van de Kamp in January 1973. In August 1975 van de Kamp reported that Barnard's Star (Munich 15040) possibly had two planets equivalent in mass to Jupiter and Saturn.

Listening operations ("Project Ozma") on *Tau Ceti* and *Epsilon Eridani* were maintained from 4 April 1960 to March 1961, using an 85-ft *25,90 m* radio telescope at Deer Creek Valley, Green Bank, West Virginia, U.S.A. The apparatus was probably insufficiently sensitive for any signal from a distance of 10.7 light-years to be received. Monitoring has been conducted from Gorkiy, U.S.S.R. since 1969.

Longest Name

The longest name for any star is *Shurnarkabtishashutu,* the Arabic for "under the southern horn of the bull".

The Great Galaxy in Andromeda, the most distant heavenly body visible with the naked eye. (See page 74)

Black Holes

The first tentative identification of a Black Hole was announced in December 1972 in the binary-star X-ray source Cygnus X-1. This is a small dark companion of some 10 solar masses from which the escape velocity tends to c (the velocity of light). The critical size has been estimated to be as low as a diameter of 3.67 miles *5,90 km*.

THE UNIVERSE

According to Einstein's Special Theory time dilation effect (published in 1905), time slows down on a moving system as measured by the system at rest, according to the Lorentz transformation

$$T = T_0 \sqrt{1 - \frac{v^2}{c^2}}$$

where T_0 = time interval when systems are at rest relatively; c = speed of light constant; v = relative velocity, and T = time measured in one system observing the other moving system.

PROGRESSIVE RECORDS OF THE MOST DISTANT MEASURED HEAVENLY BODIES

The possible existence of galaxies external to our own Milky Way system was mooted in 1789 by Sir William Herschel (1738–1822). These extra-galactic nebulae were first termed "island universes". Sir John Herschel (1792–1871) opined as early as 1835 that some were 48,000 light-years distant. The first direct measurement of any body outside our Solar System was in 1838.

Estimated Distance in Light Years[1]		Object	Method	Astronomer	Observatory	Date
nearly 11 (now 11.08)		61 Cygni	Parallax	F. Bessel	Königsberg, Germany	1838
>20 (now 26)		Vega	Parallax	F. G. W. Struve	Dorpat (now Tartu), Estonia	1840
c. 200		Limit	Parallax			by 1900
750,000 (now 2.2 m)[2]		Galaxy M31	Cepheid variable	E. P. Hubble	Mt. Wilson, Cal., U.S.A.	1923
900,000 (now 2.2 m)[2]		Galaxy M31	Cepheid variable	E. P. Hubble	Mt. Wilson, Cal., U.S.A.	1924

Millions of Light Years*	% of c					
			Red shift[3]			
250	2.5	Ursa Major Galaxy		E. P. Hubble	Mt. Wilson, Cal., U.S.A.	by 1934[4]
>350	3.6			M. L. Humason	Palomar, Cal., U.S.A.	by 1952
	>10			M. L. Humason	Palomar, Cal., U.S.A.	1954
3,000	31	Cluster 1448			Palomar, Cal., U.S.A.	1956
c. 4,500	46	3C 295 in Boötes			Palomar, Cal., U.S.A.	June 1960
5,300	54.5	QSO 3C·147			Palomar, Cal., U.S.A.	April 1964[5]
8,700	80	QSO 3C 9		M. Schmidt	Palomar, Cal., U.S.A.	May 1965
c. 10,000	81			Dr. E. M. Burbidge *et al.*	Palomar, Cal., U.S.A.	Dec. 1965
	82.2	QSO 1116 + 12		M. Schmidt	Palomar, Cal., U.S.A.	Jan. 1966
13,000	82.4	QSO PKS 0237−23		J. G. Bolton	Parkes, N.S.W., Australia	March 1967
	83.8	QSO 4C 25.5		E. Olsen	Palomar, Cal., U.S.A.	July 1968
	87.5	QSO 4C 05.34			Kitt Peak, Arizona, U.S.A.	May 1970
15,000	92	QSO OH 471		R. F. Carswell *et al.*	Steward Observatory, Arizona, U.S.A.	March 1973
15,600	95.5	QSO OQ 172		Dr. E. M. Burbidge *et al.*	Lick Observatory, Cal., U.S.A.	April 1973

Note: c is the notation for the speed of light.
[1] *Term first utilised in 1888.*
[2] *Re-estimate by W. Baade in Sept. 1952.*
[3] *Discovered by V. M. Slipher from Flagstaff, Arizona, U.S.A. 1920.*
[4] *In this year Hubble opined that the observable horizon would be 3,000 m light-years.*

[5] *Then said that QSO 3C2 and 286 might be more distant—former even 10,000 m light years.*
* *The distances are on a Euclidian model. According to the model, based on a refined (1976) value of the Hubble constant (50.3 km/sec/megaparsec) the expansion of the Universe began 19,400 million years ago.*

Outside the Milky Way galaxy, which possibly moves around the centre of the local super-cluster of 2,500 neighbouring galaxies at a speed of 1,350,000 m.p.h. *2 172 500 km/h*, there exist 10,000 million other galaxies. These range in size up to the largest known object in the Universe, the radio galaxy 3C-236 in Leo Minor announced from Westerbork Synthesis Radio Telescope, Netherlands in August 1974, which is 18.6 million light-years across. In Oct. 1976 it was suggested that 3C-123 may have a diameter of 120 million light-years. The nearest heavenly body outside our galaxy is its satellite, the ninth to be discovered, a small galaxy designated 0627 + 15, with a mass of 100 million suns, 55,000 ± 13,000 light years distant. It was announced by S. Christian Simonson III of the University of Maryland U.S.A. in July 1975.

Farthest visible object
The remotest heavenly body visible with the naked eye is the Great Galaxy in *Andromeda* (Mag. 3.47), known as Messier 31. This is a rotating nebula in spiral form, and its distance from the Earth is about 2,200,000 light-years, or about 13,000,000,000,000,000,000,000 miles *21 × 10^18 km*. It is just possible however that, under ideal seeing conditions, Messier 33, the Spiral in Triangulum (Mag. 5.79), can be glimpsed by the naked eye of keen-sighted people at a distance of 2,300,000 light-years.

Quasars
In November 1962 the existence of quasi-stellar radio sources ("quasars" or QSO's) was established. No satisfactory model has yet been constructed to account for the immensely high luminosity of bodies apparently so distant and of such small diameter. In April 1975 it was announced that 3C-279 had a measured luminosity of 2.75×10^{14} that of the sun.

Pulsars
The earliest observation of a pulsating radio source or "pulsar" CP 1919 by Dr. Jocelyn Bell Burnell was announced from the Mullard Radio Astronomy Observatory, Cambridgeshire, England, on 29 Feb. 1968. The 100th was announced from Jodrell Bank, Cheshire in June 1973. The fastest so far discovered is NP 0532 in the Crab Nebula with a pulse of 33 milli-sec. The now accepted model is that they are rotating neutron stars with an inner core density of 4.7×10^{15} g/cm³ (*74,400 million tons/in³*).

Remotest object
The interpretation of very large red shifts exhibited by quasars is controversial. The record value of 2 = 3.53 for Quasar OQ 172 (see table p. 73) has been interpreted at 15,600 million light years.

Age of the Universe
In November 1976 a refined value of Hubble's constant indicated that the age of the Universe lay between 17.5 and 21.3 billion years.

ROCKETRY AND MISSILES
Earliest uses
The origin of the rocket dates from war rockets propelled by a charcoal-saltpetre-sulphur gunpowder, made by the Chinese as early as *c.* 1100. These early rockets became known in Europe by 1258. The pioneer of military rocketry in Britain was Col. Sir William Congreve, Bt., M.P. (1772–1828), Comptroller of the Royal Laboratory, Woolwich, Greater London and Inspector of Military Machines, whose "six-pound *2,72 kg* rocket" was developed to a range of 2,000 yds *1 825 m* by 1805 and first used by the Royal Navy against Boulogne, France on 8 Oct. 1806.

The first launching of a liquid-fuelled rocket (patented 14 July 1914) was by Dr. Robert Hutchings Goddard (1882–1945) of the United States, at Auburn, Massachusetts, U.S.A., on 16 March 1926, when his rocket reached an altitude of 41 ft *12,5 m* and travelled a distance of 184 ft *56 m*. The U.S.S.R.'s earliest rocket was the semi-liquid fuelled GIRD-IX tested on 17 Aug. 1933.

Longest ranges
On 16 March 1962, Nikita Khrushchyov, then Prime Minister of the U.S.S.R., claimed in Moscow that the U.S.S.R. possessed a "global rocket" with a range of 30 000 km (*about 19,000 miles*) i.e. more than the Earth's semi-circumference and therefore capable of hitting any target from either direction.

Most powerful *World*
It has been suggested that the U.S.S.R. lunar booster which blew up at Tyuratam in the summer (? July) of 1969 had a thrust of 10 to 14 million lb. *4,5 to 6,35 million kg*. There is some evidence of a launch of a U.S.S.R. "G" class lunar booster, larger than the U.S. *Saturn V* on 11 May 1973.

The most powerful rocket that has been publicized is the *Saturn V*, used for the Project Apollo and Skylab programmes on which development began in January 1962, at the John F. Kennedy Space Center, Merritt Island, Florida, U.S.A. The rocket is 363 ft 8 in *110,85 m* tall, with a payload of 199,500 lb. *90 490 kg* in the case of *Skylab I*, and gulps 13.4 tons *13,6 tonnes* of propellant per sec for 2½ min (2,010 tons *2 042 tonnes*). Stage I (S-IC) is 138 ft *42,06 m* tall and is powered by five Rocketdyne F-1 engines, using liquid oxygen (LOX) and kerosene, each delivering 1,514,000 lb. *686 680 kg* thrust. Stage II (S-II) is powered by five LOX and liquid hydrogen Rocketdyne J-2 engines with a total thrust of 1,141,453 lb. *517 759 kg* while Stage III (designated S-IVB) is powered by a single 228,290 lb. *103 550 kg* thrust J-2 engine. The whole assembly generates 175,600,000 h.p. and weighs up to 7,600,000 lb. (3,393 tons *3 447 tonnes*) fully loaded in the case of *Apollo 17*. It was first launched on 9 Nov. 1967, from Cape Kennedy, Florida.

Highest velocity
The first space vehicle to achieve the Third Cosmic velocity sufficient to break out of the Solar System was *Pioneer 10* (see page 75). The Atlas SLV-3C launcher with a modified Centaur D second stage and a Thiokol Te-364-4 third stage left the Earth at an unprecedented 32,114 m.p.h. *51 682 km/h* on 2 March 1972. The highest velocity of any space vehicle has been 107,630 m.p.h. *173 214 km/h* by Pioneer 11 (now named Pioneer-Saturn) at 1.42 GMT on 2 Dec. 1974 in its fly-by 26,000 miles *41 840 km* distant from Jupiter.

Ion rockets
Speeds of up to 100,000 m.p.h. *160 000 km/h* are envisaged for rockets powered by an ion discharge. An ion thruster has been maintained for 9,715 hours (404 days 19 hrs) at the Lewis Research Center in Cleveland, Ohio, U.S.A. Ion rockets were first used in flight by NASA's SERT I rocket launched on 20 July 1964.

SPACE FLIGHT
The physical laws controlling the flight of artificial satellites were first propounded by Sir Isaac Newton (1642–1727) in his *Philosophiae Naturalis Principia Mathematica* ("Mathematical Principles of Natural Philosophy"), begun in March 1686 and first published in the summer of 1687. The first artificial satellite was successfully put into orbit at an altitude of 142/588 miles *228,5/946 km* and a velocity of more than 17,750 m.p.h. *28 565 km/h* from Tyuratam, a site located 170 miles *275 km* east of the Aral Sea on the night of 4 Oct. 1957. This spherical satellite *Sputnik* ("Fellow Traveller") *1*, officially designated "Satellite 1957 Alpha 2", weighed 83,6 kg *184.3 lb.*, with a diameter of 58 cm *22.8 in*, and its lifetime is believed to have been 92 days, ending on 4 Jan. 1958. It was designed under the direction of Dr. Sergey Pavlovich Korolyov (1906–1966).

Earliest successful manned satellite
The first successful manned space flight began at 9.07 a.m. (Moscow time), or 6.08 a.m. G.M.T., on 12 April 1961. Cosmonaut Flight Major (later Colonel) Yuriy Alekseyevich Gagarin (born 9 March 1934) completed a single orbit of the Earth in 89.34 min in the 4.65 ton *4,72 tonnes* space vehicle *Vostok* ('East') I. The take-off was from Tyuratam in Kazakhstan, and the landing was 108 min later near the village of Smelovka, near Engels, in the Saratov region of the U.S.S.R. The maximum speed was 17,560 m.p.h. *28 260 km/h* and the maximum altitude 327 km *203.2 miles* in a flight of 40 868,6 km *25,394.5 miles*. Major Gagarin, invested a Hero of the Soviet Union and awarded the Order of Lenin and the Gold Star Medal, was killed in a jet plane crash near Moscow on 27 March 1968.

The crew of the U.S. *Skylab* space station who undertook the longest manned space flight in history from 16 Nov. 1973 to 8 Feb. 1974. (see below) (*NASA*)

First woman in space

The first and only woman to orbit the Earth was Junior Lieutenant (now Lt.-Col.) Valentina Vladimirovna Tereshkova, now Mme. Nikolayev (b. 6 March 1937), who was launched in *Vostok 6* from Tyuratam, U.S.S.R., at 9.30 a.m. G.M.T. on 16 June 1963, and landed at 8.16 a.m. on 19 June, after a flight of 2 days 22 hrs 46 min, during which she completed over 48 orbits (1,225,000 miles *1 971 000 km*) and passed momentarily within 3 miles *4,8 km* of *Vostok 5*. She was formerly a textile worker. Her mission was variously reported to be punctuated with pleas to be brought back due to giddiness and of being extended because of her excellent performance.

First in flight fatality

Col. Vladimir Mikhailovich Komarov (b. 16 March 1927) was launched in *Soyuz* ("Union") *1* at 00.35 a.m. G.M.T. on 23 April 1967. The spacecraft was in orbit for about 25½ hrs but he impacted on the final descent due to parachute failure and was thus the first man indisputedly known to have died during space flight.

First "walk" in space

The earliest undoubted instance of an astronaut floating free outside a space vehicle was by Astronaut Edward H. White II (now Major General U.S. Air Force [retired]) for 21 min over Hawaii to the U.S. Atlantic coast on 3 June 1965 from Gemini IV. Evidence for the earlier claim of Lt.-Col. Aleksey A. Leonov from *Voshkod 2* on 18 Mar. 1965 is not internationally accepted.

Longest manned space flight

The longest time spent in the weightlessness of space has been 84 days 1 hr 15 min 30.8 sec by the third crew to man the U.S. *Skylab* space station; Lt.-Col. Gerald Paul Carr U.S.M.C. (b. Denver, Colorado 22 Aug. 1932), Lt.-Col. William Reid Pogue U.S.A.F. (b. Okemah, Oklahoma 23 Jan. 1930) and Dr. Edward George Gibson (b. Buffalo, N.Y.

PROGRESSIVE ROCKET ALTITUDE RECORDS				
Height in miles	**Height in km**	**Rocket**	**Place**	**Launch Date**
0.71	1,14	A 3-in rocket	near London, England	April 1750
1.24	2	Reinhold Tiling[1] (Germany) solid fuel rocket	Osnabruck, Germany	April 1931
3.1	5	GIRD-X liquid fuel (U.S.S.R.)	U.S.S.R.	25 Nov. 1933
8.1	13	U.S.S.R. "Stratosphere" rocket	U.S.S.R.	1935
52.46	84,42	A.4 rocket (Germany)	Peenemünde, Germany	3 Oct. 1942
c. 85	c. 136	A.4 rocket (Germany)	Heidelager, Poland	early 1944
118	190	A.4 rocket (Germany)	Heidelager, Poland	mid 1944
244	392,6	V-2/W.A.C. Corporal (2-stage) Bumber No. 5 (U.S.A.)	White Sands, N.M., U.S.A.	24 Feb. 1949
250	400	M. 104 *Raketa* (U.S.S.R.)	? Tyuratam, U.S.S.R.	1954
682	1 097	Jupiter C (U.S.A.)	Cape Canaveral, Florida U.S.A.	20 Sept. 1956
>7,800	>1 300	I.C.B.M. test flight (U.S.S.R.)	Tyuratum/Baikonur, U.S.S.R.	Aug. 1957
>2,700	>74 345	Farside No. 5 (4-stage) (U.S.A.)	Eniwetok Atoll	20 Oct. 1957
70,700	113 770	Pioneer I-B Lunar Probe (U.S.A.)	Cape Canaveral, Florida, U.S.A.	11 Oct. 1958
215,300,000*	346 480 000	Luna 1 or Mechta (U.S.S.R.)	Tyuratam, U.S.S.R.	2 Jan. 1959
242,000,000*	389 450 000	Mars 1 (U.S.S.R.)	U.S.S.R.	1 Nov. 1962
887,500,000[2]	1 420 000 000	Pioneer 10 (U.S.A.) (see page 74)	Kennedy Space Center, Cape Canaveral, Florida, U.S.A.	2 Mar. 1972

* Apogee in solar orbit.
[1] There is some evidence that Tiling may shortly after have reached 9,500 m (5.90 miles) with a solid fuel rocket at Wangerooge, East Friesian Islands, West Germany.
[2] Distance by April 1976. A distance of 3,600 million miles 5 800 million km *will be reached by 1987 on its way to crossing the orbit of Pluto and leaving the Solar System's effective gravitational field. Pioneer 11 will fly-by Saturn on c. 6 Sept. 1979 at 108,000 mph 174 000 km/h and then chase Pioneer 10 in leaving the Solar System for deep space. Mariner 11 (launch 20 Aug. 1977) and Mariner 12 (1 Sept. 1977) comprise the Jupiter-Saturn Mission. On 27 Aug. 1981 it may prove possible to re-target Mariner 11 to approach Uranus (31 Jan. 1986) and even Neptune (Sept. 1989).*

8 Nov. 1936) from 16 Nov. 1973 to 8 Feb. 1974. During this time they became the most travelled humans of all-time with a mileage of 34,469,696 miles *55 474 039 km. Skylab* had been launched on 14 May 1973. During the 1,214 orbits with an apogee of 283 miles *455 km* the crew temporarily grew 1 in *2,5 cm* each in stature.

Astronaut *Oldest and youngest*
The oldest of the 77 people in space has been Donald Kent "Deke" Slayton (b. Sparta, Wisconsin, U.S.A. 1 Mar. 1924) who was aged 51 years 145 days when he landed from the Apollo-Soyuz mission on 24 July 1975. The youngest has been Major (later Col.) Gherman Stepanovich Titov (b. 11 Sept. 1935), who was aged 25 years 329 days when launched in *Vostok 2* on 6 Aug. 1961.

Duration record on the Moon
The crew of *Apollo 17* collected a record 253 lb. *114,8 kg* of rock and soil during their 22 hrs 5 min "extra-vehicular activity". They were Capt. Eugene A. Cernan, U.S.N. (b. Chicago, 14 Mar. 1934) and Dr. Harrison H. (Jack) Schmitt (b. Santa Rosa, New Mexico 3 July 1935) who became the 12th man on the moon. The crew were on the lunar surface for 74 hrs 59½ min during this longest of lunar missions which took 12 days 13 hrs 51 min on 7–12 Dec. 1972.

First extra-terrestrial vehicle
The first wheeled vehicle landed on the Moon was *Lunokhod 1* which began its Earth-controlled travels on 17 Nov. 1970. It moved a total of 10,54 km *6.54 miles* on gradients up to 30 deg in the Mare Imbrium and did not become non-functioning until 4 Oct. 1971. The lunar speed and distance record was set by the *Apollo 16* Rover with 11.2 m.p.h. *18 km/h* downhill and 22.4 miles *33,8 km.*

above left: Aleksey A. Leonov, who is claimed to be the first astronaut to float freely outside a space vehicle on 18 Mar. 1965, but evidence of this remains controversial. (See page 75) (*Novosti Press Agency*)

above right: The youngest astronaut, Major Gherman Stepanovich Titov, aged only 25 years 329 days when launched. (*Novosti Press Agency*)

Closest Approach to the Sun
The research spacecraft *Helios* approached within 28 million miles *45 million km* of the Sun, carrying both U.S. and West German instrumentation on 18 Mar. 1975.

Largest Space Object
The heaviest object orbited is the 118 ft *35,96 m* long 12,398 ft³ *351 m³* U.S. *Skylab* weighing 89.17 tons *90 490 kg* on 14 May 1973. The 442 lb. *200 kg* U.S. R.A.E. (radio astronomy explorer) B or Explorer 49 launched on 10 June 1973 has, however, antennae 1,500 ft *415 m* from tip to tip.

Most expensive project
The total cost of the U.S. manned space programme up to and including the lunar mission of *Apollo 17* has been estimated to be $25,541,400,000 (£9,823,150,000). The first 15 years of the U.S.S.R. space programme from 1958 to Sept. 1973 has been estimated to have cost $45,000 million.

5. THE SCIENTIFIC WORLD

1. ELEMENTS

All known matter in, on and beyond the Earth is made up of chemical elements. The total of naturally-occurring elements so far detected is 94, comprising, at ordinary temperature, two liquids, 11 gases and 81 solids. They so-called "fourth state" of matter is plasma, when negatively charged electrons and positively-charged ions are in flux.

Lightest and heaviest sub-nuclear particles
By January 1976 the existence of 74 resonance "multiplets" was accepted, representing the possible eventual discovery of 160 particles and an equal number of anti-particles. Of SU(3) particles the one with the highest mass is the omega minus, announced on 24 Feb. 1964 from the Brookhaven National Laboratory, near Upton, Long Island, New York State, U.S.A. It has a mass state of 1672.2 ± 0.4 Mev and a lifetime of 1.3×10^{-10} sec. Sub-atomic concepts require that the masses of the graviton, photon, and neutrino should all be zero. Based on the sensitivities of various cosmological theories, upper limits for the masses of these particles are 10^{-67} g for the graviton, (c.f. $9,10953 \times 10^{-28}$ g for the mass of an electron.)

Newest particles
These are the "psions", two of which were announced in November 1974 [the psi particles ψ_0 (3094) and ψ (3684)] and three in July–August 1975, [the chi particles χ_0 (3410), χ_1 (3490), and χ_2 (3530)]. They are said to be mesons composed of a mixture of a "charmed" quark and an "anti-charmed" quark, although no wholly conclusive evidence has been obtained for the existence of any of 12 types of quark.

Least stable
The least stable or shortest lived nuclear particles discovered are the rho prime meson (definite proof of existence announced on 29 January 1973) and the three baryon resonances N (3030), Δ (2850) and Δ (3230), all 1.6×10^{-24} sec.

Substance smelliest
The most evil smelling substance, of the 17,000 smells so far classified, must be a matter of opinion but ethyl mercaptan (C_2H_5SH) and butyl seleno-mercaptan (C_4H_9SeH), are powerful claimants, each with a smell reminiscent of a combination of rotting cabbage, garlic, onions and sewer gas.

Most expensive perfume
The retail prices of the most expensive perfumes tend to be fixed at public relations rather than economic levels. The most expensive ingredient in perfume is pure French middle note jasmine essence at £2,900 per kg or £82.20p per oz.

Most potent poison
The rikettsial disease, Q-fever can be instituted by a *single* organism but is only fatal in 1 in 1,000 cases. Effectually the most poisonous substance yet discovered is the toxin of the bacterium *Pasteurella tularensis*. About 10 organisms can institute tulaeremia variously called alkali disease, Francis disease or deerfly fever, and this is fatal in 50 to 80 cases in 1,000.

Most powerful nerve gas
In the early 1950s substances known as V-agents, notably VX, 300 times more toxic than phosgene ($COCl_2$) used in World War I, were developed at the Chemical Defence Experimental Establishment, Porton Down, Wiltshire. V-agents are lethal at 1 mg per man. Patents were applied for in 1962 and published in February 1974.

Most powerful drugs
The most potent and, to an addict, the most expensive of all naturally-derived drugs is heroin, which is a chemically-processed form of opium from the juice of the unripe seed capsules of the white poppy (*Papaver somniferum*). An oz., which suffices for up to 1,800 hypodermic shots or "fixes", may fetch up to $10,000 (now £5,900) in the United States, or a 70,000 per cent profit over the raw material price. Producing countries include China, India, Iran, Mexico and Turkey. It has been estimated that an addict who has no income is impelled to steal $50,000 (now £29,000) worth of goods per annum to keep him or herself in "fixes". The most powerful synthetically manufactured drug is d-Lysergic Acid Diethylamide tartrate (LSD-25, $C_{20}H_{25}N_3O$) first produced in 1938 for common cold research and as a hallucinogen by Dr. Albert Hoffmann (Swiss) on 16–19 Apr. 1943. The most potent analgesic drug is Etorphine or M-99, announced in June 1963 by Dr. Kenneth W. Bentley (b. 1925) and D. G. Hardy of Reckitt & Sons Ltd. of Hull, Humberside, with almost 10,000 times the potency of morphine.

Most prescribed drug
The benzodiazepine group tranquilizing drug Valium discovered by Hoffman-La Roche is the world's most widely used drug.

THE 106 ELEMENTS

There are 94 known naturally-occurring elements comprising, at ordinary temperatures, two liquids, 11 gases, 72 metals and 9 other solids. To date the discovery of a further 12 transuranic elements (Elements 95 to 106) has been claimed of which 10 are undisputed.

Category	Name	Symbol	Discovery of Element	Record
Commonest (lithosphere)	Oxygen	O	1771 Scheele (Germany-Sweden)	46.60% by weight
Commonest (atmosphere)	Nitrogen	N	1772 Priestly (G.B.) et al.	78.09% by volume
Commonest (extra-terrestrial)	Hydrogen	H	1776 Cavendish (G.B.)	90% of all matter
Rarest (of the 94)	Astatine	At	1940 Corson (U.S.) et al.	1/100th oz. 0,35 g in Earth's crust
Lightest	Hydrogen	H	1776 Cavendish (G.B.)	0.005612 lb/ft³ 0,00008989 g/cm³
Lightest (Metal)	Lithium	Li	1817 Afrwedson (Sweden)	33.30 lb/ft³ 0,5334 g/cm³
Densest	Osmium	Os	1804 Tennant (G.B.)	1,410 lb/ft³ 22,59 g/cm³
Heaviest (Gas)	Radon	Rn	1900 Dorn (Germany)	0.6274 lb/ft³ 0,01007 g/cm³
Newest*	Element 106		1974 Ghiorso et al. (U.S.)	announced 9 Sept. 1974
Purest	Germanium	Ge	1886 Winker (Germany)	99.99999999% purity (1967)
Hardest	Carbon	C	— prehistoric	Diamond isotope, Knoop value 8,400
Most Expensive	Californium	Cf	1950 Seaborg et al. (U.S.)	Sold in 1968 for $1000 per μg
Most Stable	Tellerium	Te 130	1782 von Reichenstein (Hung.)	Half-life of 2.2×10^{21} years.
Least Stable	Lithium (isotope 5)	Li 5	1817 Afrwedson (Sweden)	Half-life of 4.4×10^{-22} sec.
Most Isotopes	Tellurium	Te	1782 von Reichenstein (Austro-Hung.)	31
Least Isotopes	Hydrogen	H	1776 Cavendish (G.B.)	3 (confirmed)
Most Ductile	Gold	Au	ante 3000 B.C.	1 oz. drawn to 43 miles 1 g/2,4 km
Highest Tensile Strength	Boron	B	1808 Gay-Lussac et al. (France)	3.9×10^6 lb f/in² 2,68 $\times 10^7$ kPa
Lowest Melting/Boiling Point	Helium	He	1895 Ramsay (G.B.)	−271,72°C under pressure 26 atm (2600 kPa) and −268.926° C
Highest Melting/Boiling Point	Tungsten	W	1783 J. J. & F. d'Elhuyar (Spain)	3 422° C and 5 730° C
Most Poisonous	Plutonium	Pu	1940 Seaborg (U.S.) et al.	1 μg or microgramme (1 thirty millionth of an oz.) inhaled or swallowed will cause cancer. With a half-life of 23,640 years, toxicity is retained for a thousand centuries

Evidence alleging the existence of Elements 116, 124 and 126 published on 17 June 1976 has subsequently been declared to have been misconceived.

CHEMICAL COMPOUNDS

It has been estimated that there are more than 4 million described chemical compounds.

Most Refractory	Tantulum Carbide TaC₀.₈₈	Melts at 4 010° ± 75 deg C
Most Refractory (plastics)	Modified polymides	900°F 482°C for short periods
Lowest Expansion	Delta prime allotrope of plutonium (disc. 1953)	$-1{,}18 \times 10^{-4}$ cm/cm/deg C
Highest Tensile Strength	Sapphire whisker Al_2O_3	6×10^6 lb/in² 4,27 $\times 10^7$ kPa
Highest Tensile Strength (plastics)	Polyvinyl alcoholic fibres	1.4×10^5 lb f/in² 10,3 $\times 10^5$ kPa
Most Magnetic	Cobalt-copper-samarium Co_3Cu_2Sm	10,500 oersted coercive force
Least Magnetic alloy	Copper nickel alloy CuNi	963 parts Cu to 37 parts Ni
Most Pungent	Vanillaldehyde	Detectable at 2×10^{-8} mg/litre
Sweetest	1n-propoxy-2-amino-4-nitro-benzene	5,600 × as sweet as 1% sucrose
Bitterest	Bitrex or Benzyl diethyl ammonium benzoate	200 × as bitter as quinine sulphate
Most Acidic[1]	Perchloric acid ($HClO_4$)	pH value of normal solution tends to 0.
Most Alkaline	Caustic soda ($NaOH$) and potash (KOH) and tetramethylammonium hydroxide ($N(CH_3)_4OH$)	pH value of normal solution is 14.
Highest Specific Impulse	Hydrogen with liquid fluorine	447 lb f/sec/lb 4382 N/sec/kg
Most Poisonous	Thiopentone (a barbituate)	Intracardiac injection will kill in 1 to 2 secs.

[1] *The most powerful acid, assessed on its power as a hydrogen-ion donor, is a solution of antimony pentafluoride in fluosulphonic acid—$SbF_5 + FSO_3H$.*

Most absorbant substance

The U.S. Department of Agriculture Research Service announced on 18 Aug. 1974 that "H-span" or Super Slurper composed of one half starch derivative and one fourth each of acrylamide and acrylic acid can when treated with iron retain water 1,300 times its own weight.

Finest powder

Particulate matter of 25 to 40 Å or $2{,}564 \times 10^{-6}$ cm was reportedly produced by an electron beam evaporation process at the Atomic Energy Establishment, Harwell in October 1972. The paper was published by Dr. P. RamaKrishnan.

2. DRINK

The strength of spirituous liquor is gauged by degrees proof. In the United Kingdom proof spirit is that mixture of ethyl alcohol (C_2H_5OH) and water which at 51° F 10,55° C weighs in air 12/13ths of an equal measure of distilled water. Such spirit in fact contains 49.28 per cent alcohol by weight, so that pure or absolute alcohol is 75.35° over proof (O.P.). In the U.S.A. proof is double the actual percentage of alcohol by volume at 60°F 15,6°C. A "hangover" is due to toxic congenerics such as amyl alcohol ($C_5H_{11}OH$).

Most alcoholic

Absolute (or 100%) alcohol is 75.35 degrees over proof (U.K.) or 200% proof spirit (U.S.). During independence (1918–1940) the Estonian Liquor Monopoly marketed 98% potato alcohol (196 proof U.S.). In 31 U.S. states *Everclear* 190 proof 95% alcohol, is marketed by the American Distilling Co. "primarily as a base for home-made cordials". Royal

A bottle of the most alcoholic drink in the World, at 95% alcohol, currently unavailable in 19 U.S. states.

Navy rum introduced in 1692, was 40° O.P. (79.8%) before 1948 but was reduced to 4.5° U.P. (under proof) or 46.3% alcohol by weight, before its abolition on 31 July 1970.

Oldest Vintage Wine

The oldest datable vintage of any wine has been a bottle of *Steinwein* 1540 from Wurzburg am Main, West Germany salvaged from the cellars of King Ludwig of Bavaria sold by Ehrmann's of Grafton Street, London and described 420 years later as "dark, feeble but definitely alive".

Beer *Strongest world*

The world's strongest and most expensive beer is EKU Kulminator Urtyp Hell from Kulmbach, West Germany which retails for up to 70p per ½ pint *28,4 cl* bottle. It is 13.2% alcohol by volume at 20° C with an original gravity of 1117.6°.

Beer *Strongest Great Britain*

The strongest beer in Britain is Thomas Hardy's Ale bottled in December 1975 by Dorchester Brewery, Dorset with 13.1% alcohol by volume and an original gravity of 1120.4°. The strongest regularly brewed nationally distributed beer in Britain is Gold Label Barley Wine brewed by Tennant Bros. of Sheffield, a subsidiary of Whitbread & Co. Ltd. It has an alcoholic content of 8.6 per cent by weight, 10.6 per cent by volume and an original gravity of 1098.06°. The strongest regularly brewed draught beer is Fuller's E.S.B. at 1055°.

Beer *Weakest*

The weakest liquid ever marketed as beer was a sweet ersatz beer which was brewed in Germany by Sunner, Colne-Kalk, in 1918. It had an original gravity of 1,000.96° and a strength 1/30th that of the weakest beer now obtainable in the United Kingdom.

Most Expensive Wine

The highest ever paid for any bottle of wine has been $14,200 (*then £8,100*) for one of the perhaps four remaining bottles of the pre-phylloxera claret *Château Lafite* Rothschild 1806 Grand Cru Classe red Bordeaux by David L. Lyons, 37 of West Hollywood, California at the auction by Heubleins Inc. in the Royal Sonesta Hotel, New Orleans, Louisiana, U.S.A. on 27 May 1976. The auction was conducted by Mr. Michael Broadbent, wine director of Christie's of London, who had discovered the bottle in Paris 4 months previously. Asked how he would transport the bottle to his cellar, Mr. Lyons replied "Very, very carefully".

Greatest Wine Auction

The largest single sale of wine took place at Christie's of King Street, St. James's, London on 25–26 Mar. 1976 when 31,000 bottles of Bordeaux wines were auctioned for £880,000.

Most expensive liqueurs

The most expensive liqueur in France is the orange-flavoured *Le Grand Marnier Coronation*. Owing to excise duties, *Elixir Végétale de la Grande Chartreuse* which is 24 degrees O.P. is sold only in miniature bottles of 2.8 fl. oz. *7,95 centilitres* at £1.98 per bottle in the United Kingdom. This liqueur has been produced since 1757, by Carthusian monks from a recipe of 1605, which reputedly contains 130 herbs including *Arnica montana*. Ancient *Chartreuse* (before 1903) has been known to fetch more than £15 per litre bottle *1,76 pints*. An 1878 bottle was sold in 1954 for this price.

Most expensive spirits

The most expensive spirit is *Grande Fine Champagne Arbellot* 1749 brandy, retailed at Fauchon, Paris, at 667 francs (*then £48.25*) per bottle. In Britain 19th century *Hennessy Grande Champagne La Sauzade* retails for £69.55 (including V.A.T.) for a standard bottle.

Largest bottles

The largest bottle normally used in the wine and spirit trade is the Jeroboam (equal to 4 bottles of champagne or, rarely, of brandy) and the Double Magnum (equal, since *c.* 1934 to 6 bottles of claret or, more rarely, red Burgundy). A complete set of Champagne bottles would consist of a ¼ bottle, through the ½ bottle, bottle, magnum, Jeroboam, Rehoboam, Methuselah, Salmanazer and Balthazar, to the Nebuchadnezzar, which has a capacity of 16 litres *38.16 pt*, and is equivalent to 20 bottles. In May 1958 a 5 ft *152 cm* tall sherry bottle with a capacity of 20½ Imperial gal *93,19 litres* was blown in Stoke-on-Trent, Staffordshire. This bottle, with the capacity of 131 normal bottles, was named an "Adelaide".

Smallest bottles

The smallest and meanest bottles of liquor sold are the bottles of Scotch whisky marketed by The Cumbrae Supply Co. of Glasgow. They contain 24 minims or 1/20 of a fl. oz. *1,42 millilitres* and retailed in 1977 for 31p (including the match box in which it is packaged).

Champagne cork flight

The longest distance for a champagne cork to fly from an untreated and unheated bottle 4 ft *1,22 m* from level ground is 102 ft 11 in *31,36 m* by Gary P. Mahan at La Habra Heights, California on 2 Aug. 1975.

Miniature Bottles

The largest reported collection of unduplicated miniature bottles is one of 1,131 amassed over 22 years to 1976 by G. H. White of Warminster, Wiltshire.

---

3. TELESCOPES

Earliest

Although there is evidence that early Arabian scientists understood something of the magnifying power of lenses, their first use to form a telescope has been attributed to Roger Bacon (c. 1214–92) in England. The prototype of modern refracting telescopes was that completed by Johannes Lippershey for the Netherlands government on 2 Oct. 1608.

Largest *Refractor*

The largest refracting (*i.e.* magnification by lenses) telescope in the world is the 62 ft *18,90 m* long 40 in *101,6 cm* telescope completed in 1897 at the Yerkes Observatory, Williams Bay, Wisconsin, and belonging to the University of Chicago, Illinois, U.S.A. In 1900 a 125 cm *49.2 in* refractor *54,85 m* *180 ft* in length was built for the Paris Exposition but its optical performance was too poor to justify attempts to use it. The largest in the British Isles is the 28 in *71,1 cm* at the Royal Greenwich Observatory (then in London) completed in 1894.

Largest *Reflector World*

The largest telescope in the world is the 6 m *236.2 in* telescope sited on Mount Semirodriki, near Zelenchukskaya in the Caucasus Mountains, U.S.S.R., at an altitude of 6,830 ft *2,080 m*. The mirror, weighing 70 tons/*tonnes* was completed in November 1967, assembled by October 1970. Regular observations were begun on 7 Feb. 1976 after 16 years work. The overall weight of the 79 m long assembly is 840 tonnes *827 tons*. Being the most powerful of all telescopes its range, which includes the location of objects down to the 25th magnitude, represents the limits of the observable Universe. Its light-gathering power would enable it to detect the light from a candle at a distance of 15,000 miles *24 000 km.*

Largest *Reflector Great Britain*

The largest reflector in the British Isles is the Isaac Newton 98.2 in *249,4 cm* reflector at the Royal Greenwich Observatory, Herstmonceux Castle, East Sussex. It was built in Newcastle upon Tyne, Tyne and Wear, weighs 92 tons *93,5 tonnes*, cost £641,000 and was inaugurated on 1 Dec. 1967. Plans are now advanced to move it to a new northern hemisphere site—probably in the Canary Islands—and refit a 100 inch *254 cm* reflector.

Radio *Largest steerable dish*

The world's largest trainable dish-type radio telescope is the 100 m *328 ft* diameter, 3,000 ton *3048 tonnes* assembly at the Max Planck Institute for Radio Astronomy of Bonn in the

Effelsberger Valley, West Germany; it became operative in May 1971. The cost of the installation begun in November 1967 was 36,920,000 DM *£6,150,000*. The earliest fully steerable radio telescope was the 82 ft *25 m* dish at Dwingeloo, The Netherlands completed in May 1956. It was announced in June 1974 that the University of Manchester Mark V radio telescope project at Meiford, Powys, Wales, for a 375 ft *120 m* instrument had been abandoned when cost estimates surpassed £17 million.

Radio *Largest Dish*
The world's largest dish radio telescope is the partially-steerable ionospheric assembly built over a natural bowl at Arecibo, Puerto Rico, completed in November 1963 at a cost of about $9,000,000 *(£3.75 million)*. The dish has a diameter of 1,000 ft *304,80 m* and covers 18½ acres *7,28 ha*. Its sensitivity was raised by a factor of 1,000 and its range to the edge of the observable Universe at some 15,000 million light-years by the fitting of new aluminium plates at a cost of $8.8 million. Re-dedication was on 16 Nov. 1974. The RATAN-600 radio telescope being built in the Northern Caucasus, U.S.S.R. will have mirror dishes on a 600 m *1,968.5 ft* perimeter.

Radio *Largest World*
The first $3 million instalment for the building of the world's largest and most sensitive radio telescope was included by the National Science Foundation in their federal budget for the fiscal year 1973. The instrument termed the VLA (Very Large Array) is Y-shaped with each arm 13 miles *20,9 km* long with 27 mobile antennae (each of 25 m *82 ft* diameter) on rails. It is 50 miles *80 km* west of Socorro in the Plains of San Augustin, New Mexico and the completion date will be late 1979 at an estimated cost of $75 million *(now £44 million)*.

Radio *Largest Great Britain*
The British Science Research Council 5 km Radio telescope at Lord's Bridge, Cambridgeshire to be operated by the Mullard Radio Astronomy Observatory of Cambridge University will utilize eight mobile 42 ft *12,80 m* rail-borne computer-controlled dish aerials, which will be equivalent to a single steerable dish 5 km *3 miles 188 yds* in diameter. The project cost more than £2,100,000 and was completed in 1973.

Solar
The world's largest solar telescope is the 480 ft *146,30 m* long McMath telescope at Kitt Peak National Observatory near Tucson, Arizona, U.S.A. It has a focal length of 300 ft *91,44 m* and an 80 in *2,03 m* heliostat mirror. It was completed in 1962 and produces an image measuring 33 in *83,8 cm* in diameter.

Observatory *Highest*
The highest altitude observatory in the world is the University of Denver's High Altitude Observatory at an altitude of 14,100 ft *4 297 m*, opened in 1973. The principal instrument is a 24 in *60,48 cm* Ealing Beck reflecting telescope.

Observatory *Oldest*
The oldest astronomical observatory building extant in the world is the Chomsong-dae built in A.D. 632 in Kyongju, South Korea and still extant.

Planetaria *World*
The ancestor of the planetarium is the rotatable Gottorp Globe, built by Andreas Busch in Denmark between 1654 and 1664 to the orders of Olearius, court mathematician to Duke Frederick III of Holstein. It is 34.6 ft *10,54 m* in circumference, weighs nearly 3½ tons/*tonnes* and is now preserved in Leningrad, U.S.S.R. The stars were painted on the inside. The earliest optical installation was not until 1923 in the Deutsches Museum, Munich, by Zeiss of Jena, Germany. The world's largest planetarium, is in Moscow, U.S.S.R., and has a diameter of 82½ ft *25,15 m*.

Planetaria *Great Britain*
The United Kingdom's first planetarium was opened at Madame Tussaud's, Marylebone Road, London, on 19 March 1958. Accurate images of 8,900 stars (some below naked eye magnitude) are able to be projected on the 70 ft *21,33 m* high copper dome.

4. PHOTOGRAPHY

CAMERAS

Earliest
The earliest photograph was taken in the summer of 1826 by Joseph Nicéphore Niepce (1765–1833), a French physician and scientist. It showed the courtyard of his country house at Gras, near St. Loup-de-Varennes. It probably took eight hours to expose and was taken on a bitumen-coated polished pewter plate measuring 7¾ in by 6½ in *20 × 16,5 cm*. The earliest photograph taken in England was one of a diamond-paned window in Laycock (or Lacock) Abbey, Wiltshire, taken in August 1835 by William Henry Fox Talbot, M.P. (1800–77), the inventor of the negative-positive process. The negative of this was donated to the Science Museum, London in 1937 by his granddaughter Matilda. The world's earliest aerial photograph was taken in 1858 by Gaspard Félix Tournachon (1820–1910), *alias* Nadar, from a balloon near Villacoublay, on the outskirts of Paris, France.

Largest
The largest camera ever built is the 27 ton Rolls Royce camera built for Product Support (Graphics) Ltd., of Derby, England completed in 1959. It measures 8 ft 10 in *2,69 m* high, 8 ft 3 in *2,51 m* wide and 35 ft *10,66 m* in length. The lens is a 63″ f 15 Cooke Apochromatic. Its value after improvements in 1971 was in excess of £100,000.

Smallest
Apart from cameras built for intra-cardiac surgery and espionage, the smallest camera that has been marketed is the circular Japanese "Petal" camera with a diameter of 1.14 in *2,9 cm* and a thickness of 0.65 in *1,65 cm*. It has a focal length of 12 mm *0.47 in*. The B.B.C. T.V. programme *Record Breakers* showed prints from this camera on 3 Dec. 1974.

Fastest
In 1972 Prof. Basor of the U.S.S.R. Academy of Sciences published a paper describing an experimental camera with a time resolution of 5×10^{-13} of a sec or ½ a picosec. The fastest production camera in the world is the Imacon 600 manufactured by John Hadland (P.I.) Ltd of Bovington, Hertfordshire which is capable of 600 million pictures per sec. Uses include lasar, ballistic, detonic, plasma and corona research.

Most expensive
The most expensive range of camera equipment in the world is the F-1 35 mm system of Canon Camera Co. Inc. of Tokyo. The 40 lenses offered range from the Fish Eye 7.5 mm F5.6 to the FL 1200 mm F11, while the accessories available number 180. The total cost of the range would exceed £30,000. A Thomas Sutton wet plate camera, *c.* 1865, was sold at auction at Sotheby's for £11,500 on 8 March 1974.

Professor Stanley Skewes of Cape Town University, South Africa, the mathematician who devised Skewes number. (See page 82)

5. GEMS AND OTHER PRECIOUS MATERIALS

PRECIOUS STONE RECORDS

Note: The carat was standardised at 205 mg in 1877. The metric carat of 200 mg was introduced in 1913.

Largest

Diamond (*pure crystallised carbon*)
3,106 metric carats (over 1¼ lb.)—*The Cullinan*, found by Capt. M. F. Wells 26 Jan. 1905 in the Premier Mine, Pretoria, South Africa.
The largest uncut diamond is *The Star of Sierra Leone* found at Kono on 14 Feb. 1972 weighing 969.1 carats. It was sold for an undisclosed amount below its reserve of some $2.6 million in Feb. 1973 to Harry Winston (U.S.).

Emerald (*green beryl*) [$Be_3Al_2(SiO_3)_6$]
125 lb. *56 kg 70* crystal (up to 15¾ in *40 cm* long and 9¾ in *24,75 cm* in diameter) from a Ural, U.S.S.R. mine.

Sapphire (*blue corundum*) (Al_2O_3)
2,302 carat stone found at Anakie, Queensland, Australia, in *c.* 1935, now a 1,318 carat head of President Abraham Lincoln (1809–65).

Ruby (*red corundum*) (Al_2O_3)
3,421 carat broken stone reported found in July 1961 (largest piece 750 carats).

Largest Cut Stone

530.2 metric carats. Cleaved from *The Cullinan* in 1908, by Jak Asscher of Amsterdam and polished by Henri Koe known as *The Star of Africa* No. 1 and now in the Royal Sceptre.
In Nov. 1975 a top blue-white uncut gem was quoted at £1,428 per carat.

2,680 carat unguent jar carved by Dionysio Miseroni in the 17th century owned by the Austrian Government. 1,350 carat of *gem* quality, the *Devonshire* stone from Muso, Columbia

1,444 carat black star stone carved from 2,097 carats in 1953–1955 into a bust of General Dwight David Eisenhower (1890–1969).

1,184 carat natural gem stone of Burmese origin.

Other records

Diamond is the *hardest* known naturally-occurring substance, being 90 times as hard as the next hardest mineral, corundum (Al_2O_3). The peak hardness value on the Knoop scale is 8,400 compared with an average diamond of 7,000. The rarest colours for diamond are blue (record—44.4 carat *Hope* diamond) and pink (record—24 carat presented by Dr. John Thoburn Williamson to H.M. The Queen in 1958). Auction record: $1,050,000 (*then £437,500*) for a 69.42 carat stone bought by Cartier on 13 Oct. 1969 and sold to Richard Burton at $1,200,000 (*then £500,000*) for Elizabeth Taylor on 24 Oct. 1969.
Miss Debbie Reynolds (U.S.) wore a tiara owned by Harry Winston, valued at $4,500,000 (*£1,875,000*) in New York on 25 Sept. 1973.

A necklace of eight major emeralds and one pendant emerald of 75.63 carats with diamonds was sold by Sotheby's in Zurich on 24 Nov. 1971 for £436,550 (*then $1,090,000*).
The Swiss customs at Geneva confirmed on 16 April 1972 the existence of an hexagonal emerald of about 20,000 carats, thus possibly worth more than $100 million.

Note: both the sapphire busts are in the custody of the Kazanjian Foundation of Los Angeles, California, U.S.A.

Since 1955 rubies have been the world's most precious gem attaining a price of up to £4,000 per carat by 1969.
The ability to make corundum prisms for laser technology up to over 12 in *30 cm* in length must now have a bearing on the gem market.

RECORDS FOR OTHER PRECIOUS MATERIALS

Largest	Where Found	Notes On Present Location, etc.
Pearl (*Molluscan consecretion*) 14 lb. 1 oz. *6,37 kg* 9½ in *24 cm* long by 5½ in *14 cm* in diameter—*Pearl of Laotze*	At Palawan, Philippines, 7 May 1934 in shell of giant clam.	In a San Francisco bank vault. It is the property since 1936 of Wilburn Dowell Cobb and was valued at $4,080,000 in July 1971.
Opal ($SiO_2.nH_2O$) Any stone: 220 troy oz. (yellow-orange). Gem stone: 17,700 carats (*Olympic Australis*)	Andamooka, South Australia Jan. 1970. Coober Pedy, South Australia, Aug. 1956.	The Andamooka specimen was unearthed by a bulldozer.
Crystal Any stone: 250 tons/*tonnes* (Beryl)	Malakialina, Madagascar reported 1964.	Note: Measures 18 m *59 ft* long and 173 m³ *226 yd³* in volume.
Ball: 106¾ lb. *40,48 kg* 12⅞ in *32,7 cm* diameter, the *Warner* sphere	Burma, (originally a 1,000 lb. *450 kg* piece).	U.S. National Museum, in Washington, D.C.
Topaz [($AlSi_2O_4)_4(F,OH)_2$] Any stone: 596 lb. *270 kg* Gem stone: 7,725 carats	Minas Gerais, Brazil.	American Museum of Natural History, New York City, since 1951. Also at the American Museum of Natural History.
Amber (*Coniferous fossil resin*) 33 lb. 10 oz. *15,25 kg.*	Reputedly from Burma acquired in 1860.	Bought by John Charles Bowing (d. 1893) for £300 in Canton, China. Natural History Museum, London, since 1940.
Turquoise monolith ($CuAl_6(PO_4)_4(OH)_8.4H_2O$) 218 lb. *98,8 kg*	Riverside County, California, 17 Jan. 1975.	Found by Chester Jastromb and Kenneth Casper. Original weight was probably *c.* 250 lb. *113,4 kg.*
Jade [$NaAl(Si_2O_6)$] Sub-marine boulder of 5 short tons *4,53 tonnes* valued at $180,000)	Off Monterey, California. Landed 5 June 1971.	Jadeite can be virtually any colour. The less precious nephrite is $Ca_2(Mg,Fe)_5(OH)_2(Si_4O_{11})_2$.
Marble (*Metamorphosed* $CaCO_3$) 90 tons/*tonnes* (single slab)	Quarried at Yule, Colorado, U.S.A.	A piece of over 45 tons/*tonnes* was dressed from this slab for the coping stone of the Tomb of the Unknown Soldier in Arlington National Cemetery, Virginia, U.S.A.
Nuggets—Gold (Au) 7,560 oz. (472½ lb. *214,32 kg*) (reef gold) *Holtermann Nugget*	Beyers & Holtermann Star of Hope Gold Mining Co., Hill End, N.S.W., Australia, 19 Oct. 1872	The purest large nugget was the *Welcome Stranger*, found at Moliagul, Victoria, Australia, which yielded 2,248 troy oz. *69,92 kg* of pure gold from 2,280¼ oz. *70,92 kg.*
Silver (Ag) 2,750 lb. troy	Sonora, Mexico	Appropriated by the Spanish Government before 1821.

Other Gems Records:
Largest Stone of Gem Quality:
A 520,000 carat (2 cwt. 5 lb. *103,8 kg*) aquamarine, $Be_3Al_2(SiO_3)_6$] found near Marambaia, Brazil in 1910. Yielded over 200,000 carats of gem quality cut stones.
Rarest:
Taaffeite ($Be_4Mg_4Al_{15}O_{32}$) first discovered in Dublin, Ireland, in November 1945. Only four of these pale mauve stones are known—the largest is of 5.35 of a carat.
Densest Gem Mineral:
Stibotantalite [$(SbO)_2(Ta,Nb)_2O_6$] a rare brownish-yellow mineral found in San Diego County, California, has a density of 7.46. The alloy platiniridium has a density of more than 22.0.

6. NUMEROLOGY

In dealing with large numbers, scientists use the notation of 10 raised to various powers to eliminate a profusion of noughts. For example, 19,160,000,000,000 miles would be written 1.916×10^{13} miles. Similarly, a very small number for example 0,0000154324 of a gramme, would be written $1,5432 \times 10^{-5}$ g. Of the prefixes used before numbers the smallest is "atto-" from the Danish atten for 18, indicating a trillionth part (10^{-18}) of the unit, and the highest is "exa" (Greek, hexa, six), symbol E, indicating six groups of 3 zeros 10^{18} or a trillion (U.K.) or a quintillion (U.S.) fold.

Highest Numbers

The highest lexicographically accepted named number in the system of successive powers of ten is the centillion, which is 10 raised to the power 600, or one followed by 600 noughts in the British system or 10^{303} in the U.S. system. The highest named number outside the decimal notation is the Buddhist *asankhyeya*, which is equal to 10^{140} or 100 tertio-virgintillions (British system) or 100 quinto-quadragintillions (U.S. system).

The number 10^{100} (10,000 sexdecillion [U.K.] or 10 duo-trigintillion [U.S.]) is designated a Googol. The term was devised by Dr. Edward Kasner (U.S.) (d. 1955). Ten raised to the power of a Googol is described as a Googolplex. Some conception of the magnitude of such numbers can be gained when it is said that the number of atoms in some models of the observable Universe does not exceed 10^{85}. Skewes' number, which arose from prime number theory, approximates to 10 to the power 10 to the power 10 to the power 10 to the power 3 and was published in 1933 by Prof. Stanley Skewes Ph.D. of Cape Town University, South Africa. The number Megiston written with symbol ⑩ is a number too great to have any physical meaning.

Prime numbers

A prime number is any positive integer (excluding 1) having no integral factors other than itself and unity, *e.g.* 2, 3, 5, 7 or 11. The lowest prime number is thus 2. The highest known prime number is $2^{19937} - 1$ (a number of 6,002 digits of which the first five are 43,154 and the last three 471) received by the American Mathematical Society on 18 March 1971 and calculated on an I.B.M. 360/91 computer in 39 mins. 26.4 sec by Dr. Bryant Tuckerman at Yorktown Heights, New York.

Perfect numbers

A number is said to be perfect if it is equal to the sum of its divisors other than itself, *e.g.* $1 + 2 + 4 + 7 + 14 = 28$. The lowest perfect number is 6 $(1 + 2 + 3)$. The highest known and the 24th so far discovered, is $(2^{19937} - 1) \times 2^{19936}$ which has 12,003 digits of which the first 3 are 931, and the last 3 are 656. It is a consequence of the highest known prime (see above).

Most Innumerate

The most innumerate people are the Nambiquara of the north west Matto Grosso of Brazil who lack any system of numbers. They do however have a verb which means "they are two alike".

Most accurate and most inaccurate version of "pi"

The greatest number of decimal places to which *pi* (π) has been calculated is 1,000,000 by the French mathematicians Jean Guilloud and Mlle. Martine Bouyer achieved on 24 May 1973 on a CDC 7600 computer but not verified until 3 Sept. 1973. The published value to a million places, in what has been described as the world's most boring 400 page book, was 3.141592653589793 ... (omitting the next 999,975 places) ... 5779458151. In 1897 the General Assembly of Indiana enacted in House Bill No. 246 that *pi* was *de jure* 4.

Earliest measures

The earliest known measure of weight is the *beqa* of the Amratian period of Egyptian civilization *c.* 3,800 B.C. found at Naqada, United Arab Republic. The weights are cylindrical with rounded ends from 188.7 to 211.2 g *6.65 to 7.45 oz.*

The unit of length used by the megalithic tomb-builders in Britain *c.* 2300 B.C. appears to have been 2.72 ± 0.003 ft *82,90 cm ± 0.09 cm.*

Time Measure *Longest*

The longest measure of time is the *kalpa* in Hindu chronology. It is equivalent to 4,320 million years. In astronomy a cosmic year is the period of rotation of the sun around the centre of the Milky Way galaxy, *i.e.* about 225,000,000 years. In the Late Cretaceous Period of *c.* 85 million years ago the Earth rotated faster so resulting in 370.3 days per year while in Cambrian times some 600 million years ago there is evidence that the year contained 425 days.

Time Measure *Shortest*

Owing to variations in the length of a day, which is estimated to be increasing irregularly at the average rate of about two milliseconds per century due to the Moon's tidal drag, the second has been redefined. Instead of being 1/86,400th part of a mean solar day, it has, since 1960, been reckoned as 1/31,556,925.9747th part of the solar (or tropical) year at A.D. 1900, January 0. 12 hrs, Ephemeris time. In 1958 the second of Ephemeris time was computed to be equivalent to $9,192,631,770 \pm 20$ cycles of the radiation corresponding to the transition of a caesium 133 atom when unperturbed by exterior fields. The greatest diurnal change recorded has been 10 milliseconds on 8 Aug. 1972 due to the most violent solar storm recorded in 370 years of observations. In a nanosecond or a milli-micro second (1.0×10^{-9} of a sec) light travels 11.8 in *29,97 cm.*

Smallest Units

The shortest unit of length is the atto-metre which is 1.0×10^{-16} of a cm. The smallest unit of area is a "shed", used in sub-atomic physics and first mentioned in 1956. It is 1.0×10^{-48} of a cm². A "barn" is equal to 10^{24} "sheds". The reaction of a neutrino occurs over the area of 1×10^{-43} of a cm².

Longest Slide Rule

The world's longest slide rule is one 12 metres *39 ft* in length completed on 24 Mar. 1976 by Clarence T. Hay, Randy R. and Jeff H. Meyer of Huron Heights Secondary School, Newmarket, Ontario, Canada.

7. PHYSICAL EXTREMES
(*Terrestrial*)

Temperature *Highest*

The highest man-made temperatures yet attained are those produced in the centre of a thermonuclear fusion bomb, which are of the order of 300,000,000 to 400,000,000° C. Of controllable temperatures, the highest effective laboratory figure reported is 50,000,000° C, for 2/100ths of a second by Prof. Lev A. Artsimovich at Tokamuk in the U.S.S.R. in 1969. At very low particle densities even higher figures are obtainable. Prior to 1963 a figure of 3,000 million ° C was reportedly achieved in the U.S.S.R. with Ogra injection-mirror equipment.

Temperature *Lowest*

The lowest temperature reached is 5×10^{-7} degree Kelvin, achieved by Professor A. Abragam (b. 1914) in collaboration with M. Chapellier, M. Goldman, and Vu Hoang Chau at the Centre d'Etudes Nucléaires, Saclay, France, in March 1969. Absolute or thermodynamic temperatures are defined in terms of ratios rather than as differences reckoned from the unattainable absolute zero, which on the Kelvin scale is $-273,15°$ C or $-459.67°$ F. Thus the lowest temperature ever attained is 1 in 5.46×10^8 of the melting point of ice (0° C or 273.15K or 32° F).

The lowest equilibrium temperature ever attained is 0.0003 K by nuclear refrigeration in a 1,4 kg *3 lb.* copper specimen by Prof. Olli V. Lounasmaa (b. 1920) and his team at the Helsinki University of Technology, Otaniemi, Finland, on 17 April 1974.

A monument depicting the site where the Welcome Stranger gold nugget was found. (See page 81)

Solar Power plant

The largest solar furnace in the world is the Laboratoire de l'Energie Solaire, at Odeillo, Pyrénées-Orientales, France. It consists of an array of 63 steerable mirrors with a total area of 2 835 m² *30,515 ft²* or seven tenths of an acre which can generate a heat of 3 725° C *6,735° F.*

Highest pressures

The highest sustained laboratory pressures yet reported are of 5,000,000 atmospheres or 5,000 kilobars *(7.25 × 10⁷ lbf/in²)*, achieved in the U.S.S.R. and announced in October 1958. Using dynamic methods and impact speeds of up to 18,000 m.p.h. *29 000 km/h,* momentary pressures of 75,000,000 atmospheres (490,000 tons/in² *7 × 10⁹ kPa*) were reported from the United States in 1958.

Highest vacuum

The highest (or 'hardest') vacuums obtained in scientific research are of the order of 10⁻¹⁴ torr at the IBM Thomas J. Watson Research Center, Yorktown Heights, New York, U.S.A. in October 1976 in a cryogenic system with temperatures down to −269° C *−452° F.* This is equivalent to depopulating (baseball sized) molecules from one metre apart to 80 km apart or from 1 yard to 50 miles.

Fastest centrifuge

The highest man-made rotary speed ever achieved and the fastest speed of any earth-bound object is 4,500 m.p.h. *7 250 km/h* by a swirling tapered 6 in *15,2 cm* carbon fibre rod in a vacuum at Birmingham University, England reported on 24 January 1975.

Most Powerful Microscope

The world's most powerful microscope was announced by Dr. Lawrence Bartell and Charles Ritz of Michigan University in July 1974 with an image magnification of 260 million fold. It uses an optical laser to decode holograms produced with 40 Kev radiation and has produced photographs of electron clouds of atoms of neon and argon.

Highest frequency

It was announced in December 1974 that D. A. Jennings, F. R. Peterson, and K. M. Evenson of the U.S. National Bureau of Standards, Boulder, Colorado, had attained a frequency of 1,4791585 × 10¹⁴ Hz (147,91585 terahertz) with a xenon laser emission.

Highest note

The highest note yet attained is one of 60,000 megahertz (60 GHz) (60,000 million vibrations/sec), generated by a 'laser' beam striking a sapphire crystal at the Massachusetts Institute of Technology in Cambridge, Massachusetts, U.S.A., in September 1964.

Loudest noise

The loudest noise created in a laboratory is 210 decibels or 400,000 acoustic watts reported by NASA from a 48 ft *14,63 m* steel and concrete horn at Huntsville, Alabama, U.S.A. in October 1965. Holes can be bored in solid material by this means.

Quietest place

The "dead room", measuring 35 ft by 28 ft *10,67 × 8,50 m* in the Bell Telephone System laboratory at Murray Hill, New Jersey, U.S.A., is the most anechoic room in the world. eliminating 99.98 per cent of reflected sound.

Finest balance

The most accurate balance in the world is the Sartorius Model 4108 manufactured in Göttingen, West Germany, which can weigh objects of up to 0,5 g to an accuracy of 0,01 µg or 0,00000001 g which is equivalent to little more than one sixtieth of the weight of the ink on this full stop .

Lowest viscosity

The California Institute of Technology, U.S.A. announced on 1 Dec. 1957 that there was no measureable viscosity, *i.e.* perfect flow, in liquid helium II, which exists only at temperatures close to absolute zero (−273,15° C or −459.67° F).

Lowest friction

The lowest coefficient of static and dynamic friction of any solid is 0.02, in the case of polytetrafluoroethylene ($[C_2F_4]_n$), called P.T.F.E.—equivalent to wet ice on wet ice. It was first manufactured in quantity by E. I. du Pont de Nemours & Co. Inc. in 1943, and is marketed from the U.S.A. as Teflon. In the United Kingdom it is marketed by I.C.I. as Fluon.

In the centrifuge at the University of Virginia a 30 lb. *13,60 kg* rotor magnetically supported has been spun at 1,000 revs/sec in a vacuum of 10⁻⁶ mm of mercury pressure. It loses only one revolution per second per day thus spinning for years.

Most powerful electric current

The most powerful electric current generated is that from the Zeus capacitor at the Los Alamos Scientific Laboratory, New Mexico, U.S.A. If fired simultaneously the 4,032 capacitors would produce for a few microseconds twice as much current as that generated elsewhere on Earth.

Most powerful particle accelerator

The 1.24 mile *2 km* diameter proton synchrotron at the Fermi National Accelerator Laboratory at Weston, Illinois, U.S.A. is the largest and most powerful "atom-smasher" in the world. By June 1976 an energy of 500 GeV was attained. Plans to double the energy to nearly 1 Tera electron volts were begun in 1971 by means of a second ring of superconducting magnets but only one sixth of this has so far been authorized.

The £32 million CERN intersecting storage rings (ISR) project near Geneva, Switzerland started on 27 Jan. 1971, using two 28 GeV proton beams, and is designed to yield the equivalent of 1,700 GeV or 1.7 Tev (1.7 million million electron volts) in its centre of mass experiments.

Largest bubble chamber

The largest bubble chamber in the world is the $7 million installation completed in October 1973 at Weston, Illinois (see above). It is 15 ft *4,57 m* in diameter and contains 7,259 gal *33 000 litres* of liquid hydrogen at a temperature of −247° C with a super-conductivity magnet of 30,000 gauss.

Heaviest magnet
The heaviest magnet in the world is one measuring 60 m *196 ft* in diameter, with a weight of 36,000 tons/*tonnes* for the 10 GeV synchrophasotron in the Joint Institute for Nuclear Research at Dubna, near Moscow, U.S.S.R. Intermagnetics General Corporation announced in 1975 plans for a 180 kG vanadium-gallium magnet.

Strongest magnetic field
The strongest magnetic field strength achieved has been one of 254 kilogauss at the Francis Bitter National Magnet Laboratory at Massachusetts Institute of Technology, announced in March 1977. The outer magnet is of superconducting niobium-titanium and it is predicted that a field of 300 kilogauss will be obtained.

The weakest magnetic field measured is one of 1.6×10^{-10} gauss in the heavily shielded room at the Francis Bitter National Magnet Laboratory, Cambridge, Massachusetts, U.S.A. It is used for research into the very weak magnetic fields generated in the heart and brain.

Finest cut
Biological specimens embedded in epoxy resin can be sectioned by a glass knife microtome under ideal conditions to a thickness of 1/875,000th of an inch $2,9 \times 10^{-5}$ mm.

Sharpest objects
The University of California Medical Center, San Francisco announced in July 1974 the ultimate in sharpness—glass electrodes more than 200 times slimmer than a diamond phonograph stylus. These can be used for exploring the cells in the eye. The points are 0.05 μm.

Most powerful "laser" beams
The first illumination of another celestial body was achieved on 9 May 1962, when a beam of light was successfully reflected from the Moon by the use of an optical "maser" (microwave amplification by stimulated emission of radiation) or "laser" (light amplification by stimulated emission of radiation) attached to a 48 in *121,9 cm* telescope at Massachusetts Institute of Technology, Cambridge, Massachusetts, U.S.A. The spot was estimated to be 4 miles *6,4 km* in diameter on the Moon. The device was propounded in 1958 by Dr. Charles Hard Townes (born 1915) of the U.S.A. A "maser" light flash is focused into liquid nitrogen-cooled ruby crystal. Its chromium atoms are excited into a high energy state in which they emit a red light which is allowed to escape only in the direction desired. Such a flash for 1/5,000th of a second can bore a hole through a diamond by vaporization at 10,000° C, produced by 2×10^{23} photons.

Brightest light
The brightest steady artificial light sources are "laser" beams with an intensity exceeding the Sun's 1,500,000 candles/in² *232 500 candelas/cm²* by a factor well in excess of 1,000. In May 1969 the U.S.S.R. Academy of Sciences announced blast waves travelling through a luminous plasma of inert gases heated to 90,000° K. The flare-up for up to 3 microseconds shone at 50,000 times the brightness of the Sun *viz.* 75,000 million candles/in². Of continuously burning sources, the most powerful is a 200 kW high-pressure xenon arc lamp of 600,000 candle-power, reported from the U.S.S.R. in 1965.

The synchrotron radiation from a 4 by 0.5 in *100 × 2,5 mm* slit in the SPEAR high energy physics plant at the end of the 2 mile *3,2 km* long Stanford Linear Accelerator, California, U.S.A. has been described as the world's most powerful light beam.

The most powerful searchlight ever developed was one produced during the 1939–45 war by the General Electric Company Ltd. at the Hirst Research Centre in Wembley, Greater London. It had a consumption of 600 kW and gave an arc luminance of 300,000 candles/in² and a maximum beam intensity of 2,700,000,000 candles from its parabolic mirror (diameter 10 ft *3,04 m*).

Most durable light
The average bulb lasts for 750 to 1,000 hrs. There is some evidence that a carbide filament bulb burning in the Fire Department, Livermore, south Alameda County, California has been burning since 1901.

Shortest wavelength
On 15 Apr. 1974 I.B.M. researchers E. Spillar and Armin Segmüller announced that X-rays with a wavelength of only $4,6 \times 10^{18}$ Hz (6,000 millionths of an inch) had been harnessed in a device, which may become a "light pipe" to guide X-rays to required locations.

Longest Echo
The longest recorded echo in any building in Great Britain is one of 15 sec. following the closing of the door of the Chapel of the Mausoleum, Hamilton, Strathclyde built in 1840–55.

Largest wind tunnel *World*
The world's largest wind tunnel is a low-speed tunnel with a 40 × 80 ft *12,19 × 24,38 m* test section built in 1944 at the Ames Research Center, Moffett Field, California, U.S.A. The tunnel encloses 800 tons/*tonnes* of air and cost approximately $7,000,000 (*then* £1,735,000). The maximum volume of air that can be moved is 60,000,000 ft³ *1 700 000 m³* per min. On 30 July 1974 NASA announced an intention to increase it in size to 80 × 120 ft *24,38 × 36,57 m* for 345 m.p.h. speeds with a 135,000 h.p. system. The most powerful is the 216,000 h.p. *219 000 c.v.* installation at the Arnold Engineering Test Center at Tullahoma, Tennessee, U.S.A. opened in September 1956. The highest Mach number attained with air is Mach 27 at the works of the Boeing Company in Seattle, Washington State, U.S.A. For periods of micro-seconds, shock Mach numbers of the order of 30 (22,830 m.p.h. *36 735 km/h*) have been attained in impulse tubes at Cornell University, Ithaca, New York State, U.S.A.

Largest wind tunnel *Great Britain*
The most powerful wind tunnel in the United Kingdom is the intermittent compressed air type installation at the B.A.C. plant at Warton, Lancashire which can be run at Mach 4, which is equivalent to 3,044 m.p.h. *4 898 km/h* at sea level.

6. THE ARTS AND ENTERTAINMENTS

1. PAINTING

Earliest

Evidence of Palaeolithic art was first found in 1834 at Chaffaud, Vienne, France by Brouillet when he recognised an engraving of two deer on a piece of flat bone from the cave, dating to *c.* 20,000 B.C. The number of stratigraphically-dated examples of cave art is very limited. The oldest known dated examples came from La Ferrassie, near Les Eyzies in the Périgord, France, where large blocks of stone engraved with animal figures and symbols were found in a layer of the Aurignacian II period dated to *c.* 25,000 B.C.

Largest World *All time*

Panorama of the Mississippi, completed by John Banvard (1815–91) in 1846, showing the river for 1,200 miles *1 930 km* in a strip probably 5,000 ft *1 525 m* long and 12 ft *3,65 m* wide, was the largest painting in the world, with an area of more than 1.3 acres *0,52 ha*. The painting is believed to have been destroyed when the rolls of canvas, stored in a barn at Cold Spring Harbor, Long Island, New York State, U.S.A., caught fire shortly before Banvard's death on 16 May 1891.

Existing

The largest known painting now in existence is *The Battle of Gettysburg*, completed in 1883, after 2½ yrs of work, by Paul Philippoteaux (France) and 16 assistants. The painting is 410 ft *125 m* long, 70 ft *21,3 m* high and weighs 5.36 tons *5,45 tonnes*. It depicts the climax of the Battle of Gettysburg, in southern Pennsylvania, U.S.A., on 3 July 1863. In 1964 the painting was bought by Joe King of Winston-Salem, North Carolina, U.S.A. after being stored by E. W. McConnell in a Chicago warehouse since 1933.

The 6,050 ft² *562 m²* painting at Colchester, which took 365 people 209 days to complete. (See page 86) (*Roy Farthing*)

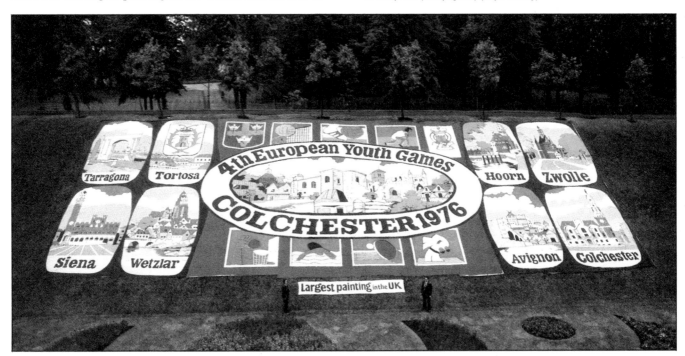

"Old Master"

The largest "Old Master" is *Il Paradiso*, painted between 1587 and 1590 by Jacopo Robusti, *alias* Tintoretto (1518–94), and his son Domenico on Wall "E" of the Sala del Maggior Consiglio in the Palazzo Ducale (Doge's Palace) in Venice, Italy. The work is 22 m *72 ft 2 in* long and 7 m *22 ft 11½ in* high and contains more than 100 human figures.

Largest *Great Britain*

The largest painting in Great Britain is the giant oval *Triumph of Peace and Liberty* by Sir James Thornhill (1676–1734), on the ceiling of the Painted Hall in the Royal Naval College, Greenwich, Greater London. It measures 106 ft *32,3 m* by 51 ft *15,4 m* and took 20 yrs (1707–1727) to complete.

A painting 6,050 ft² *562 m²* in area and weighing more than a ton was painted for the 4th European Youth Games under the direction of David A. Judge and to the design of Norman G. Warner in Colchester, Essex between 29 Oct. 1975 and 24 May 1976 by 365 people.

Smallest

The smallest paintings in the world are those executed in oils with a 4 or 5 sable hair brush on pinheads $\frac{1}{32}$ to $\frac{1}{4}$ inch *0,8–6,3 mm* in diameter by Gerard Legare of British Columbia, Canada.

Most Valuable

The "Mona Lisa" (*La Gioconda*) by Leonardo da Vinci (1452–1519) in the Louvre, Paris, was assessed for insurance purposes at the highest ever figure of $100,000,000 (*then £35.7 million*) for its move for exhibition in Washington, D.C., and New York City, N.Y., U.S.A., from 14 Dec. 1962 to 12 March 1963. However, insurance was not concluded because the cost of the closest security precautions was less than that of the premiums. It was painted in *c.* 1503–07 and measures 77 × 53 cm *30.5 × 20.9 in*. It is believed to portray Mona (short for Madonna) Lisa Gherardini, the wife of Francesco del Giocondo of Florence, who disliked it and refused to pay for it. Francis I, King of France, bought the painting for his bathroom in 1517 for 4,000 gold florins or 492 oz. *15,30 kg* of gold now worth some £30,000.

HIGHEST PRICE

Auction price *World*

The highest price ever bid in a public auction for any painting is £2,310,000 for *Portrait of Juan de Pareja*, also known as *The Slave of Velázquez*, painted in Rome in 1649 by Diego Rodríguez de Silva Velázquez (1599–1660) and sold on 27 Nov. 1970 at the salerooms of Christie, Manson & Woods, London to the Wildenstein Gallery, New York. The painting had been sold at Christie's at auction in 1801 for 39 guineas (£40.95). It was in the possession of the Earls of Radnor from May 1811 until 1970.

By British Artist

The highest auction price for the work of a British artist is the £280,000 paid by Messrs. Colnaghi's at Sotheby's for Thomas Gainsborough's painting of *Mr. and Mrs. Gravenor and their daughters Elizabeth and Dorothea*, from the estate of Major J. Townshend, on 19 July 1972. Executed in *c.* 1748, it measures 35½ in *90 cm* square. It was discovered by Mr. Andrew Festing, a Sotheby expert.

By A Woman Artist

The highest price ever paid for a painting by a female artist is $150,000 (*then £62,500*), at Parke Bernet, New York on 10 Mar. 1970, for *Summertime* by Mary Cassatt (b. Pensylvania, U.S.A., 1844—d. 1926). She worked mainly from Paris.

Miniature portrait

The highest price ever paid for a portrait miniature is the £65,100 given by an anonymous buyer at a sale held by Christie, Manson and Woods, London on 8 June 1971 for a miniature of Frances Howard, Countess of Essex and Somerset by Isaac Oliver, painted *c.* 1605. This miniature, sent for auction by Lord Derby, measured 5⅛ in *13 cm* in diameter.

Modern painting

The highest price paid for a modern painting is $2,000,000 (*£1 million*) paid by the National Gallery of Australia, Canberra, Australia in 1973 for the 83 × 192½ in *210,8 × 488,9 cm* canvas *Blue Poles* painted in 1953 by Jackson Pollock (1912–1956) of New York.

Living artist *World*

The highest price paid for paintings in the lifetime of the artist is $1,950,000 (*then £812,500*) paid for the two canvases *Two Brothers* (1905) and *Seated Harlequin* (1922) by Pablo Diego José Francisco de Paula Juan Nepomuceno Crispín Crispiano de la Santisima Trinidad Ruiz y Picasso (1881–1973) of Spain. This was paid by the Basle City Government to the Staechelin Foundation to enable the Basle Museum of Arts to retain the painting after an offer of $2,560,000 (*£1,066,666*) had been received from the United States in December 1967.

British and Irish

The highest price for any painting by a living United Kingdom born artist is $160,000 (*then £89,890*) for the painting *Reclining Man with Sculpture* by Francis Bacon (b. Dublin, Ireland, 1909, then part of the United Kingdom) sold on 27 May 1976 at Sotheby, Parke Bernet, New York City, U.S.A.

Drawing

The highest price ever attached to any drawing is £804,361 for the cartoon *The Virgin and Child with St. John the Baptist and St. Anne*, measuring 54½ in by 39¼ in *137 by 100 cm*, drawn in Milan, probably in 1499–1500, by Leonardo da Vinci (1452–1519) of Italy, retained by the National Gallery in 1962. Three United States bids of over $4,000,000 (*then £1,428,570*) were reputed to have been made for the cartoon.

Most Prolific *Painter*

Picasso was the most prolific of all painters in a career which lasted 78 years. It has been estimated that Picasso produced about 13,500 paintings or designs, 100,000 prints or engravings, 34,000 book illustrations and 300 sculptures or ceramics. His life-time *oeuvre* has been valued at £500 million.

HIGHEST-PRICED PAINTINGS—Progressive records

Price	Equivalent 1977 Value	Painter, title, sold by and sold to	Date
£6,500	£117,000	Antonio Correggio's *The Magdalen Reading* (in fact spurious) to Elector Friedrich Augustus II of Saxony.	1746
£8,500	£146,000	Raphael's *The Sistine Madonna* to Elector Friedrich Augustus II of Saxony.	1759
£16,000	£158,000	Van Eycks' *Adoration of the Lamb*, 6 outer panels of Ghent altarpiece by Edward Solby to the Government of Prussia.	1821
£24,600*	£357,000	Murillo's *The Immaculate Conception* by estate of Marshall Soult to the Louvre (against Czar Nicholas I) in Paris.	1852
£70,000	£1,580,000	Raphael's *Ansidei Madonna* by the 8th Duke of Marlborough to the National Gallery.	1885
£100,000	£2,282,000	Raphael's *The Colonna Altarpiece* by Seldemeyer to J. Pierpoint Morgan.	1901
£102,880	£1,814,000	Van Dyck's *Elena Grimaldi-Cattaneo* (portrait) by Knoedler to Peter Widener (1834–1915).	1906
£102,880	£1,498,000	Rembrandt's *The Mill* by 6th Marquess of Lansdowne to Peter Widener.	1911
£116,500	£1,697,000	Raphael's smaller *Panshanger Madonna* by Joseph (later Baron) Duveen (1869–1939) to Peter Widener.	1913
£310,400	£4,496,000	Leonardo da Vinci's *Benois Madonna* to Czar Nicholas II in Paris.	1914
£821,429*	£2,106,000	Rembrandt's *Aristotle Contemplating the Bust of Homer* by estate of Mr. and Mrs. Alfred W. Erickson to New York Metropolitan Museum of Art.	1961
£1,785,714	£4,739,000	Leonardo da Vinci's *Ginerva de' Benci* (portrait) by Prince Franz Josef II of Liechtenstein to National Gallery of Art, Washington, D.C., U.S.A.	1967
£2,310,000*	£5,090,000	Velázquez's *Portrait of Juan de Pareja* by the Earl of Radnor to the Wildenstein Gallery, New York.	1970

Indicates price at auction, otherwise prices were by private treaty.

Portraitist
John A. Wismont Jr. (b. New York City, 20 Sept. 1941), formerly of Disneyland, Annaheim, California, painted 44,372 water colour paintings in his career including 9,853 in 1976.

Most Repetitious Painter
Antonio Bin of Paris has painted the *Mona Lisa* on some 300 occasions. These sell for up to £1,000 apiece.

Oldest and youngest R.A.
The oldest ever Royal Academician has been (Thomas) Sidney Cooper C.V.O., who died on 8 Feb. 1902 aged 98 yrs 136 days, having exhibited 266 paintings over the record span of 69 consecutive years (1833–1902). The youngest ever R.A. has been Mary Moser (1744–1819) (later Mrs. Hugh Lloyd), who was elected on the foundation of the Royal Academy in 1768 when aged 24.

Youngest exhibitor
The youngest ever exhibitor at the Royal Academy of Arts Annual Summer Exhibition has been Lewis Melville "Gino" Lyons (b. 30 Apr. 1962). His *Trees and Monkeys* was painted on 4 June 1965, submitted on 17 Mar. 1967 and exhibited to the public on 29 Apr. 1967.

Largest gallery
The world's largest art gallery is the Winter Palace and the neighbouring Hermitage in Leningrad, U.S.S.R. One has to walk 15 miles *24 km* to visit each of the 322 galleries, which house nearly 3,000,000 works of art and objects of archaeological interest.

MURALS
Earliest
The earliest known murals on man-made walls are those at Catal Hüyük in southern Anatolia, Turkey, dating from *c.* 5850 B.C.

Largest
The largest logo and mural painting in the world is the American Revolution Bicentennial symbol, on the curved roof of the Arizona Veterans Memorial Coliseum, Phoenix, Arizona. It occupies 110,000 ft² *10 219 m²* or more than 2½ acres *1,0 ha*. It will be painted over in 1977. After being outlined by aid of a computer, it took 45 man days, under the supervision of its designer John M. Glitsos, to apply the necessary 870 gallons *3 955 l* of patriotic (red, white and blue) paint on 18–26 Aug. 1973.

A ground mural measuring 1,400 ft *426,7 m* long by 100 ft *30,4 m* named Yellow Brick Road—Leisure Time painted on a disused runway near the Tamiami Stadium, South Dade, Florida U.S.A. was completed on 18 Mar. 1976.

Largest mosaic
The world's largest mosaic is on the walls of the central library of the Universidad Nacional Autónomao de México, Mexico City. There are four walls, the two largest measuring 12,949 ft² *1 203 m²* each representing the pre-Hispanic past.

The largest Roman mosaic in Britain is the Woodchester Pavement, Gloucestershire of *c.* A.D. 325, excavated in 1793, now recovered with protective earth until its 8th showing due in 1983. It measures 48 ft 10 in *14,88 m* square comprising 1½ million tesserae.

Largest cartoon
The largest cartoon ever exhibited was one covering five storeys (50 × 150 ft *15 × 45 m*) of a University of Arizona building drawn by Dr. Peter A. Kesling for Mom 'n Dad's Day 1954.

MUSEUMS
Oldest
The oldest museum in the world is the Ashmolean Museum in Oxford built in 1679.

Largest
The largest museum in the world is the American Museum of Natural History on 77th to 81st Streets and Central Park West, New York City, N.Y., U.S.A. Founded in 1874, it comprises 19 interconnected buildings with 23 acres *9 ha* of floor space. The largest museum in the United Kingdom is the British Museum (founded in 1753), which was opened to the public in 1759. The main building in Bloomsbury, London, was built in 1823 and has a total floor area of 17.57 acres *7,11 ha*.

2. SCULPTURE

Earliest *World*
The earliest known examples of sculpture are the so-called Venus figurines from Aurignacian sites, dating to *c.* 25,000–22,000 B.C., *e.g.* the famous Venus of Willendorf from Austria and the Venus of Brassempouy (Landes, France). A piece of ox rib found in 1973 at Pech de l'Aze, Dordogne, France in an early Middle Palaeolithic layer of the Riss glaciation *c.* 105,000 B.C. appears to have several intentional engraved lines on one side.

Great Britain
The earliest British art object is an engraving of a horse's head on a piece of rib-bone from Robin Hood Cave, Creswell Crag, Derbyshire. It dates from the Upper Palaeolithic period (*c.* 15,000 to 10,000 B.C.). The earliest Scottish rock carving from Lagalochan, Strathclyde dates from *c.* 3,000 B.C.

Most expensive *World*
The highest price ever paid for a sculpture is the $750,000 (*then* £326,000) given at Sotheby's Parke-Bernet New York salerooms, on 1 May 1974 for Constantin Brancusi's polished bronze *Negresse Blonde* of 1926.

Ancient
The highest price paid for any work of art from any ancient civilization is $260,000 (£140,000) given by the Metropolitan Museum of Art, New York City for the 18th dynasty turquoise glazed Egyptian faience 9⅞ in *24,9 cm* figure of Pharoah Amenhotep III (*c.* 1410–1320 B.C.) at Sotheby Parke-Bernet, New York on 2 May 1972.

Living sculptor
The highest price paid for the work of a living sculptor is the $260,000 (£104,000) given at Sotheby's Parke-Bernet Galleries, New York on 1 March 1972 by Fischer Fine Arts of London for the 75 in *189 cm* long wooden carving *Reclining Figure* by Henry Moore, O.M., C.H. (b. Castleford, West Yorkshire, 30 July 1898) sold by Cranbrook Academy, Bloomfield Hills, Michigan, U.S.A.

Largest
The world's largest sculptures are the mounted figures of Jefferson Davis (1808–89), Gen. Robert Edward Lee (1807–70) and Gen. Thomas Jonathan ("Stonewall") Jackson (1824–63), covering 1.33 acres *0,5 ha* on the face of Stone Mountain, near Atlanta, Georgia. They are 90 ft *27,4 m* high and took from 1958 to May 1970 to sculpt. Roy Faulkner was on the mountain face for 6 years with a thermo-jet torch working with the sculptor Walker Kirtland Hancock. When completed the world's largest sculpture will be that of the Indian chief Tashunca-Uitco (*c.* 1849–1877), known as Crazy Horse, of the Oglala tribe of the Dakota or Nadowessioux (Sioux) group. The sculpture was begun on 3 June 1948 near Mount Rushmore, South Dakota, U.S.A. A projected 561 ft *170 m* high and 641 ft *195 m* long, it will require the removal of 5,800,000 tons *5 890 000 tonnes* of stone and is the life work of one man, Korczak Ziolkowski. The work will take until at least 1978.

Ground figures
In the Nazca Desert, south of Lima, Peru there are straight lines (one more than 7 miles *11,2 km* long), geometric shapes and of plants and animals drawn on the ground sometime between 100 B.C. and A.D. 700 for an uncertain but probably religious or astronomical purpose by a still unknown civilization. They were first detected from the air in *c.* 1928.

Hill figures

In August 1968 a 330 ft *100 m* tall figure was found on a hill above Tarapacár, Chile.

The largest human hill carving in Britain is the "Long Man" of Wilmington, East Sussex, 226 ft *68 m* in length. The oldest of all White Horses in Britain is the Uffington White Horse in Oxfordshire, dating from the late Iron Age (*c.* 150 B.C.) and measuring 374 ft *114 m* from nose to tail and 120 ft *36 m* from ear to heel.

Most Massive Mobile

The most massive recorded mobile is *Quest* by Jerome Kirk installed at TRW Inc., Redondo Beach, California U.S.A. in Sept. 1968. It is a 32 ft *9,75 m* long wind-driven pivotal mobile weighing 5.35 tons *5 442 kg*. The term mobile was coined to contrast with "stabile" sculpture by Marcel Duchamp in 1932.

3. LANGUAGE

Earliest

Anthropologists have evidence that the truncated pharynx of Neanderthal man precluded his speaking anything akin to a modern language any more than an ape or a modern baby. Cro-Magnon man of 40,000 B.C. had however developed an efficient vocal tract. Clay tablets of the neolithic Danubian culture discovered in Dec. 1966 at Tartaria, Moros River, Romania have been dated to the fifth or fourth millennium B.C. The tablets bear symbols of bows and arrows, gates and combs. In 1970 it was announced that writing tablets bearing an early form of the Elamite language dating from 3,500 B.C. had been found in south-eastern Iran. The scientist Alexander Marshack (U.S.) maintains that marked Upper Palaeolithic artifacts, such as a Cro-Magnon bone from 30,000 B.C. in the Musée des Antiquités Nationales, outside Paris with 69 marks with 24 stroke changes, are not random but to him of possibly lunar or menstrual cycle significance.

Oldest

The written language with the longest continuous history is Egyptian from the earliest hieroglyphic inscriptions on the palette of Narmer dated to *c.* 3,100 B.C. to Coptic used in Churches at the present day more than 5,000 years later. Hieroglyphs were used until A.D. 394 and thus may be overtaken by Chinese characters as the most durable script in the 21st century.

Oldest words in English

Some as yet unpublished research indicates four words of an Indo-European substrate survive in English—apple (apal), bad (bad), gold (gol) and tin (tin).

Commonest language

Today's world total of languages and dialects still spoken is about 5,000 of which some 845 come from India. The language spoken by more people than any other is Northern Chinese, or Mandarin, by an estimated 68 per cent of the population hence 575 million people in 1975. The so-called national language (*Guóyǔ*) is a standardized form of Northern Chinese (*Běifanghuà*) as spoken in the Peking area. This was alphabetized into *zhùyīn fùhào* of 37 letters in 1918. In 1958 the *pīnyīn* system, which is a phonetic pronunciation guide, was introduced. The next most commonly spoken language and the most widespread is English, by an estimated 360,000,000 in mid-1975. English is spoken by 10 per cent or more of the population in 34 sovereign countries.

In Great Britain and Ireland there are five indigenous tongues: English, Scots Gaelic, Welsh, Irish Gaelic, and Romany (Gipsy). Of these English is, of course, predominant. Manx followed Cornish (whose last fluent speaker, John Davey, died in 1891) into extinction, when Mr. Edward (Ned) Maddrell (1877–1974) of Glen Chass, Port St. Mary, Isle of Man, died as the last islander whose professed tongue was Manx. In the Channel Islands, apart from Jersey and Guernsey *normand*, there survive words of Sarkese or *Sèrtchais* in which a prayer book was published in 1812, but of which there are very few speakers left.

Rarest Language

There are believed to be 20 or more languages including 6 Indian languages in North America in which no-one can converse because there is only one speaker left. Eyak is still spoken in South east Alaska by two aged sisters if they meet.

Most complex

The following extremes of complexity have been noted: Chippewa, the North American Indian language of Minnesota, U.S.A., has the most verb forms with up to 6,000; Tillamook, the North American Indian language of Oregon, U.S.A., has the most prefixes with 30; Tabassaran, a language in Daghestan, U.S.S.R., uses the most noun cases with 35, while Eskimaux use 63 forms of the present tense and simple nouns have as many as 252 inflections. In Chinese the 40 volume *Chung-wén Tà Tź'u-tien* dictionary lists 49,905 characters. The fourth tone of "i" has 84 meanings, varying as widely as "dress", "hiccough" and "licentious". The written language provides 92 different characters of "i". The most complex written character in Chinese is that representing *xiè* consisting of 64 strokes meaning "talkative". The most complex in current use is *yù* with 32 strokes meaning to urge or implore.

Most and least irregular verbs

Esperanto was first published by Dr. Ludwig Zamenhof (1859–1917) of Warsaw in 1887 without irregular verbs and is now estimated (by text book sales) to have a million speakers. Swahili has a strict 6-class pattern of verbs and no verbs which are irregular to this pattern. According to the more daunting grammars published in West Germany, English has 194 irregular verbs though there are arguably 214.

Rarest and commonest sounds

The rarest speech sound is probably the sound written ř in Czech which occurs in very few languages and is the last sound mastered by Czech children. In the southern Bushman language !xo there is a click articulated with both lips, which is written ⊙. The *l* sound in the Arabic word *Allah*, in some contexts, is pronounced uniquely in that language. The commonest sound is the vowel *a* (as in the English father); no language is known to be without it.

Vocabulary

The English language contains about 490,000 words plus another 300,000 technical terms, the most in any language, but it is doubtful if any individual uses more than 60,000. Those in Great Britain who have undergone a full 16 years of education use perhaps 5,000 words in speech and up to 10,000 words in written communications.

Greatest linguist

According to some uncompleted and hence as yet unpublished researches, the most proficient linguist in history was Sir John Bowring (1792–1872), who was said to be able to read 200 languages and speak 100. The greatest living linguist is probably Georges Schmidt (b. Strasbourg, France in 1915) of the United Nations Translation Department in New York City, U.S.A. who can reputedly speak fluently in 30 languages and has been prepared to embark on the translation of 36 others.

ALPHABET

Earliest

The development of the use of an alphabet in place of pictograms occurred in the Sinaitic world between 1700 and 1500 B.C. This western Semitic language developed the consonantal system based on phonetic and syllabic principles. The oldest letter is "O", unchanged in shape since its adoption in the Phoenician alphabet *c.* 1300 B.C. The newest letters in the English alphabet, are "j" and "v" which are of post Shakespearean use *c.* 1630. There are 65 alphabets now in use.

Longest and shortest

The language with most letters is Cambodian with 72 (including useless ones) and Rotokas in central Bougainville Island has least with 11 (just a, b, e, g, i, k, o, p, ř, t and u). Amharic has 231 formations from 33 basic syllabic forms, each of which has seven modifications, so this Ethiopian language cannot be described as alphabetic.

Most and least consonants and vowels

The language with most consonantal sounds is the Caucasian language Ubyx, with 80 and that with least is Rotokas, with only 6 consonants. The language with the most vowels is Sedang, a central Vietnamese language with 55 distinguishable vowel sounds and those with the least are the Caucasian languages Abaza and Kabardian with two such. The Hawaiian word for "certified" has 8 consecutive vowels—hooiaioia—while the English record is 6 in the musical term *euouae*. The Estonian word jäääärne, meaning the edge of the ice, has the same 4 consecutively. The Latin genitive for Aeneas's island consists solely of 6 vowels—aeaeae. The English word "latchstring" has 6 consecutive consonants.

Largest letter

The largest permanent letters in the world are the giant 600 ft *183 m* letters spelling READYMIX on the ground in the Nullarbor near East Balladonia, Western Australia. This was constructed in Dec. 1971. In sky-writing (normally at *c.* 8,000 ft *2 400 m*) a seven letter word may stretch for 6 miles *9 km* in length and can be read from 50 miles *80 km*. The world's earliest example was over Epsom racecourse, Surrey on 30 May 1922 when Cyril Turner "spelt out" "London Daily Mail" from an S.E.5A biplane.

WORDS

Longest words *World*

The longest word ever to appear in literature occurs in *The Ecclesiazusae*, a comedy by Aristophanes (448–380 B.C.). In the Greek it is 170 letters long but transliterates into 182

letters in English, thus: lopadotemachoselachogaleokranio-leipsanodrimhypotrimmatosilphioparaomelitokatakechy menokichlepikossyphophattoperisteralektryonopteke phalliokigklopeleiolagoiosiraiobaphetraganopterygon. The term describes a fricassee of 17 sweet and sour ingredients including mullet, brains, honey, vinegar, pickles, marrow and ouzo (a Greek drink laced with anisette).

English

The longest word in the Oxford English Dictionary is floccipaucinihilipilification (alternatively spelt in hyphenated form with "n" in seventh place), with 29 letters, meaning "the action of estimating as worthless", first used in 1741, and later by Sir Walter Scott (1771–1832). Webster's Third International Dictionary lists among its 450,000 entries pneumonoultramicroscopicsilicovolcanoconiosis (45 letters) the name of a miners' lung disease.

The nonce word used by Dr. Edward Strother (1675–1737) to describe the spa waters at Bristol was aequeosalinocalcalinoceraceoaluminosocupreovitriolic of 52 letters.

The longest regularly formed English word is praetertrans-substantiationalistically (37 letters), used by Mark McShane in his novel *Untimely Ripped*, published in 1963. The medical term hepaticocholangiocholecystenterostomies (39 letters) refers to the surgical creations of new communications between gallbladders and hepatic ducts and between intestines and gallbladders. The longest word in common use is disproportionableness (21 letters).

Longest palindromes

The longest known palindromic word is *saippuakivikauppias* (19 letters), the Finnish word for a dealer in lye (i.e. caustic soda). The longest in the English language is *redivider* (9 letters), while another nine-letter word, *Malayalam*, is a proper noun given to the language of the Malayali people in Kerala, southern India. The nine letter word ROTAVATOR is a registered trade mark belonging to Howard Machinery Ltd. The contrived chemical term *detartrated* has 11 letters. Some baptismal fonts in Greece and Turkey bear the circular 25 letter inscription NIΨON ANOMHMATA MH MONAN OΨIN meaning "wash (my) sins not only (my) face". This appears at St. Mary's Church Nottingham, St. Paul's, Woldingham, Surrey and other churches. The longest palindromic composition devised is one of 10,689 words completed by Edward Benbow of Bewdley, England in April 1977. It begins "Now, Norris, Sir, I mail a new opus. So be it." . . . and hence predictably ends . . . ". . . Tie boss up, Owen. Al, I am Iris. Sir, Ron won."

Longest chemical name

The longest chemical term is that describing Bovine NADP-specific Glutamate Dehydrogenase, which contains 500 amino-acids and a resultant name of some 3,600 letters.

Longest anagrams

The longest non-scientific English words which can form anagrams are the 17-letter transpositions "misrepresentation" and "representationism". The case has also been argued for the 19 letter "transsubstantiation" and "transubstantiations".

Longest abbreviation

The longest known abbreviation is S.O.M.K.H.P.B.K.J.C.-S.S.D.P.M.W.D.T.B., the initials of the Sharikat Orang-Orang Melayu Kerajaan Hilir Perak Berkerjasama-Serker-jasama Kerana Jimat Chermat Serta Simpanon Dan Pinjam Meminjam Wang Dengan Tanggonnan Berhad. This is the

LONGEST WORDS IN VARIOUS LANGUAGES	
Only the first 7 are to be found in standard dictionaries	
French	Anticonstitutionnellement (25 letters) —anticonstitutionally.
Croatian	Prijestolenaslijednikovica (26 letters) —wife of an heir apparent.
Italian	Precipitevolissimevolmente (26 letters) —as fast as possible.
Portuguese	inconstitucionalissimamente (27 letters) —the highest degree of unconstitutionality.
Japanese	Ryágū-no-otohime-no-motoyui-no-kirihazushi (36 letters) —a seaweed, literally of small pieces of the paper hair streamers of the underwater princess.
Hungarian	Legengedelmeskedhetetlenségeskedéseitekért (41 letters) —because of your continued greatest disobedience.
Russian	ryentgyenoelyektrokardiografichyeskogo (33 Cyrillic letters, transliterating as 38) —of the radioelectrocardiographic.
Dutch	Rijksluchtvaartdienstweerschepenpersoneel (41 letters) —Government aviation department weather ship personnel.
Turkish	Cekoslovakyalilastiramadiklarimizdanmiymissiniz (47 letters) —"are you not of that group of persons that we were said to be unable to Czechoslovakanise?"
Mohawk*	tkanuhstasrihsranuhwe'tsraaksahsrakaratattsrayeri' (50 letters) —the praising of the evil of the liking of the finding of the house is right.
German†	Donaudampfschifffahrtselectricitaetenhauptbetriebswerkbauunterbeamtengesellschaft (81 letters) —The club for subordinate officials of the head office management of the Danube steamboat electrical services (Name of a pre-war club in Vienna).
Swedish	Spårvagnsaktiebolagsskensmutsskjutarefackföreningspersonalbeklädnadsmagasinsförrådsförvaltaren (94 letters) —Manager of the depot for the supply of uniforms to the personnel of the track cleaners' union of the tramway company

* Mohawk forms words of limitless length. Above is an example.
† The longest dictionary word in every day usage is Kraftfahrzeugreparaturwerkstatten (33 letters or 34 if the ä is written as ae) meaning motor vehicle repair shops (or service garages).

Malay name for the Lower Perak Malay Government Servant's Co-operative Thrift and Loan Society Limited, in Telok Anson, Perak State, West Malaysia (formerly Malaya). The abbreviation for this abbreviation is not recorded.

Longest Acronym

The longest acronym is ADCOMSUBORDCOMPHIB-SPAC (22 letters) used in the U.S. Navy to denote the Administrative Command; Amphibious Forces, Pacific Fleet, Subordinate Command.

Commonest words and letters

In written English the most frequently used words are in order: the, of, and, to, a, in, that, is, I, it, for *and* as. The most used in conversation is I. The commonest letter is 'e' and the commonest initial letter is 'T'.

Most meanings

The most over-worked word in English is the word *set* which has 58 noun uses, 126 verbal uses and 10 as a participial adjective.

Most Homophones

The most homophonous sounds in English are *air* and *sol* which, according to the researches of Dora Newhouse of Los Angeles, both have 38 homophones. The homonym with most variant spellings is *Air* with Aire, Are, Ayr, E'er, Eir, Ere, Err, Erre, Eyre, Heir, Eire, Eyr *and* Ore.

Most accents

Accents were introduced in French in the reign of Louis XIII (1601–43). The word with most accents is *hétérogénéité*, meaning heterogeneity. An atoll in the Pacific Ocean 320 miles *516 km* E.S.E. of Tahiti is named Héréhérétué.

Shortest holoalphabetic sentence

The contrived headline describing the reaction of despicable vandals from the valley thwarted by finding a block of quartz with carvings (already) upon it as "Quartz glyph job vex'd cwm finks" represents the ultimate in containing all 26 letters in 26 letters. This was devised by Jeff Grant of Hastings, New Zealand.

Longest sentence

A sentence of 1300 words appears in "Absolam Absolam" by William Faulkner and one of 3,153 words in *History of the Church of God* composed by Sylvester Hassell of Wilson, North Carolina, U.S.A., *c.* 1884 with 86 semi-colons and 390 commas. The longest sentence recorded to have got past the editor of a major newspaper is one of 1,030 words in the *Chicago Tribune* T.V. column by Clarence G. Petersen in the issue of 19 Aug. 1970. The Report of the President of Columbia University 1942–43 contained a sentence of 4,284 words. The first 40,000 words of *The Gates of Paradise* by George Andrzeyevski (Panther) appear to lack any punctuation. Some authors such as James Joyce (1882–1941) appear to eschew punctuation altogether.

PLACE-NAMES

Earliest

The earliest recorded British place-name is Belerion, the Penwith peninsula of Cornwall, referred to as such by Pytheas of Massalia in *c.* 308 B.C. The name Salakee on St. Mary's, Isles of Scilly is however arguably of a pre Indo-European substrate meaning *tin island*. The earliest distinctive name for what is now Great Britain was Albion by Himilco *c.* 500 B.C. The oldest name among England's 46 counties is Kent, first mentioned in its Roman form of Cantium (from the Celtic *canto*, meaning a rim, *i.e.* a coastal district) from the same circumnavigation by Pytheas. The earliest mention of England is the form *Angelcynn*, which appeared in the Anglo-Saxon Chronicle in A.D. 880.

Longest *World*

The official name for Bangkok, the capital city of Thailand, is Krungtep Mahanakhon. The full name is however: Krungthep Mahanakhon Bovorn Ratanakosin Mahintharayutthaya Mahadilokpop Noparatratchathani Burirom Udomratchanivetmahasathan Amornpiman Avatarnsathit Sakkathattiyavisnukarmprasit (167 letters) which in its most

scholarly transliteration emerges with 175 letters. The longest place-name now in use in the world is Taumata-whakatangihangakoauauotamatea(turipukakapikimaungahoronuku)pokaiwhenuakitanatahu, the unofficial 85-letter version of the name of a hill (1,002 ft above sea-level) in the Southern Hawke's Bay district of North Island, New Zealand. This Maori name means "the place where Tamatea, the man with the big knee who slid, climbed and swallowed mountains, known as Traveller (or Land eater) played on his flute to his loved one". The official version has 57 letters (1 to 36 and 65 to 85).

Great Britain

The longest place-name in the United Kingdom is the concocted 58-letter name Llanfairpwllgwyngyllgogerychwyrndrobwllllantysiliogogogoch, which is translated: "St. Mary's Church in a hollow by the white hazel, close to the rapid whirlpool, by the red cave of St. Tysilio". This is the name used for the reopened (April 1973) village railway station in Anglesey, Gwynedd, Wales, but the *official* name consists of only the first 20 letters of what the Welsh would regard as a 51 letter word since "ll" and "ch" may be regarded as one. The longest genuine Welsh place-name listed in the Ordnance Survey Gazetteer is Lower Llanfihangel-y-Creuddyn (26 letters), a village near Aberystwyth, Dyfed, Wales.

England

The longest single word (unhyphenated) place-name in England is Blakehopeburnhaugh, a hamlet between Burness and Rochester in Northumberland, of 18 letters. The hyphenated Sutton-under-Whitestonecliffe, North Yorkshire has 27 letters on the Ordnance Survey but with the insertion of "the" and the dropping of the final "e" 29 letters in the Post Office List. The longest multiple name is North Leverton with Habbelsthorpe (30 letters), Nottinghamshire, while the longest parish name is Saint Mary le More and All Hallows with Saint Leonard and Saint Peter, Wallingford (68 letters) in Oxfordshire formed on 5 April 1971.

Scotland

The longest single word place-names in Scotland are Claddochknockline, on the island of North Uist, Western Isles and the nearby Claddochbaleshare both with 17 letters. Kirkcudbrightshire (18 letters) became merged into Dumfries and Galloway on 16 May 1975. A 12-acre *5 ha* loch 9 miles *14 km* west of Stornoway on Lewes, Western Isles is named Loch Airidh Mhic Fhionnlaidh Dhuibh (31 letters).

Ireland

The longest place-name in Ireland is Muckanagheder-dauhaulia (22 letters), 4 miles *6 km* from Costello in Camus Bay, County Galway. The name means "soft place between two seas".

Shortest

The shortest place names in the world are the French village of Y (population 143), so named since 1241; the Norwegian village of Å (pronounced "Aw"), the Swedish place Å in Vikholandet, U in the Caroline Islands, Pacific Ocean; and the Japanese town of Sosei which is alternatively called Aioi or O-o or even O. There was once a 6 in West Virginia, U.S.A. The shortest place-names in Great Britain are the two-lettered villages of Ae (population 199 in 1961) Dumfries and Galloway; Oa on the island of Islay, Strathclyde and Bu on Wyre, Orkney Islands. In the Shetland Islands there are skerries called Ve and two stacks called Aa. The island of Iona was originally I. The River E flows into the southern end of Loch Mhór, Inverness-shire, and O Brook flows on Dartmoor, Devon. The shortest place-name in Ireland is Ta (or Lady's Island) Lough, a sea-inlet on the coast of County Wexford. Tievelough, in County Donegal, is also called Ea.

PERSONAL NAMES

Earliest

The earliest personal name which has survived is possibly N'armer, the father of Men (Menes), the first Egyptian Pharaoh, dating from *ante* 3100 B.C. The earliest known name of any resident of Britain is Divitiacus, King of the Suessones, the Gaulish ruler of the Kent area *c.* 75 B.C. under the name

A sign displaying the name of a village in France—one of the shortest place names in the World. (See page 90)

Prydhain. Scotland, unlike England, was never conquered by the Roman occupiers (A.D. 43–410). Calgācus (b. c. A.D. 40), who led this last resistance was the earliest native of Scotland whose name has been recorded.

Longest Pedigree

The only non-Royal English pedigree that can with certainty show a clear pre-Conquest descent is that of the Arden family. It is claimed on behalf of the Clan Mackay that their clan can be traced to Loarn, the Irish invader of south west Pictland, now Strathclyde, c. A.D. 501.

Longest Single name

The longest Christian or given name on record is Napuamahalaonaonekawehiwehionakuahiweanenawawakehoonkakehoaalekeeaonanainananiakeao'-Hawaiikawao (94 letters) in the case of Miss Dawn N. Lee so named in Honolulu, Hawaii, U.S.A. in February 1967. The name means "The abundant, beautiful blossoms of the mountains and valleys begin to fill the air with their fragrance throughout the length and breadth of Hawaii".

Longest Surname *World*

The longest name used by anyone is Adolph Blaine Charles David Earl Frederick Gerald Hubert Irvin John Kenneth Lloyd Martin Nero Oliver Paul Quincy Randolph Sherman Thomas Uncas Victor William Xerxes Yancy Zeus Wolfeschlegelsteinhausenbergerdorff, Senior, who was born at Bergedorf, near Hamburg, Germany, on 29 Feb. 1904. On printed forms he uses only his eighth and second Christian names and the first 35 letters of his surname. The full version of the name of 590 letters appeared in the 12th edition of *The Guinness Book of Records*. He now lives in Philadelphia, Pennsylvania, U.S.A., and has shortened his surname to Mr. Wolfe + 585, Senior.

United Kingdom

The longest surname in the United Kingdom was the six-barrelled one borne by the late Major L.S.D.O.F. (Leone Sextus Denys Oswolf Fraudati filius) Tollemache-Tollemache de Orellana Plantagenet Tollemache Tollemache, who was born in 1884 and died of pneumonia in France on 20 Feb. 1917. Of non-repetitious surnames, the last example of a five-barrelled one was that of the Lady Caroline Jemima Temple-Nugent-Chandos-Brydges-Grenville (1858–1946). The longest single English surname is Featherstonehaugh, correctly pronounced on occasions (but improbably on the correct occasion) Featherstonehaw or Festonhaw or Fessonhay or Freestonhugh or Feerstonhaw or Fanshaw.

Scotland

In Scotland the surname nin (feminine of mac) Achinmacdholicachinskerray (29 letters) was recorded in an 18th century parish register.

Most Christian names

The French composer Louis Jullien (1812–1860) had 36 Christian names because all 36 members of a Philharmonic Society insisted on being godfathers.

Most versions

Mr. C. Mazillius of Pinner, Middlesex, England has collected 133 different versions of the spelling of his name from 1959 to 1977. Mzili Kazi of Zululand (b. c. 1795) had his name chronicled in 325 spellings, according to researches by Dr. R. Kent Rasmussen.

Shortest

The single letter surname O, of which 13 examples appear in the telephone directory in Brussels, besides being the commonest single letter name is the one obviously causing most distress to those concerned with the prevention of cruelty to computers. There are two one-lettered Burmese names E (calm), pronounced aye and U (egg), pronounced Oo. U before the name means "uncle". There exist among the 47,000,000 names on the Dept. of Health & Social Security index 5 examples of a one-lettered surname. Their identity has not been disclosed, but they are "A", "B", "J", "N" and "O". Two-letter British surnames include By and On have recently been joined by Oy and Za.

Commonest Surname *World*

The commonest surname in the world is the Chinese name Chang which is borne according to estimates, by between 9.7% and 12.1% of the Chinese population, so indicating even on the lower estimate that there are at least some 75,000,000 Changs—more than the entire population of all but 7 of the 158 other sovereign countries of the world.

English

The commonest surname in the English-speaking world is Smith. The most recent published count showed 671,550 nationally insured Smiths in Great Britain, of whom 7,081 were plain John Smith and another 22,550 were John (plus one or more given names) Smith. Including uninsured persons there were over 800,000 Smiths in England and Wales alone, of whom 90,000 were called A. Smith. There were an estimated 2,382,509 Smiths in the U.S.A. in 1973.

"Macs"

There are, however, estimated to be 1,600,000 persons in Britain with M', Mc or Mac (Gaelic "son of") as part of their surnames. The commonest of these is Macdonald which accounts for about 55,000 of the Scottish population.

Commonest Christian name

From the latest available full year (1975) birth registrations for England and Wales at St. Catharine's House (formerly Somerset House), the most favoured first forename choice of parents bearing the 29 commonest surnames are boys Stephen/Steven with a very slight lead over Paul and girls Sarah/Sara with a fair lead over Claire/Clare/Clair. This massive survey of 75,000 names was carried out by C. V. Appleton. From 1196 to at least 1925 William and John were first and second but by 1971 John had sunk to 17th and William failed to make the Top 50.

Most contrived name

The palm for the most determined attempt to be last in the local telephone directory must now be awarded to Mr. Zachary Zzzzra of San Francisco, California. He outdid the previous occupant who was a mere Mr. Zeke Zzzypt. In September 1970 Mr. Zero Zzyzz (rhymes with "fizz") was ousted by Mr. Vladimir Zzzyd (rhymes with "outdid") in the Miami directory. In Los Angeles a private enterprise company surpassed all being the ZZZZZZZ Co. The alpha and omega of Britain's 62 directories are Mrs. Maude E. Aab of Hull, Humberside and Mr. P. Zyzniewski of Northampton.

TEXTS AND BOOKS

Oldest

The oldest known written text is the pictographic expression of Sumerian speech (see Earliest Language, p. 88). The Samarian papyri, written in Aramaic, found 8½ miles *13,7 km* north of Jerico are dated 375–335 B.C.

Oldest printed

The oldest surviving printed work is a Korean scroll or *sutra* from wooden printing blocks found in the foundations of the Pulguk Sa pagoda, Kyongju, Korea, on 14 Oct.

1966. It has been dated no later than A.D. 704. It was claimed in November 1973 that a 28 page book of Tang dynasty poems at Yonsei University, Korea was printed from metal type *c.* 1160.

Oldest Mechanically printed

It is widely accepted that the earliest mechanically printed full length book was the 42-line Gutenberg Bible, printed at Mainz, Germany, in *c.* 1455 by Johann Henne zum Gensfleisch zur Laden, called "zu Gutenberg" (*c.* 1398 - *c.* 1468). Work on water marks published in 1967 indicates a copy of a surviving printed "Donatus" Latin grammar was made from paper in *c.* 1450. The earliest exactly dated printed work is the Psalter completed on 14 Aug. 1457 by Johann Fust (*c.* 1400–1466) and Peter Schöffer (1425–1502), who had been Gutenberg's chief assistant. The earliest printing by William Caxton (*c.* 1422–1491) though undated would appear to be The Recuyel of the Historyes of Troye in late 1473 to spring 1474.

Largest *Book*

The largest book in the world is the *Super Book* measuring 9 ft × 10 ft 2⅛ in *2,74 × 3,07 m* weighing 557 lb. *252,6 kg* consisting of 300 pages published in Denver, Colorado, U.S.A. in 1976.

Publication

The largest publication in the world is the 1,112 volume set of *British Parliamentary Papers* published by the Irish University Press in 1968–1972. A complete set weighs 3¼ tons *3,3 tonnes*, costs £21,000 and would take 6 years to read at 10 hours per day. The production involved the death of 34,000 Indian goats, and the use of £15,000 worth of gold ingots. The total print is 500 sets.

Dictionary

The largest dictionary now published is the 12-volume Royal quarto *The Oxford English Dictionary* of 15,487 pages published between 1884 and 1928 with a first supplement of 963 pages in 1933 with a further 4-volume supplement, edited by R. W. Burchfield, in which the third and fourth volumes covering O–S and T–Z have yet to appear. The work contains 414,825 words, 1,827,306 illustrative quotations and reputedly 227,779,589 letters and figures.

Smallest Book

The smallest bound book with cursive material printed in movable metal type (as opposed to any micro-photographic process) is one of 3,5 × 3,5 mm *0.14 × 0.14 in* printed for the Gutenberg Museum, Mainz, West Germany. It comprises the Lord's Prayer in seven languages.

Longest novel

The longest important novel ever published is *Les hommes de bonne volonté* by Louis Henri Jean Farigoule (b. 26 Aug. 1885), *alias* Jules Romains, of France, in 27 volumes in 1932–46. The English version *Men of Good Will* was published in 14 volumes in 1933–46 as a "novel-cycle". The novel *Tokuga-Wa Ieyasu* by Sohachi Yamaoka has been serialised in Japanese daily newspapers since 1951. When completed it will run to 40 volumes.

Encyclopaedias *Earliest*

The earliest known encyclopaedia was compiled by Speusippas (*post* 408–*c.* 388 B.C.) a nephew of Plato, in Athens *c.* 370 B.C. The earliest encyclopaedia compiled by a Briton was *Liber exerptionum* by the Scottish monk Richard (d. 1173) at St. Victor's Abbey, Paris *c.* 1140.

Largest

The largest encyclopaedia ever compiled was the *Great Standard Encyclopaedia* of Yung-lo ta tien of 22,937 manuscript chapters (370 still survive), written by 2,000 Chinese scholars in 1403–08.

Most comprehensive

The most comprehensive present day encyclopaedia is the *Encyclopaedia Britannica*, first published in Edinburgh, Scotland, in Dec. 1768–1771. A group of booksellers in the United States acquired reprint rights in 1898 and completed ownership in 1899. In 1943 the *Britannica* was given to the University of Chicago, Illinois, U.S.A. The current 30-volume 15th edition contains 33,141 pages and 43,000,000 words from 4,277 contributors. It is now edited in Chicago and in London.

Maps *Oldest*

The oldest known map of any kind is a clay tablet depicting the river Euphrates flowing through northern Mesopotamia, Iraq, dated *c.* 3800 B.C. The earliest surviving product of English map-making is the Anglo Saxon *mappa mundi*, known as the Cottonian manuscript from the late 10th century. The earliest printed map in the world dates from Isodore of Sevillés *Etymologlarum* of 1472. The earliest printed map of Britain was Ptolemy's outline printed in Bologna, Italy in 1477.

Most valuable *Book*

The most valuable printed books are the three surviving perfect vellum copies of the Gutenberg Bible, printed in Mainz, Germany, in 1452–56 by Gutenberg (see page 92). The United States Library of Congress copy, bound in three volumes, was obtained in 1930 from Dr. Otto Vollbehr, who paid about $330,000 (*then £68,000*) for it. During 1970 a paper edition in the hands of the New York book dealer, Hans Peter Kraus, was privately bought for $2,500,000 (*then £1,041,666*). Only 48 examples, many of them missing some of the 324 pages, of the *c.* 200 printed, have survived. The most recent discoveries were in Mons, France in 1950 and Immenhausen, West Germany in 1958.

Broadsheet

The highest price ever paid for a broadsheet has been $404,000 (*then £168,333*) for one of the 16 known copies of *The Declaration of Independence*, printed in Philadelphia in 1776 by Samuel T. Freeman & Co., and sold to a Texan in May 1969.

Manuscripts

The highest value ever paid for any manuscript is £219,780 paid at Sotheby's Zurich, Switzerland on 5 Nov. 1975 for the autograph of Maimonides, the great Jewish philosopher. This was a study, written *c.* 1160, on the rabinnical law *Mishna Torah* from the collection of David Sassoon bought by the Hebrew University of Jerusalem.

BIBLE
Oldest

Biblical texts in Hebrew are known to have become stabilized as early as A.D. 70. The oldest leather and papyrus Dead Sea Scrolls date from *c.* 250 B.C. The oldest known bible is the *Codex Vaticanus* written in Greek *ante* A.D. 350 and preserved in the Vatican Museum, Rome. The earliest Bible printed in English was one edited by Miles Coverdale, Bishop of Exeter (*c.* 1488–1569), while living in Antwerp, and printed in 1535. William Tyndale's New Testament in English had, however, been printed in Cologne and in Worms, Germany in 1525.

Longest and Shortest books

The longest book in the Authorized version of the Bible is the Book of Psalms, while the longest book including prose is the Book of the Prophet Isaiah, with 66 chapters. The shortest is the Third Epistle of John, with 294 words in 14 verses. The Second Epistle of John has only 13 verses but 298 words.

Longest Psalm, verse sentence and name

Of the 150 Psalms, the longest is the 119th, with 176 verses and the shortest is the 117th, with two verses. The shortest verse in the Authorized Version (King James) of the Bible is verse 35 of Chapter XI of the Gospel according to St John, consisting of the two words "Jesus wept". The longest is verse 9 of Chapter VIII of the Book of Esther, which extends to a 90-word description of the Persian empire. The total number of letters in the Bible is 3,566,480. The total number of words depends on the method of counting hyphenated words, but is usually given as between 773,692 and 773,746. The word "and" according to Colin McKay Wilson of the Salvation Army appears 46,227 times. The longest personal name in the Bible is Maher-shalal-hash-baz, the symbolic name of the second son of Isaiah (Isaiah, Chapter VIII, verses 1 and 3). The caption of Psalm 22, however, contains a Hebrew title sometimes rendered Al-'Ayyeleth Hash-Shahar (20 letters).

LETTERS

Longest
The longest personal letter based on a word count is one of 1,113,747 words written in 8 months ending May 1976, by Miss Jacqueline Jones of Lindale, Texas, to her sister, Mrs. Jean Stewart, of Springfield, Maine, U.S.A.

To an editor *Longest*
The longest recorded letter to an editor was one of 13,000 words (a third of a modern novel) written to the editor of the *Fishing Gazette* by A.R.I.E.L. and published in 7-point type spread over two issues in 1884.

Most
Britain's, and seemingly the world's, most indefatigable writer of letters to the editors of newspapers is Raymond L. Cantwell, 52, of Oxford, who since 1948 claims 27,809 letters published in print or on the air. His peak production has been 425 in 36 hours non-stop in aid of charity.

Shortest
The shortest correspondence on record was that between Victor Marie Hugo (1802–85) and his publisher Hurst and Blackett in 1862. The author was on holiday and anxious to know how his new novel *Les Misérables* was selling. He wrote " ?". The reply was "!".

Most Personal Mail
The highest confirmed mail received by any private citizen in a year is 900,000 letters by the baseball star Hank Aaron reported by the US Postal Department in June 1974. About a third were letters of hate engendered by his bettering of Babe Ruth's career record for "home runs". (See Chap. 12.)

Pen Pals Most Durable
The longest sustained correspondence on record is one of 61 years, since 1916, between Mrs. L. M. West of Canvey Island, Essex, and the sisters Mrs. A. Krebs of Brisbane, Australia and Mrs. W. Lane, who lives in Malaysia.

AUTOGRAPHS AND SIGNATURES

Earliest English Regal
The earliest English sovereign whose handwriting is known to have survived is Edward III (1327–1377). The earliest full signature extant is that of Richard II (dated 26 July 1386). The Magna Carta does not bear even the mark of King John (reigned 1199–1216), but carries only his seal. An attested cross of King Cnut (1016–1035) has survived.

The earliest full Royal signature—that of Richard II in 1386. See *The Guinness Book of World Autographs* by Ray Rawlins (Published Sept. 1977 at £7.95).

Most expensive
The highest price ever paid on the open market for a single autograph letter signed is $51,000 (*then £10,500*), paid in 1927 for a letter written by the Gloucestershire-born Button Gwinnett (1732–77), one of the three men from Georgia to sign the United States' Declaration of Independence in Philadelphia beginning on 4 July 1776. Such an item would today probably attract bids of $250,000 (*£135,000*). If one of the six known signatures of William Shakespeare (1564–1616) were to come on the market or a new one was discovered the price would doubtless set a record.

AUTHORS

Most prolific
The most prolific writer for whom a word count has been published was Charles Hamilton, *alias* Frank Richards (1875–1961), the Englishman who created Billy Bunter. At his height in 1908 he wrote the whole of the boys' comics *Gem* (founded 1907) and *Magnet* (1908–1940) and most of two others, totalling 80,000 words a week. His lifetime output has been put at 100,000,000 words. He enjoyed the advantages of the use of electric light rather than candlelight and of being unmarried. The champion of the goose quill era was Jósef Ignacy Kraszewski (1812–1887) of Poland who produced more than 600 volumes of novels and historical works.

Most Novels
The greatest number of novels published by any author is 904 by Kathleen Lindsay (Mrs. Mary Faulkner) (1903–1973) of Somerset West, Cape Province, South Africa. She wrote under six pen names, two of them masculine. After receiving a probable record 743 rejection slips the British novelist John Creasey M.B.E. (1908–1973), under his own name and 13 *noms de plume* had 564 books totalling more than 40,000,000 words published from 1932 to his death on 9 June 1973. The British authoress with the greatest total of full length titles is Miss Ursula Harvey Bloom (b. Chelmsford, Essex 1892) (Mrs. A. C. G. Robinson, formerly Mrs. Denham-Cookes), who reached 500 by December 1975, starting in 1924 with *The Great Beginning* and including the best sellers *The Ring Tree* (novel) and *The Rose of Norfolk* (non-fiction). Enid Mary Blyton (1898–1968) (Mrs. Darrell Waters) completed 600 titles of children's stories many of them brief with 59 in the single year 1955. She was translated into a record 128 languages.

Most Text Books
Britain's most successful writer of text books is the ex-schoolmaster Ronald Ridout (b. 23 July 1916) who between 1948 and May 1976 had 334 titles published with sales of 56,500,000. His *The First English Workbook* has sold 3,974,000 copies.

Highest paid
In 1958 a Mrs. Deborah Schneider of Minneapolis, Minnesota, U.S.A., wrote 25 words to complete a sentence in a competition for the best blurb for Plymouth cars. She won from about 1,400,000 entrants the prize of $500 (*£178*) every month for life. On normal life expectations she would have collected $12,000 (*£4,285*) per word. No known anthology includes Mrs. Schneider's deathless prose.

Top selling
It was announced on 13 March 1953 that 672,058,000 copies of the works of Marshal Iosif Vissarionovich Dzhugashvili, *alias* Stalin (1879–1953), had been sold or distributed in 101 languages.

The all-time estimate of book sales by Erle Stanley Gardner (1889–1970) (U.S.) to 1 Jan. 1977 were 304,000,000 copies in 23 languages. The top selling authoress, has been Dame Agatha Christie (*née* Miller) (later Lady Mallowan) (1890–1976) whose 80 crime novels sold an estimated 300,000,000 in 103 languages.

Highest selling title
The authors who have written the highest selling title are Norris Dewar McWhirter (b. 12 Aug. 1925) and his twin brother Alan Ross McWhirter (k. 27 Nov. 1975), editors and compilers of *The Guinness Book of Records* first published from 107 Fleet Street, London in October 1955. Global sales in 16 languages by May 1977 reached over 32,000,000 copies.

Most rejections
The greatest recorded number of publisher's rejections for a manuscript is 106 for "World Government Crusade" by

Gilbert Young (b. 1906) since 1958. His public meeting in Bath, England in support of his parliamentary candidature as a World Government Candidate, however, drew a crowd of one.

Oldest authoress

The oldest authoress in the world is Mrs. Alice Pollock (*née* Wykeham-Martin, b. 2 July 1868) of Haslemere, Surrey, whose book "Portrait of My Victorian Youth" (Johnson Publications) was published in March 1971 when she was aged 102 years 8 months.

Youngest

The youngest recorded commercially published author is Dorothy Straight (b. 25 May 1958) of Washington D.C., who wrote *How the World Began* in 1962 aged 4 which was published in August 1964 by Pantheon Books, New York.

Longest Literary Gestation

The standard German dictionary *Deutsches Wörterbuch*, begun by the brothers Grimm in 1854, was finished in 1971. *Acta Sanctorum* begun by Jean Bolland in 1643, arranged according to saints' days, reached the month of November in 1925 and an introduction for December was published in 1940.

Poet Laureate *Youngest and oldest*

The youngest Poet Laureate was Laurence Eusden (1688–1730), who received the bays on 24 Dec. 1718 at the age of 30 years and 3 months. The greatest age at which a poet has succeeded is 73 in the case of William Wordsworth (1770–1850) on 6 April 1843. The longest lived Laureate was John Masefield, O.M., who died on 12 May 1967, aged 88 years 345 days. The longest which any poet has worn the laurel is 41 years 322 days, in the case of Alfred (later the 1st Lord) Tennyson (1809–92), who was appointed on 19 Nov. 1850 and died in office on 6 Oct. 1892.

Longest poem

The longest poem ever written was the *Mahabharata* which appeared in India in the period *c.* 400 to 150 B.C. It runs to 220,000 lines and nearly 3,000,000 words.

The longest poem ever written in the English language is one on the life of King Alfred by John Fitchett (1766–1838) of Liverpool which ran to 129,807 lines and took 40 years to write. His editor Robert Riscoe added the concluding 2,585 lines

Most Successful Sloganeer

"Think Mink" invented by Jack Gasnick (b. 25 Mar. 1918) in 1929 has sold in metal, celluloid and ribbon 50 million since 1950. His "*Cross at the Green . . . not in Between Enterprises*" of New York City has sold 55 million buttons, badges and tabs and 40 million other pieces.

HIGHEST PRINTINGS
World

The world's most widely distributed book is the Bible, portions of which have been translated into 1,603 languages. This compares with 222 languages by Lenin. It has been estimated that between 1815 and 1975 some 2,500,000,000 copies were printed of which 1,500,000,000 were handled by Bible Societies. The total distribution of complete Bibles by the United Bible Societies (covering 150 countries) in the year 1976 was 7,083,825.

It has been reported that 800,000,000 copies of the red-covered booklet *Quotations from the Works of Mao Tse-tung* were sold or distributed between June 1966, when possession became virtually mandatory in China, and Sept. 1971 when their promoter Marshal Lin Piao was killed. The *American Spelling Book* by Noah Webster was distributed in some 75,000,000 copies.

Non fiction

The total disposal through non-commercial channels by Jehovah's Witnesses of the 190 page hard bound book *The Truth That Leads to Eternal Life* published by the Watch-tower Bible and Tract Society of Brooklyn, New York, on 8 May 1968, reached 89 million in 102 languages by 5 May 1977.

BEST SELLERS

The world's all-time best *selling* book is the annual reference work *The World Almanac & Book of Facts* first published in 1868 and currently edited by George E. Delury. Its cumulative sale to October 1977 is estimated at 37 million copies increasing by 1,100,000 each year.

Fiction

The novel with the highest sales has been *Valley of the Dolls* (first published March 1966) by Jacqueline Susann (Mrs. Irving Mansfield) (1921–1974) with a world wide total of 20,230,000 to 28 Apr. 1977. In the first 6 months Bantam sold 6.8 million. In the United Kingdom the highest print order has been 3,000,000 by Penguin Books Ltd. for their paperback edition of *Lady Chatterley's Lover*, by D. H. (David Herbert) Lawrence (1885–1930). The total sales to April 1977 were 3,928,000.

Slowest seller

The accolade for the world's slowest selling book (known in U.S. publishing as slooow-sellers) probably belongs to David Wilkins's Translation of the New Testament from Coptic into Latin published by Oxford University Press in 1716 in 500 copies. Selling an average of one each 139 days it was in print for 191 years.

Largest Publisher *World*

The largest publisher in the world is the United States Government Printing Office (founded 1860) in Washington, D.C., U.S.A. The Superintendents of Documents Division dispatches more than 150,000,000 items of 27,000 titles every year. The annual list of new titles and annuals is about 6,000.

Great Britain

In terms of new titles per annum Britain's most prolific publisher was Robert Hale Ltd. (founded 1936) with 631 in 1976. The U.K. published a record 35,604 book titles in 1975 of which 8,361 were reprints. The highest figure for reprints was 9,977 in 1970. The 1976 total was 34,434.

Largest Printer *World*

The largest printers in the world are R. R. Donnelly & Sons Co. of Chicago, Illinois, U.S.A. The company, founded in 1864 has plants in ten main centres, turning out $584,000,000 (*£343 million*) worth of work per year. More than 60,000 tons of inks and 1,000,000 tons of paper and board are consumed every year.

Print order

The initial print order for the 49th Automobile Association Members' Handbook (1976–77) was 3,700,000 copies. The total print since 1908 has been 67,710,000. It is currently printed by web offset by Petty & Sons of Leeds.

LIBRARIES
Largest *World*

The largest library in the world is the United States Library of Congress (founded on 24 Apr. 1800), on Capitol Hill, Washington, D.C. By 1976 it contained 72,000,000 items, including 18,000,000 volumes and pamphlets. The buildings contain 35 acres *14,0 ha* of floor space and contain 327 miles *526 km* of shelving. The James Madison Memorial Extension began in 1971 is due for completion in 1980.

The Lenin State Library in Moscow, U.S.S.R., (founded 1862), claims to house more than 27,000,000 books, but this total is understood to include periodicals.

The largest non-statutory library in the world is the New York Public Library (founded 1895) on Fifth Avenue with a floor space of 525,276 ft² *48 800 m²* and 80 miles *128 km* of shelving. Its collection including 83 branch libraries embraces 8,605,610 volumes 10,683,105 manuscripts and 317,183 maps.

Great Britain

The largest library in the United Kingdom is that in the British Museum, London. It contains more than 9,000,000 books, about 115,000 manuscripts and 101,000 charters on 158 miles *254 km* of shelving. There are spaces for 370 readers in the domed Reading Room, built in 1854. The largest public library in the United Kingdom will be the extended Mitchell Library, North Street, Glasgow with a floor area of 510,000 ft² *47 380 m²* or 11.7 acres *4,7 ha* and an ultimate capacity for 4,000,000 volumes. The oldest public library in Scotland is in Kirkwall, Orkney, founded in 1683.

Overdue books

The most overdue book taken out by a known borrower was one reported on 7 Dec. 1968, checked out in 1823 from the University of Cincinnati Medical Library on Febrile Diseases (London, 1805 by Dr. J. Currie). This was returned by the borrower's great-grandson Richard Dodd. The fine calculated to be $22,646 (*then £9,435*) was waived.

PERIODICALS

Oldest *World*

The oldest continuing periodical in the world is *Philosophical Transactions of the Royal Society*, published in London, which first appeared on 6 Mar. 1665.

Great Britain

The Botanical Magazine has been in continuous publication since 1787, as several "parts" a year forming a series of continuously numbered volumes. Britain's oldest weekly periodical is *Lancet* first published in 1823. The Scottish monthly *Blackwood's Magazine* has not missed an issue since the first in April 1817. The Editor has always been a Blackwood. Since 1948 it has been Douglas Blackwood great great-grandson of the founder. The *Scots Magazine* began publication in 1739 and ran till 1826, and with three breaks has been produced continuously since 1924.

Largest circulation *World*

The largest circulations of any weekly periodical is that of *TV Guide* (U.S.A.) which in 1974 became the first magazine in history to sell a billion (1,000 million) copies in a year. The weekly average for Jul.–Dec. 1976 was 20,226,757. In its 30 basic international editions *The Reader's Digest* (established February 1922) circulates 29,110,000 copies monthly in 13 languages, including a United States edition of more than 17,750,000 copies and a United Kingdom edition (established 1939) of 1,380,892 copies (av. Jan.–Dec. 1976).

Great Britain

The highest circulation of any periodical in Great Britain is that of the *Radio Times* (instituted on 28 Sept. 1923). The average weekly sale for July–December 1976 was 3,614,730 copies with a readership of 9,553,000. The highest sale of any issue was 9,778,062 copies for the Christmas issue of 1955. *T.V. Times* averaged sales of 3,458,014 in the period July–Dec. 1976 with an estimated readership of 9,897,000 (Jan.–Dec. 1976).

Annual

Old Moore's Almanack has been published annually since 1697, when it first appeared as a broadsheet, by Dr. Francis Moore (1657–1715) of Southwark, London to advertise his "physiks". The annual sale certified by its publishers W. Foulsham & Co. Ltd. of Slough England is 1,150,000 copies and its aggregate sale is estimated to be 106 million.

NEWSPAPERS

Oldest *World*

The oldest existing newspaper in the world is the Swedish official journal *Post och Inrikes Tidningar*, founded in 1644. It is published by the Royal Swedish Academy of Letters. The oldest existing commercial newspaper is the *Haarlems Dagblad/Oprechte Haarlemsche Courant*, published in Haarlem, in the Netherlands. The *Courant* was first issued as the *Weeckelycke Courante van Europa* on 8 Jan. 1656 and a copy of issue No. 1 survives.

Great Britain

The oldest continuously produced newspaper in the United

Mr. Robert Edwards, the only person to have been appointed editor of a national newspaper four times.

Kingdom is *Berrow's Worcester Journal* (originally the *Worcester Post Man*), published in Worcester. It was traditionally founded in 1690 and has appeared weekly since June 1709. The oldest newspaper title is that of the *Stamford Mercury* dating back to at least 1714 and traditionally to 1695. The oldest daily newspaper in the United Kingdom is *Lloyd's List*, the shipping intelligence bulletin of Lloyd's London, established as a weekly in 1726 and as a daily in 1734. The *London Gazette* (originally the *Oxford Gazette*) was first published on 16 Nov. 1665. The oldest Sunday newspaper in the United Kingdom is *The Observer*, first issued on 4 Dec. 1791.

Largest and Smallest

The most massive single issue of a newspaper was the 7½ lb. *3,40 kg New York Times* of Sunday 17 Oct. 1965. It comprised 15 sections with a total of 946 pages, including about 1,200,000 lines of advertising. The largest page size ever used has been 51 in by 35 in *130 cm by 89 cm* for *The Constellation*, printed in 1859 by George Roberts as part of the Fourth of July celebrations in New York City, N.Y., U.S.A. The *Worcestershire Chronicle* was the largest British newspaper. A surviving issue of 16 Feb. 1859 measures 32¼ in by 22½ in *82 cm by 57 cm*. The smallest recorded page size has been 3 × 3¾ in *7,6 × 9,5 cm* of the *Daily Banner* (25 cents per month) of Roseberg, Oregon, U.S.A., issues of which, dated 1 and 2 Feb. 1876, survive. The *Answers to Correspondents* published by Messrs Carr & Co., Paternoster Square, London in 1888 was 3½ × 4½ in *9 × 11 cm*.

Most Expensive

Britain's most expensive paper is *The Sunday Times* at 22p or 4s 4.8d in the money prior to 15 Feb. 1971.

Most

The United States had 1,630 English language daily newspapers at 1 Jan. 1976. They had a combined net paid circulation of 60,203,329 copies per day at 30 Sept. 1975. The peak year for U.S. newspapers was 1910, when there were 2,202. The leading newspaper readers in the world are the people of Sweden, where 515 newspapers were sold for each 1,000 compared with the U.K. figure of 488.

Longest editorship

The longest editorship of any national newspaper has been more than 59 years by C. P. Scott (1846–1932) of the (then Manchester) *Guardian*, who was appointed aged 25 in 1872 and died on 1 Jan. 1932. John Watson was editor of the South Australian newspaper *The Border Watch* from 1863 to Dec. 1925—a span of 62 years.

Robert Edwards was 4 times appointed editor of a national paper—*Daily Express* (1961); *Daily Express* (1963); *Sunday People* (1966) and *Sunday Mirror* (1972).

Miss Rhona Chesters ("Auntie Rhona"), who has been contributing weekly to the Peterborough Standard without intermission for over 50 years. (*Peterborough Standard*)

Most durable feature

The longest lasting feature in the British national press from one pen is *Your Stars* by Edward Lyndoe. It has run since 1 Oct. 1933 in *The Sunday People*. "Auntie Rhona" (Miss Rhona Chesters b. 14 Feb. 1900) has contributed her Children's Corner in the *Peterborough Standard* since 2 Oct. 1925.

Longest lived strip

The most durable newspaper comic strip has been the Katzenjammer Kids (Hans and Fritz) created by Rudolph Dirks and first published in the *New York Journal* on 12 Dec. 1897 and perpetuated by his son John. The earliest strip was The Yellow Kid, which first appeared in the New York *Journal* on 18 Oct. 1896. The most widely syndicated is *Blondie* (originated in 1930) appearing in 1,600 newspapers in 50 countries.

CIRCULATION

Earliest 1,000,000

The first newspaper to achieve a circulation of 1,000,000 was *Le Petit Journal*, published in Paris, France, which reached this figure in 1886, when selling at 5 centimes. The *Daily Mail* first reached a million in May 1900.

Highest *World*

The highest circulation for any newspaper in the world is that for the *Asahi Shimbun* (founded 1879) of Japan which attained a figure of 11,814,265 copies in April 1977. This is achieved by totalling the figures for editions published in various centres with a morning figure of 7,233,996 and an evening figure of 4,580,269. The highest circulation of any single newspaper in Britain is that of the Sunday newspaper *The News of the World*, printed in Bouverie Street, London. Single issues have attained a sale of 9,000,000 copies with an estimated readership of more than 19,000,000. The paper first appeared on 1 Oct. 1843, and surpassed the million mark in 1905. The latest sales figure is 5,113,517 copies per issue (average for 1 July to 31 Dec. 1976), with an estimated readership of 13,562,000.

Great Britain

The highest daily net sale of any newspaper in the United Kingdom is that of *The Daily Mirror*, founded in London in 1903. A print of 7,161,704 was sold out on 3 June 1953. The latest sales figure is 3,864,119 (July–Dec. 1976), with an estimated readership of 12,329,000.

Evening

The highest circulation of any evening newspaper is that of *The Evening News*, established in London in 1881. The latest weekday figure is 573,420 copies per issue (average for Oct. 1976 to Mar. 1977), with an average readership of 1,758,000.

Most read

The newspaper which achieves the closest to a saturation circulation is *The Sunday Post*, established in Glasgow in 1914. In 1976 its estimated readership in Scotland of 2,806,000 represented 74 per cent of the entire population aged 15 and over.

CROSSWORDS

First

The earliest crossword was one with 32 clues invented by Arthur Wynne (b. Liverpool, England, d. 1945) and published in the *New York World* on 21 Dec. 1913. The first crossword published in a British newspaper was one furnished by C. W. Shepherd in the *Sunday Express* of 2 Nov. 1924.

Largest

The largest crossword ever published is one with 2,631 clues across and 2,922 clues down, compiled by Hank Koval (U.S.), assistant producer of the ABC T.V. show "Let's Make a Deal" between 22 Feb. 1974 and 1 Oct. 1975. It measures 16.66 ft² *1,54 m²* and is published by Price/Stern/Sloan Publishers Inc. of Los Angeles, California. The largest crosswords regularly published are "Mammoth" crosswords based on grids of 73 × 73 (5,329) squares with up to 828 clues by First Features Ltd of Hastings, East Sussex since 1 May 1970. Edward Akenhead, *The Times* Crossword Editor, succeeded in 1971 in including in a puzzle the word honorificabilitudinitatibus.

Fastest and slowest solution

The fastest recorded time for completing *The Times* crossword under test conditions is 3 min 45.0 sec by Roy Dean, 43 of Bromley, Greater London in the B.B.C. "Today" radio studio on 19 Dec. 1970. In May 1966 *The Times* of London received an announcement from a Fijian woman that she had just succeeded in completing their crossword No. 673 in the issue of 4 Apr. 1932. Dr. John Sykes won the Cutty Sark/*Times* championship 4 times (1972–1975). The only woman to reach a final has been Mrs. Morar Ryton.

Most Durable Compilers

Adrian Bell (b. 4 Oct. 1901) of Barsham, Suffolk contributed a record 4,327 crosswords to *The Times* from 2 Jan. 1930 to 1 Mar. 1975. R. J. Baddock of Plymouth (b. 30 Oct. 1894) has been a regular contributor to national newspapers since 13 Aug. 1926. Mrs. Phyllis Harvey, 82, of Brighton from December 1924 to December 1976 completed 52 years of contributions to the *Evening News* Junior Cross Word (now Quick crossword).

ADVERTISING RATES

The highest ever price for a single page has been $84,100 (£35,040) for a four-colour back cover in the now defunct *Life* magazine (circulation 8½ million per week) from Jan. 1969 to Jan. 1971. The current record is $66,295 (then £39,000) for a four colour page in the U.S. edition of *The Reader's Digest* effective from Jan. 1977.

The highest expenditure ever incurred on a single advertisement in a periodical is $1,028,410 (then £510,000) by the Bicentennial Commission of Pennsylvania for a detachable 48-page insert in the March 1976 issue of the U.S. edition of *The Reader's Digest*. The British record is some £100,000 for a 20-page colour supplement by Woolsworths in *The Radio Times* of 16 Nov. 1972. The colour rate for a single page in *The Radio Times* reached £9,930 in Oct.–Dec. 1976.

The world's highest advertising rate is 21,000,000 Yen (£44,210) for a full page in the morning edition and 17,000,000 Yen (£35,790) for the evening edition of the *Asahi Shimbun* of Tokyo (April 1977). The highest rate in Britain is a full page in *The Sunday Express* at £14,940 (April 1977).

Christmas cards

The greatest number of personal Christmas cards sent out is believed to be 62,824 by Mr. Werner Erhard of San Francisco, California in December 1975.

4. MUSIC

The Guinness Book of Music Facts and Feats, by Robert and Celia Dearling with Brian Rust (£6.50) contains a more detailed treatment of musical facts and superlatives.

Origins

The world's oldest surviving musical notation date from *c.* 1800 B.C. A heptonic scale deciphered from a clay tablet by Dr. Duchense-Guillemin in 1966–67 was found at a site in Nippur Sumer, now Iraq. An Assyrian love song also *c.* 1800 B.C. to an Ugarit god from a tablet of notation and lyric was reconstructed for an 11 string lyre at the University of California, Berkeley on 6 Mar. 1974. Musical history is, however, able to be traced back to the 3rd millennium B.C., when the yellow bell (*huang chung*) had a recognised standard musical tone in Chinese temple music. Whistles and flutes made from perforated phalange bones have been found at Upper Palaeolithic sites of the Aurignacian period (*c.* 25,000–22,000 B.C.) *e.g.* at Istallóskö, Hungary and in Molodova, U.S.S.R.

INSTRUMENTS

Piano Earliest

The earliest pianoforte in existence is one built in Florence, Italy, in 1720 by Bartolommeo Cristofori (1655–1731) of Padua, and now preserved in the Metropolitan Museum of Art, New York City.

Piano Grandest

The grandest grand piano built was one of $1\frac{1}{4}$ tons/*tonnes* 11 ft 8 in *3,55 m* in length made by Chas. H. Challen & Son Ltd. of London in 1935. The longest bass string measured 9 ft 11 in *3,02 m* and the tensile stress on the $6\frac{1}{2}$ cwt *330 kg* frame was 30 tons/*tonnes*.

Organ Largest *World*

The largest and loudest musical instrument ever constructed is the now only partially functional Auditorium Organ in Atlantic City, New Jersey, U.S.A. Completed in 1930, this heroic instrument has two consoles (one with seven manuals and another movable one with five), 1,477 stop controls and 33,112 pipes ranging in tone from $\frac{3}{16}$ of an inch *4,7 mm* to the 64 ft *19 m* tone. It is powered with blower motors of 365 horsepower *370 cv*, cost $500,000 (*then £102,880*) and has the volume of 25 brass bands, with a range of seven octaves. The grand organ at Wannamaker's Store, Philadelphia, installed in 1911, was enlarged until by 1930 it had 6 manuals and 30,067 pipes including a 64 ft *19 m* tone Gravissima. The world's largest church organ is that in Passau Cathedral, Germany. It was completed in 1928 by D. F. Steinmeyer & Co. It was built with 16,000 pipes and five manuals. The world's only five-manual electric organ was installed in the Carnegie Hall, New York City in Sept. 1974.

Great Britain

The largest organ in Great Britain is that completed in Liverpool Anglican Cathedral on 18 Oct. 1926, with two five-manual consoles of which only one is now in use, and 9,704 speaking pipes (originally 10,936) ranging from tones of $\frac{3}{4}$ in to 32 feet *1,9 cm to 9,75 m*.

Organists *Most Durable*

The longest recorded reign as an organist has been 81 years in the case of Charles Bridgeman (1779–1873) of All Saints Parish Church, Hertford, England, who was appointed in 1792 and who was still playing in 1873. The year in which he reached his crescendo was not recorded.

Loudest Organ stop

The loudest organ stop in the world is the Ophicleide stop of the Grand Great in the Solo Organ in the Atlantic City Auditorium (see above). It is operated by a pressure of 100 in *254 cm* of water ($3\frac{1}{2}$ lb./in² *24 kPa*) and has a pure trumpet note of ear-splitting volume, more than six times the volume of the loudest locomotive whistles.

Brass instrument *Largest*

The largest recorded brass instrument is a tuba standing $7\frac{1}{2}$ ft *2,28 m* tall, with 39 ft *11,8 m* of tubing and a bell 3 ft 4 in *1 m*

across. This contrabass tuba was constructed for a world tour by the band of John Philip Sousa (1854–1932), the United States composer, in *c.* 1896–98, and is still in use. This instrument is now owned by a circus promoter in South Africa.

Alphorn *Longest*

The longest alphorn is one of 13,4 m *43 ft 11½ in* built from a spruce log by Herr Stocker in Switzerland in 1976. It weighs 32 kg *70½ lb.*

Stringed instrument *Largest*

The largest movable stringed instrument ever constructed was a pantaleon with 270 strings stretched over 50 ft² *4,6 m²* used by George Noel in 1767. The greatest number of musicians required to operate a single instrument was the six required to play the gigantic orchestrion, known as the Apollonican, built in 1816 and played until 1840.

Guitar *Largest and Most Expensive*

The largest and presumably also the loudest playable guitar in the world is one 8 ft 10 in *2,6 m* tall, weighing 80 lb. *36 kg* and with a volume of 16,000 in³ *262 200 cm³* (*c.f.* the standard 1,024 in³ *16 780 cm³*) built by The Harmony Company of Chicago and completed in April 1970 and is priced at $15,000 (*now £8,100*). The most expensive standard sized guitar is the German chittara battente by Jacob Stadler, dated 1624, which was sold for £10,500 at Christies, London on 12 June 1974.

Double bass *Largest*

The largest bass viol ever constructed was an octobass 13 ft *3,96 m* tall, built in 1849 by J. B. Vuillaume (1798–1875) of France. Because of the span between the rope-like strings, it was fitted with foot levers to assist in "stopping".

Violin *Most valuable*

The highest recorded price for a violin is the $250,000 (*then £104,166*) paid by a private buyer to Harry A. Duffy for the Cessole Stradivarius of 1716 in December 1972. On this valuation the "Messie" Stradivarius in the Ashmolean Museum at Oxford, England, is now worth at least £200,000.

An inventory of 700 known or recorded string instruments made by Antonio Stradivari (1644–1737) is contained in the *Violin Iconography* by Herbert K. Goodkind of which those made between 1720–1730 reached a "tonal zenith".

Underwater Violinist

The only violinist to surmount the problems of playing the violin underwater has been Mark Gottlieb. Submerged in Evergreen State College swimming bath in Olympia, Washington, U.S.A. in March 1975 he gave a submarine rendition of Handel's Water Music. He is still working on both his bow speed and his *détaché.*

Most Durable Fiddler

Otto E. Funk, 62, walked 4,165 miles *6 702 km* from New York City to San Francisco, California playing his Hopf violin every step of the way westward. He arrived on 16 June 1929 after 183 days on the road.

Drum *Largest*

The largest drum in the world is the Disneyland Big Bass Drum with a diameter of 10 ft 6 in *3,2 m* and a weight of 450 lb. *204 kg.* It was built in 1961 by Remo Inc. of North Hollywood, California, U.S.A. and is mounted on wheels and towed by a tractor.

Fastest Drummer

Michael Loftus of Livonia, Michigan, U.S.A. on 30 June 1975, achieved a rate of 40 beats per second (24 with hands and 16 with feet) in his "controlled thunder" routine.

Highest and lowest notes

The extremes of orchestral instruments (excluding the organ) range between a handbell tuned to g^v (6,272 cycles/sec) and the sub-contrabass clarinet, which can reach C_{11} or 16.4 cycles/sec. The highest note on a standard pianoforte is c^v (4,186 cycles/sec), which is also the violinist's limit. In 1873 a sub double bassoon able to reach B_{111} ♯ or 14.6 cycles/sec was constructed but no surviving specimen is known. The extremes for the organ are g^{vi} (the sixth G above middle c) (12,544 cycles/sec) and C_{111} (8.12 cycles/sec) obtainable from ¾ in *1,9 cm* and 64 ft *19 m* pipes respectively.

ORCHESTRAS

Largest

The most massive orchestra ever recorded were those assembled on Band Day at the University of Michigan, U.S.A. In some years between 1958 and 1965 the total number of instrumentalists reached 13,500. On 17 June 1872, Johann Strauss the younger (1825–99) conducted an orchestra of 987 pieces supported by a choir of 20,000, at the World Peace Jubilee in Boston, Massachussetts, U.S.A. The number of first violinists was 400:

Marching band

The largest marching band on record was one of 1,976 musicians and 54 drill majors, flag bearers and directors who marched 2 miles *3,2 km* down Pennsylvania Avenue in President Nixon's Inaugural Parade on 20 Jan. 1973.

Most Successful Brass band

Most British Open Championship titles (inst. 1853) have been won by the Black Dyke Mills Band which has won 22 times from 1862 to 1974 including three consecutive wins in 1972–74.

Greatest attendance

The greatest attendance at any classical concert has been 150,000 for the New York Philharmonic Orchestra, conducted by Andre Kostelanetz, at Sheep Meadow in Central Park, New York City, N.Y., U.S.A., on 29 July 1975.

Pop Festival *Attendance*

The greatest claimed attendance at a Pop Festival has been 600,000 for the "Summer Jam" at Watkins Glen, New York, U.S.A., on Sunday 29 July 1973 of whom about 150,000 actually paid. There were 12 "sound towers". The attendance at the third Pop Festival at East Afton Farm, Freshwater, Isle of Wight, England on 30 Aug. 1970 was claimed by its promoters, Fiery Creations, to be 400,000.

Highest gross and audience

The highest recorded paid attendance for a single pop recording group is 76,229 attenders for the concert by the British group Led Zeppelin at the Silver Dome, Pontiac, Michigan, U.S.A. on 30 Apr. 1977.

COMPOSERS

Most prolific

The most prolific composer of all time was probably Georg Philipp Telemann (1681–1767) of Germany. He composed 12 complete sets of services (one cantata every Sunday) for a year, 78 services for special occasions, 40 operas, 600 to 700 orchestral suites, 44 Passions, plus concertos and chamber music. The most prolific symphonist was Johann Melchior Molter (c. 1695–1765) of Germany who wrote 165. Joseph Haydn (1732–1809) of Austria wrote 104 numbered symphonies some of which are regularly played today.

Most rapid

Among composers of the classical period the most prolific was Wolfgang Amadeus Mozart (1756–91) of Austria, who wrote *c.* 1,000 operas, operettas, symphonies, violin sonatas, divertimenti, serenades, motets, concertos for piano and many other instruments, string quartets, other chamber

An aerial view of the 1970 East Afton Pop Festival on the Isle of Wight. The attendance was estimated by its promoters to be 400,000 (see above). (*Illustrated London News*)

music, masses and litanies, of which only 70 were published before he died aged 35. His opera *The Clemency of Titus* (1791) was written in 18 days and three symphonic master-pieces, *Symphony No. 39 in E flat major, Symphony in G minor* and the *Jupiter Symphony in C*, were reputedly written in the space of 42 days in 1788. His overture *Don Giovanni* was written in full score at one sitting in Prague in 1787 and finished on the day of its opening performance.

Longest symphony

The longest of all single classical symphonies is the orchestral symphony No. 3 in D minor by Gustav Mahler (1860–1911) of Austria. This work, composed in 1895, requires a con-tralto, a women's and boys' choir and an organ, in addition to a full orchestra. A full performance requires 1 hour 34 min, of which the first movement alone takes 45 min. The Sym-phony No. 2 (the Gothic, or No. 1), composed in 1919–22 by Havergal Brian (1876–1972) has been performed only twice, on 24 June 1961 and 30 Oct. 1966. The total *ensemble* included 55 brass instruments, 31 wood wind, six kettle-drummers playing 22 drums, four vocal soloists, four large mixed choruses, a children's chorus and an organ. The symphony is continuous and required, when played as a recording on 27 Nov. 1967, 100 min. Brian wrote an even vaster work based on Shelley's "Prometheus Unbound" lasting 4 hrs 11 min but the full score has been missing since 1961. He wrote 27 symphonies, 4 grand operas and 7 large orchestral works between 1948 when he was 72 and 1968.

The symphony *Victory at Sea* written by Richard Rodgers and arranged by Robert Russell Bennett for N.B.C. T.V. in 1952 lasted for 13 hours.

Longest piano composition

The longest continuous non-repetitious piece for piano ever composed has been the Opus Clavicembalisticum by Kaikhosru Shapurji Sorabji (b. 1892). The composer himself gave it its only public performance on 1 Dec. 1930 in Glasgow, Scotland. The work is in 12 movements with a theme and 44 variations and a Passacaglia with 81 and a playing time of 2¾ hours.

The longest musical composition of any kind is all 40,320 possible permutations of the C major scale for piano or organ. The score is a computer print out in 16 volumes named *Sadist Factory* by its organiser Philip Crevier. The premiere was in Trinity College Chapel, Hartford, Connecticut, U.S.A. on 9–13 Aug. 1973 and required 9 players to play for exactly 100 hrs to reach the best part—the end.

Longest silence

The most protracted silence in a modern sheet music is one entitled *4 minutes 33 seconds* in a totally silent *opus* by John Cage (U.S.A.). Commenting on this trend among young composers, Igor Fyodorovich Stravinsky (1882–1971) said that he looked forward to their subsequent compositions being "works of major length".

HIGHEST PAID MUSICIANS

Pianist

Liberace (b. West Allis, Wisconsin, U.S.A., 16 May 1917) earns more than $2 million each 26 week season with a peak of $138,000 *(then £49,285)* for a single night's performance at Madison Square Gardens, New York City, U.S.A. in 1954.

The highest paid classical concert pianist was Ignace Jan Paderewski (1860–1941), Prime Minister of Poland (1919–20), who accumulated a fortune estimated at $5,000,000, of which $500,000 *(then £110,000)* was earned in a single season in 1922–23.

Singer *Most Successful*

Of great fortunes earned by singers, the highest on record are those of Enrico Caruso (1873–1921), the Italian tenor, whose estate was about $9,000,000 *(then £1,875,000)* and the Italian-Spanish coloratura soprano Amelita Galli-Curci (1889–1963), who received about $3,000,000 *(£750,000)*. In 1850, up to $653 was paid for a single seat at the concerts given in the United States by Johanna ("Jenny") Maria Lind, later Mrs. Otto Goldschmidt (1820–87), the "Swedish Nightingale". She had a range from g to e''' of which the

middle register is still regarded as unrivalled. The tenor Count John Francis McCormack (1884–1945) of Ireland gave up to 10 concerts to capacity audiences in a single season in New York City.

Worst

While no agreement exists as to the identity of history's greatest singer, there is unanimity on the worst. The excur-sions of the soprano Florence Foster Jenkins (1868–1944) into lieder and even high coloratura culminated on 25 Oct. 1944 in her sell-out concert at the Carnegie Hall, New York, U.S.A. The diva's (already high) high F was said to have been made higher in 1943 by a crash in a taxi. It is one of the tragedies of musicology that Madame Jenkins' *Clavelitos*, accompanied by Cosme McMoon, was never recorded for posterity.

Violinist

The Austrian-born Fritz Kreisler (1875–1962) is reputed to have received more than £1,000,000 in his career.

OPERA

Longest

The longest of commonly performed operas is *Die Meister-singer von Nürnberg* by Wilhelm Richard Wagner (1813–83) of Germany. A normal uncut performance of this opera as performed by the Sadler's Wells company between 24 Aug. and 19 Sept. 1968 entailed 5 hrs 15 min of music. An opera *The Life and Times of Joseph Stalin* performed in 7 acts at the Brooklyn Academy of Music, U.S.A. on 14–15 Dec. 1973 required 13 hrs 25 min. Act 7 was deemed by some to be the best.

Shortest

The shortest opera written was *The Deliverance of Thesus* by Darius Milhaud (b. Sept. 1892) first performed in 1928 which lasts for 7 min 27 secs.

Aria

The longest single aria, in the sense of an operatic solo, is is Brünnhilde's immolation scene in Wagner's *Gotterdam-merung*. A well-known recording of this has been precisely timed at 14 minutes 46 seconds.

Opera houses *Largest*

The largest opera house in the world is the Metropolitan Opera House, Lincoln Center, New York City, N.Y., U.S.A., completed in September 1966 at a cost of $45,700,000 *(then £16,320,000)*. It has a capacity of 3,800 seats in an audi-torium 451 ft *137 m* deep. The stage is 234 ft *71 m* in width and 146 ft *44,5 m* deep. The tallest opera house is one housed in a 42-storey building on Wacker Drive in Chicago, Illinois, U.S.A.

Most tiers

The Teatro della Scala (La Scala) in Milan, Italy, shares with the Bolshoi Theatre in Moscow, U.S.S.R., the distinction of having the greatest number of tiers. Each has six, with the topmost in Moscow being termed the Galurka.

Opera Singers *Youngest and Oldest*

The youngest opera singer in the world has been Jeanette Gloria La Bianca, born in Buffalo, New York on 12 May 1934, who sang Rosina in *The Barber of Seville* at the Teatro dell'Opera, Rome on 8 May 1950 aged 15 years 361 days, having appeared as Gilda in *Rigoletto* at Velletri 45 days earlier. Ginetta La Bianca was taught by Lucia Carlino and managed by Angelo Carlino. The tenor Giovanni Martinelli sang Emperor Altoum in *Turandot* in Seattle, Washington, U.S.A. on 4 Feb. 1967 when aged 81.

SONG

Oldest

The oldest known song is the *shaduf* chant, which has been sung since time immemorial by irrigation workers on the man-powered pivoted-rod bucket raisers of the Nile water mills (or *saqiyas*) in Egypt (now the United Arab Republic). The English song *Sumer is icumen in* dates from *c.* 1240.

National anthems

The oldest national anthem is the *Kimigayo* of Japan, in which the words date from the 9th century. The anthem of

Greece constitutes the first four verses of the Solomos poem, which has 158 stanzas. The shortest anthems are those of Japan, Jordan and San Marino, each with only four lines. Of the 23 wordless national anthems the oldest is that of Spain dating from 1770.

Longest rendering

"God Save the King" was played non-stop 16 or 17 times by a German military band on the platform of Rathenau Railway Station, Brandenburg, on the morning of 9 Feb. 1909. The reason was that King Edward VII was struggling inside the train with the uniform of a German Field-Marshal before he could emerge.

Top songs of all time

The most frequently sung songs in English are *Happy Birthday to You* (based on the original *Good morning to all*), by Mildred and Patty S. Hill of New York (published in 1935 and in copyright until 2010); *For He's a Jolly Good Fellow* (originally the French *Malbrouk*), known at least as early as 1781, and *Auld Lang Syne* (originally the Strathspey *I fee'd a Lad at Michaelmass*), some words of which were written by Robert Burns (1759–96). *Happy Birthday* was sung in space by the Apollo IX astronauts on 8 Mar. 1969.

Top selling sheet music

Sales of three non-copyright pieces are known to have exceeded 20,000,000 namely *The Old Folks at Home, Listen to the Mocking Bird* (1855) and *The Blue Danube* (1867). Of copyright material the two top-sellers are *Let Me Call You Sweetheart* (1910, by Whitson and Friedman) and *Till We Meet Again* (1918, by Egan and Whiting) each with some 6,000,000 by 1967.

Most successful songwriter

In terms of sales of single records, the most successful of all song writers has been Paul McCartney (see also Gramophone, Fastest sales, p. 103) formerly of the Beatles and now of Wings. Between 1962 and 1 Jan. 1977 he wrote jointly or solo 53 songs which sold a million or more.

Eurovision Contest

In the 22 contests since 1956 France has won 4 (1958–60–62–77) and shared in 1969. Luxembourg also won outright 4 times (1961–65–72–73). The U.K. won in 1967 (Sandie Shaw, *Puppet On A String*) and 1976 (Brotherhood of Man, *Save Your Kisses For Me*) and shared in 1969 (Lulu, *Boom, Bang-a-Bang*).

HYMNS

Earliest

There are believed to be more than 500,000 Christian hymns in existence. "Te Deum Laudamus" dates from about the 5th century, but the earliest exactly datable hymn is the French one "Jesus soit en ma teste et mon entendement" from 1490 translated into the well-known "God be in my head" in 1512.

Longest and shortest

The longest hymn is "Hora novissima tempora pessima sunt; vigilemus" by Bernard of Cluny (12th century), which runs to 2,966 lines. In English the longest is "The Sands of Time are sinking" by Mrs. Anne Ross Cousin, *née* Cundell (1824–1906), which is in full 152 lines, though only 32 lines in the Methodist Hymn Book. The shortest hymn is the single verse in Long Metre "Be Present at our Table Lord", anonymous but attributed to "J. Leland".

Most prolific hymnists

Mrs. Frances (Fanny) Jane Van Alstyne *née* Crosby (1820–1915), (U.S.A.) wrote 8,500 hymns although she had been blinded at the age of 6 weeks. She is reputed to have knocked off one hymn in 15 min. Charles Wesley (1707–88) wrote about 6,000 hymns. In the seventh (1950) edition of *Hymns Ancient and Modern* the works of John Mason Neale (1818–66) appear 56 times.

BELLS

Oldest *World*

The oldest bell in the world is reputed to be that found in the Babylonian Palace of Nimrod in 1849 by Mr. (later Sir) Austen Henry Layard (1817–94). It dates from *c*. 1000 B.C.

The most prolific hymnist of all-time, the blind Fanny Crosby (US) whose life-time score was 8,500. (*Bettmann Archive*)

Great Britain

The oldest *dated* bell in England is one hanging in Lissett church, near Bridlington, Humberside discovered in Oct. 1972 to bear the date MCCLIIII (1254). The oldest inscribed bell is at Caversfield church, Oxfordshire and may be dated *c*. 1210. The uninscribed bell, at the Parish Church of St. Nicholas, Lanark, Strathclyde in daily use was originally founded in 1110 and refounded in 1659, 1740 and 1835.

Heaviest *World*

The heaviest bell in the world is the Tsar Kolokol, cast in 1733 in Moscow, U.S.S.R. It weighs 193 tons *196 tonnes* measures 22 ft 8 in *6,9 m* diameter and over 19 ft *5,8 m* high, and its greatest thickness is 24 in *60 cm*. The bell is cracked, and a fragment, weighing about 11 tons/*tonnes* was broken from it. The bell has stood, unrung, on a platform in the Kremlin, in Moscow, since 1836.

The heaviest bell in use is the Mingun bell, weighing 55,555 viss or *90,52 tons* with a diameter of 16 ft 8½ in *5,09 m* at the lip, in Mandalay, Burma, which is struck by a teak boom from the outside. It was cast at Mingun late in the reign of King Bodawpaya (1782–1819). The heaviest swinging bell in the world is the Petersglocke in Cologne Cathedral, Germany, cast in 1923 with a diameter of 3,40 m *11 ft 1¾ in* weighing 25,4 tonnes *25.0 tons*.

The heaviest change ringing peal in the world is the ring of 13 bells, cast in 1938–39, weighing 16½ tons *16,7 tonnes*, in Liverpool Anglican Cathedral. The tenor bell, Emmanuel, weighs 82 cwt. 11 lb. *4 170,8 kg*.

Great Britain

The heaviest bell hung in Great Britain is "Great Paul" in St. Paul's Cathedral, London. It was cast in 1881, weighs 16 tons 14 cwt. 2 qrs. 19 lb. *17 tonnes* and has a diameter of 9 ft 6½ in *2,9 m*. "Big Ben", the hour bell in the clock tower of the House of Commons, was cast in 1858 and weighs 13 tons 10 cwt. 3 qrs. 15 lb. *13 761 kg*.

The heaviest bell ever cast in England and the heaviest tuned bell in the world is the bourdon bell of the Laura Spelman Rockefeller Memorial carillon in Riverside Church, New York City, N.Y., U.S.A. It weighs 18 tons 5 cwt. 1 qr. 18 lb. *18,5 tonnes* and is 10 ft 2 in *3 m* in diameter.

Carillon *Largest*

The largest carillon in the world is the Laura Spelman Rockefeller Memorial carillon in Riverside Church, New York City, U.S.A. with 74 bells weighing 102 tons.

Heaviest

The heaviest carillon in Great Britain is in St. Nicholas Church, Aberdeen, Scotland. It consists of 48 bells, the total weight of which is 25 tons 8 cwt. 2 qrs. 13 lb. *25 838 kg*. The bourdon bell weighs 4 tons 9 cwt. 3 qrs. 26 lb. *4 571 kg* and the carillon comprises four octaves, less the bottom semi-tone.

Bell Ringing

Eight bells have been rung to their full "extent" (a "Bob Major" of 40,320 changes) only once without relays. This took place in a bell foundry at Loughborough, Leicestershire, beginning at 6.52 a.m. on 27 July 1963 and ending at 00.50 a.m. on 28 July, after 17 hrs 58 min. The peal was composed by Kenneth Lewis of Altrincham, Greater Manchester, and the eight ringers were conducted by Robert B. Smith, aged 25, of Marple, Greater Manchester. Theoretically it would take 37 years 355 days to ring 12 bells (maximus) to their full extent of 479,001,600 changes. The greatest number of peals (minimum of 5,040 changes, all in tower bells) rung in a year is 209 by Mark William Marshall of Ashford, Kent in 1973. The late George E. Fearn rang 2,666 peals from 1928 to May 1974.

5. THEATRE

Origins

Theatre in Europe has its origins in Greek drama performed in honour of a god, usually Dionysus. The earliest amphitheatres date from the 5th century B.C. and the largest of all known is one at Megalopolis in central Greece, where the auditorium reached a height of 75 ft *23 m* and had a capacity of 17,000. The first stone built theatre in Rome erected in 55 B.C. could accommodate 40,000 spectators.

Oldest *World*

The oldest indoor theatre in the world is the Teatro Olimpico in Vicenza, Italy. Designed in the Roman style by Andrea di Pietro, *alias* Palladio (1508–80), it was begun three months before his death and finished in 1582 by his pupil Vicenzo Scamozzi (1552–1616). It is preserved today in its original form.

Great Britain

The earliest London theatre was James Burbage's "The Theatre", built in 1576 near Finsbury Fields, London. The oldest theatre still in use in Great Britain is The Royal, Bristol. The foundation stone was laid on 30 Nov. 1764, and the theatre was opened on 30 May 1766 with a "Concert of Music and a Specimen of Rhetorick". The City Varieties Music Hall, Leeds was a singing room in 1762 and so claims to outdate the Theatre Royal. Actors were legally rogues and vagabonds until the passing of the Vagrancy Act in 1824. The oldest amateur dramatic society is the Amateur Dramatic Club (A.D.C.) in Cambridge founded in the Hoop Hotel, Jesus Lane by F. C. Burnand in May 1855.

Largest *World*

The world's largest building used for theatre is the National People's Congress Building (*Ren min da hui tang*) on the west side of Tian an men Square, Peking, China. It was completed in 1959 and covers an area of 12.9 acres *5,2 ha*. The theatre seats 10,000 and is occasionally used as such as in 1964 for the play "The East is Red". The largest regular theatre in the world has been Radio City Music Hall in Rockefeller Center, New York City, N.Y., U.S.A. with a seating capacity of more than 6,200 people and thus 8 million per annum. The stage is 144 ft *44 m* wide and 66 ft 6 in *20,26 m* deep, equipped with a revolving turntable 43 ft *13,10 m* in diameter and three elevator sections, each 70 ft *21 m* long.

The greatest seating capacity of any regular theatre in the world is that of the "Chaplin" (formerly the "Blanquita") in Havana, Cuba. It was opened on 30 Dec. 1949 and has 6,500 seats.

Great Britain

The highest capacity theatre is the Odeon, Hammersmith, Greater London, with 3,485 seats in 1975. The largest theatre stage in Great Britain is the Opera House in Blackpool, Lancashire. It was re-built in July 1939 and has seats for 2,975 people. Behind the 45 ft *14 m* wide proscenium arch the stage is 110 ft *33 m* high, 60 ft *18 m* deep and 100 ft *30 m* wide, and there is dressing room accommodation for 200 artistes.

Britain's largest open air theatre is at Scarborough, North Yorkshire opened in 1932 with a seating capacity of 7,000 plus standing room for 9,000 and a 182 ft *55 m* long stage.

Smallest

The smallest regularly operated professional theatre in Great Britain is the Mull Little Theatre, Tobermory, Isle of Mull, Strathclyde, Scotland with a capacity of 36 seats.

Largest amphitheatre

The largest amphitheatre ever built is the Flavian amphitheatre or Colosseum of Rome, Italy, completed in A.D. 80. Covering 5 acres *2 ha* and with a capacity of 87,000, it has a maximum length of 612 ft *187 m* and maximum width of 515 ft *175 m*.

Longest runs

The longest continuous run of any show in the world is by *The Mousetrap* by Dame Agatha Mary Clarissa Christie, D.B.E. (*née* Miller, later Lady Mallowan) (1890–1976). This thriller opened on 25 Nov. 1952, at the Ambassadors Theatre (capacity 453) and moved after 8,862 performances "down the road" to St. Martin's Theatre on 25 Mar. 1974. The Silver Jubilee performance on 25 Nov. 1977 will be the 10,390th.

Revue

The greatest number of performances of any theatrical presentation is 40,200 (to July 1977) in the case of *The Golden Horseshoe Revue*—a show staged at Disneyland Park, Anaheim, California, U.S.A. The show was first put on on 17 July 1955. The three main performers Fulton Burley, Walley Baag and Betty Taylor play as many as five houses a day in a routine lasting 45 minutes. In Britain, the Brighton Corporation's variety show *Tuesday Night at the Dome* reached its 1,429th performance in 31 years on 3 May 1977.

Broadway

The Broadway record is 3,242 performances by *Fiddler on the Roof* which closed, after its first run, on 3 July 1972. It had opened on 22 Sept. 1964. Paul Lipson played 1,811 times as Tevye during which time he had ten "wives" and 58 "daughters". The world gross earnings reached $64,300,000 (£25.7 million) on an original investment of $375,000 (then £133,928). The off-Broadway musical show *The Fantasticks* by Tom Jones and Harvey Schmidt achieved its 7,072nd performance as it entered its 18th year at the Sullivan Street Playhouse, Greenwich Village, New York City on 3 May 1977. It has been played in a record 3,788 productions in 55 countries.

Musical shows

The longest-running musical show ever performed in Britain was *The Black and White Minstrel Show* later *Magic*

101

of the Minstrels. The aggregate number of performances was 6,464 with a total attendance of 7,794,552. The show opened at the Victoria Palace, London on 25 May 1962 and closed on 4 Nov. 1972. It re-opened for a season in June 1973 at the New Victoria and finally closed on 8 Dec. 1973.

One-man shows

The longest run of one-man shows is 849 by Victor Borge in his *Comedy in Music* from 2 Oct. 1953 to 21 Jan. 1956 at the Golden Theatre, Broadway, New York City. The world aggregate record for one-man shows is 1,700 performances of *Brief Lives* by Roy Dotrice (b. Guernsey, 5 May 1923) including 400 straight at the Mayfair Theatre, London ending on 20 July 1974. He was on stage for more than 2½ hours per performance of this 17th century monologue and required 3 hours for make up and 1 hour for removal of make-up so aggregating 40 weeks in the chair.

Most Durable Leading Actress

Dame Anna Neagle, D.B.E., played the lead role in *Charlie Girl* at the Adelphi Theatre, London for 2,062 of 2,202 performances between 15 Dec. 1965 and 27 Mar. 1971. She played the role a further 327 times in 327 performances in Australasia.

Shortest runs *World*

The shortest run on record was that of *The Intimate Revue* at the Duchess Theatre, London, on 11 March 1930. Anything which could go wrong did. With scene changes taking up to 20 min apiece, the management scrapped seven scenes to get the finale on before midnight. The run was described as "half a performance". In a number of Broadway productions the opening and closing nights have coincided.

Broadway

Of the many Broadway shows for which the opening and closing nights coincided, one of the more costly was *Kelly*, a musical costing $700,000 which underwent the double ceremony on 6 Feb. 1965.

Longest play

O'Casey by Patrick Funge played at the Lantern Theatre, Dublin, lasted 6 hrs 45 min playing time, opening on 24 July 1972 at 3 p.m. and finishing at 11.15 p.m. with a 90 min meal interval. George Begley was never off the stage. The 15th century Cornish Cycle of Mystery Plays was revived in English in July 1969, at the earthwork theatre, St. Piran's Round, Piran, near Perranporth, Cornwall, by the Drama Department of Bristol University. Three parts, *Origo Mundi*, *Passio*, and *Resurrectio*, ran for 12 hrs with two intermissions.

Shakespeare

The first all amateur company to have staged all 37 of Shakespeare's plays was The Southsea Shakespeare Actors, Hampshire, England (founded 1947), when in October 1966 they presented *Cymbeline*. The amateur director throughout was Mr. K. Edmonds Gateloy, M.B.E. Ten members of the Abbey Theatre Company, St. Albans, Hertfordshire, completed a dramatic reading of all the 37 plays, 154 sonnets and five narrative poems in 37 hours 52 mins on 11–12 Oct. 1975. The longest is *Hamlet* with 4,042 lines and 29,551 words. Of Shakespeare's 1,277 speaking parts the longest is Hamlet with 11,610 words.

Longest chorus line

The world's longest permanent chorus line is that formed by the Rockettes in the Radio City Music Hall, which opened in December 1932 in New York City, U.S.A. The 36 (now 30) girls danced precision routines across its 144 ft *43,9 m* wide stage. They have 10 reserves for vacations and other absences.

Cabaret fee

The highest night club fee in history has been $100,000 (then *£40,000*) collected by Liza Minnelli for the New Year's Eve show at the Colonie Hill Club, Long Island, New York on 1 Jan. 1975. Patrons paid $150 (*£65*) per seat.

Ice shows

Holiday on Ice Production Inc., founded by Morris Chalfen in 1945, stages the world's most costly live entertainment with up to seven productions playing simultaneously in several of 75 countries drawing 20,000,000 spectators paying $40 million (*£22.2 million*) in a year. The total skating and other staff exceeds 900. The most prolific producer of Ice Shows is Gerald Palmer with 132 since 1945 including 30 consecutive shows at Empire Pool, Wembley, London with attendances up to 537,000. Hazel Wendy Jolly (b. 1933) has appeared in the Wembley Winter Pantomime for 26 years.

Most Ardent Theatregoers

It has been estimated by the press that H. Howard Hughes (b. 1904) of Fort Worth, Texas, had seen 4,160 shows in the period 1956–1976. Britain's leading "first nighter" Edward Sutro (b. 1900) was reputed by the press to have attended his 3,000th first night as long ago as 1958. The highest firmly recorded number of theatre attendances in Britain is 3,112 shows in 24 years from 28 Mar. 1953 to 28 Mar. 1977 by John Iles of Salisbury, Wiltshire. He estimates he has travelled 128,860 miles *207 380 km* and seen 111,724 performers in 7,976 hours (47½ weeks) inside theatres.

Fashion Shows

The most prolific producer and most durable commentator of fashion shows is Adalene Ross of Palo Alto, California with totals about 4,500 in both categories to mid-1977.

6. GRAMOPHONE

Origins

The gramophone (phonograph) was first *conceived* by Charles Cros (1842–1888) a French poet and scientist, who described his idea in sealed papers deposited in the French Academy of Sciences on 30 Apr. 1877. However the realisation of a practical device was first *achieved* by Thomas Alva Edison (1847–1931) of the U.S.A. The first successful machine was constructed by his mechanic, John Kruesi on 4–6 Dec. 1877, demonstrated on the 7 Dec. and patented on the 19 Feb. 1878. Pre-recorded tapes were first marketed by Recording Associates in New York City, U.S.A. in 1950.

Earliest

The first practical hand cranked, wax coated cylinder phonograph was manufactured in the United States by Chichester Bell and Charles Sumner Tainter in 1886. The forerunner of the modern disc gramophone was patented in 1887 by Emile Berliner (1851–1929), a German immigrant to the U.S.A. Although a toy machine based on his principle was produced in Germany in 1889, the gramophone was not a serious commercial competitor to the cylinder phonograph until 1896.

Most Record Players

The country with the greatest number of record players is the United States, with a total of more than 72,000,000 by Dec. 1974. A total of more than half a billion dollars (*now £192 million*) is spent annually on 500,000 juke boxes in the United States.

In the United States retail sales of discs and tapes reached $2,277 million in 1975 which included sales for L.P.'s, cassettes and cartridges. The sale of units was 564 million.

Oldest Records

The B.B.C. record library, contains over 750,000 records, including 5,250 with no known matrix. An Edison solid wax cylinder, recorded in Edison's laboratory and dated 26 June 1888 is the oldest record in the library which also contains a collection of early Berliner discs.

Earliest jazz records

The earliest jazz record made was *Indiana* and *The Dark Town Strutters Ball*, recorded for the Columbia label in New York City, N.Y., U.S.A., on or about 30 Jan. 1917, by the Original Dixieland Jazz Band, led by Dominick (Nick) James La Rocca (1889–1961). This was released on 31 May 1917. The first jazz record to be released was the O.D.J.B.'s *Livery Stable Blues* (recorded 24 Feb.), backed by *The Dixie*

Jass Band One-Step (recorded 26 Feb.), released by Victor on 7 March 1917.

Smallest Record

The smallest functional gramophone record is one 1⅜ in *3,5 cm* in diameter of "God Save the King" of which 250 were made by HMV Record Co. in 1924.

Most successful solo recording artist

On 9 June 1960 the Hollywood Chamber of Commerce presented Harry Lillis (*alias* Bing) Crosby, Jr. (b. 2 May 1904 at Tacoma, Washington) with a platinum disc to commemorate a sale of 200,000,000 records from the 2,600 singles and 125 albums he had recorded. On 15 Sept. 1970 he received a second platinum disc for selling 300,650,000 discs with Decca. His global life-time sales on 179 labels have totalled, according to his royalty reports, 400,000,000 to July 1975. His first commercial recording was "*I've Got the Girl*" recorded on 18 Oct. 1926 (master number W142785 [Take 3] issued on the Columbia label).

The greatest recorded success in a single year has been the sale of 13.7 million albums in 1966 by the ex-Army trumpeter Herb Alpert (b. Los Angeles, 31 Mar. 1937) with his Tijuana Brass Band.

Most Successful group

The singers with the greatest sales of any group have been the Beatles. This group from Liverpool, Merseyside, comprised George Harrison, M.B.E. (b. 25 Feb. 1943), John Ono (formerly John Winston) Lennon, M.B.E. (b. 9 Oct. 1940), James Paul McCartney, M.B.E. (b. 18 June 1942) and Richard Starkey, M.B.E. *alias* Ringo Starr (b. 7 July 1940). Between February 1963 and June 1972 their group sales were estimated at 545 million in singles' equivalents. This included 85 million albums. The 40,000 strong Beatles Fan Club had been closed down on 31 Mar. 1972.

Golden Discs *Earliest*

The earliest recorded piece eventually to aggregate a total sale of a million copies were performances by Enrico Caruso (b. Naples, Italy, 1873, and d. 2 Aug. 1921) of the aria *Vesti la giubba* (*On with the Motley*) from the opera *I Pagliacci* by Ruggiero Leoncavallo (1858–1919), the earliest version of which was recorded with piano on 12 Nov. 1902. The first single recording to surpass the million mark was Alma Gluck's *Carry me back to old Virginny* on the Red Seal Victor label on the 12-inch *30,48 cm* single faced (later backed) record 74420. The first actual golden disc was one sprayed by R.C.A. Victor for presentation to the U.S. trombonist and band-leader Alton "Glen" Miller (1904–44) for his *Chattanooga Choo Choo* on 10 Feb. 1942.

Most

The only *audited* measure of million-selling records within the United States, is certification by the Recording Industry Association of America introduced 14 Mar. 1958. Out of the 1,899 R.I.A.A. gold record awards made to 1 Jan. 1977, the most have gone to The Beatles with 38 (plus one with Billy Preston) as a group. McCartney has 14 more awards outside the group and with Wings. The most awards to an individual is 28 to Elvis Aron Presley (b. Tupelo, Mississippi, U.S.A., 8 Jan. 1935) spanning 1958 to 1 Jan. 1977.

Most recorded song

Two songs have each been recorded between 900 and 1,000 times in the United States alone—*St. Louis Blues*, written in 1914 by W. C. (William Christopher) Handy (b. Florence, Alabama 1873 and d. 1958), and *Stardust*, written in 1927 by Hoagland ('Hoagy') Carmichael (b. Bloomington, Indiana, 22 Nov. 1899).

Most recordings

Miss Lata Mangeshker (b. 1928) between 1948 and 1974 has reportedly recorded not less than 25,000 solo, duet and chorus backed songs in 20 Indian languages. She frequently had 5 sessions in a day and has "backed" 1,800 films to 1974.

Biggest sellers

The greatest seller of any gramophone record to date is *White Christmas* by Irving Berlin (b. Israel Bailin, at Tyumen,

The most successful pop group in history, the Beatles. In 1955 John Lennon formed the Quarry Men. Paul McCartney and George Harrison later joined the group. Ringo Starr was added to the line up who made their first record as the Beatles in 1962. (*Popperfoto*)

Russia, 11 May 1888). First recorded in 1941, it reached 135,000,000 by December 1974. The highest claim for any "pop" record is an unaudited 25,000,000 for *Rock Around the Clock*, copyrighted in 1953 by James E. Myers under the name Jimmy DeKnight and the late Max C. Freedman and recorded on 12 Apr. 1954 by Bill Haley and the Comets. The top-selling British record of all-time is *I Want to Hold Your Hand* by the Beatles, released in 1963, with world sales of over 13,000,000.

Best sellers' charts

Best sellers' charts were first published in the U.S. periodical *Billboard* on 27 July 1940. The longest stay in the L.P. charts in the U.S.A. has been 490 weeks from late in 1958 to July 1968 by the Columbia album *Johnny's Greatest Hits* (Johnny Mathis). The first album ever to enter the *Billboard* list at No. 1 is *Captain Fantastic and the Brown Dirt Cowboy* by Elton John (b. Reg Dwight) in June 1975. The longest in the U.K. has been *Sound of Music* (sound track) with 362 weeks to April 1973. The longest reign at No. 1 in British singles charts has been 11 weeks for *Rose Marie* by Slim Whitman from 29 May 1955. *Release Me* by Englebert Humperdinck stayed in for 56 consecutive weeks from 26 Jan. 1967 and *My Way* by Frank Sinatra for 122 weeks between 2 Apr. 1969 to 1 Jan. 1972.

Top-selling L.P.

The best-selling L.P. is the 20th Century Fox album *Sing We now of Christmas*, issued in 1958 and re-entitled *The Little Drummer Boy* in 1963. Its sales were reported to be more than 14,000,000 by Nov. 1972. Carole King's *Tapestry* was in Billboard's Top 100 list in the period 1970–75 selling 13 million on the Ode label and grossing $65 million. The first British L.P. to sell 1,000,000 copies was *With the Beatles* (Parlophone), from November 1963 to January 1964 in the United States and to September 1965 in Britain. The top-selling British L.P. has been the double (4-sided) *Jesus Christ Superstar* by Andrew Lloyd Webber (b. 22 Mar. 1948) and Tim Rice (b. 10 Nov. 1944) released on 10 Oct. 1970. Sales are now approaching 6 million.

Top-selling L.P. sound track

The all-time best-seller among long-playing records of musical film shows is *The Sound of Music* sound track album, released by Victor in U.S.A. on 2 Mar. and in Britain on 9 Apr. 1965, with more than 19,000,000 to 1 Jan. 1973. In Britain it was No. 1 in the L.P. Charts for 69 weeks.

The collaborators in Britain's most successful L.P., Jesus Christ Superstar by Tim Rice (lyrics) and Andrew Lloyd Webber (music) (see page 103)

Fastest selling L.P.s

The fastest selling record of all time is *John Fitzgerald Kennedy—A Memorial Album* (Premium Albums), an L.P. recorded on 22 Nov. 1963, the day of Mr. Kennedy's assassination, which sold 4,000,000 copies at 99 cents (*then 35p*) in six days (7–12 Dec. 1963), thus ironically beating the previous speed record set by the satirical L.P. *The First Family* in 1962–63. The fastest selling British record has been the Beatles' double album *The Beatles* (Apple) with "nearly 2 million" in its first week in November 1968.

Advance sales

The greatest advance sale was 2,100,000 for *Can't Buy Me Love* by the Beatles, released in the United States on 16 Mar. 1964. The Beatles also equalled their British record record of 1,000,000 advance sales, set by *I want to Hold Your Hand* (Parlophone transferred to Apple Aug. 1968) on 29 Nov. 1963, with this same record on 20 Mar. 1964. The U.K. record for advance sales of an L.P. is 750,000 for the Parlophone album *Beatles for Sale* released on 4 Dec. 1964.

Top-selling classical L.P.

The first classical long-player to sell a million was a performance featuring the pianist Harvey Lavan (Van) Cliburn, Jr. (b. Kilgore, Texas, U.S.A., 12 July 1934) of the *Piano Concerto No. 1* by Pyotr Ilyich Tchaikovsky (1840–93) (more properly rendered Chaykovskiy) of Russia. This recording was made in 1958 and sales reached 1,000,000 by 1961, 2,000,000 by 1965 and about 2,500,000 by January 1970.

Longest L.P. set

The longest long-playing record is the 137-disc set of the complete works of William Shakespeare (1564–1616). The recordings, which were made in 1957–1964, cost £260.62½ per set, and are by the Argo Record Co. Ltd., London, S.W.3. The Vienna Philharmonic's playing of Wagner's "The Ring" covers 19 L.P.s, was eight years in the making and requires 14½ hrs playing time.

Loudest *Pop Group*

The amplification at *The Who* concert at Charlton Athletic Football Ground, London on 31 May 1976 provided by a Tasco P.A. System had a total power of 76,000 watts from eighty 800 W Crown D.C. 300 A Amplifiers and twenty 600 W Phase Linear 200's. The readings at 50 metres from the front of the sound system were 120 db.

Longest Silence

The earliest commercially released silent record was *Three Minutes of Silence* by C.B.S. engineers Hamilton M. O'Hara and Don Foster in 1953. It received rave notices and was rated a "coin grabber" in juke boxes. The longest silent L.P. *Auditory Memory* runs for 52 min 10 sec "recorded" in November 1974 by Jerry Cammarata of Staten Island, N.Y. and played on ABC network TV on 21 May 1976.

7. CINEMA

FILMS

Origins

The greatest impetus in the development of cinematography came from the inventiveness of Etienne Jules Marey (1830–1903) of France in the 1870's.

Earliest silent showings

The earliest demonstration of a celluloid cinematograph film on a screen was given at 44 Rue de Rennes, Paris on 22 Mar. 1895 by Auguste Marie Louis Nicolas Lumière (1862–1954) and Louis Jean Lumière (1864–1948). The film was entitled *La Sortie des Ouvriers de l'Usine Lumière* taken probably in August or September 1894 outside the factory gates at Lyons. Louis Aimé Augustin Le Prince, according to evidence in *The Shell Book of Firsts*, achieved dim moving outlines on a whitewashed wall at the Institute for the Deaf, Washington Heights, New York, U.S.A. as early as 1885.

Earliest 'Talkie'

The earliest sound-on-film motion picture was achieved by Eugene Augustin Lauste (b. Paris 17 Jan. 1857) who patented his process on 11 Aug. 1906 and produced a workable system using a string galvanometer in 1910 in London. The event is more usually attributed to Dr. Lee de Forest (1873–1961) in New York City, N.Y., U.S.A., on 13 March 1923. The first all-talking picture was *Lights of New York*, shown at The Strand, New York City, on 6 July 1928.

Most expensive film

The most expensive film ever made is the 6 hr 13 min long *War and Peace*, the U.S.S.R. government adaptation of the masterpiece of Tolstoy directed by Sergei Bondarchuk (b. 1921) over the period 1962–67. The total cost has been officially stated to be more than £40,000,000. More than 165,000 uniforms had to be made. The re-creation of the Battle of Borodino (7 Sept. 1812) involved 120,000 Red Army "extras" at 3 roubles (£1.38) per month.

Most expensive film rights

The highest price ever paid for film rights is $5,500,000 (*£2,000,000*) paid on 6 Feb. 1962 by Warner Brothers for *My Fair Lady*, which cost $17,000,000 (*£6,000,000*) thus making it the most expensive musical film then made.

Longest film

The longest film ever shown is *The Human Condition*, directed in three parts by Masaki Kobayashi of Japan. It lasts 8 hrs 50 min, excluding two breaks of 20 min each. It was shown in Tōkyō in October 1961 at an admission price of 250 yen (24½p). The longest film ever released was **** by Andy Warhol (b. Cleveland, Ohio, 1931) which lasted 24 hrs. It proved not surprisingly, except reportedly to its creator, a commercial failure and was withdrawn and re-released in 90 min form as *The Loves of Ondine*.

Highest box office gross

The film which has had the highest world gross earnings (amount paid by cinema owners) is *Jaws*, which in its first 78 days from 20 June 1975 grossed $124 million (*£55 million*) in North America alone. The film, based on a novel by Peter Benchley, cost some $8 million to make.

Highest earnings by an actor

The highest rate of pay in cinema history is $3,700,000 (*£2.2 million*) for 12 days work playing father to *Superman* by producer Ilya Salkind in advance of an 11.3% share of gross box-office receipts to Marlon Brando.

Largest Studios

The largest complex of film studios in the world are those at Universal City, South California. The Back Lot contains 561 buildings and there are 34 sound stages.

Walt Disney, creator of Mickey Mouse and Donald Duck, surrounded by his unrivalled collection of Oscars and other awards.

Oscars *Most*

Walter (Walt) Elias Disney (1901–1966) won more "Oscars" —the awards of the United States Academy of Motion Picture Arts and Sciences, instituted on 16 May 1929 for 1927–28—than any other person. The physical count is 29 including posthumous awards. The only actress to win three Oscars in a starring rôle has been Miss Katharine Hepburn, formerly Mrs. Ludlow Ogden Smith (b. Hartford, Conn., 9 Nov. 1909) in *Morning Glory* (1932–3), *Guess Who's Coming to Dinner* (1967) and *The Lion in Winter* (1968). Oscars are named after Mr. Oscar Pierce of Texas, U.S.A. The films with most awards have been *Ben Hur* (1959) with 11, followed by *Gone With the Wind* (1939) with 10 and *West Side Story* (1961) with 10. The film with the highest number of nominations was *All About Eve* (1950) with 14. It won four.

Newsreels

The world's most durable newsreel commentator has been Bob Danvers-Walker (b. Cheam, Surrey, 11 Oct. 1906), who commentated for Pathé "Gazette" from June 1940 until its demise in February 1970.

CINEMAS

Oldest

The earliest cinema was the "Electric Theatre", part of a tented circus in Los Angeles, California, U.S.A. It opened on 2 April 1902. The oldest building designed as a cinema is the Biograph Cinema in Wilton Road, Victoria, London. It was opened in 1905 and originally had seating accommodation for 500 patrons. Its present capacity is 700.

Largest *World*

The largest cinema in the world is the Radio City, New York City, with a capacity of 6,200 (see Theatres largest, page 101).

Great Britain

Great Britain's largest cinema is the Odeon Theatre, Hammersmith, Greater London, with 3,485 seats. The Playhouse, Glasgow had 4,235 seats.

Most cinema seats

The Falkland Islands and the Cook Islands have more cinema seats per total population than any other country in the world, with 250 seats for each 1,000 inhabitants. The Central African Republic has 2 cinemas and hence one seat per 4,100 people.

Highest cinema going

The people of Taiwan go to the cinema more often than those of any other country in the world with an average of 66 attendances per person per annum according to the latest data. The Soviet Union has the most cinemas in the world, with 147,200 in 1970 including those projecting only 16 mm film. The number of cinemas in the U.K. declined from 4,542 in 1953 to 1,565 screens on 31 Mar. 1977. The average weekly admissions declined from 24,700,000 in 1953 to 2,060,000 in 1976. The most persistent known cinema-goer is Paul Morgan 92, a retired car paint sprayer. Since 1949 he has attended the Rio cinema Theatre, Miami, Florida every day including Sundays although the programme is not changed more than thrice weekly. The manager states Mr. Morgan is always "first in line".

8. RADIO BROADCASTING

Origins

The earliest description of a radio transmission system was written by Dr. Mahlon Loomis (U.S.A.) (b. Fulton County, N.Y., 21 July 1826) on 21 July 1864 and demonstrated between two kites more than 14 miles *22 km* apart at Bear's Den, Loudoun County, Virginia in October 1866. He received U.S. patent No. 129,971 entitled Improvement in Telegraphing on 20 July 1872. He died in 1886.

Earliest patent

The first patent for a system of communication by means of electro-magnetic waves, numbered No. 12039, was granted on 2 June 1896 to the Italian-Irish Marchese Guglielmo Marconi, G.C.V.O. (Hon.) (1874–1937). A public demonstration of wireless transmission of speech was, however, given in the town square of Murray, Kentucky, U.S.A. in 1892 by Nathan B. Stubblefield. He died destitute on 28 March 1928. The first permanent wireless installation was at The Needles on the Isle of Wight, by Marconi's Wireless Telegraph Co., Ltd., in November 1896.

Earliest broadcast *World*

The world's first advertised broadcast was made on 24 Dec. 1906 by the Canadian born Prof. Reginald Aubrey Fessenden (1868–1932) from the 420 ft *128 m* mast of the National Electric Signalling Company at Brant Rock, Massachusetts, U.S.A. The transmission included Handel's *Largo*. Fessenden had achieved the broadcast of speech as early as November 1900 but this was highly distorted.

Great Britain

The first experimental broadcasting transmitter in Great Britain was set up at the Marconi Works in Chelmsford, Essex, in December 1919, and broadcast a news service in February 1920. The earliest regular broadcast was made from the Marconi transmitter "2 MT" at Writtle, Essex, on 14 Feb. 1922.

Transatlantic transmissions

The earliest transatlantic wireless signals (the letter S in Morse Code) were received by Marconi, George Stephen Kemp and Percy Paget from a 10 kw station at Poldhu, Cornwall, at Signal Hill, St. John's, Newfoundland, Canada, at 12.30 p.m. on 12 Dec. 1901. Human speech was first heard across the Atlantic in November 1915 when a transmission from the U.S. Navy station at Arlington, Virginia was received by U.S. radio-telephone engineers on the Eiffel Tower.

Earliest Radio-Microphones

The radio-microphone, which was in essence also the first "bug", was devised by Reg. Moores (G.B.) in 1947 and first used on 76 MHz in the ice show *Aladdin* at Brighton Sports Stadium, East Sussex in Sept. 1949.

Longest broadcast

The longest B.B.C. national broadcast was the reporting of the Coronation of Queen Elizabeth II on 2 June 1953. It began at 10.15 a.m. and finished at 5.30 p.m., after 7 hrs 15 min. The longest local radio transmission has been 12 hrs 5 min by B.B.C. Radio Bristol's programme "Mid Night Rally" on 25–26 Feb. 1977. The staff worked with students from their "I-level" programme.

The longest continuous broadcast (excluding disc-jockeying) has been one of 222 hrs 22 min by Bob Reitman on WQFM, Milwaukee, Wisconsin, U.S.A., on 12–21 Aug. 1976.

Most durable programmes *B.B.C.*

The most durable B.B.C. radio series is *The Week's Good Cause* beginning on 24 Jan. 1926. The longest running record programme is *Desert Island Discs* which began on 21 Jan. 1942 and on which programme the only guests to be thrice stranded have been Arthur Bowden Askey, O.B.E. (b. 6 June 1900) and Robertson Hare (b. 17 Dec. 1891). The *Desert Island* programme has been presented since its inception by Roy Plomley, O.B.E. who devised the idea. The longest running solo radio feature is *Letter from America* by (Alfred) Alistair Cooke, Hon. K.B.E. (b. Manchester 20 Nov. 1908), first commissioned as a series of 13 talks on 6 March 1946. The longest running radio serial is *The Archers* which was created by Godfrey Baseley and was first broadcast on 7 June 1950. Up to 1 Jan. 1977 the signature tune *Borwick Green* had been played 28,462 times. The only one of 363 roles which has been played without interruption from the start has been that of Philip Archer by Norman Painting O.B.E. (b. Leamington Spa 23 Apr. 1924).

Earliest Antipodal Reception

Frank Henry Alfred Walker (b. 11 Nov. 1904) on the night of 12 Nov. 1924 received on his home-made 2 valve receiver on 75 metres signals from Marconi's yacht *Electra* (call sign ICCM) in Australian waters at Crown Farm, Cuttimore Lane, Walton-on-Thames, Surrey, England.

Most stations

The country with the greatest number of radio broadcasting stations is the United States, where there were 7,426 authorized broadcast stations in 1974 of which 4,305 were AM (Amplitude modulation) and 2,413 FM (Frequency modulation).

Highest listenership

The peak recorded listenership on B.B.C. Radio was 30,000,000 adults on 6 June 1950 for the boxing fight between Lee Savold (U.S.) and Bruce Woodcock (G.B.).

Highest Response

The highest recorded response from a radio show occurred on 27 Nov. 1974 when on a 5 hour talk show on WCAU, Philadelphia, U.S.A., Howard Sheldon, the astrologist registered a call count of 388,299 calls on the "Bill Corsair Show".

9. TELEVISION

Invention

The invention of television, the instantaneous viewing of distant objects by electrical transmissions, was not an act but a process of successive and inter-dependent discoveries. The first commercial cathode ray tube was introduced in 1897 by Karl Ferdinand Braun (1850–1918), but was not linked to "electric vision" until 1907 by Boris Rosing of Russia in St. Petersburg (now Leningrad). A. A. Campbell Swinton F.R.S. published the fundaments of television transmission

A. A. Campbell Swinton whose paper on television published in 1908 was the earliest landmark in the ultimate invention of present day TV systems.

on 18 June 1908. The earliest public demonstration of television was given on 27 Jan. 1926 by John Logie Baird (1888–1956) of Scotland, using a development of the mechanical scanning system suggested by Paul Nipkov in 1884. A patent application for the Iconoscope (Number 2,141,059) had been filed on 29 Dec. 1923 by Dr. Vladimir Kosma Zworykin (born in Russia on 30 July 1889, became a U.S. citizen in 1924), and a short range transmission of a model windmill had been made on 13 June 1925 by C. Francis Jenkins in Washington, D.C., U.S.A. The first experimental transmission in Britain was on 30 Sept. 1929. Public transmissions on 30 lines were made from 22 Aug. 1932 until 11 Sept. 1935.

Earliest service

The world's first high definition (*i.e.* 405 lines) television broadcasting service was opened from Alexandra Palace, Haringey, Greater London, on 2 Nov. 1936, when there were about 100 sets in the United Kingdom. The Chief Engineer was Mr. Douglas Birkinshaw. A television station in Berlin, Germany, made a low definition (180 line) transmission from 22 March 1935. The transmitter burnt out in Aug. 1935.

Transatlantic transmission

The earliest transatlantic transmission by satellite was achieved at 1 a.m. on 11 July 1962, *via* the active satellite *Telstar 1* from Andover, Maine, U.S.A., to Pleumeur Bodou, France. The picture was of Mr. Frederick R. Kappell, chairman of the American Telephone and Telegraph Company, which owned the satellite. The first "live" broadcast was made on 23 July 1962 and the first woman to appear was the *haute couturière*, Ginette Spanier, directrice of Balmain, the next day. On 9 Feb. 1928 the image of J. L. Baird (see above) and of a Mrs. Howe was transmitted from Station 2 KZ at Coulsdon, Surrey, England to Station 2 CVJ, Hartsdale, N.Y., U.S.A.

Longest telecast

The longest pre-scheduled telecast on record was a continuous transmission for 163 hours 18 mins by GTV 9 of Melbourne, Australia covering the Apollo XI moon mission on 19–26 July 1969. The longest continuous TV transmission under a single director was the Avro Television Production *Open Het Dorpe* transmitted in the Netherlands on 26–27 November 1962 for 23 hrs 20 min under the direction of Theo Ordaman.

Most durable show

The world's most durable T.V. show is N.B.C.'s *Meet the Press* first transmitted on 6 Nov. 1947 and weekly since 12 Sept. 1948 originated by Lawrence E. Spivak, who appeared weekly as either moderator or panel member until 1975.

Most durable B.B.C. programme

The longest running T.V. programme on B.B.C. is *Panorama* which was first transmitted, introduced by Patrick Murphy, on 11 Nov. 1953. *Andy Pandy* was first transmitted on 11 July 1950 but consisted of repeats of a cycle of 26 shows until 1970. The seasonal programme *Come Dancing* was first transmitted on 12 Nov. 1951. "The News" started on 23 Mar. 1938.

Most sets

In 1975 the total estimated number of television transmitters in use or under construction was 19,870 serving 363,770,000 sets (91 for each 1,000 of the world population). Of these, about 121,000,000 were estimated to be in use in the United States where 99 per cent of the population is reached. The number of colour sets in the U.S.A. has grown from 200,000 in 1960 to 51,250,000 (74%) by Oct. 1975. The number of licences current in the United Kingdom was 18,056,058 on 31 Mar. 1977 of which 9,957,672 (55.14%) were for colour sets. Black and white sets became rarer than colour sets in 1976.

Greatest audience

The greatest estimated number of viewers for a televised event is 1,000 million for the live and recorded transmissions of the XXth Olympic Games in Munich, West Germany from 26 Aug. to 11 Sept. 1972.

Dean Martin in the year in which he signed the largest ever television contract for $34,000,000 (see below). (*BBC*)

Largest Contracts *World*

The largest T.V. contract ever signed was one for $34,000,000 (*then £14,166,666*) in a three-year no-option contract between Dino Paul Crocetti (b. 7 June 1917) otherwise Dean Martin, and N.B.C. in 1968.

Currently television's highest-paid performer is Johnny Carson the host of *The Tonight Show*. His current 3-year N.B.C. contract calls for annual payments of some $1,000,000 (*now £588,250*) for forty 4 day weeks with 12 week's vacation with perhaps double that in percentages on commercial fees. The talk show host Mike Douglas has a contract reported to be for $2 million (*£1,176,000*) for his syndicated show. The highest-paid current affairs or news performer is Barbara Walters of ABC *The Evening News* programme, who signed a 5-year $1 million a year contract on or about 21 Apr. 1976.

Mary Tyler Moore as head of her own production company will reputedly earn some $2,250,000 (*£1,325,000*) in the last series of the show in which she stars.

Great Britain

The largest contract in British television was one of a reported £9,000,000, inclusive of production expenses, signed by Tom Jones (b. Thomas Jones Woodward, 7 June 1940) of Treforest, Mid Glamorgan, Wales in June 1968 with ABC-TV of the United States and ATV in London for 17 one-hour shows per annum from January 1969 to January 1974.

Largest T.V. prizes *World*

The greatest amount won by an individual in T.V. prizes was $264,000 (*then £94,286*) by Teddy Nadler (b. 1910) of St. Louis, Missouri on quiz programmes in the United States up to September 1958. He reputedly had to pay $155,000 in federal and state taxes and has been unemployed since. On 24 July 1975 WABC-TV, New York City transmitted the first televised Grand Tier draw of the State Lottery in which the winner took the grand prize of $1,000,000 (*now £540,500*). This was however taxable.

Great Britain

The largest T.V. prize won in the U.K. is £5,580 by Bernard Davis, aged 33, on Granada T.V.'s "Twenty-one" quiz programme, reached on 24 Sept. 1958.

Most successful appeal

The greatest amount raised by any Television Appeal has been £1,520,000 raised by Jonathan Dimbleby for the Ethiopian and African Drought Appeal on both B.B.C. T.V. and I.B.A. (Thames T.V.) on 30 Oct. 1973.

Earliest T.V. critic

The first man in the world appointed to be a T.V. critic and correspondent was Leonard Marsland Gander (b. 27 June 1902) by the London *Daily Telegraph* in 1935—the year before the B.B.C.'s 405 line transmissions. He retired in July 1970 after spanning 35 yrs with T.V. and 44 yrs with radio.

Biggest sale

The greatest number of episodes of any T.V. programme ever sold has been 1,144 episodes of "Coronation Street" by Granada Television to CBKST Saskatoon, Saskatchewan, Canada, on 31 May 1971. This constituted 20 days 15 hrs 44 min continuous viewing.

Most prolific scriptwriter

The most prolific television writer in the world is the Rt. Hon. Lord Willis (b. 13 Jan. 1918), who in the period 1949–74 has created 21 series, including the first seven years and 2,250,000 words of *Dixon of Dock Green* which has been running since 1955, 20 plays and 21 features films. He had 18 plays produced. His total output since 1945 can be estimated at 15,000,000 words.

Highest T.V. advertising rates

The highest T.V. advertising rate has been $250,000 (*£104,000*) per minute for N.B.C. network prime time during the transmission of Paramount Pictures, *Godfather* bought by the network for $10 million (*£4,166,000*) on 30 July 1974. In Great Britain the I.B.A. peak time weekday network 30 sec spots rate was fixed in autumn 1975 at £11,580 or £386 per sec.

Most takes

The highest number of "takes" for a T.V. commercial is 28 in 1973 by Pat Coombs, the commedienne, who has supported Dick Emery on B.B.C. T.V. Her explanation was "Everytime we came to the punch line I just could not remember the name of the product".

Highest Paid TV Actor

Peter Falk, the disarmingly persistent detective *Columbo*, was paid from $300,000 to $350,000 (*£176,000–£205,000*) for a single episode of his series of six so totalling $1,950,000 (*£1,147,000*) in 1976.

Most Exposed Star on Commercials

JoAnn Cameron (b. 1951) appeared on 94 nationally programmed T.V. commercials in the United States in 1969–75 representing at least $100 million worth of advertising expenditure. "Katie" (real name Mary) Holland appeared in Britain's Brooke Bond Oxo commercials for 18 years (1958–1976).

Captions from top to bottom:

Marlon Brando whose rate of pay in *Superman* is an all-time record, a guaranteed $308,333 (*£181,372*) per day (see page 104). (*Cinema International Corp*)

Katie Holland who graced Independent Television's commercials for Oxo for an unrivalled 18 years. (*Bill McKenzie*)

The United State's most familiar face on television commercials, JoAnn Cameron.

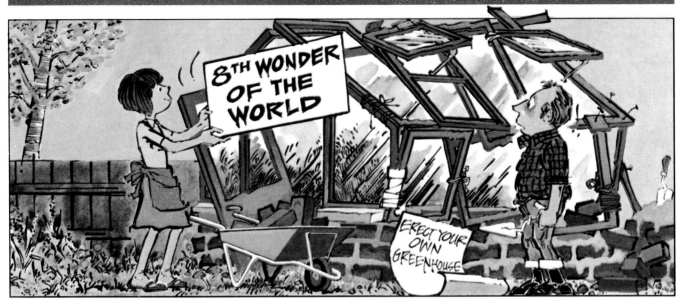

7. THE WORLD'S STRUCTURES

Note—Guinness Superlatives has published civil engineering records in greater detail in the more specialist publication, *Guinness Book of Structures — Bridges, Towers, Tunnels, Dams...* (£6.50) by John H. Stephens.

EARLIEST STRUCTURES

World

The earliest known human structure is a rough circle of loosely piled lava blocks found in 1960 on the lowest cultural level at the Lower Paleolithic site at Olduvai Gorge in Tanzania. The structure was associated with artifacts and bones and may represent a work-floor, dating to *c.* 1,750,000 B.C. The earliest evidence of *buildings* yet discovered is that of 21 huts with hearths or pebble-lined pits and delimited by stake holes found in October 1965 at the Terra Amata site in Nice, France thought to be belonging to the Acheulian culture of 120,000 years ago. Excavation carried out between 28 June and 5 July 1966 revealed one hut with palisaded walls with axes of 49 ft *15 m* and 20 ft *6 m*. The oldest free standing structures in the world are now believed to be the megalithic temples at Mgarr and Skarba in Malta and Ggantija in Gozo dating from *c.* 3,250 B.C.

Great Britain

A rudimentary platform of birch branches, stones and wads of clay thrown down on the edge of a swamp at Star Carr, south of Scarborough, North Yorkshire, may possibly represent the earliest man-made "dwelling" yet found in Britain (Mesolithic, 7607 B.C. ± 210). Remains of the earliest dated stone shelter and cooking pit were discovered in 1967 at Culver Well, Isle of Portland, Dorset (Mesolithic, 5200 B.C. ± 135). On the Isle of Jura, Strathclyde, Scotland a hearth consisting of three linked stone circles has been dated to the Mesolithic period 6013 ± 200 B.C.

Ireland

The earliest known structures in Ireland date from the Mesolithic period *c.* 6850–6500 B.C. A series of pits associated with post-holes have been excavated at a living site at Mount Sandel, Co. Derry.

---

1. BUILDINGS FOR WORKING

LARGEST BUILDINGS

Commercial *World*

The greatest ground area covered by any building in the world is that by the Ford Parts Redistribution Center, Pennsylvania Avenue, Brownstown Township, Michigan, U.S.A. It encloses a floor area of 3,100,000 ft² or 71.16 acres *28,8 ha.* It was opened on 20 May 1971 and employs 1,400 people. The fire control system comprises 70 miles *112 km* of pipelines with 37,000 sprinklers. The building with the largest cubic capacity in the world is the Boeing Company's main assembly plant at Everett, Washington State, U.S.A. completed in 1968 with a capacity of 200 million ft³ *5,6 million m³.*

Great Britain

The largest building in Britain is the Ford Parts Center at Daventry, Northamptonshire, which measures 1,978 × 780 ft *602 × 237 m* and 1.6 million ft² or 36.7 acres *14,86 ha.* It was opened on 6 Sept. 1972 at a cost of nearly £8 million. It employs 1,600 people and is fitted with 14,000 fluorescent lights.

Scientific

The most capacious scientific building in the world is the Vehicle Assembly Building (VAB) at Complex 39, the selected site for the final assembly and launching of the Apollo moon spacecraft on the Saturn V rocket, at the John F. Kennedy Space Center (KSC) on Merritt Island, Cape Canaveral, Florida, U.S.A. It is a steel-framed building measuring 716 ft *218 m* in length, 518 ft *158 m* in width and 525 ft *160 m* high. The building contains four bays, each with its own door 460 ft *140 m* high. Construction began in April 1963 by the Ursum Consortium. Its floor area is 343,500 ft² (7.87 acres *3,18 ha*) and its capacity is 129,482,000 ft³ *3 666 500 m³.* The building was "topped out" on 14 Apr. 1965 at a cost of $108,700,000 (*then £38.8 million*).

Administrative

The largest ground area covered by any office building is that of the Pentagon, in Arlington County, Virginia, U.S.A. Built to house the U.S. Defense Department's offices it was completed on 15 Jan. 1943 and cost an estimated $83,000,000 (*then £20,595,000*). Each of the outermost sides of the Pentagon is 921 ft *281 m* long and the perimeter of the building is about 1,500 yds *1 370 m*. The five storeys of the building enclose a floor area of 6,500,000 ft² *604 000 m²* (149.2 acres). During the day 29,000 people work in the building. The telephone system of the building has over 44,000 telephones connected by 160,000 miles *257 500 km* of cable and its 220 staff handle 280,000 calls a day. Two restaurants, six cafeterias and ten snack bars and a staff of 675 form the catering department of the building. The corridors measure 17 miles *27 km* in length and there are 7,748 windows to be cleaned.

Office

The largest office buildings in the world are The World Trade Center in New York City, U.S.A. with a total of 4,370,000 ft^2 (100.32 acres *40,6 ha*) of rentable space in each of the twin towers of which the taller is 1,350 ft *411,48 m.*

Single Office *Great Britain*

The largest single office in the United Kingdom is that of West Midlands Gas at Solihull, West Midlands, built by Spooners (Hull) Ltd. in 1962. It now measures 753 ft by 160 ft *230 by 49 m* (2.77 acres *1,12 ha*) in one open plan room accommodating 2,170 clerical and managerial workers.

TALLEST BUILDINGS

World

The tallest inhabited building in the world is the Sears Tower, the national headquarters of Sears, Roebuck & Co. in Wacker Drive, Chicago, Illinois with 110 storeys rising to 1,454 ft *443 m* and begun in March 1970. Its gross area is 4,400,000 ft^2 (101.0 acres *40,8 ha*). It was "topped out" on 4 May 1973. It surpassed the World Trade Center in New York City in height at 2.35 p.m. on 6 Mar. 1973 with the first steel column reaching to the 104th storey. The addition of two T.V. antennae brought the total height to 1,800 ft *548,64 m.* The building's population is 16,700 served by 103 elevators and 18 escalators. It has 16,000 windows.

Great Britain

The tallest office block in Britain is The National Westminster tower block in Bishopsgate, City of London due for completion in spring 1979. It has 49 storeys and 3 basement levels and is 600 ft 4 in *183 m* tall. The gross floor area is 636,373 ft^2 *59 121 m^2* or 14.6 acres.

HABITATIONS

Greatest altitude

The highest inhabited buildings in the world are those in the Indian–Tibet border fort of Bāsisi at *c.* 19,700 ft *5 988 m.* In April 1961, however, a 3-room dwelling was discovered at 21,650 ft *6 600 m* on Cerro Llullaillaco (22,058 ft *6 723 m*), on the Argentine-Chile border, believed to date from the late pre-Columbian period *c.* 1480. An unnamed settlement on the T'e-li-mo trail in southern Tibet is at an apparent altitude of 19,800 ft *6 019 m.*

Northernmost

The most northerly habitation in the world is the Danish Scientific station set up in 1952 in Pearyland, northern Greenland, over 900 miles *1 450 km* north of the Arctic Circle. Eskimo hearths dated to before 1000 B.C. were discovered in Pearyland in 1969. The U.S.S.R. and the United States have maintained research stations on ice floes in the Arctic. The U.S.S.R.'s "North Pole 15", which drifted 1,250 miles *2 000 km,* passed within 1¼ miles *2,8 km* of the North Pole in December 1967.

The most northerly continuously inhabited place is the Canadian Department of National Defence outpost at Alert on Ellesmere Island, Northwest Territories in Lat 82 ° 30' N. Long. 62 ° W set up in 1950.

Southernmost

The most southerly permanent human habitation is the United States' Scott-Amundsen South Polar Station (see page 61) completed in 1957 and replaced in 1975.

The City of London's tallest office block, the 600 ft *183 m* National Westminster Building in Bishopsgate. (*Panorama Commercial*)

above: The world's largest inhabited castle at Windsor, Berkshire, England constructed mainly in the 12th Century. (*John Rivers*)

below: Britain's largest Royal Palace at Hampton Court, Greater London. It was used by 13 British Monarchs. (*John Rivers*)

EMBASSIES AND CIVIC BUILDINGS
Largest
The largest embassy in the world is the U.S.S.R. embassy on Bei Xiao Jie, Peking, China, in the north-eastern corner of the Northern walled city. The whole 45 acre *18,2 ha* area of the old Orthodox Church mission (established 1728), now known as the *Bei guan*, was handed over to the U.S.S.R. in 1949. The largest in Great Britain is the United States of America Embassy in Grosvenor Square, London. The Chancery Building, completed in 1960, alone has 600 rooms for a staff of 700 on seven floors with a usable floor area of 255,000 ft² (5.85 acres *2,37 ha*).

Great Britain
The oldest municipal building in Britain is the Exeter Guildhall first referred to in a deed of 1160. The Tudor front was added in 1593.

INDUSTRIAL STRUCTURES
Tallest chimneys *World*
The world's tallest chimney is the $5.5 million International Nickel Company's stack 1,245 ft 8 in *379,6 m* tall at Copper Cliff, Sudbury, Ontario, Canada, completed in 1970. It was built by Canadian Kellogg Ltd., in 60 days and the diameter tapers from 116.4 ft *35,4 m* at the base to 51.8 ft *15,8 m* at the top. It weighs 38,390 tons *39 006 tonnes* and became operational in 1971. The world's most massive chimney and Europe's tallest is of 1,148 ft *350 m* at Puentes, Spain built by M. W. Kellogg Co. It contains 20,600 yd³ *15 750 m³* of concrete and 2.9 million lb. *1 315 tonnes* of steel and has an internal volume of 6.7 million ft³ *189 720 m³*.

Great Britain
The tallest chimney in Great Britain is one of 850 ft *259 m* at Drax Power Station, North Yorkshire, begun in 1966 and topped out on 16 May 1969. It has an untapered diameter of 87 ft 9 in *26 m* and has the greatest capacity of any chimney. The architects were Clifford Tee & Gale of London. The oldest known industrial chimney in Britain is the Stonedge Chimney, near Chesterfield, Derbyshire built to a height of 55 ft *16,76 m ante* 1771.

Cooling towers
The largest cooling tower in the world is that adjacent to the nuclear power plant at Uentrop, West Germany which is 590 ft *179,8 m* tall. It was completed in 1976. The largest in the United Kingdom are the Ferrybridge "C" power station, West Yorkshire, type measuring 375 ft *114 m* tall and 300 ft *91 m* across the base.

HANGARS
Largest *World*
The world's largest hangar is the Goodyear Airship hangar at Akron, Ohio, U.S.A. which measures 1,175 ft *358 m* long, 325 ft *99 m* wide and 200 ft *61 m* high. It covers 364,000 ft² (8.35 acres *3,38 ha*) and has a capacity of 55,000,000 ft³ *1,6 million m³*. The world's largest single fixed-wing aircraft hangar is the Lockheed-Georgia engineering test center at Marietta, Georgia measuring 630 ft by 480 ft *192 by 146 m* (6.94 acres *2,8 ha*) completed in 1967. The maintenance hangar at Frankfurt/Main Airport, West Germany has a slightly lesser area but a frontage of 902 ft *275 m*. The cable supported roof has a span of 130 m *426.5 ft.* Delta Air Lines' jet base on a 140 acre *56,6 ha* site at Hartsfield International Airport, Atlanta, Georgia, has 36 acres *14,5 ha* under roof.

Great Britain
The largest hangar building in the United Kingdom is the Britannia Assembly Hall at the former Bristol Aeroplane Company's works at Filton, Avon, now part of the British Aircraft Corporation. The overall width of the Hall is 1,054 ft *321 m* and the overall depth of the centre bay is 420 ft *128 m*. It encloses a floor area of 7½ acres *3,0 ha*. The cubic capacity of the Hall is 33,000,000 ft³ *934 000 m³*. The building was begun in April 1946 and completed by September 1949.

GRAIN ELEVATOR
Largest
The world's largest single-unit grain elevator is that operated by the C-G-F-Grain Company at Wichita, Kansas, U.S.A.

Consisting of a triple row of storage tanks, 123 on each side of the central loading tower or "head house", the unit is 2,717 ft *828 m* long and 100 ft *30 m* wide. Each tank is 120 ft *37 m* high, with an inside diameter of 30 ft *9 m* giving a total storage capacity of 20,000,000 bushels *7,3 million hl* of wheat. The largest collection of elevators in the world are the 23 at City of Thunder Bay, Ontario, Canada, on Lake Superior with a total capacity of 103.9 million bushels *37,4 million hl*.

GARAGES
Largest *World*
The world's largest parking garage is at O'Hare Airport, Chicago with 6 levels and a capacity for 9,250 cars. It is operated by Allright Auto Parks Inc., the world's largest parking company.

Great Britain
Great Britain's highest capacity underground car park is that under the Victoria Centre, Nottingham with a capacity of 1,650 cars opened in June 1972.

Private
The largest private garage ever built was one for 100 cars at the Long Island, New York mansion of William Kissam Vanderbilt (1849–1920).

Parking lot
The world's largest parking lot is believed to be that at the Lakewood Center, California with a capacity of 12,500 cars. (See page 159).

Filling station
The largest filling station of the 36,000 in the United Kingdom is the Esso service area on the M4 at Leigh Delamere, Wiltshire, opened on 3 Jan. 1972. It has 48 petrol and diesel pumps and extends over 43 acres *17,4 ha*. It cost £650,000, has a staff of 280 and can service two million vehicles a year.

SEWAGE WORKS
Largest *World*
The largest single full treatment sewage works in the world is the West-Southwest Treatment Plant, opened in 1940 on a site of 501 acres *203 ha* in Chicago, Illinois, U.S.A. It serves an area containing 2,940,000 people. It treated an average of 835,000,000 gal *3 795 million litres* of wastes per day in 1973. The capacity of its sedimentation and aeration tanks is 1 280 000 m³ *1.6 million yds³*.

Great Britain
The largest full treatment works in Britain and probably in Europe is the G.L.C. Beckton Works which serves a 2,966,000 population and handles a daily flow of 207 million gal *941 million litres* in a tank capacity of 757,000 ft³ *21 400 m³*.

GLASSHOUSE
Largest *Great Britain*
The largest glasshouse in the United Kingdom is one covering 7.34 acres *2,97 ha* owned by Van Heyningen Bros. at Holland Nurseries, Littlehampton, West Sussex.

WOODEN BUILDING
Largest
The world's largest building in timber is the asbestos fibre storage building completed in 1971 at Deception Bay, Quebec Roverie, Canada. It measures 760 ft *231,6 m* long with a clear span of 305 ft *92,96 m* and is 144 ft *43,89 m* high.

---

2. BUILDINGS FOR LIVING

WOODEN BUILDINGS
Oldest
The oldest wooden buildings in the world are those comprising the Pagoda, Chumanar gate and the Temple of Horyu (Horyu-ji), at Nara, Japan, dating from A.D. 607. The largest wooden building in the world, the nearby Daibutsu-den, built in 1704–11, once measured 285.4 ft long, 167.3 ft wide and 153.3 ft tall *87 × 51 × 46,75 m*. The present dimensions are 187 × 165.6 × 159.7 ft *57 × 50,5 × 48,7 m*.

CASTLES

Earliest *World*

Castles existed in all the great early civilizations, including that of ancient Egypt from 3,000 B.C. Fortified castles in the more accepted sense only existed much later. The oldest in the world is that at Gomdan, in the Yemen, which originally had 20 storeys and dates from before A.D. 100.

Great Britain

The oldest stone castle extant in Great Britain is Richmond Castle, Yorkshire, built in *c.* 1075. Iron Age relics from the first century B.C. or A.D. have been found in the lower levels of the Dover Castle site.

Ireland

The oldest Irish castle is Ferrycarrig near Wexford dating from *c.* 1180. The oldest castle in Northern Ireland is Carrickfergus Castle, County Antrim, Northern Ireland, which dates from before 1210.

Largest *United Kingdom and Ireland*

The largest inhabited castle in the world is the Royal residence of Windsor Castle at New Windsor, Berkshire. It is primarily of 12th century construction and is in the form of a waisted parallelogram 1,890 ft by 540 ft *576 by 164 m.* The total area of Dover Castle however covers 34 acres *13,75 ha* with a width of 1,100 ft *335,2 m* and a curtain wall of 1,800 ft *550 m* or if underground works are taken in, 2,300 ft *700 m.* The overall dimensions of Carisbrooke Castle (450 ft by 360 ft *110 by 137 m*), Isle of Wight, if its earthworks are included, are 1,350 ft by 825 ft *411 m by 251 m.* The largest castle in Scotland is Edinburgh Castle with a major axis of 1,320 ft *402 m* and measuring 3,360 ft *1 025 m* along its perimeter wall including the Esplanade. The most capacious of all Irish castles is Carrickfergus (see above) but that with the most extensive fortifications is Trim Castle, County Meath, built in *c.* 1205 with a curtain wall 1,455 ft *443 m* long.

Forts *Largest*

The largest ancient castle in the world is Prague Castle, Czechoslovakia originating in the 9th century. It is a very oblong irregular polygon with an axis of 570 m *1,870 ft* and an average traverse diameter of 128 m *420 ft* with a surface area of 7,28 hectares *18 acres.* Fort George, Ardersier, Highland built in 1748–1769 measures 2,100 ft *640 m* in length and has an average width of 620 ft *189 m.* The total site covers 42½ acres *17,2 ha.*

Thickest walls

The walls of Babylon north of Al Hillah, Iraq, built in 600 B.C., were up to 85 ft *26 m* in thickness. The walls of the Great Tower or Donjon of Flint Castle, built in 1277–80 are 23 ft *7,01 m* thick. The largest Norman keep in Britain is that of Colchester Castle measuring 152½ ft *46 m* by 111½ ft *34 m.*

PALACES

Largest *World*

The largest palace in the world is the Imperial Palace (*Gu gong*) in the centre of Peking (*Bei jing*, the northern capital), China, which covers a rectangle 1,050 yds by 820 yds *960 by 750 m* an area of 177.9 acres *72 ha.* The outline survives from the construction of the third Ming Emperor Yong le of 1307–20, but due to constant re-arrangements most of the intra-mural buildings are 18th century. These consist of 5 halls and 17 palaces of which the last occupied by the last Empress was the Palace of Accumulated Elegance (*Chu xia gong*) until 1924.

Residential

The largest residential palace in the world is the Vatican Palace, in the Vatican City, an enclave in Rome, Italy. Covering an area of 13½ acres *5,5 ha* it has 1,400 rooms, chapels and halls, of which the oldest date from the 15th century.

Great Britain

The largest palace in the United Kingdom in Royal use is Buckingham Palace, London, so named after its site, bought in 1703 by John Sheffield, the 1st Duke of Buckingham and Normandy (1648–1721). Buckingham House was reconstruc-

ted in the Palladian style between 1835 and 1836, following the design of John Nash (1752–1835). The 610 ft *186 m* long East Front was built in 1846 and refaced in 1912. The Palace, which stands in 39 acres *15,8 ha* of garden, has 600 rooms including a ballroom 111 ft *34 m* long.

The largest ever Royal palace has been Hampton Court Palace, Greater London, acquired by Henry VIII from Cardinal Wolsey in 1525 and greatly enlarged by the King and later by William III, Anne and George I, whose son George II was its last resident monarch. It covers 4 acres *1,6 ha* of a 669 acre *270,7 ha* site.

Largest moat

The world's largest moats are those which surround the Imperial Palace in Peking (see above). From plans drawn by French sources it appears to measure 54 yds *49 m* wide and have a total length of 3,600 yds *3 290 m.* The city's moats total in all 23½ miles *38 km.*

FLATS

Largest

The largest block of private flats in Britain is Dolphin Square, London, covering a site of 7½ acres *3 ha.* The building occupies the four sides of a square enclosing gardens of about three acres *1,2 ha.* Dolphin Square contains 1,220 separate and self-contained flats, an underground garage for 300 cars with filling and service station, a swimming pool, eight squash courts, a tennis court and an indoor shopping centre. It cost £1,750,000 to build in 1936 but was sold to Westminster City Council for £4,500,000 in January 1963. Its nine storeys house 3,000 people.

The Hyde Park development in Sheffield, South Yorkshire, comprises 1,322 dwellings and an estimated population of 4,675 persons. It was built between 1959 and 1966.

Tallest *World*

The tallest block of flats in the world are Lake Point Towers of 70 storeys, and 645 ft *197 m* in Chicago, Illinois, U.S.A.

Great Britain

The tallest residential block in Great Britain is the Shakespeare Tower in the Barbican in the City of London, which has 116 flats and rises to a height of 419 ft 2½ in *127,77 m* above the street. The first of the three towers was "topped out" in May 1971.

HOTELS

Largest *World*

The hotel with most rooms in the world is the 12 storey Hotel Rossiya in Moscow, U.S.S.R., with 3,200 rooms providing accommodation for 5,350 guests opened in 1967. It would thus require more than 8½ years to spend one night in each room. In addition there is a 21 storey "Presidential" tower in the central courtyard. The hotel employs about 3,000 people, and has 93 lifts. The ballroom is reputed to be the world's largest. Muscovites are not permitted as residents while foreigners are charged 16 times more than the very low rate charged to U.S.S.R. officials.

The largest commercial hotel building in the world, is the Waldorf Astoria, on Park Avenue, New York City, N.Y., U.S.A. It occupies a complete block of 81,337 ft² (1.87 acres *0,75 ha*) and reaches a maximum height of 625 ft 7 in *191 m.* The Waldorf Astoria has 47 storeys and 1,900 guests rooms and maintains the largest hotel radio receiving system in the world. The Waldorf can accommodate 10,000 people at one time and has a staff of 1,700. The restaurants have catered for parties up to 6,000 at a time. The coffee-maker's daily output reaches 1,000 gal *4 546 litres.* The electricity bill is $2,000,000 each year. The hotel has housed 6 Heads of States simultaneously and has both a resident gynaecologist and mortician.

Great Britain

The greatest sleeping capacity of any hotel in Great Britain is 1,859 in the London Penta Hotel, Cromwell Road, London S.W.7 with a staff of 419. It was opened in 1973. The Regent Palace Hotel, Piccadilly Circus, London, opened 20 May 1915, has however 225 more rooms totalling 1,140. The largest hotel is the Grosvenor House Hotel, Park Lane, London, which was opened in 1929. It is of 8 storeys covering 2½ acres *1 ha* and caters for more than 100,000 visitors per year in 470 rooms. The Great Room is the largest hotel room measuring 181 ft by 131 ft *55 by 40 m* with a height of 23 ft *7 m*. Banquets for 1,500 are frequently handled.

Tallest

The tallest hotel in the world, measured from the street level of its main entrance to the top, is the 723 ft *220,3 m* tall 70 storey Peachtree Center Plaza, Atlanta, Georgia, U.S.A. The $50 million 1,100 room hotel is operated by Western International Hotels and owned by Portman Properties. Their Detroit Plaza measuring from the rear entrance level is however 748 ft *227,9 m* tall. Britain's tallest hotel is the 27 storey 380 ft *132,24 m* tall London Penta Hotel (see p. 112).

Most expensive

The world's costliest hotel accommodation is The Celestial Suite on the ninth floor of the Astroworld Hotel Houston, Texas which is rented for $2,500 (*now £1,350*) a day. It makes the official New York City Presidential Suite in the Waldorf Astoria at $850 (*now £500*) a day seem positively lower middle-class.

The most expensive hotel suites in Britain are the luxury suites in the London Hilton, Park Lane, London W.1. A suite for two is £291 60p (incl. V.A.T.) per night in mid-1977. Breakfast is extra. A single suite at the Inter-Continental, Park Lane costs £237 60p.

Spas

The largest spa in the world measured by number of available hotel rooms is Vichy, Allier, France, with 14,000 rooms, Spas are named after the watering place in the Liège province of Belgium where hydropathy was developed from 1626. The highest French spa is Baréges, Hautes-Pyrénées, at 4,068 ft *1 240 m* above sea level.

HOUSING
Largest estate

The largest housing estate in the United Kingdom is the 1,670-acre *675 ha* Becontree Estate, on a site of 3,000 acres *1 214 ha* in Barking and Redbridge, Greater London, built between 1921 and 1929. The total number of homes is 26,822, with an estimated population of nearly 90,000.

New towns

Of the 23 new towns being built in Great Britain that with the largest eventual planned population is Milton Keynes, Buckinghamshire, with 250,000 planned for 1992.

Largest house *World*

The largest private house in the world is the 250-room Biltmore House in Asheville, North Carolina, U.S.A. It is owned by George and William Cecil, grandsons of George Washington Vanderbilt II (1862–1914). The house was built between 1890 and 1895 in an estate of 119,000 acres *48 160 ha*, at a cost of $4,100,000 (now (*£1,708,333*) and now valued at $55,000,000 with 12,000 acres *4 856 ha*. The most expensive private house ever built is The Hearst Ranch at San Simeon, California, U.S.A. It was built in 1922–39 for William Randolph Hearst (1863–1951), at a total cost of more than $30,000,000 (*then £6,120,000*). It has more than 100 rooms, a 104 ft *32 m* long heated swimming pool, an 83 ft *25 m* long assembly hall and a garage for 25 limousines. The house required 60 servants to maintain it.

Great Britain

The largest house in Great Britain was Wentworth Wood-house, near Rotherham, South Yorkshire, formerly the seat of the Earls Fitzwilliam and now a teacher's training college. The main part of the house, built over 300 years ago, has more than 240 rooms with over 1,000 windows, and its principle façade is 600 ft *183 m* long. The Royal residence, Sandringham House, Norfolk, has been reported to have had 365 rooms before the demolition of 73 surplus rooms in 1975. The largest house in Ireland is Castletown in County Kildare, owned by the Hon. Desmond Guinness and is the headquarters of the Irish Georgian Society. Scotland's largest house is Hopetoun House, West Lothian, built between 1696 and 1756 with a west façade 675 ft *206 m* long.

Smallest

The smallest house in Britain is the 19th century fisherman's cottage on Conway Quay, Gwynedd. It has a 72 in *182 cm* frontage, is 122 in *309 cm* high and has two tiny rooms and a staircase.

Most expensive *House*

The Georgian town house in Grafton Street, Mayfair, City of Westminster, formerly the home of Lord Brougham, was sold to the Irish Life Assurance Co. on 28 Aug. 1973 for £3,350,000. It is now let to Mr. Henry Ford II. The highest asking price for a private furnished house is £3,800,000 by Mr. Ravi Tikkóó, for Kenstead Hall, The Bishop's Avenue, Hampstead, London. The buyer by private treaty on 6 Apr. 1977 was reported to be King Khaled of Saudi Arabia for his nephew Prince Faisal.

Penthouse

The world's most expensive penthouse is the four storey Galleria International penthouse on 57th Street between Park and Lexington Avenue, Manhattan, New York City with 4 main bedrooms, a 22 ft swimming pool, a library, a sauna and several solariums. It was on the market in March 1976 for £1,750,000.

Stately home most visited

The most visited stately home, for which precise figures are published in the United Kingdom, is Beaulieu, Hampshire, owned by Lord Montagu of Beaulieu with 528,217 (1975/76) visitors. The figures for Woburn Abbey, Bedfordshire, owned by the Duke of Bedford, have not been published since 1963 but the annual attendance including that of the Woburn Wild Animal Kingdom exceeds 1,000,000.

Barracks

The oldest purpose built barracks in the world are believed to be Collins Barracks, formerly the Royal Barracks, Dublin Ireland completed in 1704 and still in use.

---

3. BUILDINGS FOR ENTERTAINMENT

STADIUM
Largest *World*

The world's largest stadium is the Strahov Stadium in Praha (Prague), Czechoslovakia. It was completed in 1934 and can accommodate 240,000 spectators for mass displays of up to 40,000 Sokol gymnasts.

Football

The largest football stadium in the world is the Maracaña Municipal Stadium in Rio de Janeiro, Brazil, where the football ground has a normal capacity of 205,000, of whom 155,000 may be seated. A crowd of 199,854 was accommodated for the World Cup final between Brazil and Uruguay on 16 July 1950. A dry moat, 7 ft *2,13 m* wide and more than 5 ft *1,5 m* deep, protects players from spectators and *vice versa*. Britain's most capacious football stadium is Hampden Park, Glasgow opened on 31 Oct. 1903 and once surveyed to accommodate 184,000 compared with an attendance of 149,547 on 17 Apr. 1937 and the present licensed limit of 135,000.

Covered

The Azteca Stadium, Mexico City, Mexico, opened in 1968, has a capacity of 107,000 of whom nearly all are under cover. The largest covered stadium in Britain is the Empire Stadium Wembley, Brent, Greater London, opened in April 1923. It was the scene of the 1948 Olympic Games and the final of the 1966 World Cup. In 1962–63 the capacity under cover was increased to 100,000 of whom 45,000 may be seated. The original cost was £1,250,000.

Largest Roof

The transparent acryl glass "tent" roof over the Munich Olympic Stadium, West Germany measures 914,940 ft² (21.0 acres *8,5 ha*) in area resting on a steel net supported by masts. The roof of longest span in the world is the 680 ft

207,2 m diameter of the Louisiana Superdome (see below). The major axis of the eliptical Texas Stadium completed in 1971 at Irving, Texas is however 240 m *787 ft 4 in.*

Indoor

The world's largest indoor stadium is the 13 acre $173 million (*then £75 million*) 273 ft *83,2 m* tall Superdome in New Orleans, Louisiana completed in May 1975. Its maximum seating capacity for conventions is 97,365 or 76,791 for football. Box suites rent for $35,000 excluding the price of admission. A gondola with six 312 inch *7,92 m* T.V. screens produces instant replay.

Largest ballroom

The largest ballroom in the United Kingdom is Tiffany's, Purley, Croydon, Greater London. The room is over 200 ft *60 m* long and 117 ft *35,7 m* wide, and has a total floor area of 23,320 ft² *2 170 m²*. When laid out for dance championships, the floor of the Earl's Court Exhibition Hall, Kensington, London is 256 ft *78 m* in length

Amusement resort

The world's largest amusement resort is Disney World in 27,443 acres *11 105 ha* of Orange and Osceola counties, 20 miles *32 km* south of west of Orlando in central Florida. It was opened on 1 Oct. 1971. This $400 million investment attracted 10,700,000 visitors in its first year. The most attended resort in the world is Disneyland, Anaheim, California where the total number of visitors reached 144,000,000 by 1 Oct. 1976.

Holiday Camps

The largest holiday camp in Britain is that at Filey, North Yorkshire owned by Butlins Ltd. It extends over 500 acres *200 ha* and can house 10,600 residents.

Largest Pleasure Beach

The largest pleasure beach in the world is Virginia Beach, Virginia, U.S.A. It has 28 miles *45 km* of beach front on the Atlantic and 10 miles *16 km* of estuary frontage. The area embraces 255 miles² *660 km²* and 134 hotels and motels.

Longest pleasure pier

The longest pleasure pier in the world is Southend Pier at Southend-on-Sea in Essex. It is 1.34 miles *2,15 km* in length. It was first opened in August 1889 with final extensions made in 1929. It is decorated with more than 75,000 lamps. The peak attendance was 5,750,000 in 1949–50.

Earliest Fair

The earliest major international fair was the Great Exhibition of 1851 in the Crystal Palace, Hyde Park, City of Westminster, Greater London which in 141 days attracted 6,039,195 admissions.

Largest Fair

The largest ever fair ground was that for the New York World's Fair, covering 1,216½ acres *492 ha* of Flushing Meadow Park, Queens Borough, Long Island, New York, U.S.A. between 20 April 1939 and 21 Oct. 1940 with 25,817,265 admissions. In 1964–65 there was an attendance of 51,607,037 for the second fair staged there.

Record Fair attendance

The record attendance for any fair was 65,000,000 for Expo 70 held on an 815 acre *330 ha* site at Osaka, Japan from March to 13 Sept. 1970. It made a profit of more than £11,000,000.

Big Wheel

The original Ferris Wheel, named after its constructor, George W. Ferris (1859–96), was erected in 1893 at the Midway, Chicago, Illinois, at a cost of $385,000 (*then £79,218*) It was 250 ft *76 m* in diameter, 790 ft *240 m* in circumference, weighed 1,070 tons *1 087 tonnes* and carried 36 cars each seating 60 people, making a total of 2,160 passengers. The structure was removed in 1904 to St. Louis, Missouri, and was eventually sold as scrap for $1,800 (*then £370*). In 1897 a Ferris Wheel with a diameter of 300 ft *91 m* was erected for the Earl's Court Exhibition, London. It had ten 1st-class and 30 2nd-class cars. The largest wheel now operating is the Riesenrad in the Prater Park, Vienna, Austria with a diameter of 197 ft *60 m*. It was built by the British engineer Walter Basset in 1896 and carried 15 million people in its first 75 years to 13 June 1971.

Fastest switchback

The maximum speeds claimed for switchbacks, scenic railways or roller coasters tend to be exaggerated for commercial reasons. The world's highest are the 110 ft *33,5 m* high "The Racer" in Chapultepec Park, Mexico City and "The Screamin' Eagle" at Eureka, Missouri, U.S.A. Even the highest of all-time, the 120 ft *36,5 m* now demolished "Blue Streak" in Woodcliffe Pleasure Park, Poughkeepsie, New York, could produce only 57 m.p.h. *91,7 km/h.*

The longest roller-coaster is "The Comet" at Crystal Beach Park, Ontario, Canada with a track of 4,800 ft *1,46 km.*

Restaurant *Highest*

The highest restaurant in Great Britain is the Ptarmigan Observation Restaurant at 3,650 ft *1 112 m* above sea-level on Cairngorm (4,084 ft *1 244 m*) near Aviemore, Highland, Scotland.

Kitchen *Largest*

The largest kitchen ever set up has been the Indian Government field kitchen set up in April 1973 at Ahmadnagar, Maharashtra in the famine area which daily provided 1.2 million subsistence meals.

Night Club *Oldest*

The earliest night club (*boite de nuit*) was "Le Bal des Anglais" at 6 Rue des Anglais, Paris, 5e France. It was founded in 1843 but closed c. 1960.

Largest

The largest night club in the world is Gilley's Club (formerly Shelly's) built in 1955 and extended in 1971 on Spencer Highway, Houston, Texas, U.S.A. with a seating capacity of more than 3,000 and a total capacity of 5,500. In the more classical sense the largest night club in the world is "The Mikado" in the Akasaka district of Tōkyō, Japan, with a seating capacity of 2,000. It is "manned" by 1,250 hostesses, some of whom earn an estimated £6,000 per annum. A binocular is essential to an appreciation of the floor show.

Lowest

The lowest night club is the "Minus 206" in Tiberias, Israel on the shores of the Sea of Galilee. It is 206 m *676 ft* below sea-level. An alternative candidate is "Outer Limits", opposite the Cow Palace, San Francisco, California which was raided for the 151st time on 1 Aug. 1971. It has been called "The Most Busted Joint" and "The Slowest to Get the Message".

PUBLIC HOUSES
Oldest

There are various claimants to the title of the United Kingdom's oldest inn. A foremost claimant is "The Fighting Cocks", St. Albans, Hertfordshire (an 11th century structure on an 8th century site). The timber frame of The Royalist Hotel, Digbeth Street, Stow-on-the-Wold, Gloucestershire has been dated to 1,000 years before the present. It was the inn "The Eagle and the Child" in the 13th century and known to exist in A.D. 947. An origin as early as A.D. 560 has been claimed for "Ye Olde Ferry Boat Inn" at Holywell, Cambridgeshire. There is some evidence that it antedates the local church, built in 980, but the earliest documents are not dated earlier than 1100. There is evidence that the "Bingley Arms", Bardsey, near Leeds, West Yorkshire, restored and extended in 1738 existed as the "Priest's Inn" according to Bardsey Church records dated 905.

Largest *World*

The largest beer-selling establishment in the world is the Mathäser, Bayerstrasse 5, München (Munich), West Germany, where the daily sale reaches 84,470 pts *48 000 litres*. It was established in 1829, was demolished in World War II and re-built by 1955 and now seats 5,500 people.

The through-put at the Dube beer halls in the Bantu township of Soweto, Johannesburg, South Africa may, however, be higher on some Saturdays when the average consumption of 6,000 gal (48,000 pts *27 280 litres*) is far exceeded.

Great Britain

The largest public house in Great Britain is "The Swan" at Yardley, West Midlands. It has eight bars with a total drinking area of 13,852 ft² *1 287 m²* with 58 taps and 2 miles *3,2 km* of piping. The sale of beer is equivalent to 31,000 bottles per week. The pub can hold well over 1,000 customers and 320 for banqueting. The permanent staff totals 60 with seven resident. "The Swan" is owned by Allied Breweries and administered by Ansells Limited.

Smallest

The smallest pub in Great Britain is the 17th century "The Nutshell", Bury St. Edmunds, Suffolk with maximum dimensions of 15 ft 10 in by 7 ft 6 in *4,82 × 2,28 m*.

Longest bars *World*

The longest permanent bar with beer pumps is that built in 1938 at the Working Men's Club, Mildura, Victoria, Australia. It has a counter 298 ft *90,8 m* in length, served by 27 pumps. Temporary bars have been erected of greater length. The Falstaff Brewing Corp. put up a temporary bar 336 ft 5 in *102 m* in length on Wharf St., St. Louis, Missouri, U.S.A., on 22 June 1970.

United Kingdom and Ireland

The longest bar in the United Kingdom with beer pumps is the French Bar (198 ft 5½ in *60,5 m*) at Butlin's Holiday Camp, Filey, North Yorkshire. It has 20 beer pumps, 12 tills and stillage for 30 barrels, and is operated by 30 barmaids, 20 floor waiters and 20 other hands. The longest bar in a pub is the 45 ft *13,72 m* counter in "Downham Tavern" Bromley, Greater London. The Grand Stand Bar at Galway Racecourse, Ireland completed in 1955, measures 210 ft *64 m*.

Highest

The highest public house in the United Kingdom is the "Tan Hill Inn" in Yorkshire. It is 1,732 ft *528 m* above sea-level, on the moorland road between Reeth, North Yorkshire and Brough, Cumbria. The highest pub open the year round is the "Cat and Fiddle" in Cheshire, near Buxton, Derbyshire at 1,690 ft *515 m*. The White Lady Restaurant, 2,550 ft *777 m* up on Cairngorm (4,084 ft *1 244 m*) near Aviemore, Highland, Scotland is the highest licensed restaurant.

Longest name

The English pub with the longest name was the 39 letter "The Thirteenth Mounted Cheshire Rifleman Inn", at Stalybridge, Greater Manchester. The word "Mounted" is now omitted making "The London, Chatham and Dover Railway Tavern" (37 letters), the champion.

Shortest name

Public houses in the United Kingdom with a name of only two letters include the "C.B." Hotel Arkengarthdale, near Richmond, North Yorkshire, The "H.H." at Cheriton, Hampshire and the "Ox" in Lebberston, near Filey, North Yorkshire.

Commonest name

The commonest pub name in Britain is "Red Lion" of which there are probably just more than 1,000.

Wine cellar

The largest wine cellars in the world are at Paarl, those of the Ko-operative Wijnbouwers Vereeniging, known as K.W.V. near Cape Town, in the centre of the wine-growing district of South Africa. They cover an area of 25 acres *10 ha* and have a capacity of 30,000,000 gal *136 million litres*. The largest blending vats have a capacity of 45,700 gal *207 750 litres* and are 17 ft *5 m* high, with a diameter of 26 ft *8 m*.

above: Britain's tallest hotel, the 380 ft *132 m* London Penta Hotel (see pages 112–113).

below: The Nutshell, Bury St. Edmunds, Suffolk, the smallest of the United Kingdom's 73,000 pubs. (*Henry A. Kiddy*)

4. TOWERS AND MASTS

TALLEST STRUCTURES
World

The tallest structure in the world is the guyed Warszawa Radio mast at Konstantynow near Gabin and Płock 60 miles *96 km* north-west of the capital of Poland. It is 646,38 m *2,120 ft 8 in* tall or more than four tenths of a mile. The mast was completed on 18 July 1974 and put into operation on 22 July 1974. It was designed by Jan Polak and weighs 550 tons/*tonnes*. The mast is so high that anyone falling off the top would reach their terminal velocity and hence cease to be accelerating before hitting the ground. Work was begun in July 1970 on this tubular steel construction, with its 15 steel guy ropes. It recaptured for Europe a record held in the U.S.A. since the Chrysler Building surpassed the Eiffel Tower in 1929.

Great Britain

The tallest structure in the United Kingdom is the Independent Broadcasting Authority's mast at Belmont, north of Horncastle, Lincolnshire completed in 1965 to a height of 1,265 ft *385 m* with 7 ft *2,13 m* added by meteorological equipment installed in September 1967. It serves Anglia T.V. and weighs 210 tons.

TALLEST TOWERS
World

The tallest self-supporting tower (as opposed to a guyed mast) in the world is the $44 million CN Tower in Metro Centre, Toronto, Canada, which rises to 1,815 ft 5 in *553,33 m*. Excavation began on 12 Feb. 1973 for the 130,000 ton structure of reinforced, post-tensioned concrete topped out on 2 Apr. 1975. The 400-seat restaurant revolves in the Sky Pod at 1,140 ft *347,5 m* from which the visibility extends to 74½ miles *120 km*.

The tallest tower built before the era of television masts is the Eiffel Tower, in Paris, France, designed by Alexandre Gustav Eiffel (1832–1923) for the Paris exhibition and completed on 31 March 1889. It was 300,51 m *985 ft 11 in* tall, now extended by a T.V. antenna to 320,75 m *1,052 ft 4 in* and weighs 7 340 tonnes *7,224 tons*. The maximum sway in high winds is 12,7 cm *5 in*. The whole iron edifice which has 1,792 steps, took 2 years, 2 months and 2 days to build and cost 7,799,401 francs 31 centimes.

Great Britain

The tallest self-supported tower in Great Britain is the 1,080 ft *329,18 m* tall Independent Broadcasting Authority transmitter at Emley Moor, West Yorkshire, completed in September 1971. The structure, which cost £900,000, has an enclosed room at the 865 ft *263,65 m* level and weighs with its foundations more than 15,000 tons/*tonnes*. The tallest tower of the pre-television era was the New Brighton Tower of 562 ft *171,29 m* built on Merseyside in 1897–1900 and dismantled in 1919–1921.

5. BRIDGES

Oldest *World*

Arch construction was understood by the Sumerians as early as 3200 B.C. and a reference exists to a Nile bridge in 2650 B.C. The oldest surviving dateable bridge in the world is the slab stone single arch bridge over the River Meles in Smyrna (now Izmir), Turkey, which dates from *c.* 850 B.C.

Great Britain

The clapper bridges of Dartmoor and Exmoor (*e.g.* the Tarr Steps over the River Barle, Exmoor, Somerset) are thought to be of prehistoric types although none of the existing examples can be certainly dated. They are made of large slabs of stone placed over boulders. The Romans built stone bridges in England and remains of these have been found at Corbridge (Roman, Corstopitum), Northumberland dating to the 2nd century A.D.; Chester, Northumberland and Willowford, Cumbria. Remains of a very early wooden bridge, have been found at Ardwinkle, Northamptonshire.

LONGEST
Cable suspension *World*

The world's longest single span bridge is the Verrazano-Narrows Bridge stretching across the entrance to New York City Harbour from Richmond, Staten Island to Brooklyn. Work on the $305,000,000 (*then £109 million*) project began on 13 Aug. 1959 and the bridge was opened to traffic on 21

A PROGRESSIVE RECORD OF THE TALLEST STRUCTURES IN THE WORLD

Height in ft	m	Structure	Location	Material	Building or Completion Dates
204	62	Djoser step pyramid (earliest Pyramid)	Saqqâra, Egypt	Tura limestone	c. 2650 B.C
294	89	Pyramid of Meidun	Meidun, Egypt	Tura limestone	c. 2600 B.C.
c. 336	102	Snefru Bent pyramid	Dahshûr, Egypt	Tura limestone	c. 2600 B.C.
342	104	Snefru North Stone pyramid	Duhshûr, Egypt	Tura limestone	c. 2600 B.C.
480.9[1]	146,5	Great Pyramid of Cheops (Khufu)	El Gizeh, Egypt	Tura limestone	c. 2580 B.C.
525[2]	160	Lincoln Cathedral, Central Tower	Lincoln, England	lead sheathed wood	c. 1307–1548
489[3]	149	St. Paul's Cathedral spire	City of London, England	lead sheathed wood	1315–1561
465	141	Minster of Notre Dame	Strasbourg, France	Vosges sandstone	1420–1439
502[4]	153	St. Pierre de Beauvais spire	Beauvais, France	lead sheathed wood	–1568
475	144	St. Nicholas Church	Hamburg, Germany	stone and iron	1846–1847
485	147	Rouen Cathedral spire	Rouen, France	cast iron	1823–1876
513	156	Köln Cathedral spires	Cologne, West Germany	stone	–1880
555[5]	169	Washington Memorial	Washington, D.C., U.S.A.	stone	1848–1884
985.9[6]	300,5	Eiffel Tower	Paris, France	iron	1887–1889
1,046	318	Chrysler Building	New York City, U.S.A.	steel and concrete	1929–1930
1,250[7]	381	Empire State Building	New York City, U.S.A.	steel and concrete	1929–1930
1,572	479	KWTV Television Mast	Oklahoma City, U.S.A.	steel	Nov. 1954
1,610[8]	490	KSWS Television Mast	Roswell, New Mexico, U.S.A	steel	Dec. 1956
1,619	493	WGAN Television Mast	Portland, Maine, U.S.A.	steel	Sept. 1959
1,676	510	KFVS Television Mast	Cape Girardeau, Missouri, U.S.A.	steel	June 1960
1,749	533	WTVM & WRBL Television Mast	Columbus, Georgia, U.S.A.	steel	May 1962
1,749	533	WBIR-TV Mast	Knoxville, Tennessee, U.S.A.	steel	Sept. 1963
2,063	628	KTHI-TV Mast	Fargo, North Dakota, U.S.A.	steel	Nov. 1963
2,120.6	646,38	Warszawa Radio Mast	Płock, Poland	galvanised steel	July 1974

[1] *Original height. With loss of pyramidion (topmost stone) height now 449 ft 6 in 137 m.*
[2] *Fell in a storm.*
[3] *Struck by lightning and destroyed 4 June 1561.*
[4] *Fell April 1573, shortly after completion.*
[5] *Sinking at a rate of 0.0047 ft per annum or 5 in 12,7 cm since 1884.*

[6] *Original height. With addition of T.V. antenna in 1957, now 1,052 ft in 320,75 m.*
[7] *Original height. With addition of T.V. tower on 1 May 1951 now 1,427 ft 449 m. On 11 Oct. 1972 it was revealed that the top 15 storeys might be replaced by 33 to give the old champion 113 storeys and a height of 1,494 ft 455,37 m.*
[8] *Fell in gale in 1960.*

The north tower at Hessle, Humberside of what will be the world's longest suspension bridge. It will be 1⅝ in *40 mm* out of parallel with the south tower at Barton to allow for the curvature of the earth (see right above). (*Freeman Fox and Partners*)

The main span of the £54 million Humber Estuary Bridge, England will be the longest in the world at 4,626 ft *1 410 m* when completed in March 1979. Work began on 27 July 1972. The towers are 162,5 m *533 ft 1⅝ in* tall from datum and are 1⅝ in *40 mm* out of parallel, to allow for the curvature of the Earth. Including the Hessle and the Barton side spans the bridge stretches 2 220 m or 1.37 miles.

The double-deck road-rail Akashi-Kaikyo bridge linking Honshu and Shikoku, Japan is expected to be completed in 1988. The main span will be 5,840 ft *1 780 m* in length with an overall suspended length with side spans totalling 11,680 ft *3 560 m*.

Great Britain

The longest span bridge in Great Britain is the Firth of Forth Road Bridge with a main channel span of 3,300 ft *1 006 m* and side spans of 1,340 ft *408 m* each, opened on 4 Sept. 1964. The main towers each stand 512 ft *156 m* high. It is the seventh longest span in the world and cost £11,000,000 including the viaducts. The approach roads cost £9 million.

Cantilever *World*

The Quebec Bridge (Pont de Québec) over the St. Lawrence River in Canada has the longest cantilever truss span of any in the world—1,800 ft *549 m* between the piers and 3,239 ft *987 m* overall. It carries a railway track and 2 carriageways. Begun in 1899, it was finally opened to traffic on 3 Dec. 1917 at a cost of 87 lives, and $Can.22,500,000 (*then £4,623,000*).

Great Britain

The longest cantilever bridge in Great Britain is the Forth Bridge. Its two main spans are 1,710 ft *521 m* long. It carries a double railway track over the Firth of Forth 156 ft *47,5 m* above the water level. Work commenced in November 1882 and the first test trains crossed on 22 Jan. 1890 after an expenditure of £3 million. It was officially opened on 4 March 1890. Of the 4,500 workers who built it, 57 were killed in various accidents.

Steel arch *World*

The longest steel arch bridge in the world is the New River Gorge bridge, near Fayetteville, West Virginia, U.S.A., completed in 1977 with a span of 1,700 ft *518,2 m*.

Great Britain

The longest steel arch bridge in Great Britain is the Runcorn-Widnes bridge, Cheshire opened on 21 July 1961. It has a span of 1,082 ft *329,8 m*.

Floating bridge

The longest floating bridge in the world is the Second Lake Washington Bridge, Seattle, Washington State, U.S.A. Its total length is 12,596 ft *3 839 m* and its floating section measures 7,518 ft *2 291 m* (1.42 miles *2,29 km*). It was built at a total cost of $15,000,000 (*then £5,357,000*) and completed in August 1963.

Covered bridge

The longest covered bridge in the world is that at Hartland, New Brunswick, Canada measuring 1,282 ft *390,8 m* completed in 1899.

Railway bridge

The longest railway bridge in the world is the Huey P. Long Bridge, Metairie, Louisiana, U.S.A. with a railway section 22,996 ft *7 009 m* (4.35 miles *7 km*) long. It was completed on 16 Dec. 1935 with a longest span of 790 ft *241 m*. It is sometimes claimed that the Yangtse River Bridge, completed in 1968 in Nanking, China is the world's longest railway bridge if the rail deck of 6 772 m *4.20 miles* is added to the road deck (4 589 m *2.85 miles*) to make 11 361 m *7.05 mile*.

Great Britain

The longest railway bridge in Britain is the second Tay Bridge (11,653 ft *3 552 m*), Tayside, Scotland opened on 20 June 1887. Of the 85 spans, 74 (length 10,289 ft *3 136 m*) are over the waterway.

Nov. 1964. It measures 1.26 miles *2 039 m* between anchorages and carries two decks, each of six lanes of traffic. The centre span is 4,260 ft *1 298 m* and the main towers are 690 ft *210 m* tall.

The Mackinac Straits Bridge between Mackinaw City and St. Ignace, Michigan, U.S.A., is the longest suspension bridge in the world measured between anchorages (1.58 miles *2 543 m*) and has an overall length, including viaducts of the bridge proper measured between abutment bearings, of 3.63 miles *5 853,79 m*. It was opened in November 1957 (dedicated 28 June 1958) at a cost of $100 million (*then £35,700,000*) and has a main span of 3,800 ft *1 158 m*.

HIGHEST
World
The highest bridge in the world is the bridge over the Royal Gorge of the Arkansas River in Colorado, U.S.A. It is 1,053 ft *321 m* above the water level. It is a suspension bridge with a main span of 880 ft *268 m* and was constructed in 6 months, ending on 6 Dec. 1929. The highest railway bridge in the world is the single track span at Fades, outside Clermont-Ferrand, France. It was built in 1901–09 with a span of 472 ft *144 m* and is 435 ft *132,5 m* above the River Sioule.

Great Britain
The highest railway bridge in Great Britain is the Ballochmyle viaduct over the River Ayr, Strathclyde built 169 ft *51,5 m* over the river bed in 1846–48 with the then world's longest masonry arch span of 181 ft *55,16 m*.

Widest World
The world's widest long-span bridge is the 1,650 ft *502,9 m* span Sydney Harbour Bridge, Australia (160 ft *48 m* wide). It carries two electric overhead railway tracks, 8 lanes of roadway and a cycle and footway. It was officially opened on 19 Mar. 1932. The Crawford Street Bridge in Providence, Rhode Island, U.S.A., has a width of 1,147 ft *350 m*. The River Roch is bridged for a distance of 1,460 ft *445 m* where the culvert passes through the centre of Rochdale, Greater Manchester and this is sometimes claimed to be a breadth.

Longest bridging
The world's longest bridging is the Second Lake Pontchartrain Causeway, completed on 23 March 1969, joining Lewisburg and Metairie, Louisiana, U.S.A. It has a length of 126,055 ft *38 422 m* (23.87 miles). It cost $29,900,000 (*then £12.45 million*) and is 228 ft *69 m* longer than the adjoining First Causeway completed in 1956. The longest railway viaduct in the world is the rock-filled Great Salt Lake Railroad Trestle, carrying the Southern Pacific Railroad 11.85 miles *19 km* across the Great Salt Lake, Utah, U.S.A. It was opened as a pile and trestle bridge on 8 Mar. 1904, but converted to rock fill in 1955–60.

The longest stone arch bridging in the world is the 3,810 ft *1 161 m* long Rockville Bridge north of Harrisburg, Pennsylvania, U.S.A., with 48 spans containing 196,000 tons/*tonnes* of stone and completed in 1901.

AQUEDUCTS
World longest *Ancient*
The greatest of ancient aqueducts was the Aqueduct of Carthage in Tunisia, which ran 87.6 miles *141 km* from the springs of Zaghouan to Djebel Djougar. It was built by the Romans during the reign of Publius Aelius Hadrianus (A.D. 117–138). By 1895, 344 arches still survived. Its original capacity has been calculated at 7,000,000 gal *31,8 million litres* per day. The triple-tiered aqueduct Pont du Gard, built in A.D. 19 near Nîmes, France, is 160 ft *48 m* high. The tallest of the 14 arches of Aguas Livres Aqueduct, built in Lisbon, Portugal, in 1784 is 213 ft 3 in *65 m*.

World longest *Modern*
The world's longest aqueduct, in the modern sense of a water conduit, as opposed to an irrigation canal, is the California State Water Project aqueduct, completed in 1974, to a length of 826 miles *1329 km* of which 385 miles *619 km* is canalized.

Great Britain *longest*
The longest aqueduct in Great Britain is the Pont Cysylltau in Clwyd on the Frankton to Llantisilio branch of the Shropshire Union Canal. It is 1,007 ft *307 m* long, has 19 arches up to 121 ft *36 m* high above low water on the Dee. It was designed by Thomas Telford (1757–1834) of Scotland, and was opened for use in 1805.

---

6. CANALS

Earliest *World*
Relics of the oldest canals in the world, dated by archaeologists *c.* 4000 B.C., were discovered near Mandali, Iraq early in 1968.

Earliest *Great Britain*
The first canals in Britain were undoubtedly cut by the Romans. In the Midlands the 11 mile *17 km* long Fossdyke Canal between Lincoln and the River Trent at Torksey was built in about A.D. 65 and was scoured in 1122. Part of it is still in use today. Though the Exeter canal was cut as early as 1564–68, the first wholly artificial major navigation canal in the United Kingdom was the Bridgewater canal dug in 1759–61. It ran from Worsley, Greater Manchester. Parts of the Sankey Canal from St. Helens, Merseyside to Widnes, Cheshire were, however, dug before the Bridgewater Canal.

Longest *World*
The longest canalized system in the world is the Volga-Baltic Canal opened in April 1965. It runs 1,850 miles *2 300 km* from Astrakhan up the Volga, *via* Kuybyshev, Gor'kiy and Lake Ladoga, to Leningrad, U.S.S.R. The longest canal of the ancient world has been the Grand Canal of China from Peking to Hangchou. It was begun in 540 B.C. and not completed until 1283 by which time it extended (including canalized river sections) for 1,107 miles *1 781 km*. The estimated work force at one time reached 5,000,000. Having been allowed by 1950 to silt up to the point that it was in no place more than 6 ft *1,8 m* deep, it is now, however, plied by ships of up to 2,000 tons/*tonnes*.

The Beloye More (White Sea) Baltic Canal from Belomorsk to Povenets, in the U.S.S.R., is 141 miles *227 km* long with 19 locks. It was completed with the use of forced labour in 1933 and cannot accommodate ships of more than 16 ft *5 m* in draught.

The world's longest big ship canal is the Suez Canal linking the Red and Mediterranean Seas, opened on 16 Nov. 1869 but inoperative from June 1967 to June 1975. The canal was planned by the French diplomatist Count Ferdinand de Lesseps (1805–94) and work began on 25 April 1859. It is 100.6 miles *161,9 km* in length from Port Said lighthouse to Suez Roads and 197 ft *60 m* wide. The construction work force was 8,213 men and 368 camels.

The busiest big ship canal is the Panama first transited on 15 Aug. 1914. In 1974 there were a record 14,304 ocean-going transits. The largest liner to transit is *Queen Elizabeth 2* (66,851 gross tons) on 25 Mar. 1975 for a toll of $42,077.88. The ships with the greatest beam to transit have been the *Acadia Forest* and the *Atlantic Forest* of 106.9 ft *32,58 m*. The lowest toll was 36 U.S. cents by the swimmer Richard Halliburton in 1928. The fastest transit has been 4 hr 38 min by the destroyer *U.S.S. Manley*.

Longest *Great Britain*
Inland Waterways in Great Britain, normally defined as non-tidal (except for a few tidal "links" on the Thames, Trent and Yorkshire Ouse) rivers and canals, consist of 2,390 miles *3 846 km* with 106 miles *170,5 km* being restored. Of this total 2,121 miles *3 413 km* are inter-linked.

The longest possible journey on the system would be one of 408¼ miles *657,0 km* and 153 locks from above Roxton, on the Great Ouse near Bedford to near Ripon, North Yorkshire.

Largest seaway
The world's longest artificial seaway is the St. Lawrence Seaway (189 miles *304 km* long) along the New York State-Ontario border from Montreal to Lake Ontario, which enables 80 per cent of all ocean-going ships, and bulk carriers with a capacity of 26,000 tons *26 400 tonnes* to sail 2,342 miles *3 769 km* from the North Atlantic, up the St. Lawrence estuary and across the Great Lakes to Duluth, Minnesota, U.S.A., on Lake Superior (602 ft *183 m* above sea level). The project cost $470,000,000 (*then £168 million*) and was opened on 25 Apr. 1959.

Irrigation canal
The longest irrigation canal in the world is the Karakumskiy Kanal, stretching 528 miles *850 km* from Haun-Khan to Ashkhabad, Turkmenistan, U.S.S.R. In September 1971 the "navigable" length reached 280 miles *450 km*. The length of the £370 million project will reach 930 miles *1 300 km*.

Canals

LOCKS

Largest *World*

The world's largest single lock is that connecting the Schelde with the Kanaaldok system at Zandvliet, west of Antwerp, Belgium. It is 500 m *1,640 ft* long and 57 m *187 ft* wide and is an entrance to an impounded sheet of water 18 km *11.2 miles* long.

Largest *Great Britain*

The largest lock on any canal system in the United Kingdom is the Eastham Large Lock, Eastham, Merseyside, on the Manchester Ship Canal. It can handle craft up to 600 ft *182 m* long and 80 ft *24 m* beam.

Deepest *World*

The world's deepest lock is the John Day dam lock on the Columbia river, Oregon and Washington, U.S.A. completed in 1963. It can raise or lower barges 113 ft *34,4 m* and is served by a 982 ton *998 tonne* gate.

Deepest *Great Britain*

The deepest lock in Britain is the rebuilt Lock 8/9 at Bath on the Kennet and Avon Canal which will lower boats 19½ ft *5,94 m*.

Longest flight

The world's highest lock elevator is at Arzwiller-Saint Louis in France. The lift was completed in 1969 to replace 17 locks on the Marne-Rhine canal system. It drops 146 ft *44,5 m* over a ramp 383.8 ft *116,9 m* long on a 41 degree gradient.

The longest flight of locks in the United Kingdom is on the Worcester and Birmingham Canal at Tardebigge, Hereford and Worcester, where in a 2½ mile *4 km* stretch there are the Tardebigge (30) and Stoke (6) flights which together drop the canal 259 ft *78,9 m*.

Largest cut

The Gaillard Cut (known as "the Ditch") on the Panama Canal is 270 ft *82 m* deep between Gold Hill and Contractor's Hill with a bottom width of 500 ft *152 m*. In one day in 1911 as many as 333 dirt trains each carrying 357 tons *363 tonnes* left this site. The total amount of earth excavated for the whole Panama Canal was 8,910,000 tons *9 053 000 tonnes* which total will be raised by the further widening of the Gaillard Cut.

7. DAMS

Earliest

The earliest dam ever built was the Sadd al-Kafara, seven miles *11,3 km* south-east of Helwan, United Arab Republic. It was built in the period 2950 to 2750 B.C. and had a length of 348 ft *106 m* and a height of 37 ft *11 m*.

Most massive

Measured by volume, the largest dam in the world is the 98 ft *29,8 m* high New Cornelia Tailings earthfill dam, Arizona, U.S.A. with a volume of 274,026,000 yd³ *209 506 000 m³* completed in 1973 to a length of 6.74 miles *10,85 km*.

Largest concrete

The world's largest concrete dam, and the largest concrete structure in the world, is the Grand Coulee Dam on the Columbia River, Washington State, U.S.A. Work on the dam was begun in 1933, it began working on 22 Mar. 1941 and was completed in 1942 at a cost of $56 million. It has a crest length of 4,173 ft *1 272 m* and is 550 ft *167 m* high. It contains 10,585,000 yds³ *8 092 000 m³* of concrete and weighs about 19,285,000 tons *19 595 000 tonnes*. The hydro-electric power plant (now being extended) will have a capacity of 9,780,000 kw.

Highest

The highest dam in the world is the Grande Dixence in Switzerland, completed in September 1961 at a cost of 1,600 million Swiss francs (£151,000,000). It is 932 ft *284 m*

from base to rim, 2,296 ft *700 m* long and the total volume of concrete in the dam is 7,792,000 yds³ *5 957 000 m³*. The earth fill Nurek dam on the Vakhsh-Amu Darya river, U.S.S.R. will be 1,017 ft *310 m* high, have a crest length of 2,390 ft *730 m* and a volume of 70,806,000 yds³ *54 million m³*. Work began in 1961 but completion has so far slipped from 1967 to 1979. The concrete Ingurskaya dam in western Georgia, U.S.S.R., was planned to have a final height of 988 ft *301 m*, a crest length of 2,390 ft *728 m* but may be completed only to 892 ft *271 m*.

Longest

The longest river dam in the world is the 62 ft *19 m* high Kiev dam on the river Dnepr, U.S.S.R. which was completed in 1964 to a length of 33.6 miles *54,1 km*. In the early 17th century an impounding dam of moderate height was built in Lake Hungtze, Kiangsu, China, to a reputed length of 100 km *62 miles*.

The longest sea dam in the world is the Afsluitdijk, stretching 20.195 miles *32,5 km* across the mouth of the Zuider Zee in two sections of 1.553 miles *2,499 km* (mainland of North Holland to the Isle of Wieringen) and 18.641 miles *30 km* from Wieringen to Friesland. It has a sea-level width of 293 ft *89 m* and a height of 24 ft 7 in *7,5 m*.

Strongest

The world's strongest structure will be the Sayano-Shusenskaya dam on the River Yenisey, U.S.S.R. which is under construction and designed to bear a load of 18 000 000 tonnes from a fully-filled reservoir.

United Kingdom

The most massive (5,630,000 yds³ *4 304 000 m³*), and longest (2,050 ft *625 m* crest length) high dam in the United Kingdom is the 240 ft *73 m* high Scammonden Dam, West Yorkshire, begun in November 1966 and completed in the summer of 1970. This rock fill dam carries the M62 on its crest and was built by Sir Alfred McAlpine. The cost of the project together with the 6½ miles *10 km* motorway was £8,400,000. There are longer low dams or barrages of the valley cut-off type notably the Hanningfield Dam, Essex, built from July 1952 to August 1956 to a length of 6,850 ft *2 088 m* and a height of 64.5 ft *19,7 m*. The rock fill Llyn Brianne Dam, Dyfed is Britain's highest dam reaching 298½ ft *91 m* in Nov. 1971 and becoming operational on 20 July 1972.

Largest Reservoir *World*

The most voluminous man-made is Bratsk reservoir (River Angara) U.S.S.R., with a volume of 137,214,000 acre-ft *169 250 million ha-m*. The dam was completed in 1964.

The world's largest artificial lake measured by surface area is Lake Volta, formed by the Akosombo dam completed in 1965. By 1969 the lake had filled to an area of 3,275 miles² *8 482 km²* with a shoreline 4,500 miles *7 250 km* in length.

The completion in 1954 of the Owen Falls Dam near Jinja, Uganda, across the northern exit of the White Nile from the Victoria Nyanza marginally raised the level of that *natural* lake by adding 166,000,000 acre-ft *204 750 million ha-m*, and technically turned it into a reservoir with a surface area of 17,169,920 acres *6,9 million ha* (26,828 miles² *69 484 km²*).

Largest Reservoir *Great Britain*

The largest wholly artificial reservoir in Great Britain is the Queen Mary Reservoir, built from August 1914 to June 1925, at Littleton, near Staines, Surrey, with an available storage capacity of 8,130 million gal. *36 960 million litres* and a water area of 707 acres *286 ha*. The length of the perimeter embankment is 20,766 ft *6 329 m* (3.93 miles *6,32 km*). Of valley cut-off type reservoirs the most capacious is Llwyn Celyn, Gwynedd with a capacity of 17,800 million gals *809 million hectolitres*. The capacity of Haweswater, Cumbria, was increased by 18,660 million gal *6 786 million litres* by the building in 1929–41 of a 1,540 ft *470 m* long concrete buttress dam 120 ft *36 m* high. The natural surface area was trebled to 1,050 acres *425 ha*. The deepest reservoir in Europe is Loch Morar, Highland, Scotland, with a maximum depth of 1,017 ft *310 m* (see also page 65).

Largest polder

The largest of the five great polders in the old Zuider Zee, Netherlands, will be the 149,000 acre *60 300 ha* (232.8 miles² *602,9 km²*) Markerwaard. Work on the 66 mile *106 km* long surrounding dyke was begun in 1957. The water area remaining after the erection of the 1927–32 dam (20 miles *32 km* in length) is called IJssel Meer, which will have a final area of 487.5 miles² *1 262,6 km²*

Largest levees

The most massive levees ever built are the Mississippi levees begun in 1717 but vastly augmented by the U.S. Federal Government after the disastrous floods of 1927. These extend for 1,732 miles *2 787 km* along the main river from Cape Girardeau, Missouri, to the Gulf of Mexico and comprise more than 1,000 million yds³ *765 million m³* of earthworks. Levees on the tributaries comprise an additional 2,000 miles *3 200 km.*

8. TUNNELS

LONGEST

Water supply *World*

The world's longest tunnel of any kind is the New York City West Delaware water supply tunnel begun in 1937 and completed in 1944. It has a diameter of 13 ft 6 in *4,1 m* and runs for 105 miles *168,9 km* from the Rondout Reservoir into the Hillview Reservoir, in the northern part of Manhattan Island, New York City, N.Y., U.S.A.

Water supply *Great Britain*

The longest water supply tunnel in the United Kingdom is the Thames water tunnel from Hampton-on-Thames to Walthamstow, Greater London, completed in 1960 with a circumference of 26 ft 8 in *8,1 m* and a length of 18.8 miles *30,3 km.*

Railway *World*

The world's longest main-line tunnel is the Simplon II Tunnel, completed after 4 year's work on 16 Oct. 1922. Linking Switzerland and Italy under the Alps, it is 12 miles 559 yds *19,82 km* long. Over 60 were killed boring this and the Simplon I (1898–1906), which is 22 yds *20 m* shorter. Its greatest depth below the surface is 7,005 ft *2 135 m*. The Dai-Shimizu tunnel in Japan will, when completed, be 22,3 km *13 miles 1,507 yds* long.

Railway *Great Britain*

Great Britain's longest main-line railway tunnel is the Severn Tunnel (4 miles 628 yds *6 km*), linking Avon and Gwent completed with 76,400,000 bricks between 1873 and 1886.

Sub-aqueous

The 33.49 mile *53,9 km* long Seikan Rail Tunnel will be 240 m *787 ft* beneath sea level and 100 m *328 ft* below the sea bed of the Tsugaru Strait between Tappi Saki, Honshū, and Fukushima, Hokkaidō, Japan. Once due to be completed by March 1979 at a cost of Yen 200,000 million, major flooding on 6 May 1976 has put back completion beyond 1982. Tests started on the sub-aqueous section (14.5 miles *23,3 km*) in 1963 and construction in June 1972. Currently the world's longest sub-aqueous rail tunnel is the Shin Kanmon Tunnel, completed in May 1974 which runs 11.55 miles *18,6 km* from Honshū to Kyūshū, Japan.

Subway

The world's longest continuous vehicular tunnel is the London Transport Executive underground railway line from Morden to East Finchley, *via* Bank. In use since 1939, it is 17 miles 528 yds *27,8 km* long and the diameter of the tunnel is 12 ft *3,7 m* and the station tunnels 22.2 ft *6,8 m.*

Road *World*

The longest road tunnel is the tunnel 7.2 miles *11,6 km* long under Mont Blanc (15,771 ft *4 807 m*) from Pèlerins, near Chamonix, France, to Entrèves, near Courmayeur in Valle d'Aosta, Italy, on which work began on 6 Jan. 1959. The holing through was achieved on 14 Aug. 1962 and it was opened on 16 July 1965, after an expenditure of £22,800,000. The 29½ ft *9 m* high tunnel with its carriage-way of two 12 ft *3,7 m* lanes is expected to carry 600,000 vehicles a year. There were 23 deaths during tunnelling.

Great Britain

The longest road tunnel in the United Kingdom is the Mersey Tunnel, joining Liverpool and Birkenhead, Merseyside. It is 2.13 miles *3,43 km* long, or 2.87 miles *4,62 km* including branch tunnels. Work was begun in December 1925 and it was opened by H.M. King George V on 18 July 1934. The total cost was £7¾ million. The 36 ft *11 m* wide 4-lane roadway carries nearly 7½ million vehicles a year. The first tube of the second Mersey Tunnel was opened on 24 June 1971.

Largest

The largest diameter road tunnel in the world is that blasted through Yerba Buena Island, San Francisco, California, U.S.A. It is 76 ft *23 m* wide, 58 ft *17 m* high and 540 ft *165 m* long. More than 35,000,000 vehicles pass through on its two decks every year.

Hydro-Electric or Irrigation *World*

The longest irrigation tunnel in the world is the 51.5 mile *82,9 km* long Orange-Fish Rivers Tunnel, South Africa, begun in 1967 at an estimated cost of £60 million. The boring was completed in April 1973. The lining to a minimum thickness of 9 inches *23 cm* will give a completed diameter of 17 ft 6 in *5,33 m*. The total work force was at times more than 5,000. Some of the access shafts in the eight sections descend more than 1,000 feet *305 m.*

Great Britain

The longest in Great Britain is that at Ben Nevis, Highland, which has a mean diameter of 15 ft 2 in *4,6 m* and a length of 15 miles *24 km*. It was begun in June 1926 and was holed through into Loch Treig on 3 Jan. 1930 for hydro-electric use. The greatest diameter water tunnel is the 23 ft *7,01 m* tunnel at Clunie, Tayside.

A PROGRESSIVE LIST OF THE WORLD'S LONGEST TUNNELS

Miles	km	Date	Location	Purpose
0·6	*0,9*	c 2100 B.C.	*Euphrates, Babylon, Iraq	Vehicular
0·6	*0,9*	c. 550 B.C.	Isle of Samos, Greece	Water tunnel
1·4	*2,2*	c. 250 B.C.	Cazlona, Spain	Silver mining
3·5	*5,6*	c. A.D. 45	Lake Fucinus (near Rome, Italy)	Lake draining
4	*6,4*	1608	N.W. of Mexico City, Mexico	Drainage
7·45	*12,0*	1822	Noirieu, France	Saint Quentin Canal
7·79	*12,79*	1857–71	Mont Cenis, France–Italy	Rail Tunnel
9·3	*15*	1872–82	St. Gotthard, Switzerland	Rail Tunnel
12·30	*19,80*	1898–1906	Simplon I Brigue, Switzerland–Iselle, Italy	Rail Tunnel
12·31	*19,82*	1918–22	Simplon II Brigue, Switzerland–Iselle, Italy	Rail Tunnel
18·1	*29,1*	1923	Shandaken, New York, U.S.A.	Water supply
105	*168,9*	1937–44	Delaware Aqueduct, N.Y. U.S.A.	Water supply

* Some accounts indicate this was only an arched cut across a dry river bed

Bridge Tunnel

The world's longest bridge-tunnel system is the Chesapeake Bay Bridge-Tunnel, extending 17.65 miles *28,40 km* from Eastern Shore, Virginia Peninsula to Virginia Beach, Virginia, U.S.A. It cost $200,000,000 (*then £71,4 million*) and was completed after 42 months and opened to traffic on 15 Apr. 1964. The longest bridged section is Trestle C (4.56 miles *7,34 km* long) and the longer tunnel is the Thimble Shoal Channel Tunnel (1.09 miles *1,75 km*).

Canal Tunnels *World*

The world's longest canal tunnel is that on the Rove canal between the port of Marseilles, France and the river Rhône, built in 1912–27. It is 4.53 miles *7,29 km* long, 72 ft *22 m* wide and 50 ft *15 m* high, involving 2¼ million yds³ *1,7 million m³* of excavation.

Great Britain

The longest canal tunnel in Great Britain is the Standedge (more properly Stanedge) Tunnel in West Yorkshire on the Huddersfield Narrow Canal built from 1794 to 4 Apr. 1811. It measures 3 miles 418 yds *5,21 km* in length and was closed on 21 Dec. 1944. The longest *continuous* tunnel of the 43 still in use is the 3,056 yd *2 794 m* long Blisworth on the Grand Union. The now closed Huddersfield Narrow Canal is also the highest in the United Kingdom, reaching a height at one point of 638 ft *194 m* above sea-level.

Tunnelling records

The world's records for rapid tunnelling were set on 18 March 1967 in the 8.6 mile *13,8 km* long Blanco Tunnel, in Southern Colorado when the "mole" (giant boring machine) crew advanced the 10 ft *3 m* diameter heading 375 ft *114 m* in one day, and on 26 June 1972 in the 20½ ft *6,95 m* diameter Navajo Tunnel 3 project, New Mexico with an advance of 247 lineal ft *75,28 m*.

9. SPECIALISED STRUCTURES

Seven Wonders of the World

The Seven Wonders of the World were first designated by Antipater of Sidon in the 2nd century B.C. They included the Pyramids of Giza, built by three Fourth Dynasty Egyptian Pharaohs, Hwfw (Khufu or Cheops), Kha-f-Ra (Khafre, Khefren or Chepren) and Menkaure (Mycerinus) near El Giza (El Gizeh), south-west of El Qâhira (Cairo) in Egypt (now the United Arab Republic). The Great Pyramid ("Horizon of Khufu") was finished *c.* 2580 B.C. Its original height was 480 ft 11 in *146,5 m* (now, since the loss of its topmost stone or pyramidion, reduced to 449 ft 6 in *137 m*) with a base line of 756 ft *230 m* and thus covering slightly more than 13 acres *5 ha*. It has been estimated that a permanent work force of 4,000 required 30 years to manoeuvre into position the 2,300,000 limestone blocks averaging 2½ tons/*tonnes* each, totalling about 5,750,000 tons *5 840 000 tonnes* and a volume of 90,700,000 ft³ *2 568 000 m³*. A costing exercise published in Dec. 1974. indicated that it would require 405 men 6 years at a cost of $1.13 billion (*then £500 million*).

Of the other six wonders only fragments remain of the Temple of Artemis (Diana) of the Ephesians, built in *c.* 350 B.C. at Ephesus, Turkey (destroyed by the Goths in A.D. 262), and of the Tomb of King Mausolus of Caria, built at Halicarnassus, now Bodrum, Turkey, in *c.* 325 B.C. No trace remains of the Hanging Gardens of Semiramis, at Babylon, Iraq (*c.* 600 B.C.); the 40 ft *12 m* tall marble, gold and ivory statue of Zeus (Jupiter), by Phidias (5th century B.C.) at Olympia, Greece (lost in a fire at Istanbul); the 117 ft *35 m* tall statue by Chares of Lindus of the figure of the god Helios (Apollo) called the Colossus of Rhodes (sculptured 292–280 B.C., destroyed by an earthquake in 224 B.C.); or the 400 ft *122 m* tall world's earliest lighthouse built by Sostratus of Cnidus *c.* 270 B.C. as a pyramidically shaped tower of white marble (destroyed by earthquake in A.D. 1375) on the island of Pharos (Greek, *pharos* = lighthouse), off the coast of El Iskandariya (Alexandria), Egypt.

Britain's tallest flag pole, the 225 ft *68 m* tall Douglas fir at Kew Gardens, erected in 1958. (*Barratt's Photo Press*)

Pyramid Oldest

The oldest known pyramid is the Djoser step pyramid at Saqqâra, Egypt constructed to a height of 204 ft *62 m* of Tura limestone in *c.* 2650 B.C. The oldest New World pyramid is that on the island of La Venta in south-eastern Mexico built by the Olmec people *c.* 800 B.C. It stands 100 ft *30 m* tall with a base diameter of 420 ft *128 m*.

Pyramid Largest

The largest pyramid, and the largest monument ever constructed, is the Quetzalcóatl at Cholula de Rivadahia, 63 miles *101 km* south-east of Mexico City, Mexico, It is 177 ft *54 m* tall and its base covers an area of nearly 45 acres *18,2 ha*. Its total volume has been estimated at 4,300,000 yds³ *3 300 000 m³* compared with 3,360,000 yds³ *2,5 million m³* for the Pyramid of Cheops (see above). The pyramid-building era here was between the 2nd and 6th centuries A.D.

Flagstaff Tallest *World*

The tallest flagstaff ever erected was that outside the Oregon Building at the 1915 Panama-Pacific International Exposition in San Francisco, California, U.S.A. Trimmed from a Douglas fir, it stood 299 ft 7 in *91 m* in height and weighed 45 tons *47 tonnes*. The tallest unsupported flag pole in the world is a 220 ft *67 m* tall metal pole weighing 28,000 lb. *12 700 kg* erected in 1955 at the U.S. Merchant Marine Academy in King's Point, New York, U.S.A. The pole, built by Kearney-National Inc., tapers from 24 in to 5½ in *61 cm to 14 cm* at the jack.

Great Britain

The tallest flagstaff in Great Britain is a 225 ft *68 m* tall Douglas fir staff at Kew, Richmond upon Thames, Greater London. Cut in Canada, it was shipped across the Atlantic and towed up the River Thames on 7 May 1958, to replace the old 214 ft *65 m* tall staff of 1919.

Totem Pole Tallest

A totem pole 173 ft *52,73 m* tall was raised on 6 June 1973 at Alert Bay, British Columbia, Canada. It tells the story of the Kwakiutl and took 36 man-weeks to carve.

Maypole

The tallest reported Maypole erected in England was one of Sitka spruce 105 ft 7 in *32,12 m* tall put up in Pelynt, Cornwall on 1 May 1974.

Monument Prehistoric *Largest*

Britain's largest megalithic prehistoric monuments are the 28½ acre *11,5 ha* earthworks and stone circles of Avebury, Wiltshire, rediscovered in 1646. The earliest calibrated date in the area of this neolithic site is *c.* 4200 B.C. The whole work is 1,200 ft *365 m* in diameter with a 40 ft *12 m* ditch around the perimeter and required an estimated 15 million man-hours of work. The largest trilithons exist at Stonehenge, to the south of Salisbury Plain, Wiltshire, with single sarsen blocks weighing over 45 tons/*tonnes* and requiring over 550 men to drag them up a 9° gradient. The earliest stage of the construction of the ditch has been dated to 2180 ± 105 B.C. Whether Stonehenge was a lunar calendar or an eclipse-predictor remains debatable.

Earthworks Largest *World*

The largest earthworks in the world carried out prior to the mechanical era were the Linear Earth Boundaries of the Benin Empire in the Mid Western state of Nigeria. These were first reported in 1903 and partially surveyed in 1967. In April 1973 it was estimated by Mr Patrick Darling that the total length of the earthworks was probably between 4,000 and 8,000 miles *6 400–12 800 km* with the total amount of earth moved estimated at from 500 to 600 million yds³ *380–460 million m³*.

Earthworks Largest *Great Britain*

The greatest prehistoric earthwork in Britain is Wansdyke, originally Woden's Dyke, which ran 86 miles *138 km* from Portishead, Avon to Inkpen Beacon and Ludgershall, south of Hungerford, Berkshire. It is believed to have been built by the pre-Roman Wessex culture. The most extensive single site earthwork is the Dorset Curses near Gussage St. Michael, dating from *c.* 1900 B.C. The workings are 6 miles *9,7 km* in length, involving an estimated 250,000 yds³ *191 000 m³* of excavations. The largest of the Celtic hill-forts is that known as Mew Dun, or Maiden Castle, 2 miles *3 km* south-west of Dorchester, Dorset. It covers 115 acres *46,5 ha* and was abandoned shortly after A.D. 43.

Mound Largest *World*

The gravel mound built as a memorial to the Seleucid King Antiochus I (reigned 69–34 B.C.) on the summit of Nemud Dagi (8,205 ft *2 494 m*) south east of Malatya, Eastern Turkey measures 197 ft *59,8 m* tall and covers 7.5 acres *3 ha.*

Mound Largest *United Kingdom*

The largest artificial mound in Europe is Silbury Hill, 6 miles *9,7 km* west of Marlborough, Wiltshire, which involved the moving of an estimated 670,000 tons *681 000 tonnes* of chalk to make a cone 130 ft *39 m* high with a base of 5½ acres *2 ha*. Prof. Richard Atkinson in charge of the 1968 excavations showed that it is based on an innermost central mound, similar to contemporary round barrows, and is now dated to 2,745 ± 185 B.C. The largest long barrow in England is that inside the hill-fort at Maiden Castle (see above). It originally had a length of 1,800 ft *548 m* and had several enigmatic features such as a ritual pit with pottery, limpet shells, and animal bones. The longest long barrow containing a mega-lithic chamber is that at West Kennet (*c.* 2200 B.C.), near Silbury, measuring 385 ft *117 m* in length.

Henges

There are in Britain some 80 henges built *c.* 2500 B.C. of which the largest was Durrington Walls, Wiltshire with an average diameter of 1,550 ft *472 m*. It has been obliterated by road building.

Monument Tallest

The world's tallest monument is the stainless steel Gateway to the West Arch in St. Louis, Missouri, U.S.A., completed on 28 Oct. 1965 to commemorate the westward expansion after the Louisiana Purchase of 1803. It is a sweeping arch spanning 630 ft *192 m* and rising to the same height of 630 ft *192 m* and costing $29,000,000 (*then £10.35 million*). It was designed in 1947 by Eero Saarinen (died 1961).

The tallest monumental column in the world is that commemorating the battle of San Jacinto (21 Apr. 1836), on the bank of the San Jacinto river near Houston, Texas, U.S.A. General Sam Houston (1793–1863) and his force of 743 Texan troops killed 630 Mexicans (out of a total force of 1,600) and captured 700 others, for the loss of nine men killed and 30 wounded. Constructed in 1936–39, at a cost of $1,500,000 (*then £372,000*), the tapering column is 570 ft *173 m* tall, 47 ft *14 m* square at the base, and 30 ft *9 m* square at the observation tower, which is surmounted by a star weighing 196.4 tons *199,6 tonnes*. It is built of concrete, faced with buff limestone, and weighs 31,384 tons *31 888 tonnes*.

Obelisk (Monolithic) Oldest

The longest an obelisk has remained *in situ* is that at Helio-polis, near Aswan, Egypt, erected by Senusret I *c.* 1750 B.C.

Obelisk (Monolithic) Largest

The largest standing obelisk in the world is that in the Piazza of St. John in Lateran, Rome, erected in 1588. It came originally from the Circus Maximus (erected A.D. 357) and before that from Heliopolis, Egypt (erected *c.* 1450 B.C.). It is 110 ft *33 m* in length and weighs 450 tons *457 tonnes*. The largest obelisk in the United Kingdom is Cleopatra's Needle on the Embankment, London, which is 68 ft 5½ in *20 m* tall and weighs 186.36 tons *189,35 tonnes*. It was towed up the Thames from Egypt on 20 Jan. 1878.

Tomb Largest

The largest tomb in the world is that of Emperor Nintoku (died *c.* A.D. 428) south of Osaka, Japan. It measures 1,594 ft *485 m* long by 1,000 ft *305 m* wide by 150 ft *45 m* high.

Ziqqurat Largest

The largest surviving ziqqurat (from the verb *zaqaru*, to build high) or stage-tower is the Ziqqurat of Ur (now Muqqayr, Iraq) with a base 200 ft by 150 ft *60 by 45 m* built to at least three storeys of which the first and part of the second now survive to a height of 60 ft *18 m*. It has been variously dated between *c.* 2,050 B.C. and *c.* 2,800 B.C.

Statue Tallest

The tallest free-standing statue in the world is that of "Motherland", an enormous pre-stressed concrete female figure on Mamayev Hill, outside Volgograd, U.S.S.R., designed in 1967 by Yevgenyi Vuchetich, to commemorate victory in the Battle of Stalingrad (1942–43). The statue from its base to the tip of the sword clenched in her right hand measures 270 ft *82,30 m*.

The U.S. sculptor Felix de Welton has announced a plan to replicate the Colossus of Rhodes to a height of 308 ft *93,87 m*.

Statue Longest

Near Bamiyan, Afghanistan there are the remains of the recumbent Sakya Buddha, built of plastered rubble, which was "about 1,000 ft *305 m*" long and is believed to date from the 3rd or 4th century A.D.

Dome Largest *World*

The world's largest dome is the Louisiana Superdome, New Orleans, U.S.A. It has a diameter of 680 ft *207,26 m*. (See pages 113–114 for further details.) The largest dome of ancient architecture is that of the Pantheon, built in Rome in A.D. 112, with a diameter of 142½ ft *43 m*.

Dome Largest *Great Britain*

The largest dome in Britain is that of the Bell Sports Centre, Perth, Scotland, with a diameter of 222 ft *67 m* designed by D. B. Cockburn and constructed in Baltic whitewood by Muirhead & Sons Ltd. of Grangemouth, Central, Scotland.

Column Tallest

The tallest columns (as opposed to obelisks) in the world are the sixteen 82 ft *25 m* tall pillars in the Palace of Labour in Torino (Turin), Italy, for which the architect was Pier Luigi Nervi (born 21 June 1891). They were built of concrete and steel in only 8 days. The tallest load-bearing stone columns in the world are those measuring 69 ft *21 m* in the Hall of Columns of the Temple of Amun at Karnak, opposite Thebes on the Nile, the ancient capital of Upper Egypt. They were built in the 19th dynasty in the reign of Rameses II in *c.* 1270 B.C.

Jetty Longest

The longest deep water jetty in the world is the Quai Hermann du Pasquier at Le Havre, France, with a length of 5,000 ft

1 524 m. Part of an enclosed basin, it has a constant depth of water of 32 ft *9,8 m* on both sides.

Pier Longest *World*

The world's longest pier is the Damman Pier, Saudi Arabia, on the Persian Gulf. A rock-filled causeway 4.84 miles *7,79 km* long joins the steel trestle pier 1.80 miles *2,90 km* long, which joins the Main Pier (744 ft *226 m* long), giving an overall length of 6.79 miles *10,93 km*. The work was begun in July 1948 and completed on 15 Mar. 1950.

Pier Longest *Great Britain*

The longest pier in Great Britain is the Bee Ness Jetty, completed in 1930, which stretches 8,200 ft *2 500 m* along the west bank of the River Medway, 5 to 6 miles *8 to 9,6 km* below Rochester, at Kingsnorth, Kent.

Breakwater Longest *World*

The world's longest breakwater system is that which protects the ports of Long Beach and Los Angeles, California, U.S.A. The combined length of the four breakwaters is 43,602 ft (8.26 miles *13,29 km*) of which the Long Beach section, built between 1941 and February 1949, is the longest at 13,350 ft (2.53 miles *4,07 km*). The North breakwater at Tuticorin, Madras Province, Southern India on which construction began in 1968 extends to 13,589 ft *4,14 km*.

Breakwater Longest *Great Britain*

The longest breakwater in Great Britain is the North Breakwater at Holyhead, Anglesey, Gwynedd which is 9,860 ft (1.86 miles *3 005 m*) in length and was completed in 1873.

Dry Dock Largest *World*

The largest dry dock in the world is that at Koyagi, Nagasaki, Japan completed in 1972. It measures 970 m *3,182 ft* long; 100 m *328 ft* in width and has a maximum depth of 14,5 m *47.6 ft*.

The largest shipbuilding dry dock in the U.K. is the Belfast Harbour Commission and Harland and Wolff building dock at Belfast, Northern Ireland. It was excavated by Wimpey's to a length of 1,825 ft *556 m* and a width of 305 ft *93 m* and could accommodate tankers of 1,000,000 tons deadweight. Work was begun on 26 Jan. 1968 and completed on 30 Nov. 1969 and involved the excavation of 400,000 yds³ *306 000 m³*. (See also Largest crane.) The dry dock under construction at Port Rashid, Dubai, Persian Gulf, due for completion in 1978 will measure 1,722 by 328 ft *525 × 100 m*.

Dock Gate

The world's largest dock gate is that at Nigg Bay, Cromarty Firth, Highlands, Scotland first operated in March 1974. It measures 408 ft *124 m* long, 50 ft *15,2 m* high with a 4 ft *1,21 m* thick base, is made of reinforced concrete and weighs 16,000 tons *16 257 tonnes* together with its sill, quoins and roundheads. The builders were Brown and Root-Wimpey Highland Fabricators.

Lighthouse Brightest *World*

The lighthouse with the most powerful light in the world is Créac'h d'Ouessant lighthouse, established in 1638 and last altered in 1939 on l'Ile d'Ouessant, Finistère, Brittany, France. It is 163 ft *50 m* tall and, in times of fog, has a luminous intensity of up to 500 million candelas.

The lights with the greatest visible range are those 1,092 ft *332 m* above the ground on the Empire State Building, New York City, N.Y., U.S.A. Each of the four-arc mercury bulbs has a rate candlepower of 450,000,000, visible 80 miles *130 km* away on the ground and 300 miles *490 km* away from aircraft. They were switched on on 31 Mar. 1956.

Lighthouse Brightest *Great Britain*

The lighthouse in Great Britain with the most powerful light is the shorelight Orfordness, Suffolk. It has an intensity of 7,500,000 candelas. The Irish light with the greatest intensity is Aranmore on Rinrawros Point, County Donegal.

Lighthouse Tallest

The world's tallest lighthouse is the steel tower 348 ft *106 m* tall near Yamashita Park in Yokohama, Japan. It has a power of 600,000 candles and a visibility range of 20 miles *32 km*.

Lighthouse Remotest *Great Britain*

The most remote Trinity House lighthouse is The Smalls, about 16 sea miles (18.4 statute miles *29,6 km*) off the Dyfed coast. The most remote Scottish lighthouse is Sule Skerry, 35 miles *56 km* off shore and 45 miles *72 km* north-west of Dunnet Head, Highland. The most remote Irish light is Blackrock, 9 miles *14 km* off the Mayo coast.

Windmill Earliest

The earliest recorded windmills are those used for grinding corn in Iran (Persia) in the 7th century A.D.

The earliest known in England was the post-mill at Bury St. Edmunds, Suffolk, recorded in 1191. The oldest Dutch mill is the towermill at Zedden, Gelderland built in *c.* 1450. The oldest working mill in England is the post-mill at Outwood, Surrey, built in 1665, though the Ivinghoe Mill in Pitstone Green Farm, Buckinghamshire, dating from 1627, has been restored.

Windmill Largest

The largest Dutch windmill is the Dijkpolder in Maasland built in 1718. The sails measure 95¾ ft *29 m* from tip to tip. The tallest windmill in the Netherlands is De Walvisch in Schiedam built to a height of 108 ft *33 m* in 1794. The largest conventional windmill in England is a disused one at Sutton, Norfolk.

Waterwheel Largest *World*

The largest waterwheel in the world is the Mohammadieh Noria wheel at Hama, Syria with a diameter of 131 ft *40 m* dating from Roman times. The Lady Isabella wheel at Laxey, Isle of Man is the largest in the British Isles and was built for draining a lead mine and completed on 27 Sept. 1854, and dis-used since 1929. It has a circumference of 228 ft *69 m*, a diameter of 72½ ft *22 m* and an axle weighing 9 tons/*tonnes*. The largest waterwheel in England is claimed to be the pitch-back indoor wheel of 45 ft *13,70 m* diameter which provided power from 1862–1932 for the mill of James Wilson & Son Ltd. of Keighley, West Yorkshire.

Barn Largest

The largest barn in Britain is one at Manor Farm, Cholsey, near Wallingford, Oxfordshire. It is 303 ft *92 m* in length and 54 ft *16 m* in breadth (16,362 ft² *1 520 m²*). The Ipsden Barn, Oxfordshire, is 385½ ft *117 m* long but 30 ft *9 m* wide (11,565 ft² *1 074 m²*). The longest tithe barn in Britain is one measuring 268 ft *81 m* long at Wyke Farm, near Sherborne, Dorset.

Nudist Camp

The oldest nudist resort is Der Freilichtpark, Klingberg, West Germany established in 1903. The largest such camp in the world is the Centre Helio-Marin, Montalivet, near Bordeaux, France extending over 1¼ miles *2 km* of coast and 420 acres *170 ha* with 1,200 chalets and 50,000 visitors per annum.

Wall Longest *World*

The Great Wall of China, completed during the reign of Shih Huang-ti (246–210 B.C.), has main line length of 2,150 miles *3 460 km* with a further 1,780 miles *2 860 km* of branches and spurs, with a height of from 15 to 39 ft *4,5 to 12 m* and up to 32 ft *9,8 m* thick. It runs from Shanhaikuan, on the Gulf of Pohai, to Chiayukuan in Kansu and was kept in repair up to the 16th century.

Wall Longest *Great Britain*

The longest of the Roman Walls built in Britain was the 15–20 ft *4,5–6 m* tall Hadrian's Wall, built in the period A.D. 122–126. It ran across the Tyne-Solway isthmus for 74½ miles *120 km* from Bowness-on-Solway, Cumbria, to Wallsend-on-Tyne, Tyne and Wear, and was abandoned in A.D. 383.

Fence Largest

The longest fence in the world is the dingo-proof fence enclosing the main sheep areas of Queensland, Australia. The wire fence is 6 ft *1,8 m* high, one foot *30 cm* underground and stretches for 3,437 miles *5 531 km.*

Door Largest *World*

The largest doors in the world are the four in the Vehicle Assembly Building near Cape Kennedy, Florida, with a height of 460 ft *140 m* (see page 109).

Door Largest *Great Britain*

The largest doors in Great Britain are those to the Britannia Assembly Hall, at Filton airfield, Avon. The doors are 1,035 ft *315 m* in length and 67 ft *20 m* high, divided into three bays each 345 ft *105 m* across. The largest simple hinged door in Britain is that of Ye Old Bull's Head, Beaumaris, Anglesey, Gwynedd, which is 11 ft *3,35 m* wide and 13 ft *3,96 m* high.

Door Oldest

The oldest doors in Britain are those of Hadstock Church, Essex, which date from *c.* 1040 A.D. and exhibit evidence of Danish workmanship.

Window Largest

The largest sheet of glass ever manufactured was one of 50 m² *538.2 ft²*, or 20 m *65 ft 7 in* by 2,5 m *8 ft 2½ in*, exhibited by the Saint Gobian Company in France at the *Journées Internationales de Miroiterie* in March 1958. The largest single windows in the world are those in the Palace of Industry and Technology at Rondpoint de la Défense, Paris, with an extreme width of 218 m *715,2 ft* and a maximum height of 50 m *164 ft.*

Stairs Longest *World*

The world's longest stairs are reputedly at the Mår power station, Øverland, western Norway. Built of wood, these are 4,101 ft *1 250 m* in length, rising in 3,875 steps at an angle of 41 degrees inside the pressure shaft. The T'ai Chan temple stairs of 6,600 steps in the Shantung Mountains, China ascend 4,700 feet in 5 miles *1 428 m* in *8 km.*

Stairs Longest *Great Britain*

The longest stairs in Britain are those from the transformer gallery to the surface 1,065 ft *324 m* in the Cruachan Power Station, Argyll, Scotland. They have 1,420 steps and the Work Study Dept. allows 27 mins 41.4 sec for the ascent.

Marquee Largest *World*

The largest tent ever erected was one covering an area of 188,368 ft² (4.32 acres *17 500 m²*) put up by the firm of Deuter from Augsburg, West Germany, for the 1958 "Welcome Expo" in Brussels, Belgium.

Marquee Largest *Great Britain*

The largest marquee in Britain is one made by Piggot Brothers in 1951 and used by the Royal Horticultural Society at their annual show (first held in 1913) in the grounds of the Royal Hospital, Kensington and Chelsea, Greater London. The marquee is 310 ft *94 m* long by 480 ft *146 m* wide and consists of 18¾ miles *30 km* of 36 in *91 cm* wide canvas covering a ground area of 148,800 ft² *13 820 m².* A tent 390 ft *119 m* long was erected in one lift by the Army for the Colchester Tattoo in Kings Head Meadow with 135 men in July 1970.

Vats Largest

The largest vat in the world is named "Strongbow" used by H. P. Bulmer Ltd., the cider makers of Hereford, England. It measures 64½ ft *19,65 m* in height and 75½ ft *23,0 m* in diameter with a capacity of 1,630,000 gallons *74 099 hectolitres.*

Advertising sign Largest

The greatest advertising sign ever erected was the electric Citroën sign on the Eiffel Tower, Paris. It was switched on on 4 July 1925, and could be seen 24 miles *38 km* away. It was in six colours with 250,000 lamps and 56 miles *90 km* of electric cables. The letter "N" which terminated the name "Citroën" between the second and third levels measured 68 ft 5 in *20,8 m* in height. The whole apparatus was taken down after 11 years in 1936. For the largest ground sign see Chapter 6, page 89—Letters, largest.

The Leeds Playhouse opened in 1970 in Calverley Street, Leeds, West Yorkshire. The letters "PLAYHOUSE" formed Britain's largest illuminated sign. Each of the nine letters is 9 ft 3 in *2,81 m* high and 42 neon tubes are used.

The world's largest neon sign was that owned by the Atlantic Coast Line Railroad Company at Port Tampa, Florida, U.S.A. It measured 387 ft 6 in *118 m* long and 76 ft *23 m* high, weighed 175 tons *178 tonnes* and contained about 4,200 ft *1 280 m* of red neon tubing. It was demolished on 19 Feb. 1970. Broadway's largest billboard in New York City is 11,426 ft² *1 062 m²* in area—equivalent to 107 ft *32,6 m* square. Britain's largest illuminated sign is the word PLAY-HOUSE extending 90 ft *27 m* across the frontage of the new theatre in Leeds, West Yorkshire opened in 1970.

The world's largest working sign was that in Times Square, at 44 & 45th Streets, New York City, U.S.A., in 1966. It showed two 42½ ft *13 m* tall "bottles" of Haig Scotch Whisky and an 80 ft *24 m* long "bottle" of Gordon's Gin being "poured" into a frosted glass.

Advertising sign Highest *World*
The highest advertising sign in the world are the four Bank of Montreal logos atop the 72 storey 935 ft *285 m* tall First Canadian Place, Toronto. Each sign, built by Claude Neon Industries Ltd., measures 20 × 22 ft *6,09 × 6,70 m* and was lifted by helicopter.

Advertising sign Highest *Great Britain*
The highest advertising sign in Great Britain was the revolving name board of the contractors "Peter Lind" on the Post Office Tower, London. The illuminated letters were 12 ft *3,7 m* tall and 563 to 575 ft *171 to 175 m* above the street.

Gasholder Largest *World*
The world's largest gasholder is that at Fontaine l'Eveque, Belgium, where disused mines have been adapted to store up to 500 million m³ *17,650 million ft³* of gas at ordinary pressure. Probably the largest conventional gasholder is that at Wein-Simmering, Vienna, Austria, completed in 1968, with a height of 274 ft 8 in *84 m* and a capacity of 10.59 millions ft³ *300 000 m³*.

Gasholder Largest *Great Britain*
The largest gasholder ever constructed in Great Britain is the East Greenwich Gas Works No. 2 Holder built in 1891 with an original capacity for 12,200,000 ft³ *346 000 m³*. As constructed its capacity is 8.9 million ft³ *252 000 m³* with a water tank 303 ft *92 m* in diameter and a full inflated height of 148 ft *45 m*. The No. 1 holder (capacity 8.6 million ft³ *243 500 m³*) has a height of 200 ft *61 m*. The River Tees Northern Gas Board's 1,186 ft *361 m* deep underground storage in use since January 1959 has a capacity of 330,000 ft³ *9 300 m³*.

Fountain Tallest *World*
The world's tallest fountain is the Fountain at Fountain Hills, Arizona built at a cost of $1,500,000 for McCulloch Properties Inc. At full pressure of 375 lb./in² *26,3 km/cm²* and at a rate of 5,928 Imp. gal/min *26 500 litres/min* the 560 ft *170 m* tall column of water weighs more than 8 tons/*tonnes*. The nozzle speed achieved by the three 600 h.p. pumps is 46.7 m.p.h. *75 km/h*.

Fountain Tallest *Great Britain*
The tallest fountain in Great Britain is the Emperor Fountain at Chatsworth, Bakewell, Derbyshire. When first tested on 1 June 1844, it attained the then unprecedented height of 260 ft *79 m*. Since the war it has not been played to more than 250 ft *76 m* and rarely beyond 180 ft *55 m*.

Globe Largest revolving
The world's largest revolving globe is the 21½ton/*tonnes* 27 ft 11 in *8,50 m* diameter sphere in the Coleman Map Building, Wellesley, Massachusetts, U.S.A. completed at a cost of $200,000 (then £71,425) in 1956.

Bonfire Largest
The largest recorded bonfire constructed in Britain was the Coronation bonfire using 600 tons *608 tonnes* of timber and 2,000 gallons *9 100 litres* of petroleum built to a height of 120 ft *36,6 m* in Whitehaven, Cumbria in 1902.

Cemetery Largest
The world's largest cemetery is that in Leningrad, U.S.S.R., which contains over 500,000 of the 1,300,000 victims of the German army's siege of 1941–42. The largest cemetery in the United Kingdom is Brookwood Cemetery, Brookwood, Surrey. It is owned by the London Necropolis Co. and is 500 acres *200 ha* in extent with more than 225,000 interments.

Crematorium Earliest
The oldest crematorium in Britain is one built in 1879 at Woking, Surrey. The first cremation took place there on 20 March 1885, the practice having been found legal after the cremation of Iesu Grist Price on Caerlan fields on 13 Jan. 1884.

Crematorium Largest
The largest crematorium in the world is at the Nikolo-Arkhangelskoye Cemetery, East Moscow, with 7 twin cremators of British design, completed in March 1972. It has several Halls of Farewell for atheists. Britain's largest is the City of London Crematorium, E.12, which extends over 165 acres *66,77 ha* and in 1976 undertook a peak 5,290 cremations.

Biggest Garbage Dump
Reclamation Plant No. 1, Fresh Kills, Staten Island, opened in March 1974, is the world's largest sanitary landfill. In its first 4 months 450,000 tons of refuse from New York City was dumped on the site by 700 barges.

Scaffolding
The greatest scaffolding structure ever erected was one comprising 750,000 ft (152 miles *228,5 km*) of tubing up to 486 ft *148 m* in height used in the reconstruction of Guy's Hospital, London in 1971.

10. BORINGS AND MINES

PROGRESSIVE RECORDS IN DEEP DRILLING

Depth in ft	m	Location	Date
2,000	600	Szechwan, China	c.150B.C.
5,735	1 748	Schladebach, Germany	1886
6,570	2 002	Schladebach, Germany	1893
7,230	2 203	Schladebach, Germany	1909
8,046	2 452	Olinda, Calif.	1927
8,523	2 597	Big Lake, W. Texas	1928
9,280	2 828	Long Beach, Calif.	1929
9,753	2 972	Midway, Calif.	1930
10,030	3 057	Rinconfield, Calif.	1931
10,585	3 226	Vera Cruz, Mexico	1931
10,944	3 335	Kettleman Hills, Calif.	1933
11,377	3 467	Belridge, Calif.	1934
12,786	3 897	Gulf McElroy, W. Texas	1935
15,004	4 573	Wasco, Calif.	1938
15,279	4 657	Pecos County, W. Texas	1944
16,246	4 951	S. Coles, Levee, Calif.	1944
16,655	5 076	Brazos County, Texas	1945
16,668	5 080	Miramonte, Calif.	1946
17,823	5 432	Caddo County, Oklahoma	1947
18,734	5 710	Ventura County, Calif.	1949
20,521	6 254	Sublette County, Wyoming	1949
21,482	6 547	Bakersfield, Calif.	1953
22,570	6 879	Plaquemines, Louisiana	1956
25,340	7 723	Pecos County, W. Texas	1958
25,600	7 802	St. Bernard Parish, Louisiana	1970
28,500	8 686	Pecos County, W. Texas	1972
30,050	9 159	Beckham County, Oklahoma	1972
31,441	9 583	Washita County, Oklahoma	1974

Deepest *World*
Man's deepest penetration into the Earth's crust is under Rig No. 32 gas well at No. 1 Bertha Rogers Field, Washita County, Oklahoma, U.S.A. After 503 days drilling the Loffland Brothers Drilling Co. reached 31,441 ft *9 583 m* (5.95 miles *9,58 km*) on 3 Apr. 1974. The hole temperature at the bottom was 475° F. *246° C*. A conception of the depth

above and right: Man's deepest penetration into the earth has now reached the point that the bore holes are deeper than Everest is high. The current record is held by Loffland Brothers Drilling Co, one of whose rigs and drilling crews are here seen in action in Oklahoma. (*Loffland Brothers Co.*)

of this $6 million (then £2,500,000) hole can be gained by the realization that it was sufficient in depth to lower the CN Tower down it more than 17 times (see page 116).

In May 1976 drilling was begun at Saatly, Azerbaijan, U.S.S.R. in an attempt to reach the Mohorovičić discontinuity. The target here was announced to be 15 km *49,212 ft.*

Deepest *Ocean Drilling*
The deepest recorded drilling into the sea bed by the *Glomar Challenger* of the U.S. Deep Sea Drilling Project is one of 5,709 ft *1 740 m* off N.W. Spain in 1976 and the deepest site is one 20,483 ft *6 243 m* below the surface.

Oil Fields
The largest oil field in the world is the Ghawar field, Saudi Arabia developed by ARAMCO which measures 150 miles by 22 miles *240 km by 35 km*. It has been asserted that the Groningen gas field in the Netherlands will prove to be the largest discovered. The area of the designated parts of the U.K. Continental shelf as at 1 Apr. 1975 was 223,550 miles^2 *579 000 km^2* with total recoverable reserves of 3,000 to 4,500 million tonnes *2950 to 4425 million tons* of oil and 51,000,000 million cubic feet *1 443 000 million m^3* of gas. Gas was first discovered in the West Sole Field in October 1965 and oil in the Forties Field at 11,000 ft *3 352 m* announced from the drilling barge *Sea Quest* on 7 Oct. 1970, though a small gasfield was detected near Whitby, N. Yorkshire in 1937. The most productive oil field is expected to be Brent (found in July 1971) with 22 million tons *22,3 million tonnes* per year attainable by 1981.

Gusher Greatest

The most prolific wildcat recorded is the 1,160 ft *353 m* deep Lucas No. 1, at Spindletop, about 3 miles *4,8 km* south of Beaumont, Texas, U.S.A., on 10 Jan. 1901. The gusher was heard more than a mile *1,6 km* away and yielded 800,000 barrels during the 9 days it was uncapped. The surrounding ground subsequently yielded 142,000,000 barrels.

Flare Greatest

The greatest gas fire was that which burnt at Gassi Touil in the Algerian Sahara from noon on 13 Nov. 1961 to 9.30 a.m. on 28 Apr. 1962. The pillar of flame rose 450 ft *137 m* and the smoke 600 ft *182 m*. It was eventually extinguished by Paul Neal ("Red") Adair, aged 47, of Austin, Texas, U.S.A., using 550 lb. *245 kg* of dynamite. His fee was understood to be about $1,000,000 (*then £357,000*).

Water Well Deepest *World*

The world's deepest water bore is the Stensvad Water Well 11-W1 of 7,320 ft *2 231 m* drilled by the Great Northern Drilling Co. Inc. in Rosebud County, Montana, U.S.A. in October-November 1961. The Thermal Power Co. geothermal steam well begun in Sonoma County, California in 1955 is now down to 9,029 ft *2 752 m*.

Water Well Deepest *Great Britain*

The deepest well in Great Britain is a water table well 2,842 ft *866 m* deep in the Staffordshire coal measures at Smestow. The deepest artesian well in Britain is that at the White Heather Laundry, Stonebridge Park, Brent, Greater London, bored in 1911 to a depth of 2,225 ft *678 m*. The deepest private well is probably that of Friningham Farm, Thurnham, Kent sunk to 415 ft *126,5 m* and deepened by bore to 818 ft *249,3 m* in 1940.

Water Well *Greatest Flow*

The highest recorded flow rate of any artesian well is 20,000 U.S. gallons (16,650 Imp. galls) per min *757 hectolitres/min* certified in 1973 for a well 20 miles *32 km* north west of Orlando, Florida by the Wekiva river.

MINES

Earliest

The earliest known mining operations were in the Ngwenya Hills of the Hhohho District of north-western Swaziland where haematite (iron ore) was mined for body paint *c.* 41,000 B.C. The earliest known mines in England are the Neolithic flint mines at Church Hill, Findon, West Sussex dated to 3390 B.C. ± 150.

Deepest *World*

The world's deepest mine is the Western Deep Levels Mine at Carletonville, South Africa. A depth of 12,600 ft *3 840 m* (2.38 miles) was attained by May 1975. At such extreme depths where the rock temperature attains temperatures of 131° F *55° C* refrigerated ventilation is necessary. The other great hazard is rock bursts due to the pressures.

above: The greatest wildcat 'gusher' in the history of the oil industry at Spindletop in Texas in full spate in January 1901. (*Photo Reportage Ltd.*)

below left and right: The world's most productive artesian well in Florida, U.S.A. switched off and switched on. Its output exceeds 16,000 gallons a minute.

Deepest *Great Britain*

The all-time record depth is 4,132 ft *1 259 m* in the Arley Seam of the Parsonage Colliery, Leigh, Greater Manchester in February 1949. The all-time deepest working in Scotland is at Frances Colliery, Dysant, Fife, (sunk 1877). The Bowhouse seam is under the sea, 3,118 ft *950,36 m* below sea level. The deepest present mine workings are the Fickershaw Colliery, Greater Manchester at 3,690 ft *1 127 m*. The deepest ever shaft in England, is that of the Cleveland Potash Ltd. at Boulby, North Yorkshire at 3,754 ft *1 144 m* completed in February 1973 and the deepest in Scotland is Monktonhall No. 1, Lothian, which is 3,048 ft *929 m* to the sump. The deepest Cornish tin mine was Dolcoath mine, near Camborne. The Williams shaft was completed in 1910 to 550 fathoms (3,300 ft *1 005 m*) from adit or approximately 3,600 ft *1 097 m* from the surface.

Gold Mine Largest area

The largest goldmining area in the world is the Witwatersrand gold field extending 30 miles *48 km* east and west of Johannesburg, South Africa. Gold was discovered there in 1886 by George Harrison and by 1944 more than 45 per cent of the world's gold was mined there by 320,000 Bantu and 44,000 Europeans. In 1976 73.9% of the free world's supply came from this area whose production reached a peak 999 857 kg *984 tons* in 1970.

Copper Mine

Historically the world's most productive copper mine has been the Bingham Canyon Mine (see below) belonging to the Kennecott Copper Corporation with over 9,000,000 short tons *8 million tonnes* in the 65 years 1904–68. Currently the most productive is the Chuquicamata mine of the Anaconda Company 150 miles *240 km* north of Antofagasta, Chile, with more than *300 000 tonnes*.

The world's largest underground copper mine is at El Teniente, 50 miles *80 km* south-east of Santiago, Chile with more than 200 miles *320 km* of underground workings and an annual output of nearly 11,000,000 tons *11 176 000 tonnes* of ore.

Silver, lead and zinc Mine

The world's largest lead, zinc and silver mine is the Kidd Creek Mine of Texasgulf Canada Ltd., located at Timmins, Ontario, Canada. Since 1970 the world's leading lead mine has been the Viburnum Trend, S.E. Missouri, U.S.A. with 489,397 short tons *443 700 tonnes* in 1972, from which is extracted some 10% of the world's output of lead. The world's largest zinc smelter is the Cominco Ltd. plant at Trail, British Columbia, Canada which has an annual capacity of 263,000 tons *267 000 tonnes* of zinc and 800 tons *813 tonnes* of cadmium.

Gold Mine Largest *World*

The largest goldmine in area is the East Rand Proprietary Mines Ltd., whose 8,785 claims cover 12,100 acres *4 900 ha*. The largest, measured by volume extracted, is Randfontein Estates Gold Mine Co. Ltd. with 170 million yds³ *129 million m³*—enough to cover Manhattan Island to a depth of 8 ft *2,4 m*. The main tunnels if placed end to end would stretch a distance of 2,600 miles *4 184 km*.

Gold Mine Largest *Great Britain and Ireland*

The most productive goldmine in Britain was Clogan St. David's, Powys, Wales, in which county gold was discovered in 1836. This mine yielded 120,000 fine oz. in 1854–1914. Alluvial gold deposits are believed to have been worked in the Wicklow Mountains, Ireland, as early as 1800 B.C.

Gold Mine Richest

The richest goldmine has been Crown Mines with nearly 49.4 million ounces *1 400 million g* and still productive. The richest in yield per year in 1976 was West Driefontein with 22,59 grams per tonne milled *0.80 oz. per ton*) in November 1968 by flooding.

Iron Mine

The world's largest iron-mine is at Lebedinsky, U.S.S.R., in the Kursk Magnetic Anomaly which has altogether an estimated 20,000 million tons *20 320 million tonnes* of rich (45–65 per cent) ore and 10,000,000 million tons *10,16 × 10¹² tonnes* of poorer ore in seams up to 2,000 ft *610 m* thick. The world's greatest reserves are, however, those of Brazil, estimated to total 58,000 million tons *58 930 million tonnes* or 35 per cent of the world's total surface stock.

Tungsten Mine

The largest tungsten mine with published output figures is the Union Carbide mine in Mount Morgan, near Bishop, California opened in 1937 with a capacity of 2,000 tons/*tonnes* per day and a work force of 420.

Spoil heap

The world's largest artificial heap is the sand dump on the Randfontein Estates Gold Mines, South Africa, which comprises 42 million tons *42,6 million tonnes* of crushed ore and rock waste and has a volume six times that of the Great Pyramid. The largest colliery tip in Great Britain covers 114 acres *46 ha* (maximum height 130 ft *40 m*) with 18 million tons *18,3 million tonnes* of slag at Cutacre Clough, Lancashire.

Quarry Largest *World*

The world's largest excavation is the Bingham Canyon Copper Mine, 30 miles *48 km* south of Salt Lake City, Utah, U.S.A. From 1906 to mid-1976 the total excavation has been 3,700 million short tons *3 355 million tonnes* over an area of 2.81 miles² *7,21 km²* to a depth of 2,540 ft *774 m*. This is seven times the amount of material moved to build the Panama Canal. Three shifts of 900 men work round the clock with 39 face shovels, 113 dump trucks and 67 locomotives and 17 drilling machines for the 28 tons/*tonnes* of explosive used daily. The record extraction in 24 hours is 504,167 short tons *457 372 tonnes* on 13 Oct. 1974.

The world's deepest open pit is the Kimberley Open Mine in South Africa, dug over a period of 43 years (1871 to 1914) to a depth of nearly 1,200 ft *365 m* and with a diameter of about 1,500 ft *457 m* and a circumference of nearly a mile, covering an area of 36 acres *14,5 ha*. Three tons/*tonnes* (14,504,566 carats) of diamonds were extracted from the 21,000,000 tons *21 337 000 tonnes* of earth dug out. The inflow of water has now made the depth 845 ft *257 m* to the water surface. The "Big Hole" was dug by pick and shovel.

Quarry Largest *England*

The deepest quarry in England is the Old Delabole Slate Quarry, Cornwall, which has been worked since *c*. 1570 and now has a circumference of 1.63 miles *2,6 km* and a depth of 500 ft *152 m*. The largest limestone quarry in Britain is the Imperial Chemical Industries Ltd.'s Tunstead Quarry, near Buxton, Derbyshire. The working face is 1.6 miles *2,57 km* long and up to 180 ft *54,8 m* high. It is producing 6,000,000 long tons of limestone per annum.

Largest stone

The largest mined slab of quarried stone on record is one of 1,800 tons of slate from Spouterag Quarry, Larrydale Valley, Cumbria, England in May 1969.

Open Cast Mining

The world's largest open cast mine is the Fortuna-Garsdorf lignite mine near Bergheim, West Germany.

8. THE MECHANICAL WORLD

1. SHIPS

EARLIEST BOATS

Evidence for sea faring between the Greek mainland and Melos to trade obsidian *c.* 7250 B.C. was published in 1971. Oars found in bogs at Magle Mose, Sjaelland, Denmark and Star Carr, North Yorkshire, England, have been dated to the eighth millenium B.C.

The oldest surviving boat is the 142 ft *43,4 m* long 40 ton Nile boat buried near the Great Pyramid of Khufu, Egypt *c.* 2515 B.C. and now re-assembled.

The oldest shipwreck ever found is one of a Cycladic trading vessel located off the islet of Dhákos, near the Greek island of Hydra reported in May 1975 and dated to 2450 B.C. ± 250.

Earliest power

Propulsion by steam engine was first achieved when in 1783 the Marquis Jouffroy d'Abbans ascended a reach of the river Saône near Lyon, France, in the 180 ton *182 tonnes* paddle steamer *Pyroscaphe*.

The tug *Charlotte Dundas* was the first successful power-driven vessel. She was a paddle-wheel steamer built in Scotland in 1801–02 by William Symington (1763–1831), using a double-acting condensing engine constructed by James Watt (1736–1819). The earliest regular steam run was by the paddle-wheeler *Clermont*, built by Robert Fulton (1765–1815), a U.S. engineer, using a Boulton and Watt engine. She maintained a service from New York to Albany (150 miles *240 km* in 32 hrs) from 17 Aug. 1807.

Oldest Steam vessel *Great Britain*

The 48 ton Bristol steam driven dredger *Bertha* of 50 ft *15,42 m* was designed by I. K. Brunel in 1844 and is afloat at Exeter, Devon, England. Mr. G. H. Pattinson's 40 ft *12,20 m* steam launch, raised from Ullswater, Cumbria, in 1962 and now on Lake Windermere, may date from a year or two earlier. The oldest motor vessel afloat in British waters is the *Proven* on the run from the Clyde to the Inner Hebrides. She was built in Norway in 1866.

World

The world's oldest active steam ship is the *Skibladner*, which has plied Lake Mjøsa, Norway since 1856. She has had two major refits and was built in Motala, Sweden.

Earliest turbine

The first turbine ship was the *Turbinia*, built in 1894 at Wallsend-on-Tyne, Tyne and Wear, to the design of the Hon. Sir Charles Algernon Parsons, O.M., K.C.B. (1854–1931). The *Turbinia* was 100 ft *30,48 m* long and of 44½ tons *45,2 tonnes* displacement with machinery consisting of three steam turbines totalling about 2,000 shaft horsepower. At her first public demonstration in 1897 she reached a speed of 34.5 knots (39.7 m.p.h. *63,9 km/h*).

PASSENGER LINERS
Largest active

The world's largest liner is R.M.S. *Queen Elizabeth 2* of 66,851 gross tons and with an overall length of 963 ft *293 m* completed for the Cunard Line Ltd. in 1969. She set a "turn round" record of 8 hrs 3 min at New York on 17 May 1972. In her 96 day Pacific cruise to 32 ports 16 Jan. to 22 Apr. 1978 the price of the Trafalgar and Queen Anne suites will be £91,675 (*$155,850*).

Largest ever

The R.M.S. *Queen Elizabeth* (finally 82,998 but formerly 83,673 gross tons), of the Cunard fleet, was the largest passenger vessel ever built and had the largest displacement of any liner in the world. She had an overall length of 1,031 ft *314 m* and was 118 ft 7 in *36 m* in breadth and was powered by steam turbines which developed 168,000 h.p. Her last passenger voyage ended on 15 Nov. 1968. In 1970 she was removed to Hong Kong to serve as a floating marine university and renamed *Seawise University*. On 9 Jan. 1972 she was fired by 3 simultaneous outbreaks and was gutted.

WARSHIPS
Battleships *Largest World*

The largest battleship in the world is now the U.S.S. *New Jersey* with a full load displacement of 59,000 tons *59 900 tonnes* and an overall length of 888 ft *270 m*. She was the last fire support ship on active service in the world and was de-commissioned on 17 Dec. 1969.

Largest all-time

The Japanese battleships *Yamato* (completed on 16 Dec. 1941 and sunk south west of Kyūshū, Japan, by U.S. planes on 7 Apr. 1945) and *Musashi* (sunk in the Philippine Sea by 11 bombs and 16 torpedoes on 24 Oct. 1944) were the largest battleships ever commissioned, each with a full load displacement of 72,809 tons *73 977 tonnes*. With an overall length of 863 ft *263 m*, a beam of 127 ft *38,7 m* and a full load draught of 35½ ft *10,8 m* they mounted nine 460 mm *18,1 in* guns and three triple turrets. Each gun weighed 162 tons *164,6 tonnes* and was 75 ft *22,8 m* in length firing a 3,200 lb. *1 451 kg* projectile.

Largest Great Britain
Britain's largest ever and last battleship was H.M.S. *Vanguard* with a full load displacement of 51,420 tons *52 245 tonnes*, overall length 814 ft *248,1 m*, beam 108½ ft *33,07 m*, with a maximum draught of 36 ft *10,9 m*. She mounted eight 15 in *38 cm* and sixteen 5.25 in *13,33 cm* guns. A shaft horsepower of 130,000 gave her a sea speed of 29½ knots (34 m.p.h. *54 km/h*). The *Vanguard* was laid down in John Brown & Co. Ltd.'s yard at Clydebank, Strathclyde, on 20 Oct. 1941, launched on 30 Nov. 1944 and completed on 25 April 1946. She was sold in August 1960 for scrap, having cost a total of £14,000,000.

Guns
The largest guns ever mounted in any of H.M. ships were the 18 in *45 cm* pieces in the light battle cruiser (later aircraft carrier) H.M.S. *Furious* in 1917. In 1918 they were transferred to the monitors H.M.S. *Lord Clive* and *General Wolfe*. The thickest armour ever carried was in H.M.S. *Inflexible* (completed 1881), measuring 24 in *60 cm* backed by teak up to a maximum thickness of 42 in *106,6 cm*.

Fastest destroyer
The highest speed attained by a destroyer was 45.02 knots (51.84 m.p.h. *83,42 km/h*) by the 3,750 ton *3 810 tonnes* French destroyer *Le Terrible* in 1935. She was powered by four Yarrow small tube boilers and two geared turbines giving 100,000 shaft horse-power. She was removed from the active list at the end of 1957.

AIRCRAFT CARRIERS
Largest *World*
The warship with the largest full load displacement in the world is the $1,880 million (*now £1,105 million*) aircraft carrier U.S.S. *Nimitz* at 91,400 tons *92 800 tonnes*. She is 1,092 ft *332 m* in length overall and has a speed well in excess of 30 knots *56 km/h*. U.S.S. *Enterprise* is, however, 1,123 ft *341,3 m* long and thus still the longest warship ever built. When completed the U.S.S. *Dwight D. Eisenhower*, sister ship to the *Nimitz*, will have cost more than $2 billion (£1,176 million) and will have a crew of 6,100.

The largest warship ever built, the U.S. Aircraft Carrier *Nimitz* whose flight deck could accommodate more than 70 tennis courts (see above).

Largest *Great Britain*
Britain's largest ever aircraft carrier is H.M.S. *Ark Royal*, completed on 25 Feb. 1955, with a full load displacement of 50,786 tons *51 601 tonnes* (previously 53,340 tons *54 196 tonnes*), 845 ft *257,5 m* overall, 166 ft *50,5 m* wide, maximum draught 36 ft *10,9 m*, with a full complement of 2,640 and a capacity of 30 naval jet aircraft and 6 helicopters. Her 152,000 shaft horse-power gives her a maximum speed of 31.5 knots (36.27 m.p.h. *58,37 km/h*).

SUBMARINES
Largest
The world's largest ever submarine will be the nuclear powered submarine U.S.S. *Ohio* due to be commissioned in 1979 with 24 Trident missiles of 4,600 mile *7 400 km* range and a submerged displacement of 18,400 tons *18 700 tonnes*. The U.S.S.R. Delta II class submarines with 16 SSN 8 missiles, may be substantially larger. Four or five were in service by Jan. 1977 when even larger submarines were reported under construction. The largest submarines ever built for the Royal Navy are the four atomic-powered nuclear missile R class boats with a surface displacement of 7,500 tons *7 620 tonnes* and 8,400 tons *8 534 tonnes* submerged, a length of 425 ft *129,5 m* a beam of 33 ft *10 m* and a draught of 30 ft *9,1 m*.

Fastest
The world's fastest submarines are the U.S. Navy's tear-drop hulled nuclear vessels of the Los Angeles class. They have been listed officially as capable of a speed of "30 plus knots" (34 plus m.p.h. *55 plus km/h*) but the true figure is believed to be dramatically higher. The first 4 were commissioned in 1975/76 with a further 19 by 1979–80.

Deepest
The two U.S.N. vessels able to descend 12,000 ft *3 650 m* are the 3 man *Trieste II* (DSV I) of 303 tons recommissioned in November 1973 and the DSV 2 (Deep submergence vessel) U.S.S. *Alvin*. The *Trieste II* was reconstructed from the record-breaking bathyscaphe *Trieste* but without the Krupp built sphere, which enabled it to descend to 35,820 ft *10 917 m*. (see Chapter 11, Greatest ocean descent).

TANKERS
Largest
The world's largest tanker and ship of any kind is the 550,000 ton *558,800 tonnes* deadweight *Bellamya* completed in St. Nazaire, France for Shell in February 1977 and sailing under the French flag. She is 400 m *1,312.3 ft* long with a beam of 63 m *206.6 ft* and a draught of 28,5 m *93.5 ft* powered by a 64,800 metric h.p. engine she can maintain a speed of 16.7 knots *19.2 m.p.h.*

Globtik Tankers U.S. Inc. expect to take delivery of the first of three 600,000 d.wt. ton nuclear-powered tankers from Newport News Shipbuilding and Dry Dock Co. at £187 million each in 1985. These 1,303 ft *397,15 m* long tankers will have an annual carrying capacity of 25 million barrels or 5 million tons of crude oil at 22 knots.

Largest propeller
The largest ship's propeller ever cast has been one for the Kuwaiti oil tanker *Al Rawdatain* (328,000 d.wt. tons) building at Chantiers Navals de la Ciotat, France which weighs 73.33 long tons *76 160 kg* with a diameter of 31 ft 8 in *9 650 mm*, constructed by Heliphoc of Marseille, France in 1976.

CARGO VESSELS
Largest
The largest vessel in the world capable of carrying dry cargo is the Swedish ore/oil carrier *Svealand* of 282,450 d.wt. tons *152,068 g.r.t.* with a length of 1,109 ft *338,03 m* and a beam of 179 ft *54 m* owned by Angt. A/B. Tirfing completed in 1973. The largest British ore/oil carrier is the P & O's *Nordic Conqueror*, built in Japan in 1972, of 268,728 d.wt. tons, *143,959 g.r.t.* and a length of 1,101 ft *335,6 m*.

Largest cable ship
The world's largest cable-laying ship is the American Telephone & Telegraph Co.'s German-built *Long Lines* (11,200

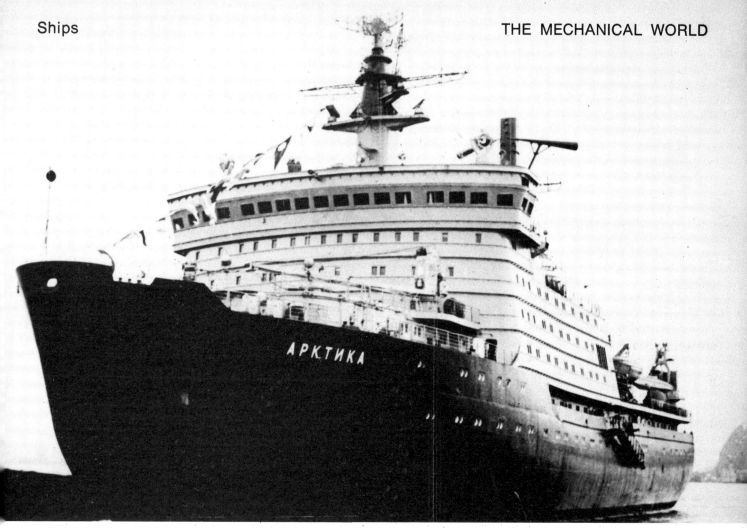

The world's most powerful purpose-built ice-breaker, the U.S.S.R.'s *Arktika* which can smash through ice 7 ft *2,1 m* thick. *(Novosti Press Agency)*

gross tons), completed by Deutsche Werft of Hamburg in April 1963, at a cost of £6,800,000. She has a fully-laden displacement of 17,000 tons, measures 511 ft 6 in *156 m* overall and is powered by twin turbine electric engines.

Largest whale factory

The largest whale factory ship is the U.S.S.R.'s *Sovietskaya Ukraina* (32,034 gross tons), with a summer deadweight of 46,000 tons *46 738 tonnes* completed in October 1959. She is 714.6 ft *217,8 m* in length and 84 ft 7 in *25,8 m* in the beam.

Most powerful tugs

The world's largest and most powerful tug is the *S. A. Wolraad Waltemade* of 2,822 g.r.t. rated at 19,200 horse-power and with a bollard pull of 150 tons. She has an overall length of 278 ft 10 in *85 m* and a beam of 49 ft 10 in *15,2 m*. She was built at Leith, Lothian, to handle the largest tankers and was completed in Apr. 1976.

Largest car ferry

The world's largest car and passenger ferry is the 502 ft *153 m* long MV *Norland* (12,998 g.r.t.), which made its maiden voyage on 10 June 1974. She can carry 520 cars and has a service speed of 18½ knots (21 m.p.h. *34 km/h*) and was built by A. G. Weser of Bremen, West Germany.

Largest hydrofoil

The world's largest naval hydrofoil is the 212 ft *65 m* long *Plainview* (310 tons *314 tonnes* full load), launched by the Lockheed Shipbuilding and Construction Co. at Seattle, Washington, U.S.A., on 28 June 1965. She has a service speed of 50 knots (57 m.p.h. *92 km/h*). Three 165 ton Supramar PTS 150 Mk III hydrofoils carrying 250 passengers

at 40 knots *74 km/h* ply the Malmö–Copenhagen crossing. They were built by Westermoen Hydrofoil Ltd. of Mandal, Norway. A 500 ton wing ground effect vehicle capable of carrying 900 tons has been reported in the U.S.S.R.

Most powerful icebreaker

The world's most powerful icebreaker is the U.S.S.R. atomic powered *Arktika*, able to go through ice 7 ft *2,1 m* thick at 4 knots *7 km/h*. She completed trials in December 1974.

The largest *converted* icebreaker has been the 1,007 ft *306,9 m* long S.S. *Manhattan* (43,000 s.h.p.), which was converted by the Humble Oil Co. into a 150,000 ton *152 407 tonnes* ice-breaker with an armoured prow 69 ft 2 in *21,08 m* long. She made a double voyage through the North-West Passage in arctic Canada from 24 Aug. to 12 Nov. 1969. The North-West Passage was first navigated in 1906.

The Norwegian shipbuilders Aker of Oslo announced in May 1975 plans for a 250,000 deadweight ton semi-submarine 121,000 h.p. ice-breaker capable of smashing through ice *3,8 m 12½ ft* thick.

Largest dredger

The world's most powerful dredger is the 470 ft *143 m* long *Prins der Nederlanden*. She can dredge 20,000 tonnes of sand from a depth of 35 m *115 ft* via two suction tubes in less than an hour.

Wooden ship

The heaviest wooden ship ever built was the *Richelieu*, 333 ft 8 in *101,70 m* long and of 8,534 tons launched in Toulon, France on 3 Dec. 1873. H.M. Battleship *Lord Warden*, completed in 1869, displaced 7,940 tons *8 060 tonnes*. The longest modern wooden ship ever built was the New York built *Rochambeau* (1867–1872) formerly *Dunderberg*. She measured 377 ft 4 in *115 m* overall. It should be noted that the biblical length of Noah's Ark was 300 cubits or, at 18 inches *45,7 cm* to a cubit, 450 ft *137 m* (but see Junks p. 132).

Longest dug-out

The world's longest canoe is the 117 ft *35,7 m* long 20 ton Kauri wood Maori war canoe Nga Toki Matawhaorua built by adzes at Kerikeri Inlet, New Zealand in 1940 for a crew of 70 or more.

SAILING SHIPS

Largest

The largest sailing vessel ever built was the *France II* (5,806 gross tons), launched at Bordeaux in 1911. The *France II* was a steel-hulled, five-masted barque (square-rigged on four masts and fore and aft rigged on the aftermost mast). Her hull measured 418 ft *127,4 m* overall. Although principally designed as a sailing vessel with a stump topgallant rig, she was also fitted with two steam engines. She was wrecked in 1922. The only seven masted sailing schooner ever built was the 375.6 ft *114,4 m* long *Thomas W. Lawson* (5,218 gross tons) built at Quincy, Massachusetts, U.S.A. in 1902 and lost in the English Channel on 15 Dec. 1907.

The largest sailing vessel under the Red Ensign is the three-masted topgallant schooner *Captain Scott* of 144 ft *43,8 m* overall and displacing 380 tons/*tonnes* completed in September 1971 and based in Loch Eil, Highland, Scotland.

The world's only surviving First Rate Ship-of-the-Line is the Royal Navy's 104 gun battleship H.M.S. Victory laid down at Chatham, Kent on 23 July 1759 constructed from the wood of some 2,200 oak trees. She bore the body of Admiral Nelson from Gibraltar to Portsmouth arriving 44 days after serving as his victorious flagship at the Battle of Trafalgar on 21 Oct. 1805. In 1922 she was moved to No. 2 dock, Portsmouth—site of the world's oldest graving dock. The total length of her cordage (both standing and running rigging) is 100,962 ft (19.12 miles *30,77 km.*)

Largest junks

The largest junk on record was the sea-going *Cheng Ho*, flagship of Admiral Cheng Ho's 62 treasure ships, of *c.* 1420, with a displacement of 3,100 tons *3 150 tonnes* and a length variously estimated up to 538 ft *164 m* and believed to have had 9 masts.

A river junk 361 ft *110 m* long, with treadmill-operated paddle-wheels, was recorded in A.D. 1161. In *c.* A.D. 280 a floating fortress 600 ft *182,8 m* square, built by Wang Chün on the Yangtze took part in the Chin-Wu river war. Present day junks do not, even in the case of the Chiangsu traders, exceed 170 ft *51,8 m* in length.

Longest day's run under sail

The longest day's run by any sailing ship was one of 465 nautical miles (535.45 statute miles *861,72 km*) by the clipper *Champion of the Seas* (2,722 registered tons) of the Liverpool Black Ball Line running before a north-westerly gale in the south Indian Ocean under the command of Capt. Alex. Newlands. The elapsed time between the fixes was 23 hrs 17 min giving an average of 19.97 knots *37,00 km/h.*

Greatest speed

The highest speed by a sailing merchantman is 22 knots (25.3 m.p.h. *40,7 km/h*) in 4 consecutive watches, by *Lancing* (ex *La Péreire*) when "running her easting down" on a passage to Melbourne in 1890/91. She was the last 4 masted full-rigged ship (36 sails) and at 405 ft *123,4 m* the longest. Her main and mizzen masts were 203 ft *61,8 m* from keelson to truck with yards 98 ft 9 in *30,09 m* across. In February 1916 she sighted Cape Wrath, Scotland 6 days 18 hrs out of New York.

Largest sails

The largest spars ever carried were those in H.M. Battleship *Temeraire*, completed at Chatham, Kent, on 31 Aug. 1877. The fore and main yards measured 115 ft *35 m* in length. The mainsail contained 5,100 ft *1 555 m* of canvas, weighing 2 tons *2,03 tonnes* and the total sail area was 25,000 ft² *2 322 m²*.

Largest Oil Platforms

The largest fixed leg drilling platforms are the four B.P. Forties Field platforms. The overall height from below the mud line to the top of the drilling rig is 686 ft *209 m*. Each weighs 57,000 tons. Their foundation piles penetrate 100 m *330 ft* into the sea bed and are the deepest foundations in the world.

The world's most massive oil platform is Shell-Esso's 230,000 ton deadweight Condeep Brent B Field platform built in Stavanger, Norway and positioned in June 1975. The tallest platform is one 750 ft *228,6 m* in height built by Redpath Dorman Long for Shell-Esso at Methil, Fife and moved to the Brent Field in April 1976.

The concrete production and storage platform for the Ninian Field under construction at the Loch Kishorn site Highland, Scotland will have an overall height of 820 ft *250 m* and will in 1977 when moved to its station become the heaviest mobile object ever constructed with a ballasted weight of some 600,000 tons/*tonnes* (see photograph page 149).

Largest wreck

The largest ship ever wrecked has been the £25 million tanker *Olympic Bravery* (275,000 tons deadweight) which ran aground off Ushant Is, N.W. France on 24 Jan. 1976 on her maiden voyage. She broke in two on 12 Mar. 1976. The largest vessel ever to be wrecked in British waters has been the 965 ft *294 m* long tanker, *Torrey Canyon*, of 61,275 tons gross and 118,285 tons deadweight, which struck the Pollard Rock of the Seven Stones Reef between the Isles of Scilly and Land's End, Cornwall, England, at 08.50 on 18 Mar. 1967. The resultant oil pollution from some 30,000 tons *30 481 tonnes* of Kuwait crude was "on a scale which had no precedent anywhere in the world". In an attempt to fire the remaining oil, the ship was bombed to virtual destruction on 28–30 Mar. 1967.

Oldest salvaged vessel

The oldest wreck to be salvaged has been a 45 ft *13,7 m* merchant vessel, which had sunk in 100 ft *30,5 m* of water off Kyrenia, Cyprus *c.* 250 B.C. It was spotted in 1965 and raised after 7 years work.

OCEAN CROSSINGS

Atlantic *Earliest*

The earliest crossing of the Atlantic by a power vessel, as opposed to an auxiliary engined sailing ship, was a 22-day voyage begun in April 1827, from Rotterdam, Netherlands, to the West Indies by the *Curaçao*. She was a 127 ft *38,7 m* wooden paddle boat of 438 tons, built in Dundee, Tayside, in 1826 and purchased by the Dutch Government for the West Indian mail service. The earliest Atlantic crossing entirely under steam (with intervals for desalting the boilers) was by H.M.S. *Rhadamanthus* from Plymouth to Barbados in 1832. The earliest crossing of the Atlantic under continuous steam power was by the condenser-fitted packet ship *Sirius* (703 tons *714 tonnes*) from Queenstown (now Cóbh), Ireland, to Sandy Hook, New Jersey, U.S.A., in 18 days 10 hours on 4–22 Apr. 1838.

Atlantic Fastest *World*

The fastest Atlantic crossing was made by the *United States* (then, 51,988, now 38,216 gross tons), former flagship of the United States Lines. On her maiden voyage between 3 and 7 July 1952 from New York City N.Y., U.S.A., to Le Havre, France, and Southampton, England, she averaged 35.59 knots, or 40.98 m.p.h. *65,95 km/h* for 3 days 10 hrs 40 min (6.36 p.m. G.M.T. 3 July to 5.16 a.m. 7 July) on a route of 2,949 nautical miles *5 465 km* from the Ambrose Light Vessel to the Bishop Rock Light, Isles of Scilly, Cornwall. During this run, on 6–7 July 1952, she steamed the greatest distance ever covered by any ship in a day's run (24 hrs)—868 nautical miles *1 609 km*, hence averaging 36.17 knots (41.65 m.p.h. *67,02 km/h*). Her maximum speed was 41.75 knots (48 m.p.h. *77,24 km/h*) on a full power of 240,000 shaft horse-power.

Most Atlantic crossings

Between 1856 and June 1894 Captain Samuel Brooks (1832–1904) crossed the North Atlantic 690 times—equal to 2,437,712 statute miles *3 923 117 km*. In 1850–51 he had sailed in the brig *Bessie* as an Able Bodied seaman round The

Horn to Panama coming home to Liverpool as her master. His life-time sailing distance was at least 2,513,000 miles *4 044 000 km.*

John D. Hunter, Boatswain of the container vessel *Sea-Land McLean* made 45 North Atlantic return voyages and steamed 328,500 miles *528 600 km* in the year 6 Oct. 1972 to 7 Oct. 1973.

Fastest Pacific crossing
The fastest crossing of the Pacific Ocean is 4 days 21 hrs 24 min (Shionomisaki, Japan to Race Rock, B.C.) by the container ship *Sea-Land Commerce* (50,315 tons) on 27 May 1973. On 6 July 1973 she completed the 4,840 nautical miles *8 960 km* from Yokohama to Long Beach, California at a higher average of 33.27 knots (38.31 m.p.h. *61,65 km/h*).

EXTREMITIES REACHED
Northernmost
The farthest north ever attained by a surface vessel is 86° 39′ N. in 47° 55′ E. by the drifting U.S.S.R. icebreaker *Sedov* on 29 Aug. 1939. She was locked in the Arctic ice floes from 23 Oct. 1937 until freed on 13 Jan. 1940.

Southernmost
The farthest south ever reached by a ship was achieved on 15 Feb. 1912 when the *Fram* reached Lat. 78° 41′ S. off the Antarctic coast.

Deepest anchorage
The deepest anchorage ever achieved is one of 24,600 ft *7 498 m* in the mid-Atlantic Romanche Trench by Capt. Jacques-Yves Cousteau's research vessel *Calypso*, with a 5½ mile *8,9 km* long nylon cable, on 29 July 1956.

Greatest Roll
The ultimate in rolling was recorded in heavy seas off Coos Bay, Oregon, U.S.A. on 13 Nov. 1971, when the U.S. Coast Guard motor lifeboat *Intrepid* made a 360 degree roll.

2. ROAD VEHICLES

Guinness Superlatives has now published automotive records in greater detail in the more specialist publication *Car Facts and Feats* (price £4.95).

COACHING
Before the advent of the McAdam road surfaces in *c.* 1815 coaching was slow and hazardous. The zenith was reached on 13 July 1888 when J. Selby, Esq., drove the "Old Times" coach 108 miles *173 km* from London to Brighton and back with 8 teams and 14 changes in 7 hrs 50 min to average 13.79 m.p.h. *22,19 km/h.* Four-horse carriages could maintain a speed of 21⅓ m.p.h. *34 km/h* for nearly an hour. The *Border Union* stage coach, built *c.* 1825, ran 4 in hand from Edinburgh to London (393 miles *632 km*). When it ceased in 1842 the allowed schedule was 42 hours 23 mins.

MOTOR CARS
Earliest automobiles *Model*
The earliest automobile of which there is record is a two-foot-long steam-powered model constructed by Ferdinand Verbiest (d. 1687) a Belgian Jesuit priest, and described in his *Astronomia Europaea.* His model of 1668 was possibly inspired either by Giovanni Branca's description of a steam turbine, published in his *La Macchina* in 1629, or by writings on "fire carts" or *Nan Huai-Jen* during the Chu dynasty (*c.* 800 B.C.) in the library of the Emperor Khang-hi of China, to whom he was an astronomer during the period *c.* 1665–80.

Earliest automobiles *Passenger-carrying*
The earliest mechanically-propelled passenger vehicle was the first of two military steam tractors, completed at the Paris Arsenal in 1769 by Nicolas-Joseph Cugnot (1725–1804). This reached 2¼ m.p.h. *3,6 km/h.* Cugnot's second, larger tractor, completed in May 1771, today survives in the *Conservatoire Nationale de Arts et Métiers* in Paris. Britain's first steam carriage carried eight passengers on 24 Dec. 1801 in Camborne, Cornwall and was built by Richard Trevithick (1771–1833).

Nelson's flagship H.M.S. *Victory*, the world's last surviving First Rate Ship-of-the-Line now 218 years old (see page 132).

Earliest automobiles *Internal combustion*
The first true internal-combustion engined vehicle was that built by the Londoner Samuel Brown (Patent 5350, 25 Apr. 1826) whose 4 h.p. *4,05 c.v.* two cylinder atmospheric gas 88 litre engined carriage climbed Shooters Hill, Blackheath, Kent in May 1826. The first successful petrol-driven car, the Motor-wagen, built by Karl-Friedrich Benz (1844–1929) of Karlsruhe, ran at Mannheim, Germany, in late 1885. It was a 5 cwt. *250 kg* 3-wheeler reaching 8–10 m.p.h. *13–16 km/h.* Its single cylinder 4-stroke chain-drive engine (bore 91.4 mm., stroke 160 mm.) delivered 0.85 h.p. *0,86 c.v.* at 200 r.p.m. It was patented on 29 Jan. 1886. Its first 1 kilometre road test was reported in the local newspaper, the *Neue Badische Landeszeitung,* of 4 June 1886, under the heading "Miscellaneous". Two were built in 1885 of which one has been preserved in "running order" at the Deutsches Museum, Munich.

Earliest automobile *British*
In Britain Edward Butler (1863–1940) built a 1,042 c.c. twin-cylinder 2-stroke petrol-engined tricycle at Erith, Kent in 1888 but the earliest successful British built car with an internal combustion engine was the Bremer car built at Walthamstow, Greater London, by the engineer Frederick William Bremer (1872–1941) which first took the road in December 1894 though the body was not completed until the following month. The car has a single cylinder horizontal, water cooled 600 c.c. engine with a two speed chain drive and tiller steering. The maximum speed is about 15 m.p.h. and the car in 1964 completed the London-to-Brighton run. It is now housed in the Vestry House Museum, London E.17. Henry Hewetson drove an imported Benz Velo in the south-eastern suburbs of London in November 1894.

Earliest registrations

The world's first plates were probably introduced by the Parisian police in France in 1893. Registration plates were introduced in Britain in 1903. The original A1 plate was secured by the 2nd Earl Russell (1865–1931) for his 12 h.p. *12,1 c.v.* Napier. This plate, willed in September 1950 to Mr. Trevor T. Laker of Leicester, was sold in August 1959 for £2,500 in aid of charity. It was reported in April 1973 that a "cherished" number plate changed hands for £14,000 in a private deal.

FASTEST CARS

Rocket-engined

The highest speed attained by any wheeled land vehicle is 631.367 m.p.h. *1 016,086 km/h* over the first measured kilometre by *The Blue Flame*, a rocket powered 4-wheeled vehicle driven by Gary Gabelich (b. San Pedro, California 29 Aug. 1940) on the Bonneville Salt Flats, Utah, U.S.A. on 23 Oct. 1970. Momentarily Gabelich exceeded 650 m.p.h. *1 046 km/h*. The car was powered by a liquid natural gas/hydrogen peroxide rocket engine developing a maximum 22,000 lb.s.t. and thus theoretically capable of 900 m.p.h. *1 448 km/h*.

Jet-engined

The highest speed attained by any jet-engined car is 613.995 m.p.h. *988,129 km/h* over a flying 666.386 yds *609,342 m* by the 34 ft 7 in *10,5 m* long 9,000 lb. *4 080 kg Spirit of America —Sonic I*, driven by Norman Craig Breedlove (b. Los Angeles, California, 23 Mar. 1938) on Bonneville Salt Flats, on 15 Nov. 1965. The car was powered by a General Electric J79 GE-3 jet engine, developing 15,000 lb.s.t. *6 080 kg* at sea-level.

Wheel-driven

The highest speed attained by a wheel-driven car is 429.311 m.p.h. *690,909 km/h* over a flying 666.386 yds *609,342 m* by Donald Malcolm Campbell, C.B.E. (1921–67), a British engineer, in the 30 ft *9,10 m* long *Bluebird*, weighing 9,600 lb. *4 354 kg* on the salt flats at Lake Eyre, South Australia, on 17 July 1964. The car was powered by a Bristol-Siddeley Proteus 705 gas-turbine engine developing 4,500 s.h.p. Its *peak* speed was *c.* 445 m.p.h. *716 km/h*. It was rebuilt in 1962, after a crash at about 360 m.p.h. *579 km/h* on 16 Sept. 1960.

Piston-engined

The highest speed attained by a piston-engined car is 418.504 m.p.h. *673,516 km/h* over a flying 666.386 yds *609,342 m* by Robert Sherman Summers (born Omaha, Nebraska, 4 Apr. 1937) in *Goldenrod* on Bonneville Salt Flats on 12 Nov. 1965. The car, measuring 32 ft *9,75 m* long and weighing 5,500 lb. *2 494 kg* was powered by four fuel-injected Chrysler Hemi engines (total capacity 27,924 c.c.) developing 2,400 b.h.p.

Racing car

The world's fastest racing car yet produced was the Porsche 917/30 Can-Am Car powered by a 5,374 c.c. flat 12 turbocharged engine developing 1,100 b.h.p. On the Paul Ricard circuit near Toulon, France, in Aug. 1973 Mark Donohue (U.S.A.) reached 257 m.p.h. *413,6 km/h*. The two models built took 2.2 secs for 0–60 m.p.h. *0–96 km/h*, 4.3 secs for 0–100 m.p.h. *0–160,9 km/h* and 12.6 secs for 0–200 m.p.h. *0–321,8 km/h*. In 1973 the UOP Shadow Can-Am car's 8.1 litre turbocharged Chevrolet V-8 engine developed 1,240 b.h.p.

Road cars

The fastest production road cars, capable of 300 km/h *186 m.p.h.*, are the Lamborghini Countach P400 and the Ferrari BB Berlinetta Boxer and GTB4 Daytona. The word "countach" is Piedmontese for "cor!". Various detuned track cars have been licensed in some countries for road use but are not purchasable production models. The fastest 0 to 60 m.p.h. *96,5 km/h* acceleration achieved in *Autocar* road tests is 5.4 secs by the Daytona and the Aston Martin Vantage, which has also reached 100 m.p.h. *160,9 km/h* in 13.0 secs.

Fastest lorry

The U.S. stock truck class A diesel record was set at 132.154 m.p.h. *212,635 km/h* on the Bonneville Salt Flats on 9 Sept.

The world's longest car, the 26 ft 7 in *8,10 m* long Cadillac special of Mr. Leo Weiser of New York City.

1975 by Harold Miller, 26 and Larry Lange, 38 in a 17,500 lb *7 937 kg* rig powered by a 1150 in³ *18 845 cm³* Cummins turbocharged diesel engine.

LARGEST CARS

World

Of cars produced for private road use, the largest has been the Bugatti "Royale" type 41, known in Britain as the "Golden Bugatti", of which only six (not seven) were made at Molsheim, France by the Italian Ettore Bugatti, and some survive. First built in 1927, this machine has an 8-cylinder engine of 12.7 litres capacity, and measures over 22 ft *6,7 m* in length. The bonnet is over 7 ft *2 m* long. The special Cadillac built for Leo Weiser, President of Automobile Club of America Inc. completed in Sept. 1976 measures 26 ft 7 in *8,10 m* in length. It weighs 9,000 lb. *4 080 kg* and carries 43 U.S. gals *162,7 litres* of fuel. It carries circular couches, television, stereo, bar, refrigerator, telephones, video tape recorder and 3 anti-theft systems. The longest present-day limousine is the Stageway Coaches Inc. 10 door Travelall 18 seat model measuring 25 ft 4¼ in *7,7 m* overall. (For cars not intended for private use, see Largest engines.)

Heaviest

The heaviest standard production car is the U.S.S.R.'s Zil 114, which weighs 7,000 lb. (3.12 ton *3 175 kg*.)

Largest Engines

Cars are compared on the basis of engine capacity. Distinction is made between those designed for normal road use and machines specially built for track racing and outright speed records.

Largest Engines *All-time record*

The world's most powerful piston engine car is "Quad Al." It was designed and built in 1964 by Jim Lytle and was first shown in May 1965 at the Los Angeles Sports Arena. The car featured four Allison V12 aircraft engines with a total of 6 840 in³ *112,087* c.c. displacement and 12,000 h.p. The car has 4-wheel drive, 8 wheels and tyres, and dual six-disc clutch assemblies. The wheelbase is 160 in *406,4 cm*, and weighs 5,860 lb. *2 658 kg*. It has 96 spark plugs and 96 exhaust pipes.

The largest car ever used was the "White Triplex", sponsored by J. H. White of Philadelphia, Pennsylvania, U.S.A. Completed early in 1928, after two year's work, the car weighed about 4 tons *4,06 tonnes* and was powered by three Liberty V12 aircraft engines with a total capacity of 81,188 c.c., developing 1,500 b.h.p. at 2,000 r.p.m. It was used to break the world speed record but crashed at Daytona, Florida on 13 Mar. 1929.

Largest Engines *Production car*

The highest engine capacity of a production car was $13\frac{1}{2}$ litres *824 in³*, in the case of the U.S. Pierce-Arrow 6-66 Raceabout of 1912–18, the U.S. Peerless 6-60 of 1912–14 and the Fageol of 1918. The largest currently available is the V8 engine of 500.1 in³ *8,195 c.c.*, developing 235 b.h.p. net, used in the 1972 Cadillac Fleetwood Eldorado.

Petrol consumption

The world record for fuel economy on a closed circuit course (one of 14.076 miles *22,00 km*) was set by Ben Visser (U.S.) in a highly modified 1.5 litre *90.8 in³* 1959 Opel Caravan station wagon in the annual Shell Research Laboratory contest at Wood River, Illinois, driven by Ben and Carolyn Visser on 2 Oct. 1973 with 451.90 ton miles per U.S. gal. and 376.59 miles *606,0 km* on one U.S. gal. i.e. *3,78 litres*. These figures are equivalent to 542.70 ton miles and 452.26 miles *727,84 km* on an imperial gallon i.e. *4,54 litres*. The tyre pressure was 200 lb/in² and the maximum speed was 12 m.p.h. *19,3 km/h.*

The 10 miles in an hour four stroke 3 wheel record is 1,141 miles per gallon *403,9 km per litre* by Brian W. Beattie and Brian Toft of the Shell Thornton Research Centre, Cheshire on 28 June 1976. They used a 50 c.c. Honda-engined sawn down tricycle.

Engine Change Record

The fastest time recorded for taking out a car engine and replacing it is 52 secs for a Mini-car by an R.A.F. team of 5 from Wattisham, Suffolk at Colchester, Essex on 3 Aug. 1974.

Champion Mechanic

Leopold Alfonso Villa O.B.E. (b. London 30 Nov. 1899) acted as racing mechanic or chief engineer for Sir Malcolm Campbell and Donald Campbell at 10 land and 11 water speed world records from 1924 to 1964.

Most Durable Car

The highest recorded mileage for a car is 789,000 miles *1 270 000 km* for a 1953 Mercedes 170SD in 23 years to 1976. It is owned by Warren Angstadt of Wernersville, Pennsylvania, U.S.A.

Taxis

The largest taxi fleet was that of New York City, which amounted to 29,000 cabs in October 1929, compared with the present figure of 12,500 plus an equal number of "gypsies". London's most durable "cabby" was F. Fuller, who drove from 26 Oct. 1908 until he handed in his badge on 16 Sept. 1966—57 years later. In May 1977 there were 12,000 cabs and 16,000 drivers in London.

Longest Taxi Ride

Mrs. Ann Drache, 60 and Mrs. Nesta Sgro, 57 hired a Hoboken, New Jersey taxi (driver, Jack Keator) on 9 Sept. and drove for an agreed fare of $2500 (£1,470) 6,752 miles *10 866 km* through 15 U.S. States arriving back on 6 Oct. 1976.

MOST EXPENSIVE CARS

Special

The most expensive car to build has been the U.S. Presidential 1969 Lincoln Continental Executive delivered to the U.S. Secret Service on 14 Oct. 1968. It has an overall length of 21 ft 6.3 in *6,56 m* with a 13 ft 4 in *4,06 m* wheel-base and with the addition of two tons *2,03 tonnes* of armour plate, weighs 5.35 tons *5,43 tonnes* (12,000 lb. *5 443 kg*). The estimated research, development and manufacture cost was $500,000 (*then £208,000*) but it is rented at $5,000 (*now £2,940*) per annum. Even if all four tyres were shot out it can travel at 50 m.p.h. *80 km/h* on inner rubber-edged steel discs.

Jack Keator (right) midway through his 6,752 mile *10 866 km* long taxi hiring with his two "fares" Mrs. Ann Drache and Mrs. Nesta Sgro (see above). (*David Ranns*)

Standard

The most expensive British standard car is the Rolls-Royce 8 cylinder 6,230 c.c. Phantom VI, quoted in the *Autocar New Car Price List* at £43,389 (incl. tax). Among more expensive custom built models are the Rolls-Royce Landaulette quoted at £78,000 in June 1977.

Used

The greatest price paid for any used car has been $280,000 (then *£121,740*) for a Rolls-Royce Phantom by an undisclosed Kentucky coal merchant from Chas. Schmitt & Co. of St. Louis, Missouri reported on 30 Nov. 1974. The car was "one previous owner, chauffeur driven" and was part of a job lot of seven Rolls-Royces. The previous owner was Queen Juliana. The greatest collection of vintage cars is the William F. Harrah Collection of 1,700, estimated to be worth more than $4 million (*£2·3 million*), at Reno, Nevada, U.S.A. Mr. Harrah is still looking for a Chalmer's Detroit 1909 Tourabout, an Owen car of 1910–12 and a Nevada Truck of 1915.

Most inexpensive

The cheapest car of all-time was the 1½ h.p. single cylinder Smith Flyer built by A. O. Smith Corp. of Milwaukee, Wisconsin, in 1916–1919 selling for $140. The cheapest of the 598 models listed in *Autocar's* New Car Prices feature on 7 May 1977 was the 988 c.c. Skoda S100 at £1,225 (incl. tax). The early models of the King Midget cars were sold in kit form for self-assembly for as little as $100 (*then £24 16s.*) as late as 1948.

Longest production

The longest any car has been in production is 42 years (1910–52), including wartime interruptions, in the case of the "Flat Twin" engined Jowett produced in Britain. The Ford Model T production record of 15,007,033 cars (1908–1927) was surpassed by the Volkswagen "Beetle" series, originally designed by Ferninand Porsche, when their 15,007,034th car since May 1938 came off the production line on 17 Feb. 1972. Production by May 1977 had reached 19,113,000. Britain's all-time champion is the Mini, originally sold for £496 19s 2d (incl. Purchase Tax) in Aug. 1959. The 4 millionth sold on 22 Nov. 1976 and reached 4,061,476 by May 1977.

Round the World Driving

The fastest circumnavigation embracing more than an equator's length of driving (26,514.43 road miles *42 670 km*) is one in 102 days 18 hrs 26 min 54.7 secs by Johnnie Parsons in the U.S. Bicentennial Global Record Run from 4 July to 15 Oct. 1976 in a Pontiac G.P. He averaged 47.22 m.p.h. *75,99 km/h*. Paula Murphy *née* Mulhauser finishing on 17 Oct. 1976 drove her Pontiac Sunbird 26,412.30 road miles *42,506 km* in 105 days 2 hrs 29 min 25.0 secs averaging 47.49 m.p.h. *76,42 km/h* also through 28 countries.

Mountain Driving

Cars have been driven up Ben Nevis, Highland, Scotland (4,406 ft *1 342 m*) on 4 occasions. The record times are 7 hr 23 min (ascent) and 1 hr 55 min (descent) by George F. Simpson in an Austin 7 on 6 Oct. 1928. Henry Alexander accomplished the feat twice in May 1911 (Model T Ford) and on 13 Sept. 1928 (Model A Ford).

Driving in Reverse

Charles Creighton (1908–1970) and James Hargis of Maplewood, Missouri, U.S.A., drove their Ford Model A 1929 roadster in reverse from New York City 3,340 miles *5 375 km* to Los Angeles, California on 26 July–13 Aug. 1930 without once stopping the engine. They arrived back in New York in reverse on 5 Sept. so completing 7,180 miles *11 555 km* in 42 days.

Oldest driver

Roy M. Rawlins (b. 10 July 1870) of Stockton, California, U.S.A., was warned for driving at 95 m.p.h. *152 km/h* in a 55 m.p.h. *88,5 km/h* zone in June 1974. On 25 Aug. 1974 he was awarded a California State licence valid till 1978 when he will be 108. Mrs. Maude Tull of Inglewood, California, who took to driving aged 91 after her husband died, was issued a renewal on 5 Feb. 1976 when aged 104. Britain's only recorded centenarian driver was Herbert Warren (1874–1975) of Whatlington, Norfolk, who drove a 1954 Standard 10. The oldest age at which anyone has passed the then Ministry of Transport driving test was on 20 Sept. 1969 at Sutton-in-Derwent, Yorkshire, when Mr. Arthur Daniel (b. 7 Feb. 1884) passed at his second attempt aged 85. The highest year number ever displayed on a Veteran Motorist's badge was "75" by Walter Herbert Weake, who started his accident free career in 1894 and drove daily until his death in 1969, aged 91.

Youngest driver

Instances of drivers passing their test in Britain on their 17th birthday are periodically reported. Gordon John Graham of Clydebank, Strathclyde passed his advanced driving test aged 17 years 18 days on 20 Nov. 1973.

"L" test *Most failures*

The record for persistence in taking the Ministry of Transport's Learners' Test is held by Mrs. Miriam Hargrave, 62, of Wakefield. West Yorkshire, who failed her 39th driving test in eight years on 29 Apr. 1970 after "crashing" a set of red lights. She triumphed at her 40th attempt on 3 Aug. 1970. The examiner was alleged not to have known about her previous 39 tests.

Buses *Earliest*

The first municipal motor omnibus service in the world was inaugurated on 12 April 1903 between Eastbourne railway station and Meads, East Sussex, England.

Longest

The longest buses in the world are the 76 ft *23,16 m* long articulated buses, with 121 passenger seats, built by the Wayne Corporation of Indiana, U.S.A. for use in the Middle East.

Longest route

The longest regularly scheduled bus route is the Greyhound "Supercruiser" Miami, Florida, to San Francisco, California, route over 3,240 miles *5 214 km* in 81 hours 50 min (average speed of travel 39.59 m.p.h. *63,71 km/h*). The total Greyhound fleet numbers 5,500 buses.

Longest motor caravan journey

The longest motor caravan tour on record is one 88,607 miles *142 600 km* in a Volkswagen by Jonathan and Theresa Hewat between Jan. 1973 and June 1976 through 56 countries.

Most massive vehicles

The most massive vehicle ever constructed is the Marion eight-caterpillar crawler used for conveying *Saturn V* rockets to their launching pads at the John F. Kennedy Space Center, Florida (See Chapter 4, Most powerful rocket). It measures 131 ft 4 in *40 m* by 114 ft *34,7 m* and the two built cost $12,300,000 (*then £5,125,000*). The loaded train weight is 8,036 tons *8 165 tonnes*. Its windscreen wipers with 42 in *106 cm* blades are the world's largest.

Bulldozers *Largest*

The world's most powerful bulldozer is the 136.16 ton *138,3 tonne* VCON V220 diesel electric bulldozer completed by the Marion Power Shovel Co. Inc. of Dallas, Texas in 1975. The blade is 26 ft *7,9 m* wide and can push 90 yd³ *68,8 m³* of earth. The machine is 52 ft *15,8 m* long and 23½ ft *7,16 m* high with 500 h.p. on each of the four 10 ft 2 in *3,09 m* diameter wheels.

Largest Earth Mover

The world's largest earth mover is the Balderson "Double Dude" plow (plough) harnessed to a Caterpillar SXS D9H 820 flywheel horsepower tractor. It can cast 14,185 yd³ *10 845 m³* per hour.

Dumper Truck *Largest*

The world's largest dump truck is the Terex Titan 33–19 manufactured by the Terex Division of General Motors Corporation. It has a loaded weight of 539.9 tons *548,6 tonnes* and a capacity of 312½ tons *317,5 tonnes*. When tipping its height is 56 ft *17,06 m*. The 16 cylinder engine delivers 3,300 h.p. The fuel tank holds 1,300 Imperial gallons *5 904,6 litres*. It went into service in Nov. 1974.

Load Heaviest and largest *World*

The world's record road load is one of 400 short tons *363 tonnes*. This reactor was moved from Avila Beach for 10 miles *16 km* to Diablo Canyon, California in November 1970. The conveyance called "Atlas", built by the Bigge Drayage Co. itself weighs 211 short tons *191 tonnes* has 192 wheels in 16 groups of twelve.

Great Britain

The heaviest road load moved in the United Kingdom has been a stator frame of 310 tons *315,06 tonnes* moved by Robert Wynn & Sons for export order for G.E.C. Stafford to Pomona Dock, Manchester on 23–27 May 1976. The longest load moved on British roads has been a 192 ft *58,5 m* 143 ton Belgian made main wash column to I.C.I. Wilton on 29 July 1976. The greatest weight moved on wheels anywhere in the world was a 1,400 ton *1 422 tonne* oil platform module from Whessoe Ltd. at Middlesbrough, Cleveland on 400 wheels by Wynn's onto a barge on 18 Apr. 1976. It measured 260 ft *79,2 m* in length.

Largest Steam Traction Engine

The largest automobile steam traction engine is the 25 ton Showman's Road Locomotive Supreme with a 10 h.p. Super Lion coal-fired engine built by John Fowler of Leeds, West Yorkshire, England in 1934 for £3,250. The best of the three surviving is owned by S. J. Wharton.

Amphibious vehicle circumnavigation

The only trans-Atlantic crossing by an amphibious vehicle was achieved by Ben and Elinore Carlin (Australia and U.S.A. respectively) in an amphibious jeep "Half-Safe". He completed the last leg of the Atlantic crossing (the English Channel) on 24 Aug. 1951. He arrived back in Montreal, Canada on 8 May 1958 having completed a circumnavigation of 39,000 miles *62 765 km* over land and 9,600 miles *15 450 km* by sea and river.

Go-kart circumnavigation

The only recorded instance of a go-kart being driven round the world was a circumnavigation by Stan Mott, of New York, U.S.A., who drove a Lambretta engined 175 c.c. Italkart, with a ground clearance of 2 in *5 cm*, 23,300 land miles *37 500 km* through 28 countries from 15 Feb. 1961 to 5 June 1964, starting and finishing in New York, U.S.A.

Skid marks Longest

The longest recorded skid marks on a public road have been those 950 ft *290 m* long left by a Jaguar car involved in an accident on the M1 near Luton, Bedfordshire, on 30 June 1960. Evidence given in the High Court case *Hurlock* v. *Inglis and others* indicated a speed "in excess of 100 m.p.h. *160 km/h*" before the application of the brakes. The skid marks made by the jet-powered *Spirit of America*, driven by Craig Breedlove, after the car went out of control at Bonneville Salt Flats, Utah, U.S.A., on 15 Oct. 1964, were nearly 6 miles *9,6 km* long. (see Jet-engined record p. 134)

Tyres Largest

The world's largest tyres are manufactured in Topeka, Kansas by the Goodyear Co. for giant dumper trucks. They measure 11 ft 11 in *3,63 m* in diameter and weigh 8,000 lb. *3 628 kg*. A tyre 17 ft *5,18 m* in diameter is believed to be the limitation of what is practical.

Petrol Station

The largest gallonage sold claimed through a single pump is 7,399.3 gal. *33 638,2 litres* in 24 hours on 24 Nov. 1974 at the Downtown Service Station, Auckland, N.Z.

Tow Longest

The longest tow on record was one of 4,759 miles *7 658 km* from Halifax, Nova Scotia to Canada's Pacific Coast, when Frank J. Elliott and George A. Scott of Amherst persuaded 168 passing motorists in 89 days to tow their Model T Ford (in fact engineless) to win a $1,000 bet on 15 Oct. 1927.

MOTORCYCLES
Earliest and Largest

The earliest internal combustion-engined motorized bicycle was a wooden-framed machine built at Bad Constatt in Nov. 1885 by Gottlieb Daimler (1834–1900) of Germany and first ridden by Wilhelm Maybach (1846–1929). It had a top speed of 12 m.p.h. *19 km/h* and developed one-half of one horse-power from its single-cylinder 264 c.c. four-stroke engine at 700 r.p.m. The first motorcycles of entirely British production were the 1,046 c.c. Holden flat-four and the 2¾ h.p. Clyde single both produced in 1898. The earliest factory which made motorcycles in quantity was opened in 1894 by Heinrich and Wilhelm Hildebrand and Alois Wolfmüller at Munich, West Germany. In its first two years this factory produced over 1,000 machines, each having a water-cooled 1,488 c.c. twin-cylinder four-stroke engine developing about 2.5 b.h.p. at 600 r.p.m.—the largest ever motor cycle put into production.

Absolute Speed Record

The highest speed ever achieved on a motorcycle is 307.692 m.p.h. *495,183 km/h* by Don Vesco (U.S.) on his *Silver Bird* at Bonneville Salt Flats, Utah, U.S.A. on 28 Sept. 1975 in a flying quarter mile (see further details Chapter 12, Motorcycling.)

Fastest road machine

The fastest production motorcycle ever made is the Dunstall Kawasaki powered by a four-cylinder 1,100 c.c. engine developing 85 b.h.p. Road test maxima have been 138 m.p.h. *222 km/h* (mean) and 147.4 m.p.h. *237,2 km/h* (one-way).

Fastest racing machine

The fastest racing motorcycle ever is the 748 c.c. 130 b.h.p. Yamaha OW 31 four cylinder two-stroke which is capable of 186.4 m.p.h. *300 km/h*. Of British machines the fastest ever were the 741 c.c. 3-cylinder B.S.A. Rocket 3 and Triumph Trident racers used in the "Daytona 200" on 14 Mar. 1971. They developed 84 b.h.p. and were capable of 170 m.p.h. *273 km/h*.

Duration Record

The longest time a solo motorcycle has been kept in non-stop motion is 466 hr 10 min by Noel Mallyon, Malcolm Mallyon and Ken Bland, riding a Yamaha RD 400 in Emerald, Queensland, Australia on 2–21 Oct. 1976. They covered approximately 25,000 km *15,534 miles*.

Most on One Machine

The Huntingdon Park Elks stunt and drill team from California mounted and rode 17 men on a 1200 c.c. Harley Davidson in April 1974. The feat was repeated at Sydney Showground, Australia on 21 May 1976 when Sgt. Henry Brennan drove a Police 750 c.c. Honda 535 metres *585 yd* with 13 other policemen and 3 police women aboard totalling 1,412 kg *1.38 tons*.

Most expensive

The most expensive road motorcycle in current production is the 790 c.c. in-line four cylinder Italian built M.V.—Agusta 750 S America which retailed in Britain for £3,765 in February 1977.

BICYCLES
Earliest

The first design for a machine propelled by cranks and pedals, with connecting rods has been attributed to Leonardo da Vinci (1452–1519) or one of his pupils dated *c* 1493. The earliest such design actually built was in 1839–40 by Kirkpatrick Macmillan (1810–78) of Dumfries, Scotland. It is now in the Science Museum, Kensington and Chelsea, Greater London.

Longest

The longest tandem "bicycle" ever built is the 1⅓ ton *1 360 kg* Vestergaard multipede built in Koege, Denmark in April 1976. It seats 35 and measures 72 feet *21,94 m* in length and has an additional stabilizing wheel.

Smallest

The world's smallest wheeled rideable bicycle is one with
2⅛ in *5,4 cm* wheels weighing 2 lb. *900 g* built and ridden by
Charlie Charles at Circus Circus Hotel, Las Vegas, Nevada
U.S.A.

Largest

A classic Ordinary bicycle with wheels of 64 in *162,5 cm*
diameter front and 20 in *50,8 cm* back was built *c.* 1886 by
the Pope Manufacturing Co. of Massachusetts, U.S.A.
It is now owned by Paul Niquette of Connecticut.

Unicycle records

The tallest unicycle ever mastered in one 39 ft 10 in *12,14 m*
tall ridden (with a safety belt or mechanic) by Jim Petty, 29
in Grand Junction, Colorado on 19 Nov. 1976. Walter J.
Watts (Canada) (b. 2 Oct. 1948) set a duration record when
he completed in 93 days the trans-Canadian leg of 4,550
miles *7 322 km* of his round the world tour from Vancouver
(26 May) to Halifax (27 Aug. 1973). The unicycle marathon
record is 85 miles *136,7 km* in 14 hr 35 min covered by Tim
Burns of Princetown Junction, New Jersey, U.S.A. on 18
Aug. 1976.

Penny-Farthing record

The record for riding from Land's End to John o'Groats on
Ordinary Bicycles, more commonly known in the 1870's as
Penny-Farthings, is 13 days (123½ hours riding) by Brian
Thompson, 34 in 1970.

Lawn Mower Largest

The widest gang mower in the world is the 5 ton 60 ft *18,28 m*
wide 27 unit Big Green Machine used by the sod farmer
Jay Edgar Frick of Monroe, Ohio. It mows an acre in
60 secs.

The world's only acre-a-minute grass mower, owned by sod farmer Jay Frick. (*Middletown Journal*)

3. RAILWAYS

Guinness Superlatives has now published railway records in much greater detail
in the more specialist publication *Guinness Book of Rail Facts and Feats* (price
£4.95).

TRAINS

Earliest

Railed trucks were used for mining as early as 1550 at
Leberthal, Alsace and at the Broseley colliery, Salop in
October 1605, but the first self-propelled locomotive ever to
run on rails was that built by Richard Trevithick (1771–1833)
and demonstrated over 9 miles *14 km* with a 10 ton *10,2
tonnes* load and 70 passengers in Penydarren, Mid Glamorgan,
on 21 Feb. 1804. The earliest established railway to have a
steam powered locomotive was the Middleton Colliery Railway, set up by an Act of 9 June 1758 running between
Middleton Colliery and Leeds Bridge, Yorkshire. This line
went over to the use of steam locomotives (gauge 4 ft 1 in)
built by Matthew Murray (1765–1826), in 1812. The Stockton and Darlington Railway, Cleveland, which ran from
Shildon through Darlington to Stockton, opened on 27 Sept.
1825. The 7 ton *7,1 tonnes* *Locomotion I* (formerly *Active*)
could pull 48 tons *48,7 tonnes* at a speed of 15 mp.h. *24 km/h.*
It was designed and driven by George Stevenson (1781–
1848). The first regular steam passenger run was inaugurated
over a one mile section (between Bogshole Farm and South
Street) on the 6¼ mile *10,05 km* track between Canterbury
and Whitstable, Kent, on 3 May 1830 hauled by the engine
Invicta. The first electric railway was Werner von Siemen's
600 yds *548 m* long Berlin electric railway opened for the
Berlin Trades' Exhibition on 31 May 1879.

Fastest *Electric*

The world rail speed record was set up by the U.S. Federal
Railroad Administration LIMRV (Linear Induction Motor
Research Vehicle) built by the Garrett Corporation on the
6.2 mile *9,97 km* long Pueblo test track, Colorado, U.S.A.
when a speed of 234.2 m.p.h. *376,9 km/h* was attained on
28 Mar. 1974.

*A progressive table of railway speed records from 1829 to date
was published in the 23rd edition on page 141.*

Steam

The highest speed ever ratified for a steam locomotive was
126 m.p.h. *202 km/h* over 440 yds *402 m* by the L.N.E.R.
4-6-2 No. 4468 *Mallard* (later numbered 60022), which
hauled seven coaches weighing 240 tons *243 tonnes* gross,
down Stoke Bank, near Essendine, between Grantham,
Lincolnshire, and Peterborough, Cambridgeshire on 3 July
1938. Driver Joseph Duddington was at the controls with
Fireman Thomas Bray. The engine suffered severe damage.
On 12 June 1905 a speed of 127.06 mp.h. *204,48 km/h* was
claimed for the "Pennsylvania Special" near Ada, Ohio,
U.S.A. but has never been accepted by leading experts.

Regular run *World*

The fastest point-to-point schedule in the world is that of the

"New Tokaido" service of the Japanese National Railways from Osaka to Okayama, inaugurated on 15 Mar. 1972. The train covers 99.9 miles *160,7 km* in 58 mins, averaging 103.3 m.p.h. *166,2 km/h.* The peak speed attainable with a 950 ton *965 tonnes* 16 car train is 159 m.p.h. *255,9 km/h.*

Great Britain

British Rail inaugurated their HST (High Speed Train) daily services between London–Bristol and South Wales on 4 Oct. 1976. On 7 May 1977 one covered the 117¾ miles *189,5 km* between Bristol and Paddington, London in 68 min 20 sec to average 103.38 m.p.h. *166,37 km/h.* The peak speed is 125 m.p.h. *201 km/h.* The prototype British Rail gas turbine APT-E (Advanced Passenger Train-Experimental) attained 152 m.p.h. *244,6 km/h,* between Swindon and Reading on the Bristol-London line on 10 Aug. 1975.

Longest Non-Stop

The world's longest daily non-stop run is that on Amtrak's "Silver Meteor" 1,377 miles *2 216 km* from New York City to Miami, Florida. The 659 mile *1 060 km* section between Richmond, Virginia and Jacksonville, Florida is run entirely without stops. The longest run on British Rail without any advertised stop is the Night Motorail Service from Olympia, Kensington and Chelsea, Greater London to Inverness inaugurated in May 1973. The distance is 565 miles *909 km* and the time taken is 13 hours 20 min.

Most Powerful World

The world's most powerful steam locomotive, measured by tractive effort, was No. 700, a triple articulated or triplex 2-8-8-8-4, the Baldwin Locomotive Co. 6-cylinder engine built in 1916 for the Virginian Railway. It had a tractive force of 166,300 lb. *75 432 kg* working compound and 199,560 lb. *90 518 kg* working simple. The most powerful locomotives measured on a potential horsepower basis were the Northern Pacific 2-8-8-4 "Mallets" first built in 1928 with a tractive effort of 145,930 lb. *66 193 kg* with a booster adding 13,400 lb. *6 078 kg.* Probably the heaviest train ever hauled by a single engine was one of 15,300 tons *15 545 tonnes* made up of 250 freight cars stretching 1.6 miles *2,5 km* by the *Matt H. Shay* (No. 5014), a 2-8-8-8-2 engine which ran on the Erie Railroad from May 1914 until 1929.

Longest freight train

The longest and heaviest freight train on record was one about 4 miles *6 km* in length consisting of 500 coal cars with three 3,600 h.p. diesels pulling and three more pushing on the Iaeger, West Virginia to Portsmouth, Ohio stretch of 157 miles *252 km* on the Norfolk and Western Railway on 15 Nov. 1967. The total weight was nearly 42,000 tons *42 674 tonnes.*

Greatest load

The heaviest single piece of freight ever conveyed by rail was a 1,230,000 lb. *557 918 kg* (549.2 ton *558 tonnes*) 106 ft *32,3 m* tall hydrocracker reactor which was carried from Birmingham, Alabama, to Toledo, Ohio, U.S.A., on 12 Nov. 1965.

The heaviest load carried by British Rail was a 122 ft *37,1 m* long boiler drum, weighing 275 tons *279 tonnes* which was carried from Immingham Dock to Killinghome, Humberside in September 1968.

The heaviest load ever moved on rails is the 10,700 ton Church of the Virgin Mary built in 1548 in the village of Most, Czechoslovakia in Oct.-Nov. 1975 because it was in the way of coal deposits. It was moved 800 yds *730 m* at 0.0013 m.p.h. *0,002 km/h* over 4 weeks at a cost of £9 million.

TRACKS
Longest line

The world's longest run is one of 9 334 km *5,799 miles* on the Trans Siberian line from Moscow to Nakhodka, U.S.S.R. in the Soviet Far East. There are 97 stops. The Baykal-Amur Magistral (BAM) northern line, begun with forced labour in 1938, is expected to be open in 1982 and will cut

British Rail's High Speed Train, which, in May 1977, first averaged more than 100 m.p.h. for more than 100 miles *160 km* (see left).

500 km *310 miles* off the route round the southern end of Lake Baykall. A total of 10,000 million ft³ *283,000,000 m³* of earth has to be moved.

Longest straight

The longest straight in the world is on the Commonwealth Railways Trans Australian line over the Nullarbor Plain from Mile 496 between Nurina and Loongana, Western Australia, to Mile 793 between Ooldea and Watson, South Australia, 297 miles *478 km* dead straight although not level. The longest straight on British Rail is the 18 miles *29 km* between Balley and Staddlethorpe Junctions on the Selby, North Yorkshire to Kingston-upon-Hull, Humberside line.

Widest and Narrowest

The widest gauge in standard use is 5 ft 6 in *1,676 m.* This width is used in India, Pakistan, Bangladesh, Sri Lanka (Ceylon), Argentina and Chile. In 1885 there was a lumber railway in Oregon, U.S.A., with a gauge of 8 ft *2,4 m.* The narrowest gauges in use are 1 ft 3 ins *0,381 m* on the Ravenglass & Eskdale Railway, Cumbria (7 miles *11,2 km*) and the Romney, Hythe & Dymchurch line in Kent (14 miles *22,53 km*).

Highest *World*

The highest standard gauge (4 ft 8½ in *1,43 m*) track in the world is on the Peruvian State Railways at La Cima, on the Morocoha Branch at 15,806 ft *4 817 m* above sea-level. The highest point on the main line is 15,688 ft *4 781 m* in the Galera tunnel.

Great Britain

The highest point of the British Rail system is at the pass of Druimnachdar on the former Perth-Inverness border, where the track reaches an altitude of 1,484 ft *452 m* above sea-level. The highest railway in Britain is the Snowdon Mountain Railway, which rises from Llanberis, Gwynedd to 3,493 ft *1 064 m* above sea-level, just below the summit of Snowdon (Yr Wyddfa). It has a gauge of 2 ft 7½ in *800 mm.*

Lowest

The lowest point on British Rail is in the Severn Tunnel—144 ft *43,8 m* below sea-level.

Steepest Gradient *World*

The world's steepest standard gauge gradient by adhesion is 1:11 between Chedde and Servoz on the SNCF Chamonix line, France.

Great Britain

The steepest sustained adhesion-worked gradient on main line in the United Kingdom is the two-mile Lickey incline of 1:37.7 in Hereford and Worcester. From the tunnel bottom to James Street, Liverpool, on the former Mersey Railway, there is a stretch of 1:27; and between Folkestone Junction and Harbour a mile *1,6 km* of 1:30.

Shallowest Gradient

The shallowest gradient posted on the British Rail system is one indicated as 1 in 14,400 between Pirbright Junction and Farnborough, Hampshire. This could be described alternatively as England's most obtuse summit.

Busiest Rail system

The world's most crowded rail system is the Japanese National Railways, which by 1971 carried 16,495,000 passengers daily. Professional pushers are employed on the Tōkyō Service to squeeze in passengers before the doors can be closed. Among articles lost in 1970 were 419,929 umbrellas, 172,106 shoes, 250,630 spectacles and hats and also assorted false teeth and artificial eyeballs.

Greatest mileage

The greatest mileage covered with a 7 day all-line roving ticket on British Rail is 10,306½ miles *16 586,7 km* on 18–24 Apr. 1977 by J. Jeffrey of Maidstone, Kent. He carried on another week to reach 19,912½ miles *32 046,0 km.*

Most Countries in a Day

Dr. Kurt Kauffmann of Lucerne, Switzerland on 19 Feb. 1976 (his 76th birthday) travelled by rail in 8 countries— West Germany, Austria, Liechtenstein, Switzerland, France, Luxemburg, Belgium and the Netherlands.

STATIONS
Largest *World*

The world's largest railway station is Grand Central Terminal, Park Avenue and 43rd Street, New York City, N.Y., U.S.A., built 1903–13. It covers 48 acres *19 ha* on two levels with 41 tracks on the upper level and 26 on the lower. On average more than 550 trains and 180,000 people per day use it, with a peak of 252,288 on 3 July 1947.

Great Britain

The largest railway station in extent on the British Rail system is the 17-platform Clapham Junction, London covering 27¾ acres *11,22 ha* with a total face of 11,185 ft *3 409 m.* The station with the largest number of platforms is Waterloo, London (24½ acres *9,9 ha*), with 21 main line and two Waterloo and City Line platforms, with a total face of 15,352 ft *4 679 m.* Victoria Station (21¾ acres *8,80 ha*) with 17 platforms has, however, a total face length of 18,412 ft *5 611 m.* The oldest station in Britain is Liverpool Road Station, Greater Manchester, first used on 15 Sept. 1830.

Busiest

The world's busiest station is reputedly the main Moscow Station, U.S.S.R. which in 1972 handled some 2,740,000 passengers daily. The busiest railway junction in Great Britain is Clapham Junction, Wandsworth, Greater London on the Southern Region of British Rail, with an average of 2,392 trains passing through each 24 hours (June, 1977).

Highest

The highest station in the world is Condor, Bolivia at 15,705 ft *4 786 m* on the metre gauge Rio Mulato to Potosi line. The highest passenger station on British Rail is Corrour, Highland, at an altitude of *1,347* ft *410,5 m* above sea-level.

Waiting rooms

The world's largest waiting rooms are those in Peking Station, Chang'an Boulevard, Peking, China, opened in September 1959, with a capacity of 14,000.

Longest platform

The longest railway platform in the world is the Kharagpur platform, West Bengal, India, which measures 2,733 ft *833 m* in length. The State Street Center subway platform staging on "The Loop" in Chicago, Illinois, U.S.A., measures 3,500 ft *1 066 m* in length.

The longest platform in the British Rail system is the 1,981 ft *603,8 m* long platform at Colchester, Essex.

UNDERGROUND RAILWAYS
Most extensive

The most extensive and earliest (opened 10 Jan. 1863) underground or rapid transit railway system of the 67 in the world is that of the London Transport Executive, with 252 miles *405 km* of route, of which 77 miles *123 km* is bored tunnel and 22 miles *35 km* is "cut and cover". This whole Tube system is operated by a staff of 10,500 serving 279 stations. The 591 trains comprising 4,368 cars carried 638,750,000 passengers in 1975. The greatest depth is 221 ft *67,3 m* near Hampstead on the Northern Line. The longest journey without a change is Epping to West Ruislip—34.1 miles *54,8 km.* The record for touring the then 277 stations was 15 hours precisely by Leslie R. V. Burwood on 3 Sept. 1968.

Busiest

The busiest subway in the world is the New York City Transport Authority (opened on 27 Oct. 1904) with a total of 230.64 route miles *371,17 km* and 2,081,810,464 passengers in 1970. The 460 stations are closer set than London's. The record for travelling the whole system is 21 hours 8½ min by Mayer Wiesen and Charles Emerson on 8 Oct. 1973.

MODEL RAILWAYS
Duration Record

The non-stop duration record for a model train is 273.84 miles *440,70 km* by a Rovex-Hornby *Princess* hauling 6 bogie coaches over 23,570 circuits at Mevagissey, Cornwall, England, taking 194 hrs 27 mins from 31 July to 8 Aug. 1973. The scale speed was 107 m.p.h. *172,2 km/h.*

TRAMS
Longest tram journey

The longest tramway journeys now possible are in the Rhein-Ruhr area of West Germany from Dinslaken to Krefeld, a distance of 64 km *40 miles.* The record journeys in the United Kingdom have been by the famous illuminated car from Edgehill Works, Merseyside *via* Knotty Ash, St. Helens, Greater Manchester, Atherton, Leigh, Salford and then branching off to Ashton-under-Lyne on 13 Dec. 1925 and alternatively to Stockport on 14 Nov. 1926. Both journeys were of some 40 miles *64 km* in length.

MONORAIL
Highest Speed

The highest speed ever attained on rails is 3,090 m.p.h. *4 972 km/h* (Mach 4.1) by an unmanned rocket-powered sled on the 6.62 mile *10,65 km* long captive track at the U.S. Air Force Missile Development Center at Holloman, New Mexico, U.S.A., on 19 Feb. 1959. The highest speed reached carrying a chimpanzee is 1,295 m.p.h. *2 084 km/h.*

The highest speed attained by a tracked hovercraft is 235 m.p.h. *378 km/h* by the jet-powered *L'Aérotrain*, invented by Jean Bertin.

---

4. AIRCRAFT

Guinness Superlatives has published aircraft records in much greater detail in the specialist publication *Guinness Book of Air Facts and Feats* (3rd edition) (price £6.50).

Note—The use of the Mach scale for aircraft speeds was introduced by Prof. Acherer of Zürich, Switzerland. The Mach number is the ratio of the velocity of a moving body to the local velocity of sound. This ratio was first employed by Dr. Ernst Mach (1838–1916) of Vienna, Austria in 1887. Thus Mach 1.0 equals 760.98 m.p.h. *1 224,67 km/h* at sea-level at 15°C, and is assumed, for convenience, to fall to a constant 659.78 m.p.h. *1 061,81 km/h* in the stratosphere, *i.e.* above 11,000 m *36,089 ft.*

EARLIEST FLIGHTS
World

The first controlled and sustained power-driven flight occurred near the Kill Devil Hill, Kitty Hawk, North Carolina, U.S.A., at 10.35 a.m. on 17 December 1903, when Orville Wright (1871–1948) flew the 12 h.p. chain-driven *Flyer I* for a distance of 120 ft *36,5 m* at an airspeed of 30 m.p.h. *48 km/h,* a ground speed of 6.8 m.p.h. *10,9 km/h* and an altitude of 8–12 ft *2,4–3,6 m* for about 12 sec watched by his brother Wilbur (1867–1912), three life savers and two others. Both brothers, from Dayton, Ohio, were bachelors because, as Orville put it, they had not the means to "support a wife as well as an aeroplane". The *Flyer* is now in the National Air and Space Museum at the Smithsonian Institution, Washington D.C.

The first man-carrying powered aeroplane to fly, but not entirely under its own power, was the monoplane with a hot-air engine built by Félix Du Temple de la Croix (1823–90), a French naval officer, and piloted by a young sailor who made a short hop after taking off, probably down an incline at Brest, France, in c. 1874. The first hop by a man-carrying aeroplane entirely under its own power was made when Clément Ader (1841–1925) of France flew in his *Eole* for about 50 m *164 ft* at Armainvilliers, France, on 9 Oct. 1890. The earliest "rational design" according to the Royal Aeronautical Society, for a flying machine was that published by Emanuel Swendenborg (1688–1772) in Sweden in 1717.

Great Britain
The first officially recognised flight in the British Isles was made by the U.S. citizen Samuel Franklin Cody (1861–1913) who flew 1,390 ft *423 m* in his own biplane at Farnborough, Hampshire, on 16 Oct. 1908. Horatio Frederick Phillips (1845–1924) almost certainly covered 500 ft *152 m* in his Phillips II "*Venetian blind*" aeroplane at Streatham, in 1907. The first resident British citizen to fly in a powered 'plane was Griffith Brewer (1867–1948), as a passenger of Wilbur Wright, on 8 Oct. 1908 at Auvours, France.

Cross-Channel
The earliest cross-Channel flight by an aeroplane was made on Sunday, 25 July 1909 when Louis Blériot (1872–1936) of France flew his *Blériot XI* monoplane, powered by a 23 h.p. Anzani engine, 26 miles *41,8 km* from Les Baraques, France, to Northfall Meadow near Dover Castle, England, in 36½ minutes, after taking off at 4.41 a.m.

Jet-engined *World*
Proposals for jet propulsion date back to Captain Marconnet (1909) of France, and Henri Coanda (1886–1972) of Romania and to the turbojet proposals of Maxime Guillaume in 1921. The earliest test bed run was that of the British Power Jets Ltd.'s experimental W.U. (Whittle Unit) on 12 Apr. 1937, invented by Flying Officer (now Air Commodore Sir) Frank Whittle (b. Coventry, 1 June 1907), who had applied for a patent on jet propulsion in 1930. The first flight by an aeroplane powered by a turbojet engine was made by the Heinkel He 178, piloted by Flug Kapitan Erich Warsitz, at Marienehe, Germany, on 27 Aug. 1939. It was powered by a Heinkel S3B engine (834 lb. s.t. as installed with long tail-pipe) designed by Dr. Hans 'Pabst' von Ohain and first tested in August 1937.

Great Britain
The first British jet flight occurred when Fl. Lt. P. E. G. "Jerry" Sayer, O.B.E., (k. 1942) flew the Gloster-Whittle E.28/39 (wing span 29 ft *8,83 m*, length 25 ft 3 in *7,69 m*) fitted with an 860 lb. *390 kg* s.t. Whittle W-1 engine for 17 min at Cranwell, Lincolnshire, on 15 May 1941. The maximum speed was c. 350 m.p.h. *560 km/h*.

Supersonic flight
The first supersonic flight was achieved on 14 Oct. 1947 by Capt. (later Brig.-Gen) Charles ("Chuck") Elwood Yeager, U.S.A.F. retd. (b. 13 Feb. 1923), over Edwards Air Force Base, Muroc, California, U.S.A., in a Bell XS-1 rocket plane ("Glamorous Glennis"), with Mach 1.015 (670 m.p.h. *1 078 km/h*) at an altitude of 42,000 ft *12 800 m*.

The first British aeroplane, and the first turbojet-powered aeroplane in the world, to achieve supersonic speed was a de Havilland D. H. 108 tailless research aircraft which, piloted by John Derry, recorded a Mach number between 1.0 and 1.1 in a dive on 6 Sept. 1948.

Trans-Atlantic
The first crossing of the North Atlantic by air was made by Lt-Cdr. (later Rear Admiral) Albert Cushion Read (1887–1967) and his crew (Stone, Hinton, Rodd, Rhoads and Breese) in the 84 knot *155 km/h* U.S. Navy/Curtiss flying-boat NC-4 from Trepassey Harbour, Newfoundland, *via* the Azores, to Lisbon, Portugal, on 16 to 27 May 1919. The whole flight of 4,717 miles *7 591 km* originating from Rockaway Air Station, Long Island, N.Y. on 8 May, required 53 hours 58 min, terminating at Plymouth, England, on 31 May.

The Newfoundland-Azores flight of 1,200 miles *1930 km* took 15 hrs 18 min at 81.7 knots *151,4 km/h.*

Non-stop
The first non-stop trans-Atlantic flight was achieved from 4.13 p.m. G.M.T. on 14 June 1919, from Lester's Field, St. John's, Newfoundland, 1,960 miles *3 154 km* to Derrygimla bog near Clifden, County Galway, Ireland, at 8.40 a.m. G.M.T., 15 June, when the pilot Capt. John William Alcock, D.S.C. (1892–1919), and the navigator Lt. Arthur Whitten Brown (1886–1948) flew across in a Vickers *Vimy*, powered by two 360 h.p. Rolls-Royce *Eagle VIII* engines. Both men were created K.B.E. on 21 June 1919 when Alcock was aged 26 years 227 days, and won the *Daily Mail* prize of £10,000.

Solo
The 79th man to achieve a trans-Atlantic flight but the first to do so solo was Capt. (later Brig.) Charles Augustus Lindbergh (1902–1974) who took off in his 220 h.p. Ryan monoplane "Spirit of St. Louis" at 12.52 p.m. G.M.T. on 20 May 1927 from Roosevelt Field, Long Island, N.Y., U.S.A. He landed at 10.21 p.m. G.M.T. on 21 May 1927 at Le Bourget airfield, Paris, France. His flight of 3,610 miles *5 810 km* lasted 33 hours 29½ min and he won a prize of $25,000 (*then £5,300*).

Trans-Pacific
The first trans-Pacific flight was made from Oakland Field, San Francisco, California to Eagle Farm, Brisbane *via* Honolulu and Suva, Fiji by Capt. (later Sir) Charles Kingsford Smith and C.T.P. Ulm (pilots), accompanied by Harry Lyon (navigator) and James Warner (radio operator) on 31 May–9 June 1928. The flying time for the 7,389 miles *11 891 km* was 83 hr. 38 min. The aircraft used, a Fokker F. VIIB-3m, named "Southern Cross', is preserved and displayed at Eagle Farm airport.

Circumnavigational Flights
Strict circumnavigation requires passing through two antipodal points thus with a minimum distance of 24,859.75 miles *40 007,89 km*. The F.A.I. permits flights which exceed the length of the Tropic of Cancer or Capricorn viz 22,858.754 miles *36 787,599 km*.

The earliest such flight of 26,345 miles *42 398 km* was by two U.S. Army Douglas amphibians in 57 "hops". The "Chicago" was piloted by Lt. Lowell H. Smith and Lt. Leslie P. Arnold and the "New Orleans" was piloted by Lt. Erik H. Nelson and Lt. John Harding between 6 Apr. and 28 Sept. 1924 ending at Seattle, Washington, U.S.A.

The earliest solo claim was by Wiley Hardemann Post (1898–1935) (U.S.) in the Lockheed Vega "Winnie Mae" starting and finishing at Floyd Bennett Field, New York City on 15–22 July 1933 in 10 "hops". The distance of 15,596 miles *25 099 km* with a flying time of 115 hrs 36 min was however at too high a latitude to qualify.

The fastest flight has been the non-stop eastabout flight of 45 hrs 19 min by three flight-refuelled USAF B-52's led by Maj-Gen. Archie J. Old Jr. They covered 24,325 miles *39 147 km* on 16–18 Jan. 1957 finishing at March Air Force Base, Riverside California, having averaged 525 m.p.h. *844 km/h* with four in-flight refuellings by KC-97 aerial tankers.

The first circum-polar flight was solo by Capt. Elgen M. Long, 44, in a Piper Navajo on 5 Nov.–3 Dec. 1971. He covered 38,896 miles *62 597 km* in 215 flying hours. The cabin temperature sank to −40° C −40° F over Antarctica.

Circumnavigation *Smallest*
The smallest aircraft to complete a circumnavigation is the 20 ft 11 in *6,37 m* single-engined 180 h.p. Thorp T-18 built in his garage by its pilot Don Taylor of Sage, California. His 26,190 mile *42 148 km* flight in 37 stages took 176 flying hours ending at Oshkosh, Wisconsin on 30 Sept. 1976.

Heaviest and Most Powerful (*Commercial*)

The greatest weight at which an aeroplane has taken off is 840,200 lb. (375.09 tons *381,11 tonnes*), achieved by the first production Boeing Model 747-236B commercial transport to be powered by four Rolls-Royce RB.211 turbofan engines, at the Moore Naval Air Section, California, on 1 Nov. 1976. William J. Allsopp was the pilot in command (see Airliner, Largest below). This version of the Boeing 747 has a wing span of 195 ft *59,64 m* and is 231 ft 4 in *70,51 m* long. Each of its RB 211-524B engines gives a thrust of 50,100 lb. *22,725 kg*. It entered service with British Airways in mid-1977.

Largest wing span

The aircraft with the largest wing span ever constructed was the $40 million Hughes H.2 *Hercules* flying-boat, which was raised 70 ft *21,3 m* into the air in a test run of 1,000 yds *914 m*, piloted by Howard Hughes (1905–1976), off Long Beach Harbor, California, U.S.A., on 2 Nov. 1947. The eight-engined 190 ton *193 tonnes* aircraft had a wing span of 320 ft *97,53 m* and a length of 219 ft *66,75 m* and never flew again. It was not scrapped until April 1976.

Most Powerful (*Military*)

The third Boeing E-4A advanced airborne command post version of the Boeing 747-200B transport flew for the first time on 6 June 1974 powered by 4 General Electric F103-GE-100 turbofan engines with a total thrust of 210,000 lb. *95 250 kg*.

Lightest

The lightest powered aeroplane ever flown is the Birdman TL-1, a single-place monoplane designed and built by Emmet M. Tally III (*k.* 1976) of Daytona Beach, Florida and first flown on 25 Jan. 1975. It has a wing span of 34 ft *10,36 m*, a weight of 100 lb. *45 kg* empty, and 288 lb. *131 kg* at normal take-off weight. It is powered by a 15 h.p. Tally aircraft M.C. 101DT single cylinder two-stroke engine, driving a pusher propeller and has a maximum speed of 60 m.p.h. *97 km/h* and a range of 200 miles *322 km* on 4 U.S. gallons (15 litres) of fuel. The pilot sits on an open seat. Many more Birdmans are being built from kits supplied by the Birdman company.

The lightest and smallest twin-engined aeroplane is the prototype MC 10 Cricri single-seat monoplane designed and built by Michel Colomban of Rueil-Malmaison, France, and first flown on 19 July 1973 by 68-year-old Robert Buisson. It has a wing span of 16 ft 4¾ in *5,00 m*, an empty weight of 139 lb. *63 kg* and take-off weight of 375 lb. *170 kg*, including this pilot. Two 9 h.p. Rowena two-stroke engines give it a maximum speed of 130 m.p.h. *210 km/h* and a range of 248 miles *400 km*. The Cricri is aerobatic.

Smallest

The smallest aeroplane ever flown is the Stits *Skybaby* biplane, designed and built by Ray Stits at Riverside, California, U.S.A., and first flown by Robert H. Starr on 26 May 1952. It was 9 ft 10 in *3 m* long, with a wing span of 7 ft 2 in *2,18 m*, and weighed 452 lb. *205 kg* empty. It was powered by an 85 h.p. Continental C85 engine, giving a top speed of 185 m.p.h. *297 km/h*.

Bombers *Heaviest*

The world's heaviest bomber is the eight-jet swept-wing Boeing B-52H *Stratofortress*, which has a maximum take-off weight of 488,000 lb. (217.86 tons *221,35 tonnes*). It has a wing span of 185 ft *56,38 m* and is 157 ft 6¾ in *48,02 m* in length, with a speed of over 650 m.p.h. *1 046 km/h*. The B-52 can carry twelve SRAM thermonuclear short range attack missiles or twenty four 750 lb. *340 kg* bombs under its wings and eight more SRAMS or eighty four 500 lb. *226 kg* bombs in the fuselage. The ten-engined Convair B-36J, weighing 183 tons *185 tonnes*, had a greater wing span, at 230 ft *70,10 m* but it is no longer in service. It had a top speed of 435 m.p.h. *700 km/h*.

Fastest

The world's fastest operational bombers are the French Dassault *Mirage IV*, which can fly at Mach 2.2 (1,450 m.p.h. *2 333 km/h*) at 36,000 ft *11 000 m*; the American General Dynamics FB-111A, with a maximum speed of Mach 2.5; and the Soviet swing-wing Tupolev Tu-26 known to N.A.T.O. as "Backfire", which has an estimated over-target speed of Mach 2.0 and a combat radius of up to 3,570 miles *5 745 km*.

Most Expensive

Although estimated costs for the U.S. Rockwell International B-1 supersonic bomber, first flown on 23 Dec. 1974, vary widely, it is clearly the most expensive aircraft ever produced. An official Departmental of Defense estimate of $22,850 million (*£13,400 million*) for 244 was published in 1977—a cost of $93.6 million (*then £55 million*) per aircraft.

Airliner Largest *World*

The highest capacity jet airliner is the Boeing 747 "Jumbo

The actual Boeing 747-236B with Rolls-Royce RB211 engines, which set the aviation record for the heaviest flying object at 375.09 tons *381,11 tonnes*. (John W. R. Taylor)

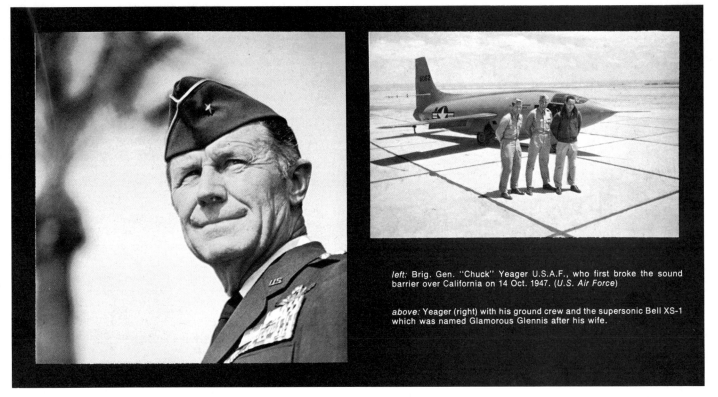

left: Brig. Gen. "Chuck" Yeager U.S.A.F., who first broke the sound barrier over California on 14 Oct. 1947. (*U.S. Air Force*)

above: Yeager (right) with his ground crew and the supersonic Bell XS-1 which was named Glamorous Glennis after his wife.

Jet", first flown on 9 Feb. 1969 (see Heaviest aircraft, p. 142) and has a capacity of from 385 to 500 passengers with a maximum speed of 608 m.p.h. *978 km/h.* Its wing span is 195.7 ft *59,64 m* and its length 231.3 ft *70,5 m.* It entered service on 22 Jan. 1970.

Great Britain

The heaviest United Kingdom airliner in service is the B.A.C. Super VC10, which first flew on 7 May 1964. It weighs 335,000 lb. (149.5 tons) *151,8 tonnes* and is 171.7 ft *52,33 m* long, with a wing span of 146.2 ft *44,56 m.* The largest ever British aircraft was the experimental Bristol Type 167 *Brabazon*, which had a maximum take-off weight of 129.4 tons *131,4 tonnes*, a wing span of 230 ft *70,10 m* and a length of 177 ft *53,94 m.* This eight-engined aircraft first flew on 4 Sept. 1949. The *Concorde* (see below) has a maximum take-off weight of 400,000 lb. *181 435 kg* (178.5 tons).

Airliner Fastest *World*

The U.S.S.R.'s Tu-144 supersonic airliner, with a capacity of 140 passengers, first flew on 31 Dec. 1968, and "went" supersonic on 5 June 1969. It first exceeded Mach 2 on 26 May 1970. During later flight trials it attained Mach 2.4 (1,585 m.p.h. *2 550 km/h*). The Tu-144 is claimed to have opened the first scheduled supersonic airline service on 26 Dec. 1975 with 2 return flights weekly between Moscow and Alma Ata (2,190 miles *3 520 km*) carrying freight and mail. It may yet enter passenger service in late 1977 at an average speed of 1,245 m.p.h. *2 000 km/h* (Mach 1.9).

Great Britain

The supersonic BAC/Aerospatiale *Concorde*, first flown on 2 Mar. 1969, with a capacity of 128 passengers, cruises at up to Mach 2.2 (1,450 m.p.h. *2 334 km/h*). It flew at Mach 1.05 on 10 Oct. 1969, exceeded Mach 2 for the first time on 4 Nov. 1970 and became the first supersonic airliner used on passenger services on 21 Jan. 1976 when Air France and British Airways opened services simultaneously between, respectively, Paris–Rio de Janeiro and London–Bahrain. In a flight on 13 June 1974 a Concorde flew from Paris to Boston in 3 hrs 9 min.

Largest cargo compartment

The largest cargo compartment of any aircraft is the 39,000 ft³ *1 104 m³* of the American Aero Spacelines Guppy-201 which was put into service in September 1971. The compartment is more than 25 ft *7,6 m* in diameter.

Largest propeller

The largest aircraft propeller ever used was the 22 ft 7½ in *6,89 m* diameter Garuda propeller, fitted to the Linke-Hofmann R II built in Wroclaw, Poland, which flew in 1919. It was driven by four 260 h.p. Mercedes engines and turned at only 545 r.p.m.

Scheduled flights *Longest*

The longest distance scheduled non-stop flight is the weekly Pan-Am Sydney-San Francisco non-stop 13 hr 25 min Flight 816, in a Boeing 747 SP, opened in December 1976, over 7,475 statute miles *12 030 km.* The longest delivery flight by a commercial jet is 8,950 nautical miles or 10,305 statute miles *16 560 km* from Seattle, Washington, U.S.A. to Cape Town, South Africa by the South African Airway's Boeing 747 SP (Special performer) "Matrousberg" with 178 400 kg *175.5 tons* of pre-cooled fuel in 17 hr 22½ min on 23–29 Mar. 1976.

Shortest

The shortest scheduled flight in the world is that by Loganair between the Orkney Islands of Westray and Papa Westray which has been flown with Britten-Norman Islander twin-engined 10-seat transports since September 1967. Though scheduled for 2 min, in favourable wind conditions it has been accomplished in 69 secs by Capt. Andrew Alsop.

HIGHEST SPEED
Official record

The official air speed record is 2,193.167 m.p.h. *3 529,56 km/h* by Capt. Eldon W. Joersz and Maj. George T. Morgan, Jr., in a Lockheed SR-71A near Beale Air Force Base, California, U.S.A. over a 15/25 km course on 28 July 1976.

Air-launched record

The fastest fixed-wing aircraft in the world was the U.S. North American Aviation X-15A-2, which flew for the first time (after modification from X-15A) on 28 June 1964 powered by a liquid oxygen and ammonia rocket propulsion system. Ablative materials on the airframe once enabled a temperature of 3,000° F. to be withstood. The landing speed was 210 knots (242 m.p.h. *389,1 km/h*) momentarily. The highest speed attained was 4,534 m.p.h. *7 297 km/h* (Mach 6.72) when piloted by Major William J. Knight, U.S.A.F. (b. 1930), on 3 Oct. 1967. An earlier version piloted by Joseph A. Walker (1920–66), reached 354,200 ft *107 960 m* (67.08 miles) also over Edwards Air Force Base, California, U.S.A., on 22 Aug. 1963. The programme was suspended after the final flight of 24 Oct. 1968.

Potentially the fastest aircraft ever flown is the Space Shuttle Orbiter built for N.A.S.A. by Rockwell International Corporation and first flown piggyback atop a converted Boeing 747 on 18 Feb. 1977. When flown into space, from 1979, the Orbiter will take off like a rocket, operate in orbit as a spacecraft, at up to 17,600 m.p.h. *28 325 km/h*, and land at an airfield like a conventional aeroplane.

Fastest jet

The world's fastest jet aircraft is the U.S.A.F. Lockheed SR-71 reconnaissance aircraft (see Official record above) which was first flown on 22 Dec. 1964 and is reportedly capable of attaining an altitude ceiling of close to 100,000 ft *30 480 m*. The SR-71 has a wing span of 55.6 ft *16,94 m* and a length of 107.4 ft *32,73 m* and weighs 170,000 lb. (75.9 tons *77,1 tonnes*) at take-off. Its reported range is 2,982 miles *4 800 km* at Mach 3 at 78,750 ft *24 000* m. At least 30 are believed to have been built and 9 had been lost by April 1969. The fastest combat aircraft in the world is the U.S.S.R. Mikoyan MiG-25 fighter (code name "Foxbat"). The reconnaissance "Foxbat-B" has been tracked by radar at about Mach 3.2 (2,110 m.p.h. *3 395 km/h*). When armed with four large underwing air-to-air missiles known to N.A.T.O. as "Acrid", the fighter "Foxbat-A" is limited to Mach 2.8 (1,845 m.p.h. *2 975 km/h*). The single-seat "Foxbat-A" spans 45 ft 9 in *13,95 m*, is 73 ft 2 in *22,3 m* long and has a take-off weight of about 77,150 lb. *35 000 kg*.

Fastest biplane

The fastest recorded biplane was the Italian Fiat C.R.42B, with a 1,010 h.p. Daimler-Benz DB601A engine, which attained 323 m.p.h. *520 km/h* in 1941. Only one was built.

Fastest piston-engined aircraft

The fastest speed at which a piston-engined aeroplane has ever been measured was for a cut-down privately owned Hawker *Sea Fury* which attained 520 m.p.h. *836 km/h* in level flight over Texas, U.S.A., in August 1966 piloted by Mike Carroll (k. 1969) of Los Angeles. The official record for a piston-engined aircraft is 482.462 m.p.h. *776,449 km/h* over Edwards AFB California by Darryl C. Greenamyer, 33, (U.S.) in a modified Grumman F8F-2 *Bearcat* on 16 Aug. 1969.

Fastest propeller-driven aircraft

The Soviet Tu-114 turboprop transport is the world's fastest propeller-driven aeroplane. It has achieved average speeds of more than 545 m.p.h. *877 km/h* carrying heavy payloads over measured circuits. It is developed from the Tupolev Tu-95 bomber, known in the West as the "Bear", and has 14,795 h.p. engines. The turboprop-powered Republic XF-84H prototype U.S. Navy fighter which flew on 22 July 1955 had a top *design* speed of 670 m.p.h. *1 078 km/h* but was abandoned.

Fastest Trans-Atlantic flight

The trans-Atlantic flight record is 1 hr. 54 min. 56.4 secs. by Major James V. Sullivan, 37 and Major Noel F. Widdifield, 33 flying a Lockheed SR-71A eastwards on 1 Sept. 1974. The average speed, slowed by refuelling by a KC-135 tanker aircraft, for the New York–London stage of 3,461.53 miles *5 570,80 km* was 1,806.963 m.p.h. *2 908,026 km/h*.

Fastest circumnavigation (*Flights longer than Tropic of Cancer*)*

The fastest circumnavigation of the globe was achieved by three U.S.A.F. B-52 *Stratofortresses*, led by Maj.-Gen. Archie J. Old, Jr. from Castle Air Force Base, Merced, California, arriving 45 hours 19 min later at March Air Force Base, Riverside, California, on 18 Jan. 1957, after a flight of 24,325 miles *39 147 km*. The commercial record was set by a Pan Am Boeing 747 SP (Capt. Walter H. Mullikin) New York–Delhi–Tokyo–New York on 1–3 May 1976 in 46 hrs 50 sec for the 23,230.3 miles *37 385,5 km*, equivalent to a speed of 502.84 m.p.h. *809,24 km/h*. *22,858.754 miles *31 787,599 km*.

Altitude *Official record*

The official world altitude record by an aircraft taking off from the ground under its own power is 118,897 ft (22.51 miles *36,24 km*) by Aleksandr Fedotov (U.S.S.R.) in a Mikoyan E.266 (MiG-25) aircraft, powered by two 24,250 lb. *11 000 kg* thrust turbojet engines, on 25 July 1973. For Milestones in absolute human altitude see front end paper.

The greatest recorded height by any pilot without a pressure cabin or even a pressure suit has been 49,500 ft *15 085 m* by Sq./Ldr. G. W. H. Reynolds, D.F.C. in a Spitfire Mark 5C over Libya in 1942.

Duration

The flight duration record is 64 days, 22 hours, 19 min and 5 sec, set up by Robert Timm and John Cook in a Cessna 172 "Hacienda". They took off from McCarran Airfield, Las Vegas, Nevada, U.S.A., just before 3.53 p.m. local time on 4 Dec. 1958, and landed at the same airfield just before 2.12 p.m. on 7 Feb. 1959. They covered a distance equivalent to six times the world with continued refuellings, without landing.

The record for duration without refuelling is 84 hrs 32 min, set by Walter E. Lees and Frederic A. Brossy in a Bellanca

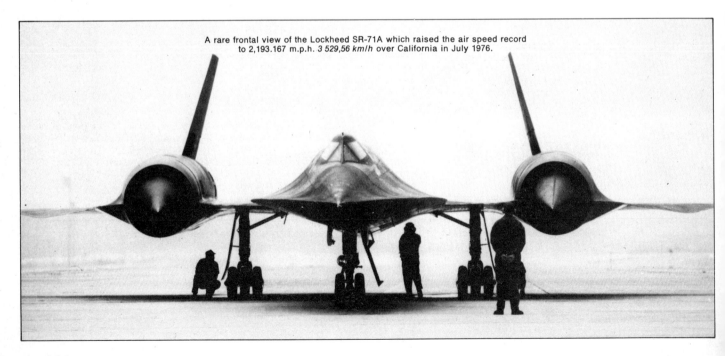

A rare frontal view of the Lockheed SR-71A which raised the air speed record to 2,193.167 m.p.h. *3 529,56 km/h* over California in July 1976.

A side view of the U.S. Rockwell International Space Shuttle Orbiter, which is expected to fly at 17,600 m.p.h. *28 325 km/h* outside the atmosphere in 1979/80. The road load also qualified as a record.

monoplane with a 225 h.p. Packard Diesel engine, at Jacksonville, Florida, on 25–28 May 1931.

AIRPORTS

Largest *World*

The world's largest airport is the Dallas/Fort Worth Airport, Texas, U.S.A., which extends over 17,500 acres *7 080 ha* in the Grapevine area, midway between Dallas and Fort Worth. It was opened in January 1974 at an initial cost of $700 million. The present 3 runways and 4 terminal buildings are planned to be extended to 9 runways and 13 terminals with 260 gates with an ultimate capacity for 60 million passengers. The total airport reserve area of Mirabel, Montreal's airport, Canada, is 88,000 acres *35 600 ha* of which 17,000 acres *6 880 ha* is operational.

Great Britain

Seventy-three airline companies from 68 countries operate scheduled services into Heathrow Airport—London (2,819 acres *1 142 ha*), and during 1976 there was a total of 275,109 air transport movements handled by a staff of 52,620 employed by the various companies and the British Airports Authority. The total number of passengers, both incoming and outgoing, was 23,612,990. The most flights yet handled by Heathrow in a day was 986 on 19 July 1974 and the largest number of passengers yet handled in a day was 95,816 on 31 July 1976. Aircraft fly to more than 90 countries.

Busiest

The world's busiest airport is the Chicago International Airport, O'Hare Field, Illinois, U.S.A. with a total of 718,147 movements and 38,000,000 passengers in Fiscal Year 1975. This represents a take-off or landing every 44.03 seconds round the clock. Heathrow Airport—London handles more international traffic than any other.

The busiest landing area ever has been Bien Hoa Air Base, south Vietnam, which handled more than 1,000,000 take-offs and landings in 1970. The world's largest "helipad" was An Khe, south Vietnam.

Highest and lowest

The highest airport in the world is El Alto, near La Paz, Bolivia, at 13,599 ft *4 150 m* above sea-level. Ladakh airstrip in Kashmir has, however, an altitude of 14,270 ft *4 349 m.*

The highest landing ever made by a fixed-wing 'plane is 6 080 m *19,947 ft* on Dhaulagri, Himalaya by a Pilatus Porter, named "Yeti", supplying the 1960 Swiss Expedition. The lowest landing field is El Lisan on the east shore of the Dead Sea, 1,180 ft *360 m* below sea-level, but the lowest international airport is Schiphol, Amsterdam, at 13 ft *3,9 m* below sea-level.

Longest Runway *World*

The longest runway in the world is one of 7 miles *11 km* in length (of which 15,000 ft *4 572 m* is concreted) at Edwards Air Force Base on the bed of Rogers Dry Lake at Muroc, California, U.S.A. The whole test centre airfield extends over 65 miles² *168 km²*. In an emergency an auxiliary 12 mile *19 km* strip is available along the bed of the Dry Lake. The world's longest civil airport runway is one of 16,076 ft (3.04 miles *4,89 km*) at Upington, South Africa.

Great Britain

The longest runway available normally to civil aircraft in the United Kingdom is No. 1 at Heathrow Airport—London, measuring 12,799 ft (2.42 miles *3,89 km*).

HELICOPTERS

Fastest

A Bell YUH-1B Model 533 compound research helicopter, boosted by two auxiliary turbojet engines, attained an unofficial speed record of 316.1 m.p.h. *508,7 km/h* over Arlington, Texas, U.S.A., in April 1969. The official world speed record for a pure helicopter is 220.885 m.p.h. *355 485 km/h* by a Sikorsky S-67 *Blackhawk*, flown by test pilot Kurt Cannon (1934–74), between Milford and Branford, Connecticut, U.S.A. on 19 Dec. 1970.

Largest

The world's largest helicopter is the Soviet Mil *Mi-12* ("Homer"), also known as the V-12, which set up an international record by lifting a payload of 88,636 lb. (39.5 tons *40,2 tonnes*) to a height of 7,398 ft *2 255 m* on 6 Aug. 1969. It is powered by four 6,500 h.p. turboshaft engines and has a span of 219 ft 10 in *67 m* over its rotor tips with a length of 121 ft 4½ in *37,00 m* and weighs 103.3 tons *105 tonnes.*

Highest

The altitude record for helicopters is 40,820 ft *12 442 m* by an Aérospatiale SA315B *Lama*, over France on 21 June

1972. The highest landing has been at 23,000 ft *7 010 m* below the South-East face of Everest in a rescue sortie in May 1971.

AUTOGYROS
Earliest
The autogyro or gyroplane, a rotorcraft with an unpowered rotor turned by the airflow in flight, preceded the practical helicopter with engine-driven rotor. Juan de la Cierva (Spain), made the first successful autogyro flight with his model C.4 (commercially named an *Autogiro*) at Getafe, Spain, on 9 Jan. 1923. On 6 Dec. 1955, Dr. Igor B. Bensen (U.S.A.) flew his very simple open-seat Gyro-Copter and then made the design available in kit form to amateur constructor/pilots.

Speed Altitude and Distance Records
Wing Cdr. Kenneth H. Wallis (G.B.) holds the straight-line distance record of 543.27 miles *874,32 km* set in his WA-116 F autogyro on 28 Sept. 1975 non-stop from Lydd, Kent to Wick, Highland. Wg. Cdr. Wallis flew his WA-116, with 72 h.p. McCulloch engine, to a record altitude of 15,220 ft *4 639 m* on 11 May 1968, and to a record speed of 111.2 m.p.h. *179 km/h* over a 3 km straight course on 12 May 1969.

FLYING-BOAT
Fastest
The fastest flying-boat ever built has been the Martin XP6M-1 *Seamaster*, the U.S. Navy 4 jet engined minelayer flown in 1955–59 with a top speed of 646 m.p.h. *1 040 km/h*. In Sept. 1946 the Martin JRM-2 *Mars* flying-boat set a payload record of 68,327 lb. *30 992 kg*.

The official flying-boat speed record is 566.69 m.p.h. *912 km/h*, set up by Nikolai Andrievsky and crew of two in a Soviet Beriev M-10, powered by two AL-7 turbojets, over a 15/25 km course on 7 Aug. 1961. The M-10 holds all 12 records listed for jet-powered flying-boats, including an altitude of 49,088 ft *14 962 m* set by Georgiy Buryanov and crew over the Sea of Azov on 9 Sept. 1961.

AIRSHIPS
Earliest
The earliest flight in an airship was by Henri Giffard from Paris in his coal-gas 88,300 ft³ *2 500 m³* 144 ft *43,8 m* long airship on 24 Sept. 1852. The earliest British airship was a 20,000 ft³ *566 m³* 75 ft *22,8 m* long craft built by Stanley Spencer whose maiden flight was from Crystal Palace, Bromley, Greater London on 22 Sept. 1902. The latest large airship to be assembled in Britain is the 202,700 ft³ *5 739 m³* 192½ ft *56,67 m* long *Europa* built at Cardington, Bedfordshire by the Goodyear Tyre & Rubber Co. which first flew on 8 Mar. 1972.

Largest *Rigid*
The largest rigid airship ever built was the German *Graf Zeppelin II* (LZ 130), with a length of 245 m *803.8 ft* and a capacity of 7,062,100 ft³ *199 977 m³*. She made her maiden flight on 14 Sept. 1938 and in May and August 1939 made radar spying missions in British air space. She was dismantled in April 1940. Her sister ship *Hindenburg* was 5.6 ft *1,70 m* longer.

British
The largest British airship was the R101 built by the Royal Airship Works, Cardington, Bedfordshire, which first flew on 14 Oct. 1929. She was 777 ft *236,8 m* in length and had a capacity of 5,508,800 ft³ *155 992 m³*. She crashed near Beauvais, France, killing 48 aboard on 5 Oct. 1930.

Non-Rigid
The largest non-rigid airship ever constructed was the U.S. Navy ZPG 3-W which had a capacity of 1,516,300 ft³ *42 937 m³*, was 403.4 ft *122,9 m* long and 85.1 ft *25,93 m* in diameter, with a crew of 21. She first flew on 21 July 1958, but crashed into the sea in June 1960.

Greatest Passenger Load
The most people ever carried in an airship was 207 in the U.S. Navy *Akron* in 1931. The trans-Atlantic record is 117 by the German *Hindenburg* in 1937. The distance record for

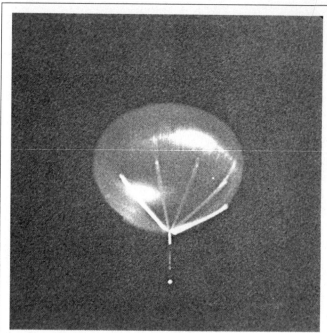

An unmanned Winzen balloon photographed at high altitude. The company set the record for both size and altitude at 32.19 miles *51,8 km*.

airships is 3,967.3 miles *6 384,5 km*, set up by the German *Graf Zeppelin*, captained by Dr. Hugo Eckener, between 29 Oct. and 1 Nov. 1928.

BALLOONING
Earliest
The earliest recorded ascent was with a hot air balloon invented by Father Bartolomeu de Gusmão (*né* Lourenço) (b. Santos, Brazil, 1685), which was first flown indoors at the Casa da India, Terreiro do Paço, Portugal on 8 Aug. 1709.

Distance record
The record distance travelled by a balloon is 2,520 miles *4 055 km* in 107 hr 35 min by *Silver Fox* piloted by Ed Yost (U.S.) from the U.S. landing 200 miles *320 km* east of the Azores in Oct. 1976. Col. Thomas L. Gatch's lost balloon *Light Heart* was sighted over the Atlantic some 3,000 miles *4 800 km* from its take-off point at Harrisburg, Pennsylvania, U.S.A. on 19 Feb. 1974.

Highest *Unmanned*
The highest altitude attained by an unmanned balloon was 170,000 ft *51 815 m* by a Winzen balloon of 47.8 million ft³ *1,35 million m³* launched at Chico, California in October 1972.

Manned
The greatest altitude reached in a manned balloon is the unofficial 123,800 ft (23.45 miles *37 735 m*) by Nicholas Piantanida (1933–66) of Bricktown, New Jersey, U.S.A., from Sioux Falls, South Dakota, U.S.A., on 1 Feb. 1966. He landed in a cornfield in Iowa but did not survive. The official record is 113,740 ft *34 668 m* by Cdr. Malcolm D. Ross, U.S.N.R. and the late Lt.-Cdr. Victor E. Prather, U.S.N. in an ascent from the deck of U.S.S. *Antietam* on 4 May 1961, over the Gulf of Mexico.

Largest
The largest balloon ever to fly is one with an inflated volume of 70 million ft³ *2 million m³* built by Winzen Research Inc. flown in the autumn of 1975.

Ballooning (*Hot-Air*)
The world's distance record for hot-air ballooning is 337.2 miles *542,7 km* by Matt Wiederkehr, 43, in a Raven S-55A from St. Paul, Minnesota to Butte, Nebraska on 7 Mar. 1974. The altitude record is 45,837 ft *13 971 m* by Julian Nott and co-pilot Felix Pole (both G.B.) over Bhopal, India on 25 Jan.

1974 in *Daffodil II*, the 375,000 ft³ *10618 m³* Cameron A-375 balloon. The largest hot-air balloon ever built is the U.K. Cameron A-500 500,000 ft³ *14158 m³* *Gerard A. Heineken* first flown on 18 Aug. 1974. The endurance record is 18 hrs 56 min from Melbury Bubb, Dorset to Angers, France by Donald Allan Cameron (G.B.) and Le Comte Jean Costa de Beauregard (France) in a Cameron A-500 on 21–22 Nov. 1975.

HOVERCRAFT (Skirted Air Cushion Vehicles)
Earliest
The inventor of the ACV (air-cushion vehicle) is Sir Christopher Sydney Cockerell, C.B.E., F.R.S. (b. 4 June 1910), a British engineer who had the idea in 1954, published his Ripplecraft Report 1/55 on 25 Oct. 1955 and patented it on 12 Dec. 1955. The earliest patent relating to an air-cushion craft was applied for in 1877 by John I. Thornycroft (1843–1928) of Chiswick, London. The first flight by a hovercraft was made by the 4 ton/*tonnes* Saunders-Roe SR-N1 at Cowes on 30 May 1959. With a 1,500 lb. *680 kg* thrust Viper turbo-jet engine, this craft reached 68 knots *126 km/h* in June 1961. The first hovercraft public service was run across the Dee Estuary by the 60 knot *111 km/h* 24-passenger Vickers-Armstrong's VA-3 between July and September 1962.

Largest
The largest is the 200 ton *203 tonne* Westland SR-N4, *Mountbatten*, Mark II. It has a top speed of 77 knots *142 km/h* powered by 4 Bristol Siddeley Marine Proteus engines with 19 ft *5,7 m* propellers. The U.S.N. Bell Aerospace 2K SES (Surface Effect Ship) Weapons' Test Platform prototype is expected to be of 2,800 tons/*tonnes* measuring about 250 ft × 110 ft *76,2 m × 33,5 m.*

Fastest warship
The world's fastest warship is the 78 ft *23,7 m* long 100 ton/*tonnes* U.S. Navy test vehicle SES-100B. She attained 88.88 knots *102.35 m.p.h.* in speed trials in 1976. A contract for a 3,000 ton Large Surface Effect Ship (LSES) was placed by the U.S. Department of Defense with Bell Aerospace in September 1977 for delivery in mid-1981.

Longest flight
The longest hovercraft journey was one of 5,000 miles *8 047 km* through eight West African countries between 15 Oct. 1969 and 3 Jan. 1970 by the British Trans-African Hovercraft Expedition.

Greatest Load
The heaviest object moved by "hover flotation" is 700 tons *711 tonnes* by Mears Construction Ltd., in Feb. 1975 for Shell Francaise near Bordeaux.

Highest
The greatest altitude at which a hovercraft is operating is on Lago Titicaca, Peru, where since 1975 an HM2 Hoverferry is hovering 12,506 ft *3 811 m* above sea level.

MODEL AIRCRAFT
Altitude, Speed and Duration
The world record for altitude is 26,929 ft *8 208 m* by Maynard L. Hill (U.S.A.) on 6 Sept. 1970 using a radio-controlled model. The free flight speed record is 213.70 m.p.h. *343,92 km/h* by V. Goukoune and V. Myakinin (both U.S.S.R.) with a radio-controlled model at Klementyeva, U.S.S.R., on 21 Sept. 1971. The record duration flight is one of 25 hrs 44 min 8 sec by Myakinin with a radio-controlled glider on 30 Sept.– 1 Oct. 1973.

Cross Channel
The first cross channel model helicopter flight was achieved by an 11 lb. *5,00 kg* model Bell 212 radio controlled by Dieter Zeigler for 32 miles *52 km* between Ashford, Kent and Ambleteuse, France on 17 July 1974.

Indoor
An indoor distance of 109 ft 2 in *33,27 m* was recorded by Brian Baumann in the Gill Coliseum, Corvallis, Oregon, U.S.A. on 22 Apr. 1976.

Paper Aircraft
The flight duration record for a paper aircraft over level ground is 15.0 sec by William Harlan Pryor in the Municipal Auditorium, Nashville, Tennessee, U.S.A. on 26 Mar. 1975. A paper plane was reported and witnessed to have flown 1¼ miles *2,0 km* by "Chick" C. O. Reinhart from a 10th storey office window at 60 Beaver Street, New York City across the East River to Brooklyn in August 1933. It was helped by a thermal from a coffee-roasting plant.

PERSONAL AVIATION RECORDS
Most Flying Hours
Max Conrad, 70 (U.S.A.) between 1928 and mid-1974 totalled 52,929 hr 40 min logged flight—more than 6 years.

Most Landings
Tony Cattle and David R. Shevloff in a Cessna 172 took off and landed at 65 airfields in southern England in 16 hrs 19 min in daylight on 19 June 1974 for a British record.

Oldest and Youngest Pilots
The youngest age at which anyone has ever qualified as a military pilot is 15 yrs 5 months in the case of Sgt. Thomas Dobney (b. 6 May 1926) of the R.A.F. He had overstated his age (14 years) on entry. Miss Betty Bennett took off, flew and landed solo at the age of 10 on 4 Jan. 1952 in Cuba. A number of pilots have been reported to have qualified on their 17th birthdays. The world's oldest pilot in March 1976 was probably Cecile Raymond Sinclair (b. 8 Apr. 1888) of Muskegon, Michigan, U.S.A. aged 87 years 11 months who soloed in 1915. Maurice Tabiteau of Issey les Moulineaux, Seine, France is also believed to have been born in 1888. Glenn E. Messer of Birmingham, Alabama has been flying "steady" since 13 May 1911. Theodore Julius Caesar of Tuakau, New Zealand was issued with his PPL aged 74 years 359 days on 25 Mar. 1974.

Human-powered flight
The greatest distance achieved in human-powered flight is 3,175 yds *2,9 km* by Takashi Kato in the 68 ft 11 in *21,0 m* span Nihon University Stork in 4 min 27 sec at Shimofusa naval airfield, northeast of Tokyo, Japan on 2 Jan. 1977.

5. POWER PRODUCERS

Oldest Steam Engine
The oldest steam engine in working order is the 1812 Boulton & Watt 26 h.p. 42 in bore beam engine on the Kennet & Avon Canal at Great Bedwyn, Wiltshire. It was restored by the Crofton Society in 1971.

Earliest Atomic Pile
The world's first atomic pile was built in a disused squash court at Stagg Field, University of Chicago, Illinois, U.S.A. It went "critical" at 3.25 p.m. on 2 Dec. 1942.

Power Plant Largest *World*
The world's largest power station is the U.S.S.R.'s hydro-electric station at Krasnoyarsk on the river Yenisey, Siberia, U.S.S.R. with a power of 6,096 MW. Its third generator turned in March 1968 and the twelfth became operative in December 1970. The turbine hall, completed in June 1968, is 1,378 ft *420 m* long. The reservoir backed up by the dam was reported in Nov. 1972 to be 240 miles *386 km* in length.

The largest planned power plant is the Itaipu on the river Paraná on the Brazil–Paraguay border with an ultimate 12,600,000 kW.

Great Britain
The power station with the greatest installed capacity in Great Britain is Longannet, Fife, Scotland which attained 2,400 MW by December 1972. At Drax, North Yorkshire, the first stage of 3 × 660 MW sets have been commissioned and there is provision, to double this figure to 3,960 MW. A 3,300 MW oil fired installation on the Isle of Grain, Kent, is planned to be completed in 1980.

The largest hydro-electric plant in the United Kingdom is the North of Scotland Hydro-electricity Board's Power Station at Loch Sloy, Central. The installed capacity of this station is 130 MW. The Ben Cruachan Pumped Storage Scheme was opened on 15 Oct. 1965 at Loch Awe, Strathclyde, Scotland. It has a capacity of 400 MW and cost £24,000,000. The 1,880 MW underground pumped storage scheme at Dinorwic, Gwynedd will be the largest built in Europe with a head of 1,739 ft *530 m* and a capacity of 13,770 ft³/sec *390 m³/sec*. Completion is due in 1981.

The nuclear power station which has generated the largest quantity of electricity in the world is Dungeness "A", Kent with a cumulative generation of 38,144 net GWh by 1 May 1977.

Nuclear Power Station *Largest*
The world's largest atomic power station is the Ontario Hydro's Pickering station which in 1973 attained full output of 2,160 MW.

Nuclear Reactor *Largest*
The largest single nuclear reactor in the world is the 1,098 MW Browns Ferry Unit 1 General Electric boiling water type reactor located on the Wheeler Reservoir, near Decatar, Alabama which became operative in 1973. The Grand Gulf Nuclear Station at Port Gibson, Mississippi will have a capacity of 1,290 MW in 1979.

Tidal Power Station
The world's first major tidal power station is the *Usine marèmotrice de la Rance*, officially opened on 26 Nov. 1966 at the Rance estuary in the Golfe de St. Malo, Brittany, France. It was built in five years at a cost of 420,000,000 francs (£34,685,000), and has a net annual output of 544,000,000 kWh. The 880 yd *804 m* barrage contains 24 turbo alternators. This harnessing of the tides has imperceptibly slowed the Earth's rate of revolution. The $1,000 million (£540 million) Passamaquoddy project for the Bay of Fundy in Maine, U.S.A., and New Brunswick, Canada, is not expected to be operative before 1978.

Boiler *Largest*
The largest boilers ever designed are those ordered in the United States from The Babcock & Wilcox Company (U.S.A.) with a capacity of 1,330 MW so involving the evaporation of 9,330,000 lb. *4 232 000 kg* of steam per hour. The largest boilers now being installed in the United Kingdom are the three 660 MW units for the Drax Power Station (see p. 147) designed and constructed by Babcock & Wilcox Ltd.

Generator *Largest*
Generators in the 2,000,000 kW (or 2,000 MW) range are now in the planning stages both in the U.K. and the U.S.A. The largest under construction is one of 1,300 MW by the Brown Boveri Co. of Switzerland for the Tennessee Valley Authority.

Turbines *Largest*
The largest turbines are those rated at 820,000 h.p. with an overload capacity of 1,000,000 h.p., 32 ft *9,7 m* in diameter with a 401 ton *407 tonnes* runner and a 312½ ton *317,5 tonnes* shaft installed at the Grand Coulee "Third Powerplant".

Pump
The world's largest integral reversible pump-turbine is that made by Allis-Chalmers for the $50,000,000 Taum Sauk installation of the Union Electric Co. in St. Louis, Missouri, U.S.A. It has a rating of 240,000 h.p. as a turbine and a capacity of 1,100,000 gallons *5 000 559 litres*/min as a pump. The Tehachapi Pumping Plant, California (1972) pumps 18,300,000 gal/min *83,2 million litres/min* over 1,700 ft *518 m* up.

Gas Works *Largest*
The flow of natural gas from the North Sea is diminishing the manufacture of gas by the carbonisation of coal and the re-forming process using petroleum derivatives. Britain's largest ever gasworks 300 acres *120 ha* were at Beckton, Newham. Currently the most productive gasworks are at the oil re-forming plant at Greenwich, Greater London, with an output of 420.5 million ft³ *11 907 298 m³* per day.

Biggest black-out
The greatest power failure in history struck seven northeastern U.S. States and Ontario, Canada, on 9–10 Nov. 1965. About 30,000,000 people in 80,000 miles² *207 200 km²* were plunged into darkness. Only two were killed. In New York City the power failed at 5.27 p.m. Supplies were eventually restored by 2 a.m. in Brooklyn, 4.20 a.m. in Queens, 6.58 a.m. in Manhattan and 7 a.m. in the Bronx.

6. ENGINEERING

Oldest Machinery *World*
The earliest machinery still in use is the *dâlu*—a water raising instrument known to have been in use in the Sumerian civilization which originated *c.* 3500 B.C. in Lower Iraq even earlier than the *Saqiyas* on the Nile.

Great Britain
The oldest piece of machinery (excluding clocks) operating in the United Kingdom is the snuff mill driven by a water wheel at Messrs. Wilson & Co.'s Sharrow Mill in Sheffield, South Yorkshire. It is known to have been operating in 1797 and more probably since 1730.

Press *Largest*
The world's two most powerful production machines are forging presses in the U.S.A. The Loewy closed-die forging press, in a plant leased from the U.S. Air Force by the Wyman-Gordon Company at North Grafton, Massachusetts, U.S.A. weighs 9,469 tons *9 620 tonnes* and stands 114 ft 2 in *34,79 m* high, of which 66 ft *20,1 m* is sunk below the operating floor. It has a rated capacity of 44,600 tons *45 315 tonnes*, and went into operation in October 1955. The other similar press is at the plant of the Aluminium Company of America at Cleveland, Ohio. There has been a report of a press in the U.S.S.R. with a capacity of 75 000 tonnes *73,800 tons* at Novo Kramatorsk. The Bêché and Grohs counterblow forging hammer, manufactured in West Germany are rated at 60,000 tonnes. The most powerful press in Great Britain is the closed-die forging and extruding press installed in 1967 at the Cameron Iron Works, Livingston, Lothian. The press is 92 ft *28 m* tall (27 ft *8,2 m* below gound) and exerts a force of 30,000 tons *30 481 tonnes*.

Lathe *Largest*
The world's largest lathe is the 72 ft *21,9 m* long 385 ton *391 tonnes* giant lathe built by the Dortmunder Rheinstahl firm of Wagner in 1962. The face plate is 15 ft *4,57 m* in diameter and can exert a torque of 289,000 ft/lb. *39 955 m/kg f* when handling objects weighing up to 200 tons *203 tonnes*.

Excavator *Largest*
The world's largest excavator is the 13,000 tonne bucket wheel excavator being assembled at the open cast lignite-mine of Hambach, West Germany with a rating of 200 000 m³ *260,000 yd³* per 20 hour working day. It is 210 m *690 ft* in length and 82 m *269 ft* tall. The wheel is 67,88 m *222 ft* in circumference with 5 m³ *6,5 yd³* buckets.

Dragline *Largest World*
The Ural Engineering Works at Ordzhonikidze, U.S.S.R., completed in March 1962, has a dragline known as the ES-25(100) with a boom of 100 m *328 ft* and a bucket with a capacity of 31.5 yds³ *24 m³*. The world's largest walking dragline is the Bucyrus-Erie 4250W with an all-up weight of 12,000 tons *12 192 tonnes* and a bucket capacity of 220 yds³ *168 m³* on a 310 ft *94,4 m* boom. This machine, the world's largest mobile land machine is now operating on the Central Ohio Coal Company's Muskingum site in Ohio, U.S.A.

Great Britain
The largest dragline excavator in Britain is "Big Geordie", the Bucyrus-Erie 1550W 6250 gross h.p., weighing 3,000

tons *3 048 tonnes* with a forward mast 160 ft *48,7 m* high. On open-cast coal workings at Butterwell, Northumberland in September 1975, it proved able to strip 100 tons *101 tonnes* of overburden in 65 secs with its 65 yard³ *49,7 m³* bucket on a 265 ft *80,7 m* boom. It is owned by Derek Crouch (Contractors) Ltd. of Peterborough, Cambridgeshire.

Crane Most Powerful *World*
The world's most powerful crane is the 53,000 tons 584 ft *178 m* long converted tanker *Odin* owned by Heerema Engineering Service of The Hague, Netherlands. On 26 May 1976 she made a test lift on 3000 tonnes *3,048 tons* at a radius maximum of 105 ft *32 m* in the Calard Canal, Europoort.

Gantry Crane Most Powerful
The 92.3 ft *28,14 m* wide Rahco (R. A. Hanson Disc. Ltd.) gantry crane at the Grand Coulee Dam Third Powerplant was tested to lift a load of 2,232 long tons *2 268 tonnes* in 1975. It lowered a 3,944,000 lb. *1789 tonne* generator rotor with an accuracy of $\frac{1}{32}$ inch *0,8 mm*.

Crane Tallest Mobile
The tallest mobile crane in the world is the 810 tonnes Rosenkranz K10001 with a lifting capacity of 1 000 tonnes *948 tons*, a combined boom and jib height of 202 m *663 ft*. It is carried on 10 trucks each limited to 75 ft 8 in *23,06 m* and an axle weight of 118 tonnes *116 tons*. It can lift 30 tonnes *29.5 tons* to a height of 160 m *525 ft*.

Greatest Lift
The heaviest lifting operation in engineering history was the 41,000 short ton (36,607 long tons *37 194 tonnes*) roof of the Velodrome in Montreal, Canada in 1975. It was raised by jacks some 4 in *10 cm* to strike its centering.

Blast Furnace Largest
The world's largest blast furnace is one with an inner volume of 5000 m³ *176,570 ft³* at the Krivoi Rog Iron and Steel Works, Ukraine, U.S.S.R. completed in December 1974 with an annual capacity of 4,000,000 tons *4 064 000 tonnes*.

Forging Largest
The largest forging on record is one of a 450,600 lb. *204,4 tonnes* 55 ft *16,76 m* long generator shaft for Japan, forged by the Bethlehem Steel Corp. Pennsylvania in Oct. 1973.

Pipeline Longest *Oil*
The longest crude oil pipeline in the world is the Interprovincial Pipe Line Company's installation from Edmonton, Alberta, to Buffalo, New York State, U.S.A., a distance of 1,775 miles *2 856 km*. Along the length of the pipe 13 pumping stations maintain a flow of 6,900,000 gal *31 367 145 litres* of oil per day.

The eventual length of the Trans-Siberian Pipeline will be 2,319 miles *3 732 km*, running from Tuimazy through Omsk and Novosibirsk to Irkutsk. The first 30 mile *48 km* section was opened in July 1957.

Submarine Pipelines
The longest submarine pipeline is the Ekofisk-Emden line stretching 260 miles *418 km* under the North Sea and completed in July 1975. The deepest North Sea pipeline is that from the Cormorant Field to Firths Voe, Shetland at 530 ft *162 m*.

Natural Gas
The longest natural gas pipeline in the world is the Trans-Canada Pipeline which by 1974 had 5,654 miles *9 099 km* of pipe up to 42 in *106,6 cm* in diameter.

Pipeline Most Expensive
The world's most expensive pipeline is the Alaska pipeline running 798 miles *1 284 km* Prudhoe Bay to Valdez. By completion of the first phase in 1977 it had cost at least $6,000 million (£3,250 million). The pipe is 48 in *1,21 m* in diameter and will eventually carry up to 2 million barrels of crude oil per day.

The world's most massive ever mobile object—the Ninian Field North Sea Oil Platform of 600,000 tons under construction in Loch Kishorn, Scotland (see p. 132).

Oil Tank Largest
The largest oil tank ever constructed is the Million Barrel Ekofisk Oil Tank completed in Norway in 1973 and implanted in the North Sea measuring 92 × 92 × 102 m high (*301.8 ft square and 335 ft high*) and containing 8 000 tonnes *7,873 tons* of steel and 202 000 tonnes *198,809 tons* of concrete. The capacity of 160 000 m³ *209,272 yds³* is equivalent to 1.42 times the amount of oil which escaped from the *Torrey Canyon*.

Cat Cracker Largest
The world's largest catalyst cracker is the Exxon Co's Bayway Refinery plant at Linden, New Jersey, U.S.A. with a fresh feed rate of 5,040,000 U.S. galls *19 077 000 litres* per day.

Nut Largest
The largest nuts ever made weigh 29.5 cwt. (1.475 tons *1,50 tonnes*) each and have an outside diameter of 43½ in *110,5 cm* and a 26 in *66 cm* thread. Known as the Pilgrim Nuts, they are manufactured by Doncaster Moorside Ltd. of Oldham, Greater Manchester for securing propellers.

Valve Largest
The world's largest valve is the 14 ft *4,26 m* diameter Pratt-Triton XL butterfly valve made in Aurora, Illinois, U.S.A. for water and power systems.

Transformer Largest
The world's largest single phase transformers are rated at 1,500,000 kVa of which 8 are in service with the American Electric Power Service Corporation. Of these five stepdown from 765 to 345 kV. Britain's largest transformers are those

149

rated at 1,000,000 kVa 400/275 kV built by Hackbridge & Hewittic Co. Ltd., Walton-on-Thames, Surrey first commissioned for the CEGB in Oct. 1968.

Ropeway or Telepherique Highest *World*

The highest and longest aerial ropeway in the world is the Teleférico Mérida (Mérida téléphérique) in Venezuela, from Mérida City (5,379 ft *1 639,5 m*) to the summit of Pico Espejo (15,629 ft *4 763,7 m*), a rise of 10,250 ft *3 124 m*. The ropeway is in four sections, involving 3 car changes in the 8 mile ascent in one hour. The fourth span is 10,070 ft *3 069 m* in length. The two cars work on the pendulum system—the carrier rope is locked and the cars are hauled by means of three pull ropes powered by a 230 h.p. *233 c.v.* motor. They have a maximum capacity of 45 persons and travel at 32 ft *9,7 m* per sec (21.8 m.p.h. *35,08 km/h*). The longest single span ropeway is the 13,500 ft *4 114 m* long span from the Coachella Valley to Mt. San Jacinto (10,821 ft *3 298 m*), California U.S.A., inaugurated on 12 Sept. 1963.

Great Britain

Britain's longest cabin lift is that at Llandudno, Gwynedd, opened in June 1969. It has 42 cabins with a capacity of 1,000 people per hour and is 5,320 ft *1 621 m* in length.

Passenger Lift Fastest *World*

The fastest domestic passenger lifts in the world are the express lifts to the 103rd floor or 1,340 ft *408 m* level in the 110 storey Sears Tower in Chicago, Illinois, U.S.A. They operate at a speed of 1,800 ft per min. 20.45 m.p.h. *32,91 km/h*. Much higher speeds are achieved in the winding cages of mine shafts. A hoisting shaft 6,800 ft *2 072 m* deep, owned by Western Deep Levels Ltd. in South Africa, winds at speeds of up to 40.9 m.p.h. *65,8 km/h* (3,595 ft *1 095 m* per min).

Great Britain

The longest lift in the United Kingdom is one 930 ft long inside the B.B.C. T.V. tower at Bilsdale, West Moor, North Yorkshire, built by J. L. Eve Construction Co. Ltd. It runs at 130 ft *39,6 m*/min. The longest fast lifts are the two 15-passenger cars in the Post Office Tower, Maple Street, London W1 which travel 540 ft *164 m* up at up to 1,000 ft *304 m*/min.

Escalator Longest

The term was registered in the U.S. on 28 May 1900 but the earliest "Inclined Escalator" was installed by Jesse W. Reno on the pier at Coney Island, New York in 1896. The first installation in Britain was at Harrods, Knightsbridge, London in Nov. 1898. The escalators on the Leningrad Underground, U.S.S.R. have a vertical rise of 195 ft *59,4 m*. The longest escalators in Britain are the four in the Tyne Tunnel, Tyne and Wear installed in 1951. They measure 192 ft 8 in *58,7 m* between combs with a vertical lift of 85 ft *25,9 m* and a step speed of up to 1.7 m.p.h. *2,7 km/h.*

The world's longest "moving sidewalks" are those installed in 1970 in the Neue Messe Centre, Dusseldorf, West Germany which measure 225 m *738 ft* between comb plates. The longest in Great Britain is the 375 ft *114,3 m* long Dunlop Starglide at London Airport Terminal 3 installed in March–May 1970.

Printer Fastest

The world's fastest printer is the Radiation Inc. electro-sensitive system at the Lawrence Radiation Laboratory, Livermore, California. High speed recording of up to 30,000 lines each containing 120 alphanumeric characters per minute is attained by controlling electronic pulses through chemically impregnated recording paper which is rapidly moving under closely spaced fixed styli. It can thus print the wordage of the whole Bible (773,692 words) in 65 sec—3,333 times as fast as the world's fastest typist.

Transmission Lines *Longest*

The longest span between pylons of any power line in the world is that across the Sogne Fjord, Norway, between Rabnaberg and Flatlberg. Erected in 1955 by the Whitecross Co. Ltd. of Warrington, Cheshire, England as part of the high-tension power cable from Refsdal power station at Vik, it has a span of 16,040 ft *4 888 m* and a weight of 12 tons/*tonnes*. In 1967 two further high tensile steel/aluminium lines 16,006 ft *4 878 m* long, and weighing 33 tons *33,5 tonnes*, manufactured by Whitecross and B.I.C.C. were erected here. The longest in Britain are the 5,310 ft *1 618 m* lines built by J. L. Eve Co. across the Severn with main towers each 488 ft *148 m* high.

Highest

The world's highest are those across the Straits of Messina, with towers of 675 ft *205 m* (Sicily side) and 735 ft *224 m* (Calabria) and 11,900 ft *3 627 m* apart. The highest lines in Britain are those made by British Insulated Callender's Cables Ltd. at West Thurrock, Essex, which cross the Thames estuary suspended from 630 ft *192 m* tall towers at a minimum height of 250 ft *76 m*, with a 130 ton *132 tonnes* breaking load. They are 4,500 ft *1 371 m* in length.

The most expensive jewelled watch on the market—the $47,500 (£27,940) Piaget watch sold by Van Cleef & Arpels of New York City.

Part of the world's longest 9 mile *14 km* long single-flight conveyor belt at Uniontown, Kentucky, U.S.A. (*Cable Belt Ltd., Camberley, Surrey*)

Highest voltages

The highest voltages now carried are 1,330,000 volts 1,224 miles *1 970 km* on the D.C. Pacific Inter-tie in the United States. The Ekibastuz D.C. transmission lines in Kazakhstan, U.S.S.R. are planned to be 2400 *km 1,490 miles* long with 1,500,000 volt capacity.

Conveyor Belt Longest

The world's longest single flight conveyor belt is one of 9 miles *14 km* installed near Uniontown, Kentucky, U.S.A. by Cable Belt Ltd. of Camberley, Surrey. It has a weekly capacity of 140,000 short tons *142 247 tonnes* of coal on a 42 in *1,06 m* wide 800 ft *243 m*/min belt and forms part of a 12½ miles *20 km* long system. The longest installation in Great Britain is also by Cable Belt Ltd. and of 5½ miles *8,9 km* underground at Longannet Power Station, Fife, Scotland. The world's longest multi-flight conveyor is one of 100 km *62 miles* between the phosphate mine near Bucraa and the port of El Aaiun, Morocco, built by Krupps and completed in 1972. It has 11 flights of between 9 and 11 km *5.6–6,8 miles* and is driven at 4,5 m/sec *10.06 m.p.h.*

Wire Rope Longest

The longest wire rope ever spun in one piece was one measuring 46,653 ft *14 219 m* (8.83 miles) long and 3⅛ in *7,93 cm* in circumference, with a weight of 28½ tons *28,9 tonnes*, manufactured by British Ropes Ltd. of Doncaster, South Yorkshire. The heaviest reported is one 7 inches *17,8 cm* in circumference, 3.94 miles *6,34 km* long weighing 81 tons

made by Martin-Black & Co. (Wire Ropes) Ltd. at Coatbridge, Strathclyde in 1973.

TIME PIECES

Clock *Oldest*

The earliest mechanical clock, that is one with an escapement, was completed in China in A.D. 725 by I Hsing and Liang Ling-tsan.

The oldest surviving working clock in the world is the faceless clock dating from 1386, or possibly earlier, at Salisbury Cathedral, Wiltshire, which was restored in 1956 having struck the hours for 498 years and ticked more than 500 million times. Earlier dates, ranging back to *c.* 1335, have been attributed to the weight-driven clock in Wells Cathedral, Somerset, but only the iron frame is original. A model of Giovanni de Dondi's heptagonal astronomical clock of 1348–64 was completed in 1962.

Clock Largest *World*

The world's most massive clock is the Astronomical Clock in Beauvais Cathedral, France, constructed between 1865 and 1868. It contains 90,000 parts and measures 40 ft *12,1 m* high, 20 ft *6,09 m* wide and 9 ft *2,7 m* deep. The Su Sung clock, built in China at K'aifeng in 1088–92, had a 20 ton *20,3 tonnes* bronze armillary sphere for 1½ tons *1,52 tonnes* of water. It was removed to Peking in 1126 and was last known to be working in its 40 ft *12,1 m* high tower in 1136.

Public

The largest four-faced clock in the world is that on the building of the Allen-Bradley Company of Milwaukee, Wisconsin, U.S.A. Each face has a diameter of 40 ft 3½ in *12,28 m* with a minute hand 20 ft *6,09 m* in overall length. The tallest four-faced clock in the world is that of the Williamsburgh Savings Bank in Brooklyn, New York City, N.Y., U.S.A. It is 430 ft *131 m* above street level.

Great Britain

The largest clock in the United Kingdom is that on the Royal Liver Building (built 1908–11) with dials 25 ft *7,62 m* in diameter and the 4 minute hands each 14 ft *4,26 m* long. The mechanism and dials weigh 22 tons and are 220 ft *67 m* above street level.

Longest stoppage

The longest stoppage of the clock in the House of Commons clock tower, London since the first tick on 31 May 1859 has been 13 days from noon 4 Apr. to noon 17 Apr. 1977. In 1945 a host of starlings slowed the minute hand by 5 minutes.

Clock Most accurate

The most accurate and complicated clockwork in the world is the Olsen clock, installed in the Copenhagen Town Hall, Denmark. The clock, which has more than 14,000 units, took 10 years to make and the mechanism of the clock functions in 570,000 different ways. The celestial pole motion of the clock will take 25,753 years to complete a full circle and is the slowest moving designed mechanism in the world. The clock is accurate to 0.5 of a second in 300 years—50 times more accurate than the previous record.

Clock Most expensive

The highest auction price for any portable English clock is £62,500 (*250,000 Swiss francs*), for Thomas Mudge's marine

The ultimate in animated cuckoo clocks, the 23½ ft *7,16 m* high clock designed by Karl Schleutermann in 1962 and completed in May 1975 at Wilmot, Ohio, U.S.A.

timekeeper in a green shagreen case completed in 1779, at Christie's in Geneva on 8 Nov. 1976.

Watch Oldest

The oldest watch (portable clock-work time-keeper) is one made of iron by Peter Helein (or Hele) in Nürnberg (Nuremberg), Bavaria, Germany, in *c.* 1504 and now in the Memorial Hall, Philadelphia, Pennsylvania, U.S.A. The earliest wrist watches were those of Jacquet-Droz and Leschot of Geneva, Switzerland, dating from 1790.

Watch Smallest

The smallest watches in the world are produced by Jaeger Le Coultre of Switzerland. Equipped with a 15-jewelled movement they measure just over half-an-inch *1,2 cm* long and three-sixteenths of an inch *0,476 cm* in width. The movement, with its case, weighs under a quarter of an oz. *7 g*.

Watch Most expensive

Excluding watches with jewelled cases, the most expensive standard men's pocket watch is the Swiss *Grande Complication* by Audemars-Piguet which retails for £22,500. On 1 June 1964, a record £27,500 was paid for the Duke of Wellington's watch made in Paris in 1807 by Abraham Louis Bréguet, (1747–1823) at the salerooms of Sotheby & Co., London, by the dealers Messrs. Ronald Lee for a Portuguese client.

The Patek Phillippe 18 carat gold minute-repeater, perpetual calendar pocket watch launched by Tiffany's, New York on 28 Sept. 1976 is priced at $48,000 (£28,250).

Time Measurer Most accurate *World*

The most accurate time-keeping devices are the twin atomic hydrogen masers installed in 1964 in the U.S. Naval Research Laboratory, Washington, D.C. They are based on the frequency of the hydrogen atom's transition period of 1,420,450,751,694 cycles/sec. This enables an accuracy to within one sec/1,700,000 years.

Great Britain

The most accurate measurer in the United Kingdom is the 14 ft *4,2 m* long rubidium resonance Standard Atomic Clock at the National Physical Laboratory, Teddington, Richmond upon Thames, Greater London, devised by Dr. Louis Essen, O.B.E. and Mr. J. V. L. Parry and completed in 1962. It is accurate to within one second in 1,000 years.

Radar Installation *Largest*

The largest of the three installations in the U.S. Ballistic Missile Early Warning System (B.M.E.W.S.) is that near Thule, in Greenland, 931 miles *1 498 km* from the North Pole, completed in 1960 at a cost of $500,000,000 (*then £178.5 million*). Its sister stations are one at Cape Clear, Alaska, U.S.A., completed in 1961, and a $115,000,000 (*then £41.07*

The geocentric mechanism of the Olsen clock which enables eclipses of both the sun and moon to be indicated (see above). (*Jorgensen & Co., Copenhagen*)

The IBM System 370 Model 168 MP which has the largest memory of any computer built in Britain.

million) installation at Fylingdales Moor, North Yorkshire, completed in June 1963. The largest scientific radar installation is the 21 acre *84 000 m²* ground array at Jicamarca, Peru.

Tubing Smallest

The smallest tubing in the world is made by Accles and Pollock, Ltd. of Warley, West Midlands. It is of pure nickel with an outer and inner diameter of 0.0005 in and 0.00013 in and was announced on 9 Sept. 1963. The average human hair measures from 0.002 to 0.003 of an inch *0,05–0,075 mm* diameter. The tubing, which is stainless, can be used for the artificial insemination of bees and for the medical process of "feeding" nerves, and weighs only 5 oz. *141 gr* per 100 miles *160 km.*

COMPUTERS

The modern computer was made possible by the invention of the point-contact transistor by John Bardeen and Walter Brattain announced in July 1948, and the junction transistor by R. L. Wallace, Morgan Sparks and Dr. William Shockley in early 1951.

Oldest

The oldest operative computer in Britain and probably the world is Witch built at Harwell in 1949–50 and last in service at the Polytechnic, Wolverhampton whence it was transferred in 1973 to the Museum of Science and Industry, Birmingham in full operational condition. It has 827 "Dekatron" cathode tubes.

Most Powerful and Fastest *World*

The world's most powerful and fastest computer is the CRAY-1 designed by Seymour R. Cray for Cray Research Inc. of Minneapolis, Minnesota, U.S.A. The clock period is 12.5 nanoseconds and memory range up to 1,048,000 64-bit words resulting in a capability of 5.6×10^8 results per sec. With 32 Cray DD-19 disk storage units it has a storage capacity of 7.7568×10^{10} bits. Floating point numbers may vary between 10^{-5000} to 10^{2500}. The cost of a mid-range system is $5.5 million £3.25 million. The IBM 3850 mass storage device launched in 1977 is the world's most capacious with a thousand terabit memory or 4×10^{15} bits of information.

Great Britain

The computer with the largest memory built in the United Kingdom is the International Business Machines' I.B.M. System/370 Model 168 MP which is a multiprocessing computer with 16,777,216 bytes of main storage. A 'byte' is a unit of storage comprising 8 'bits' collectively equivalent to one alphabetic letter or two numerals. This machine is produced at Havant, Hampshire. ICL has proposed a computer with 576 separate streams which would be 50 times faster than ILLIAC IV.

Fastest Switch

An electronic device that can be switched in less than one 10-billionth of a second (10^{-11} sec) was announced on 18 Jan. 1973. It utilizes the prediction of the English physicist Brian Josephson (b. 1940) in 1962 that ultra-thin insulators can be made superconductive.

9. THE BUSINESS WORLD

1. COMMERCE

The $(US) has in this chapter been converted at a fixed mean rate of $1.70 to the £ Sterling for mid 1977 and at the relevant rates at other dates.

The *Guinness Book of the Business World* by Henry Button and Andrew Lampert (£6.50) contains a more detailed treatment of records and facts in the world of commerce and industry.

Oldest Industry

Agriculture is often described as "the oldest industry in the world", whereas in fact there is no evidence that it was practised before *c.* 11,000 B.C. The oldest known industry is flint knapping, involving the production of chopping tools and hand axes, dating from about 1,750,000 years ago. Salt panning is of comparable antiquity.

Oldest Company *World*

The oldest company in the world is the Faversham Oyster Fishery Co., referred to in the Faversham Oyster Fishing Act 1930, as existing "from time immemorial", *i.e.* in English law from before 1189.

Great Britain

The Royal Mint has origins going back to A.D. 287. The Shore Porters Society, 12 Virginia Street, Aberdeen in the haulage and removal business, carry the legend "Established in 1498". This is a reference to a town council minute of 22 June 1498 but the society was most probably in being in the harbour in the 12th century. The Whitechapel Bell Foundry of Whitechapel Road, London, E.1, has been in business since 1570. The retail business in Britain with the oldest history is the Cambridge bookshop, which, though under various ownership, has traded from the site of 1 Trinity Street since 1581 and since 1907 under its present title Bowes & Bowes. R. Durtnell & Sons, builders, of Brasted, Kent, has been run by the same family since 1591. The first bill of adventure signed by the English East India Co., was dated 21 March 1601.

Greatest Assets *World*

The business with the greatest amount in physical assets is the Bell System, which comprises the American Telephone and Telegraph Company, with headquarters at 195 Broadway, New York City, N.Y., U.S.A., and its subsidiaries. The group's total assets on the consolidated balance sheet at 31 Dec. 1976 were valued at $86,717,000,000 (*then £51,000 million*). The plant involved included 123.13 million telephones. The number of employees is 927,000. A total of 20,109 shareholders attended the Annual Meeting in April 1961, thereby setting a world record.

The first company to have assets in excess of $1 billion was the United States Steel Corporation with $1,400 million (*then £287.73 million*) at the time of its creation by merger in 1900.

Great Britain

The enterprise in the United Kingdom, excluding banks, with the greatest capital employed is the Electricity Council and the Electricity Boards in England and Wales with £6,012,000,000 in 1976. This ranks tenth in the western world.

The biggest British industrial company is Imperial Chemical Industries Ltd. with assets employed of £3,519 million as at 31 Dec. 1976. Its staff and payroll averaged 192,000 during the year. The company, which has 509 U.K. and overseas subsidiaries, was formed on 7 Dec. 1926 by the merger of four concerns—British Dyestuffs Corporation Ltd.; Brunner, Mond & Co. Ltd.; Nobel Industries Ltd. and United Alkali Co. Ltd. The first chairman was Sir Alfred Moritz Mond (1868–1930), later the 1st Lord Melchett.

The net assets of The "Shell" Transport and Trading Company, Ltd., at 31 Dec. 1976 were £2,744,937,015 comprising mainly its 40% share in the net assets of the Royal Dutch/Shell Group of Companies which stood at £6,576 million. Group companies employ 153,000. "Shell" Transport was formed in 1897 by Marcus Samuel (1853–1927), later the 1st Viscount Bearsted.

Greatest sales

The first company to surpass the $1 billion (U.S.) mark in annual sales was the United States Steel Corporation in 1917. Now there are 183 corporations with sales exceeding £1,000 million (128 U.S., 42 European, 11 Japanese and 2 Canadian. The list is headed by Exxon of New York with $48,630,817,000 (*£28,606 million*) in 1976.

Greatest profit and loss

The greatest net profit ever made by an industrial company in a year is $3,142 million (*£1,366 million*) by Exxon in 1974.

The Coat of Arms of Britain's oldest family firm, the 386 year old R. Durtnell & Sons, builders, of Brasted, Kent.

The greatest loss ever sustained by a commercial concern in a year is $431.2 million (£179.6 million) by Penn Central Transportation Co. in 1970—a rate of $13.67 (then £5.69) per second. The top gross profits in the United Kingdom in 1976 were British Petroleum with £1,626.4 million which, after all charges and extraordinary items, including £1,323.2 million in overseas tax, resulted in a net profit of £166.2 million. The biggest loss maker in *The Times 1,000 1976–77* was Chrysler United Kingdom with £24,506,000.

The greatest loss ever recorded by any enterprise in a year was £309,700,000 by the Post Office in the United Kingdom for 1974–75. Of nationalized industries the record cost to the taxpayer in a year was £567,600,000 or £1,079 per minute in 1975 by British Rail.

Biggest work force

The greatest payroll of any single civilian organisation in the world is that of the U.S.S.R. National Railway system with a total work force of 1,996,600. The biggest employer in the United Kingdom is the Post Office with 455,627 employees (incl. part time workers and sub postmasters) on 31 Mar. 1976.

Largest Take-Over

The largest take-over in commercial history has been the bid of £438,000,000 by Grand Metropolitan Hotels Ltd., for the brewers Watney Mann on 17 June 1972. The value of the consideration was £378.2 million.

Largest Merger

The largest merger ever mooted in British business was that of the Hill Samuel Group (£768 million assets) and Slater,

Walker Securities (£469 million) in April 1973 with combined assets of £1,237 million. This plan was called off on 19 June 1973.

Biggest Write Off

The largest reduction of assets in corporate history was the $800 million *£347 million* write off of Tristar aircraft development costs announced on 23 Nov. 1974.

Companies

The number of companies on the register in Great Britain at 31 Dec. 1976 was 621,683 of which 15,585 were public and the balance private companies. The smallest company on the register is Frank Davies Ltd., of Hemel Hempstead, Hertfordshire incorporated on 22 Aug. 1924 with a nominal capital of $\frac{1}{2}$d divided into two one farthing shares.

Most directorships

The record for directorships was set in 1961 by Hugh T. Nicholson, formerly senior partner of Harmood Banner & Co., London who as a liquidating chartered accountant became director of all 451 companies of the Jasper group in 1961 and had 7 other directorships.

Advertising Agent

The largest international single-name advertising agency in the world is J. Walter Thompson Co., which in 1976 had total world wide billings of $1,039.0 million (£611.1 million).

Biggest advertiser

The world's biggest advertiser is Sears Roebuck and Co., with $419,460,000 (£246 million) in 1976 excluding its catalogue.

Aircraft manufacturer

The world's largest aircraft manufacturer is the Boeing Company of Seattle, Washington, U.S.A. The corporation's sales totalled $3,918,535,000 (£2,305 million) in 1976 and it had 63,400 employees and assets valued at $1,279,988,000 (then 752.9 million) at 1 Apr. 1977. Cessna Aircraft Company of Wichita, Kansas, U.S.A., produced 7,673 civil aircraft (55 models) in the year 1975, with total sales of $492 million (then £240 million). The company has produced more than 130,000 aircraft since Clyde Cessna's first was built in 1911. Their record year was 1965–66 with 7,922 aircraft completed.

The world's most productive aircraft manufacturers, the Cessna Aircraft Co., which has produced more than 130,000 aircraft since 1911.

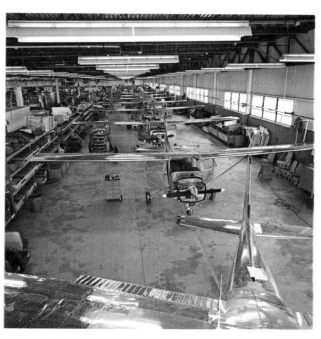

Airline *Largest*

The largest airline in the world is the U.S.S.R. State airline "Aeroflot", so named since 1932. This was instituted on 9 Feb. 1923, with the title of Civil Air Fleet of the Council of Ministers of the U.S.S.R., abbreviated to "Dobrolet". It operates 1,300 aircraft over about 560,000 miles *900 000 km* of routes, employs 400,000 people and carries 100 million passengers to 67 countries. The commercial airline carrying the greatest number of passengers in 1976 was United Airlines of Chicago, Illinois, U.S.A. (formed 1926) with 34,001,564 passengers. The company had 49,922 employees and a fleet of 365 jet planes. In March 1976 British Airways were operating a fleet of 189 aircraft, with 14 on order. Staff employed on airline activities totalled 58,200 and 13.8 million passengers were carried in 1975–76 on 396,434 miles *638,000 km* of unduplicated routes.

Oldest

The oldest existing national airline is Koninklijke-Luchtvaart-Maatschappij N.V. (KLM) of the Netherlands, which opened its first scheduled service (Amsterdam-London) on 17 May 1920, having been established on 7 Oct. 1919. One of the original constituents of B.O.A.C., Handley-Page Transport Ltd., was founded in May 1919 and merged into Imperial Airways in 1924. Delag (Deutsche Luftschiffahrt A.G.) was founded at Frankfurt am Main on 16 Nov. 1909 and started a scheduled airship service June 1910. Chalk's International Airline has been flying amphibians between Miami, Florida and the Bahamas since July 1919. Albert "Pappy" Chalk flew from 1911 to 1975.

Aluminium producer

The world's largest producer of primary aluminium is Alcan Aluminium Limited, of Montreal, Quebec, Canada. With its affiliated companies, the company had an output of 1,673,000 short tons *1 518 000 tonnes* in 1976. The company's principal subsidiary, the Aluminium Company of Canada Ltd., owns the largest aluminium smelter in the western world, at Arvida, Quebec, with a capacity of 465,000 short tons *422 000 tonnes* per annum. Alcoa of Pittsburgh, U.S.A. has the highest sales with $2,924,400,000 (*£1,720 million*).

Art auctioneering

The largest and oldest firm of art auctioneers in the world is Sotheby Parke-Bernet of London and New York, founded in 1744. The turnover in 1975–76 was $175,000,000 (*£103 million*). The highest total for any house sale auction was theirs on 18–27 May 1977 at the 6th Earl of Roseberg's home at Mentmore, Buckinghamshire which reached £6,389,933 or *$10,9 million*. H.M. Government had turned down an offer of £2 million.

Bank

The International Bank for Reconstruction and Development (founded 27 Dec. 1945), the United Nations "World Bank" at 1818 H Street N.W., Washington, D.C., U.S.A., has an authorized share capital of $27,000 million (*£10,800 million*). There were 128 members with a subscribed capital of $25,586,300,000 (*£15,050 million*) at 31 Dec. 1976. The International Monetary Fund in Washington, D.C., U.S.A. has 129 members with total quotas of SDR 29,213,300,000 (*$33,751 million* or *£19,853 million*) at 28 Feb. 1977.

The private bank with the greatest deposits is the Bank of America National Trust and Savings Association, of San Francisco, California, U.S.A., with $61,749,814,000 (*£36,323,420,000*) at 31 Dec. 1976. Its total assets were $73,912,940,000 (*£43,480 million*). Barclays Bank (with Barclays Bank International and other subsidiary companies) had over 5,100 branches in 70 countries (3,090 in the United Kingdom) in December 1976. Deposits totalled £18,163,316,000 and assets £19,320,053,000. The largest bank in the United Kingdom is the National Westminster with total assets of £17,070,044,000 and 3,300 branches as at 31 Dec. 1976.

Bank building

The world's tallest bank building is the Bank of Montreal's First Bank Tower, Toronto, Canada which has 72 stories and stands 935 ft *284,98 m*. The largest bank vault in the world, measuring 350 × 100 × 8 ft *106,7 × 30,4 × 2,4 m* and

above: Richard Booth, the world's leading second hand bookseller, with a stock of a million volumes.

below: The Headquarters' building of the world's largest building society at Halifax, West Yorkshire.

weighing 879 tons *893 tonnes* is in the Chase Manhattan Building, New York City, completed in May 1961. Its six doors weigh up to 40 tons *40,6 tonnes* apiece but each can be closed by the pressure of a forefinger.

Banquet Greatest *Outdoors*

The greatest banquet ever staged was that by President Loubet, President of France, in the gardens of the Tuileries, Paris, on 22 Sept. 1900. He invited every one of the 22,000 mayors in France and their deputies. With the Gallic *penchant* for round numbers, the event has always been referred to as "le banquet des 100,000 maires".

Indoors

The greatest number of people served indoors at a single sitting was 13,383 at the Indiana State Fairgrounds, Indianapolis, U.S.A. on 17 Mar. 1976. The meal was served in 53 mins at $3.21 (*£1.88*) per plate.

Most expensive

The menu for the main 5½ hr banquet at the Imperial Iranian 2500th Anniversary gathering at Persepolis in October 1971 was probably the most expensive ever compiled. It comprised quail eggs stuffed with Iranian caviar, a mousse of crayfish tails in Nantua sauce, stuffed rack of roast lamb, with a main course of roast peacock stuffed with *foie gras*, fig rings and raspberry sweet champagne sherbet, with wines including *Château Lafite-Rothschild* 1945 at £40 per bottle from the cellars of Maxime, Paris.

Barbers

The largest barbering establishment in the world is Norris of Houston, 3303 Audley, Houston, Texas, U.S.A. which employs 60 barbers.

Bicycle factory

The 64-acre *25,9 ha* plant of TI-Raleigh Industries Ltd. at Nottingham is the largest cycle factory in the world producing complete bicycles, components and wheeled toys. The company employs 10,000 and in 1976 had targets to make 850,000 wheeled toys and more than 2 million bicycles.

Book shop

The book shop with most titles and the longest shelving (30 miles *48 km*) in the world is W. & G. Foyle Ltd., City of Westminster, Greater London. First established in 1904 in a small shop in Islington, the company is now at 119–125 Charing Cross Road. The area on one site is 75,825 ft² *7 044 m²*. The most capacious bookstore in the world measured by square footage is Barnes & Noble Bookstore of Fifth Ave. at 17th Street, New York City, U.S.A. with 154,250 ft² *14 330 m²* and with 12.87 miles *20,71 km* of shelving.

The world's largest second-hand booksellers are Richard Booth (Bookseller) Ltd., of Hay-on-Wye, Powys, Wales with 8.12 miles *13,07 km* of shelving and a running stock of 900,000 to 1,100,000 in 30,091 ft² *2 795 m²* of selling space.

Brewer *Oldest*

The oldest brewery in the world is the Weihenstephan Brewery, Freising, near Munich, West Germany, founded in A.D. 1040.

Largest World

The largest single brewer in the world is Anheuser-Busch, Inc. in St. Louis, Missouri, U.S.A. In 1975 the company sold 35,196,180 U.S. barrels, equivalent to 7,267 million Imperial pints, the greatest annual volume ever produced by a brewing company. The company's St. Louis plant covers 95 acres *38,4 ha* and has a capacity of 10,500,000 U.S. barrels *2,168 million Imperial pints*. The largest brewery on a single site is Adolph Coors Co. of Golden, Colorado, U.S.A. which is scheduled to produce 14,650,000 U.S. barrels *2,967 million Imperial pints* in 1977.

Europe

The largest brewery in Europe is the Guinness Brewery at St. James's Gate, Dublin, Ireland, which extends over 60.44 acres *24,64 ha*. The business was founded in 1759.

Great Britain

The largest brewing company in the United Kingdom based on its 8,985 public houses, 944 off-licenses and 60 hotels, is Bass Charington Ltd. The company has net assets of £577,200,000, 62,449 employees (including bar-staff) and controls 12 breweries. Their sales figure for the year ending 30 Sept. 1976 was £801,700,000.

Greatest exports

The largest exporter of beer, ale and stout in the world is Arthur Guinness, Son & Co. Ltd., of Dublin, Ireland. Exports of Guinness from the Republic of Ireland in the 52 weeks ending 12 Mar. 1977 were 954,300 bulk barrels (bulk barrel = 36 Imperial gallons), which is equivalent to 1,510,101 half pint glasses *1,430,065 30-centilitre glasses* per day.

Brickworks

The largest brickworks in the world is the London Brick Company plant at Stewartby, Bedfordshire. The works, established in 1898, now cover 221 acres *90 ha* and has a production capacity of 17,000,000 bricks and brick equivalent each week.

Building contractors

The largest construction company in the United Kingdom is George Wimpey & Co. Ltd. (founded 1880), of London, who undertake building, civil, mechanical, electrical and chemical engineering work. With gross assets of £425,187,000 and 28,000 employees, the turnover of work was £652,000,000 in 35 countries in 1976.

Building societies

The biggest building society in the world is the Halifax Building Society of Halifax, West Yorkshire. It was established in 1853 and has total assets exceeding £5,400,000,000. It has over 7,000 employees and over 340 branches and 1,200 agencies. The smallest was the Southgate and Palmers Green Building Society in the Greater London Borough of Enfield founded in 1955 with assets of £2 but was deregistered in 1976.

Chemist shop chain

The largest chain of chemist shops in the world is Boots The Chemists, which has 1,250 retail branches. The firm was founded by Jesse Boot (b. Nottingham, 1850), later the 1st Baron Trent, who died in 1931.

Chocolate factory

The world's largest chocolate factory is that built by Hershey Foods Corp. in Hershey, Pennsylvania, U.S.A. in 1903–1905. It now has 2,000,000 ft² *185,800 m²* of floor space.

Computer Company

The world's largest computer firm is International Business Machines (IBM) Corporation of New York which in a 1975 court decision was held to have a 36.7% share in the value of "electronic computers and peripheral equipment, except parts" based on 1971 shipments. In 1976 assets were $17,723,326,000 and sales were $16,304 million (£9,590 million).

Department Stores *World*

The largest department store chain, in terms of number of stores, is J. C. Penney, Company Inc., founded in Wyoming, U.S.A., in 1902. The company operates 2,089 retail units in the U.S.A., Belgium and Italy, with net selling space of 62.4 million ft² *5,59 million m²*. Its turnover was $8,353.8 million (£4,914 million) in the year ending 29 Jan. 1977 the twenty first consecutive year of record sales.

Great Britain

The largest department store in the United Kingdom is Harrods Ltd. of Knightsbridge, Royal Borough of Kensington and Chelsea, Greater London named after Henry Charles Harrod, who opened a grocery in Knightsbridge Village in 1849. It has a total selling floor space of 16 acres *6,4 ha*, employs 4,000 people and had a total of 16,700,000 transactions in 1976.

Most profitable

The department store with the fastest-moving stock in the world is the Marks & Spencer premier branch, known as "Marble Arch" at 458 Oxford Street, City of Westminster, Greater London. The figure of £750 worth of goods per square foot of selling space per year is believed to be an understatement when the selling area was raised to 97,400 ft² *9 048 m²* in August 1976. The company has 254 branches in the U.K. and operates on over 6 million ft² *558 000 m²* of selling space and now has stores on the Continent and Canada.

Distillery

The world's largest distilling company is The Seagram Company Ltd., of Canada. Its sales in the year ending 31 July 1976 totalled U.S. $2,048,970,000 (£1,205 million) of which $1,723,684,000 (*£1,013 million*) were from sales by Joseph E. Seagram & Sons, Inc. in the United States. The group employs about 17,000 people, including about 12,500 in the United States.

The largest of all Scotch whisky distilleries is Carsebridge at Alloa, Central Region, Scotland, owned by Scottish Grain Distillers Limited. This distillery is capable of producing more than 20,000,000 proof gallons per annum. The largest establishment for blending and bottling Scotch whisky is owned by John Walker & Sons Limited at Kilmarnock, Strathclyde, where over 2½ million bottles are filled each week. "Johnnie Walker" is the world's largest-selling brand of Scotch whisky. The largest malt Scotch whisky distillery is the Tomatin Distillery, Highland, established at 1,028 ft *313 m* above sea level in 1897, with an annual capacity 4.75 million proof gallons. The world's largest-selling brand of gin is Gordon's.

Fisheries
The world's highest recorded catch of fish was 65 700 000 tonnes in 1973. Peru had the largest ever national haul with 12 160 000 tonnes in 1970 comprising mostly anchoveta. The United Kingdom's highest figure was 1 206 000 tonnes in 1948. The world's largest fishmongers are MacFisheries, a subsidiary of Unilever Ltd., with 252 retail outlets as at April 1977.

Largest Net
The largest net yet manufactured is one that can fish 6.8 million m³ *8.8 million yd³* per hour announced from West Germany in March 1974.

Grocery stores
The largest grocery chain in the world is Safeway Stores Incorporated of Oakland, California, U.S.A. with sales in 1976 of $10,442,531,000 (*£6,142 million*) and total current assets valued at $957,863,000 (*£563 million*) as at 1 Jan. 1977. The company has 2,438 stores totalling 53,223,000 ft² *4 944 417 m²*. The total payroll is 133,035.

Hotelier
The top revenue-earning hotel business is Holiday Inns Inc., with a 1976 revenue of $965,626,000 (*£568 million*), from 1,708 inns (277,932 rooms) at 1 March 1977 in 50 countries. The business was founded by Charles Kemmons Wilson with his first inn in Summer Avenue, Memphis, Tennessee in 1952.

Insurance *Company Largest World*
The company with the highest volume of insurance in force in the world is the Prudential Insurance Company of America of Newark, New Jersey with $258,000 million (*£151,764 million*) at 31 Dec. 1976, which is more than double the U.K. National Debt figure. The admitted assets are $43,700 million.

Great Britain
The largest insurance company in the United Kingdom is the Prudential Assurance Co. Ltd. At 1 Jan. 1977 the tangible assets were £4,495,827,000 and the total amount assured was £28,116,100,000.

Life policies Largest
The largest life assurance policy ever written was one of £10,000,000 $25,000,000 for James Derrick Slater (b. 13 Mar. 1929), Chairman of Slater, Walker Securities, the City of London Investment bankers. The existence of the policy was made known on 3 June 1971.

Highest pay-out
The highest pay-out on a single life has been some $14 million (*£5.6 million*) to Mrs. Linda Mullendore, wife of an Oklahoma rancher, reported on 14 Nov. 1970. Her murdered husband had paid $300,000 in premiums in 1969.

Marine
The largest ever marine insurance loss was the 125,000 grt VLCC (Very Large Crude Carrier), *Olympic Bravery*. This vessel which was insured at Lloyds and valued at £25 m, ran aground off Ushant on 24 Jan. 1976. The new 60,000 g.r.t. LNG (Liquid Natural Gas) Carrier *Angus Aquarius* built by General Dynamics Corporation, Massachusetts, U.S.A. is currently insured for $175 million *£103 million*. This vessel is owned by Cryogenic Energy Transportation Inc., U.S.A., and chartered to the Burmah Oil Co., Ltd.

Land *Owner*
The world's largest landowner is the United States Government, with a holding of 760,999,000 acres (1,189,060 miles² *3 079 651 km²*) which is nearly the area of India. The United Kingdom's greatest ever private landowner was the 3rd Duke of Sutherland, George Granville Sutherland-Leveson-Gower, K.G. (1828–92), who owned 1,358,000 acres *549 560 ha* in 1883. Currently the largest landholder in Great Britain is the Forestry Commission (instituted 1919) with 3,041,737 acres *1 230 948 ha*. The longest tenure is that by St. Paul's Cathedral of land at Tillingham, Essex, given by King Ethelbert before A.D. 616. Currently the landowner with the largest known acreage is the 9th Duke of Buccleuch (b. 1923) with 336,000 acres *136 035 ha*.

Value Highest
Currently the most expensive land in the world is that in the City of London. The freehold price on small prime sites reached £1,950/ft² (*£21,230/m²*) in mid 1973. In February 1964 a woman paid $510 (*£212.50*) for a triangular piece of land measuring 3 by 6½ by 5¾ in, *7,6 × 16,5 × 14,6 cm* at a tax lien auction in North Hollywood, California, U.S.A. —equivalent to $365,182,470 (*£152.1 million*) per acre. The real estate value per square metre of the two topmost French vineyards, Grande and Petite Cognac vineyards in Bordeaux, has not been recently estimated.

Greatest auction
The greatest auction was that at Anchorage, Alaska on 11 Sept. 1969 for 179 tracts 450,858 acres *182 455 ha* of the oil-bearing North Slope, Alaska. An all-time record bid of $72,277,133 for a 2,560 acre *1 036 ha* lease was made by the Amerada Hess Corporation—Getty Oil consortium. This £30,115,472 bid indicated a price of $28,233 (*then £11,763*) per acre.

Highest rent
The highest record rentals in the world are for modern office accommodation in the prime areas of the City of London. In mid-1975 figures of £24/ft² *£304/m²* were reached exclusive of rates and services. For main thoroughfare ground floor banking halls figures up to £43/ft² *£494/m²* have been under negotiation.

Mineral water
The world's largest mineral firm is Source Perrier, near Nimes, France with an annual production of more than 1,800,000,000 bottles, of which 640,000,000 now come from Contrexeville. The French drink about 50 litres *88 pts* of mineral water per person per year.

Motor Car Manufacturer *Largest World*
The largest manufacturing company in the world is General Motors Corporation of Detroit, Michigan, U.S.A. During its peak year of 1976 world wide sales totalled $47,181,000,000 (*£27,753 million*). Its assets at 31 Dec. 1976 were valued at $24,442,400,000 (*£14,377 million*). Its total 1976 payroll was $12,908,500,000 (*£7,593 million*) to an average of 748,000 employees. Dividends paid in 1976 were a record $1,603,400,000 (*£943 million*).

Great Britain
The largest British manufacturer was British Leyland Ltd. with 981,000 vehicles produced and a sales turnover of £2,892 million of which 54.4% or £1,576 million was overseas sales in 180 markets in 1976.

Largest plant
The largest single automobile plant in the world is the Volkswagenwerk, Wolfsburg, West Germany, with 47,000 employees and a capacity for 4,000 vehicles daily. The surface

One of the newest additions at Rivermont, to Holiday Inns' world-wide chain of 1,708 hotels in 50 countries.

area of the factory buildings is 356 acres *144 ha* and that of the whole plant 4,991 acres *2 020 ha* with 43.5 miles *70 km* of rail sidings.

Salesmanship
The all-time record for automobile salesmanship in units sold individually is 1,425 in 1973 by Joe Girard of Detroit, U.S.A., winner of the No. 1 Car Salesman title each year since 1966. His commissions in 1976 totalled $180,000 (*£105,880*) when his total was 1,285. (His lifetime total is 12,147 sales, all retail.)

Oil Company
The world's largest oil company is the Exxon Corporation (formerly Standard Oil Company [New Jersey]), with 135,500 employees and assets valued at $36,331,364,000 (*£21,371 million*) on 1 Jan. 1977.

Oil refineries *Largest*
The world's largest refinery is the Amuya Bay refinery in Venezuela, operated by Lagoven with a capacity of 31.5 million tons *32,0 million tonnes*. The largest oil refinery in the United Kingdom is the Esso Refinery at Fawley, Hampshire, Opened in 1921 and much expanded in 1951, it has a capacity of 19,500,000 tons *19,8 million tonnes* per year. The total investment on the 1,300 acre *526 ha* site is £159,000,000.

Paper mills
The world's largest paper mill is that established in 1936 by the Union Camp Corporation at Savannah, Georgia, U.S.A., with an all-time record output in 1974 of 1,002,967 short tons *909 829 tonnes*. The largest paper mill in the United Kingdom is the Bowater's Kemsley Mill near Sittingbourne, Kent with a complex covering an area of 500 acres *202 ha* and a capacity in excess of 300,000 tons/*tonnes* a year.

Pop-corn plant
The largest pop-corn plant in the world is The House of Clarks Ltd. (instituted 1933) of Dagenham, Barking, which in 1975/76 produced 65,000,000 packets of "Butterkist".

Public relations
The world's largest public relations firm is Hill and Knowlton, Inc. of 633 Third Avenue, New York City, N.Y., U.S.A. and ten other U.S. cities. The firm employs a full-time staff of more than 560 and also maintains offices in 27 overseas cities. The world's pioneer public relations publication is *Public Relations News*, founded by Mrs. Denny Griswold in 1944 and which now circulates in 77 countries.

Publishing
The publishing company generating most net revenue is Time Inc. of New York City with $1,038.2 million (*£610.7 million*) in 1976. Britain's largest publisher is I.P.C. Ltd., a subsidiary of Reed International Ltd., with a publishing turnover of £200 million as at March 1977. The largest book publishing concern in the world is the Book Division of McGraw-Hill Inc. of New York with sales of $255,713,000 (*£150.4 million*) in 1976.

Restaurateurs
The largest restaurant chain in the world is that operated by McDonald's Corporation of Oakbrook, Illinois, U.S.A., founded on 15 Apr. 1955 in Des Plaines, Chicago by Ray A. Kroc B.H. (Bachelor of Hamburgerology). By late 1977 the number of McDonald's restaurants licensed and owned in 23 countries reached 4,400 with an aggregate throughput of 22 billion 100% beef hamburgers under the motto "Q.S.C. & V."—for quality, (fast) service, cleanliness and value. Sales systemwide in 1976 were $3,000 million (*£1,764 million*). The largest hotel, catering and leisure group in the United Kingdom is Trust Houses Forte who employ up to 48,647 full and part-time staff in the U.K. 13,591 overseas, and who had a turnover of £451,700,000 in 1975–76. They had 888 hotels world-wide.

Retailer
The largest retailing firm in the world is Sears, Roebuck and Co. (founded by Richard Warren Sears in North Redwood railway station, Minnesota in 1886) of Chicago, Illinois, U.S.A. The net sales were $14,950,000,000 (*£8,795 million*) in the year ending 31 Jan. 1977 when the corporation had 859 retail stores and 2,920 catalogue, retail and telephone sales offices and independent catalogue merchants in the U.S.A. and total assets valued at $12,711,476,000 (*£7,470 million*).

The world's largest public enterprise merchandiser is The Defense Logistics Service Center, Battle Creek, Michigan which sells off surplus U.S. Federal material.

Ship-building
In 1976 there were 33,922,193 tons gross of ships, excluding sailing ships, barges and vessels of less than 100 tons, completed throughout the world, excluding the U.S.S.R., Romania and China. Japan completed 15,867,828 tons gross (46.78 per cent of the world total). The United Kingdom ranked fifth with 1,500,139 tons gross.

The world's leading shipbuilding firm in 1976 was the Ishikawajima-Harima Heavy Industries Co. of Japan, which launched 47 merchant ships of 3,350,400 gross tons from five shipyards.

Physically the largest shipyard in the United Kingdom is Harland and Wolff Ltd. of Queen's Island, Belfast, which covers some 300 acres *120 ha*.

Shipping line
The largest shipping owner and operator in the world is the Royal Dutch/Shell Group of Companies (see page 154) which on 31 Dec. 1976 owned and managed 132 oil tankers totalling 15,033,000 d.wt. tonnes and had on charter 155 totalling 18,167,000 d.wt. tonnes. In addition the fleet has 11 gas carriers owned or on charter with a combined capacity of 731,601 m³.

Shoe shop
The largest shoe shop in the world is that of Lilley & Skinner, Ltd. at 360–366 Oxford Street, City of Westminster, Greater London. The shop has a floor area of 76,000 ft² *7 060 m²* spread over four floors. With a total staff of more than 180 people it offers, in ten departments, a choice of 125,000 pairs of shoes. Every week, on average, over 45,000 people visit this store.

Shopping Centre
The world's largest shopping centre is the Lakewood Center, California with a gross building area of 2,451,438 ft² *227 745 m²* on a 165 acre *66,7 ha* site with parking for 12,500 cars. Britain's largest shopping centre is The Victoria Centre, Nottingham opened in 1972 which extends over 13 acres *5,2 ha*. The world's first was "Suburban Square" in Ardmore, Pennsylvania built in 1928. The world's largest market

centre is that on Stemmons Freeway, Dallas, Texas with 4.85 million ft² *450 000 m²* in six buildings (opened 1955–1976) on a 135 acre *54 ha* site housing 2,256 permanent wholesale showrooms.

Soft drinks

The world's top-selling soft drink is Coca-Cola with over 185,000,000 drinks sold per day at the end of 1976 in more than 130 countries. Coke was launched as a tonic by Dr. John S. Pemberton of Atlanta, Georgia in 1886. The Coca-Cola Company was formed in 1892 and the famous bottle patented in 1915.

Steel Company *World*

The world's largest producer of steel is Nippon Steel of Tōkyō, Japan which produced 83.9 million tons *85.2 million tonnes* of steel, steel products and pig iron in 1975. The Fukuyama Works of Nippon Kokan has a capacity of more than 16 000 000 tonnes per annum.

Great Britain

Currently the largest single British plant is the Port Talbot works of the British Steel Corporation, West Glamorgan, which extends for 4½ miles *7,2 km*, with an area of 2,600 acres *1 050 ha*. The total number employed at this plant is 13,100 and its capacity is 3 000 000 tonnes *2,950,000 tons*. Plans were announced in March 1977 to double output to 6 000 000 tonnes *5,900,000 tons*. The £240 million Anchor Complex, Scunthorpe, Humberside, which went into production in 1973 is planned to have an ultimate capacity of 5.2 million tonnes/*tons*.

STOCK EXCHANGES

The oldest Stock Exchange in the world is that at Amsterdam, in the Netherlands, founded in 1602. There were 138 throughout the world as of 22 June 1976.

Most markings

The highest number of markings received in one day on the London Stock Exchange was 32,665 on 14 Oct. 1959 following the 1959 General Election. The record for a year is 4,396,175 "marks" in the year ending 31 Mar. 1960. There were 8,434 securities (gilt-edged 1,522, company 6,912) listed at 31 Dec. 1976. Their total nominal value was £86,580 million (gilt-edged £50,154 million, company £36,426 million) and their market value was £295,288 million (gilt-edged £37,673 million, company £257,615 million).

The highest figure of *The Financial Times* Industrial Ordinary share index (1 July 1935 = 100) was 543.6 on 19 May 1972. The lowest figure was 49.4 on 26 June 1940. The greatest rise in a day has been 23.7 points to 315.5 on 1 July 1975 in anticipation of anti-inflationary measures, and the greatest fall in a day was 24.0 to 313.8 on 1 Mar. 1974 on the realisation of a fourth post-war Labour Government.

Highest and lowest par values

The highest denomination of any share quoted in the world is a single share in F. Hoffmann–La Roche of Basel worth Sw. Fr. 101 000 (£21,992) on 23 Apr. 1976. The record for the London Stock Exchange is £100 for preference shares in Baring Brothers & Co. Ltd., the bankers.

U.S. records

The highest index figure on the Dow Jones average (instituted 8 Oct. 1896) of selected industrial stocks at the close of a day's trading was 1,051.70 on 11 Jan. 1973, when the average of the daily "highs" of the 30 component stocks was 1,067.20. The old record trading volume in a day on the New York Stock Exchange of 16,410,030 shares on 29 Oct. 1929, the "Black Tuesday" of the famous "crash" was unsurpassed until April 1968. The Dow Jones industrial average, which had reached 381.71 on 3 Sept. 1929, plunged 30.57 points in the day, on its way to the Depression's lowest point of 41.22 on 8 July 1932. The largest decline in a day, 38.33 points, occurred on 28 Oct. 1929. The total lost in security values from 1 Sept. 1929 to 30 June 1932 was $74,000 million (*then £23,000 million*). The greatest paper loss in a year was $209,957 million (*then £87,500 million*) in 1974. The record

daily increase of 28.40 on 30 Oct. 1929 was beaten on 16 Aug. 1971, when the index increased 32.93 points to 888.95. The record day's trading was 44,512,860 shares on 20 Feb. 1976. The largest transaction on record "share-wise" was on 14 Mar. 1972 for 5,245,000 shares of American Motors at $7.25 each. The record for one block was $76,135,026 for 730,312 shares of American Standard Class A Preferred shares at $104.25 a share. The largest deal "value-wise" was for two 2,000,000 blocks of Greyhound shares at $20 each sold to Goldman, Sachs and Salomon Brothers on 9 Feb. 1971. The highest price paid for a seat on the N.Y. Stock Exchange was $515,000 (*then £214,580*) in 1969. The lowest 20th century price was $17,000 in 1942.

Largest equity

The greatest aggregate market value of any corporation is $33.5 billion (£16,420 million) assuming a closing price of $206⅝ multiplied by the 149,533,813 shares of IBM extant on 31 Dec. 1975.

Greatest Personal Loss

The highest recorded personal paper losses on stock values have been those of Ray A. Kroc, Chairman of McDonald's Corporation with $64,901,718 (*then £27 million*) on 8 July 1974 and Edwin H. Land, President of Polaroid Corporation with $59,397,355 on 28–29 May 1974, when Polaroid stock closed $12.12 down at 43¼ on the day.

Largest new issue

The American Telegraph & Telephone Company offered $1,375 million's worth of shares in a rights offer on 27,500,000 shares of convertible preferred stock on the New York market on 2 June 1971. The largest offering on the London Stock Exchange by a United Kingdom company was the £76 million rights offer of Lloyds Banks Ltd. on 6 Feb. 1976.

Largest investment house

The largest investment company in the world, and also once the world's largest partnership with 124 partners, before going public in 1959 is Merrill, Lynch, Pierce, Fenner & Smith Inc. (founded 6 Jan. 1914) of New York City, U.S.A. It has assets of $6.6 billion, 19,715 employees, 326 offices and 1,600,000 separate accounts. The firm is referred to in the United States stock exchange circles as "We" or "We, the people" or "The Thundering Herd".

Largest store

The world's largest store is R. H. Macy & Co. Inc. at Broadway and 34th Street, New York City, N.Y., U.S.A. It covers 50.5 acres *20,3 ha* and employs 11,000 who handle 400,000 items. The sales of the company and its subsidiaries in 1976 were $1,469,363,000 (£864 million). Mr. Rowland Hussey Macy's sales on his first day at his fancy goods store on 6th Avenue, on 27 Oct. 1858, were recorded as $11.06 (*then £2.20*).

Largest supermarket

The largest supermarket building in the United Kingdom is the Woolco One-Stop Shopping Centre opened in Bournemouth, Dorset on 29 Oct. 1968. Currently it has an area of 114,000 ft² *10 590 m²* and parking space for 2,300 cars.

Tobacco company

The world's largest tobacco company is the British-American Tobacco Company Ltd. (founded in London in 1902). The Company's subsidiaries and affiliates operate 128 tobacco factories in 51 countries: consolidated turnover in 1975/76 was £4,791 million and total assets were £2,635 million at 30 Sept. 1976. The Group's sales in 1976 topped 500,000 million cigarettes.

The world's largest cigarette plant is the $200 million Philip Morris plant at Richmond, Virginia, U.S.A. opened in October 1974 with a payroll of 2,700 producing 200 million cigarettes a day.

Toy manufacturer

The world's largest toy manufacturer is Mattel Inc. of Hawthorne, Los Angeles, U.S.A. founded in 1945. Its 1976 sales were $386,273,000 (*then £227 million*).

Toy shop *World*

The world's biggest toy store is F.A.O. Schwartz, 745 Fifth Avenue at 58th Street, New York City, N.Y., U.S.A. with 50,000 ft² *4 645 m²* on three floors. Schwartz have 17 branch stores with a further 140,000 ft² *13 006 m²*.

Great Britain

Britain's biggest toy shop is that of Hamley of Regent Street Ltd., founded in 1760 in Holborn and removed to Regent Street, London, W.1. in 1901. It has selling space of 28,000 ft² *2 600 m²* on 11 floors, over 300 employees during the Christmas season and a world-wide mail order catalogue. It was taken over by Debenhams on 12 May 1976 and 3 further branches were opened in 1977.

Vintners

The oldest champagne firm is Ruinart Père et Fils founded in 1729. The oldest cognac firm is Augier Frères & Co., established in 1643.

2. MANUFACTURED ARTICLES

Guinness Superlatives Ltd. publishes fine art books in colour on *English and Irish Glass, English Pottery and Porcelain; English Furniture;* (2 Volumes) and *Militaria.*

Antique *Largest*

The largest antique ever sold has been London Bridge in March 1968. The sale was made by Mr. Ivan F. Luckin of the Court of Common Council of the Corporation of London to the McCulloch Oil Corporation of Los Angeles, California, U.S.A. for $2,460,000 (*then £1,029,000*). The 10,000 tons/ *tonnes* of facade stonework were re-assembled at a cost of £3 million, at Lake Havasu City, Arizona and "re-dedicated" on 10 Oct. 1971.

Armour

The highest auction price paid for a suit of armour is £25,000 paid in 1924 for the Pembroke suit of armour, made at Greenwich in the 16th century, for the 2nd Earl of Pembroke.

Beds *Largest*

In Bruges, Belgium, Philip, Duke of Burgundy had a bed 12½ ft wide and 19 ft long *3,81 × 5,79 m* erected for the perfunctory *coucher officiel* ceremony with Princess Isabella of Portugal in 1430. The largest bed in Great Britain is the Great Bed of Ware, dating from *c.* 1580, from the Crown Inn, Ware, Hertfordshire, now preserved in the Victoria and Albert Museum, London. It is 10 ft 8½ in wide, 11 ft 1 in long and 8 ft 9 in tall *3,26 × 3,37 × 2,66 m.* The largest bed currently marketed in the United Kingdom is the Super Size Diplomat bed, 9 ft wide by 9 ft long, *2,74 m²* which sells for £1,350 (inc. VAT).

Heaviest

The world's most massive bed is the four poster slate bed in Penrhyn Castle, Bangor, Gwynedd, Wales. It measures 7 ft 3 in *2,21 m* long and 6 ft 2 in *1,88 m* wide and weighs 2,070 lb. *938 kg.*

Beer cans

Beer cans date from a test marketing by Krueger Beer of Richmond, Virginia on 24 Jan. 1935. The largest collection is claimed by John F. Ahrens of Mount Laurel, New Jersey with 11,000 *different* cans.

Beer mats

The world's largest collection of beer mats is owned by Leo Pisker of Vienna, who had collected more than 64,000 different mats by July 1976. The largest collection of purely British mats is 17,728 by Charles M. Schofield of Glasgow by 5 Apr. 1977.

Carpets and Rugs *Earliest*

The earliest carpet known is a woollen pile-knitted carpet, red on white ground excavated at Pazyryk, U.S.S.R. in 1947, dated to the 5th century B.C. and now preserved in Leningrad.

Largest

Of ancient carpets the largest on record was the gold-enriched silk carpet of Hashim (dated A.D. 743) of the Abbasid caliphate in Baghdad, Iraq. It is reputed to have measured 180 by 300 ft *54,86 × 91,44 m.*

The world's largest carpet now consists of 88,000 ft² (over two acres *or 0,81 ha*) of maroon carpeting in the Coliseum exhibition hall, Columbus Circle, New York City, N.Y., U.S.A. This was first used for the International Automobile Show on 28 Apr. 1956.

Most expensive

The most magnificent carpet ever made was the Spring carpet of Khusraw made for the audience hall of the Sassanian palace at Ctesiphon, Iraq. It was about 7,000 ft² *650 m²* of silk, gold thread and encrusted with emeralds. It was cut up as booty by a Persian army in A.D. 635 and from the known realisation value of the pieces must have had an original value of some £100,000,000. The highest price ever paid at auction for a carpet is the $200,000 (*then £116,957*) given at Sotheby Parke Bernet, New York City on 3 Feb. 1977 for a 125 year old rust and blue Heriz Persian carpet in mint condition measuring 9 × 12½ ft *2,7 × 3,8 m* by Emmanuel Antiques and sold by the estate of Emily Stifel of West Virginia, U.S.A.

Most finely woven

The most finely woven carpet known is one with more than 2,490 knots per in² *386 per cm²* from a fragment of an Imperial Mughal prayer carpet of the 17th century now in the Altman collections in the Metropolitan Museum of Art, New York City, N.Y., U.S.A.

Ceramics

The auction record for any ceramic object is £420,000 for the 16¼ in *41,2 cm* Ming blue and white bottle dated 1403–24 acquired by Mrs. Helen Glatz, a London dealer, at Sotheby Parke Bernet, London on 2 Apr. 1974. The Greek urn painted by Ueuphromios and thrown by Euxitheos in *c.* 530 B.C. was bought by private treaty by the Metropolitan Museum of Art, New York for $1.3 million (*then £541,666*) in August 1972.

Chair *Largest*

The world's largest chair is the 1.33 ton *1 360 kg* mahogany chair 20 ft 7 in *6,27 m* built in 1976 by Leon La Plante for the Rotary Club of Gardner, Massachusetts, U.S.A.

The largest chair in the world in Gardner, Massachusetts, U.S.A., which stands the height of a two storey building.

161

Most expensive

The highest price ever paid for a single chair is $85,000 (*then £35,000*) for the John Brown Chippendale mahogany corner chair attributed to John Goddard of Newport, Rhode Island, U.S.A. and made in *c.* 1760. This piece was included in the collection of Mr. Lansdell K. Christie dispersed by Sotheby Parke Bernet, New York on 21 Oct. 1972.

Cigars *Largest*

The largest cigar in existence is one 5 ft 4½ in *1,63 m* long and 10½ in *26,6 cm* in diameter made by Abraham & Gluckstein, London and now housed at the Northumbrian University Air Squadron. The largest standard cigar in the world is the 9¾ in *24,1 cm* long "Partagas Visible Immensas". The Partagas factory in Havana, Cuba, manufactures special gift cigars 50 cm *19.7 in* long, which retail in Europe for £7.

Most expensive

The most expensive standard cigar in the world is the Monte Cristo 'A', which retails in Britain at £4.25.

Most voracious smokers

Scott Case smoked 110 cigarettes simultaneously for 30 secs at the Oddball Olympics in Los Angeles in May 1974. Paul Mears (University of Winnipeg, Manitoba, Canada) won a contest in smoking 35 full-size cigars simultaneously in 1975.

Cigarettes *Consumption*

The heaviest smokers in the world are the people of the United States, where 607,000 million cigarettes (an average of 4,300 per adult) were consumed at a cost of about $13,000 million (*£6,350 million*) in 1975. The peak consumption in the United Kingdom was 3,230 cigarettes per adult in 1973. The peak volume was 243,100,000 lb. *110,2 million kg* in 1961, compared with 205,400,000 lb. *93,1 million kg* in 1976, when 130,600 million cigarettes were sold.

In the United Kingdom 62 per cent of adult men and 43 per cent of adult women smoke. Each cigarette is alleged to reduce the life span by 5½ minutes.

Tar/Nicotine Content

Of the 121 brands most recently analysed for the Dept. of Health and Social Security the one with highest tar/nicotine content is *Capstan Full Strengh* with 35/3.6 *mg* per cigarette *Silk Cut Extra Mild*, *Embassy Ultra Mild* and *Player's Mild de Luxe* with <4/0.3 are at the safer end of the league table.

Most popular

The world's most popular cigarette is "Marlboro", a filter cigarette made by Philip Morris, which sold 136,000 million in 1975. The largest selling British cigarette in 1976 was John Player and Sons of Nottingham's "Player's No. 6 Filter". The Wills brand "The Three Castles" was introduced in 1878.

Longest and shortest

The longest cigarettes ever marketed were "Head Plays", each 11 in *27,9 cm* long and sold in packets of 5 in the United States in about 1930, to save tax. The shortest were "Lilliput" cigarettes, each 1¼ in *31,7 mm* long, and ⅛ in *3 mm* in diameter, made in Great Britain in 1956.

Largest collection

The world's largest collection of cigarettes is that of Robert E. Kaufman, M.D., of 950 Park Avenue, New York City 28, N.Y., U.S.A. In April 1977 he had 7,015 different kinds of cigarettes from 166 countries. The oldest brand represented is "Lone Jack", made in the U.S.A. in *c.* 1885. Both the longest and shortest (see above) are represented.

Cigarette cards

The earliest known and most valuable cigarette card is that

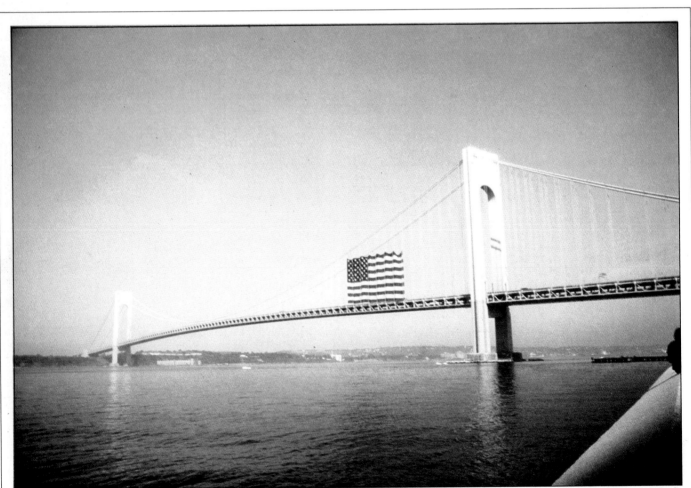

The world's largest flag which flew briefly on the world's longest span bridge in New York City. It measured more than 1½ acres *0,66 ha* in area (see p. 163).

bearing the portrait of the Marquess of Lorne published in the United States c. 1879. The only known specimen is in the Metropolitan Museum of Art, New York City. The earliest British example appeared c. 1883 in the form of a calendar issued by Allen & Ginter, of Richmond, Virginia, trading from Holborn Viaduct, City of London. The largest known collection is that of Mr. Edward Wharton-Tigar (b. 1913) of London with a collection of more than 500,000 cigarette and trade cards in about 25,000 sets. The highest price paid for a set is £2,000 at Murray's Auction, London on 11 Oct. 1975 for Taddy's "Clowns" by Ian Graham of Leeds.

Cigarette lighter *Most expensive*
The most expensive cigarette pocket lighter in the world is a hand made solid gold and silver lighter by Iwan Ries Co. of Chicago, Illinois, depicting a Japanese garden scene and selling for $10,000 (£5,880) in 1977. The 18 carat lighthouse table lighter, made by Alfred Dunhill Ltd. of St. James's, City of Westminster, Greater London, set on an island of amethyst retails for a record £32,500.

Cigarette packets
The earliest surviving cigarette packet is the Finnish "Petit Canon" packet for 25, made by Tollander & Klärich in 1860, from the Ventegodt Collection. The rarest is the Latvian 700-year anniversary (1201–1901) Riga packet, believed to be unique, from the same collection.

Chandelier *Largest*
The world's largest chandelier, named *Walküre*, designed by Pietro Canta, the Milanese sculptor, was completed in October 1974 for a client in Borneo. It measures 16 m *52 ft 6 in* in circumference 4,5 m *14 ft 9 in* in height with 900 bulbs and 15,000 crystal pieces.

Christmas cracker
The largest cracker ever constructed was one 45 ft *13,71 m* in length and 8 ft *2,43 m* in diameter built for the BBC TV Christmas *Record Breakers* Show transmitted on 27 Dec. 1974.

Credit card collection
The largest collection of credit cards is one of 864 (all different) by Walter Cavanagh (b. 1943) of Santa Clara, California, U.S.A. The cost of acquisition to "Mr. Plastic Fantastick" was nil.

Curtain
The largest curtain ever built has been the bright orange-red 4 ton *4 064 kg* 185 ft *56 m* high curtain suspended 1,350 ft *411 m* across the Rifle Gap, Grand Hogback, Colorado, U.S.A. by the Bulgarian-born sculptor Christo, 36 (*né* Javacheff) on 10 Aug. 1971. It blew apart in a 50 m.p.h. *80 km/h* gust 27 hrs later. The total cost involved in displaying this work of art was $750,000 (*then £312,500*).

Dinner service
The highest price ever paid for a silver dinner service is £207,000 for the Berkeley Louis XV Service of 168 pieces, made by Jacques Roettiers between 1736 and 1738, sold at the salerooms of Sotheby & Co., City of Westminster, Greater London, in June 1960.

Dolls
The highest price paid at auction for dolls is £16,000 for a pair of William and Mary painted wooden dolls in original clothes 22 in *55,8 cm* high at Sotheby's, London on 19 Apr. 1974. After an export licence was refused they were purchased, following a public subscription, by Victoria and Albert Museum, London.

Dress *Most expensive*
The dress with the highest price tag ever exhibited by a Paris fashion house was one in the Schiaparelli spring/summer collection on 23 Jan. 1977. "The Birth of Venus" designed by Serge Lepage with 512 diamonds was priced at Fr. 7,500,000 (*£880,000*).

Fabrics *Earliest and Most expensive*
The oldest surviving fabric discovered from Level VIA at Catal Hüyük, Turkey has been radio-carbon dated to 5900 B.C.

The most expensive fabric obtainable is an evening-wear fabric 40 in *101,6 cm* wide, hand embroidered and sequinned on a pure silk ground in a classical flower pattern. It has 194,400 tiny sequins per yard, *21 per cm²* and is designed by Alan Hershman of Duke St., London; it cost £250 per metre or £225 per yard in May 1977.

Finest cloth
The most expensive cloth, the brown-grey throat hair of Indian goats, is Shatoosh (or Shatusa), finer, and more expensive than Vicuña. It is sold by Nieman-Marcus of Dallas, Texas, U.S.A., at $108 £61 per linear foot.

Firework
The most powerful firework obtainable is the Bouquet of Chrysanthemums *hanabi*, marketed by the Marutamaya Ogatsu Fireworks Co. Ltd., of Tōkyō, Japan. It is fired to a height of over 3,000 ft *915 m* from a 36 in *914 mm* calibre mortar. Their chrysanthemum and peony flower shells produce a spherical flower with "twice-thrice changing colours", 2,000 ft *610 m* in diameter. The largest firework produced in Britain is one fired on 8 June 1946 from Brock's 25 in *635 mm*, 22 cwt. *1 117 kg* mortar. The shell weighs 200 lb. *90,7 kg* and is 6½ ft *1,98 m* in circumference and was first used in Lisbon in 1886. The world's lowest firework was George Plimpton's 40½ in *102 cm* 720 lb. *325 kg* Roman candle "Fat Man" intended to break the Japanese record over Long Island, N.Y. in February 1975. It sizzled, hissed and exploded leaving a crater 10 ft *3 m* deep.

Flags *Oldest*
The crest in the centre of the Austrian flag has its origins in the 11th century while that of Malta dates from 1090. The origins of the Iranian flag, with its sword-carrying lion and sun, are obscure but "go beyond the 12th century".

Largest
The largest flag in the world, the "Stars and Stripes", was displayed by the Great American Flag Co. of Warren, Vermont on the Verranzano Narrows Bridge, New York, U.S.A. on 28 June 1976. It measured 193 ft *58,82 m* by 366½ ft *101,7 m* or 1.64 acres *0,66 ha* weighing about 1½ tons with 15 ft *4,57 m* wide stripes and stars 11 ft *3,35 m* in diameter. The largest Union Flag (or Union Jack) was one 11,520 ft² (144 by 80 ft *43,89 × 23,38 m*) used at a military tattoo in the Olympic Stadium, West Berlin in September 1967. The largest flag *flown* from a public building in Britain is a Union Flag measuring 40 ft *12,19 m* by 20 ft *6,09 m* first flown from the Civic Offices, Newcastle-under-Lyme, Staffordshire on 21 Apr. 1977. The study of flags is known as vexicollogy.

Float
The largest float used in any street carnival is the 200 ft *60 m* long dragon *Sun Loon* used in Bendigo, Victoria, Australia. It has 65,000 mirror scales. Six men are needed to carry its head alone.

Furniture *Most expensive*
The highest price ever paid for a single piece of furniture is £240,000 for a French Louis XVI ormolu mounted ebony *bureau plat* and *cartonnier* 5 ft 4½ in *1,63 m* high by 3 ft 1½ in *95 cm* wide at Sotheby Parke Bernet, New Bond Street, London on 13 Dec. 1974. At Mentmore, Buckinghamshire on 18 May 1977 a bureau *en pente* of c. 1735 by Bernard van Risen Burgh was bought in at £280,000.

Oldest British
The oldest surviving piece of British furniture is a three-footed tub with metal bands found at Glastonbury, Somerset, and dating from between 300 and 150 B.C.

Largest Piece
The largest item of furniture in the world is the Long Sofa—a wooden bench for old seafarers—measuring 72 m *236 ft* in length at Oscarshamn, Sweden.

Glass

The most priceless example of the art of glass-making is usually regarded as the glass Portland Vase which dates from late in the 1st century B.C. or 1st century A.D. It was made in Italy, and was in the possession of the Barberini family in Rome from at least 1642. It was eventually bought by the Duchess of Portland in 1792 but smashed while in the British Museum in 1847. The auction record is £68,200 for an Archaemenid Persian pale green bowl (diameter 6¾ in *17 cm*) sold at Sotheby's, London on 13 July 1976.

Gold plate

The world's highest auction price for a single piece of gold plate is £40,000 for a 20 oz. 4 dwt. *628,3 g* George II teapot made by James Ker of Edinburgh for the King's Plate Horse race for 100 guineas at Leith, Scotland in 1736. The sale was by Christie's, City of Westminster, Greater London on 13 Dec. 1967 to a dealer from Boston, Massachusetts, U.S.A.

The gold coffin of the 14th century B.C. Pharaoh Tutankhamun discovered by Howard Carter on 16 Feb. 1923 in Luxor, western Thebes, Egypt weighed 2,448 lb. *1 110 kg*. The exhibition at the British Museum attracted 1,656,151 people (of whom 45.7% bought catalogues) from 30 Mar. to 30 Dec. 1972 resulting in a profit of £657,731.22.

Guns

The highest price ever paid for a single gun is £125,000 given by the London dealers F. Partridge for a French flintlock fowling piece made for Louis XIII, King of France in *c.* 1615 and attributed to Pierre le Bourgeoys of Lisieux, France (d. 1627). This piece was included in the collection of the late William Goodwin Renwick of the United States sold by Sotheby's, London on 21 Nov. 1972. (see also Pistols)

Hat *Most expensive*

The highest price ever paid for a hat is 165,570 francs (*then £14,032*) (inc. tax) by Moët et Chandon at an auction by Maîtres Liery, Rheims et Laurin on 23 Apr. 1970 for one last worn by Emperor Napoleon I (1769–1821) on 1 Jan. 1815.

Jade

The highest price ever paid for an item in jade is 1,250,000 Swiss Francs (*then £156,250*) for a necklace set with 31 graduated beads of Imperial green jade. This was sold by Christie's at the Hotel Richmond, Geneva, Switzerland, on 9 May 1973. The highest price paid for a single piece of jade sculpture is £71,000 for a massive Ming jade buffalo sold by Sotheby's on 15 Mar. 1973.

Jig-saw

The largest jig-saw ever made is one 48 ft 0 1/16 in × 24 ft 0⅛ in *14,63 × 7,31 m* built with 9,111 pieces by the 75th Field Artillery Group, U.S. Army at Fort Sill, Oklahoma and exhibited on 3 Nov. 1975. The *Festival of Britain* jig-saw by Efroc Ltd., now in Montserrat though of much lesser area contains an estimated 40,000 pieces.

Matchbox labels

The oldest match label is that of John Walker, Stockton-on-Tees, Cleveland, England in 1827. Collectors of labels are phillumenists, of bookmatch covers philliberumenists and of matchboxes cumyxaphists. Several labels are only uniquely known such as the Byron Match from Roche & Co., Marseilles and the Canadian Allumettes Frontenac from the Eddy Match Co. both in the Frank J. Mrazik Collection in Quebec, Canada.

Medal or Decoration

The highest price paid at auction for an order or decoration is £14,700 for an Order of the Golden Fleece sold at Christie's London on 27 June 1974. The record for a British order is £11,000 for the insignia of the Most Noble Order of the Garter (K.G.) of the 2nd Earl of Talbot sold at Sotheby's, London on 26 Jan. 1977.

Nylon Sheerest

The lowest denier nylon yarn ever produced is the 6-denier used for stockings exhibited at the Nylon Fair in London in February 1956. The sheerest stockings normally available are 9-denier. An indication of the thinness is that a hair from the average human head is about 50 denier.

Paperweight

The highest price ever paid for a paperweight is £8,500 at Sotheby & Co., of London on 16 Mar. 1970 for a 19th century Clichy lily-of-the-valley glass weight. The earliest were made in Italy in the 15th century.

Penknife

The penknife with the greatest number of blades is the Year Knife made by the world's oldest firm of cutlers, Joseph Rodgers & Sons Ltd., of Sheffield, England, whose trade mark was granted in 1682. The knife was built in 1822 with 1,822 blades but now has 1,973 to match the year of the Christian era until A.D. 2000, beyond which there will be no further space. It was acquired by Britain's largest hand tool manufacturers, Stanley Works (Great Britain) Ltd. of Sheffield, South Yorkshire in 1970.

Pens *Most expensive*

The most expensive writing pens are the 18 carat pair of pens (one fibre-tipped and one ballpoint) capped by diamonds of 3.88 carats sold by Alfred Dunhill (see Cigarette lighter above) for £9,943 the pair (incl. V.A.T.).

Pipe *Most expensive*

The most expensive smoker's pipe is the four bowl Danish Preben Holm pipe of Corsican briar wood marketed in the U.S. at $5,500 (*then £2,600*) in 1975.

Pistols *Most expensive*

The highest price paid for a pair of pistols at auction is the £78,000 given by the London dealer Howard Ricketts at Sotheby Parke Bernet, London on 17 Dec. 1974 for a pair of English Royal flintlock holster pistols made *c.* 1690–1700 by Pierre Monlong. They were sent for sale by Anne, Duchess of Westminster.

Porcelain and Pottery English

The highest price ever paid for a single piece of English porcelain is £32,000 for a Chelsea Boar's Head (of the red anchor period) sold at Sotheby's on 13 Nov. 1973. The pottery record is £15,015 for a Staffordshire 18th century salt-glaze pew group sold at Christie's on 15 Dec. 1975.

The world's most expensive paperweight, the 19th century Clichy lily-of-the-valley piece sold for £8,500.

Ropes largest and longest

The largest rope ever made was a coir fibre launching rope with a circumference of 47 in *119 cm* made in 1858 for the British liner *Great Eastern* by John and Edwin Wright of Birmingham. It consisted of four strands, each of 3,780 yarns. The longest fibre rope ever made without a splice was one of 10,000 fathoms or 11.36 miles *18 288 m* of 6½ in *16,5 cm* circumference manila by Frost Brothers (now British Ropes Ltd.) in London in 1874.

Shoes *Most expensive*

The most expensive standard shoes obtainable are mink-lined golf shoes with 18 carat gold embellishments and ruby-tipped spikes made by Stylo Matchmakers International Ltd., of Northampton, England which retail for £2,700 or $6,500 per pair in the U.S.A.

Largest

Excluding cases of elephantiasis, the largest shoes ever sold are a pair size 42 built for the giant Harley Davidson of Avon Park, Florida, U.S.A. The normal limit is Size 14.

Silver

The highest price ever paid for a single piece of silver is 2,000,000 Swiss Francs (*then £363,636*) for a pair of Jardinières and stands by Thomas Germain of Paris dated *c.* 1727, sold by Christie's in Geneva on 11 Nov. 1975. In the same place on 27 Apr. 1976 a pair of silver soup tureens and covers, by the same maker, made 1.8 million Swiss Francs, which, with a 14% commission was equivalent to £446,000.

Snuff *Most expensive*

The most expensive snuff obtainable in Britain is "Café Royale" sold by G. Smith and Sons (est. 1869) of 74, Charing Cross Road, City of Westminster, Greater London. It sells at £1.20 per oz.

Box

The highest price ever paid for a snuff box is £89,250 paid by Kenneth Snowman of Wartski's in a sale at Christie's, London on 26 June 1974. This was for the gold and lapis lazuli example uniquely signed by Juste-Oreille Meissonnier (d. 1750) the French master goldsmith and dated Paris 1728. It was made for Marie-Anne de Vaviere-Neubourg, wife of Charles II of Spain. It measures 83 × 57 mm *3¼ × 2¼ in*. It was sent in for sale from the Ortiz-Patino collection.

Spoons Apostle

The highest price ever paid for a set of 12 apostle spoons is £70,000 paid by Mrs. How in a sale at Christie's, London on 26 June 1974. They are Elizabethan silver-gilt spoons, made by Christopher Wace in 1592, known as the "Tichborne Celebrities".

Stuffed bird

The highest price ever paid for a stuffed bird is £9,000. This was given on 4 Mar. 1971 at Messrs Sotheby & Co., London by the Iceland Natural History Museum for a specimen of the Great Auk (*Alca impennis*) in summer plumage, which was taken in Iceland *c.* 1821; this particular specimen stood 22½ in *57 cm* high. The Great Auk was a flightless North Atlantic seabird, which was finally exterminated on Eldey, Iceland in 1844, becoming extinct through hunting. The last British sightings were at Co. Waterford in 1834 and St. Kilda, Highland *c.* 1840.

Sword

The highest price paid for a sword is the $145,000 (*then £85,800*) paid for the gold sword of honour presented by the Continental Congress of 1779 to General Marie Jean Joseph Lafayette at Sotheby Parke Bernet, New York City, U.S.A. on 20 Nov. 1976.

Table cloth

The world's largest table cloth is one 219 yds *200 m* long by 2 yds *1,8 m* wide double damask made by John S. Brown & Sons Ltd. of Belfast and shipped to a royal palace in the Middle East. There was also an order for matching napkins for 450 places.

Tapestry *Earliest*

The earliest known examples of tapestry weaved linen are three pieces from the tomb of Thutmose IV, the Egyptian Pharaoh and dated to 1483–1411 B.C.

Largest

The largest single piece of tapestry ever woven is "Christ in His Majesty", measuring 72 ft by 39 ft *21,94 × 11,88 m* designed by Graham Vivian Sutherland O.M. (b. 24 Aug. 1903) for an altar hanging in Coventry Cathedral, West Midlands. It cost £10,500, weighs ¾ ton *760 kg* and was delivered from Pinton Frères of Felletin, France, on 1 Mar. 1962.

Longest Embroidery

An uncompleted 8 in *20,3 cm* deep 800 ft *243 m* embroidery of scenes from C. S. Lewis's Narnia children's stories has been woven by Mrs. Margaret Pollard of Truro, Cornwall to the order of Mr. Michael Maine. The famous Bayeux *Telle du Conquest, dite tapisserie de la reine Mathilde*, a hanging 19½ in *49,5 cm* wide by 231 ft *70,40 m* in length. It depicts events of the period 1064–1066 in 72 scenes and was probably worked in Canterbury, Kent, in *c.* 1086. It was "lost" from 1476 until 1724.

Most expensive

The highest price paid for a set of tapestries is £200,000 for four Louis XV pieces at Sotheby & Co., London on 8 Dec. 1967.

Tartan *Earliest*

The earliest evidence of tartan is the so-called Falkirk tartan, found stuffed in a jar of coins in Bells Meadow, north of Callendar Park, Scotland. It is of a dark and light brown pattern and dates from *c.* A.D. 245. The earliest reference to a specific named tartan has been to a Murray tartan in 1618 although Mackay tartan was probably worn earlier.

Time Capsule

The world's largest time capsule is a sealed crypt entitled the Crypt of Civilization at Oglethorpe University, Atlanta, Georgia, U.S.A. measuring 20 × 10 × 10 ft *6,09 × 3,04 × 3,04 m* sealed on 28 May 1940 and intended to remain so for 7,193 years. None of the artifacts is of gold, silver or precious stones so vandals are not tempted.

Wig

The largest wig yet made is that by Bergmann of 5th Avenue, New York City in 1975. It measures 15 ft *4,57 m* in length.

Wreath *Most expensive*

The most expensive wreath on record was that sent to the funeral of President Kennedy in Washington, D.C. on 25 Nov. 1963 by the civic authority of Paris. It was handled by Interflora Inc. and cost $1,200 (*then £428*). The only rival was a floral tribute sent to the Mayor of Moscow in 1970 by Umberto Formichello, general manager of Interflora which is never slow to scent an opportunity.

Writing paper

The most expensive writing paper in the world is that sold by Cartier Inc. on Fifth Avenue, New York City at $8,000 (*now £4,570*) per 100 sheets with envelopes. It is of hand made paper from Tervakoski Osakeyhtiö, Finland, with deckle edges and a "personalized" portrait watermark. Second thoughts and mis-spellings tend to be costly.

3. AGRICULTURE

Origins

It has been estimated that only 21 per cent of the world's land surface is cultivable and that of this only two-fifths is cultivated. Evidence adduced in 1971 from Nok Nok Tha and Spirit Cave, Thailand tends to confirm plant cultivation and animal domestication was part of the Hoabinhian culture *c.* 11,000 B.C. Reindeer may have been domesticated as early as *c.* 18,000 B.C. but definite evidence is still lacking.

The earliest attested evidence for the cultivation of grain comes from Ali Kosh, Iran and Jericho, by c. 7000 B.C. Goat was domesticated at Asiab, Iran by c. 8050 B.C. and dog at Star Carr, North Yorkshire by c. 7700 B.C.: the earliest definite date for sheep is c. 7200 B.C. at Argissa-Magula, Thessaly, Greece and for pig and cattle c. 7000 B.C. at the same site. The earliest date for horse is c. 4350 B.C. from Dereivka, Ukraine, U.S.S.R.

FARMS

Earliest

The earliest dated British farming site is a neolithic one, enclosed within the Iron Age hill-fort at Hembury, Devon, excavated during 1934–5 and now dated to 4210–3990 B.C. Pollen analysis from two sites Oakhanger, Hampshire, and Winfrith Heath, Dorset (Mesolithic c. 4300 B.C.) indicates that Mesolithic man may have had herds which were fed on ivy during the winter months.

Largest *World*

The largest farms in the world are collective farms in the U.S.S.R. These have been reduced in number from 235,500 in 1940 to only 36,000 in 1969 and have been increased in size so that units of over 60,000 acres *25 000 ha* are not uncommon. The pioneer farm of Laucidio Coelho near Campo Grande, Mato Grosso, Brazil in c. 1901 was 3,358 miles² *8 700 km²* 2.15 million acres with 250,000 head of cattle at the time of his death in 1975.

Great Britain

The largest farms in the British Isles are Scottish hill farms in the Grampians. The largest arable farm is that of Elveden, Suffolk, farmed by the Earl of Iveagh. Here 11,251½ acres *4 553 ha* are farmed on an estate of 22,918 acres *9 274 ha*, the greater part of which was formerly derelict land. The 1976 production included 1,576,429 gal. *7 166 288 litres* of milk, 2,520 tons *2 560 tonnes* of grain and 16,025 tons *16 282 tonnes* of sugar beet. The livestock includes 3,441 cattle, 950 ewes and 4,230 pigs.

Cattle station

The world's largest cattle station is Alexandria Station, Northern Territory, Australia, selected in 1873 by Robert Collins, who rode 1,600 miles *2 575 km* to reach it. It has 82 working bores, a staff of 90 and originally extended over 7,207,608 acres *2 916 818 ha*—more than the area of England's four largest counties of North Yorkshire, Cumbria, Devon and Lincoln put together. The present area is 6,500 miles² *16 835 km²* which is stocked with 60,000 shorthorn cattle. Until 1915 the Victoria River Downs Station, Northern Territory, was over three times larger, with an area of 22,400,000 acres (35,000 miles² *90 650 km²*).

Sheep station

The largest sheep station in the world is Commonwealth Hill, in the north-west of South Australia. It grazes between 70,000 and 90,000 sheep, c. 700 cattle and 25,000 uninvited kangaroos in an area of 4,080 miles² *10 567 km²* i.e. larger than the combined area of Norfolk and Suffolk.

The largest sheep move on record occurred when 27 horsemen moved a mob of 43,000 sheep 40 miles *64 km* from Barcaldine to Beaconsfield Station, Queensland, Australia, in 1886.

Turkey farm

The world's largest turkey farm is that of Bernard Matthews Ltd., centred at Gt. Witchingham, Norfolk, with 700 workers tending 4,000,000 turkeys.

Chicken ranch

The world's largest chicken ranch is the 520 acre *210 ha* "Egg City" Moorpark, California established by Jules Goldman in 1961. Some 2 million eggs are laid daily by 3.1 million chickens.

Piggery

The world's largest piggery is the Sljeme pig unit in Yugoslavia which is able to process 300,000 pigs in a year. Even larger units may exist in Romania but details are at present lacking.

Cow shed

The longest cow shed in Britain is that of the Yorkshire Agricultural Society at Harrogate, North Yorkshire. It is 456 ft *139 m* in length with a capacity of 686 cows. The National Agricultural Centre, Kenilworth, Warwickshire, completed in 1967, has, however, capacity for 782 animals.

Foot-and-mouth disease

The worst outbreak of foot-and-mouth disease in Great Britain was that from Salop on 25 Oct. 1967 to 25 June 1968 in which there were 2,364 outbreaks and 429,632 animals slaughtered at a direct and consequential loss of £150,000,000. The outbreak of 1871, when farms were much smaller, affected 42,531 farms. The disease first appeared in Great Britain at Stratford near London in August 1839.

Sheep Shearing

The highest recorded speed for sheep shearing in a working day was that of G. Phillips who machine-sheared 694 lambs (average 77.1 per hour) in 9 hrs at Tymawr Farm, Libanus, Powys on 25 June 1975. The blade (*i.e.* handshearing) record in a 9 hr working day is 350, set in 1899. The female record is held by Mrs. Pamela Warren, aged 21, who machine-sheared 337 Romney Marsh ewes and lambs at Puketutu, near Piopio, North Island, New Zealand in January 1972. In a shearing marathon, four men machineshore 1,019 sheep in 24 hrs at Northam, near Perth, Western Australia on 21–22 Aug. 1976.

Great Britain

British records for 9 hrs have been set at 555 by Roger Poyntz-Roberts (300) and John Savery (255) on 9 June 1971 (sheep caught *by* shearers), and 610 by the same pair (sheep caught *for* shearers) in July 1970.

Lifetime Total

The sheep shearer with the largest life-time total is believed to be LaVor Taylor (b. 27 Feb. 1896) of Ephraim, Utah, U.S.A., who with annual totals varying between 8,000 and 22,000 sheep sheared 510,000 head in 60 years.

Mushroom farm

The largest mushroom farm in the world is the Butler County Mushroom Farm, Inc., founded in 1937 in a disused limestone mine near West Winfield, Pennsylvania, U.S.A. It employs over 1,000 in a maze of underground galleries 110 miles *177 km* long, producing over 42,000,000 lb. *19 056 tonnes* of mushrooms per year.

Largest wheat field

The largest single fenced field sown with wheat was one of 35,000 acres *14 160 ha* sown in 1951 south west of Lethbridge, Alberta, Canada.

Largest vineyard

The world's largest vineyard is that extending over the Mediterranean façade between the Rhône and the Pyrenees in the *départments* Hérault Gard Aude, and Pyrenées-Orientales in an area of 840 000 ha *2,075,685 acres* of which 52.3% is *monoculture viticole*.

Largest hop field

The largest hop field in the world is one of 790 acres *319 ha* at Toppenish, Washington State, U.S.A. It is owned by John I. Haas, Inc., the world's largest hop growers, with hop farms in British Columbia (Canada), California, Idaho, Oregon and Washington, with a total net area of 3,765 acres *1 522 ha*.

Crop Yields *Wheat*

Crop yields for highly tended small areas are of little significance. The British record is 86.10 cwt/acre *10 808 kg/ha* on a field of 28.53 acres *11,54 ha* by Brian Reynolds of Stanaway Farm, Otley, Suffolk in 1974 using Maris Huntsman winter wheat.

Barley

A yield of 82.61 cwt./acre *10 371 kg/ha* of Clermont Spring Barley was achieved in 1972 by John Graham of Kirkland Hall, Wigton, Cumbria from a 13.52 acre *5,47 ha* field.

The world's largest turkey farm, that of Bernard Matthews Ltd., centred at Great Witchingham, Norfolk with a population sometimes reaching 4 million (see p. 166).

The world's largest hop field measuring 787 acres *3.18 km²* at Toppenish, Washington State, U.S.A. (See page 166) (*John I. Haas Inc.*)

Record Harvest
 Britain's all-time record harvest was achieved in 1972 with 15,750,000 tons of grain.

Sugar beet
 The highest recorded yield for sugar beet is 62.4 short tons (55.71 long tons) per acre *1 139,8 tonnes/ha* by Andy Christensen and Jon Giannini in the Salinas Valley, California.

Ploughing
 The world championship (instituted 1953) has been staged in 17 countries and won by ploughmen of ten nationalities of which the United Kingdom has been most successful with 6 championships. The only man to take the title three times has been Hugh Barr of Northern Ireland in 1954–55–56.

 The fastest recorded time for ploughing an acre *0,404 ha* (minimum 32 right-hand turns and depth 9 in *22 cm*) is 15 min 30 sec by John Binning using a Bamford 5 furrow 14 in *35,5 cm* plough towed by a Ford 9,600 tractor at Oxfordshire Young Farmers' County Show held at Besselsleigh, Nr. Oxford on 22 May 1976.

 The greatest recorded acreage ploughed in 24 hrs is 115 acres *46,53 ha* at North Barn Farm, Dorchester, Dorset on 22–23 Nov. 1971 with a County Eleven Twenty Four tractor with a Bamford Kverneland 7 furrow plough to a depth of 6 in *15 cm*. John Sephton at Clare Park Farm, Crondall, Hampshire ploughed for 50 hours on 1–3 Nov. 1974.

LIVESTOCK
Heaviest *Cattle*
 Of heavyweight cattle the heaviest on record was a Hereford-Shorthorn named "Old Ben", owned by a Mike and John Murphy of Miami, Indiana, U.S.A. When he died at the age of 8, in February 1910, he had attained a length of 16 ft 2 in *4,92 m* from nose to tail, a girth of 13 ft 8 in *4,16 m*, a height of 6 ft 4 in *1,93 m* at the forequarters and a weight of 4,720 lb. *2 140 kg*. The stuffed and mounted steer is displayed in Highland Park, Kokomo, Indiana, as proof to all who would otherwise have said "there ain't no such animal". The British record is the 4,480 lb. *2 032 kg* of "The Bradwell Ox" owned by William Spurgin of Bradwell, Essex. He was 15 ft *4,57 m* from nose to tail and had a girth of 11 ft *3,35 m* when 6 years old in 1830. The largest breed of heavyweight cattle is the Chianini brought to Italy from the Middle East in pre Roman times. Mature bulls stand 6 ft *1,83 m* at the forequarters and weigh 26–27 cwt *1 323–1 374 kg*.

 The highest recorded birthweight for a calf is 225 lb. *102 kg* from a British Friesian cow at Rockhouse Farm, Bishopston, Swansea, West Glamorgan, in 1961.

Pigs

The heaviest pig ever recorded is "Big Boy", a hog of 1,904 lb. (17 cwt) *863,6 kg* bred by B. Liles and H. A. Sanders of Black Mountain, North Carolina, U.S.A. weighed on 5 Jan. 1939. The British record is a hog of 12 cwt. 66 lb. *639,5 kg* bred by Joseph Lawton of Astbury, Cheshire. In 1774 it stood 4 ft 8½ in *1,43 m* in height and was 9 ft 8 in *2,94 m* long. The highest recorded weight for a piglet at weaning (8 weeks) is 81 lb. *36,7 kg* for a boar, one of nine piglets farrowed on 6 July 1962 by the Landrace gilt "Manorport Ballerina 53rd", alias "Mary", and sired by a Large White named "Johnny" at Kettle Lane Farm, West Ashton, Trowbridge, Wiltshire.

Sheep

The highest recorded birthweight for a lamb in the world is 38 lb. *17,2 kg* at Clearwater, Miner County near Howard, Kansas, U.S.A. in 1975 but neither this lamb nor the ewe survived.

Prolificacy *Cattle*

On 25 Apr. 1964 it was reported that a cow named "Lyubik" had given birth to seven calves at Mogilev, U.S.S.R. A case of five live calves at one birth was reported in 1928 by T. G. Yarwood of Manchester. The life-time prolificacy record is 30 in the case of a cross-bred cow owned by G. Page of Warren Farm, Wilmington, East Sussex, which died in November 1957, aged 32. A cross-Hereford calved in 1916 and owned by A. J. Thomas of West Hook Farm, Marloes, Dyfed, Wales, produced her 30th calf in May 1955 and died in May 1956, aged 40.

Pigs

The highest recorded number of piglets in one litter is 34, thrown on 25–26 June 1961 by a sow owned by Aksel Egedee of Denmark. In February 1955 a Wessex sow owned by Mrs. E. C. Goodwin of Paul's Farm, Leigh, near Tonbridge, Kent, had a litter of 34, of which 30 were born dead. A litter of 32 piglets (26 live born) was thrown in February 1971 by a British saddleback owned by Mr. R. Spencer of Toddington, Gloucestershire. A sow, "Bessie" owned by Mr L. Witt of Bath, Avon farrowed litters of 19 (1 stillborn) on 12 Nov. 1975, 19 (3 stillborn) on 5 Apr. 1976 and 21 (3 stillborn) on 16 Sept. 1976 making 59 in a year (52 reared).

Sheep

A case of eight lambs at a birth was reported by D. T. Jones of Priory Farm, Gwent, in June 1956, but none lived. A case of a sheep living to 26 years was recorded in flock book records by H. Poole, Wexford, Ireland. A Greyface ewe at Moss Side Farm, Longtown Cumbria gave birth to live sextuplets in March 1977.

Egg-laying

The highest authenticated rate of egg-laying is by "Princess Te Kawau", a Black Orpington, owned by Mrs. D. M. Waddell, with 361 eggs in 364 days in an official test at Taranaki, New Zealand, ending on 31 Mar. 1930. The U.K. record is 353 eggs in 365 days in a National Laying Test at Milford, Surrey in 1957 by a Rhode Island Red owned by W. Lawson of Welham Grange, Retford, Nottinghamshire.

The heaviest egg reported is one of 16 oz. *454 g*, with double yolk and double shell, laid by a white Leghorn at Vineland, New Jersey, U.S.A., on 25 Feb. 1956. The largest recorded was one of "nearly 12 oz." for a 5 yolked egg 12¼ in *31 cm* around the long axis and 9 in *22,8 cm* around the shorter axis laid by a Black Minorca at Mr. Stafford's Damsteads Farm, Mellor, Lancashire in 1896.

The highest recorded annual average for a flock is 313 eggs in 52 weeks from a flock of 1,000 Warren-Stadler SSL layers (from 21 weeks of age) by Eric Savage, White Lane Farm, Albury, Surrey, England in 1974–75.

Most yolks

The highest claim for the number of yolks in a chicken's egg is 9 reported by Mrs. Diane Hainsworth of Hainsworth Poultry Farms, Mount Morris, New York, U.S.A. in July 1971.

Milk Yields *Cows*

The world lifetime record yield of milk is 340,578 lb. (152.04 tons *154 479 kg*) at 3.3 per cent butter fat by the U.S. Holstein cow "Or-Win Masterpiece Riva" owned by Willard and Gary Behm at Adrian, Michigan up to 10 Apr. 1975. The greatest yield of any British cow was that given by the British Friesian "Guillyhill Janna 2nd", owned by S. H. West. This cow yielded 330,939 lb. *150 111 kg* up to 1973. The greatest recorded yield for one lactation (365 days) is 50,759 lb. *23 023,8* by "Mowry Prince Corinne" a Holstein at Roaring Springs, Pennsylvania, U.S.A. ending on 8 Dec. 1974. The British and probably world record for milk yield in a day is 198¼ lb. *89,92 kg* by R. A. Pierson's British Friesian "Garsdon Minnie" in 1948.

Hand milking

Andy Faust at Collinsville, Oklahoma, U.S.A. in 1937 achieved 120 U.S. gallons *99.92 U.K. galls* in 12 hours.

Goats

The highest recorded milk yield for any goat is 7,546 lb. *3 422 kg* in 365 days by "Waiora Frill Q*" bred by Mr. & Mrs. E. L. Collins of Swanson, Auckland, New Zealand in 1972.

Butter fat yield

The world record lifetime yield is 13,607 lb. *6 172 kg* from 308,569 lb. *139 964 kg* by the U.S. Brown Swiss cow "Ivetta" (1954–71) in the herd of W. E. Naffziger at Pekin, Illinois, U.S.A. in 4,515 days. The British record butter fat yield in a lifetime is 12,166 lb. *5 518 kg* by the Ayrshire cow "Craighead Welma" owned by W. Watson Steele from 273,072 lb. at 4.45%. The highest recorded lactation (365 days) yield reported is 1,956 lb. *887 kg* from 31,870 lb. *14 455 kg* of milk at 6.14% by Mr. Vincent A. Machin's "Crookgate Aylwinia 7" at Penley, near Wrexham, Clwyd ending on 7 July 1973. This is sufficient to produce 2,386 lb. *1 082,4 kg* of butter. The United Kingdom record for butter fat in one day is 9.30 lb. *4,218 kg* (79 lb. *35,8 kg* milk at 11.8%) by Queens Letch Farms' Guernsey Cow "Thisbe's Bronwen of Trewollack".

Cheese

The most active cheese-eaters are the people of France, with an annual average in 1975 of 34 lb. *15,4 kg* per person. The world's biggest producer is the United States with a factory production of 998,800 tons *1 014 827 tonnes* in 1970. The U.K. cheese consumption in 1975 was 13.7 lb. *6,2 kg* per head.

Oldest

The oldest and most primitive cheeses are the Arabian *kishk*, made of dried curd of goats' milk. There are today 450 named cheeses of 18 major varieties, but many are merely named after different towns and differ only in shape or the method of packing. France has 240 varieties.

Most expensive

The most expensive French cheese in France is the ewe's milk mountain cheese Laruns from the Bearn area of the Pyrenees, France, which is marketed in Paris, at times, for 38 francs per kg (*£1.42 per lb.*) Britain's most costly cheeses are Blue Cheshire and Blue Wensleydale at £1.16 per lb. in April 1977. In the U.S. Imported Brie from France may cost $5.80 (*£2.32*) per lb. or *£5.11 kg* retail.

Largest

The largest cheese ever made was a cheddar of 34,591 lb. *15 190 kg* made in 43 hrs on 20–22 Jan. 1964 by the Wisconsin Cheese Foundation for exhibition at the New York World's Fair, U.S.A. It was transported in a specially designed refrigerated tractor trailer "Cheese Mobile" 45 ft *13,71 m* long.

Longest sausage

The longest sausage ever recorded was one 7,480 ft *2 279 m* long, made by J. M. Schneiders Inc. of Kitchener, Ontario, Canada in October 1976. It was made with pork and seasonings and weighed 3,084 lb. *1 398,8 kg 1.37 tons*.

The world's largest hunk of cheese, the 15.4 ton cheddar aboard its refrigerated trailer, the "Cheese Mobile" in the U.S.A. in 1964 (see p. 168). (*Hank Lefebvre*)

LIVESTOCK PRICES

Note: Some exceptionally high livestock auction sales are believed to result from collusion between buyer and seller to raise the ostensible price levels of the breed concerned.

Highest Priced *Bull*

The highest price ever paid for a bull is $2,500,000 (£1,087,000) for the beefalo (a ⅜th buffalo, ⅜ charolais, ¼ Hereford) *Joe's Pride* sold by D. C. Basolo of Burlingame, California to the Beefalo Cattle Co. of Canada of Calgary, Alberta, Canada on 9 Sept. 1974.

The highest price ever paid for a bull in Britain is 60,000 guineas (£63,000), paid on 5 Feb. 1963 at Perth, Scotland, by James R. Dick (1928–74) co-manager of Black Watch Farms, for "Lindertis Evulse", an Aberdeen-Angus owned by Sir Torquil and Lady Munro of Lindertis, Kirriemuir, Tayside, Scotland. This bull failed a fertility test in August 1963 when 20 months old thus becoming the world's most expensive piece of beef.

Cow

The highest price ever paid for a cow is $Can. 235,000 (£131,200) for the Holstein-Friesian "Hanover Hill Barb" by a U.S.-Canadian syndicate at the Sale of Stars, Oakville, Ontario, Canada on 8 Nov. 1976. The British record is £14,910 for "Fairthwaite Indiana", a pure-bred Chianina in-calf heifer sold to Mr. Christopher Reeves of Taunton, Somerset by Harrison & Hetherington Ltd. in Carlisle, Cumbria on 21 Sept. 1974.

Sheep

The highest price ever paid for a sheep is $A46,000 (£30,000) for a Merino ram from John Collins & Sons, Mount Bryan, South Australia by Mrs. P. L. Puckridge of White River, Port Lincoln, South Australia at the Royal Adelaide Show on 2 Sept. 1976.

The British auction record is £13,000 paid by A. C. Campbell & Co. of Creetown, Dumfries & Galloway for Graham McClymont's Scottish Blackface ram in Oct. 1976.

The highest price ever paid for wool is $A46 per kg (£11.09 per lb.) for a bale of superfine Merino fleece from the Launceston, Tasmania sales in February 1973 set by Mr. C. Stephen of Mount Morriston estate.

Pig

The highest price ever paid for a pig is $38,000 (£16,520) for a champion Duroc owned by Forkner Farms, Horton, Missouri by Soga-No-Yo Swine Farms, Hiratosuka, Japan at Austin, Minnesota, U.S.A. on 11 Sept. 1973. The U.K. record is 3,300 guineas (£3,465), paid by Malvern Farms for the Swedish Landrace gilt "Bluegate Ally 33rd" owned by Davidson Trust in a draft sale at Reading, Berkshire on 2 Mar. 1955.

Horse

The highest price for a draught horse is $47,500 (*then £9,970*) paid for the 7 year old Belgian stallion *Farceur* by E. G. Good at Cedar Falls, Iowa on 16 Oct. 1917.

Donkey

Perhaps the lowest ever price for livestock was at a sale at Kuruman, Cape Province, South Africa in 1934 where donkeys were sold for less than 2p each.

Turkey

The highest price ever paid for a turkey is $1,600 (*then £760*) for a 44 lb. *19,9 kg* bird bought at the Pasadena Rodeo Show, Texas, U.S.A. from Billy R. Petty Jr. on 25 Sept. 1975.

Chicken Plucking

The record time for plucking 12 chickens clean by a team of 4 women at the annual Chicken Plucking Championship at Marsaryktown, Florida, U.S.A. is 47.8 seconds set on 4 Oct. 1975 by Sammie Alexsuk, Lottie Nemcovic, Irene Walker and Janice Oravec.

10. THE HUMAN WORLD

1. POLITICAL AND SOCIAL

The land area of the Earth is estimated at 57,270,000 miles² *148 328 000 km²* (including inland waters), or 29.08 per cent of the world's surface area.

Largest political division

The British Commonwealth of Nations, a free association of 36 independent sovereign states together with their dependencies, covers an area of 13,095,000 miles² *33 915 000 km²* and has a latest estimated population of 948.8 million (1976).

COUNTRIES

Total

The total number of separately administered territories in the world is 223, of which 160 are independent countries. Of these 32 sovereign and 49 non-sovereign are insular countries. Only 26 sovereign and 1 non-sovereign countries are entirely without a seaboard.

Largest

The country with the greatest area is the Union of Soviet Socialist Republics (the Soviet Union), comprising 15 Union (constituent) Republics with a total area of 22 402 000 km² *8,649,500 miles²*, or 15.0 per cent of the world's total land area, and a total coastline (including islands) of 106 360 km *66,090 miles*. The country measures 8 980 km *5,580 miles* from east to west and 4 490 km *2,790 miles* from north to south.

The United Kingdom covers 94,221 miles² *244 030 km²* (including 1,197 miles² *3 100 km²* of inland water), or 0.16 per cent of the total land area of the world. Great Britain is the world's eighth largest island, with an area of 84,186 miles² *218 040 km²* and a coastline 4,928 miles *7 930 km* long, of which Scotland accounts for 2,573 miles *4 141 km*, Wales 426 miles *685 km* and England 1,929 miles *3 104 km*.

Smallest

The smallest independent country in the world is the State of the Vatican City or Holy See (Stato della Città del Vaticano), which was made an enclave within the city of Rome, Italy on 11 Feb. 1929. It has an area of 44 hectares *108.7 acres*. The maritime sovereign country with the shortest coastline is Monaco with 3.49 miles *5,61 km* excluding piers and breakwaters.

The world's smallest republic is Nauru, less than 1 degree south of the equator in the Western Pacific, which became independent on 31 Jan. 1968, has an area of 5,263 acres *2 129 ha* and a population of 7,000 (latest estimate mid-1974).

The smallest colony in the world is Pitcairn Island with an area of 960 acres *388 ha* and a population of 82 (Dec. 1973).

The official residence, since 1834, of the Grand Master of the Order of the Knights of Malta totalling 3 acres *1,2 ha* and comprising the Villa del Priorato di Malta on the lowest of Rome's seven hills, the 151 ft *46 m* Aventine, retains certain diplomatic privileges as does 68 Via Condotti. The order has accredited representatives to foreign governments and is hence sometimes cited as the smallest state in the world.

Most Frontiers

The country with the most land frontiers is China, with 13 —Mongolia, U.S.S.R., North Korea, Hong Kong, Macau, Vietnam, Laos, Burma, India, Bhutan, Nepal, Pakistan and Afghanistan. France, if all her *Départments d'outre-mer* are included, may, on extended territorial waters, have 20 frontiers.

Longest and Shortest Frontier

The longest *continuous* frontier in the world is that between Canada and the United States, which (including the Great Lakes boundaries) extends for 3,987 miles *6 416 km* (excluding 1,538 miles *2 547 km* with Alaska). The frontier which is crossed most frequently is that between the United States and Mexico. It extends for 1,933 miles *3 110 km* and there are more than 120,000,000 crossings every year. The Sino-Soviet frontier, broken by the Sino-Mongolian border, extends for 4,500 miles *7 240 km* with no reported figure of crossings. The "frontier" of the Holy See in Rome measures 2.53 miles *4,07 km*. The land frontier between Gibraltar and Spain at La Linea, closed since 1969, measures 1,672 yds *1,53 km*.

Most impenetrable boundary

The "Iron Curtain" (858 miles *1 380 km*) dividing the Federal Republican (West) and the Democratic Republican (East) parts of Germany, utilises 2,230,000 land mines and 50,000 miles *80 500 km* of barbed wire, much of it of British manufacture, in addition to many watch-towers containing detection devices. The whole strip of 270 yds *246 m* wide occupies 133 miles² *344 km²* of East German territory.

POPULATIONS
World
Estimates of the human population of the world have largely hinged on the accuracy of the component figure for the population of the People's Republic of China, which has published no census since that of 30 June 1953. On 25 Aug. 1974 the Hsinhua Official News Agency announced that the figure was "nearly 800 million"—at least 29 million lower than the U.N. estimate. The world total at mid-1976 was estimated to be 4,061 million, giving an average density of 29.9 people per km^2 *76,4 per mile*^{2} of land (including inland waters). This excludes Antarctica and uninhabited island groups. The daily increase in the world's population was running at 174,600 in 1976–77. It is estimated that 204 are born and 83 die every minute in 1976–77. The world's population has doubled in the last 49 years and is expected to double again in the next 42 years. It is now estimated that the world's population in the year 2000 will be more than 6,000 million. The recent population "explosion" was of such a magnitude that it has been fancifully calculated that, *if* it had continued unabated, there would have been one person to each square yard by A.D. 2600, and humanity would have weighed more than Earth itself by A.D. 3700. It is estimated that 75,000,000,000 humans have been born and died in the last 600,000 years.

Date	Millions	Date	Millions
8000 B.C.	7		
4000 B.C.	85		
A.D. 1	c.300	1960	2,986
1650	c.500–550	1970	3,650
1750	770	1975	3,996
1800	1,000	1976	4,061[1]
1850	1,300	1977	4,126[2]
1900	1,680	1980	4,817*
1920	1,862	2000	6,254
1930	2,070	2007	7,600
1940	2,295	2070	25,000†
1950	2,543		

* U.N. Forecasts made on medium variants.

† Some demographers maintain that the figure will (or must) stabilize at 10 to 15,000 million but above 8,000 million during the 21st century.

[1] Estimate on 1.64% growth rate.

[2] Estimate on 1.6% growth rate.

Most populous country
The largest population of any country is that of the People's Republic of China (see above). The mid-1976 U.N. estimate was 854 million. The rate of natural increase is now believed to be 16.6 per 1,000 or 36,000 per day.

Least populous
The independent state with the smallest population is the Vatican City or the Holy See (see Smallest country, page 170), with 704 inhabitants at 23 Nov. 1974 and a nil birth rate.

Most densely populated
The most densely populated territory in the world is the Portuguese province of Macau (or Macao), on the southern coast of China. It has an estimated population of 271,000 (mid-1975) in an area of 6.2 miles^2 *16,05 km*^{2} giving a density of 43,700 per mile^2 *16 870 per km*^{2}.

The Principality of Monaco, on the south coast of France, has a population of 23,035 (30 June 1975) in a area of 369,9 acres *149,6 ha* giving a density of 39,855/mile^2 *15 388/km*^{2}. This is being relieved by marine infilling which will increase her area to 447 acres *180 ha*. Singapore has 2,278,000 (mid-1976 estimate) people in an inhabited area of 73 miles^2 *189 km*^{2}.

Of territories with an area of more than 200 miles^2 *518 km*^{2}, Hong Kong (398¼ miles^2 *1 031,4 km*^{2}) contains 4,367,000 (estimated mid-1975), giving the territory a density of 10,950/mile^2 *4 230/km*^{2}. Hong Kong is now the most populous of all colonies. The transcription of the name is from a local pronunciation of the Peking dialect version of Xiang gang (a port for incense). About 80 per cent of the population lives in the urban areas of Hong Kong island and Kowloon, on the mainland, and the density there is greater than 200,000/mile^2 *518 000/km*^{2}. On the Wah Fu estate there are 55,000 people living on 24 acres giving an unsurpassed spot density of 1,466,600 per mile^2 *566 280/km*^{2}. In 1959, at the peak of the housing crisis, it was reported that in one house designed for 12 people the number of occupants was 459, including 104 in one room and 4 living on the roof.

Of countries over 1,000 miles^2 *2 589 km*^{2} the most densely populated is Bangladesh with a population of 76,815,000 (mid 1975, estimate) living in 55,126 miles^2 *142 775 km*^{2} at a density of 1,392/mile^2 *537/km*^{2}. The Indonesian island of Java (with an area of 48,763 miles^2 *126 295 km*^{2}) had a population of 69,037,000 (1971), giving a density of 1,415/mile^2 *547/km*^{2}.

The United Kingdom (94,221 miles^2 *244 030 km*^{2}) had an estimated home population of 55,928,000 at 30 June 1976, giving a density of 594.4 people/mile^2 *229,5/km*^{2}. The projected population figures for 1980 and 2000 are 57,519,000 and 62,794,000 respectively. The population density for England alone (50,869 miles^2 *131 750 km*^{2}) is 962.0/mile^2 *371,4/km*^{2}, while that of south-eastern England is more than 1,640/mile^2 *630/km*^{2}.

Most sparsely populated
Antarctica became permanently occupied by relays of scientists from October 1956. The population varies seasonally and reaches 1,500 at times.

The least populated territory, apart from Antarctica, is Greenland, with a population of 54,000 (estimated mid 1975) in an area of 840,000 miles^2 *2 175 000 km*^{2} giving a density of one person to every 15.44 miles^2 *39,9 km*^{2}. Some 84.3% of the island comprises an ice-cap.

Emigration
More people emigrate from the United Kingdom than from any other country. A total of 236,400 emigrated from the U.K. in 1975. The largest number of emigrants in any one year was 360,000 in 1852, mainly from Ireland after the Great Famine.

Immigration
The country which regularly receives the most immigrants is the United States, with 386,194 in 1975. It has been estimated that in the period 1820–1975, the U.S.A. has received 47,098,939 *official* immigrants. One in 26 of the U.S. population is an *illegal* immigrant. The peak year for immigration into the United Kingdom was the 12 months from 1 July 1961 to 30 June 1962, when about 430,000 Commonwealth citizens arrived. The number of immigrants who were permitted to settle in 1975 were 40,428.

Tourism
In 1976 the United Kingdom received a record 10 million visitors, who spent an estimated £1,550,000,000 excluding fares to British carriers.

Birth Rate *Highest and Lowest*
The highest 1970–75 figure is 52.2 for the Niger Republic. The rate for the whole world was 31.5 per 1,000 in 1975.

Excluding Vatican City, where the rate is negligible, the lowest recorded rate is 7.8 for Monaco (1973).

171

The 1976 rate in the United Kingdom was 12.1/1,000 (11.9 in England and Wales, 12.5 in Scotland and 17.1 in Northern Ireland), while the 1975 rate for the Republic of Ireland was 21.6 registered births per 1,000. The highest number of births in England and Wales (since registration in 1837) has been 957,782 in 1920 and the lowest this century 579,091 in 1941. The figure has fallen each year since 1964 (875,972) to 1976 (585,600 est.).

Death Rate *Highest and Lowest*
The highest of the latest available recorded death rates is 28.1 deaths per each 1,000 of the population in Bangladesh in 1970–75. The rate for the whole world was 12.8 per 1,000 in 1975.

The lowest of the latest available recorded rates is 3.2 deaths/ 1,000 in Tonga in 1971.

The 1976 rate in the United Kingdom was 12.2/1,000 (12.2 in England and Wales, 12.5 in Scotland and 11.0 in Northern Ireland). The highest S.M.I. (Standard Mortality Index where the national average is 100) is in Salford, Greater Manchester with a figure of 133. The 1975 rate for the Republic of Ireland was 10.7 registered deaths per 1,000.

Natural Increase
The highest of the latest available recorded rates of natural increase is 38.3 (45.6 − 7.3 in 1970)/1,000 in the U.S. Virgin Island. The rate for the whole world was 31.5 − 12.8 = 18.7 per 1,000 in 1973.

The 1976 rate for the United Kingdom was a decrease of 0.1/1,000 (nil in England and Wales, nil in Scotland and 5.9 increase in Northern Ireland). The figure for the Republic of Ireland was 10.9/1,000 in 1975. The rate for the first time in the first and fourth quarters of 1975 became ones of natural decrease.

The lowest rate of natural increase in any major independent country is in France (birth rate 10.8 death rate 14.3) with a negative figure thus of −3.5 per 1,000 for 1975.

Marriage ages
The country with the lowest average ages for marriage is India, with 20.0 years for males and 14.5 years for females. At the other extreme is Ireland, with 31.4 for males and 26.5 for females. In the People's Republic of China the *recommended* age for marriage for men is 28 and for women 25. In England and Wales the peak age for marriages are 22.8 years (male) and 19.6 years (female).

Divorces
The country with most divorces is the United States with a total of 1,026,000 in 1975—a rate of 48.2% on the current annual total of marriages or 4.8 per thousand.

Sex Ratio
The country with the largest recorded shortage of males is the U.S.S.R., with 1,169 females to every 1,000 males at 15 Jan. 1970. The country with the largest recorded woman shortage is Pakistan, with 936 to every 1,000 males in 1972. The figures are, however, probably under-enumerated due to *purdah*. The ratio in the United Kingdom was 1,054.7 females to every 1,000 males at 30 June 1976, and is expected to be 1,014.2/1,000 by A.D. 2000.

Infant Mortality
Based on deaths before one year of age, the lowest of the latest available recorded rates is 8.3 deaths per 1,000 live births in the Channel Islands and in Sweden both in 1975. The world rate in 1975 was 98.

The highest recorded infant mortality rate reported has been 195 to 300 for Burma in 1952 and 229 for Gabon. Many countries have apparently ceased to make returns. Among these is Ethiopia, where the infant mortality rate was unofficially estimated to be nearly 550/1,000 live births in 1969.

The United Kingdom figure for 1975 was 14.1/1,000 live births (England and Wales 12.9, Scotland 14.7, Northern Ireland 17.8). The Republic of Ireland figure for 1972 was 18.0.

Life Expectation
There is evidence that life expectation in Britain in the 5th century A.D. was 33 years for males and 27 years for females. In the decade 1890–1900 the expectation of life among the population of India was 23.7 years.

Based on the latest available data, the highest recorded expectation of life at age 12 months is 72.11 years for Swedish males and 77.6 years for Norwegian females (1973).

The lowest recorded expectation of life at birth is 27 years for both sexes in the Vallée du Niger area of Mali in 1957 (sample survey, 1957–58). The figure for males in Gabon was 25 years in 1960–61 but 45 for females.

The latest available figures for England and Wales (1974) are 69.3 years for males and 75.5 years for females; for Scotland (1968–70) 66.9 years for males and 73.08 years for females; for Northern Ireland (1969–71) 67.9 years for males and 73.7 years for females and for the Republic of Ireland (1970–72) 68.77 years for males and 73.52 years for females. The British figure for 1901–1910 was 48.53 years for males and 52.83 years for females.

Standards of Living
The world average per capita Gross National Product in 1976 was $963 £566. The country with the highest average income per native citizen in 1977 was Abu Dhabi, with some $70,000 £41,200. In 1976 the average income per head in the United Kingdom was £1,813 $3,082.

Housing
For comparison, dwelling units are defined as a structurally separated room or rooms occupied by private households of one or more people and having separate access or a common passageway to the street.

The country with the greatest recorded number of private housing units is India, with 100,251,000 occupied in 1972.

Great Britain comes fourth among reporting countries, with a stock of 20,350,000 dwellings as at 1 Jan. 1976. The record number of permanent houses built has been 425,800 in 1968.

Physicians
The country with the most physicians is the U.S.S.R., with 831,300, or one to every 307 persons. China has more than a million para-medical personnel known as "bare foot doctors". In England and Wales there were 85,000 hospital doctors, general practitioners and dentists working within the National Health Service in 1975.

The country with the lowest recorded proportion is Upper Volta, with 58 physicians (one for every 92,759 people) in 1970.

Dentists
The country with the most dentists is the United States, where 122,000 were registered members of the American Dental Association in 1975.

Psychiatrists
The country with the most psychiatrists is the United States. The registered membership of the American Psychiatric Association was 22,426 in 1976. The membership of the American Psychological Association was 42,000 in 1976.

Hospital Largest *World*
The largest medical centre in the world is the District Medical Center in Chicago, Illinois, U.S.A. It covers 478 acres *193 ha* and includes five hospitals, with a total of 5,600 beds, and eight professional schools with more than 3,000 students.

The largest mental hospital in the world is the Pilgrim State Hospital, on Long Island, New York State, U.S.A., with 12,800 beds. It formerly contained 14,200 beds.

172

BRITISH AND IRISH LARGEST AND SMALLEST PRIMARY LOCAL GOVERNMENT AREAS—By size and population									
	By Area (in acres/hectares)					By Home Population			
	Largest			Smallest			Most Populous		Least Populous	
England	North Yorkshire	2,055,109	831 661	Isle of Wight	94,141	38 096	Greater London	7,028,200	Isle of Wight	111,000
Wales	Dyfed	1,424,668	576 534	South Glamorgan	102,807	41 604	Mid Glamorgan	540,100[2]	Powys	100,800
Scotland[3]	Highland[4]	6,214,400	2 514 880	Orkney	217,600	88 059	Strathclyde[5]	2,504,909	Orkney	17,675
Northern Ireland	Tyrone	779,520	315 460	North Down	18,174	7 354	Belfast City	368,200[1]	Moyle	13,400
Republic of Ireland	Cork	1,843,408	745 990	Louth	202,806	82 071	Dublin County	799,048	Longford	28,250

[1] *Figures based on 1971 Census.*
[2] *The most populous town in Wales—the City of Cardiff (pop. 284,400)—is in South Glamorgan.*
[3] *Scotland's 33 Counties were replaced on 16 May 1975 by nine regions and three Island Areas.*
[4] *The inclusion by Act of Parliament on 10 February 1972 of Rockall in the District of Harris in Western Isles put the extremities of that Authority at the record distance apart of 302 miles 486 km.*
[5] *Includes the most populous town in Scotland—the City of Glasgow (pop. 880,617).*

The busiest maternity hospital in the world is the Mama Yemo Hospital, Kinshasa, Zaire with 41,930 deliveries in 1976. The record "birthquake" occurred on a day in May 1976 with 175 babies born. It has 599 beds.

Great Britain

The largest hospitals of any kind in Great Britain are the Rainhill Hospital near Liverpool, with 2,250 staffed beds, and St. Bernard's Hospital, Southall, Ealing, Greater London, which has 1,785 staffed beds for mental patients.

The largest general hospital in the United Kingdom is the St. James Hospital, Leeds, West Yorkshire, with 1,413 available staffed beds.

The largest maternity hospital in the United Kingdom is the Mill Road Maternity Hospital, Liverpool with 177 staffed beds.

The largest children's hospital in the United Kingdom is Queen Mary's Hospital for Children, at Carshalton, Sutton, Greater London, with 686 staffed beds.

Longest stay in hospital

Miss Martha Nelson was admitted to the Columbus State Institute for the Feeble-Minded in Ohio, U.S.A. in 1875. She died in January 1975 aged 103 years 6 months in the Orient State Institution, Ohio after spending more than 99 years in institutions.

CITIES
Oldest *World*

The oldest known walled town in the world is Arīhā (Jericho). The latest radio-carbon dating on specimens from the lowest levels reached by archaeologists indicate habitation there by perhaps 3,000 people as early as 7800 B.C. The village of Zawi Chemi Shanidar, discovered in 1957 in northern Iraq, has been dated to 8910 B.C. The oldest capital city in the world is Dimashq (Damascus), the capital of Syria. It has been continuously inhabited since c. 2500 B.C.

Great Britain

The oldest town in Great Britain is often cited as Colchester, the old British Camulodunum, headquarters of Belgic chiefs in the 1st century B.C. However, the tin trading post Salakee, St. Mary's Isles of Scilly is believed to be pre-Celtic and hence *ante* 550 B.C.

Most populous *World*

The most populous city in the world is Tōkyō, Japan with a population in 1976 of 8,586,900. At the census of 1975 the "Keihin Metropolitan Area" (Tōkyō-Yokohama Metropolitan Area) of 1,081 miles[2] *2 800 km*[2] however contained 17,037,300 people.

The world's largest city not built by the sea or on a river is Greater Mexico City, (Ciudad de Mexico), Mexico, with a population (1976 estimate) of 11,943,100.

Great Britain

The largest conurbation in Britain is Greater London (established on 1 Apr. 1965), with a population of 7,028,200 (mid-1976). The residential population of the City of London (677.3 acres *274 ha* plus 61.7 acres *24,9 ha* foreshore) is 5,304 compared with 128,000 in 1801. The peak figure for Greater London was 8,615,050 in 1939.

Largest in area

The world's largest town, in area, is Mount Isa, Queensland, Australia. The area administered by the City Council is 15,822 miles[2] *40 978 km*[2]. The largest conurbation in the United Kingdom is the county of Greater London with an area of 609.8 miles[2] *1 579,5 km*[2]. The designated area of the district of the city of Carlisle in Cumbria is 398.36 miles[2] *1 031,77 km*[2].

Smallest town and hamlet

The smallest place with a town council is Caerwys, Clwyd, Wales with a population of 801. The town has a charter dated 1284. The only hamlet in Great Britain with an official population of one in the 1961 census was Gallowhill in the parish of Inveravon, Grampian, Scotland. The population (Miss Jessie Ann Stuart aged 74) died in 1969.

Highest *World*

The highest capital in the world, before the domination of Tibet by China, was Lhasa, at an elevation of 12,087 ft *3 684 m* above sea-level. La Paz, the administrative and *de facto* capital of Bolivia, stands at an altitude of 11,916 ft *3 631 m* above sea-level. The city was founded in 1548 by Capt. Alonso de Mendoza on the site of an Indian village named Chuquiapu. It was originally called Ciudad de Nuestra Señora de La Paz (City of Our Lady of Peace), but in 1825 was renamed La Paz de Ayacucho, its present official

WORLD'S MOST POPULOUS CITIES—PROGRESSIVE LIST			
Population	Name		Date
c. 150	Chemi Shanidar	Iraq	8910 B.C.
3,000	Jericho (Arīcha)	Samaria	7800 B.C.
50,000	Uruk (Erech) (now Warka)	Iraq	3000 B.C.
250,000	Greater Ur	Iraq	2200 B.C.
350,000	Babylon (now al-Ḥillah)	Iraq	600 B.C.
500,000	Pataliputra (Palna) Bihār	India	400–185 B.C.
600,000	Seleukia (near Baghdad)	Iraq	300–165 A.D.
1,100,000	Rome	Italy	133 B.C.
1,500,000	Ankor	Cambodia	900 A.D.
1.0–1.5 million	Hang Chow	China	1279
707,000	Peking (Cumbaluc)	China	1578
1,117,290	Greater London	United Kingdom	1801
8,615,050	Greater London (peak)	United Kingdom	1939
8,586,900	Tōkyō	Japan	1976

Note: The 1975 estimates for the metropolitan areas of Tōkyō-Yokohama and for New York are 17,037,300 (census) and 16,848,000. The U.N. projection for A.D. 2000 for Greater Mexico City and Tōkyō-Yokohama are 31,616,000 and 26,128,000.

name. Sucre, the legal capital of Bolivia, stands at 9,301 ft *2 834 m* above sea-level. The new town of Wenchuan, founded in 1955 on the Chinghai-Tibet road, north of the Tangla range is the highest in the world at 5 100 m *16,732 ft* above sea-level. The highest dwellings in the world are those at Bāsisi, India near the Tibet border at *c.* 19,700 ft *5 988 m.*

Great Britain
The highest village in England is Flash, in northern Staffordshire, at 1,518 ft *462 m* above sea-level. The highest in Scotland is Wanlockhead, in Dumfries and Galloway at 1,380 ft *420 m* above sea-level.

Lowest
The settlement of Ein Bokek, which has a synagogue, on the shores of the Dead Sea is the lowest in the world at 1,299 ft *395,9 m* below sea-level.

Northernmost
The world's most northerly town with a population of more than 10,000 is the Arctic port of Dikson, U.S.S.R. in 73° 32′ N. The northernmost village is Ny Ålesund (78° 55′ N.), a coalmining settlement on King's Bay, Vest Spitsbergen, in the Norwegian territory of Svalbard, inhabited only during the winter season. The northernmost capital is Reykjavik, the capital of Iceland, in 64° 06′ N. Its population was estimated to be 84,772 in 1 Dec. 1974. The northernmost permanent human occupation is the base at Alert (82° 31′ N.), on Dumb Bell Bay, on the north-east coast of Ellesmere Island, northern Canada.

Southernmost
The world's southernmost village is Puerto Williams (population about 350), on the north coast of Isla Navarino, in Tierra del Fuego, Chile, about 680 miles *1 090 km* north of Antarctica. Wellington, North Island, New Zealand is the southernmost capital city on 41° 17′ S. The world's southernmost administrative centre is Port Stanley (51° 43′ S.), in the Falkland Islands, off South America.

Most remote from the sea
The largest town most remote from the sea is Wulumuch'i (Urumchi) formerly Tihwa, Sinkiang, capital of the Uighur Autonomous Region of China, at a distance of about 1,400 miles *2 250 km* from the nearest coastline. Its population was estimated to be 320,000 in 1974.

2. ROYALTY AND HEADS OF STATE

Oldest ruling house
The Emperor of Japan, Hirohito (born 29 Apr. 1901), is the 124th in line from the first Emperor, Jimmu Tenno or Zinmu, whose reign was traditionally from 660 to 581 B.C., but probably from *c.* 40 to *c.* 10 B.C. His Imperial Majesty Muhammad Rizā Shāh Pahlavi of Iran (b. 26 Oct. 1919) claims Cyrus the Great (reigned *c.* 559–530 B.C.) as an ancestor.

Her Majesty Queen Elizabeth II (b. 21 Apr. 1926) represents dynasties historically traceable at least back until the 5th century A.D.; notably that of Elesa of whom Alfred The Great was a 13 great grandson and the Queen is therefore a 49 great granddaughter.

Reigns *Longest*
The longest recorded reign of any monarchy is that of Pepi II, a Sixth Dynasty Pharaoh of ancient Egypt. His reign began in *c.* 2,310 B.C., when he was aged 6, and lasted *c.* 94 years. Musoma Kanijo, chief of the Nzega district of western Tanganyika (now part of Tanzania), reputedly reigned for more than 98 years from 1864, when aged 8, until his death on 2 Feb. 1963. The 6th Japanese Emperor Koo-an traditionally reigned for 102 years (from 392 to 290 B.C.), but probably his actual reign was from about A.D. 110 to about A.D. 140. The reign of the 11th Emperor Suinin was traditionally from 29 B.C. to A.D. 71 (99 years), but probably from

A.D. 259 to 291. The longest reign in European history was that of King Louis XIV of France, who ascended the throne on 14 May 1643, aged 4 years 231 days, and reigned for 72 years 110 days until his death on 1 Sept. 1715, four days before his 77th birthday.

Currently the longest reigning monarch in the world is King Sobhuza II, K.B.E. (b. 4 July 1899), the *Ngwenyama* (Paramount Chief) of Swaziland, under United Kingdom protection since December 1899, and independent since 6 Sept. 1968. At the last published count in 1972 he had 112 wives. Hirohito (see above) has been Emperor in Japan since 25 Dec. 1926.

Roman Occupation
During the 369 year long Roman occupation of England, Wales and parts of Scotland there were 40 sole and 27 co-Emperors of Rome. Of these the longest reigning was Constantinus I (The Great) from 31 Mar. 307 to 22 May 337—30 years 2 months.

Shortest
The shortest recorded reign was that of Jean I, King of France, who was born posthumously on 15 Nov. 1316 and died aged 4 days on 19 Nov. 1316.

Highest post-nominal numbers
The highest post-nominal number ever used to designate a member of a Royal House was 75 briefly enjoyed by Count Heinrich LXXV Reuss (1800–1801). All male members of this branch of this German family are called Heinrich and are successively numbered from I upwards *each* century.

The highest British regnal number is 8, used by Henry VIII (1509–1547) and by Edward VIII (1936) who died as H.R.H. the Duke of Windsor, K.G., K.T., K.P., G.C.B., G.C.S.I., G.C.M.G., G.C.I.E., G.C.V.O., G.B.E., I.S.O., M.C. on 28 May 1972. Jacobites liked to style Henry Benedict, Cardinal York (born 1725), the grandson of James II, as Henry IX in respect of his "reign" from 1788 to 1807 when he died the last survivor in the male line of the House of Stuart.

Longest lived 'Royals'
The longest life among the Blood Royal of Europe has been that of the late H.R.H. Princess Alicia of Bourbon who was born on 29 June 1876 and died on 20 Jan 1975 aged 98 years 206 days. The greatest age among European Royal Consorts is the 99 years 110 days of H.S.H. Princess Marie Felixovna Romanovsky-Krassinsky, who was born 19 Aug. 1872 and died in Paris 7 Dec. 1971. The longest-lived Queen on record has been the Queen Grandmother of Siam, Queen Sawang (b. 10 Sept. 1862), 27th daughter of King Mongkut (Rama IV), who died on 17 Dec. 1955 aged 93 years 3 months.

Youngest King and Queen
Of the world's 26 monarchies that with the youngest King is Bhutan where King Jigme Singye Wangchuk was born 11 Nov. 1955, succeeded on 24 July 1972.

Heaviest Monarch
The world's heaviest monarch is the 6 ft 3 in *1,90 m* tall King Taufa'ahau of Tonga who in Sept. 1976 was weighed on the only adequate scales in the country at the airport recording 33 st. *462 lb. 209,5 kg.*

Most Prolific
The most prolific monogamous "royals" have been Prince Hartmann of Liechtenstein (1613–1686) who had 24 children, of whom 21 were live born, by Countess Elisabeth žu Salm—Reifterscheidt (1623–1688). H.R.H. Duke Roberto I of Parma also had 24 children but by two wives.

Head of State oldest and youngest
The oldest head of state in the world is H.E. Hon. Mzee Jomo Kenyatta born, as he says "approximately 1889". The youngest non-royal head of state is Jean-Claude Duvalier, (b. 3 July 1951) President of Haiti since 21 Apr. 1971.

BRITISH MONARCHY RECORDS

	Kings	Queens Regnant	Queens Consort
Longest Reign or tenure	59 years 96 days[1] George III 1760-1820	63 years 216 days Victoria 1837-1901	57 years 70 days Charlotte 1761 1818 (Consort of George III)
Shortest Reign or tenure	77 days[2] Edward V 1483	13 days Jane, July 1553	154 days Yoleta (1285–1286) (2nd consort of Alexander III of Scotland)
Longest lived	81 years 239 days[3] George III (b.1738–d.1820)	81 years 243 days Victoria (b. 1819–d. 1901)	85 years 303 days Mary of Teck (b.1867 d.1953) (Consort of George V)
Most children (legitimate)[4]	18 Edward I 1272-1307	9[5] Victoria (b.1819–d.1901)	15 Eleanor (c 1244-1290) and Charlotte (b. 1744-d. 1818)
Oldest to start reign or consortship	64 years 10 months William IV 1830–1837	37 years 5 months Mary I 1553-1558	56 years 53 days Alexandra (b 1844 d 1925) (Consort of Edward VII)
Youngest to start reign or consortship	269 days Henry VI in 1422	6 or 7 days Mary, Queen of Scots in 1542	6 years 11 months Isabella (second consort of Richard II in 1396)
Most married	6 times Henry VIII 1509–1547	3 times Mary, Queen of Scots 1542-1567 (executed 1587)	4 times Catharine Parr (b c.1512 d.1548) (sixth consort of Henry VIII)

Notes (Dates are dates of reigns or tenures unless otherwise indicated).
[1] James Francis Edward, the Old Pretender, known to his supporters as James VIII, styled his reign from 16 Sept. 1701 until his death 1 Jan. 1766 (i.e. 64 years 109 days).
[2] There is the probability that in pre-Conquest times Sweyn 'Forkbeard', the Danish King of England, reigned for only 40 days in 1013–1014.
[3] Richard Cromwell (b. 4 Oct. 1626), the 2nd Lord Protector from 3 Sept. 1658 until his abdication on 24 May 1659, lived under the alias John Clarke until 12 July 1712 aged 85 years 9 months and was thus the longest lived Head of State.
[4] Henry (b. 1068—d. 1135) in addition to one (possibly two) legitimate sons and a daughter had at least 20 bastard children (9 sons, 11 daughters), and possibly 22 by six mistresses.
[5] Queen Anne (b. 1665—d. 1714) had 17 pregnancies, which produced only 5 live births.

Her Majesty Queen Elizabeth II, whose dynasty is historically traceable for 49 generations back to the 5th century (see p. 174). (*Popperfoto*)

3. LEGISLATURES

PARLIAMENTS—WORLD

Earliest and Oldest
The earliest known legislative assembly was a bicameral one in Erech, Iraq *c.* 2800 B.C. The oldest legislative body is the *Alpingi* (Althing) of Iceland founded in A.D. 930. This body, which originally comprised 39 local chieftains, was abolished in 1800, but restored by Denmark to a consultative status in 1843 and a legislative status in 1874. The legislative assembly with the oldest continuous history is the Tynwald Court in the Isle of Man, which is believed to have originated more than 1,000 years ago.

Largest
The largest legislative assembly in the world is the National People's Congress of the People's Republic of China. The fourth Congress, which met in March 1969, had 3,500 members.

Smallest quorum
The House of Lords has the smallest quorum, expressed as a percentage of eligible voters, of any legislative body in the world, namely less than one-third of one per cent. To transact business there must be three peers present, including the Lord Chancellor or his deputy. The House of Commons quorum of 40 M.P.'s, including the Speaker or his deputy, is 20 times as exacting.

Highest paid legislators
The most highly paid of all the world's legislators are Members of the U.S. Congress who receive a basic annual salary of $42,500 (now £24,285). Of this, up to $3,000 (£1,715) is exempt from taxation. In addition up to $157,092 (£89,766) per annum is allowed for office help, with a salary limit of $30,600 (*now* £17,485) for any one staff member (limited to 16 in number). Senators also enjoy free travel, telephones, postage, medical care, telegrams, stationery (limited to 480,000 envelopes per year), flowers and haircuts. They also command very low rates for filming, speech and ratio transcriptions and, in the case of women senators, beauty treatment. When abroad they have access to "counterpart funds". A retiring President electing to take also his congressional pension would enjoy a combined pension of $103,500 (£60,882) per annum.

Longest membership

The longest span as a legislator was 83 years by József Madarász (1814–1915). He first attended the Hungarian Parliament in 1832–36 as *oblegatus absentium* (*i.e.* on behalf of an absent deputy). He was a full member in 1848–50 and from 1861 until his death on 31 Jan. 1915.

Best Attendance Record

U.S. Congressman William H. Natcher (Democrat) of Bowling Green, Kentucky completed more than 20 years (1954–1975) without missing a single call or vote (3,353 quorum calls and 4,723 roll call votes).

Filibusters

The longest continuous speech in the history of the United States Senate was that of Senator Wayne Morse of Oregon on 24–25 Apr. 1953, when he spoke on the Tidelands Oil Bill for 22 hrs 26 min without resuming his seat. Interrupted only briefly by the swearing-in of a new senator, Senator Strom Thurmond (South Carolina, Democrat) spoke against the Civil Rights Bill for 24 hrs 19 min on 28–29 Aug. 1957. The United States national record duration for a filibuster is 43 hrs by Texas State senator Bill Meier against non-disclosure of industrial accidents in May 1977.

Treaty *Oldest*

The world's oldest treaty is the Anglo-Portuguese Treaty of Alliance signed in London over 600 years ago on 16 June 1373. The text was confirmed "with my usual flourish" by John de Banketre, Clerk.

PARLIAMENTS—UNITED KINGDOM

Earliest

The earliest known use of the term "parliament" in an official English royal document, in the meaning of a summons to the King's council, dates from 19 Dec. 1241.

The Houses of Parliament of the United Kingdom in the Palace of Westminster, London, had 1,762 members (House of Lords 1,127, House of Commons 635) in June 1975.

Longest

The longest English Parliament was the "Pensioners" Parliament of Charles II, which lasted from 8 May 1661 to 24 Jan. 1679, a period of 17 years 8 months and 16 days. The longest United Kingdom Parliament was that of George V, Edward VIII and George VI, lasting from 26 Nov. 1935 to 15 June 1945, a span of 9 years 6 months and 20 days.

Shortest

The parliament of Edward I, summoned to Westminster for 30 May 1306, lasted only one day. The parliament of Charles II at Oxford from 21–28 March 1681 lasted 7 days. The shortest United Kingdom Parliament was that of George III, lasting from 15 Dec. 1806 to 29 Apr. 1807, a period of only 4 months and 14 days.

Longest sittings

The longest sitting in the House of Commons was one of 41½ hrs from 4 p.m. on 31 Jan. 1881 to 9.30 a.m. on 2 Feb. 1881, on the question of better Protection of Person and Property in Ireland. The longest sitting of the Lords has been 19 hrs 16 min from 2.30 p.m. on 29 Feb. to 9.46 a.m. on 1 Mar. 1968 on the Commonwealth Immigrants Bill (Committee stage).

Longest speech

The longest recorded continuous speech in the House of Commons was that of Henry Peter Brougham (1778–1868) on 7 Feb. 1828, when he spoke for 6 hrs on Law Reform. He ended at 10.40 p.m. and the report of this speech occupied 12 columns of the next day's edition of *The Times*. Brougham, created the 1st Lord Brougham and Vaux on 22 Nov. 1830, also holds the House of Lords record, also with six hours on 7 Oct. 1831, when speaking on the second reading of the Reform Bill. The longest back bench speech since 7 Feb. 1828 has been one of 3 hrs 16 min by Sir Bernard Braine (b. 1914) the Conservative member for Essex, South East concerning Canvey Island on 23–24 July 1974.

The longest speech in Stormont, Northern Ireland was one of 9½ hours by Tommy Henderson M.P. on the Appropriations Bill on 26–27 May 1936.

Greatest parliamentary petition

The greatest petition was supposed to be the Great Chartist Petition of 1848 but of the 5,706,000 "signatures" only 1,975,496 were valid. The all time largest was for the abolition of Entertainment Duty with 3,107,080 signatures presented on 5 June 1951.

Most time consuming legislation

The most profligate use of parliamentary time was on the Government of Ireland Bill of 1893–4, which required 82 days in the House of Commons of which 46 days was in Committee. The record for a standing committee is 58 sessions for the Aircraft and Shipbuilding Industries bill which was represented to the House of Commons on 8 June 1976 after the notorious 303–303 tied vote of 27 May 1976.

Divisions

The record number of divisions in the House of Commons is 43 in the single session of 20–21 March 1907. The largest division was one of 350–310 on a vote of confidence in 1892.

ELECTIONS—WORLD

Largest

The largest election ever held was that for the Indian *Lok Sabha* (House of the People) on 1–10 Mar. 1971. About 152,720,000 of the electorate of 272,630,000 chose from 2,785 candidates for 518 seats.

Most expensive

The cost of the 1972 Presidential election in the United States was estimated at $49.07 million by the Republicans, who won 49 of the 50 States, and $45.0 million by the Democrats.

Closest

The ultimate in close general elections occurred in Zanzibar (now part of Tanzania) on 18 Jan. 1961, when the Afro-Shirazi Party won by a single seat, after the seat of Chake-Chake on Pemba Island had been gained by a single vote.

Most one-sided

North Korea recorded a 100 per cent. turn-out of electors and a 100 per cent vote for the Worker's Party of Korea in the general election of 8 Oct. 1962. The previous record had been set in the Albanian election of 4 June 1962, when all but seven of the electorate of 889,875 went to the polls—a 99.9992 per cent turn-out. Of the 889,868 voters, 889,828 voted for the candidates of the Albanian Party of Labour, *i.e* 99.9955 per cent of the total poll.

Most Bent

In his book *Journey Without Maps* Graham Greene quotes the case of the Liberian presidential election of 1928 in which President Charles D. B. King was returned with a majority over his opponent Mr Thomas J. Faulkner of the People's Party officially announced as 600,000. The total electorate at the time was less than 15,000.

Highest personal majority

The highest ever personal majority by any politician has been 424,545 by Ram Bilas Paswan, the Janata candidate for Hajipur in Bihar, India in March 1977. The electorate was 625,179.

Communist parties

The largest national Communist party outside the Soviet Union (15,000,000 members in 1975) and Communist states has been the Partito Communista Italiano (Italian Communist Party), with a membership of 2,300,000 in 1946. The total was 1,700,000 in 1976. The membership in mainland China was estimated to be 28,000,000 in 1974. The Communist Party of Great Britain, formed on 31 July 1920 in Cannon Street Station Hotel, London, attained its peak membership of 56,000 in December 1942, compared with 28,529 in April 1976.

Most parties

The country with the greatest number of political parties is Italy with 73 registered for the elections of 19 May 1968. These included "Friends of the Moon" with one candidate.

Voting Age Extremes

The eligibility for voting is 15 years of age in the Philippines and 25 years in Andorra.

PRIME MINISTERS—WORLD

Oldest

The longest lived Prime Minister of any country is believed to have been Chrisopher Hornsrud, Prime Minister of Norway from 28 Jan. to 15 Feb. 1928. He was born on 15 Nov. 1859 and died on 13 Dec. 1960, aged 101 years 28 days.

El Hadji Muhammad el Mokri, Grand Vizier of Morocco, died on 16 Sept. 1957, at a reputed age of 116 Muslim (*Hijri*) years, equivalent to 112.5 Gregorian years.

Longest term of office

Prof. Dr. António de Oliveirar Salazar, G.C.M.G. (Hon.) (1889–1970) was the President of the Council of Ministers (*i.e.* Prime Minister) of Portugal from 5 July 1932 until 27 Sept. 1968—36 years 84 days. He was superseded 11 days after going into coma.

ELECTORATES—UNITED KINGDOM

Largest and smallest

The largest electorate of all time was the estimated 217,900 for Hendon, Barnet, Greater London, prior to the redistribution in 1941. The largest electorate for a seat in Great Britain is 97,364 for Meriden (1974 Register). In Antrim South, Northern Ireland the figure is 117,834. The smallest electorate of all-time was in Old Sarum (number of houses nil, population nil since *c.* 1540) in Wiltshire, with eight electors who returned two members in 1821, thus being 54,475 times as well represented as the Hendon electorate of 120 years later. There were no contested elections in Old Sarum for the 536 years from 1295 to 1831. The smallest electorate for any seat is Western Isles with 24,477 electors.

Referendum

On the Common Market referendum of 5 June 1975 the electorate was 40,086,677 of whom 25,848,654 cast effective votes. The highest "Yes" vote was 76.3% in North Yorkshire and highest "No" vote was 70.5% in the Western Isles. The highest turnout was 75.0% in the Isles of Scilly and the lowest was 47.1% in Shetland.

MAJORITIES—UNITED KINGDOM

Party

The largest party majorities were those of the Liberals, with 307 seats in 1832 and 356 seats in 1906. In 1931 the Coalition of Conservatives, Liberals and National Labour candidates had a majority of 491. The narrowest party majority was that of the Whigs in 1847, with a single seat.

The largest majority on a division was one of 463 (464 votes to 1), on a motion of "no confidence" in the conduct of World War II, on 29 Jan. 1942. Since the war the largest has been one of 461 (487 votes to 26) on 10 May 1967, during the debate on the government's application for Britain to join the European Economic Community (the "Common Market").

Largest personal *All-time*

The largest individual majority of any Member of Parliament was the 62,253 of Sir A. Cooper Rawson, M.P. (Conservative) at Brighton in 1931. He polled 75,205 votes against 12,952 votes for his closer opponent the Labour Candidate, Lewis Coleman Cohen, later Lord Cohen of Brighton (1897–1966), from an electorate of 128,779. The largest majority of any woman M.P. was 38,823 in the same General Election by the Countess of Iveagh (*née* Lady Gwendolen Florence Mary Onslow), C.B.E. (1881–1966), the Conservative member for Southend-on-Sea, Essex, from November 1927 to October 1935.

Current

The largest majority in the October 1974 Parliament is 38,432

The finest economy of electoral effort. Sir Harmar-Nicholls (Con.), right, winning the Peterborough Election of 1966 at the seventh recount from Michael J. Ward (Lab.), left, by three votes. (*Peterborough Citizen and Advertiser*)

held by James H. Molyneaux (United Ulster Unionist Council) in Antrim South where he received 48,892 votes. The highest figure for Great Britain is 34,481 by T. Alec Jones (Lab.) in Rhondda, Wales.

Narrowest personal *All-time*

The closest result occurred in the General Election of 1886 at Ashton-under-Lyne, Greater Manchester when the Conservative and Liberal candidates both received 3,049 votes. The Returning Officer, Mr. James Walker, gave his casting vote for John E. W. Addison (Con.), who was duly returned while Alexander B. Rowley (Gladstone-Liberal) was declared unelected. On 13 Oct. 1892 there was a by-election at Cirencester, Gloucestershire, which resulted in an election petition after which the number of votes cast for the Conservative and Liberal were found to have been equal. A new election was ordered.

Two examples of majorities of one have occurred. At Durham in the 1895 General Election, Matthew Fowler (Lib.) with 1,111 votes defeated the Hon. Arthur R. D. Elliott (Liberal-Unionist) (1,110 votes) after a recount. At Exeter in the General Election of December 1910 a Liberal victory over the Conservatives by 4 votes was reversed on an election petition to a Conservative win by H. E. Duke K.C. (later the 1st Lord Merrivale) (Unionist) with 4,777 votes to R. H. St. Maur's (Lib.) 4,776 votes.

The smallest majority since "universal" franchise was one of two votes by Abraham John Flint (b. 1903), the National Labour candidate at Ilkeston, Derbyshire, in the 1931 General Election. He received 17,587 votes, compared with 17,585 for G. H. Oliver, D.C.M. (Labour).

Current

The finest economy of effort in getting elected by any member of the present Parliament was a majority of 22 by Mrs. Margaret A. Bain M.P. (Scot. Nat.) with 15,551 votes in Dunbartonshire East over J. S. Barry Henderson (Con.).

Most recounts

The greatest recorded number of recounts has been 7 in the case of Brighton, Kemptown on 16 Oct. 1964 when Dennis H. Hobden (Labour) won by 7 votes and at Peterborough on 31 Mar–1 Apr. 1966 when Sir Harmar-Nicholls Bt. (Conservative) won by 3 votes. The counts from the point of view of the loser Michael J. Ward (Labour) went +163, +163, +2, −2, −6, +1, −2, −3. Lord Harmar-Nicholls, whose final majority was 22, suffered 21 counts in 8 elections as an M.P.

Most Lost Deposits

The highest number of lost deposits is 12 (costing £1,800) by Harold Smith of Oldham (More Prosperous Britain Party) who averaged only 177 votes in the 12 constituencies in which he stood in October 1974.

Most rapid change of fortune

On 3 July 1874 Hardinge Stanley Giffard (Con.), later the 1st Earl of Halsbury (1823–1921), received one vote at Launceston, Cornwall. In 1877 he was returned unopposed for the same seat.

Greatest swing

The greatest swing, at least since 1832, was at the Dartford, Kent by-election when on 27 Mar. 1920 Labour turned a Coalition majority of 9,370 to a win by 9,048. This represented a swing of 38.7 per cent. In 1970 in Antrim, North an Ulster Unionist majority of 22,986 was turned into a Protestant Unionist majority of 2,679 over the sitting Member by Ian Richard Kyle Paisley (b. 8 Apr. 1926). Since there was no Protestant Unionist candidate in 1966 no swing figure was therefore calculable. He gained 41.3% of the poll.

Highest poll

The highest poll in any constituency since "universal" franchise was 93.42 per cent in Fermanagh and South Tyrone, Northern Ireland, at the General Election of 25 Oct. 1951, when there were 62,799 voters from an electorate of 67,219. The Anti-Partition candidate, Mr. Cahir Healy (1877–1970), was elected with a majority of 2,635 votes. The highest poll in any constituency in the Oct. 1974 General Election was 88.68 per cent in Fermanagh and South Tyrone. The highest figure in Great Britain was 85.60 per cent in Carmarthen and the lowest in Chelsea with 49.97%.

HOUSE OF LORDS

Oldest Member

The oldest member ever was the Rt. Hon. the 5th Baron Penrhyn, who was born on 21 Nov. 1865 and died on 3 Feb. 1967, aged 101 years 74 days. The oldest now is the Rt. Hon. Walter Egerton George Lucian Keppel, M.C., ninth Earl of Albemarle (b. 28 Feb. 1882). The oldest peer to make a maiden speech was Lord Maenan (1854–1951) aged 94 years 123 days. (see Oldest creation, Chapter 11)

Youngest Member

The youngest present member of the House of Lords has been H.R.H. the Prince Charles Philip Arthur George, K.G., K.T., G.C.B., the Prince of Wales (b. 14 Nov. 1948). All Dukes of Cornwall, of whom Prince Charles is the 24th, are technically eligible to sit, regardless of age—in his case from his succession on 6 Feb. 1952, aged 3. The 20th and 21st holders, later King George IV (b. 1762) and King Edward VII (b. 1841), were technically entitled to sit from birth. The youngest creation of a life peer under the Peerage Act 1958 has been that of Lord Tanlaw, formerly the Hon. Simon Brooke Mackay (b. 30 Mar. 1934) at the age of 37 years 8 days. However Lady Masham (b. 14 Apr. 1935) was created Baroness Masham of Ilton at the age of 34 years 262 days.

POLITICAL OFFICE HOLDERS

Premiership *Longest term*

No United Kingdom Prime Minister has yet matched in duration the continuous term of office of Great Britain's first Prime Minister the Rt. Hon. Sir Robert Walpole, K.G., later the 1st Earl of Orford (1676–1745), First Lord of the Treasury and Chancellor of the Exchequer for 20 years 326 days from 3 Apr. 1721 to 12 Feb. 1742. The office was not, however, officially recognised until 1905, since when the longest tenure has been that of Herbert Henry Asquith, later the 1st Earl of Oxford and Asquith (1852–1928), with 8 years 243 days from 8 Apr. 1908 to 7 Dec. 1961. This was 7 days longer than the three terms of Sir Winston Churchill, between 1940 and 1955.

Shortest term

The Rt. Hon. William Pulteney, the Earl of Bath (1684–1764) held office for 3 days from 10–12 Feb. 1746 but was unable to form a ministry. The shortest term of any ministry was that of the 1st Duke of Wellington, K.G., G.C.B., G.C.H. (1769–1852), whose third ministry survived only 22 days from 17 Nov. to 9 Dec. 1834.

Most times

The only Prime Minister to have accepted office five times was the Rt. Hon. Stanley Baldwin, later the 1st Earl Baldwin of Bewdley (1867–1947). His ministries were those of 22 May 1923 to 22 Jan. 1924, 4 Nov. 1924 to 5 June 1929, 7 June 1935 to 21 Jan. 1936, from then until the abdication of 12 Dec. 1936 and from then until 28 May 1937.

H.R.H. Prince Charles, Prince of Wales, who was eligible to sit in the House of Lords as Duke of Cornwall since the age of three when his mother succeeded in 1952. (*Associated Press*)

above: The Rt. Hon. Stanley Baldwin (1867–1947), the only one of Britain's 50 Prime Ministers to accept office five times (see p. 178). *(Mansell)*

right: Andrew Mackay (Con.) the youngest MP, elected on 31 Mar. 1977 at the Stechford by-election aged 27 yrs 216 days.

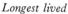

Longest lived

The longest lived Prime Minister of the United Kingdom has been the Rt. Hon. Sir Winston Leonard Spencer-Churchill, K.G., O.M., C.H., T.D., (b. 30 Nov. 1874), who surpassed the age of the Rt. Hon. William Ewart Gladstone (1809–98) on 21 Apr. 1963 and died on 24 Jan. 1965, aged 90 years 55 days. Gladstone's last day in office on 3 Mar. 1894 was when he was 84 years 64 days—having been elected on 18 Aug. 1892.

Youngest

The youngest of Great Britain's 50 Prime Ministers has been the Rt. Hon. the Hon. William Pitt (b. 28 May 1759), who accepted the King's invitation to be First Lord of the Treasury on 19 Dec. 1783, aged 24 years 205 days. He had previously declined on 27 Feb. 1783, when aged 23 years 275 days.

Chancellorship *Longest and shortest tenures*

The Rt. Hon. Sir Robert Walpole, K.G., later the 1st Earl of Orford (1676–1745), served 22 years 5 months as Chancellor of the Exchequer, holding office continuously from 12 Oct. 1715 to 12 Feb. 1742, except for the period from 16 Apr. 1717 to 2 Apr. 1721. The briefest tenure of this office was 26 days in the case of the Baron (later the 1st Earl of) Mansfield (1705–93), from 11 Sept. to 6 Oct. 1767. The only man with four terms in this office was the Rt. Hon. William Ewart Gladstone (1809–98) in 1852–55, 1859–66, 1873–74 and 1880–82.

Foreign Secretaryship *Longest tenures*

The longest term of office of any Foreign Secretary has been the 10 years 196 days of the Most Hon. Robert Stewart, Marquis of Londonderry, formerly Viscount Castlereagh (1769–1822) from 4 Mar. 1812 until his suicide on 16 Sept. 1822. The Most Hon. Robert Arthur Talbot Gascoyne-Cecil, Marquis of Salisbury, K.G., G.C.V.O., in two spells in 1887–92 and 1895–1900 aggregated 11 years 87 days in this office. The longest tenure during this century has been 11 years 75 days by the Rt. Hon. Sir (Robert) Anthony Eden, Earl of Avon, K.G., M.C. (1897–1977) in three spells in 1935–38, 1940–45 and 1951–55.

Colonial Secretaryship *Longest tenures*

The longest term of office has been 19 years 324 days by the Rt. Hon. Henry Bathurst, Earl Bathurst (1762–1834), who was Secretary of State for the Colonial and War Department from 11 June 1812 to 1 May 1827. The longest tenure this century has been the 5 years 61 days of the Rt. Hon. Alan Tindal Lennox-Boyd, Viscount Boyd of Merton, C.H. (b. 18 Nov. 1904) during 1954 to 1959.

Speakership *Longest*

Arthur Onslow (1691–1768) was elected Mr. Speaker on 23 Jan. 1728, at the age of 36. He held the position for 33 years 43 days, until 18 Mar. 1761 allowing for the "lost" 11 days (3–13 Sept. 1752).

M.P.s *Youngest*

Edmund Waller (1606–1687) was the Member of Parliament for Amersham, Buckinghamshire, in the Parliament of 1621, in which year he was 15. The official returns, however, do not show him as actually having taken his seat until two years later when, in the Parliament of 1623–24, he sat as Member for Ilchester, Somerset. In 1435 Henry Long (1420–1490) was returned for an Old Sarum seat also at the age of 15. His precise date of birth is unknown. Minors were debarred in law in 1695 and in fact in 1832. Since that time the youngest Member of Parliament has been the Hon. Esmond Cecil Harmsworth (now the 2nd Viscount Rothermere) who was elected for the Isle of Thanet, Kent, on 28 Nov. 1919, when 21 years 183 days. The youngest M.P. is Andrew James Mackay (b. 27 Aug. 1949) (Conservative) elected on 31 Mar. 1977 at 27 years 216 days for Stechford, Birmingham.

Oldest

The oldest of all members was Samuel Young (b. 14 Feb. 1822), Nationalist M.P. for East Cavan (1892–1918), who died on 18 Apr. 1918, aged 96 years 63 days. The oldest "Father of the House" in Parliamentary history was the Rt. Hon. Charles Pelham Villiers (b. 3 Jan. 1802), who was the Member for Wolverhampton when he died on 16 Jan. 1898, aged 96 years 13 days. He was a Member of Parliament for 63 years 6 days, having been returned at 16 elections. The longest sitting member in the present Parliament is the Rt.

Hon. George Russell Strauss (b. 18 July 1901), Labour member for Lambeth, Vauxhall, who has sat continuously since 1934 and also from 1929–31. He missed election in 1924 by 29 votes. The oldest member is David Weitzman Q.C., M.P. (b. 18 June 1898), member (Labour) for Hackney North, and Stoke Newington.

Longest span

The longest span of service of any M.P., is 63 years 10 months (1 Oct. 1900 to 25 Sept. 1964) by the Rt. Hon. Sir Winston Leonard Spencer-Churchill, K.G., O.M., C.H., T.D. (1874–1965), with a break only from November 1922 to October 1924. The longest unbroken span was that of C.P. Villiers (see above). The longest span in the Palace of Westminster (both Houses of Parliament) has been 73 years by the 10th Earl of Wemyss and March G.C.V.O., who, as Sir Francis Wemyss-Charteris-Douglas, served as M.P. for East Gloucestershire (1841–46) and Haddingtonshire (1847–83) and then took his seat in the House of Lords, dying on 30 June 1914, aged 95 years 330 days.

Women M.P.s *Earliest*

The first woman to be elected to the House of Commons was Mme. Constance Georgine Markievicz (*née* Gore Booth). She was elected as member (Sinn Fein) for St. Patrick's Dublin, in December 1918. The first woman to take her seat was the Viscountess Astor, C. H. (1879–1964) (b. Nancy Witcher Langhorne at Danville, Virginia, U.S.A.; formerly Mrs. Robert Gould Shaw), who was elected Unionist member for the Sutton Division of Plymouth, Devon, on 28 Nov. 1919, and took her seat three days later.

Longest Serving

The longest ever serving woman M.P. has been Baroness Irene Mary Bewick Ward C.H., D.B.E., who fought all 12 General elections (1924–1970) and who served as member for Wallsend (1931–45) and for Tynemouth (1950–74). She shared also the 20th century record for introducing 4 Private Members Bills which became Acts with Sir Robert Gower (1880–1953).

Heaviest

The heaviest M.P. of all-time is believed to have been Cyril Smith M.B.E., Liberal member for Rochdale since October 1972, whose peak reported weight in early 1976 was 29 st. 12 lb. *189,60 kg.*

---

4. MILITARY AND DEFENCE

WAR

Guinness Superlatives Ltd. has published specialist volumes entitled *The Guinness History of Land Warfare* (£4.95) by Kenneth Macksey, *History of Sea Warfare* (£4.95) by Gervis Frere-Cook and Macksey, and *History of Air Warfare* by David Brown, Christopher Shores and Macksey (£6.50).

Longest

The longest of history's countless wars was the "Hundred Years War" between England and France, which lasted from 1338 to 1453 (115 years), although it may be said that the Holy War, comprising the nine Crusades from the First (1096–1104) to the Ninth (1270–91), extended over 195 years.

Shortest

The shortest war on record was that between the United Kingdom and Zanzibar (now part of Tanzania) from 9.02 to 9.40 a.m. on 27 Aug. 1896. The U.K. battle fleet under Rear-Admiral (later Admiral Sir) Harry Holdsworth Rawson (1843–1910) delivered an ultimatum to the self-appointed Sultan Sa'īd Khalid to evacuate his palace and surrender. This was not forthcoming until after 38 minutes of bombardment. Admiral Rawson received the Brilliant Star of Zanzibar (first class) from the new Sultan Hamud ibn Muhammad. It was proposed at one time that elements of the local populace should be compelled to defray the cost of the ammunition used.

Bloodiest

By far the most costly war in terms of human life was World War II (1939–45), in which the total number of fatalities, including battle deaths and civilians of all countries, is estimated to have been 54,800,000 assuming 25 million U.S.S.R. fatalities and 7,800,000 Chinese civilians killed. The country which suffered most was Poland with 6,028,000 or 22.2 per cent of her population of 27,007,000 killed.

In the case of the United Kingdom, however, the heaviest armed forces fatalities occurred in World War I (1914–18), with 765,399 killed out of 5,500,000 engaged (13.9 per cent), compared with 265,000 out of 5,896,000 engaged (4.49 per cent) in World War II. The total death roll from World War I was only 17.7 per cent of that of World War II, *viz* 9,700,000.

In the Paraguayan war of 1864–70 against Brazil, Argentina and Uruguay, their population was reduced from 1,400,000 to 220,000 of whom only 30,000 were adult males.

Bloodiest civil

The bloodiest civil war in history was the T'ai-p'ing ("Great Peace") rebellion, in which peasant sympathizers of the Southern Ming dynasty fought the Manchu Government troops in China from 1851 to 1864. The rebellion was led by the deranged Hung Hsiu-ch'üan (executed) who imagined himself to be a younger brother of Jesus Christ. His force was named *T'ai-p'ing T'ien Kuo* (Heavenly Kingdom of Great Peace). According to the best estimates, the loss of life was between 20,000,000 and 30,000,000, including more than 100,000 killed by Government forces in the sack of Nanking on 19–21 July 1864.

Most costly

The material cost of World War II far transcended that of the rest of history's wars put together and has been estimated at $1.5 million million. The total cost to the Soviet Union was estimated semi-officially in May 1959 at 2,500,000,000,000 roubles (£100,000 million) while a figure of $530,000 million has been estimated for the U.S.A. In the case of the United Kingdom the cost of £34,423 million was over five times as great as that of World War I (£6,700 million) and 158.6 times that of the Boer War of 1899–1902 (£217 million).

Last battle on British soil

The last pitched land battle in Britain was at Culloden Field, Drummossie Moor, near Inverness, Highland, on 16 Apr. 1746. The last Clan battle in Scotland was between Clan Mackintosh and Clan MacDonald at Mulroy, Highland in 1689. The last battle on English soil was the Battle of Sedgemoor, Somerset, on 6 July 1685, when the forces of James II defeated the supporters of Charles II's illegitimate son, James Scott (formerly called Fitzroy or Crofts), the Duke of Monmouth (1649–85). During the Jacobite rising of 1745–46, there was a skirmish at Clifton Moor, Cumbria, on 18 Dec. 1745, when the British forces under Prince William, the Duke of Cumberland (1721–65), brushed with the rebels of Prince Edward Stuart (1720–88) with about 12 killed on the King's side and 5 Highlanders. This was a tactical victory for the Scots under Lord George Murray.

Bloodiest battle *Modern*

The battle with the greatest recorded number of fatalities was the First Battle of the Somme, France from 1 July to 19 Nov. 1916, with more than 1,030,000—614,105 British and French and c. 420,000 (*not* 650,000) German. The gunfire was heard on Hampstead Heath, London. The greatest battle of World War II and the greatest ever conflict of armour was the Battle of Kursk and Oryol which raged for 50 days on 5 July–23 Aug. 1943 on the Eastern front, which involved 1,300,000 Red Army troops with 3,600 tanks, 20,000 guns and 3,130 aircraft in repelling a German Army Group which had 2,700 tanks. The final investment of Berlin by the Red Army on 16 Apr.–2 May 1945 involved 3,500,000 men; 52,000 guns and mortars; 7,750 tanks and 11,000 aircraft on both sides.

Ancient

Modern historians give no credence to the casualty figures attached to ancient battles, such as the 250,000 reputedly killed at Plataea (Greeks v. Persians) in 479 B.C. or the 200,000 allegedly killed in a single day.

British

The bloodiest battle fought on British soil was the Battle of Towton, in North Yorkshire, on 29 Mar. 1461, when 36,000 Yorkists defeated 40,000 Lancastrians. The total loss has been estimated at between 28,000 and 38,000 killed. A figure of 80,000 British dead was attributed by Tacitus to the battle of A.D. 61 between Queen Boudicca (Boadicea) of the Iceni and the Roman Governor of Britain Suetonius Paulinus, for the reputed loss of only 400 Romans in an army of 10,000. The site of the battle is unknown but may have been near Borough Hill, Daventry, Northamptonshire, or more probably near Hampstead Heath, Greater London. Prior to this battle the Romans had lost up to 70,000 in Colchester and London.

Greatest naval battle

The greatest number of ships and aircraft ever involved in a sea-air action was 231 ships and 1,996 aircraft in the Battle of Leyte Gulf, in the Philippines. It raged from 22 to 27 Oct. 1944, with 166 Allied and 65 Japanese warships engaged, of which 26 Japanese and 6 U.S. ships were sunk. In addition 1,280 U.S. and 716 Japanese aircraft were engaged. The greatest naval battle of modern times was the Battle of Jutland on 31 May 1916, in which 151 Royal Navy warships were involved against 101 German warships. The Royal Navy lost 14 ships and 6,097 men and the German fleet 11 ships and 2,545 men. The greatest of ancient naval battles was the Battle of Salamis, Greece on 23 Sept. 480 B.C. There were an estimated 800 vessels in the defeated Persian fleet and 310 in the victorious Greek fleet with a possible involvement of 190,000 men.

Invasion Greatest *Seaborne*

The greatest invasion in military history was the Allied land, air and sea operation against the Normandy coasts of France on D-day, 6 June 1944. Thirty-eight convoys of 745 ships moved in on the first three days, supported by 4,066 landing craft, carrying 185,000 men and 20,000 vehicles, and 347 minesweepers. The air assault comprised 18,000 paratroopers from 1,087 aircraft. The 42 available divisions possessed an air support from 13,175 aircraft. Within a month 1,100,000 troops, 200,000 vehicles and 750,000 tons of stores were landed. The Allied invasion of Sicily on 10–12 July 1943 involved the landing of 181,000 men in 3 days.

Airborne

The largest airborne invasion was the Anglo-American assault of three divisions (34,000 men), with 2,800 aircraft and 1,600 gliders, near Arnhem, in the Netherlands, on 17 Sept. 1944.

Last on the soil of Great Britain

The last invasion of Great Britain occurred on 12 Feb. 1797, when the Irish-American adventurer General Tate landed at Carreg Gwastad with 1,400 French troops. They surrendered near Fishguard, Dyfed, to Lord Cawdor's force of the Castlemartin Yeomanry and some local inhabitants armed with pitchforks. The U.K. Crown Dependency of the Channel Islands were occupied by German armed forces from 30 June 1940 to 8 May 1945.

Greatest evacuation

The greatest evacuation in military history was that carried out by 1,200 Allied naval and civil craft from the beach-head at Dunkerque (Dunkirk), France, between 27 May and 4 June 1940. A total of 338,226 British and French troops were taken off.

Worst sieges

The worst siege in history was the 880-day siege of Leningrad, U.S.S.R. by the German Army from 30 Aug. 1941 until 27 Jan. 1944. The best estimate is that between 1.3 and 1.5 million defenders and citizens died. The longest recorded siege was that of Azotus (now Ashdod), Israel which according to Herodotus was invested by Psamtik I of Egypt for 29 years in the period 664–610 B.C.

DEFENCE

The estimated level of spending on armaments throughout the world in 1974 was $225,000 million £97,825 *million*. This represents £24.76p per person per annum, or more than 6 per cent of the world's total production of goods and services. It was estimated in 1974 that there were 15.5 million full-time armed force regulars or conscripts.

The budgetted expenditure on defence by the U.S. government for the year ending 30 June 1977 was $101,100 million (£57,700 *million*) or 6.9 per cent of the country's Gross National Product.

Western estimates of the U.S.S.R.'s defence expenditure in 1975 were drastically raised following an inadvertent publication in *Finanzy* SSR that the budget heading "other" included "state reserves" which in turn included military hardware. The 1975 total was revised to 60–63 billion roubles, or some 13% of G.N.P.

At the other extreme is Andorra, whose defence budget, voted in 1972, was reduced to £2.00.

ARMED FORCES

Largest

Numerically, the country with the largest regular armed force is the U.S.S.R., with 3,650,000 at mid-1976 compared with the U.S.A.'s 2,086,000 at the same date. With the end of conscription this is likely to sink to 1,800,000 during 1977. The Chinese People's Liberation Army, which includes naval and air services, has 3,525,000 regulars, but there is also a civilian home guard militia once claimed to be 200 million strong but regarded by the Institute of Strategic Studies to have an effective element of about 5,000,000.

Navies *Largest*

The largest navy in the world in terms of man power is the United States Navy, with a manpower of 539,650 and 196,000 Marines in mid-1977. The active strength in 1977 included 13 aircraft carriers, 41 Strategic Missile Submarines, 64 attack nuclear submarines and 9 diesel attack submarines, 71 Guided Missile Warships (26 cruisers, 39 destroyers and 6 frigates) and 60 amphibious warfare ships.

The U.S.S.R. navy has a larger submarine fleet of 390 boats of which 125 are nuclear powered, 55 of them carrying strategic atomic missiles. It has more than 2,600 vessels of all kinds.

The strength of the Royal Navy in mid-1977 included an aircraft carrier, 4 nuclear submarines with strategic atomic missiles; 9 fleet and 19 patrol submarines; 2 helicopter and 8 light cruisers, 3 destroyers, 61 frigates and 2 assault ships among a total fleet of 500 of all types. The uniformed strength was 76,200 including Fleet Air Arm and Royal Marines in mid-1976. In 1914 the Royal Navy had 542 warships including 72 capital ships with 16 building.

Armies *Oldest*

The oldest army in the world is the 83-strong Swiss Guard in the Vatican City, with a regular foundation dating back to 21 Jan. 1506. Its origins, however, extend back before 1400.

Largest

Numerically, the world's largest army is that of the People's Republic of China, with a total strength of about 3,000,000 in mid-1976. The total size of the U.S.S.R.'s army in mid-1975 was estimated at 1,825,000 men, believed to be organised into about 168 divisions with a maximum strength of 12,000 each. The strength of the British Army was 177,600 on 30 Apr. 1976. The NATO agreement requires not less than 55,000 in West Germany. The basic strength maintained in Northern Ireland is 14,500 but this fluctuates.

Oldest and Youngest soldiers

The oldest old soldier of all time was probably John B. Salling of the army of the Confederate States of America and the last accepted survivor of the U.S. Civil War (1861–65). He died in Kingsport, Tennessee, U.S.A., on 16 Mar. 1959, aged 113 years 1 day. The oldest Chelsea pensioner, based *only* on the evidence of his tombstone, was the 111-year-old William Hiseland (b. 6 Aug. 1620, d. 7 Feb. 1732). The

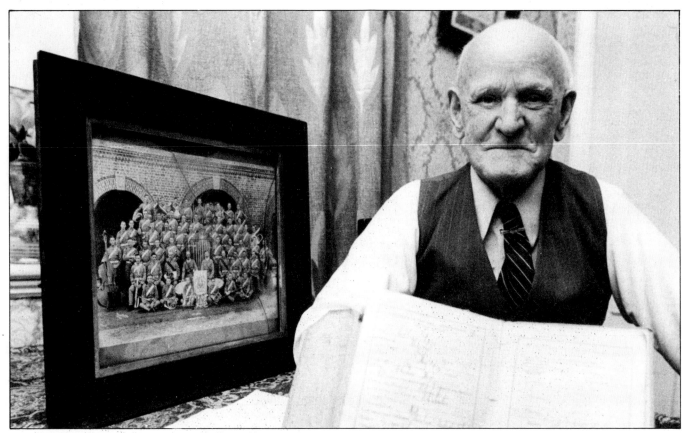

Britain's youngest enlisted soldier, William Price, among his souvenirs. He joined the army at Aldershot nine days before his 12th birthday.

longest serving British soldier has been Field Marshall Sir William Maynard Gomm G.C.B. (1784–1875), who was an ensign in 1794 and as Constable of the Tower to his death aged 91.

William Frederick Price (b. 1 June 1891) was enlisted into the Army at Aldershot on 23 May 1903 aged 11 years 356 days.

Youngest Conscripts

President Francisco Macias Nguema of Equatorial Guinea decreed in March 1976 compulsory military service for all boys between 7 and 14. Any parent refusing to hand over his or her son "will be imprisoned or shot".

Tallest soldiers

The tallest soldier of all time was Väinö Myllyrinne (1909–63) who was inducted into the Finnish Army when he was 7 ft 3 in *2,21 m* and later grew to 8 ft 1¼ in *2,47 m*. The British Army's tallest soldier was Benjamin Crow who was signed on at Lichfield in November 1947 when he was 7 ft 1 in *2,15 m* tall. Edward Evans (1924–58), who later grew to 7 ft 8½ in *2,34 m* was in the Army when he was 6 ft 10 in *2,08 m*.

British regimental records

The oldest regular regiment in the British Army is the Royal Scots, raised in French service in 1633, though the Buffs (Royal East Kent Regiment) can trace back their origin to independent companies in Dutch pay as early as 1572. The Coldstream Guards, raised in 1650, were, however, placed on the establishment of the British Army before the Royal Scots and the Buffs. The oldest armed body in the United Kingdom is the Queen's Bodyguard of the Yeoman of the Guard formed in 1495. The Honourable Artillery Company, formed from the Finsbury Archers, received its charter from Henry VIII in 1537 but this lapsed until reformed in 1610. The infantry regiment with most battle honours is The Queen's Lancashire Regiment with 188.

The most senior regiment of the Reserve Army is The Royal Monmouthshire Royal Engineers (Militia) formed in 1572 and never disbanded.

Longest march

The longest march in military history was the famous Long March by the Chinese Communists in 1934–35. In 368 days, of which 268 days were of movement, from October to October, their force of 90,000 covered 6,000 miles *9 650 km* from Kiangsi to Yenan in Shensi *via* Yünnan. They crossed 18 mountain ranges and six major rivers and lost all but 22,000 of their force in continual rear-guard actions against Nationalist Kuo-min-tang (K.M.T.) forces.

Most rapid march

The most rapid recorded march by foot-soldiers was one of 12 Spanish leagues (42 miles *67 km*) in 26 hours on 28–29 July 1809, by the Light Brigade under Brigadier- (later Major-) General Robert Craufurd (1764–1812), coming to the relief of Lieut-Gen. Sir Arthur Wellesley, later Field Marshall the 1st Duke of Wellington (1769–1852), after the Battle of Talavera (Talavera de la Reina, Toledo, Spain) in the Peninsular War.

Air Forces *Oldest*

The earliest autonomous air force is the Royal Air Force whose origin began with the Royal Flying Corps (created 13 May 1912); the Air Battalion of the Royal Engineers (1 Apr. 1911) and the Corps of Royal Engineers Balloon Section (1878) which was first operational in Bechuanaland (now Botswana) in 1884.

Largest

The greatest Air Force of all time was the United States Army Air Force (now called the U.S. Air Force), which had 79,908 aircraft in July 1944 and 2,411,294 personnel in March 1944. The U.S. Air Force including strategic air forces had 645,000 personnel and 5,000 combat aircraft in mid-1974. The U.S.S.R. Air Force, including Air Defence Forces, with about 900,000 men in mid-1974, had 8,000 combat aircraft. In addition, the U.S.S.R.'s Offensive Strategic Rocket

The 189 ton German World War II Panzer Kampfwagen Maus II, the heaviest tank ever built. (*Illustration by Mike Roffe*)

Forces had about 350,000 operational personnel in mid-1974. The strength of the Royal Air Force was 98,200 with some 500 combat aircraft in mid 1974.

BOMBS
Heaviest
The heaviest conventional bomb ever used operationally was the Royal Air Force's "Grand Slam", weighing 22,000 lb. *9 975 kg* and measuring 25 ft 5 in *7,74 m* long, dropped on Bielefeld railway viaduct, Germany, on 14 Mar. 1945. In 1949 the United States Air Force tested a bomb weighing 42,000 lb. *19 050 kg* at Muroc Dry Lake, California, U.S.A.

Atomic
The two atom bombs dropped on Japan by the United States in 1945 each had an explosive power equivalent to that of 20,000 short tons *20 kilotons* of trinitrotoluene ($C_7H_5O_6N_3$), called T.N.T. The one dropped on Hiroshima, known as "Little Boy", was 10 ft *3,04 m* long and weighed 9,000 lb. *4 080 kg*. The most powerful thermo-nuclear device so far tested is one with a power equivalent to 57,000,000 short tons of T.N.T., or 57 megatons, detonated by the U.S.S.R. in the Novaya Zemlya area at 8.33 a.m. G.M.T. on 30 Oct. 1961. The shock wave was detected to have circled the world three times, taking 36 hours 27 min for the first circuit. Some estimates put the power of this device at between 62 and 90 megatons. On 9 Aug. 1961, Nikita Khrushchyov, then the Chairman of the Council of Ministers of the U.S.S.R., declared that the Soviet Union was capable of constructing a 100-megaton bomb, and announced the possession of one in East Berlin, Germany, on 16 Jan. 1963. It has been estimated that such a bomb would make a crater 19 miles *30 km* in diameter and would cause serious fires at a range of from 36 to 40 miles *58–64 km*. The atom bomb became inevitable with the meso-thorium experiments of Otto Hahn, Fritz Strassman and Lise Meitner on 17 Dec. 1938. Work started in the U.S.S.R. on atomic bombs in June 1942 although their first chain reaction was not achieved until December 1945 by Dr. Igor Vasilyevich Kurchatov. The patent for the fusion or H bomb was filed in the United States on 26 May 1946 by Dr. Janos (John) von Neumann (1903–57), a Hungarian-born mathematician, and Dr. Klaus Julius Emil Fuchs (born in Germany 29 Dec. 1911), the defector physicist.

Largest nuclear arsenal
The International Institute for Strategic Studies estimate that if 3 of the 4 known new ICBM (Inter-Continental Ballistic Missiles) systems now being developed in the U.S.S.R. are fully deployed their capacity would be to deliver 7,000 separately-targeted nuclear warheads in the megaton range from 1,527 ICBM's and 845 SLBM's (submarine launched).

No official estimate has been published of the potential power of the device known as Doomsday, but this far surpasses any

tested weapon. A 50,000 megaton cobalt-salted device has been mooted which could kill the entire human race except those who were deep underground and who stayed there for more than five years.

Largest "conventional" explosion
The largest use of conventional explosive was for the demolition of German U-Boat pens at Heligoland on 18 Apr. 1947. A charge of 3,997 tons *4 061 tonnes* was detonated by E. C. Jellis aboard H.M.S. *Lassoe* lying 9 miles *14,4 km* out to sea.

TANKS
Note—Guinness Superlatives Ltd. has published a specialist volume entitled *The Guinness Book of Tank Facts and Feats* (2nd edition) by Kenneth Macksey (£4.95). This work deals with all the aspects of the development and history of the tank and other armoured fighting vehicles in greater detail.

Earliest
The first fighting tank was "Mother" *alias* "Big Willie" built by William Foster & Co. Ltd. of Lincoln, and completed on 8 Sept. 1915. Tanks were first taken into action by the Machine Gun Corps (Heavy Section), which later became the Royal Tank Corps, at the battle of Flers, in France, on 15 Sept. 1916. The Mark I Male tank, which was armed with a pair of 6-pounders guns and two machine-guns, weighed 28 tons *28,4 tonnes* and was driven by a motor developing 105 horse-power which gave it a maximum road speed of 3 to 4 m.p.h. *4,8–6,4 km/h*.

Heaviest
The heaviest tank ever constructed was the German Panzer Kampfwagen Maus II, which weighed 189 tons *192 tonnes*. By 1945 it had reached only the experimental stage and was not proceeded with.

The heaviest operational tank used by any army was the 81.5 ton *82,8 tonnes* 13-man French Char de Rupture 2C bis of 1923. It carried a 155 mm. howitzer and had two 250 h.p. engines giving a maximum speed of 8 m.p.h. *12 km/h*. On 7 Nov. 1957, in the annual military parade in Moscow, U.S.S.R., a Soviet tank possibly heavier than the German Jagd Tiger II (71.7 tons *72,8 tonnes*), built by Henschel, and certainly heavier than the Stalin III, was displayed.

The heaviest British tank ever built was the 78-ton *79 tonnes* prototype "Tortoise". With a crew of seven and a designed speed of 12 m.p.h. *19 km/h*, this tank had a width two inches *5 cm* less than that of the one-time operational 65-ton *66 tonnes* "Conqueror". The most heavily armed is the 52-ton *52,8 tonnes* "Chieftain", put into service in November 1966, with a 120 mm gun.

GUNS
Earliest
Although it cannot be accepted as proved, the best opinion is that the earliest guns were constructed in North Africa,

possibly by Arabs, in *c.* 1250. The earliest representation of an English gun is contained in an illustrated manuscript dated 1326 at Oxford. The earliest anti-aircraft gun was an artillery piece on a high angle mounting used in the Franco-Prussian War of 1870 by the Prussians against French balloons.

Largest

The remains of the most massive gun ever constructed were found near Frankfurt am Main, Germany, in 1945. It was the 'Schwerer Gustav" or "Dora", which had a barrel 94.7 ft *28,87 m* long, with a calibre of 800 mm (31.5 in), and a breech weighing 108 tons *109 tonnes*. The maximum charge was 4,409 lb. *2 000 kg* of cordite to fire a shell weighing 4.7 tons *4 800 kg* a distance of 34 miles *55 km*. The maximum projectile was one of 7 tons/*tonnes* with a range of 22 miles *35 km*. Each gun with its carriage weighed 1,323 tons *1 344 tonnes* and required a crew of 1,500 men.

During the 1914–18 war the British army used a gun of 18 in *457 mm* calibre. The barrel alone weighed 125 tons *127 tonnes*. In World War II the "Bochebuster", a train-mounted howitzer with a calibre of 18 in *457 mm* firing a 2,500 lb. *1 133 kg* shell to a maximum range of 22,800 yds *20 850 m*, was used from 1940 onwards as part of the Kent coast defences.

Greatest range

The greatest range ever attained by a gun was achieved by the H.A.R.P. (High Altitude Research Project) gun consisting of two 16.5 in *419 mm* calibre barrels in tandem in Barbados. In 1968 a 200 lb. *90 kg* projectile was fired to a height of 400,000 ft (75¾ miles *121,9 km*). The static V.3 underground firing tubes built in 50 degree shafts near Mimoyecques, near Calais, France to bombard London were never operative due to R.A.F. bombing.

The famous long range gun, which shelled Paris in World War I, was the *Kaiser Wilhelm geschütz* with a calibre of 220 mm (*8.66 in*), a designed range of 79.5 miles *127,9 km* and an achieved range of 76 miles *122 km* from the Forest of Cérpy in March 1918. The Big Berthas were of greater calibre and of lesser range.

Mortars

The largest mortars ever constructed were Mallets mortar (Woolwich Arsenal, London, 1857), and the "Little David" of World War II, made in the U.S.A. Each had a calibre of 36¼ in *920 mm*, but neither was ever used in action. The heaviest mortar used was the German 600 mm *23.6 in* railway-mounted siege piece known as "Karl" before Stalingrad, U.S.S.R.

Largest cannon

The highest calibre cannon ever constructed is the *Tsar Puchka* (King of Cannons), now housed in the Kremlin, Moscow, U.S.S.R. It was built in the 16th century with a bore of 36 in *915 mm* and a barrel 17 ft *5,18 m* long. It was designed to fire cannon balls weighing 2 tons but was never used. The Turks fired up to seven shots per day from a bombard 26 ft *7,92 m* long, with an internal calibre of 42 in *1 066 mm* against the walls of Constantinople (now Istanbul) from 12 Apr. to 29 May 1453. It was dragged by 60 oxen and 200 men and fired a stone cannon ball weighing 1,200 lb. *544 kg*.

Military engines

The largest military catapults, or onagers, were capable of throwing a missile weighing 60 lb. *27 kg* a distance of 500 yds *457 m*.

5. JUDICIAL

LEGISLATION AND LITIGATION

Statutes *Oldest*
The earliest known judicial code was that of King Ur-Hammu

during the third dynasty of Ur, Iraq, in *c.* 2145 B.C. The oldest English statute in the Statute Book is a section of the Statute of Marlborough of 1267, retitled in 1948 "The Distress Act, 1267". Some statutes enacted by Henry II (d. 1189) and earlier kings are even more durable as they have been assimilated in to the Common Law. An extreme example is Ine's Law concerning the administration of shires *c.* 8 A.D.

Longest in the United Kingdom
Measured in bulk the longest statute of the United Kingdom, is the Income Tax and Corporation Tax Act, 1970, which ran to 540 sections, 15 schedules and 670 pages. It is 1½ in *37 mm* thick and costs £2.80. However, its 540 sections are surpassed in number by the 748 of the Merchant Shipping Act, 1894.

Of old statutes, 31 George III XIV, the Land Tax Act of 1791, written on parchment, consists of 780 skins forming a roll 1,170 ft *360 m* long.

Shortest
The shortest statute is the Parliament (Qualification of Women) Act, 1918, which runs to 27 operative words—"A woman shall not be disqualified by sex or marriage from being elected to or sitting or voting as a Member of the Commons House of Parliament". Section 2 contains a further 14 words giving the short title.

Most inexplicable
Certain passages in several Acts have always defied interpretation and the most inexplicable must be a matter of opinion. A Judge of the Court of Session of Scotland has sent the Editors his candidate which reads, "In the Nuts (unground), (other than ground nuts) Order, the expression nuts shall have reference to such nuts, other than ground nuts, as would but for this amending Order not qualify as nuts (unground) (other than ground nuts) by reason of their being nuts (unground)."

Earliest English patent

The earliest of all known English patents was that granted by Henry VI in 1449 to Flemish-born John of Utyman for making the coloured glass required for the windows of Eton College. The peak number of applications for patents filed in the United Kingdom in any one year was 63,614 in 1969. The shortest, concerning a harrow attachment, of 48 words was filed on 14 May 1956 while the longest, comprising 2,318 pages of text and 495 pages of drawings, was filed on 31 Mar. 1965 by I.B.M. to cover a computer.

Most protracted litigation

The longest contested law suit ever recorded ended in Poona, India on 28 Apr. 1966, when Balasaheb Patloji Thorat received a favourable judgment on a suit filed by his ancestor Maloji Thorat 761 years earlier in 1205. The points at issue were rights of presiding over public functions and precedences at religious festivals.

The dispute over the claim of the Prior and Convent (now the Dean and Chapter) of Durham Cathedral to administer the spiritualities of the diocese during a vacancy in the See grew fierce in 1283. It flared up again in 1672 and 1890; an attempt in November 1975 to settle the issue, then 692 years old, was unsuccessful. Neither side admit the legitimacy of writs of appointment issued by the other even though identical persons are named.

Longest British trial

The longest trial in the annals of British justice was the Tichborne personation case. The civil trial began on 11 May 1871, lasted 103 days and collapsed on 6 Mar. 1872. The criminal trial went on for 188 days, resulting in a sentence on 28 Feb. 1874 for two counts of perjury (two 7 year consecutive terms of imprisonment with hard labour) on the London-born Arthur Orton, *alias* Thomas Castro (1834–98), who claimed to be Roger Charles Tichborne (1829–54), the elder brother of Sir Alfred Joseph Doughty-Tichborne, 11th Bt. (1839–66). The whole case, thus spanned 1025 days. The jury were out for only 30 minutes.

The impeachment of Warren Hastings (1732–1818), which began in 1788, dragged on for seven years until 23 Apr. 1795, but the trial lasted only 149 days. He was appointed a member of the Privy Council in 1814.

The longest criminal trial held at the "Old Bailey" (opened in 1907) has been that of 6 men and 1 woman before Mr. Justice Swanwick which opened on 11 Nov. 1976. They were charged with the murders of William Moseley and Michael Cornwall. By the 112th day on 9 May 1977 the evidence had run into 3,200,000 words.

The £21 million claim against the U.K. government by the Ocean Islanders, Pacific before Mr. Justice Megarry finished after 226 days on 3 Dec. 1976 with 7,000,000 words on evidence.

Murder

The longest murder trial in Britain was that of Reginald Dudley, 51 and Robert Maynard, 46 in the Torso Murder of Billy Moseley and Micky Cornwall which ran from November 1976 to 17 June 1977 with 136 trial days. Both men were sentenced to life (minimun 15 years) imprisonment. The costs were estimated to exceed £500,000.

The shortest recorded British murder hearings were *R. v. Murray* on 28 Feb. 1957 and *R. v. Cawley* at Winchester Assizes on 14 Dec. 1959. The proceedings occupied only 30 sec on each occasion.

Divorce

The longest trial of a divorce case in Britain was *Gibbons v. Gibbons and Roman and Halperin*. On 19 Mar. 1962, after 28 days, Mr. Alfred George Boyd Gibbons was granted a decree *nisi* against his wife Dorothy for adultery with Mr. John Halperin of New York City, N.Y., U.S.A.

Longest address

The longest address in a British court was in *Globe and Phoenix Gold Mining Co. Ltd. v. Amalgamated Properties of Rhodesia*. Mr. William Henry Upjohn, K.C. (1853–1941) concluded his speech on 22 Sept. 1916, having addressed the court for 45 days.

The Hon. Justice Sir Robert Megarry who tried the £75,000, 226 day long Ocean Island case in 1975–76. He is also the author of the famous book "Miscellany at Law". (*UPI*)

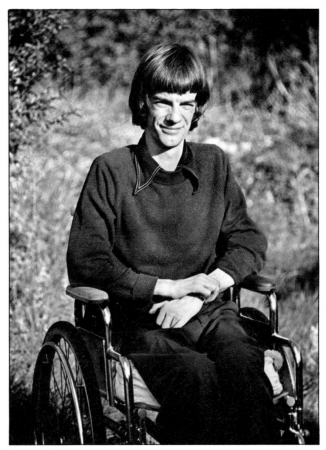

Max Bowker, the recipient of the highest damages ever awarded for personal injury by a British court, £132,970, for a car accident in 1971 (see p. 186).

Highest bail *World*

The highest amount ever demanded as bail was $46,500,000 (*then £16,608,333*) against Antonio De Angelis in a civil damages suit by the Harbor Tank Storage Co. filed in the Superior Court, Jersey City, New Jersey, U.S.A. on 16 Jan. 1964 in the Salad Oil Swindle. He was released on 4 June 1972.

Great Britain

The highest bail figure in a British court is £250,000 granted to the former Hong Kong policeman, chief superintendent Peter Godber, 52 at Bow Street Court, Greater London on 16 May 1974 when charged with bribery. This consisted of a maximum of four sureties aggregating £200,000 and £50,000 in his own recognisance.

Longest arbitration

The longest arbitration (under the 1950 Act) on record has been the Royce Arbitration. It lasted 239 days and concerned the Milchell Construction Co. and the East Anglian Regional Hospital Board over the building of Peterborough Hospital.

Best attended trial

The greatest attendance at any trial was that of Major Jesús Sosa Blanco, aged 51, for an alleged 108 murders. At one point in the 12½ hr trial (5.30 p.m. to 6 a.m., 22–23 Jan. 1959), 17,000 people were present in the Havana Sports Palace, Cuba.

Shortest Trial

An ill-founded prosecution under the Air Navigation Order, 1974 against a pilot at Edinburgh airport was timed at No. 1 Sheriff Court, Edinburgh on 1 Mar. 1977 to have lasted 7 seconds. Sheriff Skae uttered two words—"Not Guilty".

Greatest Damages *Personal injury World*

The greatest personal injury damages ever awarded were to Janelle Lynn Stearns, 12, against Park Avenue Hospital Inc.

185

and an anaesthetist Dr. Howard K. Gifford in settlement for alleged medical malpractice resulting in severe brain damage following a tonsillectomy at Pomona, California in May 1973. If she lives to the average expectation of 63.9 additional years the payments will total $26,541,832. The single payment personal injuries record was $6,300,000 (*then £3 million*) awarded to Thomas Hooks, 18, of Venice, Illinois for diving off a faultily constructed board in a hotel swimming pool and thereby paralysing himself in Washington on 27 May 1975.

The highest damages ever actually paid have been $14,387,674, following upon the crash of a private aircraft at South Lake, Tahoe, California, U.S.A. on 21 Feb. 1967, to the sole survivor Ray Rosendin, 45, by the Santa Clara Superior Court on 8 Mar. 1972. Rosendin received *inter alia* $1,069,374 for the loss of both legs and disabling arm injuries; $1,213,129 for the loss of his wife and $10,500,000 punitive damages against Avco-Lyconing Corporation which allegedly violated Federal regulations when it rebuilt the aircraft engine owned by Rosendin Corporation.

Great Britain

The highest damages for personal injury ever awarded in the United Kingdom court were for £132,970.00 in the Queen's Bench Division by Mr. Justice Talbot on 17th February 1977 to Mr. Max Bowker of Reading against Mrs. Vivienne Jean Rose in whose car he was travelling when it was involved in an accident in 1971. He had been effectually paralysed below the waist.

On 5 Feb. 1960, the Dublin High Court awarded £87,402 damages for motor injuries to Mr. Kevin P. McMorrow, aged 38, of County Leitrim, against his driver Mr. Edward Knott. It is understood that, after an appeal, a settlement was made out of court for £50,000.

Breach of contract

The greatest damages ever awarded for a breach of contract were £610,392, awarded on 16 July 1930 to the Bank of Portugal against the printers Waterlow & Sons Ltd., of London, arising from their unauthorized printing of 580,000 five-hundred escudo notes in 1925. This award was upheld in the House of Lords on 28 Apr. 1932. One of the perpetrators, Arthur Virgilio Alves Reis, served 16 years (1930–46) in gaol.

Breach of promise

The largest sum involved in a breach of promise suit in the United Kingdom was £50,000, accepted in 1913 by Miss Daisy Markham, *alias* Mrs. Annie Moss (d. 20 Aug. 1962, aged 76), in settlement against the 6th Marquess of North-ampton (b. 6 Aug. 1885).

Defamation *World*

A sum of $16,800,000 (£6,720,000) was awarded to Dr. John J. Wild, 58, at the Hennepin District Court, Minnesota, U.S.A., on 30 Nov. 1972 against The Minnesota Foundation and others for defamation, bad-faith termination of a contract, interference with professional business relationship and $10.8 million in punitive damages. These amounts are unappealed.

The greatest damages for defamation ever awarded in the United Kingdom were £117,000, awarded on 21 July 1961 in *The Rubber Improvement Co. Ltd. v. Associated Newspapers Ltd.* for 51 words which appeared in the *Daily Mail* of 23 Dec. 1958. The company was represented by Colin Duncan, M.C. (now a Q.C.) and Mr. (now Sir) Helenus Patrick Joseph Milmo, Q.C. (b. 24 Aug. 1908), who since became a judge. After appeal proceedings by both sides this action was settled out of court for a substantially smaller amount.

The largest libel settlement made has been one for $600,000 (*then £343,000*) by the San Francisco Examiner's publishers, the Hearst Corporation in response to a $32 million (*£18 million*) suit by the Synanon Foundation Inc. and its founder Charles E. Dederich on 1 July 1976 for adverse news articles.

Greatest compensation

William De Palma (b. 1938) of Whittier, California, agreed to a $750,000 settlement for 16 months wrongful imprisonment in McNeil Island Federal Prison, on 12 Aug. 1975 after a 15 year sentence for armed robbery in Buena Park on forged finger print evidence in 1968. The greatest Crown compensation in Britain for wrongful imprisonment has been £17,500 paid to Laszio Virag, 35, who had been sentenced to 10 years imprisonment at Gloucester assizes in 1969 for theft and shooting and wounding a police officer. His acceptance of this sum was announced on 23 Dec. 1974 after his having been released in April 1974 on grounds of mistaken identification.

Greatest Alimony

The highest alimony awarded by a court has been $2,261,000 (*then £983,000*) against George Storer Sr., 74, in favour of his third wife Dorothy, 73, in Miami, Florida on 29 Oct. 1974. Mr Storer, a broadcasting executive, was also ordered to pay his ex-wife's attorney $200,000 (*then £86,950*) in fees.

Greatest Divorce Settlement

The greatest amount ever paid in a divorce settlement is $9,500,000 (*then £3,393,000*) paid by Edward J. Hudson to Mrs. Cecil Amelia Blaffer Hudson, aged 43. This award was made on 28 Feb. 1963 at the Domestic Relations Court, Houston, Texas, U.S.A. Mrs. Hudson was, reputedly, already worth $14,000,000 (*then £5,000,000*).

Patent case

The greatest settlement ever made in a patent infringement suit is $9,250,000 (*then £3,303,000*), paid in April 1952 by the Ford Motor Company to the Ferguson Tractor Co. for a claim filed in January 1948.

Largest Suit

The highest amount of damages ever sought is $675,000,000,000,000 (equivalent to more than 10 times the U.S. national wealth) in a suit by Mr. I. Walton Bader brought in the U.S. District Court, New York City on 14 Apr. 1971 against General Motors and others for polluting all 50 states.

Highest Costs

The highest costs in English legal history arose from the alleged infringement of a patent owned by General Tire and Rubber Co. of America by the Firestone Tyre and Rubber Co. The case was heard by 17 judges over 5½ years ending on 16 Apr. 1975 in a reduction of damages from £1,388,000 to £311,000 but costs were an estimated £500,000.

Income tax *Highest reward*

The greatest amount paid for information concerning a case of income tax delinquency was $79,999.93 (*then £28,571*) paid by the United States Internal Revenue Service to a group of informers. Payments are limited to 10 per cent of the amount recovered as a direct result of information laid. Informants are often low-income accountants or women scorned.

Greatest lien

The greatest lien ever imposed by a court is 40,000 million lire (£27 million) on 9 Apr. 1974 upon Vittorio and Ida Riva in Milan for back taxes allegedly due on a chain of cotton mills around Turin, Italy, inherited by their brother Felice (now safe in Beirut) in 1960.

Wills *Shortest*

The shortest valid will in the world is "Vše zene", the Czech for "All to wife", written and dated 19 Jan. 1967 by Herr Karl Tausch of Langen, Hesse, Germany. The shortest will contested but subsequently admitted to probate in English law was the case of *Thorn v. Dickens* in 1906. It consisted of the three words "All for Mother".

Longest

The longest will on record was that of Mrs. Frederica Cook (U.S.A.), in the early part of the century. It consisted of four bound volumes containing 95,940 words.

Judge Oldest *World*

The oldest recorded active judge was Judge Albert R. Alexander (1859–1966) of Plattsburg, Missouri, U.S.A. He was the magistrate and probate judge of Clinton County until his retirement aged 105 years 8 months on 9 July 1965.

Great Britain
The greatest recorded age at which any British judge has sat on a bench was 93 years 9 months in the case of Sir William Francis Kyffin Taylor, G.B.E., K.C. (later Lord Maenan), who was born on 9 July 1854 and retired as presiding judge of the Liverpool Court of Passage in April 1948, having held that position since 1903. The greatest age at which a House of Lords judgment has been given is 92 in the case of the 1st Earl of Halsbury (b. 3 Sept. 1823) in 1916.

Judge Youngest
No collated records on the ages of judicial appointments exist. However Thomas J. Boynton (b. Amherst, Ohio on 31 Aug. 1838) is known to have been appointed Federal Judge at Key West, Florida on 20 Jan. 1864 aged 25 years 142 days. The youngest certain age at which any English judge has been appointed is 31, in the case of Sir Francis Buller (b. 17 Mar. 1746), who was appointed Second Judge of the County Palatine of Chester on 27 Nov. 1777, and Puisne Judge of the King's Bench on 6 May 1778, aged 32 years 1 month.

Youngest English Q.C.
The earliest age at which a barrister has taken silk since 1900 is 33 years 8 months in the case of Mr. (later the Rt. Hon. Sir) Francis Raymond Evershed (1899–1966) in April 1933. He was later Lord Evershed, Master of the Rolls.

Highest paid lawyer
It was estimated that Jerry Giesler (1886–1962), an attorney in Los Angeles, California, U.S.A., averaged $50,000 (then £17,850) in fees for each case which he handled during the latter part of his career. Currently, the most highly paid lawyer is generally believed to be Louis Nizer (b. London 6 Feb. 1902) of New York City, N.Y., U.S.A.

Most successful advocate
Sir Lionel Luckhoo K.C.M.G., C.B.E. senior partner of Luckhoo and Luckhoo of Georgetown, Guyana succeeded in getting his 200th successive murder charge acquittal by 1 Mar. 1977.

Deadliest Prosecutor
Joe Freeman Britt, District Attorney, Sixteenth Judicial District, North Carolina, U.S.A. obtained 23 death verdicts in 28 months to mid-1976 when he had 13 defendants on death row.

CRIME
Mass Killings China
The greatest massacre ever imputed by the government of one sovereign nation against the government of another is that of 26,300,000 Chinese during the regime of Mao Tse-tung between 1949 and May 1965. This accusation was made by an agency of the U.S.S.R. Government in a radio broadcast on 7 Apr. 1969. The broadcast broke down the figure into four periods:—2.8 million (1949–52); 3.5 million (1953–57); 6.7 million (1958–60); and 13.3 million (1961–May 1965). The highest reported death figures in single monthly announcements on Peking radio were 1,176,000 in the provinces of Anhwei, Chekiang, Kiangsu, and Shantung, and 1,150,000 in the Central South Provinces. Po I-po, Minister of Finance, is alleged to have stated in the organ For a lasting peace, for a people's democracy "in the past three years (1950–52) we have liquidated more than 2 million bandits". General Jacques Guillermaz, a French diplomat estimated the total executions between February 1951 and May 1952 at between 1 million and 3 million. In April 1971 the Executive cabinet or Yuan of the implacably hostile government of The Republic of China in Taipei, Taiwan announced its official estimate of the mainland death roll in the period 1949–69 as "at least 39,940,000". This figure, however, excluded "tens of thousands" killed in the Great Proletarian Cultural Revolution, which began in late 1966. The Walker Report published by the U.S. Senate Committee of the Judiciary in July 1971 placed the parameters of the total death roll since 1949 between 32.25 and 61.7 million.

U.S.S.R.
The total death roll in the Great Purge, or Yezhovshchina, in the U.S.S.R., in 1936–38 has, not surprisingly, never been published. Evidence of its magnitude may be found in population statistics which show a deficiency of males from before the outbreak of the 1941–45 war. The reign of terror was administered by the Narodny Kommissariat Vnutrennykh Del (N.K.V.D.), or People's Commissariat of Internal Affairs, the Soviet security service headed by Nikolay Ivanovich Yezhov (1895–?1939), described by Nikita Khrushchyov in 1956 as a "degenerate". S. V. Utechin, an expert on Soviet affairs, regards estimates of 8,000,000 or 10,000,000 victims as "probably not exaggerations".

Nazi Germany
Obersturmbannführer (Lt.-Col.) Karl Adolf Eichmann (b. Solingen, West Germany 19 Mar. 1906) of the S.S. was hanged in a small room inside Ramleh Prison, near Tel Aviv, Israel, at just before midnight (local time) on 31 May 1962, for his complicity in the deaths of an indeterminably massive number of Jews during World War II, under the instruction given in April 1941 by Adolf Hitler (1889–1945) for "the Final Solution" (Endlösung).

At the S.S. (Schutzstaffel) extermination camp (Vernichtungslager) known as Auschwitz-Birkenau (Oswiecim-Brzezinka), near Oswiecim (Auschwitz), in southern Poland, where a minimum of 920,000 people (Soviet estimate is 4,000,000) were exterminated from 14 June 1940 to 18 Jan. 1945, the greatest number killed in a day was 6,000. The man who operated the release of the "Zyklon B" cyanide pellets into the gas chambers there during this time was Sgt. Major Moll (variously Mold). The Nazi (Nationalsozialistiche Deutsche Arbeiter Partei) Commandant during the period 1940–43 was Rudolph Franz Ferdinand Höss who was tried in Warsaw from 11 Mar. to 2 Apr. 1947 and hanged, aged 47, at Oswiecim on 15 Apr. 1947.

Forced Labour
No official figures have been published of the death roll in Corrective Labour Camps in the U.S.S.R., first established in 1918. The total number of such camps was known to be more than 200 in 1946 but in 1956 many were converted to less severe Corrective Labour Colonies. An estimate published in the Netherlands puts the death roll between 1921 and 1960 at 19,000,000. The camps were administered by the Cheka until 1922, the O.G.P.U. (1922–34), the N.K.V.D. (1934–46), the M.V.D. (1946–53) and the K.G.B. since 1953. Solzhenitsyn's aggregate best estimate is that the number of inmates has been 66 million. In China there are no published official statistics on the numbers undergoing Lao Jiao (Education through Labour) nor Lao Dong Gai Zao (Reform through manual labour). An estimate published by Bao Ruo-wang, who was released in 1964 due to his father having been a Corsican, was 16,000,000 which approached 3 per cent of the population.

Largest criminal organization
The largest syndicate of organized crime is the Mafia or La Cosa Nostra, which has infiltrated the executive, judiciary and legislature of the United States. It consists of some 3,000 to 5,000 individuals in 24 "families" federated under "The Commission", with an annual turnover in vice, gambling, protection rackets, cigarettes, bootlegging, hijacking, narcotics, loan-sharking and prostitution estimated in the Time magazine survey of May 1977 at $48,000 million per annum of which $25.3 billion were profit—9½ times more than Exxon. The origin in the U.S. dates from the lynching of 11 Mafiosi in New Orleans in 1890 for which a naïve U.S. government paid $30,000 compensation to widows which was seized as the initial funding to prime the whole operation. The biggest Mafia (meaning swank from a Sicilian word for beauty or pride) killing was on 11–13 Sept. 1931 when the topmost man Salvatore Maranzano, Il Capo di Tutti Capi, and 40 allies were liquidated.

Murder rate Highest
The country with the highest recorded murder rate is Mexico, with 46.3 registered homicides per each 100,000 of the population in 1970. It has been estimated that the total

number of murders in Colombia during *La Violencia* (1945–62) was about 300,000, giving a rate over a 17-year period of more than 48 a day. A total of 592 deaths was attributed to one bandit leader, Teófilo ("Sparks") Rojas, aged 27, between 1948 and his death in an ambush near Armenia on 22 Jan. 1963. Some sources attribute 3,500 slayings to him.

The highest homicide rates recorded in New York City have been 58 in a week in July 1972 and 13 in a day in August 1972. In 1973 the total for Detroit, Michigan (pop. then 1.5 million) was 751.

Lowest
The country with the lowest officially recorded rate in the world is Spain, with 39 murders (a rate of 1.23 per each million of the population) in 1967, or one murder every 9 days. In the Indian state of Sikkim, in the Himalayas, murder is, however, practically unknown, while in the Hunza area of Kashmir, in the Karakoram, only one definite case by a Hunzarwal has been recorded since 1900.

Great Britain
In Great Britain the total number of homicides and deaths from injuries purposely inflicted by other persons in the year 1975 was 515. This figure compares with a murder total of 124 in 1937 and 125 in 1958.

Most Prolific Murderers *World*
It was established at the trial of Buhram, the Indian thug, that he had strangled at least 931 victims with his yellow and white cloth strip or *ruhmal* in the Oudh district between 1790 and 1840. It has been estimated that at least 2,000,000 Indians were strangled by Thugs (*burtotes*) during the reign of the Thugee cult (pronounced tugee) from 1550 until its final suppression by the British *raj* in 1853. The greatest number of victims ascribed to a murderess has been 610 in the case of Countess Erszebet Bathory (1560–1614) of Hungary. At her trial which began on 2 Jan. 1611 a witness testified to seeing a list of her victims in her own handwriting totalling this number. All were alleged to be young girls from the neighbourhood of her castle at Csejthe where she died on 21 Aug. 1614. She had been walled up in her room for the 3½ years after being found guilty.

20th century
The 20th century's most prolific one-at-a-time murderer has been Bruno Lüdke (Germany) (b. 1909), who confessed to 85 murders of women between 1928 and 29 Jan. 1943. He was executed by injection without trial in a hospital in Vienna on 8 Apr. 1944.

Frans Hooymayers, 40, a male nurse at the Luckerheide Geriatric Clinic, Kerkrade, Netherlands admitted to 14 murders of patients in August 1976. In his section since November 1969 there were 245 other deaths of a suspicious nature and an inordinately high consumption of insulin and Valium.

Great Britain
The total number of victims of the cannibalistic cave-dwelling Bean family in Galloway, Scotland in the 15th century is not known but may have run as high as 50 per year. Sawney Bean, head of the family, his wife, 8 sons, 6 daughters and 32 grandchildren were taken by a militia detachment to Edinburgh and executed without process.

Six men were each charged with 21 murders at Lancaster Crown Court on 9 June 1975 concerning the bombing of the two Birmingham public houses Mulberry Bush and Tavern in the Town on 21 Nov. 1974. They were John Walker, Patrick Hill, Robert Hunter, Noel McIlkenny, William Power and Hugh Callaghan.

Judith Minna Ward, 25 of Stockport, Cheshire was convicted on 11 separate murder charges on 4 Nov. 1974 making 12 in all arising from the explosion in an army coach on the M.62 near Drighlington, West Yorkshire on 4 Feb. 1974. Mary Ann Cotton (*née* Robson) (b. 1832, East Rainton, County Durham), hanged in Durham Jail on 24 Mar. 1873 is believed to have poisoned 14, possibly 20, people.

Gang murders
During the period of open gang warfare in Chicago, Illinois, U.S.A., the peak year was 1926, when there were 76 unsolved killings. The 1,000th gang murder in Chicago since 1919 occurred on 1 Feb. 1967. Only 13 cases have ended in convictions.

"Smelling out"
The greatest "smelling out" recorded in African history occurred before Shaka (1787–1828) and 30,000 Nguni subjects near the River Umhlatuzana, Zululand (now Natal, South Africa) in March 1824. After 9 hrs, over 300 were "smelt out" as guilty of smearing the Royal *Kraal* with blood, by 150 witch-finders led by the hideous female *isangoma* Nobela. The victims were declared innocent when Shaka admitted to having done the smearing himself to expose the falsity of the power of his diviners. Nobela poisoned herself with atropine ($C_{17}H_{23}NO_3$), but the other 149 witch-finders were thereupon skewered or clubbed to death.

Suicide
The estimated daily total of suicides throughout the world surpassed 1,000 in 1965. The country with the highest suicide rate is Hungary, with 36.9 per each 100,000 of the population in 1973. The country with the lowest recorded rate is Jordan with a single case in 1970 and hence a rate of 0.04 per 100,000.

In England and Wales there were 3,689 suicides in 1975, or an average of 10.1 per day. In the northern hemisphere April and May tend to be peak months.

Robbery
The greatest recorded art robbery by market valuation was the removal of 19 paintings, valued at £8,000,000 taken from Russborough House, Blessington, County Wicklow, Ireland, the home of Sir Alfred and Lady Beit by 4 men and a woman on 26 Apr. 1974. They included the £3 million Vermeer "Lady Writing a Letter with her maid". The paintings were recovered on 4 May near Glandore, County Cork. Dr. Rose Bridgit Dugdale (b 1941) was convicted. It is arguable that the value of the *Mona Lisa* at the time of its theft from The Louvre, Paris on 21 Aug. 1911 was greater than this figure. It was recovered in Italy in 1913 when Vincenzo Perruggia was charged with its theft. On 1 Sept. 1964 antiquities reputedly worth £10,000,000 were recovered from 3 warehouses near the Pyramids, Egypt.

Bank
During the extreme civil disorder prior to 22 Jan. 1976 in Beirut, Lebanon, a guerilla force blasted the vaults of the British Bank of the Middle East in Bab Idriss and cleared out safe deposit boxes with contents valued by former Finance Minister, Lucien Dahadah, at $50 million and by another source as an 'absolute minimum' of $20 million.

Britain's greatest ever robbery was of an estimated £8,000,000 from the Bank of America, Mayfair, London on 24 Apr. 1975. On 16 Nov. 1976 five men were jailed for between 12 and 23 years. Leonard "The Twirler" Wilde, 51 was the locksmith.

Train
The greatest recorded train robbery occurred between about 3.03 a.m. and 3.27 a.m. on 8 Aug. 1963, when a General Post Office mail train from Glasgow, Scotland, was ambushed at Sears Crossing and robbed at Bridego Bridge near Mentmore, Buckinghamshire. The gang escaped with about 120 mailbags containing £2,631,784 worth of bank notes being taken to London for destruction. Only £343,448 had been recovered by 9 Dec. 1966.

Bullion
The greatest bullion robbery was that of the Reichbank reserves by a civilian—U.S. military consortium near Einsiedel, Bavaria on 7 June 1945. The gold alone at current values was worth more than £18½ million.

Jewels

The greatest recorded theft of jewels was from safe deposits in Palm Towers, Palm Beach, Florida on 14 Apr. 1976 estimated by the police at about $6,000,000 (then £3.4 million) and $1 million for other items. The haul from Carrington & Co. Ltd. of Regent Street, London, on 21 Nov. 1965 was estimated to be £500,000. Jewels are believed to have constituted a major part of the Hotel Pierre "heist" on Fifth Avenue, New York City, U.S.A. on 31 Dec. 1971. An unofficial estimate ran as high as $5,000,000 (*then £2,000,000*).

Greatest kidnapping ransom

Historically the greatest ransom paid was that for Atahualpa by the Incas to Francisco Pizarro in 1532–33 at Cajamarca, Peru which constituted a hall full of gold and silver worth in modern money some $170 million (*£95 million*).

The greatest ransom ever exported is 1,500 m pesos (*£25,300,000*) for the release of the brothers Jorge Born, 40 and Juan Born, 39, of Bunge and Born, paid to the left wing urban guerilla group Montoneros in Buenos Aires, Argentina on 20 June 1975.

The youngest person kidnapped has been Carolyn Wharton born at 12.46 p.m. on 19 Mar. 1955 in the Baptist Hospital, Texas, U.S.A. and kidnapped, by a woman disguised as a nurse, at 1.15 p.m. aged 29 minutes.

Greatest hijack ransom

The highest amount ever paid to hijackers has been £2,000,000 in small denomination notes by the West German government to Popular Front for the Liberation of Palestine representatives 30 miles outside Beirut, Lebanon on 23 Feb. 1972. In return a Lufthansa Boeing 747, hijacked an hour out of New Delhi and bound for Athens which had been forced down at Aden, and its 14 crew members were released. The longest air piracy has been one of 8,800 miles *14 160 km* by three Filipino Moslem separatists from Southern Philippines in a BAC 111 changing to a DC8 at Bangkok and arriving at Benghazi, Libya a week later on 14 Apr. 1976.

Largest narcotics haul

The heaviest recorded haul of narcotics was made in The Bahamas on 16 Aug. 1975 when 1049 sacks of high grade Columbian marijuana was discovered with a weight of 86,280 lb 43.14 short tons *38,85 tonnes* worth an estimated $24 million. The most valuable ever haul was of 937 lb *425 kg* of pure heroin worth $106¼ million (*then £44 million*) retail seized aboard the 60 ton shrimp boat *Caprice des Temps* at Marseille, France on 28 Feb. 1972. The captain, Louis Boucan, 57, who tried to commit suicide was sentenced to 15 years on 5 Jan. 1973.

It was revealed on 31 Jan. 1973 that 398 lb. *180,5 kg* of heroin and cocaine with a street value of $73 million (*then £29.2 million*) had been stolen from the New York Police Department—a record for any law enforcement agency.

Largest bribe

An alleged bribe of £30,000,000 offered to Shaikh Zaid ibn Sultan of Abu Dhabi, United Arab Emirates, by a Saudi Arabian official in August 1955, is the highest on record. The affair concerned oil concessions in the disputed territory of Buraimi on the Persian Gulf.

Greatest forgery

The greatest forgery was the German Third Reich government's forging operation, code name "Bernhard", engineered by SS Sturmbannfuhrer Alfred Naujocks of the Technical Dept. of the German Secret Service Amt VI F in Berlin in 1940–41. It involved £150,000,000 worth of £5 notes.

Biggest fraud

The largest amount of money named in a defalcation case has been a gross £33,000,000 at the Lugano branch of Lloyd's Bank International Ltd. in Switzerland on 2 Sept. 1974. Mr. Mark Colombo was arrested pending charges including falsification of foreign currency accounts and suppression of evidence.

The murderess Mrs. Ruth Ellis, the fourteenth and last woman hanged in Britain this century (see page 190). (*Mirrorpic*)

Computer Fraud

Between 1964 and 1973, 64,000 fake insurance policies were created on the computer of the Equity Funding Corporation involving $2,000 million.

Welfare swindle

The greatest welfare swindle yet worked was that of the gypsy Anthony Moreno on the French Social Security in Marseilles. By forging birth certificates and school registration forms, he invented 197 fictitious families and 3,000 children on which he claimed benefits from 1960 to mid-1968. Moreno, nicknamed "El Chorro" (the fountain), was last reported free of extradition worries and living in luxury in his native Spain having absquatulated with an estimated £2,300,000.

CAPITAL PUNISHMENT

Capital punishment was first abolished *de facto* in 1798 in Liechtenstein. The death penalty for murder was formally abolished in Britain on 18 Dec. 1969. Between the 5-4 Supreme Court decision against capital punishment in June 1972 and April 1975, 32 of the 50 States of the U.S.A. voted to restore it.

Capital punishment in the British Isles dates from A.D. 450, but was abolished by William I and re-imposed by Henry I, reaching a peak in the reign of Edward VI (1547–1553), when an average of 560 persons were executed annually at Tyburn alone. Even into the 19th century, there were 223 capital crimes, though people were, in practice, hanged for only 25 of these. Between 1830 and 1955 the most murderers hanged in a year was 27 (24 men, 3 women) in 1903. The least was 5 in 1854, 1921 and 1930. In 1956 there were no hangings in England, Wales or Scotland, since when the highest number in any year to 1964 was 5.

Largest hanging

The most people hanged from one gallows was 38 Sioux Indians by William J. Duly outside Mankato, Minnesota, U.S.A. for the murder of unarmed citizens on 26 Dec. 1862.

Last hangings

The last public execution in England took place outside Newgate Prison, London at 8 a.m. on 26 May 1868, when Michael Barrett was hanged for his part in the Fenian bomb outrage on 13 Dec. 1867, when 12 were killed outside the Clerkenwell House of Detention, London. The earliest non-public execution was of the murderer Thomas Wells on 13 Aug. 1868. The last public hanging in Scotland was that of the murderer Joe Bell in Perth in 1866. The last in the United States occurred at Owensboro, Kentucky in 1936. The last hangings were those of Peter Anthony Allen (b. 4 Apr. 1943) at Walton Prison, Liverpool, and John Robson Walby (b. 1 Apr. 1940), *alias* Gwynne Owen Evans, at Strangeways Gaol, Manchester both on 13 Aug. 1964. They had been found guilty of the capital murder of John Alan West, on 7 Apr. 1964. The 14th and last woman executed this century was Mrs. Ruth Ellis (*née* Neilson), 28, for the murder of David Blakely, 25, shot outside The Magdala, Hampstead, on 10 Apr. 1955. She was executed on 13 July at Holloway.

Last from yard-arm

The last naval execution at the yard-arm was the hanging of Private John Dalliger, Royal Marines, aboard H.M.S. *Leven* in the River Yangtze, China, on 13 July 1860. Dalliger had been found guilty of two attempted murders.

Last public guillotining

The last person to be publicly guillotined in France was the murderer Eugen Weidmann before a large crowd at Versailles, near Paris, at 4.50 a.m. on 17 June 1939. The last person guillotined in a French prison was the Tunisian child murderer Ali Benyanès, 34 at Marseille on 12 May 1973. It was the 74 year old executioner's 364th successful execution. Dr. Joseph Ignace Guillotin (1738–1812) died a natural death. He had advocated the use of the machine designed by Dr. Antoine Louis in 1789 in the French constituent assembly.

Youngest

Although the hanging of persons under 18 was expressly excluded only in the Children's and Young Person's Act, 1933 (Sec. 33), no person under that age was, in fact executed more recently than 1887. The lowest satisfactorily recorded age was of a boy aged 8 "who had malice, cunning and revenge" in firing two barns and who was hanged at Abingdon, Oxfordshire in the 17th century. The youngest persons hanged since 1900 have been 18 years old, the most recent of whom was Francis Robert George ("Flossie") Forsyth on 10 Nov. 1960.

Oldest

The oldest person hanged in the United Kingdom since 1900 was a man of 71 named Charles Frembd (*sic*) at Chelmsford Gaol on 4 Nov. 1914, for the murder of his wife at Leytonstone, Waltham Forest, Greater London. In 1822 John Smith, said to be 80, of Greenwich, Greater London, was hanged for the murder of a woman.

Most attempts

In 1803 it was reported that Joseph Samuels was reprieved in Sydney, Australia after three unsuccessful attempts to hang him in which the rope twice broke.

Death Row Longest Stay

The longest stay on "death row" in the United States has been one of more than 14 years by Edgar Labat, aged 44, and Clifton A. Paret, aged 38, in Angola Penitentiary, Louisiana, U.S.A. In March 1953 they were sentenced to death, after being found guilty of rape in 1950. They were released on 5 May 1967, only to be immediately re-arrested on a local jury indictment arising from the original charge. Caryl Whittier Chessman, aged 38 and convicted of 17 felonies, was executed on 2 May 1960 in the gas chamber at the California State Prison, San Quentin, California, U.S.A. In 11 years 10 months and one week on "death row", Chessman had won eight stays.

Executioner

The longest period of office of a Public Executioner was that of William Calcraft (1800–1879), who was in office from 1828 to 1871 and officiated at nearly every hanging outside and later inside Newgate Prison, London. On 2 Apr. 1868 he hanged the murdress Mrs. Frances Kidder, 25 outside Maidstone Jail, Kent—the last public execution of a woman.

Albert Pierrepoint officiated at the execution of 433 men and 17 women during his career.

Bloodiest Assizes

In the West Country Assizes of 1685 (Winchester to Wells), George Jeffreys, the 1st Baron Jeffreys of Wem (1645–1689), sentenced 330 persons to be hanged, 841 to be transported for periods of ten or more years and larger numbers to be imprisoned, flogged, pilloried, mutilated or fined. These sentences followed the Duke of Monmouth's insurrection.

Longest sentences *World*

The longest recorded prison sentence is one of 7,109 years awarded to a pair of confidence tricksters by an Iranian court on 15 June 1969. The duration of sentences are proportional to the amount of the defalcations involved. A sentence of 384,912 years was demanded at the prosecution of Gabriel March Grandos, 22, at Palma de Mallorca, Spain on 11 Mar. 1972 for failing to deliver 42,768 letters.

Juan Corona, a Mexican-American was sentenced to 25 consecutive life terms, for murdering 25 farm workers in 1970–71 around Feather River, Yuba City, California, at Fairfield on 5 Feb. 1973. His U.S. 20th century record for victims was surpassed with the discovery on 13 Aug. 1973 of the body of the 27th victim of the pervert Dean Corll, 33 of Houston, Texas.

Great Britain

Mr. Justice Chapman at Oxford Assizes on 15 Oct. 1971 jailed the police murderer Arthur William Skingle, 25, of London for life with the first recommendation that "life should mean for life".

The longest single period served by a reprieved murderer in Great Britain this century was 40 years 11 months by John Watson Laurie, the Goat Fell or Arran murderer, who was reprieved on the grounds of insanity in November 1889 and who died in Perth Penitentiary on 4 Oct. 1930.

The longest specific minimum period recommended by a judge under the Murder (Abolition of Death Penalty) Act 1965 has been 35 years in the case of Patrick Armstrong and Michael Hill on 22 Oct. 1975 for pub bombings (7 killed, 99 injured) at Guildford and Woolwich in 1974.

The longest prison sentence ever passed under British law was one of three consecutive and two concurrent terms

George Blake (*né* Behar), who was sprung in 1966 from Wormwood Scrubs Prison after serving less than 5½ years of his record sentence of 42 years for treachery (see p. 191). (*Central Press*)

The scene at Trafalgar Square on 17 September 1961, when 1,314 unilateral nuclear disarmament demonstrators were arrested for unlawful forms of demonstration. (*Popperfoto*)

of 14 years, thus totalling 42 years, imposed on 3 May 1961 on George Blake (b. Rotterdam, 11 Nov. 1922 of an Egyptian-born Jewish-British father and a Dutch mother as George Behar), for treachery. Blake, formerly U.K. vice-consul in Seoul, South Korea, had been converted to Communism during 34 months' internment there from 2 July 1950 to April 1953. It had been alleged that his betrayals may have cost the lives of up to 42 British agents. He was "sprung" from Wormwood Scrubs Prison, Greater London, on 22 Oct. 1966.

The longest single sentence passed on a woman under English law was 20 years for Mrs. Lona Teresa Cohen *née* Petra (b. 1913) at the Old Bailey, City of London on 2 Mar. 1961 for conspiring to commit a breach of the Official Secrets Act, 1911. The sentence of this K.G.B. agent was remitted by the Foreign Secretary on no known lawful authority on 24 July 1969. Ward (see Most Prolific Murderers) was sentenced to 20 years for a single offence and an aggregate 30 years on 4 Nov. 1974.

Longest Time Served
Johnson VanDyke Grigsby, who began serving a life sentence for second degree murder on 5 Aug. 1908, was discharged from Indiana State Prison on 9 Dec. 1974 after 66 years 126 days. He believed he was 89 or 90. He complained of the bad language of "modern" prisoners.

Longest in Broadmoor
The longest period for which any person has been detained in the Broadmoor hospital for the criminally insane, near Crowthorne, Berkshire, is 76 years in the case of William Giles. He was admitted as an insane arsonist at the age of 11 and died there on 10 Mar. 1962, at the age of 87.

The longest escape from Broadmoor was one of 39 years by the Liverpool wife murderer James Kelly, who got away on 28 Jan. 1888, using a pass key made from a corset spring. After an adventurous life in Paris, in New York and at sea he returned in April 1927, to ask for re-admission. After some difficulties this was arranged. He died in 1930.

Oldest prisoner
The oldest known prisoner in the United States is John Weber, 95, at the Chillicothe Correctional Institute, Ohio who began his 44th year in prison on 29 Oct. 1970.

Most Appearances
There are no collected records on the greatest number of convictions on an individual but the highest recently reported is 1,433 for the gentlemanly but alcoholic Edward Eugene Ebzery, who died in Brisbane Jail, Queensland, Australia on 23 Sept. 1967.

Most Parking Offences
Henry Rabin, 40 of Skókie, Chicago, U.S.A. was arrested in July 1975 for failing to pay 468 parking tickets in 2½ years. This top "scofflaw" was fined $5,000 (*then £2,375*).

Most "Obstructive"
The third generation "buskers" Henry and Bert Hollis with their one-man band Charlie Hillard were arrested more than 500 times under Sect. 73 of the Highway Act, 1835 in 30 years usually in Leicester Square, London. Part of their routine was to enter the police van by one door and leave by another.

Greatest mass arrest
The greatest mass arrest in the United Kingdom occurred on 17 Sept. 1961, when 1,314 demonstrators supporting the unilateral nuclear disarmament of the United Kingdom were arrested for wilfully disregarding the directions of the police and thereby obstructing highways leading to Parliament Square, London, by sitting down. As a consequence of the 1926 General Strike there were 3,149 prosecutions: incitement (1,760) and violence (1,389).

Lynching
The worst year in the 20th century for lynchings in the United States has been 1901, with 130 lynchings (105 Negroes, 25 Whites), while the first year with no reported cases was 1952. The last lynching recorded in Britain was that of Panglam Godolan, a Pakistani and a suspected murderer, in London on 27 Oct. 1958. The last case previous to this was of a kidnapping suspect in Glasgow in 1922.

FINES
A fine equivalent to £10,686,000 was levied on Jean Pierre Pilato (France) by a court in Valencia, Spain on 6 Feb. 1972

Britain's most capacious prison with 1,208 cells, known to both inmates and "screws" as "The Scrubs" (see below). (*David L. Roberts*)

for attempting to smuggle 250 lb *113,6 kg* of heroin worth £16 million from France *via* Spain to the U.S. He was arrested on 5 June 1971 and is serving a 10 year sentence plus 4 years if the fine is unpaid.

Heaviest

The heaviest fine ever imposed in the United Kingdom was one of £277,500, plus £3,717 costs, on I. Hennig & Co. Ltd., the London diamond merchants, at Clerkenwell Magistrates' Court, London, on 14 Dec. 1949. The amount was later reduced on appeal.

Rarest prosecution

There are a number of crimes in English law for which there have never been prosecutions. Among unique prosecutions are *Rex v. Crook* in 1662 for the praemunire of disputing the King's title and *Rex v. Gregory* for selling honours under the Honours (Prevention of Abuses) Act, 1924, on 18 Feb. 1933. John Maundy Gregory (d. 3 Oct. 1941 in France as "Sir" "Arthur" Gregory) was an honours broker during 6 administrations from 1919 to 1932 and was sentenced to two months in Wormwood Scrubs, London.

PRISONS

Largest *World*

The largest prison in the world is Kharkov Prison, in the U.S.S.R., which has at times accommodated 40,000 prisoners.

Great Britain

The largest prison in Great Britain is Wormwood Scrubs, West London, with 1,208 cells. The highest prison walls in Great Britain are those of Lancaster Prison measuring 36 to 52 ft *11–15,85 m.*

The largest prison in Scotland in Barlinnie, Glasgow, with 753 single cells. Ireland's largest prison is Mountjoy Prison, Dublin, with 808 cells.

Penal camps

The largest penal camp systems in the world were those near Karaganda and Kolyma, in the U.S.S.R., each with a population estimated in 1958 at between 1,200,000 and 1,500,000. The largest labour camp is now said to be the Dubrovlag Complex of 15 camps centred on Pot'ma, Mordovian S.S.R. The official N.A.T.O. estimate for all Soviet camps was "more than one million" in March 1960 compared with a peak of probably 12 million during the Stalinist era.

Devil's Island

The largest French penal settlement was that of St. Laurent du Maroni, which comprised the notorious Îles du Diable, Royale and St. Joseph (for incorrigibles) off the coast of French Guiana, in South America. It remained in operation for 99 years from 1854 until the last group of repatriated prisoners, including Théodore Rouselle, who had served 50 years, was returned to Bordeaux on 22 Aug. 1953. It has been estimated that barely 2,000 *bagnard* (ex-convicts) of the 70,000 deportees ever returned. These, however, include the executioner Ladurelle (imprisoned 1921—37), who was murdered in Paris in 1938.

Highest population

The peak prison population, including Borstals and detention centres, for England and Wales was the figure for 1 May 1977 of 41,912. In Scotland the prison population on 17 May 1977 was 4,988 and in Northern Ireland 2,828 as at 22 May 1977.

Most secure prison

After it became a maximum security Federal prison in 1934, no convict was known to have lived to tell of a successful escape from the prison of Alcatraz Island in San Francisco Bay, California, U.S.A. A total of 23 men attempted it but 12 were recaptured, 5 shot dead, one drowned and 5 presumed drowned. On 16 Dec. 1962, just before the prison was closed on 21 Mar. 1963 one man reached the mainland alive, only to be recaptured on the spot. John Chase held the record with 26 years there.

Most Expensive Prison

Spandau Prison, Berlin built 100 years ago for 600 prisoners is now used solely for the Nazi war criminal Rudolf Hess (b. 26 Apr. 1894). The cost of maintenance of the staff of 105 has been estimated at $415,000 £245,000 per annum.

Longest Escape

The longest recorded escape by a recaptured prisoner was that of Leonard T. Fristoe, 77, who escaped from Nevada State Prison, U.S.A., on 15 Dec. 1923 and was turned in by his son on 15 Nov. 1969 at Compton, California. He had had 46 years of freedom under the name Claude R. Willis. He had killed two sheriff's deputies in 1920. The longest period of freedom achieved by a British gaol breaker is more than 20 years by Irish-born John Patrick Hannan, who escaped from Verne Open Prison at Portland, Dorset, on 22 Dec. 1955 and was still at large in June 1976. He had served only 1 month of a 21-month term for car-stealing and assaulting two policemen.

Greatest gaol break

On 19 Apr. 1974 50 prisoners escaped from Rio di Janeiro Jail, Brazil. Thirty were re-captured on the same day.

The greatest gaol break in Britain was that from Brixton Prison, Lambeth, Greater London on 30 May 1973 when 20 men got out using a rubbish tipping lorry as a battering ram. Eighteen were captured immediately and one other 5 weeks later, nine staff were injured.

---

6. ECONOMIC

MONETARY AND FINANCE

Largest budget *World*

The greatest annual expenditure budgeted by any country has been $447,100 million (£263,000 million) by the United States government for the fiscal year ending 30 June 1978. The highest budgeted revenue in the United States has been $405,700 million (£238,650 million) for 1977–78.

In the United States, the greatest surplus was $8,419,469,844 in 1947–48, and the greatest budgeted deficit was $59,200,000,000 (£34,820 million) in 1976–77.

Largest budget *Great Britain*

The greatest budgeted current expenditure of Great Britain has been £56,606 million for the fiscal year 1977–78. The highest budgeted current revenue has been £56,956 million after the budget changes of 29 Mar. 1977.

Foreign aid
The total net foreign aid given by the United States government between 1 July 1945 and 1 Jan. 1976 was $164,990 million. The country which received most U.S. aid in 1975 was Israel with $803 million. U.S. foreign aid began with $50,000 to Venezuela for earthquake relief in 1812.

Least taxed
The lowest income taxed nations in the world include Bahrain, Kuwait and Quatar where the rate regardless of income is nil.

There is no income tax paid by residents on Lundy Island off North Devon, England. This 1,062.4 acre *429,9 ha* island issued its own unofficial currency of Puffins and Half Puffins between the Wars for which offence the owner was prosecuted.

Highest Taxation Rates
The country with the most confiscatory taxation is Norway where in January 1974 the Labour Party and Socialist Alliance abolished the 80 per cent limit so that some 2,000 citizens have to pay more than 100 per cent of their taxable income. The shipping magnate Hilmar Reksten was assessed at 491 per cent. The highest rate in the United Kingdom, is the 1976–77 rate for taxable incomes over £20,000 at 83 per cent with an additional surcharge on investment incomes in excess of £2,000 of 15 per cent making a rate of 98 per cent. In 1967–68 a "special charge" of up to 9s. (45p) in the £ additional to surtax brought the top rate to 27s 3d. (or 136%) in the £ on investment income.

Highest and lowest rates in Great Britain
Income tax was first introduced in Great Britain in 1799 for incomes above £60 per annum. It was discontinued in 1815, only to be re-introduced in 1842 at the rate of 7d. (3p) in the £. It was at its lowest at 2d. (0.83p) in the £ in 1875, gradually climbing to 1s. 3d. (6p) by 1913. From April 1941 until 1946 the record peak of 10s. (50p) in the £ was maintained to assist in financing of World War II. Death Duties (introduced in 1894) began at 8 per cent (1894–1907) and were raised to a peak of 80 per cent on millionaire estates by 1949. These have been replaced by a Capital Transfer Tax.

National Debt
The largest national debt of any country in the world is that of the United States, where the gross federal public debt of the Federal Government surpassed the half trillion dollar mark in 1975 and budgetted to reach $784,973 billion (£411 billion) by 30 June 1978. This amount in dollar bills would make a pile 42,594 miles *68,548 km* high, weighing 596,723 tons *606 308 tonnes*.

The National Debt in Great Britain was less than £1 million during the reign of James II in 1687. It was £54,041 million or £966 per person at 31 March 1977. This amount placed in a pile of brand new £1 notes would be 3,293.1 miles *5 299 km* in height.

Gross National Product
The country with the largest Gross National Product is the United States with $2,038 billion in 1977–78. The estimated G.N.P. of the United Kingdom was £108,404 million for 1976.

National Wealth
The richest nation, measured by average per capita is Abu Dhabi with $70,000 (US) (£41,175) in 1976. The U.S.A. which took the lead in 1910 is now (1976) sixth behind also Switzerland, Sweden and Denmark. The United Kingdom stands 20th with $3,455 (£2,032) per head. It has been estimated that the value of all physical assets in the U.S.A. in 1976 was $6·2 trillion ($10^{12}$) or $28,800 (£16,950) per head. The comparative figure for the United Kingdom was £193,700 million (1972) or £3,472 per head.

Poorest Country
The lowest published annual income per caput of any country in the world is Rwanda, with $70 (£41).

National Savings—Premium Bonds
Mr. Arthur Ellis of Saltergate, Chesterfield between 1958 and his death in June 1971 won one £250, two £100 and 39 £25 premium bond draw prizes. All his winnings were donated to the local parish church.

Gold Reserves *World*
The country with the greatest monetary gold reserve is the United States, whose Treasury had $11,238 million (*then £5,350 million*) on hand in January 1976. The United States Bullion Depository at Fort Knox, 30 miles *48 km* south-west of Louisville, Kentucky, U.S.A. is the principal Federal depository of U.S. gold. Gold is stored in standard mint bars of 400 troy ounces *12,441 kg* measuring 7 by 3⅝ by 1⅝ in, *17,7 × 9,2 × 4,1 cm* and each worth $16,888.

The greatest accumulation of the world's central banks' $50,000 million of gold bullion is now in the Federal Reserve Bank at 33 Liberty Street, New York City, N.Y., U.S.A. Some $17,000 million or 14,000 tons is stored 85 ft *25,90 m* below street level, in a vault 50 ft *15,24 m* by 100 ft *30,48 m* behind a steel door weighing 89 tons/*tonnes*.

Gold and Dollar Reserves *Great Britain*
The lowest published figure for the sterling area's gold and convertible currency reserves was $298,000,000 (*then £74 million*) on 31 Dec. 1940. A peak valuation of $11,572 million (£6,727 million at $1.72 to the £) was announced for 30 June 1977.

Minimum Lending Rate
The highest ever figure for the British bank rate (since 13 Oct. 1972, the Minimum Lending Rate) has been 15% from 7 Oct. to 19 Nov. 1976. The longest period without a change was the 12 years 13 days from 26 Oct. 1939 to 7 Nov. 1951, during which time the rate stayed at 2 per cent. This record low rate was first attained on 22 Apr. 1852.

Balance of Payments
The most unfavourable current balance of payments figure for the United Kingdom has been a deficit of £3,650 million in 1974 with the 4th quarter being the worst with £965 million. The greatest surplus for a quarter has been £172 million for the 3rd quarter of 1971. Monthly figures are regarded as too erratic to be significant.

Worst Inflation *World*
The world's worst inflation occurred in Hungary in June 1946, when the 1931 gold pengö was valued at 130 trillion (1.3 × 10^{20}) paper pengös. Notes were issued for szazmillio billion (100 trillion or 10^{20}) pengös on 3 June and withdrawn on 11 July 1946. Notes for 1,000 trillion or 10^{21} pengös were printed but not circulated. On 6 Nov. 1923 the circulation of Reichsbank marks reached 400,338,326,350,700,000,000. *Pick's World Currency Report* of May 1977 listed the worst inflation in the period 1950–75 as the Chilean escudo at 11,318,874% and the £ sterling in 22nd place at 345%.

Worst Inflation *Great Britain*
The United Kingdom's worst rate in a year has been for Aug. 1974 to Aug. 1975 when inflation ran at a rate of 26.9% compared with 17.2% from June 1976 to June 1977. At a sustained 20% inflation rate the £ will be worth 1p (1977 value) sometime during the year 2002—only 25 years hence.

PAPER MONEY
Earliest
Paper money is an invention of the Chinese first tried in A.D. 910 and prevalent by A.D. 970. The world's earliest bank notes were issued by the Stockholms Banco, Sweden, in July 1961. The oldest surviving banknote is one for 5 dalers dated 6 Dec. 1662. The oldest surviving printed Bank of England note is one for £555 to bearer, dated 19 Dec. 1699 (4½ × 7½ in, *11,4 × 19,6 cm*).

Largest and smallest

The largest paper money ever issued was the one kwan note of the Chinese Ming dynasty issue of 1368–99, which measured 9 by 13 in *22,8 × 33,0 cm*. The smallest bank note ever issued was the 10 bani note of the Ministry of Finance of Romania, issued in 1917. It measured (printed area) 27,5 × 38 mm *1.09 × 1.49 in.*

Highest denominations *World*

The highest denomination notes in circulation are U.S. Federal Reserve Bank notes for $10,000 (£5,555). They bear the head of Salmon Portland Chase (1808–73). None has been printed since July 1944 and the U.S. Treasury announced in 1969 that no further notes higher than $100 would be issued. Only some 400 $10,000 bills remain in circulation.

Great Britain

Two Bank of England notes for £1,000,000 still exist, dated before 1812, but these were used only for internal accounting. The highest issued denominations were £1,000 notes, first printed in 1725, discontinued on 22 Apr. 1943 and withdrawn on 30 April 1945. A total of 62 of these notes were still unretired up to May 1973 (last data). Of these only 3 or 4 are known to be in the hands of collectors.

Lowest denomination *World*

The lowest denomination banknote issued is the 1 cent Hong Kong note which is worth 1/12th of one new penny.

Great Britain

The lowest denomination Bank of England notes ever printed were half-crown (2s 6d) black on pale blue notes in 1941, signed by K. O. Peppiatt. Very few examples have survived and they are now valued at from £750.

The world's highest priced coin, the unique 1907 U.S. $20 gold piece from the Dr. Wilkison Collection valued at $900,000 £530,000. (see p. 195).

Highest circulation

The highest ever Bank of England note circulation in the United Kingdom was £6,858 million in Dec. 1976—equivalent to a pile of £1 notes 395.58 miles *636,62 km* high.

CHEQUES
Largest *World*

The greatest amount paid by a single cheque in the history of

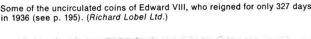

Some of the uncirculated coins of Edward VIII, who reigned for only 327 days in 1936 (see p. 195). *(Richard Lobel Ltd.)*

The legendary Edward VIII Collection

banking has been one for Rs. 16,640,000,000 equivalent to £852,791,660 handed over by Hon. Daniel P. Moynihan, Ambassador of the U.S.A. to India in New Delhi on 18 Feb. 1974. An internal U.S. Treasury check for $4,176,969,623.57 was drawn on 30 June 1954.

Largest *Great Britain*
The largest cheque drawn in Britain was one for £119,595,645, drawn on 24 Jan. 1961 by Lazard Brothers & Co. Ltd., and payable to the National Provincial Bank, in connection with the takeover of the British Ford Motor Company.

COINS
Oldest *World*
The earliest certainly dated coins are the electrum (alloy of gold and silver) staters of Lydia, in Asia Minor (now Turkey), which were coined in the reign of King Gyges (c. 685–652 B.C.). Primitive uninscribed "spade" money of the Chou dynasty of China is now *believed* to date from c. 770 B.C. A discovery at Tappeh Nush-i-jan, Iran of silver ingot currency in 1972 has been dated to as early as 760 B.C. Laos and Paraguay are the only countries today without coins.

Oldest *Great Britain*
The earliest coins to circulate in Britain were Gallo-Belgic gold imitations of the Macedonian staters of Philip II (359–336 B.C.). The Bellovaci type has been tentatively dated c. 130 B.C. The earliest date attributed to coins minted in Britain is c. 95 B.C. for the Westerham type gold stater of which 51 examples are known.

Heaviest
A Swedish 10 daler copper plate of 1644 attained a weight of 43 lb 7¼ oz. *19,710 kg.* Of primitive exchange tokens, the most massive are the holed stone discs, or *Fé*, from the Yap Islands, in the western Pacific Ocean, with diameters of up to 12 ft *3,65 m* and weighing up to 185 lb. *84 kg.* A medium-sized one was worth one Yapese wife or an 18 ft *5,18 m* canoe.

Smallest
The smallest coins in the world have been the Nepalese ¼ dam or Jawa struck c. 1740 in silver in the reign of Jeya Prakash Malla. The Jawa of between 0.008 and 0.014 g measuring about 2 × 2 mm were sometimes cut into ½ and even ¼ Jawa of 0.002 g or 14,000 to the oz.

Highest denomination *World*
The 1654 Indian gold 200 Mohur (£500) coin of the Mughal Emperor Khurram Shihāb-ud-dīn Muhammad, Shāh Jahān (reigned 1628–57), is both the highest denomination coin and that of the greatest intrinsic worth ever struck. It weighed 2 177 g *70 troy oz.* and hence has an intrinsic worth of £2,800. It had a diameter of 5⅜ in *136 mm.* The only known example disappeared in Patna, Bihar, India, in c. 1820, but a plaster-cast of this coin exists in the British Museum, London.

Highest denomination *Great Britain*
Gold five-guinea pieces were minted from the reign of Charles II (1660–1685) until 1753 in the reign of George II. A pattern 5 guinea piece of George III dated 1777 also exists.

Lowest denomination *Great Britain*
Quarter farthings (sixteen to the penny) were struck in copper at the Royal Mint, London, in the Imperial coinage for use in Sri Lanka (then Ceylon), in 1839 and 1851–53.

Rarest *World*
There are numerous coins of which but a single example is known. An example of a unique coin of threefold rarity (in alloy, denomination and reign) is one of the rare admixture of bronze with inlaid gold of Kaleb I of Axum (c. A.D. 500). Only 700 Axumite coins of any sort are known.

Rarest *Modern British*
Single examples of a Victoria farthing of 1889, a George VI half-crown of 1952 and an Elizabeth II penny of 1954 are known. They were probably struck to test dies but escaped into circulation.

Most expensive *World*
The highest price paid at auction for a single coin is $272,000 (*then* £113,000) or $314,000 inclusive of commission for an Athenian silver decadrachm in Zurich, Switzerland on 30 June 1974 by Constantinople Fine Arts Inc. Steven C. Markoff of A-Mark Coin Co. Inc., Beverly Hills, California paid about $900,000 (£530,000) for the unique U.S. 1907 $20 gold Double Eagle pattern from the Dr. Wilkison collection in June 1976.

Most expensive *Great Britain*
The highest auction price paid for a British coin is $67,500 (*then* £33,000) for a James VI of Scotland £20 gold piece of 1576 at the auction of the Dundee Collection by Spink/Bowers & Ruddy in Los Angeles on 19 Feb. 1976. On 24 Nov. 1972 one of the eight 1933 bronze pennies minted was auctioned at Sotheby's for £7,000. Only one other is in private hands.

An unissued silver Crown (5 shillings) piece of Edward VIII owned by Richard Lobel & Co. in London, is the most valuable item in a set, dated 1937, insured for $500,000.

Legal tender coins *Oldest*
The oldest legal tender Imperial coins in circulation are the now rare silver shillings (now 5p) and sixpences (now 2½p) of the reign of George III, dated 1816. All gold coinage of or above the least current weight dated onward from 1838 is still legal tender. Scotland's separate coinage dates between 1135 and 1709.

Legal tender coins *Heaviest and highest denomination*
The gold five-pound (£5) piece or quintuple sovereign is both the highest current denomination coin in the United Kingdom and also, at 616.37 grains *1.4066 oz.* the heaviest. The most recent specimens made available to the public were dated 1937, of which only 5,501 were minted. (See Colour photographs 20th edition.)

Legal tender coins *Lightest and smallest*
The silver Maundy (new) penny piece is the smallest of the British legal tender coins and, at 7.27 grains (just under 1/60th of an ounce), the lightest. These coins were so used since 1670 and exist for each date since 1822 and are 0.453 in *11,5 mm* in diameter.

Greatest collection
The highest price paid for a coin collection has been $7,300,000 (*then* £3,550,000) for a hoard of 407,000 U.S. silver dollars from the La Vere Redfield estate in a courtroom auction in Reno, Nevada on 27 Jan. 1976 by Steven C. Markoff of A-Mark Coin Co. Inc. of Beverly Hills, California.

Largest Hoards
The largest hoard ever found was one of about 80,000 aurei in Brescello near Modena, Italy in 1814 believed to have been deposited c. 37 B.C. The numerically largest hoard ever found was the Brussels hoard of 1908 containing c. 150,000 coins. The Blackmoor hoard of 1873 containing 29,802 3rd and 4th century Roman bronze coins is the largest found in Britain.

The greatest hoard of gold of unknown ownership ever recovered is one valued at about $3,000,000 (£1,070,000) from the lost $8,000,000 (£2,860,000) carried in 10 ships of a Spanish bullion fleet which was sunk by a hurricane off Florida, U.S.A., on 31 July 1715. The biggest single haul was by the diver Kip Wagner on 30 May 1965.

Largest mint
The largest mint in the world is the U.S. Treasury's mint built in 1965–69 on Independence Mall, Philadelphia, covering 11½ acres *4,65 ha* with an annual capacity on a 3 shift seven day week production of 8,000 million coins. A single stamping machine can produce coins at a rate of 10,000 per minute.

Largest charity collection
The most valuable column of coins amassed for charity was a column of 62,906 two pence pieces totalling £1,258.12p "knocked over" for the Coundon Cockerels youth football

teams at the Coundon Hotel, Coventry on 8 Nov. 1976 and collected by the manager Michael Keane. The *longest* line of pennies laid was one of 1 mile 432 yds *2 005 m* (98,700 coins) by 198 children of Icknield Primary School, Sawston, Cambridgeshire in 24 hrs on 1–2 Oct. 1976. The most valuable charity fund-raising line of coins was one of 2p pieces of 1,925 yards *1,76 km* laid in under 10 hrs by the Lions Club in Chippenham Wiltshire on 7 Aug. 1976. The 70,011 coins weighed 9.91 cwt *503 kg* and were worth £1,400.22p. The worlds greatest "penny-collector" is Mr. Ray Edwards of Edmonton, Alberta, who in 1967–76 donated 188,682 Canadian one cent pieces to 6 charities.

LABOUR

Trade Union Oldest *Great Britain*
The oldest of the 150 trade unions affiliated to the Trades Union Congress (founded 1868) is the National Society of Brushmakers and General Workers (current membership 1,620) founded in 1747.

Trade Union Largest *World*
The world's largest union is the Industrie-Gewerkschaft Metall (Metal Workers' Union) of West Germany, with a membership of 2,581,340 on 1 July 1977. The union with the longest name is probably the International Association of Marble, Slate and Stone Polishers, Rubbers and Sawyers, Tile and Marble Setters' Helpers and Marble Mosaic and Terrazzo Worker's Helpers of Washington D.C., U.S.A.

Trade Union Largest *Great Britain*
The largest union in the United Kingdom is the Transport and General Workers' Union, with 1,929,834 members at 1 Apr. 1977.

Trade Union Smallest
The smallest T.U.C. affiliated union is the Wool Shear Workers' Trade Union of Sheffield with a membership of 27. The unaffiliated London Handforged Spoon and Fork Makers' Society instituted in July 1874, has a last reported membership of 6.

Labour Dispute *Earliest*
A labour dispute concerning monotony of diet and working conditions was recorded in 1153 B.C. in Thebes, Egypt. The earliest recorded strike was one by an orchestra leader from Greece named Aristos in Rome *c.* 309 B.C. The cause was meal breaks.

Labour Dispute *Largest*
The most serious single labour dispute in the United Kingdom was the General Strike of 4–12 May 1926, called by the Trades Union Congress in support of the Miners' Federation. During the nine days of the strike 1,580,000 people were involved and 14,500,000 working days were lost.

During the year 1926 a total of 2,750,000 people were involved in 323 different labour disputes and the working days lost during the year amounted to 162,300,000, the highest figure ever recorded. The figure for 1976 was 3,286,000 working days involving 658,000 workers.

Labour Dispute *Longest*
The world's longest recorded strike ended on 4 Jan. 1961, after 33 years. It concerned the employment of barbers' assistants in Copenhagen, Denmark. The longest recorded major strike was that at the plumbing fixtures factory of the Kohler Co. in Sheboygan, Wisconsin, U.S.A., between April 1954 and October 1962. The strike is alleged to have cost the United Automobile Workers' Union about $12,000,000 (£4.8 million) to sustain.

Longest Dispatch to Coventry
The longest recorded instance of a worker being "sent to Coventry" by his fellow workers is 4 years 11 months endured by Mr. Tommy Seddon of Droylsden, Greater Manchester from 9 Dec. 1970 until 7 Nov. 1975 at the Wellman Gas Engineering Co.

Unemployment *Highest*
The highest recorded unemployment in Great Britain was on 23 Jan. 1933, when the total of unemployed persons on the Employment Exchange registers was 2,903,065, representing 22.8 per cent of the insured working population. The highest figure for Wales was 244,579 (39.1 per cent) on 22 Aug. 1932.

Unemployment *Lowest*
In Switzerland in December 1973 (pop. 6.6 million), the total number of unemployed was reported to be 81. The lowest recorded peace-time level of unemployment in Britain was 0.9 per cent on 11 July 1955, when 184,929 persons were registered. The peak figure for the total working population in the United Kingdom has been 26,290,000 in September 1966.

Association *Largest*
The largest single association in the world is the Blue Cross, the U.S.-based medical insurance organization with a membership of 83,943,610 on 1 Jan. 1977. Benefits paid out exceeded $12.9 billion (£7,580 million). The largest association in the United Kingdom is the Automobile Association (formed 1905) with a membership which reached 5,190,000 on 1 Jan. 1977.

CONSUMPTION

Calories
Of all countries in the world, based on the latest available data, Ireland has the largest available total of calories per person. The net supply averaged 3,450 per day in 1968. The United Kingdom average was 3,180 per day in 1968–69. It has been estimated that Britons eat 7¼ times their own weight in food per annum or 70,000 tons/*tonnes* per day. The highest calorific value of any foodstuff is that of pure animal fat, with 930 calories per 100 g *3.5 oz*. Pure alcohol provides 710 calories per 100 g.

Protein
Australia and New Zealand have the highest recorded consumption of protein per person, an average of 106 g *3.79 oz*. per day in 1969. The United Kingdom average was 88 g *3.1 oz*. per day in 1968–69.

The lowest *reported* figures are 1,730 calories per day in the Libyan Arab Republic in 1960–62 and 33 g *1.47 oz*. of protein per day in Zaire in 1964–66.

Cereals
The greatest consumers of cereal products—flour, milled rice, etc.—are the people of Egypt, with an average of 501 lb. per person *600 g/day* in 1966–67. The United Kingdom average was 160.9 lb. *199 g/day* in 1968–69 and the figure for the Republic of Ireland was 210 lb. *260 g/day* in 1968.

Starch
The greatest eaters of starchy food (e.g. bananas, potatoes, etc.) are the people of Gabon, who consumed 4.02 lb. *1,823 g* per head per day in 1964–66. The United Kingdom average was 9.77 oz. *276 g* per day in 1970. The average for Ireland was 12.30 oz. *348 g* in 1968.

Sugar
The greatest consumers of sugars are the people of Israel, with an average of 5.85 oz. *166 g* per person per day in 1974. The lowest consumption is 0.45 oz. *13,1 g* per day reported for China. The average was 5.26 oz. *149 g* for Scotland in 1974.

Meat
The greatest meat eaters in the world—figures include offal and poultry—are the people of Uruguay, with an average consumption of 10.93 oz. *309 g* per person per day in 1964–1966. The lowest consumption is 0.16 oz. *0,45 g* in Sri Lanka (formerly Ceylon) in 1968. The United Kingdom average was 5.6 oz. *158 g* in 1973 and the Irish average was 5.52 oz. *208 g* in 1970.

Sweets
The biggest sweet eaters in the world are the people of Britain with 7.8 oz. *221 g* of confectionery per person per week in 1971. The figure for Scotland was more than 9 oz. *255 g* in 1968.

Tea

The most expensive tea marketed in the United Kingdom is "Oolong Leaf Bud", specially imported for Fortnum and Mason of Piccadilly, City of Westminster, Greater London, where in May 1977, it retailed for £11.20 per lb. or £2.47/ *100 g.* It is blended from very young Formosan leaves. In Britain the *per caput* consumption of tea in 1976 was 129.7 oz. *3 678 g.*

Coffee

The world's greatest coffee drinkers are the people of Sweden, who consumed 13,37 kg *29.47 lb.* of coffee per person in 1976. This compared with 1,86 kg *4.1 lb.* for the United Kingdom in 1976. The most expensive coffee is Jamaica Blue Mountain retailed in the U.S. but not in the United Kingdom.

Fresh water

The world's greatest consumers of fresh water are the people and industry of the United States, whose average daily consumption reached 317,540 million Imperial gal *14 435 million hectolitres* in 1974 or 1,855 U.S. gal *7 021 litres* per head per day.

Beer

Of reporting countries, the nation with the highest beer consumption per person is Western Germany, with 147,0 litres *258.7 pints* per person in 1975. The equivalent figure for the United Kingdom in 1976 is 208.0 pints *118,2 litres* per person. In the Northern Territory of Australia, however, the annual intake has been estimated to be as high as 416 pints *236 litres* per person. A society for the prevention of alcoholism in Darwin had to disband in June 1966 for lack of support.

Wine

The consumption of wine in Britain (84.4% imported) in 1976 reached an all-time high of 72.36 million gallons *328,9 million litres* or 10.33 pints *6,43 litres* per person.

Spirits

The U.K. consumption in 1976 of 35.64 million proof gallons at 5.09 pints *2,89 litres* per head was however only half the level of gin consumption in 1742.

Prohibition

The longest lasting imposition of prohibition has been 26 years in Iceland (1908–34). Other prohibitions have been Russia, later U.S.S.R. (1914–24) and U.S.A. (1920–33). The Faroe Islands have had a public (as opposed to private licensed) prohibition since 1918.

Biggest round

The largest round of drinks ever recorded was one for 1,222 people stood by the *Sunday Sun* and shouted by Jack Amos in Newcastle upon Tyne, England in October 1974 at the conclusion of the Jack o' Clubs road show.

Largest dish

The largest menu item in the world is roasted camel, prepared occasionally for Bedouin wedding feasts. Cooked eggs are stuffed in fish, the fish stuffed in cooked chickens, the chickens stuffed into a roasted sheep carcass and the sheep stuffed into a whole camel.

Most expensive food

The most expensive non-seasonal food is white truffle of Alba which fetch, according to seasonal rarity, up to $200 per lb. $440 or £250 per kg on the U.S. market. Truffles from oak roots in the Périgord district of France require drought between mid-July and mid-August. Only 7 of Europe's 70 species of this hypogeous mycorrhizal fungus are considered edible.

Longest banana split

The longest Banana split ever made was one of 1 700 m *1 mile 99 yds* in length embracing 11,333 bananas; 34,000 scoops of ice cream; 260 gal *1 181 litres* of topping, 160 lb. *72,59 kg* of chopped nuts and 100 gal *453 litres* of whipped cream at the annual fete of the Cleveland State High School, Queensland, Australia on 20 Nov. 1976.

Largest beefburger

The largest beefburger on record is one of 2,859 lb. *1 293 kg* 27½ ft *8,38 m* in circumference exhibited by Tip Top Butchers and Noonan's Bakery Pty. Ltd. at the Perth Royal Show, Western Australia on 24 Sept. 1975.

Largest cake

The largest cake ever assembled was the Baltimore City Bicentennial Cake on 4 July 1976 with ingredients weighing 69,860 lb. or 31.18 tons *31,69 tonnes.* An estimated 10,000 dozen eggs, 21,600 lb. *9 797 kg* of sugar and a 415 lb. *188 kg* pinch of salt were used. The tallest recorded self-supporting wedding cake was one of 29 tiers 15 ft *4,57 m* tall baked for Alberina Larkham (now Mrs. Ball) in Sydney Australia in June 1976.

Largest Easter egg

The largest Easter egg ever made was one 9 ft *2,74 m* high and 18 ft *5,48 m* in circumference weighing over a ton, made by Messrs Buszard of Oxford Street, London for the trousseau of a South African millionaire's daughter in 1897.

Largest haggis

The largest haggis (encased in cows stomach linings) on record was one weighing 170 lb. *77,11 kg* made by Baxters of Speyside, Fochabers, Scotland, for the Food Exhibition at Olympia in 1965.

Longest loaf

The longest one-piece loaf ever baked was one of 464 ft *141,4 m* baked by Leonard W. Gentieu on 4th Street Taft, California, U.S.A. on 17 Oct. 1975. The bake used more than 1,000 lb. *453 kg* of charcoal and the finished sandwich weighed 1,494 lb. *677 kg.*

Largest apple pie

The largest apple pies ever baked were those in a 12 ft *3,65 m* diameter dish at the Orleans Country Fair, New York State, U.S.A. of 1928 and 1929. Baking time of the 125 bushels of apples, 600 lb. *272 kg* of sugar and 600 lb. of flour was 24 hours.

Largest cherry pie

The largest cherry pie ever made was one weighing a total of 6¼ tons *6 350 kg* and containing 4,950 lb. *2 245 kg* of cherries. It measured 14 ft 4 in *4,36 m* in diameter, 24 in *60,96 cm* in depth, and was baked in the grounds of the Medusa Cement Corporation, Charlevoix, Michigan on 15 May 1976, as part of the town's contribution to America's Bicentennial celebrations.

Largest meat pie

The largest meat pie ever baked weighed 5¾ tons, measuring 18 × 6 ft and 18 in deep *5,48 × 1,83 × 0,45 m,* the eighth in the series of Denby Dale, West Yorkshire pies, to mark four royal births, baked on 5 Sept. 1964. The first was in 1788 to celebrate King George III's return to sanity but the fourth (Queen Victoria's Jubilee, 1887) went a bit "off" and had to be buried in quick-lime.

Largest mince pie

The largest mince pie recorded was one of 2,260 lb. *1 025 kg* 20 × 5 ft *6,09 × 1,52 m,* baked at Ashby-de-la-Zouch, Leicestershire on 15 Oct. 1932.

Largest omelette

The largest verified omelette in the world was one made of 6,720 eggs in a frying pan 5,0 m *16 ft 5 in* in diameter with 30 litres *52¾ pints* of oil by 6 chefs in 2 hrs 18 min. at Kruishoutem, Belgium on 19 Apr. 1976.

Largest pancake

The largest pancake ever flipped intact on any griddle was one of 5 ft 3½ in *1,61 m* diameter at a Venturer-Explorer Scouts breakfast at Escondido, California on 19 June 1976.

Largest pizza pie

The largest pizza ever baked was one measuring 25 ft 1 in *7,64 m* in diameter, hence 494 ft² *45,8 m²* in area and 1,200 lb.

544 kg in weight at the Pizza Inn, Little Rock, Arkansas, U.S.A. on 4 Sept. 1974. It was commissioned by the KARN radio station.

Largest Iced Lollipop

The world's largest iced lollipop was one of 5,750 lb. *2 608 kg* constructed for the Westside Assembly of God Church, Davenport, Iowa, U.S.A. on 7 Sept. 1975.

Blackpool rock

The mightiest piece of Blackpool lettered rock ever produced was a piece weighing more than 3 cwt *152 kg* delivered on 16 Apr. 1975 to the Royal Variety Club of Great Britain in London by Ashton Candy Co. Ltd. of Blackpool.

Largest salami

The largest salami on record was one of 11 ft *3,35 m* long with a circumference of 20 in *58 cm* weighing 142½ lb. *64,6 kg* made at St. Kilda, Melbourne, Australia in November 1974.

Largest spit roast

The most monumental barbeque has been one for over 4,000 people at Brisbane, California on 16 Sept. 1973 with a rotisserie with 12 ft *3,65 m* spit length impaling 7 buffalo with a dressed weight of 3,755 lb. *1 703 kg*. John De Marco supervised the 26 hour roast.

Largest sundae

The most monstrous ice cream sundae ever concocted is one of 5,475 lb. *2 483 kg* constructed by K. Wayne Johnson at the Annual Riverlade Carnival, Sioux City, Iowa on 24 July 1976.

Largest Yorkshire Pudding

The largest Yorkshire Pudding on record is one measuring 12 ft 8½ in by 3 ft 10 in *3,87 × 1,16 m* baked at Northallerton Rugby Club, Yorkshire, on 28 Aug. 1972.

Top Selling Sweet

The world's top selling sweets (candies) are Life Savers with 25,000 million rolls between 1913 and 14 Nov. 1973. The aggregate depth of the "hole in the middle" exceeds 1,000,000 miles *1,6 million km*. One has been made to last 87 mins.

Spice *Most expensive*

The most expensive of all spices is Mediterranean saffron (*Crocus sativus*). It takes 96,000 stigmas and therefore 32,000 flowers to make a pound *453 g*. Packets of 8 grains are retailed in the United Kingdom for 59p—equivalent to £32.26 per oz. *£1.13 per gramme*.

Spice "Hottest"

The hottest of all spices is the capsicum hot pepper known as Tabasco, first reported in 1868 by Mr. Edmund McIlhenny on Avery Island, Louisiana, U.S.A.

Most Expensive Fruit

On 5 Apr. 1977 John Synnott of Ashford, Co. Wicklow, Ireland sold 1 lb. *453 g* of strawberries (a punnet of 30 berries) to the restauranteur Mr. Leslie Cooke in the Dublin Fruit Market for £530 or £17.70 a berry.

Rarest condiment

The world's most prized condiment is Cà Cuong, a secretion recovered in minute amounts from beetles in northern Vietnam. Owing to war conditions, the price rose to $100 (*now £57*) per ounce *28 g* before supplies virtually ceased in 1975.

Energy Consumption

To express the various forms of available energy (coal, liquid fuels and water power, etc., but omitting vegetable fuels and peat), it is the practice to convert them all into terms of coal. On this basis the world average consumption was the equivalent of 2 054 kg (*40.4 cwt*) of coal, or its energy equivalents, per person in 1974.

The highest consumption in the world is in the United States, with an average of 11 485 kg *226.0 cwt* per person in 1974. The United Kingdom average was 5 464 kg *107.5 cwt* per person in 1976. The lowest recorded average for 1974 was 13 kg *28,6 lb*. per person in Rwanda.

MASS COMMUNICATIONS

Airline

The country with the busiest airlines system is the United States of America where 162,917,214,000 revenue passenger miles were flown on scheduled domestic and local services in 1974. This was equivalent to an annual trip of 770.6 miles *1 240,3 km* for every one of the inhabitants of the U.S.A. The United Kingdom airlines flew 317,628,790 miles *511,174,000 km* and carried 27,506,703 passengers in 1976.

Merchant Shipping

The world total of merchant shipping excluding vessels of less than 100 tons gross, sailing vessels and barges was 65,887 vessels of 371,999,926 tons gross on 1 July 1976. The largest merchant fleet in the world as at mid-1976 was that under the flag of Liberia with 2,600 ships of 73,477,326 tons gross. The U.K. figure for mid-1976 was 3,549 ships of 32,923,308 tons gross.

Largest and busiest ports

Physically, the largest port in the world is New York Harbor, N.Y., U.S.A. The port has a navigable waterfront of 755 miles *121,5 km* (295 miles *474 km* in New Jersey) stretching over 92 miles² *238 km²*. A total of 261 general cargo berths and 130 other piers give a total berthing capacity of 391 ships at one time. The total warehousing floor space is 422.4 acres *170,9 ha*. The world's busiest port and largest artificial harbour is the Rotterdam-Europoort in the Netherlands which covers 38 miles² *100 km²*. It handled 31,993 sea-going vessels carrying a total of 288 million tonnes of sea-going cargo, and about 200,000 barges in 1976. It is able to handle 310 sea-going vessels simultaneously of up to 300,000 tonnes and 72 ft *21,94 m* draught.

Railways

The country with the greatest length of railway is the United States, with 201,067 miles *323 585 km* of track at 1 Jan. 1974.

Britain's Narrowest Thoroughfare—Parliament Street, Exeter, Devon which narrows to 26 in *66 cm* (see p. 199). (*Alan Stone*)

The farthest anyone can get from a railway on the mainland island of Great Britain is 110 miles *177 km* by road in the case of Southend, Mull of Kintyre.

The number of journeys made on British Rail in 1976 was 708,474,000, compared with the peak year of 1957, when 1,101 million journeys (average 20.51 miles *33 km*) were made.

Road *Oldest*

The oldest trackway yet discovered in the world is the Sweet track, Shapwick, Somerset which has been dated to 4,000 B.C. The first sod on Britain's first motorway, the M6 Preston By-Pass, was cut by bulldozer driver Fred Hackett on 12 June 1956.

The country with the greatest length of road is the United States (all 50 States), with 3,815,807 miles *6 140 946 km* of graded roads at 1 Jan. 1974. Regular driving licences are issuable at 15, without a driver education course only in Hawaii and Mississippi. Thirteen U.S. States issue restricted juvenile licences at 14.

The United Kingdom has 220,690 miles *355 035 km* of road including 1,261 miles *2 029 km* of motorway at 1 April 1975 and 17,864,372 vehicles in September 1975. A total of 22,400,000 vehicles by 1985 has been forecast. The longest uninterrupted dual carriageway is from Hendon, Barnet, Greater London, for more than 425 miles *683 km via* M.1, M6, A74, M74, to the Stirling by-pass on to the A9, in Scotland.

Traffic Volume *Highest*

The highest traffic volume of any point in the world is at the Harbor and Santa Monica Freeways interchange in Los Angeles, California, U.S.A. with a 24-hour average on week-days of 425,000 vehicles in 1974. The most heavily travelled stretch of road is between 43rd and 47th Street on the Dan Ryan Expressway, Chicago with an average daily volume of 254,700 vehicles.

The territory with the highest traffic density in the world is Hong Kong. By 1 Jan. 1977 there were 190,746 motor vehicles on 674.1 miles *1085 km* of serviceable roads giving a density of 6.22 yds *5,69 m* per vehicle. The comparative figure for Great Britain in 1975 was 21 yds 2 ft 2½ in *19,88 m.*

The greatest traffic density at any one point in Great Britain is at Hyde Park Corner, London. The average daytime 8 a.m.–8 p.m. flow in 1970 (last census) was 164,338 vehicles every 12 hours. The busiest Thames bridge in 1976 was Putney Bridge, with a 24-hour average of 63,000 vehicles. The greatest reported aggregation of London buses was 52, bumper to bumper, along Oxford Street on 13 February 1976. The longest traffic jam reported in Britain was one of 35 miles *56 km* out of 42.5 miles *75,6 km* road length between Torquay and Yarcombe, Devon, on 25 July 1964 and 35 miles *56 km* on the A30 between Egham, Surrey and Micheld-ever, Hampshire on 23 May 1970.

Road *Widest*

The widest street in the world is the Monumental Axis running for 1½ miles *2,4 km* from the Municipal Plaza to the Plaza of the Three Powers in Brasilia, the capital of Brazil. The six-lane Boulevard was opened in April 1960 and is 250 m *273.4 yds* wide. The B Bridge Toll Plaza has 23 lanes (17 west bound) serving the Bay Bridge, San Francisco, California.

The only instance of 17 carriageway lanes side by side in Britain occurs on the M61 at Linnyshaw Moss, Worsley, Greater Manchester.

Road *Narrowest*

The world's narrowest street is St. John's Lane in Rome, with a width of 19 in *48 cm*. In Port Isaac, Cornwall, Temple Bar at its junction with Dolphin Street is of similar width. It is popularly known as "Squeeze-belly alley".

Roads *Longest straight*

The longest straight road in the United Kingdom was a stretch of 22¾ miles *33,6 km* between Bailgate in the City of Lincoln and Broughton Village, Humberside. Part of the

The world's busiest traffic point—the Santa Monica-Harbor Freeway interchange in Los Angeles, California. An average of 295 cars pass each minute round the clock. *(Popperfoto)*

Roman road Ermine Street, it now comprises sections of Class I (A15), Class III and unclassified road, with only two slight deviations of less than 50 ft *15 m* from the true straight line. Part of the road was closed for an airfield, reducing the straight section to 16½ miles *26,5 km.*

Road *Longest*

The longest motorable road in the world is the Pan-American Highway, which will stretch 17,018 miles *27 387 km* from North West Alaska, to southernmost Chile. There remains a gap known as the Tapon del Darién, in Panama and the Atrato Swamp, Colombia. This was first crossed in 101 days by a Jeep and a Land Rover in the 1960 National Geographic Society expedition, Richard Bevier (Canada) and Terence Whitfield (Australia).

Most complex interchange

The most complex interchange on the British road system is that at Gravelly Hill, north of Birmingham on the Midland Link Motorway section of the M6 opened on 24 May 1972. There are 18 routes on 6 levels together with a diverted canal and river, which consumed 26,000 tons/*tonnes* of steel, 250,000 tons/*tonnes* of concrete, 300,000 tons/*tonnes* of earth and cost £8,200,000.

Street *Longest World*

The longest designated street in the world is Yonge Street running north and west from Toronto, Canada. The first stretch completed on 16 Feb. 1796 ran 34 miles 53 chains *55,783 km*. Its official length now extended to Rainy River at the Manitoba-Minnesota border is 1,178.3 miles *1 896,2 km.*

Longest Great Britain

The longest designated road in Great Britain is the A1 from London to Edinburgh of 404 miles *650 km*. The longest Roman roads were Watling Street, from Dubrae (Dover) 215 miles *346 km* through Londinium (London) to Viroconium (Wroxeter), and Fosse Way, which ran 218 miles *350 km* from Lindum (Lincoln) through Aquae Sulus (Bath) to Isca Dumnoniorum (Exeter). However, a 10 mile *16 km* section of Fosse Way between Ilchester and Seaton remains indistinct. The commonest street name in Greater London is Park Road, of which there are 46.

Shortest

The shortest reported measurement of a street in Britain is 58 ft *17,67 m* of Tolbooth Street, Falkirk, Central, Scotland.

Steepest
The steepest streets in the world are Filbert Street, Russian Hill and 22nd Street, Dolores Heights, San Francisco with gradients of 31.5% or 1 in 3.17. Lombard Street between Leavenworth and Hyde with 5 consecutive hairpins is described as the "Crookedest street in the world".

Longest hill
The longest steep hill on any road in the United Kingdom is on the road westwards from Lochcarron towards Applecross in Highland, Scotland. In 6 miles *9,6 km* this road rises from sea-level to 2,054 ft *626 m* with an average gradient of 1 in 15.4, the steepest part being 1 in 4.

Of the five unclassified roads with 1 in 3 gradients the most severe is Hard Knott Pass between Boot and Ambleside, Cumbria.

Road *Highest World*
The highest trail in the world is an 8 mile *13 km* stretch of the Kang-ti-suu between Khaleb and Hsin-chi-fu, Tibet which in two places exceeds 20,000 ft *6 080 m*. The highest carriageable road in the world is one 1,180 km *733.2 miles* long between Tibet and south western Sinkiang, completed in October 1957, which takes in passes of an altitude up to 18,480 ft *5 632 m* above sea-level. Europe's highest pass (excluding the Caucasian passes) is the Col de Restefond (9,193 ft *2 802 m*) completed in 1962 with 21 hairpins between Jausiers and Saint Etienne-de-Tinée, France. It is usually closed between early October and early June. The highest motor road in Europe is the Pico de Veleta in the Sierra Nevada, southern Spain. The shadeless climb of 36 km *22.4 miles* brings the motorist to 11,384 ft *3 469 m* above sea-level and became, on completion of a road on its southern side in Summer 1974, arguably Europe's highest "pass".

Road *Highest Great Britain*
The highest road in the United Kingdom is the A6293 tarmac extension at Great Dun Fell, Cumbria, (2,780 ft *847 m*) leading to a Ministry of Defence radar installation. A permit is required to use it. The highest classified road in England is the B6293 at Killhope Cross (2,056 ft *626 m*) on the Cumbria-Durham border near Nenthead. The highest classified road in Scotland is the A93 road over the Grampians through Cairnwell, a pass between Blairgowrie, Tayside, and Braemar, Grampian, which reaches a height of 2,199 ft *670 m*. The highest classified road in Wales is the Rhondda-Afan Inter-Valley road (A4107), which reaches 1,750 ft *533 m* 2½ miles *4 km* east of Abergwynfi, Mid Glamorgan. An estate track exists to the summit of Ben a'Bhuird (3,860 ft *1 176 m*) in Grampian, Scotland. The highest motorway in Great Britain is the trans-Pennine M62, which, at the Windy Hill interchange, reaches an altitude of 1,220 ft *371 m*. Its Dean Head cutting is the deepest roadway cutting in Europe at 183 ft *55,7 m*.

Road *Lowest*
The lowest road in the world is that along the Israeli shores of the Dead Sea, 1,290 ft *393 m* below sea-level. The lowest surface roads in Great Britain are just below sea-level in the Holme Fen area of Cambridgeshire. The world's lowest "pass" is Rock Reef Pass, Everglades National Park, Florida which is 3 ft *91 cm* above sea-level.

Longest viaduct
The longest elevated road viaduct on the British road system is the 2.97 mile *4 779 m* Gravelly Hill to Castle Bromwich section of the M6. It was completed in May 1972.

Biggest square
The Tian an men (Gate of Heavenly Peace) Square in Peking, described as the navel of China, extends over 98 acres *39,6 ha*. The Maiden e Shah in Isfahan, Iran extends over 20.1 acres *8,1 ha*. The oldest London Square is Bloomsbury Square planned in 1754.

Traffic lights
Semaphore-type traffic *signals* had been set up in Parliament Square, London in 1868 with red and green gas lamps for night use. It was not an offence to disobey traffic signals until assent was given to the 1930 Road Traffic Bill. Traffic *lights* were introduced in Great Britain with a one day trial in Wolverhampton on 11 Feb. 1928. They were first permanently operated in Leeds, West Yorkshire on 16 Mar. and in Edinburgh, Scotland on 19 Mar. 1928. The first vehicle-actuated lights were installed at the Cornhill-Gracechurch Junction, City of London in 1932.

Parking meters
The earliest parking meters ever installed were those put in the business district of Oklahoma City, Oklahoma, U.S.A., on 19 July 1935. They were the invention of Carl C. Magee (U.S.A.) and reached London in 1958.

In Jan. 1977 Mr. Derek Shaw of Edinburgh was required to answer a summons for a parking ticket in Hong Kong. It was found that he did not own that vehicle and was unable to drive.

Worst driver
It was reported that a 75-year-old *male* driver received 10 traffic tickets, drove on the wrong side of the road four times, committed four hit-and-run offences and caused six accidents, all within 20 minutes, in McKinney, Texas, U.S.A., on 15 Oct. 1966. The most heavily banned driver in Britain was John Hogg, 28, who, in the High Court, Edinburgh on 27 Nov. 1975, received 5¾ years in gaol and his 3rd, 4th and 5th life bans for drunken driving in a stolen car while disqualified. For his previous 40 offences he had received bans of 71½ years plus two life bans.

Milestone
Britain's oldest milestone *in situ* is a Roman stone dating from A.D. 150 on the Stanegate, at Chesterholme, near Bardon Mill, Northumberland.

Longest Ford
The longest ford in any classified road in England is that at Bilbrook, Old Cleeve parish, Somerset which measures 90 yds *82 m* in width.

Inland Waterways
The country with the greatest length of inland waterways is Finland. The total length of navigable lakes and rivers is about 50,000 km *31,000 miles*. In the United Kingdom the total length of navigable rivers and canals is 3,940 miles *6 340 km*.

Longest navigable river
The longest navigable natural waterway in the world is the River Amazon, which sea-going vessels can ascend as far as Iquitos, in Peru, 2,236 miles *3 598 km* from the Atlantic seaboard. On a National Geographic Society expedition ending on 10 Mar. 1969, Helen and Frank Schreider navigated downstream from San Francisco, Peru, a distance of 3,845 miles *6 187 km* to Bélem.

TELECOMMUNICATIONS
Telephones
There were 379,524,000 telephones in the world at 1 Jan. 1976 as estimated by The American Telephone & Telegraph Co. The country with the greatest number was the United States, with 149,011,000 instruments, equivalent to 694.9 for every 1,000 people, compared with the United Kingdom figure of 21,035,602 (third largest in the world to the U.S.A. and Japan), or 375.1 per 1,000 people, at 31 Mar. 1976. The territory with fewest reported telephones is Pitcairn Island with 41.

The country with the most telephones per head of population is Monaco, with 840.7 per 1,000 of the population at 1 Jan. 1976. The country with the least was Bangladesh with 0.11 of a telephone per 1,000.

The greatest total of calls made in any country is in the United States, with 204,645 million (940 calls per person) in 1975. The United Kingdom telephone service connected 16,091,917,000 calls in the year 1975–76, an average of 287.7 per person.

The city with most telephones is New York City, N.Y., U.S.A., with 5,965,684 (791 per 1,000 people) at 1 Jan. 1976. In 1975 Washington D.C. reached the level of 1,404 telephones per 1,000 people though in some small areas there are still higher densities such as Beverly Hills, west of Los Angeles with a return of about 1,600 per 1,000.

Telephones *Busiest Phone*
The pay phone with the heaviest usage in the world is one in the Greyhound bus terminal, Chicago, which averages 270 calls a day thus used each 5 min 20 secs round the clock all year.

Telephones *Longest call*
The longest telephone connection on record was one of 1,000 hours from 12 Mar.–23 Apr. 1975 on the campus of Western Michigan University, Kalamazoo, Michigan. Students worked one hour shifts for the 41½ days in the fund-raising effort for a burns unit in a medical centre.

Telephones *Longest telephone cable*
The world's longest submarine telephone cable is the Commonwealth Pacific Cable (COMPAC), which runs for more than 9,000 miles *14 480 km* from Australia, *via* Auckland, New Zealand and the Hawaiian Islands to Port Alberni, Canada. It cost about £35,000,000 and was inaugurated on 2 Dec. 1963.

Telephones *Bill Most Incorrect*
On 18 Aug. 1975 the landlord of the Blue Bell Inn, Lichfield Staffordshire received a bill for £1,494,000,000. The Post Office admitted it contained "an arithmetical error".

Postal Services
The country with the largest mail in the world is the United States, whose population posted 901,000 million letters and packages in 1974 when the U.S. Postal Service employed 710,000 people. The United Kingdom total was 9,903 million letters and 170.0 million parcels in the year ending 31 Mar. 1976.

The United States also takes first place in the average number of letters which each person posts during one year. The figure was 413 in 1970. The United Kingdom figure was 177 per head in 1975–76. Of all countries the greatest discrepancy between incoming and outgoing mail is for the U.S.A. whence in 1970 only 887 million items were mailed in response to 1,477 million items received from foreign sources.

The pair of 2 cent "Cotton Reel" stamps of British Guiana (now Guyana) auctioned for £75,000 in 1970. (*Robson Lowe Ltd. (New York)*)

The rarest United Kingdom stamp ever issued—the Edward VII 6d purple overprinted IR (for Inland Revenue) of which only 11 or 12 exist. (*Stanley Gibbons Limited*)

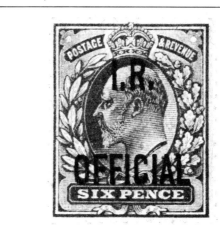

POSTAGE STAMPS

Earliest	Issued 1 May 1840	1d Black of Great Britain, Queen Victoria, 68,158,080 printed. Put on sale 6 May 1840 two days before the 2d Blue.
Highest Price (Auction) (World)	$280,000 (*then £116,666*)	1 cent black on magenta, British Guiana (now Guyana) of 1856 sold by F. T. Small to Irwin Weinberg by Robson Lowe in New York City, U.S.A. on 24 Mar. 1970.
Highest Price (Auction) (U.K.)	£50,000 £50,000	1d "Perot" of Bermuda, 1854, at Stanley Gibbons, London on 4 Oct. 1973. 1d orange-red of Mauritius, 1847, by M. René Berlingen at Stanley Gibbons, London on 25 Nov. 1976.
Largest (Special purpose) (Standard postage)	9¾ × 2¾ in 247,5 × 69,8 mm 4¾ × 3½ in 111 × 90 mm	Express Delivery of China, 1913. 250 mils of Cyprus, 2 July 1974.
Smallest	0.31 × 0.37 in 8 × 9,5 mm	10 cent and 1 peso Colombian State of Bolivar, 1863–66.
Highest Denomination (World) (U.K.)	£100 £5	Red and black, George V, of Kenya, 1925–27. Orange, Victoria, issued 21 Mar. 1882.
Lowest Denomination	3,000 pengö of Hungary	Issued 1946 when 150 million million pengö = 1p.
Rarest (World)	Unique examples include	British Guiana (now Guyana) 1 cent black on magenta of 1856 above, Swedish 3 skilling banco yellow colour error of 1857.
Rarest (U.K.)	11 or 12	6d dull purple Inland Revenue Edward VII, issued and withdrawn on 14 May 1904. Only unused specimen in private hands from W. H. Harrison-Cripps sold by Stanley Gibbons for £10,000 on 27 Oct. 1972.
Highest Price (Philatelic Item) (World)	$380,000 (*then £158,333*)	Two 1d orange-red "Post Office" stamps of Mauritius, at Harmer's Inc., New York by Raymond H. Weil Co. on 21 Oct. 1968. Item bought in an Indian Bazaar by Charles Williams in 1897 for less than £1.
Highest Price (Philatelic Item) (U.K.)	£75,000	Pair of 2 cent "Cotton Reels" of British Guiana (now Guyana) on envelope dated 26 Nov. 1851 sold by F. T. Small, by Robson Lowe at Christie's, London on 21 Mar. 1970.

Postal Address *Highest numbering*

The practice of numbering houses began in 1463 on the Pont Notre Dame, Paris, France. The highest numbered house in Britain is No. 2,679 Stratford Road, Hockley Heath, West Midlands, owned since 1964 by Mr. & Mrs. Howard Hughes. The highest numbered house in Scotland is No. 2,629 London Road, Mount Vernon, Glasgow, which is part of the local police station.

Pillar-boxes *Oldest*

The oldest site on which one is still in service is one dating from 8 Feb. 1853 in Union Street, St. Peter Port Guernsey though the present box is not the original. The oldest original box in Great Britain is another Victorian example at Barnes Cross, Holwell, near Sherborne, Dorset, also dating from probably later in 1853.

Post Offices

The Post Office's northernmost post office is at Haroldswick, Unst, Shetland Islands. The most southerly in the British Isles is at Samarès, Jersey. The oldest is at Sanquhar, Dumfries and Galloway which was first referred to in 1763. In England the Post Office at Shipton-Under-Wychwood, Oxfordshire dates back to April 1845.

Telegrams

The country where most telegrams are sent is the U.S.S.R., whose population sent 422,224,000 telegrams in 1974. The United Kingdom total was 21,036,000 including 16,806,000 sent overseas, in the year ending 31 Mar. 1976.

7. EDUCATION

Illiteracy

Literacy is variously defined as "ability to read simple subjects" and "ability to read and write a simple letter". The looseness of definition and the scarcity of data for many countries preclude anything more than approximations, but the extent of illiteracy among adults (15 years old and over) is estimated to have been 34.7 per cent in 1969. The continent with the greatest proportion of illiterates is Africa, where 81.5 per cent of adults are illiterate. The last published figure for Mali in 1960 showed 97.8 per cent of people over 15 were unable to read.

University Oldest *World*

Probably the oldest educational institution in the world is the University of Karueein, founded in A.D. 859 in Fez, Morocco.

University Oldest *Great Britain*

The oldest university in the United Kingdom is the University of Oxford, which came into being in *c.* 1167. The oldest of the existing colleges is probably University College (1249), though its foundation is less well documented than that of Merton College in 1264. The earliest college at Cambridge University is Peterhouse, founded in 1284. The largest college at either university is Trinity College, Cambridge. It was founded in 1546. The oldest university in Scotland is the University of St. Andrews, Fife. It was established in 1411.

University *Greatest enrolment*

The university with the greatest enrolment in the world is the City University of New York, U.S.A., with 269,929 students and 15,116 appointed teachers in 1976. It was founded in 1847 and has ten colleges. By May 1976 it had run into economic crisis. Britain's largest university is the University of London with 37,053 internal students (1976–77) and 27,760 external students (at 31 Mar. 1977) so totalling 64,813.

University *Largest building*

The largest university building in the world is the M. V. Lomonosov State University on the Lenin Hills, south of Moscow, U.S.S.R. It stands 240 m *787.4 ft* tall, has 32 storeys and contains 40,000 rooms, It was constructed in 1949–53.

Professor *Youngest*

The youngest at which anybody has been elected to a chair in a university is 19 years in the case of Colin MacLaurin (1698–1746), who was admitted to Marischal College, Aberdeen as Professor of Mathematics on 30 Sept. 1717. In 1725 he was made Professor of Mathematics at Edinburgh University on the recommendation of Sir Isaac Newton. In July 1967 Dr. Harvey Friedman, Ph.D., was appointed Assistant Professor of Mathematics at Stanford University, California, U.S.A. aged just 19 years.

Professor *Most durable*

The longest period for which any professorship has been held is 63 years in the case of Thomäs Martyn (1735–1825), Professor of Botany at Cambridge University from 1762 until his death. His father, John Martyn (1699–1768), had occupied the chair from 1733 to 1762.

Senior Wranglers

Since 1910 the Wranglers (first class honours students in the Cambridge University mathematical Tripos, part 2) have been placed in alphabetical order only. In 1890 Miss P. G. Fawcett of Newnham was placed "above the Senior Wrangler".

Most Eternal Students

George A. Goulty J.P. of Guildford, Surrey in July 1977 submitted a thesis for a Ph.D. after 23 years as a student. He was already an M.A. M.Sc., M.Phil., A.A.Dipl., A. R.I.B.A., D.p. T.P., M.R.T.P.I., A.I.L.A. etc. Mrs. Sarah Ann Raw joined Hendon College, Greater London on 29 Sept. 1976 for further education in lip-reading aged 102 years 9 months.

Miss Mabel Fitzgerald received an honorary M.A. degree from Oxford University on 14 Dec. 1972 aged 100 years 113 days in recognition of work on the 19th century before the School of Physiology was open to women.

Youngest undergraduate and graduate

The most extreme recorded case of undergraduate juvenility was that of William Thomson (1824–1907), later Lord Kelvin, O.M., G.C.V.O., who entered Glasgow University aged 10 years 4 months in October 1834 and matriculated on 14 Nov. 1834. Dr. Merrill Kenneth Wolf (b. 28 Aug. 1931) of Cleveland, Ohio took his B.A. in music from Yale University in Sept. 1945 in the month of his 14th birthday.

School *Oldest in Britain*

The title of the oldest existing school in Britain is contested. It is claimed that King's School in Canterbury, Kent, was a foundation of Saint Augustine, some time between his arrival in Kent in A.D. 597 and his death in *c.* 604. Cor Tewdws (College of Theodosius) at Llantwit Major, South Glamorgan, reputedly burnt down in A.D. 446, was refounded after an elapse of 62 years, by St. Illtyd in 508 and flourished into the 13th century.

School Largest *World*

At the time of its highest enrolments the largest school in the world was the De Witt Clinton High School in the Bronx, New York City, N.Y., U.S.A., with a peak of 12,000 in 1934. It was founded in 1897 and now has an enrolment of 6,000.

Great Britain

The school with the most pupils in Great Britain was Exmouth Comprehensive, Devon with 2,364 (Jan. 1976). The highest enrolment in Scotland is at Our Lady's Roman Catholic High School, Motherwell, Strathclyde with 2,279 (Jan. 1977). The total in Holy Child School, Belfast, Northern Ireland reached 2,752 in 1973 before being split up.

School *Longest*

Britain's most attenuated school is the Wensleydale School, Leyburn, North Yorkshire. Some pupils have to be "bussed" 13.0 miles *20,9 km* between class-rooms of the two most separated elements of this comprehensive.

School Most Expensive *World*

The Oxford Academy at Westbrook, Connecticut, U.S.A. charges annual tuition fees of $9,600 (£4,500).

The world's most massive single university building at the University of Mihail Lomonosov in the Lenin Hills south of Moscow. The tower is 240 m *787 ft* in height (see page 202). (*Tim Roberts*)

Great Britain

The most expensive school in Great Britain is Millfield in Street, Somerset, founded by R. J. O. Meyer in 1937. The terminal fee for boarding entries under 17 for the winter term 1977 is £960 indicating an annual rate of some £2,880. The most expensive girls' school in 1977–78 was Roedean, East Sussex (founded 1885) with annual fees of £1,869.

Oldest old school tie

The practice of wearing distinctive neckties bearing the colours of registered designs of schools, universities, sports clubs, regiments, etc., appears to date from *c.* 1880. The practice originated in Oxford University, where boater bands were converted into use as "ribbon ties". The earliest definitive evidence stems from an order from Exeter College for college ties, dated 25 June, 1880.

Most Schools

The greatest documented number of schools attended by a pupil is 265 by Wilma Williams, now Mrs. R. J. Horton, from 1933–43 when her parents were in show business in the U.S.A.

Most "O" and "A" levels

Francis L. Thomason of Tottenham, London had by January 1977 accumulated 37 "O", 8 "A" and 1 "S" levels making a total of 46. A. F. Prime, a prisoner in H.M. Prison Portsmouth, has a total of 10 A's and 33 O's to July 1977. Environmental difficulties make study far harder in prison than elsewhere.

Robert Pidgeon (b. 7 Feb. 1959) of St. Peter's School, Bournemouth, secured 13 "O" level passes at Grade A at one sitting in the summer of 1975.

Youngest headmaster

The youngest headmaster of a major public school was Henry Montagu Butler (b. 2 July 1833), appointed Headmaster of Harrow School on 16 Nov. 1859, when aged 26 years 137 days. His first term in office began in January 1860.

Most Durable Teachers

James Boucher, J.P. (born in Fife, Scotland, 1851) served as a schoolmaster for 72 years from 1866 to January 1939. He began as a pupil teacher in his village school in Ladybank, Fife and ended his career as Headmaster of Garvald Public School for 55 years (1884–1939). Col. Ernest Achay Loftus C.B.E., T.D. (b. 11 Jan. 1884) served as a teacher over a span of 73 years from September 1901 in York, England until 18 Feb. 1975 in Zambia retiring as the world's oldest civil servant aged 91 years 38 days. Miss Nellie Collier (b. 1889) taught at Enborne School, Berkshire from 1902 to 1960 and from then to May 1968 as a Meals supervisor to complete 75 years. As a teacher no pupil left unable to read or write.

8. RELIGIONS

Oldest

The oldest major formal religion is Hinduism. Its Vedic precursor was brought to India by Aryans *c.* 1500 B.C. The Rig Veda Hindu hymnal was codified *c.* 900 B.C. or earlier.

Largest

Religious statistics are necessarily only approximate. The test of adherence to a religion varies widely in rigour, while many individuals, particularly in the East, belong to two or more religions.

Christianity is the world's prevailing religion, with some 1,050,000,000 adherents in 1977. The Vatican computer reported that for 1971 there were 665,700,000 Roman Catholics. The largest non-Christian religion is Islam (Muslim) with some 540,000,000 followers.

In the United Kingdom the Anglicans comprise members of the Established Church of England, the Dis-established Church in Wales, the Episcopal Church in Scotland and the Church of Ireland. In mid 1973 there were 27,484,000 (58.9%

of the home population) baptized in the Church of England, which has two provinces (Canterbury and York), 43 dioceses, 12,009 full-time diocesan clergymen (1976) and 13,950 parish churches (1976).

In Scotland the most numerous group is the Church of Scotland (46 Presbyteries), which had 1,061,706 members as at 1 Jan. 1975.

Largest clergies

The world's largest religious organization is the Roman Catholic Church, with 717,000,000 members, 425,000 professional priests and 900,000 nuns. The total number of cardinals, patriarchs, metropolitans, archbishops, bishops, abbots and superiors is 4,000. There are about 420,000 churches. The total number holding Aaronic and Melchizedek priesthood in the Latter-day Saint Church (Mormon Church) as at 1 Jan. 1977 was 906,180.

Jews

The total of world Jewry was estimated to be 14.6 million in 1975. The highest concentration is in the United States, with 5.9 million, of whom 2,100,000 are in the New York area. The total in Israel is 3,450,000. The total of British Jewry is 460,000 of whom 285,000 are in Greater London, and 13,750 in Glasgow. The total in Tokyo, Japan, is less than 1,000.

PLACES OF WORSHIP

Oldest *World*

The earliest known shrine dates from the proto-neolithic Natufian culture in Jericho, where a site on virgin soil has been dated to the ninth millennium B.C. A simple rectilinear red-plastered room with a niche housing a stone pillar believed to be the shrine of a Pre-Pottery fertility cult dating from c. 6500 B.C. was also uncovered in Jericho (now Arihā) in Jordan. The oldest surviving Christian church in the world is Qal'at es Salihige in eastern Syria, dating from A.D. 232.

Oldest *Great Britain*

The oldest ecclesiastical building in the United Kingdom is a 6th century cell built by St. Brendan in A.D. 542 on Eileachan Naoimh (pronounced Noo), Garvelloch Islands, Strathclyde. The Church in the United Kingdom with the oldest origins is St. Martin's Church in Canterbury, Kent. It was built in A.D. 560 on the foundations of a 1st century Roman church. The

oldest church in Ireland is the Gallerus Oratory, built in c. 750 at Ballyferriter, near Kilmalkedar, County Kerry, Britain's oldest nunnery is St. Peter and Paul Minster, on the Isle of Thanet, Kent. It was founded in c. 748 by the Abbess Eadburga of Bugga. The oldest wooden church in Great Britain is St. Andrew's, Greensted, near Ongar, Essex dating to A.D. 845 though some of the timbers date to the original building of c. A.D. 650.

Temple Largest

The largest religious structure ever built is Angkor Wat (City Temple), enclosing 402 acres *162,6 ha* in Cambodia, south-east Asia. It was built to the God Vishnu by the Khmer King Suryavarman II in the period 1113–50. Its curtain wall measures 1,400 by 1,400 yds *1 280 × 1 280 m* and its population before it was abandoned in 1432, was 80,000. The largest Buddhist temple in the world is Borobudur, near Joyjakarta, Indonesia built in the 8th century.

Cathedral Largest *World*

The world's largest cathedral is the cathedral church of the Diocese of New York, St. John the Divine, with a floor area of 121,000 ft^2 *11 240 m^2* and a volume of 16,822,000 ft^3 *476 350 m^3*. The corner stone was laid on 27 Dec. 1892, and the Gothic building was still uncompleted in 1977. In New York it is referred to as "Saint John the Unfinished". The nave is the longest in the world, 601 ft *183,18 m* in length, with a vaulting 124 ft *37,79 m* in height.

The cathedral covering the largest area is that of Santa Mariá de la Sede in Sevilla (Seville), Spain. It was built in Spanish Gothic style between 1402 and 1519 and is 414 ft *126,18 m* long, 271 ft *82,60 m* wide and 100 ft *30,48 m* high to the vault of the nave.

Cathedral Largest *Great Britain*

The largest cathedral in the British Isles is the Anglican Cathedral of Liverpool. Built in modernized Gothic style, work was begun on 18 July 1904, and when completed will have cost over £3,000,000. The building encloses 100,000 ft^2 *9 300 m^2* and has an overall length of 671 ft *204,52 m*. The Vestey Tower is 331 ft *100,88 m* high.

The largest church in the world, St. Peter's in Rome. Its construction spanned the whole of the 16th century (see p. 205). (*Popperfoto*)

Cathedral Smallest

The smallest cathedral in the world is the Pro-Cathedral Church of St. John the Baptist, Murray Bridge, South Australia. It was dedicated on 2 Feb. 1887 and has had the cathedra of the Bishop of The Murray since 16 Apr. 1970. It measures 1,025 ft² *95,2 m²* and has a capacity for only 130. The smallest cathedral in use in the United Kingdom (of old foundation) is St. Asaph in Clwyd, Wales. It is 182 ft *55,47 m* long, 68 ft *20,72 m* wide and has a tower 100 ft *30,48 m* high. Oxford Cathedral in Christ Church (College) is 155 ft *47,24 m* long. The nave of the Cathedral of the Isles on the Isle of Cumbrae, Strathclyde measures only 40 × 20 ft *12,19 × 6,09 m*. The total floor area is 2,124 ft² *197,3 m²*.

Church Largest *World*

The largest church in the world is the basilica of St. Peter, built between 1492 and 1612 in the Vatican City, Rome. The length of the church, measured from the apse, is 611 ft 4 in *186,33 m*. The area is 162,990 ft² *15 142 m²*. The inner diameter of the famous dome is 137 ft 9 in *41,98 m* and its centre is 119 m *390 ft 5 in* high The external height is 457 ft 9 in *139,52 m*.

The elliptical Basilique of St. Pie X at Lourdes, France, completed in 1957 at a cost of £2,000,000 has a capacity of 20,000 under its giant span arches and a length of 200 m *656 ft*.

The crypt of the underground Civil War Memorial Church in the Guadarrama Mountains, 45 km *28 miles* from Madrid, Spain, is 260 m *853 ft* in length. It took 21 years (1937–58) to build, at a reported cost of £140,000,000 and is surmounted by a cross 150 m *492 ft* tall.

Church Largest *Great Britain*

The largest church in the United Kingdom used as a parish church (since 1548) is the Church of SS John and Martin at Beverley, Humberside, known as Beverley Minster, which is 365 ft *111,25 m* long and 169 ft *51,5 m* across the large transept with a 64 ft *19,5 m* wide nave and a calculated floor area of 29,840 ft² *2 772 m²*.

Church Smallest *World*

The world's smallest church is the Union Church at Wiscasset, Maine, U.S.A., with a floor area of 31½ ft² *2,92 m²* (7 × 4½ ft *2,13 × 1,37 m*). Les Vauxbalets Church in Guernsey has an area of 16 × 12 ft *4,87 × 3,65 m*, room for one priest and a congregation of two.

Church Smallest *Great Britain*

The smallest church in use in England is Bremilham Church, Cowage Farm, Foxley near Malmesbury, Wiltshire which measures 12 × 12 ft *3,65 × 3,65 m* and is used for service once a year. The smallest completed medieval English church in regular use is that at Culbone, Somerset, which measures 35 × 12 ft *10,66 × 3,65 m*. The smallest Welsh chapel is St. Trillo's Chapel, Rhôs-on-Sea (Llandrillo-yn-Rhos), Clwyd, measuring only 12 × 6 ft *3,65 × 1,83 m*. The smallest chapel in Scotland is St. Margaret's, Edinburgh, measuring 16½ × 10½ ft *5,02 × 3,20 m*, giving a floor area of 173¼ ft² *16,09 m²*.

Synagogue Largest *World*

The largest synagogue in the world is the Temple Emanu-El on Fifth Avenue at 65th Street, New York City, N.Y., U.S.A. The temple, completed in September 1929, has a frontage of 150 ft *45,72 m* on Fifth Avenue and 253 ft *77,11 m* on 65th Street. The Sanctuary proper can accommodate 2,500 people, and the adjoining Beth-El Chapel seats 350. When all the facilities are in use, more than 6,000 people can be accommodated.

Synagogue Largest *Great Britain*

The largest synagogue in Great Britain is the Edgware Synagogue, Barnet, Greater London, completed in 1959, with a capacity of 1,630 seats. That with highest active membership is Ilford Synagogue with 2,699 at 1 Jan. 1977.

Mosque Largest

The largest mosque ever built was the now ruinous al-Malawiya mosque of al-Mutawakil in Samarra, Iraq built in A.D. 842–852 and measuring 9.21 acres *3,72 ha* with dimensions of 784 × 512 ft *238,9 × 156,0 m*. The world's largest mosque in use is the Jama Masjid (1644–58) in Delhi, India, with an area of more than 10,000 ft² *929 m²* and two minarets 108 ft *32,91 m* tall. The largest mosque will be the Merdeka Mosque in Djakarta, Indonesia, which was begun in 1962. The cupola will be 45 m *147.6 ft* in diameter and the capacity in excess of 50,000 people.

Minaret Tallest

The world's tallest minaret is the Qutb Minar, south of New Delhi, India, built in 1194 to a height of 238 ft *72,54 m*.

Pagoda Tallest

The world's tallest pagoda is the Shwe Dogon Pagoda in Rangoon, Burma which was increased to its present height of 326 ft *99,36 m* and perimeter of 1,420 ft *432,8 m* by Hsinbyushin, King of Ava (1763–1776). The tallest Chinese temple is the 13-storey Pagoda of the Six Harmonies (*Liu he t'a*) outside Hang-chow. It is "nearly 200 ft [*61 m*] high".

Nave Longest

The longest nave in the United Kingdom is that of St. Albans Cathedral, Hertfordshire, which is 285 ft *86,86 m* long compared with 266½ ft *81,22 m* for the nave of Winchester Cathedral, which is 8 ft *1,82 m* longer overall with 556 ft *169,46 m*.

Spire Tallest *World*

The tallest cathedral spire in the world is that of the Protestant Cathedral of Ulm in Germany. The building is early Gothic and was begun in 1377. The tower, in the centre of the west façade, was not finally completed until 1890 and is 160,90 m *528 ft* high. The world's tallest church spire is that of the Chicago Temple of the First Methodist Church on Clark Street, Chicago, Illinois, U.S.A. The building consists of a 22-storey skyscraper (erected in 1924) surmounted by a parsonage at 330 ft *100,5 m*, a "Sky Chapel" at 400 ft *121,92 m* and a steeple cross at 568 ft *173,12 m* above street level.

Great Britain

The highest spire in Great Britain is that of the church of St. Mary, called Salisbury Cathedral, Wiltshire. The Lady Chapel was built in the years 1220–25 and the main fabric of the cathedral was finished and consecrated in 1258. The spire was added later, 1334–65, and reaches a height of 404 ft *123,13 m*. The Central Spire of Lincoln Cathedral completed in c. 1307 and which fell in 1548 was 525 ft *160,02 m* tall.

Stained glass *Oldest*

The oldest stained glass in the world represents the Prophets in a window of the cathedral of Augsburg, Bavaria, Germany, dating from c. 1050. The oldest datable stained glass in the United Kingdom is represented by 12th century fragments in the Tree of Jesse in the north aisle of the nave of York Minster, dated c. 1150, and medallions in Rivenhall Church, Essex which appear to date from the first half of that century. Dates late in the previous century have been attributed to glass in a window of the church at Compton, Surrey, and a complete window in St. Mary the Virgin, Brabourne, Kent.

Stained glass *Largest*

The largest stained glass window is the complete mural of The Resurrection Mausoleum in Justice, Illinois, measuring 22,381 ft² *2 079 m²* in 2,448 panels completed in 1971. The largest single stained glass window in Great Britain is the East window in Gloucester Cathedral measuring 72 × 38 ft *21,94 × 11;58 m*, set up to commemorate the Battle of Crécy (1346), while the largest area of stained glass is 125 windows, totalling 25,000 ft² *2 322 m²* in York Minster.

Brasses

The world's oldest monumental brass is that commemorating Bishop Ysowilpe in St. Andrew's Church, Verden, near Hanover, West Germany, dating from 1231. The oldest in Great Britain is of Sir John D'Abernon at Stoke D'Abernon, near Leatherhead, Surrey, dating from 1277.

CHURCH PERSONNEL
Saints

There are 1,848 "registered" saints of whom 628 are Italians, 576 French and 271 from the British Isles. The total includes 15 Popes. The first U.S. born saint is Mother Elizabeth Ann Bayley Seton (1774–1821) canonized 14 Sept. 1975.

Most and least rapidly Canonized
The shortest interval that has elapsed between the death of a Saint and his canonization was in the case of St. Anthony of Padua, Italy, who died on 13 June 1251 and was canonized 352 days later on 30 May 1252. The other extreme is represented by St. Bernard of Thiron for 20 years Prior of St. Sabinus, who died in 1117 and was made a Saint in 1861—744 years later.

Pope *Reign Longest and Shortest*
The longest reign of any of the 262 Popes has been that of Pius IX (Giovanni Maria Mastai-Ferretti), who reigned for 31 years 236 days from 16 June 1846 until his death aged 85, on 7 Feb. 1878. Pope Stephen II was elected on 24 Mar. 752 and died two days later.

Pope *Oldest*
It is recorded that Pope St. Agatho (reigned 678–681) was elected at the age of 103 and lived to 106, but recent scholars have expressed doubts. The oldest of recent Pontiffs has been Pope Leo XIII (Gioacchino Pecci), who was born on 2 Mar. 1810, elected Pope at the third ballot on 20 Feb. 1878 and died on 20 July 1903, aged 93 years 140 days.

Pope *Youngest*
The youngest of all Popes was Pope Benedict IX (d. 1056) (Theophylact), who had three terms as Pope; 1032–44; April to May 1045; and 8 Nov. 1047 to 17 July 1048. It would appear that he was aged only 11 or 12 in 1032, though the Catalogue of the Popes admits only to his "extreme youth".

Last non-Italian, ex-Cardinalate and English Popes
The last non-Italian Pope was the Utrecht-born Cardinal Priest Adrian Dedel (1459–1523) of the Netherlands. He was elected on 9 Jan. 1522, crowned Pope Adrian VI on 31 Aug. 1522 and died on 14 Sept. 1523. The last Pope elected from outside the College of Cardinals was Bartolomeo Prignano (1318–89), Archbishop of Bari, who was elected Pope Urban VI on 8 April 1378. The only Englishman to be elected Pope was Nicholas Breakspear (born at Abbots Langley, near Watford, Hertfordshire, in *c.* 1100), who, as Cardinal Bishop of Albano, was elected Pope Adrian IV on 4 Dec. 1154, and died on 1 Sept. 1159.

Last married Pope
The first 37 Popes had no specific obligation to celibacy. Pope Hormisdas (514–523) was the father of Pope Silverius (536–537). The last married Pope was Adrian II (867–872). Rodrigo Borgia was the father of at least four children before being elected Pope Alexander VI in 1492.

Slowest papal election
After 31 months without declaring *Habemus Papam* ("We have a Pope"), the cardinals were subjected to a bread and water diet and the removal of the roof of their conclave by the Mayor of Viterbo before electing Tabaldo Visconti (*c.* 1210–1276), the Archbishop of Liège, as Pope Gregory X on 1 Sept. 1271. The papacy was, however, vacant for at least 3 years 214 days in A.D. 304–308. The shortest conclave was that of 21 Oct. 1503 for the election of Pope Julius II on a first ballot.

Cardinal *Oldest*
By 2 Feb. 1973 the Sacred College of Cardinals contained a record 145 declared members compared with 138 in June 1976. The oldest is the 96 year old Cardinal José da Costa Nuñes (born Cardelaria, Portugal, 15 Mar. 1880). The record length of service of any cardinal has been 60 years 10 days by the Cardinal York, a grandson of James VII of Scotland and II of England, from 3 July 1747 to 13 July 1807. The oldest Cardinal of all time was probably Giorgio da Costa (b. Portugal, 1406), who died in Rome on 18 Sept. 1508 aged 102.

Cardinal *Youngest*
The youngest Cardinal of all time was Luis Antonio de Borbon (b. 25 July 1727) created on 19 Dec. 1735 aged 8 years 147 days. His son Luis was also made a Cardinal but aged 23. The youngest Cardinal is Emile Biayenda, Archbishop of Brazzaville (b. 1927). Antonio Ribeiro, Patriarch of Lisbon, was named on 2 Feb. 1973 aged 45.

Bishopric *Longest tenures*
The longest tenures of any Church of England bishopric is 57 years in the case of the Rt. Rev. Thomas Wilson, who was consecrated Bishop of Sodor and Man on 16 Jan. 1698 and died in office on 7 Mar. 1755. Of English bishoprics the longest tenure, if one excludes the unsubstantiated case of Aethelwulf, reputedly Bishop of Hereford from 937 to 1012, are those of 47 years by Jocelin de Bohun (Salisbury) 1142–1189 and Nathaniel Crew or Crewe (Durham) 1674–1721.

Bishop *Oldest*
The oldest serving bishop (excluding Suffragans and Assistants) in the Church of England at 1 July 1977 was the Rt. Rev. Ronald Ralph Williams who was born on 14 Oct. 1906 and has been Bishop of Leicester since 1953.

The oldest Roman Catholic bishop in recent years was Mgr. Ernesto Alfonso Carinci (b. 9 Nov. 1862), who was titular Archbishop of Seleucia, in Isauria, from 1945 until his death on 6 Dec. 1963, at the age of 101 years 27 days. He had celebrated Mass about 24,800 times. Bishop Herbert Welch of the United Methodist Church who was elected a bishop for Japan and Korea in 1916 died on 4 Apr. 1969 aged 106.

Bishop *Youngest*
The youngest bishop of all time was H.R.H. The Duke of York and Albany K.G., G.C.B., G.C.H., the second son of George III, who was elected Bishop of Osnabrück, through his father's influence as Elector of Hanover, at the age of 196 days on 27 Feb. 1764. He resigned after 39 years' enjoyment.

The youngest serving bishop (excluding Suffragans and Assistants) in the Church of England at 1 July 1977 was the Rt. Rev. David Stuart Sheppard (b. 6 Mar. 1929), Bishop of Liverpool. He played 22 times for England in Test cricket.

Longest incumbency
The longest incumbency on record is one of 76 years by the Rev. Bartholomew Edwards, Rector of St. Nicholas, Ashill, Norfolk from 1813 to 1889. There appears to be some doubt as to whether the Rev. Richard Sherinton was installed at Folkestone from 1524 or 1529 to 1601. If the former is correct it would surpass the Norfolk record. The parish of Farrington, Hampshire had only two incumbents in the 122 year period from 28 Mar. 1797 to 5 Apr. 1919.

Longest serving chorister
Alfred Ernest Pick (d. 23 Dec. 1973, aged 95) served in the choir of St. Helen's Church, Sandal, Wakefield, West Yorkshire from August 1886 to April 1973—a stretch of 86¾ years. Having become a choirster in 1876 at the age of 9, Thomas Rogers was appointed vicar's warden in 1966 at Montacute, Somerset.

Oldest parish register
The oldest part of any parish register surviving in England is a sheet from that of Alfriston, East Sussex recording a marriage on 10 July 1504. Scotland's oldest surviving register is that for Anstruther-Wester, Fife, with burial entries from 1549.

Crowds *Largest*
The greatest recorded number of human beings assembled with a common purpose was an estimated 12,700,000 at the Hindu festival of Kumbh-Mela, which was held at the confluence of the Yamuna (formerly called the Jumna), the Ganges and the invisible "Sarasviti" at Allahabad, Uttar Pradesh, India, on 19 Jan. 1977. The holiest time during this holiest day since 1833 was during the planetary alignment between 9.28 and 9.40 a.m. during which only 200,000 achieved immersion.

Largest funeral
The greatest attendance at any funeral is the estimated 4 million who thronged Cairo, Egypt, for the funeral of President Gamal Abdel Nasser (1918–1970) on 1 Oct. 1970.

Biggest demonstrations
A figure of 2.7 million was published from China for the demonstration against the U.S.S.R. in Shanghai on 3–4 Apr. 1969 following the border clashes, and one of 10 million for the May Day celebrations of 1963 in Peking.

ACCIDENTS & DISASTERS Death Tolls

WORST IN THE WORLD

Category	No.	Description	Date
Pandemic	75,000,000	The Black Death (bubonic, pneumonic and septicaemic plague)	1347–1351
	21,640,000	Influenza	April–Nov. 1918
Famine	9,500,000[1]	Northern China	Feb. 1877–Sept. 1878
Flood	3,700,000	Hwang-ho River, China	Aug. 1931
Circular Storm[2]	1,000,000	Ganges Delta Islands, Bangladesh	12–13 Nov. 1970
Earthquake	830,000	Shensi Province, China (duration 2 hours)	23 Jan. 1556
Landslide	180,000	Kansu Province, China	16 Dec. 1920
Atomic Bomb	141,000	Hiroshima, Japan	6 Aug. 1945
Conventional Bombing[3]	135,000	Dresden, Germany	13–15 Feb. 1945
Marine (single ship)	c. 7,700	Wilhelm Gustloff (24,484 tons) German liner torpedoed off Danzig by U.S.S.R. submarine S-13	30 Jan. 1945
Aluvian Flood	c. 25,000[4]	Yungay, Huascarán, Peru	31 May 1970
Panic	c. 4,000	Chungking (Zhong qing) China air raid shelter	c. 8 June 1941
Dam Burst	2,209	South Fork Dam, Johnstown, Pennsylvania	31 May 1889
Explosion	1,963[5]	Halifax, Nova Scotia, Canada	6 Dec. 1917
Fire[6] (single building)	1,670	The Theatre, Canton, China	May 1845
Mining[7]	1,572	Honkeiko Colliery, China (coal dust explosion)	26 April 1942
Riot	c. 1,200	New York City anti-conscription riots	13–16 July 1863
Crocodiles	c. 900	Japanese soldiers, Ramree Is., Burma (disputed)	19–20 Feb. 1945
Fireworks	>800	Dauphine's Wedding, Seine, Paris	16 May 1770
Tornado	689	South Central States, U.S.A.	18 Mar. 1925
Aircraft (Civil)	582	KLM-Pan Am Boeing 747 ground crash, Tenerife	27 Mar. 1977
Railway	543	Modane, France	12 Dec. 1917
Man-eating Animal[8]	436	Champawat district, India, tigress shot by Col. Jim Corbett	
Hail	246	Moradabad, Uttar Pradesh, India	20 April 1888
Submarine	129	U.S.S. Thresher off Cape Cod, Massachusetts, U.S.A.	10 April 1963
Road (single vehicle)[9]	127	Bus crashed into irrigation canal, Egypt	9 Aug. 1973
Helicopter	54	Israeli military "Sea Stallion", West Bank	10 May 1977
Mountaineering	40[10]	U.S.S.R. Expedition on Mount Everest	Dec. 1952
Ski Lift (Cable car)	42	Cavalese resort, Northern Italy	9 Mar. 1976
Lightning (single bolt)	21	Hut in Chinamasa Kraal nr. Umtali, Rhodesia	23 Dec. 1975
Space Exploration	3	Apollo oxygen fire, Cape Kennedy, Fla., U.S.A.	27 Jan. 1967
	3	Soyuz II re-entry over U.S.S.R.	29 June 1971

WORST IN THE UNITED KINGDOM

Category	No.	Description	Date
Pandemic	800,000	The Black Death (bubonic, pneumonic and septicaemic plague)	1347–1350
	225,000	Influenza	Sept.–Nov. 1918
Famine	1,500,000[11]	Ireland (famine and typhus)	1846–1851
Flood	c. 2,000[12]	Severn Estuary	20 Jan. 1606
Circular Storm	c. 8,000	"The Channel Storm"	26 Nov. 1703
Earthquake	4	East Anglian Earthquake	22 April 1884
Landslide	144	Pantglas coal tip No. 7, Aberfan, Mid Glamorgan	21 Oct. 1966
Conventional Bombing	1,436	London	10–11 May 1941
Marine (single ship)	c. 800[13]	H.M.S. Royal George, off Spithead	29 Aug. 1782
Aluvian Flood	8	Lewes, East Sussex (snowdrifts)	27 Dec. 1836
Panic	183	Victoria Hall, Sunderland, Tyne and Wear	16 June 1883
Dam Burst	250	Bradfield Reservoir, Dale Dyke, near Sheffield, South Yorkshire (embankment burst)	12 Mar. 1864
Explosion	134[14]	Chilwell, Notts. (explosives factory)	1 July 1918
Fire (single building)	188[15]	Theatre Royal, Exeter	5 Sept. 1887
Mining	439	Universal Colliery, Senghenydd, Mid Galmorgan	14 Oct. 1913
Riot	565 (min)	London anti-Catholic Gordon riots	2–13 June 1780
Tornado	60	Widecombe, Devon (casualty figure)	21 Oct. 1638
Aircraft (Civil)	118[16]	B.E.A. Trident 1C, Staines, Surrey	18 June 1972
Railway	227[17]	Triple collision, Quintins Hill, Dumfries & Galloway	22 May 1915
Submarine	99	H.M.S. Thetis, during trials, Liverpool Bay	1 June 1939
Road (single vehicle)	33	Coach crash, River Dibb, nr. Grassington, North Yorks	27 May 1975
Mountaineering	6	On Cairngorm, Scotland (4,084 ft)	21 Nov. 1971
Lightning (single bolt)	31	Worst year on record (annual av. 12)	1914

Footnotes

[1] In 1770 the great Indian famine carried away a proportion of the population estimated as high as one third, hence a figure of tens of millions. The figure for Bengal alone was also probably about 10 million. It has been estimated that more than 5,000,000 died in the post-World War I famine of 1920–21 in the U.S.S.R. The U.S.S.R. government in July 1923 informed Mr. (later President) Herbert Hoover that the A.R.A. (American Relief Administration) had since August 1921 saved 20,000,000 lives from famine and famine diseases.

[2] This figure published in 1972 for the East Pakistan disaster was from Dr. Afzal, Principal Scientific Officer of the Atomic Energy Authority Centre, Dacca. One report asserted that less than half of the population of the 4 islands of Bhola, Charjabbar, Hatia and Ramagati (1961 Census 1.4 million) survived. The most damaging hurricane recorded was the billion dollar Betsy (name now retired) in 1965 with an estimated insurance pay-out of $750 million.

[3] The number of civilians killed by the bombing of Germany has been put variously at 593,000 and "over 635,000". A figure of c. 140,000 deaths in the U.S.A.F. fire raid on Tokyo of 10 Mar. 1945 has been attributed. Total Japanese fatalities were 600,000 (conventional) and 220,000 (nuclear).

[4] A total of 10,000 Austrian and Italian troops is reported to have been lost in the Dolomite valley of Northern Italy on 13 Dec. 1916 in more than 100 snow avalanches. The total is probably exaggerated though bodies were still being found in 1952.

[5] Some sources maintain that the final death roll was over 3,000 on 6–7 Dec.

[6] Worst ever hotel fire 162 killed. Hotel Taeyonkak, Seoul, South Korea 25 Dec. 1971.

[7] The worst gold mining disaster in South Africa was 152 killed due to flooding in the Witwatersrand Gold Mining Co. Gold Mine in 1909. Between 500 and 800 died in the Torro Tunnel, Leon, Spain on 3 Jan. 1944.

[8] In the period 1941–42 c. 1,500 Kenyans were killed by a pride of 22 man-eating lions. Eighteen of these were shot by a hunter named Rushby.

[9] The worst ever years for road deaths in the U.S.A. and the U.K. have been respectively 1969 (56,400) and 1941 (9,169). The global aggregate death roll was put at 25 million in Sept. 1975. The greatest pile-up on British roads was on the M6 near Thelwall Interchange, near Thelwall, involving 200 vehicles on 13 Sept. 1971 with 11 dead and 60 injured.

[10] According to Polish sources, not confirmed by the U.S.S.R. Also 23 died on Mount Fuji, Japan, in blizzard and avalanche on 20 Mar. 1972.

[11] Based on the net rate of natural increase between 1841 and 1851, a supportable case for a loss of population of 3 million can be made out if rates of under-enumeration of 25 per cent (1841) and 10 per cent (1851) are accepted. Potato rot (Phytophthora infestans) was first reported on 13 Sept. 1845.

[12] Death rolls of 100,000 were reputed in England and Holland in the floods of 1099, 1421 and 1446.

[13] c. 4,000 were lost on H.M. Troopship Lancastria 16,243 tons off St. Nazaire on 17 June 1940.

[14] H.M. Armed Cruiser Natal blew up off Invergordon killing 428 on 30 Dec. 1915.

[15] In July 1212, 3,000 were killed in the crush, burned or drowned when London Bridge caught fire at both ends. The death roll in the Great Fire of London of 1666 was only 8. History's first "fire storm" occurred in the Quebec Yard, Surrey Docks, Southwark, London during the 300-pump fire in the Blitz on 7–8 Sept. 1940. Dockland casualties were 306 killed.

[16] The worst crash by a U.K. operated aircraft was that of the B.O.A.C. Boeing 707 which broke up in mid-air near Mount Fuji, Japan, on 5 March 1966. The crew of 11 and all 113 passengers (total 124) were killed. The cause was violent CAT (Clear Air Turbulence).

[17] The 213 yd long troop train was telescoped to 67 yds. Signalmen Meakin and Tinsley were sentenced for manslaughter. Britain's worst underground train disaster was the Moorgate Tube disaster of 28 Feb. 1975 when 43 were killed.

11. HUMAN ACHIEVEMENTS

1. ENDURANCE AND ENDEAVOUR

Lunar conquest

Neil Alden Armstrong (b. Wapakoneta, Ohio, U.S.A. of Scoto-Irish and German ancestry, on 5 Aug. 1930), command pilot of the Apollo XI mission, became the first man to set foot on the Moon on the Sea of Tranquillity at 02.56 and 15 sec G.M.T. on 21 July 1969. He was followed out of the Lunar Module *Eagle* by Col. Edwin Eugene Aldrin, Jr. U.S.A.F. (b. Montclair, New Jersey, U.S.A. of Swedish, Dutch and British ancestry, on 20 Jan. 1930), while the Command Module *Columbia* piloted by Lt.-Col. Michael Collins, U.S.A.F. (b. Rome, Italy, of Irish and pre-Revolutionary American ancestry, on 31 Oct. 1930) orbited above.

Eagle landed at 20.17 hours 42 sec G.M.T. on 20 July and lifted off at 17.54 G.M.T. on 21 July, after a stay of 21 hours 36 min. The Apollo XI had blasted off from Cape Canaveral, Florida at 13.32 G.M.T. on 16 July and was a culmination of the U.S. space programme, which, at its peak, employed 376,600 people and attained in the year 1966–67 a peak budget of $5,900,000,000 (*then £2,460 million*).

Altitude *Man*

The greatest altitude attained by man was when the crew of the ill-fated Apollo XIII were at apocynthion (*i.e.* their furthest point) 158 miles *254 km* above the lunar surface and 248,655 miles *400 187 km* above the Earth's surface at 1.21 a.m. B.S.T. on 15 Apr. 1970. The crew were Capt. James Arthur Lovell, U.S.N. (b. Denver, Colorado, 30 Aug. 1931), Frederick Wallace Haise Jr. (b. Cleveland, Ohio, 25 Mar. 1928) and John L. Swigert Jr. (b. Biloxi, Miss. 14 Nov. 1933).

Altitude *Woman*

The greatest altitude attained by a woman is 231 km *143.5 miles* by Jnr. Lt. (now Lt. Col.) Valentina Vladimirovna Tereshkova-Nikolayev (b. 6 Mar. 1937) of the U.S.S.R., during her 48-orbit flight in *Vostok 6* on 16 June 1963. The record for an aircraft is 24 336 m *79,842 ft* by Natalia Prokhanova (U.S.S.R.) (b. 1940) in an E-33 jet, on 22 May 1965.

Speed *Man*

The fastest speed at which any human has travelled is 24,791 m.p.h. *39 897 km/h* when the Command Module of Apollo X carrying Col. Thomas P. Stafford, U.S.A.F. (b. Weatherford, Okla. 17 Sept. 1930), and Cdrs. Eugene Andrew Cernan (b.

Chicago, 14 Mar. 1934) and John Watts Young, U.S.N. (b. San Francisco, 24 Sept. 1930), reached this maximum value at the 400,000 ft *121,9 km* altitude interface on its trans-Earth return flight on 26 May 1969 (see also page 2).

Speed *Woman*

The highest speed ever attained by a woman is 28 115 km/h *17,470 m.p.h.* by Jnr. Lt. (now Lt. Col.) Valentina Vladimirovna Tereshkova-Nikolayev (b. 6 Mar. 1937) of the U.S.S.R. in *Vostok 6* on 16 June 1963. The highest speed ever achieved by a woman aircraft pilot is 2 687,42 km/h *1,669.89 m.p.h.* by Svetlana Savitskaya (U.S.S.R.) reported on 2 June 1975.

Land Speed *Man*

The highest speed ever achieved on land is 650 m.p.h. *1 046 km/h* momentarily during the 627.287 m.p.h. *1 009,520 km/h* run of *The Blue Flame* driven by Gary Gabelich (b. San Pedro, California, 29 Aug. 1950) on Bonneville Salt Flats, Utah, U.S.A., on 23 Oct. 1970 (see Mechanical World, page 134). The car built by Reaction Dynamics Inc. of Milwaukee, Wisconsin, is designed to withstand stresses up to 1,000 m.p.h. *1 600 km/h* while the tyres have been tested to speeds of 850 m.p.h. *1 365 km/h*.

Land Speed *Woman*

The highest land speed recorded by a woman is 524.016 m.p.h. *843,323 km/h* by Mrs. Kitty Hambleton *née* O'Neil (U.S.) in the 48,000 h.p. rocket-powered 3 wheeled S.M.1 *Motivator* over the Alvard Desert, Oregon, U.S.A. on 6 Dec. 1976. Her official two-way record was 512.710 m.p.h. *825,126 km/h* and she probably touched 600 m.p.h. *965 km/h* momentarily.

Water Speed *Unofficial*

The highest speed ever achieved on water is 328 m.p.h. *527,8 km/h* by Donald Malcolm Campbell, C.B.E. (1921–67) of the U.K., on his last and fatal run in the turbo-jet engined 2¼ ton *2 285 kg Bluebird* K7, on Coniston Water, Cumbria, England, on 4 Jan. 1967.

Official

The official record is 285.213 m.p.h. *459,005 km/h* (average of two 1 mile runs) by Lee Taylor, Jr. (b. 1934) of Downey, California, U.S.A., in the hydroplane *Hustler* on Lake Guntersville, Alabama, U.S.A., on 30 June 1967. He is currently experimenting with his 38 ft *11,58 m* jet powered *U.S. Discovery*.

Kitty O'Neil the fastest woman on land, who probably momentarily touched 600 m.p.h. *965 km/h* during her record run in December 1976 (see p. 208).

The 48,000 h.p. rocket-powered vehicle S.M.1. *Motivator* in which Kitty O'Neil broke the feminine land speed record (see p. 208).

Water speed *Propeller driven*

The world record for propeller-driven craft is 202.42 m.p.h. *325,76 km/h* set by Larry Hill in his supercharged hydroplane *Mr. Ed* off Long Beach, California. On a one-way run *Climax* recorded 205.19 m.p.h. *330,22 km/h*.

Most travelled *Man*

The man who has visited more countries than anyone is Jesse Hart Rosdail (b. 1914) of Elmhurst, Illinois, U.S.A., a teacher of children in the 5th grade. Since 1934, of the 160 sovereign countries and 61 non-sovereign territories, listed by the *U.N. Population Report*, making a total of 221, he has visited all but two, namely North Korea, and French Antarctic Territories. He estimated his mileage as 1,626,605 statute miles *2 617 766 km* at July 1977.

Though he has not visited so many *currently* existing countries, Mehmet S. Ersöz (b. 1904 in Turkey) has travelled much more widely within some 210 countries. Mrs. Ersöz may well also prove to be the most travelled woman.

Disabled Person

The most countries visited by a disabled person is 115 sovereign and 59 non-sovereign countries by Professor Daniel J. Crowley of Davis, California, U.S.A. who has been confined to a wheelchair since March 1946.

The late Donald Campbell (G.B.), who in 1967 touched 328 m.p.h. *527,8 km/h* just before his *Bluebird* K7 hydroplane became airborne (see p. 208). (*Popperfoto*)

Horseback

The most travelled man in the horseback era was probably the Methodist preacher Francis Asbury (b. Birmingham, England), who travelled 264,000 miles *424 850 km* in North America from 1771–1815 preaching 16,000 sermons.

Space

The most travelled men in history are the third crew of the U.S. *Skylab* space station with 34,469,696 miles *55 474 039 km* (see details pages 75–76).

Passport Records

The world's most expensive passports are those from the U.S.S.R. which in 1974 at the official rate of exchange were priced at £225 payable in advance. If applications involved a whole family or travel to the West however the necessary accompanying visa was refused, 996 times in each 1,000 applications.

Round the World

The fastest time for a round the world trip on commercial flights for a true circumnavigation is 46 hrs 8 mins (flying time) and 65 hrs 58 mins elapsed time by Gordon Banks (Australia) westabout Sydney *via* London, New York to Sydney in June 1973.

The F.A.I. allows any flight taking off and landing at the same point, which is as long as the Tropic of Cancer (viz 22,858.754 miles *36 787,599 km*) as a circumnavigational flight.

MARINE CIRCUMNAVIGATION RECORDS (Compiled by Sq. Ldr. D. H. Clarke, D.F.C., A.F.C.)

A true circumnavigation entails passing through two antipodal points (which are at least 12,429 statute miles *20 000 km* apart).

CATEGORY	VESSEL	NAME	START PLACE AND DATE	FINISH DATE AND DURATION
Earliest	*Vittoria* Expedition of Fernão de Magalhães, c. 1480–k. 1521	Juan Sebastion de Elcano or Del Cano (d. 1526) and 17 crew	Seville, Spain 20 Sept. 1519	San Lucur, 6 Sept. 1522 30,700 miles *49 400 km*
Earliest British	*Golden Hind* (ex *Pelican*) 100 tons/tonnes	Francis Drake (c. 1540–1596)· (Knighted 4 April 1581)	Plymouth, 13 Dec. 1577	26 Sept. 1580
Earliest Woman	*Etoile*	Crypto-female valet of M. de Commerson, named Baré	St. Malo, 1766	1769
Earliest Solo	*Spray* 36¾ ft *11,20 m* gaff yawl	Capt. Joshua Slocum, 51, (U.S.) (a non-swimmer)	Newport, Rhode Island, U.S.A. *via* Magellan Straits, 24 Apr. 1895	3 July 1898 46,000 miles *74 000 km*
Earliest Solo Eastabout *via* Cape Horn	*Lehg II* 31¼ ft *9,52 m* Bermuda Ketch	Vito Dumas (Argentina)	Buenos Aires, 27 June 1942	7 Sept. 1943 (272 ex436 days) 20,400 miles *32 830 km*
Smallest Boat	*Ahadori II* 20 ft 8 in *6,3 m* Bermudan Yawl	Hiroshi Aoki (Japan)	Osaka, Japan, 13 June, Cape Horn 12 Jan. 1973	Osaka, Japan 29 July 1974
Earliest Submerged	*U.S. Submarine Triton*	Capt. Edward L. Beach U.S.N. plus 182 crew	New London, Connecticut 16 Feb. 1960	10 May 1960 30,708 miles *49 422 km*
Earliest Solo with One Stop Over	*Gipsy Moth IV* 53 ft *16,15 m* Bermudan Yawl 11½ tons	Sir Francis Chichester K.B.E. (1901–72)	Plymouth to Sydney 27 Aug. 1966	Sydney to Plymouth 28 May 1967 29,626 miles *47 678 km*
Earliest non-stop Solo (Port to Port)	*Suhaili* 32.4 ft *9,87 m* Bermuda Ketch	Robin Knox Johnston C.B.E. (b. 1939)	Falmouth, 14 June 1968	22 Apr. 1969 (312 days) Longest alone at sea
Fastest Solo	*Manureva* (ex *Pen Duick IV*) 70 ft *21,33 m* Trimaran	Alain Colas (France)	Saint Malo *via* Sydney	29 Mar. 1974 (167 days)
Fastest	*Great Britain II* 72 ft *21,94 m* Ketch	1st Mike Gill (13 crew) 2nd R. Mullender (15 crew)	Thames 31 Aug. 1975 *via* Sydney (Change crews)	67 days 5 hrs 19 min 66 days 22 hrs 31 min 26,380 miles 209.9 m.p.h.
Fastest Solo Westabout (*via* Cape Horn)	*Mermaid III* 28 ft *8,80 m* sloop	Kenichi Horie (Japan) (b. 1939)	Osaka 1 Aug. 1973	5 May 1974 (275 days 13 hrs)

North Pole conquest

The claims of neither of the two U.S. Arctic explorers, Dr. Frederick Albert Cook (1865–1940) nor Cdr. (later Rear Ad.) Robert Edwin Peary (1856–1920), of the U.S. Naval Civil Engineering branch in reaching the North Pole are subject to positive proof. Cook, accompanied by the Eskimos, Ah-pellah and Etukishook, two sledges and 26 dogs, struck north from a point 60 miles *96,5 km* north of Svartevoeg, on Axel Heiberg Is., Canada, 460 miles *740 km* from the Pole on 21 Mar. 1908, allegedly reaching Lat. 89° 31′ N on 19 April and the Pole on 21 April. Peary, accompanied by his negro assistant, Matthew Alexander Henson (1866–1955) and the four Eskimos, Ooqueah, Eginwah, Seegloo, and Ootah (1875–1955), struck north from his Camp Bartlett (Lat. 87° 44′ N.) at 5 a.m. on 2 Apr. 1909. After travelling another 134 miles *215 km*, he allegedly established his final camp, Camp Jessup, in the proximity of the Pole at 10 a.m. on 6 April and marched a further 42 miles *67,5 km* quartering the sea-ice before turning south at 4 p.m. on 7 April. On excellent pack ice Wally Herbert's 1968–69 Expedition (see below) attained a best day's route mileage of 23 miles *37 km* in 15 hours. Cook claimed 26 miles *41,8 km* twice while Peary claimed a surely unsustainable average of 38 miles *61 km* for 8 consecutive days.

The earliest indisputable attainment of the North Pole over the sea-ice was at 3 p.m. (Central Standard Time) on 19 Apr. 1968 by Ralph Plaisted (U.S.) and three companions after a 42-day trek in four Skidoos (snow-mobiles). Their arrival was independently verified 18 hours later by a U.S. Air Force weather aircraft. The sea bed is 13,410 ft *4 087 m* below the North Pole.

Arctic crossing

The first crossing of the Arctic sea-ice was achieved by the British Trans-Arctic Expedition which left Point Barrow, Alaska on 21 Feb. 1968 and arrived at the Seven Island Archipelago north-east of Spitzbergen 464 days later on 29 May 1969 after a haul of 2,920 statute miles *4 699 km* and a drift of 700 miles *1 126 km* compared with the straight line distance of 1,662 miles *2 674 km*. The team was Wally Herbert (leader), 34, Major Ken Hedges, 34, R.A.M.C., Allan Gill, 38, and Dr. Roy Koerner, 36 (glaciologist), and 40 huskies. This was the longest sustained journey ever made on polar pack ice and the first indisputable attainment of the North Pole by sledge. Temperatures sank to −47° F *−43,8° C* during the trek.

South Pole conquest

The first ships to cross the Antarctic circle (Lat. 66° 30′ S.) were the 193 crew of the *Resolution* (462 tons) (Capt. James Cook R.N. (1728–79)) and *Adventure* (336 tons) (Lt. T. Furneaux) on 17 Jan. 1773 in 39° E. The first person to sight the Antarctic *mainland*—on the best available evidence and against claims made for British and Russian explorers—was Nathaniel Brown Palmer (U.S.) (1799–1877). On 17 Nov. 1820 he sighted the Orleans Channel coast of the Palmer Peninsular from his 45 ton/*tonnes* sloop *Hero*.

The South Pole (alt. 9,186 ft *2 799 m* on ice and 336 ft *102 m* bed rock) was first reached at 3 p.m. on 14 Dec. 1911 by a Norwegian party led by Capt. Roald Amundsen (1872–1928), after a 53-day march with dog sledges from the Bay of Whales, to which he had penetrated in the *Fram*. Olav Olavson Bjaaland, the first to arrive, was the last survivor, dying in June 1961, aged 88. The others were the late Helmer Hanssen, Sverre H. Hassell and Oskar Wisting.

Women

The first woman to set foot on Antarctica was Mrs. Klarius Mikkelsen on 20 Feb. 1935. No woman stood on the South Pole until 11 Nov. 1969. On that day Lois Jones, Kay Linsay, Eileen McSavenay, Jean Pearson, Tarry Lee Tickhill and Pam Young, all of U.S.A. arrived by air.

Antarctic crossing

The first crossing of the Antarctic continent was completed at 1.47 p.m. on 2 Mar. 1958, after a trek of 2,158 miles *3 473 km* lasting 99 days from 24 Nov. 1957, from Shackleton Base to Scott Base *via* the Pole. The crossing party of twelve was led by Dr. (now Sir) Vivian Ernest Fuchs (born 11 Feb. 1908).

A unique moment in polar history made on 10 Jan. 1913. Rear Admiral Robert Peary, the proclaimed conqueror of the North Pole meeting Roald Amundsen, 13 months after the Norwegian's conquest of the South Pole. (*Gilbert Grosvenor, Collection* Courtesy *National Geographic Society*)

Longest sledge journeys

The longest totally self-supporting Polar sledge journey ever made, was one of 1,080 miles *1 738 km* from West to East across Greenland on 18 June to 5 Sept. 1934 by Capt. M. Lindsay (now Sir Martin Lindsay, Bt., C.B.E., D.S.O.); Lt. Arthur S. T. Godfrey, R.E., (later Lt. Col., k. 1942), Andrew N. C. Croft (later Col., D.S.O.) and 49 dogs. The same crossing was first made but with man hauled sledges by the inter Services 1974 Trans Greenland Expedition, led by Flt. Lt. D. R. Gleed in 36 days.

The longest dog hauled sledge journey in history has been that by the Japanese mountaineer and adventurer Naomi Uemura (b. 1941) from Greenland across northern Canada to Kotzebue, Alaska—a distance of reportedly 4,475 miles *7 200 km* in 490 days. He started on the west coast of Greenland in January 1975 and reached Kaktovik, Alaska in early May 1976.

Greatest Ocean Descent

The record ocean descent was achieved in the Challenger Deep of the Marianas Trench, 250 miles *400 km* south-west of Guam, in the Pacific Ocean, when the Swiss-built U.S. Navy bathyscaphe *Trieste*, manned by Dr. Jacques Piccard (b. 1914) (Switzerland) and Lt. Donald Walsh, U.S.N., reached the ocean bed 35,820 ft (6.78 miles *10 917 m*) down, at 1.10 p.m. on 23 Jan. 1960 (see page 59). The pressure of the water was 16,883 lbf/in² *1 183 kg f/cm²* and the temperature 37.4° F *3° C*. The descent required 4 hours 48 min and the ascent 3 hours 17 min.

Deep diving records

The record depth for the extremely dangerous activity of breath-held diving is 282 ft *85,9 m* by Jacques Mayol (France) off Elba, Italy, on 9 Nov. 1973 for men and 147½ ft *45 m* by Guiliana Treleani (Italy) off Cuba in September 1967 for women. The pressure on Mayol's thorax was 136.5 lb f/in² *9,6 kg/cm²* and his pulse fell to 36. Enzo Maiorca (Italy) surfaced unconscious from a dive of 87 m *285 ft* off Sorrento, Italy on 27 Sept. 1974. The record dive with Scuba (self-contained under-water breathing apparatus) is 437 ft *133 m* by John J. Gruener and R. Neal Watson (U.S.A.) off Freeport, Grand Bahama on 14 Oct. 1968. The record dive utilizing gas mixtures is a simulated dive of 2,001 ft *609 m* in a dry chamber by Patrice Chemin and Robert Gauret (France) at

TRANS-ATLANTIC MARINE RECORDS (Compiled by Sq. Ldr. D. H. Clarke, D.F.C., A.F.C.)

Earliest rowing (partial)	Six British deserters from garrison	Ship's boat c. 20 ft 6,1 m	St. Helena (10 June)	Belmonte, Brazil	28 days (83 m.p.d.)	1799
Earliest crossing (2 men)	C. R. Webb + 1 crew (U.S.)	Charter Oak 43 ft 13,1 m	New York	Liverpool	35 days	1857
Earliest Trimaran	John Mikes + 2 crew (U.S.)	Non Pareil, 25 ft 7,62 m	(New York 4 June)	Southampton	51 days	1868
Earliest Solo Sailing	Alfred Johnson (U.S.)	Centennial 20 ft 6,09 m	Glos., Mass	Wales	46 days	1876
Earliest Woman (with U.S. husband)	Mrs. Joanna Crapo (b. Scotland)	New Bedford 20 ft 6,09 m	Chatham, Mass.	Newlyn, Cornwall	51 days	1877
Earliest Single-handed race	J. W. Lawlor (U.S.) (winner)	Sea Serpent 15 ft 4,57 m	Boston (21 June)	Coverack, Cornwall	45 days	1891
Earliest Rowing by 2 men (Northern)	George Harbo and Frank Samuelson (U.S.)	Richard K. Fox 18⅛ ft 5,58 m	New York City (6 June)	Isles of Scilly (1 Aug.)	55 days (56 m.p.d.)	1897
Fastest Sailing Ship	Captain and crew	Lancing 4 masts	New York	Cape Wrath, Scot.	6 days 18 hours	1916
Fastest Solo Sailing West–East	J. V. T. McDonald (G.B.)	Inverarity 38 ft 11,58 m	Nova Scotia	Ireland	16 days	1922
Earliest Canoe (with sail)	F. Romer (Germany)	Deutscher Sport 21½ ft 6,55 m	Las Palmas (2 June)	St. Thomas, West Indies	58 days (47 m.p.d.)	1928
Fastest Solo Sailing East West (Northern)	Cdr. R. D. Graham R.N. (G.B.)	Emanuel 30 ft 9,14 m	Bantry, Ireland	St. John's, Newfoundland	24.35 days	1934
Earliest Woman Solo (East–West)	Mrs. Ann Davison (G.B.)	Felicity Ann 23 ft 7,01 m	Plymouth (18 May 1952)	Miami, Florida (13 Aug. 1953)	454 days	1952/ 1953
Earliest Woman Solo (West–East)	Gladys Gradely (U.S.)	Lugger 18 ft 5,5 m	Nova Scotia	Hope Cove, Devon	60 days	1903
Fastest Woman Solo	Clare Francis (G.B.)	Robertson's Golly 37½ ft 11,43 m	Plymouth	Newport, R.I.	29 days 1 hr 52 mins	1976
Longest Non-Stop Woman Solo	Anna Woolf (S.Af.)	Zama Zulu 43 ft 13,10 m	Cape Town Ascension Is.	Ascension Is. Bowling, Scot.	1,800 miles 29 days 7,120 miles 80 days	1976
Smallest (across 2 oceans)	John Riding (G.B.)	Sjo Ag 12 ft 3,65 m	Plymouth via Panama	New Zealand, 1973	Lost in Tasman Sea	1964/ 1974
Smallest West–East	William Verity (U.S.)	Nonoalca 12 ft 3,65 m	Ft. Lauderdale, Florida	Tralee, Kerry (12 July)	68 days	1966
Smallest East–West (Southern)	Hugo S. Vihlen (U.S.)	The April Fool 5 ft 11⅞ in 1,83 m	Casablanca (29 Mar.)	Ft. Lauderdale, Florida (21 June)	85 days	1968
Fastest Crossing Sailing (multihull)	Eric Tabarly (France) + 2 crew	Pen Duick IV 67 ft 20,42 m	Tenerife	Martinique	251.4 miles 404,5 km/ day (10 days 12 hours)	1968
Fastest Crossing Sailing (Monohull)	Wilson Marshall (U.S.) & crew	Atlantic 185 ft 56,38 m	Sandy Hook, N.J.	Lizard, Cornwall (3,054 miles)	12 days 4 hr (fastest noon to noon 341 miles)	1905
Fastest Solo East–West (Northern) (monohull)	Jean-Yves Terlain (France)	Vendredi 13, 128 ft 39 m	Plymouth 13 June	Newport R.I. 8 July	21 days 5¼ hr	1972
Fastest Solo East–West (Southern) (monohull)	Sir Francis Chichester K.B.E. (G.B.)	Gipsy Moth V 57 ft 17,37 m	Portuguese Guinea	Nicaragua	179.1 miles 288,2 km/ day (22.4 days)	1970
Fastest Solo East–West (Northern) (multihull)	Alain Colas (France)	Pen Duick IV 70 ft 21,33 m trimaran	Plymouth (17 June)	Newport, Rhode Is. (7 July)	20 days 13¼ hrs	1972
Fastest Solo Rowing East–West	Sidney Genders, 51 (G.B.)	Khaggavisana 19¾ ft 6,02 m	Penzance, Cornwall	Miami, Florida via Antigua	37.3 miles 60 km/day 162 days 18 hr	1970
Earliest Solo Rowing East–West	John Fairfax (G.B.)	Britannia 22 ft 6,70 m	Las Palmas (20 Jan.)	Ft. Lauderdale, Florida (19 July)	180 days	1969
Earliest Solo Rowing West–East	Tom McClean (Ireland)	Super Silver 20 ft 6,90 m	St. John's, Newfoundland (17 May)	Black Sod Bay, Ireland (27 July)	70.7 days	1969

TRANS-PACIFIC MARINE RECORDS

Fastest	Bill Lee	Merlin 67 ft 20,42 m sloop	Los Angeles, Cal.	Honolulu, Hawaii	8 days 11 hr 1 min	1977
Earliest Solo (Woman)	Sharon Sites Adams	Sea Sharp II 31 ft 9,45 m	Yokohama, Japan	San Diego, Cal.	75 days (5,911 miles)	1969
Earliest Rowing	John Fairfax (G.B.) Sylvia Cook (G.B.)	Britannia II 35 ft 10,66 m	San Francisco, Cal. 26 Apr. 1971	Hayman Is. Australia 22 Apr. 1972	362 days	1971/ 1972
Earliest Rowing Solo	Anders Sveland (Sweden)	Roslagena 20 ft 6,10 m	Chile	Samoa	118 days	1974

N.B.—The earliest single-handed Pacific crossings were achieved East–West by Bernard Gilboy (U.S.) in 1882 in the 18 ft 5,48 m double-ender Pacific and West–East by Fred Rebel (Latvia) in the 18 ft 5,48 m Elaine, and Edward Miles (U.S.) in the 36¾ ft 11,2 m Sturdy II both in 1932.

the Comex Chamber, Marseille, France reported in June 1972. Some divers have survived free swimming for short intervals at depths of 1,400 ft 426 m.

Deepest Underwater Escape
The deepest underwater rescue achieved was of the Pisces III in which Roger R. Chapman, 28 and Roger Mallinson, 35 were trapped for 76 hours when it sank to 1,575 ft 480 m 150 miles 240 km south-east of Cork, Ireland on 29 Aug. 1973. She was hauled to the surface by the cable ship John Cabot after work by Pisces V, Pisces II and the remote control recovery vessel U.S. C.U.R.V. on 1 Sept. The greatest depth of an actual escape without any equipment has been from 198 ft 60,3 m by Sub. Lt. W. Morrison, R.N.V.R. and E.R.A. Swatton from H.M. Submarine X.E.11 in Loch Striven, Strathclyde on 6 Mar. 1945.

Deepest salvage
The greatest depth at which salvage has been achieved is 16,500 ft 5 029 m by the bathyscaphe Trieste II (Lt.-Cdr. Mel Bartels U.S.N.) to attach cables to an "electronic package" on the sea bed 400 miles 645 km north of Hawaii on 20 May 1972. Project Jennifer by U.S.S. Glomar Explorer in June/July 1974 to recover a Golfclass U.S.S.R. submarine, 750 miles 1 200 km N.W. of Hawaii, cost $550 million but was not successful.

Flexible dress divers
The deepest salvaging operation ever carried out was on the wreck of the S.S. Niagara, sunk by a mine in 1940, 438 ft 133,5 m down off Bream Head, Whangarei North Island, New Zealand. All but 6 per cent of the £2,250,000 of gold in her holds was recovered in 7 weeks. The record recovery was that from the White Star Liner Laurentic, which was mined in 132 ft 40,2 m of water off Malin Head, Donegal, Ireland, in 1917, with £5,000,000 of gold ingots in her Second Class baggage room. By 1924, 3,186 of the 3,211 gold bricks had been recovered with immense difficulty.

Greatest penetration into the Earth
Man's deepest penetration made into the ground is in the Western Deep Levels Mine at Carltonville, Transvaal, South Africa. By May 1975 a record depth of 12,600 ft 3 840 m had been attained. The rock temperature at this depth is 131° F 55° C.

Shaft sinking record
The one month (31 days) world record is 1,251 ft 381,3 m for a standard shaft 26 ft 7,92 m in diameter at Buffelsfontein Mine, Transvaal, South Africa, in March 1962. The British record of 410 ft 124,9 m of 18 ft 1 in 5,51 m diameter shaft was set in the Boulby Mine, Whitby, North Yorkshire on 18

Jan.–17 Feb. 1971 (30 days). The rock shaft at this potash mine at 3,765 ft *1 147,5 m* is the deepest in Great Britain.

Longest on a raft

The longest recorded survival alone on a raft is 133 days (4½ months) by Second Steward Poon Lim (born Hong Kong) of the U.K. Merchant Navy, whose ship, the S.S. *Ben Lomond*, was torpedoed in the Atlantic 565 miles *910 km* west of St. Paul's Rocks in Lat. 00° 30′ N Long. 38° 45′ W at 11.45 a.m. on 23 Nov. 1942. He was picked up by a Brazilian fishing boat off Salinópolis, Brazil, on 5 April 1943 and was able to walk ashore. In July 1943, he was awarded the B.E.M. and now lives in New York City.

Maurice and Maralyn Bailey survived 118⅓ days in an inflatable dinghy 4½ ft *1,37 m* in diameter in the north-east Pacific from 4 Mar. to 30 June 1973.

Most Marriages *World*

The greatest number of marriages accumulated in the monogamous world is 19 by Glynn de Moss Wolfe (U.S.) (b. 1908) who married for the 19th time since 1931 his 17th wife Gloria, aged 23, on 22 Feb. 1969. His total number of children is, he says, 34. He keeps two wedding dresses (different sizes) in his closet for ready use. He has additionally suffered 16 mothers-in-law. The most often marrying millionaire was Thomas F. Manville (1894–1967) who contracted his 13th marriage to his 11th wife Christine Erdlen Popa (1940–71) aged 20, in New York City, U.S.A., on 11 Jan. 1960 when aged 65. His shortest marriage (to his seventh wife) effectively lasted only 7½ hours. His fortune of $20 million came from asbestos, neither of which he could take with him.

Mrs. Beverly Nina Avery, then aged 48 a bar-maid from Los Angeles, California, U.S.A., set a monogamous world record in October 1957 by obtaining her sixteenth divorce from her fourteenth husband, Gabriel Avery. She alleged outside the court that five of the 14 had broken her nose.

Great Britain

Seven times married individuals in Britain include Sir Francis Ferdinand Maurice Cook, 4th baronet (b. 21 Dec. 1907) and Mr. Lionel Birch.

Oldest Bride and Bridegroom

The British record was set by Edward Reuben Simpson, (1873–1973), who married Mrs. Eva. J. Midwinter, 83, at Swindon, Wiltshire, on 8 Dec. 1971 when aged 98 years 10 months.

Dyura Avramovich, 101, married Yula Zhivich, 95, in Belgrade, Yugoslavia in November 1963.

Longest Engagements

The longest engagement on record is one of 67 years between Octavio Guillen, 82 and Adriana Martinez, 82. They finally took the plunge in June 1969 in Mexico City, Mexico.

Longest Marriage *World*

The longest recorded marriage is one of 86 years between Sir Temulji Bhicaji Nariman and Lady Nariman from 1853 to 1940 resulting from a cousin marriage when both were five. Sir Temulji (b. 3 Sept. 1848) died, aged 91 years 11 months, in August 1940 at Bombay. The only reliable instance of an 83rd anniversary celebrated by a couple marrying at normal ages is that between the late Edd (105) and Margaret (99) Hollen, who celebrated their 83rd anniversary on 7 May 1972. They were married in Kentucky on 7 May 1889.

Great Britain

James Frederick Burgess (born 3 March 1861, died 27 Nov. 1966) and his wife Sarah Ann, *née* Gregory (born 11 July 1865, died 22 June 1965) were married on 21 June 1883 at St. James's, Bermondsey, London, and celebrated their 82nd anniversary in 1965.

The most recent example of a marriage with both partners being centenarians was that of Samuel Stanton (b. 25 Jan. 1875) and Emma (b. 3 Jan. 1877) of Goldthorpe, South Yorkshire, who celebrated their 76th anniversary on 11 Sept. 1976.

Shortest Marriage

The shortest marriage on record occurred on 11 Sept. 1976 at the Fort Palmer United Presbyterian Church, Greensberg, Pennsylvania, U.S.A. when the bridegroom Robert Neiderhiser, 39 collapsed at the altar just as he and the former Miss Naomi Nicely, 46 were prounced to be man and wife.

Most married

Jack V. and Edna Moran of Seattle, Washington, U.S.A. have married each other 40 times since the original and only really necessary occasion on 27 July 1937 in Seaside, Oregon. Subsequent ceremonies have included those at Banff, Canada (1952), Cairo, Egypt (1966) and Westminster Abbey, London (1975).

Mass ceremony

The largest mass wedding ceremony was one of 1,800 couples officiated over by Sun Myung Moon of the Holy Spirit Association for the Unification of World Christianity in Seoul, South Korea on 14 Feb. 1975. The response to the question "Will you swear to love your spouse for ever?" is "Ye".

Eating out

The world champion for eating out is Fred E. Magel of Chicago, Illinois, U.S.A. who since 1928 has dined in 39,900 restaurants in 60 nations as a restaurant grader (to July 1977). He asserts the one serving the largest helpings is Zehnder's Hotel, Frankenmuth, Michigan, U.S.A. Mr. Magel's favourite dishes are South African rock lobster and mousse of fresh English strawberries.

Party giving

The most expensive private party ever thrown was that of Mr. and Mrs. Bradley Martin of Troy, N.Y., U.S.A. staged at the Waldorf Hotel, Manhattan in February 1897. The cost to the host and hostess was estimated to be $369,200 in the days when dollars were made of gold.

Toastmasters

The Guild of Professional Toastmasters (founded 1962) has only 12 members. Its founder and President, Ivor Spencer, listened to a speech in excess of 2 hours by the maudlin subject of a retirement luncheon. The Guild also elects the most boring speaker of the year, but for professional reasons, will not publicize the winner's name until A.D. 2000. Red coats were introduced by the pioneer professional, William Knight-Smith (d. 1932) *c.* 1900.

Lecture Agency

The world's largest lecture agency is the American Program Bureau of Boston, Mass., U.S.A., with 400 Personalities on 40 Topics and a turnover of some $5 million. The top rate is $4,000 (£1,600) per hour commanded by Ralph Nader (b. Winsted, Connecticut, 27 Feb. 1934). This is $66.66 (£26.66) per min.

Working week

Dr. Adrian Cox of Norfolk and Norwich Hospital, gave evidence in November 1971, that some housemen and registrars in hospitals have an active working week in extreme cases of 139 hours, allowing only 4 hours 8½ mins sleep per night. Some contracts for University lecturers call for a 3 hour week or a 72 hour year spread over 24 weeks.

Working career

The longest recorded working career in one job in Britain was that of Miss Polly Gadsby who started work with Archibald Turner & Co. of Leicester aged 9. In 1932, after 86 years service, she was still at her bench wrapping elastic, at the age of 95. Mr. Theodore C. Taylor (1850–1952) served 86 years with J. T. & T. Taylor of Batley, West Yorkshire including 56 years as chairman.

Milkman, Longest serving

Britain's longest serving milkman was Mr. John Baggs (b. August 1884) of Horndean, near Portsmouth, Hampshire, who had been on his round for over 80 years ("I don't like sitting about"). He was assisted by his boy John Baggs Junior, aged 64.

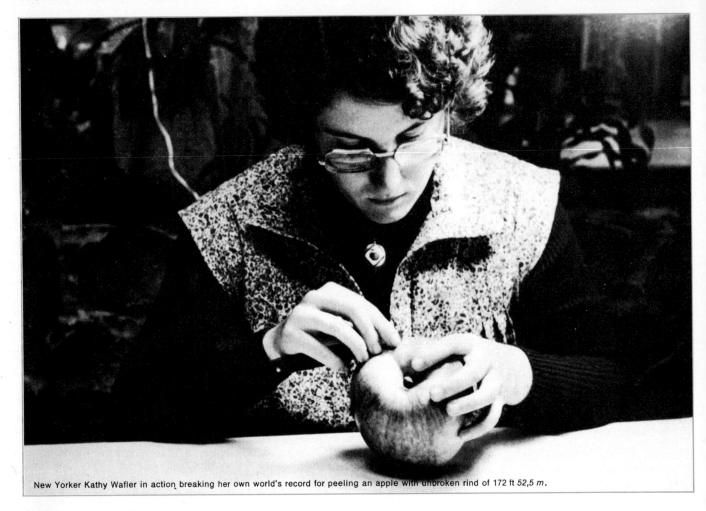

New Yorker Kathy Wafler in action breaking her own world's record for peeling an apple with unbroken rind of 172 ft *52,5 m*.

Most Durable Coal Miner

David Davies (*né* David) (b. 19 Feb. 1842 Pontrhyfen, Afan Valley, South Wales) worked underground as a collier for 73 years from 1849 to 1922 from the age of 7 to his retirement aged 80.

Longest pension

Miss Millicent Barclay, daughter of Col. William Barclay was born posthumously on 10 July 1872 and became eligible for a Madras Military Fund pension to continue until her marriage. She died unmarried on 26 Oct. 1969 having drawn the pension for every day of her life of 97 years 3 months.

Most jobs

The greatest number of different paid jobs recorded in a working life is the 125 accumulated by D. H. "Nobby" Clarke, the yachting author, of Ipswich, Suffolk.

Doctors *Oldest*

Dr. Frederick Walter Whitney Dawson (b. 22 Oct. 1876 in Hobsonville, New Zealand) was the first doctor to be registered this century in London on 1 Jan. 1901. He was still practising on his 100th birthday in Whangarei, New Zealand.

Doctors *Most in a family*

David L. Bernie, M.D. of Dayton, Ohio numbers 5 sons and a daughter and 11 other members of his family who are qualified M.D.'s.

MISCELLANEOUS ENDEAVOURS

Accordian Playing

Norman English of Weston-super-Mare, Avon, played an electric accordian for 54 hrs 1 min on 7–9 Mar. 1977. Bert Thomas of Eccles, Lancs. and Robert McGuffin of Balbriggan, Co. Dublin, Eire, have each completed 54 hours.

Apple peeling

The longest single unbroken apple peel on record is one of

172 ft 4 in *52,51 m* peeled by Kathy Wafler, 17 of Wolcott, New York, U.S.A. in 11 hours 30 min at Long Ridge Mall, Rochester, N.Y. on 16 Oct. 1976. The apple weighed 20 oz *567 g*.

Apple picking

The greatest recorded performance is 341 U.S. bushels (330.4 Imperial bushels *120,14 hectolitres*) picked in 8 hours by Geoffrey Cash at N. & E. Hides, Batlow, N.S.W., Australia on 3 Apr. 1977.

Bag carrying

The greatest non-stop bag-carrying feat carrying 1 cwt. *50,8 kg* of household coal in an open bag is 22.2 miles *35,72 km* by Brian Newton, 29 from Leicester to Rearsby and back in 6 hr 7 mins on 12 Nov. 1976.

Bag-pipes

The longest duration pipe has been one of 100 hours by Neville Workman, Clive Higgins, Patrick Forth and Paul Harris of Churchill School Pipe Band, Salisbury, Rhodesia on 9–13 July 1976.

Balancing on one foot

The longest recorded duration for continuous balancing on one foot is 12 hours by Gary Shaw of Lexington, Kentucky, U.S.A. on 4 March 1977. The disengaged foot may not be rested on the standing foot nor may any sticks be used for support or balance.

The record allowing 5 min breaks per hour is 14 hours by Wendy Morrell of Poole Technical College, Poole, Dorset on 25 March 1977.

Ball punching

Ron Renaulf (Australia) equalled his own world duration ball punching record of 125 hours 20 min at 10.20 p.m. on 31 Dec. 1955, at the Esplanade, Southport, Australia.

Geraldine Williams ("Miranda") in action breaking the female bed of nail duration record with 30 hours in Welwyn Garden City, England (see p. 216). (*Stephen Austin Newspapers Ltd.*)

Balloon flights

The longest reported toy balloon flight is one of 9,000 miles *14 500 km* from Atherton, California (released by Jane Dorst on 21 May 1972) and found on 10 June at Pietermaritzburg, South Africa. The longest recorded hydrogen-filled balloon flight from the geographical British Isles is one of 5,880 miles *9 460 km* from Jersey which was returned from Camps Bay, Cape Province, South Africa on 28 Apr. 1974, 43 days after release by Gerard Wankling.

Balloon racing

The largest balloon release on record has been one of 130,000 helium balloons at Baltimore Memorial Stadium, Baltimore, Maryland, U.S.A. on 10 Oct. 1976.

Band marathons

The longest recorded "blow-in" is 100 hrs 2 min by the Du Val Senior High School, Lanham, Maryland, U.S.A. on 13–17 May 1977. The record for a one-man band is 16 hours (no breaks) by Joe Littlefield of McNavy High School, Salem, Oregon on 10 Nov. 1974.

Band One-Man

Don Davis of Hollywood, California is the only one-man band able to play 4 melody and 2 percussion instruments simultaneously without electronics. For his rendition of the 4th movement of Beethoven's Fifth, he utilizes his unique 8-prong pendular perpendicular piano pounder and semi-circular chromatic radially-operated centrifugally sliding left-handed glockenspiel. The greatest number of instruments played in a single tune in 3 minutes is 58 by Christopher Critchlów of Darlington, County Durham, England at the Cockerton Band Club on 18 Dec. 1975. Ron Ruedi played his one man band (which must include at least 3 instruments played simultaneously) for 29 hrs 1 min on 3–4 Dec. 1976 at Barnums Restaurant, Columbia, Maryland, U.S.A.

Barrel jumping

The greatest reported distance achieved by a barrel-jumper on ice skates is 32 ft *9,75 m* (over 13 barels) by T. Karl Milne (b. 1900) at Albany, N.Y., U.S.A. on 31 Jan. 1930.

Barrel rolling

The record for rolling a 36 gallon metal beer barrel over a measured mile is 12 min 29.5 secs by "The Fletch" A team in Coventry, West Midlands on 13 Oct. 1974.

Barrow pushing

The heaviest loaded barrow pushed for a minimum 20 ft (actually 21 ft 9½ in *6,64 m*) is one loaded with 290 bricks weighing 15 cwt 60 lb. *743,8 kg* by Peter King at Ventnor, Isle of Wight in November 1975.

Bath Tub Racing

The record for the annual international 36 miles *57,9 km* Nanaimo to Vancouver, British Columbia bath tub race is 1 hr 35 min 4 secs by Phil Holt (Australia) on 18 July 1976. Tubs are limited to 75 in *1,90 m* and 6 h.p. motors. The greatest distance for a hand propelled bath tub in 24 hours is 36 miles 1,072 yds *58,91 km* by 25 scouts at Priory Park, Malvern, Hereford and Worcester on 10–11 May 1975.

Baton Twirling

Five Portland High School Maine, U.S.A. majorettes Lucinda Haney, Sharan Harkins, Diane Heal, Susan Leiter and Laurie Orfaly twirled for 44 hours accompanied by their school band on 26–28 June 1975.

Bed making

The record time set under the rigorous rules of the Australian Bedmaking Championships is 29.74 secs by Wendy Wall, 33, of Hebersham, Sydney, N.S.W. on 6 June 1977.

The British record with 1 blanket, 2 sheets, 2 uncased pillows, 1 counterpane and "hospital" corners is 2 min 00.8 sec by Staff Nurse Roberta Godwin (St. George's Hospital) in an inter-hospital contest on B.B.C. T.V. *Record Breakers* on 28 Oct. 1975.

Bed of nails

Note: Now that weights in Bed of Nails contests have attained ¾ ton 762 kg it is felt that this category should be retired. No further claims for publication will henceforward be examined.

The duration record for non-stop lying on a bed of nails (sharp 6-inch *15,2 cm*; 2 in *5 cm* apart) is 65 hours 43 min. by Tom Robinson (Strombo, The Maniac) at Oral House Theatre Club, London, on 16–19 June 1977. The female record is 30 hours (non-stop) set by Geraldine Williams (Miranda, Queen of the fakirs) of Welwyn Garden City, Hertfordshire, on 18–19 Mar. 1977. Much longer durations are claimed by uninvigilated *fakirs*— the most extreme case being *Silki* who claimed 111 days in São Paulo, Brazil ending on 24 Aug. 1969. The ultimate weight in an Iron Maiden, being sandwiched between two beds of nails, is 1,642½ lb. *745,02 kg* endured by Komar (Vernon E. Craig) at Old Chicago Towne, Chicago, Illinois on 6 Mar. 1977.

Bed pushing
The longest recorded push of a normally sessile object is of 1,776 miles *2 858 km* in the case of a wheeled hospital bed by a team of 12 at the Greensburg Recreational Board, Greensburg, Pa, U.S.A. on 10–27 Aug. 1975.

Bed race
The record time for the annual Knaresborough Bed Race (established 1966) in North Yorkshire is 14 min 9.0 sec for the 2½ mile *4 km* course crossing the River Nidd by the Harrogate Athletic Club on 14 June 1975.

Beer Label Collecting
The greatest collection of British Beer labels is 20,600 different by Keith Osborne, Hon. Sec. of The Labologists Society (founded by Guinness Exports Ltd in 1958). His oldest is a Bass label of 1869.

Beer Mat Flipping
Lack of standardisation of the size and weight of beer mats has bedevilled the chronicling of records in this international pursuit.

Best man
The world's champion "best man" is Mr. Wally Gant, a bachelor fishmonger from Wakefield, West Yorkshire, who officiated for the 50th time since 1931 in December 1964.

Big Wheel riding
The endurance record for riding a Big Wheel is 29 days by six teenagers at Long Branch Pier, New Jersey, U.S.A. on 9 Aug.–8 Sept. 1976.

Billiard table jumping
Joe Darby (1861–1937) cleared a full-sized 12 ft *3,65 m* billiard table lengthwise, taking off from a 4 in *10 cm* high solid wooden block, at Wolverhampton, West Midlands on 5 Feb. 1892.

Bomb defusing
The highest reported number of unexploded bombs defused by any individual is 8,000 by Werner Stephan in West Berlin, Germany, in the 12 years from 1945 to 1957. He was killed by a small grenade on the Grunewald blasting site on 17 Aug. 1957.

Bond signing
The greatest historical feat of bond signing was that performed by L. E. Chittenden (d. 1902), the Registrar of the United States Treasury. In 48 hours (20–22 March 1863) he signed 12,500 bonds worth $10,000,000 (*now £4 million*), which had to catch a steam packet to England. He suffered years of pain and the bonds were never used.

Boomerang throwing
The earliest mention of a word similar to *boomerang* is *wo-mur-rang* in Collins *Acct. N.S. Wales Vocab.* published in 1798. The earliest certain Australian account of a returning boomerang (term established, 1827) was in 1831 by Major (later Sir Thomas) Mitchell. Curved throwing sticks for wild fowl hunting were found in the tomb of Tutankhamun dating from the mid 14th century B.C.

World championships and codified rules were not established until 1970. Jeff Lewry has won in 1970–71–72–73 and also the Australian title in 1974. The Boomerang Association of

Australia's champion boomerang thrower, Bob Burwell, who has achieved a distance of 110 yds *100,58m.*

Australia's official record for distance reached from the thrower before the boomerang returns is 82 m *89.67 yd* by Jeff Lewry at Albury, N.S.W., on 16 July 1972. Bob Burwell, 32 won a contest at Albany Creek, Queensland with a throw of 110 yds *100,58 m* in 1976.

Braille Writing
Braille was invented in 1825 by Louis Braille (France) aged 16. The highest speed recorded by a braillist (using contracted braille) is 100 words/min using repetitive copy on a Stainsby writer by William P. Rowland at Claremont Civic Centre, Cape Town, South Africa on 19 June 1975.

Brick carrying
The greatest distance achieved for carrying a brick 8 lb. 15 oz. *4,053 kg* in a nominated ungloved hand in an uncradled downward pincher grip is 43.57 miles *70,11 km* by Ken Gormley and Paul Schweibinz of Pittsburg, Pennsylvania U.S.A. on 5 July 1975.

The feminine record for an 9 lb. 12 oz. *4,422 kg* brick is 19.5 miles *30,89 km* by Cynthia Ann Smolko of Denville, New Jersey, U.S.A. on 14 May 1977. The British record for a 6 lb. *2,72 kg* smooth-sided brick is 2.24 miles *3,60 km* by Mrs. Jane Reynolds of Salisbury, Wiltshire at the B.B.C. T.V. Centre London on 10 Nov. 1974.

Bricklaying Records
Publication of achievements in this field has been delayed until standardization of conditions has been agreed between the organizers of contests.

Brick Racing
The record times recorded at the Annual N.F.B.T.E. Young Builders Dry-brick championship in Leicester are 100 metres: 1 min 50.0 secs + 14 penalty points giving a gross 2 min 04.0 secs by James Blenkin in 1974, and 1 mile (team): 25 mins 24 secs + 38 penalties by Stoneygate F.C. on 22 May 1977.

Brick throwing
The greatest reported distance for throwing a standard 5 lb. *2 kg 268* building brick is 142 ft 6 in *43,43 m* by Robert

Gardner at Stroud, Gloucestershire, England in the 1971 Champion of Champions contest.

Burial alive
In June 1951 a groundless story was published that two men had emerged from an underground bunker at Babie Doly, near Gdynia, Poland which had been demolished and blocked by the retreating German army in January 1945.

Voluntary burial alive (for which claims up to 217 days have been published) are inadmissible unless the depth of the coffin is a minimum 2 m *6 ft 6¾ in* below ground; the coffin has maximum dimensions of 200 × 70 × 100 cms *6 ft 6¾ in × 27½ in × 39½ in* and the aperture for communication and feeding is a maximum 10 cm or *4 inches*.

Camping Out
Graeme Hurry (38th Coventry Central Scout Group) completed three years sleeping out on 19 June 1977. He had earlier shared first place in the *Scouting* magazine national contest on 19 June 1975 but just carried on.

Card Throwing
Ricky Jay (U.S.) of Venice, California threw a standard playing card 135 ft *41,1 m* at the BBC T.V. Centre on 4 Nov. 1976.

Car Wrecking
The greatest number of cars wrecked in a stunting career is 1,314 to 1 July 1977 by Dick Sheppard of Gloucester, England.

Cat's Cradle
Jane Muir and Robyn Lawrick completed 22,700 cat's cradles in 21 hours at Calgary Market Mall, Calgary, Alberta, Canada on 25 August 1976.

Champagne Fountain
The tallest successfully filled column of champagne glasses is one 18 high filled from the top by Frank Dettmer of Oakland, California on 2 Aug. 1975.

Clapping
The duration record for continuous clapping (sustaining an average of 140 claps per min audible at 100 yd *91 m*) is 38 hrs 14 min by Andrea McClure and Julie Scribner of Glendale, California, U.S.A. on 7–8 Aug. 1976.

Club swinging
Bill Franks set a world record of 17,280 revolutions (4.8 per sec) in 60 min at Webb's Gymnasium, Newcastle, N.S.W., Australia on 2 Aug. 1934. M. Dobrilla swung continuously for 144 hours at Cobar, N.S.W. finishing on 15 Sept. 1913.

Coal cutting
The first coal mine in Britain to achieve more than 5 tons output per man-shift for a whole year has been Bagworth Colliery, Leicestershire announced on 5 Apr. 1975. The individual record for filling is 218 tons in a week of 5 shifts by Jim Morley (b. 1914) at East Walbottle Colliery, Tyne and Wear, England in 1949. This included 47½ tons in 6 hours.

Coal shovelling
The record for filling a half-ton *508 kg* hopper with coal is 47.4 sec by R. Hughes of Westport, New Zealand in February 1974.

Coin balancing
The greatest recorded feat of coin-balancing is the stacking of 126 coins on top of a silver U.S. dollar on edge by Alex Chervinsky, 65 of Lock Haven, Pennsylvania on 16 Sept. 1971 after 23 years practice.

Coin snatching
The greatest number of 10p pieces clean caught from being flipped from the back of a forearm is 60 by Dennis Cole, 18 in Newry, County Down, Northern Ireland on 20 May 1976. The North American record using 25 cent pieces or "quarters" is 74 by Timothy B. Throckmorton at the University of Maine campus, Maine, U.S.A. on 1 Feb. 1977.

Competition winnings
The largest individual competition prize win on record is $307,500 (*then £109,821*) by Herbert J. Idle, 55, of Chicago in an encyclopaedia contest run by Unicorn Press Inc. on 20 Aug. 1953. The highest value first prize offered in Britain has been a £21,000 cash alternative to a $50,000 New York spending spree offered by Soft Blue Band Luxury Margarine in a contest which closed on 30 Nov. 1971. It was won by Mrs. Susan B. Jenkins of Kirkby, Merseyside, who took the cash.

Complainer Most successful
Ralph Charell (b. 3 Dec. 1929), author of *How I Turn Ordinary Complaints into Thousands of Dollars*, between January 1963 and July 1973 amassed a total of $76,919.31 (*£33,443*) ranging between $6.95 and $25,000 in refunds and compensations. A recent complaint was against this publication for failing to list his 51 consecutive profitable transactions in "option trading".

Cow Chip tossing
The record distance for throwing a dried cow chip is 291.7 ft *88,91 m* by Carl G. Engel and the feminine record is 115 ft 4 in *35,15 m* by Linda Reece, 17 both made at the 1973 Texas State Championship at Odessa. These increasing distances are anxiously studied by party political campaign managers who are also in support of a rule which precludes the mixing of cement into the cow feed prior to contests.

Crawling
The longest continuous voluntary crawl (progression with one or other knee in unbroken contact with the ground) on record is 10.1 miles *16,25 km* by Gerhard Leopold Kroll of Stafford, Staffs on 27 May 1977. A crawl of 27.9 miles *44,9 km* in 43 hours from Swindon, to Oxford, England was performed by Hormoz Tabar Heydar of Iran on 28–30 March 1971. It is chronicled that Hugh Glass crawled 100 miles *160 km* dragging a broken leg in South Dakota, U.S.A. in 1823.

Crochet
The longest recorded crocheted chain is one of 4 ply wool measuring 11,09 miles *17,84 km* completed between October 1976 and 19 Feb. 1977 by Mrs. Betty Tafat of Cuyahoga Falls, Ohio, U.S.A.

Mrs. Betty Tafat (U.S.A.) completing her 11 mile *17,8 km* long crochet chain after 4 months. (*Akron Beacon Journal*)

Cucumber slicing

Norman Johnson of Blackpool College of Art and Technology set a record of 24.2 sec for slicing a 12 in cucumber 1½ in diameter at 20 slices to the inch (total 240 slices) on B.B.C. T.V. *Record Breakers* on 28 Sept. 1973.

Custard Pie throwing

The most times champion in the annual World Custard Pie Championships at Coxheath, Kent (instituted 1967) have been the "The Birds" and the Coxheath Man each with 3 wins. The target (face) must be 8 ft 3⅞ in *2,53 m* from the thrower who must throw a pie no more than 10¾ in *27,3 cm* in diameter. Six points are scored for a square hit full in the face.

DANCING
Largest Dance

The largest dance ever staged was that put on by the Houston Livestock Show at the Astro Hall, Houston, Texas, U.S.A. on 8 Feb. 1969. The attendance was more than 16,500 with 4,000 turned away.

Marathon dancing must be distinguished from dancing mania, which is a pathological condition. The worst outbreak of dancing mania was at Aachen, Germany, in July 1374, when hordes of men and women broke into a frenzied and compulsive choreomania in the streets which lasted for hours till injury or complete exhaustion ensued.

The most severe marathon dance staged as a public spectacle in the U.S.A. was one lasting 4,152½ hours (24 weeks 5 days) completed by Tony Alteriri and Vera Mikus (now Mrs. Oglesby of Springdale, Pennsylvania) at Motor Square Garden, Pittsburgh from 6 June to 30 Nov. 1932. The rest allowance of 15 min per hour was progressively cut to 10, 7, 6, 5, and in the final weeks to 3 min. per hour until this Marathon Dance "Classic" was finally stopped by the authorities. The prize of $1,000 was equivalent to 24 cents per hour.

Ballet

In the *entrechat* (a vertical spring from the fifth position with the legs extended criss-crossing at the lower calf), the starting and finishing position each count as one such that in an *entrechat douze* there are *five* crossings and uncrossings. This was performed by Wayne Sleep for the B.B.C. *Record Breakers* programme on 7 Jan. 1973. He was in the air for 0.71 of a second.

Ballet *Most turns*

The greatest number of spins called for in classical ballet choreography is the 32 *fouettés rond de jambe en tournant* in "Swan Lake" by Pyotr Ilyich Chaykovskiy (Tschaikovsky) (1840–1893). Miss Rowena Jackson (later Chatfield), M.B.E. (b. Invercargill, N.Z., 1925) achieved 121 such turns at her class in Melbourne, Victoria, Australia, in 1940.

Ballet *Most curtain calls*

The greatest recorded number of curtain calls ever received by ballet dancers is 89 by Dame Margaret Evelyn Arias, D.B.E. *née* Hookham (born Reigate, Surrey, 19 May 1919), *alias* Margot Fonteyn, and Rudolf Hametovich Nureyev (born on a train near Irkutsk, U.S.S.R., 17 Mar. 1938) after a performance of "Swan Lake" at the Vienna Staatsoper, Austria, in October 1964.

Ballet *Largest Cast*

The largest number of ballet dancers used in a production in Britain has been 2,000 in the London Coster Ballet of 1962, directed by Lillian Rowley, at the Royal Albert Hall, London.

Ballroom *Marathon*

The individual continuous world record for ballroom dancing is 106 hours 5 min 10 sec by Carlos Sandrini in Buenos Aires, Argentina, in September 1955. Three girls worked shifts as his partner.

Ballroom *Champions*

The world's most successful professional ballroom dancing

champions have been Bill Irvine, M.B.E. and Bobbie Irvine, M.B.E., who won 13 world titles between 1960 and 1972.

The most consecutive national titles won is 10 in the New Zealand Old Time Championship by Mr. Maurice Fox and his wife Royce (*née* Miles) of Palmerston North in 1959–68.

The oldest competitive ballroom dancer is Albert J. Sylvester C.B.E., J.P. (b. 24 Nov. 1889) of Corsham, Wiltshire. In 1976 he won the Imperial Society of Teachers of Dancing annual award for Latin American dancing.

Belly Dancing

The longest recorded belly dance was one of 66 hrs 40 mins by Sabra Starr at the Crab's Claw Restaurant, Atlantic City, New Jersey, U.S.A. on 8–11 Jan. 1977.

The world's most durable belly dancer, Sabra Starr, who gyrated for 66 hours 40 mins in Atlantic City, New Jersey.

Charleston
The Charleston duration record is 37½ hours by Terri Fry, Roberta Gatto, Mary McPeak, and Scotty Parker all of Parkrose High School, Portland, Oregon, U.S.A., on 28–30 May 1976.

Conga
The longest recorded conga was one comprising a "snake" of 5562 visitors and residents at Sidmouth, Devon, on 14 July 1977.

Flamenco
The fastest flamenco dancer ever measured is Solero de Jerez aged 17 who in Brisbane, Australia in September 1967 in an electrifying routine attained 16 heel taps per second or a rate of 1,000 a minute.

Go-go
The duration record for go-go dancing (Boogoloo or Reggae) is 113 hrs 35 min by Julie Skubala of the Affair Club, Swindon, Wiltshire on 7–12 Apr. 1977.

High Kicking
The world record for high kicks is 8,005 in 4 hrs 40 min by Veronica Evans (née Steen), (b. Liverpool, 20 Feb. 1910) at the Pathétone Studios, Wardour Street, London in summer 1939.

Jiving
The duration record for non-stop jiving is 58 hrs 4 min by Eric Brennan of Winnipeg, Manitoba, U.S.A. on 21–23 Feb. 1977.

Limbo
The lowest height for a bar under which a limbo dancer has passed under a flaming bar is 6⅛ in 15,5 cm off the floor by Marlene Raymond, 15 at the Port of Spain Pavilion, Toronto, Canada on 24 June 1973. Strictly no part of the body other than the sole or side of the foot should touch the ground though the brushing of a shoulder blade does not in practice usually result in disqualification.

Modern
The longest recorded dancing marathon in modern style is one of 144 hours by Albert Harding at the Inn Cognito, Middlesbrough, Cleveland on 23–29 Apr. 1977.

Tap
The fastest rate ever measured for any tap dancer has been 1,440 taps per min (24 per sec) by Roy Castle on the B.B.C. T.V. Record Breakers programme on 14 Jan. 1973.

Twist
The duration record for the twist is 102 hours 28 mins 37 sec by Roger Guy English at La Jolla, California, U.S.A. on 11–16 July 1973.

Dance band
The most protracted session for a dance band is one of 321 hours (13 days 9 hours) by the Black Brothers of West Germany at Bonn ending on 2 Feb. 1968. Never less than a quartet were in action during the marathon.

Demolition work
Fifteen members of the International Budo Association (Japanese martial arts) led by Phil Milner (3rd Dan Karate) demolished, a 6-roomed early Victorian house at Idle, Bradford, West Yorkshire by head, foot and empty hand in 6 hours on 4 June 1972. On completion they bowed to the rubble.

Disc-Jockey
The longest continuous period of acting as a disc-jockey is 800 hours by Mark Gondelman of Woodstock, New York, U.S.A. on 4 July–7 Aug. 1975. L.P.'s are limited to 50% of total playing time.

Domino Toppling
The greatest number of dominoes toppled is 33,266 by Mike

Cairney and his team from Leeds University at Chelsea College, London on 30 Mar. 1977.

Drumming
The world's duration drumming record is 320 hours by Jim Purol of Livonia, Michigan, U.S.A. on 19 June–2 July 1976 beating the existing record of 270 hours set up by Jim Moore of McCall, Idaho, U.S.A. on 11–22 June, 1975.

Ducks and Drakes
The best accepted ducks and drakes (stone-skipping) record is 24 skips (10 plinkers and 14 pitty-pats) by Warren Klope, 20 of Troy, Michigan with a 4 in 10 cm thin flat limestone at the annual Mackinac Island, Michigan, U.S.A. stone skipping tournament on 5 July 1975.

Egg dropping
The greatest height from which fresh eggs have been dropped and remained intact is 600 ft 182 m by David Donaghue and John Cartwright from a helicopter on 8 Feb. 1974.

Egg and spoon racing
Gerry O'Kane, 21, from Carfin, Motherwell, Strathclyde completed a 27-mile 43,45 km fresh egg and dessert spoon marathon in 5 hours 27 min on 7 Apr. 1977.

Egg shelling
Two kitchen hands, Harold Witcomb and Gerald Harding shelled 1,050 dozen eggs in a 7¼ hour shift at Bowyers, Trowbridge, Wiltshire on 23 Apr. 1971. Both are blind.

Egg throwing
The longest recorded distance for throwing a fresh hen's egg without breaking is 316 ft 5¾ in at their 11th exchange between David Barger and Craig Finley at Lamar High School, Missouri on 2 May 1974.

Escapology
The most renowned of all escape artists has been Erich Weiss alias Harry Houdini (1874–1926), who pioneered underwater escapes from locked, roped and weighted containers while handcuffed and shackled with irons. The fastest reported time for an escape dangling from a helicopter is 19.9 secs by Jimmy Dixon 200 ft 61 m above Circus Circus Hotel/Casino Las Vegas, Nevada, U.S.A. on 15 Dec. 1976. Stephen B. Burke performed an escape from a strait jacket when dangling upside down below a helicopter 1,400 ft 425 m from the ground over St. Augustine airport, Florida, U.S.A. on 12 Sept. 1976. Burke escaped from standard strait jacket at the Friendship Fountain, Jacksonville, Florida in 10.0 secs on 28 Aug. 1976.

Reynir Oern Léossen (born 1938) succeeded in breaking out of a cell in Keflavik prison, Iceland on 23 Sept. 1972 from a cell in which he had been locked with three handcuffs behind his back and his hands tied by 5 mm chains each able to withstand a force of 1 270 kg 2,800 lb. His feet were fastened with footcuffs and he was further loaded with 5 mm and 10 mm (tensile strenth 6 050 kg) chains weighing in all 20 kg 44 lb. Léossen broke out in five hours and 50 min and emerged through a 28 mm 1.1 in thick 15 cm 5.9 in wide glass window which he had "extended" by breaking some of the adjoining brickwork. In a laboratory on 24 May 1972 he demonstrated the ability of parting 10 mm 0.4 in chain which had a tensile strength of 6 100 kg 13,448 lb. or 6.00 tons.

Family Tree
The largest family tree on record is the Borton tree measuring 18 × 15 ft 5,48 × 4,57 m compiled by Nelleray Borton Holt of Union Gap, Washington, U.S.A. over 16 years. It contains 6,820 names extending back to 1562. She also constructed a 340 ft 103,6 m long pedigree chart covering 16 generations commissioned by Maxine Bremerman.

Fashion Show longest
The longest fashion show ever recorded was one which lasted 44 hrs at Huntingdon Center Mall, Huntingdon, California, U.S.A. on 18–20 Mar. 1977. Debbi Ubaldini, Susan Lister, and Myra Robinson all completed 28.5 miles 45,86 km on the cat walk.

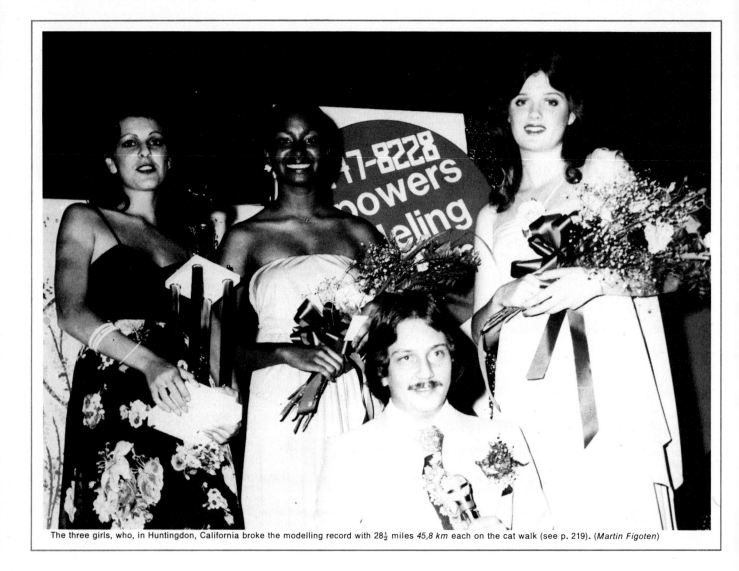

The three girls, who, in Huntingdon, California broke the modelling record with 28½ miles *45,8 km* each on the cat walk (see p. 219). (*Martin Figoten*)

Faux Pas

If measuring by financial consequence, the greatest *faux pas* on record was that of the young multi-millionaire, James Gordon Bennett, committed on 1 Jan. 1877 at the family mansion of his demure fiancée one Caroline May, in Fifth Avenue, New York City. Bennett arrived in a two-horse cutter late and obviously in wine. By dint of intricate footwork, he gained the portals to enter the withdrawing room where he was the cynosure of all eyes. He mistook the fireplace for a plumbing fixture more usually reserved for another purpose. The May family broke the engagement and Bennett (1841–1918) was obliged to spend the rest of his foot-loose and fancy-free life based in Paris with the resultant non-collection of millions of tax dollars by the U.S. Treasury.

Feminine Beauty

Female pulchritude being qualitative rather than quantitative does not lend itself to records. It has been suggested that, if the face of Helen of Troy (*c.* 1200 B.C.) was capable of launching 1,000 ships, a unit of beauty sufficient to launch one ship should be a millihelen. The pioneer beauty contest was staged at Atlantic City, New Jersey, U.S.A. in 1921 and was won by a blue-eyed blonde with a 30 in *76,2 cm* chest, Margaret Gorman. The Miss World contest began in London in July 1951. The maximum dimensions of any winner were those of Miss Egypt, Antigone Costanda, in 1954 whose junoesque characteristics were at 40-26-38 in *101-66-96 cm* in advance of the classic Western idea of allure. The United Kingdom is the only country to have produced four winners. They were Rosemarie Frankland (1961); Ann Sidney (1964); Lesley Langley (1965) and Helen Morgan (1974), who resigned. The maximum number of contestants was 68 in November 1975.

Victor Malafronte, who awaits ratification by the International Frisbee Association of a throw of 538 ft *163,98 m* in Golden Gate Park, San Francisco, California on 15 May 1977.

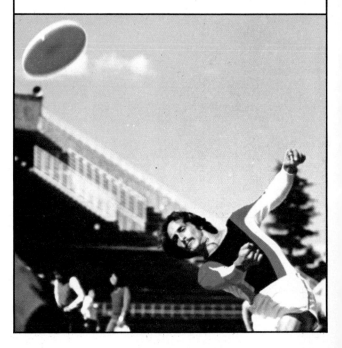

The world's largest beauty pageant is the annual Miss Universe contest inaugurated in Long Beach California in 1952. The most successful country has been the U.S.A. with winners in 1954–56–60–67. The number of countries represented has reached 75 with Miss Trinidad reigning in 1977.

Fire Pump pulling
The longest unaided tow of a fire appliance in excess of 10 cwt *508 kg* is 155.2 miles *249,7 km* on 7–8 June 1975 around Yeovilton airfield by the Somerset Fire Brigade and the Fleet Air Arm Fire Service.

Flute marathon
The longest recorded marathon by a flautist is 48 hours by Joe Silmon on H.M.S. *Dolphin* in Gosport, Hampshire on 19–20 Feb. 1977.

Frisbee throwing
A Frisbee is a concave plastic throwing plate. Competitive Frisbee throwing began in 1957. The International Frisbee Association indoor records are Men: 277 ft 2 in *84,48 m* by Dave Johnson and Women: 209 ft 2 in *63,75 m* Monika Lou both in Los Angeles on 20 Aug. 1975. The throw, run and catch record is 234 ft *71,3 m* by John Kirkland, at Boulder Colorado, U.S.A., on 17 July 1976. Johnson's outdoor record is 412 ft *125,5 m* at Boston, Mass., U.S.A. The marathon record is 475 hrs 18 min on the Munich campus, West Germany of the University of Maryland on 8–28 Oct. 1975.

Gold panning
The fastest time recorded for "panning" 8 planted gold nuggets in a 10 in *25,4 cm* diameter pan is 15.4 sec by Larry Bertles of Fallon, Nevada and 18.9 sec by Carolyn J. Box of Ahwahnee, California in the 1976 16th World Gold Panning Championships held at Tropico Gold Mine, Rosamond, California on 7 Mar. 1976. Ms Lilly Szcrupa, a school teacher, took the award for the "world's worst gold panner" in 1974.

Golf Ball Balancing
Mark Baumen of Grand Island, Nebraska, U.S.A., on 21 Nov. 1974 succeeded in balancing 5 new golf balls vertically without adhesive.

Grape catching
The longest recorded distance for catching a thrown grape in the mouth is 243 ft *74,06 m* by Arden Chapman at Northeast Louisiana University, U.S.A. on 6 May 1977. The grape thrower was Benny D. Jones.

Grave digging
It is recorded that Johann Heinrich Karl Thieme, sexton of Aldenburg, Germany, dug 23,311 graves during a 50-year career. In 1826 *his* understudy dug his grave.

Guitar playing
The longest recorded solo guitar playing marathon is one of 128 hrs 21 min by Steve Owens of Kingswear, Devon on 9–14 Dec. 1976.

Gum Boot throwing
The longest recorded distance (a Size 8 Challenger Dunlop Boot) for "Wellie wanging" is 155 ft 10 in *47,50 m* by Howard Payne at the National Exhibition Centre, Birmingham on 31 May 1976. His wife Rosemary established the feminine record at Cannon Hill Park, Birmingham on 21 June 1975 with 129 ft 11 in *39,60 m*.

Gun running
The record for the Royal Tournament naval gun run competition (instituted 1900, with present rules since 1919) is 2 min 4.7 sec by the Portsmouth "Pompey" Crew at Earl's Court, Kensington & Chelsea, Greater London in 1973. The barrel alone weighs 8 cwt. *406 kg*. The wall is 5 ft *1,52 m* high and the chasm 28 ft *8,53 m* across. The Portsmouth crew returned 2 min 40.7 sec in a training practice run at Whale Island, Portsmouth, Hampshire in 1972.

Hair-dressing
Louis Sanft of Fall River, Massachusetts, U.S.A. cut, set and styled hair continuously for 200 hours on 27 May–4 June 1976.

Hair splitting
The greatest reported achievement in hair splitting has been that of Alfred West (b. London, 14 Apr. 1901) who has succeeded in splitting a human hair 14 times into 15 parts in 1977.

Handbell ringing
The longest recorded handbell ringing recital has been one of 41 hours by the Potomac Handbell Ringers of Washington, U.S.A. on 19–20 Feb. 1977.

Handshaking
A world record for handshaking was set up by Theodore Roosevelt (1858–1919), President of the U.S.A., when he shook hands with 8,513 people at a New Year's Day, White House Presentation in Washington, D.C., U.S.A. on 1 Jan. 1907. Outside public life the record has become meaningless because aspirants merely tend to arrange circular queues or wittingly or unwittingly shake the same hands repetitively.

Hand writing
The longest recorded hand written letter writing marathon is one of 317 hours and more than 2,900 letters with their envelopes by Raymond L. Cantwell of Littlemore, Oxford, England in raising money for The Churchill Hospital, on 26 Apr.– 9 May 1977.

High Diving
The highest regularly performed dive is that of professional divers from La Quebrada ("the break in the rocks") at Acapulco, Mexico, a height of 118 ft *36 m*. The leader of the 27 divers in the exclusive Club de Clavadistas is Raul Garcia (b. 1928) with more than 35,000 dives. The base rocks, 21 ft *6,40 m* out from the take-off, necessitate a leap of 27 ft *8,22 m* out. The water is 12 ft *3,65 m* deep. The *Wide World of Sports* record is 130 ft 6 in *39,77 m* jointly set by Donnie Vick, Pat Sucher and John Tobler in March 1974.

On 8 May 1885, Sarah Ann Henley, aged 24, jumped from the Clifton Suspension Bridge, which crosses the Avon, England. Her 250 ft *76 m* fall was slightly cushioned by her voluminous dress and petticoat acting as a parachute. She landed, bruised and bedraggled, in the mud on the north bank and was carried to hospital by four policemen. On 11 Feb. 1968 Jeffrey Kramer, 24, leapt off the George Washington Bridge 250 ft *76 m* above the Hudson River, New York City, N.Y. and survived. Of the 511 (to 25 Apr. 1974) people who have made 240 ft *73 m* suicide dives from the Golden Gate Bridge, San Francisco, California, U.S.A. since 1937 seven survived. On 10 July 1921 a stuntman named William H. Bailey leapt from a seaplane into the Ohio River at Louiselle, Kentucky. The alleged altitude was 310 ft *94,5 m*.

Samuel Scott (U.S.A.) is reputed to have made a dive of 497 ft *151,48 m* at Pattison Fall (now Manitou Falls) in Wisconsin, U.S.A., in 1840, but this would have entailed an entry speed of 86 m.p.h. *138 km/h*. The actual height was probably 165 ft *50,30 m*. Col. Harry A. Froboess (Switzerland) jumped 110 m *360 ft* into the Bodensee from the airship *Graf Hindenberg* on 22 June 1936.

The greatest height reported for a dive into a flaming tank is one of 100 ft *20,4 m* into 7½ ft *2,28 m* by Bill McGuire, 48 at the Holiday Inn, Chicago City Center, Michigan, U.S.A. on 14 Aug. 1975.

Ron Nix dived into flaming 5 ft *1,52 m* tall cardboard boxes from 66 ft *20,1 m* above the street outside Vine Street Theatre, Los Angeles, California for a David Frost TV show on 7 May 1975.

Highest Shallow Dive
Henri La Mothe (b. 1904) set a record by diving 40 ft *12,20 m* into 12½ in *31,7 cm* of water in a child's paddling pool on Broadway, New York City on 5 Apr. 1974. He decelerates at 70 g.

Steve McPeak, making his hazardous high wire crossing at Circus Circus, Las Vegas, Nevada, on a 41 ft *12,49 m* tall unicycle, on a high wire 40 ft *12,19 m* above the ground. (*Franklin Berger*)

High-wire act *Highest*

The greatest drop beneath any high wire performance has been from a 140 ft *42,6 m* wire between the 1,350 ft *411 m* twin towers of the World Trade Center, New York City by Phillipe Petit, 24 of Nemours, France on 7 Aug. 1974. He was charged with criminal trespass after a 75 minute display of at least 7 crossings. The police psychiatrist opined "Anyone who does this 110 storeys up can't be entirely right".

Steve McPeak, 31 made a 225 ft *68,58 m* unicycle crossing on a high wire 2,550 ft *777,2 m* above the Yosemite Falls, California, U.S.A. on 12 July 1976.

Hitch-hiking

The title of world champion hitch-hiker is claimed by Devon Smith who from 1947 to 1971 thumbed lifts totalling 291,000 miles *468 300 km*. In 1957 he covered all the then 48 U.S. States in 33 days. It was not till his 6,013th "hitch" that he got a ride in a Rolls-Royce. The hitch-hiking record for the 873 miles *1 405 km* from Land's End, Cornwall, to John o'

Groats, Highland, Scotland, is 23 hours 24 min by Miranda Brooks and Margaret Allinson of New Hall College, Cambridge on 28 Feb.–1 Mar. 1977. The time before the first "hitch" on the first day is excluded. The fastest time recorded for the round trip is 54 hours 40 min by Peter W. Ford of Cheltenham, Gloucestershire on 1–3 June 1976.

Hod Carrying

Bernie Gill of Old Coulsdon, Surrey carried fifty 4.4 lb. *2 kg* Fletton bricks totalling 220 lb. *100 kg* up a 10 ft *3,048 m* ladder in BBC TV's *Record Breakers* on 27 Oct. 1976.

Hoop rolling

In 1968 it was reported that Zolilio Diaz (Spain) had rolled a hoop 600 miles *965 km* from Mieres to Madrid and back in 18 days.

Hop Scotch

The longest recorded hop scotch marathon is one of 39 hours by 2 pairs, Donna Gardiner and Joan Popilia, Raewyn Gavet and Kimina Styche, all of Tokoroa High School, Tokoroa, New Zealand on 18–19 March 1977.

Hot Water Bottle Bursting

The highest lung power measurement in bursting hot water bottles is $28\frac{1}{2}$ lb./in² *139 kg/m²* by Mel Robson of Newcastle upon Tyne in February 1977. He and Stuart Hughes have both extended a Super-Suba Seal Safety Bottle to 5 ft 6 in *1,67 m* before rupture.

House of cards

The greatest number of storeys achieved in building houses of playing cards is 43 in the case of a tower using 2,500 cards by Bruce Marchese of San Dimas, California on 14 May 1976. The highest house with alternate 8 and 6 card storeys is 30 achieved by Julian Bardo in St. John's College, Cambridge on 14 June 1974. He used 4 packs and a plumb-line.

Hula hooping

The record for sustaining gyrating hoops is 28 set by DeAnn Deluna of Los Angeles winning the U.S. National championship on 27 May 1974. The longest recorded marathon is 10 hr 47 min by Mary Jane Freeze aged 8 of West Laurel, Maryland, U.S.A. on 19 Aug. 1976.

Human cannonball

The record distance for firing a human from a cannon is 175 ft *53,3 m* in the case of Emanuel Zacchini in the Ringling Bros. and Barnum & Bailey Circus, Madison Square Gardens, New York City, U.S.A., in 1940. His muzzle velocity has been estimated at 54 m.p.h. *86,9 km/h.* On his retirement the management were fortunate in finding that his daughter Florinda was of the same calibre.

In the Halifax explosion of 6 Dec. 1917 (see page 209) A. B. William Becker, A.M. (d. 1969) was blown some 1,600 yd *1,46 km* but was found breathing in a tree.

Human Fly

The greatest climb achieved on the vertical face of a building occurred on 26 May 1977 when George Willig, 27, scaled the outside of the 1,350 ft *411,48 m* high World Trade Center, New York City in $3\frac{1}{2}$ hours at a rate of 6.4 ft/min *1,95m/min.* On descending by elevator he was led to a waiting police car.

Joke cracking

Johnny Kay of Cheadle, Cheshire cracked jokes unremittingly for 9 hours 15 min on 23 June 1977. The duration record for a duo is 52 hours by Wayne Malton and Mike Hamilton at the Howard Johnson Motor Hotel, Toronto airport, Ontario, Canada on 13–16 Nov. 1975.

right: Bruce Marchese of San Dimas, California, who completed a 43 storey house of cards, having used 2,500 cards.

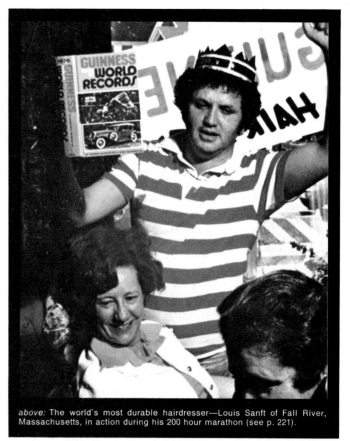

above: The world's most durable hairdresser—Louis Sanft of Fall River, Massachusetts, in action during his 200 hour marathon (see p. 221).

George Willig, the Human Fly, during his gravity-defying 110 storey ascent of the vertical wall of New York's 1,350 ft *411,48 m* World Trade Center (see p. 223). (*Jerry Brooks*)

Juggling

The only juggler in history able to juggle—as opposed to "shower"—10 balls or eight plates was the Italian Enrico Rastelli, who was born in Samara, Russia, on 19 Dec. 1896 and died in Bergamo, Italy, on 13 Dec. 1931.

Jumble Sale

Britain's largest permanent Jumble Sale, opened on 18 Nov. 1975, is the Oxfam Wastesaver Centre, Milford St., Huddersfield, West Yorkshire. Annual running costs of the 8,000 ft² *743 m²* warehouse are estimated at £150,000 and the projected revenue for 1978 is £250,000.

Karate Chop

Claims for breaking bricks and wooden slats etc. are unsatisfactory because of the lack of any agreed standards upon which comparisons can be made.

Kiss of Life

Five members of the 2nd/1st Battalion Medical Section R.N.Z.I.R., Burnham Camp, Christchurch, New Zealand on 4–6 Nov. 1976 maintained a "Kiss of life" for 48 hours with 43,086 "inflations". The "patient" was a dummy.

Kissing

The most prolonged osculatory marathon in cinematic history is one of 185 sec by Regis Toomey and Jane Wyman in *You're In the Army Now* released in 1940. In a "Smoochathon" at Springfield, Virginia, U.S.A., Candy Wessling and Klaus Wagner kissed for 124 hours 51 mins. Jeffrey R. Henzler of Indiana, Pennsylvania kissed 3,225 girls in 8 hours at Regency Hall, Indiana on 5 Mar. 1977—a rate of one per 8.93 secs.

Kite Flying *Largest*

The largest kite on record was built in Naruto City, Japan in

1936 of 3,100 panes of paper weighing 8½ tons/*tonnes*. The largest hand-launched kite was one 83 ft *25,3 m* long and of 820 ft² *76 m²* by Robert Bartlett at Grant Park, Chicago, Illinois, U.S.A. on 28 Apr. 1974.

Kite Flying *Greatest number*
The most kites flown on a single line is 1,050 by Kazuhiko Asaba, 52 at Kama Kura, Japan on 4 Apr. 1976. The topmost kite reached an estimated 4,000 ft *1 220 m.*

Kite Flying *Altitude*
The single kite record is 22,500 ft (min)–28,000 ft (max) *6 860 to 8 535 m* by Prof. Phillip R. Kunz and Jay P. Kunz at Laramie, Wyoming, U.S.A. on 21 Nov. 1967. A claim for a chain of 8 kites reaching 31,955 ft *9 470 m* was made from Lindenburg, East Germany on 1 Aug. 1919.

Kite Flying *Duration*
The longest recorded flight is one of 169 hours by the Sunrise Inn team, Fort Lauderdale, Florida managed by Will Yolen on 30 Apr.–7 May 1977.

Knitting
The world's most prolific hand-knitter of all time has been Mrs. Gwen Matthewman of Featherstone, West Yorkshire, who in 1975 knitted 885 garments involving 10,530 oz. *298,52 kg* of wool (equivalent to the fleece of 85 sheep). She had been timed to average 108 stitches per min in a 30-min test. Her technique has been filmed by the world's only Professor of Knitting—a Japanese. The longest recorded knitting marathon is one of 100 hrs by Mrs. Ann Whitbrown of Market Drayton, Salop (with 5 min time out allowances per hour), on 11–15 Apr. 1976.

The winner of the 1976 *Pins and Needles* magazine speed contest was Mrs. Margaret Collins of Bournemouth, who knitted 139 rows (3,336 stitches) in 45 min (74.1 garter stitches per min).

Knot-tying
The fastest recorded time for tying the six Boy Scout Handbook Knots (square knot, sheet bend, sheep shank, clove hitch, round turn and two half hitches and bowline) on individual ropes is 8.1 sec by Clinton R. Bailey Sr., 52, of Pacific City, Oregon, on 13 Apr. 1977.

Leap frogging
Fourteen members of the Hoover Apprentices Association Merthyr Tydfil, Mid Glamorgan covered 399¼ miles in 96 hours on 11–15 Aug. 1975.

Life Saving
In November 1974 the City of Galveston, Texas and the Noon Optimist Club unveiled a plaque to the deaf-mute lifeguard Leroy Colombo (1905–1974) who saved 907 people from drowning in the waters around Galveston Island from 1917 to his death.

Lightning most times struck
The only living man in the world to be struck by lightning 7 times is ex-Park Ranger Roy C. Sullivan (U.S.), the human lightning conductor of Virginia. His attraction for lightning began in 1942 (lost big toe nail), and was resumed in July 1969 (lost eyebrows), in July 1970 (left shoulder seared), on 16 Apr. 1972 (hair set on fire), on 7 Aug. 1973 (new hair refired and legs seared), on 5 June 1976 ankle injured, and sent to hospital with chest and stomach burns on 26 June 1977.

Lion-taming
The greatest number of lions mastered and fed in a cage by an unaided lion-tamer was 40, by "Captain" Alfred Schneider in 1925. Clyde Raymond Beatty handled more than 40 "cats" (mixed lions and tigers) simultaneously. Beatty (b. Bainbridge, Ohio, 10 June 1903, d. Ventura, California, 19 July 1965) was the featured attraction at every show he appeared with for more than 40 years. He insisted upon being called a lion-trainer. Twenty-one lion-tamers have died of injuries since 1900.

Alfred Schneider, who first proved his ability to feed 40 lions unaided in a cage in 1925.

Log rolling
The most protracted bout in the famous contest on Chequamegon Bay, Wisconsin, U.S.A. on 4 July 1900 was 11¾ min between Ronald Macdonald (winner) and James Oliver. The record number of International Championships is 10 by Jubiel Wickheim (Canada) between 1956 and 1969.

Merry Go Round
The longest merry go round marathon on record is one of 312 hours 43 min by Gary Mandau, Chris Lyons and Dana Dover in Portland, Oregon, U.S.A. on 20 Aug.–2 Sept. 1976.

Message in a bottle
The longest recorded interval between drop and pick up is 64 years between 7 Aug. 1910 ("please write to Miss Gladys Potter") in Grand Lake and August 1974 from Lake Huron. Miss Potter was traced as Mrs. Oliver Scheid, 76 of Columbus, Ohio. A bottle apparently bearing a message written on 19 Nov. 1899 by Capt. Charles Weieerishen of the S.S. "Crown Princess Cecilia" off Varberg, Sweden was reportedly picked up on the coast of Victoria, B.C. Canada on 9 Dec. 1936.

Milk Bottle Balancing
The greatest distance walked by a person continuously balancing a full pint milk bottle on the head is 15 miles 1,738 yds. *25,729 km* by William Charlton at Davenport, Tasmania on 4 June 1972.

Model *Highest Paid*
The longest contract in the history of modelling was for $1,000,000 *£588,200* between Fabergé and Miss Margaux Hemingway (b. 1955) of Ketchum, Idaho, U.S.A. on 20 May 1975. She is described as "corn-fed pretty" and describes her own height as "five foot twelve".

225

Morse

The highest recorded speed at which anyone has received morse code is 75.2 words per minute—over 17 symbols per second. This was achieved by Ted R. McElroy of the United States in a tournament at Asheville, North Carolina, U.S.A. on 2 July 1939.

Musical Chairs

The largest game on record was one starting with 1,162 participants and 900 chairs and ending with Donna Deakins, 12 on the last chair at Forster Memorial Park, Catford, London on 4 Apr. 1977.

Needle threading

The record number of strands of cotton threaded through a number 13 needle (eye ½ in by $\frac{1}{16}$ of an in *12,7 mm × 1,6 mm*) in 2 hours is 3,795 times by Miss Brenda Robinson of the College of Further Education, Chippenham, Wiltshire on 20 Mar. 1971.

Noodle making

Stephen Yim (b. Shanghai, China, 1949) made 256 noodle strings (over 5 ft *1,52 m*) in 63 sec on the B.B.C. T.V. *Record Breakers* programme on 21 Oct. 1973.

Onion Peeling

The record for onion peeling is 42 lb. *19,05 kg* in 45 min by Cameron Simpson, then of the *Sunday Post* at Foresthall Hospital, Glasgow on 29 Oct. 1976.

Omelette making

The greatest number of two-egg omelettes made in 30 min is 188 by Jeffrey Neese, a short order cook at the Palace Restaurant, Taylor, Chicago, Michigan, U.S.A. on 23 Dec. 1975. He used 6 pans and 6 burners. The single pan record of 105 in 26 min 25 sec was set by Clement Rapphael Freud (later M.P.) at The Victoria, Nottingham on 15 July 1971.

Organ

The longest recorded electric organ marathon is one of 411 hours by Vince Bull at the Comet Hotel, Scunthorpe, South Humberside on 2–29 June 1977.

Parachuting *Longest fall without*

The greatest altitude from which anyone has bailed out without a parachute and survived is 6 700 m *21,980 ft*. This occurred in January 1942, when Lt. (now Lt.-Col.) I. M. Chisov (U.S.S.R.) fell from an Ilyushin 4 which had been severely damaged. He struck the ground a glancing blow on the edge of a snow-covered ravine and slid to the bottom. He suffered a fractured pelvis and severe spinal damage. It is estimated that the human body reaches 99 per cent of its low level terminal velocity after falling 1,880 ft *573 m* which takes 13 to 14 sec. This is 117–125 m.p.h. *188–201 km/h* at normal atmospheric pressure in a random posture, but up to 185 m.p.h. *298 km/h* in a head down position. Vesna Vulovic, 23 a Jugoslavenski Aerotransport hostess, survived when her DC9 blew up at 33,330 ft *10 160 m* over the Czechoslovak village of Ceská Kamenice on 26 Jan. 1972. She fell inside a section of tail unit. She attended hospital for 17 months.

The British record is 18,000 ft *5 485 m* by Flt.-Sgt. Nicholas Stephen Alkemade, aged 21, who jumped from a blazing R.A.F. *Lancaster* bomber over Germany on 23 Mar. 1944. His headlong fall was broken by a fir tree and he landed without a broken bone in a snow bank 18 in *45 cm* deep.

Piano-playing

The longest piano-playing marathon has been one of 1,091 hours (45 days 11 hours) playing 22 hours every day (with 5 min intervals each playing hour) from 11 Oct. to 24 Nov. 1970 by James Crowley, Jr., 30 at Scranton, Pennsylvania, U.S.A. The British record is 200 hours 35 min (with 5 min breaks each hour) set by Michael George of Cheadle Heath, Stockport in a music shop in Edgware Road, London on 12–21 Aug. 1974. The women's world record in the discontinued non-stop category was 133 hours (5 days 13 hours) by Mrs. Marie Ashton aged 40, in a theatre in Blyth, Northumberland, on 18–23 Aug. 1958.

Piano smashing

The record time for demolishing an upright piano and passing the entire wreckage through a circle 9 in *22,8 cm* in diameter is 2 min 26 sec by six men representing Ireland led by Johnny Leydon of Sligo, at Merton, Greater London on 7 Sept. 1968. Messrs Anthony Fukes, Mike Newman, Terry Cullington and Malcolm Large smashed a piano with bare hands in 7 min in Nottingham on 6 June 1977.

Piano tuning

The record time for pitch raising (one semi-tone or 100 cents) and then returning a piano to a musically acceptable quality is 20 min 50 sec by Harry Buyce of the Western Michigan Chapter of the Piano Technicians' Guild Inc. in Kalamazoo on 14 Apr. 1977.

Pillar box standing

The record number of people to pile on top of a pillar box (oval top of 6 ft² *0,55 m²*) is 29, all students of the City of

PARACHUTING RECORDS

First from Tower	Sébastien Lenormand	quasi-parachute	Lyon, France		1783
First from Balloon	André-Jacques Garnerin (1769–1823)	2,230 ft *680 m*	Monceau Park, Paris	22 Oct.	1797
First from Aircraft (man)	Capt. Albert Berry	U.S. Army	St. Louis, Missouri	1 Mar.	1912
(woman)	Mrs. Georgina 'Tiny' Broadwick (b. 1893)		Griffith Park, Los Angeles	21 June	1913
	Mrs. Georgina 'Tiny' Broadwick	Pilot Glenn L. Martin	North Island, San Diego, California	13 Sept.	1914
Lowest Escape	S/Ldr. Terence Spencer, D.F.C., R.A.F.	30–40 ft *9–12 m*	Wismer Bay, Baltic	19 April	1945
Longest Duration Fall	Lt. Col. Wm. H. Rankin U.S.M.C.	40 min due to thermals	North Carolina	26 July	1956
Highest Escape	Flt. Lt. J. de Salis and Fg. Off. P. Lowe, R.A.F.	56,000 ft *17 068 m*	Monyash, Derby	9 April	1958
Longest Delayed Drop (man)	Capt. Joseph W. Kittinger[1]	84,700 ft 16.04 miles *25 816 m* from balloon at 102,800 ft *31 333 m*	Tularosa, New Mexico	16 Aug.	1960
(woman)	O. Kommissarova (U.S.S.R.)	14 100 m *46,250 ft*	over U.S.S.R.	21 Sept.	1965
(civilian, over U.K)	John Noakes (G.B.)	22,000 ft from 25,000 ft *7 620 m*	Salisbury Plain, Wiltshire	15 May	1973
(civilian, world)	R. W. K. Beckett (G.B.) Harry Ferguson (G.B.)	30,000 ft *9 144 m* from 32 000 ft *9 753 m*	D. F. Malan Airport, Capetown	23 Nov.	1969
Most Southerly	T/Sgt. Richard J. Patton (d. 1973)	Operation Deep Freeze	South Pole	25 Nov.	1956
Most Northerly	Ray Munro (Canada)	−39° F (−39,4° C)	In 89° 39′ N	31 Mar.	1969
Career Total	Lt.-Col. Ivan Savkin (U.S.S.R.)	More than 5,000	over U.S.S.R.	12 Aug.	1967
	Patty Wilson	More than 1,000	Elsinore paracenter, California	Nov.	1973
Highest Landing	Ten U.S.S.R. parachutists[2]	23,405 ft *7 133 m*	Lenina Peak	May	1969
Heaviest Load	U.S.A.F. C-130 Hercules	22.52 tons *22,88 tonnes* steel plates 6 parachutes	El Centro, California	28 Jan.	1970
Highest from Bridge	Donald R. Boyles	1,053 ft *320 m*	Royal Gorge, Colorado	7 Sept.	1970
Highest Tower Jump	Herbert Leo Schmidtz (U.S.A.)	KTUL-TV Mast 1,984 ft *604 m*	Tulsa, Oklahoma	4 Oct.	1970
Biggest Star	33	Connected free fall (3 sec. min)	Elsinore, California	24 July	1974
Most Travelled	Kevin Seaman from a Cessna Skylane (pilot Charles E. Merritt)	12,186 miles *19 611 km*	Jumps in all 50 U.S. States	26 July–15 Oct.	1972
Oldest Man	Bob Broadbere (G.B.)	85 years (broke glasses)	Honiton, Devon, England	10 July	1977
Woman	Mrs. Cecilia M. Reeser (U.S.)	aged 62 years	Flint, Michigan, U.S.A.	15 Aug.	1972
24 Hour Total	Jean Pierre Blanchet (Canada)	232 in 24 hrs	Quebec City, Canada	9–10 Sept.	1972

[1] *Maximum speed in rarified air was 614 m.p.h. 988 km/h.*
[2] *Four were killed.*

London College, Moorgate, in Finsbury Circus, City of London on 21 Oct. 1971.

Pin Ball marathon
The most protracted pin ball game was one of 92 hours played simultaneously by Ian Jamieson and Phil Wain at Brisbane, Queensland, Australia on 4–8 May 1977.

Pipe smoking
The duration record for keeping a pipe (3.3 g *0.1 oz* of tobacco) continuously alight with only an initial match is 253 min 28 sec by Yrjö Pentikäinen of Kuopio, Finland on 15–16 Mar. 1968.

Plate spinning
The greatest number of plates spun simultaneously is 44 by Holley Gray, on the *Blue Peter* T.V. show at the B.B.C. T.V. Centre, Hammersmith, Greater London on 18 May 1970.

Pogo Stick Jumping
The greatest number of jumps achieved in the now discontinued category *without* rest breaks is 70,076 in 10 hrs 1 min by William Hanrahan of Waterford, Connecticut, U.S.A. on 9 Oct. 1976. Douz Ziegler of Allentown, Pennsylvania, U.S.A. achieved 80,080 jumps in 11 hrs 5 min (taking five minutes break per hour).

Pole-squatting
Modern records do not, in fact, compare with that of St. Simeon the Younger, (*c.* 521–597 A.D.) called Stylites (Greek, *stylos* = pillar) a monk who spent his last 45 years up a stone pillar on The Hill of Wonders, near Antioch, Syria. This is probably the earliest example of record setting.

There being no international rules, the "standards of living" atop poles vary widely. The record squat is 399 days by Frank Perkins from 1 June 1975–4 July 1976 in 8 × 8 ft *2,43 × 2,43 m* box atop a 50 ft *15,24 m* telegraph pole in San Jose, California, U.S.A.

The British record is 32 days 14 hours by John Stokes, aged 32, of Moseley, West Midlands in a barrel on a 45 ft *13,70 m* pole in Birmingham, ending on 27 June 1966. This is claimed as a world record for a barrel.

"Pond" baling
The record for baling a "village pond" with a No. 1 size sewing thimble is 1 024 litres *225.17 gal* in 12 hrs by a team of 12 from Tokoroa High School, Tokoroa, New Zealand on 19 Mar. 1977.

Pop group
The duration record for a 4-man pop-playing group is 144 hours by "Rocking Ricky and the Velvet Collars" at The Talardy Hotel, St. Asaph, Clwyd, North Wales on 12–18 Nov. 1976. The group at no time sank below a trio.

Potato peeling
An inaugural achievement of peeling 120 lb 8 oz *54,65 kg* of potatoes to an institutional cookery standard by 5 sub teenage children with standard kitchen knives in 60 minutes was set by five boys of the 2nd Bletchley Company of the Boys' Brigade at Manor Fields, Bletchley, Bucks. on 28 June 1975.

Pram pushing
The greatest distance covered in pushing a pram in 24 hours is 319 miles *513 km* on a track by a 60 strong team from the White Horse Sports and Social Club, Stony Stratford, Buckinghamshire on 19–20 May 1973. A team of 10 with an adult "baby" from "Flore Moderns" covered 226.1 miles *363,8 km* at Flore, Northamptonshire in 24 hours on 28–29 June 1975.

"Psychiatrist" fastest
The world's fastest "psychiatrist" was Dr. Albert L. Weiner of Erlton, New Jersey, U.S.A., who was trained solely in osteopathy but who dealt with up to 50 psychiatric patients a day in four treatment rooms. He relied heavily on narcoanalysis, muscle relaxants and electro-shock treatments. In December 1961 he was found guilty on 12 counts of manslaughter from using unsterilized needles.

The world's highest paid model, Margaux Hemmingway, grand-daughter of Ernest (see p. 225). *(Francesco Scarullo)*

Quoit throwing
The world's record for rope quoit throwing is an unbroken sequence of 4,002 pegs by Bill Irby, Snr. of Australia in 1968.

Ramp Jumping
The longest distance claimed for motor cycle long jumping over cars is 178 ft *54,25 m* on a Triumph over 15 buses by Joe Einhorn at Lancaster National Speedway on 5 June 1976. The pioneer Evel Knievel (b. Robert Craig Knievel, 17 Oct. 1938 at Butte, Montana, U.S.A.) had suffered 433 bone fractures by his 1975 season. His ramp jump of 110 ft *33,52 m* over 12 of the 13 buses provided at Wembley Stadium, London on 26 May 1975 was the longest attempted in Britain. His abortive attempt to cross the Snake River Canyon, Idaho on 8 Sept. 1974 in a rocket reputedly increased his life-time earnings by $6 million (*then £2½ million*) The longest car jump recorded is one of 62 metres *203 ft* into water by the stuntman Roland van de Putte (Belgium) at 174 km/h *108.1 m.p.h.* in a Volvo on 11 Aug. 1968.

Riding in armour
The longest recorded ride in full armour is one of 147.6 miles *237,5 km* around East Grinstead, West Sussex in 3 days 40 min (riding time 24 hrs 25 min) by John Asmus and John Waller on 26–30 Aug. 1976.

Riveting
The world's record for riveting is 11,209 in 9 hours by J. Moir at the Workman Clark Ltd. shipyard, Belfast, Northern Ireland, in June 1918. His peak hour was his seventh with 1,409, an average of nearly 23½ per min.

Rocking chair
The longest recorded duration of a "Rockathon" is 432 hours by Mrs. Maureen Weston of Petreburgh Athletics Club, Peterborough, Cambridge on 14 Apr.–2 May 1977.

Rolling pin
The record distance for a woman to throw a 2 lb. *907 g* rolling pin is 157 ft 6 in *48,00 m* by Janet Thompson at West London Stadium, Wormwood Scrubs, Greater London on 6 July 1975.

Rope tricks
The only man to demonstrate the ability to spin 12 ropes

simultaneously has been Roy Vincent (b. 1910) of Gloversville, N.Y. in the period 1933–53.

Scooter riding
The greatest distance covered by a team of 25 in 24 hours is 326.15 miles *524,88 km* by the Warracknabeal High School, Victoria, Australia 16–17 Aug. 1973.

Search *Longest*
In October 1972 Frank Jones of Lowestoft, Suffolk ended a 68 year long search by locating his missing brother Arthur Jones.

See-saw
George Partridge and Tamara Marquez of Auburn High School, Washington, U.S.A. on a suspension see-saw completed 1,101 hrs 40 min (indoor) on 28 Mar.–13 May 1977. Georgia Chaffin and Tammy Adams of Goodhope Jr. High School, Cullman Alabama, U.S.A. completed 730 hrs 30 min (outdoor) on 25 June–25 July 1975.

Sermon
The longest church sermon on record was delivered by the Rev. Tony Leyva of West Palm Beach, Florida, U.S.A. on 10–13 Feb. 1977 for 72 hours. From 31 May to 10 June 1969 the 14th Dalai Lama (b. 6 July 1934) the exiled ruler of Tibet, completed a sermon on Tantric Buddhism for five to seven hours per day to total 60 hours in India.

Shaving
The fastest demon barber on record is Gerry Harley, who shaved 130 men in 60 min with a cut-throat razor at The Plough, Gillingham, Kent on 1 Apr. 1971. In an attempt to set a marathon he ran out of volunteer subjects.

Sheaf tossing
The world's best performance for tossing an 8 lb. *3 kg 620* sheaf for height is 56 ft *17,06 m* by C. R. Wiltshire of Geelong, Victoria, Australia in 1956. Contests date from 1914.

Shoeshine Boys
In this category (limited to a team of 4 teenagers; duration of 8 hours; shoes 'on the hoof') the record is 6,334 pairs by the Bedford North (Newnham) Scout Group on 16 July 1977.

Shorthand fastest
The highest recorded speeds ever attained under championship conditions are: 300 words per min (99.64 per cent accuracy) for five minutes and 350 w.p.m. (99.72 per cent accuracy, that is, two insignificant errors) for two minutes by Nathan Behrin (U.S.A.) in tests in New York in December 1922. Behrin (b. 1887) used the Pitman system invented in 1837. Morris I. Kligman, official court reporter of the U.S. Court House, New York has taken 50,000 words in five hours (a sustained rate of 166.6 w.p.m.). Rates are much dependent upon the nature, complexity and syllabic density of the material. Mr. G. W. Bunbury of Dublin, Ireland held the unique distinction of writing at 250 w.p.m. for 10 min on 23 Jan. 1894.

Currently the fastest shorthand writer in Britain is Mrs. June Meader (*née* Swan) of North Finchley, Barnet, Greater London with a Pitman's Certificate for 230 w.p.m. She demonstrated the ability to write at the *rate of* 260 w.p.m. with a syllabic density of 1.5, on the B.B.C. T.V. Show *Record Breakers* on 31 Dec. 1972.

In Great Britain only four shorthand writers have passed the official Pitman test at 250 w.p.m. for five min:

Miss Edith Ulrica Pearson of London, on 30 June 1927.
Miss Emily Doris Smith of London, on 22 Mar. 1934.
Miss Beatrice W. Solomon of London, in March 1942.
Mrs. Audrey Boyes (*née* Bell) of Finchley, Barnet, Greater London, in 1956.

Shouting
The greatest number of wins in the national town criers' contest is 11 by Ben Johnson of Fowey, Cornwall, who won in 1939, 1949–55, 1966, 1969 and 1973. (See also Longest-ranged voice, Chapter I page 19.)

Showering
The most prolonged continuous shower bath on record is one of 202 hours by Michael Speed of Sydney, Australia on 19–27

Feb. 1977. The feminine record is 98 hours 1 min by Paula Glenn, 18 and Margaret Nelson, 20 in Britain on 24 Nov. 1971. Desquamation can be a positive danger.

Singing
The longest recorded solo singing marathon is one of 105 hours by Eamonn McGirr at The Bower Club, Stalybridge, Manchester on 5–10 Aug. 1974. The marathon record for a choir has been 41 hours by pupils from Bingley Beckfoot Grammar School, Bingley, West Yorkshire on 13–15 July 1977.

Skate Boarding
"World" championships have been staged intermittently since 1966. Activity was revived in 1975 with the marketing of aluminium boards with 4 urethane "stoker" wheels.

Records set at Signal Hill, Long Beach California are 4 ft 7 in *1,39 m* by Ernie Martin in Sept. 1976 and 57 m.p.h. *91,7 km/h* by David Dillberg and Henry Hester on 20 Mar. 1977.

Skipping
The longest recorded non-stop skipping marathon was one of 5 hrs 37 mins (49,299 turns) by Kazuya Shiozaki in Fukuyama, Japan on 25 Apr. 1976.

Other records made without a break:

Most turns in one jump	5 by Katsumi Suzuki, Tokyo, early 1968
Most turns in 1 min	287 by a A. Rayner, Wakefield, W. Yorks., 6 July 1976
Most turns in 10 secs	68 by A. Rayner, Wakefield, W. Yorks, 6 July 1976
Most doubles (with cross)	56 by G. K. Brooks
Double turns	3,001 by Katsumi Suzuki, Tokyo, 4 July 1976
Treble turns	138 by Katsumi Suzuki, Tokyo, 4 July 1976
Quadruple turns	15 by Katsumi Suzuki, Tokyo, 4 July 1976
Duration	1,264 miles *2 034 km* by Tom Morris, Brisbane–Cairns, Queensland, 1963
Most children, single rope (11 turns)	52 by Ogallala Girls Team, Nebraska, U.S.A., 14 May 1977

Slinging
The greatest distance recorded for a sling-shot is 1,147 ft 4 in *349,70 m* using a 34 in *86 cm* long sling and a 7½ oz. *212 g* stone by Melvyn Gaylor on Newport Golf Course, Shide Isle of Wight on 25 Sept. 1970.

Smoke ring blowing
The highest recorded number of smoke rings formed from a single pull of a cigarette is 257 rings by Jan Formann, 21 of Copenhagen, Denmark at *The Evening Argus* offices, Brighton, East Sussex on 12 July 1977.

Snakes and Ladders
The longest recorded game of Snakes and Ladders has been one of 204 hours by a team of six (four always in play) from Baulkham Hills High School, Baulkham Hills, N.S.W., Australia on 15–23 June 1976.

Snow Shoeing
The fastest officially recorded time for covering a mile *1 609,34 m* is 6 min 23.8 sec by Richard Lemay (Frontenac Club, Quebec, Canada) at Manchester, New Hampshire, U.S.A. in 1973.

Spinning
The duration record for spinning a clock balance wheel by hand is 5 min 26.8 sec by Philip Ashley, aged 16, of Leigh, Greater Manchester on 20 May 1968.

Spitting
The greatest distance achieved at the annual tobacco spitting classic (instituted 1955) at Raleigh, Mississippi is 31 ft 1 in *9,47 m* by Don Snyder, 28 on 26 July 1975. In the 3rd International Spittin', Belchin' and Cussin' Triathlon Harold Fielden reached 34 ft 0¼ in *10,36 m* at Central City, Colorado U.S.A. on 13 July 1973. Distance is dependent on the quality of salivation, absence of cross wind, two finger pucker and the coordination of the back arch and neck snap. Sprays or wads smaller than a dime are not measured. The record for projecting a melon seed is under WCWSSCA rules is 59 ft 1½ in *18,02 m* by Brian Dunne at Savemore Centre, Yeppoon,

Queensland, Australia on 11 Dec. 1976. The highest reported distance for a cherry stone is 47 ft 7½ in *14,51 m* by Richard Hahn at Eau Claire, Michigan, U.S.A. on 24 July 1976. Spitters who care about their image wear 12 in *30,4 cm* block-ended boots so practice spits can be measured without a tape.

Stair Climbing
The 100 storey record for stair climbing was set by Dr. Randolph W. Seed in the Hancock Building, Chicago on 27 Feb. 1972 at 14 min 29 sec. His record for the vertical mile (5 round trips) was 2 hrs 53 min 16 sec on 15 Nov. 1970.

Standing
The longest period on record that anyone has continuously stood is 17 years in the case of Swami Maujgiri Maharij when performing the *Tapasya* or penance from 1955 to November 1973 in Shahjahanpur Uttar, Pradesh, India. When sleeping he would lean against a plank.

Stilt-walking
The highest stilts ever successfully mastered were more than 21 ft *6,40 m* from the ankle to the ground by Henry Edward Yelding ("Harry Sloan") 1902–1971 of Great Yarmouth, Norfolk. Hop stringers use stilts up to 15 ft *4.57 m*. In 1892 M. Garisoain of Bayonne stilt-walked the last 8 km *4,97 miles* into Biarritz in 42 min to average 11,42 km/h *7.10 m.p.h.* In 1891 Sylvain Dornon stilt-walked from Paris to Moscow *via* Vilno in 50 stages for the 1,830 miles *2 945 km*. Another source gives his time as 58 days.

Stretcher bearing
The longest recorded carry of a stretcher case with a 10 st. *63,5 kg* "body" is 80.4 miles *129,36 km* in 24 hours 25 min by two 4 men teams from 1 Field Ambulance, Canadian Forces Base, Calgary, Alberta, Canada on 24–25 June 1975.

The record limited to Venture Scouts (under 20) and 8 hours carrying is 35.4 miles *56,97 km* by 8 members of the Vulcan Venture Scout Unit, Marlow, Bucks on 26 March 1977.

String Ball Largest
The largest balls of string on record are ones both of 11 ft *3,35 m* in diameter, weighing 4½ tons/*tonnes* amassed by Francis A. Johnson of Darwin, Minnesota, U.S.A., since 1950 and Frank Stoeber of Cawker City, Kansas since at least 1962.

Stowaway
The most rugged stowaway was Socarras Ramirez who escaped from Cuba on 4 June 1969 by stowing away in an unpressurized wheel well in the starboard wing of a Boeing 707 from Havana to Madrid in a 5,600 mile *9 010 km* Iberian Airlines flight. He survived 8 hours at 30,000 ft *9 145 m* where temperatures were −8° F *−22,2° C*.

Submergence
The most protracted underwater endurance record (excluding the use of diving bells) is 126 hrs 30 min established at the 1961 Canadian National Sportmen's Show, Toronto by Patrick Morrison of Toronto; Joe Mangus of Ohio, U.S.A. and Mrs. Alberta Jones of Miami, Florida, U.S.A.

The British record for a wet suit is 88 hours 2 min continuously by Brian Foulds, 23 of the Blackpool & Fylde Sub-Aqua Club in fresh water at the Imperial Hotel on 4–8 May 1975.

Suggestion boxes
The most prolific example on record of the use of any suggestion box scheme is that of John Drayton (b. 18 Sept. 1907) of Newport, Gwent who has plied British Rail and the companies from which it was formed with a total of 27,632 suggestions from 1924 to June 1977 of which one in seven were accepted.

The U.S. Postal Service champion John Kingston has had an acceptance rate of one in 5.3 (284 out of 1,500) to January 1976.

Swinging
The record duration for continuous swinging is 170 hours

by Jeffrey Lucas of Southville, Ontario, Canada, on 9–16 Aug. 1976.

Switchback riding
The endurance record for rides on a roller coaster is 74 hours by five DJ's (Doug Benton, Doug Shane, Bill Barron, Kris Van Dyke, and Kelly McCann) at Panama City Beach, Florida, U.S.A., on 27–30 May 1977.

Tailoring
The highest speed in which the making of a 2 piece suit has been made from sheep to finished article is 1 hour 52 min 18.5 sec to the order of Bud Macken of Mascot, N.S.W., Australia on 23 Dec. 1931. The shearing took 35 sec, the carding and teasing 19 min and weaving 20 min.

Talking
The world record for non-stop talking is 144 hours 4 min by Tim Harty of Coon Rapids, Minnesota, U.S.A. on 27 Jan.–2 Feb. 1975. The longest continuous political speech on record was one of 30 hours by Marvin A. Eakman in Minneapolis, Minnesota, U.S.A. on 10–11 June 1976. The longest recorded lecture was one of 45 hours on "The Christian Faith and its Response" by the Rev. Roger North, 26, at Hartley Victoria Methodist College, Greater Manchester on 15–17 May 1971.

A feminine non-stop talking record was set by Mrs. Mary E. Davis, who on 2–7 Sept. 1958 started at a radio station in Buffalo, New York and did not draw breath until 110 hours 30 min 5 secs later in Tulsa, Oklahoma U.S.A.

The longest recorded after-dinner speech with unsuspecting victims was one of 3 hours by the Rev. Henry Whitehead (d. March 1896) at the Rainbow Tavern, Fleet Street, London on 16 Jan. 1874. Ted Harrison addressed the Canterbury Ladies' Circle, Kent, England for 4 hrs 40 min 52 sec on 20 Nov. 1976 at a charity dinner.

T-bone dive
The so-called T-bone dives or Dive Bomber crash by cars off ramps over and on to parked cars are often measured by the number of cars, but owing to their variable size and that their purpose is purely to cushion the shock, distance is more significant. The longest recorded distance is 176 ft *53,6 m* by Dusty Russell in a 1963 Ford Falcon at Athens, Georgia in April 1973.

Teeth-pulling
The man with "the strongest teeth in the world" is "Hercules" John Massis (b. Wilfried Oscar Morbée, 4 June 1940) of St Amandsberg, Belgium, who on 19 Oct. 1976 demonstrated the ability to pull a British Rail locomotive and a truck weighing 121 tons on a level track at Park Royal, London N.W.10 with a bit in his teeth. At Evry, France on 19 Mar. 1977 Massis raised a weight of 233 kg *513⅝ lb.* 15 cm *6 in* from the ground with a teeth bit.

John "Hercules" Massis of Belgium, the man with the iron jaw (see above).

CIRCUS RECORDS (See also page 231)

The following circus acrobatic feats represent the greatest performed, either for the first time or, if marked with an asterisk, uniquely. A "mechanic" is a safety harness.

Flying Trapeze	Earliest Act	Jules Léotard (France)	Circus Napoléon, Paris	12 Nov. 1859
	Double back somersault	Eddie Silbon	Paris Hippodrome	1879
	Triple back somersault (female)	Lena Jordan (Latvia) to Lew Jordan (U.S.A.)	Sydney, Australia	April 1897
	Triple back somersault (male)	Ernest Clarke to Charles Clarke	Publiones Circus, Cuba	1909
	Triple and half back somersault	Tony Steel to Lee Strath Marilees	Durango, Mexico	30 Sept. 1962
	Quadruple back somersault (in practice)	*Ernest Clarke to Charles Clarke	Orrin Bros. Circus, Mexico City, Mexico	1915
	Triple back somersault (with 1½ twists)	Terry Cavarette Lemus (b. 6 Mar. 1953, Buffalo, N.Y.)	Circus Circus, Las Vegas	16 Mar. 1969
	Head to head stand on swinging bar (no holding)	*Ed and Ira Millette (née Wolf)	Various	1910–20
	Upward circles or "Muscle grinding"	308 by Denise La Grassa (U.S.)	Circus World Museum, Baraboo, Wisconsin	9 May 1976
Horse back	Running leaps on and off	*26 by "Poodles" Hanneford	New York	1915
	Three-high column without "mechanic"	*Willy, Baby and Rene Fredianis	Nouveau Cirque, Paris	1908
	Double back somersault mounted	(John or Charles) Frederic Clarke	Various	c. 1905
	Double back somersault from a 2-high to a trailing horse with "mechanic"	Aleksandr Sergey	Moscow Circus	1956
Fixed Bars	Pass from 1st to 3rd bar with a double back somersault	Phil Shevette, Andres Atayde	Woods Gymnasium, New York, European tours	1925–27
	Triple fly-away to ground (male)	Phil Shevette	Folies Bergere, Paris	May 1896
	Triple fly-away to ground (female)	Loretto Twins, Ora and Pauline	Los Angeles	1914
Giant Spring Board	Running forward triple back somersault	John Cornish Worland (1855–1933) of the U.S.A.	St. Louis, Missouri	1874
Risley (Human Juggling)	Back somersault feet to feet	Richard Risley Carlisle (1814–74) and son (U.S.A.)	Theatre Royal, Edinburgh	Feb. 1844
Teeter Board	Quadruple back somersault to a chair	Sylvester Mezzetti (voltiger) to Butch Mezzetti (catcher)	New York Hippodrome	1915–17
	Six man high perch pyramid	Emilia Ivanova (Bulgaria) of Kehaiovi Troupe	Inglewood, California	21 July 1976
Aerialist	One arm swings or planges 305 (no net)	Janet May Klemke (U.S.A.)	Medina Shrine Circus, Chicago	Jan 1938
Risley	Seat to seat triple back somersault	The 5 Draytons		1896
Wire-Juggling	16 hoops (hands and feet)	Ala Naito (Japan) (female)	Madison Square Garden, N.Y.	1937
Low Wire (7 ft 2 m)	Feet to feet forward somersault	Con Colleano	Empire Theatre, Johannesburg	1923
		Ala Naito (Japan) (female)	Madison Square Garden, N.Y.	1937
High Wire (30–40 ft 9–12 m)	Four high column (with mechanic)	*The Solokhin Brothers (U.S.S.R.)	Moscow Circus	1962
	Three layer, 7 man pyramid	Great Wallendas (Germany)	U.S.A.	1961
Ground Acrobatics	Stationary double back somersault	Francois Gouleau (France)		1905
	Four high column	The Picchianis (Italy)		1905
	Five high column	The Yacopis (Argentina) with 3 understanders, 3 second layer understanders, 1 middleman, 1 upper middleman and a top mounter	Ringling Bros., Barnum & Bailey circuit	1941
Hand to Hand Balance	Longest horizontal dive 22 ft 6,7 m	Harry Berry (top mounter) to Nelson Soule (understander)	Bell-Thazer troupe, State Fair in the U.S.	1908–17

Tightrope walking

The greatest 19th century tightrope walker was Jean François Gravelet, *alias* Charles Blondin (1824–1897), of France, who made the earliest crossing of the Niagara Falls on a 3 in *76 mm* rope, 1,100 ft *335 m* long, 160 ft *48,75 m* above the Falls on 30 July 1855. He also made a crossing with Harry Colcord, pick-a-back on 15 Sept. 1860. Though other artists still find it difficult to believe, Colcord was his agent.

Tightrope walking *Endurance*

The world tightrope endurance record is 185 days by Henri Rochetain (b. 1926) of France on a wire 394 ft *120 m* long, 82 ft *25 m* above a supermarket in Saint Etienne, France, on 28 Mar.–29 Sept. 1973. His ability to sleep on the wire has left doctors puzzled. He walked some 500 km *310 miles* on the wire to keep fit.

Tightrope walking *Longest*

The longest walk by any funambulist was achieved by Henri Rochetain (b. 1926) of France on a wire 3,790 yds *3 465 m* long slung across a gorge at Clermont Ferrand, France on 13 July 1969. He required 3 hours 20 min to negotiate the crossing.

The first crossing of the River Thames was achieved by Charles Elleano (b. 1911) of Strasbourg, France on a 1,050 ft *320 m* wire 60 ft *18,2 m* above the river in 25 min on 22 Sept. 1951.

Treasure finding

The most successful treasure hunter has been C. Fred Ahrendt of Dayton, Ohio, who by August 1976 has found with his metal detector 175 class rings (earliest, 1890) and 179 wedding rings of 14 or more carats. Employees of crematoria are officially excluded from competition.

Tree-climbing

The fastest speed climb up a 100 ft *30,4 m* fir spar pole and return to the ground is one of 31.3 sec by Marvin Trudeau of Squamish, B.C. at Haywood, Wisconsin, U.S.A. in 1974.

Tree-sitting

The duration record for sitting in a tree is 61 days 21 hrs 56 min by Jim Sparks 14 in a fruitless mulberry in his father's backyard in Visalia, California, U.S.A. from 25 June to 25 Aug. 1975.

Tunnel of fire

The significance of the length of a tunnel of fire depends largely upon its dimensions. A height and width of 6 ft 8 in *2,03 m* is now becoming standard. All previous records were eclipsed in February 1974 near Johannesburg, South Africa when the stuntman Ed Kannemeyer (b. 1950) forsook the usual motor cycle for a "push bike". Blinded by flames after 137 ft *41,75 m* he ran the remaining 84½ ft *25,75 m* emerging after 15 sec. Fatalities have occurred.

Typewriting *Fastest*

The highest recorded speeds attained with a ten-word penalty per error on a manual machine are:

One Min: 170 words, Margaret Owen (U.S.A.) (Underwood Standard), New York, 21 Oct. 1918.
One Hour: 147 words (net rate per min) Albert Tangora (U.S.A.) (Underwood Standard), 22 Oct. 1923.

The official hour record on an electric machine is 9,316 words (40 errors) on an I.B.M. machine, giving a net rate of

149 words per min, by Margaret Hamma, now Mrs. Dilmore (U.S.A.), in Brooklyn, New York City, N.Y., U.S.A. on 20 June 1941. Mrs. Barbara Blackburn of Lee's Summit, Missouri can maintain 150 w.p.m. for 50 min (37,500 key strokes) and attain speeds of 170 w.p.m. using the Dvorak Simplified Keyboard (D.S.K.) system.

In an official test in 1946 Stella Pajunas now Mrs. Garnard attained a rate of 216 words in a minute on an I.B.M. machine.

Typewriting *Slowest*
Chinese typewriters were so complex that even the most skilled operator could not select loose characters from the fount of 1,500 offered at a rate of more than 11 words a minute. The Hoang "typewriter" first produced in 1962 now has 5,850 Chinese characters. The keyboard is 2 ft *60 cm* wide and 17 in *43 cm* high.

Typewriting *Longest*
The world duration record for typewriting on an electric machine is 162 hrs 1 min by Robert Heil of Sherman E. Burroughs High School, Ridgecrest, Calif. U.S.A. on 6–13 April 1976. Mrs. Marva Drew, 51, of Waterloo, Iowa, U.S.A. between 1968 and 30 Nov. 1974 typed number 1 to 1,000,000 in words on a manual typewriter on 2,473 pages. Asked why she replied "But I love to type".

The longest duration typing marathon on a manual machine is 120 hours 15 min by Mike Howell, a 23 year-old blind office worker from Greenfield, Oldham, Greater Manchester on 25–30 Nov. 1969 on an Olympia manual typewriter in Liverpool. In aggregating 561,006 strokes he performed a weight movement of 2,482 tons *2 521 tonnes* plus a further 155 tons *157 tonnes* on moving the carriage for line spacing.

Tyre Lifting
The greatest number of motor tyres lifted is 51 by Geoffrey Capes, the Champion shot putter, in the BBC *Record Breakers* programme on 4 Oct. 1976. The total weight was 765 lb. *347 kg.* The tyres used were Michelin ZX155 × 13.

Unsupported Circle
The highest recorded number of people who have demonstrated the physical paradox of all being seated without a chair is an unsupported circle of 3,333 for 60 sec from the Air Force Cadet Wing U.S.A.F. Academy, Colorado, U.S.A. on 28 Oct. 1976.

Walking on hands
The duration record for walking on hands is 1 400 km *871 miles* by Johann Hurlinger, of Austria, who in 55 daily 10-hour stints, averaged 1.58 m.p.h. *2,54 km/h* from Vienna to Paris in 1900. Cadet Thomas P. Hunt of the U.S.A.F. Academy, Colorado Springs, U.S.A. completed an inverted 50 yd *45,72 m* sprint in 19.1 secs on 27 Jan. 1977.

Wall of death
The greatest endurance feat on a wall of death was 3 hours 4 min by the motorcyclist Louis W. "Speedy" Babbs (1908–1976) on a silo, 32 ft *9,75 m* in diameter refuelling in motion, at the Venice Amusement Pier, California on 11 Oct. 1929. In 1934 Babbs performed in a globe 18 ft *5,48 m* at Ocean Park Pier, California, U.S.A. Britain's most durable performer is Doug. Murphy of Colne, Lancashire who completed his 30th season in 1975 billed in West Germany as *Der Welte bester steilwand faher.*

Wallpapering
Robert Marshall, 34, of Smethwick, West Midlands demonstrated the ability to hang 38½ rolls of wallpaper in 4¼ hrs on 23 April 1977. His rate averages 298.9 ft *91,11m* per hour.

Whip cracking
The longest stock whip ever "cracked" (*i.e.* the end made to travel above the speed of sound—760 m.p.h. *1 223 km/h* is one of 80 ft first cracked by Frank Dean (U.S.) at North Dakota State Fair in 1939.

Wood-cutting
The earliest competitions date from Tasmania in 1874. The

---

records set at the Lumberjack World Championships at Hayward, Wisconsin (founded 1960) are

Power Saw	11.55 sec	Ron Johnson (U.S.)	1976
One-Man Bucking	23.06 sec	Ron Hartill (N.Z.)	1976
Standing Block Chop	26.9 sec	Ron Wilson (Aust.)	1973
Underhand Block Chop	20.3 sec	Jim Alexander (Aust.)	1973
Two-Man Bucking	10.40 sec	Dave Green and	1976
		Rudy Dettmer (U.S.)	

White pine logs 14 in *35,5 cm* diameter are used for chopping and 20 in *50,8 cm* for sawing.

Writing Minuscule
Larry R. Yates of McMinnville, Oregon, U.S.A. has manually engraved the Lord's Prayer within a square millimetre 1/645th in² with a pivot-arm device of his own invention. William R. Woodbridge, 46 of Harrow, England demonstrated in November 1974 the ability without mechanical or optical aid to write the Lord's Prayer 10 times (2,700 letters) within the size of a definitive U.K. postage stamp (viz. 0.84 × 0.71 of an inch *21,1 × 18,2 mm*.

Writing under handicap
The ultimate feat in "funny writing" would appear to be the ability to write extemporaneously and decipherably backwards, upside down, laterally inverted (mirror-style) while blindfolded with both hands simultaneously. Several close approaches to this have been reported.

Yodelling
The most protracted yodel on record was that of Donn Reynolds for 7 hrs 29 min in Brampton, Ontario, Canada on 27 Nov. 1976.

Yo-yo
The yo-yo originates from a Filipino jungle fighting weapon recorded in the 16th century weighing 4 lb. with a 20 ft *6 m* thong. The word means "come-come". Though illustrated in a book in 1891 as a bandalore the craze did not begin until it was started by Donald F. Duncan of Chicago, U.S.A. in 1926. The most difficult modern yo-yo trick is the "Whirlwind" incorporating both inside and outside horizontal loop-the-loops. The individual continuous endurance record is 100 hours by Tim Harty of Coon Rapids, Minnesota, U.S.A. on 11–15 July 1976. Dr. Allen Bussey in Waco, Texas on 23 Apr. 1977 completed 20,302 loops in 3 hours (including 6,886 in a single 60 min period). He used a Duncan Imperial with a 34½ in *87,6 cm* nylon string.

CIRCUS RECORDS
Largest circus
The world's largest permanent circus is Circus Circus Las Vegas, Nevada, U.S.A. opened on 18 Oct. 1968 at a cost of $15,000,000 (*then £6,250,000*). It covers an area of 129,000 ft² *11 984 m²* capped by a tent-shaped flexiglass roof 90 ft *27,43 m* high. The largest travelling circus is the Circus Vargas in the U.S.A. which can accommodate 5,000 people under its Big Top. (see also page 230).

Most on One Cycle
The cyclist troupe from the Chinese Acrobatic Theatre from Shanghai regularly perform tricks involving up to 12 members simultaneously riding one bicycle.

WEALTH AND POVERTY
The measurement of extreme personal wealth is beset with intractable difficulties. Quite apart from reticence and the element of approximation in estimating the valuation of assets, as Mr. Getty (see below) once said "if you can count your millions you are not a billionaire". The term millionaire was invented *c.* 1740 and billionaire in 1861. The earliest dollar billionaires were John Davison Rockefeller (1839–1937); Henry Ford (1863–1947) and Andrew William Mellon (1855–1937). In 1937, the last year in which all 3 were alive, a billion U.S dollars were worth £205 million but that amount of sterling would today have a purchasing power of in excess £1,680 million.

Richest Men *World*
There are currently only two surviving proclaimed U.S. dollar billionaires (a billion dollars is now £588,000,000) John

Donald MacArthur (b. Pittston, Pennsylvania, 6 Mar. 1897) and Daniel K. Ludwig (b. South Haven, Mich., June 1897). The researches of Francis P. Antel indicated that Mr. MacArthur's assets in 1974/75 were an unencumbered $1,720 million at a minimum valuation. H. Ross Perot of Texas (b. Texarkana, Texas, 1930) was in December 1969 worth in excess of a billion dollars on paper.

The wealthiest newly married couple are believed to be Alexander Andreadis and Christina Onassis, whose combined assets were estimated at $1,158 million in Sept. 1975.

Europeans with family assets in excess of the equivalent of a billion dollars, include the Wallenburg family in Sweden. The wealthiest United Kingdom citizen, at the time of his death, was Sir John Reeves Ellerman 2nd Bt. (1909–73), whose fortune was estimated at £600 million ($1.5 billion).

Richest Man *Great Britain*
The richest man in Great Britain is reputed to be John Moores, the football pool pioneer in 1923. In 1973 he was estimated to be worth about £400 million. His first job after leaving school at 14 was as a telephone operator. He was born in Eccles, Lancashire in 1896.

Highest Incomes
The greatest incomes derive from the collection of royalties per barrel by rulers of oil-rich sheikhdoms, who have not abrogated personal entitlement. Before his death in 1965, H. H. Sheikh Sir Abdullah as-Salim as-Sabah G.C.M.G., C.I.E. (b. 1895), the 11th Amir of Kuwait was accumulating royalties payable at a rate of £2.6 million per week or £145 million a year.

The highest gross income ever achieved in a single year by a private citizen is an estimated $105,000,000 (*then £21½ million*) in 1927 by the Neopolitan born Chicago gangster Alphonse ("Scarface Al") Capone (1899–1947). This was derived from illegal liquor trading and alky-cookers (illicit stills), gambling establishments, dog tracks, dance halls, "protection" rackets and vice. On his business card Capone described himself as a "Second Hand Furniture Dealer".

Highest Paid Executive
In 1976, according to the *Business Week* survey, 7 U.S. businessmen had 7 figure remunerations, headed by Harry Grey, President of United Technologies with $1,662,000 (£977,650).

Proved Wills and Death Duties
Sir John Reeves Ellerman, 2nd Bt., (1909–1973) left £53,238,370 on which all-time record death duties will be payable. This is the largest will ever proved in the United Kingdom. The greatest will proved in Ireland was that of the 1st Earl of Iveagh (1847–1927), who left £13,486,146.

Millionairesses
The world's wealthiest woman was probably Princess Wilhelmina Helena Pauline Maria of Orange-Nassau (1880–1962), formerly Queen of the Netherlands from 1890 to her abdication, 4 Sept. 1948, with a fortune which was estimated at over £200 million. The largest amount proved in the will of a woman in the United Kingdom has been the £4,075,550 (duty paid £3,233,454) of Miss Gladys Meryl Yule, daughter of Sir David Yule, Bt. (1858–1928), in August 1957. Mrs. Anna Dodge (later Mrs. Hugh Dillman) who was born in Dundee, Scotland, died on 3 June 1970 in the United States, aged 103, and left an estate of £40,000,000.

The cosmetician Madame Charles Joseph Walker *née* Sarah Breedlove (b. Louisiana Delta, U.S.A. 23 Dec. 1867) is reputed to have become the first self-made millionairess. She was an uneducated negro orphan scrub-woman whose fortune was founded on a hair straightener.

Millionaire and Millionairess *Youngest*
The youngest person ever to accumulate a million dollars was the child film actor Jackie Coogan (b. Los Angeles, 1914) co-star with Sir Charles Chaplin (b. London, 1889) in "The Kid" made in 1920. Shirley Temple (b. Santa Monica, California 23 Apr. 1928), formerly Mrs. John Agar, Jr., now Mrs. Charles Black accumulated wealth exceeding $1,000,000

(*then £209,000*) before she was 10. Her child actress career spanned the years 1934–39.

Richest families *World*
It has been tentatively estimated that the combined value of the assets nominally controlled by the du Pont family of some 1,600 members may be of the order of $150,000 million. The family arrived penniless in the U.S.A. from France on 1 Jan. 1800.

Largest dowry
The largest recorded dowry was that of Elena Patiño daughter of Don Simón Iturbi Patiño (1861–1947), the Bolivian tin millionaire, who in 1929 bestowed £8,000,000 from a fortune at one time estimated to be worth £125,000,000.

Greatest miser
If meanness is measurable as a ratio between expendable assets and expenditure then Henrietta (Hetty) Howland Green (*née* Robinson) (1835–1916), who kept a balance of over $31,400,000 (*then £6.2 million*) in one bank alone, was the all-time world champion. Her son had to have his leg amputated because of her delays in finding a *free* medical clinic. She herself lived off cold porridge because she was too thrifty to heat it and died of apoplexy in an argument over the virtues of skimmed milk. Her estate proved to be of $95 million (*then £19 million* [*and now worth £200 million*]).

Return of cash
The largest amount of *cash* ever found and returned to its owners was $500,000 (U.S.) found by Lowell Elliott, 61 on his farm at Peru, Indiana, U.S.A. It had been dropped in June 1972 by a parachuting hi-jacker.

Greatest bequests
The greatest bequests in a life-time of a millionaire were those of the late John Davison Rockefeller (1839–1937), who gave away sums totalling $750,000,000 (*now £312.5 million*). The greatest benefactions of a British millionaire were those of William Richard Morris, later the Viscount Nuffield, G.B.E., C.H. (1877–1963), which totalled more than £30,000,000 between 1926 and his death on 22 Aug. 1963. The Scottish-born U.S. citizen Andrew Carnegie (1835–1919) is estimated to have made benefactions totalling £70 million during the last 18 years of his life. These included 7,689 church organs and 2,811 libraries. He had started life in a bobbin factory at $1.20 per week.

The largest bequest made in the history of philanthropy was the $500,000,000 (£178,570,000) gift, announced on 12 Dec. 1955, to 4,157 educational and other institutions by the Ford Foundation (established 1936) of New York City, N.Y., U.S.A. The assets of the Foundation had a book value of $3,140,000,000 (*now £1,800 million*) in 1974.

Salary Highest *World*
The highest salary paid in the United States in 1976 was to the President of the United Technologies, Harry Grey with $1,662,000 (£977,650). The United States highest salaried woman executive was believed to be Mary Wells Lawrence, Chairman of the advertising firm Wells, Rich, Greene, Inc. of New York, $385,000 (£160,400) in 1973. She is the mother of five and has an earning husband—Harding L. Lawrence, chairman of Braniff Airways.

Salary Highest *Great Britain*
Britain's highest paid business executive has been Mr. Richard Tompkins, Chairman of Green Shield Trading Stamp Company which he founded in 1958. His service agreement entitled him to 15 per cent of profits which for the year ending 31 Oct. 1971 would have earned him £395,000. He waived £135,000. On 1972–73 full standard taxation rates it has been calculated that £185,600 of the £260,000 would be payable in income tax and surtax. His present salary is believed to be less than 6 figures.

The highest straight salary paid in British business was the £91,842 payable to the highest paid director of Shell Trading and Transport in 1975. The 1976 figure was £2,677 less.

Golden Handshake
The highest carat handshake in Britain has been one of £139,000 for Basil Glass 64, Honorary President of Vantora textile company resident in Monaco, in October 1974.

Lowest Incomes

The poorest people in the world are the Tasaday tribe of cave-dwellers of central Mindanao, Philippines who were "discovered" in 1971 without any domesticated animals, agriculture, pottery, wheels or clothes.

GLUTTONY RECORDS

Records for eating and drinking by trenchermen do not match those suffering from the rare disease of bulimia (morbid desire to eat) and polydipsia (pathological thirst). Some bulimia patients have to spend 15 hours a day eating, with an extreme consumption of 384 lb. 2 oz. *174,236 kg* of food in six days by Matthew Daking, aged 12, in 1743 (known as Mortimer's case). Some polydipsomaniacs have been said to be unsatisfied by less than 96 pints *54,55 litres* of liquid a day. Miss Helge Andersson (b. 1908) of Lindesberg, Sweden was reported in January 1971 to have been drinking 40 pints *22,73 litres* of water a day since 1922—a total of 87,600 gal *3 982 hectolitres*.

The world's greatest trencherman has been Edward Abraham ("Bozo") Miller (b. 1909) of Oakland, California, U.S.A. He consumed up to 25,000 calories per day or more than 11 times that recommended. He stands 5 ft 7½ in *1,71 m* tall but weighs from 20 to 21½ st. *127–139 kg* with a 57 in *144 cm* waist. He had been undefeated in eating contests since 1931 (see below). The bargees on the Rhine are reputed to be the world's heaviest eaters with 5,200 calories a day. However the New Zealand Sports Federation of Medicine reported in December 1972 that a long-distance road runner consumed 14,321 calories in 24 hours.

While no healthy person has been reported to have succumbed in any contest for eating or drinking non-alcoholic or non-toxic drinks, such attempts, from a medical point of view, must be regarded as *extremely inadvisable*, particularly among young people. Gluttony record attempts should aim at improving the *rate* of consumption rather than the *volume*. Guinness Superlatives will not list any records involving the consumption of more than 2 litres *3.52 Imperial pints* of beer nor any at all involving spirits. Nor will records for such potentially dangerous categories as live ants, chewing gum, marsh mallow or raw eggs with shells be published.

Specific records have been claimed as follows:

Baked Beans
1,840 cold baked beans one by one with a cocktail stick in 30 min by Michael Reynolds of Chelmsford, Essex on 29 July 1976.
Bananas
70 in 8 min 31 sec by Joshua Bevelyn in St. Lucia, West Indies on 9 July, 1977.
Beer
Steven Petrosino drank one litre of beer in 1.3 sec on 22 June 1977 at "The Gingerbreadman", Carlisle, Pennsylvania.
Peter G. Dowdeswell (b. London 29 July 1940) of Earls Barton, Northampton-shire holds the following two records:
2 pints—2.3 sec Zetters Social Club, Wolverton, Bucks 11 June 1975
2 litres—6.0 sec Carriage Horse Hotel, Higham Ferrars, Northants 7 Feb. 1975
Yards of Ale
2½ pints—5.0 sec R.A.F. Upper Heyford, Oxfordshire 4 May
3 pints—5.4 sec Corby Town S.C., Northamptonshire 23 Jan. 1976
Upsidedown
2 pints—6.4 sec Top Rank Club, Northants 25 May
Champagne
1,000 bottles per annum by Bobby Acland of the "Black Raven", Bishopsgate, City of London.
Cheese
16 oz. *453 g* of Cheddar in 2 min 15 sec by Peter Dowdeswell (see above) at Little Ilford School, London E.12 on 12 Mar. 1977.
Chicken
27 (2 lb. *907 g* pullets) by "Bozo" Miller (see above) at a sitting at Trader Vic's, San Francisco, California, U.S.A. in 1963.
Clams
424 (Littlenecks) in 8 min by Dave Barnes at Port Townsend Bay, Washington, U.S.A. on 3 May 1975.
Doughnuts
29 in 7 min 16 sec by Hany Rizk of Chedstone, Melbourne, Australia on 10 Apr. 1976. (total weight 2 lb. 12½ oz.).
Eels
1 lb. *453 g* of elvers (1,300) in 43 secs by Leslie Cole, 37 at Frampton-on-Severn, Gloucestershire on 13 Apr. 1971.
Eggs
(Hard Boiled) 14 in 58 sec by Peter Dowdeswell (see above) at the Stardust Social Club, Corby, Northants on 18 Feb. 1977.
(Soft Boiled) 32 in 130 secs by Douglas L. Burch at Korbets Restaurants, Mobile, Alabama, U.S.A. on 9 May 1975.
(Raw) 13 in 3.8 sec by James Lindop in Manchester on 29 Sept. 1973.
Frankfurters
23 (2 oz. *56,6 g*) in 3 min 10 sec by Lynda Kuerth, 21, at the Veterans Stadium, Philadelphia, on 12 July 1977.
Gherkins
1 lb. *453 g* in 43.6 sec by Rex Barker of Elkhorn, Nebraska, U.S.A. on 30 Oct. 1975.
Grapes
3 lb. 1 oz. of grapes in 34.6 sec by Jim Ellis of Montrose, Michigan, U.S.A. on 30 May 1976.
Haggis
24 oz. *680 g* in 2 min 14 sec by Peter Dowdeswell at Corby, Northamptonshire on 24 Jan. 1977.
Hamburgers
14 hamburgers (3½ oz. *99,2 g* with buns) (49 oz. *1,389 kg* of meat) in 30 min by Kirk Stout of Albany, Indiana, U.S.A. on 1 June 1976.
Ice Cream
11 lb. *4,989 kg* in 8 min 15 sec by Ken Redding at Pyramid Mall, Saratoga Springs, New York, U.S.A. on 27 Apr. 1976.

Kippers
25 (self-filleted) in 60 min by Bob Ibbotson at Scarborough, North Yorkshire on 10 Aug. 1973.
Lemons
12 quarters (3 lemons) whole (including skin and pips) in 24 sec by Bob Blackmore of Lexington, Kentucky, U.S.A. on 2 Mar. 1977.
Meat
One whole roast ox in 42 days by Johann Ketzler of Munich, Germany in 1880.
Meat Pies
19 five oz. *141 g* in a 30 min session by Geoffrey Heeman in Arbroath, Tayside, Scotland on 25 Oct. 1972.
Milk
2 pt (1 Imperial quart or *113.5 centilitres*) in 3.2 sec by Peter Dowdeswell (see above) at Dudley Top Rank Club, West Midlands on 31 May 1975.
Oysters
684 in 20 min 30 sec by Vernon Bass at Walt's Fish Market, Sarasota, Florida, U.S.A. on 21 Nov. 1976. The record for opening oysters is 100 in 3 min 1 sec by Douglas Brown, 26 at Christchurch, New Zealand on 29 Apr. 1974.
Pancakes
(6 in *15,2 cm* diameter buttered and with syrup) 62 in 6 min 58.5 sec by Peter Dowdeswell (see above) at The Drapery, Northampton on 9 Feb. 1977.
Peanuts
100 (whole) singly in 56.1 sec by Rudi Wesheim at Pembroke College, Cambridge on 16 Feb. 1977.
Pickled Onions
91 pickled onions in 1 min 19 sec by David S. Newburg of Lexington, Kentucky on 2 Mar. 1977.
Potatoes
3 lb. *1,360 g* in 1 min 45 sec by Leslie Carter of Blisworth, Northants on 12 Oct. 1976.
Potato Crisps
30 2 oz. *56,6 g* bags in 24 min 33.6 sec, without a drink, by Paul G. Tully of Brisbane University in May 1969. The largest naturally occurring crisp on record is one measured to be 5¾ × 3½ in *14,6 × 8,8 cm* found by Joan Manageri of Newark, N.J. in June 1976.
Prunes
130 in 105 sec by Dave Man at Eastbourne on 16 June 1971.
Ravioli
324 (first 250 in 70 min) by "Bozo" Miller (see above) at Rendezvous Room, Oakland, California, U.S.A. in 1963.
Sandwiches
40 in 39 min (jam "butties" 6 × 3¾ × ½ in *15,2 × 9,5 × 1,2 cm*) by Steve Street in Edmonton, Greater London on 10 Apr. 1974.
Sausage Meat
96 1 oz. *28,3 g* sausages in 6 min by Steve Meltzer of Brooklyn, New York, U.S.A. on 14 Oct. 1974. No "Hot Dog" contests results have been remotely comparable.
Shrimps
2½ lb. *1,133 kg* in 7 min 32 sec by Jimmy Davenport of Lexington, Kentucky on 2 Mar. 1977.
Snails
124 in 15 mins (Moroccan snails) by Mrs. Nicky Bove at 6th Great Escargot Eating Contest, Houston, Texas, U.S.A. 1 Apr. 1974. The style prize was won by Rex Miller.
Spaghetti
100 yds *91,44 m* in 28.73 sec by Steve Weldon of Austin, Texas, U.S.A., on 1 May 1977.
Tortilla
74 by Tom Nall in the 2nd World Championship at Mariano's Mexican Restaurant, Dallas, Texas, U.S.A. on 16 Oct. 1973.
Whelks
81 (unshelled) in 15 min by William Corfield, 35 at the Helyar Arms, East Coker, Somerset on 6 Sept. 1969.

2. HONOURS, DECORATIONS AND AWARDS

Oldest Order

The earliest of the orders of chivalry is the Venetian order of St. Marc, reputedly founded in A.D. 831. The Castilian order of Calatrava has an established date of foundation in 1158. The prototype of the princely Orders of Chivalry is the Most Noble Order of the Garter founded by King Edward III in c. 1348. A date of A.D. 809 has been attributed to the Most Ancient Order of the Thistle but is of doubtful provenance.

Eponymous record

The largest object to which a human name is attached is the super cluster of galaxies known as Abell 7, after the astronomer Dr. George O. Abell of the University of California, U.S.A. The group of clusters has an estimated linear dimension of 300,000,000 light years and was announced in 1961. The human who has had most objects named after him is William Prout (1785–1850) who, in 1814 enunciated (the incorrect) Prout's Law that all the atomic weights of all the elements are multiples of the atomic weight of hydrogen. Ernest (later Lord) Rutherford in 1911 named the positively charged nucleus of the atom a Proton (after Prout). It is estimated that there are some 10^{85} protons in the observable universe.

Most titles
The most titled person in the world is the 18th Duchess of Alba (Albade Termes), Doña Maria del Rosario Cayetana Fitz-James Stuart y Silva. She is 8 times a duchess, 15 times a marchioness, 21 times a countess and is 19 times a Spanish grandee.

Versatility
The only person to win a Victoria Cross and an Olympic Gold Medal has been Lt. Gen. Sir Philip Neame V.C., K.B.E., C.B., D.S.O. (b. 12 Dec. 1888). He won the V.C. in 1914 and was an Olympic gold medalist for rifle shooting in 1924.

Most expensive
The highest auction price for any British gallantry decoration is £7,500 for a V.C. group given at Sotheby's, London on 22 June 1977 by The Returned Services League for the medals of Lt. L. Keysor, V.C., A.I.F., won at Gallipoli on 7 Aug. 1915.

Victoria Cross *Most bars*
The only three men ever to have been awarded a bar to the Victoria Cross (instituted 1856) are:

Surg.-Capt. (later Lt.-Col.) Arthur Martin-Leake, V.C.*, V.D., R.A.M.C. (1874–1953) (1902 and bar 1915).
Capt. Noel Godfrey Chavasse, V.C.*, M.C., R.A.M.C. (1884–1917) (1916 and bar posthumously 14 Sept. 1917).
Second Lieut. (later Capt.) Charles Hazlett Upham, V.C.*, N.Z.M.F. (born 1911) (1941 and bar 1942).

Victoria Cross *Youngest*
The lowest established age for a V.C. is 15 years 100 days for Hospital Apprentice Andrew (wrongly gazetted as Arthur) Fitzgibbon (born at Peteragurh, northern India, 13 May 1845) of the Indian Medical Services for bravery at the Taku Forts in northern China on 21 Aug. 1860. The youngest living V.C. is Lance-Corporal Rambahadur Limbu (b. Nepal, 1939) of the 10th Princess Mary's Own Gurkha Rifles. The award was for his courage while fighting in the Bau district of Sarawak, East Malaysia, on 21 Nov. 1965.

Victoria Cross *Longest lived*
The longest lived of all the 1,349 winners of the Victoria Cross was Captain (later General Sir) Lewis Stratford Tolle-mache Halliday, V.C. K.C.B., of the Royal Marine Light Infantry. He was born on 14 May 1870, won his V.C. in China in 1900, and died on 9 Mar. 1966, aged 95 years 299 days.

George Cross
The highest award ever given to a woman is the George Cross. The oldest recipient was Miss Emma Josie Townsend (formerly E.G.M.) aged 53 in 1932 and the youngest is Mrs. Doreen Ashburnham-Ruffner (formerly A.M.) aged 11 in 1916.

Order of Merit
The Order of Merit (instituted on 23 June 1902) is limited to 24 members. Up to 30 June 1977 there have been 124 awards including only 3 women, plus 9 honorary awards to non-British citizens. The longest lived holder has been the Rt. Hon. Bertrand Arthur William Russell, 3rd Earl Russell, who died on 2 Feb. 1970 aged 97 years 260 days. The oldest recipient was Admiral of the Fleet the Hon. Sir Henry Keppel, G.C.B., O.M. (1809–1904), who received the Order aged 93 years 56 days on 9 Aug. 1902. The youngest recipient has been H.R.H. the Duke of Edinburgh, K.G., K.T., O.M., G.B.E. who was appointed on his 47th birthday on 20 June 1968.

RECORD NUMBER OF BARS (repeat awards) EVER GAZETTED TO BRITISH GALLANTRY DECORATIONS
* = a bar or repeat award

V.C.*
A first bar has been three times awarded to the Victoria Cross (see above).
D.S.O.***
A third bar was 16 times awarded to the Distinguished Service Order.
R.R.C.*
Over 100 first bars have been awarded to the Royal Red Cross, but of these Dame Sarah Elizabeth Oram, D.B.E., R.R.C.* (1860–1946) uniquely was gazetted *twice* (1896 and 1901) before receiving a bar in 1918, thus indicating 3 awards.

D.S.C.***
A third bar was uniquely awarded to the Distinguished Service Cross won by Cdr. Norman Eyre Morley, R.N.V.R.
M.C.***
A third bar has been four times awarded to the Military Cross.
D.F.C.**
A second bar has been 54 times awarded to the Distinguished Flying Cross.
A.F.C.**
A second bar has been 12 times awarded to the Air Force Cross.
D.C.M.**
A second bar has been 11 times awarded to the Distinguished Conduct Medal.
C.G.M.*
A first bar has been uniquely awarded to the Conspicuous Gallantry Medal (Naval) won by C.P.O. Arthur Robert Blore, M.M. (1890–1947) and a second medal to Able Seaman D. Barry.
G.M.**
A first bar has been 25 times awarded to the George Medal.
K.P.M.**
A second bar has been uniquely awarded to the King's/Queen's Police Medal for Gallantry won by Supt. Frederick William O'Goreman, C.I.E., O.B.E. (d. 1949).
E.M.*
A first bar has twice been awarded to the Edward Medal (1st Class or in Silver).
D.S.M.***
A third bar has been uniquely awarded to the Distinguished Service Medal won by Petty Officer William Henry Kelly.
M.M.***
A third bar has been uniquely awarded to the Military Medal won by Cpl. Ernest Albert Correy (1888–1972).
D.F.M.**
A second bar has been uniquely awarded to the Distinguished Flying Medal won by Flt.-Sgt. (now Group Capt.) Donald Ernest Kingsby, D.S.O., A.F.C.
A.F.M.*
A first bar has been 8 times awarded to the Air Force Medal.
S.G.M.*
A first bar has been uniquely awarded to the Sea Gallantry Medal won by Chief Officer James Whiteley.
B.E.M.*
A first bar has been 4 times awarded to the British Empire Medal for Gallantry (as instituted in 1957 but abolished in 1974).
Q.G.M.*
A first bar was awarded to the Queen's Gallantry Medal on 7 Dec. 1976 to P.C. Ryan Kenneth David.

No bars have yet been awarded to the George Cross (G.C.), or the Conspicuous Gallantry Medal (Flying) (C.G.M.). No bars were ever awarded to the now obsolete Albert Medal in Gold (A.M.), the Albert Medal (A.M.), the Edward Medal (in bronze) (E.M.) or the Empire Gallantry Medal (E.G.M.), which have all been superceded by the G.C.

Most mentions in despatches
The record number of "mentions" is 24 by Field Marshal the Rt. Hon. Sir Frederick Sleigh Roberts Bt., the Earl Roberts, V.C., K.G., K.P., G.C.B., O.M., G.C.S.I., G.C.I.E., V.D. (1832–1914).

Most post-nominal letters
Lord Roberts was the only subject with 8 sets of *official* post-nominal letters. Currently the record number is seven by Admiral of the Fleet the Earl Mountbatten of Burma (born 25 June 1900) K.G., G.C.B., O.M., G.C.S.I., G.C.I.E., G.C.V.O., D.S.O.

U.S.S.R.
The U.S.S.R.'s highest award for valour is the Gold Star of a Hero of the Soviet Union. Over 10,000 were awarded in World War II. Among the 109 awards of a second star were those to Marshall Iosif Vissarionovich Dzhugashvili, *alias* Stalin (1879–1953) and Lt.-General Nikita Sergeyevich Khrushchyov (1894–1971). The only war-time triple awards were to Marshal Georgiy Konstantinovich Zhukov, Hon. G.C.B. (1896–1974) (subsequently awarded a fourth Gold Star unique until Mr. Khrushchyov's fourth award) and the leading air aces Guards' Colonel (now Aviation Maj.-Gen.) Aleksandr Ivanovich Polkyrshkin and Aviation Maj.-Gen. Ivan Nikitaevich Kozhedub. Zhukov also had the Order of Victory, twice, the Order of Lenin 4 times and the Order of the Red Banner, thrice.

Germany
The only man to be awarded the Knight's Cross of the Iron Cross with swords, diamonds and golden oak-leaves was Col. Hans-Ulrich Rudel.

U.S.A.
The highest U.S. decoration is the Congressional Medal of Honor. Five marines received both the Army and Navy Medals of Honor for the same acts in 1918 and 14 officers and men from 1863 to 1915 have received the medal on two occasions.

Top Scoring Air Aces (World Wars I and II)
World
80 Rittmeister Manfred, Freiherr (Baron) von Richthofen (Germany).
352[1] Major Erich Hartman (Germany).
United Kingdom
73[2] Capt. (acting Major) Edward Mannock, V.C., D.S.O.**, M.C.*.
38[3] Wg.-Cdr. (now Air Vice Marshal) James Edgar Johnson, C.B., C.B.E., D.S.O.**, D.F.C.*.
A compilation of the top air aces of 13 combatant nations in World War I and of 22 nations in World War II was included in the 13th edition of *The Guinness Book of Records*.

[1] *All except one of the aircraft in this unrivalled total were Soviet combat aircraft on the Eastern Front in 1942–45. The German air ace with most victories against the R.A.F. was Oberleutnant Hans-Joachim Marseille (killed 30 Sept. 1942), who in 388 actions shot down 158 Allied aircraft, 151 of them over North Africa.*

[2] *Recent research suggests that Mannock's total may have been lower than that of Major James Thomas Byford McCudden, V.C., D.S.O.*, M.C.*, M.M. (57 victories).*

[3] *The greatest number of successes against flying bombs (V.1's) was by Sqn. Ldr. Joseph Berry, D.F.C.** (b. Nottingham, 1920, killed 2 Oct. 1944). who brought down 60 in 4 months. The most successful R.A.F. fighter pilot was Sqn. Ldr Marmaduke Thomas St. John Pattle, D.F.C.*, of South Africa, with a known total of at least 40.*

Top jet ace

The greatest number of kills in jet to jet battles is 16 by Capt. Joseph Christopher McConnell, Jr., U.S.A.F. (b. Dover, New Hampshire, 30 Jan. 1922) in the Korean war (1950–53). He was killed on 25 Aug. 1954. It is possible that an Israeli ace may have surpassed this total in the period 1967–70 but the identity of pilots is subject to strict security.

Top woman ace

The record score for any woman fighter pilot is 12 by Jnr. Lt. Lydia Litvak (U.S.S.R.) (b. 1921) on the Eastern Front between 1941 and 1943. She was killed in action on 1 Aug. 1943.

Anti Tank successes

Major Hans-Ulrich Rudel, the German *Stuka* pilot, in 2,530 combat missions destroyed 519 Soviet armoured vehicles and was uniquely awarded the golden oak-leaves to the Knight's Cross of the Iron Cross on 1 Jan. 1945. (see above).

Anti-submarine successes

The highest number of U-boat kills attributed to one ship in the 1939–45 war was 13 to H.M.S. *Starling* (Capt. Frederick J. Walker, C.B., D.S.O.***, R.N.). Captain Walker was in overall command of the sinking of a total of 25 U-boats between 1941 and the time of his death on 9 July 1944. The U.S. Destroyer Escort *England* sank six Japanese submarines in the Pacific between 18 and 30 May 1944.

Most successful U-boat captain

The most successful of all World War II submarine commanders was Leutnant Otto Kretschmer, captain of the U.23 and U.99 who up to March 1940 sank one destroyer and 44 Allied merchantmen totalling 266,629 gross registered tons.

In World War I Kapitän-Leutnant Lothar von Arnauld de la Periere, in the U.35 and U.139, sank 194 allied ships totalling 453,716 gross tons. The most successful boats were U.48, which in World War I sank 54 ships of 90,350 g.r.t. in a single voyage and 535,900 g.r.t. all told, and U.53 which sank 53 ships of 318,111 g.r.t. in World War II.

NOBEL PRIZE

The Nobel Foundation of £3,200,000 was set up under the will of Alfred Bernhard Nobel (1833–96), the unmarried Swedish chemist and chemical engineer, who invented dynamite, in 1866. The Nobel Prizes are presented annually on 10 December, the anniversary of Nobel's death and the festival day of the Foundation. Since the first Prizes were awarded in 1901, the highest cash value of the award, in each of the six fields of Physics, Chemistry, Medicine and Physiology, Literature, Peace and Economics (inst. 1969) was $160,000 (£94,100) in 1976.

Most awards by countries (shared awards count as one)

The United States has shared in the greatest number of awards (including those made in 1976) with a total of 103 made up of 28 for Physics, 16 for Chemistry, 31 for Medicine-Physiology, 6 for Literature, 15 for Peace and 7 for Economics.

The United Kingdom has shared in 62 awards, comprising 17 for Physics, 17 for Chemistry, 13 for Medicine-Physiology, 6 for Literature, 8 for Peace and 1 for Economics.

By classes, the United States holds the record for Medicine-Physiology with 31, for Physics with 28, for Peace with 15 and Economics with 6; Germany for Chemistry with 21; and France for Literature with 12.

Individuals

Individually the only person to have won two Prizes outright is Dr. Linus Carl Pauling (b. 28 Feb. 1901), Professor of

Supreme among the United Kingdom's 22 gallantry decorations—the Victoria Cross to which only 3 first bars have ever been awarded in 121 years (see p. 234).

Chemistry at the California Institute of Technology, Pasadena, California, U.S.A. since 1931. He was awarded the Chemistry Prize for 1954 and the Peace Prize for 1962. The only other persons to have won two prizes are Madame Marie Curie (1867–1934), who was born in Poland as Marja Sklodowska. She shared the 1903 Physics Prize with her husband Pierre Curie (1859–1906) and Antoine Henri Becquerel (1852–1908), and won the 1911 Chemistry Prize outright. Professor John Bardeen (b. 23 May 1908) shared the Physics Prize in 1956 and 1972. The Peace Prize has been awarded three times to the International Committee of the Red Cross (founded 29 Oct. 1863), of Geneva, Switzerland, namely in 1917, 1944 and in 1963, when it was shared with the International League of Red Cross Societies.

Oldest

The oldest prizeman has been Professor Francis Peyton Rous (1879–1970) of the United States. He shared the Medicine Prize in 1966, at the age of 87.

Youngest

The youngest laureate has been Professor Sir William Lawrence Bragg, C.H., O.B.E., M.C. (1890–1971), of the U.K., who at the age of 25, shared the 1915 Physics Prize with his father, Sir William Henry Bragg, O.M., K.B.E. (1862–1942), for work on X-rays and crystal structures. Bragg and also Theodore William Richards (1868–1928) of the U.S.A., who won the 1914 Chemistry Prize, carried out their prize work when aged 23. The youngest Literature prizeman has been Joseph Rudyard Kipling (1865–1936) at the age of 41 in 1907. The youngest Peace prize-winner has been the Rev. Dr. Martin Luther King, Jr. (1929–68) of the U.S.A., in 1964.

Most statues

The world record for raising statues to oneself was set by Generalissimo Dr. Rafael Leónidas Trujillo y Molina (1891–1961), former President of the Dominican Republic. In March 1960 a count showed that there were "over 2,000".

The country's highest mountain was named Pico Trujillo (now Pico Duarte). One province was called Trujillo and another Trujillo Valdez. The capital was named Ciudad Trujillo (Trujillo City) in 1936, but reverted to its old name of Santo Domingo de Guzmán on 23 Nov. 1961. Trujillo was assassinated in a car ambush on 30 May 1961, and 30 May is now celebrated annually as a public holiday. The man to whom most statues have been raised is undoubtedly Vladimir Ilyich Ulyanov, *alias* Lenin (1870–1924), busts of whom have been mass-produced as also in the case of Mao Tse-tung (b. 26 Dec. 1893) and Hô Chi Minh (1890–1969).

PEERAGE

Most ancient
The oldest extant peerage is that of the premier Earl of Scotland, the Rt. Hon. Margaret of Mar, the Countess of Mar and 31st holder of this Earldom, (b. 19 Sept. 1940), who is the heir-at-law of Roderick or Rothri, 1st Earl (or Mormaer) of Mar, who witnessed a charter in 1114 or 1115 as "Rothri *comes*".

Oldest creation
The greatest age at which any person has been raised to the peerage is 93 years 337 days in the case of Sir William Francis Kyffin Taylor, G.B.E., K.C. (b. 9 July 1854), who was created Baron Maenan of Ellesmere, County Salop (Shropshire), on 10 June 1948, and died, aged 97, on 22 Sept. 1951, when the title became extinct.

Longest lived peer
The longest lived peer ever recorded was the Rt. Hon. Frank Douglas-Pennant, the 5th Baron Penrhyn (b. 21 Nov. 1865), who died on 3 Feb. 1967, aged 101 years 74 days. The oldest peeress recorded was the Countess Desmond, who was alleged to be 140 when she died in 1604. This claim is patently exaggerated but it is accepted that she may have been 104. Currently the oldest holder of a peerage, and the oldest Parliamentarian, is the Rt. Hon. Walter Egerton George Lucian Keppal M.C., the 9th Earl of Albemarle who was born on 28 Feb. 1882.

Youngest peers
Twelve Dukes of Cornwall became (in accordance with the grant by the Crown in Parliament) peers at birth as the eldest son of a Sovereign; and the 9th Earl of Chichester posthumously inherited his father's (killed 54 days previously) earldom at his birth on 14 Apr. 1944. The youngest age at which a person has had a peerage conferred on them is 7 days old in the case of the Earldom of Chester on H.R.H. the Prince George (later George IV) on 19 Aug. 1762.

Longest and shortest peerages
The peer who has sat longest in the House of Lords was Lt.-Col. Charles Henry FitzRoy, O.B.E., the 4th Baron Southampton (b. 11 May 1867), who succeeded to his father's title on 16 July 1872, took his seat on 23 Jan. 1891, 18 months before Mr. W. E. Gladstone's fourth administration began, and died, aged 91, on 7 Dec. 1958, having held the title for 86 years 144 days.

The shortest enjoyment of a peerage was the "split second" by which the law assumes that the Hon. Wilfrid Carlyle Stamp (b. 28 Oct. 1904), the 2nd Baron Stamp, survived his father, Sir Josiah Charles Stamp, G.C.B., G.B.E., the 1st Baron Stamp, when both were killed as a result of German bombing of London on 16 Apr. 1941. Apart from this legal fiction, the shortest recorded peerage was one of 30 minutes in the case of Sir Charles Brandon, K.B., the 3rd Duke of Suffolk, who died, aged 13 or 14, just after succeeding his brother, Sir Henry, the 2nd Duke, when both were suffering a fatal illness, at Buckden, Cambridgeshire, on 14 July 1551.

Highest numbering
The highest succession number borne by any peer is that of the present 35th Baron Kingsale (John de Courcy, b. 27 Jan. 1941), who succeeded to the then 746-year-old Barony on 7 Nov. 1969.

Most creations
The largest number of new hereditary peerages created in any year was the 54 in 1296. The record for all peerages (including 40 life peerages) is 55 in 1964. The greatest number of extinctions in a year was 16 in 1923 and the greatest number of deaths was 44 in 1935.

Most prolific
The most prolific peers of all time are believed to be the 1st Earl Ferrers (1650–1717) and the 3rd Earl of Winchelsea (*c.* 1620–1689) each with 27 legitimate children. In addition, the former reputedly fathered 30 illegitimate children. Currently the peer with the largest family is the Rt. Hon. Bryan Walter Guinness, 2nd Baron Moyne (b. 27 Oct. 1905) with 6 sons and 5 daughters.

The most prolific peeress is believed to be Elizabeth (*née* Barnard), who bore her husband, Lord Chandos of Sudeley (1642–1714), 22 children.

Oldest baronet
The greatest age to which a baronet has lived is 101 years 188 days, in the case of Sir Fitzroy Donald Maclean, 10th Bt., K.C.B., (1835–1936). He was the last survivor of the Charge of the Light Brigade at Balaclava in the Crimea.

Knight *Youngest and oldest*
The youngest age for the conferment of a knighthood is 29 days for H.R.H. the Prince Albert Edward (b. 9 Nov. 1841) (later Edward VII) by virtue of his *ex officio* membership of the Order of the Garter (K.G.) consequent upon his creation as Prince of Wales on 8 Dec. 1841. The greatest age for the conferment of a knighthood is 98 years 167 days in the case of Sir Alfred Hamish Reed, C.B.E., born Hayes, Kent 30 Dec. 1875. the author-explorer who lives in New Zealand whose knight bachelorhood was announced 15 June 1974.

Queen's Award for Export and Technology
The record number of awards (instituted in 1966) for export achievement in their sole right is six by Glaxo Laboratories Ltd. (1967 to 1972). The record number of awards for technological achievement in their sole right is three by Decca Radar Ltd. (1968–71–72) and the Kelvin Hughes division of Smiths Industries (1967–68–75).

Most freedoms
Probably the greatest number of freedoms ever conferred on any man was 57 in the case of Andrew Carnegie (1835–1919), who was born in Dumfermline, Fife but emigrated to the United States in 1848. The most freedoms conferred upon any citizen of the United Kingdom is 42, in the case of Sir Winston Churchill, (1874–1965).

Most honorary degrees
The greatest number of honorary degrees awarded to any individual is 89, given to Herbert Clark Hoover (1874–1964), former President of the United States (1929–33).

Greatest vote
The largest monetary vote made by Parliament to a subject was the £400,000 given to the 1st Duke of Wellington (1769–1852) on 12 Apr. 1814. He received in all £864,000. The total received by the 1st, 2nd and 3rd Dukes to January 1900 was £1,052,000.

Who's Who
The longest entry in *Who's Who* (founded 1848) was that of the Rt. Hon. Sir Winston Leonard Spencer Churchill, K.G., O.M., C.H., T.D. (1874–1965), who had 211 lines in the 1965 edition. Currently the longest entry is that of Lord Cohen of Birkenhead C.H. (b. 1900), with 113 lines. The longest feminine entry is that of Barbara Cartland, the romantic novelist, with 96 lines. Apart from those who qualify for inclusion by hereditary title, the youngest entry has been Yehudi Menuhin, Hon. K.B.E. (b. New York City, U.S.A. 22 Apr. 1916), the concert violinist, who first appeared in the 1932 edition aged 15. The longest entry of the 66,000 entries in *Who's Who in America* is that of Prof. Richard Buckminster Fuller, Jr. (b. 12 July 1895) whose all-time record of 139 lines compares with the 23 line sketch on ex-President Nixon.

Most brothers
The most brothers having entries in *Who's Who* is five in the case of the Barrington-Wards: Frederick Temple (1880-1938), Sir Lancelot (1884–1953), Sir Michael (1887–1972) Robert McGowan (1891–1948) and John Grosvenor (1894-1946). Their father Canon Mark James (died 1924) of Duloe Cornwall was himself in *Who's Who*.

12. SPORTS, GAMES AND PASTIMES

ALL SPORTS

Earliest
The origins of sport stem from the time when self-preservation ceased to be the all-consuming human preoccupation. Archery was a hunting skill in mesolithic times (by *c.* 8000 B.C.), but did not become an organized sport until *c.* A.D. 300, among the Genoese. The earliest dated evidence for sport is *c.* 2450 B.C. for fowling with throwing sticks, similar to return boomerangs, and hunting. Ball games by girls depicted on Middle Kingdom murals at Ben Hasan, Egypt have been dated to *c.* 2050 B.C.

Fastest
The governing body for aviation, *La Fédération Aéronautique Internationale*, records maximum speeds in lunar flight of up to 24,791 m.p.h. *39 897 km/h.* However, these achievements, like all air speed records since 1923, have been para-military rather than sporting. The highest speed reached in a non-mechanical sport is in sky-diving, in which a speed of 185 m.p.h. *298 km/h* is attained in a head-down free falling position, even in the lower atmosphere. In delayed drops speeds of 614 m.p.h. *988 km/h* have been recorded at high rarefied altitudes. The highest projectile speed in any moving ball game is *c.* 160 m.p.h. *260 km/h* in pelota. This compares with 170 m.p.h. *273 km/h* (electronically-timed) for a golf ball driven off a tee.

Slowest
In wrestling, before the rules were modified towards "brighter wrestling", contestants could be locked in holds for so long that a single bout could have lasted for 11 hrs 40 min. In the extreme case of the 2 hrs 41 min pull in the regimental tug o' war in Jubbulpore, India, on 12 Aug. 1889, the winning team moved a net distance of 12 ft *3,6 m* at an average speed of 0.00084 m.p.h. *0,00135 km/h.*

Longest
The most protracted sporting test was an automobile duration test of 222,618 miles *358 268 km* by Appaurchaux and others in a Ford Taunus. This was contested over 142 days in 1963. The distance was equivalent to 8.93 times around the equator.

The most protracted non-mechanical sporting event is the *Tour de France* cycling race. In 1926 this was over 3,569 miles *5 743 km* lasting 29 days. The total damage to the French national economy of this annual event, now reduced to 23 days, is immense. If it is assumed that one-third of the total working population works for only two-thirds of the time during the currency of *Le Tour* this would account for a loss of more than three-quarters of one per cent of the nation's annual Gross National Product. In 1976 this loss would have been in excess of £1,000,000,000.

Competitors in the Tour de France, with Eddy Merckx in the *maillot jaune* worn by the race leader. (*Tony Duffy, All-Sport Photographic*)

Largest stadium
For details of the world's largest stadium see p. 113.

Largest pitch
The largest pitch of any ball game is that of polo, with 12.4 acres *5,0 ha,* or a maximum length of 300 yd *274 m* and a width, without side boards, of 200 yd *182 m.* Twice a year in the Parish of St. Columb Major, Cornwall, England, a game called Hurling (not to be confused with the Irish game) is played on a "pitch" which consists of the entire Parish, approximately 25 square miles *64,7 km².*

Largest trophy
The world's largest trophy for a particular sport is the Bangalore Limited Handicap Polo Tournament Trophy. This

massive cup is 6 ft *1,83 m* tall and was presented in 1936 by the Raja of Kolanka.

Heaviest sportsmen
The heaviest sportsman of all-time was the wrestler William J. Cobb of Macon, Georgia, U.S.A., who in 1962 was billed as the 802 lb. (57 st. 4 lb. *363 kg*) "Happy Humphrey". The heaviest player of a ball-game has been Bob Pointer, the U.S. Football tackle formerly on the 1967 Santa Barbara High School Team, California, U.S.A. and still playing in 1972 at 480 lb. (34 st. 4 lb. *217 kg*).

Youngest world record breaker
The youngest age at which any person has broken a world record is 12 years 328 days in the case of Karen Yvette Muir (b. 16 Sept. 1952) of Kimberley, South Africa, who broke the women's 110 yds backstroke world record with 1 min 08.7 sec at Blackpool on 10 Aug. 1965.

Oldest world record breaker
Gerhard Weidner of West Germany (b. 15 Mar. 1933) broke the world 20 miles track walking record at Hamburg, West Germany, in 2 hr 30 min 38.6 sec when aged 41 years 71 days.

Youngest and oldest internationals
The youngest age at which any person has won international honours is eight years in the case of Joy Foster, the Jamaican singles and mixed doubles table tennis champion in 1958. The youngest British international has been diver Beverley Williams (b. 5 Jan. 1957), who was 10 yr 268 days old when she competed against the U.S.A. at Crystal Palace, London, on 30 Sept. 1967. It would appear that the greatest age at which anyone has actively competed for his country was 72 years 280 days in the case of Oscar G. Swahn (Sweden) (1847–1927) who won a silver medal for shooting in the Olympic Games at Antwerp on 26 July 1920. He qualified for the 1924 Games but was unable to participate due to illness.

Most versatile
All-round ability is measured by level of attainment in highly varied pursuits. By these parameters Charlotte (Lottie) Dod (1871–1960) stands supreme. She won the Wimbledon Singles title five times between 1887 and 1893, the British Ladies Golf Championship in 1904, an Olympic silver medal for archery in 1908, and represented England at hockey in 1899. Among current sportsmen, Chief Petty Officer Alan Robert Cronin (b. 20 Sept. 1946) has represented Great Britain in track and field (hurdles), karate, and bobsleigh.

Youngest and oldest champions
The youngest successful competitor in a world title event was a French boy, whose name is not recorded, who coxed the Netherlands' Olympic pair at Paris on 26 Aug. 1900. He was not more than ten and may have been as young as seven. The youngest individual Olympic winner was Marjorie Gestring (U.S.A.), who took the springboard diving title at the age of 13 years 9 months at the Olympic Games in Berlin in 1936. On retirement as undefeated world real tennis champion in 1955, Pierre Etchebaster (b. France, 1893) was 62 yr old, an age which is not known to have been surpassed by any other Olympic or World champion.

Longest reign
The longest reign as a world champion is 27 years (1928–1955) by Pierre Etchebaster at real tennis.

The longest reign as a British champion is 41 years by the archer Alice Blanche Legh (1855–1948) who first won the Championship in 1881 and for the 23rd and final time in 1922 aged 67.

Greatest earnings
The greatest fortune amassed by an individual in sport is an estimated £17,000,000 by the late Sonja Henie of Norway (1912–1969), the triple Olympic figure skating champion (1928, 1932, 1936), when later (1936–56) a professional ice skating promoter starring in her own ice shows and 11 films. The highest paid woman athlete in the world is ice skater Janet

Lynn (U.S.A.) (b. 6 Apr. 1953), who, in 1974, signed a $1.5 million £652,000 three year contract. In 1974 she earned more than $750,000 £325,000. The greatest purse won for a single sports contest is $6½ million by Muhammad Ali Haj (U.S.A.) when he defeated Ken Norton (U.S.A.) in New York on 28 Sept. 1976. (For Ali's career total see p. 250.)

Most expensive
The most expensive of all sports is the racing of large yachts —"J" type boats, last built in 1937, and International 12-metre boats. The owning and racing of these is beyond the means of individual millionaires and is confined to multi-millionaires or syndicates.

Largest crowd
The greatest number of live spectators for any sporting spectacle is the estimated 1,500,000 who lined the route of the 81st Boston Marathon on 18 Apr. 1977. The race was won by Jerome Drayton of Canada. However, spread over 23 days, it is estimated that more than 10,000,000 see the annual *Tour de France* along the route (see also above).

The largest crowd travelling to any sporting venue is "more than 400,000" for the annual *Grand Prix d'Endurance* motor race on the Sarthe circuit near Le Mans, France. The record stadium crowd was one of 199,854 for the Brazil v. Uruguay match in the Maracaña Municipal Stadium, Rio de Janeiro, Brazil, on 16 July 1950.

Most participants
The annual *Figaro* cross country race in the Bois de Boulogne, Paris, France, attracted 23,657 entries on 23–24 Dec. 1976. In May 1971, the "Ramblin' Raft Race" on the Chattahoochee River, at Atlanta, Georgia, U.S.A., attracted 37,683 competitors on 8,304 rafts.

Largest following
The sport with most regular participants in Britain is angling with 2¾ million. Over 21 million spectators watched Association Football matches in Britain in 1976–77. The largest television audience for a single sporting event was 75.9 million who saw the telecast of the seventh game of the 1975 Baseball World Series. (See also p. 107).

Most sportsmen
According to a report issued in April 1971, 28,400,000 men and 15,200,000 women are actively involved in 209,000 physical culture and sports groups in the U.S.S.R. where there are 6.1 million track athletes, 5.6 million volleyball players, 3.9 million footballers and 891,000 weightlifters. The report lists 2,918 stadiums, 430 indoor and 475 outdoor swimming pools for 791,000 swimmers.

Worst disasters
The worst sports disaster in recent history was when an estimated 604 were killed after some stands at the Hong Kong Jockey Club racecourse collapsed and caught fire on 26 Feb. 1918. During the reign of Antoninus Pius (A.D. 138–161) the upper wooden tiers in the Circus Maximus, Rome, collapsed during a gladiatorial combat killing some 1,112 spectators. Britain's worst sports disaster was when 66 were killed and 145 injured at the Rangers v. Celtic football match at Exit 13 of Ibrox Park stadium, Glasgow on 2 Jan. 1971.

Best attended sporting funeral
A crowd estimated at between 60–70,000 people attended the funeral of the 1960 and 1964 Olympic marathon champion Abebe Bikila (Ethiopia) (1932–1973) at Addis Ababa in October 1973.

AEROBATICS
Earliest
The first aerobatic manoeuvre is generally considered the achievement of Célestin-Adolphe Pégoud, at Juvisy, France in 1913, but claims are made that Lieut. Peter Nesterov, of the Imperial Russian Air Service, performed a loop a few weeks previously.

Sidney Lanier's poem "The Song of the Chattahoochee" never visualised the river hosting the record breaking "Ramblin' Raft Race". (*American Rafting Association*)

World Championships

Held biennially since 1960 (excepting 1974), scoring is based on the system devised by Col José Aresti of Spain. The competitions consist of two compulsory and two free programmes.

Most titles

The world championships Team competition has been won on four occasions by the USSR. No individual has won more than one title, the most successful competitor being Igor Egorov (USSR) who won in 1970, was second in 1976, fifth in 1972 and eleventh in 1968. The most successful in the women's competition has been Lidia Leonova (USSR) with first place in 1976, third in 1972 and fifth in 1970. The only medal achieved by Britain has been a bronze in the team event at Kiev, USSR in 1976. The highest individual placing by a Briton is fourth by Neil Williams in 1976.

ANGLING

Catch *Largest Single*

The largest officially ratified fish ever caught on a rod is a man-eating great white shark (*Carcharodon carcharias*) weighing 2,664 lb. *1 208 kg* and measuring 16 ft 10 in *5,13 m* long, caught on a 130 lb. *58 kg* test line by Alf Dean at Denial Bay, near Ceduna, South Australia, on 21 Apr. 1959. A white pointer shark weighing 3,388 lb. *1 537 kg* was caught by Clive Green off Albany, Western Australia, on 26 Apr. 1976 but will remain unratified as whale meat was used as bait. The biggest ever rod-caught fish by a British angler is a 1,260 lb. *571,5 kg* black marlin caught by Edward A. Crutch off Cairns, Queensland, Australia on 19 Oct. 1973.

Capt. Frank Mundus (U.S.A.) harpooned a 17 ft *5,18 m* long 4,500 lb. *2,040 kg* great white shark off Montauk Point, New York, U.S.A. on 6 June 1964 and, assisted by Peter Brandenberg, Jerome Mallow, Frank Bloom and Harvey Ferster, landed it after a five hour battle.

The largest marine animal ever killed by *hand* harpoon was a blue whale 97 ft *29,56 m* in length, killed by Archer Davidson in Twofold Bay, New South Wales, Australia, in 1910. Its tail flukes measured 20 ft *6,09 m* across and its jaw bone 23 ft 4 in *7,11 m*. To date this has provided the ultimate in "fishing stories".

Catch *Smallest*

The smallest fish to win a competition is a smelt, weighing $\frac{1}{16}$ of an ounce *1 dram*, caught by Peter Christian at Buckenham Ferry, Norfolk, England on 9 Jan. 1977, in defeating 107 other competitors. For details of the smallest full-grown fish see p. 40.

Spear fishing

The largest fish ever taken underwater was an 804 lb. *364 kg* giant black grouper or jewfish by Don Pinder of the Miami Triton Club, Florida, U.S.A., in 1955. The British spearfishing record is 89 lb. *40,36 kg* for an angler fish by J. Brown (Weymouth Association Divers) in 1969.

Championship records *World*

The *Confederation Internationale de la Pêche Sportive* championships were inaugurated as European championships in 1953. They were recognised as World Championships in 1957. France won eight times between 1956 and 1976 and Robert Tesse (France) the individual title uniquely three times, in 1959–60, 1965.

Championship records *British*

The National Angling Championship (instituted 1906) has been won seven times by Leeds (1909–10, 1914, 1928, 1948–49, 1952). Only James H. R. Bazley (Leeds) has ever won the individual title twice (1909, 1927). The record catch is 76 lb. 9 oz. *34 kg 720* by David Burr (Rugby) in the Huntspill, Somerset in 1965. The largest single fish caught in the Championships is a carp of 14 lb. 2 oz. *6 kg 406* by J. C. Essex in Sept. 1975. The team record is 136 lb. 15¼ oz. *62 kg 120* by Sheffield Amalgamated also in the Huntspill in 1955.

Casting records

The longest freshwater cast ratified under I.C.F. (International Casting Federation) rules is 175,01 m *574 ft 2 in* by

Walter Kummerow (West Germany), for the Bait Distance Double-Handed 30 g event held at Lenzerheide, Switzerland in the 1968 Championships. The British National record is 148,78 m *488 ft 1 in* by A. Dickison on the same occasion. The longest Fly Distance Double-Handed cast is 78,38 m *257 ft 2 in* by S. Scheen (Norway), also at Lenzerheide in 1968, when Peter Anderson set a British National professional record of 69,80 m *229 ft.*

Longest fight

The longest recorded individual fight with a fish is 32 hrs 5 min by Donal Heatley (b. 1938) (New Zealand) with a broadbill (estimated length 20 ft *6,09 m* and weight 1,500 lb. *680 kg*) off Mayor Island off Tauranga, North Island on 21–22 Jan. 1968. It towed the 12 ton/*tonnes* launch 50 miles *80 km* before breaking the line.

Rarest fish

The burbot or eel-pout, the rarest British freshwater fish, is "almost extinct", so it has been agreed that no record for this species should be published, at least until November 1979, in the interests of conservation.

Marathon

Richard Schreiber and George Martin, of Silver Springs Shores, Fla., U.S.A. fished for 360 hr from a boat on 1–16 Aug. 1976.

A latter-day Izaak Walton, James Bazley, the only angler to win the British Championship twice. (*Angling News Services*)

WORLD RECORDS

(Selected Sea fish [All Tackle] from the complete list ratified by the International Game Fish Association to 30 June 1977. Selected Freshwater fish from the complete list ratified by "Field & Stream" are marked*)

Species	Weight lb. oz.	kg/g	Name of Angler	Location	Date
Amberjack	149 0	67,585	Peter Simons	Bermuda	21 June 1964
Barracuda[1]	83 0	37,648	K. J. W. Hackett[2]	Lagos, Nigeria	13 Jan. 1952
Bass (Giant Sea)	563 8	255,599	James D. McAdam Jr.	Anacapa Is., California, U.S.A.	20 Aug. 1968
Black Runner (Cobia)	110 5	50,035	Eric Tinworth	off Mombasa, Kenya	8 Sept. 1964
*Carp[3]	55 5	25,089	Frank J. Ledwein	Clearwater Lake, Minnesota, U.S.A.	10 July 1952
Cod	98 12	44,792	Alphonse J. Bielevich	Isle of Shoals, New Hampshire, U.S.A.	8 June 1969
Marlin (Black)	1,560 0	707,604	Alfred C. Glassell, Jr.	Cabo Blanco, Peru	4 Aug. 1953
Marlin (Atlantic Blue)	1,142 0	518,002	Jack Herrington	Nags Head, North Carolina, U.S.A.	26 July 1974
Marlin (Pacific Blue)	1,153 0	522,992	Greg D. Perez	Ritidian Point, Guam	21 Aug. 1969
Marlin (Striped)	415 0	188,240	B. C. Bain	Cape Brett, New Zealand	31 Mar. 1964
Marlin (White)	174 3	79,000	Otavia Cunha Reboucas	Vitoria, Brazil	1 Nov. 1976
*Pike (Northern)	46 2	20,921	Peter Dubuc	Sacandaga Reservoir, N.Y., U.S.A.	15 Sept. 1940
Sailfish (Atlantic)	128 1	58,088	Harm Steyn	Luanda, Angola	27 Mar. 1974
Sailfish (Pacific)	221 0	100,243	C. W. Stewart	Santa Cruz Is., Galapagos Is.	12 Feb. 1947
*Salmon (Chinook)	92 0	41,730	Heinz Wichman	Skeena River, British Columbia, Canada	19 July 1959
Shark (Blue)	410 0	185,972	Richard C. Webster	Rockport, Massachusetts, U.S.A.	1 Sept. 1960
	410 0	185,972	Martha C. Webster	Rockport, Massachusetts, U.S.A.	17 Aug. 1967
Shark (Shortfin Mako)[5]	1,061 0	481,261	James B. Penwarden	Mayor Island, New Zealand	17 Feb. 1970
Shark (White or Man-eating)	2,664 0	1 208,370	Alfred Dean	Denial Bay, Ceduna, South Australia	21 Apr. 1959
Shark (Porbeagle)	465 0	210,920	Jorge Potier	Padstow, Cornwall, England	23 July 1976
Shark (Thresher)[6]	739 0	335,204	Brian Galvin	Tutukaka, New Zealand	17 Feb. 1975
Shark (Tiger)	1,780 0	807,394	Walter Maxwell	Cherry Grove, South Carolina, U.S.A.	14 June 1964
*Sturgeon (White)	360 0	163,293	Willard Cravens	Snake River, Idaho, U.S.A.	24 Apr. 1956
Swordfish	1,182 0	536,146	L. E. Marron	Iquique, Chile	7 May 1953
Tarpon	283 0	128,366	M. Salazar	Lago de Maracaibo, Venezuela	19 Mar. 1965
*Trout (Lake)[7]	65 0	29,483	Larry Daunis	Great Bear Lake, N.W.T., Canada	8 Aug. 1970
Tuna (Allison or Yellowfin)	308 0	139,706	Harold J. Tolson	San Benedicto Is., Mexico	18 Jan. 1973
Tuna (Atlantic bigeye)	352 11	160,000	Dr. Michael Margoulies	Arguineguin, Canary Islands	8 Sept. 1976
Tuna (Pacific bigeye)	435 0	197,312	Dr. Russel V. A. Lee	Cabo Blanco, Peru	17 Apr. 1957
Tuna (Bluefin) Tunny	1,200 0	544,310	Leslie Vibert	Chaleur Bay, N.B., Canada	22 Sept. 1976
Wahoo	149 0	67,585	John Pirovano	Cat Cay, Bahamas	15 June 1962

[1] *A barracuda weighing 48 lb. 6 oz. 21 kg 942, was caught barehanded by Thomas B. Pace at Panama City Beach, Florida, U.S.A. on 19 April 1974.*
[2] *Aged 11 yrs 137 days at the time.*
[3] *A carp weighing 83 lb. 8 oz. 37 kg 874 was taken (not by rod) near Pretoria, South Africa.*
[4] *A salmon weighing 126 lb. 8 oz. 57 kg 379 was taken (not by rod) near Petersburg, Alaska, U.S.A.*

[5] *A 1,295 lb. 587 kg specimen was taken by two anglers off Natal, South Africa on 17 Mar. 1939 and a 1,500 lb. 680 kg specimen harpooned inside Durban Harbour, South Africa in 1933.*
[6] *W. W. Dowding caught one of 922 lb. 418 kg in 1937 on an untested line.*
[7] *A 102 lb. 46 kg 266 trout was taken from Lake Athabasca, northern Saskatchewan, Canada, on 8 Aug. 1961.*

BRITISH RECORDS

SEA FISH
(Selected from the complete list ratified by the British Record [rod-caught] Fish Committee of the National Anglers' Council to 30 June 1977)

Species	Weight lb oz. dr.	kg/g	Name of Angler	Location	Year
Angler Fish	82 12	37,534	K. Ponsford	off Mevagissey, Cornwall	1977
Bass	18 6	8,334	R. G. Slater	off Eddystone Reef	1975
Bream (Black)	6 7 12	2,941	J. L. D. Atkins	off Eastern Blackstone Rocks, Devon	1973
Bream (Red)	9 8 12	4,330	B. H. Reynolds	Mevagissey, Cornwall	1974
Brill	16 0	7,257	A. H. Fisher	Derby Haven, Isle of Man	1950
Bull Huss	21 3	9,610	J. Holmes	Hat Rock, Looe, Cornwall	1955
Coalfish	30 12	13,947	A. F. Harris	South of Eddystone	1973
Cod	53 0	24,039	G. Martin	off Start Point, Devon	1972
Conger	109 6	49,609	Robin. W. Potter	S. E. of Eddystone	1976
Dab	2 12 4	1,254	Robert Islip	Gairloch, Wester Ross	1975
Dogfish (Lesser Spotted)	4 8	2,040	J. Beattie	off Ayr Pier, Strathclyde	1969
Flounder	5 11 8	2,593	A. G. L. Cobbledick	Fowey, Cornwall	1956
Garfish	2 13 14	1,300	S. Claeskens	off Newton Ferrers, Devon	1971
Greater Weever	2 4	1,020	P. Ainslie	Brighton, East Sussex	1927
Gurnard (Red)	5 0	2,268	B. D. Critchley	off Rhyl, Clwyd	1973
Gurnard (Yellow)	12 3	5,528	G. J. Reynolds	Langland Bay, Wales	1976
Haddock	12 10 1	5,727	Sub. Lt. K. P. White	Falmouth Bay, Cornwall	1975
Hake	25 5 8	11,494	H. W. Steele	Belfast Lough, N. Ireland	1962
Halibut	212 4	96,270	J. A. Hewitt	off Dunnet Head, Highland	1975
John Dory	10 12	4,876	B. Perry	Porthallow, Cornwall	1963
Ling	57 2 8	25,924	H. Solomons	off Mevagissey, Cornwall	1975
Lumpsucker	14 3	6,435	W. J. Burgess	Felixstowe Beach, Suffolk	1970
Mackerel	5 6 8	2,452	S. Beasley	N. of Eddystone Lighthouse	1969
Megrim	3 12 8	1,715	Paul Christie	Gairloch, Wester Ross	1973
Monkfish	66 0	29,936	G. C. Chalk	Shoreham, West Sussex	1965
Mullet (Red)	3 10	1,644	J. E. Martel	St. Martin's, Guernsey	1967
Mullet (Thick Lipped)	10 1	4,564	P/O. P. C. Libby	Portland, Dorset	1952
Plaice	10 3 8	4,635	Master H. Gardiner	Longa Sound, Scotland	1974
Pollack	25 0	11,339	R. J. Hosking	off Eddystone Lighthouse	1972
Pouting	5 8	2,494	R. S. Armstrong	off Berry Head, Devon	1969
Ray (Spotted)	5 5 14	2,433	R. A. Croft	Falmouth Estuary, Cornwall	1976
Ray (Sting)	59 0	26,761	J. M. Buckley	Clacton-on-Sea, Essex	1952
Ray (Thornback)	38 0	17,236	J. Patterson	Rustington, East Sussex	1935
Rockling (Three bearded)	3 2	1,417	N. Docksey	off Portand Breakwater, Dorset	1976
Scad	3 4 8	1,488	D. O. Cooke	Mewstone, Plymouth	1971
Shad (Allis)	3 4 8	1,488	B. H. Sloane	Torquay, Devon	1964
Shad (Thwaite)	3 2	1,417	T. Hayward	Deal, Kent	1949
	3 2	1,417	S. Jenkins	Tor Bay, Devon	1954
Shark (Blue)	218 0	98,878	N. Sutcliffe	Looe, Cornwall	1959
Shark (Mako)	500 0	226,786	Mrs. J. Yallop	off Eddystone Lighthouse	1971
Shark (Porbeagle)	see world record list				
Shark (Thresher)	280 0	127,000	H. A. Kelly	Dungeness, Kent	1933
Skate (Common)	226 8	102,733	R. S. Macpherson	Dury Voe, Shetland	1970
Sole	4 3 8	1,913	R. Wells	off Redcliffe Beach, Dorset	1974
Spurdog	20 3	9,156	J. Newman	off Needles Lighthouse	1972
Tope	74 11	33,876	A. B. Harries	Caldy Island, Dyfed	1964
Tunny (Tuna bluefin)	851 0	385,989	L. Mitchell-Henry	Whitby, North Yorkshire	1933
Turbot	32 4	14,628	Derrick Dyer	off Plymouth, Devon	1976
Whiting	6 4	2,834	S. Dearman	West Bay, Bridport, Dorset	1977
Wrasse (Ballan)	8 6 6	3,808	R. W. Le Page	Bordeaux Beach, Guernsey, C.I.	1976

FRESHWATER FISH

Barbel	13 12	6,237	J. Day	Royalty Fishery, Christchurch, Dorset	1962
Bleak	0 3 15	0,111	D. Pollard	Staythorpe, Nottinghamshire	1971
Bream (Common)	12 14	5,840	G. J. Harper	Stour, Great Cornard, Suffolk	1971
Carp	44 0	19,957	Richard Walker	Redmire Pool, Hereford and Worcester	1952
Carp (Crucian)	5 10 8	2,565	G. Halls	near King's Lynn, Norfolk	1976
Chub	7 6	3,345	W. L. Warren	River Avon, Hampshire	1957
Dace	1 4 4	0,574	J. L. Gasson	Little Ouse, Thetford, Norfolk	1960
Eel	8 10	3,912	A. Dart	Hunstrete Lake, Somerset	1969
Gudgeon	0 4	0,118	M. Morris	Susworth Roach Ponds, Lincolnshire	1971
Gwyniad (Whitefish)	1 4	0,567	J. R. Williams	Llyn Tegid, Gwynedd	1965
Loch Lomond Powan	1 7	0,652	J. M. Ryder	Loch Lomond, Strathclyde/Central	1972
Perch	4 12	2,154	S. F. Baker	Oulton Broad, Suffolk	1962
Pike[1]	40 0	18,143	Peter D. Hancock	Horsey Mere, Norfolk	1967
Roach	4 1	1,842	Richard G. Jones	Gravel pits, Colwich, Notts.	1975
Rudd	4 8	2,041	Rev. E. C. Alston	Mere, near Thetford, Norfolk	1933
Ruffe	0 4	0,113	B. B. Poyner	River Stour, Warwickshire	1969
Salmon[2]	64 0	29,029	Miss G. W. Ballantyne	River Tay, Tayside	1922
Tench	10 1 2	4,567	L. W. Brown	Brick pit, Peterborough	1975
Trout (Brown)[3]	19 4 8	8,745	T. Chartres	Lower Lough Erne, N. Ireland	1974
Trout (Rainbow)	19 2	8,674	Roy W. Hopkins	Avington Trout Fisheries, Itchen Abbas, Hampshire	1977

[1] A pike of allegedly 52 lb. 23 kg was recovered when Whittlesea Mere, Cambridgeshire was drained in 1851. A pike of reputedly 72 lb. 32 kg 650 was landed from Loch Ken, Dumfries and Galloway, by John Murray in 1777.
[2] The 8th Earl of Home is recorded as having caught a 69¾ lb. 31 kg 638 specimen in the River Tweed in 1730. J. Wallace claimed a 67-pounder 30 kg at Barjarg, Dumfries and Galloway in 1812.
[3] In 1866 W. C. Muir caught a 39½ lb. 17 kg 916 specimen in Loch Awe, Strathclyde and in 1816 a 36 lb 16 kg specimen was reported from the R. Colne, near Watford, Hertfordshire.

IRISH RECORDS

(Selected from the complete list as ratified by the Irish Specimen Fish Committee to 1 Jan 1977)

Species SEA FISH	Weight lb. oz.	kg/g	Name of Angler	Location	Date
Angler Fish	71 8	32,431	Michael Fitzgerald	Cork (Cóbh) Harbour	5 July 1964
Bass	16 6	7,427	James McClelland	Causeway Coast	13 Nov. 1972

continued on p. 242

continued from p. 241

Species SEA FISH	Weight lb. oz.	kg/g	Name of Angler	Location	Date
Sea Bream (Red)	9 6	4,252	P. Maguire	Valentia, Kerry	24 Aug. 1963
Coalfish	24 7	11,084	J. E. Hornibrook	Kinsale, Cork	26 Aug. 1963
Cod	42 0	19,050	I. L. Stewart	Ballycotton, Cork	1921
Conger	72 0	32,658	J. Greene	Valentia, Kerry	June 1914
Dab	1 12½	0,807	Ian V. Kerr	Kinsale, Cork	10 Sept. 1963
Dogfish (Greater Spotted)	21 4	9,638	Drew Alexander	Mallin Head, Co. Donegal	3 Sept. 1975
Dogfish (Spur)	16 4	7,370	Crawford McIvor	Strangford Lough, Co. Down	20 June 1969
Flounder	4 3	1,899	J. L. McMonagle	Killala Bay, Co. Mayo	5 Aug. 1963
Garfish	3 10¼	1,651	Evan G. Bazzard	Kinsale, Cork	16 Sept. 1967
Gurnard (Grey)	3 1	1,389	Brendan Walsh	Rosslare Bay	21 Sept. 1967
Gurnard (Red)	3 9½	1,630	James Prescott	Belmullet, Co. Mayo	17 July 1968
Gurnard (Tub)	12 3½	5,542	Robert J. Seaman	Achill, Co. Mayo	8 Aug. 1973
Haddock	10 13½	4,918	F. A. E. Bull	Kinsale, Cork	15 July 1964
Hake	25 5½	11,495	Herbert W. Steele	Belfast Lough	28 Apr. 1962
Halibut	156 0	70,760	Frank Brogan	Belmullet, Co. Mayo	23 July 1972
John Dory	7 1	3,203	Stanley Morrow	Tory Island, Co. Donegal	6 Sept. 1970
Ling	46 8	21,092	Andrew J. C. Bull	Kinsale, Cork	26 July 1965
Mackerel	3 8	1,587	Roger Ryan	Clogherhead Pier, Co. Louth	1 July 1972
Monkfish	69 0	31,297	Mgr, Michael Fuchs	Westport, Co. Mayo	1 July 1958
Mullet (Grey)	7 12	3,515	Colm Quinn	Brittas Bay, Co. Wicklow	7 Sept. 1975
Plaice	10 8	4,762	James Stafford	Achill, Co. Mayo	3 Sept. 1973
Pollack	19 3	8,703	J. N. Hearne	Ballycotton, Cork	1904
Pouting	4 10	2,097	W. G. Pales	Ballycotton, Cork	1937
Ray (Blonde)	36 8	16,556	D. Minchin	Cork (Cóbh) Harbour	9 Sept. 1964
Ray (Sting)	51 0	23,133	John K. White	Kilfenora Strand, Fenet	8 Aug. 1970
Ray (Thornback)	37 0	16,782	M. J. Fitzgerald	Kinsale, Cork	28 May 1961
Shark (Blue)	206 0	93,440	J. L. McMonagle	Achill, Co. Mayo	7 Oct. 1959
Shark (Porbeagle)	365 0	165,561	Dr. M. O'Donel Browne	Keem Bay, Achill, Co. Mayo	28 Sept. 1932
Skate (Common)	221 0	100,243	T. Tucker	Ballycotton, Cork	1913
Skate (White)	165 0	74,842	Jack Stack	Clew Bay, Westport, Co. Mayo	7 Aug. 1966
Tope	60 12	27,555	Crawford McIvor	Strangford Lough, Co. Down	12 Sept. 1968
Turbot	26 8	12,020	J. F. Eldridge	Valentia, Kerry	1915
Whiting	4 8½	2,055	Eddie Boyle	Kinsale, Cork	4 Aug. 1969
Wrasse (Ballan)	7 6	3,345	Anthony J. King	Killybegs, Donegal	26 July 1964
FRESHWATER FISH					
Bream	11 12	5,329	A. Pike	River Blackwater, Co. Monaghan	July 1882
Carp	18 12	8,504	John Roberts	Abbey Lake	6 June 1958
Dace	1 2	0,510	John T. Henry	River Blackwater, Cappoquin	8 Aug. 1966
Eel (River)	5 15	2,693	Edmund Hawksworth	River Shannon, Clondra	25 Sept. 1968
Perch	5 8	2,494	S. Drum	Lough Erne	1946
Pike (River)[1]	42 0	19,050	M. Watkins	River Barrow	22 Mar. 1964
Roach	2 13½	1,289	Lawrie Robinson	River Blackwater, Cappoquin	11 Aug. 1970
	2 13½	1,289	Ronald Frost	River Blackwater, Cappoquin	29 Aug. 1972
Rudd	3 1	1,389	A. E. Biddlecombe	Kilglass Lake	27 June 1959
Rudd-Bream hybrid	5 13½	2,650	P. J. Dighton	River Shannon, Lanesboro, Co. Longford	12 Apr. 1975
Salmon[2]	57 0	25,854	M. Maher	River Suir	1874
Tench	7 13¼	3,550	R. Webb	River Shannon, Lanesboro, Co. Longford	25 May 1971
Brown Trout (Lake)[3]	26 2	11,850	William Meares	Lough Ennell	15 July 1894
Brown Trout (River)	20 0	9,071	Major Hugh Ll. Place	River Shannon, Corbally	22 Feb. 1957
Sea Trout	14 3	6,435	Dr. Eoin Bresnihan	Dooagh Beach, Achill, Co. Mayo	8 June 1973

[1] *A pike in excess of 92 lb. 41 kg is reputed to have been landed from the Shannon at Portumna, County Galway, in c. 1796.*

[2] *A 58 lb. 26 kg salmon was reported from the River Shannon in 1872 while one of 62 lb. 28 kg was taken in a net on the lower Shannon on 27 Mar. 1925.*

[3] *A 35½ lb. 16 kg 102 brown trout is reputed to have been caught at Turlaghvan near Tuam, in August 1738. "Pepper's Ghost", the 30 lb. 8 oz. 13 kg 834 fish caught by J. W. Pepper in Lough Derg in 1860 has now been shown to have been a salmon.*

ARCHERY

Earliest references

The discovery of stone arrow heads at Border Cave, Northern Natal, South Africa in deposits exceeding the Carbon 14 dating limit indicates the invention of the bow as *ante* 46,000 B.C. Archery developed as an organized sport at least as early as the 4th century A.D. The oldest archery body in the British Isles is the Royal Company of Archers, the Sovereign's bodyguard for Scotland, dating from 1676, though the Ancient Scorton Arrow meeting in North Yorkshire was first staged in 1673. The world governing body is the *Fédération Internationale de Tir à l'Arc* (FITA), founded in 1931.

World records

The world records for a single FITA Round are: men 1,316 points (possible 1,440) by Darrell Pace (U.S.A.) at Oxford, Ohio on 5–6 Aug. 1975, and women 1,282 points (possible 1,440) by Luann Ryon (U.S.A.) at Montreal, on 29–30 July 1976.

Highest Championship scores

There are no world records for Double FITA Rounds but the highest scores achieved in either a world or Olympic championship were: men, 2,571 points (possible 2,880) by Darrell Pace (U.S.A.) at the 1976 Olympic Games in Montreal, Canada, on 29–30 July 1976; and women, 2,515 points by Luann Ryon (U.S.A.) at Canberra, Australia, 11–12 Feb. 1977.

British records

York Round (6 dozen at 100 yds, 4 dozen at 80 yds and 2 dozen at 60 yds)—possible 1,296 pts.
Single Round, 1,108 John W. Snelling on 7 Sept. 1975.
Double Round, 2,150 David Pink at Oxford on 23–24 June 1976.
Hereford (Women) (6 dozen at 80 yds, 4 dozen at 60 yds and 2 dozen at 50 yds)—possible 1,296 pts.
Single Round, 1,118 Pauline M. Edwards at London on 26 Aug. 1973.
Double Round, 2,200 Pauline M. Edwards at Oxford, 27–28 June 1973.
FITA Round (Men) (3 dozen each at 90, 70, 50 and 30 m).
Single Round, 1,241 David Pink at Stoneleigh, Warwick, 22–23 May 1976.
Double Round, 2,406 David Pink at Stoneleigh, Warwick, 22–23 May 1976.
FITA Round (Women's) (3 dozen each at 70, 60, 50 and 30 m).
Single Round, 1,218, Barbara A. Gould (formerly Strickland) at Zagreb, Yugoslavia 24–25 Aug. 1974.
Double Round, 2,314 P. Conway at Stoneleigh, Warwick, 22–23 May 1976.

Most titles *World*

The greatest number of world titles (instituted 1931) ever won by a man is four by Hans Deutgen (Sweden) in 1947–50. The greatest number won by a woman is seven by Janina Spychajowa-Kurkowska (Poland) in 1931–34, 1936, 1939 and 1947. Oscar Kessels (Belgium) has participated in 21 world championships since 1931.

Most titles, *Olympic*

Hubert van Innis (1866–1961) won six gold and three silver

medals in archery events at the 1900 and 1920 Olympic Games.

Most titles *British*
The greatest number of British Championships is 12 by Horace Alfred Ford (1822–1880) in 1849–59 and 1867, and 23 by Alice Blanche Legh (1855–1948) in 1881, 1886–1892 1895, 1898–1900, 1902–09, 1913 and 1921–22. Miss Legh was inhibited from winning from 1882 to 1885—because her mother Piers Legh was Champion—and also for four further years 1915 to 1918 because there were no Championships held owing to the first World War.

Flight shooting
Sultan Selim III shot 1,400 Turkish *Pikes* or *gez* near Istanbul, Turkey in 1798. The equivalent is arguably between 953–972 yd *871–888 m*. The longest recorded distance ever shot is 1 mile 268 yd *1 854,40 m* in the unlimited footbow class by the professional Harry Drake (b. 7 May 1915) of Lakeside, California, U.S.A. at Ivanpah Dry Lake, California on 24 Oct. 1971. Bruce Odle (b. 13 July 1953) set the flight record for the handbow with 1,077 yd 3 in *985,05 m* at Wendover, Utah, U.S.A. on 11 Sept. 1976. Drake holds the crossbow flight record with 1,359 yds 2 ft 5 in *1 243,4 m* at Ivanpah Dry Lake on 14–15 Oct. 1967.

The British record (Men) is 695 yd 2½ in *635,57 m* by Alan Webster at York on 21 Apr. 1974 and (Women) 446 yd *407,82 m* by Monica Thorley at Burton Constable, nr Hull, Humberside in 1976.

Greatest draw
Gary Sentman, of Roseburg, Oregon, U.S.A. drew a longbow weighing a record 176 lb. *79,83 kg* to the maximum draw on the arrow of 28¼ in *72 cm* at Forksville, Penn., on 20 Sept. 1975.

Marathon
The highest recorded score over 24 hours by a pair of archers is 45,454 during 42 Portsmouth Rounds (60 arrows at 20 yds *18,28 m* with a 2 in *5 cm* diameter 10 ring) shot by Stan Kiehl and Greg Shumaker at the S. & R. Sports Haven, Greentown, Ohio, U.S.A. on 21–22 June 1975.

BADMINTON

Origins
The game was devised *c.* 1863 at Badminton Hall in Avon, the seat of the Dukes of Beaufort. The oldest club is the Newcastle Badminton Club formed as the Armstrong College Club on 24 Jan. 1900.

Thomas Cup
The International Championship or Thomas Cup (instituted 1948) has been won six times by Indonesia in 1957–58, 1960–61, 1963–64, 1969–70, 1972–73 and 1975–76.

Uber Cup
The Ladies International Championship or Uber Cup (instituted 1956) has been won three times by Japan (1966, 1969 and 1972), and the U.S.A. (1957, 1960 and 1963).

Inter County Championships
The most successful county has been Surrey with 19 wins between 1955 and 1975. The championships were instituted on 30 Oct. 1930.

Most titles
The men's singles in the All-England Championships (instituted 1899) have been won a record eight times by Rudy Hartono (Indonesia) (b. 1949) in 1968–74 and 1976. The greatest number of championships won (incl. doubles) is 21 by G. A. Thomas (later Sir George Alan Thomas, Bt.) (1881–1972) between 1903 and 1928. The women's title has been won ten times by Judy Hashman (*née* Devlin) (U.S.A.) (b. 1935) in 1954, 1957–58, 1960–64, 1966–67. She also equalled the greatest number of championships won of 17 by M. Lucas (later Mrs. King Adams) from 1899 to 1910.

Shortest game
In the 1969 Uber Cup in Jakarta, Indonesia, Noriko Takagi (later Mrs. Nakayama) (Japan) beat P. Tumengkol in 9 min.

Longest hit
Frank Rugani drove a shuttlecock 79 ft 8½ in *24,29 m* in tests at San Jose, California, U.S.A., on 29 Feb. 1964.

Marathon
The longest doubles marathon has been one of 318 hrs maintained by eight players from the Muslim Youth Association on 18–30 July 1974 at the Mill Lane Youth Centre, Newcastle-upon-Tyne, Tyne and Wear, England.

MOST INTERNATIONAL APPEARANCES		
	Times	Men
England	100	Anthony Derek Jordan, M.B.E., 1951 to 1970
Ireland	45	K. Carlisle, 1954 to 1970
Scotland	67	Robert S. McCoig, M.B.E., 1956 to 1976
Wales	43	David Colmer, 1964 to 1976
	Times	Women
England	65	Gillian M. Gilks (*née* Perrin), 1966 to 1977
Ireland	57	Yvonne Kelly, 1955 to 1976
Scotland	32	Christine Stewart (*née* Evans), 1970 to 1976
Wales	43	Angela Dickson, 1964 to 1976

BASEBALL

Earliest game
A woodcut of "Base-Ball" of English provenance dated 1744 is the earliest known reference. On 4 Feb. 1962, it was claimed in *Nedelya*, the weekly supplement to the Soviet newspaper *Izvestiya*, that "Beizbol" was an old Russian game. The earliest baseball game under the Cartwright (Alexander Joy Cartwright Jr. 1820–1892) rules was at Hoboken, New Jersey, U.S.A., on 19 June 1846, with the New York Nine beating the Knickerbockers 23–1 in four innings.

Highest batting average
The highest average in a career is .367 by Tyrus Raymond Cobb (1886–1961), the "Georgia Peach" of Augusta, Anniston, Detroit (1905–26) and Philadelphia (1927–28). During his career Ty Cobb made 2,244 runs from a record 4,191 hits made during a record 11,429 times at bat in a record 3,033 major league games. Lin Wen-Nsiung (Taiwan) is reported to have an average of .727.

Home runs *Most*
Henry Louis "Hank" Aaron (Atlanta Braves) (b. 5 Feb. 1934) surpassed the career home run record of George Herman "Babe" Ruth (1895–1948) when he struck his 715th homer at the Atlanta, Georgia stadium on 8 Apr. 1974. On his retirement in 1976 his lifetime total was 755. Babe Ruth's major league record for home runs in one year is 60 in 154 games between 15 Apr. and 30 Sept. 1927. Roger Eugene Maris (b.

All-England badminton champion in 1972, Noriko Takagi (Japan) holds the record for the shortest ever game. (*Press Association*)

Though Roger Maris set a season's homer record, the authorities decreed that the figure must have an asterisk, 61*, to differentiate from Babe Ruth's previous record achieved in less games. (*Syndication International*)

George Zaharias) (U.S.) (1914–56) at Jersey City, New Jersey, U.S.A. on 25 July 1931.

Fastest base runner
The fastest time for circling bases is 13.3 sec by Ernest Evar Swanson (1902–73) at Columbus, Ohio, in 1932, at an average speed of 18.45 m.p.h. *29,70 km/h.*

Pitching
The first "perfect game" (no hits, no runs, no walks) pitched in a World Series was by Don Larsen (New York Yankees) (b. 7 Aug. 1929) with 97 pitches (71 in the strike zone) against Brooklyn Dodgers on 8 Oct. 1956.

Fastest pitcher
The fastest pitcher in the world is Lynn Nolan Ryan (California Angels) (b. 31 Jan. 1947) who, on 20 Aug. 1974 at Anaheim Stadium, California, U.S.A., was measured to pitch at 100.9 m.p.h. *162,3 km/h.*

Highest earnings
The greatest earnings of a baseball player is $1,091,477 amassed by Babe Ruth between 1914 and 1938. On 31 Dec. 1974, Jim "Catfish" Hunter (b. 8 Apr. 1946) signed a contract with the New York Yankees worth $3.7 million over the following five years.

Record attendances and receipts
The World Series record attendance is 420,784 (six games with total receipts of $2,626,973.44) when the Los Angeles (ex-Brooklyn) Dodgers beat the Chicago White Sox 4–2 on 1–8 Oct. 1959. The single game record is 92,706 for the fifth game (receipts $552,774.77) at the Memorial Coliseum, Los Angeles, California, on 6 Oct. 1959. The record net receipts for a series has been $3,954,542 from a paid attendance of 363,149 who saw the Oakland A's beat the Cincinnati Reds 4–3 on 14–22 Oct. 1972. The highest seating capacity in a baseball stadium is 76,977 in the Cleveland Municipal Stadium, Ohio, U.S.A.

An estimated 114,000 spectators watched a game between Australia and an American Services team in a "demonstration" event during the Olympic Games at Melbourne, 1 Dec. 1956.

The all-time season record for attendances for both leagues has been 29,193,417 in 1971.

Youngest player
The youngest major league player of all time was the Cincinnati pitcher, Joseph Henry Nuxhall (b. 30 July 1928) who started his career in June, 1944, aged 15 years 10 months 11 days.

10 Sept. 1934) (New York Yankees) hit 61 homers in a 162-game schedule in 1961. Joshua Gibson (1911–1947) of Homestead Grays and Pittsburgh Crawfords, Negro League clubs, achieved a career total of 800 homers and 84 in one season, and in 1972 was elected to the Hall of Fame.

BATTING RECORDS (see also above)

Batting av., season	.438	Hugh Duffy	1894
Base hits, season	257	George Harold Sisler	1920
RBI's, season	190	Lewis Robert "Hack" Wilson	1930
RBI's, career	2,297	Henry Louis "Hank" Aaron	1954–76
Stolen bases, season	118	Louis Clark Brock	1974
Stolen bases, career	892	Tyrus Raymond "Ty" Cobb	1905–28
Runs, season	196	William Robert Hamilton	1894

PITCHING RECORDS

Games won, season	60	Charles Gardner Radbourn	1884
Games won, career	511	Denton True "Cy" Young	1890–1911
Strikeouts, season	383	Lynn Nolan Ryan	1973
Strikeouts, career	3,508	Walter Perry Johnson	1907–27
Shutouts, season	16	George W. Bradley	1876
	16	Grover Cleveland Alexander	1916
Shutouts, career	113	Walter Perry Johnson	1907–27
No-hit games, career	4	Sandford "Sandy" Koufax	1962, 63, 64, 65
	4	Lynn Nolan Ryan	1973 (2), 74, 75

Longest run
The longest home run ever measured was one of 618 ft *188,4 m* by Roy Edward "Dizzy" Carlyle (1900–56) in a minor league game at Emeryville Ball Park, California, U.S.A., on 4 July 1929. In 1919 Babe Ruth hit a 587 ft *178,9 m* homer in a Boston Red Sox *v.* New York Giants match at Tampa, Florida, U.S.A.

Longest throw
The longest throw (ball weighs 5–5¼ oz *141–148 g*) is 445 ft 10 in *135,88 m* by Glen Edward Gorbous (b. Canada 8 July 1930) on 1 Aug. 1957. The longest throw by a woman is 296 ft *90,2 m* by Mildred "Babe" Didrikson (later Mrs.

BASKETBALL
Origins
The game of "Pok-ta-Pok" was played in the 10th century B.C., by the Olmecs in Mexico, and closely resembled basketball in its concept. "Ollamalitzli" was a variation of this game played by the Aztecs in Mexico as late as the 16th century. If the solid rubber ball was put through a fixed stone ring the player was entitled to the clothing of all the spectators. Modern basketball was devised by the Canadian-born Dr. James A. Naismith (1861–1939) at the Training School of the International Y.M.C.A. College at Springfield, Massachusetts, U.S.A., in mid-December 1891. The first game played under modified rules was on 20 Jan. 1892. The game is now a global activity. The International Amateur Basketball Federation (F.I.B.A.) was founded in 1932, and the English Basket Ball Association was founded in 1936.

Most titles *Olympic*
The U.S.A. won all seven Olympic titles from the time the sport was introduced to the Games in 1936 until 1968, without losing a single match. In 1972 in Munich their run of 64 consecutive victories in matches in the Olympic Games was broken when they lost 50–51 to the U.S.S.R. in the Final match. They won their eighth title in 1976.

Most titles *World*
Brazil and the U.S.S.R. are the only countries to win the World Men's Championship (instituted 1950) on more than

one occasion. Brazil won in 1959 and 1963, the U.S.S.R. in 1967 and 1974. In 1975 the U.S.S.R. won the Women's Championship (instituted 1953) for the fifth consecutive time since 1959.

Most titles *European Cups*
The most European Champions Cup (instituted 1957) wins is five by Real Madrid, Spain, and Mobilgirgi (formerly Ignis) of Varese, Italy. The women's title has been won 16 times by Dangawa, Riga, U.S.S.R. The most wins in the European Nations Cup for men is 11 by the U.S.S.R., and in the Women's event 13 also by the U.S.S.R.

Most titles *British*
England and Scotland have each won five British Championship titles, out of the 12 competitions (now biennial) since the tournament was introduced in 1960.

Most titles *American Professional*
The most National Basketball Association titles (instituted 1947), played for between the leading professional teams in the United States, have been won by the Boston Celtics with 13 victories between 1957 and 1976.

Most titles *English National Cup*
The most English National Championship Cup wins (instituted 1936) have been by London Central Y.M.C.A., with eight wins in 1957–58, 1960, 1962–64, 1967 and 1969. On 6 Apr. 1974 Sutton and Crystal Palace beat Embassy All Stars in a record score for the final of 120–100.

Most titles *English Women's Cup*
Most English Women's titles (instituted 1965) have been won by the Malory Club, and Tigers (Dacorum) with four wins each.

Highest score *NBA match*
The highest aggregate score in an N.B.A. match is 316 in a match between the Philadelphia Warriors (169 points) and the New York Knickerbockers (147 points) at Hershey, Pennsylvania on 2 Mar. 1962, and in a match between the Cincinnati Royals (165 points) and the San Diego Rockets (151 points) on 12 Mar. 1970. In an A.B.A. match between the San Diego Conquistadors (176 points) and the New York Nets (166 points) on 14 Feb. 1975, the score totalled 342 points after four periods of overtime.

Highest score *International*
The highest score recorded in an international match is 164 by Romania against Wales (50) on 15 May 1975, in the European Men's Championship at Hagen, West Germany. The highest by a women's team is 153 by U.S.S.R. against Switzerland (25) on 4 June 1956 in the European Championships. The highest in a British Championship is 116 by England when beating Wales (60) on 29 Mar. 1975.

Highest score *United Kingdom*
The highest score recorded in a match is 250 by the Nottingham Y.M.C.A. Falcons *v.* Mansfield Pirates at Nottingham, England on 18 June 1974. It was a handicap competition and Mansfield received 120 points towards their total of 145.

Highest score *Individual*
Mats Wermelin, 13, (Sweden) scored all 272 points in a 272–0 win in a regional boys' tournament in Stockholm, Sweden on 5 Feb. 1974.

The highest single game score in an N.B.A. game is 100 points by Wilton Norman Chamberlain (b. 21 Aug. 1936) for Philadelphia *v.* New York on 2 Mar. 1962. The most in a college game is 150 points by Clarence Francis, of Rio Grande, Ohio in 1954.

The highest individual score in an English National League or Cup match is 57 points by Alan Bunting, of Magnet Wicksteed Metros (Romford) at Aycliffe, Co. Durham on 6 Mar. 1977.

Free throw expert, Florida's Ted St. Martin, who scored 1,704 times in a row.

Most points
Wilt Chamberlain, scored a career total of 31,419 points in N.B.A. matches between 1960–73. The record for the most points scored in a college season, is 4,065 by Travis Grant for Kentucky State in 1971–1972.

Tallest players
The tallest player of all time has been Emili Rached of Brazil, who competed in the 1971 Pan American Games when measuring 233 cm *7 ft 7⅝ in.* The tallest woman player is Iuliana Semenova (U.S.S.R.) (b. 1951) reputed to be 7 ft 2 in *2,18 m* tall and weighing 281 lb. *127,4 kg.* The tallest British player has been the 7 ft 5¼ in *226,6 cm* tall Christopher Greener (see p. 8) of London Latvians whose International debut for England was *v.* France on 17 Dec. 1969.

Most expensive

In 1976 the Philadelphia 76ers contracted to pay Julius ("Dr. J") Erving (b. 22 Feb. 1950) $600,000 a year for six years, making him the sport's highest paid player.

Most accurate

The greatest goal shooting demonstration has been by Ted St. Martin of Jacksonville, Florida, who, on 28 Feb. 1975, scored 1,704 consecutive free throws. In a 24 hour period, 31 May to 1 June 1975 Fred L. Newman of San José, California, U.S.A. scored 12,874 baskets out of 13,116 throws (98.15% accuracy). John T. Sebastian holds the record for consecutive blindfold free throws with 63 straight at Maine Township High School East, Park Ridge, Illinois on 18 May 1972.

Longest recorded goal

The longest recorded field goal in a match is a measured 86 ft *26,22 m* by Barry Hutchings at Sutherlin High School, Sutherlin, Oregon on 22 March 1976. In practice in 1953, Larry Slinkard at Arlington Heights High School, Illinois, scored with a shot from 88 ft *26,82 m*.

Most travelled team

The Harlem Globetrotters (U.S.A.) have travelled over 6,000,000 miles *9 600 000 km*, visited 94 countries on six continents, and have been watched by an estimated 80,000,000. The team was founded by the London-born Abraham M. Saperstein (1903–66) of Chicago, Illinois, U.S.A., and their first game was played at Hinckley, Illinois on 7 Jan. 1927. In the fifty years since then the team have recorded over 12,000 victories, with fewer than 350 defeats, but they have been entertainers rather than competitive players for much of their existence.

Largest ever gate

The Harlem Globetrotters (U.S.A.) played an exhibition in front of 75,000 in the Olympic Stadium, West Berlin, Germany, in 1951. The largest indoor basketball attendance was at the Astrodome, Houston, Texas, U.S.A., where 52,693 watched the match between University of Houston and University of California at Los Angeles (U.C.L.A.), on 20 Jan. 1968.

Marathon

The longest recorded marathon is 66 hr 2 min by two teams of five (no substitutes) from Valparaiso University, Indiana, U.S.A., 31 Mar.–3 Apr. 1977.

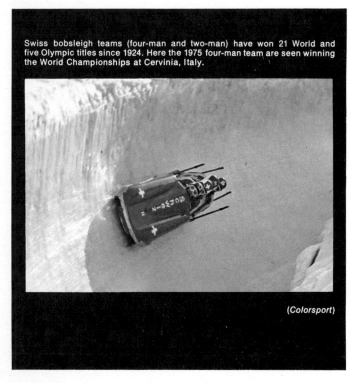

Swiss bobsleigh teams (four-man and two-man) have won 21 World and five Olympic titles since 1924. Here the 1975 four-man team are seen winning the World Championships at Cervinia, Italy.

(Colorsport)

In the nineteenth century "The Billiard Table" caught the attention of social caricaturist Thomas Rowlandson. (*The Mansell Collection*)

BILLIARDS

Earliest mention

The earliest recorded mention of billiards was in France in 1429, and it was mentioned in England in 1588 in inventories of the Duke of Norfolk's Howard House and the Earl of Leicester's property at Wanstead House, Redbridge, Greater London. The first recorded public billiards room in England was the Piazza, Covent Garden, London, in the early part of the 19th century. Rubber cushions were introduced in 1835 and slate beds in 1836.

Most titles *Professional*

The greatest number of world championship titles (instituted 1870) won by one player is eight by John Roberts, Jnr. (England) in 1870 (twice), 1871, 1875 (twice), 1877 and 1885 (twice). The greatest number of United Kingdom titles (instituted 1934) won by any player is seven (1934–39 and 1947) by Joe Davis, O.B.E. (b. 15 Apr. 1901) (England), who also won four world titles (1928–30 and 1932) before the series was discontinued in 1934. William F. Hoppe (U.S.A.) (1887–1959) won 51 "world" titles in the United States variant of the game between 1906 and 1952.

Most titles *Amateur*

The record for world amateur titles is four by Robert Marshall (Australia) in 1936, 1938, 1951 and 1962. The greatest number of English Amateur Championships (instituted 1888) ever won is eight by Sidney H. Fry between 1893 and 1925, A. Leslie Driffield (1952–54, 1957–59, 1962 and 1967) and Norman Dagley (1965–66, 1970–75). The record number of women's titles is nine by Maureen Baynton (*née* Barrett) between 1955 and 1968.

Highest breaks

Tom Reece (1873–1953) made an unfinished break of 499,135, including 249,152 cradle cannons (two points each), in 85 hrs 49 min against Joe Chapman at Burroughes' Hall, Soho Square, London, between 3 June and 6 July 1907. This was not recognized because press and public were not continuously present. The highest certified break made by the anchor cannon is 42,746 by W. Cook (England) from 29 May to 7 June 1907. The official world record under the then baulk-line rule is 1,784 by Joe Davis, O.B.E. in the United Kingdom Championship on 29 May 1936. Walter Lindrum O.B.E. (Australia) (1898–1960) made an official break of 4,137 in 2 hrs 55 min against Joe Davis at Thurston's on 19–20 Jan. 1932, before the baulk-line rule was in force. Davis has an unofficial personal best of 2,502 (mostly pendulum cannons) in a match against Tom Newman (1894–1943) (England) in Manchester in 1930. The amateur record is 859 by Mohammed Lafir (Sri Lanka) in the world amateur championships in Bombay, India on 5 Dec. 1973.

Fastest century

Walter Lindrum, O.B.E. of Australia made an unofficial 100 break in 27.5 sec in Australia on 10 Oct. 1952. His official record is 100 in 46.0 sec set in Sydney in 1941.

BAR BILLIARDS

Highest scoring rate

Thomas Morrison Clayton of Earlsfield, Greater London scored 11,700 in 10 min on a timed table at the Greyhound, Battersea High Street on 18 June 1974. The record scoring rate in a league match has been 24,590 in 21 min (1,170.9 per min) by Tegid Hughes (Bold Forester) at the "Sportsmans Rest", Portsmouth on 24 Sept. 1969.

Marathon

The duration record for bar billiards is 262 hours by a team of four from the "Five Bells", Colne Engaine, Essex ending on 5 Aug. 1975.

POOL

Pool or championship pocket billiards with numbered balls began to become standardized *c.* 1890. The greatest exponents were Ralph Greenleaf (U.S.A.) (b. 1899 d. 15 Mar. 1950) won the "world" professional title 19 times (1919–1937) and William Mosconi (U.S.A.) who dominated the game from 1941–1957.

The greatest number of balls pocketed in 24 hours is 8,133 (a rate of one per 10.62 secs) by Michael Hendrickson at Family Billiards, Las Vegas, Nevada, U.S.A. on 15–16 Apr. 1977.

Marathon

The longest recorded game is by four players with 393 hr at the "Bechers", Sale, Greater Manchester, 30 Mar.–15 Apr. 1977. (In future this category will only apply to a two-man record). The longest game by two players is 101 hr by Mike Hammer and Richard Becker of New York, U.S.A., on 10–14 Feb. 1976.

3 CUSHION

This pocketless variation dates back to 1878. The world governing body, the *Union Mondiale de Billiard* (U.M.B.) was formed in 1928. The most successful exponent spanning the pre and post international era from 1906–1952 was Willie Hoppe who won 51 billiards championships in all forms. Most U.M.B. titles have been won by Raymond Ceulemans (Belgium) with 11 consecutive (1963–73) with a peak average of 1,479 in 1973, and a twelfth title in 1976.

BOBSLEIGH

Origins

The oldest known sledge is dated *c.* 6500 B.C. and came from Heinola, southern Finland. Modern world championships were inaugurated in 1924. Four-man bobs were included in the first Winter Olympic Games at Chamonix in 1924 and two-man boblets from the third Games at Lake Placid, U.S.A., in 1932.

Most titles *Olympic*

The Olympic four-man bob title has been won four times by Switzerland (1924, 1936, 1956 and 1972). The U.S.A. (1932, 1936), Italy (1956, 1968) and West Germany (1952 and 1972) have won the Olympic boblet event twice. The most medals won by an individual is six (two gold, two silver, two bronze) by Eugenio Monti (Italy) (b. 23 Jan. 1928) from 1956 to 1968.

Most titles *World*

The world four-man bob title has been won 12 times by Switzerland (1924, 1936, 1939, 1947, 1954–57, 1971–73 and 1975). Italy won the two-man title 14 times (1954, 1956–63, 1966, 1968–69, 1971 and 1975). Eugenio Monti has been a member of eleven world championship crews.

TOBOGGANING

Cresta Run

The word toboggan comes from the Micmac American Indian word *tobaakan*. The oldest toboggan club in the world is the St. Moritz Tobogganing Club, Switzerland, founded in 1887. It is the home of the Cresta Run, which dates from 1884 and the introduction of the skeleton one-man racing toboggan. On the 3,977 ft *1212,25 m* long Cresta Run the record is 53.24 sec (av. 50.92 m.p.h. *81,96 km/h*) by Poldi

Berchtold of Switzerland in Jan. 1975. The record from the Junction (2,913 ft *888 m*) is 42.96 sec, also by Berchtold in Jan. 1975. Momentary speeds of 90 m.p.h. *145 km/h* are attained.

The greatest number of wins in the Cresta Run Grand National (inst. 1885) is eight by the 1948 Olympic champion Nino Bibbia (Italy) (b. 9 Sept. 1924) in 1960–64, 1966, 1968 and 1973. The greatest number of wins in the Cresta Run Curzon Cup (inst. 1910) is eight by Bibbia in 1950, 1957–58, 1960, 1962–64, and 1969, who hence won the Double in 1960 1962 and 1963–64. The greatest number of descents made in a season is 7,832 during 1976.

LUGEING

In lugeing the rider adopts a sitting, as opposed to a prone position. It was largely developed by British tourists at Klosters, Switzerland, from 1883. The first European championships were at Reichenberg, East Germany, in 1914 and the first world championships at Oslo, Norway, in 1953. The International Luge Federation was formed in 1957. Lugeing became an Olympic sport in 1964.

Most titles *World and Olympic*

The most successful rider in the world championships is Thomas Köhler (East Germany) (b. 25 June 1940), the only double Olympic gold medallist, who won the single-seater title in 1962, 1964 (Olympic), 1966 and 1967 and shared the two seater title in 1967 and 1968 (Olympic). In the women's championship Margit Schumann (East Germany) (b. 14 Sept. 1952) has won five times, in 1973–75, 1976 (Olympic) and 1977.

Highest speed

The fastest luge run is at Krynica, Poland, where speeds of more than 80 m.p.h. *128 km/h* have been recorded.

BOWLING (TENPIN)

Origins

The ancient German game of nine-pins was exported to the United States in the early 17th century. In about 1845 the Connecticut and New Haven State Legislatures prohibited the game so a tenth pin was added to evade the ban; but there is some evidence of ten pins being used in Suffolk about 300 years ago.

In the United States there were 8,607 bowling establishments with 143,380 bowling lanes and 65,000,000 bowlers in 1976. The world's largest bowling centre is the Tōkyō World Lanes Centre, Japan with 252 lanes. The largest in Europe is the Nottingham Bowl at Nottingham, England, where the game was introduced in 1960, with 48 lanes on two floors (24 on each floor).

World championships

The world (Fédération Internationale des Quilleurs) championships were instituted in 1954. The highest pinfall in the individual men's event is 5,963 (in 28 games) by Ed Luther (U.S.) at Milwaukee, Wisconsin, in 1971. In the women's championships (instituted 1963) the record is 4,615 pins (in 24 games) by Annedore Haefker (West Germany) at Tolworth, Surrey in 1975.

Highest scores *World*

The highest individual score for three sanctioned games (possible 900) is 886 by Albert "Allie" Brandt of Lockport, New York, U.S.A., on 25 Oct. 1939. The record by a woman is 818 by Bev Ortner in Galva, Iowa, U.S.A. in 1968. The record for consecutive strikes in sanctioned match play is 33 by John Pezzin (b. 1930) at Toledo, Ohio, U.S.A. on 4 Mar. 1976. The highest number of sanctioned 300 games is 26 (till 1975) by Elvin Mesger of Sullivan, Missouri, U.S.A. The maximum 900 for a three-game series has been recorded three times in unsanctioned games—by Leo Bentley at Lorain, Ohio, U.S.A., on 26 Mar. 1931; by Joe Sargent at Rochester, New York State, U.S.A., in 1934, and by Jim Margie in Philadelphia, Pennsylvania, U.S.A., on 4 Feb. 1937. Such series must have consisted of 36 consecutive strikes (*i.e.* all pins down with one ball).

The highest average for a season attained in sanctioned competition is 239 by Jim Lewis, of Schenectady, N.Y., U.S.A., for 88 games in 1975–76.

Highest scores *Great Britain*
The United Kingdom record for a three-game series is 775 by Geoffrey Liddiard at Harrow, Greater London on 3 Oct. 1971. The record score for a single game is 300, first achieved by Albert Kirkham (b. 1931) of Burslem, Staffordshire, on 5 Dec. 1965, which has since been equalled on several occasions. The best by a woman is 299 by Carole Cuthbert at the Airport Bowl, West London on 16 Mar. 1972. The three-game series record for a woman player is 724 by Joyce Presland at the Humber Bowl, Ilkeston, Derby on 8 Oct. 1974.

Longest career
William H. Bailey (b. 4 Jan. 1891) has been bowling for 70 consecutive years in the Hamilton City Ten Pin League, Ontario, Canada.

Marathon
Thomas Mogavero of Leroy, New York, U.S.A., bowled for 130 hrs 50 min on 22–28 Oct. 1975. He bowled 861 games with a 16 lb. ball. Richard Dewey, 46, of Omaha, Nebraska, bowled 1,472 consecutive games in 114½ hours, 5–10 June 1975.

SKITTLES
Hood skittles
The highest hood skittle score in 24 hr is 107,487 pins by 12 players from the Plume of Feathers, Daventry, Northamptonshire, on 19–20 Mar. 1976.

Table skittles
The highest score claimed in 24 hr is 148,048 skittles by 12 players from the Alleyn Old Boys Athletic Club, Herne Hill, Greater London, on 20–21 Nov. 1976.

Nine-pin marathon
The duration record for knocking down skittles (9-pins) is 120 hr by seven skittlers from the Rotaract Club of Bristol North-West, Avon, England ending on 4 May 1977.

BOWLS
OUTDOOR
Origins
Bowls can be traced back to at least the 13th century in England. The Southampton Town Bowling was formed in 1299. A green dating back to 1294 is claimed by the Chesterfield Bowling Club. After falling into disrepute, the game was rescued by the bowlers of Scotland who, headed by W. W. Mitchell, framed the modern rules in 1848–49.

Most titles *World*
In the inaugural World Championship held in Sydney, Australia in October 1966 the singles title was won by David John Bryant M.B.E. (b. 1931) (England) and the team title (Leonard Cup) by Australia. In the second Championships at Worthing in 1972 the singles was won by Malwyn Evans (Wales) and Scotland won the Leonard Cup. At Johannesburg, South Africa, in February 1976, the South African team achieved an unprecedented clean sweep of all four titles and the Leonard Cup.

Most titles *International Championship*
In the annual International Championships (instituted 1903) Scotland have won 31 times to England's 19. The most consecutive wins are 11 by Scotland from 1965 to 1975.

Most titles *English*
The record number of English Bowls Association (founded 8 June 1903) championships is 14 won or shared by David Bryant, M.B.E., including six singles, three pairs wins (1965, 1969 and 1974), a triples win (1966), who uniquely was involved in all four titles with four rinks or fours championships (1957, 1968, 1969 and 1971). He has also won six British Isles titles (four singles, one pairs, one fours) in the period 1957–74.

Most international appearances
The greatest number of international appearances by any bowler is 78 reached by Syd Thompson for Ireland in 1973.

Oldest player
Tom Fatherson (1870–1975) (Long Beach Club) was still playing daily in California until two months before he died aged 104 yr 6 months in May 1975.

Marathon
The most protracted bowls marathon has been one of 58 hr by a fours team, playing against 13 other teams, from the Magazine B.C., Wallasey, Merseyside, 3–5 June 1977.

INDOOR
The English Indoor Bowling Association became an autonomous body in 1971. Prior to that it was part of the English Bowling Association.

Most titles
The four-corner international championship was first held in 1936. England have won most titles with 16 wins. The National Singles title (inst. 1960) has been won most often by David Bryant M.B.E. with six wins (1960, 1966, 1971–3, 1975).

Highest score
The highest score in a British International match is 52 by Scotland v. Wales (3) at Teeside in 1972.

Marathon
Two fours teams played for 60 hours 4 min at Abergavenny Leisure Centre, Gwent, on 28–30 May 1976.

BOXING
Earliest references
Boxing with gloves was depicted on a fresco from the Isle of Thera, Greece which has been dated 1520 B.C. The earliest prize-ring code of rules was formulated in England on 16 Aug. 1743 by the champion pugilist Jack Broughton (1704–1789), who reigned from 1729 to 1750. Boxing, which had, in 1867, come under the Queensberry Rules formulated for John Sholto Douglas, 9th Marquess of Queensberry (1844–1900) was not established as a legal sport in Britain until after the ruling, R. v. Roberts and Others, of Mr. Justice Grantham, following the death of Billy Smith (Murray Livingstone) as the result of a fight on 24 Apr. 1901.

Longest fights
The longest recorded fight with gloves was between Andy Bowen of New Orleans (k. 1894) and Jack Burke in New Orleans, Louisiana, U.S.A., on 6–7 Apr. 1893. The fight lasted 110 rounds and 7 hr and 19 min from 9.15 p.m. to 4.34 a.m., but was declared a no contest when both men were unable to continue. The longest recorded bare knuckle fight was one of 6 hr 15 min between James Kelly and Jack Smith at Fiery Creek, Dalesford, Victoria, Australia on 3 Dec. 1855. The longest bare knuckle fight in Britain was one of 6 hr 3 min (185 rounds) between Bill Hayes and Mike Madden at Edenbridge, Kent, on 17 July 1849. The greatest recorded number of rounds is 276 in 4 hr 30 min when Jack Jones beat Patsy Tunney in Cheshire in 1825.

Shortest fights
There is a distinction between the quickest knock-out and the shortest fight. A knock-out in 10½ sec (including a 10 sec count) occurred on 26 Sept. 1946, when Al Couture struck Ralph Walton while the latter was adjusting a gum shield in his corner at Lewiston, Maine, U.S.A. If the time was accurately taken it is clear that Couture must have been more than half-way across the ring from his own corner at the opening bell. The shortest fight on record appears to be one in a Golden Gloves tournament at Minneapolis, Minnesota, U.S.A., on 4 Nov. 1947 when Mike Collins floored Pat Brownson with the first punch and the contest was stopped, without a count, four secs after the bell.

The fastest officially timed knock-out in British boxing is 11 sec (including a doubtless fast 10 sec count) when Jack Cain beat Harry Deamer, both of Notting Hill, Greater London at the National Sporting Club on 20 Feb. 1922.

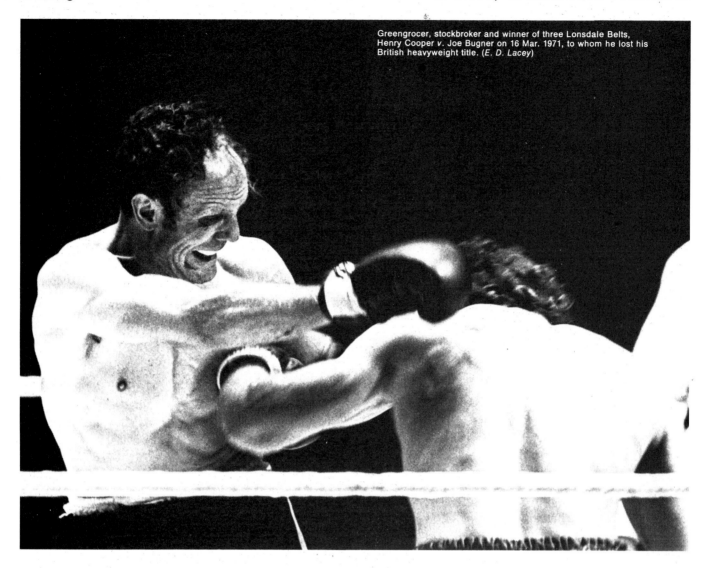

Greengrocer, stockbroker and winner of three Lonsdale Belts, Henry Cooper v. Joe Bugner on 16 Mar. 1971, to whom he lost his British heavyweight title. (E. D. Lacey)

The shortest world heavyweight title fight occurred when Tommy Burns (b. Noah Brusso) (1881–1955) of Canada knocked out Jem Roche in 1 min 28 sec in Dublin, Ireland, on 17 Mar. 1908. The duration of the fight between Cassius Clay (b. Louisville, Kentucky, U.S.A., 17 Jan. 1942 who later took the name Muhammed Ali Haj) and Charles "Sonny" Liston (1932–1970) at Lewiston, Maine, U.S.A., on 25 May 1965 was 1 min 52 sec (including the count) as timed from the video tape recordings, despite a ringside announcement giving a time of 1 min. The shortest world title fight was when Al McCoy knocked out George Chip in 45 sec for the middleweight crown in New York on 7 Apr. 1914. The shortest ever British title fight was one of 40 sec (including the count), when Dave Charnley knocked out David "Darkie" Hughes in a lightweight championship defence in Nottingham on 20 Nov. 1961.

Most British titles

The most defences of a British heavyweight title is 14 by "Bombardier" Billy Wells (b. 31 Aug. 1889–1967) from 1911 to 1919. The only British boxer to win three Lonsdale Belts outright has been Henry William Cooper, O.B.E. (b. Camberwell, London, 3 May 1934), heavyweight champion (1959–69, 1970–71). He retired after losing to Joe Bugner (b. Hungary, 13 Mar. 1950), having held the British heavyweight title from 12 Jan. 1959 to 28 May 1969 and from 24 Mar. 1970 to 16 Mar. 1971.

Tallest

The tallest boxer to fight professionally was Gogea Mitu (b. 1914) of Romania in 1935. He was 7 ft 4 in 223 cm and weighed 23 st. 5 lb. 148 kg (327 lb.). John Rankin, who won

a fight in New Orleans, Louisiana, U.S.A., in November 1967, was reputedly also 7 ft 4 in 223 cm.

Longest career

The heavyweight Jem Mace (G.B.), known as "the gypsy" (1831–1910), had a career lasting 35 years from 1855 to 1890, but there were several years in which he had only one fight. Bobby Dobbs (U.S.A.) (1858–1930) is reported to have had a 39 yr career from 1875 to 1914. Walter Edgerton, the "Kentucky Rosebud", knocked out John Henry Johnson aged 45 in four rounds at the Broadway A.C., New York City, N.Y., U.S.A., on 4 Feb. 1916, when aged 63.

Most fights

The greatest recorded number of fights in a career is 1,024 by Bobby Dobbs (U.S.A.) (see above). Abraham Hollandersky, alias Abe the Newsboy (U.S.A.) is reputed to have had up to 1,309 fights from 1905 to 1918, but many of them were exhibition bouts.

Most fights without loss

Hal Bagwell, a lightweight, of Gloucester, England, was reputedly undefeated in 180 consecutive fights, of which only five were draws, between 15 Aug. 1938 and 29 Nov. 1948. His record of fights in the war-time period (1939–46), is however very sketchy. He never contested a British title. Of boxers with complete records Packey McFarland (1888–1936) had 97 fights in 1905–1915 without a defeat.

Most knock-outs

The greatest number of finishes classed by the rules prevailing as "knock-outs" in a career (1936 to 1963) is 141 by

Archie Moore (b. Archibald Lee Wright, Collinsville, Illinois, U.S.A., 13 Dec. 1913 or 1916). The record for consecutive K.O.'s is 44, set by Lamar Clark of Utah at Las Vegas, Nevada, U.S.A., on 11 Jan. 1960. He knocked out six in one night (five in the first round) at Bingham, Utah, on 1 Dec. 1958.

Largest purse
The greatest purse won is a reported $6,500,000 by Muhammad Ali Haj for his heavyweight title fight against Ken Norton (U.S.A.) in the Yankee Stadium, New York on 28 Sept. 1976.

Highest bare knuckle stake
The largest stake ever fought for in this era was $22,500 *then* £4,633 in the 27-round fight between Jack Cooper and Wolf Bendoff at Port Elizabeth, South Africa on 29 July 1889.

Highest earnings in career
The largest known fortune ever made in a fighting career is an estimated $49¾ million amassed by Muhammad Ali to July 1977.

Attendances *Highest*
The greatest paid attendance at any boxing fight has been 120,757 (with a ringside price of $27.50) for the Tunney *v.* Dempsey world heavyweight title fight at the Sesquicentennial Stadium, Philadelphia, Pennsylvania, U.S.A., on 23 Sept. 1926. The indoor record is 37,321 at the Clay *v.* Ernie Terrell fight in the Astrodome, Houston, Texas, on 6 Feb. 1967. The British attendance record is 82,000 at the Len Harvey *v.* Jock McAvoy fight at White City, London, on 10 July 1939.

The highest non-paying attendance is 135,132 at the Tony Zale *v.* Billy Pryor fight at Juneau Park, Milwaukee, Wisconsin, U.S.A., on 18 Aug. 1941.

Attendances *Lowest*
The smallest attendance at a world heavyweight title fight was 2,434 at the Clay *v.* Liston fight at Lewiston, Maine, U.S.A., on 25 May 1965.

WORLD HEAVYWEIGHT CHAMPIONS
Earliest title fight
The first world heavyweight title fight, with gloves and three min rounds, was that between John Lawrence Sullivan (1858–1918) and "Gentleman" James J. Corbett (1866–1933) in New Orleans, Louisiana, U.S.A., on 7 Sept. 1892. Corbett won in 21 rounds.

Longest and shortest reigns
The longest reign of any world heavyweight champion is 11 years 8 months and 7 days by Joe Louis (b. Joseph Louis Barrow, Lafayette, Alabama, 13 May 1914), from 22 June 1937, when he knocked out James J. Braddock in the eighth round at Chicago, Illinois, U.S.A., until announcing his retirement on 1 Mar. 1949. During his reign Louis made a record 25 defences of his title. The shortest reign was by Primo Carnera (1906–67) (Italy) for 350 days from 29 June 1933 to 14 June 1934. However, if the disputed title claim of Marvin Hart is allowed, his reign from 3 July 1905 to 23 Feb. 1906 was only 235 days.

Oldest and youngest
The oldest man to win the heavyweight crown was Jersey Joe Walcott (b. Arnold Raymond Cream, 31 Jan. 1914 at Merchantville, New Jersey, U.S.A.) who knocked out Ezzard Mack Charles (1921–1975) on 18 July 1951 in Pittsburgh, Pennsylvania, when aged 37 years 168 days. Walcott was the oldest holder at 38 years 7 months 23 days losing his title to Rocky Marciano (1923–69) on 23 Sept. 1952. The youngest age at which the world title has been won is 21 years 331 days by Floyd Patterson (b. Waco, North Carolina, 4 Jan. 1935). After the retirement of Marciano, Patterson won the vacant title by beating Archie Moore in five rounds in Chicago, Illinois, U.S.A., on 30 Nov. 1956.

Most recaptures
Patterson and Muhammad Ali Haj are the only two men to

regain the heavyweight championship. Patterson defeated Ingemar Johansson (Sweden) on 20 June 1960 having lost to him on 26 June 1959. Muhammad Ali defeated George Foreman on 30 Oct. 1974 having been stripped of the title by the world boxing authorities on 28 Apr. 1967.

Undefeated
Rocky Marciano (b. Rocco Francis Marchegiano) (1923–1969) is the only world heavyweight champion to have been undefeated during his entire career (1947–56).

Heaviest and lightest
The heaviest world champion was Primo Carnera of Italy, the "Ambling Alp", who won the title from Jack Sharkey in six rounds in New York City, N.Y., U.S.A., on 29 June 1933. He scaled 267 lb. *121 kg* for this fight but his peak weight was 270 lb. *122 kg*. He had an expanded chest measurement of 53 in *134 cm*, the longest reach at 85½ in *217 cm* (finger tip to finger tip) and also the largest fists with a 14¾ in *37 cm* circumference. The lightest champion was Robert James (Bob) Fitzsimmons (1863–1917), from Helston, Cornwall, England, who at a weight of 167 lb. *75 kg*, won the title by knocking out James Corbett in 14 rounds at Carson City, Nevada, U.S.A., on 17 Mar. 1897.

The greatest differential in a world title fight was 86 lb. *39 kg* between Carnera (270 lb. *122 kg*) and Tommy Loughran (184 lb. *83 kg*) of the U.S.A., when the former won on points at Miami, Florida, U.S.A., on 1 Mar. 1934.

Tallest and shortest
The tallest world champion according to measurements by the Physical Education Director of the Hemingway Gymnasium, Harvard University, was Carnera at 6 ft 5.4 in *196,59 cm* although he was widely reported and believed to be up to 6 ft 8½ in *204 cm*. Jess Willard, who won the title in 1915, often stated to be 6 ft 6¼ in *199 cm* was in fact 6 ft 5.25 in *196,21 cm*. The shortest was Tommy Burns of Canada, world champion from 23 Feb. 1906 to 26 Dec. 1908, who stood 5 ft 7 in *170 cm* and weighed 179 lb. *81 kg*.

WORLD CHAMPIONS (any weight)
Longest and shortest reign
Joe Louis's heavyweight duration record of 11 years 252 days stands for all divisions. The shortest reign has been 54 days by the French featherweight Eugène Criqui (1893–1977) from 2 June to 26 July 1923. The disputed flyweight champion Emile Pladner (France) (b. 2 Sept. 1906) reigned only 47 days from 2 Mar. to 18 Apr. 1929, as did also the disputed featherweight champion Dave Sullivan, from 26 Sept. to 11 Nov. 1898.

Youngest and oldest
The youngest age at which any world championship has been won is 17 years 180 days by Wilfredo Benitez (b. 8 Sept. 1958) of Puerto Rico, who won the W.B.A. light welterweight title in San Juan, P.R., on 6 Mar. 1976. The oldest world champion was Archie Moore who was recognized as a light heavyweight champion up to 10 Feb. 1962 when his title was removed. He was then believed to be between 45 and 48. Bob Fitzsimmons had the longest career of any official world titleholder with over 32 years from 1882 to 1914. He won his last world title aged 40 years 183 days in San Francisco, California on 25 Nov. 1903. He was an amateur from 1880 to 1882.

Longest fight
The longest world title fight (under Queensberry Rules) was that between the lightweights Joe Gans (1874–1910), of the U.S.A., and Oscar Matthew "Battling" Nelson (1882–1954), the "Durable Dane", at Goldfield, Nevada, U.S.A., on 3 Sept. 1906. It was terminated in the 42nd round when Gans was declared the winner on a foul.

Most recaptures
The only boxer to win a world title five times at one weight is "Sugar" Ray Robinson (b. Walker Smith, Jr., in Detroit, 3 May 1920) of the U.S.A., who beat Carmen Basilio (U.S.A.) in the Chicago Stadium on 25 Mar. 1958, to regain the world middleweight title for the fourth time. The

other title wins were over Jake LaMotta (U.S.A.) in Chicago on 14 Feb. 1951, Randolph Turpin (United Kingdom) in New York on 12 Sept. 1951, Carl "Bobo" Olson (U.S.A.) in Chicago on 9 Dec. 1955, and Gene Fullmer (U.S.A.) in Chicago on 1 May 1957. The record number of title bouts in a career is 33 or 34, at bantam and featherweight, by George Dixon (1870–1909), *alias* "Little Chocolate", of Canada, between 1890 and 1901.

Greatest weight span

The only man to hold world titles at three weights *simultaneously* was Henry "Homicide Hank" Armstrong (b. 12 Dec. 1912), now the Rev. Henry Jackson, of the U.S.A., at featherweight, lightweight and welterweight from August to December 1938.

Greatest "tonnage"

The greatest "tonnage" recorded in any fight is 700 lb. *317 kg* when Claude "Humphrey" McBride (Oklahoma) 340 lb. *154 kg* knocked out Jimmy Black (Houston), who weighed 360 lb. *163 kg* in the third round at Oklahoma City on 1 June 1971. The greatest "tonnage" in a world title fight was 488¾ lb. *221 kg 690*, when Carnera, then 259¼ lb. *117 kg 590* fought Paolino Uzcuden 229½ lb. *104 kg 090* of Spain in Rome on 22 Oct. 1933.

Smallest champion

The smallest man to win any world title has been Pascual Perez (b. Mendoza, Argentina, 4 Mar. 1926) who won the flyweight title in Tōkyō on 26 Nov. 1954 at 107 lb. *48 kg 500* and 4 ft 11½ in *1,51 m*. Jimmy Wilde who held the flyweight title from 1916–23 was reputed never to have fought above 108 lb. *49 kg*.

Most knock-downs in Title fights

Vic Toweel (South Africa) knocked down Danny O'Sullivan of London 14 times in ten rounds in their world bantamweight fight at Johannesburg on 2 Dec. 1950, before the latter retired.

AMATEUR
Most Olympic titles

The only amateur boxer to win three Olympic gold medals is the southpaw László Papp (b. 25 Mar. 1926) (Hungary), who took the middleweight (1948) and the light-middleweight titles (1952 and 1956). The only man to win two titles in one celebration was Oliver L. Kirk (U.S.A.), who took both the bantam and featherweight titles in St. Louis, Missouri, U.S.A., in 1904, when the U.S. won all the titles. In 1908 Great Britain won all the titles. Harry W. Mallin (1892–1969) (G.B.) was in 1924 the first boxer ever to defend successfully an Olympic title in retaining the middleweight title.

Olympic middleweight champion Harry Mallin (G.B.), five-time A.B.A. winner, successfully defended his title in 1924 despite being bitten on the chest by an opponent. (*Radio Times Hulton Picture Library*)

Oldest gold medallist

Richard K. Gunn (b. 1870) (G.B.) won the Olympic featherweight gold medal on 27 Oct. 1908 in London aged 38.

Most A.B.A. titles

The greatest number of A.B.A. titles won by any boxer is six by Joseph Steers at middleweight and heavyweight between 1890 and 1893. Trevor Andrews (Battersea Club) has uniquely won four successive National Schools titles and two A.B.A. Junior titles in 1972–73. In 1975, Kevin John Woolnough (b. 20 Feb. 1959), of St. Georges A.B.C. became the first boxer to win the National Schools, National Association of Boys Clubs, and A.B.A. Junior titles.

Longest span

The greatest span of A.B.A. title-winning performances is that of the heavyweight H. Pat Floyd, who won in 1929 and gained his fourth title 17 years later in 1946.

MOST A.B.A. TITLES WON IN EACH CLASS

Class	Instituted	Wins	Name	Years
Light-Flyweight (7st. 7lb. *47 kg 600* or under)	1971	3	M. Abrams	1971–73
Flyweight (8 st. *50 kg 800* or under)	1920	5	T. Pardoe	1929–33
Bantamweight (8 st. 7 lb. *54 kg* or under)	1884	4	W. W. Allen	1911–12, 1914, 1919
Featherweight (9 st. *57 kg* or under)	1884	5	G. R. Baker	1912–14, 1919, 1921
Lightweight (9 st 7 lb. *60 kg* or under)	1881	4	M. Wells	1904–7
		4	F. Grace	1909, 1913, 1919–20
Light-Welterweight (10 st. *63 kg 500* or under)	1951	2	D. Stone	1956–57
		2	R. Kane	1958–59
		2	L/Cpl. B. Brazier	1961–62
		2	R. McTaggart	1963, 1965
Welterweight (10 st. 8 lb. *67 kg* or under)	1920	3	N. Gargano	1954–56
		3	T. Waller	1970, 1973–74
Light-Middleweight (11 st. 2 lb. *70 kg* or under)	1951	2	B. Wells	1953–54
		2	B. Foster	1952, 1955
		2	S. Pearson	1958–59
		2	T. Imrie	1966, 1969
Middleweight (11 st. 11 lb. *74 kg* or under)	1881	5	R. C. Warnes	1899, 1901, 1903, 1907, 1910
		5	H. W. Mallin	1919–23
		5	F. Mallin	1928–32
Light-Heavyweight (12 st. 10 lb. *80 kg* or under	1920	4	H. J. Mitchell	1922–25
Heavyweight (any weight)	1881	5	F. Parks	1899, 1901–02, 1905–06

BULLFIGHTING

Earliest

In the latter half of the Second Millenium B.C. bull leaping was practised in Crete. Bullfighting in Spain was first reported by the Romans in Baetica (Andalusia) in the third century B.C.

The first renowned professional *espada* was Francisco Romero of Ronda, in Andalusia, Spain, who introduced the *estoque* and the red muleta *c.* 1700. Spain now has some 190 active matadors. Since 1700, 42 major matadors have died in the ring.

Most successful matadors

The most successful matador measured by bulls killed was Lagartijo (1841–1900), born Rafael Molina, whose lifetime total was 4,867. The longest career as a full matador was by Bienvenida (1922–1975), born Antonio Mejías, from 1942 to 1974. Recent Spanish law requires compulsory retirement at 55 years of age.

Most kills in a day

In 1884 Romano set a record by killing 18 bulls in a day in Seville and in 1949 El Litri (Miguel Báes) set a Spanish record with 114 *novilladas* in a season.

Highest paid

The highest paid bullfighter in history was El Cordobes (b. Manuel Benítez Pérez, probably on 4 May 1936, Palma del Rio, Spain), who became a sterling millionaire in 1966, when he fought 111 *corridas* up to 4 October of that year. In

In the 17 years since he took the *alternativa* Paco Camino has become the world's highest paid matador. (*Club Taurino*)

1970 he received an estimated £750,000 for 121 fights. Paco Camino (b. 19 Dec. 1941) has received up to 2,000,000 pesetas £16,000 for a *corrida*.

Largest stadiums

The world's largest bullfighting ring, the Plaza, Mexico City, with a capacity of 48,000, was closed in Mar. 1976. The largest of Spain's 312 bullrings is Las Ventas, Madrid with a capacity of 24,000.

CANOEING

Origins

The acknowledged pioneer of canoeing as a sport was John Macgregor, a British barrister, in 1865. The Canoe Club was formed on 26 July 1866.

Most titles *Olympic*

Gert Fredriksson (b. 21 Nov. 1919) of Sweden has won most Olympic gold medals with six: the 1,000 m Kayak singles in 1948, 1952 and 1956, the 10,000 m Kayak singles in 1948 and 1956 and the 1,000 m Kayak doubles in 1960. The most by a woman is three by Ludmila Pinayeva (*née* Khvedosyuk) (b. 14 Jan. 1936) (U.S.S.R.), in the 500 m K.1, 1964 and 1968, and 500 m K.2 in 1972.

Most titles *World*

In addition to his six Olympic championships Gert Fredriksson has three other world titles in non-Olympic years: 1,000 m K.1 in 1950 and 1954 and 500 m K.1 in 1954, for a record total of nine. The Olympic 1,000 m best performance of 3 min 06.46 sec by the 1976 Spanish K.4 represents an average speed of 11.99 m.p.h. *19,30 km/h* and a striking rate of about 125 strokes per min.

The only British canoeists to win world titles have been

the late Paul Farrant of Chalfont Park Canoe Club, who won the canoe slalom at Geneva, Switzerland, in August 1959, and Alan Emus, who won the canoe sailing at Hayling Island, Hampshire, in August 1961 and on the Boden See (Lake of Constance) in August 1965.

Most titles *British*

The most British Open titles (instituted 1936) ever won is 32 by John Laurence Oliver (Lincoln Canoe Club) (b. 12 Jan. 1943) from 1966 to 1976 including 12 individual events. David Mitchell (Chester S. & C.C.) won eight British slalom titles in 1963–68, 1970–71.

Longest journey

The longest journey ever made by canoe is one of 7,516 miles *12 096 km* around the eastern U.S.A. by paddle and portage, from Lake Itasca, Minn. via New Orleans, Miami, New York and Lake Ontario, by Randy Bauer (b. 15 Aug. 1949) and Jerry Mimbach (b. 22 May 1952) of Coon Rapids, Minn. from 8 Sept. 1974 to 30 Aug. 1976.

The longest journey without portages or aid of any kind is one of 6,102 miles *9 820 km* by Richard H. Grant and Ernest "Moose" Lassy circumnavigating the eastern United States via Chicago, New Orleans, Miami, New York and the Great Lakes from 22 Sept. 1930 to 15 Aug. 1931.

DOWNSTREAM CANOEING

River	Miles	Km	Name and Country	Route	Date	Duration
Rhine	714	*1 149*	Sgt. Charles Kavanagh (G.B.)	Chur, Switzerland to Willemstad, Neth.	13 Feb.–2 Apr. 1961	17½ days
	714	*1 149*	Four Royal Marine Reservists (G.B.)	Chur to Willemstad	9–14 Mar. 1974	10 days 11 hr.
Murray-Darling	1,980	*3 186*	Six students of St. Albert's College, UNE. (Australia)	Gunnedah, N.S.W. to Lake Alexandrina, S.A.	Dec. 1975	—
Mississippi	2,245	*3 612*	Dr. Gerald Capers, Charles Saunders, Joseph Tagg Jr. (U.S.)	Lake Itasca, Minnesota to New Orleans, Louisiana	4 July–8 Aug. 1937	56 days
Zaire (Congo)	2,600	*4 185*	John and Julie Batchelor (G.B.)	Moasampanga to Banana	8 May–12 Sept. 1974	128 days
Amazon	3,400	*5 470*	Stephen Z. Bezuk (U.S.) (Kayak)	Atalaya to Ponta do Céu	21 June–4 Nov. 1970	136 days
Nile	4,000	*6 500*	John Goddard (U.S.), Jean Laporte and André Davy (France)	Kagera to the Delta	Nov. 1953–July 1954	9 months

Cross-Channel

The singles record for canoeing across the English Channel is 3 hr 33 min 47 sec by Andrew William Dougall Samuel, of Glasgow, from Shakespeare Bay, Dover, to Wissant, France, on 5 Sept. 1976. The doubles record is 3 hr 20 min 30 sec by Capt. William Stanley Crook and the late Ronald Ernest Rhodes in their glass-fibre K.2 *Accord*, from St. Margaret's Bay, Dover, to Cap Blanc Nez, France on 20 Sept. 1961.

The record for a double crossing is 12 hr 47 min in K.1 canoes by nine members of the Canoe Camping Club, G.B., on 7 May 1976.

North Sea

On 4–5 June 1976, Derek Hutchinson, Tom Caskey and Dave Hellawell paddled their kayaks from Felixstowe, Suffolk to Ostend, Belgium, over 100 miles *160 km* across open sea, in 31 hours.

Devizes-Westminster

The Senior Class record for the annual Devizes-Westminster Challenge Cup race (instituted officially 1949) over 125 miles *201 km* with 77 locks is 16 hrs 56 min 25 sec by John Fowler and Brian Greenaway (Royal Canoe Club) to win the 1977 race. The Junior Class record is 16 hr 6 min 7 sec by I. White

and C. Gale (Sussex Police Cadets) to win the 1975 race from 66 crews. Junior crews have three compulsory night stops.

Loch Ness

The fastest time for a K.1 from Fort Augustus to Lochend (22.7 miles *36,5 km*) is 3 hrs 33 min 4 sec by Andrew Samuel (Trossachs Canoe and Boat Club) on 19 Oct. 1975.

Highest altitude

In Sept. 1976 Dr. Michael Jones and Michael Hopkinson of the British Everest Canoe Expedition canoed down the River Dudh Kosi, Nepal from an altitude of 17,500 ft *5 334 m*.

Texas Water Safari

The longest regularly held canoe race in the U.S.A. is the Texas Water Safari (inst. 1963), 419 miles *674 km* from San Marcos to Seadrift on the San Marcos and Guadalupe rivers. John Nabors and Mike Wooley set a record of 38 hr 5 min on 7–8 June 1975.

Eskimo rolls

The record for Eskimo rolls is 1,004 in 107 min 12 sec by David Ansell, 19 at Bedford, England on 29 May 1972. A "hand-rolling" record of 100 rolls in 3 min 58.7 sec was set in the Bootham School Pool, York on 14 June 1975 by David A. Clapham, 15. (In future, records must be set at 1,000 rolls and 100 rolls, respectively).

CAVING

Duration (trogging)

The endurance record for staying in a cave is 463 days by Milutin Veljkovic (b. 1935) (Yugoslavia) in the Samar Cavern, Svrljig Mountains, northern Yugoslavia from 24 June 1969 to 30 Sept. 1970. The British record is 130 days by David Lafferty, (b. 1939) of Hampstead, who stayed in Boulder Chamber, Goughs' Cave, Cheddar Gorge, Somerset, from 27 Mar. to 4 Aug. 1966. He was alone until 1 Aug. when he thought it was 7 July.

PROGRESSIVE WORLD DEPTH RECORDS

Compiled by Dr. A. C. Waltham, Trent Polytechnic, Nottingham.

ft	m	Cave	Country	Cavers	Date	
453	138	Macocha	Czechoslovakia	J. Nagel et al.		1748
741	226	Grotta di Padriciano	Italy	A. Lindner et al.		1839
1,076	328	Grotta di Trebiciano	Italy	A. Lindner et al.		1841
1,509	460	Geldloch	Austria	—		1923
1,574	480	Antro di Corchia	Italy	E. Fiorentino Club		1934
1,978	603	Trou du Glaz	France	P. Chevalier et al.		1947
2,418	737	Reseau de la Pierre St. Martin	France	G. Lepineux et al.	July	1953
2,962	903	Gouffre Berger	France	F. Petzl et al.	Sept.	1954
3,123	952	Gouffre Berger	France	L. Potié et al.	Aug.	1955
3,681	1 122	Gouffre Berger	France	F. Petzl et al.	Aug.	1956
3,715	1 133	Gouffre Berger	France	A.R.S.I.P.	July	1963
3,842	1 171	Reseau de la Pierre St. Martin	France	A.R.S.I.P.	Aug.	1966
4,370	1 332	Reseau de la Pierre St. Martin	France	A.R.S.I.P.	Aug.	1975

N.B. The Reseau de la Pierre St. Martin has been explored via a number of entrances and has never been entirely descended at any one time; consequently after Aug. 1963 the "sporting" records for the greatest descent into a cave should read:

3,743	1 141	Gouffre Berger	France	Speleo Club de Seine	July	1968

COMMONWEALTH GAMES

These quadrennial Games, second only to the Olympic Games for international participation, have been allocated as follows:

I	Hamilton, Ontario, Canada	16–23 Aug.	1930
II	London, England	4–11 Aug.	1934
III	Sydney, Australia	5–12 Feb.	1938
IV	Auckland, New Zealand	4–11 Feb.	1950
V	Vancouver, British Columbia, Canada	30 July–7 Aug.	1954
VI	Cardiff, Wales	18–26 July	1958
VII	Perth, Western Australia	22 Nov.–1 Dec.	1962
VIII	Kingston, Jamaica	4–13 Aug.	1966
IX	Edinburgh, Scotland	16–25 July	1970
X	Christchurch, New Zealand	24 Jan.–2 Feb.	1974
XI	Edmonton, Alberta, Canada	3–12 Aug.	1978

In 1977 there were 48 countries affiliated to the Commonwealth Games Federation. The record entry was 42 countries and 1,383 competitors in 1970 at Edinburgh. Of the 925 gold medals awarded 1930–74, England has won most with 255, followed by Australia with 242.

Most Gold medals

The most gold medals won is nine by Henry William Furse Hoskyns, M.B.E. (England) (b. 19 March 1931) for fencing

between 1958 and 1970 and Michael Vincent Wenden M.B.E. (Australia) (b. 17 Nov. 1949) for swimming 1966–1974. The most by a woman is seven by Australia's Marjorie Nelson, M.B.E. (*née* Jackson) (b. 13 Sept. 1931) in track and field events 1950–54. The most in individual events is five by Valerie Isobel Young (*née* Sloper) (N.Z.) (b. 10 Aug. 1937) shot putt 1958, 1962 and 1966 and discus 1962 and 1966, and five by swimmer Mike Wenden. The most at one celebration is five by Decima J. Norman (Australia) in track and field at Sydney in 1938.

Youngest Gold Medallist

Ved Prakash (India) of Delhi, who won the light flyweight wrestling title at Edinburgh in 1970, was 14 years old according to his passport but only 12 according to his fellow team members.

Most medals

The most medals won is 13 by Ivan G. Lund (Australia) with 3 gold, 6 silver and 4 bronze for fencing 1950–62 and Mike Wenden with 9 gold, 3 silver and 1 bronze in 1966–74. The record for a woman is eight medals (6 golds, 2 silver) for swimming in 1958 and 1962 by Dawn Fraser (later Mrs. Gary Ware, O.B.E.) (Australia).

MOST GOLD MEDALS BY SPORTS		
Badminton (introduced 1966)	3	Derek Talbot (England) 1970, 74 Gillian M. Gilks (*née* Perrin) (England) 1974
Bowls (lawn) (introduced 1930 but once omitted in 1966)	4	David Bryant, M.B.E. (England) 1966, 70, 74
Boxing (since 1930)	2	Anthony Madigan (Australia) 1958, 62 Eddie Blay (Ghana) 1962, 66 Sulley Shitu (Ghana) 1962, 66 Philip Waruingi (Kenya) 1966, 70 Mohamed Muruli (Uganda) 1970, 74
Cycling (introduced 1934)	3	Ian Hallam (England) 1970, 74
Fencing (introduced 1950)	9	H. W. F. Hoskyns M.B.E. (England) 1958, 66, 70
Rowing (1930 to 1962)	4	Mervyn T. Wood (Australia) 1950, 54
Shooting (1966, 1974 only)		No marksman has yet won a second gold medal
Swimming & Diving (since 1930)	9	Michael Vincent Wenden M.B.E. (Australia) 1966, 70, 74
Track & Field Athletics (since 1930)	7	Marjorie Nelson, M.B.E. (*née* Jackson) (Australia) 1950, 54
Weightlifting (introduced 1950)	3	Louis George Martin, M.B.E. (England) 1962, 66, 70 George Newton (England) 1962, 70, 74 Precious McKenzie M.B.E. (England) 1966, 70, 74
Wrestling (since 1930)	3	Richard E. Gerrard O.B.E. (Australia) 1934, 38, 1950 Muhammad Bashir (Pakistan) 1958, 62, 66 Muhammad Faiz (Pakistan) 1962, 66, 70

See also current Commonwealth Games records table at end of Chap. 12.

COURSING

Origins

The sport of dogs chasing hares was probably of Egyptian origin in *c.* 3000 B.C. and brought to England by the Normans in 1067. The first club was the Swaffham Coursing Club formed in 1776. The classic event is the annual Waterloo Cup, instituted at Altcar, Merseyside in 1836. A government bill to declare the sport illegal was "lost" owing to the dissolution

left: In a 20 year career, Bill Hoskyns has won medals in World Championships, Olympic and Commonwealth Games. (*Syndication International*)

below: A brace of greyhounds in full flight in what may be the oldest of sports. (*Radio Times Hulton Picture Library*)

of Parliament on 29 May 1970. The number of clubs in Britain had dwindled from 169 in 1873 to 25 in 1973.

Most successful dog

The most successful Waterloo Cup dog recorded was Colonel North's *Fullerton*, sired by *Greentich*, who tied for first in 1889 and then won outright in 1890–92. He died on 4 June 1899.

Longest course

The longest authenticated course is one of 4 min 10 sec, when Major C. Blundell's *Blackmore* beat *Boldon* in a Barbican Cup decider on 2 Mar. 1934.

BEAGLING

The oldest beagle hunt is the Royal Rock Beagle Hunt, Wirral, Merseyside, whose first outing was on 28 Mar. 1845. The Newcastle and District Beagles claim their origin from the municipally-supported Newcastle Harriers existing in 1787. The Royal Agricultural College beagle pack killed 79½ brace of hares in the 1968–69 season.

CRICKET

Earliest match

The earliest evidence of the game of cricket is from a drawing depicting two men playing with a bat and ball dated *c.* 1250. The game was played in Guildford, Surrey, at least as early as 1550. The earliest major match of which the score survives was one in which a team representing England (40 and 70) was beaten by Kent (53 and 58 for 9) by one wicket at the Artillery Ground in Finsbury, London, on 18 June 1744. Cricket was played in Australia as early as 1803.

BATTING RECORDS—TEAMS
Highest innings *World*

The highest recorded innings by any team was one of 1,107 runs by Victoria against New South Wales in an Australian inter-State match at Melbourne, Victoria, on 27–28 Dec. 1926.

Highest innings *England*

The highest innings made in England is 903 runs for 7 wickets declared, by England in the Fifth Test against Australia at the Oval, London, on 20, 22 and 23 Aug. 1938. The highest innings in a county championship match is 887 by Yorkshire *versus* Warwickshire at Edgbaston on 7–8 May 1896.

Lowest innings

The lowest recorded innings is 12 made by Oxford University *v.* the Marylebone Cricket Club (M.C.C.) at Oxford on 24 May 1877, and 12 by Northamptonshire *v.* Gloucestershire at Gloucester on 11 June 1907. On the occasion of the Oxford match, however, the University batted a man short. The lowest score in a Test innings is 26 by New Zealand *v.* England in the second innings of the Second Test at Auckland on 28 Mar. 1955.

The lowest aggregate for two innings is 34 (16 in first and 18 in second) by Border *v.* Natal in the South African Currie Cup at East London on 19 and 21 Dec. 1959.

Greatest victory

The greatest recorded margin of victory is an innings and 851 runs, when Pakistan Railways (910 for 6 wickets declared) beat Dera Ismail Khan (32 and 27) at Lahore on 2–4 Dec. 1964. The largest margin in England is one of an innings and 579 runs by England over Australia in the Fifth Test at the Oval on 20–24 Aug. 1938 when Australia scored 201 and 123 with two men short in both innings. The most one-sided county match was when Surrey (698) defeated Sussex (114 and 99) by an innings and 485 runs at the Oval on 9–11 Aug. 1888.

Most runs in a day *World*

The greatest number of runs scored in a day is 721 all out (ten wickets) in 5 hrs 48 min by the Australians *v.* Essex at Southchurch Park, Southend-on-Sea on the first day on 15 May 1948.

Most runs in a day *Test match*

The Test record for runs in a day is 588 at Old Trafford on 27 July 1936 when England put on 398 and India were 190 for 0 in their second innings by the close.

Fastest 200 or more

The fastest recorded exhibition of hitting occurred in a Kent *v.* Gloucestershire match at Dover on 20 Aug. 1937, when Kent scored 219 runs for two wickets in 71 min, at the rate of 156 runs for each 100 balls bowled.

BATTING RECORDS—INDIVIDUALS
Highest innings

The highest individual innings recorded is 499 in 10 hrs 40 min by Hanif Muhammad (b. Junagadh, India, now Pakistan, 21 Dec. 1934) for Karachi *v.* Bahawalpur at Karachi, Pakistan, on 8, 9 and 11 Jan. 1959. The highest score in England is 424 in 7 hrs 50 min by Archibald Campbell MacLaren (1871–1944) for Lancashire *v.* Somerset at Taunton on 15–16 July 1895. The record for a Test match is 365 not out in 10 hrs 8 min by Sir Garfield St. Aubrun Sobers (b. Bridgetown, Barbados, 28 July 1936) playing for the West Indies in the Third Test against Pakistan at Sabina Park, Kingston, Jamaica, on 27 Feb.–1 Mar. 1958. The England Test record is 364 by Sir Leonard Hutton (b. Fulneck, Pudsey, West Yorkshire, 23 June 1916) *v.* Australia in the Fifth Test at the Oval on 20, 22 and 23 Aug. 1938.

1,000 in May

The most recent example of scoring 1,000 runs *in May* was by Charles Hallows (Lancashire) (1895–1972), who made precisely 1,000 between 5–31 May 1928. Dr. William Gilbert Grace (1848–1915) 9–30 May 1895, and Walter Reginald Hammond (1903–1965) 7–31 May 1927, surpassed this feat with 1,016 and 1,042 runs. The greatest number of runs made *before the end of May* was by Thomas Walter Hayward (1871–1939) with 1,074 from 16 Apr. to 31 May in 1900.

Longest innings

The longest innings on record is one of 16 hrs 10 min for 337 runs by Hanif Muhammad (Pakistan) *v.* the West Indies in the First Test at Bridgetown, Barbados, on 20–23 Jan. 1958. The English record is 13 hrs 17 min by Len Hutton.

Most runs *Season*

The greatest number of runs ever scored in a season is 3,816 in 50 innings (8 not out) by Denis Charles Scott Compton C.B.E. (b. Hendon, Greater London, 23 May 1918) of Middlesex, in 1947. His batting average was 90.85.

Most runs *Career*

The greatest aggregate of runs in a career is 61,237 in 1,315 innings (106 not out) between 1905 and 1934 by Sir John (Jack) Berry Hobbs (1882–1963) of Surrey and England. His career average was 50.65.

Most runs *Test matches*

The greatest number of runs scored in Test matches is 8,032 in 160 innings (21 not out) by Sir Garfield Sobers of Barbados and Nottinghamshire playing for the West Indies between 1952–53 and 1973–74. His average is 57.78.

Most runs *Off an over*

The first batsman to score the possible of 36 runs off a six-ball over was Sir Garfield Sobers (Nottinghamshire) off Malcolm Andrew Nash (Glamorgan) at Swansea on 31 Aug. 1968. The ball (recovered from the last hit from the road by a small boy) resides in Nottingham's Museum.

Most runs *Off a ball*

The most runs scored off a single hit is ten by Samuel Hill Wood (later Sir Samuel Hill Hill-Wood) (1872–1949) off Cuthbert James Burnup (1875–1960) in the Derbyshire *v.*

M.C.C. match at Lord's, City of Westminster, Greater London, on 26 May 1900.

Most sixes *In an innings*
The highest number of sixes hit in an innings is 15 by John Richard Reid, O.B.E. (b. 3 June 1928), in an innings of 296, lasting 3 hrs 47 min, for Wellington v. Northern Districts in the Plunket Shield Tournament at Wellington, New Zealand, on 14–15 Jan. 1963. The Test record is ten by Walter Hammond in an innings of 336 not out for England v. New Zealand at Auckland on 31 Mar. and 1 Apr. 1933.

Most sixes *In a match*
The highest number of sixes in a match is 17 (ten in the first and seven in the second innings) by William James Stewart (b. 31 Aug. 1934) for Warwickshire v. Lancashire at Blackpool on 29–31 July 1959. His two innings were of 155 and 125.

Most boundaries in an innings
The highest number of boundaries in an innings was 68 (all in fours) by Percival Albert Perrin (1876–1945) in an innings of 343 not out for Essex v. Derbyshire at Chesterfield on 18–19 July 1904.

Highest score by a No. 11
The highest score by a No. 11 batsman is 163 by Thomas Peter Bromly Smith (1908–67) for Essex v. Derbyshire at Chesterfield in August 1947.

Most centuries *Season*
The record for the greatest number of centuries in a season is held by Denis Compton with 18 in 1947.

Most centuries *Career*
The most centuries in a career is 197 by Sir Jack Hobbs between 1905 and 1934.

Most centuries *Test matches*
The greatest number of centuries scored in Test matches is 29 by Sir Donald George Bradman (Australia) (b. Cootamundra, N.S.W., 27 Aug. 1908) between 1928 and 1948. The English record is 22 by Walter Hammond of Gloucestershire, between 1927 and 1947, and 22 by Michael Colin Cowdrey, C.B.E. (b. Bangalore, India 24 Dec. 1932) (Kent) between 1954 and 1975.

Double centuries
The only batsman to score double centuries in both innings is Arthur Edward Fagg (b. 18 June 1915), who made 244 and 202 not out for Kent v. Essex at Colchester on 13–15 July 1938.

Highest averages
The highest recorded seasonal batting average in England is 115.66 for 26 innings (2,429 runs) by Sir Donald Bradman (Australia) in England in 1938. The English record is 100.12 by Geoffrey Boycott (b. 21 Oct. 1940) of Yorkshire and England for 30 innings (2,503 runs) including 13 centuries and five times not out in 1971. The world record for a complete career is 95.14 for 338 innings (28,067 runs) by Bradman between 1927 and 1949. The record for Test matches is 99.94 in 80 innings (6,996 runs) by Bradman in 1928–48. The English career record is 56.37 for 500 innings (62 not out) by Kumar Shri Ranjitsinhji (1872–1933) later H. H. the Jam Saheb of Nawanagar, with 24,692 runs between 1893 and 1920.

Fastest *Half century*
The fastest 50 ever hit was completed in 8 min (1.22 to 1.30 p.m.) and in 11 scoring strokes by Clive C. Inman (b. Colombo, Ceylon, 29 Jan. 1936) in an innings of 57 not out for Leicestershire v. Nottinghamshire at Trent Bridge, Nottingham on 20 Aug. 1965.

Fastest *Century*
The fastest century ever hit was completed in 35 min by Percy George Herbert Fender (b. 22 Aug. 1892), when scoring 113 not out for Surrey v. Northamptonshire at Northampton on 26 Aug. 1920. The most prolific scorer of centuries in an hour or less was Gilbert Laird Jessop (1874–1955), with 11 between 1897 and 1913. The fastest Test century was one of 70 min by Jack Morrison Gregory (1895–1973) of New South Wales, for Australia v. South Africa in the Second Test at Johannesburg on 12 Nov. 1921. Edwin Boaler Alletson (1884–1963) scored 189 runs in 90 min for Nottinghamshire v. Sussex at Hove on 20 May 1911.

Fastest *Double century*
A double century in 120 min was achieved by Gilbert Jessop (286) for Gloucestershire v. Sussex at Hove on 1 June 1903 and equalled by Clive Hubert Lloyd (West Indies) (b. Georgetown, now Guyana, 31 Aug. 1944) v. Glamorgan at Swansea, West Glamorgan, on 9 Aug. 1976.

Fastest *Treble century*
The fastest treble century was completed in 181 min by Denis Compton, C.B.E. (Middlesex) who scored 300 for the M.C.C. v. North-Eastern Transvaal at Benoni on 3–4 Dec. 1948.

Slowest scoring
The longest time a batsman has ever taken to open his scoring is 1 hr 37 min by Thomas Godfrey Evans (b. Finchley, Greater London, 18 Aug. 1920) of Kent, who scored ten not out for England v. Australia in the Fourth Test at Adelaide on 5–6 Feb. 1947. Richard Gorton Barlow (1850–1919) utilized 2½ hrs to score five not out for Lancashire v. Nottinghamshire at Nottingham on 8 July 1882. During his innings his score remained unchanged for 80 min.

The slowest century on record was by Derrick John "Jackie" McGlew (b. 11 Mar. 1929) of South Africa in the Third Test v. Australia at Durban on 25 and 27 Jan. 1958. He required 9 hrs 35 min for 105, reaching the 100 in 9 hrs 5 min. The slowest double century recorded is one of 10 hrs 8 min by Robert Baddeley Simpson (b. 3 Feb. 1936) of New South Wales, during an innings of 311, lasting 12 hrs 42 min, for Australia v. England in the Fourth Test at Old Trafford on 23–25 July 1964.

Greatest partnership *World*
The record stand for any partnership is the fourth wicket stand of 577 by Gul Muhammad (b. 15 Oct. 1921), who scored 319, and Vijay Samuel Hazare (b. 11 Mar. 1915) 288 in the Baroda v. Holkar match at Baroda, India, on 8–10 Mar. 1947.

Greatest partnership *England*
The highest stand in English cricket is the first-wicket partnership of 555 by Percy Holmes (1886–1971) (224 not out) and Herbert Sutcliffe (b. 24 Nov. 1894) (313) for Yorkshire v. Essex at Leyton on 15–16 June 1932.

Longest hit
The longest measured drive is one of 175 yds *160 m* by Walter (later the Rev.) Fellows (1834–1901) of Christ Church, Oxford University, in a practice on their ground off Charles Rogers in 1856. J. E. C. Moore made a measured hit of 170 yds 1 ft 5 in *155,59 m* at Griffith, New South Wales, Australia, in February 1930.

BOWLING

Most wickets *Season*
The largest number of wickets ever taken in a season is 304 by Alfred Percy "Tich" Freeman (1888–1965) of Kent, in 1928. Freeman bowled 1,976.1 overs, of which 423 were maidens, with an average of 18.05 runs per wicket.

Most wickets *Career*
The greatest wicket-taker in history was Wilfred Rhodes (1877–1973) who took 4,187 wickets for 69,993 runs (average 16.71 runs per wicket) between 1898 and 1930. The highest percentage of wickets gained unassisted is 73.50% (1,479 from 2,012) by Schofield Haigh (1871–1921), who played for Yorkshire from 1895 to 1913.

Most wickets *Tests*
The greatest number of wickets taken in Test matches is 309 for 8,989 runs (average 29.09) by Lancelot Richard Gibbs (b. Georgetown, now Guyana, 29 Sept. 1934) in 79 Tests between 1958 and 1976. The lowest bowling average in a Test career (minimum 15 wickets) is 112 wickets for 1,205 runs (10.75 runs per wicket) by George Alfred Lohmann (1865–1901) in 18 Tests for England between 1886 and 1896.

GILLETTE CUP, JOHN PLAYER LEAGUE AND BENSON & HEDGES CUP RECORDS

	Gillette Cup (Instituted 1963)	John Player League (Instituted 1969)	Benson and Hedges Cup (Instituted 1972)
Highest Individual Innings	177—C. G. Greenidge, Hants v. Glams. Southampton 1975	155*—B. A. Richards, Hants v. Yorks. Hull, 1970	173*—C. G. Greenidge, Hants v. Minor Counties (South), Amersham, 1973
Best Individual Bowling	7–15—A. L. Dixon, Kent v. Surrey, Oval, 1967	8–26—K. D. Boyce, Essex v. Lancs. Old Trafford, 1971. N.B. A. Ward, Derby v. Sussex, Derby 1970, 4 wickets in 4 balls	6–13—M. Proctor, Gloucester v. Hants. Southampton, 1977
Highest Innings Total	371 for 4 (off 60 overs), Hants v. Glams. Southampton 1975	307 for 4 (off 38 overs) Worcs. v. Derbys. at Worcester, 1975	327 for 4 (off 55 overs), Leics. v. Warwicks, Coventry, 1972
Lowest Innings Total	41 (off 20 overs), Cambs. v. Bucks., Cambridge, 1972 41 (off 19.4 overs), Middlesex v. Essex, Westcliff, 1972 41(off 36.1 overs), Shropshire v. Essex, Wellington, 1974	23 (off 19.4 overs), Middlesex v. Yorks., Headingley, 1974	62 (off 26.5 overs), Glos. v. Hants., Bristol, 1975
Highest Partnership	227 for 1st wicket—R. E. Marshall and B. L. Reed, Hants v. Beds, Goldington, 1968	218 for 1st wicket—A. R. Butcher and G. P. Howarth, Surrey v. Gloucestershire, Oval, 1976	285* for 2nd wicket—C. G. Greenidge and D. R. Turner, Hants v. Minor Counties (South), Amersham, 1973

* Not Out

Most wickets *In an innings*

The taking of all ten wickets by a single bowler has been recorded many times but only one bowler has achieved this feat on three occasions—Alfred Freeman of Kent, against Lancashire at Maidstone on 24 July 1929, against Essex at Southend on 13–14 Aug. 1930 and against Lancashire at Old Trafford, Greater Manchester on 27 May 1931. The fewest runs scored off a bowler taking all ten wickets is ten, when Hedley Verity (1905–43) of Yorkshire dismissed (eight caught, one l.b.w., one stumped) every Nottinghamshire batsman in 118 balls at Leeds on 12 July 1932. The only bowler to have "clean bowled" a whole side out was John Wisden (1826–84) of Sussex, playing for the North v. the South at Lord's in 1850.

Most wickets *Match*

James Charles Laker (b. Frizinghall, West Yorkshire, 9 Feb. 1922) of Surrey took 19 wickets for 90 runs (9–37 and 10–53) for England v. Australia in the Fourth Test at Old Trafford, on 26–31 July 1956. No other bowler has taken more than 17 wickets in a first class match.

Most wickets *In a day*

The greatest number of wickets taken in a day's play is 17 by Colin Blythe (1879–1917) for 48 runs, for Kent against Northamptonshire at Northampton on 1 June 1907; by Hedley Verity for 91 runs, for Yorkshire v. Essex at Leyton on 14 July 1933; and by Thomas William John Goddard (1900–66) for 106 runs, for Gloucestershire v. Kent at Bristol, Avon on 3 July 1939.

Most consecutive wickets

No bowler in first class cricket has yet achieved five wickets with five consecutive balls. The nearest approach was that of Charles Warrington Leonard Parker (1884–1959) (Gloucestershire) in his own benefit match against Yorkshire at Bristol on 10 Aug. 1922, when he struck the stumps with five successive balls but the second was called as a no-ball. The only man to have taken four wickets with consecutive balls more than once is Robert James Crisp (b. 28 May 1911) for Western Province v. Griqualand West at Johannesburg on 23–24 Dec. 1931 and against Natal at Durban on 3 Mar. 1934.

Most "hat tricks"

The greatest number of "hat tricks" is seven by Douglas Vivian Parson Wright (b. 21 Sept. 1914) of Kent, on 3 and 29 July 1937, 18 May 1938, 13 Jan. and 1 July 1939, 11 Aug. 1947 and 1 Aug. 1949. In his own benefit match at Lord's on 22 May 1907, Albert Edwin Trott (Middlesex) took four Somerset wickets with four consecutive balls and then later in the same innings achieved a "hat trick".

Most expensive bowling

The greatest number of runs hit off one bowler in one innings is 362, scored off Arthur Alfred Mailey (1886–1967) in the New South Wales v. Victoria inter-State match at Melbourne on 24–28 Dec. 1926. The greatest number of runs ever con-

Barbados-born Gordon Greenidge, of Hampshire, has particularly made his mark in both the Gillette and the Benson and Hedges Cups. (*George Herringshaw*)

Included in George Lohmann's record low bowling average in Test matches is his finest feat of 9 wickets for 28 runs against South Africa. (*Radio Times Hulton Picture Library*)

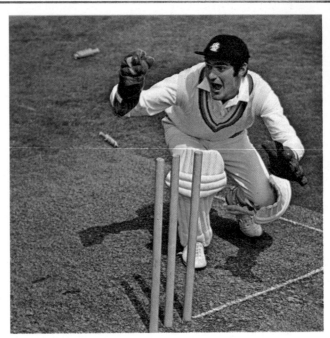

above: Apart from his wicket keeping feats, Alan Knott has scored over 4,000 runs in Test cricket—the most by any wicket keeper. (*Gerry Cranham*)

left: Though he bowls right handed, it is as a left handed batsman that Clive Lloyd has made his reputation, including a double century in record time. (*Colorsport*)

ceded by a bowler in one match is 428 by C. S. Nayudu (b. 18 Apr. 1914) in the Holkar *v.* Bombay match at Bombay on 4–9 Mar. 1945, when he also made the record number of 917 deliveries.

Most maidens
Hugh Tayfield bowled 16 consecutive eight-ball maiden overs (137 balls without conceding a run) for South Africa *v.* England at Durban on 25–27 Jan. 1957. The greatest number of consecutive six-ball maiden overs bowled is 21 (130 balls) by Ragunath G. "Bapu" Nadkarni (b. 4 Apr. 1932) for India *v.* England at Madras on 12 Jan. 1964. The English record is 17 overs (105 balls) by Horace L. Hazell (b. 30 Sept. 1909) for Somerset *v.* Gloucestershire at Taunton on 4 June 1949, and 17 (104 balls) by Graham Anthony (Tony) Richard Lock (b. 5 July 1929) of Surrey, playing for the M.C.C. *v.* the Governor-General's XI at Karachi, Pakistan, on 31 Dec. 1955. Alfred Shaw (1842–1907) of Nottinghamshire bowled 23 consecutive four-ball maiden overs (92 balls) for North *v.* the South at Nottingham in 1876.

Most balls
The greatest number of balls sent down by any bowler in one season is 12,234 (651 maidens: 298 wickets) by Alfred Freeman in 1933. The most balls bowled in an innings is 588 (98 overs) by Sonny Ramadhin (b. 1 May 1930) of Trinidad, playing for the West Indies in the First Test *v.* England at Edgbaston, West Midlands on 30 May and 1, 3 and 4 June 1957. He took two for 179.

Best average
The lowest recorded bowling average for a season is one of 8.61 runs per wicket (177 wickets for 1,525 runs) by Alfred Shaw of Nottinghamshire in 1880.

Fastest
The highest electronically measured speed for a ball bowled by any bowler is 99.7 m.p.h. *160,45 km/h* by Jeffrey Robert

Thomson (b. 16 Aug. 1950) (Australia) during the Second Test *v.* the West Indies in Dec. 1975. Albert Cotter (1883–1917) of New South Wales, Australia, is reputed to have broken a stump more than 20 times.

FIELDING
Most catches *Innings*
The greatest number of catches in an innings is seven, by Michael James Stewart (b. 16 Sept. 1932) for Surrey *v.* Northamptonshire at Northampton on 7 June 1957, and by Anthony Stephen Brown (b. 24 June 1936) for Gloucestershire *v.* Nottinghamshire at Trent Bridge, Nottingham on 26 July 1966.

Most catches *Match*
Walter Hammond held a record total of ten catches (four in the first innings, six in the second) for Gloucestershire *v.* Surrey at Cheltenham, Gloucestershire on 16–17 Aug. 1928. The record for a wicket-keeper is 11 (see wicket-keeping).

Most catches *Season and career*
The greatest number of catches in a season is 78 by Walter Hammond in 1928, and 77 by Michael James Stewart in 1957. The most catches in a career is 1,015 by Frank Edward Woolley (b. 27 May 1887) of Kent in 1906–1938. The Test record is 120 by Colin Cowdrey between 1954 and 1975.

Longest throw
The longest recorded throw of a cricket ball (5½ oz. *155 g*) is 140 yds 2 ft *128,6 m* by Robert Percival, a left-hander, on Durham Sands Racecourse on Easter Monday, 14 Apr. 1884.

WICKET KEEPING
Most dismissals *Season*
The record number of dismissals for any wicket-keeper in a season is 127 (79 caught, 48 stumped) by Leslie Ethelbert George Ames, C.B.E. (b. 3 Dec. 1905) of Kent in 1929. The record for the number stumped is 64 by Ames in 1932. The

record for catches is 96 by James Graham Binks (b. 5 Oct. 1935) of Yorkshire in 1960.

Most dismissals *Career*
The highest total of dismissals in a wicket-keeping career is 1,527 (a record 1,270 catches plus 257 stumpings) by John Thomas Murray M.B.E. (b. 1 Apr. 1935) of Middlesex between 1952 and 1975. The most stumpings in a career is 415 by Leslie Ames between 1926 and 1951. The Test record is 247 dismissals (228 catches, 19 stumpings) in 87 Tests by Alan Philip Eric Knott (b. 9 Apr. 1946) for England between 1967 and 2 Aug. 1977.

Most dismissals *Innings*
The most dismissals by a wicket-keeper in an innings is eight (all caught) by Arthur Theodore Wallace Grout (1927–68) for Queensland against Western Australia at Brisbane on 15 Feb. 1960. The most stumpings in an innings is six by Henry "Hugo" Yarnold (1917–1974) for Worcestershire v. Scotland at Broughty Ferry, Tayside, on 2 July 1951. The Test record is six (all caught) by Wally Grout (see above) in the First Australia v. South Africa Test at Johannesburg on 27–28 Dec. 1957; six (all caught) by Denis Thomson Lindsay (b. 4 Sept. 1939) of North-Eastern Transvaal, for South Africa v. Australia in the First Test at Johannesburg on 24 Dec. 1966; six (all caught) by John Murray M.B.E. for England v. India in the Second Test at Lord's on 22 June 1967; six (five caught, one stumped) by Syed Mujtaba Hussain Kirmani (b. 29 Dec. 1949) for India v. New Zealand in the Second Test at Christchurch on 9 Feb. 1976.

Most dismissals *Match*
The greatest number of dismissals by a wicket-keeper in a match is 12 by Edward Pooley (1838–1907), eight caught, four stumped, for Surrey v. Sussex at the Oval on 6–7 July 1868; nine caught, three stumped by Don Tallon (b. 17 Feb. 1916) of Australia for Queensland v. New South Wales at Sydney on 2–4 Jan. 1939; and also nine caught, three stumped by Hedley Brian Taber (b. 29 Apr. 1940) of New South Wales against South Australia at Adelaide 17–19 Dec. 1968. The record for catches is 11, seven in the first innings and four in the second, by Arnold Long (b. 18 Dec. 1940), for Surrey v. Sussex at Hove, East Sussex on 18 and 21 July 1964, and also by Rodney William Marsh (b. 11 Nov. 1947) for Western Australia v. Victoria at Perth on 15–17 Nov. 1975. The most stumpings in a match is nine by Frederick Henry Huish (1872–1957) for Kent v. Surrey at the Oval on 21–23 Aug. 1911. The Test record for dismissals is nine, eight caught, one stumped, by Gilbert Roche Andrews Langley (b. 19 Sept. 1919), playing for Australia v. England in the Second Test at Lord's on 22–26 June 1956.

TEST RECORDS
Most Test appearances
The record number of Test appearances is 114 by Colin Cowdrey C.B.E. for England between December 1954 and February 1975. The highest number of Test captaincies is 41 including 35 consecutive games by Peter Barker Howard May (b. 31 Dec. 1929) of Cambridge University and Surrey, who captained England from 1955 to 1961 and played in a total of 66 Tests. The most innings batted in Test matches is 188 in 114 Tests by Colin Cowdrey. Sir Garfield Sobers (West Indies) holds the record for consecutive Tests, with 85 from April 1955 to April 1972.

Longest match
The lengthiest recorded cricket match was the "timeless" Test between England and South Africa at Durban on 3–14 Mar. 1939. It was abandoned after ten days (eighth day rained off) because the boat taking the England team home was due to leave. The lengthiest in England have been the six-day Fifth England v. Australia Test on 6–12 Aug. 1930, when rain prevented play on the fifth day, and six-day Fifth England v. Australia Test on 10–16 Aug. 1972, when play took place on all six days.

Largest crowds
The greatest recorded attendance at a cricket match is 350,534 (receipts £30,124) for the Third Test between Australia and England at Melbourne on 1–7 Jan. 1937. For the whole series the figure was a record 933,513 (receipts £87,963). The greatest recorded attendance at a cricket match on one day was 90,800 on the second day of the Fifth Test between Australia and the West Indies at Melbourne on 11 Feb. 1961, when the receipts were £A13,132 £10,484 sterling. The English record is 159,000 for the Fourth Test between England and Australia at Headingley, Leeds, West Yorkshire, on 22–27 July 1948, and the record for one day probably a capacity of 46,000 for a match between Lancashire and Yorkshire at Old Trafford on 2 Aug. 1926. The English record for a Test series is 549,650 (receipts £200,428) for the series against Australia in 1953.

Greatest receipts
The world record for receipts from a match is £156,538.90 at the Second Test between England and the West Indies on 17–19, 21–22 June 1976. The Test series record is £474,817 paid by 375,965 for the five England v. West Indies Tests of June–August 1976.

ENGLISH COUNTY CHAMPIONSHIP
The greatest number of victories has been secured by Yorkshire with 29 outright wins up to 1976, and one shared with Middlesex in 1949. The most "wooden spoons" have been won by Northamptonshire, with ten since 1923. They did not win a single match between May 1935 and May 1939. The record number of consecutive title wins is seven by Surrey from 1952 to 1958. The greatest number of consecutive appearances for one county in county championship matches is 423 by Kenneth George Suttle (b. 25 Aug. 1928) of Sussex in 1954–69. James Graham Binks (b. 5 Oct. 1935) of Yorkshire played in every county championship match for his side between his debut in 1955 and his retirement in 1969—412 matches.

Oldest and youngest county cricketers
The youngest player to represent his county was William Wade Fitzherbert Pullen (1866–1937), for Gloucestershire against Middlesex at Lord's on 5 June 1882, when aged 15 years 346 days. The oldest regular county players have been William George Quaife (1872–1951) of Sussex and Warwickshire, who played his full season last match for Warwickshire against Hampshire at Portsmouth on 27–30 Aug. 1927, when aged 55, and John Herbert King (1871–1946) of Leicestershire, who played his last match for his county against Yorkshire at Leicester on 5–7 Aug. 1925, when aged 54.

WOMEN'S CRICKET
Earliest
The first recorded women's match took place at Gosden Common, Surrey, England on 26 July 1745. *Circa* 1807 Christina Willes is said to have introduced the roundarm bowling style. The first Test match was Australia v. England at Brisbane on 28 Dec. 1934. The International Women's Cricket Council was formed in 1958.

Batting *Individual*
The highest individual innings recorded is 224 not out by Mabel Bryant for Visitors v. Residents at Eastbourne, East Sussex, England in Aug. 1901. The highest innings in a Test match is 189 by Elizabeth Alexandra (Betty) Snowball for England v. New Zealand at Christchurch, N.Z. on 16 Feb. 1935. The highest Test innings in England is 179 by Rachael Flint (*née* Heyhoe) for England v. Australia at The Oval, Greater London on 27–28 July 1976. Rachael Flint also has scored the most runs in Test cricket with 1,432 in 19 matches from Dec. 1960 to July 1976.

Batting *Team*
The highest innings score by any team is 567 by Tarana v. Rockley, at Rockley, N.S.W., Australia in 1896. The highest Test innings is 503 for five wickets declared by England v. New Zealand at Christchurch, N.Z. on 16 Feb. 1935. The most in a Test in England is 379 by Australia v. England at The Oval, Greater London on 26–27 July 1976. The highest innings total by any team in England is 406 by South v. Australia at Hove, East Sussex in July 1937.

The lowest innings in a Test is 35 by England v. Australia at Melbourne, Australia in Feb. 1958. The lowest in a Test in England is 58 by England v. New Zealand at Edgbaston, West Midlands in July 1966.

Bowling

The greatest number of wickets taken in Test matches is 53 by Betty Wilson (Australia) in nine Tests between Jan. 1949 and March 1958.

MINOR CRICKET RECORDS
(where excelling those in First Class Cricket)

Highest individual innings

In a Junior House match between Clarke's House (now Poole's) and North Town, at Clifton College, Bristol, 22–23, 26–28 June 1899, A. E. J. Collins (b. India, 1886—k. Flanders, Nov. 1914) scored an unprecedented 628 not out in 6 hrs 50 min, over five afternoons' batting, carrying his bat through the innings of 836. The scorer, E. W. Pegler, gave the score as "628—plus or minus 20, shall we say".

Fastest individual scoring

S.K. Coen (South Africa) scored 50 runs (11 fours and one six) in 7 min for Gezira v. the R.A.F. in 1942, compared with the First Class record of 8 min. Thomas Paston Adderson (b. 4 Sept. 1909) hit a century in 23 min for Bedminster v. Long Ashton, at Bristol, Avon, on 13 May 1939. Cedric Ivan James Smith hit nine successive sixes for a Middlesex XI v. Harrow and District at Rayner's Lane, Harrow, Greater London in 1935. This feat was repeated by Arthur Dudley Nourse in a South African XI v. Military Police match at Cairo in 1942–43. Nourse's feat included six sixes in one over.

Fastest and Slowest scoring rates

In the match Royal Naval College, Dartmouth v. Seale Hayne Agricultural College in 1923, K. A. Sellar (now Cdr. "Monkey" Sellar, D.S.O., D.S.C., R.N.) and Leslie Kenneth Allen Block (now Judge Block, D.S.C.) (b. 9 Aug. 1906) were set to score 174 runs in 105 min but achieved this total in 33 min, so averaging 5.27 runs per min. Playing for Gentlemen of Leicestershire C.C. v. Free Foresters, on 19 Aug. 1963, Ian H. S. Balfour batted for 100 min without adding to his score of five runs.

Young Stephen Lane, of New Zealand, whose 14 catches in a schools' match surpasses anything achieved in first class cricket. (*Wellington Evening Post*)

Most runs off a ball

A scoring strike of 11 (all run, with no overthrows) was achieved by Lt. P. Mitford, Q.O. Cameron Highlanders, in a Governor's Cup match on 28 May 1903.

Lowest score

There are at least 60 recorded instances of sides being dismissed for 0.

Greatest stand

T. Patten and N. Rippon made a third wicket stand of 641 for Buffalo v. Whorouly at Gapsted, Victoria, Australia, on 19 Mar. 1914.

Bowling

Stephen Fleming bowling for Marlborough College "A" XI, New Zealand v. Bohally Intermediate at Blenheim, New Zealand in December 1967 took nine wickets in nine consecutive balls. In February 1931 in a schools match in South Africa Paul Hugo also took nine wickets with nine consecutive balls for Smithfield School v. Aliwal North. In August 1917 Pte. J. Leake (9th Brigade Canadian Expeditionary Force) took all ten wickets of the Canadian Army Service Corps all clean bowled in 12 balls.

In 1881 Frederick Robert Spofforth (1853–1926) in Australia clean bowled all ten wickets in *both* innings. J. Bryant for Erskine v. Deaf Mutes in Melbourne on 15 and 22 Oct. 1887, and Albert Rimmer for Linwood School v. Cathedral G.S. at Canterbury, New Zealand in Dec. 1925 repeated the feat. The most extreme double hat trick reported was by N. Stracey for the Belvine Club near Melbourne, Australia in late March 1903. All six deliveries struck the middle stump.

Wicket-keeping

In a Repton School match for Priory v. Mitre, the late H. W. P. Middleton caught one and stumped eight batsmen in one innings on 10 July 1930.

Fielding

In a Wellington, New Zealand secondary schools 11-a-side match on 16 Mar. 1974, Stephen Lane, 13, held 14 catches in the field (seven in each innings) for St. Patrick's College, Silverstream v. St. Bernard's College, Lower Hutt.

Marathon

A match under M.C.C. rules was played by 22 members of the Mount Eliza C.C., Melbourne, Australia, for 60 hrs 7 min on 23–25 Jan. 1977.

CROQUET

Earliest references

Croquet, in its present-day form, originated as a country-house lawn game in Ireland in the 1830's when it was called "crokey". It was introduced to Hampshire 20 years later. The first club was formed in the Steyne Gardens, Worthing, West Sussex.

Most championships

The greatest number of victories in the Open Croquet Championships (instituted at Evesham, Hereford and Worcester, 1867) is ten by John William Solomon (b. 1932) (1953, 1956, 1959, 1961, 1963–68). He has also won the Men's Championship on ten occasions (1951, 1953, 1958–60, 1962, 1964–1965, 1971 and 1972), the Open Doubles (with Edmond Patrick Charles Cotter) on ten occasions (1954–55, 1958–59, 1961–65 and 1969) and the Mixed Doubles once (with Mrs. N. Oddie) in 1954, making a total of 31 titles. Solomon has also won the President's Silver Cup (inst. 1934) on nine occasions (1955, 1957–59, 1962–64, 1968 and 1971). He has also been Champion of Champions on all four occasions that this competition has been run (1967–70).

Dorothy Dyne Steel (1884–1965), fifteen times winner of the Women's Championship (1919–39), won the Open Croquet Championship four times (1925, 1933, 1935–36). She had also five Doubles and seven Mixed Doubles titles making a total of 31 titles.

International trophy

The MacRobertson International Shield (instituted 1925) has been played for ten times. It has been won most often by Great Britain with six wins (in **1925**, 1937, 1956, 1963, 1969 and 1974). The players to make five international appearances are J. C. Windsor (Australia) in 1925, 1928, 1930, 1935 and 1937 and John Solomon (G.B.) in 1951, 1956, 1963, 1969 and 1974.

Lowest handicap

Historically the lowest playing handicap has been that of Humphrey Osmond Hicks (Devon) (b. 1904) with minus 5½. In 1974 the limit was however fixed at minus 5. The player holding the lowest handicap is G. Nigel Aspinall with minus 5.

Largest club

The largest number of courts at any one club is eleven, at the Sussex County (Brighton) Croquet and Lawn Tennis Club.

Marathon

The longest croquet match on record is one of 88 hours by Don Lancaster, Kevin Burke, Jonathan Pye and Andrew Parkinson of Durham University, Durham, on 12–15 June 1976.

CROSS-COUNTRY RUNNING

International championships

The earliest recorded international cross-country race took place over 14,5 km *9 miles 18 yds* from Ville d'Avray, outside Paris, on 20 Mar. 1898, between England and France (England won by 21 points to 69). The inaugural International Cross-Country Championships took place at the Hamilton Park Racecourse, Glasgow, on 28 Mar. 1903. The greatest margin of victory is 56 sec or 390 yds *356 m* by Jack T. Holden (England) at Ayr Racecourse, Scotland, on 24 Mar. 1934. The narrowest win was that of Jean-Claude Fayolle (France) at Ostend, Belgium, on 20 Mar. 1965, when the timekeepers were unable to separate his time from that of Melvyn Richard Batty (England), who was placed second. Since 1973 the race has been run under the auspices of the International Amateur Athletic Federation.

The greatest team wins have been those of England, with a minimum of 21 points (the first six runners to finish) on two occasions, at Gosforth Park, Newcastle, Tyne and Wear, on 22 Mar. 1924, and at the Hippodrome de Stockel, Brussels, Belgium, on 20 Mar. 1932.

Most international appearances

The runners of participating countries with the largest number of international championship appearances are:

Belgium	20	M. Van de Wattyne, 1946–65
Wales	14	D. Phillips, 1922, 1924, 1926–37
England	12	J. T. Holden, 1929–39, 1946
Spain	14	M. Haro, 1962–65, 1967–69, 1971–76, 1977
Scotland	14	J. N. C. Alder, 1962, 1964–1976
France	14	N. Tijou, 1963–1975, 1977

Most wins

The greatest number of victories in the International Cross-Country Race is four by Jack Holden (England) in 1933–35 and 1939, by Alain Mimoun-o-Kacha (France) in 1949, 1952, 1954 and 1956 and Gaston Roelants (Belgium) in 1962, 1967, 1969 and 1972. England have won 43 times to 1977.

English championship

The English Cross-Country Championship was inaugurated at Roehampton, Wandsworth, Greater London, in 1877. The greatest number of individual titles achieved is four by P. H. Stenning (Thames Hare and Hounds) in 1877–80 and Alfred E. Shrubb (1878–1964) (South London Harriers) in 1901–04. The most successful club in the team race has been Birchfield Harriers from Birmingham with 27 wins and one tie between 1880 and 1953. The largest field was the 1,458 starters in 1977 at Parliament Hill Fields, Greater London, of whom all but 90 finished.

Largest field

The largest recorded field was one of 1,815 starters (1,020 completed the course) at Gosforth Park, Newcastle, Tyne and Wear in the summer of 1916. It was staged by the Northern Command of the Army and was won by Sapper G. Barber in 35 min 7.2 sec, by a margin of over 40 yd *36 m.*

CURLING

Origins

The earliest illustration of the sport was in one of the Flemish painter Pieter Bruegel's winter scenes *c.* 1560. The club with the earliest records, dating back to 1716, is that of Kilsyth, Strathclyde which was resuscitated in 1954. The game was introduced into Canada in 1807. Organized administration began in 1838 with the formation of the Grand (later Royal) Caledonian Curling Club, the international legislative body based in Edinburgh. The first indoor ice rink to introduce curling was at Southport, Merseyside in 1879.

The U.S.A. won the first Gordon International Medal series of matches, between Canada and the U.S.A., at Montreal in 1884. The first Strathcona Cup match between Canada and Scotland was won by Canada in 1903. Although demonstrated at the Winter Olympics of 1924, 1932 and 1964, curling has never been included in the official Olympic programme.

Most titles

The record for international team matches for the Scotch Cup and Air Canada Silver Broom (instituted 1959) is 12 wins by Canada, in 1959–64, 1966, 1968–72. The most Strathcona Cup wins is seven by Canada (1903, 1909, 1912, 1923, 1938, 1957, 1965) against Scotland.

Perfect games

A unique achievement is claimed by Bernice Fekete, of Edmonton, Alberta, Canada, who skipped her rink to two consecutive eight-enders on the same sheet of ice at the Derrick Club, Edmonton, on 10 Jan. and 6 Feb. 1973.

Largest bonspiel

The largest bonspiel in the world is the Manitoba Bonspiel held in Winnipeg, Canada. There were 728 teams, or rinks, of four players in the Feb. 1977 tournament.

Largest rink

The world's largest curling rink is the Big Four Curling Rink, Calgary, Alberta, Canada opened in 1959 at a cost of $Can. 2,250,000 *£867,050*. Each of the two floors has 24 sheets of ice, the total accommodating 96 teams and 384 players.

Marathons

The longest recorded curling match is one of 60 hours by eight members of the Glendale Golf and Curling Club, Hamilton, Ont., Canada on 2–4 Apr. 1976.

The duration record for two curlers is 14 hr 23 min by Timothy Moreton, 21 and Robert Maddock, 23 in Toronto, Canada on 16–17 Apr. 1973. The weight handled was 10.8 tons each.

CYCLING

Earliest race

The earliest recorded bicycle race was a velocipede race over 2 km *1.24 miles* at the Parc de St. Cloud, Paris, on 31 May 1868, won by James Moore (G.B.).

Highest speed

The highest speed ever achieved on a bicycle is 140.5 m.p.h. *226.1 km/h* by Dr. Allan V. Abbott, 29, of San Bernadino, California, U.S.A., behind a wind-shield mounted on a 1955 Chevrolet over ¾ mile *1,2 km* at Bonneville Salt Flats, Utah, U.S.A. on 25 Aug. 1973. His speed over a mile *1,6 km* was 138.674 m.p.h. *223.174 km/h.* It should be noted that considerable help is provided by the slipstreaming effect of the lead vehicle. The first Mile a Minute was achieved by Charles Minthorne Murphy (b. 1872) behind a pacing locomotive on the Long Island Railroad on 30 June 1899 in 57⅘ sec for an average of 62.28 m.p.h. *100.23 km/h.* Allan Abbott recorded an official unpaced 9.22 sec for 200 m

A rare photograph of Belgium's Leon Vanderstuyft, whose paced one hour record, set in 1928, still stands today. (*John Massis*)

(48.52 m.p.h. *78,08 km/h*) on a streamlined bicycle at Ontario, California, U.S.A., on 30 Apr. 1977.

The greatest distance ever covered in one hour is 122,862 km *76 miles 604 yd* by Leon Vanderstuyft (Belgium) (1890–1964) on the Montlhery Motor Circuit, France, on 30 Sept. 1928. This was achieved from a standing start paced by a motor-

cycle. The 24 hr record behind pace is 860 miles 367 yds *1 384,367 km* by Hubert Opperman in Australia in 1932.

Most titles *World*
The greatest number of world titles for a particular event won since the institution of the amateur championships in 1893 and the professional championships in 1895 are:

Amateur Sprint	7	Daniel Morelon (France)	1966–67, 1969–71, 1973, 1975
Amateur 100 km Paced	7	Leon Meredith (U.K.)	1904–05, 1907–09, 1911, 1913
Amateur Road Race	2	Giuseppe Martano (Italy)	1930, 1932
	2	Gustave Schur (East Germany)	1958–59
Professional Sprint	7	Jeff Scherens (Belgium)	1932–37, 1947
	7	Antonio Maspes (Italy)	1955–56, 1959–62, 1964
Amateur Pursuit	3	Guido Messina (Italy)	1947–48, 1953
	3	Tiemen Groen (Netherlands)	1964–66
Professional Pursuit	4	Hugh Porter (U.K.)	1968, 1970, 1972–3
Professional 100 km Paced	6	Guillermo Timoner (Spain)	1955, 1959–60, 1962, 1964–65
Professional Road Race	3	Alfredo Binda (Italy)	1927, 1930, 1932
	3	Henri (Rik) Van Steenbergen (Belgium)	1949, 1956–57
	3	Eddy Merckx (Belgium)	1967, 1971, 1974
Women's titles	7	Beryl Burton, O.B.E. (U.K.)	1959–60, 1962–63, 1966 (pursuits) 1960, 1967 (Road)
	7	Yvonne Reynders (Belgium)	1961, 1964–65 (pursuits) 1959, 1961, 1963, 1966 (Road)

Most titles *Olympic*
Cycling has been on the Olympic programme since the revival of the Games in 1896. The most gold medals won is three by Paul Masson (France) in 1896, Francisco Verri (Italy) in 1906 and Robert Charpentier (France) in 1936. In the "unofficial" 1904 cycling programme, Marcus Hurley (U.S.A.) won four events.

Most titles *British*
Beryl Burton, O.B.E. (b. 12 May 1937), 18 times British all-round time trial champion (1959–76), has won 12 B.C.F. road race titles, 14 track pursuit titles and 53 R.T.T.C. titles. Mrs. Burton's career overshadows all male achievements. Albert White (b. 1890) gained 12 individual National track championships from the $\frac{1}{4}$ mile to 25 miles in 1920–25. Frederick Harry Wyld (1900–76) of Derby, won 14 National titles, 11 of them individual, between 1924 and 1929, including five in one year.

Tour de France
The greatest number of wins in the Tour de France (inaugurated 1903) is five by Jacques Anquetil (b. 8 Jan. 1934) of France, 1957, 1961–64 and by Eddy Merckx (b. Belgium, 1945), 1969–72 and 1974. The closest race ever was that of 1968 when after 4 665 km *2,898.7 miles* over the 25 days (27 June–21 July) Jan Janssen (Netherlands) (b. 1940) beat Herman van Springel (Belgium) in Paris by 38 sec. The fastest average speed was 37,3 km/h *23.2 m.p.h.* by Anquetil in 1962.

Tour of Britain (Milk Race)
Three riders have won the Tour of Britain twice each—Bill Bradley (1959–60), Les West (1965, 1967) and Fedor den Hertog (Netherlands) (1969, 1971). The closest race ever was in 1976 when after 1,035 miles *1 665,67 km* over 14 days (30 May–12 June) Bill Nickson (G.B.) (b. 30 Jan. 1953) beat Joe Waugh (G.B.) by 5 sec. Den Hertog recorded the fastest

average speed of 25.20 m.p.h. *40,55 km/h* in the 1971 race (1,096 miles *1 763,84 km*). The longest Milk Race was in 1969 (1,515 miles *2 438,16 km*) although the longest ever Tour of Britain was in 1953 (1,631 miles *2 624,84 km* starting and finishing in London) under *Daily Express* sponsorship.

Land's End to John o' Groats

The "end to end" record for the 879 miles *1 414 km* is 1 day 23 hr 46 min 35 sec (average speed 18.40 m.p.h. *29,61 km/h*) by Richard W. E. (Dick) Poole (b. 1932) on 14–16 June 1965. After a break of half an hour he completed 1,000 miles *1 609 km* in 2 days 8 hrs 6 min. The equivalent feminine records (2 days 11 hr 7 min and 3 days 1 hr respectively) were set by Eileen Sheridan (b. 1925) on 9–11 June 1954.

Endurance

Tommy Edward Godwin (1912–1975) (G.B.) in the 365 days of 1939 covered 75,065 miles *120 805 km* or an average of 205.65 miles *330,96 km* per day. He then completed 100,000 miles *160 934 km* in 500 days on 14 May 1940.

The greatest mileage amassed in a cycle tour was more than 402,000 miles *643 700 km* by the itinerant lecturer Walter Stolle (b. Sudetenland, 1926) from 24 Jan. 1959 to 12 Dec. 1976. He visited 159 countries starting from Romford, Essex, England. Among his many misadventures were over 1,000 punctures. From 1922 to 25 Dec. 1973 Tommy Chambers (b. 1903) of Glasgow, had ridden a verified total of 799,405 miles *1 286 517 km*. On Xmas Day he was badly injured and has not ridden since.

Ray Reece (b. 13 July 1930), of Alverstoke, Hants, circumnavigated the world (13,325 road miles *21 444 km*) between 14 June and 5 Nov. (143 days) in 1971. Visiting every continent, John W. Hathaway (b. England, 13 Jan. 1925) of Vancouver, Canada covered 50,600 miles *81 300 km* from 10 Nov. 1974–6 Oct. 1976. Paul Cornish, 25, of Santa Ana, California rode from Los Angeles to New York City in a record 13 days 5 hrs 20 min on 4–17 Mar. 1973, averaging 225 miles *362 km* a day. Stan N. Kuhl (b. 31 Dec. 1955) and Steve Jeschien (b. 6 Aug. 1956) of Sunnyvale, Calif. travelled 8,026.7 miles *12,918 km* on a tandem around the United States from 29 June–3 Oct. 1976 to celebrate the Bicentennial.

Cyclo-cross

The greatest number of world championships (inst. 1950) have been won by Eric de Vlaeminck (Belgium) (b. 23 Aug. 1945) with the amateur and Open in 1966 and six professional titles in 1968–73. British titles (inst. 1955) have been won most often by John Atkins (b. 1942) with five amateur (1961–62, 1966–68), seven professional (1969–75) and one pro-am title in 1977.

Pennine Way

John Rawnsley (b. 7 Apr. 1937) of Shipley, West Yorkshire, cycled or carried his machine along the 270 mile *434,5 km*

Britain's outstanding cyclo-cross competitor, John Atkins. (*All-Sport Photographic*)

Pennine Way from Edale, Derbyshire to Kirk Yetholm, Borders in 2 days 23 hrs 27 min on 1–4 July 1976.

Slow cycling

William Van Puyenbroeck (b. 15 Sept. 1954) of Zaffelare, Belgium, stayed stationary without support for 5 hr 52 min on 19 June 1976.

Roller cycling

The greatest recorded distance registered by an individual in a 24 hr roller cycling test is 717.77 miles *1 155,13 km* by Len Vreeland (U.S.A.) at Trexlertown, Penn., U.S.A. The eight-man 24 hr record is 1,259.58 miles *2 027,09 km* by the Brunswick Amateur C.C. at Melbourne, Vic., Australia on 25–26 Oct. 1976.

WORLD RECORDS (*In events contested by professional and amateur riders only the better mark is given*)

OPEN AIR TRACKS

MEN

Distance	min sec	Name and Country	Place	Date
Professional unpaced standing start:				
5 km	5:51.6	Ole Ritter (Denmark)	Mexico City	4 Oct. 1968
10 km	11:53.2	Eddy Merckx (Belgium)	Mexico City	25 Oct. 1972
20 km	24:06.8	Eddy Merckx (Belgium)	Mexico City	25 Oct. 1972
100 km	2hr 14:02.5	Ole Ritter (Denmark)	Mexico City	15 Nov. 1971
1 hour	30 miles 1,258 yd *49 431 m*	Eddy Merckx (Belgium)	Mexico City	25 Oct. 1972
Professional motor-paced:				
100 km	1hr 03:40.0	Walter Lohmann (W. Germany)	Wuppertal, W. Germany	24 Oct. 1955
1 hour	58 miles 737 yd *94 015 m*	Walter Lohmann (W. Germany)	Wuppertal, W. Germany	24 Oct. 1955
Amateur unpaced standing start:				
1 km	1:02.4	Pierre Trentin (France)	Zürich, Switzerland	15 Nov. 1970
Amateur unpaced flying start:				
200 metres	10.61	Omari Phakadze (U.S.S.R.)	Mexico City	22 Oct. 1967
500 metres	27.85	Pierre Trentin (France)	Mexico City	21 Oct. 1967
1,000 metres	1:01.14	Luigi Borghetti (Italy)	Mexico City	21 Oct. 1967

continued on page 264

WOMEN

Distance	min sec	Name and Country	Place	Date
Unpaced standing start:				
1 km	1:15.1	Irena Kirichenko (U.S.S.R.)	Yerevan, U.S.S.R.	8 Oct. 1966
5 km	7:00.1	Maria Cressari (Italy)	Mexico City	24 Nov. 1972
10 km	14:19.9	Maria Cressari (Italy)	Mexico City	22 Nov. 1972
20 km	28:51.4	Maria Cressari (Italy)	Mexico City	22 Nov. 1972
100 km	2hr 41:32.6	Maria Cressari (Italy)	Milan, Italy	17 Oct. 1974
1 hour	25 miles 1,354 yd *41 471 m*	Maria Cressari (Italy)	Mexico City	25 Nov. 1972
Unpaced flying start:				
200 metres	12.3	Lyubov Razuvayeva (U.S.S.R.)	Irkutsk, U.S.S.R.	17 July 1955
500 metres	32.8	Lyubov Razuvayeva (U.S.S.R.)	Irkutsk, U.S.S.R.	17 July 1955
1,000 metres	1:12.9	Lyubov Razuvayeva (U.S.S.R.)	Irkutsk, U.S.S.R.	17 July 1955

INDOOR TRACKS

MEN

Distance	min sec	Name	Place	Date
Professional unpaced standing start:				
5 km	6:05.6	Ferdinand Bracke (Belgium)	Grenoble, France	5 Dec. 1964
1 hour	29 miles 192 yd *46 847 m*	Siegfried Adler (W. Germany)	Zürich, Switzerland	2 Aug. 1968
Professional unpaced flying start:				
500 metres	28.6	Oscar Plattner (Switzerland)	Zürich, Switzerland	17 Aug. 1956
1,000 metres	1:01.23	Patrick Sercu (Belgium)	Antwerp, Belgium	3 Feb. 1967
Professional motor-paced:				
100 km	1hr 23:59.8	Guillermo Timoner (Spain)	San Sebastian, Spain	12 Sept. 1965
1 hour	76 miles 669 yd *74 641 m*	Guy Solente (France)	Paris, France	13 Feb. 1955
Amateur unpaced standing start:				
1 km	1:06.76	Patrick Sercu (Belgium)	Brussels, Belgium	12 Dec. 1964
10 km	12:26.2	Xavier Kurmann (Switzerland)	Zürich, Switzerland	1 Dec. 1968
20 km	25:14.6	Ole Ritter (Denmark)	Zürich, Switzerland	30 Oct. 1966
Amateur unpaced flying start:				
200 metres	10.72	Daniel Morelon (France)	Zürich, Switzerland	4 Nov. 1967
500 metres	28.89	Pierre Trentin (France)	Zürich, Switzerland	4 Nov. 1967

WOMEN

Distance	min sec	Name	Place	Date
Unpaced standing start:				
1,000 metres	1:15.5	Elizabeth Eicholz (E. Germany)	E. Berlin, E. Germany	4 Mar. 1964
Unpaced flying start:				
200 metres	13.2	Karla Günther (E. Germany)	E. Berlin, E. Germany	7 Mar. 1964
500 metres	35.0	Karla Günther (E. Germany)	E. Berlin, E. Germany	7 Mar. 1964

BRITISH RECORDS (*Where a rider set up one or more intermediate records during the same attempt, only the figure for the final distance has been given.*)

OPEN AIR TRACKS

MEN

Distance	min sec	Name	Place	Date
Professional unpaced flying start:				
500 metres	31.8	Trevor Bull	Leicester, Leicestershire	12 Aug. 1976
Professional unpaced standing start:				
10 km	13:18.8	Phil Bayton	Leicester, Leicestershire	12 Aug. 1976
20 km	27:24.4	Phil Bayton	Wolverhampton, W. Midlands	10 June 1975
Amateur unpaced standing start:				
1 km	1:11.0	Ian Hallam	Leicester, Leicestershire	31 July 1973
1 hour	27 miles 414 yd *43 830 m*	Graham Webb	Birmingham, W. Midlands	11 July 1966
Amateur motor-paced standing start:				
50 km	42:58.0	Rik Notley	Leicester, Leicestershire	31 July 1976
1 hour	43 miles 1,426 yd *70 506 m*	Rik Notley	Leicester, Leicestershire	31 July 1976

WOMEN

Distance	min sec	Name	Place	Date
Unpaced standing start:				
3 km	4:14.9	Beryl Burton, O.B.E.	Newcastle-under-Lyme, Staffordshire	18 July 1964
5 km	7:19.0	Carol Barton	Leicester, Leicestershire	13 Aug. 1976
20 km	30:11.8	Carol Barton	Leicester, Leicestershire	10 Oct. 1973
1 hour	24 miles 979 yd *39 520 m*	Carol Barton	Leicester, Leicestershire	10 Oct. 1973

ROAD CYCLING RECORDS
(British) as recognized by the Road Time Trials Council (out and-home records)

MEN

Distance	min sec	Name	Course area	Date
10 miles	20:27	Ian White	Blyth, Nottinghamshire	9 Aug. 1975
25 miles	51:00	Alf Engers	Catterick, North Yorkshire	30 Aug. 1969
30 miles	1hr 02:27	Alf Engers	Basildon, Essex	24 Aug. 1975
50 miles	1hr 43:46	John Watson	Boroughbridge, North Yorkshire	23 Aug. 1970
100 miles	3hr 46:22	Phil Griffiths	Boroughbridge, North Yorkshire	15 Aug. 1976
12 hours	281.87 miles *453,62 km*	John Watson	Blyth, Nottinghamshire	7 Sept. 1969
24 hours[1]	507.00 miles *815,93 km*	Roy Cromack	Cheshire	26–27 July 1969

[1] *On 10 Sept. 1974 Teuvo Luohivuori (Finland) cycled from Tampere to Kolari, 830,1 km 515.8 miles in 24 hours—an unofficial world's best performance.*

continued on page 265

WOMEN				
Distance	min sec	Name	Course area	Date
10 miles	21:25	Beryl Burton, O.B.E.	Blyth, Nottinghamshire	29 Apr. 1973
25 miles	53:21	Beryl Burton, O.B.E.	Catterick, North Yorkshire	17 June 1976
30 miles	1hr 12:20	Beryl Burton, O.B.E.	St. Neots, Cambridgeshire	3 May 1969
50 miles	1hr 51:30	Beryl Burton, O.B.E.	Boroughbridge, North Yorkshire	25 July 1976
100 miles	3hr 55:05	Beryl Burton, O.B.E.	Essex	4 Aug. 1968
12 hours	277.25 miles *446,19 km*	Beryl Burton, O.B.E.	Wetherby, West Yorkshire	17 Sept. 1967
24 hours	427.86 miles *688,57 km*	Christine Minto (*née* Moody)	Cheshire	26–27 July 1969

ROAD RECORDS ASSOCIATION'S STRAIGHT-OUT DISTANCE RECORDS					
Distance	hr	min	sec	Name	Date
25 miles		47	0	Peter Crofts	10 Oct. 1971
50 miles	1	35	45	David Lloyd	26 Oct. 1974
100 miles	3	28	40	Ray Booty	28 Sept. 1956
1,000 miles	2 days 8	6	0	Richard W. E. Poole	14–16 June 1965

PLACE TO PLACE RECORDS					
(British) as recognized by the Road Records Association					
London to Edinburgh (380 miles *610 km*)	18	49	42	Cliff Smith	2 Nov. 1965
London to Bath and back (212 miles *341 km*)	9	07	05	Les West	28 July 1973
London to York (197 miles *317 km*)	7	41	13	Bob Addy	6 Aug. 1972
London to Brighton and back (107 miles *172 km*)	4	18	18	Les West	3 Oct. 1970
Land's End to London (287 miles *461 km*)	12	34	0	Robert Maitland	17 Sept. 1954
Land's End to John O'Groats (879 miles *1 414 km*)	1 day 23	46	35	Richard W. E. Poole	16 June 1965

EQUESTRIAN SPORTS

Origins

Evidence of horse-riding dates from an Anatolian statuette dated *c.* 1400 B.C. Pignatelli's academy of horsemanship at Naples dates from the 16th century. The earliest show jumping was in Paris in 1886. Equestrian events have been included in the Olympic Games since 1912.

Most Olympic medals

The greatest number of Olympic gold medals is five by Hans-Günter Winkler (West Germany) (b. 24 July 1926) who won four team gold medals as captain in 1956, 1960, 1964 and 1972 and won the individual Grand Prix in 1956. The most team wins in the Prix des Nations is five by Germany in 1936, 1956, 1960, 1964 and 1972. The lowest score obtained by a winner was no faults by Frantisek Ventura on *Eliot* (Czechoslovakia) in 1928. Pierre Jonqueres d'Oriola (b. 1 Feb. 1920) (France) is the only two time winner of the individual gold medal in 1952 and 1964. Richard John Hannay Meade, O.B.E. (b. 4 Dec. 1938) (Great Britain) is the only British rider to win three gold medals—as an individual in 1972 and team titles in 1968 and 1972, all in the 3-day event.

Most titles *World*

The men's world championships (inst. 1953) have been won twice by Hans-Günter Winkler (W. Germany) (1954–55) and Raimondo d'Inzeo (Italy) (1956 and 1960). The women's title (inst. 1965) has been won twice by Janou Tissot (*née* Lefebvre) (France) on *Rocket* (1970 and 1974).

Most titles *B.S.J.A.*

The most B.S.J.A. championships won is five by Alan Oliver (1951, 1954, 1959, 1969–70). The only horses to have won twice are *Maguire* (Lt.-Col. Nathaniel Kindersley) in 1945 and 1947, *Sheila* (Seamus Hayes) in 1949–50, *Red Admiral* (Oliver) in 1951 and 1954 and *Stroller* (Marion Mould) in 1968 and 1971. The record for the Ladies' Championship is eight by Patricia Smythe (b. 22 Nov. 1928), now Mrs. Samuel Koechlin, O.B.E. (1952–53, 1955, 1957–59, 1961–62). She won on *Flanagan*, owned by Robert Hanson, C.B.E., in 1955, 1958 and 1962—the only three time winner.

George V Gold Cup and Queen Elizabeth II Cup

Four men have thrice won this premier award (first held in 1911): the late Lt.-Col. J. A. Talbot-Ponsonby (1930, 1932, 1934), Lt.-Col. (later Sir) Henry Morton (Harry) Llewellyn, C.B.E. (1948, 1950, 1953), on *Foxhunter*, Piero d'Inzeo (Italy) (1957, 1961–62) and David Broome (b. 1 Mar. 1940) in 1960 on *Sunsalve*, 1966 on *Mister Softee* and 1972 on *Sportsman*. The Queen Elizabeth II Cup, (first held in 1949)

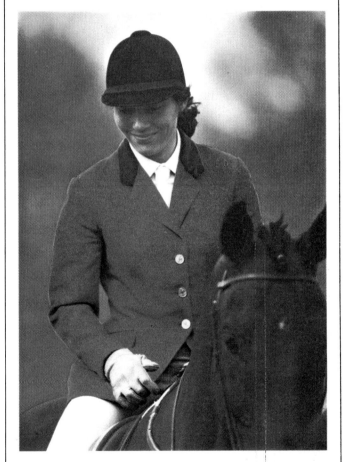

Double world champion, Janou Tissot, was the youngest ever Olympic show jumper when she won her first of two silver medals at Tokyo in 1964. (*E. D. Lacey*)

the premier award for women, has been won outright three times by Marion Mould (*née* Coakes) (G.B.) (1965, 1971) on *Stroller* and 1976 on *Elizabeth Ann*. The only horse to win both these trophies is *Sunsalve* in 1957 (with Elisabeth Anderson) and 1960.

Three-day event
The Badminton Three-Day Event (inst. 1949) has been won three times by Sheila Waddington (*née* Willcox) in 1957–59, Lt. (later Capt.) Mark Anthony Peter Phillips C.V.O. (b. 29 Sept. 1948) in 1971–72 and 1974, and Lucinda Prior-Palmer (b. 7 Nov. 1953) in 1973, 1976–77.

Jumping records
The official *Fédération Equestre Internationale* high jump record is 8 ft 1¼ in *2,47 m* by *Huasó*, ridden by Capt. Alberto Larraguibel Morales (Chile) at Vina del Mar, Santiago, Chile, on 5 Feb. 1949, and 27 ft 2¾ in *8,30 m* for long jump over water by *Amado Mio* ridden by Lt.-Col. Lopez del Hierro (Spain), at Barcelona, Spain on 12 Nov. 1951. *Heatherbloom*, ridden by Dick Donnelly was reputed to have covered 37 ft *11,28 m* in clearing an 8 ft 3 in *2,51 m puissance* jump at Richmond, Virginia, U.S.A. in 1903. H. Plant on *Solid Gold* cleared 36 ft 3 in *11,05 m* over water at the Wagga Show, New South Wales, Australia on 28 Aug. 1936. The official Australian record is 32 ft 10 in *10,00 m* by *Monarch* in Brisbane in 1951. *Jerry M.* allegedly cleared 40 ft *12,19 m* over the water at Aintree in 1912.

At Cairns, Queensland, *Golden Meade* ridden by Jack Martin cleared an unofficially measured 8 ft 6 in *2,59 m* on 25 July 1946. *Ben Bolt* was credited with clearing 9 ft 6 in *2,89 m* at the 1938 Royal Horse Show, Sydney, Australia. The Australian record is 8 ft 4 in *2,54 m* by *Flyaway* (Colin Russell) in 1939 and *Golden Meade* (A. L. Payne) in 1946. The world's unofficial best for a woman is 7 ft 5½ in *2,27 m* by Miss B. Perry (Australia) on *Plain Bill* at Cairns, Queensland, Australia in 1940. The greatest recorded height reached bareback is 6 ft 7 in *2,00 m* by *Silver Wood* at Heidelberg, Victoria, Australia, on 10 Dec. 1938.

The highest British performance is 7 ft 6¼ in *2,29 m* by the 16.2 hands *167 cm* bay gelding *Swank*, ridden by Donald Beard, at Olympia, Greater London, on 25 June 1937. On the same day, the Lady Wright (*née* Margery Avis Bullows) set the best recorded height for a British equestrienne on her liver chestnut *Jimmy Brown* at 7 ft 4 in *2,23 m*. These records were over the now unused sloping poles.

Longest ride
In 1911, two Texans, Temple and Louie Abernathy, rode 3,619 miles *5 824,2 km* from Coney Island, New York to San Francisco, in 62 days. Temple was nine and his older brother 11 years old, and had they taken two days less they would have won a $10,000 prize. The Bicentennial "Great American Horse Race", begun 31 May 1976, from Saratoga Springs, N.Y. to Sacramento, Cal. (3,500 miles *5 632 km*) was won by Virl Norton on *Lord Fauntleroy*—a mule—98 days later. His actual riding time was 315.47 hours.

Horseriding marathon
The duration record in the saddle is 245 hr 15 min by Wally Eaglesham in Wagga Wagga, N.S.W., Australia on 24 Sept. –4 Oct. 1976. Marathons of this kind stipulate that mounts must be changed at least each six hours.

Horsemanship marathon
Wally Eaglesham of Australia rode at all paces (including jumping) for 52 hr 53 min at Rockhampton, Queensland on 14–16 June 1977.

Driving
The biennial World Driving Championships have been held three times since 1972. Great Britain won the team gold medal in 1972 and 1974. The best individual performance by a Briton has been a silver medal won by Col. Sir John Miller in 1972.

FENCING
Origins
"Fencing" (fighting with single sticks) was practised as a sport in Egypt as early as *c.* 1360 B.C. The first governing body for fencing in Britain was the Corporation of Masters of Defence founded by Henry VIII before 1540 and fencing

As well as fencing Henry VIII excelled at a number of other sports, notably hunting, wrestling and throwing the hammer. (*Radio Times Hulton Picture Library*)

has been practised as sport, notably in prize fights, since that time. The foil was the practice weapon for the short court sword from the 17th century. The épée was established in the mid-19th century and the light sabre was introduced by the Italians in the late 19th century.

Most titles *World*
The greatest number of individual world titles won is four by d'Oriola (see details in table), but note that he also won two Individual Olympic titles. Of the three women foilists with three world titles, Heléne Mayer (Germany) (1929, 1931, 1937), Ellen Muller-Preiss (Austria) (1947, 1949, 1950) and Ilona Schacherer-Elek (Hungary) 1934–35, 1951), only Elek won two individual Olympic titles (1936 and 1948).

Most titles *Olympic*
The greatest number of individual Olympic Gold Medals won is three by Ramón Fonst (Cuba) (b. 1883) in 1900 and 1904 (two) and by Nedo Nadi (Italy) (1894–1952) in 1912 and 1920 (two). Nadi also won three team gold medals in 1920 making a then unprecedented total of five gold medals at one celebration. Edoardo Mangiarotti (Italy) (b. 7 Apr. 1919) with six gold, five silver and two bronze holds the record of 13 Olympic medals. He won them for foil and épée from 1936 to 1960. The women's record is seven medals (two gold, three silver, two bronze) by Ildikó Sagine-Retjöo (formerly Ujlaki-Retjö) (Hungary) (b. 11 May 1937) from 1960 to 1976.

British Olympic records
The only British fencer to win three Olympic medals has been Edgar Seligman with silver medals in the épée team event in 1906, 1908 and 1912. Henry William Furse Hoskyns M.B.E. (b. 19 Mar. 1931) has competed most often for Great Britain with six Olympic appearances, 1956–1976.

MOST OLYMPIC AND WORLD FENCING TITLES

Event	Olympic Gold Medals		World Championships (not held in Olympic years)	
Men's Foil, Individual	2	Christian d'Oriola (France) (b. 3 Oct. 1928) 1952, 56	4	Christian d'Oriola (France) (b. 3 Oct. 1928) 1947, 49, 53–54
	2	Nedo Nadi (Italy) (1894–1952) 1912, 20		
Men's Foil, Team	5	France 1924, 32, 48, 52, 68	12	Italy 1929–31, 33–35, 37–38, 49–50, 54–55
Men's Epée, Individual	2	Ramón Fonst (Cuba) (1883–1959) 1900, 04	3	Georges Buchard (France) (b. 21 Dec. 1893) 1927, 31, 33
			3	Aleksey Nikanchikov (U.S.S.R.) (1940–72) 1966–67, 70
Men's Epée Team	6	Italy 1920, 28, 36, 52, 56, 60	10	Italy 1931, 33, 37, 49–50, 53–55, 57–58
Men's Sabre, Individual	2	Dr. Jenö Fuchs (Hungary) (b. 29 Oct 1882) 1908, 12	3	Aladár Gerevich (Hungary) (b. 16 Mar. 1910) 1935, 1951, 1955
	2	Rudolf Kárpáti (Hungary) (b. 17 July 1920) 1956, 60	3	Jerzy Pawlowski (Poland) (b. 25 Oct. 1932) 1957, 65–66
	2	Jean Georgiadis (Greece) (b. 1874) 1896, 1906	3	Yakov Rylsky (U.S.S.R.) (b. 25 Oct. 1928) 1958, 1961, 1963
Men's Sabre, Team	9	Hungary 1908, 12, 28, 32, 36, 48, 52, 56, 60	14	Hungary 1930–31, 33–35, 37, 51, 53–55, 57–58, 66, 73
Women's Foil, individual	2	Ilona Schacherer-Elek (Hungary) (b. 1907) 1936, 48	3	Helène Mayer (Germany) (1910–53) 1929, 31, 37
			3	Ilona Schacherer-Elek (Hungary) (b. 17 May 1907) 1934–35, 51
			3	Ellen Muller-Preiss (Austria) (b. 6 May 1912) 1947, 49, 50 (shared)
Women's Foil, Team	4	U.S.S.R. 1960, 68, 72, 76	11	Hungary 1933–35, 37, 53–55, 59, 62, 67, 73

MOST AMATEUR FENCING ASSOCIATION TITLES

Foil	(Instituted 1898)	7	John Emrys Lloyd	1928, 1930–33, 1937–38
Epée	(Instituted 1904)	5	Robert Montgomerie	1905, 1907, 1909, 1912, 1914
Sabre	(Instituted 1898)	6	Dr. Roger F. Tredgold	1937, 1939, 1947–49, 1955
Foil (Ladies)	(Instituted 1907)	10	Gillian M. Sheen (now Mrs. R. G. Donaldson)	1949, 1951–58, 1960

FIVES

ETON FIVES

A handball game against the buttress of Eton College Chapel was recorded in 1825, but a court existed at Lord Weymouth's School (now Warminster School), Wiltshire, as early as 1773 and a handball game against the church wall at Babcary, Somerset, was recorded in June 1765. New courts were built at Eton in 1840, the rules were codified in 1877, rewritten laws were introduced in 1931 and the laws were last drawn up in 1950. There are courts in several countries besides England, with more than a dozen in Northern Nigeria.

Most titles

Only one pair have won the Amateur Championship (Kinnaird Cup) eight times—Anthony Hughes and Arthur James Gordon Campbell (1958, 1965–68, 1971, 1973 and 1975). Hughes was also in the winning pair in 1963 making nine titles in all.

RUGBY FIVES

As now known, this game dates from c. 1850 with the first inter-public school matches recorded in the early 1870s. The Oxford v. Cambridge contest was inaugurated in 1925 and the Rugby Fives Association was founded in the home of Dr. Cyriax, in Welbeck Street, City of Westminster, Greater London, on 29 Oct. 1927. The dimensions of the Standard Rugby Fives court were approved by the Association in 1931.

Most titles

The greatest number of Amateur Singles Championships (instituted 1932) ever won is five by Wayne Enstone in 1973–77. The record for the Amateur Doubles Championship (instituted 1925) is seven shared by John Frederick Pretlove (1952, 1954, 1956–59, 1961) and David E. Gardner (1960, 1965–66, 1970–72, 1974).

FOOTBALL (ASSOCIATION)

Origins

A game with some similarities termed *Tsu-chin* was played in China in the 3rd and 4th centuries B.C. The earliest clear representation of the game is an Edinburgh print dated 1672–73. It became standardized with the formation of the Football Association in England on 26 Oct. 1863. A 26-a-side game, however, existed in Florence, Italy, as early as 1530, for which rules were codified in *Discorsa Calcio* in 1580. The oldest club is Sheffield F.C., formed on 24 Oct. 1857. Eleven per side was standardized in 1870.

PROFESSIONAL

Longest match

The duration record for first class fixtures was set in the Copa Libertadores in Santos, Brazil, on 2–3 Aug. 1962, when Santos drew 3–3 with Penarol F.C. of Montevideo, Uruguay.

The game lasted $3\frac{1}{2}$ hours (with interruptions), from 9.30 p.m. to 1 a.m. A match between Simon Fraser Univ. Clansmen and Quincy College Hawks lasted 4 hr 25 min (221 min 43 sec playing time) at Pasadena, Cal., U.S.A. in Nov. 1976.

The longest British match on record was one of 3 hours 25 min between Stockport County and Doncaster Rovers in the second leg of the Third Division (North) Cup at Edgeley Park, Stockport, Greater Manchester on 26 Mar. 1946.

HIGHEST SCORES

Teams

The highest score recorded in a British first-class match is 36. This occurred in the Scottish Cup match between Arbroath and Bon Accord on 5 Sept. 1885, when Arbroath won 36–0 on their home ground. But for the lack of nets and the consequent waste of retrieval time the score would have been even higher.

Internationals

The highest margin recorded in an international match is 17. This occurred in the England v. Australia match at Sydney on 30 June 1951, when England won 17–0. This match is not listed by England as a *full* international. The highest in the British Isles was when England beat Ireland 13–0 at Belfast on 18 Feb. 1882.

F.A. Cup

The highest score in an F.A. Cup match is 26, when Preston North End beat Hyde 26–0 at Deepdale, Lancashire on 15 Oct. 1887. This is also the highest score between English clubs. The biggest victory in a final tie is six when Bury beat Derby County 6–0 at Crystal Palace on 18 Apr. 1903, in which year Bury did not concede a single goal in the five Cup matches.

League match

The highest score by one side in a Football League (Division I) match is 12 goals when West Bromwich Albion beat Darwen 12–0 at West Bromwich, West Midlands on 4 Mar. 1892; when Nottingham Forest beat Leicester Fosse by the same score at Nottingham on 21 Apr. 1909; and when Aston Villa beat Accrington 12–2 at Perry Barr, West Midlands on 12 Mar. 1892.

League match aggregate

The highest aggregate in League Football was 17 goals when Tranmere Rovers beat Oldham Athletic 13–4 in a Third Division (North) match at Prenton Park, Merseyside, on Boxing Day, 1935. The record margin in a League match has been 13 in the Newcastle United 13, Newport County 0 (Division II) match on 5 Oct. 1946 and in the Stockport County 13, Halifax 0 (Division III (North)) match on 6 Jan. 1934.

League season

The highest number of goals by any British team in a professional league in a season is 142 in 34 matches by Raith Rovers (Scottish Division II) in the 1937–38 season. The

English League record is 134 in 46 matches by Peterborough United (Division IV) in 1960–61.

Individual

The most scored by one player in a first-class match is 16 by Stanis for Racing Club de Lens v. Aubry-Asturies, in Lens, France, in a wartime game on 13 Dec. 1942. The record for any British first-class match is 13 by John Petrie in the Arbroath v. Bon Accord Scottish Cup match in 1885 (see above). The record in League Football is ten by Joe Payne (1914–77) for Luton Town v. Bristol Rovers in a Third Division (South) match at Luton on 13 Apr. 1936. The English First Division record is seven goals by Ted Drake (b. Southampton, 1912) for Arsenal v. Aston Villa at Birmingham on 14 Dec. 1935, and James Ross for Preston North End v. Stoke at Preston on 6 Oct. 1888. The Scottish First Division record is eight goals by James McGrory for Celtic v. Dunfermline Athletic at Celtic Park, Glasgow, on 14 Jan. 1928.

The record number of goals scored by one player in an international match is ten by Gottfried Fuchs for Germany who beat Russia 16–0 in the 1912 Olympic tournament (consolation event) in Sweden.

The record for individual goal-scoring in a British home international is six by Joe Bambrick (b. 1905) for Ireland v. Wales at Belfast on 1 Feb. 1930.

Career

Artur Friedenreich (b. 1892) is believed to have scored an undocumented 1,329 goals in Brazilian football, but the greatest total of goals scored in a specified period is 1,216 by Edson Arantes do Nascimento (b. Baurú, Brazil, 23 Oct. 1940), known as Pelé, the Brazilian inside left from 7 Sept. 1956 to 2 Oct. 1974 in 1,254 games. His best year was 1958 with 139 and the *milesimo* (1,000th) came in a penalty for his club Santos in the Maracaña Stadium, Rio de Janeiro on 19 Nov. 1969 when playing his 909th first-class match. He came out of retirement in 1975 to add to his total with New York Cosmos and by 26 June 1977 his total had reached 1,271, including 91 hat-tricks. Franz "Bimbo" Binder (b. 1911) scored 1,006 goals in 756 games in Austria and Germany between 1930 and 1950.

The best season League records are 60 goals in 39 League games by William Ralph "Dixie" Dean (b. Birkenhead, Cheshire, 1906) for Everton (Division I) in 1927–28 and 66 goals in 38 games by Jim Smith for Ayr United (Scottish Division II) in the same season. With three more in Cup ties and 19 in representative matches Dean's total was 82.

The international career record for England is 49 goals by Robert (Bobby) Charlton, O.B.E. (b. Ashington, Northumberland, 11 Oct. 1937). His first was v. Scotland on 19 Apr. 1958 and his last on 20 May 1970 v. Colombia.

The greatest number of goals scored in British first-class football is 550 (410 in Scottish League matches) by James McGrory of Glasgow Celtic (1922–38). The most scored in League matches is 434, for West Bromwich Albion, Fulham, Leicester City and Shrewsbury Town, by George Arthur Rowley (b. Wolverhampton, West Midlands, 1926) between 1946 and April 1965. Rowley also scored 32 goals in the F.A Cup and one for England "B".

Fastest goals

The fastest goal on record was one scored in 6 sec. by Albert Mundy for Aldershot in a Fourth Division match v. Hartlepools United at Victoria Ground, Hartlepool, Cleveland on 25 Oct. 1958. The same time was recorded by Keith Smith of Crystal Palace in a Second Division match v. Derby County at the Baseball Ground, Derby on 12 Dec. 1964. A hat-trick in 1 min 50 sec is claimed for Maglioni of Independiente v. Gimnasia y Escrima de la Plata in Argentina on 18 March 1973. John McIntyre (Blackburn Rovers) scored four goals in 5 min v. Everton at Ewood Park, Blackburn, Lancashire on 16 Sept. 1922. W. 'G.' (Ginger) Richardson (West Bromich Albion) scored four goals in 5 min against West Ham United at Upton Park on 7 Nov. 1931. Frank Keetley scored six goals in 21 min in the 2nd half of the Lincoln City v. Halifax Town league match on 16 Jan. 1932.

The international record is three goals in 3½ min by Willie Hall (Tottenham Hotspur) for England against Ireland on 16 Nov. 1938 at Old Trafford, Greater Manchester.

Fastest own goal

Torquay United's Pat Kruse equalled the fastest goal on record when he headed the ball into his own net only 6 sec after kick-off v. Cambridge United on 3 Jan. 1977.

Goal-less streak

In Oct.–Dec. 1919 Coventry played 11 successive games without scoring.

F.A. CHALLENGE CUP
Wins

The greatest number of F.A. Cup wins is seven by Aston Villa in 1887, 1895, 1897, 1905, 1913, 1920 and 1957 (nine final appearances). Of the six-time winners Newcastle United have been in the final 11 times. The highest aggregate scores have been 6–1 in 1890, 6–0 in 1903 and 4–3 in 1953.

The greatest number of Scottish F.A. Cup wins is 25 by Celtic in 1892, 1899, 1900, 1904, 1907–08, 1911–12, 1914, 1923, 1925, 1927, 1931, 1933, 1937, 1951, 1954, 1965, 1967, 1969, 1971, 1972, 1974, 1975 and 1977.

Youngest player

The youngest player in a F.A. Cup Final was Howard Kendall (b. 22 May 1946) of Preston North End, who played against West Ham United on 2 May 1964, 20 days before his 18th birthday. Note however, that Derek Johnstone (Rangers) (b. 4 Nov. 1953) was 16 years 11 months old when he played in the Scottish League Cup Final against Celtic on 24 Oct. 1970. The youngest goal scorer in the F.A. Cup Final was John Sissons (b. 30 Sept. 1945) who scored for West Ham United v. Preston North End on 2 May 1964. The youngest player ever in the F.A. Cup competition was David Fry who was only 15 yrs 321 days old when he played in goal for Weymouth v. Gillingham in Nov. 1975.

Most medals

Three players have won five F.A. Cup Winner's Medals: James Forrest (Blackburn Rovers) (1884–86, 1890–91); the Hon. Sir Arthur Fitzgerald Kinnaird, K.T. (Wanderers) (1873, 1877–78) and Old Etonians (1879, 1882) and C. H. R. Wollaston (Wanderers) (1872–73, 1876–78).

Longest tie

The most protracted F.A. Cup tie in the competition proper was that between Stoke City and Bury in the third round with Stoke winning 3–2 in the fifth meeting after 9 hours 22 min of play in January 1955. The matches were at Bury (1–1) on 8 January; Stoke on Trent on 12 January (abandoned after 22 min of extra time with the score 1–1); Goodison Park (3–3) on 17 January; Anfield (2–2) on 19 January; and finally at Old Trafford on 24 January. In the 1972 final qualifying round Alvechurch beat Oxford City after five previous drawn games.

MOST LEAGUE CHAMPIONSHIPS
World

The world record number of successive national League championship wins is nine by Celtic (Scotland) 1966–74, C.S.K.A., Sofia (Bulgaria) 1954–62 and M.T.K. Budapest (Hungary) 1917–25. The Sofia club hold a European post-war record of 19 league titles.

English

The greatest number of League Championships (Division I) is ten by Liverpool in 1901, 1906, 1922, 1923, 1947, 1964, 1966, 1973, 1976 and 1977. The record number of points in Division I is 67 by Leeds United in 1968–9. The lowest in the League has been eight by Doncaster Rovers (Division II) in 1904–5. Doncaster Rovers scored 72 points from 42 games in Division III (North) in 1946–7. Lincoln City achieved 74 points from 46 games in Division IV in 1975–6.

"Double"

The only F.A. Cup and League Championship "doubles" are those of Preston North End in 1889, Aston Villa in 1897,

Ten times League champions, Liverpool, in 1977, became the third British team to win the European Cup. (*Syndication International*)

Tottenham Hotspur in 1961 and Arsenal in 1971. Preston won the League without losing a match and the Cup without having a goal scored against them throughout the whole competition. Glasgow Rangers have won the Scottish League Championship 35 times between 1899 and 1976 and were joint champions on another occasion. Their 76 points in the Scottish First Division in 1920–1 represents a record in any division.

Closest win
In 1923–24 Huddersfield won the Division I championship over Cardiff by 0.02 of a goal with a goal average of 1.81.

Most durable player
The most durable player in League history has been Terence Lionel Paine M.B.E. (b. 23 Mar. 1939) who made 824 league appearances from 1957 to 1977 playing for Southampton F.C. and Hereford Utd. F.C. Jimmy Dickinson (b. Alton, Hampshire, 1925) made 764 appearances for one club, Portsmouth, between 1946 and 1965.

TOURNAMENT RECORDS
World Cup
The *Fédération Internationale de Football* (F.I.F.A.) was founded in Paris on 21 May 1904 and instituted the World Cup Competition on 13 July 1930, in Montevideo, Uruguay.

The only country to win three times has been Brazil in 1958, 1962 and 1970. Brazil was also third in 1938 and second in 1950, and is the only one of the 45 participating countries to have played in all ten competitions. Antonio Carbajal (b. 1923) played for Mexico in goal in the five competitions from 1950 to 1966. The record goal scorer has been Just Fontaine (b. Marrakesh, Morocco, 18 Aug. 1933) (France) with 13 goals in six games in the final stages of the 1958 competition in Sweden. The most goals scored in a final is three by Geoffrey Charles Hurst (b. Ashton-under-Lyne, Greater Manchester, 1941) (West Ham United) for England v. West Germany on 30 July 1966. Gerd Müller (b. 3 Nov. 1945) (West Germany) holds the aggregate record for goals scored in the World Cup Finals with 14 in 1970 and 1974.

World Club Championship
This club tournament was started in 1960 between the winners of the European Cup and the Copa Libertadores, the South American equivalent. Three clubs have won it twice: Penarol, Uruguay in 1961, 1966; Santos, Brazil in 1962, 1963; and Inter-Milan in 1964, 1965.

European Championship (*formerly Nations Cup*)
The European equivalent of the World Cup started in 1958 and is staged every four years. Each tournament takes two years to run with the semi-finals and final in the same country. The U.S.S.R. won the first when they beat Yugoslavia 2–1 in Paris on 10 July 1960 followed by Spain (1964), Italy (1968), West Germany (1972) and Czechoslovakia in 1976.

European Champion Clubs Cup
The European Cup for the League champions of the respective nations was approved by F.I.F.A. on 8 May 1955 and was run by the European governing body U.E.F.A. (Union of European Football Associations) which came into being in the previous year. Real Madrid won the first final, and have won a record six times, including five times consecutively, 1956–60, 1966.

Glasgow Celtic became the first British club to win the Cup when they beat Inter-Milan 2–1 in the National Stadium, Lisbon, Portugal, on 25 May 1967. At the same time they established the record of being the only British club to win the European Cup and the two senior domestic tournaments (League and Cup) in the same season.

European Cup Winners Cup
A tournament for the national Cup winners started in 1960–61 with ten entries. Fiorentina beat Glasgow Rangers 4–1 on aggregate in a two-leg final in May 1961. Tottenham Hotspur were the first British club to win the trophy, beating Atletico Madrid 5–1 in Rotterdam in 1963.

U.E.F.A. Cup
Originally known as the International Inter-City Industrial Fairs Cup, this club tournament began in 1955. The first

competition lasted three years, the second two years. In 1960–61 it became an annual tournament and since 1971–72 has been replaced by the U.E.F.A. Cup. The first British club to win the trophy were Leeds United in 1968.

PLAYERS
Most international appearances
Robert Frederick (Bobby) Moore, O.B.E. (b. Barking, Greater London, 12 Apr. 1941) of West Ham United and Fulham set up a new record of full international appearances by a British footballer by playing in his 108th game for England v. Italy on 14 Nov. 1973 at Wembley. His first appearance was v. Peru on 20 May 1962 and he retired from professional football on 14 May 1977 on his 1,000th appearance in all matches.

Most appearances *England*
The greatest number of appearances for England secured in the International Championship is 38 by William (Billy) Ambrose Wright, C.B.E. (b. Ironbridge, Salop, 6 Feb. 1924) in 1946–1959.

Most appearances *Wales*
The record number of appearances for Wales in the International Championship is 48 by William Henry (Billy) Meredith (1874–1958) (Manchester City and United) in the longest international span of 26 years (1895–1920). This is a record for any of the four home countries. Ivor Allchurch, M.B.E. (b. 29 Dec. 1929) of Swansea, Newcastle, Cardiff City and Worcester City played 68 times for Wales, including 37 times against the home countries, between 15 Nov. 1950 and Feb. 1968.

Most appearances *Scotland*
The Scottish record for International Championship matches is 30 by Alan Morton (Queen's Park and Glasgow Rangers) from 1920 to 1932. Morton also had a single foreign international making a total of 31 caps. Denis Law (b. Aberdeen 24 Feb. 1940) (Huddersfield Town, Manchester City (twice), Torino (Italy), Manchester United) has a record total of 55 appearances for Scotland between October 1958 and June 1974.

Most appearances *N. Ireland*
The greatest number of appearances for Ireland is 68 by Patrick Jennings (b. Newry, 1945) (Watford and Tottenham Hotspur) 1964 to 1977.

Oldest cap
The oldest cap has been Billy Meredith who played outside right for Wales v. England at Highbury, Islington, Greater London, on 15 Mar. 1920 when aged 45 years 229 days.

Youngest caps
The youngest cap in the four home countries internationals has been Norman Kernoghan (Belfast Celtic) who played for Ireland v. Wales in 1936 aged 17 years 80 days. It is possible, however, that W. K. Gibson (Cliftonville) who played for Ireland v. Wales in 1894 at 17 was slightly younger. England's youngest home international was Duncan Edwards (b. Dudley, West Midlands, 1 Oct. 1936, d. 21 Feb. 1958, 15 days after the Munich air crash) the Manchester United left half, against Scotland at Wembley on 2 Apr. 1955, aged 18 years 183 days. The youngest Welsh cap was John Charles (b. Swansea, 27 Dec. 1931) the Leeds United centre half, against Ireland at Wrexham on 8 Mar. 1950, aged 18 years 71 days. Scotland's youngest international has been Denis Law of Huddersfield Town, who played against Wales on 18 Oct. 1958, aged 18 years 236 days. Jackie Robinson played for England v. Finland in 1937 aged 17 years 9 months. Research remains to be completed on the date of birth of David Black of Hurlford, Strathclyde, who may have been 17 when he played for Scotland v. Ireland in 1889.

Transfer fees *World*
The world's highest transfer fee has been £922,300 paid by F.C. Barcelona, Spain to Ajax Amsterdam, Netherlands, for Johan Cruyff, (b. 25 Apr. 1947) announced on 20 Aug. 1973. On transfer (Sept.) he received a record signing fee of c. £400,000. It is reported that Napoli, Italy paid Bologna, Italy

around £1.4 m for centre forward Guiseppe Savoldi on 11 July 1975. Two other players were included in this deal.

Transfer fees *British*
British transfer fee "records" have become of progressively less significance because fiscal and public relations considerations tend to distort published figures.

The British aggregate record is held by the centre forward Tony Hateley (b. Derby, 1942) who in six moves from July 1963 to 28 Oct. 1970 was reportedly valued at £393,500.

Most successful national coach
The most successful national coach has been George Raynor (b. Hoyland, West Yorkshire, 1907) for Sweden. His teams won the 1948 Olympic competition and were second in the 1958 World Cup and third in both the 1950 World Cup and in the 1952 Olympic competition.

Heaviest goalkeeper
The biggest goalkeeper in representative football was the England international Willie J. "Fatty" Foulke (1874–1916), who stood 6 ft 3 in *1,90 m* and weighed 22 st. 3 lb. *141 kg*. His last games were for Bradford, by which time he was 26 st. *165 kg*. He once stopped a game by snapping the cross bar.

Greatest crowds
The greatest recorded crowd at any football match was 205,000 (199,854 paid) for the Brazil v. Uruguay World Cup match in the Maracaña Municipal Stadium, Rio de Janeiro, Brazil on 16 July 1950. The record attendance for a European Cup match is 136,505 at the semi-final between Glasgow Celtic and Leeds United at Hampden Park, Glasgow on 15 Apr. 1970.

The British record paid attendance is 149,547 at the Scotland v. England international at Hampden Park, Glasgow, on 17 Apr. 1937. It is, however, probable that this total was exceeded (estimated 160,000) on the occasion of the F.A. Cup Final between Bolton Wanderers and West Ham United at Wembley Stadium on 28 Apr. 1923, when the crowd broke in on the pitch and the start was delayed 40 min until the pitch was cleared. The counted admissions were 126,047.

The Scottish Cup record attendance is 146,433 when Celtic played Aberdeen at Hampden Park on 24 Apr. 1937. The record attendance for a League match in Britain is 118,567 for Rangers v. Celtic at Ibrox Park, Glasgow on 2 Jan. 1939.

For details of the largest football stadiums, see p. 113.

Smallest crowd
The smallest crowd at a full home international was 4,946 for the Northern Ireland v. Wales match of 19 May 1973 at Goodison Park, Everton, Merseyside. The smallest crowd at a Football League fixture was for the Stockport County v. Leicester City match at Old Trafford, Greater Manchester, on 7 May 1921. Stockport's own ground was under suspension and the "crowd" numbered 13.

Greatest receipts
The record gross F.A. Cup receipts at Wembley, Brent, Greater London, is £420,000 (excluding radio and television fees) for the finals on 1 May 1976 and 21 May 1977. The "gate" at the first F.A. Cup Final at Kennington Oval on 16 Mar. 1872 was £100.

The greatest receipts at any World Cup final were £204,805, from an attendance of 96,924 for England v. West Germany at Wembley, on 30 July 1966.

The record for a British international match is £303,000 for the England v. Scotland match at Wembley on 4 June 1977 (attendance 100,000). The receipts for the Manchester United v. Benfica match at Wembley on 29 May 1968 were £118,000 (attendance 100,000).

Most peripatetic fan
In a period of 227 days (3 Aug. 1974–17 Mar. 1975) Noel Conway, of London, viewed matches at all 93 English Football League grounds (incl. Berwick Rangers F.C.).

above: The cheerful faces of Dublin's Home Farm Football Club, who hold the record of winning 79 consecutive soccer matches.

left: Billy Wright captained England 90 times in his 105 international appearances from 1946 to 1959. (*Don Morley, All-Sport Photographic*)

AMATEUR AND MINOR LEAGUES

Most Olympic wins

The only country to have won the Olympic football title three times is Hungary in 1952, 1964 and 1968. The United Kingdom won the unofficial tournament in 1900 and the official tournaments of 1908 and 1912. The highest Olympic score is Denmark 17 v. France "A" 1 in 1908.

Highest scores *Teams*

The highest aggregate score in a home Amateur International is 11 goals in the England v. Scotland match (8–3) at Dulwich on 11 Mar. 1939. The foreign record was when England beat France 15–0 in Paris on 1 Nov. 1906.

The highest score in an F.A. Amateur Cup Final was eight when Northern Nomads beat Stockton 7–1 at Sunderland, Tyne and Wear in 1926, and when Dulwich Hamlet beat Marine (Liverpool) by the same score at Upton Park in 1932.

In 1975, in a Scottish ladies league match, Edinburgh Dynamos F.C. beat Lochend Thistle 42–0.

In an under-14 league match between Midas F.C. and Courage Colts, in Kent, England on 11 Apr. 1976, the full time score after 70 min play was 59–1. Top scorer for Midas was Kevin Graham with 17 goals. Courage had scored the first goal.

Highest scores *Individual*

The highest individual scores in amateur internationals are six by William Charles Jordan for England v. France (12–0) at Park Royal, Ealing, Greater London on 23 Mar. 1908; six by Vivian John Woodward (1879–1954) for England v. Holland (9–1) at Stamford Bridge, Hammersmith, Greater London, on 11 Dec. 1909; and six also by Harold A. Walden (1889–1949) for Great Britain v. Hungary, in Stockholm, Sweden, on 1 July 1912. Kim Barker, 11, of South Hobart, Tasmania, Australia scored 21 goals in his team's 25–0 win over Hutchins in the under-12 competition on 11 May 1974.

Highest scores *International Schoolboys*

The most prolific schoolboy international scorer has been Richard Smith Bell (England) who in the 1935–36 season scored 12 goals in three internationals: three v. Scotland, three v. Wales and six v. Ireland.

Highest scores *Season*

The greatest number of goals in a season reported for an individual player in junior league football is 96 by Tom Duffy, who played centre forward professionally for Ardeer Thistle F.C., Strathclyde in the 1960–61 season. The highest season figure reported in any class of competitive football for an individual is 294 goals in 67 matches by centre forward Michael Jones for Afan Lido F.C., St. Joseph's School and Port Talbot Boys XI in 1972–73. His total (65 headers, 120 right boot and 109 left boot) included an 11, a ten and six triple hat-tricks.

Fastest goals

Wind-aided goals in 3 sec after kick-off have been scored by Kenny McKenzie, Carrickvale Thistle v. Longstone Hearts, 27 Dec. 1975, and by Andrew Meadows, Riley H.S., Hull v. Kelvin Hall H.S. on 4 Mar. 1977. Tony Bacon, of Schalmont H.S. scored three goals v. Icabod Crane H.S. in 63 sec at Schenectady, New York, U.S.A. on 8 Oct. 1975.

Fastest own goal

The fastest own goal on record was one in 5 sec "scored" by Peter Johnson of Chesham United in a match against Wycombe Wanderers on 21 Feb. 1976.

Most caps

The record number of England amateur caps is held by Rod Haider, the Hendon captain and half-back, who made his 65th amateur international appearance for England v. Scotland on 5 Apr. 1974.

Most F.A. Amateur Cup wins

The greatest number of F.A. Amateur Cup (1893–1974) wins is ten by Bishop Auckland who won in 1896, 1900, 1914, 1921–22, 1935, 1939, 1955–57.

Most and Least successful teams

The Home Farm F.C., Dublin, Ireland, between 12 Oct. 1968 and 10 Oct. 1970 won 79 consecutive matches. Donnington Wood F.C., Shropshire completed a run of 92 league games without defeat to 1976. The Nomads F.C. who participate in the Norwich Lads and Minor League lost 20 out of 20 matches in 1972–73 with a score of 11–431 (a goal average of minus 21.55) despite buying a new goalkeeper for 25p. The club was awarded the League's Best Sportsmen Cup.

Longest ties

The aggregate duration of ties in amateur soccer have not

been collated but it is recorded that in the London F.A. Intermediate Cup first qualifying round Highfield F.C. Reserves had to meet Mansfield House F.C. on 19 and 26 September and 3, 10 and 14 Oct. 1970 to get a decision after 9 hours 50 min play with scores of 0–0, 1–1, 1–1, 3–3, and 0–2.

In the Hertfordshire Intermediate Cup, London Colney beat Leavesden Hospital after 12 hours 41 min play and seven ties from 6 Nov. to 17 Dec. 1971.

Most disciplined

Coleridge F.C. of the Cambridgeshire F.A. completed 23 years without a single member having been cautioned, sent off or otherwise disciplined since its formation in 1954.

Most indisciplined

In the local Cup match between Tongham Youth Club, Surrey and Hawley, Hampshire, England on 3 Nov. 1969 the referee booked all 22 players including one who went to hospital, and one of the linesmen. The match, won by Tongham 2–0, was described by a player as "A good, hard game".

In a Gancia Cup match at Waltham Abbey, Essex on 23 Dec. 1973, the referee, M. J. Woodhams, sent off the entire Juventus-Cross team and some club officials. Glencraig United, Faifley, nr. Clydebank, had all 11 team members and two substitutes for their match against Goldenhill Boy's Club on 2 Feb. 1975 booked in the dressing room before a ball was kicked. The referee, Mr. Tarbet of Bearsden, took exception to the chant which greeted his arrival. It was not his first meeting with Glencraig. The teams drew 2–2.

Oldest player

Jack Whattam (b. 7 Jan. 1909) of Cleethorpes played weekly for Burtons F.C. and Weelsby Rovers at the age of 67.

Largest crowd

The highest attendance at an amateur match has been 120,000 in Senayan Stadium, Jakarta, Indonesia, on 26 Feb. 1976 for the Pre-Olympic Group II final, North Korea v. Indonesia.

Ball control

Adrian Walsh, of Galway, Ireland juggled a regulation soccer ball for 2 hr 3½ min non-stop at Salthill Park, Galway on 22 Mar. 1977. He did 12,104 repetitions with feet, legs and head without the ball ever touching the ground.

The highest recorded number of repetitions for heading a ball is 12,100 in 54 min 22 sec by Michael Helliwell, 17, of Elland on 14 Dec. 1973.

Marathon *11-a-side*

The longest recorded 11-a-side football match played under F.A. rules without substitutes has been one of 42 hr 6 min

Ireland's champion ball juggler, Adrian Walsh, with his idol, Brazil's Pelé. (*Jerry Liebman*)

by two teams from The Brush High School, Lyndhurst, Ohio, U.S.A. on 27–29 May 1977.

Marathon *5-a-side*

The longest recorded authenticated 5-a-side games have been: outdoors: 59 hr 45 min by two teams (no substitutes) from the R.A.F. Hospital, Ely, Cambridge, England on 4–6 Aug. 1976 and indoors: 81 hr 2 min by two teams (no substitutes) from Carlow Regional Technical College, Ireland on 1–4 Mar. 1977.

FOOTBALL (GAELIC)

Earliest references

The game developed from inter-parish "free for all" with no time-limit, no defined playing area nor specific rules. Standardisation came with the formation of the Gaelic Athletic Association in Thurles, Ireland, on 1 Nov. 1884.

Most titles

The greatest number of All Ireland Championships ever won by one team is 23 by Ciarraidhe (Kerry) between 1903 and 1975. The greatest number of successive wins is four by Wexford (1915–18) and four by Kerry (1929–32).

Inter-provincials

The province of Leinster has won most championships (Railway Cup) with 18 between 1928 and 1974. Sean O'Neill (Down) holds the record of eight medals with Ulster (1960–71).

Highest scores *Team*

The highest score in an All-Ireland final was when Cork (3 goals, 17 points) beat Galway (2 goals, 13 points) in 1973. The highest combined score was also in this game. A goal equals three points.

Highest scores *Individual*

The highest recorded individual score in an All-Ireland final has been 2 goals, 5 points by Frank Stockwell (Galway) in the match against Cork in 1956.

Lowest scores

In four All-Ireland finals the combined totals have been 7 points; 1893 Wexford (1 goal, till 1894 worth 5 points, 1 point) v. Cork (1 point); 1895 Tipperary (4 points) v. Meath (3 points); 1904 Kerry (5 points) v. Dublin (2 points); 1924 Kerry (4 points) v. Dublin (3 points).

Most appearances

The most appearances in All-Ireland finals is ten by Dan O'Keeffe (Kerry) of which seven (a record) were on the winning side.

Largest crowd

The record crowd is 90,556 for the Down v. Offaly final at Croke Park, Dublin, in 1961.

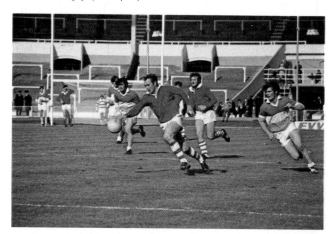

Cork v. Offaly, two of the great teams of Gaelic Football, a game akin to both Soccer and Rugby. (*Colorsport*)

FOOTBALL (RUGBY LEAGUE)

Origins
The Rugby League was formed originally in 1895 as "The Northern Rugby Football Union" by the secession of 22 clubs in Lancashire and Yorkshire from the parent Rugby Union. Though payment for loss of working time was a major cause of the breakaway the "Northern Union" did not itself embrace full professionalism until 1898. A reduction in the number of players per team from 15 to 13 took place in 1906 and the present title of "Rugby League" was adopted in 1922.

Most titles
There have been seven World Cup Competitions. Australia were winners in 1957, 1968, 1970 and 1975. Great Britain won in 1954, 1960 and 1972.

Under the one-league Championship system (1907–62 and 1965–71) the club with the most wins was Wigan with nine (1909, 1922, 1926, 1934, 1946, 1947, 1950, 1952 and 1960).

In the Rugby League Challenge Cup (inaugurated 1896–97) the club with the most wins is Leeds with nine in 1910, 1923, 1932, 1936, 1941–42 (wartime), 1957, 1968 and 1977. Oldham is the only club to appear in four consecutive Cup Finals (1924–27).

Only three clubs have won all four major Rugby League trophies (Challenge Cup, League Championship, County Cup and County League) in one season: Hunslet in 1907–08, Huddersfield in 1914–15 and Swinton in 1927–28.

In addition to the three "All Four Cup clubs", on only five other occasions has a club taken the Cup and League honours in one season: Broughton Rangers (1902); Halifax (1903); Huddersfield (1913); Warrington (1954); and St. Helens (1966). Warrington (1974) and St. Helens (1976) have won the Cup and the newly constituted Club championship.

HIGHEST TEAM SCORES
World Cup
The record aggregate score in a World Cup match is 72 points when Great Britain beat New Zealand at Hameau Stadium, Pau, France by 53 points to 19 on 4 Nov. 1972.

Senior match
The highest aggregate score in Cup or League football in a game where a senior club has been concerned, was 121 points, when Huddersfield beat Swinton Park Rangers by 119 points (19 goals, 27 tries) to 2 points (one goal) in the first round of the Northern Union Cup on 28 Feb. 1914.

Cup Final
The record aggregate in a Cup Final is 47 points when Featherstone Rovers beat Bradford Northern 33–14 at Wembley, Brent, Greater London, on 12 May 1973.

The greatest winning margin was 34 points when Huddersfield beat St. Helens 37–3 at Oldham on 1 May 1915.

Touring teams
The record score for a British team touring the Commonwealth is 101 points by England v. South Australia (nil) at Adelaide in May 1914.

The record for a Commonwealth touring team in Britain is 92 points (10 goals, 24 tries) by Australia against Bramley's 7 points (2 goals, 1 try) at the Barley Mow Ground, Bramley, near Leeds, on 9 Nov. 1921.

HIGHEST INDIVIDUAL SCORES
Most points Cup
C. H. "Tich" West of Hull Kingston Rovers scored 53 points (10 goals and 11 tries) in a First Round Challenge Cup-tie v. Brookland Rovers on 4 Mar. 1905.

Most points League
Michael Stacey (Leigh) scored 2 tries and kicked 15 goals (36 points) against Doncaster on 28 Mar. 1976. In the following two games Stacey scored 2 tries and 13 goals—a total of 68 points in three games.

Most points Season
The record number of points in a season was scored by B. Lewis Jones (Leeds) with 496 in season 1956–57 (he also scored 9 points in a friendly game). David Watkins (Salford) (b. 5 Mar. 1942) scored 493 points in season 1972–73 (he also scored 14 points in two friendly games).

Most points Career
Jim Sullivan (Wigan) (b. 2 Dec. 1903) scored 6,192 points (2,955 goals and 94 tries) in a senior Rugby League career extending from 1921 to 1946.

Most tries Season
Albert Aaron Rosenfeld (1885–1970) (Huddersfield), an Australian-born wing-threequarter, scored 80 tries in the 1913–14 season.

Most tries Career
Brian Bevan (b. Australia, 1924) a wing-threequarter, scored 834 tries in League, Cup, representative or charity games in the 18 seasons (16 with Warrington, two with Blackpool Borough) from 1946 to 1964.

Most goals Season
The record number of goals in a season is 228 by David Watkins (Salford) in the 1972–73 season. His total was made up of 221 in League, Cup, other competitions, and a Salford v. New Zealand match, plus seven in two pre-season friendly fixtures.

Fast scoring
David Watkins scored 13 points (3 tries, 2 conversions) in 5 min for Salford v. Barrow on 1 Dec. 1972.

Longest kick
In April 1940 Martin Hodgson (Swinton) kicked a goal on the Rochdale ground, later measured to be 77¾ yd 71 m to the goal posts. It thus probably carried another 20 yd or so.

Most international appearances
Test Matches between Great Britain (formerly England) and Australia are regarded as the highest distinction for a R.L. player in either hemisphere and Jim Sullivan the Wigan full-back and captain, holds the Test record for a British player with 15 appearances in these games between 1924 and 1933, though Mick Sullivan (no kin) of Huddersfield, Wigan, St. Helens and York, played in 16 G.B. v. Australia games in 1954–64, of which 13 were Tests and three World Cup matches.

In all Tests, including those against New Zealand and France, Mick Sullivan made the record number of 47 appearances and scored 43 tries.

Most Cup Finals
Two players have appeared in seven Cup Finals: Alan Edwards (Salford, Dewsbury, and Bradford Northern) between 1938 and 1949, and Eric Batten (Leeds, Bradford Northern and Featherstone Rovers) between 1941 and 1952.

Eric Ashton, M.B.E. (b. 24 Jan. 1935), Wigan and Great Britain centre has the distinction of captaining Wigan at Wembley in six R.L. Cup Finals in nine years 1958–66, taking the trophy three times (1958, 1959 and 1965).

Youngest player
The youngest player in a Cup Final was Reg Lloyd (Keighley) who was 17 years 8 months when he played at Wembley on 8 May 1937.

Most durable player
David Watkins (Salford) played and scored in every club game during seasons 1972–73 and 1973–74—a total of 92 games contributing 41 tries and 403 goals—a total of 929 points. Together with seasons 1970–71 and 1971–72 he played 140 consecutive games.

Robert Fleay (Swinton) (b. 15 Jan. 1949) played in 151 consecutive games (four full seasons) from 20 Aug. 1972 to 25 Apr. 1976.

Least successful team

Doncaster hold the unenviable record of losing 40 consecutive League games from 16 Nov. 1975 to 21 Apr. 1977.

Record transfer fees

The highest R.L. transfer fee is £20,000 paid to Dewsbury for Michael Stephenson by Penrith, Australia on 17 July 1973. David Watkins (Welsh R.U.) received an £11,000 signing fee and a guaranteed £1,000 p.a. for five years from Salford in October 1967.

Greatest crowds

The greatest attendance at any Rugby League match is 102,569 for the Warrington v. Halifax Cup Final replay at Odsal Stadium, Bradford, on 5 May 1954.

Greatest receipts

The highest receipts for a match in the world have been £247,211.26p for the Leeds v. Widnes Cup Final at Wembley on 7 May 1977.

RUGBY LEAGUE
HIGHEST SCORES

The highest aggregate scores in international Rugby League football are:

Match	Points	Score
Great Britain v. Australia (Test Matches)	62	Australia won 50–12 (Swinton, 9 Nov. 1963)
Great Britain v. New Zealand (Test Matches)	72	Great Britain won 52–20 (Wellington, 30 July 1910)
Great Britain v. France (Test Matches)	65	Great Britain won 50–15 (Leeds, 14 Mar. 1959)
England v. Wales	63	England won 40–23 (Leeds, 18 Oct. 1969)
England v. France	55	France won 42–13 (Marseilles, 25 Nov. 1951)
England v. Other Nationalities	61	England won 34–27 (Workington, 30 Mar. 1933)
Wales v. France	50	France won 29–21 (Bordeaux, 23 Nov. 1947)
Wales v. Other Nationalities	48	Other Nationalities won 27–21 (Swansea, 31 Mar. 1951)
Australia v. Great Britain	76	Australia won 63–13 (Paris, 31 Dec. 1933)
Australia v. Wales	70	Australia won 51–19 (Wembley, 30 Dec. 1933)
Australia v. France (Test Matches)	62	Australia won 56–6 (Brisbane, 2 July 1960)
Australia v. New Zealand (Test Matches)	74	New Zealand won 49–25 (Brisbane, 28 June 1952)
New Zealand v. France (Test Matches)	53	France won 31–22 (Lyon, 15 Jan. 1956)

FOOTBALL (RUGBY UNION)

Records are determined in terms of present day scoring values, i.e. a try at 4 points; a dropped goal, penalty or goal from a mark at 3 points; and a conversion at 2 points. The actual score, in accordance with which ever of the eight earlier systems was in force at the time, is also given, in brackets.

Origins

Though there are records of a game with many similarities to Rugby dating back to the Roman occupation, the game is traditionally said to have originated from a breach of the rules of the football played in November 1823 at Rugby School by William Webb Ellis (later the Rev.) (c. 1807–72). This handling code of football evolved gradually and was known to have been played at Cambridge University by 1839. The Rugby Football Union was not founded until 1871.

Most Olympic Gold Medals

Rugby Football was included four times in the Olympic Games: 1900, 1908, 1920 and 1924. Four United States players, in the 1920 winning team won second gold medals in 1924: Charles W. Doe, John T. O'Neil, John C. Patrick and Rudolph J. Scholz. Daniel B. Carroll, who was in the winning Australian team in 1908, won a second gold medal in the 1920 U.S. team.

HIGHEST TEAM SCORES
Internationals

The highest score in any full International was when Wales beat Japan by 82 points (10 goals, 4 tries, 2 penalties) to 6 points (2 penalties) in Tokyo, on 24 Sept. 1975.

The International Championship record is 75 points when Wales beat France at Swansea in 1910 by 59 points (8 goals, 1 penalty goal, 2 tries) to 16 (1 goal, 2 penalty goals and 1 try) (49–14).

The highest aggregate score for any International match between the Four Home Unions is 69 when England beat Wales by 69 points (7 goals, 1 drop goal and 6 tries) to 0 at Blackheath, Greenwich, Greater London in 1881. (Note: there was no point scoring in 1881).

The highest score by any Overseas side in an International in the British Isles is 53 points (7 goals, 1 drop goal and 2 tries) to 0 when South Africa beat Scotland at Murrayfield, Edinburgh, on 24 Nov. 1951 (44–0).

Tour match

The record score for any international tour match is 125–0 (17 goals, 5 tries and 1 penalty goal) (103–0) when New Zealand beat Northern New South Wales at Quirindi, Australia, on 30 May 1962.

Inter-club

In Denmark, Comet beat Lindo by 194–0 on 17 Nov. 1973.

Schools

Scores of over 200 points have been recorded in school matches, for example Radford School beat Hills Court 214 points (31 goals and 7 tries) to 0 (100–0) on 20 Nov. 1886.

Season

The highest number of points accumulated in a season by a rugby club is 1,454 points by Pontypridd R.F.C., Mid Glamorgan, in 1975–76. In 1970–71 Solihull R.U.F.C's 1st XV scored a record 247 tries.

Besides his record 49 Welsh caps Gareth Edwards has played for the British Lions on ten occasions, the most notable being the first defeat of New Zealand in 1971. (*Colorsport*)

HIGHEST INDIVIDUAL SCORES

Internationals

The highest individual points score in any match between members of the International Board is 24 by William Fergus "Fergie" McCormick (b. 1940)—1 drop goal, 3 conversions and 5 penalty goals for New Zealand against Wales at Auckland on 14 June 1969.

Ian Scott Smith (Scotland) (1903–1972) scored a record six consecutive international tries in 1925; last three v. France and first three v. Wales two weeks later.

Career

Fergie McCormick of Canterbury, New Zealand scored 2,153 points in his first class rugby career of 307 games from 1957 to 1974 (56 tries, 483 conversions, 312 penalty goals, 9 dropped goals).

Senior Inter [Open] Club

Chris Scotford (Solihull) contributed 41 points (7 tries, 1 penalty and 5 conversions) in a 48–7 win over Esher on 14 Dec. 1974.

Schools

In a junior house match in February 1967 at William Ellis School, Edgware, Greater London, between Cumberland and Nunn, Thanos Morphitis, 12, contributed 90 points (13 tries and 19 conversions) (77) to Cumberland's winning score.

Season

The first class rugby scoring record for a season is 581 points by Samuel Arthur Doble (b. 9 Mar. 1944) of Moseley, in 52 matches in 1971–72. He also scored 47 points for England in South Africa out of season.

Most international appearances

The totals below are limited to matches between the seven member countries of the "International Rugby Football Board" and France. Including a record 17 appearances for the British Lions, Willie John McBride (b. 6 June 1940) played in 80 international matches.

Ireland	63	Willie John McBride, M.B.E.	1962–75
New Zealand	55	Colin Earl Meads	1957–71
France	51	Walter Spanghero	1964–77
Wales	49	Gareth Owen Edwards	1967–77
Scotland	49	Alexander 'Sandy' B. Carmichael M.B.E.	1967–77
England	41	John Vivian Pullin	1966–76
Australia	39	Peter G. Johnson	1958–72
	39	Gregory Victor Davis	1963–72
South Africa	38	Frederick Christoffel Hendrick Du Preez	1960–71

County Championships

The County Championships (instituted in 1889) have been won most often by Gloucestershire with 13 titles (1910, 1913, 1920–22, 1930–32, 1937, 1972, 1974, 1975 and 1976).

Seven-a-sides *Origins*

Seven-a-side rugby dates from 28 Apr. 1883 when Melrose R.F.C., Borders in order to alleviate the poverty of a club in such a small town staged a Seven-a-side tournament. This idea was that of Ned Haig, the town's butcher. The bitter rivals Melrose and Galashiels tied in the final. In extra time, Melrose scored and absquatulated with the trophy declaring themselves to be the winners. Hence the present day tradition of "sudden death" extra-time.

Middlesex Seven-a-sides

The Middlesex Seven-a-sides were inaugurated in 1926. The most successful sides have been Harlequins with seven wins (1926–29, 1933, 1935, 1967) and London Welsh (1930–31, 1956, 1968, 1971–73).

The only players to be in five winning "sevens" have been the late N. M. Hall (St. Mary's Hospital 1944, 1946 and Richmond 1951, 1953, 1955), and J. A. P. Shackleton and I. H. P. Laughland both of London Scottish (1960–63, 1965).

Greatest crowd

The record paying attendance is 104,000 for Scotland v. Wales at Murrayfield, Edinburgh, on 1 Mar. 1975. Scotland won 12 points to 10.

Highest posts

The world's highest Rugby Union goal posts are reputed to be over $98\frac{1}{2}$ ft *30 m* high at the Railway Rugby Club, Nelspruit, South Africa. The posts at Kilmarnock R.F.C., Strathclyde, are 53 ft *16,15 m* high and made of three 20 ft *6,09 m* tubular steel lengths each.

Longest kicks

The longest recorded successful drop-goal is 90 yd *82 m* by Gerry Brand for South Africa v. England at Twickenham, Greater London, in 1932. This was taken 7 yd *6 m* inside the England "half" 55 yd *50 m* from the posts and dropped over the dead ball line.

The place kick record is reputed to be 100 yd *91 m* at Richmond Athletic Ground, Richmond upon Thames, Greater London, by D. F. T. Morkell in an unsuccessful penalty for South Africa v. Surrey on 19 Dec. 1906. This was not measured until 1932.

In the match Bridlington School 1st XV v. an Army XV at Bridlington, Humberside in 1944, Ernie Cooper, captaining the school, landed a penalty from a measured 81 yd *74 m* from the post with a kick which carried over the dead ball line.

Most tries

On 26 Mar. 1977 Andy Hill scored his 250th try for Llanelli, a British Club Rugby record, since his debut on 3 Nov. 1967.

Longest try

The longest "try" ever executed is by 15 members of Newtown Rugby Football Club, Powys, Wales, who scored at the Maesydail ground, Newtown, on 10 July 1977 from a "move" which carried the ball 602 miles *968,8 km* over a period of 72 hr 10 min. There were no forward passes or knock-ons, and the ball was touched down between the posts in the prescribed manner (Law 12). The "try" was touched down by club captain, Denzil Jones and converted by Dai Thomas.

ALL TIME SCORING RECORDS—AGGREGATE and MARGIN of VICTORY in the ten annual matches in the "International Championship" Note: Headnote on page 274 on Scoring systems				
		Aggregate Record Present Day pts. value		**Record Margin** Present Day pts. Value
England v. Scotland	Scotland (28) beat England (19) in 1931	57	England (19) beat Scotland (0) in 1924	21
			England (24) beat Scotland (5) in 1947	21
England v. Ireland	England (36) beat Ireland (14) in 1938	61	Ireland (22) beat England (0) in 1947	27
England v. Wales	England beat Wales by 7 goals, 1 drop goal and 6 tries to nil in 1881	69*	England beat Wales by 7 goals, 1 drop goal and 6 tries to nil in 1881	69
England v. France	England (49) beat France (15) in 1907	64	England (37) beat France (0) in 1911	44
Scotland v. Ireland	Scotland (29) beat Ireland (14) in 1913	51	Scotland beat Ireland by 6 goals and 2 tries to nil in 1877	44
Scotland v. Wales	Scotland (20) beat Wales (0) in 1887	56	Scotland (20) beat Wales (0) in 1887	56
Scotland v. France	Scotland (31) beat France (3) in 1912	41	Scotland (31) beat France (3) in 1912	33
Ireland v. Wales	Wales (34) beat Ireland (9) in 1976	43	Wales (29) beat Ireland (0) in 1907	34
Ireland v. France	France (27) beat Ireland (6) in 1964	40	Ireland (24) beat France (0) in 1913	30
Wales v. France	Wales (49) beat France (14) in 1910	75	Wales (47) beat France (5) in 1909	52

* Point scoring was not introduced until 1886.

FOXHUNTING

Earliest references

Hunting the fox in Britain became popular only towards the end of the 18th century though it is mentioned as early as 1278. Prior to that time hunting was confined principally to the deer, the hare, or the boar. It is estimated that foxhunters account for 10,000 of the 50,000 foxes killed each year.

Pack *Oldest*

The Old Charlton Hunt in West Sussex, now extinct, the Mid-Devon and the Duke of Buckingham in north Yorkshire, hunted foxes in the 1670s.

Pack *Largest*

The pack with the greatest number of hounds has been the Duke of Beaufort's hounds maintained at Badminton, Avon, since *c.* 1780. At times hunting eight times a week, this pack once had 120 couples.

Longest hunt

The longest recorded hunt was one led by Squire Sandys which ran from Holmbank, northern Lancashire, to Ulpha, Cumbria, a total of nearly 80 miles *128 km* in reputedly only six hours, in January or February 1743. The longest hunt in Ireland was probably a run of 24 miles *38 km* made by the Scarteen Hunt, County Limerick, from Pallas to Knockoura in 1914. The longest duration hunt was one of 10 hours 5 min by the Charlton Hunt of West Sussex, which ran from East Dean Wood at 7.45 a.m. to a kill over 57¼ miles *92 km* away at 5.50 p.m. on 26 Jan. 1738.

Largest fox

The largest fox ever killed by a hunt in England was a 23¾ lb. *10 kg 770* dog on Cross Fell, Cumbria, by an Ullswater Hunt in 1936. A fox weighing 28 lb. 2 oz. *12 kg 750* measuring 54 in *137 cm* from nose to the tip of the brush was shot on the Staffordshire-Worcestershire border on 11 Mar. 1956.

GAMBLING

World's biggest win

The world's biggest gambling win is £1,065,891 for a bet of two cruzeiros (25p) in the Brazilian football pools Loteria Esportiva by Miron Vieira de Sousa, 30, of Ivolandia, Brazil on the results of 13 games in October 1975. The first thing he bought was a set of false teeth. By winning a state lottery in January 1976, Eric C. Leek, of North Arlington, New Jersey, U.S.A., won $1,776 a week for life. Aged 26, he will receive a total of $4.6 million should he live a further 50 years.

World's biggest loss

An unnamed Italian industrialist was reported to have lost £800,000 in five hours at roulette in Monte Carlo, Monaco on 6 Mar. 1974. A Saudi Arabian prince was reported to have lost more than $1 million in a single session at the Metro Club, Las Vegas, U.S.A. in December 1974.

Largest casino

The largest casino in the world is the Casino, Mar del Plata, Argentina with average daily attendances of 14,500 rising to 25,000 during carnivals. The Casino has more than 150 roulette tables running simultaneously.

BINGO

Origins

Bingo is a lottery game which, as keno, was developed in the 1880s from lotto, whose origin is thought to be the 17th century Italian game *tumbule*. It has long been known in the British Army (called Housey-Housey) and the Royal Navy (called Tombola). The winner was the first to complete a random selection of numbers from 1–90. The U.S.A. version called Bingo differs in that the selection is from 1–75. There are six million players in the United Kingdom.

Largest house

The largest 'house' in Bingo sessions was staged at the Empire Pool, Wembley, Brent, Greater London, on 25 Apr. 1965 when 10,000 attended.

Earliest and latest Full House

A "Full House" call occurred on the 26th number by Mrs.

B. Johnstone at the Top Rank Club, Rutherglen, Glasgow on 29 Sept. 1976. "House" was not called until the 82nd number at the Telstar Club, Bransholme, Hull, Humberside on 13 Nov. 1976. 28 people won £2 each.

Largest prize

Prizes have been controlled since 1 July 1970 by the Betting and Gaming Act 1968. Prior to limitation, prizes in linked games between more than 50 clubs reached £16,000. The largest in a single game was £5,000 won in the Mecca National Rally at the Empire Pool, Wembley on 29 Mar. 1970.

Most cards

The highest recorded number of cards played simultaneously (with a call rate of 31.7 secs per call) has been 346 by Robert A. Berg at Pacific Beach, California on 16 Nov. 1973.

Marathon

A session of 128 hr 10 min was held at the Top Rank Club, Sketty, Swansea, on 11–16 July 1977 with John Barber and Tony John calling.

FOOTBALL POOLS

The winning dividend paid out by Littlewoods Pools in their first week in February 1923 was £2 12s 0d (£2.60). In April 1937 a record £30,780 was paid to R. Levy of London on four away wins, and in April 1947 a record £64,450 was paid for a 1d points pool.

Progressive list of individual record winnings

Amount	Recipient	Date
£75,000	P.C. Frank H. Chivers, 54, Aldershot, Hampshire	6 Apr. 1948
£91,832	George A. Borrett, Huyton, Merseyside	26 Sept. 1950
£94,335	Thomas A. Wood, 42, Carlisle	10 Oct. 1950
£104,990	Mrs. Evelyn Knowlson, 43, Manchester	7 Nov. 1950
£75,000 (limit)	(45 limit winners)	from 20 Nov. 1951 to 10 Sept. 1957
£205,235	Mrs. Nellie McGrail (now Mrs. Albert Cooper), 37, of Reddish, Greater Manchester	5 Nov. 1957
£206,028	W. John Brockwell, 29, Epsom, Surrey	18 Feb. 1958
£209,079	Tom Riley, 58, of Horden, Co. Durham	1 Apr. 1958
£209,837	Ronald Smith of Liverpool	23 Dec. 1958
£260,104	John Dunn, 45, of Chelsea, Greater London	27 Oct. 1959
£265,352	Arthur Webb, 70, of Scarborough, North Yorkshire	24 Nov. 1959
£301,739.45	Lawrence Freedman, 54, of Willesden, Brent, Greater London	8 Dec. 1964
£338,356.80	Percy Harrison, 52, of East Stockwith, Lincolnshire	30 Aug. 1966
£401,792	Albert Crocker, 54, of Dobwalls, Cornwall	20 Apr. 1971
£512,683	Cyril Grimes, 62, of Liss, Hampshire	7 Mar. 1972
£542,252	James Wood, 56, of Bradford, West Yorkshire	27 Feb. 1973
£547,172	A London woman	6 Mar. 1973
£629,801	Colin Carruthers, 24, of Kirkintilloch, Strathclyde	20 Mar. 1973
£680,697	Mrs. Nell Fletcher, 32, of Furnace, Strathclyde	19 Feb. 1974

In order to earn £680,697 post tax in 1976/77 a single man would have to be paid a salary of £3,970,511.47p

The odds for selecting 8 draws (if there are 8 draws) from 54 matches for an all-correct line are 1,040,465,790 to 1 against. (In practice, the approximate odds of winning a dividend of any size on Littlewoods Pools are 80 to 1.)

SLOT MACHINES

The world's biggest slot machine (or one armed bandit) is Super Bertha (555 ft³ *15,71 m³*) installed by Si Redd at the Four Queens Casino, Las Vegas, U.S.A. in September 1973. Once in every 25,000 million plays it may yield $1 million for a $10 feed. The total gambling "take" in 1976 in Nevada casinos was estimated at $1,190,000,000. The biggest beating handed to a "one-armed bandit" was $180,886 by Rodolfo Jose Salak, of San Francisco, at Harolds Club, Reno, Nevada on 9 Apr. 1977.

HORSE RACING

Highest ever odds

The highest recorded odds ever secured were 1,099,299 to 1 by a backer from Otley, West Yorkshire on a seven horse accumulator on 10 May 1975. On a stake of £1.76 in penny bets, he won a total of £12,578.14. The world record odds on a "double" are 24,741 to 1 secured by Mr. Montague Harry Parker at Windsor, England, for a £1 each-way "double" on *Ivernia* and *Golden Sparkle* with William Hill.

THE FOUR QUEENS PRESENTS
WITH '5' PLAYED 77777777 WITH 5 PLAYED **wins super**
$50,000.00
THE WORLDS LARGEST JACKPOT ON THE WORLDS LARGEST MACHINE

The biggest "bandit" of them all—Super Bertha in Las Vegas—where eight sevens adds up to a great deal more than 56. (*Las Vegas News Bureau*)

Biggest tote win

The best recorded tote win was one of £341 2s 6d to 2s (*£341.12½ to 10p*) representing odds of 3,410¼ to 1, by Mrs. Catharine Unsworth of Blundellsands, Liverpool at Haydock Park on a race won by *Coole* on 30 Nov. 1929. The highest odds in Irish tote history were £184 7s 6d on a 2s 6d (*£184.37½ on a 12½p*) stake, *viz.* 1,474 to 1 on *Hillhead VI* at Baldoyle on 31 Jan. 1970.

Most complicated bet

The most complicated bet is the Harlequin, a compound wager on four horses with 2,028 possible ways of winning. It was invented by Monty H. Preston of London who has been reputed to be the fastest settler of bets in the world. He once completed 3,000 bets in a 4½-hour test.

Largest bookmaker

The world's largest bookmaker is Ladbroke's of London with a turnover for 1976 of £319 million. The largest chain of betting shops is that of the William Hill Organization with between 980 and 1,020 shops in the United Kingdom.

Topmost tipster

The only recorded instance of a racing correspondent forecasting ten out of ten winners on a race card was at Delaware Park, Wilmington, Delaware, U.S.A. on 28 July 1974 by Charles Lamb of the *Baltimore News American*.

Greatest pay-out

The greatest published "pay-out" on a single bet is £69,375 by Ladbroke's to the late Bernard Sunley on the Derby victory of *Santa Claus* in 1964. On 12 Dec. 1976 Mr. Lim Chooi Seng won Malasian $1,112,400 £258,700 on *Freedom Fighter* in the sixth race at Penang.

ROULETTE

The longest run on an ungaffed (*i.e.* true) wheel reliably recorded is six successive coups (in No. 10) at El San Juan

Hotel, Puerto Rico on 9 July 1959. The odds with a double zero were 1 in 38^6 or 3,010,936,383 to 1.

Longest marathon

The longest "marathon" on record is one of 31 days from 10 Apr. to 11 May 1970 at The Casino de Macao, to test the validity or invalidity of certain contentions in 20,000 spins.

ELECTIONS

Ladbroke's biggest turnover is on General Elections. The highest ever individual bet was £50,000 on Labour to win the 1964 Election by Sir Maxwell Joseph. He made £37,272 on the odds offered. A bet of £5,000 at 200–1 was placed by Frank Egerton in April 1975 that his political Centre Party would win the next General Election.

GLIDING

Emanuel Swedenborg (1688–1772) of Sweden made sketches of gliders *c.* 1714. (see under I.Q. levels, page 17).

The earliest man-carrying glider was designed by Sir George Cayley (1773–1857) and carried his coachman (possibly John Appleby) about 500 yd *457 m* across a valley near Brompton Hall, North Yorkshire in the summer of 1853. Gliders now attain speeds of 168 m.p.h. *270 km/h* and the Jastrzab aerobatic sailplane is designed to withstand vertical dives at up to 280 m.p.h. *450 km/h.*

Highest standard

A gold C with three diamonds (for goal flight, distance and height) is the highest standard in gliding. This has been gained by 78 British pilots up to July 1977.

Most titles *World*

World individual championships (inst. 1948) have been won

SELECTED WORLD RECORDS (Single-seaters)		BRITISH NATIONAL RECORDS[1] (Single-seaters)	
Distance 907.7 miles *1 460,8 km*	Hans-Werner Grosse (W. Germany) in an ASW-12 on 25 Apr. 1972 from Lübeck to Biarritz	460.5 miles *741 km*	Peter D. Lane in a Skylark 3F, Geilenkirchen to Hiersac, Germany on 1 June 1962
Declared Goal Flight 765.4 miles *1 231,8 km*	Hans-Werner Grosse (W. Germany) in an ASW-17 on 16 Apr. 1974 from Lübeck to Marmande	360 miles *579,36 km*	H. C. N. Goodhart in a Skylark 3, Lasham, Hants, to Portmoak, Scotland on 10 May 1959
Absolute Altitude 46,266 ft *14 102 m*	Paul F. Bikle, Jr. (U.S.A.) in a Schweizer SGS 1-23E over Mojave, California (released at 3,963 ft *1 207 m*) on 25 Feb. 1961 (also record altitude gain—42,303 ft *12 894 m*)	37,050 ft *11 293 m*	H. C. N. Goodhart in a Schweizer 1-23 over California, U.S.A. on 12 May 1955
Goal and Return 1,004 miles *1 616 km*	Karl H. Striedieck (U.S.A.) in an ASW 17 from Lock Haven, Penn. to Tennessee. on 9 May 1977	497.7 miles *801,3 km*	Christopher Garton in a Kestrel 19, Lasham to Durham on 22 July 1976
Speed over Triangular Course 100 km 108.73 m.p.h. *175,00 km/h*	Klaas Goudriaan (S. Africa) in an ASW 17 over South Africa on 22 Nov. 1975	88.99 m.p.h. *143,3 km/h*	E. P. Hodge in a Standard Cirrus over Rhodesia on 30 Oct. 1976
300 km 95.95 m.p.h. *153,43 km/h*	Walter Neubert (W. Germany) in a Kestrel 604 over Kenya on 3 Mar. 1972	91.2 m.p.h. *146,8 km/h*	Edward Pearson in a Nimbus 2 over S.W. Africa on 30 Nov. 1976
500 km 88.82 m.p.h. *143.04 km/h*	Edward Pearson in a Nimbus 2 over Namibia on 27 Nov. 1976	88.82 m.p.h. *143.04 km/h*	Edward Pearson in a Nimbus 2 over Namibia on 27 Nov. 1976
750 km 83.26 m.p.h. *134.00 km/h*	Robert John Rowe (Australia) from Narromine Airfield on 15 Feb 1977.	68.2 m.p.h. *109,8 km/h*	Michael R. Carlton in a Kestrel 19 over South Africa on 5 Jan. 1975.
1000 km 61.13 m.p.h. *98,44 km/h*	Hans-Werner Grosse (W. Germany) in an ASW-17) over Waikerie, Australia on 18 Jan. 1977	[1] *British National Records may be set up by British pilots in any part of the world*	

five times by West Germans. There have been three British wins by Philip Aubrey Wills (b. 1907) (1952), H. C. Nicholas Goodhart and F. Foster (2-seater, 1956) and D. George Lee (b. 7 Nov. 1945) (1976).

Most titles *British*
The British national championship (instituted 1939) has been won most often by Philip A. Wills (b. 26 May 1907), in 1948–50 and 1955. The first woman to win this title was Mrs. Anne Burns of Farnham, Surrey on 30 May 1966.

PARASCENDING
The longest flight is 15 hr 22 min by Douglas Wray (G.B.), towed by John Terry, over Lake Windermere, Cumbria, England on 2 May 1977.

HANG GLIDING
Origins
In the eleventh century the monk, Elmer, is reported to have flown from the 60 ft *18,3 m* tower of Malmesbury Abbey, Wiltshire. The earliest modern pioneer was Otto Lilienthal (1848–96) (Germany) with numerous flights between 1893 and 1896. In the 1950's Professor Francis Rogallo of the

National Space Agency, U.S.A., developed a "wing" from his space capsule re-entry researches.

Championships
At the First World Championships, held at Kössen, Austria in Sept. 1976, the overall champion was Terry Delore (N.Z.). The 1976 British champion was Robert Wisely.

Greatest distance
The furthest distance covered in a hang glider, in free flight, is 61.68 miles *99,27 km* by Robert Pruitt (U.S.A.) in an Olympus 180 on 14 June 1977. The best in Britain is 22 miles *35,4 km* by Nigel Milnes in a Phoenix 6B over Hereford on 15 May 1977.

Greatest ascent and descent
The greatest height gain is by Phil Warrender (U.S.A.) from 11,980 ft *3 651 m* to 19,000 ft *5 791 m* over Telluride, Colorado, U.S.A. on 14 Aug. 1976.

The greatest altitude from which a hang-glider has descended is 31,600 ft *9 631 m* by Bob McCaffrey, 18, (U.S.A.) in an experimental design from a balloon over the Mojave Desert, California, U.S.A. on 21 Nov. 1976.

GOLF
Origins
The earliest mention of golf occurs in a prohibiting law passed by the Scottish Parliament in March 1457 under which "golfe be utterly cryed downe". The Romans had a cognate game called *paganica* which may have been carried to Britain before A.D. 400. In February 1962 the Soviet newspaper *Izvestiya* claimed that the game was of 15th century Danish origin while the Chinese Nationalist Golf Association claim the game is of Chinese origin ("the ball hitting game") in the 3rd or 2nd century B.C. Gutta percha balls succeeded feather balls in 1848 and by 1902 were in turn succeeded by rubber-cored balls, invented in 1899 by Haskell (U.S.A.). Steel shafts were authorized in 1929.

Club *Oldest*
The oldest club of which there is written evidence is the Gentlemen Golfers (now the Honourable Company of Edinburgh Golfers) formed in March 1744—ten years prior to the institution of the Royal and Ancient Club of St. Andrews, Fife. The oldest existing club in North America is the Royal Montreal Club (1873).

Club *Largest*
The only club in the world with 15 courses is the Eldorado Golf Club, California, U.S.A. The club with the highest

membership in the British Isles is Wentworth Club, Virginia Water, Surrey, with 1,850 members. The Royal and Ancient Golf Club of St. Andrews, Fife, Scotland has 1,750 members and the largest in Ireland is Royal Portrush, Co. Antrim with 1,215 members.

Course *Highest*
The highest golf course in the world is the Tuctu Golf Club in Morococha, Peru, which is 4 369 m *14,335 ft* above sea-level at its lowest point. Golf has, however, been played in Tibet at an altitude of over 4 875 m *16,000 ft*.

The highest golf course in Great Britain is one of nine holes at Leadhills, Strathclyde, 1,500 ft *457 m* above sea-level.

Course *Lowest*
The lowest golf course in the world was that of the Sodom and Gomorrah Golfing Society at Kallia, on the north-eastern shores of the Dead Sea, 380 m *1,250 ft* below sea-level. The clubhouse was burnt down in 1948 but the game is now played on Kallia Hotel course.

Longest hole
The longest hole in the world is the 17th hole (par 6) of 745 yd *681 m* at the Black Mountain Golf Club, North Carolina, U.S.A. It was opened in 1964. In August 1927 the sixth hole

at Prescott Country Club in Arkansas, U.S.A., measured 838 yd *766 m*. The longest hole on a championship course in Great Britain is the sixth at Troon, Strathclyde, which stretches 580 yds *530 m*.

Largest green
Probably the largest green in the world is the fifth green at Runaway Brook G.C. Bolton, Massachusetts, U.S.A. with an area greater than 28,000 ft² *2 600 m²*.

Biggest bunker
The world's biggest bunker (called a trap in the U.S.A.) is Hell's Half Acre on the seventh hole of the Pine Valley course, New Jersey, U.S.A., built in 1912 and generally regarded as the world's most trying course.

Longest course
The world's longest course is at Dub's Dread G.C. Piper, Kansas, U.S.A. and is a 78-par 8,101 yd *7 407 m*. Floyd Satterlee Rood used the United States as a course, when he played from the Pacific surf to the Atlantic surf from 14 Sept. 1963 to 3 Oct. 1964 in 114,737 strokes. He lost 3,511 balls on the 3,397.7 mile *5 468 km* trail.

Longest drives
In long-driving contests 330 yd *300 m* is rarely surpassed at sea level. In officially regulated long driving contests over level ground the greatest distance recorded is 392 yd *358 m* by William Thomas (Tommie) Campbell (Foxrock Golf Club) made at Dun Laoghaire, Co. Dublin, in July 1964. On an airport runway Valentin Barrios (Spain) drove a Slazenger B51 ball 568½ yd *520 m* at Palma, Majorca on 7 Mar. 1977. The greatest recorded drive on an ordinary course is one of 515 yd *471 m* by Michael Hoke Austin (b. 17 Feb. 1910) of Los Angeles, California, U.S.A., in the U.S. National Seniors Open Championship at Las Vegas, Nevada, on 25 Sept. 1974. Austin, 6 ft 2 in *1,88 m* tall and weighing 210 lb. *92,250 kg* drove the ball to within a yard of the green on the par-4 450 yd *412 m* fifth hole of the Winterwood Course and it rolled 65 yd *59 m* past the flagstick. He was aided by an estimated 35 m.p.h. *56 km/h* tailwind.

A drive of 2,640 yd *2 414 m* (1½ miles) across ice was achieved by an Australian meteorologist named Nils Lied at Mawson Base, Antarctica, in 1962. Arthur Lynskey claimed a drive of 200 yd *182 m* horizontal and two miles *3 200 m* vertical off Pikes Peak, Colorado (14,110 ft *4 300 m*) on 28 June 1968. On the Moon the energy expended on a mundane 300 yd *274 m* drive would achieve, craters permitting, a distance of one mile *1,6 km*.

Longest hitter
The golfer regarded as the longest consistent hitter the game has ever known is the 6 ft 5 in *195 cm* tall, 17 st 2 lb. *108 kg* 86 George Bayer (U.S.A.), the 1957 Canadian Open Champion. His longest measured drive was one of 420 yd *384 m* at the fourth in the Las Vegas Invitational, Nevada, in 1953. It was measured as a precaution against litigation since the ball struck a spectator. Bayer also drove a ball pin high on a 426 yd *389 m* hole at Tucson, Arizona in 1955. Radar measurements show that an 87 m.p.h. *140 km/h* impact velocity for a golf ball falls to 46 m.p.h. *74 km/h* in 3 seconds.

Longest putt
The longest recorded holed putt in a major tournament was one of 86 ft *26 m* on the vast 13th green at the Augusta National, Georgia by Cary Middlecoff (b. January 1921) (U.S.A.) in the 1955 Masters' Tournament. Robert Tyre (Bobby) Jones Jr. (1902–71) was reputed to have holed a putt in excess of 100 ft *30 m* at the fifth green in the first round of the 1927 British Open at St. Andrews.

SCORES
Lowest 9 holes and 18 holes *Men*
The lowest recorded score on any 18-hole course with a par score of 70 or more is 55 (15 under bogey) first achieved by A. E. Smith, the Woolacombe professional, on his home course on 1 Jan. 1936. The course measured 4,248 yd *3 884 m*. The detail was 4, 2, 3, 4, 2, 4, 3, 4, 3 = 29 out, and 2, 3, 3, 3, 3, 2, 5, 4, 1 = 26 in. E. F. Staugaard (U.S.A.) also scored 55 on the 6,419 yd *5 870 m* course of the Montebello Park Golf Club, California, U.S.A., in 1935. The lowest recorded score

on a long course (over 6,000 yd *5 486 m*) in Britain is 58 by Harry Weetman (1920–72) the British Ryder Cup golfer, for the 6,171 yd *5 642 m* Croham Hurst Course, Croydon, on 30 Jan. 1956.

Nine holes in 25 (4, 3, 3, 2, 3, 3, 1, 4, 2) was recorded by A. J. "Bill" Burke in a round in 57 (32 + 25) on the 6,389 yd *5 842 m* par 71 Normandie course St. Louis, Missouri, U.S.A. on 20 May 1970. This feat equalled that of Daniel E. Cavin (3, 3, 3, 3, 3, 3, 2, 3, 2) on the 2,880 yd *2 633 m* par 36 Bill Brewer Course, Greggton, Texas, on 27 Sept. 1959.

The United States P.G.A. tournament record for 18 holes is 59 (30 + 29) by Al Geiberger (b. 1 Sept. 1937) in the second round of the Danny Thomas Classic, on the 72-par 7,249 yd *6 628 m* course at Memphis, Tennessee on 10 June 1977. Two golfers have recorded 59 over 18 holes in non-P.G.A. tournaments; Samuel Jackson Snead (b. 27 May 1912) in the third round of the Sam Snead Festival at White Sulphur Springs, West Virginia, U.S.A. on 16 May 1959 and Gary Player (South Africa) (b. 1 Nov. 1936) in the second round of the Brazilian Open in Rio de Janeiro on 29 Nov. 1974.

Lowest 9 holes and 18 holes *Women*
The lowest recorded score on an 18-hole course (over 6,000 yd *5 486 m*) for a woman is 62 (30 + 32) by Mary "Mickey" Kathryn Wright (b. 14 Feb. 1935) of Dallas, Texas, on the Hogan Park Course (6,282 yd *5 747 m*) at Midland, Texas, U.S.A., in November 1964. Wanda Morgan recorded a score of 60 (31 + 29) on the Westgate-on-Sea and Birchington Golf Club course over 18 holes (5,002 yd *4 573 m*) on 11 July 1929.

Lowest 9 holes and 18 holes *Great Britain*
The British Tournament 9-hole record is 28 by John Panton (b. 1917) in the Swallow-Penfold Tournament at Harrogate, North Yorkshire, in 1952; by Bernard John Hunt (b. 2 Feb. 1930) of Hartsbourne in the Spalding Tournament at Worthing, West Sussex, in August 1953; and by Lionel Platts (b. 10 Oct. 1934, Yorkshire) of Wanstead in the Ulster Open at Shandon Park, Belfast, on 11 Sept. 1965. The lowest score recorded in a first class professional tournament on a course of more than 6,000 yd *5 486 m* in Great Britain was set at 61 (29 + 32), by Thomas Bruce Haliburton (1915–1975) of Wentworth G.C. in the Spalding Tournament at Worthing, West Sussex, in June 1952. Peter J. Butler (b. 25 Mar. 1932) equalled this record with 61 (32 + 29) in the Bowmaker Tournament on the Old Course at Sunningdale, Berkshire, on 4 July 1967.

Lowest 36 holes
The record for 36 holes is 122 (59 + 63) by Snead in the 1959 Sam Snead Festival on 16–17 May 1959. Horton Smith (1908–1963), a U.S. Masters Champion, scored 121 (63 + 58) on a short course on 21 Dec. 1928. The lowest score by a British golfer has been 126 (61 + 65) by Tom Haliburton.

Lowest 72 holes
The lowest recorded score on a first-class course is 257 (27 under par) by Mike Souchak in the Texas Open at Brackenridge Park, San Antonio in February 1955, made up of 60 (33 + 27), 68, 64, 65 (average 64.25 per round) exhibiting, as one critic said: "up and down" form, for a 27 under par with 27 birdies. The temperature on the fourth day was 27 °F — 2.8 °C

Horton Smith scored 245 (63, 58, 61 and 63) for 72 holes on the 4,700 yd *4 297 m* course (par 64) at Catalina Country Club, California, U.S.A., to win the Catalina Open on 21–23 Dec. 1928.

The lowest 72 holes in a national championship is 262 (67, 66, 66, 63) by Percy Alliss (G.B.) (1897–1975) in the 1932 Italian Open at San Remo, and by Liang Huan Lu (Taiwan) (b. 1936) in the 1971 French Open at Biarritz. Kelvin D. G. Nagle (b. 21 Dec. 1920) of Australia shot 261 in the Hong Kong Open in 1961. The lowest for four rounds in a British first class tournament is 262 (66, 63, 66 and 67) by Bernard Hunt in the Piccadilly Stroke Play tournament on Wentworth East Course, Virginia Water, Surrey on 4–5 Oct. 1966.

Eclectic record

The lowest recorded eclectic (from the Greek *eklektikos* = choosing) score, i.e. the sum of a player's all-time personal low scores for each hole, for a course of more than 6,000 yd *5 486 m* is 33 by the club professional Jack McKinnon on the 6,538 yd *5 978 m* Capilano Golf and Country Club course, Vancouver, British Columbia, Canada. This was compiled over the period 1937–1964 and reads 2-2-2-1-2-2-2-2-1 (16 out) and 2-1-2-2-1-2-2-2-3 (17 in) = 33. The British record is 38 by Alan Victor Muhr (b. 14 June 1906) at Seaton Carew Golf Club, Cleveland (6,604 yd *6 038 m*) from 1917–76. This is made up of 2, 4, 1, 2, 2, 2, 2, 2, 2 (19 out) and 2, 2, 1, 3, 3, 1, 2, 3, 2 (19 in).

Highest score

The highest score for a single hole in the British Open is 21 by a player in the inaugural meeting at Prestwick in 1860. Double figures have been recorded on the card of the winner only once, when Willie Fernie (1851–1924) scored a ten at Musselburgh, Lothian, in 1883. Ray Ainsley of Ojai, California, took 19 strokes for the par-4 16th hole during the second round of the U.S. Open at Cherry Hills Country Club, Denver, Colorado, on 10 June 1938. Most of the strokes were used in trying to extricate the ball from a brook. Hans Merell of Mogadore, Ohio, took 19 strokes on the par-3 16th (222 yd *203 m*) during the third round of the Bing Crosby National Tournament at Cypress Point Club, Del Monte, California, U.S.A., on 17 Jan. 1959. It is recorded that Chevalier von Cittern went round 18 holes in 316, averaging 17.55 per hole, at Biarritz, France in 1888. Stephen Ward took 222 strokes for the 6,212 yd *5 680 m* Pecos Course, Reeves County, Texas, U.S.A., on 18 June 1976—but he was only aged 3 yr 286 days.

Most shots for one hole

A woman player in the qualifying round of the Shawnee Invitational for Ladies at Shawnee-on-Delaware, Pennsylvania, U.S.A., in *c.* 1912, took 166 strokes for the short 130 yd *118 m* 16th hole. Her tee shot went into the Binniekill River and the ball floated. She put out in a boat with her exemplary, but statistically minded husband at the oars. She eventually beached the ball 1½ miles *2,4 km* downstream but was not yet out of the wood. She had to play through one on the home run.

Rounds fastest *Individual*

With such variations in lengths of courses, speed records, even for rounds under par, are of little comparative value. Bob Williams at Eugene, Oregon, U.S.A., completed 18 holes (6,010 yd *5 495 m*) in 27 min 48.2 sec in 1971 but this test permitted the striking of the ball whilst still moving. The record for a still ball is 31 min 22 sec by Len Richardson, the South African Olympic athlete at Mowbray, Cape Town (6,248 yd *5 713 m*) in November 1931.

Rounds fastest *Team*

Forty-three players representing Borger High School, Texas, U.S.A., completed the 18 hole 6,109 yd *5 586 m* Huber Golf Course in 10 min 11.4 sec on 11 June 1976.

Rounds slowest

The slowest stroke play tournament round was one of 6 hours 45 min taken by South Africa in the first round of the 1972 World Cup at the Royal Melbourne G.C., Australia. This was a four-ball medal round, everything holed out.

Seven countries in one day

The only golfers to have played 9 hole rounds in seven "countries" in a day are Dr. Gerry W. Donaldson of Newry and Edward S. "Skip" Wilson on 3 July 1974. They played on courses in Jersey, Channel Islands, Wales, England, Scotland, Isle of Man, Ireland and Northern Ireland.

Most rounds in a day

The greatest number of rounds played on foot in 24 hours is 22 rounds and five holes (401 holes) by Ian Colston, 35, at Bendigo G.C. Victoria (6,061 yd *5 542 m*) on 27–28 Nov. 1971. The most holes played on foot in a week (168 hr) is 1,102 by David Shepardson (U.S.A.) 17, at Maple Grove G.C., Wisconsin in Aug. 1976.

Playing a hole in an average 9 min, young David Shepardson walked about 350 miles *563 km* in his record week's play.

Throwing the golf ball

The lowest recorded score for throwing a golf ball round 18 holes (over 6,000 yd or 5 500 m) is 82 by Joe Flynn, 21, at the 6,228 yd *5 694 m* Port Royal Course, Bermuda, on 27 Mar. 1975.

CHAMPIONSHIP RECORDS

The Open

The Open Championship was inaugurated in 1860 at Prestwick, Strathclyde, Scotland. The lowest score for 9 holes is 29 by Tom Haliburton (Wentworth) and Peter W. Thomson, M.B.E. (Australia) (b. 23 Aug. 1929) in the first round of the Open on the Royal Lytham and St. Anne's course at Lytham St. Anne's, Lancashire on 10 July 1963 and by Tony Jacklin, O.B.E. in the first round of the Open at St. Andrews, Fife, on 8 July 1970.

The lowest round in The Open itself has been 63 by Mark Hayes (U.S.A.) at Turnberry, Strathclyde, in the second round on 7 July 1977. Thomas Henry Cotton, M.B.E. (b. Holmes Chapel, Cheshire, 26 Jan. 1907) at Royal St. George's Sandwich, Kent completed a 36-hole record of 132 (67 + 65) on 27 June 1934. The lowest 72-hole aggregate is 268 (68, 70, 65, 65) by Tom Watson (b. 1950) (U.S.A.) at Turnberry, Strathclyde, ending on 9 July 1977.

British Amateur

The lowest score for nine holes in the British Amateur Championship (inaugurated in 1885) is 29 by Richard Davol Chapman (b. 23 Mar. 1911) of the U.S.A. at Sandwich in 1948.

Michael Francis Bonallack, O.B.E. (b. 31 Dec. 1934) shot a 61 (32 + 29) on the par-71 6,905 yd *6 313 m* course at Ganton, North Yorkshire, on 27 July 1968 in the first 18 of the 36 holes in the final round of the English Amateur championship.

U.S. Open

The United States Open Championship was inaugurated in 1894. The lowest 72-hole aggregate is 275 (71, 67, 72 and 65) by Jack Nicklaus on the Lower Course (7,015 yd *6 414 m*) at Baltusrol Country Club, Springfield, New Jersey, on 15–18 June 1967 and 275 (69, 68, 69 and 69) by Lee Trevino (b. near Horizon City, Texas, 1 Dec. 1939) at Oak Hill Country Club, Rochester, N.Y., on 13–16 June 1968. The lowest score for 18 holes is 63 by John Miller (b. 29 Apr. 1947) on the 6,921 yd *6 328 m* par-71 Oakmont Country Club course, Pennsylvania on 17 June 1973.

U.S. Masters'

The lowest score in the U.S. Masters' (instituted on the par-72 6,980 yd *6 382 m* Augusta National Golf Course, Georgia, in 1934) has been 271 by Jack Nicklaus in 1965 and Raymond Floyd (b. 4 Sept. 1942) in 1976. The lowest rounds have been 64 by Lloyd Mangrum (1914–74) (first round, 1940), Jack

MOST TITLES

The most titles won in the world's major championships are as follows:

The Open	Harry Vardon (1870–1937)	6	1896, 1898–99, 1903, 11, 14
British Amateur	John Ball (1861–1940)	8	1888, 90, 92, 94, 99, 1907, 10, 12
U.S. Open	Willie Anderson (1880–1910)	4	1901, 1903–05
	Robert Tyre Jones, Jr. (1902–71)	4	1923, 26, 1929–30
	Ben William Hogan (b. 13 Aug. 1912)	4	1948, 1950–51, 1953
U.S. Amateur	Robert Tyre Jones, Jr. (1902–71)	5	1924–25, 1927-28, 1930
P.G.A. Championship (U.S.A.)	Walter Charles Hagen (1892–1969)	5	1921, 1924–27
Masters' Championship (U.S.A.)	Jack William Nicklaus (b. 21 Jan. 1940)	5	1963, 1965–66, 1972, 1975
U.S. Women's Open	Elizabeth (Betsy) Earle-Rawls (b. 4 May 1928	4	1951, 1953, 1957, 1960
	''Mickey'' Wright (b. 14 Feb. 1935)	4	1958–59, 1961, 1964
U.S. Women's Amateur	Glenna C. Vare (née Collett) (b. 20 June 1903)	6	1922, 1925, 1928–30, 1935
British Women's	Charlotte Cecilia Pitcairn Leitch (b. 13 Apr. 1891)	4	1914, 1920–21, 1926
	Joyce Wethered (b. 17 Nov. 1901) (now Lady Heathcoat-Amory)	4	1922, 1924–25, 1929

Note: Nicklaus is the only golfer to have won five different major titles (the Open, U.S. Open, Masters, A. P.G.and U.S. Amateur titles) twice and a record 16 all told (1962–75).

Winner of the 1969 U.S. P.G.A. title and 1976 U.S. Masters, Ray Floyd, at 6 ft. 1 in *1,85 m* and 196 lb. *88,90 kg*, casts a big shadow on the world golf scene. (*Don Morley, All-Sport Photographic*)

Nicklaus (third round, 1965), and Maurice Bembridge (G.B.) (b. 21 Feb. 1945) (fourth round, 1974).

Most club championships

D. H. R. (Doug) Adams (b. 16 Oct. 1916) has won 29 club championships at the Port Pirie G.C., South Australia, from 1939–68, including 26 consecutively. The British record for amateur club championships is 20 consecutive wins (1937–39 and 1946–62) by the late R. W. H. Taylor at the Dyke Golf Club, Brighton, East Sussex, who retired unbeaten in July 1963, and by Edward Christopher Chapman (b. 9 Apr. 1909), who won the Tunbridge Wells G.C. Scratch Championship for 20 consecutive years from 1951 to 1971.

World Cup (formerly Canada Cup)

The World Cup (instituted as the Canada Cup in 1953) has been won most often by the U.S.A. with 12 victories in 1955–56, 1960–64, 1966–67, 1969, 1971 and 1973. The only men to have been on six winning teams have been Arnold Palmer (1960, 1962–64, 1966–67) and Jack Nicklaus (1963–64, 1966–67, 1971 and 1973). Only Nicklaus has taken the individual title three times (1963–64, 1971). The lowest aggregate score for 144 holes was 545 by Australia (Bruce Devlin (b. 10 Oct. 1937) and David Graham) at San Isidro, Buenos Aires, Argentina on 12–15 Nov. 1970. The lowest individual score has been 269 by Roberto de Vicenzo (b. Buenos Aires, Argentina, 14 Apr. 1923) also in 1970.

Ryder Trophy

The biennial Ryder Cup professional match between U.S.A. and the British Isles or Great Britain was instituted in 1927. The U.S.A. have won 17½ to 3½ to date. William Earl (Billy) Casper (b. San Diego, California, U.S.A., 24 June 1931) has the record of winning most matches in the Trophy with 20 in 1961–1975. Christy O'Connor Sr. (G.B.) played in ten matches up to 1973.

Walker Cup

The U.S.A. *v.* G.B. series instituted in 1921 (for the Walker Cup since 1922 and now biennially) has been won by the U.S.A. 23½–2½ to date. Joseph Boynton Carr (G.B. & I.) (b. February 1922) played in ten contests (1947–67).

Youngest and oldest champions

The youngest winner of the British Open was Tom Morris, Jr. (1850–1875) at Prestwick, Strathclyde in 1868 aged 18. The youngest winner of the British Amateur title was John Charles Beharrel (b. 2 May 1938) at Troon, Strathclyde, on 2 June 1956, aged 18 years 1 month. The oldest British Open Champion was "Old Tom" Morris (1821–1908), who was aged 46 when he won at Prestwick in 1867. In recent times the 1967 champion, Roberto de Vicenzo was aged 44 years 93 days. The oldest winner of the British Amateur was the Hon. Michael Scott at Hoylake, Merseyside in 1933, when 54. The oldest United States Amateur Champion was Jack Westland (b. 1905) at Seattle, Washington, in 1952 aged 47.

Argentinian golfer Roberto de Vicenzo had been in the first three finishers of the British Open five times in 20 years before he finally won the title in 1967, at the age of 44. (*Colorsport*)

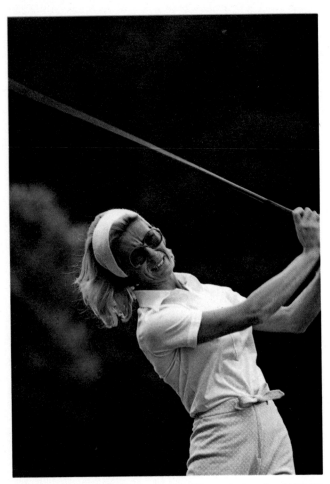

Judy Rankin's 1976 earnings set a new record for women's golf and added to her reputation of being the most consistent professional player—male or female—in golf. (*Don Morley, All-Sport Photographic*)

Record tie

The longest delayed result in any National Open Championship occurred in the 1931 U.S. Open at Toledo, Ohio. George von Elm and Billy Burke (b. 1902) tied at 292, then tied the first replay at 149. Burke won the second replay by a single stroke after 72 extra holes.

Largest tournament

The annual Ford Amateur Golf Tournament in Great Britain attracted a record 91,000 competitors in 1977.

Richest prizes

The greatest first place prize money was $100,000 (total purse $500,000) in the World Open played at Pinehurst, North Carolina, U.S.A., over 144 holes on 8–17 Nov. 1973 won by Miller Barber, (b. 1931), of Texas, U.S.A. The highest British prize was £25,000 in the John Player Golf Classic at Hollinwell, Nottinghamshire, England on 3–6 Sept. 1970 won by Christy O'Connor Sr.

Highest earnings

The all time professional money-winner is Jack Nicklaus who, up to 8 July 1977, has won $3,022,552. The record for a year is $353,021 then £153,475 by Johnny Miller in 1974. The record for a woman is $150,734 by Judy Rankin (*née* Torluemke) (b. 1945) (U.S.A.) in 1976. The record career earnings for a woman is $707,801 by Kathy Whitworth (U.S.A.) (b. 27 Sept. 1938) up to 8 July 1977. The most won in a year by a British golfer is £32,127 by Peter Oosterhuis (b. 3 May 1948) in 1974.

Most tournament wins

The record for winning tournaments in a single season is 19 (out of 31) by Byron Nelson (b. 4 Feb. 1912) of Fort Worth, Texas, in 1945. Of these 11 were consecutive, including the P.G.A., Canadian P.G.A. and Canadian Open, from 16 March to 15 August. He was a money prize winner in 113

consecutive tournaments. Kathy Whitworth won 76 professional tournaments to August 1976.

Biggest winning margin

The greatest margin of victory in a major tournament is 16 strokes by J. Douglas Elder in the Canadian Open Championship of 1919.

HOLES IN ONE

Longest

The longest straight hole ever holed in one shot is the tenth (406 m *444 yd*) at Miracle Hills Golf Club, Omaha, Nebraska, U.S.A. by Robert Mitera (b. 1944) on 7 Oct. 1965. Mitera stands 5 ft 6 in *1,68 m* tall and weighs 165 lb. *74,842 kg* (11 st. 11 lb.). He is a two handicap player who can normally drive 245 yd *224 m*. A 50 m.p.h. *80 km/h* gust carried his shot over a 290 yd *265 m* drop-off. The longest "dog-leg" hole achieved in one is the 480 yd *439 m* fifth at Hope Country Club, Arkansas by L. Bruce on 15 Nov. 1962. The feminine record is 393 yd *359 m* by Marie Robie on the first hole of the Furnace Brook Golf Club, Wollaston, Mass., U.S.A., on 4 Sept. 1949. The longest hole in one performed in the British Isles is the seventh (393 yd *359 m*) at West Lancashire G.C. by Peter Parkinson in 1972.

In 1975 *Golf Digest* magazine recorded 26,267 "aces" which averages over 71 per day.

Most

The greatest number of holes-in-one in a career is 41 by Art Wall, Jr. (b. 23 Nov. 1923) between 1936 and 1973. The British record is 31 by Charles T. Chevalier (1902–1973) of Heaton Moor Golf Club, Stockport, Greater Manchester between 20 June 1918 and 1970. Douglas Porteous, 28, holed-in-one four times over 36 consecutive holes (3rd and 6th on 26 Sept.; 5th on 28 Sept. at Ruchill Golf Club, Glasgow; 6th at the Clydebank and District Golf Course on 30 Sept. 1974). Robert Taylor (Leicestershire) holed the 188 yd *172 m* 16th at Hunstanton, Norfolk on three successive days—31 May, 1 and 2 June 1974—in the Eastern Inter-Counties foursomes. Joe Lucius (U.S.A.), 59, holed the 138 yd *126 m* 15th at the Mohawk Golf Club, Tiffin, Ohio, in one for the eighth time on 16 Nov. 1974.

Consecutive

There are at least 15 cases of "aces" being achieved in two consecutive holes of which the greatest was Norman L. Manley's unique "double albatross" on the par-4 330 yd *301 m* seventh and par-4 290 yd *265 m* eighth holes on the Del Valle Country Club Course, Saugus, California, on 2 Sept. 1964. The only woman to record consecutive "aces" is Sue Prell, on the 13th and 14th holes at Chatswood Golf Club, Sydney, Australia on 29 May 1977.

There is no recorded instance of a golfer performing three consecutive holes in one. The closest to achieving it was by the Rev. Harold Snider (b. 4 July 1900) who aced the 8th, 13th and 14th holes of the par-3 Ironwood course, Arizona, U.S.A. on 9 June 1976.

Youngest and oldest

The youngest golfer recorded to have shot a hole-in-one was Tommy Moore (6 years 36 days) of Hagerstown, Maryland on the 145 yd *132 m* fourth at the Woodbrier Golf Course, Martinsburg, West Virginia, on 8 Mar. 1968. The oldest golfers to have performed the feat are George Miller, 93 at the 11th at Anaheim G.C., California on 4 Dec. 1970 and Charles Youngman, 93 at the Tam O'Shanter Club, Toronto in 1971.

Shooting your age

The record for scoring one's age in years over an 18-hole round is held by Weller Noble (1891–1977) who from 1955 (scoring 64 aged 64) amassed over 800 "age scores" on the Claremont Country Club, Oakland, California par-68 course of 5,375 yd *4 915 m*. The course is considered harder than many of 6,000 yd *5 486 m* or more on which to produce low scores.

The oldest player to score under his age is C. Arthur Thompson (1869–1975) of Victoria, British Columbia, Canada, who scored 103 on the Uplands course of 6,215 yd *5 682 m* aged 103 in 1973. He was reported to be still in action about twice a week until a few weeks before his death. The youngest player to score his age is Robert Leroy Klingaman (b. 22 Oct. 1914) who shot a 58 when aged 58 on the 5,654 yd *5 170 m* course at the Caledonia G.C., Fayetteville, Penn., U.S.A., on 31 Aug. 1973.

GREYHOUND RACING

Earliest meeting
In September 1876 a greyhound meeting was staged at Hendon, North London with a railed hare operated by a windlass. Modern greyhound racing originated with the perfecting of the mechanical hare by Owen Patrick Smith at Emeryville, California, U.S.A., in 1919. The earliest greyhound race behind a mechanical hare in the British Isles was at Belle Vue, Manchester, opened on 24 July 1926.

Derby
The only two dogs to have won the English Greyhound Derby twice (instituted 1928 over 525 yd *480 m*, now over 500 m *546 yd*) are *Mick the Miller* (whelped in Ireland, June 1926 and died 1939) on 25 July 1929, when owned by Albert H. Williams, and on 28 June 1930 (owned by Mrs. Arundel H. Kempton), and *Patricia's Hope* on 24 June 1972 (when owned by Gordon and Basil Marks and Brian Stanley) and 23 June 1973 (when owned by G. & B. Marks and J. O'Connor). The highest prize was £17,500 to *Balliniska Band* for the Derby on 25 June 1977. The only dogs to win the English, Scottish and Welsh Derby "triple" are *Trev's Perfection*, owned by Fred Trevillion, in 1947, *Mile Bush Pride*, owned by Noel W. Purvis, in 1959, and *Patricia's Hope* in 1972. The only dog to win the American Greyhound Derby, at Taunton, Mass., twice was *Real Huntsman* in 1950–51.

Grand National
The only dog to have won the Greyhound Grand National (inst. 1927) three times over 525 yd *480 m* and four flights is *Sherry's Prince*, a 75 lb. *32 kg* dog whelped in April 1967, owned by Mrs. Joyce Mathews of Sanderstead, Surrey. He won in 1970, 1971 (record 29.22 sec) and 1972 when he won by 6¼ lengths.

Fastest greyhound
The highest speed at which any greyhound has been timed is 41.72 m.p.h. *67,14 km/h* (410 yd *374 m* in 20.1 sec) by *The Shoe* on the then straightaway track at Richmond, N.S.W., Australia on 25 Apr. 1968. It is estimated that he covered the last 100 yds *91,44 m* in 4.5 sec or at 45.45 m.p.h. *73,14 km/h*. The highest speed recorded for a greyhound in Great Britain is 39.13 m.p.h. *62,97 km/h* by *Beef Cutlet*, when covering a straight course of 500 yds *457 m* in 26.13 sec at Blackpool, Lancashire, on 13 May 1933.

Fastest 525 yd timings
The fastest *photo*-timing is 28.17 sec or 38.12 m.p.h. *61,34 km/h* by *Easy Investment* on 30 June 1973. The fastest *photo*-timing over 525 yds *480 m* hurdles is 29.10 sec (36.90 m.p.h. *59,38 km/h*) by *Sherry's Prince* on 8 May 1971.

Winning streak
Westpark Mustard, owned by Mr. & Mrs. Cyril Scotland, set a British record of 20 consecutive wins between 7 Jan. and 28 Oct. 1974. The world record is 28 consecutive victories by an American greyhound *Real Huntsman* in 1950–51.

GYMNASTICS

Earliest references
A primitive form of gymnastics was practised in ancient Greece during the period of the ancient Olympic Games (776 B.C. to A.D. 393) but the modern sport developed from *c.* 1780.

Most titles *World*
The greatest number of individual titles won by a man in the World Championships is ten by Boris Shakhlin (b. 27 Jan. 1932) (U.S.S.R.) between 1954 and 1964. He also won three

team titles. The female record is ten individual wins and five team titles by Larissa Semyonovna Latynina (b. 27 Dec. 1934, retired 1966) of the U.S.S.R., between 1956 and 1964.

Most titles *Olympic*
Japan (1960, 1964, 1968, 1972 and 1976) have won the men's team title most often. The U.S.S.R. have won the women's title seven times (1952–1976)

The only man to win six individual gold medals is Boris Shakhlin (U.S.S.R.), with one in 1956, four (two shared) in 1960 and one in 1964. He was also a member of the winning Combined Exercises team in 1956.

Vera Caslavska-Odlozil (b. 3 May 1942) (Czechoslovakia), has won most individual gold medals with seven, three in 1964 and four (one shared) in 1968. Larissa Latynina won six individual gold medals and was in three winning teams in 1956–64 making nine gold medals. She also won five silver and four bronze medals making 18 in all—an Olympic record for either sex in any sport.

Highest score
Nadia Comaneci (b. Romania, 12 Nov. 1961) achieved seven perfect scores of 10.00 at the Montreal Olympics in July 1976. Nelli Kim (b. U.S.S.R., 29 July 1957) was awarded two such scores on the same occasion.

Most titles *British*
The British Gymnastic Championship was won ten times by Arthur J. Whitford in 1928–36 and 1939. He was also in four winning teams. Wray "Nik" Stuart, M.B.E. (b. 20 July 1927) equalled the record of nine successive wins, 1956–64. The women's record is eight by Margaret Hirst (1947, 1949–50 and 1952–56). Margaret Bell (b. 23 Feb. 1945) won the title five times in succession, 1965–69.

Most titles *World Cup*
In the first World Cup Competition, in London in 1975, Ludmilla Tourischeva (b. 7 Oct. 1952) (U.S.S.R.) won all five gold medals available.

A combination of skill, precision and nerve made Nadia Comaneci, at 14 years of age, the nearest thing to perfection yet seen in gymnastics. (*Colorsport*)

Rope climbing
The United States Amateur Athletic Union records are tantamount to world records: 20 ft *6,09 m* (hands alone) 2.8 sec, Don Perry (U.S.A.) at Champaign, Illinois, U.S.A., on 3 Apr. 1954; 25 ft *7,62 m* (hands alone) 4.7 sec, Garvin S. Smith at Los Angeles, California, U.S.A., on 19 Apr. 1947.

Chinning the bar
The greatest number of continuous chin-ups (from a dead hang position) recorded is 106 by William D. Reed at the Weightman Hall, University of Pennsylvania, on 23 June 1969. William Aaron Vaught (b. 1959) performed 20 one-arm (his right) chin-ups at Finch's Gymnasium, Houston, Texas, U.S.A., on 3 Jan. 1976. There is some doubt about whether the feminine record of 27 one-arm chin-ups, claimed for Lilian Leitzel (1892–1931) (U.S.A.) in Hermann's Gym, Philadelphia, in 1918, were achieved from a "dead hang" position. Francis Lewis (b. 1896) of Beatrice, Nebraska, U.S.A. in May 1914 achieved seven consecutive chins using only the middle finger of his left hand. His bodyweight was 158 lb. *71 kg 667* (11 st. 4 lb.).

Parallel bar dips
Rick Bernstein, of Brooklyn, New York, performed a record 117 consecutive parallel bar dips on 3 Mar. 1976.

Press-ups
The greatest recorded number of consecutive press-ups is 7,026 in 3 hrs 56 min by Robert Lewis Knecht, 13, of Minneapolis, Minnesota, U.S.A. on 5 Feb. 1976. The most in 30 min is 1,538 by Philip Howarth (b. 1951) at the Burnley Youth Theatre, Burnley, Lancs., England on 9 Mar. 1977. Among his many press-up achievements Henry Marshall, of San Antonio, Texas, did 139 press-ups on his right arm in 67 sec and 112 on his left in 57 sec on 30 Nov. 1974. James R. Ullrich (U.S.A.) did 140 finger tip press-ups in 80 sec on 11 Mar. 1974.

Sit-ups *Straight-legged*
The greatest recorded number of sit-ups without feet pinned down or knees bent is 25,222 in 11 hr 14 min by Richard John Knecht, aged 8, at the Idaho Fall High School Gymnasium, Idaho, on 23 Dec. 1972. In 2 min, under the same conditions, Dr. David G. Jones recorded 123 sit-ups at Bolling A.F.B., Maryland, U.S.A. on 20 Nov. 1975.

Jumping Jacks
The greatest recorded number of side-straddle hops is 16,062 performed in 3 hr 46 min by Alvin Ludtke (b. 14 Feb. 1952) at California State Univ., Sacramento, U.S.A., on 10 Sept. 1976.

Vertical jumps
The greatest height reached for a vertical jump (formerly known as Sargent [*sic*] Jumps) *i.e.* the differential between the height of the finger-tip reach static and in jumping is 42 in *100,6 cm* by David "Dr. D" Thompson (6 ft 4 in *1,93 m*) North Carolina, U.S.A. in 1972. Mary E. Peters (G.B.) is reported to have done 30 in *76,2 cm* in California in 1972.

Somersaults
The only gymnast to have achieved a running triple back somersault on the ground is Vadim Bindler (U.S.S.R.) (b. Minsk, 1958), in Kiev, in early March 1974.

James Chelich (b. 12 Mar. 1957, Fairview, Alberta, Canada) performed 8,450 forward rolls over 8.3 miles *13,35 km* on 21 Sept. 1974.

Ian Michael Miles (b. 6 July 1960) of Corsham, Wiltshire, made a successful dive and tucked somersault over 33 men at Harrogate, North Yorkshire, on 27 July 1977.

Largest gymnasium
The world's largest gymnasium is Yale University's Payne Whitney Gymnasium at New Haven, Connecticut, U.S.A., completed in 1932 and valued at $18,000,000 £10,285,000. The building, known as the "Cathedral of Muscle" has nine storeys with wings of five storeys each. It is equipped with four basketball courts, three rowing tanks, 28 squash courts, 12 handball courts, a roof jogging track and a 25 yd *22,8 m* by 14 yd *12,8 m* swimming pool on the first floor and a 55 yd *50,2 m* long pool on the third floor.

Largest crowd
The largest recorded crowd was approximately 18,000 people who packed the Forum, Montreal, Canada, for the final of the women's individual apparatus competitions at the XXI Olympic Games on 22 July 1976. Comparable audiences are reported for the Shanghai Stadium, People's Republic of China.

HANDBALL
Origins
Handball, similar to association football, with hands substituted for feet, was first played *c.* 1895. It was introduced into the Olympic Games at Berlin in 1936 as an 11-a-side outdoor game with Germany winning, but when re-introduced in 1972 it was an indoor game with seven-a-side, the standard size of team since 1952.

By 1977 there were some 70 countries affiliated to the International Handball Federation, (founded 1946), and an estimated ten million participants. The earliest international match was when Sweden beat Denmark on 8 Mar. 1935.

Olympic titles
The most victories in Olympic competition have been those by the U.S.S.R. in winning the men and women's titles at Montreal, Canada in 1976.

World titles
The most victories won in World championship (inst. 1938) competition are by Romania with four men's and three women's titles from 1956 to 1974.

HANDBALL (Court)
Origins
Handball played against walls or in a court is a game of ancient Celtic origin. In the early 19th century only a front wall was used but gradually side and back walls were added. The earliest international contest was in New York City, U.S.A., in 1887 between the champions of the U.S.A. and Ireland. The court is now a standardized 60 ft *18 m* by 30 ft *9 m* in Ireland, Ghana and Australia, and 40 ft *12 m* by 20 ft *6 m* in Canada, Mexico and the U.S.A. The game is played with both a hard and soft ball in Ireland and soft ball only in Australia, Canada, Ghana, Mexico and the U.S.A.

Championships
World championships were inaugurated in New York in October 1964 with competitors from Australia, Canada, Ireland, Mexico and the U.S.A. The most wins have been two by the U.S.A. in 1964 and 1967 (shared with Canada).

Most titles
The U.S. Championship 4-wall singles has been won six times by Jimmy Jacobs in 1955–57, 1960, 1964–65. He also shared in six doubles titles.

HOCKEY
MEN
Origins
A representation of two hoop players with curved snagging sticks apparently in an orthodox "bully" position was found in Tomb No. 17 at Beni Hasan, Egypt and has been dated to *c.* 2050 B.C. There is a British reference to the game in Lincolnshire in 1277. The first country to form a national association was England with the first Hockey Association founded at Cannon Street Hotel, City of London on 16 Apr. 1875.

The oldest club with a continuous history is Teddington H.C. formed in the autumn of 1871. They played Richmond on 24 Oct. 1874 and used the first recorded circle *versus* Surbiton at Bushey Park on 9 Dec. 1876. The first international match was the Wales v. Ireland match at Rhyl on 26 Jan. 1895. Ireland won 3–0.

Most Olympic medals
The Indians were Olympic Champions from the re-inception of Olympic hockey in 1928 until 1960, when Pakistan beat them 1–0 at Rome. They had their seventh win in 1964. Of the six Indians who have won three Olympic team gold medals two have also won a silver medal—Leslie Walter Claudius (b. 25 Mar. 1927) in 1948, 1952, 1956 and 1960 (silver) and Udham Singh (b. 4 Aug. 1928) in 1952, 1956, 1964 and 1960 (silver).

Highest international score
The highest score in international hockey was when India defeated the United States 24–1 at Los Angeles, California, U.S.A., in the 1932 Olympic Games. The greatest number of goals in a home international match was when England defeated France 16–0 at Beckenham on 25 Mar. 1922. The World Cup was won by Pakistan at Barcelona in 1971, the Netherlands at Amsterdam in 1973 and India at Kuala Lumpur in 1975.

Most international appearances
Avtar Singh Sohal (b. 22 Mar. 1938) represented Kenya 167 times between 1957 and 1972. The most by a home countries player is 124 by H. David Judge (b. 19 Jan. 1936) with 109 for Ireland and 15 for Great Britain from 1957 to 1977.

Ireland	109	H. David Judge	1957–77
Wales	80	D. Austin Savage (b. 15 Dec. 1940)	1968–75
England	66	Paul J. T. Svehlik (b. 15 Apr. 1947)	1969–75
Scotland	63	Frederick H. Scott (b. 29 Nov. 1932)	1955–70
	63	Dennis Hay (b. 5 Oct. 1940)	1964–74
Great Britain	56	John W. Neill (England) (b. 15 May 1934)	1959–68

Greatest scoring feats
M. C. Marckx (Bowdon 2nd XI) scored 19 goals against Brooklands 2nd XI (score 23–0) on 31 Dec. 1910. He was selected for England in March 1912 but declined due to business priorities. Between 1923 and 1958, Fred H. Wagner scored 1,832 goals for Beeston H.C., Nottingham Casuals and the Nottinghamshire county side.

Greatest goalkeeping
Richard James Allen (b. 1902) (India) did not concede a goal during the 1928 Olympic Tournament and only a total of three in the following two Olympics of 1932 and 1936.

Longest game
The longest international game on record was one of 145 min (into the sixth period of extra time), when Netherlands beat Spain 1–0 in the Olympic tournament at Mexico City on 25 Oct. 1968. The longest club match on record was one of 175 min between Perth H.C. and Aberdeen G.S.F.P. at the North Inch, Perth in the Scottish Cup quarter-final on 24 Feb. 1973.

WOMEN
Origins
The earliest women's club was East Molesey in Surrey, England formed in c. 1887. The Wimbledon Ladies Hockey Club, founded one year later, is still in existence. The first national association was the Irish Ladies' Hockey Union founded in 1894. The All England Women's Hockey Association held its first formal meeting in Westminster Town Hall, London, on 23 Nov. 1895. The first international match was an England v. Ireland game in Dublin in 1896. Ireland won 2–0. The first Championship Tournament of 21 nations was at Edinburgh, Scotland in 1975. England won and hold the Silver Quaich.

Highest international score
The highest score in a women's international match occurred when England defeated France 23–0 at Merton, Greater London, on 3 Feb. 1923.

Most international appearances
The England record is 87 caps by Valerie Robinson from 1963 to 1977. The Irish record is 58 (46 full caps and 12 touring) by Maeve Esther Enid Kyle (*née* Shankey) (b. 6 Oct. 1928) between Nov. 1947 and 1966.

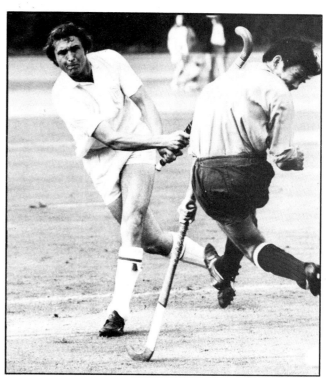

A powerful shot from England's Paul Svehlik, whose 6 ft. 2½ in *1,89 m* 189 lb. *86 kg* frame has stood him in good stead in his record 66 appearances for England. (*E. D. Lacey*)

Highest attendance
The highest attendance at a women's hockey match was 65,000 for the match between England and Wales at the Empire Stadium, Wembley, Brent, Greater London, on 8 Mar. 1969.

HORSE RACING
Origins
Horsemanship was an important part of the Hittite culture of Anatolia, Turkey dating from 1400 B.C. The 33rd ancient Olympic Games of 648 B.C. in Greece featured horse racing. The earliest horse race recorded in England was one held in about A.D. 210 at Netherby, North Yorkshire, among Arabians brought to Britain by Lucius Septimius Severus (A.D. 146–211), Emperor of Rome. The oldest race still being run annually is the Lanark Silver Bell, instituted in Scotland by William Lion (1143–1214).

The Jockey Club was formed in 1750–51; however the original Charleston Jockey Club, Virginia, U.S.A. was the first in the world, organised in 1734. The General Stud Book started in 1791. Racing colours (silks) became compulsory in 1889.

Racecourse *Largest*
The world's largest racecourse is the Newmarket course (founded 1636) on which the Beacon Course, the longest of the 19 courses, is 4 miles 397 yds *6,80 km* long and the Rowley Mile is 167 ft *50 m* wide. The border between Suffolk and Cambridgeshire runs through the Newmarket course. The world's largest grandstand is that opened in 1968 at Belmont Park, Elmont, Long Island, N.Y., U.S.A. at a cost of $30,700,000 £12.8 million. It is 110 ft *33 m* tall, 440 yd *402 m* long, contains 908 mutuel windows and seats 30,000. The highest seating capacity at any racetrack is 40,000 at Atlantic City Audit, New Jersey, U.S.A.

Racecourse *Smallest*
The world's smallest racecourse is the Lebong racecourse, Darjeeling, West Bengal, India (altitude 7,000 ft *2 125 m*), where the complete lap is 481 yd *439 m*. It was laid out c. 1885 and used as a parade ground.

285

Largest prizes

The richest race ever held is the All-American Futurity, a race for quarter-horses over 440 yds *402 m* (400 yd *366 m* before 1973) at Ruidoso Downs, New Mexico, U.S.A. The prizes in 1974 totalled $1,030,000 *£447,826*. The richest first prize for any horse race was $330,000 *£188,571* won by *Real Wind*, the winner of the 1976 All-American Futurity.

Longest race

The longest recorded horse race was one of 1,200 miles *1 925 km* in Portugal, won by a horse *Emir* bred from Egyptian-bred Blunt Arab stock. The holder of the world's record for long distance racing and speed is *Champion Crabbet*, who covered 300 miles *482 km* in 52 hr 33 min carrying 17½ st. *111,130 kg*, in 1920. In 1831 Squire George Osbaldeston (1787–1866), M.P. of East Retford covered 200 miles *321 km* in 8 hr 42 min at Newmarket, using 50 mounts, so averaging 22.99 m.p.h. *36,99 km/h*.

Most runners

The most horses in a race is 66 in the Grand National of 22 Mar. 1929. The record for the flat is 58 in the Lincolnshire Handicap on 13 Mar. 1948. The most runners at a meeting were 214 (flat) in seven races at Newmarket on 15 June 1915 and 229 (National Hunt) in eight races at Worcester on 13 Jan. 1965.

Dead heats

There is no recorded case in turf history of a quintuple dead heat. The nearest approach was in the Astley Stakes, at Lewes, England, on 6 Aug. 1880 when *Mazurka*, *Wandering Nun* and *Scobell* triple dead-heated for first place a head in front of *Cumberland* and *Thora*, who dead-heated for fourth place. Each of the five jockeys thought he had won. The only three known examples of a quadruple dead heat were between *Honest Harry*, *Miss Decoy*, *Beningbrough* and *Peteria* at Bogside, on 7 June 1808, between *Defaulter*, *Squire of Malton*, *Reindeer* and *Pulcherrima* in the Omnibus Stakes at The Hoo, Kent, England, on 26 Apr. 1851, and between *Oveneach*, *Lady Golightly*, *Gamester* and *Unexpected* at the Houghton Meeting at Newmarket on 22 Oct. 1855. Since the introduction of the photo-finish, the highest number of horses dead-heating has been three, on several occasions.

Horse *Greatest record*

The horse with the best recorded win-loss record was *Kincsem*, a Hungarian mare foaled in 1874, who was unbeaten in 54 races (1876–79), including the Goodwood Cup of 1878. *Camarero* owned by Don José Coll Vidal of Puerto Rico, foaled in 1951, had a winning streak of 56 races from 19 Apr. 1953 to 17 Aug. 1955. He died "from a colic" on 26 Aug. 1956 the day after his 73rd win in 77 starts.

Horse *Tallest*

The tallest horse ever to race is *Fort d'Or*, owned by Lady Elizabeth (Eliza) Nugent (*née* Guinness) of Berkshire, England. He stands 18.2 hands *187 cm* and was foaled in County Wexford, Ireland in April 1963 out of *Golden Sunset*, who stood only 15.1 hands.

Horse *Highest price*

The highest price ever paid for a horse is $8 million, 32 shares at $250,000 each, for the 11-year-old American stallion *What a Pleasure* in early 1976. In February 1973 the three-year-old colt *Secretariat* was syndicated in 32 shares, valued at $190,000 each. It has been estimated that, had the syndication taken place on his retirement in late 1973, he could have been sold at nearly $13 million. The highest price for a yearling is $1.5 million for a colt by *Secretariat–Charming Alibi*, subsequently named *Canadian Bound*, bought on 20 July 1976 at Keeneland, Kentucky, U.S.A.

Horse *Greatest winnings*

The greatest amount ever won by a horse is $1,977,896 *then £706,391* by *Kelso* (foaled in 1957) in the U.S.A., between 1959 and his retirement on 10 Mar. 1966. In 63 races he won 39, came second in 12 and third in two. The leading money-winning mare is *Dahlia* (foaled 1970) who, from 1972 to 1976, earned $1,535,443. The most won in a year is $860,404 *£374,088* by *Secretariat* in 1973. His total career winnings amounted to $1,316,808 in two seasons.

Horse *Shortest price*

The shortest odds ever quoted for any racehorse are 10,000 to 1 on for *Dragon Blond*, ridden by Lester Piggott O.B.E. (G.B.) (b. 5 Nov. 1935) in the Premio Naviglio in Milan, Italy on 1 June 1967. Odds of 100 to 1 on were quoted for the United States horse *Man o' War* (foaled 29 Mar. 1917, died 1 Nov. 1947) on three separate occasions in 1920, and for the two British horses, *Ormonde* (Champion Stakes, 14 Oct. 1886, three runners), and *Sceptre* (Limekiln Stakes 27 Oct. 1903, two runners).

Jockey *Wins on one card*

The greatest number of winners ridden on one card is eight by Hubert S. Jones, 17, at Caliente, California, U.S.A. on 11 June 1944, and by Oscar Barattuci, at Rosario City, Argentina, on 15 Dec. 1957. The longest winning streak is 12 by Sir Gordon Richards (b. Oakengates, Salop, 5 May 1904) (last race at Nottingham on 3 Oct., six out of six at Chepstow on 4 Oct. and the first five races next day at Chepstow) in 1933.

Jockey *Youngest and oldest*

The youngest jockey was Frank Wootton (English Champion jockey 1909–1912), who rode his first winner in South Africa aged 9 years 10 months. The oldest jockey was Levi Barlingame (U.S.A.), who rode his last race at Stafford, Kansas, in 1932 aged 80.

The greatest recorded age for a first win has been 67 years in the case of Mr. Victor Morley Lawson on *Ocean King* at Warwick on 16 Oct. 1973.

Jockey *Lightest*

The lightest recorded jockey was Kitchener (d. 1872), who won the Chester Cup on *Red Deer* in 1844 at 3 st. 7 lb. *22,226 kg*. He was said to have weighed only 2 st. 12 lb. *18,143 kg* in 1840.

Jockey *Most successful*

The most successful jockey of all time has been William Lee (Willie) Shoemaker (b. weighing 2½ lb. *1,133 kg* on 19 Aug. 1931) now weighing 98 lb. *44 kg* and standing 4 ft 11½ in *1,51 m*. From April 1949 to June 1977 he rode 7,226 winners from some 30,000 rides. His mounts earned $63 million.

The greatest amount ever won by any jockey in a year is $4,709,500 by Angel Cordero Jr. in 1976. The most winners ridden in a year is 546, from a record 2,199 mounts, by Chris McCarron (U.S.A.) (b. 1955) in 1974.

Trainers

The greatest number of wins by a trainer in one year is 494 by Jack Van Berg in 1976, when he won a record $2,972,218 in prize money.

Owners

The most winners in a year by an owner is 494 by Don R. Lasater (U.S.A.) in 1974 when he also won a record $3,022,960 in prize money.

BRITISH TURF RECORDS

Most successful *Horses*

Only fillies are eligible to win all five classics. *Sceptre* came closest in 1902 when she won the 2,000 Guineas, 1,000 Guineas, Oaks and St. Leger. In 1868 *Formosa* won the same four but dead-heated in the 2,000 Guineas. The most races won in a season is 23 by three-year-old *Fisherman* in 1856. *Catherina* (foaled 1830) won a career record 79 out of 174 races, 1833–41. The record for this century is by *Le Garcon d'Or* (foaled 1958) with 34 wins out of 181 flat races 1960–73. The only horse to win the same race in seven successive years was *Dr. Syntax* (foaled 1811) in the Preston Gold Cup (1815–21). The most successful sire was *Stockwell* (foaled 1849) whose progeny won 1,153 races (1858–76) and in 1866 set a record of 132 races won. The greatest amount ever won by an English-trained horse is £326,421 by *Grundy* (foaled 1972) 1974–75.

Most successful *Owners*

The greatest amount of stake money won is £1,025,592 from 784 races by H.H. Aga Khan III (1877–1957) from 1922 until his death. These included 35 classics, of which 17 were English classics. He was leading owner a record thirteen times between 1924 and 1952. The record for a season was set by Daniel Wildenstein, who won £244,500 in first-prize money in 1976. The most wins in a season is 115 by David Robinson in 1973. The most English classics won is 20 by the 4th Duke of Grafton, K.G. (1760–1844), from 1813 to 1831.

Most successful *Trainers*

Sir Charles Francis Noel Murless (b. Malpas, Cheshire, 24 Mar. 1910) earned more than £2,500,000 in winning money and £3,000,000 counting place money for his patrons. The record first-prize money in a season is £382,527.32p by Peter Walwyn in 1975. The most classics won by a trainer is 40 or 41 by John Scott (1794–1871) including 16 St. Leger winners between 1827 and 1862. Alec Taylor of Manton, Wiltshire headed the trainers' lists for a record 12 seasons between 1907 and 1925. In 1867 John Barham Day won 146 races.

Most successful *Jockeys*

Sir Gordon Richards won 4,870 races from 21,834 mounts from his first mount at Lingfield on 16 Oct. 1920 to 1954. His first win was on 31 Mar. 1921. In 1953, after 27 attempts, he won the Derby, six days after being knighted. In 1947 he won a record 269 races. He was champion jockey a record 26 times between 1925 and 1953. The most classic races won by a jockey is 27 by Francis (Frank) Buckle (1766–1832), between 1792 and 1827.

THE DERBY

The greatest of England's five classics is the Derby Stakes, inaugurated on 4 May 1780, and named after the 12th Earl of Derby (1752–1834). The distance was increased in 1784 from a mile to 1½ miles *2 414 m*. The race has been run at Epsom Downs, Surrey, except for the two war periods, when it was run at Newmarket, and is for three-year-olds only. Since 1884 the weights have been: colts 9 st. *57 kg*, fillies 8 st. 9 lb. *54kg 884*.

Most wins *Owners*

The only owner with five outright winners was the 3rd Earl of Egremont (1751–1837) with *Assassin* (1782), *Hannibal* (1804), *Cardinal Beaufort* (1805), *Election* (1807) and *Lapdog* (1826). H.H. Aga Khan III had four winners in *Blenheim* (1930), *Bahram* (1935), *Mahmoud* (1936) and *Tulyar* (1952) and a half-share in *My Love* (1948).

Later a successful trainer and racing manager, Sir Gordon Richards won a total of 14 Classic races in his 34 year career as a jockey. (*Sport and General Press Agency*)

Most wins *Trainers*

The only three trainers with seven winners were John Porter with *Blue Gown* (1868), *Shotover* (1882), *St. Blaise* (1883), *Ormonde* (1886), *Sainfoin* (1890), *Common* (1891) and *Flying Fox* (1899), Robert Robson with *Waxy* (1793), *Tyrant* (1802), *Pope* (1809), *Whalebone* (1810), *Whisker* (1815), *Azor* (1817), and *Emilius* (1823) and Fred Darling with *Captain Cuttle* (1922), *Manna* (1925), *Coronach* (1926), *Cameronian* (1931), *Bois Roussel* (1938), *Pont l'Evêque* (1940), and *Owen Tudor* (1941).

Most wins *Jockey*

The most successful jockey has been Lester Piggott, O.B.E. with eight wins on *Never say Die* (1954), *Crepello* (1957), *St. Paddy* (1960), *Sir Ivor* (1968), *Nijinsky* (1970), *Roberto* (1972), *Empery* (1976) and *The Minstrel* (1977).

Highest prize

The highest Derby prize and the richest prize on British Turf was £111,825.50 for *Empery* on 2 June 1976.

Record time

The record time for the Derby is 2 min 33.8 sec (average speed 35.06 m.p.h. *56 42 km/h*) by *Mahmoud* ridden by Charles James William (Charlie) Smirke (b. 1906), owned by H.H. Aga Khan III, trained by Frank Butters (1878–1957), winning at 100 to 8 by three lengths from a field of 22 in 1936. The fastest time recorded over the Derby course is, however, the hand-timed 2 min 33.0 sec by the five-year-old *Apelle* in winning the 1928 Coronation Cup. The fastest mechanically timed run was 2 min 33.31 sec by the four-year-old *Bustino* in the Coronation Cup on 7 June 1975.

Dead heats

The two instances of dead heats were in 1828, when *Cadland* beat *The Colonel* in the run off, and in 1884 between *Harvester* and *St. Gatien* (stakes divided).

Disqualifications

The two disqualifications were of *Running Rein* (race awarded to *Orlando*) in 1844 and of *Craganour* (race awarded to *Aboyeur*) in the "Suffragette Derby" on 4 June 1913, when Miss Emily Wilding Davison fatally injured herself by impeding King George V's horse *Anmer*.

Other records

The only greys to have won were *Gustavus* (1821), *Tagalie* (1912), *Mahmoud* (1936) and *Airborne* (1946). Only two black horses have ever won—*Smolensko* (1813) and *Grand Parade* (1919). The longest odds quoted on a placed Derby horse were 200–1 against for *Black Tommy*, second to *Blink Bonny* in 1857. The shortest priced winner was *Ladas* (1894) at 9–2 on and the highest priced winners were *Jeddah* (1898), *Signorinetta* (1908) and *Aboyeur* (1913), all at 100 to 1 against. The smallest field was four in 1794 and the largest 34 in 1862. The smallest winner was *Little Wonder* (14 hands 3½ in *151,12 cm*) in 1840. The largest winning margin was eight lengths when *Manna* won in 1925. The oldest winning jockey was John Forth who was over 60 yr when he rode *Frederick* in 1829. The youngest was John Parsons, believed to be only 16 yr when he rode *Caractacus* in 1862.

GRAND NATIONAL

The first official Grand National Steeplechase may be regarded as the Grand Liverpool Steeplechase of 26 Feb. 1839 though the race was not given its present name until 1847. It became a handicap in 1843. Until 1930 five-year-olds were eligible, but since then it has been for six-year-olds and above. Except for the two war periods (1916–18 and 1941–45) the race has been run at Aintree near Liverpool, since 1839, over a course of 4 miles 856 yd *7 220 m* and 30 jumps.

Most wins *Horses*

The only horse to win three times is *Red Rum* (foaled 1965) in 1973–74, and 1977. He also came second in 1975 and 1976. *Manifesto* ran eight times (1895–1904) and won twice, came third three times and fourth once.

Most wins *Owners*

The only owners with three wins are Captain Henry Machell with *Disturbance* (1873), *Reugny* (1874) and *Regal* (1876); Sir Charles Assheton-Smith (formerly Charles Duff) with

The 12 year old *Red Rum* carrying 11 st. 8 lb. *73 kg 859* made history with a third Grand National win. (*All-Sport Photographic*)

Cloister (1893), *Jerry M.* (1912) and *Covercoat* (1913); and Noel Le Mare with *Red Rum* (1973–74, 1977).

Most wins *Trainer*
The only trainer with four winners is Fred Rimell with *E.S.B.* (1956), *Nicolaus Silver* (1961), *Gay Trip* (1970) and *Rag Trade* (1976). The Hon. Aubrey Hastings won with *Ascetic's Silver* (1906), *Ally Sloper* (1915), and *Master Robert* (1924), and also won a wartime substitute race at Gatwick with *Ballymacad* (1917).

Most wins *Jockey*
The only jockey to ride five winners was George Stevens on *Free Trader* (1856), *Emblem* (1863), *Emblematic* (1864) and *The Colonel* (1869–70).

Highest prize
The highest prize and the richest ever under National Hunt rules was £41,140 for *Red Rum* on 2 Apr. 1977.

Fastest time
The record time is 9 min 1.9 sec set by *Red Rum* carrying 10 st. 5 lb. *65,770 kg* ridden by Brian Fletcher (b. 1947) owned

by Noel Le Mare (b. 1887) and trained by Donald McCain (b. 1930) of Southport on 31 Mar. 1973. This represents an average speed of 29.80 m.p.h. *47,96 km/h.*

Highest jump
The 15th jump, known as the "Chair", is 5 ft 2 in *1,57 m* high and 3 ft 9 in *1,14 m* thick. The ditch on the take-off side is 6 ft *1,83 m* wide and the guard rail in front of the ditch is 1 ft 6 in *45 cm* in height.

NATIONAL HUNT
Jockeys *Most successful*
The first National Hunt jockey to reach 1,000 wins is Stan Mellor, M.B.E. (b. Manchester, 10 Apr. 1937). This he achieved on *Ouzo* at Nottingham on 18 Dec. 1971 and retired on 18 June 1972 after 1,049 wins (incl. 14 abroad) in 20 years. He also won three flat races.

The record number of wins in a season is 125 by Ron Barry in 1972–73. The record number of National Hunt Championships is seven by Gerald Wilson (1903–68) from 1933–38 and 1941.

SPEED RECORDS

Distance	Time min. sec.	m.p.h.	km/h	Name	Age	Weight carried lb.	Course	Date
¼ mile	20.8	43.26	69,62	Big Racket (Mexico)	4	114	Mexico City, Mexico	5 Feb. 1945
¼ mile	44.4	40.54	65,24	Sonido (Venezuela)	2	111	‡ Caracas, Venezuela	28 June 1970
⅝ mile	53.6†	41.98	67,56	Indigenous (G.B.)	4	131	‡*Epsom Surrey	2 June 1960
	53.89††	41.75	67,19	Raffingora (G.B.)	5	140	‡*Epsom, Surrey	5 June 1970
	55.4	40.61	65,36	Zip Pocket (U.S.A.)	3	122	Turf Paradise, Phoenix, Arizona, U.S.A.	22 Apr. 1967
¾ mile	1:06.2	40.78	65,62	Gelding by Blink—Broken Tendril (G.B.)	2	123	*Brighton, East Sussex	6 Aug. 1929
	1:07.2	40.18	64,66	Grey Papa (U.S.A.)	6	112	Longacres, Seattle, Washington, U.S.A.	4 Sept. 1972
1 mile	1:31.8	39.21	63,10	Soueida (G.B.)	4	126	*Brighton, East Sussex	19 Sept. 1963
	1:31.8	39.21	63,10	Loose Cover (G.B.)	3	110	*Brighton, East Sussex	9 June 1966
	1:32.2	39.04	62,82	Dr. Fager (U.S.A.)	4	134	Arlington, Illinois, U.S.A.	24 Aug. 1968
1¼ miles	1:58.0	38.13	61,36	Quilche (U.S.A.)	6	115	Santa Anita, Arcadia, California, U.S.A.	23 Feb. 1970
1½ miles	2:23.0	37.76	60,76	Fiddle Isle (U.S.A.)	5	124	Santa Anita, Arcadia, California, U.S.A.	21 Mar. 1970
2 miles**	3:15.0	36.93	59,43	Polazel (G.B.)	3	142	Salisbury, Wiltshire	8 July 1924
2½ miles	4:14.6	35.35	56,90	Miss Grillo (U.S.A.)	6	118	Pimlico, Baltimore, Maryland, U.S.A.	12 Nov. 1948
3 miles	5:15.0	'34.29	55,18	Farragut (Mexico)	5	113	Agua Caliente, Mexico	9 Mar. 1941

* Epsom and Brighton courses include a sharp descent of ¼ mile.
** A more reliable modern record is 3 min 16.75 sec by Il Tempo (N.Z.) (7 yr, 130 lb.) at Trentham, Wellington, New Zealand on 17 Jan. 1970.
† Hand timed.
†† Electrically timed.
‡ Straight courses.

Capt. Kenyon Goode owned, trained and rode three successive winners under National Hunt rules at Torquay, Devon on 7 Apr. 1931.

Horse *Greatest winnings*
The greatest amount won by a British-trained jumper is £114,627 by *Red Rum* between 1969 and 1977.

HURLING

Earliest reference
A game of very ancient origin, hurling only became standardized with the formation of the Gaelic Athletic Association in Thurles, Ireland, on 1 Nov. 1884.

Most titles *All-Ireland*
The greatest number of All-Ireland Championships won by one team is 22 by Tipperary in 1887, 1895–96, 1898–1900, 1906, 1908, 1916, 1925, 1930, 1937, 1945, 1949–51, 1958, 1961–62, 1964–65 and 1971. The greatest number of successive wins is the four by Cork (1941–44).

Most titles *Inter-provincials*
Munster holds the greatest number of inter-provincial (Railway Cup) championships with 33 (1928–1976).

Most appearances
The most appearances in All-Ireland finals is ten shared by Christy Ring (Cork and Munster) and John Doyle (Tipperary). They also share the record of All-Ireland medals won with eight each. Ring's appearances on the winning side were in 1941–44, 1946 and 1952–54, while Doyle's were in 1949–51, 1958, 1961–62 and 1964–65. Ring also played in a record 22 inter-provincial finals (1942–63) and was on the winning side 18 times.

Highest score
The highest score in an All-Ireland final was in 1896 when Tipperary (8 goals, 14 points) beat Dublin (no goals, 4 points). The record aggregate score was when Cork (6 goals, 21 points) defeated Wexford (5 goals, 10 points) in 1970. A goal equals three points.

Lowest score
The lowest score in an All-Ireland final was when Tipperary (1 goal, 1 point) beat Galway (nil) in the first championship at Birr in 1887.

Highest individual score
The highest recorded individual score was by Nick Rackard (Wexford), who scored 7 goals and 7 points against Antrim in the 1954 All Ireland semi-final.

Longest stroke
The greatest distance for a "lift and stroke" is one of 129 yd *117 m* credited to Tom Murphy of Three Castles, Kilkenny, in a "long puck" contest in 1906. The record for the annual *An Poc Fada* (Long Puck) contest (instituted 1961) in the ravines of the Cooley Hills, north of Dundalk, County Louth, is 65 pucks (drives) plus 87 yd *79 m* over the course of 3 miles 320 yd *5,120 km* by Fionnbar O'Neill (Cork) in 1966. This represents an average of 84.8 yd *77,5 m* per drive.

Largest crowd
The largest crowd was 84,856 for the final between Cork and Wexford at Croke Park, Dublin, in 1954.

ICE HOCKEY

Origins
There is pictorial evidence that hockey was played on ice in the 17th century in The Netherlands. The game was probably first played in North America in 1860 at Kingston, Ontario, Canada, but Montreal and Halifax also lay claim to priority. The International Ice Hockey Federation was founded in 1908. The National Hockey League of North America was inaugurated 1917. The World Hockey Association was formed in 1971.

Olympic Games and World Championships
Canada has won the Olympic Championship six times (1920–1924–28–32–48–52) and the world title 19 times, the last being at Geneva in 1961. The longest Olympic career is that of Richard Torriani (b. 1 Oct. 1911) (Switzerland) from 1928 to 1948. The most gold medals won by any player is three achieved by Vitaliy Davidov, Anatoliy Firssov, Viktor Kuzkin and Aleksandr Ragulin of the U.S.S.R. teams that won the Olympic titles in 1964, 1968 and 1972. World amateur championships began at Antwerp, Belgium in 1920, and were first opened to professionals in 1976.

Stanley Cup
The Stanley Cup, presented by the Governor-General, Lord Stanley (original cost $48.67), became emblematic of National Hockey League supremacy 33 years after the first contest at Montreal in 1893. It has been won most often by the Montreal Canadiens with 20 wins in 1916, 1924, 1930–31, 1944, 1946, 1953, 1956–60, 1965–66, 1968–69, 1971, 1973, 1976–77.

British Leagues
The defunct British League championship (inst. 1934) was won most often by the Wembley Lions with four victories in 1936–37, 1952 and 1957. Murrayfield Racers have won the Northern League (inst. 1966) four times, 1970–72 and 1976.

Most goals *Team*
The greatest number of goals recorded in a world championship match has been 47–0 when Canada beat Denmark in Stockholm, Sweden on 12 Feb. 1949. The National Hockey League record is 21 goals when Montreal Canadiens beat Toronto St. Patrick's, at Montreal, 14–7 on 10 Jan. 1920.

Most goals *Individual*
The most goals by a professional player in a season (W.H.A.) is 83 by Anders Hedberg (b. Sweden, 25 Feb. 1951) (Winnipeg Jets) in 1976–77. Most in the N.H.L. is 80 by Reggie Leach (b. Canada, 23 Apr. 1950) (Philadelphia Flyers) in 1975–76. The most points in a season is 162 (79 goals and 83 assists) by Phil Esposito (b. Canada, 20 Feb. 1942) (Boston Bruins) in 1970–71. The North American career record for goals is 907 by Gordie Howe (b. 31 Mar. 1928) (Detroit Red Wings and Houston Aeros) in 29 seasons ending in 1976–77. On 15 Dec. 1973 he became the first major league player to aggregate 2,000 points. Two players have scored 1,000 goals in Great Britain—Chick Zamick (Nottingham Panthers and Wembly Lions) and George Beach (Wembley Monarchs and Wembley Lions).

In his thirtieth year of ice hockey Gordie Howe is still adding to his record goal scoring total, playing alongside his sons Marty and Mark. (*Syndication International*)

Most goals *British*

The highest score and aggregate in a League match has been 34–0 when Streatham beat Deeside Dragons on 1 Nov. 1975. The most individual goals scored in a game is 12 by Bernard (Bernie) Snagg (b. 1953) for Liverpool Leopards *v.* Sheffield Lancers on 27 Sept. 1975.

Fastest scoring *World*

Kim D. Miles scored a goal after only 3 sec of play for Univ. of Guelph *v.* Univ. of W. Ontario on 11 Feb. 1975. Toronto scored eight goals against the New York Americans in 4 min 52 sec on 19 Mar. 1938. Bill Mosienko (Chicago Black Hawks) scored three goals in 21 sec against New York Rangers on 23 Mar. 1952. In minor hockey three goals in 14 sec has been achieved by Kent Guest for Bay Ridges *v* Ajax, at Toronto, Ontario, Canada, on 19 Mar. 1975.

Fastest scoring *Great Britain*

Kenny Westman (Nottingham Panthers) scored a hat trick in 30 sec *v.* Brighton Tigers on 3 Mar. 1955.

Most points one game

The North American major league record for most points scored in one game is ten (3 goals, 7 assists) by Jim Harrison (b. 9 July 1947) (for Alberta, later Edmonton Oilers) in a W.H.A. match at Toronto on 30 Jan. 1973, and by Darryl Sittler (b. 18 Sept. 1950) (6 goals, 4 assists) for Toronto Maple Leafs in a N.H.L. match at Toronto on 7 Feb. 1976. In Britain, Richard Bacon scored 15 (10 goals, 5 assists) for Streatham *v.* Deeside on 1 Nov. 1975.

Most successful goaltending

The most matches played by a goaltender without conceding a goal is 103 by Terrance (Terry) Gordon Sawchuck (b. 28 Dec. 1929) of Detroit Red Wings, Toronto Maple Leafs and Los Angeles Kings, between 1950 and 1967. Gerry Cheevers (b. 2 Dec. 1940) Boston Bruins, went a record 33 games without defeat in 1971–72.

Fastest player

The highest speed measured for any player is 29.7 m.p.h. *47,7 km/h* for Bobby Hull (b. 3 Jan. 1939) of the Winnipeg Jets. The highest puck speed is also attributed to Hull, whose left-handed slap shot has been timed at 118.3 m.p.h *190,3 km/h.*

Longest match

The longest match was 2 hrs 56 min 30 sec when Detroit Red Wings eventually beat Montreal Maroons 1–0 in the sixth period of overtime at the Forum, Montreal, at 2.25 a.m. on 25 Mar. 1936.

ICE SKATING

Origins

The earliest reference to ice skating is in early Scandinavian literature referring to the 2nd century though its origins are believed, on archeological evidence, to be ten centuries earlier still. The earliest English account of 1180 refers to skates made of bone. The earliest known illustration is a Dutch woodcut of 1498. The earliest skating club was the Edinburgh Skating Club formed in 1742. The earliest artificial ice rink in the world was the "Glaciarium" in Chelsea, Greater London, in 1876. The National Skating Association of Great Britain was founded in 1879. The International Skating Union was founded in 1892.

FIGURE SKATING

Most titles *Olympic*

The most Olympic gold medals won by a figure skater is three by Gillis Gråfstrom (1893–1938) of Sweden in 1920, 1924, and 1928 (also silver medal in 1932); and by Sonja Henie (1912–1969) of Norway in 1928, 1932 and 1936.

Most titles *World*

The greatest number of world men's figure skating titles (instituted 1896) is ten by Ulrich Salchow (1877–1949) of Sweden, in 1901–05 and 1907–11. The women's record (instituted 1906) is ten titles by Sonja Henie between 1927 and 1936.

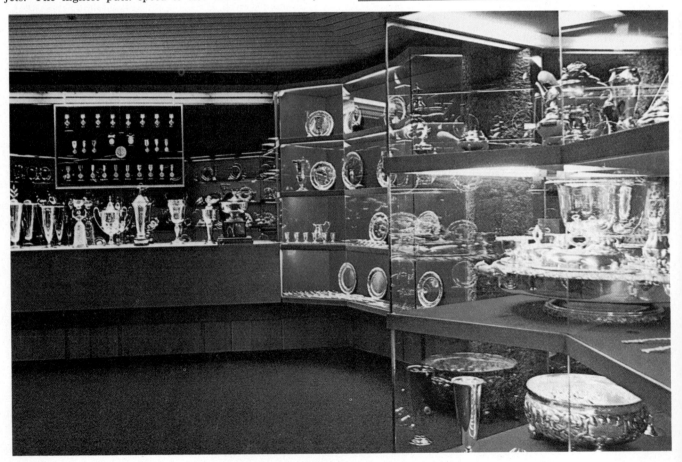

Not Aladdin's cave, but the trophy room at the Sonja Henie Museum outside Oslo, containing her many awards including ten world, three Olympic and six European gold medals. (*Sonja Henies og Niels Orstads Stiftelser*)

Most pairs titles (inst. 1908) have been won by Irina Rodnina (b. 12 Sept. 1949) (U.S.S.R.), four with Aleksiy Ulanov (b. 4 Nov. 1947) 1969–72, and five with her husband Aleksandr Zaitsev (b. 16 June 1952) 1973–77. Most ice dance titles (inst. 1950) won is six by Aleksandr Gorshkov (b. 8. Dec. 1946) and Ludmila Pakhomova (b. 31 Dec. 1946) (U.S.S.R.) 1970–74 and 1976.

Most titles British

The record number of British titles is 11 by Jack Page (Manchester S.C.) in 1922–31 and 1933, and six by Miss Cecilia Colledge (b. 28 Nov. 1920) (Park Lane F.S.C., London) in 1935–37 (two), 1938 and 1946.

Triple Crown

The only British skater to win the "Grand Slam" of World, Olympic and European titles in the same year is John Anthony Curry O.B.E. (b. 9 Sept. 1949) in 1976.

Karl Schäfer (Austria) (1909–1976) and Sonja Henie achieved double "Grand Slams", both in the years 1932 and 1936.

Highest marks

The highest number of maximum six marks awarded for one performance in an international championship was 11 to Aleksandr Zaitsev and Irina Rodnina (U.S.S.R.) in the European pairs in Zagreb, Yugoslavia, in 1974. The most by a soloist was seven to Donald Jackson (b. 2 Apr. 1940) (Canada) in the world men's championship at Prague, Czechoslovakia, in 1962.

Most successful coach

Carlo Fassi (Italy) trained both male and female World and Olympic individual figure skating champions in 1976. His pupils were Dorothy Hamill (b. 26 July 1956) (U.S.A.) and John Curry (G.B.)

Most difficult jump

The triple Axel jump has been performed by only Gordon McKellen (b. 26 Sept. 1953), the 1973 and 1974 U.S. champion. The quadruple twist lift has been performed by only one pair, Sergei Shakrai (b. 1957) and Marina Tcherkasova (b. 1962), of U.S.S.R., in international competition at Helsinki, on 26 Jan. 1977.

Marathon

The longest recorded skating marathon is one of 109 hr 5 min by Austin McKinley, of Christchurch, New Zealand on 21–25 June 1977.

Largest rink

The world's largest indoor ice rink is the quadruple rink at Burnaby, British Columbia, Canada, completed in Dec. 1972, which has an ice area of 68,000 ft² *6 317 m²*. The largest artificial outdoor rink is the Fujikyu Highland Promenade Rink, Japan opened at a cost of £335,000 in 1967 with an area of 165,750 ft² *15 400 m²* (3.8 acres *1,5 ha*).

SPEED SKATING
Most titles Olympic

The most Olympic gold medals won in speed skating is six by Lidia Skoblikova (b. 8 Mar. 1939) of Chelyaminsk, U.S.S.R., in 1960 (two) and 1964 (four). The male records are by Ivar Ballangrud (Norway) (1904–1969) with four gold, two silver and one bronze medal in 1928, 1932 and 1936, and Clas Thunberg (b. 5 Apr. 1893) (Finland) with four gold, one tied gold, one silver and one tied bronze in 1924 and 1928.

Most titles World

The greatest number of world speed skating titles (instituted 1893) won by any skater is five by Oscar Mathisen (Norway) in 1908–09 and 1912–14, and Clas Thunberg in 1923, 1925, 1928–29 and 1931. The most titles won by a woman is four by Inga Voronina (*née* Artomonova) (1936–66) of Moscow, U.S.S.R., in 1957, 1958, 1962 and 1964 and Atje Keulen-Deelstra (b. 31 Dec. 1938) (Netherlands) 1970, 1972–74.

Longest race

The longest race regularly held is the "Elfstedentocht" ("Tour of the Eleven Towns") in the Netherlands. It covers 200 km *124 miles 483 yds* and the fastest time is 7 hrs 35 min by Jeen van den Berg (b. 8 Jan. 1928) on 3 Feb. 1954.

ICE AND SAND YACHTING
Origins

The sport originated in the Low Countries from the year 1600 (earliest patent granted) and along the Baltic coast. The earliest authentic record is Dutch, dating from 1768. Land or sand yachts of Dutch construction were first reported on beaches (now in Belgium) in 1595. The earliest International championship was staged in 1914.

Highest speeds Ice

The largest known ice yacht was *Icicle*, built for Commodore John E. Roosevelt for racing on the Hudson River, New York, in *c.* 1870. It was 68 ft 11 in *21 m* long and carried 1,070 ft² *99 m²* of canvas. The highest speed officially recorded is 143

WORLD SPEED SKATING RECORDS (Ratified by the I.S.U. as at 28 May 1977)

	Distance	min. sec.	Name and Country	Place	Date
MEN	500 metres	37.00*	Evgeni Kulikov (U.S.S.R.)	Medeo, U.S.S.R.	29 Mar. 1975
	1,000 metres	1:15.33	Evgeni Kulikov (U.S.S.R.)	Medeo, U.S.S.R.	19 Mar. 1977
	1,500 metres	1:55.18	Jan Egil Storholt (Norway)	Medeo, U.S.S.R.	20 Mar. 1977
	3,000 metres	4:08.30	Ard Schenk (Netherlands)	Inzell, West Germany	2 Mar. 1972
	5,000 metres	6:56.90	Kay Stenshjemmet (Norway)	Medeo, U.S.S.R.	19 Mar. 1977
	10,000 metres	14.34.33	Viktor Leskine (U.S.S.R.)	Medeo, U.S.S.R.	3 Apr. 1977
WOMEN	500 metres	40.68	Sheila Young (U.S.A.)	Inzell, West Germany	13 Mar. 1976
	1,000 metres	1:23.46	Tatiana Averina (U.S.S.R.)	Medeo, U.S.S.R.	29 Mar. 1975
	1,500 metres	2:09.90	Tatiana Averina (U.S.S.R.)	Medeo, U.S.S.R.	11 Mar. 1975
	3,000 metres	4:31.00	Galina Stepanskaya (U.S.S.R.)	Medeo, U.S.S.R.	23 Mar. 1976

* This represents a speed of 29.43 m.p.h. 47,36 km/h.

BRITISH OUTDOOR RECORDS

	Distance	min. sec.	Name	Place	Date
MEN	500 metres	40.2	Archie Marshall	Madonna di Campilio, Italy	23 Jan. 1976
	1,000 metres	1:21.61	Archie Marshall	Madonna di Campilio, Italy	23 Jan. 1976
	1,500 metres	2:07.43	Peter R. Lake	Inzell, West Germany	10 Feb. 1975
	3,000 metres	4:34.70	John B. Blewitt	Cortina d'Ampezzo, Italy	16 Jan. 1968
	5,000 metres	7:45.26	Geoff Sandys	Herrenveen, Holland	28 Feb. 1976
	10,000 metres	16:10.49	Geoff Sandys	Inzell, West Germany	1 Feb. 1976
WOMEN	500 metres	51.90	Patricia K. Tipper	Cortina d'Ampezzo, Italy	16 Jan. 1968
	1,000 metres	1:44.20	Patricia K. Tipper	Inzell, West Germany	7 Jan. 1968
	1,500 metres	2:42.80	Patricia K. Tipper	Cortina d'Ampezzo, Italy	17 Dec. 1967
	3,000 metres	5:39.40	Patricia K. Tipper	Cortina d'Ampezzo, Italy	16 Dec. 1967

m.p.h. *230 km/h* by John D. Buckstaff in a Class A stern-steerer on Lake Winnebago, Wisconsin, U.S.A., in 1938. Such a speed is possible in a wind of 72 m.p.h. *115 km/h.*

Highest speeds *Sand*

The fastest recorded speed for a sand yacht is 57.69 m.p.h. *92,84 km/h* (measured mile in 62.4 sec) by *Coronation Year Mk. II* owned by R. Millett Denning and crewed by J. Halliday, Bob Harding, J. Glassbrook and Cliff Martindale at Lytham St. Anne's, Lancashire, England in 1956. A speed of 77.47 m.p.h. *125,11 km/h* was attained by Jan Paul Lowe (b. 15 Apr. 1936) of U.S.A. in *Sunkist* at Ivanpaugh Dry Lake, California, U.S.A. on 25 Mar. 1975.

INDOOR PASTIMES

CHESS

Origins

The name chess is derived from the Persian word *shah* (a king or ruler). It is a descendant of the game *Chaturanga*. The earliest reference is from the Middle Persian Karnamak (*c.* A.D. 590–628), though there are grounds for believing its origins are from A.D. 200 owing to the discovery, announced in December 1972, of two ivory chessmen in the Uzbek Soviet Republic dateable to that century. It reached Britain in *c.* 1255. The *Fédération Internationale des Echecs* was established in 1924. There were an estimated 7,000,000 competitive players in the U.S.S.R. in 1973.

It has been calculated that the two opening moves by each player can be made in 197,299 ways leading to some 72,000 different positions. The approximate number of different games possible is 2.5×10^{116}—a number astronomically higher than the number of atoms in the observable universe.

Most World titles

World champions have been generally recognized since 1886. The longest tenure was 27 years by Dr. Emanuel Lasker (1868–1941) of Germany, from 1894 to 1921. The women's world championship has been most often won by Vera Menchik-Stevenson (1906–44) (G.B.) in 1927, 1930–31, 1933–35, 1937 and 1939 and Nona Gaprindashvili (U.S.S.R.) 1963–76. Robert J. (Bobby) Fischer (b. Chicago, Illinois, U.S.A., 9 Mar. 1943) is reckoned on the officially adopted Elo System to be the greatest Grand Master of all-time. He became at 15 the youngest ever International Grand Master. The first British player to attain official International Grand Master status was Anthony Miles, (b. 1956), on 24 Feb. 1976.

Most British titles

Most British titles have been won by Dr. Jonathan Penrose, O.B.E. (b. 1934) of East Finchley, London with ten titles in 1958–63, 1966–69, Mrs. Rowena M. Bruce (b. 1919) of Plymouth won 11 titles in 1937 (as Miss Dew), 1950–51, 1954, 1955 (shared), 1959–60, 1962–63, 1967 (shared) and 1969 (shared).

Winning streak

Bobby Fischer won 20 games in succession in Grand Master chess from 2 Dec. 1970 *v.* Jorge Rubinetti (Argentine) to 30 Sept. 1971 *v.* Tigran Petrosian (U.S.S.R.).

Most opponents

Records by chess masters for numbers of opponents tackled simultaneously depend very much on whether or not the opponents are replaced as defeated, are in relays, or whether they are taken on in a simultaneous start. Both records are held by Vlastimil Hort (Czechoslovakia) who, in Reykjavik, Iceland on 23–24 Apr. 1977 played 550 games (winning 477 and drawing 63) in over 24 hrs of play. He started with 201 opponents who were replaced as each game ended. Georges Koltanowski (Belgium, now of U.S.A.) tackled 56 opponents "blindfold", won 50, and drew six in 9¾ hrs at the Fairmont Hotel, San Francisco, California, U.S.A., on 13 Dec. 1960.

Slowest game

The slowest recorded move (before modern rules) was one of 11 hours between Paul Morphy, the U.S. Champion of 1852–62, and the chess master Louis Paulsen.

Longest games

The master game with most moves on record was one drawn on the 191st move between H. Pilnik (Argentina) and Moshe Czerniak (Israel) at Mar del Plata, Argentina, in April 1950. The total playing time was 20 hrs. A game of 21½ hrs, but drawn on the 171st move (average over 7½ min per move), was played between Makagonov and Chekhover at Baku, U.S.S.R., in 1945.

Marathon

The longest recorded session is one of 156 hrs 2 min between Tony Togwell and Andrew Smith, in Slough, Berks., on 8–14 Nov. 1976.

CONTRACT BRIDGE

Origins

Bridge (a corruption of Biritch) is thought to be of Levantine origin, similar games having been played there in the early 1870s. The British Museum contains a pamphlet of 1886 entitled "Biritch or Russian Whist".

Auction Bridge (highest bidder names trump) was introduced in 1904 but was swamped by the Contract game, which was devised by Harold S. Vanderbilt (U.S.A.) on a Caribbean voyage in November 1925. The new version became a world-wide craze after the U.S.A. *v.* Great Britain challenge match between Ely Culbertson (b. Romania, 1891) and Lt.-Col. Walter Thomas More Buller (1886–1938) at Almack's Club, London, in Sept. 1930. The U.S.A. won the 200 hand match by 4,845 points.

Most World titles

The World Championship (Bermuda Bowl) has been won most often by Italy's Blue Team (*Squadra Azzurra*), 1957–59, 1961–63, 1965–7, 1969, 1973–75, whose team also won the Olympiad in 1964, 1968 and 1972. Giorgio Belladonna (b. 1923) was in all these winning teams.

Most master points

In 1971 a new world ranking list based on Master Points was instituted. The leading male player in the world was Giorgio Belladonna a member of Italy's Blue team with 1,765 points as at June 1977, followed by five more Italians. The leading Briton is Boris Schapiro (b. 1911) in 16th place with 353 points. The world's leading woman player is Mrs. Rixi R. Markus M.B.E. (G.B.) with 229 points to June 1977. Britain had four more women players in the Top Twenty.

Most brilliant play

Ron Klinger (Australia) was awarded the annual Bols Brilliancy Prize by the International Bridge Press Association for the most brilliant play in the 1976 World Team Olympiad on a hand in the match between Australia and U.S.A.

Perfect deals

The mathematical odds against dealing 13 cards of one suit are 158,753,389,899 to 1, while the odds against receiving a "perfect hand" consisting of all 13 spades are 635,013,559,599 to 1. The odds against each of the four players receiving a complete suit (a "perfect deal") are 2,235,197,406,895,366,368,301,559,999 to 1.

Marathon

The longest recorded session is one of 180 hr by four students at Edinburgh University on 21–28 Apr. 1972.

CRIBBAGE

Origins

The invention of the game (once called Cribbidge) is credited to the English dramatist St. John Suckling (1609–42). It is estimated that some ten million people play in the United States alone.

Combinations

Alex E. Cakebread, of Welwyn Garden City, Herts, England has listed every combination (in four cards and turn up) that produces 12,994,800 different possible crib hands.

HIGHEST POSSIBLE SCORES: BRIDGE		
Opponents bid 7 of any suit or 7 No Trumps doubled and redoubled and vulnerable		
	Opponents make no trick	
Above Line	1st undertrick	400
	12 subsequent undertricks at 600 each	7,200
	All Honours	150
		7,750
Bid 1 No Trump, doubled and redoubled, vulnerable		
Below Line	1st trick (40 × 4)	160
Above Line	6 over tricks (400 × 6)	2,400
	2nd game of 2-Game Rubber	*350
	All Honours	150
	Bonus for making redoubled contract	50
	(Highest Possible Positive Score)	3,110

* In practice, the full bonus of 700 points is awarded after the completion of the second winning game rather than 350 after each game.

DARTS

Origins

The origins of darts date from the use by archers of heavily weighted ten-inch throwing arrows for self-defence in close quarters fighting. The "dartes" were used in Ireland in the 16th century and darts was played on the *Mayflower* by the Plymouth pilgrims in 1620. Today there are an estimated 6,000,000 dart players in the British Isles—a higher participation than in any other sporting pastime. The National Darts Association of Great Britain (inst. 1953) is seeking to standardize the throwing distances and treble boards.

Most titles

Re-instituted in 1947, the annual *News of the World* England and Wales individual Championships consist of the best of three legs 501 up, "straight" start and finish on a double with an 8 ft *2,4 m* throwing distance. The only men to win twice are Tommy Gibbons (Ivanhoe Working Men's Club) of Conisbrough, South Yorkshire, in 1952 and 1958; Tom Reddington of New Inn, Stonebroom, Derbyshire in 1955 and of George Hotel, Alfreton, Derbyshire 1960; and Tom M. Barrett (Odco Sports Club, London) in 1964 and 1965.

The National Darts Association of Great Britain Individual title was won by Tom O'Regan of the Northern Star, New Southgate, Greater London in 1970–72.

Lowest possible scores

The lowest number of darts to achieve standard scores are: 201 four darts, 301 six darts, 401 seven darts, 501 nine darts, 1,001 seventeen darts. The four and six darts "possibles" have been many times achieved, the nine darts 501 occasionally but never the seventeen darts 1,001 which would require 15 treble 20's, a treble 17 and a 50. The lowest number of darts thrown for a score of 1,001 is 19 by Cliff Inglis (160, 180, 140, 180, 121, 180, 40) at the Bromfield Men's Club, Devon on 11 Nov. 1975. The lowest even number which cannot be scored with three darts (ending on a double) is 162. The lowest odd number which cannot be scored with three darts (ending on a double) is 159.

Fastest match

The fastest time taken for a match of three games of 301 is 1 min 58 sec by Ricky Fusco (G.B.) at the Perivale Residents Association Club, Middx., England on 30 Dec. 1976.

Fastest "round the board"

The record time for going round the board clockwise in "doubles" at arm's length is 9.2 sec by Dennis Gower at the Millers Arms, Hastings, East Sussex on 12 Oct. 1975 and 14.5 sec in numerical order by Jim Pike at the Craven Club, Newmarket in March, 1944. The record for this feat at the nine-feet *2,7 m* throwing distance, retrieving own darts, is 2 min 13 sec by Bill Duddy at The Plough, Hornsey Road, Harringey, Greater London on 29 Oct. 1972.

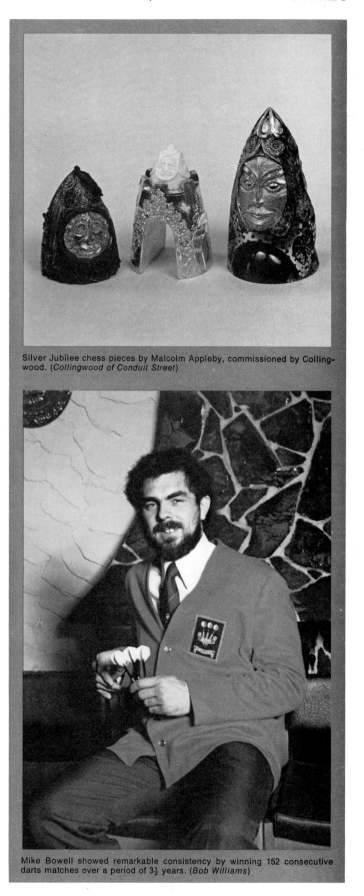

Silver Jubilee chess pieces by Malcolm Appleby, commissioned by Collingwood. (*Collingwood of Conduit Street*)

Mike Bowell showed remarkable consistency by winning 152 consecutive darts matches over a period of 3½ years. (*Bob Williams*)

Million and one up

The shortest recorded time to score 1,000,001 up *on one board*, under the rules of darts, is 6 hr 43 min by eight players from the Red Lion, Tividale, West Midlands, on 21 May 1977.

(*In future this category will only relate to number of darts and not time taken*) Under the new conditions, eight players from Little Mill, Gwent, Wales scored 1,000,001 with 57,836 darts, from 27–29 May 1977.

Ten hour scores
The record number of trebles scored in 10 hr is 2,150 (in 9,400 darts) for a percentage of 22.87 by E. Jacky Hughes at Heswell British Legion, Merseyside on 27 Sept. 1974. On 27 July 1973 Jacky Hughes scored a record 2,790 doubles (out of 9,984 darts) in 10 hr for a 27.94 percentage. The greatest score amassed in 10 hr is 451,273 by Malcolm Ellis and Bob George, at the Grove Social Club, Chudwell Heath, Ilford, Essex on 30 July 1977.

Longest unbeaten run
Mike Bowell (b. 31 May 1947) of Paulton Darts League, Avon, won 152 successive competition games from 9 Feb. 1971 to 29 Nov. 1974.

Marathon
Ron McFarland, Jim Mote, Bob Scott and Robin Davis played on a shift system non-stop for 725 hrs 6 min at the Rose and Crown Pub, Santa Ana, Calif., U.S.A., from 13 May–12 June 1976.

DOMINOES
Origins
Dominoes are known from 15th century China but remain unstandardized throughout the world. Though unknown in Europe in c. 1750, the game reached England *via* France c. 1795. The Eskimo game requires 148 pieces while that in Europe utilizes only 28.

Marathon
The longest game of dominoes is one of 168 hr 4½ min maintained by four players (in shifts) from the Royal Antediluvian Order of Buffaloes, Haverfordwest, Dyfed, on 14–21 May 1977.

DRAUGHTS
Origins
Draughts, known as checkers in North America, has origins earlier than chess. It was played in Egypt in the second millenium B.C. The earliest book on the game was by Antonio Torquemada of Valencia, Spain in 1547. There have been three U.S. *v.* Great Britain international matches—1905, 1927 and 1973—all won by the United States.

The British Championship (biennial) was inaugurated in 1926. The only man to win five titles has been Jim Marshall (Fife) in 1948, 1950, 1952, 1954 and 1966. The longest tenure of invincibility in freestyle play was that of Melvin Pomeroy (U.S.), who was internationally undefeated from 1914 until his death in 1933.

Most opponents
Newell W. Banks (b. Detroit, U.S.A., 10 Oct. 1887) played 140 games simultaneously, winning 133 and drawing seven, in Chicago, Illinois in 1933. His playing time was 145 min, so averaging about one move per sec.

Longest and shortest games
In competition the prescribed rate of play is not less than 30 moves per hour with the average game lasting about 90 min. In 1958 a match between Dr. Marian Tinsley (U.S.) and Derek Oldbury (G.B.) lasted 7½ hours. The shortest possible game is one of 21 moves composed by Alan M. Beckerson (b. 21 Feb. 1938) (G.B.) in 1964.

MONOPOLY
Origins
The patentee of Monopoly, the world's most popular proprietary board game of which Parker Bros. have sold 80,000,000 copies, was Charles Darrow (1889–1967). He invented the patented version of the game in 1933 while an unemployed heating engineer using the street names of Atlantic City, New Jersey where he spent his vacations.

Marathon
The longest game by four players ratified by the Monopoly Marathon Records Documentation Committee is 264 hr by Ray Kessinger, Tom Lashbrook, Tony Stanaró and Kirk

Hamiltons in Pinole, California, U.S.A., from 26 Dec. 1974 to 5 Jan. 1975. Sixty college students from Georgia Tech, Atlanta, Georgia, U.S.A. played for 1,176 hr ending on 11 Mar. 1976.

SCRABBLE ® Crossword Game
Origins
The crossword game was invented by Alfred M. Butts in 1931 and was developed, refined and trademarked as Scrabble ® Crossword Game by James Brunot in 1948. He sold the North American rights to Selchow & Richter Company, New York, the European rights to J. W. Spears & Sons, London, and the Australian rights to Murfett Pty. Ltd., Melbourne.

Highest scores
The highest competitive game score known is 656 by Darryl Francis (G.B.). The highest competitive single turn score recorded is between 380–390. Ronald E. Jerome, of Bracknell, Berkshire, England made an idealised single turn score of 1,961 in May 1974.

Most titles
British National Championships were instituted in 1971. Olive Behan has won twice in 1972 and 1975.

Marathon
The longest Scrabble ® Crossword Game on record is one of 120 hours set by Norman Hazeldean, Alan Giles, Tom Barton and Keith Ollett at Uckfield, East Sussex, on 4–9 Aug. 1975. This was equalled by four players in Sydney, Australia on 1 Sept. 1975.

TABLE FOOTBALL
Bar
The most protracted two-a-side table football match on record was one of 341 hours, maintained by six members of Burrow upon Soar Y.C., Leicestershire on 10–24 Apr. 1976.

Subbuteo
The longest recorded Subbuteo table soccer marathon was one of 285 hours by six boys (aged under 17) who sustained a continuous game at the Bedford Centre, Johannesburg, South Africa on 11–23 Aug. 1975.

TIDDLYWINKS
Origins
This game was only espoused by adults in 1955 when Cambridge University issued a challenge to Oxford.

National Championships
Alan Dean (Southampton) has won the singles title a record four times, 1971–3, 1976. The pairs title has been won three times by Jon Mapley (Hinkley) with different partners.

Guinness Trophy
England has remained unbeaten against Scotland, Ireland and Wales since the Trophy's inception on 7 May 1960. The closest result has been their 59½–52½ win over Wales at Warwick on 7 Apr. 1968.

Silver Wink Trophy
The *Silver Wink*, presented by H.R.H. The Duke of Edinburgh, for the British University championship has been won a record four times by both Oxford and Cambridge Universities.

Speed records
The record for potting 24 winks from 18 in *45 cm* is 21.8 sec by Stephen Williams (Altrincham Grammar School) in May 1966. Allen R. Astles (University of Wales) potted 10,000 winks in 3 hours 51 min 46 sec at Aberystwyth, Cardiganshire in February 1966.

Four Pot Relay
The greatest number of winks potted in 3 min by a relay of four is 29 by Paul Light, Paul Hoffman, Andrew James and Geoff Thorpe at "The Castle", Cambridge on 6 Dec. 1974.

Marathon
The most protracted game on record is one of 170 hr by

six players of Quinton Kynaston School, St. John's Wood, City of Westminster, Greater London, on 1–7 Jan. 1973.

WHIST
Origins
Whist, first referred to in 1529, was the world's premier card game until 1930. The rules were standardized in 1742.

Highest score
No collated records exist but the highest score notified to the editors has been—for 24 hands—209 by Mrs. E. Heslop in the Shaldon Over 60 Club, Teignmouth, Devon on 5 Jan. 1973.

Perfect hand
Mrs. Ethel Annie Cliffe on 3 Dec. 1973 at the Lache Community Centre, Chester, Cheshire picked up 13 hearts.

JUDO
Origins
Judo is a modern combat sport which developed out of an amalgam of several old Japanese fighting arts, the most popular of which was ju-jitsu (jiu-jitsu), which is thought to be of pre-Christian Chinese origin. Judo was greatly developed since 1882, when it was first devised by Dr. Jigoro Kano (1860–1938).

Most titles *World and Olympic*
World championships were inaugurated in Tōkyō on 5 May 1956. The only man to have won four world titles is Wilhelm Ruska (b. 29 Aug. 1940) (Netherlands), who won the 1967 Heavyweight, the 1971 Heavyweight and the 1972 Olympic Heavyweight and Open titles. In the European championships (instituted in 1951) only Great Britain (1957–59) and the U.S.S.R. (1972–74) have won three consecutive team titles.

Most titles *British*
The greatest number of titles (inst. 1966) won is nine by David Colin Starbrook, M.B.E. (b. 9 Aug. 1945) (5th dan) who won the middleweight title 1969–70, the light-heavy-

weight 1971–75 and the open division 1970–71. The women's championships were instituted in 1971. Christine Child (b. 1946) (4th dan) has won a record five times: the heavyweight in 1971–74 and the open division in 1973.

Highest grades
The efficiency grades in Judo are divided into pupil (*kyu*) and master (*dan*) grades. The highest awarded is the extremely rare red belt *Judan* (*10th dan*), given only to seven men so far. The Judo protocol provides for an *11th dan* (*Juichidan*) who also would wear a red belt, a *12th dan* (*Junidan*) who would wear a white belt twice as wide as an ordinary belt and the highest of all, *Shihan*, but these have never been bestowed. The highest British native Judo grades are *7th dan* by Trevor Pryce Leggett (b. 22 Aug. 1914), Charles Stuart Palmer O.B.E. (b. 1930) and Geoff Gleeson.

Marathon
The longest recorded continuous Judo marathon, by two of six Judoka in 5 min stints, is 200 hr by the Dufftown and District Judo Club, Banffshire on 9–17 July 1977.

KARATE
Origins
Based on techniques devised from the sixth century Chinese art of *Chuan-fa* (Kempo), karate (empty hand) was developed by an unarmed populace in Okinawa as a weapon against armed Japanese oppressors c. 1500. Transmitted to Japan in the 1920s by Funakoshi Gichin, the founder of modern karate, this method of combat was further refined and organized into a sport with competitive rules. The five major styles of karate in Japan are: *Shotokan, Wado-ryu, Goju-ryu, Shito-ryu* and *Kyokushinkai*, each of which place different emphasis on speed and power etc. Other styles include *Gojukai, Shotokai* and *Shukokai*. The military form of *Tae kwan-do* with nine dans is a Korean equivalent of Karate. *Wu shu* is a comprehensive term embracing all Chinese martial arts. *Kung fu* is one aspect of these arts popularised by the cinema.

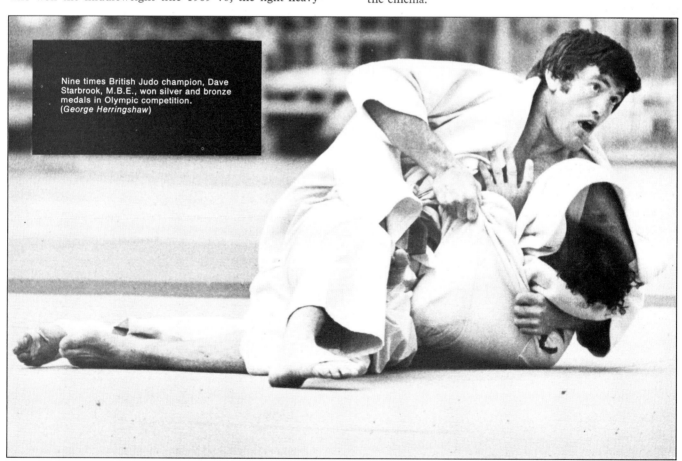

Nine times British Judo champion, Dave Starbrook, M.B.E., won silver and bronze medals in Olympic competition.
(George Herringshaw)

The Governing Body for the sport in Britain is the Martial Arts Commission upon which all the martial arts are represented.

Great Britain became the first country ever to defeat the Japanese in competition when they beat them in the 1972 World championships in Paris. They repeated the feat in the final of the 1975 World championships at Long Beach, California, U.S.A.

Most titles

The only winner of three All-Japanese titles has been Takeshi Oishi who won in 1969–71. David "Ticky" Donovan (5th dan) has won the British title on three consecutive occasions 1973–75.

Top exponents

The highest dan among karatekas is Yamaguchi Gogen (b. 1907) a 10th dan of the *Goju-ryu* Karate Do. The leading exponents in the United Kingdom are Tatsuo Suzuki (8th dan, *Wado-ryu*), chief instructor to the United Kingdom Karatedo Wadokai; Keinosuke Enoeda (7th dan, *Shotokan*), resident instructor to the Karate Union of Great Britain and Steve Arneil (6th dan, *Kyokushinkai*) British national born in South Africa.

Greatest force

Considerably less emphasis is placed on *Tamashiwara* (wood breaking etc.) than is generally supposed. Most styles use it only for demonstration purposes. However, the force needed to break a brick with the abductor *digiti quinti* muscle of the hand is 130–140 lb. *59–63 kg force* up to a maximum of 196 lb. *88 kg f.*

LACROSSE

Origins

The game is of American Indian origin, derived from the inter-tribal game *baggataway*, and was played before 1492 by Iroquois Indians in lower Ontario, Canada and upper New York State, U.S.A. It was introduced into Great Britain in 1867. The English Lacrosse Union was formed in 1892. The Oxford v. Cambridge match was instituted in 1903 and the game was included in the Olympic Games of 1908 and featured as an exhibition sport in the 1928 and 1948 Games.

Most titles *World*

The first World Tournament was held at Toronto, Canada in 1967 and the second in Melbourne, Australia in 1974. The United States won both championships.

Most titles *English*

The English Club Championship (Iroquois Cup), instituted in 1890, has been won most often by Stockport with 15 wins between 1897 and 1934.

Highest scores

The highest score in any international match was the United States' 26–15 win over Canada at Melbourne in 1974. England's highest score was their 19–11 win over Canada also at Melbourne in 1974. The highest score in the annual North of England v. South of England match has been 26–2 in 1927.

Most international appearances *Men*

The record number of international representations is 22 for England by Michael Roberts, Tom Gare (both Urmston) and Roy Higson (Mellor) to 1976.

Most international appearances *Women*

The record for women is 52 for Scotland by Caro MacIntosh (1952–1969).

Fastest scoring

Rod Burns scored only 4 sec into the game for South Manchester and Wythenshawe v. Sheffield Univ. on 6 Dec. 1975.

Longest throw

The longest recorded throw is 162.86 yds *148,91 m* by Barney Quinn of Ottawa on 10 Sept. 1892.

LAWN TENNIS

Origins

The modern game is generally agreed to have evolved as an outdoor form of the indoor game of Tennis (see separate entry). "Field Tennis" is mentioned in an English magazine —*Sporting Magazine*—of 29 Sept. 1793. The earliest club for such a game, variously called Pelota or Lawn Rackets, was the Leamington Club founded in 1872 by Major Harry Gem. The earliest attempt to commercialise the game was by Major Walter Clopton Wingfield, M.V.O. (1833–1912) who patented a form called 'sphairistike' on 23 Feb. 1874. It soon became called Lawn Tennis. Amateur players were permitted to play with and against professionals in "Open" tournaments in 1968.

Greatest domination

The grand slam is to win all four of the world's major championship singles: Wimbledon, the United States, Australian and French (on hard courts) championships. The first man to have won all four was Frederick John Perry (G.B.) (b. 18 May 1909) with the French title in 1935. The first man to hold all four championships simultaneously was John Donald Budge (U.S.A.) (b. 13 June 1915) with the French title in 1938. The first man to achieve the grand slam twice was Rodney George Laver (Australia) (b. 9 Aug. 1938) having won in 1962 as an amateur and again in 1969 when the titles were "open" to professionals.

Only two women have achieved the grand slam: Maureen Catherine Connolly (U.S.A.) (1934–69), later Mrs. Norman E. Brinker, in 1953; and Margaret Jean Court, M.B.E., (*née* Smith) (Australia) (b. 16 July 1942) in 1970.

Most Olympic titles *Men*

Lawn Tennis was part of the Olympic programme at the first eight celebrations of the Games (including the 1906 Games). The winner of most medals was Max Decugis (1882–1949) (France) with six (a record four gold, one silver and one bronze) in the 1900, 1906 and 1920 tournaments. The British male winners of most medals were Reginald Frank Doherty (1872–1910) with four (a record three gold, and one bronze) and Charles Percy Dixon (1873–1939) (one gold, one silver and two bronze).

Most Olympic titles *Women*

The most medals won by a woman player is five by Kitty McKane (later Mrs. L. A. Godfree) (b. 7 May 1897) (G.B.), with one gold, two silver and two bronze in the 1920 and 1924 tournaments. Two gold medals is the record shared by Charlotte Cooper (later Mrs. Alfred Sterry) (1871–1966) (G.B.); Edith M. Hannam (1873–1939) (G.B.); Suzanne Rachel Flore Lenglen (1899–1938) (France); Hazel Hotchkiss Wightman, C.B.E. (Hon.) (1886–1974) (U.S.A.) and Helen N. Wills (b. 6 Oct. 1905) (later Mrs. F. S. Moody and Mrs. A. Roark) (U.S.A.)

Davis Cup *Most victories*

The greatest number of wins in the Davis Cup (instituted 1900) has been (inclusive of 1976) the U.S.A., with 24 wins and Australasia/Australia with 23. The British Isles/Great Britain have won nine times, in 1903–06, 1912, 1933–36.

Davis Cup *Individual Performance*

Nicola Pietrangeli (b. 11 Sept. 1933) (Italy) played 164 rubbers, 1954 to 1972, winning 120. He played 110 singles (winning 78) and 54 doubles (winning 42). He took part in 66 ties.

Fastest service

The fastest service ever *measured* was one of 163.6 m.p.h. *263 km/h* by William Tatem Tilden (1893–1953) (U.S.A.) in 1931. Some players consider the service of Robert Falkenburg (U.S.A.) (b. 29 Jan. 1926), the 1948 Wimbledon champion, as the fastest ever produced.

Greatest crowd

The greatest crowd at a tennis match was 30,472 at the

Astrodome, Houston, Texas, on 20 Sept. 1973, when Billy-Jean King (*née* Moffitt) (b. 22 Nov. 1943) (U.S.A.) beat Robert Larimore Riggs (b. 25 Feb. 1918) (U.S.A.). The record for an orthodox match is 25,578 at Sydney, N.S.W., Australia on 27 Dec. 1954 in the Davis Cup Challenge Round (first day) Australia *v.* U.S.A.

Highest earnings
James Scott (Jimmy) Connors (b. 2 Sept. 1952) (U.S.A.) won a record $687,335 in 1976. The record for a woman player is $362,227 in 1975 by Christine Marie Evert (b. 21 Dec. 1954) (U.S.A.)

The one match record is $500,000 *£217,400* won by Jimmy Connors when he beat John Newcombe (Australia) (b. 23 May 1944) in a challenge match at Caesars Palace, Las Vegas, U.S.A. on 26 Apr. 1975.

Longest span
The championship career of C. Alphonso Smith (b. 18 Mar. 1909) of Charlottesville, Virginia, U.S.A., extended from winning the United States National Boy's title at Chicago, on 14 Aug. 1924, to winning the National 65-and-over title at Aptos, California, exactly 50 years to the day later on 14 Aug. 1974.

Marathons
The longest recorded non-stop lawn tennis singles game is one of 100 hr 10 min by Lt. C. P. Miller and Pt. A. Cloet of the Lenz Military Base, Witwatersrand Command, Johannesburg, S.A. on 14–18 July 1976. The duration record for doubles is 72 hr by four players from Shu Lin Kou Air Station (U.S.A.F.), Taiwan, on 11–14 Mar. 1976. Ron Wollenhaupt, of Omaha, Nebraska, U.S.A., played singles against a number of opponents for 87 hr on 27–31 May 1977.

WIMBLEDON RECORDS
For more details see *100 Years of Wimbledon* by Lance Tingay, published by Guinness Superlatives Ltd. (price £8.50)

Most wins *Women*
Elizabeth Montague Ryan (U.S.A.) (b. 5 Feb. 1892) won her first title in 1914 and her 19th in 1934 (a record 12 women's doubles and a record seven mixed doubles). Her total was equalled by the six time singles champion Billie-Jean King who also won nine women's doubles and four mixed doubles during the period 1961 to 1975.

Most wins *Men*
The greatest number of wins by a man at Wimbledon has been 14 by William Charles Renshaw (1861–1904) (G.B.) who won seven singles titles (1881–86, 1889) (a record for men) and seven doubles (1880–81, 1884–86, 1888–89), partnered by his twin brother James Ernest (1861–1899).

Most wins *Singles*
The greatest number of singles wins was eight by Helen N. Moody (*née* Wills), who won in 1927–30, 1932–33, 1935 and 1938.

Most wins *Doubles*
The greatest number of doubles wins by men was eight by the brothers Reginald Frank and Hugh Lawrence Doherty (1875–1919) (G.B.). They won each year from 1897 to 1905 except for 1902.

Most wins *Mixed doubles*
The male record is four wins shared by Elias Victor Seixas (U.S.A.) (b. 30 Aug. 1923) in 1953–56, Kenneth N. Fletcher (Australia) (b. 15 June 1940) in 1963, 1965–66, 1968 and Owen Keir Davidson (Australia) (b. 4 Oct. 1943) in 1967, 1971, 1973–74.

Most appearances
Arthur William Charles "Wentworth" Gore (1868–1928) (G.B.) made a record 36 appearances at Wimbledon between 1888 and 1927, and was in 1909 at 41 yr 6 months the oldest ever singles winner. In 1964, Jean Borotra (b. 13 Aug. 1898) of France, made his 35th appearance since 1922. In 1977 he appeared in the Veterans' Doubles aged 78.

Twice Wimbledon singles champion, and still playing there aged 78, Jean Borotra, one of France's "Four Musketeers", helped his country to six successive Davis Cup victories from 1927 to 1932. (*Associated Press*)

Youngest champions
The youngest Wimbledon champion was Charlotte (Lottie) Dod (1871–1960), who was 15 years 9 months when she won in 1887. Richard Dennis Ralston (b. 27 July 1942) of Bakersfield, California, U.S.A., was 25 days short of his 18th birthday when he won the men's doubles with Rafael H. Osuna (1938–1969) of Mexico in 1960. The youngest male singles champion was Wilfred Baddeley (1872–1929) who won the Wimbledon title in 1891 aged 19 years 175 days. The youngest ever player at Wimbledon is Tracy Austin (b. 12 Dec. 1962) (U.S.A.), who was only 14 yr 7 months in the 1977 tournament.

Greatest crowd
The record crowd for one day at Wimbledon is 37,393 on 22 June 1977. The record for the whole championship is 338,591 in 1975.

MARBLES
Origins
Marbles was played by the Romans who are believed to have introduced it into Britain in the 1st Century A.D. It became a competitive sport under the British Marbles Board of Control at the Greyhound Hotel, Tinsley Green, Crawley, West Sussex in 1926. The governing body now is the British Marbles Association.

Outside Europe the game is also played in Australia, Brazil (as *Gude*), Canada, China, India, Iran, New Zealand, Syria, the United States and the West Indies.

Most championships
The British Championship (established 1926) has been won most often by the Toucan Terribles with 20 consecutive titles (1956–75). Three founder members, Len Smith, Jack

and Charlie Dempsey, have played in every title win. They were finally beaten in 1976 by the Pernod Rams, captained by Len Smith's son, Paul. Len Smith (b. 13 Oct. 1917) has won the individual title 15 times (1957–64, 1966, 1968–73) but lost in 1974 to his son Alan.

Speed record

The record for clearing the ring (between 5¾ and 6¼ ft *1,75–1,90 m* in diameter) of 49 marbles is 2 min 57 sec by the Toucan Terribles at Worthing, West Sussex in 1971.

MODERN PENTATHLON

Points scores in riding, fencing, cross country and hence overall scores have no comparative value between one competition and another. In shooting and swimming (300 m) the scores are of record significance and the best achievements are shown.

The Modern Pentathlon (Riding, Fencing, Shooting, Swimming and Running) was inaugurated into the Olympic Games at Stockholm in 1912. The Modern Pentathlon Association of Great Britain was formed in 1922.

Most titles *World*

The record number of world titles won is six by András Balczó (b. 16 Aug. 1938) (Hungary) in 1963, 1965–67 and 1969. In Olympic years this title also rates as the world title, thus giving Balczó his sixth in 1972. The best British placing is the bronze medal by Sgt. (now Lieut.) Jeremy Robert "Jim" Fox, M.B.E. (b. 19 Sept. 1941) at Mexico in 1975.

Most titles *Olympic*

The greatest number of Olympic gold medals won is three by András Balczó a member of the winning team in 1960 and 1968 and the 1972 individual champion. Lars Hall (b. 30 Apr. 1927) (Sweden) has uniquely won two individual Championships (1952 and 1956). Balczó has won a record number of five medals (three gold and two silver). The best British performance is the team gold medal at Montreal, Canada 18–22 July 1976 by Jim Fox, M.B.E., Adrian Philip Parker and Daniel Nightingale. The best individual placing is fourth by Jim Fox M.B.E. at Munich in 1972.

Most titles *British*

The pentathlete with most British titles is Jim Fox, M.B.E., with ten (1963, 1965–68, 1970–74).

MODERN PENTATHLON

	World			
Shooting	1,088	Mario Medda (Italy), Munich W. Germany	29 Aug.	1972
		Jiri Adam (Czechoslovakia) Montreal, Canada	20 July	1976
Swimming	1,324	Robert L. Nieman (U.S.A.) Montreal, Canada	21 July	1976
	British			
Shooting	1,066	Robert Lawson Phelps, Leipzig E. Germany	21 Sept.	1965
Swimming	1,240	Adrian Philip Parker, Montreal, Canada	21 July	1976

MOTORCYCLE RACING

Earliest race

The first motorcycle race was held over a mile *1,6 km* on an oval track at Sheen House, Richmond, Surrey, on 29 Nov. 1897, won by Charles Jarrott (1877–1944) on a Fournier. The oldest motorcycle races in the world are the Auto-Cycle Union Tourist Trophy (T.T.) series, first held on the 15.81 mile *25,44 km* "Peel" ("St. John's") course in the Isle of Man on 28 May 1907, and still run in the island on the 37.73 mile *60,72 km* long "Mountain" circuit.

Fastest circuits *World*

The highest average lap speed attained on any closed circuit is 160.288 m.p.h. *257,958 km/h* by Yvon du Hamel (Canada) on a modified 903 c.c. four-cylinder Kawasaki Z1 at the 31 degree banked 2.5 mile *4,02 km* Daytona International Speedway, Florida, U.S.A., in Mar. 1973. His lap time was 56.149 sec.

The fastest road circuit is the Francorchamps circuit near Spa, Belgium. It is 8.74 miles *14,120 km* in length and was lapped in 3 min 50.3 sec (average speed 137.150 m.p.h. *320,721 km/h*) by Barry Stephen Frank Sheene (b. Holborn, London, 11 Sept. 1950) on a 495 c.c. four-cylinder Suzuki during the 500 c.c. Belgian Grand Prix on 3 July 1977.

Fastest circuits *United Kingdom*

The fastest circuit in the United Kingdom is the Portstewart-Coleraine-Portrush circuit in Londonderry, Northern Ireland. The lap record (10.1 mile *16,26 km* lap) is 4 min 53.2 sec (average speed 124.060 m.p.h. *199,655 km/h*) by John Glyn Williams (b. Neston, Cheshire, 27 May 1946) on a 747 c.c. four-cylinder Yamaha on lap five of the 750 c.c. event of the North West 200, on 21 May 1977.

The lap record for the outer circuit (2.767 miles *4,453 km*) at the Brooklands Motor Course, near Weybridge, Surrey (open between 1907 and 1939) was 80.0 sec (average speed 124.51 m.p.h. *200,37 km/h*) by Noel Baddow "Bill" Pope (later Major) (1909–71) of the United Kingdom on a Brough Superior powered by a supercharged 996 c.c. V-twin "8-80" J.A.P. engine developing 110 b.h.p., on 4 July 1939.

Fastest races *World*

The fastest race in the world was held at Grenzlandring, near Wegberg, W. Germany in 1939. It was won by Georg Meier (b. Germany, 1910) at an average speed of 134 m.p.h. *215 km/h* on a supercharged 495 c.c. flat-twin B.M.W.

The fastest road race is the 500 c.c. Belgian Grand Prix held on the Francorchamps circuit (see above). The record time for this ten lap (87.74 mile *141,20 km*) race is 38 min 58.5 sec (average speed 135.068 m.p.h. *217,370 km/h*) by Barry Sheene, on a 495 cc.. four-cylinder Suzuki, on 3 July 1977.

Fastest races *United Kingdom*

The fastest race in the United Kingdom is the 750 c.c. event of the North-West 200 held on the Londonderry circuit (see above). The record time for this five lap (50.52 mile *81,30 km*) race is 24 min 53.8 sec (average speed 121.751 m.p.h. *195,939 km/h*) by John Williams on a 747 c.c. four-cylinder Yamaha, on 21 May 1977.

Most successful riders *Tourist Trophy*

The record number of victories in the Isle of Man T.T. races is 12 by Stanley Michael Bailey Hailwood, M.B.E., G.M. (b. Oxford, 2 Apr. 1940) between 1961 and 1967. The first man to win three consecutive T.T. titles in two events was James A. Redman, M.B.E. (Rhodesia) (b. Hampstead, Greater London, 8 Nov. 1931). He won the 250 c.c. and 350 c.c. events in 1963–65. Mike Hailwood is the only man to win three events in one year, in 1961 and 1967.

Most successful riders *World championships*

The most world championship titles (instituted by the *Fédération Internationale Motorcycliste* in 1949) won are 15 by Giacomo Agostini (b. Lovere, Italy, 16 June 1942) 350 c.c. in 1968–1974, and 500 c.c. in 1966–1972, 1975. He is the only man to win two world championships in five consecutive years (350 and 500 c.c. titles in 1968–1972).

Agostini won 122 races in the world championship series between 24 Apr. 1965 and 29 Aug. 1976, including a record 19 in 1970, also achieved by Mike Hailwood in 1966.

Most successful riders *Trials*

Samuel Hamilton Miller (b. Belfast, Northern Ireland, 11 Nov. 1935) won eleven A.-C.U. Solo Trials Drivers' Stars in 1959–69.

Most successful riders *Scrambles*

Jeffrey Vincent Smith, M.B.E. (b. Colne, Lancashire, 14 Oct.

Britain's 1976 Olympic gold medal Modern Pentathlon champions—competitors and support team. (*Gerry Cranham*)

1934) won nine A.-C.U. 500 c.c. Scrambles' Stars in 1955–56, 1960–65 and 1967.

Joël Robert (b. Chatelet, Belgium, Nov. 1943) has won six 250 c.c. moto-cross world championships (1964, 1968–72). Between 25 Apr. 1964 and 18 June 1972 he won a record fifty 250 c.c. Grands Prix. He became the youngest moto-cross world champion on 12 July 1964 when he won the 250 c.c. championship aged 20 years 8 months.

Most successful machines
Italian M.V.-Agusta machines won 37 world championships between 1952 and 1973 and 276 world championship races between 1952 and 1976. Japanese Honda machines won 29 world championship races and five world championships in 1966. In the seven years they contested the championship (1961–67) their annual average was 20 race wins.

Youngest and oldest world champions
Alberto "Johnny" Cecotto (b. Caracas, Venezuela, 25 Jan. 1956) is the youngest to win a world championship. He was 19 years 211 days when he won the 350 c.c. title on 24 Aug.

1976 and 1977 World Champion Barry Sheene has been the fastest man on the fastest motor cycling circuit. (*All-Sport Photographic*)

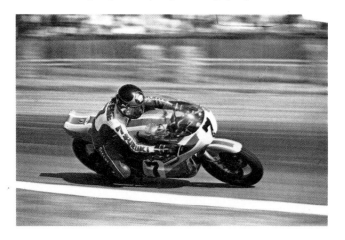

1975. The oldest was Hermann-Peter Müller (1909–76) of West Germany, who won the 250 c.c. title in 1955 aged 46.

Highest speeds
Official world speed records must be set with two runs over a measured distance made in opposite directions within a time limit. This limit is one hour for F.I.M. records and two hours for A.M.A. records.

Donald A. Vesco (b. Loma Linda, Calif., U.S.A., 8 Apr. 1939) riding his 21 ft long 1500 c.c. *Silver Bird* streamliner, powered by two Yamaha TZ750 four-cylinder engines developing 180 b.h.p., on Bonneville Salt Flats, Utah, U.S.A. on 28 Sept. 1975 set A.M.A. and F.I.M. absolute records. His average time was 11.8495 sec (303.810 m.p.h. *488,935 km/h*) for the A.M.A. record and 11.884 sec (302.928 m.p.h. *487,516 km/h*) for the F.I.M. record. (For details of the individual runs see the 23rd Edition). On the same day he covered a flying quarter mile in 2.925 sec (307.692 m.p.h. *495,183 km/h*), the highest speed ever achieved on a motorcycle.

The highest speed achieved over two runs in the U.K. is 189.873 m.p.h. *305,571 km/h* by Frederick James Cooper (b. London, 9 Mar. 1925) on his 1,267 c.c. supercharged twin-engined Triumph *Cyclotron* at R.A.F. Fairford, Glos., on 23 Sept. 1972. Average time for the flying 440 yd *402 m* runs was 4.74 sec.

The world record for 1 km *1,093.6 yd* from a standing start is 16.68 sec by Henk Vink (b. 24 July 1939) (Netherlands) on his supercharged 984 c.c. four-cylinder Kawasaki, at Elvington Airfield, North Yorkshire on 24 July 1977. The faster run was made in 16.09 secs.

The world record for 440 yd *402 m* from a standing start is 8.805 sec. by Henk Vink on his supercharged 1,132 c.c. four-cylinder Kawasaki at Elvington Airfield, North Yorkshire on 23 July 1977. The faster run was made in 8.55 sec.

The fastest time for a single run over 440 yd *402 m* from a standing start is 7.86 sec (terminal velocity 178.92 m.p.h. *287,94 km/h*) by Russ Collins of Gardena, California, U.S.A. riding his 3246 c.c. *Atchison, Topeka & Santa Fé* powered by three Honda engines, during the National Hot Rod Association's Supernationals at Ontario Motor Speedway, Ontario, California, U.S.A., on 10 Oct. 1975.

The highest terminal velocity recorded at the end of a 440 yd *402 m* run from a standing start is 182.55 m.p.h. *293,79 km/h* (elapsed time 8.12 sec) by Joe Smith of West Covina, California, U.S.A., riding his supercharged 3736 c.c. twin-engined Harley-Davidson, at the above meeting on 12 Oct. 1975.

Longest race
The longest race is the Liège 24 hours. The greatest distance ever covered is 2,761.9 miles *4 444,8 km* (average speed 115.08 m.p.h. *185,20 km/h*) by Jean-Claude Chemarin and Christian Leon, both of France, on a 941 c.c. four-cylinder Honda on the Francorchamps circuit on 14–15 Aug. 1976.

Longest circuit
The 37.73 mile *60,72 km* "Mountain" circuit, over which the two main T.T. races have been run since 1911, has 264 curves and corners and is the longest used for any motorcycle race.

MOTOR RACING
Earliest races
The first "race" was one of 12.43 miles *20 km*, held at Longchamps, Paris, in 1891, won by Georges Bouton (1847–1938) of France in his Dion steam tricycle in 41 min, at an average speed of 18.19 m.p.h. *29,27 km/h*. His only opponent broke down. The first "real" race was from Paris to Bordeaux and back (732 miles *1 178 km*) on 11–13 June 1895. The

first to finish was Emile Levassor (1844–1897) of France, in a Panhard-Levassor two-seater, with a 1.2 litre Daimler engine developing 3½ h.p. His time was 48 hr 47 min (average speed 15.01 m.p.h. *24,15 km/h*). The first closed circuit race was held over five laps of a mile *1,6 km* dirt track at Narragansett Park, Cranston, R.I., U.S.A., on 7 Sept. 1896, won by A. H. Whiting, driving a Riker electric.

The oldest motor race in the world, still being regularly run, is the R.A.C. Tourist Trophy (40th race held in 1976), first staged on 14 Sept. 1905, in the Isle of Man. The oldest continental race is the French Grand Prix (55th in 1977), first held on 26–27 June 1906.

Fastest circuits *World*
The highest average lap speed attained on any closed circuit is 221.160 m.p.h. *355,922 km/h* by Mark Donohue, Jr. (1937–75) of U.S.A., who lapped the 2.66 mile *4,28 km*, 33-degree banked tri-oval at Alabama International Motor Speedway, Talladega, Alabama, U.S.A. in 43.299 sec, driving a 5374 c.c. turbocharged Porsche 917/30 Can-Am car on 9 Aug. 1975.

The highest average race lap speed for a closed circuit is over 195 m.p.h. *313 km/h* by Richard Brickhouse (U.S.A.) driving a 1969 Dodge Daytona Charger, powered by a 6 981 c.c. 600 b.h.p. V8 engine, during a 500 mile *804 km* race on the 2.66 mile *4,28 km*, 33-degree banked tri-oval at Alabama International Motor Speedway, Talladega, Alabama, U.S.A. on 14 Sept. 1969.

The fastest road circuit was the Francorchamps circuit near Spa, Belgium, then 8.761 miles *14,100 km* in length which was lapped in 3 min 13.4 sec (average speed 163.086 m.p.h. *262,461 km/h*) on lap seven of the Francorchamps 1000 km sports car race on 6 May 1973, by Henri Pescarolo (b. Paris, France, 25 Sept. 1942) driving a 2 993 c.c. V12 Matra-Simca MS670 Group 5 sports car. The practice lap record was 3 min 12.7 sec (average speed 163.678 m.p.h. *263,414 km/h*) by Jacques-Bernard "Jacky" Ickx (b. Brussels, Belgium, 1 Jan. 1945) driving a 2 998.5 c.c. flat-12 Ferrari 312P Group 5 sports car, on 4 May 1973.

Fastest circuits *United Kingdom*
The fastest circuit in the United Kingdom is the ex-aerodrome course of 2.932 miles *4,719 km* at Silverstone, Northamptonshire (opened 1948). The race lap record is 1 min 18.81 sec (average speed 133.932 m.p.h. *215,543 km/h*) by James Simon Wallis Hunt (b. Belmont, Surrey, 29 Aug. 1947) driving a Formula One 2 993 c.c. McLaren M23 Cosworth V8 on lap 28 of the International Trophy race on 11 Apr. 1976. The practice lap record is 1 min 17.91 sec (135.479 m.p.h. *218,033 km/h*) by James Hunt on 10 Apr. 1976.

The lap record for the outer circuit (2.767 miles *4,453 km*) at the Brooklands Motor Course near Weybridge, Surrey (open between 1907 and 1939) was 1 min 9.44 sec (average speed 143.44 m.p.h. *230,84 km/h*) by John Rhodes Cobb (1899–1952) in his 3 ton *3,3 tonnes* 23 856 c.c. Napier-Railton, with a Napier *Lion* 12-cylinder aero-engine developing 450 b.h.p., on 7 Oct. 1935. His average speed over a km *0.6 mile* was 151.97 m.p.h. *244,57 km/h* (14.72 sec). The race lap record for the outer circuit at Brooklands was 1 min 9.6 sec (average speed 143.11 m.p.h. *230,31 km/h*) by Oliver Henry Julius Bertram (b. Kensington, Greater London, 26 Feb. 1910) driving a 7 963 c.c. Barnato-Hassan Special (Bentley engine), during the seven lap "Dunlop Jubilee Cup" handicap race on 24 Sept. 1938.

The Motor Industry Research Association (MIRA) High Speed Circuit (2.82 mile *4,53 km* lap with 33-degree banking on the bends) at Lindley, Warwickshire, was lapped in 1 min 2.8 sec (average speed 161.655 m.p.h. *260,158 km/h*) by David Wishart Hobbs (b. Leamington, Warwickshire, 9 June 1939) driving a 4 994 c.c. V12 Jaguar XJ13 Group 6 prototype sports car in April 1967.

Fastest races *World*
The fastest race in the world is the NASCAR Grand National 125 mile *201 km* event on the 2.50 mile *4,02 km*, 31-degree banked tri-oval at Daytona International Speedway, Daytona Beach, Florida, U.S.A. The record time for this race is 40 min 55 sec (average speed 183.295 m.p.h. *294,985 km/h*) by William Caleb "Cale" Yarborough (b. 27 Mar. 1939) of Timmonsville, S. Carolina, U.S.A., driving a 1969 Mercury V8, on 19 Feb. 1970.

The fastest road race was the Francorchamps 1000 km sports car race held on the Francorchamps circuit. The record time for this 71-lap (622.055 mile *1 001,100 km*) race was 4 hr 1 min 9.7 sec (average speed 154.765 m.p.h. *249,070 km/h*) by Pedro Rodriguez (1940–71) of Mexico, and Keith Jack "Jackie" Oliver (b. Chadwell Heath, Greater London, 14 Aug. 1942) driving a 4 998 c.c. flat-12 Porsche 917K Group 5 sports car, on 9 May 1971.

Fastest races *United Kingdom*
The fastest currently held race in the United Kingdom is the International Trophy race. The record time for this 40-lap (117.28 mile *188,74 km*) race is 53 min 4.57 sec (average speed 132.579 m.p.h. *213,366 km/h*) by James Hunt, driving a Formula One 2,993 c.c. McLaren M23-Cosworth V8, at Silverstone on 11 April 1976.

The fastest race ever held in the United Kingdom was the Broadcast Trophy Handicap held on the Brooklands outer circuit on 29 Mar. 1937. The 29 mile *46 km* race was won by John Cobb driving his 23 970 c.c. 12-cylinder Napier-Railton at an average speed of 136.03 m.p.h. *218,91 km/h*.

Fastest pit stop
Robert William (Bobby) Unser (b. Colorado Springs, Colorado, U.S.A., 20 Feb. 1934) took 4 sec to take on fuel on lap 10 of the Indianapolis 500 on 30 May 1976.

One of the reasons why Monaco is considered to be the toughest Grand Prix circuit of them all. (*Tony Duffy, All-Sport Photographic*)

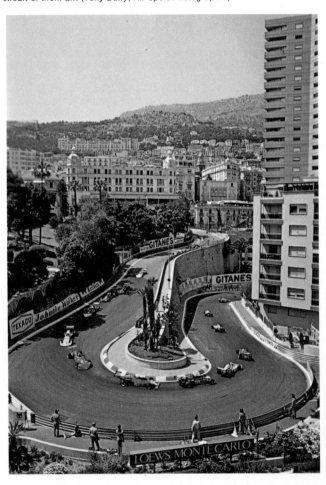

Toughest circuit *World*

The Targa Florio (first run 9 May 1906) was widely acknowledged to be the most arduous race. Held on the Piccolo Madonie Circuit in Sicily, it covered eleven laps (492.126 miles *792,000 km*) and involved the negotiation of 9,350 corners, over severe mountain gradients, and narrow rough roads. The record time was 6 hr 27 min 48.0 sec (average speed 76.141 m.p.h. *122,537 km/h*) by Arturo Francesco Merzario (b. Civenna, Italy, 11 Mar. 1943) and Sandro Munari (b. Venice, Italy, 1940) driving a 2 998.5 c.c. flat-12 Ferrari 312P Group 5 sports car in the 56th race on 21 May 1972. The lap record was 33 min 36.0 sec (average speed 79.890 m.p.h. *128,570 km/h*) by Leo Juhani Kinnunen (b. Tampere, Finland, 5 Aug. 1943) on lap 11 of the 54th race on 3 May 1970 driving a 2 997 c.c. flat-8 Porsche 908/3 Spyder Group 6 prototype sports car. The race was last held on 13 May 1973.

Toughest circuit *Grand Prix*

The most difficult Grand Prix circuit is generally regarded to be that for the Monaco Grand Prix (first run on 14 Apr. 1929), round the streets and the harbour of Monte Carlo. It is 2.058 miles *3,312 km* in length and has eleven pronounced corners and several sharp changes of gradient. The race is run over 76 laps (156.406 miles *251,712 km*) and involves on average about 1,600 gear changes. The record time for the race is 1 hr 59 min 51.47 sec (average speed 80.356 m.p.h. *129,321 km/h*) by Andreas-Nikolaus "Niki" Lauda (b. Vienna, Austria, 22 Feb. 1949) driving a 2 998.5 c.c. flat-12 Ferrari 312T2, on 30 May 1976. The race lap record is 1 min 30.28 sec (average speed 82.064 m.p.h. *132,069 km/h*) by Gianclaudio Giuseppe "Clay" Regazzoni (b. Lugano, Switz., 5 Sept. 1939) driving a similar Ferrari on lap 60 of the race held on 30 May 1976. The practice lap record is 1 min 29.65 sec (average speed 82.641 m.p.h. *132,997 km/h*) by Niki Lauda on 29 May 1976.

Le Mans

The greatest distance ever covered in the 24 hour *Grand Prix d'Endurance* (first held on 26–27 May 1923) on the Sarthe circuit at Le Mans, France is 3,315.210 miles *5 335,313 km* (average speed 138.134 m.p.h. *222,305 km/h*) by Dr. Helmut Marko (b. Graz, Austria, 27 Apr. 1943) and Jonkheer Gijs van Lennep (b. Bloemendaal, Netherlands, 16 Mar. 1942) driving a 4 907 c.c. flat-12 Porsche 917K Group 5 sports car, on 12–13 June 1971. The race lap record (8.369 mile *13,469 km* lap) is 3 min 18.7 sec (average speed 151.632 m.p.h. *244,028 km/h*) by Pedro Rodriguez driving a 4 907 c.c. flat-12 Porsche 917L on 12 June 1971. The practice lap record is 3 min 13.6 sec (average speed 155.627 m.p.h. *250,457 km/h*) by Jackie Oliver driving a similar car on 18 Apr. 1971. The pre-war record average speed was 86.85 m.p.h. *139,77 km/h* by a 3.3 litre Bugatti in 1939.

Le Mans *Most wins*

The race has been won by Ferrari cars nine times, in 1949, 1954, 1958 and 1960–65. The most wins by one man is four by Olivier Gendebien (b. 1925) (Belgium), 1958, 1960–62, and Jackie Ickx, 1969 and 1975–77.

Le Mans *British wins*

The race has been won 12 times by British cars, thus: Bentley in 1924 and 1927–30, once by Lagonda in 1935, five times by Jaguar in 1951, 1953 and 1955–57 and once by Aston Martin in 1959.

Indianapolis 500

The Indianapolis 500 mile *804 km* race (200 laps) was inaugurated in the U.S.A. on 30 May 1911. The most successful driver has been Anthony Joseph "A.J." Foyt, Jr. (b. Houston, Texas, U.S.A., 16 Jan. 1935) who won in 1961, 1964, 1967 and 1977. The record time is 3 hr 4 min 5.54 sec (average speed 162.962 m.p.h. *262,261 km/h*) by Mark Donohue, Jr. driving a 2 595 c.c. 900 b.h.p. turbocharged Sunoco McLaren M16B-Offenhauser on 27 May 1972. The race lap record is 46.71 sec (average speed 192.678 m.p.h. *310,085 km/h*) by Danny Ongais, of Costa Mesa, Calif., driving a 2.6 litre turbocharged Parnelli-Cosworth DFX on lap 42 of the race held on 29 May 1977. The practice lap

Winner of the 1969 Le Mans 24-hour race, Jackie Oliver (GB) also holds the sports car lap record at Belgium's Francorchamps circuit. (*Sport & General Press Agency*)

record is 44.86 sec (average speed 200.624 m.p.h. *322,873 km/h*) by Johnny Rutherford (b. 12 Mar. 1938) of Fort Worth, Texas, U.S.A. driving a 2.6 litre 850 b.h.p. turbocharged McLaren M24—Cosworth DFX on 13 May 1977.

The record prize fund was $1,116,807 for the 61st race on 29 May 1977. The individual prize record is $271,697.72 by Al Unser (b. Albuquerque, New Mexico, U.S.A., 29 May 1939) on 30 May 1970.

Drivers *Most successful*

Based on the World Drivers' Championship, inaugurated in 1950, the most successful driver is Juan-Manuel Fangio y Cia (b. Balcarce, Argentina, 24 June 1911) who won five times in 1951, 1954–57. He retired in 1958, after having won 24 Grand Prix races (two shared). The most successful driver in terms of race wins is Richard Lee Petty (b. Randleman, N. Carolina, U.S.A., 2 July 1937) with 180 NASCAR Grand National wins between 1960 and Feb. 1977. His best season was 1967 with 27 wins.

The most Grand Prix victories is 27 by John Young "Jackie" Stewart, O.B.E. (b. Milton, Dunbartonshire, 11 June 1939) between 12 Sept. 1965 and 5 Aug. 1973. James "Jim" Clark, O.B.E. (1936–68) of Scotland holds the record for Grand Prix victories in one year with seven in 1963. He won a record 61 Formula One and Formula Libre races between 1959 and 1968. The most Grand Prix starts is 176 (out of a possible 184) between 18 May 1958 and 26 Jan. 1975 by the British driver Norman Graham Hill, O.B.E. (1929–1975). Between 20 Nov. 1960 and 5 Oct. 1969 he took part in 90 consecutive Grands Prix.

Oldest and youngest *World champions*

The youngest world champion was Emerson Fittipaldi (b. São Paulo, Brazil, 12 Dec. 1946) who won his first world championship on 10 Sept. 1972 aged 25 years 273 days. The oldest world champion was Juan-Manuel Fangio who won his last world championship on 18 Aug. 1957 aged 46 years 55 days.

Oldest and youngest *G.P. winners and drivers*

The youngest Grand Prix winner was Bruce Leslie McLaren (1937–70) of New Zealand, who won the United States Grand Prix at Sebring, Florida, U.S.A., on 12 Dec. 1959 aged 22 years 104 days. The oldest Grand Prix winner was Tazio Giorgio Nuvolari (1892–1953) of Italy, who won the Albi Grand Prix at Albi, France on 14 July 1946 aged 53 years 240 days. The oldest Grand Prix driver was Louis Alexandre Chiron, O. St-C., L.d'H., C.d'I, (b. Monaco, 3 Aug. 1899), who finished 6th in the Monaco Grand Prix on 22 May 1955 aged 55 years 292 days. The youngest Grand Prix driver was

Christopher Arthur Amon (b. Bulls, New Zealand, 20 July 1943) who took part in the Belgian Grand Prix at Spa on 9 June 1963 aged 19 years 324 days.

Hill climbing *Pike's Peak race*
The Pike's Peak Auto Hill Climb, Colorado, U.S.A. (instituted 1916) has been won 11 times by Bobby Unser between 1956 and 1969 (nine championship, one stock and one sports car title). On 30 June 1968, in the 46th race, he set a record time of 11 min 54.9 sec in his 5 506 c.c. Chevrolet championship car for the 12.42 mile *19,98 km* course rising from 9,402 ft to 14,110 ft *2 865–4 300 m* through 157 curves.

Hill climbing *Most successful drivers*
The British National Hill Climb Championship (inaugurated in 1947) has been won six times by Anthony Ernest Marsh (b. Stourbridge, West Midlands, 20 July 1931) 1955–57, 1965–67. Raymond Mays (b. Bourne, Lincolnshire, 1 Aug. 1899) won the Shelsley Walsh hill climb, near Worcester, 19 times between 1923 and 1950.

Rallies *Earliest*
The earliest long rally was promoted by the Parisian daily *Le Matin* in 1907 from Peking, China to Paris over a route of about 7,500 miles *12 000 km*. Five cars left Peking on 10 June. The winner, Prince Scipione Borghese, of Italy, arrived in Paris on 10 Aug. 1907 in his 40 h.p. Itala accompanied by his chauffeur, Ettore, and Luigi Barzini.

Rallies *Longest*
The world's longest ever rally was the £10,000 *Daily Mirror* World Cup Rally run over 16,243 miles *26 140 km* starting from Wembley, Brent, Greater London on 19 Apr. 1970 to Mexico City *via* Sofia, Bulgaria and Buenos Aires, Argentina passing through 25 countries. It was won on 27 May 1970 by Hannu Mikkola (b. Joensuu, Finland, 24 May 1942) and Gunnar Palm (b. Kristinehamn, Sweden, 25 Feb. 1937) in a 1 834 c.c. Ford Escort RS1600. The longest held annually is the East African Safari (first run 1953), run through Kenya, Tanzania and Uganda, which is up to 3,874 miles *6 234 km* long, as in the 17th Safari held between 8–12 Apr. 1971. It has been won a record three times by Joginder Singh (Kenya) in 1965, 1974 and 1976.

Rallies *Monte Carlo*
The Monte Carlo Rally (first run 1911) has been won a record four times by Sandro Munari (Italy) in 1972, 1975, 1976 and 1977. The smallest car to win was an 851 c.c. Saab driven by Erik Carlsson (b. Sweden, 1929) and Gunnar Häggbom of Sweden on 25 Jan. 1962, and by Carlsson and Gunnar Palm on 24 Jan. 1963.

Dragging *Piston engined*
The lowest elapsed time recorded by a piston-engined dragster is 5.637 sec (terminal velocity 250.69 m.p.h. *403,45 km/h*) by Donald Glenn "Big Daddy" Garlits (b. 1932) of Seffner, Florida, U.S.A. driving his rear-engined AA/F dragster, powered by a 7 948 c.c. supercharged Dodge V8 engine, during the National Hot Rod Association's Super-nationals at Ontario Motor Speedway, Ontario, California, U.S.A., on 11 Oct. 1975. The highest terminal velocity recorded is 252.10 m.p.h. *405,72 km/h* by Shirley Muldowney (U.S.A.) in Jan. 1977.

The world record for two runs in opposite directions over 440 yd *402 m* from a standing start is 6.70 sec by Dennis Victor Priddle (b. 1945) of Yeovil, Somerset, driving his 6 424 c.c. supercharged Chrysler dragster developing 1,700 b.h.p. using nitromethane and methanol, at Elvington Airfield, North Yorkshire on 7 Oct. 1972. The faster run was made in 6.65 sec.

Dragging *Rocket or jet-engined*
The highest terminal velocity recorded by any dragster is 377.754 m.p.h. *607,936 km/h* (elapsed time 4.65 sec) by Norman Craig Breedlove (b. 23 Mar. 1938) of Los Angeles, Calif., U.S.A., in the rocket powered *English Leather Special* on Bonneville Salt Flats, Utah, U.S.A. in September 1973. The lowest elapsed time recorded by any dragster is 4.55 sec by

Samuel A. Miller (b. 15 Apr. 1945) of Wayne, N.J., in the hydrogen peroxide rocket powered *Pollution Packer* at Seattle International Raceway, Kent, Washington, U.S.A., on 31 May 1975.

Terminal velocity is the speed attained at the end of a 440 yd 402 m run made from a standing start and elapsed time is the time taken for the run.

Highest speeds
For details of the absolute land speed record see p. 134

The world speed record for compression ignition engined cars is 190.344 m.p.h. *306,328 km/h* (average of two runs in opposite directions over a measured mile *1,6 km*) by Robert Havemann of Eureka, California, U.S.A. driving his *Corsair* streamliner, powered by a turbocharged 6 981 c.c. 6-cylinder GMC 6-71 diesel engine developing 746 b.h.p., at Bonneville Salt Flats, Utah, U.S.A., in August 1971. The faster run was made at 210 m.p.h. *337 km/h*.

The most successful land speed record breaker was Major Sir Malcolm Campbell (1885–1948) of the United Kingdom. He broke the official record nine times between 25 Sept. 1924, with 146.157 m.p.h. *235,216 km/h* in a Sunbeam, and 3 Sept. 1935, when he achieved 301.129 m.p.h. *480,620 km/h* in the Rolls-Royce engined *Bluebird*.

Duration records
The greatest distance ever covered in one year is 400 000 km *248,548.5 miles* by François Lecot (1879–1949), an innkeeper from Rochetaillée, near Lyon, France, in a 1 900 c.c. 66 b.h.p. Citroën 11 sedan, mainly between Paris and Monte Carlo, from 22 July 1935 to 26 July 1936. He drove on 363 of the 370 days allowed.

The world's duration record is 185,353 miles 1,741 yd *298 298 km* in 133 days 17 hr 37 min 38.64 sec (average speed 58.07 m.p.h. *93,45 km/h*) by Marchand, Presalé and six others in a Citroën on the Montlhéry track near Paris, France, during March–July 1933.

MOUNTAINEERING

Origins
Although bronze-age artifacts have been found on the summit of the Riffelhorn, Switzerland (9,605 ft *2 927 m*) mountaineering, as a sport, has a continuous history dating back only to 1854. Isolated instances of climbing for its own sake exist back to the 14th century. The Atacamenans built sacrificial platforms near the summit of Llullaillaco (22,058 ft *6 723 m*) in late pre-Columbian times *c.* 1490. The earliest recorded rock climb in the British Isles was of Stacna Biorrach, St. Kilda by Sir Robert Moray in 1698.

Mount Everest
Mount Everest (29,028 ft *8 848 m*) was first climbed at 11.30 a.m. on 29 May 1953, when the summit was reached by Edmund Percival Hillary (b. 20 July 1919), created K.B.E., of New Zealand, and the Sherpa, Tenzing Norgay (b., as Namgyal Wangdi, in Nepal in 1914, formerly called Tenzing Khumjung Bhutia), who was awarded the G.M. The successful expedition was led by Col. (later Hon. Brigadier) Henry Cecil John Hunt, C.B.E., D.S.O. (b. 22 June 1910), who was created a Knight Bachelor in 1953 and a life Baron on 11 June 1966.

The first Britons to reach the summit were Douglas Scott (b. 29 May 1941) and Dougal Haston (1940–77) on 24 Sept. 1975. Since the first ascent, another 54 climbers have succeeded, the latest being Robert McCormack and Dr. Chris Chandler (U.S.A.) on 15 Oct. 1976. The first woman to reach the summit was Mrs. Junko Tabei (b. 1939) (Japan) on 16 May 1975.

Greatest walls
The highest final stage in any wall climb is that on the south face of Annapurna I (26,545 ft *8 091 m*). It was climbed by

The late Dougal Haston was the 50th climber, and the first Scot, to reach the top of Everest, in 1975.

The scenic grandeur of El Capitan does not obscure one of the most difficult rock climbs in the world. (*John Cleare/Mountain Camera*)

the British expedition led by Christian Bonington, C.B.E. (b. 1934) when from 2 Apr to 27 May 1970, using 18,000 ft *5 500 m* of rope, Donald Whillans (b. 1934) and Dougal Haston scaled to the summit. The longest wall climb is on the Rupal-Flank from the base camp at 3 560 m *11,680 ft* to the South Point 8 042 m *26,384 ft* of Nanga Parbat—a vertical ascent of 4 482 m *14,704 ft*. This was scaled by the Austro-Germano-Italian Expedition led by Dr. K. M. Herrligkoffer in April 1970.

Europe's greatest wall is the 6,600 ft *2 000 m* north face of the Eigerwand (Ogre wall) first climbed by Heinrich Harrer and Fritz Kasparek of Austria and Anderl Heckmair and Wiggerl Vörg of Germany on 21–24 July 1938. The northeast face of the Eiger had been climbed on 20 Aug. 1932 by Hans Lauper, Alfred Zurcher, Alexander Graven and Josef Knubel. The greatest alpine solo climb was that of Walter Bonatti (b. Bergamo, Italy, 22 June 1930) of the South West Pillar of the Dru, Montenvers now called the Bonatti Pillar, with five bivouacs in 126 hr 7 min on 17–22 Aug. 1955.

There are climbs in the Yosemite Valley, California with a severity rating of 5.12, regarded as the most demanding free climbs in the world. Warren Harding and Dean Caldwell averaged 80 vertical feet *24 m* a day in their record 27 days on the Wall of the Early Morning Light on Yosemite's El Capitan in November 1971.

Greatest fall

The greatest recorded fall survived by a mountaineer was when Christopher Timms (Canterbury University) slid 7,500 ft *2 300 m* down an ice face into a crevasse on Mt. Elie de Beaumont (10,200 ft *3 100 m*), New Zealand on 7 Dec. 1966. His companion was killed, but he survived with concussion, bruises and a hand injury.

MOUNTAIN RACING
Mount Cameroun

David Njumbe Ngou descended from the summit 13,353 ft *4 070 m* to Buea at 3,000 ft *914 m* in 84 min on 27 Feb. 1977 achieving a vertical rate of 123 ft *37,5 m* per min. In winning for the second successive year, Father Walter Stifter ran to the summit and back in a record 4 hr 18 min 55 sec in 1977.

Ben Nevis

The record time for the race from Fort William to the summit of Ben Nevis (4,406 ft *1 343 m*) and return is 1 hr 26 min 55 sec by David Cannon (b. 7 Aug. 1950) (Gateshead H.) on 4 Sept. 1976. The feminine record is 2 hr 17 min 50 sec by Joan Glass on 6 Sept. 1975. The full course by the bridle path is about 14 miles *22 km* but distance can be saved by crossing the open hillside. The mountain was first climbed in about 1720 and the earliest race was in 1895.

Skiddaw Fell

In the Skiddaw Fell Race (3,053 ft to 250 ft *930 to 107 m*) a vertical descent rate of 128 ft *39 m* per min was achieved by George Jeffrey Norman (b. 6 Feb. 1945) (Altrincham A.C.) in the 1972 race.

Peak racing

The Lakeland 24-hour record is 72 peaks achieved by Joss Naylor, M.B.E. (b. 10 Feb. 1936) of Wasdale on 22–23 June 1975. He covered 105 miles *168 km* with 40,000 ft *12 190 m* of ascents and descents in 23 hr 11 min. Naylor has won every Ennerdale mountain race over 23 miles *37 km* since it was instituted in 1968 setting a record time of 3 hr 30 min 40 sec in 1972. The Yorkshire three peak record is 2 hr 29 min 53 sec by Jeff Norman on 28 Apr. 1974.

The "Three Thousander" record over the 14 Welsh peaks of

over 3,000 ft *914 m* is 4 hr 46 min 22 sec with pacemakers, by Joss Naylor on 17 June 1973 despite misty conditions.

Three peaks record

The Three Peaks run from sea level at Fort William, Inverness-shire, to sea level at Caernarvon, *via* the summits of Ben Nevis, Scafell Pike and Snowdon, was uniquely achieved by the late Eric Beard, 37 of Leeds Athletic Club, in ten days in June 1969. Five members of the Vauxhall Motors Recreation Club, Luton, Beds., ran the distance in relay in 54 hr 57 min 47 sec, on 21–23 May 1977.

The motorised record, *under official observation*, sea level to sea level, is 14 hr 2 min by Martin Salsbury, 29, of Bradford and Airedale Canoe Club, West Yorkshire, on 11 June 1977. His time for climbing up and down the mountains totalled 5 hr 4 min. The women's record is 18 hr 45 min by Helen Butterfield, 22, of the same Club, and her mountain time was 8 hr 36 min.

(In future this category will relate *only* to the total individual time climbing up and down the mountains—car running time no longer being taken into consideration.)

Ten peaks record

The Ten Peaks race is from Barnthwaite Farm, Wasdale Head, Cumbria to the top of Skiddaw *via* England's nine other highest mountains and tops: Great Gable, Sca Fell, Scafell Pike, Ill Crags, Broad Crag, Great End, Bow Fell, Helvellyn and Lower Man. The record time is 7 hr 20 min by Derek Southworth (b. 14 Mar. 1957) and Robert Neil Banks (b. 31 Dec. 1955) in a race organized by the Cumbrian Community Trust on 15 Sept. 1974.

Pennine Way

The record for traversing the 271 mile *436 km* long Pennine Way is 3 days 1 hr 48 min by Peter Dawes (b. 1939) of Kendal A.C. on 18–21 July 1975.

Guides Race

Bill Teasdale, M.B.E., won the Guides' Race at the Grasmere Sports, Cumbria, for the eleventh time in 1966. It involves running to a turning point on Butter Crag (966 ft *294 m* above sea level) and back, a distance of about 1½ miles *2,4 km*. The record time for this race is 12 min 24.8 sec by Thomas Sedgwick on 19 Aug. 1976.

PROGRESSIVE MOUNTAINEERING ALTITUDE RECORDS

ft	m	Mountain	Climbers	Date
9,605	2 927	Riffelhorn, Zermatt, Switzerland	—	Bronze Age
14,300	4 360	Kaoshan Pass, Hindu Kush	Alexander the Great's army	327 B.C.
12,388	3 775	Fuji, Japan	—	prior A.D. 806
17,887	5 452	Popocatépetl, Mexico	Francisco Montano	1521
18,400	5 608	Mana Pass, Zaskar Range	A. de Andrade, M. Morques	July 1624
18,893	5 758	On Chimborazo, Ecuador	Dr. A. Humboldt, Goujand (France) and C. Montufar	23 June 1802
19,411	5 916	On Leo Pargyal Range, Himalaya	Gerrard and Lloyd	1818
22,260	6 784	On E. Ibi Gamih, Garhwal Himalaya	A. & R. Schlagintweit	Aug. 1855
22,606	6 890	Pioneer Peak on Baltoro Kangri	W. M. Conway, M. Zurbriggen	23 Aug. 1892
22,834	6 959	Aconcagua, Andes	M. Zurbriggen	14 Jan. 1897
23,394	7 130	On Pyramid Peak, Karakoram	W. H. Workman, J. Petigax Snr. & Jnr., C. Savoie	12 Aug. 1903
23,787	7 250	On Gurla Mandhata, Tibet	T. G. Longstaff, A. & H. Brocherel	23 July 1905
c.23,900	c.7 285	On Kabru, Sikkim-Nepal	C. W. Rubenson and M. Aas	20 Oct. 1907
24,607	7 500	On Chogolisa, Karakoram	Duke of the Abruzzi, J. Petigax, H. & E. Brocherel	18 July 1909
c.24,900	c.7 590	Camp V, Everest, Tibet-Nepal	G. L. Mallory, E. F. Norton, T. H. Somervell, H. T. Morshead	20 May 1922
26,986	8 225	On Everest (North Face), Tibet	G. L. Mallory, E. F. Norton, T. H. Somervell	21 May 1922
c.27,300	c.8 320	On Everest (North Face), Tibet	G. I. Finch, J. G. Bruce	27 May 1922
28,125	8 570	On Everest (North Face), Tibet	E. F. Norton	4 June 1924
28,125	8 570	On Everest (North Face), Tibet	P. Wyn Harris, L. R. Wager	30 May 1933
28,125	8 570	On Everest (North Face), Tibet	F. S. Smythe	1 June 1933
28,215*	8 599*	South Shoulder on Everest, Nepal	R. Lambert, Tenzing Norgay	28 May 1952
28,721	8 754	South Shoulder on Everest, Nepal	T. D. Bourdillon, R. C. Evans	26 May 1953
29,028	8 848	Everest, Nepal-Tibet	E. P. Hillary, Tenzing Norgay	29 May 1953

* Highest altitude attained without oxygen.

PROGRESSIVE LIST OF HIGHEST SUMMITS CLIMBED

The progressive list of highest summits climbed after Aconcagua in 1897 is as follows:

ft	m			
23,360	7 120	Trisul, Garhwal Himalaya	T. G. Longstaff, A. & H. Brocherel, Karbir	12 June 1907
23,385*	7 127	Pauhunri, Sikkim Himalaya	A. M. Kellas, Sonam and another porter	16 June 1911
23,383	7 127	Pik Lenin, Trans-Alai Pamir	E. Allwein, K. Wien, E. Schneider	25 Sept. 1928
23,442	7 145	Nepal Peak, Sikkim-Nepal	E. Schneider	24 May 1930
24,344	7 417	Jongsong Peak, Nepal-Sikkim-Tibet	E. Schneider, H. Hoerlin	3 June 1930
25,447	7 756	Kamet, Garhwal Himalaya	F. S. Smythe, R. L. Holdsworth, E. E. Shipton, Lewa	21 June 1931
25,645	7 816	Nanda Devi, Garhwal Himalaya	N. E. Odell, H. W. Tilman	29 Aug. 1936
26,492	8 047	Annapurna I, Nepal	M. Herzog, L. Lachenal	3 June 1950
29,028	8 848	Mount Everest, Nepal-Tibet	E. P. Hillary, Tenzing Norgay	29 May 1953

* Survey of India height now listed as 23,180 ft 7 065 m.

NETBALL

Origins

The game was invented in the U.S.A. in 1891 and introduced into England in 1895 by Dr. Toles. The All England Women's Netball Association was formed in 1926. The oldest club in continuous existence is the Polytechnic Netball Club of London founded in 1907.

Most titles *World*

World championships were inaugurated in August 1963 at Eastbourne, East Sussex and were won by Australia. The 1971 and 1975 world championships were also won by Australia.

Most titles *National*

The National Championships (inst. 1968) have been won most often by Sudbury Netball Club with five titles (1968–70, 1971 (shared) and 1973).

Most titles *County*

Surrey have won the County Championships a record 17 times 1949–64, 1966, 1969 (shared).

Most international appearances

The record number of internationals is 65 by Anne Miles (b. 9 Apr. 1942) of England 1965–1975.

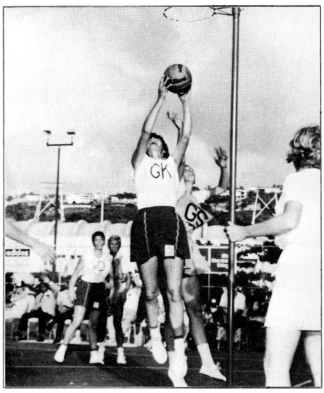

Seen here at the 1971 World Tournament in Jamaica, Anne Miles later achieved a record 65 appearances for the England netball team. (*All England Netball Association*)

Highest scores

England has never been beaten in a senior home international. The World Tournament record score was in Auckland, New Zealand in 1975 when England beat Papua New Guinea 114 goals to 16. The record number of goals in the World Tournament is 402 by Judith Heath (England) (b. 1942) in 1971. The highest international score recorded was when New Zealand beat Singapore 117–9 in Oct. 1974.

Marathon

An outdoor marathon netball match lasting 91 hours was played by six teams of seven girls of the Manly-Warringan Netball Association, Sydney, Australia on 11–15 June 1976. An indoor marathon of 72 hr was sustained by 26 girls from Brisbane State H.S., Queensland, Australia on 28–31 Jan. 1977.

OLYMPIC GAMES

Note: These records now include the un-numbered Games held at Athens in 1906, which some authorities ignore. Although inserted between the regular III Games in 1904 and the IV Games in 1908, the 1906 Games though unnumbered, were officially run by the International Olympic Committee and were of a higher standard than all three of those that preceded them.

Origins

The earliest celebration of the ancient Olympic Games of which there is a certain record is that of July 776 B.C., when Coroibos, a cook from Elis, won a foot race, though their origin dates from c. 1370 B.C. The ancient Games were terminated by an order issued in Milan in A.D. 393 by Theodosius I, "the Great" (c. 346–395), Emperor of Rome. At the instigation of Pierre de Fredi, Baron de Coubertin (1863–1937), the Olympic Games of the modern era were inaugurated in Athens on 6 Apr. 1896.

Modern celebrations

Modern celebrations have been voted for by the International Olympic Committee as follows. Dates indicate the span of Olympic competitions (excluding elimination contests). The first date is not necessarily that of the opening ceremony.

I	1896	Athens, Greece	6–15 April
II	1900	Paris, France	20 May–28 Oct.
III	1904	St. Louis, U.S.A.	1 July–23 Nov.
*	1906	Athens, Greece	22 April–2 May
IV	1908	London, England	27 April–31 Oct.
V	1912	Stockholm, Sweden	5 May–22 July
VI	1916	Berlin, Germany	not celebrated owing to war
VII	1920	Antwerp, Belgium	20 April–12 Sept.
VIII	1924	Paris, France	4 May–27 July
IX	1928	Amsterdam, Holland	17 May–12 Aug.
X	1932	Los Angeles, U.S.A.	30 July–14 Aug.
XI	1936	Berlin, Germany	1–16 Aug.
XII	1940	Tokyo, then Helsinki, Finland	not celebrated owing to war
XIII	1944	London, England	not celebrated owing to war
XIV	1948	London, England	29 July–14 Aug.
XV	1952	Helsinki, Finland	19 July–3 Aug.
XVI	1956	Melbourne, Australia[1]	22 Nov.–8 Dec.
XVII	1960	Rome, Italy	25 Aug.–11 Sept.
XVIII	1964	Tokyo, Japan	10–24 Oct.
XIX	1968	Mexico City, Mexico	12–27 Oct.
XX	1972	Munich, W. Germany	26 Aug.–10 Sept.
XXI	1976	Montreal, Canada	17 July–1 Aug.
XXII	1980	Moscow, U.S.S.R.	19 July–3 Aug.

* *This celebration (to mark the tenth anniversary of the modern Games) was officially intercalated but is not numbered.*

[1] *The equestrian events were held in Stockholm, Sweden, 10–17 June 1956.*

Separate Winter Olympics (there had been ice skating events in 1908 and 1920 and ice hockey in 1920) were inaugurated in 1924 and have been voted for as follows:

I	1924	Chamonix, France	25 Jan.–4 Feb.
II	1928	St. Moritz, Switzerland	11–19 Feb.
III	1932	Lake Placid, New York, U.S.A.	4–15 Feb.
IV	1936	Garmisch-Partenkirchen, Germany	6–16 Feb.
V	1948	St. Moritz, Switzerland	30 Jan.–8 Feb.
VI	1952	Oslo, Norway	14–25 Feb.
VII	1956	Cortina d'Ampezzo, Italy	26 Jan.–5 Feb.
VIII	1960	Squaw Valley, California, U.S.A.	18–28 Feb.
IX	1964	Innsbruck, Austria	29 Jan.–9 Feb.
X	1968	Grenoble, France	6–18 Feb.
XI	1972	Sapporo, Japan	3–13 Feb.
XII	1976	Innsbruck, Austria	4–15 Feb.
XIII	1980	Lake Placid, New York, U.S.A.	14–23 Feb.

The first Winter Games in 1924 attracted 294 competitors from 16 nations.

Most medals *Individual gold*

In the ancient Olympic Games victors were given a chaplet of wild olive leaves. Milo (Milon of Krotōn) won six titles at *palaisma* (wrestling) 540–516 B.C. The most individual gold medals won by a male competitor in the modern Games is ten by Raymond Clarence Ewry (U.S.A.) (1874–1937) (see Track and Field Athletics). The female record is seven by Vera Caslavska-Odlozil (Czechoslovakia) (see Gymnastics). The most won by a British competitor is four by Paul Radmilovic (1886–1968) in water polo 1908, 1912 and 1920 and the 4 × 200 m freestyle relay in 1908, and swimmer Henry Taylor (1885–1951) in 1906 and 1908. The Australian swimmer Ian Murray Rose, who won four gold medals, was born in Birmingham, England on 6 Jan. 1939. The only Olympian to win four consecutive individual titles in the same event has been Alfred A. Oerter (b. 19 Sept. 1936, Astoria, N.Y.) of the U.S.A., who won the discus title in 1956–68.

Most medals *National*

The total figures for most medals and most gold medals for all Olympic events (including those now discontinued) for the summer (1896–1972) and Winter Games (1924–76) and for the Art Competitions (1912–48) are:

	Gold	Silver	Bronze	Total
1. U.S.A.	658*	511½	437½	1,607
2. U.S.S.R. (formerly Russia)	309	257	244	810
3. G.B. (including Ireland to 1920)	165½	202½	178	546

* *The A.A.U. (U.S.) reinstated James F. Thorpe (1888–1953) the disqualified highest scorer in the 1912 decathlon and pentathlon events on 12 Oct. 1973 but no issue of medals has yet been authorised by the I.O.C.*

Youngest gold medallist

The youngest ever winner was a French boy (whose name is not recorded) who coxed the Netherlands pair in 1900. He was not more than ten and may have been as young as seven.

He substituted for Dr. Hermanus Brockmann, who coxed in the heats but proved too heavy. The youngest-ever female gold medal winner is Miss Marjorie Gestring (U.S.A.) (b. 18 Nov. 1922, now Mrs. Bowman), aged 13 yr 9 months, in the 1936 women's springboard event.

Longest span

The longest span of an Olympic competitor is 40 years by Dr. Ivan Osiier (Denmark) (1888–1965) who competed as a fencer in 1908–32 and 1948, totalling seven celebrations. He refused to compete in the 1936 Games on the grounds that they were Nazi-dominated. The longest feminine span is 24 years (1932–56) by the Austrian fencer Ellen Müller-Preiss (b. 6 May 1912). Raimondo d'Inzeo (b. 8 Feb. 1925) competed for Italy in equestrian events at a record eight celebrations from 1948 to 1976, gaining one gold, two silver and three bronze medals. Janice Lee York Romary (b. 6 Aug. 1928) the U.S. fencer, competed in all six Games from 1948 to 1968, and Lia Manoliu (Romania) (b. 25 Apr. 1932) competed from 1952 to 1972 winning the discus title in 1968.

The longest span of any British competitor is 28 years by Enoch Jenkins who appeared in the 1924 and the 1952 Games in the clay pigeon shooting event, and the longest feminine span is by Dorothy J. B. Tyler (*née* Odam) (b. 14 Mar. 1920) who high-jumped in 1936, 1948, 1952 and 1956. The record number of appearances for Great Britain is six by fencer Bill Hoskyns from 1956 to 1976.

Most countries and participants

The greatest number of competitors in any summer Olympic Games has been 7,356 at Montreal in 1976. A record 122 countries competed at Munich in 1972. The fewest was 311 competitors from 13 countries in 1896. In 1904 only 12 countries participated.

Ever present

Five countries have never failed to be represented at the 21 celebrations of the Games: Australia, Greece, Great Britain, Switzerland and the United States of America.

Largest team

France entered 880 men and four women in the 1900 Games at Paris.

Largest crowd

The largest crowd at any Olympic site was 150,000 at the 1952 ski-jumping at the Holmenkollen, outside Oslo, Norway. Estimates of the number of spectators of the marathon race through Tōkyō, Japan on 21 Oct. 1964 have ranged from 500,000 to 1,500,000.

ORIENTEERING

Origins

Orienteering was invented by Major Ernst Killander in Sweden in 1918. World championships were inaugurated in 1966 and are held biennially. Annual British championships were instituted in 1967 following the formation of the British Orienteering Federation.

Most titles *World*

Sweden won the world men's relay titles in 1966, 1968, 1972, 1974 and 1976 and the women's relay in 1966, 1970, 1974 and 1976. Ulla Lindkvist (Sweden) gained the women's individual titles in 1966 and 1968, and Åge Hadler (Norway) the individual titles for men in 1966 and 1972.

Most titles *British*

The most successful British team has been Edinburgh Southern Orienteering Club which won the Senior Men's title in 1969 and 1970 and the Senior Ladies' title in 1970. Geoffrey Peck (b. Blackpool, 27 Sept. 1949) (Interlopers) has won the men's individual title a record four times, 1971, 1973 1976 and 1977. Carol McNeill of the same club has won the women's title six times, 1967, 1969, 1972–76.

PARACHUTING

Origins

Parachuting graduated from pure life saving, through stunt exhibitions to a regulated sport with the institution of world championships at Lesce-Bled, Yugoslavia in 1951. A team title was introduced at the second championships at Saint Yan, France in 1954 and women's events were included at the third championships near Moscow, U.S.S.R. in 1956.

Most titles *World*

The U.S.S.R. won the men's team titles in 1954, 1958, 1960, 1966, 1972 and 1976 and the women's team title in 1956, 1958, 1966, 1968, 1972 and 1976. No individual has ever won a second world overall title.

Most titles *British*

John Meacock (Peterborough) has won the British title three times in 1969, 1971–72.

Greatest accuracy

Kumbar (Czechoslovakia) scored nine consecutive dead centre strikes (10 cm disc) in the 11th World Championships at Tahlequah, U.S.A. in 1972.

Most jumps

The greatest number of jumps completed is 232 in 24 hours by Jean-Pierre Blanchet at St. Jean Chrysostome Airport, Quebec, Canada on 9–10 Sept. 1972.

PELOTA VASCA
(Jai Alai)

Origins

The game, which originated in Italy as *longue paume* and was introduced into France in the 13th century, is said to be the fastest of all ball games with speeds of up to 160 m.p.h. *257,5 km/h.* Gloves were introduced *c.* 1840 and the *chisterak*

Carlos Lasarte probably hurls the ball faster than anyone else in Pelota, often called the fastest of all ball games. (*West Palm Beach Jai Alai Sports Theatre*)

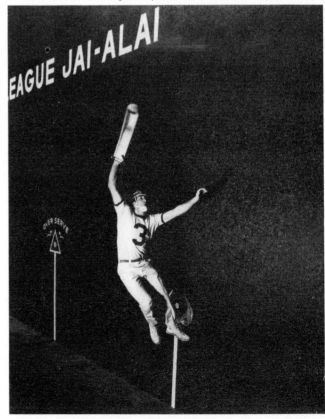

was invented *c.* 1860 by Gantchiki Dithurbide of Sainte Pée. The long *chistera* was invented by Melchior Curuchage of Buenos Aires, Argentina in 1888.

The world's largest *fronton* (the playing court) is that built (opened June 1976) for $16,000,000 at Bridgeport, Conn., U.S.A., with a seating capacity of 12,000.

Games played in a *fronton* are *frontenis*, *pelote* and *paleta* with both leather and rubber balls. The sport is governed by the International Federation of Basque Pelote.

Highest speed
An electronically measured ball velocity of 136 m.p.h. *218 km/h* was recorded by Carlos Lasarte (b. Spain, 23 Aug. 1946) at the Newport Jai Alai, R.I., U.S.A. on 18 Nov. 1976.

Longest domination
The longest domination as the world's No. 1 player was enjoyed by Chiquito de Cambo (*né* Joseph Apesteguy) (France), (1881–1955) from the beginning of the century until succeeded in 1938 by Jean Urruty (France) (b. 19 Oct. 1913).

PIGEON RACING

Earliest references
Pigeon Racing was the natural development of the use of homing pigeons for the carrying of messages—a quality utilized in the ancient Olympic Games (776 B.C.–A.D. 393). The sport originated in Belgium and came to Britain *c.* 1820. The earliest major long-distance race was from Crystal Palace, Bromley, Greater London, in 1871. The earliest recorded occasion on which 500 miles *804 km* was flown in a day was by "Motor" (owned by G. P. Pointer of Alexander Palace Racing Pigeon Club) which was released from Thurso, Scotland on 30 June 1896 and covered 501 miles *806 km* at an average speed of 1,454 yd *1 329 m* per min (49½ m.p.h. *79,6 km/h*).

Longest flights
The greatest recorded homing flight by a pigeon was made by one owned by the 1st Duke of Wellington (1769–1852). Released from a sailing ship off the Ichabo Islands, West Africa, on 8 April, it dropped dead a mile from its loft at Nine Elms, Wandsworth, Greater London on 1 June 1845, 55 days later, having flown an airline route of 5,400 miles *8 700 km*, but an actual distance of possibly 7,000 miles *11 250 km* to avoid the Sahara Desert. The official British duration record (into Great Britain) is 1,141 miles *1 836 km* in 27 days by A. Bruce's bird in the 1960 Barcelona Race. In the 1975 Patarnos Race, *The Conqueror*, owned by Alan Raeside, homed to Irvine, Strathclyde, 1,010 miles *1 625 km*, in 43 hr 56 min.

Highest speeds
In level flight in windless conditions it is very doubtful if any pigeon can exceed 60 m.p.h. *96 km/h*. The highest race speed recorded is one of 3,229 yds *2 952 m* per min (110.07 m.p.h. *177,14 km/h*) in the East Anglian Federation race from East Croydon on 8 May 1965 when the 1,428 birds were backed by a powerful south south-west wind. The winner was owned by A. Vidgeon & Son, Wickford, Essex.

The highest race speed recorded over a distance of more than 1 000 km *621.37 miles* is 2,432.70 yds *2 224,5 m* per min (82.93 m.p.h. *133,46 km/h*) by a hen pigeon in the Central Cumberland Combine race over 683 miles 147 yds *1 099,316 km* from Murray Bridge, South Australia to North Ryde, Sydney on 2 Oct. 1971.

24 hour records
The world's longest reputed distance in 24 hours is 803 miles *1 292 km* (velocity 1,525 yd *1 394 m* per min) by E. S. Petersen's winner of the 1941 San Antonio R.C. event in Texas, U.S.A.

The best 24-hour performance into the United Kingdom is 723 miles *1 163 km* by Robert White's *Jubilee Victor*, on 2 July 1977, from Nantes, France to Fraserburgh, Grampian—average speed 1,648 yd *1 507 m* per min (56.18 m.p.h. *90,41 km/h*).

Lowest speed
A pigeon *Blue Clip*, belonging to Harold Hart released in Rennes, France arrived home in its loft in Leigh, Greater Manchester, on 29 Sept. 1974, seven years and two months later. It had covered the distance of 595 km at an average speed of 0.00589 m.p.h. *0,00948 km/h* which is slower than the world's fastest snail (see page 46).

Most first prizes
Owned by R. Green, of Walsall Wood, West Midlands, *Champion Breakaway* had won a record 46 first prizes from 1972 to 20 May 1977.

Highest priced bird
The highest recorded price paid for a pigeon is £11,816 by Arthur Roger Timmermans, of Strombeek Bever, Belgium, on 30 Jan. 1977.

POLO

Earliest games
Polo is usually regarded as being of Persian origin having been played as *Pulu c.* 525 B.C. Other claims have come from Tibet and the Tang Dynasty of China A.D. 250. The earliest polo club of modern times was the Kachar Club (founded in 1859) in Assam, India. The game was introduced into England from India in 1869 by the 10th Hussars at Aldershot, Hampshire and the earliest match was one between the 9th Lancers and the 10th Hussars on Hounslow Heath, Greater London, in July 1871. The first all-Ireland Cup match was at Phoenix Park, Dublin, in 1878. The earliest international match between England and the U.S.A. was in 1886.

The game is played on the largest pitch of any ball game in the world. A ground measures 300 yd *274 m* long by 160 yd *146 m* wide with side boards, or 200 yd *182 m* wide without boards.

Most Olympic medals
Polo has been part of the Olympic programme on five occasions: 1900, 1908, 1920, 1924, and 1936. Of the 21 gold medallists, a 1920 winner, the Rt. Hon. Sir John Wodehouse, Bt., C.B.E., M.C., the 3rd Earl of Kimberly (b. 1883–k. 1941) uniquely also won a silver medal (1908).

Most international appearances
The most times any player has represented England is four in the case of Frederick Maitland Freake in 1900, 1902, 1909 and 1913. Thomas Hitchcock, Jr. (1900–44) played five times for the U.S.A. *v.* England (1921, 1924, 1927, 1930, 1939) and twice *v.* Argentina (1928 and 1936).

Highest handicap
The highest handicap based on eight 7½-min "chukkas" is ten goals introduced in the U.S.A. in 1891 and in the United Kingdom and in Argentina in 1910. The most recent additions to the select ranks of the 38 players ever to receive ten-goal handicaps are A. Heguy and A. Harriot of Argentina. The last (of six) ten-goal handicap players from Great Britain was G. Balding in 1939. A match of two 40-goal teams was staged for the first time ever, at Palermo, Buenos Aires, Argentina, in 1975.

The highest handicap of the United Kingdom's 500 players is eight, held by brothers, Julian and Howard Hipwood.

Highest score
The highest aggregate number of goals scored in an international match is 30, when Argentina beat the U.S.A. 1–92 at Meadow Brook, Long Island, New York, U.S.A., in September 1936.

Most expensive pony
The highest price ever paid for a polo pony was $22,000 by Stephen Sanford for Lewis Lacey's *Jupiter* after the U.S.A. *v.* Argentina international in 1928.

Oldest pony
The oldest known polo pony, still playing regularly, is *Rustum*, a Barb gelding aged 36 yr at Stourhead, Wiltshire, England.

Largest trophy

For details see p. 237.

Largest crowd

World record crowds of more than 50,000 have watched floodlit matches at the Sydney Agricultural Show, Australia. A crowd of 40,000 watched a game played at Jaipur, India, in 1976 using elephants instead of ponies. The length of the polo sticks used has not been ascertained.

POWERBOAT RACING

Origins

The earliest application of the petrol engine to a boat was Gottlieb Daimler's experimental powerboat on the River Seine, Paris, France, in 1887. The sport was given impetus by the presentation of an international championship cup by Sir Alfred Harmsworth in 1903, which was also the year of the first off-shore race from Calais to Dover.

Harmsworth Cup

Of the 25 contests from 1903 to 1961, the United States has won the most with 16.

The greatest number of wins has been achieved by Commodore Garfield A. Wood (1881–1971) with eight (1920–21, 1926, 1928–30, 1932–33). The only boat to win three times is *Miss Supertest III*, owned by James G. Thompson (Canada), in 1959–61. This boat also achieved the record speed of 115.972 m.p.h. *186,638 km/h* at Picton, Ontario, Canada in 1960.

Gold Cup

The Gold Cup (instituted 1903) has been one six times by Bill Muncey (b. 1929) (U.S.A.) (1956–57, 1961–62, 1972 and 1976. The record speed is 128.338 m.p.h. *206,539 km/h* for a $2\frac{1}{2}$ mile *4 km* lap by the unlimited hydroplane *Atlas Van Lines*, driven by Bill Muncey in a qualifying round on the Columbia River, Washington, U.S.A., in July 1977.

Cowes-Torquay race

The record average for the *Embassy/Daily Express* International Off-shore Race (instituted 1961) is 72.86 m.p.h. *117,26 km/h* by *UNO-Embassy* driven by Don Shead (G.B.) over the 229 mile *368,5 km* course from Cowes, Isle of Wight to Torquay, Devon and back in 3 hr 8 min 42 sec on 24 Aug. 1975. The only three time winner has been Thomas Edward Brodie (Tommy) Sopwith (b. 1933) (G.B.) in 1961, 1968, and 1970.

Highest speeds

The highest speed attained is 130.33 m.p.h. *209,74 km/h* by Tony Fahey (G.B.) in his 22 ft *6,70 m* hydroplane *Vladivar I*, powered by a 625 h.p. Jaguar V12 engine, on Lake Windermere, Cumbria, England on 23 May 1977. This is claimed as a world production-engined craft record. He also set a world R6 inboard engine record of 128.375 m.p.h. *206,599 km/h*. The Countess of Arran (b. 21 July 1918) drove her off-shore powerboat *Highland Fling* for a Class III world's record of 85.63 m.p.h. *137,80 km/h*, despite fuel trouble on the back-up run, on Windermere on 21 Oct. 1971.

Longest races

The longest race has been the Port Richborough London to Monte Carlo Marathon Off-Shore International event. The race extended over 2,947 miles *4 742 km* in 14 stages on 10–25 June 1972. It was won by *H.T.S.* (G.B.) driven by Mike Bellamy, Eddie Chater and Jim Brooks in 71 hrs 35 min 56 sec (average 41.15 m.p.h. *66,24 km/h*). The *Daily Telegraph and B.P.* Round Britain event was inaugurated on 26 July 1969 at Portsmouth with 1,403 miles *2 257 km* in ten stages west—about England, Wales and across northern Scotland *via* the Caledonian Canal. The 1969 race (26 July–7 August) was won by *Avenger Too* (Timo Makinen, Alan Pascoe Watson and Brian Hendicott) in 39 hr 9 min 37.7 sec. Of the 42 starters, 24 finished.

Longest journey

The Dane, Hans Tholstrup (b. 1946), circumnavigated

Australia (11,500 miles *18 500 km*) in a 17 ft Caribbean Couger fibreglass runabout with a single 80 h.p. Mercury outboard motor from 11 May to 25 July 1971.

Longest jump

The longest jump achieved by a powerboat has been 110 ft *32,5 m* by Jerry Comeaux (b. 1943) in a Glastron GT-150 with a 135 h.p. Evinrude Starflite on an isolated waterway in Louisiana, U.S.A. in mid-October 1972. The take-off speed was 56 m.p.h. *90 km/h*. The jump was required for a sequence in the eighth James Bond film *Live and Let Die*.

Dragsters

The first drag boat to attain 200 m.p.h. *321 km/h* was Sam Kurtovich's *Crisis* which attained 200.44 m.p.h. *322,57 km/h* in California in October 1969 at the end of a one-way run. *Climax* has since been reported to have attained 205.19 m.p.h. *330,22 km/h*.

RACKETS

Origins

There is record of the sale of a racket court at Southernhay, Exeter, Devon dated 12 Jan. 1798.

Earliest world champion

The first world rackets champion was Robert Mackay, who claimed the title in London in 1820. The first closed court champion was Francis Erwood at Woolwich in 1860. The first new court built in Great Britain since 1914 was the Second Court opened at Harrow School in 1965.

Longest reign

Of the 19 world champions since 1820 the longest reign is by British-born U.S. resident Geoffrey W. T. Atkins (b. 1922) who held the title after beating the professional James Dear in 1954 and retired after a fourth successful defence of it in April 1970.

Most Amateur titles

Since the Amateur singles championship was instituted in 1888 the most titles won by an individual is nine by Edgar M. Baerlein (1879–1971) between 1903 and 1923. Since the institution of the Amateur doubles championship in 1890 the most shares in titles has been eleven by David Sumner Milford (b. 7 June 1905), between 1938 and 1959 and John R. Thompson (b. 1918) between 1948 and 1966. Milford has also seven Amateur singles titles (1930–52), an Open title (1936) and held the World title from 1937 to 1946. Thompson has additionally won an Open singles title and five Amateur singles titles.

RODEO

Origins

Rodeo came into being in the early days of the North American cattle industry. The earliest references to the sport are from Santa Fe, New Mexico, U.S.A., in 1847. Steer wrestling came in with Bill Pickett (1870–1932) of Texas, in 1900. The other events are calf roping, bull riding, saddle and bareback bronc riding.

The largest rodeo in the world is the Calgary Exhibition and Stampede at Calgary, Alberta, Canada. The record attendance has been 1,015,682 on 9–18 July 1976. The record for one day is 141,670 on 13 July 1974.

Most world titles

The record number of all-round titles in the Association of Professional Rodeo Cowboys world championships is six by Larry Mahan (U.S.A.) (b. 21 Nov. 1943) in 1966–70 and 1973. Jim Shoulders (b. 1928) of Henryetta, Okla., has won a record 16 world championships between 1949 and 1959. The record figure for prize money in a single season is $96,913 by Tom Ferguson (b. 20 Dec. 1950) from Miami, Oklahoma, U.S.A. in 1976.

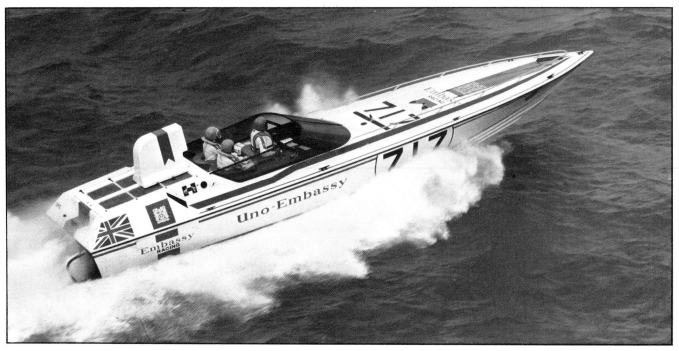

Cowes to Torquay race record holder, *UNO-Embassy*, being driven by Don Shead. (*W. D. & H. O. Wills*)

Youngest champion

The youngest winner of a world title is Metha Brorsen, of Oklahoma, who was only 11 yr when she won the International Rodeo Association Cowgirls barrel racing event in 1975.

Time records

Records for timed events, such as calf-roping and steer-wrestling, are meaningless, because of the widely varying conditions due to the size of arenas and amount of start given the stock. The fastest time recorded for roping a calf is 7.5 sec by Junior Garrison of Marlow, Oklahoma, at Evergreen, Colorado, U.S.A. in 1967, and the fastest time for overcoming a steer is 2.4 sec by James Bynum of Waxahachie, Texas, at Marietta, Oklahoma, in 1955.

The standard required time to stay on in bareback, saddle bronc and bull riding events is 8 sec. In the now discontinued ride-to-a-finish events, rodeo riders have been recorded to have survived 90+ min, until the mount had not a buck left in it.

Champion bull

The top bucking bull for 1976 was *Panda Bear* 1,500 lb. *680 kg* of cross-bred brahma. The bull, owned by Harry Vold of Fowler, Colorado, was bucked 50 times during the year in ten states and was ridden only four times for the eight seconds required.

Champion bronc

An 11 year old gelding *Sarcee Sorrell*, owned by Harry Vold of Fowler, Colorado, was named Saddle Bronc of the year in 1976. Vold bought the bronc from the Sarcee Indians in Canada in 1964 and started bucking him in 1969. The horse has twice been named the top bronc of the Canadian circuit. He was bucked 33 times in 1976 and was placed on ten times. Traditionally a bronc called *Midnight* owned by Jim McNab of Alberta, Canada was never ridden in 12 appearances at the Calgary Stampede.

ROLLER SKATING

Origins

The first roller skate was devised by Joseph Merlin of Huy, Belgium, in 1760 and first worn by him in public in London. Despite "improved" versions, a really satisfactory roller skate

did not materialize before 1866, when James L. Plimpton of New York produced the present four-wheeled type, patented it, and opened the first public rink in the world at Newport, Rhode Island, that year. The great boom periods were 1870–75, 1908–12 and 1948–54, each originating in the United States.

Most titles

Most world speed titles have been won by Alberta Vianello (Italy) with 16 between 1953 and 1965. Most world pair titles have been taken by Dieter Fingerle (W. Germany) with four in 1959, 1967–67. The records for figure titles are five by Karl Heinz Losch in 1958–59, 1961–62 and 1966, and four by Astrid Bader, also of West Germany, in 1965–68. Leslie E. Woodley of Birmingham won 12 British national individual titles over the three regulation distances (880 yds *804 m*, 1 mile *1,6 km* and 5 miles *8 km*) between 1957 and 1964. Jimmy Reed won 11 amateur and one professional title from 1929 to 1937. Chloe Ronaldson (b. 30 Nov. 1939) has won 30 ladies' titles from 1958 to 1976.

Speed skating

The fastest speed put up in an official world record is 25.78 m.p.h. *41,48 km/h* when Giuseppe Cantarella (Italy) recorded

British Ladies speed roller skating champion Chloe Ronaldson was only twelve when she won her first skating gold medal.

34.9 sec for 440 yds *402 m* on a road at Catania, Sicily on 28 Sept. 1963. The world mile record on a rink is 2 min 25.1 sec by Gianni Ferretti (Italy) at Inzell, W. Germany on 28 Sept. 1968. The greatest distance skated in one hour on a rink by a woman is 35,399 km *21.995 miles* by Marisa Danesi (Italy) at Inzell, W. Germany on 28 Sept. 1968. The men's record on a track is 37,230 km *23.133 miles* by Alberto Civolani (Italy) at Inzell, W. Germany on 28 Sept. 1968, who went on to skate 50 miles *80,46 km* in 2 hr 20 min 33.1 sec.

Roller hockey

Roller hockey (previously known as Rink Hockey in Europe) was first introduced in this country as Rink Polo, at the old Lava rink, Denmark Hill, Greater London in the late 1870s. The Amateur Rink Hockey Association was formed in 1908, and in 1913 became the National Rink Hockey (now Roller Hockey) Association. Britain won the inaugural World Championship in 1936 since when Portugal has won most titles with 11 between 1947 and 1973. The European Championship (inst. 1926) was won by Britain a record 12 times between 1926 and 1939.

Largest rink

The greatest indoor rink ever to operate was located in the Grand Hall, Olympia, Hammersmith, Greater London. Opened 1890 and closed in 1912 it had an actual skating area of 68,000 ft² *6 300 m²*. The current largest is the Fireside Roll-Arena, Illinois, U.S.A. which has a total skating surface of 26,789 ft² *2 489 m²*.

Marathon

The longest recorded continuous roller skating marathon was one of 320 hr 20 min performed by Randy Reed of Springfield, Oregon, U.S.A., on 12–26 June 1977. Clinton Shaw (b. Canada, 1942) skated from Victoria, British Columbia to St. John's Newfoundland (4,900 miles *7 900 km* on the Trans-Canadian Highway *via* Montreal) from 1 Apr. to 11 Nov. 1967. On 20 July 1974 at Santa Monica, California he completed a coast to coast 3,100 miles *4 988 km* skate having started at New York on 4 May. His longest stint in a day was 106 miles *170 km* from Clines Corners to Laguna, New Mexico, U.S.A.

ROWING

Oldest race

The earliest established sculling race is the Doggett's Coat and Badge, which was rowed on 1 Aug. 1716 over five miles *8 km* from London Bridge to Chelsea and is still being rowed every year over the same course, under the administration of the Fishmongers' Company. The first English regatta probably took place on the Thames by the Ranelagh Gardens, near Putney in 1775. Boating began at Eton in 1793, 72 years before the "song". The Leander Club was formed *c.* 1818.

Most Olympic medals

Since 1900 there have been 119 Olympic finals of which the U.S.A. have won 26, Germany (now West Germany) 15 and Great Britain 14.

Four oarsmen have won three gold medals: John B. Kelly (U.S.A.) (1889–1960), father of H.S.H. Princess Grace of Monaco, in the sculls (1920) and double sculls (1920 and 1924); his cousin Paul V. Costello (U.S.A.) (b. 27 Dec. 1899) in the double sculls (1920, 1924 and 1928); Jack Beresford, Jr., C.B.E. (G.B.) (b. 1 Jan. 1899) in the sculls (1924), coxless fours (1932) and double sculls (1936) and Vyacheslav Ivanov (U.S.S.R.) (b. 30 July 1938) in the sculls (1956, 1960 and 1964). Beresford also won two silver medals.

Boat race *Earliest*

The earliest University Boat Race, which Oxford won, was from Hambledon Lock to Henley Bridge on 10 June 1829. In the 123 races to 1977, Cambridge won 68 times, Oxford 54 times and there was a dead heat on 24 Mar. 1877.

Boat race *Record times*

The race record time for the course of 4 miles 374 yd *6,779 km* (Putney to Mortlake) is 16 min 58 sec by Oxford on 20 Mar. 1976. This represents an average speed of 14.89 m.p.h. *23,97 km/h*. The smallest winning margin was Oxford's win

Oxford University's record breaking crew of 1976, with the heaviest man ever to row in the University Boat Race at No 5. (*Christopher Blackwall*)

MEN—Fastest times over 2 000 m course				
	min sec	Country	Place	Date
Single Sculls	6:52.46	Sean Drea, Ireland	Montreal, Canada	23 July 1976
Double Sculls	6:12.48	Norway	Montreal, Canada	23 July 1976
Coxed Pairs	6:56.94	East Germany	Copenhagen, Denmark	— Aug. 1971
Coxless Pairs	6:33.02	East Germany	Montreal, Canada	23 July 1976
Coxed Fours	6:09.28	U.S.S.R.	Montreal, Canada	23 July 1976
Coxless Fours	5:53.65	East Germany	Montreal, Canada	23 July 1976
Quadruple Sculls	5:47.83	U.S.S.R.	Montreal, Canada	18 July 1976
Eights	5:32.17	East Germany	Montreal, Canada	18 July 1976

WOMEN—Fastest times over 1 000 m course				
Single Sculls	3:36.09	Christine, Scheiblich, East Germany	Montreal, Canada	19 July 1976
Double Sculls	3:21.75	U.S.S.R.	Montreal, Canada	19 July 1976
Coxless Pairs	3:31.01	West Germany	Montreal, Canada	19 July 1976
Coxed Fours	3:20.98	Bulgaria	Montreal, Canada	19 July 1976
Quadruple Sculls	3:08.49	East Germany	Montreal, Canada	19 July 1976
Eights	3:00.19	U.S.S.R.	Montreal, Canada	19 July 1976

by a canvas in 1952. The greatest margin (apart from sinking) was Cambridge's win by 20 lengths in 1900.

Boat race *Intermediate times*

The record to the Mile Post is 3 min 35 sec (Oxford 1976) an average speed of 16.74 m.p.h. *26,94 km/h*; Hammersmith Bridge 6 min 29 sec (Oxford 1976); Chiswick Steps 10 min 18 sec (Oxford 1976); and Barnes Bridge 14 min 09 sec (Oxford 1976).

Boat race *Heaviest oarsman*

The heaviest man ever to row in a University boat has been Stephen G. H. Plunkett (Queen's) the No. 5 in the 1976 Oxford boat at 16 st 5 lb. *103,872 kg*. The 1976 Oxford crew averaged a record 14 st. 0⅝ lb. *89,187 kg*.

Boat race *Lightest oarsman*

The lightest oarsman was the 1882 Oxford Stroke, A. H. Higgins, at 9 st 6½ lb *60 kg 100*. The lightest cox was F. H. Archer (Oxford) in 1862 at 5 st 2 lb *32,658 kg*.

Henley Royal Regatta

The annual regatta at Henley-on-Thames, Oxfordshire, was inaugurated on 26 Mar. 1839.

Since then the course, except in 1923, has been about 1 mile 550 yd *2 212 m* varying slightly according to the length of boat. In 1967 the shorter craft were "drawn up" so all bows start level. Prior to 1922 there were two slight angles.

Sculling

The record number of wins in the Wingfield Sculls (instituted on the Thames 1830) is seven by Jack Beresford, Jr. from 1920 to 1926. The fastest time (Putney to Mortlake) has been 21 min 11 sec by Leslie Southwood in 1933. The record number of world professional sculling titles (instituted 1831) won is seven by William Beach (Australia) between 1884 and 1887. Stuart A. Mackenzie (Great Britain and Australia) performed the unique feat of winning the Diamond Sculls at Henley for the sixth consecutive occasion on 7 July 1962. In 1960 and 1962 he was in Leander colours.

Highest speed

The highest recorded speed on non-tidal water for 2,000 m *2,187 yd* is by an East German eight in 5 min 32.17 sec (13.46 m.p.h. *21.67 km/h*) at Montreal, Canada on 18 July 1976. A team from Penn A.C., U.S.A., was timed in 5 min 18.8 sec (14.03 m.p.h. *22,58 km/h*) in the F.I.S.A. Championships on the River Meuse, Liege, Belgium, on 17 Aug. 1930.

Cross Channel

The fastest row across the channel has been 3 hr 50 min by Rev. Sidney Swann (b. 1862) in 1911.

Loch Ness

Loch Ness, the longest stretch of inland water in Great Britain (22.7 miles *36,5 km*), was rowed by George G. Parsonage, 31, of Whitehill Secondary School, Glasgow in 2 hr 43 min 34.1 sec on 17 May 1975. A coxed junior eight (average age 15 yr 7 months) from Sir Thomas Rich's School, Gloucester, rowed the distance in 2 hr 35 min 38.2 sec on 25 Aug. 1975.

Longest race

The longest annual rowing race is that over 40 miles *64 km* around the Island of Jersey, Channel Islands. The record time is 5 hr 5 min by a coxed four from the Jersey R.C. on 12 June 1976.

Oxford–London

The fastest time registered between Folly Bridge, Oxford through 33 locks and 112 miles *180 km* to Westminster Bridge, London is 14 hr 35 min 46 sec by an eight (no substitutes) of Guy's Hospital on 28 Apr. 1974.

Whaler pulling

The Isle of Wight was circumnavigated in a 60 nautical miles *111 km* pull in a 27 ft *8,22 m* naval whaler by two crews from the Southampton City Fire Brigade in 12 hr 34 min on 9 June 1973.

Punting

Punting was a sport with both amateur and professional championships instituted in the 1870s. Victorians argued about the two styles of pole planting and running *versus* pricking. W. Haines won the Professional Championship of the Thames eight times in the period 1897–1908. The longest recorded punt is one of 300 miles *482 km* from Kingston upon Thames to Cambridge via Reading, Oxford, Northampton and Ely by Peter Stickland and Chris Hampson from 10 Sept. to 3 Oct. 1973.

SHINTY

Origins

Shinty (from the Gaelic *sinteag*, a leap) was recorded in the West and Central Highlands *c.* 1790 when it was known as *lomain* (driving forward). Games were contested between whole clans or parishes without limit as to numbers or time until darkness stopped play among the walking wounded. The field of play was undelineated except by the occasional pail of *uisge-beatha* "breath of life" (i.e. whisky). In an inter-clan match a combatant who had failed to disable at least one opponent within a reasonable time had his curved stick (*caman*) confiscated as a punishment by the Chieftain so that he could only kick the ball (*cnaige*) or his opponents.

This ungovernable game was first given some rules in 1879 and the present governing body was set up by C. I. Macpherson of Balavil near Kingussie, Highland on 10 Oct. 1893.

Most titles

The most successful club has been Newtonmore, Highland which has won the Camanachd Association Challenge Cup (instituted 1896) 21 times (1896–1975).

Highest scores

The highest Cup Final score was in 1909 when Newtonmore beat Furnace 11–3 at Glasgow, Dr. Johnnie Cattanach scoring eight hails or goals. In 1938 John Macmillan Mactaggart scored ten hails for Mid-Argyll in a Camanachd Cup match.

SHOOTING

Earliest club
A target shooting club in Geneva, Switzerland has records dating back to 1474. The National Small-Bore Rifle Association, of Britain, was formed in 1901.

Most Olympic medals
The record number of medals won is 11 by Carl Townsend Osburn (U.S.A.) (b. 5 Nov. 1884) in 1912, 1920 and 1924, consisting of five gold, four silver and two bronze. Six other marksmen have won five gold medals. The only marksman to win three individual gold medals has been Gulbrandsen Skatteboe (Norway) (b. 18 July 1875) in 1906, 1908 and 1912.

Bisley
The National Rifle Association was instituted in 1859. The Queen's (King's) Prize has been shot since 1860 and has only once been won by a woman—Miss Marjorie Elaine Foster, M.B.E. (1894–1974) (score 280) on 19 July 1930. Arthur G. Fulton, M.B.E. (1887–1972) won a record three times (1912, 1926, 1931). Both his father and his son also won the Prize.

The highest score (possible 300) is 293 by Richard P. Rosling (City R.C.) and Alain Marion (Canada) on 28–29 July 1972 and by Keith Martin Pilcher on 20–21 July 1973. The record for the Silver Medal is 150 (possible 150) by M. J. Brister (City Rifle Club) and the Lord Swansea on 24 July 1971. Brister won the tie shoot.

Small Bore
The British team record (1966 target) is 1988 × 2000 by Lancashire in the Inter-County Association League, 1968–69. The British individual record is by John Palin (b. 16 July 1934) who shot 600 × 600 prone with a .22 rifle in Switzerland in 1972, and by Barry Dagger (b. 19 May 1937) at Bisley, in June 1976. The record score for a round in the British Schools' Small Bore Rifle Association (B.S.S.R.A.) contest is a team possible of 500 × 500 by Gresham's School, Holt, Norfolk in Lent Term, 1972. S. J. Carter scored 500 × 500 in the five rounds in this .22 contest.

Highest score in 24 hours
The Central Lancashire Rifle Club team of John Jepson, Graham Sharples, Derek Byron and Joseph Graham, scored 85,752 points (averaging 94.03 per card) on 26–27 Nov. 1976.

Air weapons
The individual world record for air rifle (40 shots at 10 m) is 393 by Olegario Vasquez (Mexico) at Mexico City, 1973 and for Air Pistol (40 shots at 10 m) is 393 by Harald Vollmar (East Germany) at Paris, France, in Feb. 1976.

Clay pigeon
Most world titles have been won by S. De Lamniczer (Hungary) in 1929, 1933 and 1939. The only woman to win two world titles has been Gräfin von Soden (West Germany) in 1966–67. The record number of clay birds shot in an hour is 1,904 by Tom Kreckman, 36, at Cresco, Penn., U.S.A., on 28 Sept. 1975. He used five guns and four loaders.

Bench rest shooting
The smallest group on record at 1,000 yds *914 m* is 6.125 in *155 mm* by Kenneth A. Keefer, Jr., with a 7 mm 300 Remington Action in Williamstown, Pennsylvania, U.S.A., on 22 Sept. 1974.

Revolver shooting
The greatest rapid fire feat was that of Ed McGivern (U.S.A.), who twice fired from 15 ft *4,5 m* five shots which could be covered by a silver half-dollar piece (diameter 1.205 in *3,060 cm*) in 0.45 sec at the Lead Club Range, South Dakota, U.S.A., on 20 Aug. 1932. On 13 Sept. 1932 at Lewiston, Montana, McGivern fired ten shots in 1.2 sec from two guns at the same time double action (no draw) all ten shots hitting two $2\frac{1}{4} \times 3\frac{1}{2}$ in *5,7 × 8,9 cm* playing cards at 15 ft *4,57 m*.

INDIVIDUAL WORLD RECORDS
(for Olympic Games programme events)
(as ratified by the International Shooting Union (U.I.T.)).

			Possible—Score			
Free Rifle	300 m	3 × 40 shots	1,200—1,157	Gary Lee Anderson (U.S.A.)	Mexico City, Mexico	23 Oct. 1968
Small-bore Rifle	50 m	3 × 40 shots	1,200—1,167	Lones W. Wigger (U.S.A.)	Mexico City, Mexico	Oct. 1973
Small-bore Rifle	50 m	60 shots prone	600— 599	Ho Jun Li (North Korea)	Munich, West Germany	28 Aug. 1972
				Karel Bulan (Czech.)	Thun, Switzerland	Sept. 1974
				Mircea Ilca (Romania)	Bucharest, Romania	July 1975
				Karl Heinz Smieszek (W. Ger.)	Montreal, Canada	19 July 1976
Free Pistol	50 m	60 shots	600— 573	Uwe Potteck (E. Germany)	Montreal, Canada	18 July 1976
Rapid Fire Pistol	25 m	60 shots	600— 598	Giovanni Liverzani (Italy)	Phoenix, Arizona, U.S.A.	1970
Running (Boar) Target	50 m	60 shots "normal runs"	600— 579	Alexander Gazov (U.S.S.R.)	Montreal, Canada	23 July 1976
Trap	200 birds		200— 199	Angelo Scalzone (Italy)	Munich, W. Germany	29 Aug. 1972
			200— 199	Michel Carrega (France)	Thun, Switzerland	23 Sept. 1974
Skeet	200 birds		200— 200	Yevgeniy Petrov (U.S.S.R.)	Phoenix, Arizona, U.S.A.	1970
			200— 200	Yuri Tzuranov (U.S.S.R.)	Bologna, Italy	1971
			200— 200	Tariel Zhgenti (U.S.S.R.)	Turin, Italy	1973
			200— 200	Kield Rasmussen (Denmark)	Vienna, Austria	1975
			200— 200	Wieslaw Gawlikowski (Poland)	Vienna, Austria	1975
Centre-fire Pistol	25 m	60 shots	600— 597	Thomas D. Smith (U.S.A.)	Sao Paulo, Brazil	1963

LARGEST BRITISH BAGS

Hare	1,215	11 guns	Holkham, Norfolk	19 Dec. 1877
Rabbit	6,943	5 guns	Blenheim, Oxfordshire	17 Oct. 1898
Geese (Brent)	704[1]	32 punt-guns	Colonel Russell i/c, River Blackwater, Essex	c. 1860
Grouse	1,070	1 gun	Lord Walsingham in Yorkshire	30 Aug. 1888
Grouse	2,929	8 guns	Littledale and Abbeystead, Lancashire	12 Aug. 1915
Partridge	2,015[2]	6 guns	Rothwell, Lincolnshire	12 Oct. 1952
Pheasant	3,937	7 guns[3]	Hall Barn, Beaconsfield, Buckinghamshire	18 Dec. 1913
Pigeon	561	1 gun	K. Ransford, Salop-Powys	22 July 1970
Snipe	1,108	2 guns	Tiree, Inner Hebrides	25 Oct.–3 Nov. 1906
Woodcock	228	6 guns	Ashford, County Galway, Ireland	28 Jan. 1910
Woodpigeon	550	1 gun	Major A. J. Coates, near Winchester, Hampshire	10 Jan. 1962

[1] *Plus about 250 later picked up.*
[2] *Plus 104 later picked up.*
[3] *Including H.M. King George V.*

Bob Munden's quick-draw skills may be of necessity—his wife is a record holder too.

Fast draw

Bob Graham of Houston, Texas won the World Championship of Fast Draw for a record third time at Oklahoma City, Okla., U.S.A. on 2 Oct. 1976. The official World Fast Draw Association record for the Standing Balloon event from hip is 22.9/100ths sec by Ernie Hill, of Phoenix, Arizona. Bob Munden (b. Kansas City, Missouri, 8 Feb. 1942) is reputed to be the fastest ever quick-draw exponent from the hand-on-gun position. He was timed in 1963 to hit a man-sized silhouette at 21 ft *6,40 m* in 21/100ths sec. His wife, Becky, holds various women's quick-draw records. Using the "Old West" draw style, Larry Capasso, of Godeffroy, N.Y. hit a man-sized target at 50 yd *45,72 m* in 35/100ths sec.

Block tossing

Using a pair of auto-loading Remington Nylon 66 0.22 calibre guns, Tom Frye (U.S.A.) tossed 100,010 blocks (2½ in *6 cm* pine cubes) and hit 100,004—his longest run was 32,860—on 5–17 Oct. 1959.

Trick shooting

The most renowned trick shot of all-time was Phoebe Anne Oakley Mozee (Annie Oakley) (1860–1926). She demonstrated the ability to shoot 100 × 100 in trap shooting for 35 years aged between 27 and 62. At 30 paces she could split a playing card end-on, hit a dime in mid-air or shoot a cigarette from the lips of her husband—one Frank Butler.

Record heads

The world's finest head is the 23-pointer stag head in the Maritzburg collection, Germany. The outside span is 75½ in *191 cm* the length 47½ in *120 cm* and the weight 41½ lb *18 kg 824*. The greatest number of points is probably 33 (plus 29) on the stag shot in 1696 by Frederick III (1657–1713), the Elector of Brandenburg, later King Frederick I of Prussia.

The record head for a British Red Deer is a 47-pointer (length 33½ in *85 cm*) from the Great Warnham Deer Park, West Sussex in 1892. The record for a semi-feral stag is a 20-pointer with an antler length of 45⅜ in *115 cm* from

Endsleigh Wood, Devon, found in December 1950 and owned by G. Kenneth Whitehead.

Biggest bag

The largest animal ever shot by any big game hunter was a bull African elephant (*Loxodonta africana africana*) shot by E. M. Nielsen, of Columbus, Nebraska, U.S.A., 25 miles *40 km* north-northeast of Mucusso, Angola, on 7 Nov. 1974. The animal, brought down by a Westley Richards 0.425 stood 13 ft 8 in *4,16 m* at the shoulders (see also p. 25). In November 1965 Simon Fletcher, 28, a Kenyan farmer, claimed to have killed two elephants with one 0.458 bullet.

The greatest recorded lifetime bag is 556,000 birds, including 241,000 pheasants, by the 2nd Marquess of Ripon (1867–1923). He himself dropped dead on a grouse moor after shooting his 52nd bird on the morning of 22 Sept. 1923.

Largest shoulder guns

The largest bore shoulder guns made were 2-bore. Less than a dozen of these were made by two English wildfowl gunmakers *c.* 1885. Normally the largest guns made are double-barrelled 4-bore weighing up to 26 lb *11 kg* which can be handled only by men of exceptional physique. Larger smooth-bore guns have been made, but these are for use as punt-guns.

SKIING

Origins

The earliest dated skis found in Fenno—Scandian bogs have been dated to *c.* 2500 B.C. A rock carving of a skier at Rødøy, Tjøtta, North Norway, dates from 2000 B.C. The earliest recorded military use of skiing was in Norway in 1199. Skiing did not develop into a sport until 1843 at Tromsø, Norway. The Trysil Shooting and Skiing Club, founded in Norway in 1861, claims it is the world's oldest. Skiing was not introduced into the Alps until 1883, though there is some evidence of earlier use in the Carniola district. The earliest reference to skiing in Scotland dates from 1892. The earliest formal downhill race was staged at Montana, Switzerland in 1911. The first Slalom event was run at Mürren, Switzerland, on 6 Jan. 1921. The International Ski Federation (F.I.S.) was founded on 2 Feb. 1924. The Winter Olympics were inaugurated on 25 Jan. 1924. The Ski Club of Great Britain was founded on 6 May 1903. The National Ski Federation of Great Britain was formed in 1964.

Most titles *World*

The world Alpine championships were inaugurated at Mürren, Switzerland, in 1931. The greatest number of titles won is 12 by Christel Cranz (b. 1 July 1914) of Germany, with four Slalom (1934, 1937–39), three Downhill (1935, 1937, 1939) and five Combined (1934–35, 1937–39). She also won the gold medal for the Combined in the 1936 Olympics. The most titles won by a man is seven by Anton (Toni) Sailer (b. 17 Nov. 1935) who won all four in 1956 (Giant Slalom, Slalom, Downhill and the non-Olympic Alpine Combination) and the Downhill, Giant Slalom and Combined in 1958.

In the Nordic events Sixten Jernberg (b. 6 Feb. 1929) (Sweden) won eight titles (four at 50 km, one at 30 km, and three in relays) in 1956–64. Johan Grøttumsbraaten (b. 24 Feb. 1899) of Norway won six individual titles (two at 18 km and four Combined) in 1926–32. The record for a jumper is five by Birger Ruud (b. 23 Aug. 1911) of Norway, in 1931–32 and 1935–37.

Most titles *World Cup*

The World Cup, instituted in 1967, has been won four times by Gustavo Thoeni (b. 28 Feb. 1951) (Italy) in 1971–73 and 1975. The women's cup has been won five times by the 1,67 m *5 ft 6 in* 68 kg *150 lb*. Annemarie Moser *née* Proell (b. 27 Mar. 1953) of Austria in 1971–75. In 1973 she completed a record sequence of 11 consecutive downhill wins.

Most titles *British*

The most British ski-running titles won is three by Leonard Dobbs (1921, 1923–24), William R. Bracken (1929–31) and

MOST OLYMPIC TITLES

Men Alpine	3	Anton (Toni) Sailer (Austria) (b. 17 Nov. 1935)	Downhill, slalom, giant slalom, 1956
	3	Jean-Claude Killy (France) (b. 30 Aug. 1943)	Downhill, slalom, giant slalom, 1968
Men Nordic	4[1]	Sixten Jernberg (Sweden) (b. 6 Feb. 1929)	50 km, 1956; 30 km, 1960; 50 km and 4 × 10 km, 1964
Women Alpine	2	Andrea Mead-Lawrence (U.S.A.) (b. 19 Apr. 1932)	Slalom, giant slalom, 1952
	2	Marielle Goitschel (France) (b. 28 Sept. 1945)	Giant slalom, 1964; slalom, 1968
	2	Marie-Therese Nadig (Switz.) (b. 8 Mar. 1954)	Downhill, giant slalom, 1972
	2[2]	Rosi Mittermaier (W. Germany) (b. 5 Aug. 1950)	Downhill, slalom, 1976
Women Nordic	4[3]	Galina Koulakova (U.S.S.R.) (b. 29 Apr. 1942)	5 km, 10 km and 3 × 5 km relay, 1972; 4 × 5 km relay, 1976

[1] Jernberg also won three silver and two bronze medals for a record nine Olympic medals.
[2] Also won silver medal in Giant Slalom in 1976.
[3] Koulakova also won one silver and two bronze medals in 1968 and 1976.

Jeremy Palmer-Tomkinson (b. 4 Nov. 1943) (1965–66, 1968). The most ladies' titles won is four by Isobel M. Roe (1938–39, 1948–49) and Gina Hathorn (b. 6 July 1949) (1966, 1968–70). The most wins in the British Ski-jumping championship (discontinued 1936) was three, by Colin Wyatt (1931, 1934 and 1936).

Longest jump *World*
The longest ski-jump ever recorded is one of 179 m *587 ft 3 in* by Walter Steiner (b. 15 Feb. 1951) (Switzerland) who fell on landing at Oberstdorf, W. Germany on 10 Mar. 1973. The official record is 176 m *577 ft 5 in* by Toni Innauer (b. 1 Apr. 1958) (Austria) at Oberstdorf, on 6 Mar. 1976. The record for a 70 m hill is 85,49 m *280 ft 6 in* by Tauno Käyhkö (b. 6 June 1950) (Finland) at Falun, Sweden on 19 Feb. 1973 when scoring 247.8 points for distance and style. The female record is 98 m *321 ft 6 in* jumped by Anita Wold (Norway) at Okura, Sapporo, Japan on 14 Jan. 1975.

Longest jump *British*
The British record is 61 m *200 ft 1 in* by Guy John Nixon (b. 9 Jan. 1909) at Davos on 24 Feb. 1931. The record at Hampstead, Camden, Greater London, on artificial snow is 28 m *91 ft 10 in* by Reidar Anderson (b. 20 Apr. 1911) of Norway on 24 Mar. 1950.

Highest speed
The highest speed claimed for any skier is 120.849 m.p.h. *194,489 km/h* by Tom Simons (b. 14 July 1954) (U.S.A.) above Cervinia, Italy on 11 July 1976. The average speed in the 1976 Olympic downhill race on the Iglis-Patscherkofei course, Innsbruck, Austria by Franz Klammer (b. 3 Dec. 1953) of Austria was 102,828 km/h *63.894 m.p.h.*

Highest altitude
Yuichiro Miura (Japan) (b. 1933) skied 2,5 km *1.6 miles* down Mt. Everest on 6 May 1970 starting from 26,200 ft *7 985 m*. In a run from a height of 24,418 ft *7 442 m* he reached speeds of 93.6 m.p.h. *150 km/h.*

Greatest descent
Sylvain Saudan (b. Lausanne, Switzerland, 23 Sept. 1936) became the first man to ski down Mount McKinley (20,320 ft *6 193 m*) on 10 June 1972. He took seven hours to reach the 7,000 ft *2 133 m* level and made 2,700 jump turns on the 50–55° top slopes.

The greatest reported aggregate elevation descended in 12 hr is 416,000 ft *126 796 m* by Sarah Ludwig, Scott Ludwig and Timothy B. Gaffney at Mount Brighton, Brighton, Michigan, U.S.A. on 16 Feb. 1974.

Steepest descent
The steepest descents in alpine skiing history have been by Sylvain Saudan. At the start of his descent from Mont Blanc on the north-east side down the Couloir Gervasutti from 4 248 m *13,937 ft* on 17 Oct. 1967 he skied to gradients in excess of 60°.

Longest run
The longest all-downhill ski run in the world is the Weissfluhjoch-Küblis Parsenn course, near Davos, Switzerland, which measures 12,23 km *7.6 miles*. The run from the Aiguille du Midi top of the Chamonix lift (vertical lift 2 492 m *8,176 ft* across the Vallée Blanche is 20,9 km *13 miles*.

Longest lift
The longest chair lift in the world is the Alpine Way to Kosciusko Châlet lift above Thredbo, near the Snowy Mountains, New South Wales, Australia. It takes from 45 to 75 min to ascend the 3.5 miles *5,6 km*, according to the weather. The highest is at Chacaltaya, Bolivia, rising to 5 029 m *16,500 ft.* The longest gondola ski lift, at Killington, Vermont, U.S.A., is 3.4 miles *5,48 km* long.

Largest race
The world's greatest Nordic ski race is the "Vasa Lopp", which commemorates an event of 1521 when Gustav Vasa (1496–1560), later King Gustavus Eriksson, skied 85,8 km *53.3 miles* from Mora to Sälen, Sweden. The re-enactment of this journey in reverse direction is now an annual event, with a record 10,934 starters (including King Carl Gustav) in March 1977. The fastest time is 4 hr 9 min 7 sec by Matti Kuosku on 7 Mar. 1976.

Backflip
The greatest number of skiers to perform a back layout flip while holding hands is 19 by members of the Sunset Sports Centre's "Hot Dog" team at the Grand Targhee Ski Resort, Wyoming, U.S.A. on 9 Feb. 1975.

Marathon *Nordic*
The longest non-stop skiing marathon was one lasting 48 hr by Onni Savi, aged 35, of Padasjoki, Finland, who covered 305,9 km *190.1 miles* between noon on 19 Apr. and noon on 21 Apr. 1966.

Marathon *Alpine*
Mark Filtranti (U.S.A.) completed 51 hr 2 min of alpine skiing at Bretton Woods Ski Area, New Hampshire, U.S.A., on 11–13 Feb. 1977.

Ski-Parachuting
The greatest recorded vertical descent in parachute ski-jumping is 2,300 ft *700 m* by Rick Sylvester (b. 1943) (U.S.) who on 31 Jan. 1973 skied off the 3,200 ft *975 m* sheer face of El Capitan, Yosemite Valley, California. His parachute opened at 1,500 ft *460 m*.

Skijoring
The record speed reached in aircraft skijoring (being towed by an aircraft) is 175,78 km/h *109.23 m.p.h.* by Reto Pitsch on the Silsersee, St. Moritz, Switzerland, in 1956.

Ski-Bob *Origins*
The ski-bob was invented by Mr. Stevens of Hartford, Connecticut, U.S.A., and patented (No. 47334) on 19 Apr. 1892 as a "bicycle with ski-runners". The Fédération Internationale de Skibob was founded on 14 Jan. 1961 in Innsbruck, Austria and the first world championships were held at Bad Hofgastein, Austria in 1967. The Ski-Bob Association of Great Britain was registered on 23 Aug. 1967. The highest speed attained is 166 km/h *103,4 m.p.h.* by Erich Brenter (b. 1940) (Austria) at Cervinia, Italy, in 1964.

After the 1976 Winter Olympic Games, silver medallist Toni Innauer jumped a record 176 m *192½ yd.* (*Tony Duffy, All-Sport Photographic*)

France's triple Olympic champion of 1968, Jean-Claude Killy later became a star in films with a winter sports locale. (*Popperfoto*)

Ski-Bob *World Championships*

The only ski-bobbers to retain a world championship are Alois Fischbauer (Austria) who won the men's title in 1973 and 1975, Gerhilde Schiffkorn (Austria) who won the women's title in 1967 and 1969, and Gertrude Geberth (Austria) who won in 1971 and 1973.

Snowmobile

A world record speed of 135.93 m.p.h. *218,75 km/h* was set up by Donald J. Pitzen (U.S.A.) at Union Lake, Michigan, U.S.A., on 27 Feb. 1977.

SNOOKER

Origins

Research shows that snooker was originated by Colonel Sir Neville Francis Fitzgerald Chamberlain, K.C.B., K.C.V.O. (1856–1944) as a hybrid of "black pool", "pyramids" and billiards, in the Ootacamund Club, Nilgiris, Southern India in the summer of 1875. It did not reach England until 1885, where the modern scoring system was adopted in 1891. Championships were not instituted until 1916. The World Professional Championship was instituted in 1927.

Highest breaks

It is possible if his opponent commits a foul and snookers him with 15 reds on the table that a player can exercise his option of nominating a colour as a red. If he then pots this free ball and goes on to pot the black with 15 reds still on the table, he can score 155. Alex Higgins (b. 18 Mar. 1949) (N. Ireland) became the first player ever to make a "16 red" clearance with a break of 146 at Leicester Y.M.C.A., Leicester, England in 1976. The official world record break (commonly referred to as a maximum) is 147 set by Joe Davis, O.B.E. (b. 15 Apr. 1901) against Willie Smith at Leicester Square Hall, City of Westminster, Greater London on 22 Jan. 1955, and by Rex Williams (G.B. against Manuel Francisco at Cape Town, South Africa, on 22 Dec. 1965. Some 60 other "perfect" frames have been achieved under less rigorous conditions. The world professional champion Ray Reardon (b. Tredegar, Gwent, 1932) achieved his sixth "perfect" frame on 4 Mar. 1976. Canadian professional Cliff Thorburn has made 14 breaks of 147, and three Canadian amateurs Leo Levitt (1948), Vic Kireluk (1968) and René Aubry (1973), and an English amateur, John Virgo (1976), now a professional, have also made maximums. The first man to compile a 147 break was E. J. O'Donaghue (b. New Zealand, 1901) in 1934.

The official world amateur record break is 122 set by Ratan Bader (India) in the West Bengal Championships in 1964.

Marathon

The snooker endurance record by three players (each resting for one frame in three) is one of 336 hours by Daniel Love, Thomas Hailey and Gary Neale of Beverly Hills, N.S.W., Australia, on 1–22 Jan. 1977.

SOFTBALL

Origins

Softball, the indoor derivative of baseball, was invented by George Hancock at the Parragut Boat Club of Chicago, Illinois in 1887. Rules were first codified in Minneapolis, Minnesota in 1895 as Kitten Ball. International rules were set in 1933 when the name Softball was officially adopted and the ISF was formed in 1952 as governing body for both fast pitch and slow pitch (with a minimum of a 3 ft *1 m* arch in trajectory). The world series for men was inaugurated in 1966 and for women in 1965.

Perfect game

Richard Daris (Monarchs) and Michael DeMeo (Spindrift) pitched perfect games at Springfield, Mass., on 16 May 1976 and Newport, R.I. on 16 June 1977, respectively.

Marathon

The longest fast pitch marathon is 51 hr by two teams of nine (no substitutes) from the Celtex Softball Club, Palmerston North, New Zealand on 22–24 Jan. 1977. The longest for slow pitch is 52 hr 5 min by two teams of ten players (no substitutes) from Pine Bluff P. and R.C., Arkansas, U.S.A. on 8–10 Apr. 1977.

SPEEDWAY

Origins

Motorcycle racing on large dirt track surfaces has been traced back to 1902 in the United States. The first organized "short track" races were at the West Maitland (New South Wales, Australia) Agricultural Show in November 1923. The sport evolved in Great Britain with small diameter track racing at Droylsden, Greater Manchester on 25 June 1927 and a cinder track event at High Beech, Essex, on 19 Feb. 1928. The National League was instituted in 1932. The best record is that of the Wembley Lions who won in 1932, 1946–47, 1949–53, making a record total of eight victories. Since the National Trophy knock-out competition was instituted in 1931, Belle Vue (Manchester) have been most successful with nine victories in 1933–37, 1946–47, 1949 and 1958. In 1965 the National League was replaced by the British League which Belle Vue have won three times in succession (1970–72).

Most world titles

The world speedway championship was inaugurated at Wembley, Brent, Greater London in September 1936. The only five-time winner has been Ove Fundin (Sweden) (b. Tranås, 1933) who won in 1956, 1960–61, 1963 and 1967. Ivan Gerald Mauger, M.B.E. (b. Christchurch, N.Z., 4 Oct. 1939) is the only rider to win three successive championships (1968–70). He also won in 1972. Barry Briggs, M.B.E. (b. Christchurch, N.Z., 1934) made a record 17 consecutive appearances in the finals (1954–70) and won the world title in 1957–58, 1964 and 1966. He has also scored a record 201 points in world championship competition.

Highest speed

The fastest recorded speed on a British speedway track is 54.62 m.p.h. *87,90 km/h* on the 470 yd *429 m* 2nd Division track at Crewe by Barry Meeks. This track was shortened by 40 yd *36 m* in 1970 and the current fastest track record on a British circuit is an average of 52.46 m.p.h. *84,42 km/h* on the re-shaped Crewe track by Dave Morton on 12 Aug. 1974.

Five time world speedway champion Ove Fundin (Sweden) placed in the first three for 11 years from 1956 to 1967. (*Sport & General Press Agency*)

SQUASH RACKETS

(Note: years refer to first half of season).

Earliest champion

Although rackets (U.S. spelling racquets) with a soft ball was evolved *c.* 1850 at Harrow School, Harrow, Greater London, there was no recognized champion of any country until John A. Miskey of Philadelphia won the American Amateur Singles Championship in 1906.

Most World Amateur titles

The inaugural Amateur International Federation championships were first staged in Australia in August 1967. Australians have won every individual title and the team title four times. Geoffrey B. Hunt (b. Feb. 1947) (Australia) has won the individual title three times (1967, 1969 and 1971).

World Open title

The inaugural world Open championship, held at Wembley Squash Centre, Brent, Greater London, in Feb. 1976, was won by Geoffrey Hunt (Australia).

Most titles *Open Championship*

The most wins in the Open Championship (amateurs or professionals), held annually in Britain, is seven by Hashim Khan (Pakistan) in 1950–55 and 1957.

Most titles *Amateur Championship*

The most wins in the Amateur Championship is six by Abdel Fattah Amr Bey (b. Egypt, 1910) later appointed Ambassador in London, who won in 1931–33 and 1935–37. Norman F. Borrett (b. 1919) of England won in 1946–50.

Most titles *Women*

The most wins in the Women's Squash Rackets Championship is 16 by Heather Pamela McKay, M.B.E. (*née* Blundell) (b. Australia, 31 July 1941) from 1961 to 1976.

Most titles *Professional Championship*

The most wins in the Professional Championship of Britain is ten by J. H. Giles from 1954 to 1963. He relinquished the title in 1964 undefeated.

Longest championship match

The longest recorded championship match was one of 2 hr 35 min in the British Amateur Championships at Wembley on 12 Dec. 1976 when Murray Lilley (N.Z.) beat Barry O'Connor (Kent) 9–3, 10–8, 2–9, 7–9, 10–8. The second game lasted 58 min and there were 98 lets in the match.

Most international appearances

The record for international selection is held by P. D. Stokes with 58 for Wales from 1960–1976. The record for England is 51 by P. N. Ayton from 1968 to 1976; O. L. Balfour (Scotland) gained 45 between 1954 and 1968, and D. M. Pratt totalled 48 for Ireland between 1956 and 1972.

Longest span of internationals

Sheila Macintosh (*née* Speight), the 1960 British Champion, played for England *v.* Wales in April 1949 and in December 1971—a span of 22 years. Among men P. Harding-Edgar first played for Scotland in 1938 and last played 21 years later in 1959.

Marathons

In squash marathons a rest interval of 1 min is allowed between games and 2 min between the 4th and 5th games with 5 min additional rest per hour. The rate of play must not exceed 11 games per hour. The longest squash marathon has been 76 hr 36 min by Garth Madden and Lawrie Cook at Blairgowrie, Johannesburg, South Africa, on 1–4 Apr. 1976. Snr. A/C. Mohammed "Ali" Akram, of R.A.F. Shawbury, Shropshire, England completed 100 hr 41 min against 44 opponents on 19–23 May 1977. He won 433 games out of 865 played.

SURFING

Origins
The traditional Polynesian sport of surfing in a canoe (*ehorooe*) was first recorded by Captain James Cook, R.N., F.R.S. (1728–79) on his first voyage at Tahiti in December 1771. Surfing on a board (*Amo Amo iluna ka lau oka nalu*) was first described "most perilous and extraordinary . . . altogether astonishing and is scarcely to be credited" by Lt. (later Capt.) James King, R.N., F.R.S. in March 1779 at Kealakekua Bay, Hawaii Island. A surfer was first depicted by this voyage's official artist John Webber.

The sport was revived at Waikiki by 1900. Australia's first body surfing events were run by the Bondi Surf Bathers Lifesaving Club, which was formed in February 1906. Australia's most successful champion has been Bob Newbiggin, who won the senior title in 1939–40, 1945–47 and the senior Belt Race in 1940. Hollow boards were introduced in 1929 and the light plastic foam type in 1956.

Most titles
World Championships were inaugurated in 1964 at Sydney, Australia. The first surfer to win two titles has been Joyce Hoffman (U.S.) in 1965 and 1966.

Highest waves ridden
Makaha Beach, Hawaii provides the reputedly highest consistently high waves often reaching the rideable limit of 30–35 ft *9–10 m*. The highest wave ever ridden was the *tsunami* of "perhaps 50 ft *15,24 m*", which struck Minole, Hawaii on 3 Apr. 1868, and was ridden to save his life by a Hawaiian named Holua.

Longest ride *Sea wave*
About four to six times each year rideable surfing waves break in Matanchen Bay near San Blas, Nayarit, Mexico which makes rides of c. 5,700 ft *1 700 m* possible.

Longest ride *River bore*
The longest recorded rides on a river bore have been set on the Severn bore, England. In 1968 local residents reported a ride of four to six miles *6–9 km* by Rodney Sumpter of Sussex. In September 1971 Mick Evans of Towyn Surfing Club, Gwyndd succeeded in making a run from Rea to Maisemore Weir a distance of four miles *6,4 km*

Skid boarding
The sport in which a 15 lb *7 kg* fibreglass coated plywood disc is substituted for a surfboard was introduced in 1967 on the coasts around Bournemouth, England. Speeds of 25 m.p.h. *40 km/h* and distances of 85 yds *77 m* have been achieved.

SWIMMING

Earliest references
It is recorded that inter-school swimming contests in Japan were ordered by Imperial edict of Emperor Go-Yoozei as early as 1603. Sea water bathing was fashionable at Scarborough, North Yorkshire as early as 1660. In Great Britain competitive swimming originated in London c. 1837, at which time there were five or more pools, the earliest of which had been opened at St. George's Pier Head, Liverpool in 1828.

Largest pools
The largest swimming pool in the world is the sea-water Orthlieb Pool in Casablanca, Morocco. It is 480 m *1,547 ft* long and 75 m *246 ft* wide, and has an area of 3.6 ha *8.9 acres*. The largest land-locked swimming pool with heated water was the Fleishhacker Pool on Sloat Boulevard, near Great Highway, San Francisco, California, U.S.A. It measured 1,000 × 150 ft *304,8 × 45,7 m* and up to 14 ft *4,26 m* deep and contained 7,500,000 U.S. gallons *28 390 hectolitres* of heated water. It was opened on 2 May 1925 but has now been abandoned to a few ducks. The world's largest competition pool is that at Osaka, Japan, which accommo-

dates 25,000 spectators. The largest in the United Kingdom is the Royal Commonwealth Pool, Edinburgh, completed in 1970 with 2,000 permanent seats.

Fastest swimmer
Excluding relay stages with their anticipatory starts, the highest speed reached by a swimmer is 5.19 m.p.h. *8,35 km/h* by Joe Bottom (b. 18 Apr. 1955) (U.S.A.), who recorded 19.70 sec for 50 yd *45,72 m* in a 25 yd *22,86 m* pool at Cleveland, Ohio, on 25 Mar. 1977. Jonty Skinner of South Africa set a world 100 m freestyle record of 49.44 sec at Philadelphia, Pennsylvania, U.S.A. on 14 Aug. 1976, averaging 4.524 m.p.h. *7,281 km/h*.

Most world records
Men 32, Arne Borg (Sweden) (b. 18 Aug. 1901), 1921–29. Women, 42, Ragnhild Hveger (Denmark) (b. 10 Dec. 1920), 1936–1942.

Most world titles
In the biennial world championships (inst. 1973) the greatest number of medals won is ten by Kornelia Ender (E. Germany) eight gold (100 m freestyle, 100 m butterfly, 4 × 100 m freestyle and 4 × 100 m medley in 1973 and 1975) and two silver (200 m freestyle 1975 and 200 m individual medley 1973). The most by a man is seven by James Montgomery (U.S.A.) (b. 24 Jan. 1955), six gold (100 and 200 m freestyle 1973, 4 × 100 m freestyle 1973 and 1975, 4 × 200 m freestyle and 4 × 100 m medley 1973) and a bronze (100 m freestyle 1975).

OLYMPIC RECORDS
Most gold medals *Men*
The greatest number of Olympic gold medals won is nine by Mark Andrew Spitz (U.S.A.) (b. 10 Feb. 1950):—

100 m freestyle	1972
200 m freestyle	1972
100 m butterfly	1972
200 m butterfly	1972
4 × 100 m freestyle	1968 and 1972
4 × 200 m freestyle	1968 and 1972
4 × 100 m medley	1972

All but one of these performances (the 4 × 200 m freestyle of 1968) were also new world records.

Most gold medals *Women*
The record number of gold medals won by a woman is four shared by Patricia McCormick (*née* Keller) (U.S.A.) (b. 12 May 1930) with the high and springboard diving double in 1952 and 1956 (also the female record for individual golds), Dawn Fraser, O.B.E. (later Mrs. Gary Ware) (b. Sydney, Australia, 4 Sept. 1937) with the 100 m freestyle (1956, 1960 and 1964) and the 4 × 100 m freestyle (1956) and Kornelia Ender (b. Plauen, E. Germany, 25 Oct. 1958) with the 100 and 200 m freestyle, 100 m butterfly and 4 × 100 m medley in 1976. Dawn Fraser is the only swimmer to win the same event on three successive occasions.

Most gold medals *British*
The record number of gold medals won by a British swimmer (excluding Water Polo *q.v.*) is four by Henry Taylor (1885–1951) in the mile freestyle (1906), 400 m freestyle (1908), 1,500 m freestyle (1908) and 4 × 200 m freestyle (1908). None of the seven British women who have won a gold medal won a second title.

Most medals *Men*
The most medals won is 11 by Mark Spitz who in addition to his nine golds (see above), won a silver (100 m butterfly) and a bronze (100 m freestyle) both in 1968.

Most medals *Women*
The most medals won by a woman is eight by Dawn Fraser, who in addition to her four golds (see above) won four silvers (400 m freestyle 1956, 4 × 100 m freestyle 1960 and 1964, 4 × 100 m medley 1960), Kornelia Ender (see above) who in addition to her four golds won four silvers (200 m individual medley 1972, 4 × 100 m medley 1972, 4 × 100 m freestyle 1972 and 1976) and Shirley Babashoff (U.S.A.) (b. 3 Jan. 1957), who won two golds (4 × 100 m freestyle

1972 and 1976) and six silvers (100 m freestyle 1972, 200 m freestyle 1972 and 1976, 400 m and 800 m freestyle 1976, 4 × 100 m medley 1976).

Most medals *British*
The British record is eight by Henry Taylor who in addition to his four golds (see above) won a silver (400 m freestyle 1906) and three bronzes (4 × 200 m freestyle 1906, 1912, 1920). The most medals by a British woman is four by Margaret Joyce Cooper (later Mrs. John Badcock) (b. 18 Apr. 1909) with one silver (4 × 100 m freestyle 1928) and three bronze (100 m freestyle 1928, 100 m backstroke 1928, 4 × 100 m freestyle 1932).

Most individual gold medals
The record number of individual gold medals won is four by Charles M. Daniels (U.S.A.) (1884–1973) (100 m freestyle 1906 and 1908, 220 yd freestyle 1904, 440 yd freestyle 1904); Roland Matthes (E. Germany) (b. 17 Nov. 1950) with 100 m and 200 m backstroke 1968 and 1972; Mark Spitz and Pat McCormick (see above). The most individual golds by a British swimmer is three by Henry Taylor (see above).

Closest verdict
The closest recorded win in the Olympic Games was in the Munich 400 m individual medley final of 30 Aug. 1972 when Gunnar Larsson (Sweden) (b. 12 May 1951) got the verdict over Tim McKee (U.S.A.) (b. 14 Mar. 1953) by 2/1,000th of a second in 4 min 31.981 sec to 4 min 31.983 sec—a margin of 3 mm or the length grown by a finger nail in three weeks.

DIVING
Most Olympic medals *World*
The most medals won by a diver are five (three gold, two silver) by Klaus Dibiasi (b. Austria, 6 Oct. 1947) (Italy) in four Games from 1964 to 1976. He is also the only diver to win the same event (highboard) at three successive Games (1968, 1972 and 1976). Pat McCormick (see above) won four gold medals.

Most Olympic medals *British*
The highest placing by a Briton has been the silver medal by Eileen Armstrong (b. 1896) in the 1920 highboard event. The best placings by male divers are the bronze medals by Harold Clarke (b. 1888) (plain high diving, 1924) and Brian Phelps (b. 21 Apr. 1944) (highboard, 1960).

Most world titles
Klaus Dibiasi (Italy) won two gold and two silver medals at the first two world championships held in 1973 and 1975.

Perfect dive
In the 1972 U.S. Olympic Trials, in Chicago, Illinois, Michael Finneran (b. 21 Sept. 1948) was awarded a score of 10 by all seven judges for a backward 1½ somersault, 2½ twist, free, dive from the 10 m board, an achievement without precedent.

CHANNEL SWIMMING
Earliest *Men*
The first man to swim across the English Channel (without a life jacket) was the Merchant Navy captain Matthew Webb (1848–83), who swam breaststroke from Dover, England, to Cap Gris-Nez, France, in 21 hr 45 min from 12.56 p.m. to 10.41 a.m., 24–25 Aug. 1875. He swam an estimated 38 miles *61 km* to make the 21-mile *33 km* crossing. Paul Boyton (U.S.A.) had swum from Cap Gris-Nez to the South Foreland in his patent life-saving suit in 23 hr 30 min on 28–29 May 1875. There is good evidence that Jean-Marie Saletti, a French soldier, escaped from a British prison hulk off Dover by swimming to Boulogne in July or August 1815. The first crossing from France to England was made by Enrique Tiraboschi, a wealthy Italian living in Argentina, who crossed in 16 hr 33 min on 11 Aug. 1923, to win the *Daily Sketch* prize of £1,000.

Earliest *Women*
The first woman to succeed was Gertrude Caroline Ederle (b. 23 Oct. 1906) (U.S.A.) who swam from Cap Gris-Nez, France to Dover, England on 6 Aug. 1926, in the then overall record time of 14 hr 39 min. The first woman to swim from England to France was Florence Chadwick (b. 1918) of California, U.S.A., in 16 hr 19 min on 11 Sept. 1951. She repeated this on 4 Sept. 1953 and 12 Oct. 1955. The first Englishwoman to succeed was Ivy Gill on 14 Oct. 1927.

Fastest
The official Channel Swimming Association (founded 1927) record is 8 hr 56 min by Wendy Brook (b. 1956) of Ossett, West Yorkshire, from Shakespeare Beach, Dover, England to Cap Gris-Nez, France, on 31 Aug. 1976. The fastest crossing by a relay team, from England to France is 8 hr 5 min by an Egyptian team on 5 Aug. 1976. The fastest time from France to England by a relay team is 8 hr 59 min by Hetzel's Texas Volunteers (U.S.A.), on 14 Aug. 1975.

Slowest
The slowest crossing was the third ever made, when Henry Sullivan (U.S.A.) swam from England to France in 26 hr 50 min on 5–6 Aug. 1923.

Earliest and latest
The earliest date in the year on which the Channel has been swum is 6 June by Dorothy Perkins (England) (b. 1942) in 1961, and the latest is 14 October by Ivy Gill. Both swims were from France to England.

Youngest
The youngest conqueror is David Morgan (b. 25 Sept. 1963) of Scarborough, Yorks., who swam from Dover to Wissant, France in 11 hr 5 min on 26 July 1977, when he was aged 13 yr 304 days.

Oldest
The oldest swimmer to swim the Channel has been William E. (Ned) Barnie, aged 55, when he swam from France to England in 15 hr 1 min on 16 Aug. 1951.

Double crossing *First*
Antonio Abertondo (b. Buenos Aires, Argentina, 1919), swam from England to France in 18 hr 50 min (8.35 a.m. on 20 Sept. to 3.25 a.m. on 21 Sept. 1961) and after about 4 min rest returned to England in 24 hr 16 min, landing at St. Margaret's Bay at 3.45 a.m. on 22 Sept. 1961, to complete the first "double crossing" in 43 hr 10 min. Kevin Murphy (b. Bushey Heath, Herts, 1949) completed the first double crossing by a Briton in 35 hr 10 min on 6 Aug. 1970. The first swimmer to achieve a crossing both ways was Edward H. Temme (b. 1904) on 5 Aug. 1927 and 19 Aug. 1934.

Double crossing *Fastest*
The fastest double crossing was one of 30 hrs by Jon Erikson (b. Chicago, Illinois, U.S.A., 1955) on 14–15 Aug. 1975, thereby breaking the previous record, held by his father, by three minutes.

Most conquests
The greatest number of Channel conquests is 11 by Desmond Renford, M.B.E. (b. 1928) (Australia) from 1970 to 6 July 1977 including a unique three times in 1975. Greta Andersen-Sonnichsen (b. Denmark, 1 May 1928) (U.S.A.) made five crossings in 1957–65.

Underwater
The first underwater cross-Channel swim was achieved by Fred Baldasare (b. 1924) (U.S.A.), who completed a 42 mile *67,5 km* distance from France to England with Scuba equipment in 18 hr 1 min on 10–11 July 1962. Simon Paterson (b. 1942) a frogman from Egham, Surrey, travelled underwater from France to England with an air hose attached to his pilot boat in 14 hr 50 min on 28 July 1962.

LONG DISTANCE SWIMMING
Longest ocean swim
The longest recorded ocean swim is one of 122½ miles *197.1 km* by Walter Poenisch Snr. (U.S.A.) (b. 1914) in the Florida Straits (in a shark cage) in 25 hr 8 min on 19–20 June 1976.

below: Now a coach, Pat McCormick won 17 American titles in addition to her unique four Olympic diving gold medals. (*All-Sport Photographic*)

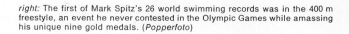

right: The first of Mark Spitz's 26 world swimming records was in the 400 m freestyle, an event he never contested in the Olympic Games while amassing his unique nine gold medals. (*Popperfoto*)

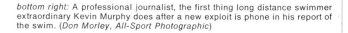

bottom right: A professional journalist, the first thing long distance swimmer extraordinary Kevin Murphy does after a new exploit is phone in his report of the swim. (*Don Morley, All-Sport Photographic*)

A unique achievement in long distance swimming was established in 1966 by the cross-Channel swimmer Mihir Sen of Calcutta, India. This was in swimming the Palk Strait from India to Sri Lanka (in 25 hr 36 min on 5–6 April); the Straits of Gibraltar (Europe to Africa in 8 hr 1 min on 24 August); the length of the Dardanelles (Gallipoli to Seddül-bahir, Turkey) in 13 hr 55 min on 12 September) and the entire length of the Panama Canal (in 34 hr 15 min on 29–31 October). He had earlier swam the English Channel in 14 hr 45 min on 27 Sept. 1958.

Irish Channel

The swimming of the 23 mile *37 km* wide North Channel from Donaghadee, Northern Ireland to Portpatrick, Scotland was first accomplished by Tom Blower of Nottingham in 15 hr 26 min in 1947. A record time of 11 hr 21 min was set by Kevin Murphy on 11 Sept. 1970. The first Irish-born swimmer to achieve the crossing was Ted Keenan on 11 Aug. 1973 in 52–56 °F *11–13° C* water in 18 hr 27 min.

Bristol Channel

The first person to achieve a crossing of the Bristol Channel was Kathleen Thomas (now Mrs. F. Day) (b. Apr. 1906) who swam from Penarth, South Glamorgan to Weston-super-Mare, Avon on 5 Sept. 1927. The record for the longer swim from Glenthorne Cove, Devon to Porthcawl, Mid-Glamorgan is 10 hr 46 min by Jane Luscombe (b. 13 Jan. 1961) of Jersey, C.I., on 19 Aug. 1976.

Solent

The fastest time for swimming the Solent (Ryde, Isle of Wight to Southsea) has been 1 hr 6 min 27 sec by Ron Evans (Wimbledon) in 1977. The greatest number of crossings has been 25 single and 2 non-stop double crossings by Richard Glynn of Cheltenham, to 1976.

Loch Ness

The fastest time for swimming the length of Great Britain's longest lake, the 22.7 mile *36,5 km* long Loch Ness, is 10 hr 30 min by Kevin Murphy in 1976.

Island circumnatation

The fastest swim round the Isle of Wight (55 miles *88 km*) is 24 hr 36 min 25 sec by Michael P. Read (Norwich) in Aug. 1976. Dr. Shaun K. O'Connell (U.S.A.) swam around Bermuda (45 miles *72 km* of shark-infested water) in 43 hr 27 min on 21–23 Aug. 1976.

Palk Strait

The first person to achieve a double crossing of the Palk Strait, between India and Sri Lanka, was V. S. C. Anandan (Sri Lanka) on 18–20 Apr. 1975.

Longest swims

The greatest recorded distance ever swum is 1,826 miles *2 938 km* down the Mississippi, U.S.A. between Ford Dam near Minneapolis and Carrollton Ave, New Orleans, Louisiana, by Fred P. Newton, (b. 1903) of Clinton, Oklahoma from 6 July to 29 Dec. 1930. He was 742 hours in the water.

The greatest distance covered in a continuous swim is 292 miles *469,9 km* by Joe Maciag (b. 26 Mar. 1956) from Billings to Glendive, Montana in the Yellowstone River in 64 hr 50 min on 1–4 July 1976.

WORLD RECORDS
recognised by the *Fédération Internationale de Natation Amateur* (as at 15 August 1977)

MEN

Event	Time Min. sec.	Name and Country	Place	Date
FREESTYLE				
100 metres	49.44	Jonty Skinner (S.A.)	Philadelphia, U.S.A.	14 Aug. 1976
200 metres	1:50.29	Bruce Furniss (U.S.A.)	Montreal, Canada	19 July 1976
400 metres	3:51.93	Brian Stuart Goodell (U.S.A.)	Montreal, Canada	22 July 1976
800 metres	8:01.54	Bobby Hackett (U.S.A.)	Long Beach, U.S.A.	21 June 1976
1,500 metres	15:02.40	Brian Stuart Goodell (U.S.A.)	Montreal, Canada	20 July 1976
4 × 100 metres	3:24.85	United States (Bruce Furniss, James Montgomery, Andrew Coan, John Murphy)	Cali, Colombia	23 July 1975
4 × 200 metres	7:23.22	United States Michael Bruner, Bruce Furniss, John Naber, James Montgomery	Montreal, Canada	21 July 1976
BREASTSTROKE				
100 metres	1:03.11	John Hencken (U.S.A.)	Montreal, Canada	20 July 1976
200 metres	2:15.11	David Andrew Wilkie M.B.E. (G.B.)	Montreal, Canada	24 July 1976
BUTTERFLY				
100 metres	54.27	Mark Andrew Spitz (U.S.A.)	Munich, West Germany	31 Aug. 1972
200 metres	1:59.23	Michael Bruner (U.S.A.)	Montreal, Canada	18 July 1976
BACKSTROKE				
100 metres	55.49	John Naber (U.S.A.)	Montreal, Canada	19 July 1976
200 metres	1:59.19	John Naber (U.S.A.)	Montreal, Canada	24 July 1976
MEDLEY				
200 metres	2:05.31	Graham Smith (Canada)	Montreal, Canada	5 Aug. 1977
400 metres	4:23.68	Rod Strachan (U.S.A.)	Montreal, Canada	25 July 1976
4 × 100 metres	3:42.22	United States (John Naber, John Hencken, Matthew Vogel, James Montgomery)	Montreal, Canada	22 July 1976

WOMEN

Event	Time Min. sec.	Name and Country	Place	Date
FREESTYLE				
100 metres	55.65	Kornelia Ender (East Germany)	Montreal, Canada	19 July 1976
200 metres	1:59.26	Kornelia Ender (East Germany)	Montreal, Canada	22 July 1976
400 metres	4:09.89	Petra Thumer (East Germany)	Montreal, Canada	20 July 1976
800 metres	8:35.04	Petra Thumer (East Germany)	Leipzig, East Germany	29 July 1977
1,500 metres	16:33.94	Jenny Turrall (Australia)	Concord, U.S.A.	25 Aug. 1974
4 × 100 metres	3:44.82	United States (Kim Peyton, Wendy Boglioli, Jill Sterkel, Shirley Babashoff)	Montreal, Canada	25 July 1976
BREASTSTROKE				
100 metres	1:10.86	Hannelore Anke (East Germany)	Montreal, Canada	22 July 1976
200 metres	2:33.35	Marina Koshevaia (U.S.S.R.)	Montreal, Canada	21 July 1976
BUTTERFLY				
100 metres	1:00.13	Kornelia Ender (East Germany)	East Berlin, East Germany	4 June 1976
		Kornelia Ender (East Germany)	Montreal, Canada	22 July 1976
200 metres	2:11.22	Rosemarie Gabriel-Kother (East Germany)	East Berlin, East Germany	5 June 1976
BACKSTROKE				
100 metres	1:01.51	Ulrike Richter (East Germany)	East Berlin, East Germany	5 June 1976
200 metres	2:12.47	Birgit Treiber (East Germany)	East Berlin, East Germany	4 June 1976
MEDLEY				
200 metres	2:16.96	Ulrike Tauber (East Germany)	Leipzig, East Germany	9 July 1977
400 metres	4:42.77	Ulrike Tauber (East Germany)	Montreal, Canada	24 July 1976
4 × 100 metres	4:07.95	East Germany (Ulrike Richter, Hannelore Anke, Andrea Pollack, Kornelia Ender)	Montreal, Canada	18 July 1976

World records can only be set in 50 m pools. FINA has not recognised records for Imperial distances since 30 Apr., 1969.

Longest duration

The longest duration swim ever achieved was one of 168 continuous hours, ending on 24 Feb. 1941, by the legless Charles Zibbelman, *alias* Zimmy (b. 1894) of the U.S.A., in a pool in Honolulu, Hawaii, U.S.A. The longest duration swim by a woman was 87 hours 27 min in a pool by Mrs. Myrtle Huddleston of New York City, N.Y., U.S.A., in 1931.

Relays

The longest recorded mileage in a 24 hr swim relay (team of five) is 76 miles 415 yds *122,8 km* by the Sarasota YMCA Sharks at Sarasota, Florida, U.S.A. on 16–17 July 1977. The fastest time recorded for 100 miles *160 km* by a team of 20 swimmers is 24 hr 24 min 21.3 sec by Inst S.C. in the short course bath of the Royal Belfast Academical Institution, N. Ireland, on 31 Mar.–1 Apr. 1977. In Buttermere, Cumbria on 18–28 July 1968 six boys, aged 13 to 15, covered 300 miles *482 km* in 230 hr 39 min.

Sponsored swimming

The greatest amount of money collected in a charity swim was £20,687.83 by the Lions Club of Jersey, C.I. on 13–15 Feb. 1976, using 1,764 swimmers.

Under-ground swimming

The longest recorded underground swim is one of 3,402 yd *3 110 m* in 87 min by David Stanley Gale through the Dudley Old Canal Tunnel, West Midlands in August 1967.

Treading water marathon

The duration record for treading water (vertical posture without touching the lane markers in an 8 ft *2,43 m* square) is 50 hr by Monnie Lewis (U.S.A.) at Winter Park, Florida, on 17–19 June 1977.

Ice swimming

The coldest temperature reported in voluntary ice swimming is 32 °F *0 °C* in the ice clogged Monongahela River, Pennsylvania, U.S.A., by the "Human Polar Bear" Gustave A. Brickner, (b. 10 Feb. 1912). The air temperature was −18 °F, *−27,7 °C* and the wind speed 40 m.p.h. *64 km/h* with a −85 °F *−65 °C* chill factor for his daily dip on 24 Jan. 1963.

Most dangerous

One of the most dangerous swims on record was the unique crossing of the Potaro River in Guyana just above the 741 ft *226 m* high Kaieteur Falls by Private Robert Howatt (the

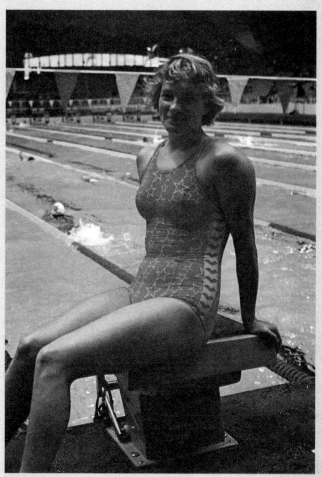

It took a world record to make Marina Koshevaia (U.S.S.R.) the only non-East German girl to win an individual Olympic swimming title at Montreal in 1976. (*Tony Duffy, All-Sport Photographic*)

Black Watch) on 17 Apr. 1955. The river is 464 ft *141 m* wide at the lip of the falls.

BRITISH NATIONAL (long course) RECORDS
as ratified by the Amateur Swimming Federation of Great Britain as at 15 Aug. 1977

MEN

Event	Time Min. sec.	Name	Place	Date
FREESTYLE				
100 metres	52.30	Brian Brinkley, M.B.E.	Coventry, England	30 Aug. 1975
200 metres	1:52.47	Gordon Downie	Montreal, Canada	19 July 1976
400 metres	4:01.00	Gordon Downie	Montreal, Canada	22 July 1976
800 metres	8:23.51†	Andrew Astbury	Leeds, England	20 July 1977
1,500 metres	15:46.60	David Parker	Montreal, Canada	19 July 1976
BREASTSTROKE				
100 metres	1:03.43	David Andrew Wilkie, M.B.E.	Montreal, Canada	20 July 1976
200 metres	2:15.11	David Andrew Wilkie, M.B.E.	Montreal, Canada	24 July 1976
BUTTERFLY				
100 metres	56.53	John Mills	Montreal, Canada	20 July 1976
200 metres	2:01.49	Brian Brinkley, M.B.E.	Montreal, Canada	18 July 1976
BACKSTROKE				
100 metres	59.60	James Carter	Montreal, Canada	22 July 1976
200 metres	2:06.87	James Carter	Long Beach, U.S.A.	1 Apr. 1976
INDIVIDUAL MEDLEY				
200 metres	2:06.25	David Andrew Wilkie, M.B.E.	Long Beach, U.S.A.	4 Apr. 1976
400 metres	4:33.56	Alan McClatchey	Pescara, Italy	15 Aug. 1976

WOMEN

FREESTYLE

100 metres	59.34	Cheryl Brazendale	Brussels, Belgium	15 May	1977
200 metres	2:06.2*	Cheryl Brazendale	Coventry, England	29 Apr.	1977
400 metres	4:24.09	Cheryl Brazendale	Rotterdam, Netherlands	17 Apr.	1977
800 metres	9:07.4*	Lindsay Heggie	Blackpool, England	9 June	1977
1,500 metres	18:19.4*	Amanda James	Cardiff, Wales	31 Oct.	1976

BREASTSTROKE

100 metres	1:13.57	Margaret Mary Kelly	Montreal, Canada	22 July	1976
200 metres	2:38.26	Debbie Rudd	Montreal, Canada	21 July	1967

BUTTERFLY

100 metres	1:03.88	Susan Jenner	Coventry, England	30 Apr.	1977
200 metres	2:19.5*	Jane Alexander	Blackpool, England	29 May	1976
	2:19.0†	Susan Jenner	Leeds, England	22 July	1977

BACKSTROKE

100 metres	1:06.41	Joy Beasley	Geneva, Switzerland	22 Jan.	1977
200 metres	2:21.18†	Sharron Davies	Leeds, England	23 July	1977

INDIVIDUAL MEDLEY

200 metres	2:22.95†	Sharron Davies	Leeds, England	21 July	1977
400 metres	4:56.28†	Sharron Davies	Leeds, England	22 July	1977

* timed to 1/10th of a second.
† to be ratified.

TABLE TENNIS

Origins

The earliest evidence relating to a game resembling table tennis has been found in the catalogues of London sports goods manufacturers in the 1880s. The old Ping Pong Association was formed in 1902 but the game proved only a temporary craze until resuscitated in 1921. The English Table Tennis Association was formed on 24 Apr. 1927.

Most English titles

The highest total of English men's titles (instituted 1921) is 20 by G. Viktor Barna (1912–72) (b. Hungary, Gyözö Braun) The women's record is 17 by Diane Rowe (b. 14 Apr. 1933), now Mrs. Eberhard Scholer. Her twin Rosalind (now Mrs. Cornett) has won nine (two in singles).

Youngest international

The youngest ever international was Joy Foster, aged 8, the 1958 Jamaican singles and mixed doubles champion.

Longest match

In the Swaythling Cup final match between Austria and Romania in Prague, Czechoslovakia, in 1936, the play lasted for 25 or 26 hours, spread over three nights.

Longest rally

In a 1936 Swaythling Cup match in Prague between Alex Ehrlich (Poland) and Paneth Farcas (Romania) the opening rally lasted 2 hr 12 min. On 2–3 July 1976 Barry Muth and Guy Frankenfield staged a 3 hr 8 min 41 sec rally at Emmaus, Penn., U.S.A.

The Rowe twins, Diane (left) and Rosalind, twice won the World ladies doubles title, as well as a record total of English championships between them. (*English Table Tennis Association*)

MOST WINS IN WORLD CHAMPIONSHIPS (Instituted 1926–27)

Event	Name and Nationality	Times	Years
Men's Singles (St. Bride's Vase)	G. Viktor Barna (Hungary)	5	1930, 1932–35
Women's Singles (G. Geist Prize)	Angelica Rozeanu (Romania)	6	1950–55
Men's Doubles	G. Viktor Barna (Hungary) with two different partners	8	1929–35, 1939
Women's Doubles	Maria Mednyanzsky (Hungary) with three different partners	7	1928, 1930–35
Mixed Doubles (Men)	Ferenc Sido (Hungary) with two different partners	4	1949–50, 1952–53
(Women)	Maria Mednyanszky (Hungary) with three different partners	6	1927–28, 1930–31, 1933–34

G. Viktor Barna gained a personal total of 15 world titles, while 18 have been won by Maria Mednyanszky.
Note: With the staging of championships biennially the breaking of the above records would now be virtually impossible.

MOST TEAM TITLES

Event	Team	Times	Years
Men's Team (Swaythling Cup)	Hungary	11	1927–31, 1933–35, 1938, 1949, 1952
Women's Team (Marcel Corbillon Cup)	Japan	8	1952, 1954, 1957, 1959, 1961, 1963, 1967, 1971

MOST WINS IN ENGLISH OPEN CHAMPIONSHIPS (Instituted 1921)

Event	Name and Nationality	Times	Years
Men's Singles	Richard Bergmann (Austria, then G.B.)	6	1939–40, 1948, 1950, 1952, 1954
Women's Singles	Maria Alexandru (Romania)	6	1963–64, 1970–72, 1974
Men's Doubles	G. Viktor Barna (Hungary, then G.B.) with five different partners	7	1931, 1933–35, 1938–39, 1949
Women's Doubles	Diane Rowe (G.B.) (now Scholer) with four different partners	12	1950–56, 1960, 1962–65
Mixed Doubles (Men)	G. Viktor Barna (Hungary, then G.B.) with four different partners	8	1933–36, 1938, 1940, 1951, 1953
(Women)	Diane Rowe (G.B.) (now Scholer) with three different partners	4	1952, 1954, 1956, 1960, 1969

Fastest counter hitting

The record number of hits in 60 sec is 162 by English Internationals Nicky Jarvis (b. 7 Mar. 1954) and Desmond Douglas (b. 20 July 1955) at the Eccentric Club, London on 1 Dec. 1976. This was equalled by Douglas and Paul Day (b. 20 Oct. 1958) at Butlins, Blackpool, Lancs., England on 21 Mar. 1977.

Highest speed

No conclusive measurements have been published but in a lecture M. Sklorz (West Germany) stated that a smashed ball had been measured at speeds up to 170 km/h *105,6 m.p.h.*

Marathons

The longest marathon singles match is 104 hr 52 min by Paul Dudmish and Paul Pells, at Holborn Telephone Exchange, Camden, Greater London, on 25–29 June 1977. Heather Cox, of Nambour, Queensland, Australia played a series of opponents for 110 hr 3 min on 7–11 Apr. 1977.

The longest marathon by four players maintaining continuous singles is 682 hours by the Lindisfarne T.T.C, on 11 Oct.–8 Nov. 1975. The longest doubles marathon is 100 hr 1 min by four players from De La Salle College, Salford, Lancs., on 12–16 Apr. 1977.

TENNIS (Real or Royal)

Origins

The game originated in French monasteries *c.* 1050.

Oldest court

The oldest of the 17 surviving Tennis Courts in the British Isles is the Royal Tennis Court at Hampton Court Palace, which was built by order of King Henry VIII in 1529–30 and rebuilt by order of Charles II in 1660. The oldest court in the world is one built in Paris in 1496. There are estimated to be 3,000 players and 31 courts throughout the world.

Most titles *World*

The first recorded World Tennis Champion was Clerge (France) *c.* 1740. Pierre Etchebaster (b. 1893) won the title at Prince's, Paris, in May 1928, last defended it in New York (winning 7–1) in December 1949 and retired undefeated in 1955, after 27 years. Etchebaster, a Basque, also holds the record for the greatest number of successful defences of his title with six.

Most titles *British*

The Amateur Championship of the British Isles (instituted 1780) has been won 13 times by Edgar M. Baerlein (1879–1971) from 1912 to 1930. Howard R. Angus (b. 1945) has won 12 consecutive titles (1966–77). He is also the first British amateur to win a World title in 1975 which he retained in 1977.

The Tudor Real Tennis Court at Hampton Court Palace, originally built by Henry VIII in 1529–30. (*Crown Copyright*)

TRACK AND FIELD ATHLETICS

Origins

Track and field athletics date from the ancient Olympic Games. The earliest accurately known Olympiad dates from 21 or 22 July 776 B.C., at which celebration Coroibos won the foot race. The oldest surviving measurements are a long jump of 7,05 m *23 ft 1½ in* by Chionis of Sparta in *c.* 656 B.C. and a discus throw of 100 cubits (about 46.30 m *152 ft*) by Protesilaus.

Earliest landmarks

The first time 10 sec ("even time") was bettered for 100 yds under championship conditions was when John Owen recorded 9⅘ sec in the United States A.A.U. Championship at Analostan Island, Washington, D.C., U.S.A., on 11 Oct. 1890. The first recorded instance of 6 ft *1,83 m* being cleared in the high jump was when Marshall Jones Brooks jumped 6 ft 0⅛ in *1,832 m* at Marston, near Oxford, England, on 17 Mar. 1876. The breaking of the "four-minute barrier" in the one mile *1 609,34 m* was first achieved by Dr. (now Sir) Roger Gilbert Bannister, C.B.E. (b. Harrow, Greater London, England, 23 Mar. 1929), when he recorded 3 min 59.4 sec on the Iffley Road track, Oxford, at 6.10 p.m. on 6 May 1954.

Fastest runner

Robert Lee Hayes (b. 20 Dec. 1942) of Jacksonville, Florida, U.S.A., may have reached a speed of over 27 m.p.h. *43,5 km/h* during his then world record run of 9.1 sec in a 100 yard event at St. Louis, Missouri, on 21 June 1963. Wyomia Tyus (b. Griffin, Georgia, U.S.A., 29 Aug. 1945) was reputed to have reached a speed of over 23 m.p.h. *37 km/h* in Kiev, U.S.S.R. on 31 July 1965.

Highest jumper

There are several reported instances of high jumpers exceeding the official world record height of 7 ft 7¾ in *2,33 m*. The earliest of these came from unsubstantiated reports of Tutsi tribesmen in Central Africa (see page 10) clearing up to 8 ft 2½ in *2,50 m*, definitely however, from inclined take-offs. The greatest height cleared above an athlete's own head is 21¼ in *54 cm* by Franklin Jacobs (U.S.) (b. 1957), who cleared 7 ft 5¼ in *2,27 m* at Los Angeles, Calif., U.S.A., on 11 June 1977. He is only 5 ft 8 in *1,73 m* tall. The greatest height cleared by a woman above her own head is 22 cm *8½ in* by Maggie Woods (b. 1960) of Canada who stands 1,58 m *5 ft 2¼ in* and jumped 1,80 m *5 ft 10¾ in* at Edmonton, Alberta, on 21 Aug. 1976.

Most Olympic titles *Men*

The most Olympic gold medals won is ten (an absolute Olympic record) by Ray C. Ewry (U.S.A.) (1874–1937) with:

Standing High Jump	1900, 1904, 1906, 1908
Standing Long Jump	1900, 1904, 1906, 1908
Standing Triple Jump	1900, 1904

Most Olympic titles *Women*

The most gold medals won by a woman is four shared by Francina E. Blankers-Koen (Netherlands) (b. 26 Apr. 1918) with 100 m, 200 m, 80 m hurdles and 4 × 100 m relay, 1948, and Betty Cuthbert (Australia) (b. 20 Apr. 1938) with 100 m, 200 m, 4 × 100 m relay, 1956 and 400 m, 1964.

Most Olympic titles *British*

The most gold medals won by a British athlete (excluding Tug of War and Walking *q.v.*) is two by: Charles Bennett (1,500 m and 5,000 m team, 1900); Alfred Tysoe (800 m and 5,000 m team, 1900); John Rimmer (4,000 m steeplechase; and 5,000 m team, 1900); Albert G. Hill (1889–1969) (800 m and 1,500 m, 1920) and Douglas Gordon Arthur Lowe (b. 7 Aug. 1902) (800 m 1924 and 1928).

Most Olympic medals *Men*

The most medals won is 12 (nine gold and three silver) by Paavo Johannes Nurmi (Finland) (1897–1973):

1920	Gold: 10,000 m; cross country, individual and team; Silver: 5,000 m.
1924	Gold: 1,500 m; 5,000 m; 3,000 m team; cross country, individual and team.

1928	Gold; 10,000 m; Silver: 5,000 m; 3,000 m steeplechase.

Most Olympic medals *Women*

The most medals won by a woman athlete is seven by Shirley de la Hunty (*née* Strickland) (Australia) (b. 18 July 1925) with three gold, one silver and three bronze in the 1948, 1952 and 1956 Games. A recently discovered photo-finish indicates that she finished third, not fourth, in the 1948 200 metres event, thus unofficially increasing her medal haul to eight. Irena Szewinska (née Kirszenstein) (Poland) (b. 24 May 1946) won three gold, two silver and two bronze in 1964, 1968, 1972 and 1976, and is the only woman athlete to win a medal in four successive games.

Most Olympic medals *British*

The most medals won by a British athlete is four by Guy M. Butler (b. 25 Aug. 1899) with a gold medal for the 4 × 400 m relay and a silver in the 400 m in 1920 and a bronze medal for each of these events in 1924. Two British women athletes have won three medals: Dorothy Hyman, M.B.E. (b. 9 May 1941) with a silver (100 m, 1960) and a bronze (200 m, 1960 and 4 × 100 m relay, 1964) and Mrs. Mary Denise Rand, M.B.E. (now Toomey, *née* Bignal), (b. 10 Feb. 1940) with a gold (long jump), a silver (pentathlon) and a bronze (4 × 100 m relay) all in 1964.

Most wins at one Games

The most gold medals at one celebration is five by Paavo Nurmi in 1924 (see above) and the most individual is four by Alvin C. Kraenzlein (U.S.A.) (1876–1928) in 1900, with 60 m, 110 m hurdles, 200 m hurdles and long jump.

World record breakers *Oldest*

The greatest age at which anyone has broken a world athletics record in a standard Olympic event is 35 years 255 days in the case of Dana Zátopkova, *née* Ingrova (b. 19 Sept. 1922) of Czechoslovakia, who broke the women's javelin record with 182 ft 10 in *55,73 m* at Prague, Czechoslovakia, on 1 June 1958.

World record breakers *Youngest*

Ulrike Meyfarth (b. 4 May 1956) of West Germany equalled the world record for the women's high jump with 1.92 m *6 ft 3½ in* in winning the gold medal on 4 Sept. 1972 at the Munich Olympics aged 16 years 4 months.

Most records in a day

Jesse Owens (b. 12 Sept. 1913) (U.S.A.) set six world records in 45 min at Ann Arbor, Michigan on 25 May 1935 with a 9.4 sec 100 yd at 3.15 p.m., a 26 ft 8¼ in *8,13 m* long jump at 3.25 p.m., a 20.3 sec 220 yd (and 200 m) at 3.45 p.m. and a 22.6 sec 220 yd low hurdles (and 200 m) at 4.00 p.m.

Most national titles

The greatest number of national A.A.A. titles (excluding those in tug of war events) won by one athlete is 14 individual and two relay titles by Emmanuel McDonald Bailey (b. Williamsville, Trinidad 8 Dec. 1920), between 1946 and 1953.

The greatest number of consecutive title wins is seven by Denis Horgan (1871–1922) (Ireland) (shot putt, 1893–99), Albert Arthur Cooper (1910–74) (2 miles walk, 1932–38), Donald Osborne Finlay, D.F.C., A.F.C. (1909–70) (120 yd hurdles, 1932–38), Harry Whittle (b. 2 May 1922) (440 yd hurdles, 1947–53) and Maurice Herriott (b. 8 Oct. 1939) (3,000 m steeplechase, 1961–67). The record for consecutive W.A.A.A. titles is eight by Judy Undine Farr (Trowbridge & District A.C.) (b. 24 Jan. 1942), who won the 1½ mile *2 500 m* walk from 1962–69.

Most international appearances

The greatest number of full Great Britain outdoor internationals won by a British male athlete is 61 by Andrew Howard Payne (b. South Africa, 17 Apr. 1931). Michael Anthony Bull (b. 11 Sept. 1946) had gained 66 full international appearances, including indoor matches, up to end July 1977. The feminine record is 63 full internationals, including indoor matches, by Brenda Bedford (*née* Sawyer) (b. 4 Sept. 1937, London) from 1961 to end July 1977.

Don Finlay had seven consecutive AAA titles and Olympic silver and bronze medals behind him when he set his last British hurdles record in 1949—at the age of forty. (*H. W. Neale*)

Oldest and youngest internationals

Of full Great Britain (outdoor) internationals the oldest have been Hector Harold Whitlock (b. 16 Dec. 1903) at the 1952 Olympic Games, aged 48 yr 218 days, and Rosemary Payne (*née* Charters) (b. 19 May 1933) in the Great Britain *v.* Sweden match, 22 Sept. 1973, aged 40 yr 126 days. The youngest have been Milton Palmer (b. 9 Sept. 1958) *v.* Finland in 1974, aged 16 yr 16 days, and Janis Walsh (b. 28 Mar. 1960) *v.* Belgium (indoor) at 60 m and 4 × 200 m relay at Cosford on 15 Feb. 1975, 41 days short of her 15th birthday.

Longest career

Duncan McLean (b. Gourock, Strathclyde, 3 Dec. 1884) set a world age—92—record of 100 m in 21.7 sec in August 1977, over 73 years after his best ever sprint of 100 yd in 9.9 sec in South Africa in February 1904. At Athens, Greece, on 10 Oct. 1976, Dimitrion Yordanidis, aged 98, completed a marathon race in 7 hr 33 min.

Ambidextrous shot putt

The best recorded distance is 121 ft 6¾ in by Allan Feuerbach (b. 14 Jan. 1948) (U.S.A.) (left 51 ft 5 in *15,67 m*, right 70 ft 1¾ in *21.38 m*) at Malmo, Sweden in 1974.

Highland Games

The weight and height of cabers (Gaelic *cabar*) vary considerably. Extreme values are 25 ft *7,62 m* and 280 lb *127 kg*. The Braemar caber (19 ft 3 in *5,86 m* and 120 lb *54,4 kg*) in Grampian, Scotland, was untossed from 1891 until 1951 when it was tossed by George Clark. The best authentic mark recorded for throwing the 56 lb. weight for height is 16 ft *4,87 m* over a bar by Geoffrey Lewis Capes (b. 23 Aug. 1949) (G.B.) at Brockwell Park, Lambeth, Greater London, on 31 May 1975.

Standing jumps

The best amateur standing high jump is 5 ft 10¾ in *1,80 m* by Rune Almen (b. 20 Oct. 1952) (Sweden) at Orebro, Sweden on 8 Dec. 1974. Joe Darby (1861–1937), the famous Victorian professional jumper reportedly cleared 6 ft *1,83 m* with

Scots-born Rosemary Payne made 48 international appearances in a career which included the current British discus record. (*Fionnbar Callanan*)

ankles tied at Church Cricket Ground, Dudley, West Midlands on 11 June 1892. Joe Darby long jumped a measured 12 ft 1½ in *3,69 m without* weights at Dudley Castle, on 28 May 1890. Johan Christian Evandt (Norway) achieved 3,65 m *11 ft 11¾ in* as an amateur in Reykjavik, Iceland on 11 Mar. 1962.

Highest one-legged jump
One legged Arnie Boldt, (b. 1958) of Saskatchewan, Canada cleared 1,93 m *6 ft 4 in* indoors at Saskatoon, Canada in 1977.

Fastest three-legged race
The fastest recorded time for a 100 yd three-legged race is 11.0 sec by Harry L. Hillman (1881–1945) and Lawson Robertson (1883–1951) at Brooklyn, New York City, N.Y., U.S.A., on 24 Apr. 1909.

Fastest run backwards
The fastest time recorded for running the 100 yd backwards is 13.3 sec by Paul Wilson (N.Z.) at Hastings, New Zealand on 10 Apr. 1977.

Fastest blind sprinting
In 1976 a blind Polish runner, Kozuck, ran 100 m *109 yd* in 11.5 sec.

Pancake race record
The annual Housewives' Pancake Race at Olney, Buckinghamshire, was first mentioned in 1445. The record for the winding 415 yd *380 m* course (three tosses mandatory) is 61.0 sec, set by Sally Ann Faulkner (b. 1958) on 26 Feb. 1974. The record for the counterpart race (inst. 1949) at Liberal, Kansas, U.S.A.-is 59.1 sec by Kathleen West, (b. 1951) on 10 Feb. 1970.

Longest runs
Mensen Ernst (1799–1846) of Norway is reputed to have run from Istanbul, Turkey, to Calcutta, in West Bengal, India, and back in 59 days in 1836, so averaging an improbable 92.4 miles *151,6 km* per day. Mark Kent, of Toronto, Canada ran 4,057.6 miles *6530 km* across Canada in 113 days from 28 June–18 Oct. 1974.

Longest non-stop run
The greatest non-stop run recorded is 186 miles *300 km* in 31 hr 33 min 38 sec by Max Telford (b. Hawick, Scotland, 2 Feb. 1935) of New Zealand at Wailuku, Hawaii, U.S.A. on 19–20 Mar. 1977.

Six-day races
The greatest distance covered by a man in six days (*i.e.* the 144 permissible hours between Sundays in Victorian times) was 623¾ miles *1 003,828 km* by George Littlewood (England), who required only 141 hr 57 min 30 sec for this feat on 3–8 Dec. 1888 at the old Madison Square Gardens, New York City, U.S.A.

Greatest mileage
The greatest life-time mileage recorded by any runner is 184,202 miles *296 444 km* by Earle Linwood Dilks (b. 1884) of New Castle, Pennsylvania, U.S.A., up to end–1975.

Longest running race
The longest race ever staged was the 1929 Trans-continental Race (3,665 miles *5 898 km*) from New York City, N.Y., to Los Angeles, California, U.S.A. The Finnish-born Johnny Salo (killed 6 Oct. 1931) was the winner in 79 days, from 31 March to 18 June. His elapsed time of 525 hr 57 min 20 sec (averaging 6.97 m.p.h. *11,21 km/h*) left him only 2 min 42 sec ahead of Englishman Peter Gavuzzi.

Oldest race
The oldest continuously held foot race is the "Red Hose Race" held at Carnwath, Lanarkshire, Scotland since 1507. The prize is a pair of hand-knitted knee length red hose.

24 hour record
The greatest distance run in 24 hours is 161 miles 545 yds *259,60 km* by Ron Bentley (b. 10 Nov. 1930) at Walton-on-Thames, Surrey, on 3–4 Nov. 1973. The best distance by a 19th century "wobbler" was 150 miles 395 yd *241 762 km* by Charles Rowell (G.B.) in 22 hr 28 min 25 sec in New York City on 27 Feb. 1882.

Fastest 100 miles
On 24 Oct. 1975 Cavin Woodward (b. 1 Aug. 1947) of Leamington, ran 100 miles *160,9 km* in a record 11 hr 38 min 54 sec at Tipton, West Midlands, England.

Mass relay records
The record for 100 miles *160,9 km* by 100 runners belonging to one club is 7 hr 56 min 55.6 sec by Shore A.C., New Jersey, U.S.A., on 5 June 1977. The feminine record is held by a team from San Francisco Dolphins Southend Running Club, U.S.A. with 10 hr 47 min 9.3 sec on 3 Apr. 1977. The best club time for a 100 × 400 metres relay is 1 hr 34 min 00.6 sec by the Tarnverein Länggasse Bern, Switzerland on 19 Apr. 1975.

A 13-man relay team from the Los Angeles Police Revolver and Athletic Club, California, U.S.A., started from the Capitol steps, Washington, D.C., on 10 May 1974, and ran 3,871.6 miles *6230,7 km* to the Los Angeles City Hall in 20 days 5 hr 20 min.

WORLD RECORDS—MEN

A list of World's Records for the 32 scheduled men's events (excluding the walking records—see under WALKING) passed by the International Amateur Athletic Federation as at 15 Aug. 1977. Fully automatic electric timing is mandatory for the six events up to the 400 metre distance.

* Denotes awaiting ratification.

RUNNING

Event	Min sec	Name and Country	Place	Date
100 metres	9.95	James Ray Hines (U.S.A.)	Mexico City, Mexico	14 Oct. 1968
200 metres	19.83	Tommie C. Smith (U.S.A.)	Mexico City, Mexico	16 Oct. 1968
400 metres	43.86	Lee Edward Evans (U.S.A.)	Mexico City, Mexico	18 Oct. 1968
800 metres	1:43.5	Alberto Juantorena (Cuba)	Montreal, Canada	25 July 1976
1,000 metres	2:13.9	Richard Charles Wohlhuter (U.S.A.)	Oslo, Norway	30 July 1974
1,500 metres	3:32.2	Filbert Bayi (Tanzania)	Christchurch, New Zealand	2 Feb. 1974
1 mile	3:49.4	John George Walker O.B.E. (N.Z.)	Gothenburg, Sweden	12 Aug. 1975
2,000 metres	4:51.4	John George Walker O.B.E. (N.Z.)	Oslo, Norway	30 June 1976
3,000 metres	7:35.2	Brendan Foster M.B.E. (G.B. & N.I.)	Gateshead, Tyne & Wear, England	3 Aug. 1974
5,000 metres	13:12.9*	Theodorus Jacobus Leonardus "Dick' Quax (N.Z.)	Stockholm, Sweden	5 July 1977
10,000 metres	27:30.5*	Samson Kimombwa (Kenya)	Helsinki, Finland	30 June 1977
20,000 metres	57:24.2	Jos Hermens (Netherlands)	Papendal, Netherlands	1 May 1976
25,000 metres	1 hr 14:16.8	Pekka Päivärinta (Finland)	Oulu, Finland	15 May 1975
30,000 metres	1 hr 31:30.4	James Noel Carroll Alder (G.B. & N.I.)	Crystal Palace, London	5 Sept. 1970
1 hour	20 944 m *13 miles 24 yd 2 ft*	Jos Hermens (Netherlands)	Papendal, Netherlands	1 May 1976

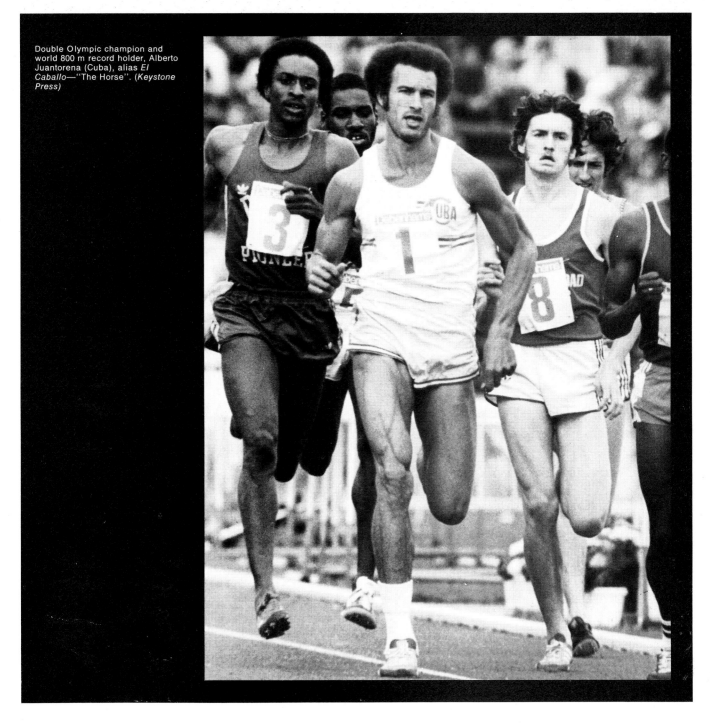

Double Olympic champion and world 800 m record holder, Alberto Juantorena (Cuba), alias *El Caballo*—"The Horse". (*Keystone Press*)

WORLD RECORDS MEN—*continued*

HURDLING

Event	Min sec	Name and Country	Place	Date
110 metres (3′ 6″ *106 cm*)	13.24	Rodney Milburn (U.S.A.)	Munich, West Germany	7 Sept. 1972
400 metres (3′ 0″ *91,4 cm*)	47.45	Edwin Corley Moses (U.S.A.)	Los Angeles, Calif., U.S.A.	11 June 1977
3,000 metres steeplechase	8:08.0	Anders Garderud (Sweden)	Montreal, Canada	28 July 1976

MARATHON

There is no offical marathon record because of the varying severity of courses. The best time recorded over 26 miles 385 yards *42,195 km* (standardised in 1924) is 2 hr 08 min 33.6 sec (av. 12.24 m.p.h. *19,69 km*) by Derek Clayton (b. 17 Nov. 1942, Barrow-in-Furness, England) of Australia, at Antwerp, Belgium, on 30 May 1969. The best time by a British international is 2 hr 09 min 12.2 sec by Ian Thompson (b. 16 Oct. 1949) at Christchurch, New Zealand, 31 Jan. 1974. The fastest time by a female is 2 hr 35 min 15.4 sec (av. 10.13 m.p.h. *16,30 km/h*) by Chantal Langlace (France) at San Sebastian, Spain, 1 May 1977. The fastest by a British woman is 2 hr 50 min 55 sec by Christine Readdy (b. 4 Jan. 1953) at Feltham, Greater London, on 16 Apr. 1976.

RELAYS

Event	Min sec	Team	Place	Date
4 × 100 metres (two turns)	38.19	United States National Team (Larry J. Black, Robert Taylor, Gerald A. Tinker, Eddie James Hart)	Munich, West Germany	10 Sept. 1972
4 × 200 metres	1:21.4†	Arizona State University, U.S.A. (Gary Burl, Anthony Darden, Gerald Burl, Herman Frazier)	Philadelphia, Pa., U.S.A.	30 Apr. 1977

327

WORLD RECORDS MEN—*continued*

Event	Time	Name and Country	Place	Date
4 × 400 metres	2:56.1	United States National Team (Vincent Edward Matthews, Ronald J. Freeman, George Lawrence James, Lee Edward Evans)	Mexico City, Mexico	20 Oct. 1968
4 × 800 metres	7:08.6	West German Team (Manfred Kinder, Walter Adams, Dieter Bogatzki, Franz-Josef Kemper)	Wiesbaden, West Germany	13 Aug. 1966
4 × 1,500 metres	14:49.0††	French Team (Gerard Vervoort, Claude Nicolas, Michel Jazy, Jean Wadoux)	St. Maur des Fosses, France	25 June 1965

† *The time of 1:20.7 (4 × 220 yd) achieved by the University of Southern California (Edesel Garrison, Lee Brown, William Deckard, Donald O'Riley Quarrie) at Fresno, California, U.S.A. on 13 May 1972 was not ratified as Quarrie is a Jamaican national.*

†† *A New Zealand team of Anthony Polhill, John G. Walker, Rodney P. Dixon and Theodorus J. L. Quax recorded a time of 14:40.4 at Oslo, Norway on 22 Aug. 1973 in a special record attempt. This was not ratified by the I.A.A.F.*

FIELD EVENTS

Event	ft	in	m	Name and Country	Place	Date
High Jump	7	7¾	2,33*	Vladimir Ilych Yashchenko (U.S.S.R.)	Richmond, Virginia, U.S.A.	3 July 1977
Pole Vault	18	8¼	5,70	David Luther Roberts (U.S.A.)	Eugene, Oregon, U.S.A.	22 June 1976
Long Jump	29	2½	8,90	Robert Beamon (U.S.A.)	Mexico City, Mexico	18 Oct. 1968
Triple Jump	58	8½	17,89	João Carlos de Oliveira (Brazil)	Mexico City, Mexico	15 Oct. 1975
Shot Putt	72	2¼	22,00	Aleksandr Baryshnikov (U.S.S.R.)	Paris, France	10 July 1976
	75	0	22,86†	Brian Ray Oldfield (U.S.A.)	El Paso, Texas, U.S.A.	10 May 1975
Discus Throw	232	6	70,86	Maurice Mac Wilkins (U.S.A.)	San José, California, U.S.A.	1 May 1976
Hammer Throw	260	2	79,30	Walter Schmidt (West Germany)	Frankfurt, West Germany	14 Aug. 1975
Javelin Throw	310	4	94,58	Miklós Németh (Hungary)	Montreal, Canada	26 July 1976

† *Note: One professional performance is superior to the I.A.A.F. mark, but the same highly rigorous rules as to measuring and weighing were not necessarily applied.*

DECATHLON

8,618 points

William Bruce Jenner (U.S.A.)
(1st day: 100 m 10.94 sec, Long Jump 7,22 m *23′ 8¼″*,
Shot Putt 15,35 m *50′4½″*, High Jump 2,03 m *6′ 8″*,
400 m 47.51 sec)

Montreal, Canada   29–30 July 1976
(2nd day: 110 m hurdles 14.84 sec,
Discus 50,04 m *164′ 2″*, Pole Vault 4,80 m *15′ 9″*,
Javelin 68,52 m *224′ 10″*, 1,500 m 4:12.61 sec)

WORLD RECORDS—WOMEN

A list of World's Records for the 19 scheduled women's events passed by the International Amateur Athletic Federation as at 15 Aug. 1977. The same stipulation about electrically timed events applies in the six events up to 400 metres as in the men's list. * Denotes awaiting ratification.

RUNNING

Event	Min sec	Name and Country	Place	Date
100 metres	10.88*	Marlies Oelsner (East Germany)	Dresden, East Germany	1 July 1977
200 metres	22.21	Irena Szewinska (*née* Kirszenstein) (Poland)	Potsdam, East Germany	13 June 1974
400 metres	49.29	Irena Szewinska (*née* Kirszenstein) (Poland)	Montreal, Canada	29 July 1976
800 metres	1:54.9	Tatyana Kazankina (U.S.S.R.)	Montreal, Canada	26 July 1976
1,500 metres	3:56.0	Tatyana Kazankina (U.S.S.R.)	Podolsk, U.S.S.R.	28 June 1976
1 mile	4:23.8*	Natalia Maracescu (*née* Andrei) (Romania)	Bucharest, Romania	22 May 1977
3,000 metres	8:27.1	Ludmila Bragina (U.S.S.R.)	College Park, Md., U.S.A.	7 Aug. 1976

HURDLING

Event	Min sec	Name and Country	Place	Date
100 metres (2′ 9″ 84 cm)	12.59	Annelie Ehrhardt (East Germany)	Munich, West Germany	8 Sept. 1972
400 metres (2′ 6″ 76 cm)	55.63*	Karin Rossley (East Germany)	Helsinki, Finland	13 Aug. 1977

RELAYS

Event	Min sec	Team	Place	Date
4 × 100 metres	42.50	East German Team (Marlies Oelsner, Renate Stecher, Carla Bodendorf, Martina Blos)	Karl Marx Stadt, East Germany	29 May 1976
4 × 200 metres	1:32.4	East German Team (Gudrun Berend, Marlies Oelsner, Bärbel Eckert, Renate Stecher)	Jena, East Germany	13 Aug. 1976
4 × 400 metres	3:19.2	East German National Team (Doris Maletzki, Brigitte Röhde, Ellen Streidt (*née* Stropahl), Christina Brehmer)	Montreal, Canada	31 July 1976
4 × 800 metres	7:52.3	U.S.S.R. National Team (Tatyana Providokhina, Valentina Gerasimova, Svetlana Styrkina, Tatyana Kazankina)	Podolsk, U.S.S.R.	16 Aug. 1976

FIELD EVENTS

Event	ft	in	m	Name and Country	Place	Date
High Jump	6	5½	1,97	Rosemarie Ackermann (*née* Witschas) (East Germany)	Helsinki, Finland	14 Aug. 1977
Long Jump	22	11¼	6,99	Sigrun Siegl (*née* Thon) (East Germany)	Dresden, East Germany	19 May 1976
Shot Putt	72	1¾†	21,99	Helena Fibingerova (Czechoslovakia)	Opava, Cz.	25 Sept. 1976
Discus Throw	231	3	70,50	Faina Melnik (U.S.S.R.)	Sochi, U.S.S.R.	24 Apr. 1976
Javelin Throw	226	9	69,12	Ruth Fuchs (*née* Gamm) (East Germany)	East Berlin, East Germany	10 July 1976

† *Helena Fibingerova set an indoor record of 22,50 m 73 ft 10 in at Jablonec, Cz. on 19 Feb. 1977.*

PENTATHLON (with 200 m)

4,932 points (1971 Scoring Tables)

Burglinde Pollak (East Germany)
(100 m hurdles 13.21 sec; Shot 15,85 m *52′ 0″*;
High Jump 1,78 m *5′ 10″*; Long Jump 6,47 m *21′ 2½″*;
200 m 23.35 sec)

Bonn, West Germany   22 Sept. 1973

right: Using the controversial rotational style, Alexander Baryshnikov (U.S.S.R.) set a world shot putt record and gained an Olympic bronze medal. (*Popperfoto*)

below: The world's greatest female hurdler, Annelie Ehrhardt, won Olympic and European championship gold medals. (*E. D. Lacey*)

PENTATHLON (with 800 m)
4,823 points (1971 Scoring Tables)

Eva Wilms (West Germany)
(100 m hurdles 13.93 sec; Shot 20,95 m *68 ft 8¾ in*; High Jump 1,74 m *5 ft 8½ in*; Long Jump 6,29 m *20 ft 7¾ in*; 800 m 2 min 19.66 sec)

Bernhausen, West Germany   19 June 1977

UNITED KINGDOM (NATIONAL) RECORDS—MEN (as at 15 Aug. 1977)
* Denotes awaiting ratification.

RUNNING

Event	Min sec	Name	Place	Date
100 metres	10.29	Peter Frank Radford	Paris, France	13 Sept. 1968
200 metres (turn)	20.66	Richard Swift Steane	Mexico City, Mexico	15 Oct. 1968
	20.66	David Andrew Jenkins	London (Crystal Palace)	27 Aug. 1973
400 metres	44.93	David Andrew Jenkins	Eugene, Oregon, U.S.A.	21 June 1975
800 metres	1:45.1	Andrew William Carter	London (Crystal Palace)	14 July 1973
1,000 metres	2:18.2	John Peter Boulter	London (Crystal Palace)	6 Sept. 1969
1,500 miles	3:36.8	Michael Kearns	Stockholm, Sweden	26 July 1977
1 mile	3:54.7	Steve Ovett	London (Crystal Palace)	26 June 1977
2,000 metres	5:02.9	Brendan Foster, M.B.E.	London (Crystal Palace)	4 July 1975
3,000 metres	7:35.2	Brendan Foster, M.B.E.	Gateshead, Tyne and Wear	3 Aug. 1974

329

UNITED KINGDOM RECORDS MEN—*continued*

5,000 metres	13:14.6	Brendan Foster, M.B.E.	Christchurch, New Zealand	29 Jan. 1974
10,000 metres	27:30.8	David Colin Bedford	London (Crystal Palace)	13 July 1973
20,000 metres	58:39.0	Ronald Hill	Leicester	9 Nov. 1968
25,000 metres	1hr 15:22.6	Ronald Hill	Bolton, Lancashire	1 July 1965
30,000 metres	1hr 31:30.4	James Noel Carroll Alder	London (Crystal Palace)	25 Sept. 1970
1 hour	12 miles 1,268 yds *20 472 m*	Ronald Hill	Leicester	9 Nov. 1968

HURDLING

Event	Min sec	Name	Place	Date
110 metres	13.69	Berwyn Price	Moscow, U.S.S.R.	18 Aug. 1973
200 metres (turn)	23.0	Alan Peter Pascoe M.B.E.	Loughborough, Leicester	5 June 1969
400 metres	48.12	David Peter Hemery, M.B.E.	Mexico City, Mexico	15 Oct. 1968
3,000 metres Steeplechase	8:19.0	Dennis Malcolm Coates	Montreal, Canada	25 July 1976

FIELD EVENTS

Event	ft	in	m	Name	Place	Date
High Jump	7	0½	2,15†	Brian Burgess	Edinburgh, Scotland	26 June 1976
Pole Vault	17	5½	5,32*	Brian Roger Leslie Hooper	Edinburgh, Scotland	22 Aug. 1976
Long Jump	27	0	8,23	Lynn Davies, M.B.E.	Bern, Switzerland	30 June 1966
Triple Jump	54	2½	16,52	Aston Llewellyn Moore	London (Crystal Palace)	11 June 1976
Shot Putt	70	8½	21,55	Geoffrey Lewis Capes	Gateshead, Tyne and Wear	28 May 1976
Discus Throw	213	1	64,94	William Raymond Tancred	Loughborough, Leicester	21 July 1974
Hammer Throw	246	0	74,98	Christopher Francis Black	Edinburgh, Scotland	6 Aug. 1976
Javelin Throw	278	7	84,92	Charles Philip Clover	Christchurch, New Zealand	2 Feb. 1974

† Michael Butterfield achieved 7 ft 1 in *2,16 m* indoors at Cosford, West Midlands on 23 Jan. 1976.
* Verification is awaited for 17 ft 8½ in *5.40 m* by Brian Hooper at Gateshead on 30 July 1977.

DECATHLON (1962 Scoring Table)

8,190 (points)	Francis Morgan (Daley) Thompson	Madrid, Spain	25–26 June 1977
	(1st day: 100 m 10.5 sec	(2nd day: 110 m Hurdles 15.1 sec,	
	Long Jump 24′ 11¼″ *7,60 m*	Discus 129′ 11″ *39,60 m*	
	Shot Putt 45′ 5¼″ *13,85 m*	Pole Vault 15′ 9″ *4,80 m*	
	High Jump 6′ 9½″ *2,07 m*	Javelin 165′ 1″ *50,32 m,*	
	400 m 47.4 sec)	1,500 m 4:29.0 sec)	

RELAYS

Event		Name	Place	Date
4 × 100 metres	39.33	United Kingdom National Team (Joseph William Speake, Ronald Jones, Ralph Banthorpe, Barrie Harrison Kelly)	Mexico City, Mexico	19 Oct. 1968
4 × 200 metres	1:24.1	Great Britain (Brian William Green, Roger Walters, Ralph Banthorpe, Martin Edward Reynolds)	Paris, France	2 Oct. 1971
4 × 400 metres	3:00.5	United Kingdom National Team (Martin Edward Reynolds, Alan Peter Pascoe, M.B.E., David Peter Hemery, M.B.E., David Andrew Jenkins)	Munich, West Germany	10 Sept. 1972
4 × 800 metres	7:17.4	United Kingdom National Team (Martin Bilham, David Cropper, Michael John Maclean, Peter Miles Browne)	London (Crystal Palace)	5 Sept. 1970
4 × 1,500 metres	15:04.6	United Kingdom Team (James McGuinness, Erwin Swag Hartel, Adrian Peter Weatherhead, Glen Arthur Barry Grant)	Athens, Greece	5 May 1976

UNITED KINGDOM (NATIONAL) RECORDS—WOMEN (as at 15 Aug. 1977)
* Denotes awaiting ratification.

RUNNING

Event	Min sec	Name	Place	Date
100 metres	11.16	Andrea Joan Caron Lynch	London (Crystal Palace)	11 June 1975
200 metres	22.81	Sonia May Lannaman	Split, Jugoslavia	2 May 1976
400 metres	51.28	Donna-Marie Louise Murray (now Hartley)	Sofia, Bulgaria	12 July 1975
800 metres	2:00.2	Rosemary Olivia Stirling (now Wright)	Munich, West Germany	3 Sept. 1972
1 mile	4:36.1	Mary Stewart	London (Crystal Palace)	18 May 1977
1,500 metres	4:04.8	Sheila Janet Carey (*née* Taylor)	Munich, West Germany	9 Sept. 1972
3,000 metres	8:55.6	Joyce Esther Smith (*née* Byatt)	London (Crystal Palace)	19 July 1974

HURDLING

Event	sec	Name	Place	Date
100 metres	13.11	Sharon Colyear	Bydgoszcz, Poland	22 June 1976
200 metres	26.7	Sharon Colyear	London (Crystal Palace)	16 July 1971
400 metres	57.84	Christine Anne Warden (*née* Howell)	London (Crystal Palace)	21 Aug. 1974

FIELD EVENTS

Event	ft	in	n	Name	Place	Date
High Jump	6	1½	1,87	Barbara Jean Inkpen (now Lawton)	London (Crystal Palace)	22 Sept. 1973
Long Jump	22	2¼	6,76	Mary Denise Rand M.B.E. (now Toomey, *née* Bignal)	Tokyo, Japan	14 Oct. 1964
Shot Putt	53	6¼	16,31†	Mary Elizabeth Peters M.B.E.	Belfast, Northern Ireland	1 June 1966
Discus Throw	190	4	58,02	Christine Rosemary Payne (*née* Charters)	Birmingham	3 June 1972
Javelin Throw	220	6	67,20*	Teresa Ione Sanderson	Dublin, Rep. of Ireland	17 July 1977

† Mary Peters achieved 53 ft 9¾ in *16,40 m* indoors at Bucharest, Romania on 28 Feb. 1970.

PENTATHLON (with 200 m)	Name	Place	Date
4,801 points (1971 Tables)	Mary Elizabeth Peters, M.B.E.	Munich, West Germany	2–3 Sept. 1972

PENTATHLON (with 800 m)
4,385 points (1971 Tables)   Susan Jane Longden (*née* Wright)   Sittard, Netherlands   31 July 1977

RELAYS

Event	Min sec	Name	Place	Date
4 × 100 metres	43.44	United Kingdom Team (Wendy Clarke, Denise Irene Ramsden, Sharon Colyear, Helen Golden)	Montreal, Canada	30 July 1976
4 × 200 metres	1:33.7	United Kingdom National Team (Verona Marolin Elder [*née* Bernard], Sharon Colyear, Donna-Marie Louise Hartley [*née* Murray], Sonia May Lannaman)	Bourges, France	19 June 1977
4 × 400 metres	3:26.6	United Kingdom National Team (Jannette Veronica Roscoe [*née* Champion], Gladys Taylor [now McCormack], Verona Marolin Elder [*née* Bernard], Donna-Marie Louise Murray [now Hartley])	Nice, France	17 Aug. 1975
4 × 800 metres	8:23.8	Great Britain (Joan Florence Allison, Sheila Janet Carey [*née* Taylor], Patricia Barbara Lowe [now Cropper], Rosemary Olivia Stirling [now Wright])	Paris, France	2 Oct. 1971

TRAMPOLINING

Origins

Trampolines were used in show business at least as early as "The Walloons" of the period 1910–12. The sport of trampolining (from the Spanish word *trampolin*, a springboard) dates from 1936, when the prototype "T" model trampoline was developed by George Nissen (U.S.A.).

Most titles

The only men to win a world title (instituted 1964) twice have been Dave Jacobs (U.S.A.) the 1967–68 champion, Wayne Miller (b. 1946) (U.S.A.), in 1966 and 1970 and Richard Tison (France) in 1974 and 1976. Judy Wills (b. 1948) (U.S.A.) won the first five women's titles (1964–68). Two European titles (1969 and 1971) have been won by Paul Luxon (b. 1952) (G.B.), the 1972 world champion. A record seven United Kingdom titles have been won by Wendy Wright (1969–70, 1972–75, 1977). The most by a man have been four by David Curtis (1966–67, 1969, 1975).

Marathons

The longest trampoline bouncing marathon is one of 1,248 hours (52 days) set by a team of six in Phoenix, Arizona, U.S.A. on 24 June to 15 Aug. 1974. The solo record is 179 hours by Geoffrey Morton, of Broken Hill, N.S.W., Australia, on 7–14 Mar. 1977.

TROTTING AND PACING

Origins

The trotting gait (the simultaneous use of the diagonally opposite legs) was first recorded in England in *c.* 1750. The sulky first appeared in harness-racing in 1829. Pacers thrust out their fore and hind legs simultaneously on one side.

Highest price

The highest price paid for a trotter is $3,000,000 for *Nevele Pride* by the Stoner Creek Stud of Lexington, Kentucky from Louis Resnick and Nevele Acres in the autumn of 1969. The highest price ever paid for a pacer is $3,600,000 for *Nero* in March 1976.

Greatest winnings

The greatest amount won by a trotting horse is $1,660,627 by *Une de Mai* up to retirement in 1973. The record for a pacing horse is $1,201,470 by *Albatross* which was retired to stud in December 1972.

Most successful driver

The most successful sulky driver in North American harness racing history has been Herve Filion (b. 1 Feb. 1940) of Quebec, Canada who reached a record 5,845 wins by the end of the 1976 season. In 1974 he set year records of 637 wins and earnings of $3,474,315 by horses he drove. He won his eighth North American championship in 1976.

Troika record

The U.S.S.R troika record for the standard 1 600 m (four laps of 400 m) is 1 min 58.0 sec by a bay trio from Nolinsk, trained by Vladimir Kuznetsov in Moscow in February 1974.

TUG OF WAR

Origins

Tug of War is a competitive sport in 14 countries. The term was first recorded in 1876 in England. It became an Olympic event in 1900 in Paris and was dropped after 1920. In 1958 a separate governing body, the Tug-of-War Association, was formed to administer Britain's 600 clubs.

Most Olympic medals

The only three men to win two gold medals (1908 and 1920) (all also won a silver medal in 1912) were James Shepherd, Frederick H. Humphreys, and Edwin A. Mills (all G.B.).

Most titles

The Wood Treatment team (formerly the Bosley Farmers) of Cheshire, have represented England since 1964, winning two World and ten European Championships at 720 kg *1,587 lb*. They have also won 15 consecutive A.A.A. Championships since 1959, Hilary Brown, Mike Eardley, George Hicton, Peter Hirst and Norman Hyde have been in every team. Trevor Thomas, of British Airways Corporation Club is the only holder of three winners medals in the European Open club championships.

Longest pulls

The longest recorded pull (prior to the introduction of A.A.A. rules) is one of 2 hrs 41 min between "H" Company and "E" Company of the 2nd Battalion of the Sherwood Foresters (Derbyshire Regiment) at Jubbulpore, India, on 12 Aug. 1889. "E" Company won. The longest recorded pull under A.A.A. Rules (in which lying on the ground or entrenching the feet is not permitted) is one of 8 min 18.2 sec for the first pull between the R.A.S.C. (Feltham) and the Royal Marines

Records against time	Trotting			Pacing		
World (mile *1 609,34 m* track)	1:54.8	Nevele Pride (driver Stanley Dancer) (U.S.) Indianapolis, Indiana	31 Aug. 1969	1:52.0	Steady Star (driver Joe O'Brien) (U.S.) Lexington, Kentucky	1 Oct. 1971
World race record (mile)	1:55.6	Noble Victory (U.S.A.) at Du Quoin, Illinois	31 Aug. 1966	1:53.2	Warm Breeze (driver Dick Farrington) (U.S.) at Sacramento, California	— June 1977

331

(Portsmouth Division) at the Royal Tournament of June 1938.

Largest pull

On 3 Nov. 1976, 1,015 students of Ajax H.S., Ontario, Canada, set a record for the most people in a tug of war match. The pull was terminated when the rope snapped.

VOLLEYBALL

Origins

The game was invented as *Minnonette* in 1895 by William G. Morgan at the Y.M.C.A. gymnasium at Holyoke, Massachusetts, U.S.A. The International Volleyball Association was formed in Paris in April 1947. The Amateur (now English) Volleyball Association of Great Britain was formed in May 1955.

Most world titles

World Championships were instituted in 1949. The U.S.S.R. has won five men's titles (1949, 1952, 1960, 1962 and 1968). The U.S.S.R. won the women's championship in 1952, 1956, 1960, 1968, 1970, and 1973.

Highest attendance

The record crowd is 60,000 for the 1952 world title matches in Moscow, U.S.S.R.

Most Olympic medals

The sport was introduced to the Olympic Games for both men and women in 1964. The only player to win four medals is Inna Ryskal (U.S.S.R.) (b. 15 June 1944), who won silver medals in 1964 and 1976 and golds in 1968, 1972 and 1976. The record for men is held by Yuriy Poyarkov (U.S.S.R.) (b. 10 Feb. 1937) who won gold medals in 1964 and 1968 and a bronze in 1972.

One-man team

Bob L. Schaffer, 50 of Suffern, New York specializes in taking on six men teams lone-handed. His latest reported lifetime score is 1,865 wins since 16 Aug. 1963 and three losses.

Marathon

The continuous volleyball marathon is one of 405 hr by four teams from Ginninderra H.S., A.C.T., Australia on 30 Sept.–17 Oct. 1976 (category now discontinued). The record by two teams is 40 hr by the Faith Christian H.S., Collingwood, New Jersey, U.S.A. on 29–30 Apr. 1977.

WALKING

Most Olympic medals

Walking races have been included in the Olympic events since 1906. The 20 kilometre event in Montreal in July 1976 was the 25th Olympic race. The only walker to win three gold medals has been Ugo Frigerio (Italy) (1901–68) with the 3,000 m and 10,000 m in 1920 and 1924. He also holds the record of most medals with four (having additionally won the bronze medal in the 50,000 m in 1932) which total is shared with Vladimir Golubnichiy (U.S.S.R.) (b. 2 June 1936), who won gold medals for the 20,000 m in 1960 and 1968, the silver in 1972 and the bronze in 1964.

The best British performance has been two gold medals by George E. Larner (1875–1949) for the 3,500 m and the 10 miles in 1908, but Ernest J. Webb (1872–1937) won three medals being twice runner up to Larner and finishing second in the 10,000 m in 1912.

Most titles

Four time Olympian, Ronald Owen Laird (b. 31 May 1938) of the New York A.C., U.S.A., won a total of 65 National titles from 1958 to 1976, plus four Canadian championships. The greatest number of National titles won by a British walker is 27 by Vincent Paul Nihill M.B.E. (b. 5 Sept. 1939) from 1963 to 1975.

Road walking

The world's best performances for road walking are: 20,000 m 1 hr 23 min 39 sec by Daniel Bautista (b. 4 Aug. 1952) (Mexico) at Warsaw, Poland, on 29 May 1976; and 50,000 m 3 hrs 52 min 44.6 sec by Bernd Kannenberg (West Germany) (b. 20 Aug. 1942) at Bremen, W. Germany on 27 May 1972.

Longest annual race

The Strasbourg–Paris event (inst. 1926 in the reverse direction) over 504–554 km *313–344 miles* is the world's longest annual race walk. The fastest performance is by Robert Rinchard (Belgium) (b. 29 May 1931) who walked 523 km *325 miles* in the 1974 race in 63 hrs 29 min (deducting 4 hrs compulsory stops). This represents an average speed of 8.24 km/h *5.12 m.p.h.* Gilbert Roger (France) (b. 1914) won six times (1949, 1953–54, 1956, 1958). The only Briton to have completed the course is Colin Young (b. 20 Jan. 1935) of Dagenham, Barking, Greater London in 1971 averaging 7.46 km/h *4.63 m.p.h.*

Greatest mileage

Dimitru Dan (b. 13 July 1890 *fl* 1976) of Romania was the only man of 200 entrants to succeed in a contest in walking 100,000 km *62,137 miles* organised by the Touring Club de France on 1 Apr. 1910. He covered 96,000 km *59,651 miles* up to 24 Mar. 1916 so averaging 43,85 km *27.24 miles* a day.

Longest walks

The first person recorded to have "walked round the world" is David Kunst, who started with his brother John from Waseca, Minnesota on 10 June 1970. John was killed by Afghani bandits in 1972. David arrived home after walking 14,500 miles *23 335 km* on 5 Oct. 1974. Georgyi Bushuyev (b. 1924) walked 6,800 miles *10 940 km* from Riga, Latvia to Vladivostok, U.S.S.R., in 238 days in 1973–74. The Trans-Canada (Halifax to Vancouver) record walk of 3,764 miles *6 057 km* is 96 days by Clyde McRae, 23, from 1 May to 4 Aug. 1973. John Lees, (b. 23 Feb. 1945) of Brighton, East Sussex, England between 11 Apr. and 3 June 1972, walked 2,876 miles *4 628 km* across the U.S.A. from City Hall, Los Angeles to City Hall, New York City in 53 days 12 hr 15 min (average 53.746 miles *86,495 km* a day). The longest continuous walk in Britain is claimed to be one of 2,043 miles *3 288 km*, linking the ten National Parks, by John N. Merrill, from 27 May to 18 Aug. 1976.

OFFICIAL WORLD RECORDS (Track Walking)
(As recognised by the International Amateur Athletic Federation)

Distance	Time hr min sec	Name and Country	Place	Date
20,000 metres	1 23 31.9	Daniel Bautista (Mexico)	Fana, Norway	14 May 1977
30,000 metres	2 12 58	Bernd Kannenberg (West Germany)	Kassel, West Germany	11 May 1974
20 miles	2 27 38	Vittorio Visini (Italy)	Vicenza, Italy	1 Nov. 1975
30 miles	3 48 23.4	Bernd Kannenberg (West Germany)	Milan, Italy	16 Nov. 1975
50,000 metres	3 56 38.2	Enrique Vera (Mexico)	Fana, Norway	16 May 1977
2 hours	27 153 m *16 miles 1,534 yd*	Bernd Kannenberg (West Germany)	Kassel, West Germany	11 May 1974

Olympic champion Daniel Bautista, the star of Mexico's record breaking walkers. (*Colorsport*)

WATER POLO

Origins

Water Polo was developed in England as "Water Soccer" in 1869 and first included in the Olympic Games in Paris in 1900.

Most Olympic titles

Hungary has won the Olympic tournament most often with six wins in 1932, 1936, 1952, 1956, 1964 and 1976. Great Britain won in 1900, 1908, 1912 and 1920.

Five players share the record of three gold medals: Britons, George Wilkinson (1879–1946) in 1900, 1908, 1912; Paulo (Paul) Radmilovic (1886–1968), and Charles Sidney Smith (1879–1951) in 1908, 1912, 1920; and Hungarians Deszo Gyarmati (b. 23 Oct. 1927) and György Kárpáti (b. 23 June 1935) in 1952, 1956, 1964. Gyarmati's wife and daughter won gold and silver medals respectively in swimming. Paul Radmilovic also won a gold medal for the 4×200 m freestyle relay in 1908.

A.S.A. championships

The club with the greatest number of Amateur Swimming Association titles is Plaistow United Swimming Club of Greater London, with eleven from 1928 to 1954. The National League (formed 1963) has been won a record eight times by London Polytechnic.

Most goals

The greatest number of goals scored by an individual in a home international is eleven by Terry Charles Miller (b. 2 Mar. 1932) (Plaistow United), when England defeated Wales 13–3 at Newport, Gwent, in 1951.

Most international appearances

The greatest number of internationals is 244 by Ozren Bonacic (b. 5 Jan. 1942) (Yugoslavia) from 1964 to Sept. 1975. The British record is 109 by Martyn Thomas, of Cheltenham, 1964–1977.

Marathon

The longest match on record is one of 63 hr between two teams of 15 from Salinas H.S. Swim Club, California, U.S.A., on 28–30 Jan. 1977. Breaks and substitutions were in accordance with the rules of the relevant governing body.

WATER SKIING

A specialist volume entitled The Guinness Guide to Water Skiing *by David Nations, O.B.E. and Kevin Desmond has been published by Guinness Superlatives Ltd. (price £8.50).*

Origins

The origins of water skiing lie in walking on planks and aquaplaning. A 19th century treatise on sorcerers refers to Eliseo of Tarentum who, in the 14th century, "walks and dances" on the water. The first report of aquaplaning was on America's Pacific coast in the early 1900's. At Scarborough, Yorks, England, on 15 July 1914, a single plankgliding contest was won by H. Storry.

The present day sport of water skiing was pioneered by Ralph W. Samuelson (b. 1904) on Lake Pepin, Minnesota, U.S.A., on two curved pine boards in the summer of 1922, though claims have been made for the birth of the sport on Lake Annecy (Haute Savoie), France at about the same time. The first world organisation, the Union Internationale de Ski Nautique, was formed in Geneva on 27 July 1946. The British Water Ski Federation was founded in London in 1954.

Most titles

World Overall championships (instituted 1949) have been won twice by Alfredo Mendoza (U.S.A.) in 1953 and 1955, Mike Suyderhoud (U.S.A.) in 1967 and 1969 and George Athans (Canada) in 1971 and 1973, and three times by Willa McGuire (*née* Worthington) of the U.S.A. in 1949–50 and 1955 and Elizabeth (Liz) Allan-Shetter (U.S.A.) in 1965, 1969 and 1975. Liz Allan-Shetter has won a record eight individual championship events. The most British Overall titles (instituted 1953) ever won by a man is four by Lance Callingham in 1959–60 and 1962–63, and Paul Seaton (b. 3 July 1951) in

"End to end"

The record for walking from John o'Groats to Land's End (route varies between 876 and 891 miles *1 409 and 1 433 km*) is 10 days 18 hrs 20 min achieved by Johnnie Savile (b. 1921) and John Ryder, both of Battersea, Wandsworth, Greater London, on 8–18 Aug. 1973. The feminine record is 17 days 7 hours by Miss Wendy Lewis ending on 15 Mar. 1960. End to end and back has twice been achieved. Frederick E. Westcott, aged 31, finished on 18 Dec. 1966 and David Tremayne (Australia), aged 27, finishing on 28 May 1971. The Irish "End to End" record over the 376 miles *605 km* from Mizen Head, Cork to Malin Head, Donegal is 7 days 22 hr 10 min, set by Tom Casey (b. 1930) on 1–9 July 1972.

London to Brighton

The record time for the London to Brighton walk is 7 hr 35 min 12 sec by Donald James Thompson, M.B.E. (b. 20 Jan. 1933) on 14 Sept. 1957. The record time for London to Brighton and back is 18 hr 5 min 51 sec by William Frederick Baker (b. 5 Apr. 1889) of Queen's Park Harriers, London, on 18–19 June 1926.

Longest non-stop walk

Thomas Patrick Benson (b. 1933) (G.B.) walked 314.33 miles *505,86 km* at Moor Park, Preston, Lancs., England in 123 hr 28 min on 11–16 Apr. 1977. He did not permit himself any stops for resting and was moving 99.41 % of the time.

24 hours

The best performance for distance walked in 24 hours is 142 miles 448 yd *228,93 km* by Jesse Castañeda (U.S.A.) at the New Mexico State Fair, Albuquerque, N.M., U.S.A., on 18–19 Sept. 1976. The best by a woman is 72 miles *115,8 km* by Dorothy Whitfield (b. 1912), of Bristol, England, on 11–12 Oct. 1975.

Walking backwards

The greatest ever exponent of reverse pedestrianism has been Plennie L. Wingo (b. 24 Jan. 1895) then of Abilene, Texas, who completed his 8,000 mile *12,875 km* trans-continental walk from Santa Monica, California to Istanbul, Turkey, from 15 Apr. 1931 to 24 Oct. 1932. He celebrated the walk's 45th anniversary by covering the 452 miles *727 km* from Santa Monica to San Francisco, backwards, in 85 days, aged 81 years. The longest distance reported for walking backwards in 24 hours is 80 miles *128,74 km* by Lindsay R. Dodd from Leeds, West Yorkshire to Kendal, Cumbria, 9–10 Apr. 1976.

1971–73 and 1975; the most by a woman is six by Karen Jane Morse (b. 1956) in 1971–76.

Jumping

The first recorded jump on water skis was made by Ralph Samuelson off a greased ramp, on Lake Pepin in 1925. The longest jump ever recorded is one of 54,86 m *180 ft* by Wayne Grimditch, (U.S.A.) at Callaway Gardens, Georgia, U.S.A. on 13 July 1975. The women's record is 39.02 m *128 ft* by Linda Giddens (U.S.A.) in Miami, Florida, U.S.A. in Aug. 1976.

The British record is 54,76 m *179 ft 8 in* by Mike Hazelwood at Nancy, France in Sept. 1976. The women's record is 35,75 m *117 ft 3 in* by Karen Morse at Thorpe Water Park, Surrey on 6 Sept. 1975.

Slalom and Tricks

The world record for slalom is 4 buoys on a 11,25 m *37 ft* line by Kris LaPoint (U.S.A.) at Horton Lake, U.S.A., on 15 July 1975, and Bob LaPoint (U.S.A.), his brother, at Miami in Aug. 1976. The record for women is 2 buoys on a 12 m *39 ft* line by Cindy Hutcherson Todd (U.S.A.) at Tomahawk, Wisconsin, in 1975. A Tricks score of 6,560 points by Russ Stifler (U.S.A.) at Lake David, Florida, on 15 Aug. 1976 is awaiting ratification. The women's record of 5,460 points by Maria Victoria Carrasco (Venezuela), was set at Thorpe Water Park, Surrey, on 6 Sept. 1975. The British record for tricks is 6,650 points by Mike Hazelwood at Jyväskylä, Finland on 6 Aug. 1977.

Highest speed

The water skiing speed record is 202,27 km/h *125.69 m.p.h.* by Danny Churchill at the Oakland Marine Stadium, California, U.S.A., in 1971. Sally Younger (b. 1953), set a feminine record of 169,20 km/h *105.14 m.p.h.* at Perris, California on 17 June 1970. The fastest recorded speed by a British skier over a measured kilometre is 131,217 km/h *81.535 m.p.h.* (average) on Lake Windermere, Cumbria on 18 Oct. 1973 by Billy Rixon. The fastest by a British woman is 107,172 km/h *66.594 m.p.h.* by Elizabeth Hobbs on Windermere, 12 Oct. 1976.

Water-ski racing

The record for the 58 mile *93 km* Cross Channel race from Greatstone-on-Sea, near New Romney, England to Cap Gris-Nez, France and back is 1 hr 37 min 30 sec by Robin Manwaring of Kent on 13 Aug. 1972.

Barefoot

The first person to water ski barefoot is reported to be Dick Pope Jr. at Lake Eloise, Florida, on 6 Mar. 1947. The barefoot duration record is 2 hr 37 min by Paul McManus (Australia). The backward barefoot record is 39 min by McManus. The British duration record is 67 min 5 sec by John Doherty on 1 October 1974. A barefoot jump of 15,40 m *50 ft 6 in* was made by John Guthrie (N.Z.) in 1976. The

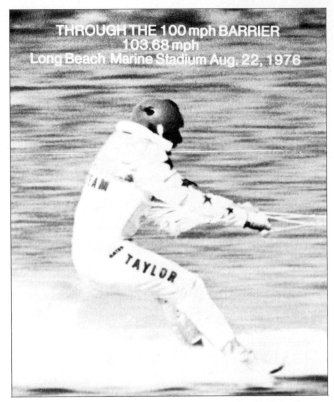

John Taylor, breaking water skiing records—without skis. (*Jack Cool*)

British barefoot jump record is 15,35 m *50 ft 4½ in* by William Stevens at Tattershall, Lincolnshire on 18 June 1977. The fastest barefoot speed, achieved wearing minimal protective foot covering, is 166,85 km/h *103.68 m.p.h.* by John Taylor (U.S.A.) at Long Beach, California, on 22 Aug. 1976. The fastest by a woman is 98 km/h *61 m.p.h.* by Haidee Jones (now Leunce) (Australia). Dennis Akins (b. 1931) (G.B.) reached 98,08 km/h *60.95 m.p.h.* at Holme Pierrepoint, Nottinghamshire on 28 Nov. 1975.

WEIGHTLIFTING

Origins

Amateur weightlifting is of comparatively modern origin and the first world championship was staged at the Cafe Monico, Piccadilly, City of Westminster, Greater London, on 28 Mar. 1891. Prior to that time, weightlifting consisted of professional exhibitions in which some of the advertised poundages were open to doubt. The first to raise 400 lb. *181 kg* was Charles Rigoulot (1903–62), a French professional, in Paris, with 402½ lb. *182,57 kg* on 1 Feb. 1929, but his barbell would not now be regarded as acceptable.

Most Olympic Medals *World*

The winner of most Olympic medals is Norbert Schemansky (U.S.A.) (b. 30 May 1924) with four: Gold, middle-heavyweight 1952; Silver, heavyweight 1948; Bronze, heavyweight 1960 and 1964. Schemansky achieved a world record—the heavyweight snatch at 361½ lb. *163,75 kg* on 28 Apr. 1962 at Detroit—at the record age of 37 years and 10 months.

Most Olympic Medals *British*

The only British lifter to win an Olympic title has been Launceston Elliott (1873–1938), the open one-handed lift champion in 1896 at Athens.

Most successful British lifter

Louis George Martin, M.B.E. (b. Jamaica, 11 Nov. 1936) won four World and European mid-heavyweight titles in 1959, 1962–63, 1965. He won an Olympic silver medal in 1964 and a bronze in 1960 and also three Commonwealth gold medals in 1962, 1966, 1970. His total of British titles was 12.

European champion and record holder Mike Hazelwood (G.B.) is only 4 in *10 cm* short of the world jumping record. (*Tony Duffy, All-Sport Photographic*)

WORLD WEIGHTLIFTING RECORDS (as at 31 July 1977)

Bodyweight Class	Lift	Lifted lb	kg	Name and Country	Place	Date
Flyweight (114½ lb. *52 kg*)	Snatch	240¼	*109*	Alexander Voronin (U.S.S.R.)	Vilnius, U.S.S.R.	18 Mar. 1977
	Jerk	310¾	*141*	Alexander Voronin (U.S.S.R.)	Montreal, Canada	18 July 1976
	Total	540	*245*	Alexander Voronin (U.S.S.R.)	Vilnius, U.S.S.R.	18 Mar. 1977
Bantamweight (123¼ lb. *56 kg*)	Snatch	265½	*120,5*	Koji Miki (Japan)	Saga, Japan	25 Oct. 1976
	Jerk	332¾	*151*	Mohammed Nassiri (Iran)	Sanandaj, Iran	2 Aug. 1973
	Total	578½	*262,5*	Norair Nurikyan (Bulgaria)	Montreal, Canada	19 July 1976
Featherweight (132¼ lb. *60 kg*)	Snatch	286½	*130*	Gyorgyi Todorov (Bulgaria)	Sofia, Bulgaria	25 May 1976
	Jerk	356	*161,5*	Nikolai Kolesnikov (U.S.S.R.)	Montreal, Canada	20 July 1976
	Total	633¾	*287,5*	Gyorgyi Todorov (Bulgaria)	Sofia, Bulgaria	25 May 1976
Lightweight (148¾ lb. *67,5 kg*)	Snatch	312	*141,5*	Alexander Aibazian (U.S.S.R.)	Minsk, U.S.S.R.	15 July 1977
	Jerk	396¾	*180*	Sergei Pevzner (U.S.S.R.)	Odessa, U.S.S.R.	16 July 1976
	Total	694¼	*315*	Sergei Pevnzer (U.S.S.R.)	Odessa, U.S.S.R.	16 July 1976
Middleweight (165¼ lb. *75 kg*)	Snatch	347	*157,5*	Yordan Vardanyan (U.S.S.R.)	Rostov, U.S.S.R.	7 May 1977
	Jerk	429¾	*195*	Vartan Militosyan (U.S.S.R.)	E. Berlin, East Germany	30 Jan. 1977
	Total	766	*347,5*	Yordan Vardanyan (U.S.S.R.)	Rostov, U.S.S.R.	7 May 1977
Light-heavyweight (181¾ lb. *82,5 kg*)	Snatch	374¾	*170*	Blagoi Blagoyev (Bulgaria)	Sofia, Bulgaria	25 May 1976
	Jerk	457½	*207,5*	Rolf Milser (W. Germany)	E. Berlin, East Germany	8 Apr. 1976
	Total	821	*372,5*	Trendafil Stoichev (Bulgaria)	Sofia, Bulgaria	25 May 1976
Middle-heavyweight (198¼ lb. *90 kg*)	Snatch	396¾	*180*	David Rigert (U.S.S.R.)	Karaganda, U.S.S.R.	14 May 1976
	Jerk	487¼	*221*	David Rigert (U.S.S.R.)	Karaganda, U.S.S.R.	14 May 1976
	Total	881¼	*400*	David Rigert (U.S.S.R.)	Karaganda, U.S.S.R.	14 May 1976
Heavyweight (242½ lb. *110 kg*)	Snatch	407¾	*185*	Valentin Khristov (Bulgaria)	E. Berlin, East Germany	10 Apr. 1976
	Jerk	523½	*237,5*	Valentin Khristov (Bulgaria)	Moscow, U.S.S.R.	22 Sept. 1975
	Total	920¼	*417,5*	Valentin Khristov (Bulgaria)	Moscow, U.S.S.R.	22 Sept. 1975
Super-heavyweight (Over 242½ lb. *110 kg*)	Snatch	440¾	*200*	Khristo Plachkov (Bulgaria)	Sofia, Bulgaria	25 May 1976
	Jerk	562	*255*	Vasili Alexeev (U.S.S.R.)	Montreal, Canada	27 July 1976
	Total	975½	*442,5*	Khristo Plachkov (Bulgaria)	Sofia, Bulgaria	25 May 1976

Greatest back lift

The greatest weight ever raised by a human being is 6,270 lb. *2 844 kg* (2.80 tons *2,84 tonnes*) in a back lift (weight raised off trestles) by the 26 st. *165 kg* Paul Anderson (U.S.A.) (b. 17 Oct. 1932), the 1956 Olympic heavyweight champion, at Toccoa, Georgia, U.S.A., on 12 June 1957. The heaviest Rolls-Royce, the Phantom VI, weighs, 5,936 lb. *2 692 kg* (2.65 tons *2,69 tonnes*). The greatest lift by a woman is 3,564 lb. *1 616 kg* with a hip and harness lift by Josephine Blatt (*née* Schauer) (1869–1923) at the Bijou Theatre, Hoboken, New Jersey, U.S.A., on 15 Apr. 1895.

Greatest overhead lifts

The greatest overhead lifts made from the ground are the clean and jerks achieved by super-heavyweights which now exceed 5 cwt (560 lb.) *254 kg*. The greatest overhead lift ever made by a woman is 286 lb. *129 kg* in a continental jerk by Katie Sandwina (*née* Brummbach, later Mrs. Max Heymann) (1884–1952) of Germany, in *c.* 1911. This is equivalent to seven 40 lb. *18 kg* office typewriters. She stood 5 ft 11 in *1,80 m* tall, weighed 210 lb. *95 kg* (15 st.) and is reputed to have unofficially lifted 312½ lb. *141,747 kg* and to have shouldered a cannon, taken from the tailboard of a Barnum and Bailey circus wagon, which allegedly weighed 1,200 lb. *544 kg*.

Greatest power lifts

Paul Anderson, as a professional, has bench-pressed 627 lb. *284 kg* and has achieved 1,200 lb. *544 kg* in a squat so aggregating, with an 820 lb. *371 kg* dead lift, a career total of 2,647 lb. *1 200 kg*. The International Powerlifting Federation records in the super-heavyweight division were all set by Donald C. Reinhoudt (U.S.A.) with squat 934 lb. *423,6 kg* (Findlay, Ohio, 10 Apr. 1976); bench press 606¼ lb. *275 kg* (31 Aug. 1975); deadlift 885½ lb. *401,5 kg* and total 2,420 lb. *1 097 kg* (3 May 1975) Britons hold: the flyweight deadlift with Precious McKenzie, M.B.E. (b. S. Africa, 6 June 1936), 490½ lb. *222,5 kg* at London, England on 1 May 1975; all the featherweight records with Eddie Pengelly, deadlift 606¼ lb. *275 kg* and total 1,372¼ lb. *622,5 kg* at Birmingham, England on 24 Apr. 1977, and the squat 507 lb. *230 kg* at Turku, Finland on 15 May 1977; the middleweight total with Ronald Collins 1,655 lb. *750,5 kg* at Liverpool on 15 Dec. 1973 (with this lift Collins, at 165 lb. *74,8 kg*, became the first man to lift a total ten times his own bodyweight); the light-

heavyweight squat 710¾ lb. *322,5 kg* and total 1,818¾ lb. *825 kg* both by Collins at Turku, Finland on 15 May 1977; the middle-heavyweight squat by Collins 716½ lb. *325 kg* in 1977.

Hermann Gorner (1891–1956) (Germany) performed a one-handed dead lift of 734½ lb. *333,1 kg* in Dresden on 20 July 1920. Peter B. Cortese (U.S.A.) achieved a one-armed dead lift of 370 lb. *167 kg i.e.* 22 lb. *9,9 kg* over triple his body-weight at York, Pennsylvania on 4 Sept. 1954.

Hermann Gorner raised 24 men weighing 4,123 lb *1 870 kg* on a plank on the soles of his feet in London on 12 Oct. 1927 and also carried on his back a 1,444 lb *654 kg* piano for 52½ ft *4,8 m* on 3 June 1921.

The highest competitive two-handed dead lift by a woman is 441 lb. *200 kg* by Jan Suffolk Todd (b. 22 May 1952) (U.S.A.) at Stephenville Crossing, Newfoundland, Canada on 4 June 1977. Mrs. Todd weighed 197½ lb. *89,7 kg*. Her three-lift total was 1,041½ lb. *472,5 kg*.

It was reported that an hysterical 8 st 11 lb *55 kg 791* woman, Mrs. Maxwell Rogers, lifted one end of a 3,600 lb *1 632 kg* (1.60 tons *1,62 tonnes*) station wagon which, after the collapsing of a jack, had fallen on top of her son at Tampa, Florida, U.S.A., on 24 Apr. 1960. She cracked some vertebrae.

A deadlifting record of 1,690,160 lb. *766 643 kg* in 24 hr was set by a 10-man team in relay, from Glendale Community College, Calif., U.S.A., on 21–22 Dec. 1976.

Cue Levering

The only man ever to have levered six 16 oz *453 g* billiard cues simultaneously by their tips through 90 degrees to the horizontal, is W. J. (Bill) Hunt of Darwen, Lancashire at the Unity Club, Great Harwood, Lancashire on 25 June 1954.

Strandpulling

The International Steel Strandpullers' Association was founded by Gavin Pearson (Scotland) in 1940. The greatest ratified poundage to date is a super-heavyweight right arm push of 815 lb. *369,5 kg* by Malcolm Bartlett, of Oldham, Lancashire. The record for the Back Press Anyhow is 645 lb. *292,5 kg* by Barry Anderson, of Leeds, in 1975.

Oldest and Youngest

Harry Sawyer (Ashford Common) set a world 12 stone dislocation record of 353 lb *160 kg* in 1972 aged 52 and David Hoar (Ossett, West Yorkshire) set a world 11 stone right arm push record of 601 lb *272,5 kg* aged 17.

WRESTLING

Origins

The earliest depictions of wrestling holds and falls are from the walls of the tomb of Ptahhotap so proving that wrestling dates from *c.* 2350 B.C. or earlier. It was the most popular sport in the ancient Olympic Games and victors were recorded from 708 B.C. The Greco-Roman style is of French origin and arose about 1860. The International Amateur Wrestling Federation (F.I.L.A.) was founded in 1912.

Most titles *Olympic*

Three wrestlers have won three Olympic titles:

Carl Westergren (Sweden) (1895–1958)	
Greco-Roman Middleweight, 75 kg	1920
Greco-Roman Light Heavyweight, 82,5 kg	1924
Greco-Roman Heavyweight over 87 kg	1932

Ivar Johansson (Sweden) (b. 31 Jan. 1903)	
Freestyle Middleweight, 79 kg	1932
Greco-Roman Welterweight, 72 kg	1932
Greco-Roman Middleweight, 79 kg	1936

Aleksandr Medved (U.S.S.R.) (b. 16 Sept. 1937)	
Freestyle Light Heavyweight	1964
Freestyle Heavyweight	1968
Freestyle Extra Heavyweight	1972

The only wrestler with more medals is Imre Polyák (Hungary) (b. 16 Apr. 1932) who won the silver medal for the Greco-Roman featherweight class in 1952, 1956, 1960 and the gold in 1964.

Most titles *World*

The greatest number of world championships won by a wrestler is ten by the freestyler Aleksandr Medved (U.S.S.R.) (b. 16 Sept. 1937) with the light-heavyweight titles in 1964 (Olympic) and 1966, the heavyweight 1967 and 1968 (Olympic), and the super-heavyweight in 1969–72 (Olympic). The only wrestler to win the same title in six successive years has been Abdullah Movahed (Iran) (b. 10 Mar. 1940) in the lightweight division in 1965–70. The record for Greco-Roman titles is five shared by Roman Rurua (U.S.S.R.) (b. 25 Nov. 1942) with the featherweight 1966–68 (Olympic), 1969 and 1970 and Victor Igumenov (U.S.S.R.) (b. 10 Mar. 1943) with the welterweight 1966–67, 1969–71.

Most titles *British*

Heavyweight	10	Kenneth Alan Richmond (b. 10 July 1926) 1949–60
Middleweight	7	Thomas Albert Baldwin (b. 27 Sept. 1905), 1942, 1944–46, 1948, 1951–52 (also Welterweight in 1941)
Welterweight	9	Joe Feeney, 1957–60, 1962, 1964–66, 1968
Lightweight	8	Arthur Thompson, 1933–40
Featherweight	8	Herbert Henry Hall, (b. 16 Mar. 1926) 1952–57, 1961, 1963 (also Lightweight 1958–59)
Bantamweight	6	Joe Reid, 1930–35

Longest span

The longest span for B.A.W.A. titles is 24 years by George Mackenzie (1890–1957) who won his first in 1909 and his last in 1933. Mackenzie represented Great Britain in five successive Olympiads from 1908 to 1928.

Most wins

In international competition, Osamu Watanabe (b. 21 Oct. 1940), of Japan, the 1964 Olympic freestyle featherweight champion, was unbeaten and unscored-upon in 187 consecutive matches.

Longest bout

The longest recorded bout was one of 11 hr 40 min between Martin Klein (Estonia representing Russia) and Armas Asikáinen (Finland) in the Greco-Roman middleweight "A" event in the 1912 Olympic Games in Stockholm, Sweden. It was won by Klein.

In Japan's national sport, Sumo wrestling, 300 lb *132 kg* opponents are not uncommon. (*Popperfoto*)

Heaviest heavyweight

The heaviest heavyweight champion in British wrestling history was A. Dudgeon (Scotland), who won the 1936 and 1937 B.A.W.A. heavyweight titles, scaling 22 st *139 kg*.

Cumberland and Westmoreland wrestling

The British amateur championships were established in 1904. The only six time champions have been J. Baddeley (middleweight in 1905–06, 1908–10, 1912) and E. A. Bacon (lightweight in 1919, 1921–23, 1928–29).

Professional wrestling

Professional wrestling dates from 1874 in U.S.A. Georges Karl Julius Hackenschmidt (U.S.S.R.) (1877–1968) was undefeated at Greco-Roman contests from 1900 to his retirement in 1911. The highest paid professional wrestler is Andre "The Giant" Roussimoff (b. France, 1946), 7 ft 4 in *2,23 m* 460 lb. *208 kg*, who earned a reported $400,000 in 1975. The heaviest ever wrestler has been William J. Cobb of Macon, Georgia, U.S.A. (b. 1926), who was billed in 1962 as the 802 lb. *363 kg* (57 st. 4 lb.) "Happy" Humphrey. Ed "Strangler" Lewis (1890–1966) *né* Robert H. Friedrich, fought 6,200 bouts in 44 years losing only 33 matches. He won world titles in 1920, 1922 and 1928. Jack Dempsey, the world heavyweight boxing champion, refused his challenge to a wrestling-boxing match.

Sumo wrestling

The sport's origins in Japan certainly date from *c.* 23 B.C. The heaviest ever *sumotori* were probably Dewagatake, a wrestler of the 1920s who was 6 ft 7¾ in *2,03 cm* tall and weighed up to 430 lb. *195 kg* and Odachi, of the 1950s, 6 ft 7½ in *2,02 cm* who weighed about 441 lb. *200 kg*. Weight is amassed by over alimentation with a high protein stew called *chankonabe*. The tallest was probably Ozora, an early 19th century performer, who stood 7 ft 3 in *220 m* tall. The most successful wrestlers have been Sadaji Akiyoshi (b. 1912) *alias* Futabayama, winner of 69 consecutive bouts in the 1930s and Koki Naya (b. 1940) *alias* Taiho ("Great Bird"), who won the Emperor's Cup 32 times up to his retirement in 1971. The youngest of the 55 men to attain the rank of *Yokozuna* (Grand Champion) was Toshimitsu Ogata (b. 16 May 1953) *alias* Kitanoumi, in July 1974 aged 21 years and two months.

YACHTING

The Guinness Book of Yachting Facts and Feats *by Peter Johnson, published by Guinness Superlatives Ltd (price £4.95) provides more data on the sport.*

Origins

Yachting in England dates from the £100 stake race between Charles II and his brother James, Duke of York, on the Thames on 1 Sept. 1661 over 23 miles from Greenwich to Gravesend. The earliest club is the Royal Cork Yacht Club (formerly the Cork Harbour Water Club), established in

When he won his first Olympic title in 1968, Rodney Pattisson (right) won five first places and a second, having been disqualified after winning the first of seven races held. (*Don Morley, All-Sport Photographic*)

Ireland in 1720. The oldest yacht club in Britain which still is active is the Starcross Yacht Club at Powderham Point, Devon. Its first regatta was held in 1772. The word yacht is from the Dutch to hunt or chase.

Most Olympic titles *World*

The first sportsman ever to win individual gold medals in four successive Olympic Games was Paul B. Elvström (b. 24 Feb. 1928) (Denmark) in the Firefly class in 1948 and the Finn class in 1952, 1956 and 1960. He has also won eight other world titles in a total of six classes. The lowest number of penalty points by the winner of any class in an Olympic regatta is three points (six wins, one disqualified and one second in seven starts) by *Superdocius* of the Flying Dutchman class (Lt. Rodney Stuart Pattisson, M.B.E., R.N. (b. 5 Aug. 1943) and Iain Somerled Macdonald-Smith, M.B.E. (b. 3 July 1945)) at Acapulco Bay, Mexico in October 1968.

Most Olympic titles *British*

The only British yacht to win two titles was *Scotia* in the Open class and Half-One Ton class at the 1900 Regatta with Lorne C. Currie, helmsman and crewed by John H. Gretton and Linton Hope. The only British yachtsman to win in two Olympic regattas is Rodney Pattisson in 1968 (see above) and again with *Superdoso* crewed by Christopher Davies (b. 29 June 1946) at Kiel, West Germany in 1972. He gained a silver medal in 1976 with Julian Brooke Houghton (b. 16 Dec. 1946).

Admiral's Cup

The ocean racing series to have attracted the largest number of participating nations (three boats allowed to each nation) is Admiral's Cup held by the Royal Ocean Racing Club in the English Channel in alternate years. In 1975 a record number of 19 nations competed. Up to 1977, Britain had won seven times, U.S.A. twice and Australia and West Germany once.

America's Cup

The America's Cup was originally won as an outright prize by the schooner *America* on 22 Aug. 1851 at Cowes and was later offered by the New York Yacht Club as a challenge trophy. On 8 Aug. 1870 J. Ashbury's *Cambria* (G.B.) failed to capture the trophy from the *Magic*, owned by F. Osgood (U.S.A.). Since then the Cup has been challenged by Great Britain in 15 contests, in 2 contests by Canada, and by Australia three times, but the United States have never been defeated. The closest race ever was the fourth race of the 1962 series, when the 12 metre sloop *Weatherly* beat her Australian challenger *Gretel* by about three and a half lengths, a margin of only 26 sec on 22 Sept. 1962. The fastest time ever recorded by a 12 metre boat for the triangular course of 24 sea miles is 2 hr 46 min 58 sec by *Gretel* in 1962.

London to Sydney

The *Great Britain II*, a 74½ ft *22,7 m* ketch manned by a British joint services crew, sailed from the Thames estuary to Sydney, Australia in 67 days 7 hrs 19 min 49 sec from 31 Aug.–7 Nov. 1975, beating the previous record of the clipper

Patriarch in 1870 by nearly two days. The return journey to Dover took only 66 days 22 hrs 31 min 35 sec. The total round-the-world passage of some 30,000 miles *42,280 km* was accomplished in a record time of 134 days 5 hrs 51 min 14 sec.

24 Hour Dinghy Race

The greatest distance covered in 24 hours is 132 nautical miles by a G.P. 14 from Bolton Sailing Club on 11–12 Sept. 1976.

Highest speeds

The official world sailing speed record is 31.60 knots (36.38 m.p.h. *58,56 km/h*) by the 73½ ft *22,40 m* proa *Crossbow II* over a 500 m *547 yd* course in Portland Harbour, Dorset, on 30 Sept. 1976. The vessel (sail area 1,400 ft² *130,06 m²*) was designed by Rod McAlpine-Downie and owned and steered by Timothy Colman. The U.S. experimental hydrofoil craft *Monitor* was reported to have attained speeds close to 40 knots (46 m.p.h. *74 km/h*) in 1956.

The fastest 24 hr-run by a sailing yacht was recorded by Nick Keig (b. 13 June 1936), of the Isle of Man, who covered 340 nautical miles single-handed in a 37½ ft *11,43 m* trimaran *Three Legs of Mann I* during the Falmouth to Punta, Azores race on 9-10 June 1975, averaging 14.16 knots (16.30 m.p.h. *26,23 km/h*). The fastest bursts of speed reached were about 25 knots (28.78 m.p.h. *46,32 km/h*).

Most successful yacht

The most successful racing yacht in history was the Royal Yacht *Britannia* (1893–1935), owned by King Edward VII, when Prince of Wales and subsequently by King George V, which won 231 races in 625 starts.

Largest yacht

The largest private yacht ever built was Emily Roebling Cadwalader's *Savarona* of 5,100 gross tons, completed in Hamburg, Germany in Oct. 1931, at a cost of $4,000,000 *now £2.28 million*. She (the yacht), with a 53 ft *16,15 m* beam and measuring 408 ft 6 in *124,50 m* overall, was sold to the Turkish government in March 1938. Operating expenses for a full crew of 107 men approached $500,000 *now £285,700* per annum. Currently she is a Turkish Navy training ship, once called "Gunes Dil", with a complement of 213.

The largest private sailing yacht ever built was the full-rigged 350 ft *106 m* auxiliary barque *Sea Cloud* (formerly *Hussar*), owned by the oft-married Marjorie Merriweather Post-Close-Hutton-Davies-May (1888–1973), one-time wife of the U.S. Ambassador in the U.S.S.R. Her four masts carried 30 sails with the total canvas area of 36,000 ft² *3 344 m²*.

Largest sail

The largest sail ever made was a parachute spinnaker with an area of 18,000 ft² *1 672 m²* (more than two-fifths of an acre *0,1 ha*) for Vanderbilt's *Ranger* in 1937.

Most numerous class

The numerically largest class of sailing boat in the world is the "Sunfish" (U.S.). The total number is in excess of 140,000. The boat is a 14 ft *1,27 m* sailing surfboard with single sail and made of plastic. The numerically largest class of centreboard sailing dinghy is the International Optimist, a 7 ft 7 in *2,31 m* wooden or plastic boat for use by children. 115,000 are claimed by the class association. It is also the smallest in size and cheapest of any recognized international yachting class of boat.

Most competitors

The most competitors ever to start in a single race was 1,261 sailing boats in the Round Zealand (Denmark) race in June 1976, over a course of 375 km *233 miles*. The greatest number to start in a race in Britain was 570 keeled yachts and multi-hulls on 25 June 1977 from Cowes in the Annual Round-the-Island race.

Highest and Lowest

In December 1970, Tristan Jones (G.B.) sailed the 27 ft *8,23 m* yawl *Barbara* on the Dead Sea 1,296 ft *395 m* b.s.l., and in January 1973 he sailed the 22 ft *6,70 m* Sea Dart on Lake Titicaca, Peru 12,500 ft *3 810 m* a.s.l.

CANADIAN SUPPLEMENT

In this second edition with a section devoted to purely Canadian records the compilers have had the benefit of helpful correspondence from many readers. The process of improving each succeeding edition is thus launched.

Continued observations and contributions from those with first hand or specialist knowledge will be most gratefully acknowledged by the compilers at their address at the front of this volume.

The Guinness Book of Records translated from the British edition is available in the French language as *Le Livre des Records*, from Editions Denoël, 19 rue de l'Université, 75007 Paris, France.

Norris McWhirter

Norris McWhirter, Editor.

THE HUMAN BEING

ORIGINS
Earliest Man
The earliest evidence of man on Canadian territory is from the discovery of a bone scraper or fleshing tool from the Old Crow Flats area of northern Yukon Territory radio carbon dated to 27,000 before the present or 25,000 B.C. This was found in July 1966 by Peter Lord working with C. R. Harington.

This artifact consists of the tibia (lower leg bone) of a caribou with a toothed working end probably for removing hair from the outside or stringy residue from the inside of a hide. A worked fragment of mammoth bone, found near-by was dated to 27,000 B.C.

Man is believed to have come to the American continent by way of the Bering Strait (now 50.0 miles *80,4 km* wide). Amino acid racemisation dating results published in March 1976 indicate that man entered North America at least 48,000 years ago and possibly by the Bering land bridge which was again exposed *c.* 70,000 B.C.

DIMENSIONS
Tallest Man
The greatest height attributed to a Canadian citizen has been 8 ft 3 in *2,51 m* in the case of Joseph Edouard Beaupré. He was born at Willow Bunch, Saskatchewan Jan 9 1881 and died aged 23 years 6 months in St. Louis, Missouri, U.S.A. scene of the Olympic Games on July 3 1904. His embalmed body is kept in the Department of Anatomy, Montreal University and measures 7 ft 1⅜ in *2,168 m* long. Though repeated in medical journals, all heights above 7 ft 9⅛ in *2,39 m* are of suspect provenance after he had become a man of the circus. Canada's and the world's tallest true giant (i.e. non-acromegalic) was Angus Macaskill, who died on Cape Breton Is., Nova Scotia in 1863 (see p. 8).

Tallest Woman
Canada's tallest giantess was Anna Hanen Swan, who was born in Nova Scotia in 1846. She was billed in exhibitions at 8 ft 1 in *2,46 m* but was actually 7 ft 5½ in *2,27 m*. In June 1871 she married the American giant Martin van Buren Bates (1845–1919), who stood 3 in *7,6 cm* shorter, at St. Martin-in-the-Fields, London, England. Anna Bates died in 1888 aged 42.

Longevity
The earliest baptismal and burial records were initiated by the Roman Catholic clergy of the French colony in 1610 and were extended to Protestant congregations in Lower Canada by an Act of 1795.

However such verification of longevity claims in Canada to an evidential standard acceptable to a lawyer or scientist is bedevilled by the "very defective" registration, particularly of births prior to 1920.

The Vital Statistics Division of Statistics Canada do not maintain a chronological record of citizens of extreme longevity. The Division further regards information on the oldest currently living Canadian citizens as "strictly confidential".

However the Chief Government Statistician, Dr. Tache, in 1870 carried out an official enquiry, which was published, into the age of Pierre Joubert (1701–1814) which provided incontestible evidence that he had lived to an age of 113 years 124 days—an age not provenly surpassed by any other human until Sept. 5 1928 when Mrs. Delina Filkins *née* Ecker (born 1815) reached that age at Richfield Springs, New York, U.S.A. and survived another 89 days to die on Dec. 4 1928 aged 113 years 214 days (see page 14).

The title of the oldest living Canadian was claimed in May 1975 for Caesar Paul (b. 1863) a retired Cree Indian trapper of Fort Coulonge, Ontario said to be aged 112 based on the federal certification of his age in 1967 at 104 years.

Sophia Rayburn (b. July 5 1867) only 4 days younger than the nation itself, died in Orangeville, Ontario on July 22 1975 aged 108 years 17 days.

REPRODUCTIVITY
Most Children
The identity of the Canadian woman who has recently borne most children, though possibly known to the Vital Statistics Section of Statistics Canada, cannot be published under the "confidentiality criteria in the Statistical Act against divulging individual information". The figure would probably be in the range of 27 to 31.

Multiple Births
The world's first all-surviving quintuple birth was to Mrs. Olivia Dionne in Callender, Ontario on May 28 1934. The five girls were Emilie (d. Aug. 6 1954 aged 20); Yvonne, Cecile (Mrs. Phillipe Langlois), Marie (Mrs. Florian Houle) and Annette (Mrs. Germain Allard) with an aggregate birthweight of 13 lb. 6 oz. *6,06 kg*. They were delivered by Dr. Allan Roy Dafoe who reported that a sixth child had earlier been stillborn.

The two children of Mr. & Mrs. John C. Oliver who could boast a full set of 8 great grandparents.

Most Descendants
For details of the 582 living descendants of Capt. Wilson Kettle (1860–1963). (see page 15).

Most Ascendants
In September 1975 the case was reported by John C. Oliver of Agincourt, Ontario of his two children being photographed with their parents, 4 grandparents and all 8 great grandparents—14 living ascendants.

Most Generations
A six generation family was reported from Alberta, Canada on June 22 1975 when 99 year old James Stevenson learnt that his great granddaughter, Mrs. Maureen Augur, 35 had become a grandmother and he had become a great-great-great-grandfather with the birth of Starla Dawn Wickham at Shaunavon Union Hospital, Saskatchewan.

THE ANIMAL KINGDOM

LONGEST
Canadian Atlantic coast waters harbour the longest of all animals—2½ times longer than the longest prehistoric dinosaur—the giant cold water jelly fish *Cyanaea artica* which has a tentacular span of some 245 ft *75 m.* (See page 23.)

LARGEST MAMMAL
Co-claimant with Kodiak bear as the world's largest land carnivore is the Polar Bear (*Ursus maritimus*). The average adult male is 850–900 lb. *386–408 kg.* but weights as high as 2,210 lb. *1 002 kg* have been claimed (see page 26).

Canada's heaviest dry land mammal is the Alaskan moose (*Alces alces gigas*). A bull standing 7 ft 8 in *2,33 m* at the withers, weighing an estimated 1,800 lb. *816 kg* was shot on the Yukon River in September 1897 (see also page 29).

RAREST MAMMAL
Five Canadian mammals which are on the "endangered species" list are Wood Bison (*Bison bison athabascae*) in Alberta; the Northern Kit Fox (*Vulpes velox hebes*); the Northern Rocky Mountain Wolf (*Canis lupus irremotus*); the Eastern Cougar (*Felis concolor cougar*) and the Black-footed Ferret (*Mustela nigripes*).

ANTLER SPAN
The recent measured span for the antlers of a moose has been 78½ in *199 cm.*

DAMS BEAVER
The interior measurement of the dome-shaped island refuges built by beavers (*Castor canadensis*) of sticks plastered with mud may exceptionally be 5 ft 10 in *1,8 m* in height. The phrase to work "like a beaver" was first recorded in 1741 and the phrase "eager beaver" was coined in 1943.

BIRDS
Largest
The largest of the 519 species currently comprising the Canadian Bird list (due to be revised upward in 1977) is the Trumpeter Swan *Olor buccinator*. Large specimens measure up to 5½ feet *1,7 m* in length with a wing span of up to 10 ft *3,05 m.*

Smallest
The smallest species is the Calliope humming bird *Stellula calliope* weighing a fraction of an ounce.

Longest Migration
The world's two longest migratory species, the Arctic tern (*Sterna paradisaea*) (see page 35) and the American golden plover (*Pluvialis dominica*) are birds of the Canadian arctic.

The largest Canadian Bird, the Trumpeter Swan, which can measure up to 5½ ft *1,7 m* in length. (*Aquila Photographics*)

Rarest

Birds on the Canadian list which are scheduled as endangered are the Bald Eagle (*Haliaetus leucocephalus*); the Whooping Crane (*Grus americana*); American Peregrine Falcon (*Falco peregrinus anatum*) the Arctic Peregrine Falcon (*F. p. tundrius*); Brown Pelican (*Pelecanus occidentalis*) and the Eskimo Curlew (*Numenuis borealis*), which last named is regarded as the rarest.

REPTILES

The longest species of snake recorded in Canadian fauna is the Black rat snake *Elaphe obsoleta*. The Royal Ontario Museum have recorded a length of 9 ft 274 cm.

Turtle Racing

The fastest time for a turtle to cover 25 ft 7,62 m under racing conditions is 23.4 secs by "Zorro", an 8 year old red-eared slider owned by Ernie McPherson of Concord, California at the 5th Annual Turtle Derby at Boissevain, Manitoba on Aug. 14 1976. The winner of the final plod-off was a local turtle "Fat Freddie" *alias* "Video" in 37.0 secs next day.

INSECTS
Largest

There are an estimated 47,000 species of insects known from Canada. According to the Biosystematics Research Institute of Agriculture Canada, Ottawa, the total may eventually reach 100,000 or 10% of the present world total. The maximum dimension of any Canadian insect is that of the cecropia moth *Hylalophora cecropia* with a wing span of 150 mm 5.90 in.

Smallest

The smallest Canadian insects are those of the Hymenoptera egg parasites. Some of these in the genera Trichogramma (family Trichogrammidae) and the genera *Anagrus*, *Mymar* or *Cleruchus* (family Mymaridae) measure only 0,4–0,8 mm $\frac{1}{64}$ to $\frac{1}{32}$ of an inch.

Moth *Largest*
(See Insect *Largest* above).

Moth *Smallest*
Canada's smallest moth is one of the species of *Nepticula* with a wing span of 3.5 mm or just over $\frac{1}{8}$ inch.

Butterfly *Largest*
The largest butterfly in Canadian fauna is the Two tailed swallowtail *Papilio multicaudata* with a wing span of 117 mm 4.60 in.

Butterfly *Smallest*
Canada's smallest butterfly is the acmon blue *Plebujus acmon* with a wing span of 17 mm 0.66 in.

MOLLUSCS
Largest

The heaviest and largest mollusc and invertebrate (back boneless) animal ever found in Canada is the Atlantic giant squid of which the largest specimen ever recovered was one captured in Thimble Tickle Bay, Newfoundland on Nov. 2 1878. It measured 55 ft 16,7 m overall including 35 ft 10,6 m tentacles and weighed an estimated 2 tons/tonnes. (See page 44).

PREHISTORIC ANIMALS
Reptiles

All four species of the earliest known reptiles have been recovered as fossils from deposits in Nova Scotia. These are Archerpeton, Hylonomus, Protoclepsybrops and Romericus all dated to 290,000,000 years ago in the Carboniferous Period.

THE PLANT KINGDOM

HEAVIEST VEGETABLE
The most massive recorded vegetable in Canada has been a 353 lb. 160,1 kg squash (*Cacurbita maxima*) grown by E. Van Wyck of Roland, Manitoba reported in 1971.

Checking the 45 ft 13,7 m circumference of the world's largest recorded burl. (see p. 341) (*Nick Yunge-Bateman*)

TREES

Tallest

The Douglas Fir reputedly of 417 ft *127,1 m* felled by George Carey in Lynn Valley, B.C. in 1895 is regarded by present day forestry experts as an unconvincing legend. It was reputedly 300 ft *91 m* to the first limb with a diameter reputedly 25 ft *7,6 m* thick, circumference 77 ft *23,46 m* and the bark 16 in *40 cm* thick. The greatest acceptably measured height of any of the 135 species of tree indigenous to Canada is 305 ft *93 m* for a Douglas Fir felled near Woss Lake on Vancouver Island, British Columbia dated to be 385 years old with a stump diameter between 80–90 in *2,03–2,28 m*.

Other very tall trees recorded by the Canadian Institute of Forestry/Institut Forestier du Canada.

286 ft	87 m	Sitka Spruce	Port McNeil, Vancouver Is. B.C. Queen Charlotte Is., B.C.
243 ft	74 m	Hemlock	Woss Lake, Vancouver Is., B.C.
>230 ft	70 m	Western Red Cedars	British Columbia
200 ft	61 m	Western White Pine	British Columbia

Oldest

The greatest reported age for any tree felled in Canada is 1,266 years a for Douglas fir felled by Jock Miller and John Weston at Cowichan Lake, Vancouver Island on June 26 1959.

Greatest Girth

The greatest diameter, excluding cases of butt swell burls recorded for a Canadian tree is 14 ft 4 in *4,36 m* for the butt end of the first log of a giant Douglas fir felled at the corner of Georgia and Granville Streets, Vancouver, B.C. in 1886.

Biggest Burl

The most massive burl on record was discovered on a 351 year old spruce found in Dec. 1976 near MacMillan Bloedel's logging camp at Port McNeill, British Columbia. It's weight was 22.47 short tons *20,38 tonnes*.

Tallest Flagpole

Canada's tallest flagpole is the 208 ft *63,3 m* tall specimen erected in 1930 at the Vancouver Court House, Vancouver, B.C. The Douglas fir flagpole at Kew Gardens, London, England, gifted by British Columbia in 1958 is however 225 ft *68,58 m* high (from a 275 ft *83,8 m* specimen felled in Copper Canyon, B.C.)

FOREST FIRES

In 1973 there were 5,524 man-caused starts and 2,081 lightning-caused starts for a total of 7,605 making 1,600 less than 1971.

Earliest National Park

Canada's first step towards a National Park was setting aside of 10 miles² *26 km²* of Sulphur Mountain, now part of Banff National Park in 1885. The earliest Federal Park is the Rocky Mountains Park of 260 miles² *675 km²* designated in 1886.

Largest Zoo

Canada's largest zoo is the Metro Toronto Zoo which covers 710 acres *287 ha* employing a full-time staff of 206 to look after 3,075 specimens of 389 species.

THE NATURAL WORLD

Largest Bay

Measured by its shoreline length rather than the distance across its mouth, Hudson Bay qualifies as the largest bay in the world, see page 59. It has a maximum chartered depth of 141 fathoms *257 m*.

Longest Strait

Canada's longest strait is the Hudson Strait which is 430 miles *692 km* long and varies in width from 37 to 120 miles *59–193 km* with a maximum charted depth of 481 fathoms *879 m*.

Greatest Tides

The greatest tides in the world surge into the Bay of Fundy between Nova Scotia and New Brunswick at Maine, U.S.A.

At Burncoat Head in the Minas Basin, Nova Scotia the mean spring range is 47.5 ft *19,50 m* and the extreme range 53.5 ft *16,30 m* (see p. 60).

Icebergs

The tallest recorded iceberg is one 550 ft *165 m above* the surface off North-West Greenland. The most southerly Arctic iceberg ever sighted was one in 30° 50′ N 45° 06′ W on June 2 1934.

Oldest Rocks

The earliest rocks found in the Canadian Shield. Some in the area of Saglek Bay, Labrador appear to pre-date 3,000 million years before the present. The only rocks of comparable age are found in the U.S.S.R., Greenland and Swaziland.

Largest Island

Baffin Island is Canada's largest and the world's fifth largest island with an area of 195,928 miles² *507 445 km²*. It measures 955 miles in length and 500 miles across at its widest point. Canada also has the world's ninth and tenth largest islands: Victoria (83,896 miles² *217 288 km²*) and Ellesmere Island (see below).

Northernmost Island

Canada's northernmost island is Ellesmere Island, which reaches Lat. 83° 07′ N and has an area of 75,767 miles² *196 235 km²*.

Lake Island

Canada and the world's largest is Manitoulin Island in Lake Huron with an area of 1,068 miles² *2 766 km²*.

Deepest Cave

The deepest cave so far discovered in Canada is the Arctomys Pot, Mount Robson, B.C. at 1,720 ft *524 m*.

Highest Mountain

Canada's highest mountain is Mount Logan in the St. Elias range, Yukon Territory, confirmed in 1925 to be 19,850 ft *6 050 m* above sea level and second only in North America to Mt. McKinley which has been climbed 12 years earlier (for details of first ascent see Chapter XII, Mountaineering).

Highest Points (by Provinces)

The highest mountains in the 10 provinces and two territories, i.e. North West Territory and Yukon are thus:

Yukon Territory	19,850 ft	6 050 m	Mount Logan
British Columbia	15,300 ft	4 663 m	Fairweather Mountain
Alberta	12,294 ft	3 747 m	Mount Columbia
North West Territory	9,062 ft	2 762 m	Mt. Sir James MacBrien
Newfoundland	5,232 ft	1 594 m	Unnamed peak is 58° 57′ N 63° 47′ W (Torngat Mts)
Quebec	5,210 ft	1 588 m	Mont D'Iberville, Torngat Mountains
Saskatchewan	4,567 ft	1 392 m	Cypress Hills
Manitoba	2,729 ft	831 m	Baldy Mountain
New Brunswick	2,690 ft	819 m	Mount Carleton
Ontario	2,275 ft	693 m	Unnamed point on 47° 20′ N 80° 44′ W in Timiskoming district.
Nova Scotia	1,747 ft	532 m	Cape Breton
Prince Edward Island	465 ft	141 m	Unnamed point is 46° 20′ N 63° 37′ W in Queen's County.

The highest insular peak is Barleau Peak on Ellesmere Island with an altitude of 8,584 ft *2 616 m*.

Canada's most mountainous area is the Canadian Cordillera which has 576.4 miles² *1 492 km²* higher than 10,000 ft.

Longest River

Canada's longest river and the eleventh longest in the world is the Mackenzie-Peace which stretches 2,635 miles *4 240 km* from the Findlay River Tatlatui Lake in the Skeera Mountain, British Columbia via the Peace and Slave rivers to the Great Slave Lake whence flows the Mackenzie (1,071 miles *1 723 km*) to the Beaufort Sea.

Greatest Flow

The highest mean discharge of any Canadian river system is 348,000 cusecs of the St. Lawrence River which waterway stretches 2,280 miles *3 669 km* from the head of Lake Superior to Belle Isle.

Largest Basin

Canada's largest basin is the Mackenzie-Peace-Findlay basin which extends over 697,000 miles² *1 805 000 km².*

Highest Waterfall

The Takakkaw Falls on the Daly Glacier, British Columbia have a total drop of 1,650 ft *502 m* with a longest leap of 1,200 ft *365 m*.

The Della Falls in Strathcona Provincial Park on Vancouver Island have an overall drop of 1,443 ft *436 m* in three cascades.

The most voluminous waterfall in Canada is the 2,500 ft *792 m* wide 162 ft *49,3 m* tall Horseshoe Fall on the Niagara River between Lakes Erie and Ontario with a mean annual flow of 212,000 cusecs (*ft³/sec*). The American Falls adjoining thr right bank are 5 ft *1,52 m* higher but have a crest length of only 1,000 ft *304 m*. The 245 ft *74,6 m* tall Grand Falls on the Hamilton river, Labrador have a flow of c. 35,000 cusecs.

Largest Lake

Of the total area of the world's largest freshwater lake, Lake Superior, 35.0% is in Ontario, Canada namely 11,100 of its 31,700 miles² (*27 750 out of 82 100 km²*). Lake Superior is additionally the deepest, 1,330 ft *405 m* and the most elevated (602 ft *183 m*) of the six Great Lakes. It measures 350 miles *563 km* by 160 miles *257 km* across. The largest lake wholly within Canada is the Great Bear Lake in North West Territories with an area of 12,096 miles² *31 328 km².*

Smallest Great Lake

Of the six Great Lakes the smallest and shallowest is St. Clair which measures 26 by 24 miles *41,8 × 38,6 km* and is 21 ft *6,4 m* deep.

Highest and Lowest Lakes

The highest major lake (i.e. more than 150 miles² *388 km²*) is the 156 miles² *404 km²* Ootsa in British Columbia at an elevation of 2,800 ft *853 m* above sea level. Chilko Lake British Columbia with an area of 75.1 miles² *194,5 km²* is 3,842 ft *1 171 m* above sea-level. Of the six Great Lakes, Lake Ontario is the lowest at 246 ft *75 m* above sea level.

WEATHER
Highest and Lowest Temperatures

The highest temperature officially recorded in Canada was 113° F *45° C* observed at Midale and Yellow Grass, Saskatchewan on July 5, 1937.

The lowest temperature ever recorded in Canada was reported to be −83° F *−63.8° C* from Snag, Yukon Territory on 3 February 1947 but a recalibration in Toronto resulted in this being marginally reduced to −81.4° F *−63° C*.

Greatest Snowfall

The 24 hr record in Canada is 44.2 in *1122,7 mm* at Kitimat Townsite, British Columbia on Feb. 18 1972. The Canadian record for one month is 202.5 in *5 143 mm* at Kemano (Kildala Pass) on Feb. 1–28 1954. The record for a season (i.e. one year) was 963.2 in *24 465 mm* at Revelstoke/Mt. Copeland, B.C. from July 1 1971 to June 30 1972.

Greatest Rainfall

The one day rainfall record for Canada is 19.26 in *489,2 mm* at Ucluelet (Brynnor Mines) on Vancouver Island, B.C. on Oct. 6 1967. The record for a month is 88.01 in *2 235 mm* at

Swanson Bay, B.C. in Nov. 1917. The record for a calendar year occurred in 1931 at Henderson Lake, B.C. when 319.78 in *8 122 mm* fell.

Highest and Lowest Barometer Pressures

The highest barometric pressure entered in Canada has been 1067.9 millibars at Mayo, Yukon Territory on Jan. 1 1971. The record low (corrected to sea-level) was 940.2 mb at St. Anthony, Newfoundland on Jan. 20 1977.

Highest Wind Speeds

The highest wind speed sustained for one hour was recorded at Cape Hopes Advance, Quebec on Nov. 18 1931 at 125 m.p.h. *201,1 km/h.*

Coldest Place in Ontario

The coldest annual mean (1960–63) recorded at Winisk, Lat. 55° 14′ N was 22.3° F *−5,3° C* in January 1960—a record for the province.

The coldest temperature ever recorded in Ontario is −73° F *−58,3° C* at Iroquois Falls on Jan. 23 1935.

Coldest Place

(See Lowest Temperature above.) The mean record for a month was at Dawson, Yukon, which averaged −51.4° F *−46,3° C* from Dec. 1 to Dec. 31 1917.

Sunshine Records

The one month sunshine record is 528 hours at Sachs Harbour, N.W.T. on June 1–30 1958, so averaging 17 hr 36 min per day.

Foggiest Place

The Grand Banks off Newfoundland average 120 days per annum of visibility below 1,000 yds *915 m*. At Yarmouth, Nova Scotia fog was reported in June, July and August 1967 on 85 of the 92 days—probably also a world's record.

Hailstones

Hailstones, measuring up to 2¾ in *7 cm* in diameter, were recorded at Montreal on Aug. 1 1969.

THE UNIVERSE AND SPACE

Earliest Recorded Eclipse

The earliest eclipse recorded in Canada was the total solar eclipse of April 19 1670 recorded by Jesuit missionaries in Quebec, where it was partial for 38 minutes.

Largest Meteorites

The heaviest meteorite specimen recovered was an iron of 386 lb. *175 kg* in Iron Creek, Alberta first recognised as such in 1869.

The heaviest stone to be recovered was one ot 237 lb. *107,5 kg* at Abec, Alberta in June 1952. A fall from which 600 lb. *272 kg* of stone were recovered but with no piece larger than 60 lb. *27,2 kg* occurred at Bruderheim, Alberta on 4 March 1960.

Largest Crater

Canada's largest crater is the New Quebec (formerly the Chubb) discovered in North Ungava in June 1943. It is 2.2 miles *3,54 km* in diameter and 1,325 ft *403 m* deep and is regarded as a water-filled vulcanoid rather than of meteoric origin. The largest astrobleme (Gk *astron*, a star; *blemma*, a glance) in Canada is Deep Bay, Saskatchewan, identified in 1956 with a diameter of 8.5 miles *13,6 km.*

Largest Star

The most massive star yet detected in the Milky Way is the fainter component of Plaskett's Star discovered by J. S. Plaskett from the Dominion Astrophysical Observatory, Victoria, B.C. *c.* 1920 with a mass 55 times that of the Sun.

Aurora Borealis

Polar lights caused by electrical solar discharges in the upper atmosphere are visible on every night of clear visibility in those regions of high geomagnetic latitude in Northern Canada near the north magnetic pole which is now estimated to be in Lat. 76° 12′ N Long. 101° W. (see page 70).

THE SCIENTIFIC WORLD

Heaviest Mineral

The mineral with the highest specific gravity of any is osmiridium with readings as high as 21.12. Apart from osmium and iridium, amounts of Rhodium, Platinum and Ruthenium are usually present. It is found in Quesnel and Simi Kameen, B.C.

Largest Crystal

The most voluminous crystal known in the world was a 90 ton *81,6 tonnes* phlogopite or brown mica discovered in Ontario of 144 m³ *5,082 ft³* measuring 33 ft *10,05 m* long and 14 ft *4,26 m* in diameter.

Largest Gold Nugget

The largest recorded Canadian gold nugget was the Kilgour nugget of 52 oz. 11 dwt 6 grains *1,634 kg* found by the Gilbert River, Beauce County, Quebec in 1865. The report of a 75 oz. *2,332 kg* nugget from the Klondike, Yukon Territory was not substantiated.

Largest Silver Nugget

The largest recorded silver nugget was one of 1,424 lb. *645,9 kg* containing 11,001 oz. *342,169 kg* of silver named the Gillies Limit Float I found *c.* 1902 6 miles *9,6 km* south of Cobalt, Ontario.

Wineries

Canada's oldest winery is Barnes Wines Ltd of St. Catharine's, Ontario (founded June 1873) which uses its original casks. Canada's largest winery is T. G. Bright & Co. with a cellar capacity of 7 million gallons *31,8 million litres*. Their Pinot is the most expensive Canadian champagne marketed.

Largest Telescope

The largest reflecting telescope in Canada is the 74 in *188 cm* David Dunlap Observatory reflector at Richmond Hill, Ontario installed in May 1935 when it ranked second to the 100 in Mount Wilson telescope at Pasadena, California.

top right: Canada's largest telescope atop Richard Hill, Ontario. (*Robert Lansdale Photography*)

right: The 74 in *188 cm* David Dunlap reflector, once the world's second largest. (*Robert Lansdale Photography*)

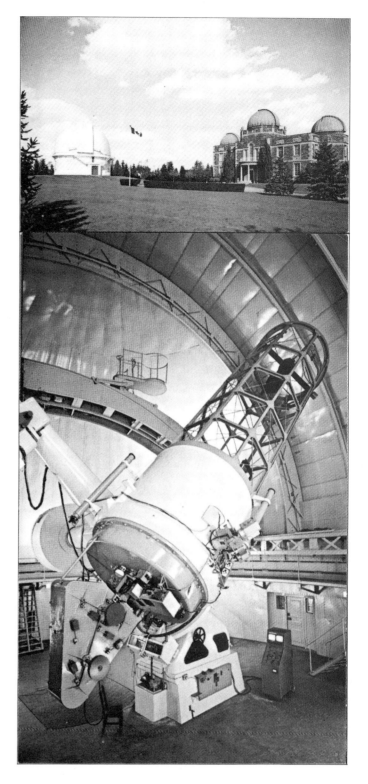

ARTS AND ENTERTAINMENTS

Most Expensive Painting

The highest price ever paid for a Canadian painting is $285,000 for a canvas by Tom Thomson by the McMichael Canadian Collection of Kleinberg, Ontario early in 1976. It is entitled "*Woodland Waterfall*" and completed in the year of Thomson's death in 1917.

Largest Gallery

Canada's largest picture gallery is the Ontario Art Gallery, Toronto incorporated in 1900. The new wing was completed in Sept. 1977.

Most Common Language

The most spoken language in Canada is English which according to the 1971 census was spoken as a first language by 60.1% of the population compared with the 28.9% who were primarily French-speaking. The largest Indian linguistic group is that of the 60,000–75,000 Cree.

Mohawk Indian is a language in which words may be formed of limitless length. A 50 letter example is tkanuhstsarihsranuhwe'tsraaksahsraksahsrakaratattsrayeri', which means, the praising of the evil of liking of the finding of the house is right.

The longest words in common use in Canada's official languages English and French are 21 letters and 25 letters respectively disproportionableness and anticonstitutionnellement.

PLACE NAMES

Oldest

The oldest Canadian place name of European origin is "Newfoundland" first noted in an entry in the Daybooks of King's Payments of Sept. 30 1502. "Cape Race", Newfoundland may be older but its earliest occurrence on a map extant is *c.* 1504. The oldest recorded name of native origin may be the river "Miramichi", New Brunswick noted by Jacques Cartier in 1535 as *Maissimeu Assi* meaning Micmac Land in Montagnais Indian.

Longest

The longest single word place name in Canada is the 17 letter Nuvursirpaaraaluk Island, N.W.T. derived from the Inuit "the thing that is farthest out and also the largest (in a line from the speaker)".

In New Brunswick there is a 45 letter (but 7 word) name *Lower North Branch Little Southwest Miramichi River* and in Quebec a 41 letter parish municipality *La-Visitation-de-la-Sainte-Vierge-de-l'Isle-du-Pads.*

Shortest

Among numerous specific single letter names in Canada may be cited two lakes, A in New Brunswick and Y in Quebec.

Personal Names

The man with the shortest name in Canada is X, formerly Mr. Scott Percy Foster, a consulting resologist in Kingston, Ontario, who changed his name on Feb. 2 1972.

"Canada" Earliest Use

The word Canada, apart from the Spanish meaning of a dale or glen between two mountains, was first recorded as "Cannaday" by Capt. Smith in his *Virginia* in 1624.

Oldest Publisher

Canada's oldest established book publisher is Gage Educational Publishing Ltd. started in 1844 as Robert and Adam Miller, Booksellers. William (later Sir) J. Gage bought the business from the estate of Adam Miller in 1880. The text book division of W. J. Gage Ltd. was changed to the present name in 1970 and acquired by Scott, Foresman and Company in 1971.

Largest Book Publisher

The highest published turnover or sales revenue of any Canadian book publisher is that of Harlequin Enterprises Ltd. of Don Mills, Ontario with consolidated sales of $53 million in 1976. In 1974 the sales income of 4 publishers exceeded $8 million.

The total number of titles published in 1974 was 6,835 (3,178 of them reprints). Of this total 4,058 were by publishers with a Canadian controlling interest.

Oldest Author

Dr. Gordon McLeod Dickie (b. Dec. 1875), a Canadian citizen, began writing verse at the age of 95 and had his first book published after his 100th birthday.

Newspaper Highest Circulation

The highest circulation of any newspaper in Canada is 763,675 (Audit Bureau of Circulations figure for Sept. 1976) for the evening paper *Toronto Star.* The highest figure for a morning paper is 314,349 for *The Globe and Mail.*

Periodical

The highest circulation for any paid circulation periodical is 1,266,969 for the *Reader's Digest* (ABC figures for Mar. 1976). The free controlled circulation consumer magazine *Homemaker's Magazine* audited by S.D.A.—Canadian Circulations Audit Board Inc. was 1,500,087 for Sept. 1976.

Advertising Rates Highest

The highest advertising page rate in Canada is the 4 color rate for *The Canadian* at $22,960 (Jan. 1977). The highest rate excluding syndicated supplements is for *Homemaker's Magazine* with $12,940 (Mar. 1977).

An historic photograph of the Italian-Irish Marchese Marconi on the day of his first Transatlantic wireless signal in St. John's, Newfoundland—Dec. 12 1901. (see page 345). (*Marconi Co. Ltd.*)

Library Largest
The largest library in volume holdings in Canada is the University of Toronto Library with 4,393,873 volumes in 1974/75.

THEATRE
Earliest
The earliest theatrical production to be performed in Canada was by the French at Port Royal, Arcadia, Nova Scotia in November 1606.

Largest
Canada's largest capacity theatre for the live arts is the O'Keefe, opened in 1960, in Toronto, Ontario with 3,155 seats.

GRAMOPHONE
Canada's most successful recording artist has been Paul Anka (b. Ottawa July 30 1941). His *Diana* (AVC Paramount) written when he was 14 also reached No. 1 in the U.S. and British Charts with global sales of 9 million. Anka's golden discs were *You Are My Destiny* (1958); *Lonely Boy* (1959) top in the U.S. for 4 weeks; *Put Your Head on My Shoulder* (1959); *Puppy Love* (1960) and *Every Time* (1964). His total sales by 1970 were said to be 40 million.

RADIO
Marconi (see page 106) received the first radio signal into Canada on Signal Hill near St. John's, Newfoundland on Dec. 12 1901. The Canadian-born Dr. Reginald Aubrey Fessenden (b. Oct. 6 1866, East Bolton, P.Q., died Bermuda, 1932) had previously achieved the world's earliest transmission of voice over one mile *1,6 km* at Cobb Island, Maryland in Dec. 1900.

The Marconi Wireless Telegraph Co. of Canada began broadcasting experiments from a now demolished factory at 173 William Street, Montreal in about Nov. 1918. It began regular programmed broadcasts under the call sign XWA in Dec. 1919 which on Nov. 4 1920 became the present day CFCF, which arguably is the oldest radio station in the world.

TELEVISION
Earliest Transmission
The first television program transmitted from Canadian soil was by CBFT, Montreal, owned and operated by CBC French, on Sept. 6 1952 CBLT (Toronto-English) transmitted two days later on Sept. 8 1952.

Highest Viewership
The highest measured viewership in Canada occurred at 7 p.m.–9 p.m. on Nov. 10 1968 when the CBC network aired a special edition of *Heidi* seen by 6,041,000 or 28.88% of the then population of 20,911,400.

STRUCTURES

Tallest Building
Canada's tallest building and the world's tallest self-supporting tower is the $44 million C.N. Tower in Metro Centre, Toronto, Canada which rises to 1,815 ft *553,33 m*. Excavation began on Feb. 12 1973 for the 130,000 ton/*tonnes* structure of reinforced, post-tensioned concrete topped out on April 2 1975. The 400-seat restaurant revolves in the Sky Pod at 1,140 ft *347,5 m* from which the visibility extends to 74½ miles *120 km*.

Tallest Office Block
The tallest office block in Canada is the 72 storey First Canadian Place, Toronto, Ontario which rises to 935 ft *285 m* and which was topped out in April 1975. The 40,000 ton steel framed tubed structure was erected in 15 months reaching a rate of 3 storeys per week.

Tallest Chimney
The International Nickel Company's chimney at Sudbury, Ontario is the tallest in the world standing 1,251 ft *381 m* in height (see page 111).

Longest Bridges
Canada's longest bridge span is the 2,190 ft *668 m* long suspension Pierre Laporte Bridge crossing the St. Lawrence River, Quebec City completed in 1970 when it ranked twelfth in the world.

Canada's longest arch span is the 1,200 ft *366 m* Port Mann Bridge (a tied arch flanked by cantilevers) across the Fraser River, British Columbia completed in 1964 and then ranking third in the world.

The Quebec Bridge (Pont du Québec) over the St. Lawrence River in Canada has the longest cantilever truss span of any in the world—1,800 ft *549 m* between the piers and 3,239 ft *987 m* overall. It carries a railway track and 2 carriageways. Begun in 1899, it was finally opened to traffic on Dec. 3 1917 at a cost of 87 lives, and $Can. 22,500,000 (*then £4,623,000*). It reigned as the world's longest bridge span of any from 1917 until the completion in 1929 of the 1,850 ft *564 m* span Ambassador Suspension Bridge across the Detroit River linking Michigan, U.S.A. with Ontario, Canada. This was then surpassed in 1931 by the George Washington Suspension Bridge across the Hudson River, New York City with a span of 3,500 ft *1 067 m*.

The Saulte Ste Marie double-leaf bascule rail bridge with a main span of 336 ft *102 m* completed in 1941 was, for 8 years till 1949, the longest of its kind in the world.

Longest Covered Bridge
The world's longest surviving covered bridge is that at Hartland, New Brunswick measuring 1,282 ft *390,8 m* completed in 1899.

Longest Canal
The St. Lawrence is the world's longest inland navigation facility for ocean-going ships extending 189 miles *304 km* along the Ontario-U.S. border from Montreal to Lake Ontario and enabling ships up to 26,000 tons to sail 2,342 miles *3,769 km* from the North Atlantic to Duluth, Minnesota, U.S.A. on Lake Superior 602 ft *183 m* above sea level. It was opened on April 25 1959 at a cost of $470,000,000.

The longest canal on the Seaway is the fourth Welland Canal completed in 1932. It is 27 miles *43 km* long with 8 locks 859 × 80 × 30 ft *262 × 24 × 9 m*. Surmounting a world record head of 326 ft *99 m*. The original Welland Canal with 40 timbered locks was begun in 1824 and in use from 1829–1845.

Largest Dam
Canada's largest dam is the Gardiner Dam, South Saskatchewan completed in 1968 to a height of 223 ft *68 m* and with a volume of 85,793,000 million yd³ *66 million m³* with a crest length of 16,700 ft *5 090 m*. It then ranked fourth largest in the world.

The highest dam in Canada is the 794 ft *242 m* Mica rockfill dam on the Columbia river, B.C. which has a crest length of 2,600 ft *792,5 m*. It is arguable that since it is regulated by a dam, Lake Ontario is a quasi-reservoir with an area of 7,550 miles² *19 554 km²* and a volume of 404.6 miles³ *1 686 km³*. Canada's largest conventional reservoir is that dammed by the Daniel Johnson dam on the Manicouagan River, Quebec filled in 1968 with 34.07 miles³ *142 km³* of water.

Longest Tunnel
Canada's longest tunnel is the Chute-des-passes hydro-electric tunnel, Quebec, completed in 1959 to a length of 11.7 miles *18,8 km* and a maximum diameter of 34 ft *10,4 m* when it ranked third in the world.

Canada's longest rail tunnel is the Connaught (Canadian Pacific) Tunnel opened on Dec. 6 1916 and 5 miles 39 yd *8,08 km* long. It is operated by the Canadian Pacific.

The Louis Hippolyte Lafontaine road tunnel, Montreal, completed in 1967 with two 3 lane immersed tubes measures 4,560 ft *1 390 m* between portals.

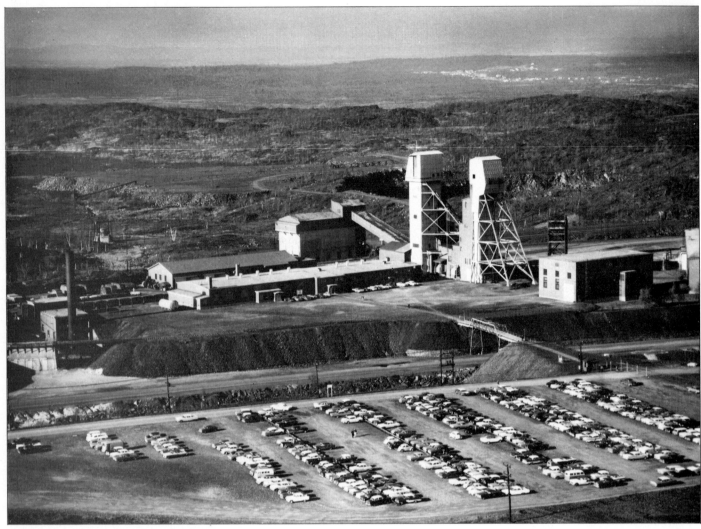

Canada's most productive nickel mine, the 90 year old Frood-Stobie mine at Sudbury, Ontario, the output of which is nearing 3 million short tons. (*George Hunter*)

The world's largest silver mine, the Kidd Creek Mine, at Timmins, Ontario, from which some 4,000 short tons of the noble metal has been extracted.

Largest Advertising Sign

The largest advertising sign in Canada is one for the Hiram Walker Distillery on their grain elevators at Walkerville, Ontario measuring 218 ft *66,44 m* long by 61½ ft *18,74 m* high.

Deepest Oil Well

The deepest well ever drilled in Canadian soil was the Union *et al* Nose Creek well 13-32-64-12 W6, located 300 miles *480 km* northwest of Edmonton, Alberta. The bore was started on Nov. 16 1972 and reached 18,677 ft *5 692 m* on Aug. 14 1973. No commercial discovery was achieved.

MINING

As a world producer of metals Canada is first (1976 figures) in nickel (262 492 tonnes), zinc (1 039 688 tonnes) and silver 1 271 7 tonnes), second in molybdenum (14 416 tonnes) and third in aluminium metal, gold (52,44 tonnes) and fourth in copper (747 135 tonnes). The earliest discovery of silver was at St. Mary's Bay, Nova Scotia by Master Simon in 1604. Copper in measurable quantities was discovered at Coppermine River, N.W.T. in 1771 and placer gold near Yale, B.C. in 1858.

Deepest Mine

The deepest continuous mine shaft in Canada is one in the Creighton Mine operated by the Inco Metals Company at more than 7,160 ft *2 182,3 m*.

LARGEST MINES

Gold

Canada's largest gold mine was The Hollinger Gold Mines of Timmins, Ontario from which 19,315,000 oz. of gold was recorded during its 58 year long operation in 1910–1968.

Silver

Canada's and the world's largest silver mine is the Kidd Creek Mine, Timmins, Ontario. In the nine years from the start-up late in 1966 to Dec. 31 1976 silver production was 3,940 short tons; 14,330 short tons of cadmium, 2,868,370 short tons of zinc and 512,970 short tons of copper. Ore reserves are estimated at 89 million short tons to the 2,800 ft *835 m* level and annual production should rise from 3.9 million to 5 million short tons in 1978.

Nickel

The largest nickel mine in Canada is the Frood-Stobie Mine, Sudbury, Ontario operated by Inco Limited. Since mining operations began in 1887, 5,800 million lb. of nickel has been produced from 247 million tons of ore.

Iron

Canada's largest open-pit iron mine is at Labrador City, Newfoundland operated by The Iron Ore Co, of Canada. It moves 56 million short tons of ore and waste each year.

THE MECHANICAL WORLD

SHIPS

Royal Canadian Navy

The first ship to be commissioned into the R.C.N. was a former British cruiser as H.M.C.S. Rainbow on Aug. 4 1910.

The largest ships ever to serve in the Maritime Command are the Operational Support Ships *Preserver* and *Protecteur* each 555 ft *169,16 m* overall with standard displacements of 24,000 tons. The largest R.C.N. warship was the former aircraft carrier H.M.C.S. Bonaventure.

Merchant Shipping

Canada's registered vessels as at Dec. 31 1976 comprised 31,593: Steam (186), Sailing (3,032) and Motor (28,375) vessels of 3,267,335 net tons or 4,374,923 tons gross.

Largest Ship

The largest Canadian registered sea-going ship is *Cape Breton Highlander*, owned by Port Weller Dry Docks Limited of St. Catherine's, Ontario with a deadweight tonnage of 51,005 tons. The largest Canadian registered lake ship is *H.M. Griffith*, owned by Niagara Finance Co. Ltd. of Toronto, Ontario with a deadweight tonnage of 31,086 tons.

Heaviest Ice Breaker

The Canadian Coast Guard's heaviest ice breaker is the 24,000 shp 13,000 ton *Louis S. St. Laurent* completed at Canadian Vickers Ltd., Montreal in October 1969.

Road Load *Longest*

The longest road load moved on Canadian roads was a 183 ft 5 in *59,93 m* long prefractionator column built for the Sun Oil Company by Sarnia Cranes Ltd. and moved from Point Edward to Sarnia, Ontario on Dec. 8 1975.

Road Speed Limits

The highest driving speed limits in Canada are 70 m.p.h. *112,65 km/h* in the provinces of Alberta, Ontario and Quebec. The lowest limits are in Alberta, British Columbia, Ontario and Prince Edward Island at 20 m.p.h. *32,18 km/h*.

RAILWAYS
Earliest

The earliest railway in Canada was the 4 ft 8½ in *1,435 m* gauge iron rail horse-drawn Coal railway at Picton, Nova Scotia opened in 1827. The first steam train to run was from Lapraire on the St. Lawrence a distance of 16 miles *25,75 km* to St. John on the Richelieu on the Champlain & St. Lawrence (5 ft 6 in *1,676 m* gauge) Railway on July 21 1836.

Trans-Continental

The Canadian Pacific line was completed at Craigellachie in Eagle Pass, B.C. on Nov. 7 1885. The mileage from Montreal to Vancouver is 2,879 miles *4 633 km*.

Highest Point

The highest altitude attained is 5,332 ft *1 625 m* above sea level on the Alberta-British Columbia boundary at the Great Divide on the Canadian Pacific Railway.

Highest Speeds

A speed of 112 m.p.h. *180,2 km/h* was achieved in a test run on one of the five Canadian Pacific Jubilee 4-4-4's. The Canadian National diesel "Rapidos" covers the 115.3 miles *185,5 km* between Dorval and Brockville in 87 mins to average 79.5 m.p.h. *127,9 km/h*.

Longest Train

The longest train ever moved on Canadian Railways was a Prairie grain train with 4 diesel locomotives at the front and three more 1¾ miles back on a 2½ mile long 250 car Canadian Pacific assembly. The train rolled into Thunder Bay from Moose Jaw on Oct. 23 1974.

AIRCRAFT
Earliest Flights

The earliest recorded flight from Canadian territory was by a hydrogen balloon manned by Richard Cowan, Charles Grimley and Charles Page which ascended from Montreal on July 31 1879.

The first sustained powered flight was made by J. A. D. McCurdy in his self-designed biplane Silver Dart over Baddeck Bay, Nova Scotia on Feb. 23 1909. He had made an earlier flight at Hammondsport, N.Y., U.S.A. in December 1908. McCurdy took up his first passenger (F. W. "Casey" Baldwin) at Petawawa, Ontario on Aug. 2 1909.

Trans Atlantic Flight

For details of the first non-stop Trans Atlantic flight see p. 141. The first flight from the Canadian mainland to Britain was by the D.H. 84 Dragon *Trail of the Caribou* flown by J. R. Ayling and Capt. L. Reid from Wasaga Beach to Heston, London in 30 hours 50 min on Aug. 8–9 1934.

POWER STATIONS

Historically the Sir Adam Beck No. 1 station on Niagara (formerly Queenston-Chippawa) became the world's largest in 1922 with 403,900 kw. In 1942 the Beauharnois Station on the St. Lawrence became operative with an ultimate power of 1,670 Mw.

Largest Hydroelectric Power Station

The world's largest underground power station is the $936 million Churchill Falls, Labrador where 2.3 million cubic yards *1,76 million m³* of rock was excavated to a depth of 984 ft *300 m*. The weight of explosive used was 2,500 short tons *2 268 tonnes* and blasting was completed in 1970 and the project was operative in 1975 with an ultimate rating of 5,225 MW, with a gross head of 1,060 ft *323 m*. The La Grande plant now under construction will have a capacity of 5,416 MW.

ENGINEERING
Largest Lift

The world's most massive lift ever accomplished was the 41,000 short ton *40 474 tonnes* roof of the Velodrome in Montreal in 1975 when this weight was jacked 4 inches *10,16 cm* to strike its centering.

Most Powerful Crane

Canada's most powerful crane is the floating crane S.L. *Herecules* owned by the St. Lawrence Seaway Authority with a 250 ton capacity.

Fastest Computer

The fastest computer installed in Canada is a Cyber 76 at the Canadian Meteorological Centre in Dorval, Quebec which executes more than 50 million calculations per second.

THE BUSINESS WORLD

Highest Sales

The top Canadian company in the 1976 *Fortune* list was Ford Motors of Canada with $4,363,311,000 sales (U.S. dollars) and 34,100 employees.

Highest Capital Employed

The Canadian company employing the greatest capital in *The Times 1000 1976–77 List* is Canadian Pacific with $5,118,544,000.

Highest Net Income

The most profitable Canadian company in the 1976 *Fortune* list was Imperial Oil with a net income of $Can 238,018,000.

Bookshop

The largest paperback bookshop in Canada is Classic Book Shop store in Montreal opened in November 1960 which carries more than 43,000 titles on 1,672 yards *1 528 m* of shelving.

Largest Engineering Contractor

Monenco Ltd. of Montreal, Quebec is Canada's largest single contractor with a 1976 payroll of 1,168.

Insurance

Canada's oldest insurance company is Halifax Insurance Co. (est. 1809). The largest in the life field is Sun Life of Canada and the largest in the Property/casualty field is Royal Insurance.

Bank

The largest Canadian commercial bank in the 1976 *Fortune* list is the Royal Bank of Canada with assets of $Can 23,993 million and deposits of $Can 21,765 million. There were 1,524 offices and 32,095 employees.

Distillery

The largest and oldest (established 1856) distillery in Canada is Hiram Walker's plant at Walkerville, Ontario.

Largest Refinery

The largest oil refinery in Canada is the Saint John, New Brunswick refinery owned by Irving Oil Ltd. and Standard Oil of California, with a capacity of 250,000 barrels per day from July 1976.

AGRICULTURE
Livestock Records

The first cow in the world to produce more than 908 kg *1 ton* of butterfat in a single year was the Holstein-Friesian "Ingholm Rag Apple President" with 952 kg *2,098 lb.* in her seventh year. She also holds the Canadian milk production record with 84,300 kg *17.07 tons* of milk in 6 lactations. She was owned by Clare Ingram of Campbellford, Ont. and died in March 1976.

The Canadian one year record is 17 463 kg *3.53 tons* with 3.93% fat by the Holstein-Friesian "Davisglen Achilles Carol" at Oak Ridges Farm, Ontario.

Highest Price

The highest price for a cow anywhere in the world was $235,000 on Nov. 8 1976 at the Sale of Stars, Hays Sales Arena, Oakville, Ontario for the Holstein-Friesian "Hanover Hill Barb" bought by a U.S.-Canadian syndicate.

THE HUMAN WORLD

Canada is the second largest country of the 223 countries in the world second only to the U.S.S.R. It is the largest in the western hemisphere with an area of 3,851,809 miles² *9 976 139 km²*.

Canada's territory comprises 27% forest and 8% farmland. Only 11% is permanently settled. Canada measures 2,875 miles *4 626 km* from the north (Cape Columbia, Ellesmere Island) in Lat. 83° 07' N to the southernmost point (Middle Island in Lake Erie) in Lat. 41° 41' N and 3,223 miles *5 186 km* from east to west at its widest point between Mount St. Elias, Yukon, in Long 141° W to Cape Spear, Newfoundland in Long. 52° 37' W.

The largest of the 10 provinces is Quebec with 594,860 miles² *1 540 675 km²* and the smallest is Prince Edward Island with 2,184 miles² *5 656 km²*. North-West Territories has however an area of 1,304,903 miles² *3 379 672 km²*.

Boundaries

The southern boundary with the United States is 3,986.8 miles *6 416,1 km* in length and that with Alaska, U.S.A. 1,539.9 miles *2 478,0 km*. Canada's Atlantic coastline is 9,843 miles *15 840 km* long, her Pacific coastline 4,363 miles *7 021 km* long and her Arctic coastline is 11,884 miles *19 125 km* in length.

Populations

The preliminary census figure for home population on Jun. 1 1976 was 22,992,604. The most populous province is Ontario with 8,132,000 and the least, Prince Edward Island with 116,250. The U.N. projection for Canada was 26,511,000 in 1985 and 31,613,000 in 2000.

Most Populous Cities

The mid-1976 estimate for the Metropolitan areas of Montreal and Toronto were 2,759,000 and 2,753,000. The respective city populations were 1,060,000 and 611,000.

Towns Northernmost and Highest

Canada's northernmost town is Inuvik, North Western Territory in Lat. 68° 21' N. Canada's highest town is Lake Louise, Alberta at 5,051 ft *1 539 m* above sea level.

above: The interior of the largest bookshop in Canada—the Classic Book Shop in Montreal, which has 1,672 yds *1 528 m* of shelving.

above right: The world's tallest chimney, that of the International Nickel Company in Sudbury, Ontario, reaching a height of 1,251 ft *381 m.* (see p. 345)

right: One of the four Bank of Montreal logos, comprising the highest advertising sign in the world, atop the 72 storey 935 ft *285 m* tall, First Canadian Place in Montreal. (See p. 125) (*Claude Neon Ltd.*)

below: The 61½ ft *18,74 m* tall advertising sign on the Hiram Walker Distillery grain elevators—Canada's largest sign. (see p. 347)

Time Zone

Canada has 6 time zones ranging over 4½ hours from the most easterly, the Newfoundland Standard Time 3½ hours behind Universal Time (U.T.) and the most westerly, Pacific Standard Time 8 hours behind U.T.

Prisons

Canada's largest prison is the maximum security institution at Laval, P.Q. with a capacity of 560. The smallest is the Oskana Centre, a minimum security Community Correctional Centre, in Regina, Saskatchewan with a capacity of 13. Canada's oldest prison is the Kingston Penitentiary, Ontario established in 1835.

Most Recent Executions

The last judicial hanging in Canada took place at Don Jail, Toronto in the early hours of Dec. 11 1962 of Ronald Turpin, who shot Constable Frederick Nash in Ontario and Arthur Lucas who had stabbed Thorland Carter.

Judge *Youngest*

The youngest recorded age for the appointment of a judge in Canada is 25 years 57 days in the case of His Honour Judge Wallace Michael Darichuk (b. St. Clements, Manitoba, May 28 1938). He was appointed by the Lt-Governor-in-Council on July 25 1963.

Hospitals

The oldest hospital in Canada is Hôtel-Dieu de Québec established in 1639. It now has 642 beds set-up and is a teaching hospital.

Canada's largest General Hospital is the Vancouver General Hospital, Vancouver, B.C. with 1,759 beds set-up. The largest children's hospital is The Hospital for Sick Children, Toronto, Ontario with 776 beds set-up and the largest mental hospital is Centre Hospitalier Robert Giffard, Beauport, Québec, P.Q. with 2,900 beds set-up.

Largest University

Canada's largest university is the third oldest, the University of Toronto with a total enrolment of 46,643 (Dec. 1 1975). The University has more than 130 buildings spread over 193 acres of land and was founded as King's College by King George IV (1820–30) in 1827 and assumed its present name when secularized in 1849.

Export-Import Trade

In 1976 The United States monopolized 67.8% of Canada's exports of $38.02 billion and 68.6% of her imports of $37.39 billion.

Postage Stamp *Highest Price*

The highest price paid for any Canadian philatelic item has been $100,000 by Robert Lyman of New York State in March 1976 for a mint pair of 12d Blacks of June 14 1851. The imperforate pair were separated and sold separately for $60,000 and $52,500 in Canada and West Germany some weeks later.

Earliest and Rarest

The first Canadian stamp was the New Carlisle, Gaspé 3 penny black of Apr. 7 1851 of which one cancelled example survives. The regular 3d red Beaver stamp was issued 16 days later.

The exterior of Canada's largest mental hospital at Beauport, Québec, which has capacity for 2,900 patients.

ROADS

Largest

The largest singly designated road is the Trans Canada Highway from St. John's Newfoundland to Victoria, B.C. stretching over 4,784 miles *7 699 km* of which 4,148 miles *6 675 km* is on the mainland. The longest street is Yonge Street (see page 199).

Highest

Canada's highest piece of carriageable roadway is between Town of High River and Kananaskis Lakes at Lat. 50° 36′ N. Long 114° 59′ W in the Rockies, Alberta at 7,250 ft 2 209 *m*.

Northernmost

Canada's most northerly piece of road is 1.5 miles *2,4 km* long at Alert, N.W.T. at Lat. 82′ 30″ N Long. 62° 20′ W.

Coin Most Valuable

The highest price paid for a Canadian coin is $110,000 for one of the two 1911 silver dollar patterns from the McKay-Clements collection at the Westbury Hotel, Toronto on May 15 1976. The purchaser was Douglas Robbins.

GOVERNORS GENERAL

Longest Lived

The longest lived of Canada's 21 Governors General was the 10th who was Field Marshall H.R.H. the Prince Arthur William Patrick Albert, 1st Duke of Connaught and Strathearn K.G., K.T., K.P., G.M.B., G.C.S.I., G.C.M.G., G.C.I.E., G.C.V.O., G.B.E., V.D., T.D. (1850–1942), a son of Queen Victoria, who died on Jan. 16 1942 aged 91 years 9 months.

Oldest in Office

The oldest in office was the 19th who was General the Rt. Hon. Georges Philias Vanier C.C., D.S.O., M.C.★, C.D. (1888–1967) who died in office aged 78 years 10 months.

Longest Span

The longest period in office was 7 years 7 months in the case of the 18th, the Rt. Hon. Vincent Massey C.C., C.H. (1887–1967) from Feb. 28 1952 to Sept. 14 1959.

Youngest

The youngest Governor General was the 4th, His Grace Sir John Douglas Sutherland Campbell Bt., K.G., K.T., G.C.M.G., G.C.V.O., V.D., 9th Duke of Argyll (1845–1914) who was 33 years 3 months old on his appointment.

PRIME MINISTERS

Longest Serving

The longest serving Canadian Prime Minister has been the 10th, the Rt. Hon. William Lyon Mackenzie King, O.M., C.M.G. (1874–1950) who uniquely had 3 terms in office in 1921–26, 1926–30 and 1935–48 aggregating a record total of 21 years 3 months.

Longest Lived and Shortest Serving

The longest lived of Canada's 15 Prime Ministers has been the Rt. Hon. Sir Charles Tupper Bt., G.C.M.G., C.B. (born July 2 1821), who died on Oct. 30 1915 aged 94 years 121 days. Ironically his tenure of 69 days in 1896 was the shortest premiership.

Youngest in Office

Canada's youngest premier was the Rt. Hon. Arthur Meighen who was 46 years and 1 month old when he achieved office on July 10 1926.

THE SENATE

The size of the Senate was increased from 102 to 104 on June 19 1975. The greatest number of seats ever held by one party has been 82 by the Liberals in 1953 for a majority of 74 over the Progressive Conservatives (8 seats). In 1956 the Progressive Conservatives held only 5 seats—the lowest ever for a principle opposition party.

Arguably the least satisfying electoral achievement on recent record was that of being beaten by a dead man. E. B. Ironside, in the Hanna council by-election in Alberta, Canada on Mar.

	SENATORS	MP'S
Oldest (all time)	102 yrs 202 days Hon Georges-Casimir Dessaulles (Liberal) b. Sept 29 1827 d. Apr. 19 1930 (Limit since June 2 1965–75 years)	86 yrs 10¾ mths William Anderson Black (1847–1934)
Younges	32 yrs 253 days Rt Hon William Miller (1835–1912) (Lib-Con) appointed Oct. 23 1867 (Legal limit 30 years)	20 yrs Claude-Andre Lachance (b. 1954) elected 1974
Longest Span (Unbroken)	48 yrs 200 days Hon. Pascal Poirier (1852–1933) (Mar. 9 1885–Sept. 25 1933) Hon. Charles Gavan Power (1888–1968) was MP and Senator for an unbroken 51 years. Hon. Hippolyte Montplaisir (1839–1927) served 53 years with a 6 day break between chambers.	41 yrs 2½ mths Sir Wilfred Laurier (1841–1933) (Nov. 28 1877–Feb. 17 1919) and (Jan. 1874–Oct. 27 1877 earlier)

2 1977, learnt that after nominations closed, his opponent Oscar Rowden had died. Nonetheless he received only 41.9% of the poll compared with the dead man's 58.1%.

M.P.'s Largest and Smallest Majorities

The largest personal majority of any M.P. is 35,437 by Pierre Elliott Trudeau (b. 1919) in Mount Royal in 1968. Six instances of majorities of one have been returned occuring between 1887 and 1930. Edouard Guilbault was returned by the deciding vote of the returning officer after a tie at Joliette on 22 Feb. 1887. On 6 Nov. 1888 he was however unseated by a judicial decision.

INDIAN AFFAIRS

The largest Indian Reserve on Canadian territory is the 349,618 acre *141 485 ha* Blood Reserve No. 148 near Fort McLeod, Alberta surveyed in 1872–73 and established by Order in Council in 1889.

The worst conflict between Indian and European settlers on Canadian territory for which a casualty estimate exists was that at Lachine in 1689 when 200 French were killed and 120 captured in a night ambush.

WORST ACCIDENTS & DISASTERS WITH DEATH ROLLS

Explosion	1,963	Ammunition ship collided in Halifax harbour.	Dec. 6 1917
Marine	1,024	Empress of Ireland in collision with a collier in St. Lawrence.	Aug. 29 1914
Aircraft	118	Trans. Canada DC 8F crashed after take-off from Montreal.	Nov. 29 1963
Fire	100	St. John, New Brunswick	June 20 1887
Railway	99	Grand Trunk Railway at Beloeil, Quebec.	June 29 1864
Road	13	Baie St. Paul, Québec bus crash	June 1 1974

HUMAN ACHIEVEMENTS

MISCELLANEOUS ENDEAVOURS

Balancing on one foot

The longest recorded duration in Canada for continuous balancing on one foot is 9 hrs 11 min by George Horning at Unicity Fashion Square, Winnipeg, Manitoba on 26 Feb. 1977.

HONOURS DECORATIONS AND AWARDS

Order of Precedence of Decorations

First in the order of wearing of decorations is the claret coloured ribbon of the Victoria Cross (V.C.), the British gallantry decoration instituted in 1856 which has been won by 90 Canadian citizens of whom 12 survive. This is followed by the blue ribboned George Cross (G.C.) instituted in 1940 held by 4 men and 1 woman. The foremost Canadian decorations are the Cross of Valour (C.V.) followed by the

Companion of the Order of Canada (C.C.) instituted on July 1 1967.

Cross of Valour
The Cross of Valour, Canada's highest decoration (created in 1972) was awarded to Mrs. Jean Swedborg of Merritt, B.C., posthumously in June 1976 for gallantry in the Valnicola Hospital fire of Sept. 1974.

Most Gallantry Awards
Wing Cmdr. John Randall Daniel Braham D.S.O.**, D.F.C.**, A.F.C., C.D. (born April 6 1920, Bath, England; died 1970) has been the most decorated Canadian serviceman having uniquely won 7 British gallantry awards. Of Canadian born serviceman, the air ace Lt. Col. William George Barker V.C., D.S.O.*, M.C.**, R.F.C. (born Nov. 3 1894 at Dauphin, Manitoba, died Mar. 12 1930 at Ottawa) won six gallantry awards.

NOBEL PRIZEMEN
Three Canadian nationals have won the Nobel Prize (instituted 1901). Sir Frederick Grant Banting K.B.E., M.C. (b. Alliston, Ont. Nov. 14 1891 and killed Newfoundland Feb. 21 1941) won the Physiology or Medicine prize in 1923 for his work on obtaining a pancreatic extract of insulin. He voluntarily shared his prize money with is co-discoverer Charles Herbert Best C.C., C.H., C.B.E. (b. Feb. 27 1899 in U.S. of Canadian parentage) at the University of Toronto. The 1971 Chemistry prize was won by the naturalized Canadian Gerhard Herzberg (b. Hamburg, West Germany Dec. 25 1904) for research into molecular geometry and electronic structure in Ottawa. In 1957 Lester Bowles Pearson (b. Toronto Apr. 23 1897) was awarded the Peace Prize.

MOST BARS (REPEAT AWARDS) BRITISH AWARDS	
WWI = World War I (1914–1918)	WWII = World War II (1939–1945)

DSO**	15 awards in WWI and 4 in WWII including Gen. Jean Victor Allard C.C., C.B.E., D.S.O.**, E.D., C.D. Maj. Gen. Bertram Meryl Hoffmeister, C.B., C.B.E., D.S.O.**, E.D. Group Capt. John Emilias Fauquier D.S.O.**, D.F.C., R.C.A.F.
R.R.C.*	4 awards all WWI Miss Edith M. Wilson Miss E. Russell Miss A. J. Hartley Miss M. H. Smith
D.S.C.**	3 awards all WWII Lt. Charles Arthur Burk, R.C.N.V.R. L.t. Cdr. Thomas George Fuller, R.C.N.V.R. Lt. Cdr. Cornelius Burke, R.C.N.V.R.
D.F.C.**	6 awards all WWII—Braham and also S./Ldr. George Urquhart Hill S./Ldr. Herbert Victor Peterson S./Ldr. Robert Wendell McNair S./Ldr. David Charles Fairbanks S./Ldr. John Todd Caine
D.C.M.**	Unique award Sgt. G. H. Soles in WWI
G.M.*	4 awards Lt. George Douglas Cook R.C.N.V.R. Lt. Cdr. James Leslie Harries O.B.E., R.C.N.V.R. Lt. Denis James Patrick O'Hagan R.C.N.V.R. Lt. George Henry Olaf Rundle R.C.N.V.R.
M.M.**	38 awards in WWI and uniquely CSM Frank Leslie Dixon in WWII.

SPORTS GAMES AND PASTIMES

ALL SPORTS

Largest crowd
The largest crowd to watch a non-Olympic event in Canada (excluding the Calgary Stampede) was one of 85,000 motor racing fans attending the Canadian Grand Prix at Mosport Park, Ontario, on Oct. 3 1976. In June 1974 an estimated 100,000 fans were at the Labatt Can-Am motor racing weekend.

Biggest stadium
For the opening of the XXI Olympic Games on July 17 1976, the Montreal Olympic Stadium held 75,860 spectators making it the largest stadium in the country. Total cost of the Olympic stadium complex is estimated at $800 million.

Most popular sport
There are an estimated four million participants in bowling in Canada—this represents one person in every six in the country. There are some 20,000 bowling lanes.

Greatest all-rounder
Canada's greatest ever all-round sportsman is generally acknowledged to be Lionel Pretoria "The Big Train" Conacher (1901–1954). He won National or Provincial championships at football (Grey Cup), hockey (Stanley Cup), lacrosse, boxing, baseball and wrestling. He died, as a Member of Parliament, playing a charity game of softball. The greatest sportswoman was Fanny "Bobbie" Rosenfeld (1903–1969). She was an Olympic gold and silver medallist athlete, as well as attaining championship status at hockey, speed skating, basketball, softball and tennis.

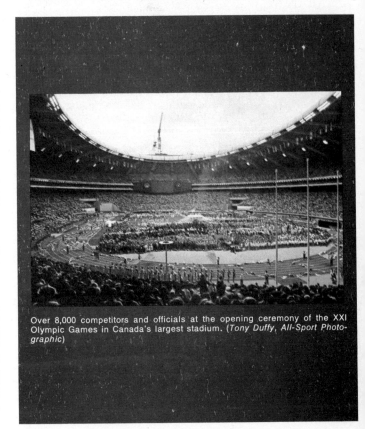

Over 8,000 competitors and officials at the opening ceremony of the XXI Olympic Games in Canada's largest stadium. (*Tony Duffy, All-Sport Photographic*)

352

ANGLING

CANADIAN RECORDS (Freshwater fish ratified by "Field and Stream", *Seawater fish ratified by International Game Fish Association)

Species	Weight lb. oz	kg/g	Name	Place	Date
Bass, Rock	3 0	1,360	Peter Gulgin	York River, Ontario	1 Aug. 1974
Char, Arctic	29 11	13,466	Jeanne P. Branson	Arctic River, N.W.T.	21 Aug. 1968
Grayling, American	5 15	2,693	Jeanne P. Branson	Katseyedie River, N.W.T.	16 Aug. 1967
Salmon, Chinook	92 00	41,730	Heinz Wichman	Skeena River, B.C.	19 July 1959
Salmon, Silver (Coho)	31 00	14,061	Mrs. Lee Halberg	Cowichan Bay, B.C.	11 Oct. 1947
Trout, Brook	14 8	6,577	Dr. W. J. Cook	Nipigon River, Ontario	July 1916
Trout, Lake¹	65 00	29,483	Larry Daunis	Great Bear Lake, N.W.T.	8 Aug. 1970
*Tuna, Bluefin	1,200 00	544,310	Leslie Vibert	Chaleur Bay, N.B.	22 Sept. 1976
Whitefish, Lake	13 00	5,896	Robert L. Stintsman	Great Bear Lake, N.W.T.	14 July 1974
Whitefish, Mountain	5 00	2,268	Orville Welch	Athabasca River, Alberta	3 June 1963

¹ See p. 240 footnote 7

ARCHERY

Earliest
The first recorded tournament was at the Yorkville Archery Club, Ontario, in 1850.

Olympic Games
The highest placing by a Canadian has been the fifth place by Lucille Lemay (Boisbriand, P.Q.) on July 29–30 1976 at Montréal, Québec.

World Championships
The only Canadians to win world titles have been Dorothy Lidstone, of Abbotsford, B.C., Target champion in 1969, and Lucille Lessard, of Loretteville, P.Q., Field champion in 1974.

Highest scores
The Canadian record for a single FITA Round is 1,267 by David Mann, (B.C.), in Aug. 1976; for the double FITA Round the record is 2,475 by Roger Lemay, (P.Q.), in 1976. The women's single Round score is 1,226 by Lucille Lessard (P.Q.) in Oct. 1974 and the double Round record is held by Dorothy Lidstone (B.C.) with 2,402 in Aug. 1975.

Oldest international
Marjory Saunders (b. Oct. 3 1913) competed in her first Olympic Games just 27 days short of her 59th birthday.

BADMINTON

Earliest
The game was being played in Canada in 1890. The first Inter-Provincial championship was won by British Columbia in 1914. Canada was a founder member of the International Badminton Federation in 1934.

All-England Championships
The only Canadian to win an All-England singles title (emblematic of the world title) is Dorothy Louise Walton (*née* McKenzie) (b. Aug. 7 1909) when she won the ladies title in 1939.

Commonwealth Games
The most successful Canadian in the Commonwealth Games has been James E. (Jamie) Paulson, who won Canada's first and so far only, gold medal at Edinburgh, Scotland in 1970 and added a silver medal four years later in Christchurch, New Zealand.

Most titles
The most National championships won have been by Marjory Shedd (b. 1926) who won seven singles, four mixed doubles, and 11 ladies doubles titles between 1953 and 1969.

Most international appearances
Marjory Shedd has played a record six times in the Uber Cup competition for the world team championship. Wayne MacDonnell has played six times in the equivalent men's competition, the Thomas Cup.

BASEBALL

Earliest
The first professional league in Canada was formed in 1885 in Ontario.

Major Leagues
For details of Major League records see p. 244.

BASKETBALL

Earliest
The modern game of basketball is credited to a Canadian (see p. 244). In the first ever game, one of the captains was T. Duncan Patton, of Montreal.

Most successful
The most successful team in Canadian basketball history was the Edmonton Grads, a ladies team, which played 24 matches on various European trips in the 1920's and 1930's and were never beaten. In 1936 they beat the acknowledged world champions 86–14 in Paris.

BILLIARDS

World Championships
The best placing in the world professional championships has been by George Chenier (1908–1970) who was twice, 1950 and 1958, runner-up to the champion Joe Davis.

BOBSLEIGH

Olympic Games
The only gold medal won by Canada was by the 1964 four-man bob team of Victor Emery, Douglas Anakin, John Emery, and Peter Kirby.

World Championships
Canadian teams have twice won the world four-man bob title. The first was the 1964 Olympic team (see above), and then in 1965 the title was successfully retained by Michael Young, Victor Emery, Gerald Presley and Peter Kirby.

BOWLING (Fivepin)

Earliest
The game was introduced in 1909 by Thomas F. Ryan (1872–1961), in Toronto, and is now the most popular participation sport in Canada with an estimated four million players.

Perfect game
The first recorded perfect game of 450 is credited to Bill Bromfield in 1921. Frank Lavigne (b. 1943) of Vancouver, set a single-season record of four perfect games between Dec. 8 1975 and Mar. 9 1976.

353

Highest scores
Frank Lavigne set a three-game series record of 1205 and a four-game record of 1605 on Apr. 19 1976, and ended the 1975–76 season with a record 329.84 average.

BOWLS (Lawn)

Earliest
It is reported that the game was first played *c.* 1734 by garrison officers at Port Royal, Nova Scotia.

Commonwealth Games
The most successful individual bowler has been W. S. Macdonald the winner of the silver medal in 1934, London, England. The pairs teams of 1930, 1934 and 1954 also gained silver medals.

BOXING

World titles
The only standard weight class in which a Canadian has never held a world professional title is the lightweight division. The youngest Canadian boxer to win a world title was George "Little Chocolate" Dixon (1870–1909) when he took the bantamweight crown on June 27 1890 aged 19 years 11 months.

Most title defences
George Dixon defended his world titles at featherweight and bantamweight on a record 19 (or possibly 20) occasions (see p. 251). World heavyweight champion Tommy Burns (b. Noah Brusso, 1881–1955) defended his title ten times in 33 months (see also pps. 249, 250).

Olympic Games
The first Canadian boxing gold medal was won by Julius Gustav Albert Schneider (b. Cleveland, U.S.A., July 1 1897) in the 1920 welterweight division. The only other gold medallist has been Horace "Lefty" Gwynne (b. 1913, Toronto) winner of the 1932 bantamweight title.

The smallest world heavyweight champion, 5 ft 7 in *1,70 m* Tommy Burns, was only knocked out once in his 60 fight, 20 year career. (*Sport & General*)

George Dixon (right) was the first black boxer to hold a world title, winning the bantamweight crown in 1890. (*The Mansell Collection*)

Six time Canadian canoeing champion, Frank Amyot, won Canada's only gold medal at the 1936 Olympic Games in Berlin. (*Alexandra Studio*)

CANOEING

Earliest
Canoes had been used by the Indians for centuries, but the birchbark developed by I. S. Stephenson in the 1850's, known as the Peterborough, was the forerunner of the Canadian Olympic Class canoe. The first sporting canoe club in Canada was Montreal's Point St. Charles Club founded in 1875.

Olympic Games
The only Canadian to win an Olympic Games gold medal for canoeing was Francis Amyot (1904–1962) when he won the 1936 Canadian Singles title at Berlin.

COMMONWEALTH GAMES

Earliest
The concept of a British Empire Games was first put forward by Melville Mark "Bobby" Robinson (1888–1974), of Hamilton, in 1928, and the first official Games were held in that city in 1930.

Most medals
From 1930 to 1974 Canada has won 129 gold, 171 silver and 161 bronze medals. The most medals won by an individual are 12 (one gold, nine silver, two bronze) by swimmer Ralph Hutton (b. May 6 1948) in 1966 and 1970.

CRICKET

Earliest
The game was played in Halifax in the latter part of the eighteenth century, and it is reported that there was a match in 1785 in Montreal. The Canadian Cricket Association was formed on March 29 1892.

International matches
There was an inter-club match between Toronto C.C. and St. George's C.C. of New York on Aug. 29 1840 but the first ever international match, in the world, was one between Canada and the United States, held in New York on Sept. 24–25 1844. It was won by Canada in front of some 5,000 spectators. Of the 57 matches played to date, the U.S.A. has won 31, Canada 18 and eight drawn.

CURLING

Earliest
The introduction of the sport to Canada is attributed to General Wolfe's soldiers in 1759. The first organised club was the Royal Montreal Curling Club founded on Jan. 22 1807 at Gillis's Coffee House, Montreal.

Strathcona and Scotch Cups
For details see p. 261.

Manitoba Bonspiel
At the Manitoba Bonspiel, held annually in Winnipeg, the record number of Grand Aggregate wins is seven by Kenneth Watson (b. 1904) skip of the Strathcona Club rink, Manitoba, in 1939, 1942–1947.

Brier Cup
The first man to win the Macdonald's Brier Tankard (the Brier Cup) on three occasions was Kenneth Watson, Strathcona Club, Manitoba, in 1936, 1942 and 1949. The Saskat-

chewan rink, composed of the Richardson family—Ernie, Arnold, Garnet and Wes—have won a record four times, in 1959, 1960, 1962 and 1963 (on the last occasion with Mel Perry in place of Wes Richardson).

Largest tournament and largest rink
For details see p. 261.

CYCLING

Earliest
The Montreal Bicycle Club was founded in 1876, some two years after the first bicycles appeared there. In 1882 the Canadian Wheelmen's Association was formed.

World Championships
Only one Canadian has won a world title, the professional H. Gibson, who won the track motor-paced championship in 1899.

Commonwealth Games
The most successful rider in the Commonwealth Games has been Jocelyn Charles Lovell (b. July 19 1950) who won the 1970 ten mile race, came second in the tandem sprint with Barry Harvey and third in the 1 000 metres time trial.

Trans-Canada
The Halifax to Vancouver, Trans-Canada (3,950 miles 6 357 km) record is 24 days 13 hr 5 min by John W. Hathaway, of Vancouver in 1957.

EQUESTRIAN SPORTS

Earliest
The first equestrian competition recorded was in 1843 in Toronto.

Olympic Games
Canada's first Olympic medal was the bronze winning team in the Three-day event at Stockholm, Sweden in 1956. The first gold medal came in the Team Jumping at Mexico City in 1968 with James Elder (b. July 27 1934), James Day (b. July 2 1946) and Thomas Gayford (b. Nov. 21 1928).

Jumping record
The Hon. C. Sifton's *Confidence* jumped 8 ft 0½ in *2,45 m* at the Ottawa Show in 1912, ridden by J. A. Hambleton.

FENCING

Commonwealth Games
The only gold medal won by Canada has been by the Sabre team of Roland Asselin, Leslie Krasa and Carl Schwende at Vancouver in 1954. The most successful fencer in the Games has been Carl Schwende who won one gold, three silver and four bronze medals from 1954 to 1962.

FOOTBALL (Association)

Earliest
The first proper soccer match was on Oct. 21 1876 between Carlton Cricket Club and Toronto Lacrosse Club, which ended in a goalless draw. However, on May 14 1874 McGill University lost to Harvard 3–0, at Cambridge, Mass., in a game which owed much to Association Football rules. The first international match was against the United States in 1886, and a team visited Great Britain in 1888.

Largest crowd
The largest attendance at a soccer match in Canada was the 71,619 who watched East Germany beat Poland 3–1 at Montreal on July 31 1976. The record number of spectators to watch a Canadian club were 26,445 who saw Vancouver Whitecaps lose 2–1 to New York Cosmos at Vancouver on July 7 1975.

National champions
The "Challenge Trophy", emblematic of the national amateur championship has been won a record eight times by New Westminster Royals (1928, 1930–31, 1936, 1953, 1955, 1958, 1960).

Youngest
The youngest N.A.S.L. player has been Peter Roe, Toronto Metros, who was only 17 years 7 months and 15 days when he played against the St. Louis Stars on May 8 1973. The youngest international player was Wes McLeod, aged 17 years and 258 days when he played against Poland in Toronto, July 9 1975.

FOOTBALL (Rugby Union)

Earliest
First reported game was at Montreal in 1865 between Army officers and civilians. The pioneer club was the Montreal F.C. formed in 1868. The Canadian Rugby Union was formed in 1882.

Most titles
British Columbia has won the Carling Bowl for the interprovincial championship a record nine times since its institution in 1958.

FOOTBALL (Canadian)

Earliest
The first championships of the new code of Canadian Football were held in 1892 and won by Osgoode Hall of Toronto, Ontario.

Grey Cup
Originally for the "Amateur rugby football championship of Canada", the Cup (costing $48) was donated by Governor-General Albert Henry George, the Fourth Earl Grey, in 1909. It was first won by the University of Toronto on Dec. 4 1909 when they beat Parkdale Canoe Club 26–6. The Cup has been won a record ten times by the Toronto Argonauts 1914, 1921, 1933, 1937–38, 1945–47, 1950, 1952. The largest margin of defeat was on Dec. 1 1923 when Queen's University beat Regina 54–0. The highest match aggregate has been 77 on Nov. 24 1956 when Edmonton Eskimos scored 50 to the 27 of Montreal Alouettes.

Largest crowd
The greatest attendance at a C.F.L. game was 68,505 for the Montreal Alouettes v. Ottawa Roughriders game in the Olympic Stadium on Sept. 26 1976. The highest gate receipts of $1,008,418 were collected for the Grey Cup game at Toronto, Nov. 28 1976.

Most touchdowns
The record number of touchdowns in a career is 137 by George Reed (b. 1940) of the Saskatchewan Roughriders, from 1963 to 1975, while the record for one season is 20 by Pat Abbruzzi of the Montreal Alouettes in 1956. The single game record of six was set by Bob McNamara for Winnipeg against the British Columbia Lions on Oct. 13 1956.

Most points
The record total of points in a career is 1,030 by Larry Robinson (b. 1942) of the Calgary Stampeders, from 1961 to 1975. The season record of 169 is held by Dave Cutler (b. Oct. 17 1945) of the Edmonton Eskimos in 1975. The most in one game was 36 by Bob McNamara for Winnipeg against B.C. Lions at Vancouver, Oct. 13 1956.

Rushing
The most yards gained in a career has been 16,116 by George Reed, 1963–1975. The season rushing record is 1,896 yards by Willie Burden, Calgary Stampeders, in 1975. Ron Stewart, Ottawa Rough Riders, rushed a single game record of 287 yards against Montreal on Oct. 10 1960. George Reed has rushed 1,000 yards in eleven seasons, 1964–69, 1971–75.

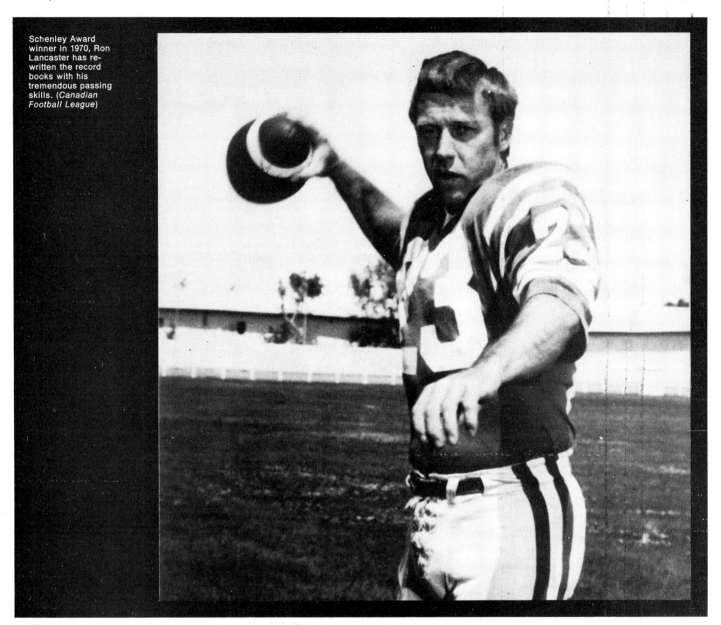

Schenley Award winner in 1970, Ron Lancaster has re-written the record books with his tremendous passing skills. (*Canadian Football League*)

Field goals

The most goals kicked in a career is 214 by Dave Cutler, Edmonton Eskimos, 1969–1976. He also holds the season record with 40 in 1975, and the game record of six. This latter was equalled by Gerry Organ (b. Dec. 4 1944), Ottawa Rough Riders. The longest field goal of 59 yd *53,94 m* was kicked by Dave Cutler at Regina on Oct. 28 1970.

Passing

Ron Lancaster (b. 1940), Ottawa Rough Riders and Saskatchewan Roughriders, holds the career records of 5,394 passes thrown, 2,924 passes completed, 44,786 yards gained passing, and 304 touchdown passes, in the period 1960–1976.

Highest score

The highest score in a major league game is the 82 points by Montreal against Hamilton at Montreal, Oct. 20 1956, when they also scored a record 12 touchdowns.

Longest punt

A punt of 102 yd *93,26 m* was kicked by Dave Mann, Toronto Argonauts against Saskatchewan Roughriders on Sept. 18 1966.

GAMBLING

Pari-mutuel

The Pari-mutuel system was introduced into Canada in 1910.

Biggest prize

On July 27 1973 Parliament approved a lottery, to benefit the Olympic Games to be held in Montreal in 1976. The first draw took place on April 15 1975 when the first prize was $1 million.

GLIDING (Soaring)

Earliest

The first recorded Canadian glider flight—towed by a boy on horseback—was by L. J. Lesh in Dominion Park, Montreal in 1907.

Records

The longest flight by a Canadian is 724,4 km *450.2 miles* from Minden, Nevada, to Malad, Idaho, U.S.A. by Richard M. Cook, on Apr. 15 1975. The greatest height attained is 12 449 m *40,843 ft* by Walter F. Chmela, over Colorado Springs, U.S.A. on Jan. 9 1974, which included a record height gain of 8 321 m *27,299 ft*. The greatest speed achieved around a 100 km Triangle course is 113,4 km *70.5 miles* at El Mirage, Ariz., U.S.A. by Richard Cook on Aug. 21 1970.

GOLF

Earliest

The oldest established club in North America is the Royal

357

Montreal Golf Club founded in 1873. The first inter-club match was in 1876 against Quebec. The first inter-provincial match was won by Quebec in 1882. The United States won the first international match in Toronto, in 1898. There are now over 1,100 courses in Canada.

World Cup
Canada has won the World Cup (formerly the Canada Cup) once, in 1968 with the team of George Knudson (b. June 28 1937, Winnipeg) and Al Balding (b. April 29 1924, Toronto). Stan Leonard (b. 1915) has been a team member on a record eight occasions.

Canadian championships
The first Open championship was held in 1904 at the Royal Montreal Club course. The most wins is four by Leo Diegel (U.S.A.) (1899–1951), 1924–25, 1928–29. Since its inauguration in 1912, the Professional Golfer's Association title has been won eight times by Stan Leonard, 1940–41, 1950–51, 1954, 1957, 1959 and 1961. The Amateur championship, inaugurated 1895 at the Royal Ottawa Club course, was won a record eight times by George Seymour Lyon (1858–1938) between 1898 and 1914.

Marlene Stewart-Streit (b. March 9 1934, Cereal, Alberta), won the women's National Open Amateur title 11 times and the Closed championship nine times. She also won the U.S. Amateur Championship in 1956, and the British Amateur title in 1953.

Longest course
The longest championship course in Canada is the London Hunt course, London, Ontario, with a par-72 for 7,168 yards *6 554 m*.

Olympic Games
Canada's only gold medal in Olympic Games competition was by George Lyon in 1904 at St. Louis, Missouri, beating a field of 87 golfers.

Oldest champion
Having won the Ladies Open Amateur title and Closed championship title five times each in her career, Ada Charlotte Mackenzie (1891–1973) went on to win eight national Senior titles, the last in 1965 aged 73 years. She later achieved a sixth place in her eightieth year.

Eclectic record
For details see p. 280.

Hole-in-one
The oldest Canadian golfer to have shot a hole-in-one was 93-year-old Charles Youngman in 1971. The youngest has been nine-year-old Maurice Regimbal at the 125 yd *114 m* 9th hole at North Bay G.C., Ont. in 1929.

GYMNASTICS

Most titles
The greatest number of wins in the National championships is by Ernestine Russell with six titles 1954–1959. The most by a male gymnast is five by Wilhelm Weiler, 1957–58, 1960, 1962 and 1966.

Somersaults
For the Canadian record for forward rolls, see p. 284.

HARNESS RACING

Most successful driver
The most successful all-round Canadian driver has been Hervé Filion (see p. 331). The most wins in a season on Canadian tracks is 246 in 1967 by Keith Gordon Waples (b. 1923). The record for most wins in a single day's racing is held by Joe O'Brien (b. 1917) who in 1966 won ten races—eight in Springfield, Illinois, and then two more in Chicago later in the day. He is the only Canadian driver to win, in 1955, the Triple Crown driving *Scott Frost.*

The uncrowned king of harness racing in North America, Hervé Filion's driving has won prizes totalling over $16 million. (*U.S. Trotting Association*)

(see also pp. 289–290)

HOCKEY (Ice)

Earliest
There is much dissension on the origin of the game in Canada. The first generally accepted instance is of a game of hockey on ice played by the Royal Canadian Rifles at Kingston, Ontario on Xmas Day 1855, although there are references to a similar game on the harbour ice at Halifax, Nova Scotia in 1851. The first properly organised game was at the Victoria Rink, Montreal on March 3, 1875.

Most points
By the end of the 1976–77 season Gordon "Gordie" Howe (b. March 31 1928, Floral, Saskatchewan) had scored a career record of 2,393 points. The most points in a season (W.H.A.) is 148 by Marc Tardif (b. Granby, P.Q., June 12 1949), Quebec Nordiques, in 81 games 1975–76.

Most goals
The greatest number of goals by a team in one game was when the Montreal Canadiens beat Quebec Bulldogs 16-3 on Mar. 3 1920. The most by an individual is seven by Joe Malone for Quebec Bulldogs *v.* Toronto St. Patricks on Jan. 31 1920.

Most shutouts
In the 1928–9 season George Hainsworth, Montreal Canadiens, played a record 22 matches without conceding a goal.

Largest arena
The Canadian arena with the largest seating capacity for an ice hockey game is the Montreal Forum which can seat 18,350 people.

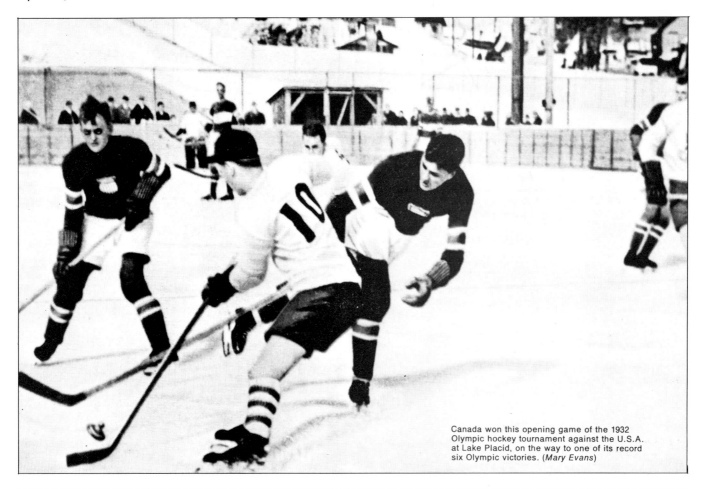

Canada won this opening game of the 1932 Olympic hockey tournament against the U.S.A. at Lake Placid, on the way to one of its record six Olympic victories. (*Mary Evans*)

HORSE RACING

Earliest

There is evidence of horse races being held in Quebec in the early 1760's. The Quebec Garrison Racing Club was founded in 1817. The first recorded steeplechase was near Montreal in 1840.

Oldest race

The oldest continuously run stakes race in North America is the Queen's Plate. It was first run in 1836 as a race for three year-olds over one and one-eighth miles *1,81 km* (now, one and one-quarter *2,01 km*). The prize is actually a gold cup, not a plate.

Most successful horse

The most successful Canadian-based horse was *Northern Dancer* (f. May 1961, Edward Plunket Taylor's Windfields Farm, Willowdale, Ontario). Victories included the 1964 Kentucky Derby (in the then record time), the Preakness Stakes, and the Queen's Plate. On retiring to stud he was named the world's leading sire in 1970.

Most successful jockey

Resident in Alberta from the age of two, Johnny Longden (b. Feb. 14 1910, Wakefield, England) set a career record of 6,032 wins from 1927 to 1966, including the American Triple Crown on *Count Fleet* in 1943. The most wins in a North American season is 515 by Sandford "Sandy" Desmond Hawley (b. April 16 1949, Oshawa, Ontario) in 1973.

Triple Crown winner, Johnny Longden, won prize money totalling $24½ million in his 39 year riding career. (*Fox Photos*)

ICE SKATING (Figure)

Earliest

The Iroquois Indians used animal shinbones tied to the feet with thongs. The first covered rink was opened in Quebec in the 1850's and the Amateur Skating Association of Canada was formed on Nov. 30 1878.

World Championships

In 1890 an unofficial world championship was held in St. Petersburg (now Leningrad), U.S.S.R., and was won by Louis Rubenstein (1861–1931) of Montreal, who had been national champion for the previous eleven years. The first Canadian to win the official men's title (instituted 1896) was Donald Jackson (b. April 2 1940, Oshawa, Ont.) in 1962. The first world title won by a Canadian was when Barbara Ann Scott (b. May 9 1928) won the 1947 Ladies title. The most successful skaters have been the pairs team of Barbara Wagner (b. May 5 1938) and Robert Paul (b. July 2 1937) winners on four consecutive occasions 1957–1960.

Olympic Games

The first gold medal by a Canadian was won by Barbara Ann Scott in 1948. The only other gold medal performance was in the pairs event of 1960 by Barbara Wagner and Robert Paul. Best individual male placing has been bronze by Montgomery Wilson (b. 1910) in 1932, Donald Jackson in 1960, and Toller Cranston (b. April 20 1949) in 1976.

National Championships

The greatest number of titles won is 15 by Constance Wilson (later Samuel) comprising nine individual and six pairs championships. Her brother, Montgomery Wilson, has also won nine individual titles but only five pairs championships.

Youngest international

When Karen Magnussen (b. April 4 1952) first competed in a world's championship meeting, at Vienna, 1967, she was aged 14 years 11 months and was unplaced. Six years later she won the title to add to her 1972 Olympic silver medal.

ICE SKATING (Speed)

Earliest

The first Canadian championships were held in 1887.

World Championships

The first Canadian world champion was Jack K. McCulloch (1872–1919) of Winnipeg, who won the 1,500, 5,000 and 10,000 metres and all-round titles in 1897. In 1976, Sylvia Burka, of Winnipeg, became the first Canadian woman to win a world title at Gjoevik, Norway.

Olympic Games

The first medal won by a Canadian was the bronze in the 500 metres at Los Angeles, on Feb. 4 1932 by Alexander Hurd (b. 1906). The highest placing has been by Cathy Priestner (b. May 27 1956) who won a silver medal over 500 metres on Feb. 6 1976 at Innsbruck, Austria. Ralf Olin, of Calgary, competed in four Olympics 1952–1964 and was Coach in 1968.

Oldest international

When he competed at the Olympic Games at Oslo, Norway in 1952, Frank Stack (b. Jan. 1 1906) was aged 46 years and 1 month. He also competed in 1932 and 1948.

SPEED SKATING
Canadian Native Records

	Distance	Time	Name	Club	Place	Date
MEN	500 m	38.97	Gaetan Boucher	Quebec Elite	Inzell, W. Germany	Feb. 21 1975
	1,000 m	1:19.05	Gaetan Boucher	Quebec Elite	Inzell, W. Germany	Feb. 21 1975
	1,500 m	2:03.63	Gaetan Boucher	Quebec Elite	Inzell, W. Germany	Feb. 21 1975
	3,000 m	4:28.71	Gaetan Boucher	Quebec Elite	Madonna di Campilio, Italy	Jan. 17 1976
	5,000 m	7:32.0	Andrew Barron	Edmonton	Inzell, W. Germany	Nov. 24 1974
	10,000 m	15:58.6	Kevin Sirois	Red Deer	Sapporo, Japan	Feb. 7 1972
WOMEN	500 m	42.15	Sylvia Burka	Winnipeg	Inzell, W. Germany	Mar. 13 1976
	1,000 m	1:25.67	Sylvia Burka	Winnipeg	Heerenveen, Netherlands	Feb. 13 1977
	1,500 m	2:12.01	Sylvia Burka	Winnipeg	Heerenveen, Netherlands	Feb. 12 1977
	3,000 m	4:44.31	Sylvia Burka	Winnipeg	Inzell, W. Germany	Mar. 14 1976

JUDO

Earliest

First practiced in Canada about 1920 by Japanese settlers in British Columbia.

Olympic Games

The most successful Canadian has been Alfred Harold Douglas Rogers (b. Jan. 26 1941) who won the silver medal in the 1964 heavyweight class at Tokyo, Japan.

LACROSSE

Earliest

Acknowledged as the oldest original sport in North America, a form of the game was played by the Indians (see p. 296) well before interest was shown by settlers in the 1830's. The first club, Montreal Lacrosse Club, was founded in 1856 and the National Lacrosse Association in 1867.

National Championships

The Mann Cup (donated in 1910 by Sir Donald Mann) has been won a record 18 times by the Salmonbellies of New Westminster, B.C. They also hold the record for the most consecutive wins, six in the period 1920–25. The most goals scored in the Cup is 60 by Bill Wilson, and the most points is 97 by Paul Parnell.

Goals

The most goals scored in a season is 89 by Bob Allan, in 1956, and the greatest number in one game is 12 by Jim Douglas on June 1 1939. The career record is held by Paul Parnell with 981, of which a record 773 were in league games. The fastest first goal of a game was scored in four seconds by Jim Rickbeil in 1974.

Points

In the 32 game season of 1971, John Davis, Peterborough, scored a record 197 points. The highest number scored in one game is 17 by Gaylord Powless, in 1970, and Rick Dudley, in 1971. The league record is 1,648 by Paul Parnell, who also holds the career record total of 1,902 points.

LAWN TENNIS

Earliest

The earliest officially recorded tournament was held at the Montreal Lacrosse Club on June 24 1878, but a club is thought to have been formed in Toronto in 1875. The L.T.A. was founded on July 2 1890 at Queen's Hotel, Toronto.

An early game of lacrosse, derived from *baggataway*, which originated with the Algonquin tribes of the St. Lawrence valley. (*Mary Evans*)

Davis Cup

Canada first entered the competition in 1913. **Dr.** Jack Wright (1903–1949), British Columbia, played on the team for eleven consecutive years, 1923–33.

Most titles

Violet Summerhayes, of Toronto, won a record six titles in the National championships (inst. 1892) 1899–1905. The most wins in the men's championships (inst. 1890) has been three by four players.

MOTORCYCLE RACING

Earliest

The British Empire Motor Club was founded in Toronto in 1928.

Hillclimbing

The only Canadian to win a world title is John Williams (b. 1939) of Markham, Ontario, when he won the B Division championship on a 400 foot *122 m* 70 degree angled hill over two eight-foot *2,43 m* ditches in a time of 7.88 seconds at Muskegan, Michigan, U.S.A. on Aug. 6 1972.

MOTOR RACING

Canadian Grand Prix

The lap record for the race (inst. 1967) of 117.84 m.p.h. *189,65 km/h* is jointly held by James Hunt (G.B.) in a McLaren and Jody Scheckter (R.S.A.) in a Tyrell, both in 1976. The practice record is 122.27 m.p.h. *196,78 km/h* by James Hunt (G.B.) in a McLaren on Oct. 2 1976. The most wins have been two by Jacky Ickx (Belgium) in 1969 and 1970, and Jackie Stewart (G.B.) in 1971 and 1972.

Drag racing

The lowest elapsed time recorded by a Canadian dragster is 5.698 sec by Gary Beck, of Edmonton, Alberta, at the National Hot Rod Association's Supernationals, at Ontario Motor Speedway, California, U.S.A., on 10 Oct. 1975.

The first of Jackie Stewart's two wins in the Canadian Grand Prix, helped him on his way to the World Drivers' Championship in 1971. (*E. D. Lacey*)

MOUNTAINEERING

Earliest

The Alpine Club of Canada was founded in 1906 but there had been a short-lived club started in 1883. There are more than 500 peaks over 10,000 ft *3 048 m*.

Progressive altitude records

The first recorded climb above the snowline was in 1827 when a botanist, David Douglas, climbed Mt. Brown, 9,156 ft *2 790 m*. Thereafter the progressive climbing record in Canada was as follows:

Date	Mountain	ft	m
1885	Mt. Avalanche	9,397	*2 864*
1887	Mt. Odaray	10,365	*3 159* †
1887	Mt. Stephen	10,495	*3 199*
1890	Mt. Selwyn	11,023	*3 360*
1898	Mt. Athabasca	11,452	*3 490*
1902	Mt. Columbia	12,294	*3 747*
1913	Mt. Robson	12,972	*3 954*
1925	Mt. Logan	19,850	*6 050* *

† J. J. McArthur was first man over 10,000 ft *3 048 m* in Canada.
* Highest point in Canada. Team led by A. H. MacCarthy and H. F. Lambert, reaching the summit on June 23.

OLYMPIC GAMES

Earliest

Canada has competed in every Olympic Games celebration since 1900, including the intercalated Games of 1906.

Medal total

The total number of medals won by Canada in the Games has been 122 in the Summer celebrations (26 gold, 43 silver, 53 bronze) and 33 in the Winter celebrations (12 gold, 7 silver, 14 bronze). This total of 155 medals places Canada sixteenth in the all-time totals by nations. The most successful Games were 1932 with 17 medals.

Gold medals

The first gold medal won by a Canadian was by George Orton (1873–1958) in the 2,500 metres steeplechase at Paris, France in 1900. The first female gold medallist was Ethel Catherwood (b. May 2 1910) when winning the high jump at Amsterdam, Netherlands, in 1928.

Most medals

The most medals won in Olympic competition are the five—all bronze—won by Guyana-born middle distance runner Dr. Philip Edwards (1907–1971) at the Games of 1928, 1932 and 1936. Additionally he achieved two fourth places and one fifth place. The most by a woman is three by Elaine Tanner (b. Feb. 22 1951) with two silver and one bronze in the 1968 swimming events at Mexico City.

Most Olympic appearances

The record for Olympic representation is held by Gilbert Boa (b. Aug. 8 1924) who competed for Canada in the shooting events in five Olympic Games, 1952–64 and 1972. The record number of appearances by a woman in the

Games is four by Abigail Hoffman (b. Feb. 11 1947), who competed in track and field athletics events in 1964 (400 m, 800 m), 1968 (800 m finalist), 1972 (800 m finalist) and 1976 (800 m).

Oldest Olympian

The oldest surviving Olympian in Canada is Petter Hol (b. Norway, Mar. 19 1883) now of Winnipeg, who won Gymnastics medals at the 1906, 1908, 1912 and 1920 Games.

PARACHUTING

Most jumps

For details see p. 306.

POWERBOAT RACING

Harmsworth Trophy

Of the 25 contests from 1903 to 1961, Canada have won three.

RODEO

Earliest

There are newspaper references to cowboy contests in the Calgary area in the 1890's, but the first organised stampede was in Alberta in 1903. The Calgary Stampede (see also p. 309) was first held in 1912, and became an annual meeting in 1923, the year that the famous Chuckwagon race was introduced.

World Saddle Bronc championship

The World Saddle Bronc title has been won on 13 occasions by Canadian cowboys between 1932 and 1976.

Most titles

The Canadian All-round championship has been won a record four times by Kenny McLean, 1967–69, 1972 and Tom Bews, 1966, 1971, 1973 and 1976. The most individual major events won in the championships has been eight by Les Brown from 1960 to 1973, and 15 (all events) by Cliff Vandergrift from 1949 to 1961.

Highest prize money

The greatest total of prize money won in one season has been $15,431 by Kenny McLean in 1972.

ROWING

Earliest

The first mention of the sport in Canada was reference to "a rowing match" at the Newfoundland Regatta of August 1816. The first true rowing regatta was on Toronto Bay in 1848. The first club was the Toronto Rowing Club founded in 1856.

World Championships

Canada's first international rowing success was at the world championships in Paris, France, in 1867 in the four-oared

CANADIAN RODEO EVENT RECORDS

Event	Name	Performance	Venue	Date
Saddle Bronc Riding	Joel Marvel, Battle Mt., Nevada	92 points	Calgary	1976
Bareback Riding	Jim Dix, West Collie, Australia	89 points	Medicine Hat	1970
	Joe Alexander, Cora, Wyoming	89 points	Calgary	1976
Bull Riding	Jim Jacobsen, Sun River, Montana	93 points	Calgary	1976
Calf Roping	Bill Reeder, Cardston, Alta; Kim Gripp, Hereford, Texas	8.0 sec	Radville, Sask.	1976
Steer Wrestling	Lee Phillips, Carseland, Alta	3.0 sec	Edmonton	1973

event. The crew, George Pirie, Robert Fulton, Samuel Hutton, and Elija Ross were thereafter nicknamed the "Paris Crew".

World Sculling Championships
Two Canadians have won the professional sculling championships of the world—Ned Hanlan (1855–1908) from 1880–84, and Jacob Gill Gaudaur (1858–1937) in 1896. Hanlan won 300 consecutive races in the period 1871–1885.

Diamond Sculls
The Diamond Sculls, at Henley Regatta, England, have been won three times by Canadian scullers; Lou Scholes in 1904, Joseph Wright Jr. in 1928, and John Schofield Guest in 1930. An Australian, Henry Robert Pearce, (b. Sept. 30 1905) represented the Leander B.C., Hamilton, when he won in 1931.

Olympic Games
Twelve Olympic medals have been won by Canadian oarsmen, of which two were gold—the 1956 Fours without cox and the 1964 pairs without cox.

National Championships
The Maple Leaf Trophy, awarded annually to the highest scoring club at the Royal Canadian Henley Regatta, has been won a record 16 years consecutively, 1960–1976, by the St. Catharine's R.C., Ontario.

Most durable record
The world record of 19 min 01.5 sec for three miles *4,8 km* with turn was set by Jacob Gill Gaudaur, of Orillia, in 1894, and has never been bettered.

SHOOTING

Earliest
The Dominion of Canada Rifle Association was founded in 1868.

Queen's Prize
The first Canadian team to compete at Bisley, England, was in 1871. The Queen's Prize has been won on 11 occasions by Canadian marksmen, the first time by Private T. H. Hayhurst in 1895. A. Narcon is co-holder of the highest score, 293 out of a possible 300, achieved July 28–29 1972.

Olympic Games
The most successful marksman has been Walter Henry Ewing, Montreal, who won the Clay Pigeon (Trap Shooting) event at London, England, in 1908 and also won silver medals in the team events of 1900 and 1908. George Patrick Genereux (b. March 1 1935) was only 17 years 4 months old when he won the 1952 Olympic Clay Pigeon event.

Highest score
When Gerald Raymond Ouellette (b. Aug. 14 1934, Windsor, Ont.) won the 1956 Olympic small-bore rifle event he scored a perfect 600 points. (The mark was never accepted as a world or Olympic record due to the range being found to be fractionally short.)

SKIING

Earliest
The first mention of skiing in Canada is at a Snow/Ice Carnival in 1759. The *Canadian Illustrated News*, Feb. 1879 had a woodcut of a Mr. Birch who skied the 170 miles *273 km* from Montreal to Quebec with the aid of a pole. The first Canadian championships were held in 1896 at Rossland, B.C.

Olympic Games
Canada's first ever medal was a bronze by Lucile Wheeler (b. Jan. 14 1935) in the 1956 Downhill race. The most successful events have been the Slalom races with gold medals by Anne Heggtveit (b. Jan. 11 1939) in 1960, Nancy Greene (b. May 11 1943) in 1968, and Kathy Kreiner (b. 1957) in 1976.

World Championships
The first Canadian winner of a world title was Lucile Wheeler, who won the Giant Slalom and Downhill titles in 1958, at Bad Gastein, Austria.

Largest club
The largest ski club in the world is Camp Fortune, near Ottawa, which had over 14,000 members in 1974.

Longest jump
The longest jump by a Canadian is 141 m *462½ ft* by Peter Wilson (b. Ottawa 1953) at Oberstdorf, W. Germany, in 1973.

SNOOKER

Highest break
For the highest break by a Canadian, see p. 315.

SNOWMOBILING

Yvon duHamel, of La Salle, P.Q., attained a record speed of 127.3 m.p.h. *204,8 km/h* on a Ski Doo XR-2 on Feb. 10 1973.

SNOWSHOEING

Earliest
The explorer, Jacques Cartier, first noted the Indians wearing snowshoes in 1534. It became a sport with the founding of the Montreal Snowshoe Club in 1840. In the 1970's the Congres International des Raquetteurs included over 100 clubs in Canada and the United States.

Fastest
The record for 100 m is 15.4 sec by Marc Nadeau (Rochambeaux) at Montreal in 1977. The female record of 18 sec was set by Deirdre Pretlove (Laurentien).

SOFTBALL

Earliest
A form of indoor baseball was played in the Knights of Columbus Hall, Hamilton, Ont., in 1896. The Ontario Amateur Softball Association was formed in 1923.

World Championships
Canada is world champion in Senior Men Fast Pitch Softball, having won the title in 1972 and successfully defended it in 1976.

Largest attendance
The greatest number of people to watch a softball game has been the 17,511 at the Hamilton Pee Gees v. Briggs Manufacturing Company, Detroit, game at Toronto in 1941.

CANADIAN SOFTBALL CHAMPIONSHIPS RECORDS		
MEN		
Most Runs Scored	7	Albert Slaunwhite (N.S.) 1973; Mickey Hancock (Ont.) 1973; Lyall Cornett (B.C.) 1974
Most Hits	10	Lyall Cornett (B.C.) 1974; Don Ross (N.S.) 1975
Most Putouts	63	Bob Solomon (Ont.) 1974
Most Innings Pitched	37	Ralph Ens (M.A.) 1972
Most Strikeouts	31	Bob Domik (Ont.) 1975; Earl Kronlund (A.A.) 1975
Longest Game (Innings)	16	Alberta (2) v. Prince Edward Island (1) 1975
WOMEN		
Most Runs Scored	9	Norma Wood (Ont.) 1975
Most Hits	13	Bonnie Cumiford (C.A.) 1975
Most Putouts	42	Francine Leger (N.B.) 1975
Most Innings Pitched	35	Mary Oakley (N.F.) 1975
Most Strikeouts	30	Rosemary Fuller (B.C.) 1975
Longest Game (Innings)	10	Quebec (4) v Alberta (3)

SWIMMING

Earliest

The Montreal Swimming Club was formed in 1876, and the Canadian Amateur Swimming Association founded in 1909.

Olympic Games

The first gold medal won by a Canadian swimmer was by George Ritchie Hodgson (b. Oct. 12 1893) who won the 1500 metres freestyle at Stockholm, Sweden, on July 10 1912. He also won the 400 metres freestyle.

Channel swimming

The first Canadian to swim the English Channel was Marilyn Bell (now Mrs. Di Lascio) (b. 1937) of Toronto, who swam from France to England in 14 hours 36 min on July 31 1955.

SWIMMING
Canadian National records

MEN

Distance	Time	Name	Place	Date	
FREESTYLE	min. sec.				
100 metres	51.87	Steve Pickell	Etobicoke	June 5	1976
200 metres	1:53.86	Stephen Badger	Montreal	July 19	1976
400 metres	4:00.14	Stephen Badger	Montreal	July 22	1976
1,500 metres	15:46.27	Stephen Badger	Vancouver	Aug. 18	1976
BACKSTROKE					
100 metres	57.58	Steve Pickell	Montreal	July 22	1976
200 metres	2:06.49	Steve Pickell	Vancouver	Aug.	1976
BUTTERFLY					
100 metres	55.56	Bruce Robertson	Munich, West Germany	Aug. 31	1972
200 metres	2:03.33	George Nagy	Montreal	July 18	1976
BREASTSTROKE					
100 metres	1:03.92	Graham Smith	Montreal	July 19	1976
200 metres	2:19.42	Graham Smith	Montreal	July 24	1976
INDIVIDUAL MEDLEY					
200 metres	2:08.37	Graham Smith	Vancouver	Aug. 21	1976
	2:08.37	William Sawchuk	Vancouver	Aug. 21	1976
400 metres	4:28.64	Graham Smith	Montreal	July 25	1976
FREESTYLE RELAYS					
4 × 100 metres	3:33.20	National Team (Bruce Robertson, Brian Phillips Tim Bach, Robert Kasting)	Munich, West Germany	Aug. 28	1972
4 × 200 metres	7:53.21	National Team (Jim Fowlie, John Van Buren, Bruce Robertson, Steve Pickell)	Cali, Columbia	July 27	1975
MEDLEY RELAY					
4 × 100 metres	3:45.94	National Team (Steve Pickell, Graham Smith, Clay Evans, Gary Macdonald)	Montreal	July 22	1976

WOMEN

Distance	Time	Name	Place	Date	
FREESTYLE					
100 metres	57.48	Anne Jardin	Etobicoke	June 1	1976
200 metres	2:02.63	Gail Amundrud	Etobicoke	June 3	1976
400 metres	4:14.60	Shannon Smith	Montreal	July 20	1976
800 metres	8:46.39	Shannon Smith	Long Beach, California, U.S.A.	April 4	1976
BACKSTROKE					
100 metres	1:03.28	Nancy Garapick	Montreal	July 20	1976
200 metres	2:15.60	Nancy Garapick	Montreal	July 25	1976
BREASTSTROKE					
100 metres	1:13.39	Robin Corsiglia	Vancouver	Aug. 21	1976
200 metres	2:36.74	Joann Baker	Etobicoke	June 3	1976
BUTTERFLY					
100 metres	1:01.54	Wendy Quirk	Montreal	July 21	1976
200 metres	2:13.68	Wendy Quirk	Montreal	July 19	1976
INDIVIDUAL MEDLEY					
200 metres	2:20.64	Becky Smith	Vancouver	Aug. 21	1976
400 metres	4:48.10	Cheryl Gibson	Montreal	July 24	1976
FREESTYLE RELAY					
4 × 100 metres	3:48.81	National Team (Gail Amundrud, Barbara Clark, Becky Smith, Anne Jardin)	Montreal	July 25	1976
MEDLEY RELAY					
4 × 100 metres	4:15.22	National Team (Wendy Hogg (née Cook), Robin Corsiglia, Susan Sloan, Anne Jardin)	Montreal	July 18	1976

top: National record holders, Shannon Smith, Becky Smith and Wendy Quirk figured in six Olympic finals between them. (*Tony Duffy, All-Sport Photographic*)

bottom: Steve Pickell set a Canadian 100 m backstroke record on the first leg of the silver medal winning medley relay team at the Montreal Olympic Games. (*Tony Duffy, All-Sport Photographic*)

Kathy Kreiner (centre) won Canada's only Olympic gold medal in 1976 with her victory in the Giant Slalom at Innsbruck, Austria. (*Tony Duffy, All-Sport Photographic*)

TRACK AND FIELD ATHLETICS

Earliest

The first recognizable track and field meeting was at the Caer Howell grounds, outside Toronto, on Sept. 11–14 1839, which had over 600 entries. Montreal A.C. was the first club, founded in 1842. Canada's first world class athlete was probably a professional runner, H. De Kelso, who was reported to have run 3 miles *4,82 km* in 13 min 11.0 sec at Barrie, Ont. on Oct. 14 1867—a performance which, if authentic, was not bettered for over ninety years.

World records

The first Canadian to hold an official I.A.A.F. world record was Earl Thomson (1895–1971) from Saskatchewan, who ran the 120 yd hurdles in 14.4 sec at Philadelphia, U.S.A. on May 29 1920. George Gray (1865–1933) had held the world's best performance in the shot from 1887 to 1898.

Olympic Games

Canadian track and field athletes have won 11 gold medals since 1900. Only one athlete has won two gold medals—Percy Williams (b. May 19 1908, Vancouver, B.C.) winner of the 100 m and 200 m in the 1928 Olympics at Amsterdam, Netherlands. The only woman to win an individual track and field gold medal has been Ethel Catherwood (b. May 2 1910) winner of the 1928 high jump.

Most titles

The most National titles won in a single afternoon was five by Walter Knox (1878–1951) who won the sprint, long jump, pole vault, shot and hammer in 1907. On another non-championship occasion he won ten firsts in a single meeting.

Olympic silver medallist Greg Joy holds the Commonwealth as well as the Canadian record for the high jump. (*Tony Duffy, All-Sport Photographic*)

365

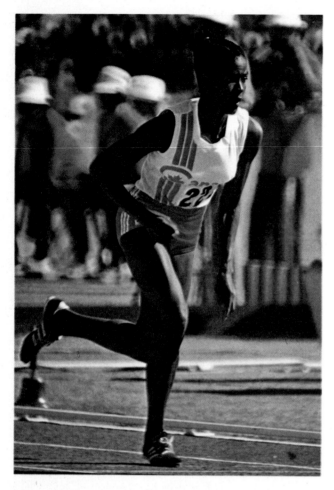

Yvonne Saunders won the 1974 Commonwealth 400 m title before moving up to break the Canadian 800 m record. (*Tony Duffy, All-Sport Photographic*)

In 1974 George Athans Jr, the son of a Commonwealth diving champion, was made a member of the Order of Canada for his water skiing exploits. (*Tony Duffy, All-Sport Photographic*)

WALKING

The most successful Canadian walker has been George Henry Goulding (1885–1966) who won the gold medal in the Olympic Games 10,000 metres *6 miles 376 yd* track walk at Stockholm, Sweden, in 1912.

WATER POLO

Earliest

The Montreal Aquatic Club, which was affiliated with the Montreal Swimming Club, laid out rules and regulations for water polo, and *c.* 1887, began to hold championships.

Olympic Games

The highest Canadian placing in the Olympic Games has been the ninth place gained at Montreal, in July 1976.

Most titles

The most National titles have been won by the Hamilton Aquatic Club with 15.

WATER SKIING

Earliest

Water skiing was first reported in Canada in 1922.

World championships

The first Canadian to win a world title was Charles Blackwell, winner of the slalom in 1953 at Toronto. The most titles won are three by George Athans Jr. (b. 1952, Kelowna, B.C.) world overall champion in 1971 and 1973, and individual slalom champion in 1973.

Most titles

The greatest number of national titles won is ten by George Athans Jr.

Longest jumps

The longest jump by a Canadian is 167 ft *50,90 m* by George Athans Jr. The best jump by a woman is 113 ft *34,44 m* by Helene Gregoire.

WEIGHTLIFTING

World championships

Douglas Hepburn (b. Sept. 16 1927, Vancouver) is the only Canadian winner of a world title, the heavyweight, in 1953.

Olympic Games

The most successful Canadian has been Gérard A. Gratton (1927–1963) of Quebec, who won a silver medal in the 1952 Olympic middleweight class in Helsinki, Finland.

Greatest lifts

Quebec strong man Louis Cyr (1863–1912)—5 ft 8½ in *1,74 m* tall, 350 lb. *158,7 kg*—is reported to have made a back lift of 4,337 lb. *1 967 kg* (18 men on a platform) in Boston on May 26 1895. In London, England, on Jan. 19 1889, before the Prince of Wales he lifted 551 lb. *250 kg* with one finger. A back lift of some 6,000 lb. *2 721 kg* attributed to Victor Delamarre (1888–1955) in Oct. 1928 is considered highly questionable—he stood 5 ft 6 in *1,68 m* tall and never weighed more than 165 lb. *74,8 kg*.

WALKING				
Track	**Time**	**Name**	**Place**	**Date**
20 miles	2hr45:50.6	Alex Oakley	Toronto	Aug. 23 1970
30 miles	4hr19:28.4	Karl Heinz Merschenz	Toronto	July 16 1972
10,000 metres	44:10.0*	Marcel Jobin	Montreal	Oct. 7 1976
20,000 metres	1hr33:52.0	Marcel Jobin	Regina	Aug. 29 1976
30,000 metres	2hr33:22.0	Alex Oakley	Toronto	Aug. 23 1970
50,000 metres	4hr29:19.4	Karl Heinz Merschenz	Toronto	July 16 1972
Road				
20,000 metres	1hr30:29.0	Marcel Jobin	Hamilton	May 16 1976
50,000 metres	4hr27:24.6	Alex Oakley	Tokyo, Japan	Oct. 18 1967

TRACK & FIELD RECORDS

MEN

RUNNING

Best performance by a Canadian as ratified by the Canadian Track & Field Association (unless marked *) as at July 31 1977. (e—indicates electric timing)

Event	min. sec.	Name	Place	Date
100 metres	10.17(e)	Harry Winston Jerome	Mexico City	Oct. 13 1968
	10.0	Harry Winston Jerome	Saskatoon	July 15 1960
200 metres	20.86(e)	Hugh Fraser	Mexico City	Oct. 15 1975
	20.4	Harry Winston Jerome	Edmonton	July 16 1975
400 metres	46.14(e)	Ross Mackenzie	Mexico City	Oct. 17 1968
	45.8	Donald Domansky	Los Angeles, U.S.A.	July 8 1967
	45.8	Donald Domansky	Winnipeg	July 30 1967
800 metres	1:45.6	William Frederick Crothers	Tokyo, Japan	Oct. 16 1964
1,000 metres	2:20.6*	William Smart	Munich, West Germany	Aug. 24 1972
1,500 metres	3:38.0	Paul Craig	Montreal	July 29 1976
1 mile	3:57.7	David Bailey	Toronto	July 22 1967
2,000 metres	5:04.8	Grant McLaren	London, England	July 20 1974
3,000 metres	7:50.4	Grant McLaren	Oslo, Norway	July 3 1975
5,000 metres	13:34.4	Grant McLaren	Warsaw, Poland	June 30 1974
10,000 metres	28:05.6	Daniel Shaughnessy	Stockholm, Sweden	June 30 1975
20,000 metres	1hr00:12.2	Tom Howard	Richmond	Apr. 3 1975
25,000 metres	1hr19:28.8	John Currie	Richmond	Apr. 3 1975
1 hour 12 miles 675 yds 2 ft *19 930 metres*		Tom Howard	Richmond	Apr. 3 1975
Marathon	2hr10:08.4	Jerome Drayton	Fukuoka, Japan	Dec. 7 1975

HURDLING

110 metres	13.89(e)*	Patrick Fogarty	Lawrence, U.S.A.	Apr. 22 1977
	13.8*	Daniel Taillon	Eschweiler, West Germany	June 4 1975
	13.8*	Daniel Taillon	Stuttgart, West Germany	June 18 1975
200 metres	23.9*	Peter Stanger	Lafayette, U.S.A.	May 24 1958
400 metres	50.99(e)	David Jarvis	London, England	July 3 1976
	50.7*	Robert McLaren	Vancouver	Sept. 22 1968
3,000 metres steeplechase	8:36.8	Joseph Sax	Toronto	Aug. 10 1974

RELAYS

4 × 100 metres	38.86(e)	Canada (Hugh Fraser, Marvin Nash, Albin Dukowski, Robert Martin)	Mexico City	Oct. 20 1975
4 × 200 metres	1:24.6	Canada (Hugh Fraser, Marvin Nash, Robert Martin, Albin Dukowski)	London, England	July 20 1974
4 × 400 metres	3:02.6	Canada (Ian Seale, Donald Domansky, Leighton Hope, Brian Saunders)	Mexico City	Oct. 20 1975
4 × 800 metres	7:34.0	Toronto Track West T.C. (Tom Potter, Gary Crossley, Steve Lincoln, Tom Lobsinger)	Etobicoke	June 14 1975
4 × 1,500 metres	16:23.0	Central Ontario T.F.A. (Neil Hendry, Henryk Kupczyk, Paul Glynn, Roger Merchant)	Kitchener	July 13 1971

FIELD EVENTS

	m	ft	in	Name	Place	Date
High Jump	2,26	7	5	Gregory Joy	Regina	Aug. 29 1976
Long Jump	7,91	25	11½	James Buchanan	Montreal	June 12 1976
Triple Jump	16,05	52	8	David Watt	Sudbury	Aug. 24 1975
Pole Vault	5,34*	17	6¼	Kirk Bryde	Scarborough	July 20 1972
Shot Putt	20,22	66	4	Bishop Dolegiewicz	Stockholm, Sweden	July 17 1975
Discus	65,40	214	7	Borys Chambul	Montreal	July 21 1976
Hammer	69.60*	228	4	Scott Neilson	Champaign, Ill., U.S.A.	June 3 1977
Javelin	87,76*	287	11	Philip Olsen	Montreal	July 25 1976

DECATHLON

7,809 points		Gerry Moro	Santa Maria, Calif., U.S.A.	May 22–23 1972

WOMEN

RUNNING

Best performance by a Canadian as ratified by the Canadian Track and Field Association (unless marked *) as at July 31 1977 (e-indicates electric timing)

Event	min. sec.	Name	Place	Date
60 metres	7.4	Patty Loverock	Vancouver	June 7 1973
100 metres	11.36(e)	Patty Loverock	Mexico City	Oct. 13 1975
	11.1	Marjorie Turner-Bailey	Irvine, U.S.A.	May 16 1976
	11.1*	Patty Loverock	Quebec City	May 29 1976
200 metres	23.03(e)	Patty Loverock	Montreal	July 26 1976
	22.6	Patty Loverock	Quebec City	May 29 1976
400 metres	51.62(e)	Joyce Sadowick-Yakubovich	Mexico City	Oct. 18 1975
	51.6	Yvonne Elaine Saunders	Athens, Greece	July 11 1974
	51.6	Joyce Sadowick-Yakubovich	Mexico City	Oct. 18 1975
800 metres	2:00.1	Yvonne Elaine Saunders	Oslo, Norway	July 3 1975
1,500 metres	4:06.7	Glenda Reiser	Munich, West Germany	Sept. 4 1972
1 mile	4:35.1	Glenda Reiser	London, England	Sept. 14 1973
3,000 metres	8:55.0	Thelma Fynn-Wright	Rome, Italy	Sept. 18 1975
Marathon	2hr57:40	JoAnn McKinty (now Heale)	Waterloo	Oct. 11 1975

HURDLING

Event	min. sec.	Name	Place	Date
100 metres	13.4	Elizabeth Damman	Dortmund, W. Germany	July 6 1975
	13.60(e)*	Elizabeth Damman	Irvine, U.S.A.	May 16 1976
200 metres	26.9	Penny May	Vancouver	Aug. 15 1971
	26.9	Penny May	Winnipeg	Aug. 22 1971
400 metres	58.2	Francine Gendron	Sudbury	Aug. 23 1975

RELAYS

Event	min. sec.	Name	Place	Date
4 × 100 metres	43.17(e)	Canada (Margot Howe, Patty Loverock, Joanne McTaggart, Marjorie Turner-Bailey)	Montreal	July 31 1976
4 × 200 metres	1:35.5*	Canada (Margaret MacGowan-Stride, Patty Loverock, Joyce Sadowick-Yacubovich, Marjorie Turner-Bailey)	Bourges, France	June 19 1977
4 × 400 metres	3:28.8	Canada (Margaret MacGowan-Stride, Joyce Sadowick-Yakubovich, Rachelle Campbell, Yvonne Elaine Saunders)	Montreal	July 30 1976
4 × 800 metres	9:04.6	Vancouver O.C. (Leslie Stubbs, Caroline Van de Poll, Maureen Crowley, Doreen Martens)	Vancouver	June 7 1973
	9:04.6	University of British Columbia (Sheila Currie, Gail Turney, Thelma Fynn-Wright, Caroline Van de Poll)	Vancouver	May 5 1974

FIELD EVENTS

	m	ft	in	Name	Place	Date
High Jump	1,91*	6	3¼	Debbie Brill	Walnut, U.S.A.	Apr. 24 1977
Long Jump	6,55*	21	6	Diane Jones	Götzis, Austria	May 22 1977
Shot Putt	16,96	55	7¾	Lucette Moreau	Mexico City	Oct. 16 1975
Discus	61,70	202	5	Jane Haist	Sondrum, Sweden	July 16 1975
Javelin	56,88	186	7	Jay Dahlgren	Winnipeg	Aug. 27 1974

PENTATHLON

	Name	Place	Date
4,673 points (with 200 m event)	Diane Jones	Sudbury	Aug. 22–23 1975
4,673 points (with 200 m event)	Diane Jones	Mexico City	Oct. 15–16 1975
4,639 points (with 800 m event)	Diane Jones	Götzis, Austria	May 22 1977

WRESTLING

Earliest
Early settlers found that the Indians wrestled with their wrists bound to each other.

Olympic Games
The first medallist was Aubert Côté (b. 1881) with a bronze in the bantamweight freestyle class at London, England, in 1908.

Commonwealth Games
The most successful team of wrestlers ever to represent Canada internationally was that at the British Empire Games at Hamilton, in 1930, which won gold medals in all seven events on the program.

Most titles
The most wins in the Canadian championships is 18 by Alfred Wurr (eight freestyle and ten Greco-Roman titles). Peter Michienzi has won ten freestyle and five Greco-Roman titles. Before the Greco-Roman style was practised in Canada, James Trifunov (b. 1903) won ten consecutive freestyle championships.

YACHTING

Earliest
The first organised club was the Halifax Yacht Club founded in July 1837 (now the Royal Nova Scotia Yacht Squadron).

America's Cup
On two occasions Canadian yachts have challenged the holders, the United States, but lost both times—in 1876 with *Countess of Dufferin*, and in 1881 with *Atalanta*.

Canada's Cup
Donated in 1895, it is now the trophy for a challenge race between Canadian and American clubs situated on the Great Lakes. It is currently held by the Bayview Yacht Club, U.S.A.

Olympic Games
The highest placing by a Canadian crew, in an event still on the Olympic program, is the bronze medal performance at Kiel, West Germany, 1972, in the Soling Class, by David Miller, John Ekels and Paul Côté. At Los Angeles in 1932, a silver medal was won in the discontinued 8-metre class.

CANADIAN WEIGHTLIFTING RECORDS

Flyweight	kg	lb.	Name	Club	Date	Place
Snatch	92,5	204	Chun Hon Chan	Palestre Nationale	Dec. 4 1971	Montreal
Jerk	112	247	Chun Hon Chan	Palestre Nationale	May 22 1971	Woodstock
Total	197	434¼	Chun Hon Chan	Palestre Nationale	Dec. 9 1972	Montreal
Bantamweight						
Snatch	105	231½	Yves Carignan	C.E.N.A.	Apr. 10 1976	Montreal
Jerk	132,5	292	Yves Carignan	C.E.N.A.	May 22 1976	New Westminster
Total	235	518	Yves Carignan	C.E.N.A.	May 22 1976	New Westminster
Featherweight						
Snatch	105	231½	Yves Carignan	Brossard W.L. Club	Jan. 18 1975	Brossard
Jerk	135	297½	Yves Carignan	Brossard W.L. Club	Jan. 18 1975	Brossard
Total	240	529	Yves Carignan	Brossard W.L. Club	Jan. 18 1975	Brossard
Lightweight						
Snatch	120	264½	Pierre Charbonneau	Palestre Nationale	May 19 1974	Edmonton
Jerk	154,5	340½	Pierre Charbonneau	Palestre Nationale	Apr. 14 1973	Germany
Total	272,5	600¾	Pierre Charbonneau	Palestre Nationale	May 19 1974	Edmonton
Middleweight						
Snatch	132,5	292	Pierre Charbonneau	Brossard W.L. Club	Jan. 18 1975	Brossard
Jerk	170	374¾	Pierre Charbonneau	Brossard W.L. Club	Jan. 18 1975	Brossard
Total	302,5	666¾	Pierre Charbonneau	Brossard W.L. Club	Jan 18 1975	Brossard
Light-heavyweight						
Snatch	150	330½	Pierre St. Jean	C.E.N.A.	Nov. 16 1975	Jonquiere
Jerk	185	407¾	Pierre St. Jean	C.E.N.A.	Feb. 28 1976	Toronto
Total	335	738½	Pierre St. Jean	C.E.N.A.	Feb. 28 1976	Toronto
Middle-heavyweight						
Snatch	140	308½	W. Smith	Eleiko	Nov. 6 1976	Stephenville
Jerk	182	401¼	W. Wilson	Spartak	May 20 1972	St Johns
Total	315	694½	Paul Bjarnason	Spartak	Aug. 4 1973	Seattle, U.S.A.
100 Kg.						
Snatch	147,5	325	Robert Santavy	Santavy A.C.	Mar. 26 1977	Sarnia
Jerk	187,5	413¼	Robert Santavy	Santavy A.C.	Mar. 26 1977	Sarnia
Total	335	738½	Robert Santavy	Santavy A.C.	Mar. 26 1977	Sarnia
Heavyweight						
Snatch	167,5	369½	Russell Prior	Trojan Barbell	July 26 1976	Montreal
Jerk	205	451¾	Russell Prior	Trojan Barbell	May 23 1976	New Westminster
Total	370	815½	Russell Prior	Trojan Barbell	May 23 1976	New Westminster
Super-heavyweight						
Snatch	162	357	Russell Prior	Trojan Barbell	May 10 1975	Ottawa
Jerk	207	456¼	Russell Prior	Trojan Barbell	May 10 1975	Ottawa
Total	360	793½	Russell Prior	Trojan Barbell	May 10 1975	Ottawa

Undefeated in public strong-man contests from 1881 to 1906, Louis Cyr inherited his strength from his mother, who stood 6 ft 1½ in *1,87 m* and weighed 267 lb. *121 kg*.

COMMONWEALTH GAMES *RECORDS*

Of the ten sports which will be on the programme of the XI Games to be held at Edmonton, Canada in 1978, five (Cycling Shooting, Swimming, Track and Field and Weightlifting) have current records as follows:

CYCLING	Time min sec	Name and Country	Place	Date	
1 000 m Sprint	11.26*	John Nicholson (Australia)	Christchurch	27 Jan.	1974
2 000 m Tandem Sprint	10.71*	England (Geoffrey Clarke, Ernest Crutchlow)	Christchurch	31 Jan.	1974
1 000 m Time Trial	1:08.69	Harry Kent (New Zealand)	Edinburgh	23 July	1970
4 000 m Individual Pursuit	4:56.6	Hugh Porter (England)	Kingston, Jamaica	10 Aug.	1966
4 000 m Team Pursuit	4:40.50	England	Christchurch	31 Jan.	1974
10 miles Track Race	20:46.72	Jocelyn B. Lowell (Canada)	Edinburgh	24 July	1970

* Time for last 200 m

SHOOTING	Score	Name and Country	Place	Date	
Full Bore Rifle (7.62 mm)[1]	394	The Rt. Hon. Sir John Hussey Hamilton Vivian Bt., 4th Baron Swansea (Wales)	Kingston, Jamaica	8 Aug.	1966
Small Bore Rifle (prone)	594	Yvonne Gowland (Australia)	Christchurch	26 Jan.	1974
Free Pistol	549	Jules Sobrian (Canada)	Christchurch	29 Jan.	1974
	549	Norman Harrison (Australia)	Christchurch	29 Jan.	1974
Rapid Fire Pistol	586	Rev. William Hare (Canada)	Christchurch	28 Jan.	1974
Centre Fire Pistol	576	James Lee (Canada)	Kingston, Jamaica	9 Aug.	1966
Shot Gun (Skeet)	194	Harry Willsie (Canada)	Christchurch	26 Jan.	1974
Shot Gun (Clay Pigeon)	196	John Primrose (Canada)	Christchurch	1 Feb.	1974

[1] Previously the .303 Rifle

SWIMMING
MEN

Event	Time min sec	Name and Country	Place	Date	
Freestyle					
100 metres	52.73	Michael Vincent Wenden M.B.E. (Australia)	Christchurch	28 Jan.	1974
200 metres	1:56.69	Michael Vincent Wenden M.B.E. (Australia)	Edinburgh	18 July	1970
400 metres	4:01.44	John Kulasalu (Australia)	Christchurch	30 Jan.	1974
1 500 metres	15:34.73	Stephen Roy Holland (Australia)	Christchurch	1 Feb.	1974
Backstroke					
100 metres	59.05[1]	Steve Pickell (Canada)	Christchurch	1 Feb.	1974
200 metres	2:06.31	Bradford Cooper (Australia)	Christchurch	28 Jan.	1974
Breaststroke					
100 metres	1:06.52	David Leigh (England)	Christchurch	1 Feb.	1974
200 metres	2:24.42	David Andrew Wilkie M.B.E. (Scotland)	Christchurch	30 Jan.	1974
Butterfly					
100 metres	56.58	Neil William Rogers (Australia)	Christchurch	31 Jan.	1974
200 metres	2:04.51	Brian Brinkley M.B.E. (England)	Christchurch	28 Jan.	1974
Individual Medley					
200 metres	2:10.11	David Andrew Wilkie M.B.E. (Scotland)	Christchurch	30 Jan.	1974
400 metres	4:35.90	Mark Treffers (New Zealand)	Christchurch	26 Jan.	1974
4 × 100 m Freestyle Relay	3:33.79	Canada (Bruce Robertson, Ian MacKenzie, Gary MacDonald, Brian Phillips)	Christchurch	25 Jan.	1974
4 × 200 m Freestyle Relay	7:50.13	Australia (John Kulasalu, Robert Nay, Stephen Badger, Michael Vincent Wenden)	Christchurch	30 Jan.	1974
4 × 100 m Medley Relay	3:52.93	Canada (Steve Pickell, William V. Mahony, Bruce Robertson, Brian Phillips)	Christchurch	1 Feb.	1974

WOMEN

Event	Time min sec	Name and Country	Place	Date	
Freestyle					
100 metres	58.87[2]	Gail Amundrud (Canada)	Christchurch	26 Jan.	1974
200 metres	2:04.27	Sonya Gray (Australia)	Christchurch	30 Jan.	1974
400 metres	4:22.09	Jennifer Lyn Turrall (Australia)	Christchurch	1 Feb.	1974
800 metres	8:55.88	Sally Lockyer (Australia)	Christchurch	25 Jan.	1974
Backstroke					
100 metres	1:04.78[1]	Wendy Cook (now Hogg) (Canada)	Christchurch	31 Jan.	1974
200 metres	2:20.31	Wendy Cook (now Hogg) (Canada)	Christchurch	31 Jan.	1974
Breaststroke					
100 metres	1:16.42	Christine Gaskell (England)	Christchurch	1 Feb.	1974
200 metres	2:42.97	Beverley Joy Whitfield (Australia)	Christchurch	25 Jan.	1974
Butterfly					
100 metres	1:05.06	Wendy Quirk (Canada)	Christchurch	28 Jan.	1974
200 metres	2:20.57	Sandra Yost (Australia)	Christchurch	31 Jan.	1974
Individual Medley					
200 metres	2:24.13	Leslie Cliff (Canada)	Christchurch	26 Jan.	1974
400 metres	5:01.35	Leslie Cliff (Canada)	Christchurch	1 Feb.	1974
4 × 100 m Freestyle Relay	3:57.14	Canada (Gail Amundrud, Anne Jardin, Becky Smith, Judy Wright)	Christchurch	26 Jan.	1974
4 × 100 m Medley Relay	4:24.77	Canada (Wendy Cook (now Hogg), Marian Stuart, Patti Stenhouse, Gail Amundrud)	Christchurch	31 Jan.	1974

[1] Set on first leg of 4 × 100 m Medley Relay [2] Set on first leg of 4 × 100 m Freestyle Relay

Scotland's dual record holder, David Wilkie M.B.E., achieved both records on the same day. (*Syndication International*)

Sally Lockyer (Australia) set an 800 m freestyle record in a heat, but was only fourth in the final. (*Tony Duffy, All-Sport Photographic*)

TRACK AND FIELD
MEN

Event	Time min sec	Name and Country	Place	Date
100 metres	10.24(wa)[1]	Donald O'Riley Quarrie (Jamaica)	Edinburgh	18 July 1970
200 metres	20.48(wa)[2]	Donald O'Riley Quarrie (Jamaica)	Edinburgh	21 July 1970
400 metres	45.01	Charles Asati (Kenya)	Edinburgh	23 July 1970
800 metres	1:43.9	John Kipkurgat (Kenya)	Christchurch	29 Jan. 1974
1 500 metres	3:32.2	Filbert Bayi (Tanzania)	Christchurch	2 Feb. 1974
5 000 metres	13:14.4	Ben Wabura Jipcho (Kenya)	Christchurch	29 Jan. 1974
10 000 metres	27:46.4	Richard John Tayler (New Zealand)	Christchurch	25 Jan. 1974
Marathon	2 hr 09:12.0	Ian Reginald Thompson (England)	Christchurch	31 Jan. 1974
4 × 100 m relay	39.31	Australia (Gregory D. Lewis, Lawrence L. D'Arcy, Andrew Ratcliffe, Graham Haskell)	Christchurch	2 Feb. 1974
4 × 400 m relay	3:02.8[3]	Trinidad and Tobago (Lennox Yearwood, Kent Bernard, Edwin M. Roberts, Wendell A. Mottley)	Kingston, Jamaica	13 Aug. 1966
110 m hurdles	13.66(wa)[4]	David Peter Hemery M.B.E. (England)	Edinburgh	18 July 1970
400 m hurdles	48.83	Alan Peter Pascoe, M.B.E. (England)	Christchurch	29 Jan. 1974
3 000 m steeplechase	8:20.8	Ben Wabura Jipcho (Kenya)	Christchurch	26 Jan. 1974
30 000 m road walk	2 hr 33:33.0	Noel F. Freeman (Australia)	Edinburgh	18 July 1970

Event	m	ft	in	Name and Country	Place	Date
High Jump	2,16	7	1	Graham P. Windeyer (Australia)	Christchurch	29 Jan. 1974
Pole Vault	5,10	16	8¾	Michael Anthony Bull (Northern Ireland)	Edinburgh	23 July 1970
Long Jump	8,06	26	5½(wa)[5]	Lyn Davies, M.B.E. (Wales)	Edinburgh	22 July 1970
Triple Jump	16,72	54	10¼	Phillip J. May (Australia)	Edinburgh	25 July 1970
Shot Putt	20,74	68	0½	Geoffrey Lewis Capes (England)	Christchurch	2 Feb. 1974
Discus Throw	63,08	206	11	Robin Tait (New Zealand)	Christchurch	31 Jan. 1974
Hammer Throw	69,56	228	2	Ian Alan Chipchase (England)	Christchurch	25 Jan. 1974
Javelin Throw	84,92	278	7	Charles Philip Clover (England)	Christchurch	2 Feb. 1974
Decathlon	7,492pts			Geoffrey J. Smith (Australia)	Edinburgh	21–22 July 1970

[1] Best legal time 10.38 by George Daniels (Ghana) and Quarrie (Jamaica) at Christchurch 1974
[2] Best legal time 20.56 by Quarrie (Jamaica) at Edinburgh 22 July 1970
[3] Actual distance was the longer 4 × 440 yards Relay
[4] Best legal time 13.69 by Fatwel Kimaiyo (Kenya) at Christchurch 26 Jan. 1974
[5] Best legal distance 7,99 m 26 ft 2¾ in by Davies (Wales) at Kingston 8 Aug. 1966

Tanzania's Filbert Bayi ran a world record 1500 m leading from start to finish. (*Colorsport*)

WOMEN

Event	Time min sec	Name and Country	Place	Date
100 metres	11.26(wa)[1]	Raelene Ann Boyle (Australia)	Edinburgh	28 July 1970
200 metres	22.50	Raelene Ann Boyle (Australia)	Christchurch	29 Jan. 1974
400 metres	51.03	Marilyn Fay Neufville (Jamaica)	Edinburgh	23 July 1970
800 metres	2:01.1	Charlene Louise Rendina (Australia)	Christchurch	29 Jan. 1974
1 500 metres	4:07.8	Glenda Reiser (Canada)	Christchurch	2 Feb. 1974
4 × 100 m relay	43.51	Australia (Jennifer Lamy, Denise Margaret Robertson, Robyn Boak, Raelene Ann Boyle)	Christchurch	2 Feb. 1974
4 × 400 m relay	3:29.2	England (Susan Pettett, Ruth Kennedy, Jannette Veronica Roscoe (née Champion), Verona Marolin Bernard (now Elder))	Christchurch	2 Feb. 1974
100 m hurdles	13.27	Pamela Kilborn, M.B.E. (now Ryan) (Australia)	Edinburgh	23 July 1970

Event	m	ft	in	Name and Country	Place	Date
High Jump	1,84	6	0½	Barbara Jean Lawton (née Inkpen) (England)	Christchurch	2 Feb. 1974
Long Jump	6,73	22	1	Sheila Sherwood (née Parkin) (England)	Edinburgh	23 July 1970
Shot Putt	16,50	54	1¾	Valerie Isobel Young (née Sloper) (New Zealand)	Kingston, Jamaica	6 Aug. 1966
Discus Throw	55,52	182	2	Jane Haist (Canada)	Christchurch	26 Jan. 1974
Javelin Throw	57,40	188	4	Anna Pazera (née Wojtaszek) (Australia)	Cardiff	24 July 1958
Pentathlon	4,524pts			Mary Elizabeth Peters, M.B.E. (Northern Ireland)	Edinburgh	21–22 July 1970

[1] Best legal time 11.27 by Boyle (Australia) at Christchurch 26 Jan. 1974

Pentathlon record-holder Mary Peters M.B.E. (Northern Ireland), began her Games career in the shot putt. (*Gerry Cranham*)

Precious McKenzie M.B.E. (England) holds records in two weight divisions. *Don Morley, All-Sport Photographic*)

WEIGHTLIFTING

Bodyweight Class	Lift	Lifted kg	Lifted lb.	Name and Country	Place	Date
Flyweight (up to 52 kg)	Snatch	92,5	203¾	Precious McKenzie M.B.E. (England)	Christchurch	25 Jan. 1974
	Jerk	122,5	270	Precious McKenzie M.B.E. (England)	Christchurch	25 Jan. 1974
	Total	215,0	473¾	Precious McKenzie M.B.E. (England)	Christchurch	25 Jan. 1974
Bantamweight (up to 56 kg)	Snatch	102,5	225¾	Chua Phung Kim (Singapore)	Perth	26 Nov. 1962
	Jerk	130,0	286¼	Precious McKenzie M.B.E. (England)	Edinburgh	24 July 1970
	Total	222,5	490½[1]	Michael Adams (Australia)	Christchurch	25 Jan. 1974
Featherweight (up to 60 kg)	Snatch	105,0	231½	Chua Phung Kim (Singapore)	Edinburgh	24 July 1970
	Jerk	140,0	308½	Mohan Lal Ghosh (India)	Kingston, Jamaica	5 Aug. 1966
	Total	237,5	523½	George Vasiliades (Australia)	Christchurch	26 Jan. 1974
Lightweight (up to 67,5 kg)	Snatch	120,0	264½	George Newton (England)	Christchurch	26 Jan. 1974
	Jerk	150,0	330½	Tan Howe Liang (Singapore)	Cardiff	23 July 1958
	Total	260,0	573	George Newton (England)	Christchurch	26 Jan. 1974
Middleweight (up to 75 kg)	Snatch	130,0	286½	John Waterworth (Australia)	Christchurch	29 Jan. 1974
	Jerk	159,0	350½	Tan Howe Liang (Singapore)	Perth	28 Nov. 1962
	Total	275,0	606½[2]	Tony Ebert (New Zealand)	Christchurch	29 Jan. 1974
Light Heavyweight (up to 82,5 kg)	Snatch	140,0	308½	Paul Wallwork (Western Samoa)	Christchurch	30 Jan. 1974
	Jerk	170,0	374¾	Tony Ford (England)	Christchurch	30 Jan. 1974
	Total	302,5	666¼[3]	Tony Ford (England)	Christchurch	30 Jan. 1974
Middle Heavyweight (up to 90 kg)	Snatch	147,5	325	Nicolo Ciancio (Australia)	Christchurch	30 Jan. 1974
	Jerk	182,5	402¼	Nicolo Ciancio (Australia)	Christchurch	30 Jan. 1974
	Total	330,0	727¼	Nicolo Ciancio (Australia)	Christchurch	30 Jan. 1974
Heavyweight (up to 110 kg)	Snatch	155,0	341½	Russell Prior (Canada)	Christchurch	31 Jan. 1974
	Jerk	197,5	435¼	Russell Prior (Canada)	Christchurch	31 Jan. 1974
	Total	352,5	776¾	Russell Prior (Canada)	Christchurch	31 Jan. 1974
Super Heavyweight (over 110 kg)	Snatch	150,0	330½	Graham May (New Zealand)	Christchurch	31 Jan. 1974
	Jerk	200,0	440¾	Donald Oliver (New Zealand)	Kingston	9 Aug. 1966
	Total	342,5	755	Graham May (New Zealand)	Christchurch	31 Jan. 1976

[1] Precious McKenzie (England) achieved a Snatch and Jerk which totalled 225 kg *496 lb.* at Edinburgh in 1970
[2] Pierre St. Jean (Canada) achieved a Snatch and Jerk which totalled 282 kg *622½ lb.* at Kingston in 1966
[3] Nicolo Ciancio (Australia) achieved a Snatch and Jerk which totalled 302,5 kg *666¾ lb.* at Edinburgh in 1970
The above mentioned performances occurred in the old style 3-lift contests and international rules do not allow such performances to be extracted to make 2-lift contest records.

STOP PRESS

CHAPTER 1

Tallest Living Giantess (page 9). Sandy Allen was medically re-measured at 7 ft 7¼ in *2,31 m* at Indiana University on 14 July 1977.

Oldest Living Man (page 14). Shigechiyo Izumi of Japan celebrated his 112th birthday on 29 June 1977.

Respirator (page 20). The harnessing of the respirator to Paul Bates was on 13 August 1954 and the estimated number of respirations received by 1 May 1977 was 162,993,000.

Motionlessness (page 21). A record for voluntary motionlessness was set by Melody Schick at North Park Center, Dallas, Texas on 9 Dec. 1976 with 5 hrs 43 min.

Fire Eating (page 21). Jack Sholomir (G.B.) raised his distance to 23 ft *7 m* at the Eardisley & District Royal British Legion Stampede at Kinnersley, Hereford and Worcester on 6 June 1977.

CHAPTER 2

Largest Land Mammals (page 25). A bull elephant measuring 13 ft 8 in *4,16 m* to the shoulder, weighing a computed 24,800 lb. 11.6 tons *11,69 tonnes* was shot on 7 Nov. 1974 in Angola (for details see Chap. XII, Shooting, Biggest Bag, page 313).

Cat and Dog Populations (page 33). The United Kingdom estimates for mid-1977 were 4.6 million and 5.3 million respectively.

Oldest Guinea Pig (page 33). Snowball, a female owned by M. A. Wall of Bingham, Nottinghamshire was still living on 20 July 1977 aged 13 years 4 months.

Popular Pet longevity (page 33). Maximum life spans have been reported thus: House mouse (*Mus musculus*) 6 years; Gerbil (*Gerbillus gerbillus*) 7 years 4 months; Golden hamster (*Mesocricetus auratus*) 10 years 2 months; European rabbit (*Oryctolagus cuniculus*) 18 years (still living in August 1977).

Longest Lived Caged Bird (page 36). "Charlie" died on 20 June 1977 aged 29 years 2 months.

Rarest Butterfly (page 44). The number of large blues was estimated to be 40 in late June 1977.

Shells (page 46). *Tethys californicus* is the largest known shell-less gastropod. The largest shelled gastropod is the Trumpet or Baler conch (*Syrinx aruanus*) of Australia. One outsized specimen collected at Bunbury, W. Australia in 1974 and now owned by Mr. Morton Hahn of Randolph, New Jersey, U.S.A., weighed 35 lb. *15,9 kg* when alive. Its shell measures 28.1 in *713,4 mm* in length and has a maximum girth of 38 in *965,2 mm*.

Largest Predator (page 47). The latest estimates for the overall length of *Tyrannosaurus* is now 35 ft *10,65 m* due to lesser estimate of its tail length.

Lemon Footnote 5 (page 52). Weight of the Mayer lemon was 6 lb. 4 oz. *2,83 kg*.

Biggest Burl (page 54). The most massive burl on record was discovered on a 351 year old spruce found in December 1976 near Port McNeill, B.C., Canada. It weighed 20.06 tons *20,38 tonnes*.

Daisy Chain (page 55). The longest daisy chain was one of 24,000 daisies, measuring 3,565 ft *1,086 m* made by 31 members of Ashcombe School, Dorking, Surrey in 7 hours on 28 May 1977.

CHAPTER 3

The Earth (page 57). 4th line: For *17 756,280 km* read *12 756,280 km*.

Earthquakes (page 58). The Tangshan shock was on 27 July 1976 (G.M.T.). People in bed were catapulted into their ceilings.

Icebergs (page 60). The U.S. Naval Weather Service reported a small iceberg in Lat. 28° 44′N Long. 48° 42′W in April 1935.
The tallest on record was one of 550 ft *167 m* sighted by U.S.C.G. icebreaker *Eastwind* in 1958.

Highest Unclimbed Mountain (page 63). Excluding subsidiary summits, the highest separate unclimbed mountain in the world is now only the 31st highest, Zemu Peak (25,526 ft *7 780 m*) in the Karakoram. The south peak of Kangchenjunga (27,848 ft *8 488 m*) is also unclimbed.

Fastest Sea Current (page 66). The 1977 Canadian Tide and Current Tables, Vol. 6, showed a current of 15.8 kts *21,1 km/h* in the Seymour Narrows, British Columbia at 11.10 hrs on 2 June 1977.

CHAPTER 4

Remotest Object (page 74). For 2 = 3.53, read Z = 3.53

Alfred M. Warden, the Command Capsule pilot of the U.S. *Apollo 15* lunar exploration of 1971 who has been separated by a greater distance from his fellow man than anyone in history. (*N.A.S.A.*)

CHAPTER 5

First Walk in Space (page 75). Edward H. White was killed in the Apollo disaster at Cape Kennedy on 27 Jan. 1967. His father is Major General U.S. Air Force (retired).

Chemical Compounds (page 78, table footnote). For fluosulphonic read fluorosulphonic.

The 106 Elements (page 78). Most stable: For Tellerium read Tellurium.

Most Expensive Spirits (page 79). The auction record for a bottle is £220 for a Grande Fine Champagne Napoleon, 1811 at Christies', London in December 1976.

Largest Bottles (page 79). In Bordeaux (claret) a Jeroboam is 6 bottles but in practice, depending on the age of bottle (whether blown or moulded), between 5 and 6½.

Miniature Bottle (page 80). Mrs. Gwen Crouch of Tenterden, Kent has a collection of 1,671 unduplicated miniatures collected in 14 years to June 1977.

Most expensive camera (page 80). The suggested retail price in Britain including VAT for the Nikon camera body together with one of each currently listed accessories is £65,791.28.

Highest Numbers (page 82). Prof. Stanley Skewes was born on 29 June 1899.

Longest Slide Rule (page 82). In July 1977 R. Clayton Brough and Ralph J. Snelson of Springville, Utah completed one measuring 204 ft 1 in *62,21 m*.

CHAPTER 6

Largest Sculptures (page 87). Roy Faulkner was on the mountain side for 8 years 174 days (12 Sept. 1963 to 3 Mar. 1972) and lost two helpers who fell to their deaths.

Longest Words (page 89). Hungarian: Megszentsegtelenithetetlenseyeskedeseitekert (44 letters). For your unprofanable actions.

Last Name in Telephone Directory (page 91). The new omega is Mr. Shamsu Zzaman, now of Northampton.

Earliest Encyclopaedia (page 92). For Speusippas read Speusippus (*Post 408–c*. 338 B.C.).

Most Text Books (page 93). To May 1977 Mr. Ridout's total number of titles had risen to 345 with sales of 60,300,000. His *The First English Workbook* has sold 4,157,000.

Library Largest (page 94). By mid-1977 there were 73,000,000 items including 18,240,295 volumes and pamphlets on 350 miles 563 km of shelving.

Overdue Books (page 95). For $22,646 read $2,646 (*then £1,102.10s*.).

Pop Concerts (page 98). The Led Zeppelin at Silverdrome, Pontiac, near Detroit, Michigan, U.S.A. on 30 Apr. 1977 played to 76,229 with a gross of $792,361 (*£446,094*).

Shortest Opera (page 99). For Thesus read Theseus.

Shakespeare (page 102). Ten students from Royal Holloway College, Englefield Green, Surrey achieved the total reading in 37 hrs 22 min on 15–16 Apr. 1977.

Acting, Most Roles (page 102). Jan Leighton of New York City, the actor with a Thousand Faces, has, since 1951 played 1,077 roles of famous, infamous or fabled historic figures on film, television, stage or other media.

First Nights (page 102). Edward Sutro (G.B.) had seen 3,000 in 40 years to 1956.

Most Golden Discs (page 103). Elvis Presley died on 16 Aug. 1977.

Longest Silence (page 104). Only "extracts" were played on A.B.C. network.

Oscars Most (page 105). Disney's total of statuettes is 17 with 12 certificates and plaques for special awards and special recognition.

CHAPTER 7

Tallest Towers (page 116). The tallest self-supporting tower, the CN Tower, Toronto was increased in height by 6 ft 7 in *2,00 m* on 11 June 1977 with the addition of meteorological equipment.

Windmill Earliest (page 123). For Zedden read Zeddam.

CHAPTER 8

Fastest Pacific Crossing (page 133). The passage time at 33.27 knots was 6 days 1 hr 27 min.

Northernmost (page 133). The U.S.S.R. Icebreaker *Arktika* (page 131) reached the North Pole on 17 Aug. 1977.

Petrol Consumption (page 135). Beattie raised his record to 1,298 miles *2 088,9 km* per gallon at Mallory Park on 5 July 1977.

Petrol Station (page 137). This record was raised to 7,813.77 gal. *35 521,4 litres* in 24 hours on 25 June 1977 at Mornington Motors Ltd., Dunedin, N.Z.

Motorcycle Duration Record (page 137). The duration record is now 500 hr by Owen Fitzgerald, Richard Kennett and Don Mitchell who covered 8,432 miles *13 570 km* between 10–31 July 1977 in Western Australia.

Penny Farthing Bicycling (page 138). James Richard Moir, 37 of St. Leonards-on-Sea, East Sussex covered the distance in 10 days 7 hrs 12 min on 5–15 June 1977.

Train Longest Non-stop (page 139). The "Silver Meteor" now stops at 9 stations on the 1,377 mile *2 216 km* run.

Aircraft Heaviest (page 142). The all-up weight of the three highly converted $117 million Boeing 747 Presidential Doomsday H.Q. Command aircraft designated E-4A has been reported to be 425 U.S. tons *385,61 tonnes*.

Busiest Airport (page 145). For 38,000,000 read 41,735,454.

Ballooning Distance (page 146). For 2,520 miles *4 055 km* read 2,740 miles *4 409 km*. Ed. Yost landed on 10 Oct. and took off from Milbridge, Maine, U.S.A. 107 hrs *37 min* earlier on 6 Oct. 1976.

Most Take-Offs and Landings (page 147). Dr. Bruce L. Odsu of Montebello, California took off and landed at 124 airfields in California in 14 hrs 6 min of daylight on 10 June 1977.

Hovercraft Largest (page 147). The 2 KESES project for a 2,800 ton craft has been discontinued.

Oldest First Flying Licence (page 147). Alton Frank Shaver (b. 11 Sept. 1897) qualified for his Private Pilot's Licence on 13 Apr. 1977 aged 79 years 7 months.

Nut Largest (page 149). The company's new "Morthrust" nut weighs up to *2 390 kg* with a 31½ in *80 cm* thread and an outside diameter of 50½ in *128,2 cm* for securing propellers and similar applications.

Watch, Most Expensive (page 152). The price of the *Grande Complication* was £26,000 in June 1977.

Computer Fastest (page 153). The Control Data STAR-100 averaged 9.78×10^8 results per sec in 5 runs at Arden Hills, Minnesota, U.S.A. on 15 Sept. 1976.

CHAPTER 9

Greatest Sales (page 154). Corporations with sales exceeding £1000 million in the 1977 *Fortune* List totalled 260, (128 U.S., 91 European, 26 Japanese, 9 Canadian and 6 others).

Greatest Profit and loss (page 155). The all time record for declared profits has been by the state owned National Iranian Oil Co. In 1976 net income was $17,175,182,000.

Advertising (page 155). It was estimated in June 1977 that the number of reproductions of the face and signature of King C. Gillette (1855–1932) used for advertising razor blades since 1903 had well exceeded 200,000,000,000.

Sheep Shearing (page 166). Four men machine-shore 1,649 sheep in 24 hours at Brecon, Powys, Wales on 13–14 July 1977.

Highest Rents (page 158). A rental of Singapore $1,488 £348 per square metre £32,33 per ft² was paid by Messrs Boen & Co. for renting the tourist shop at Paya Lebor Airport, Singapore in May 1977.

Motor Car Manufacturers (page 158). British Leyland production of 981,000 vehicles related to the 15 months to 31 Dec. 1976.

Retailer, Largest (page 159). For $14,950,000,000 read $12,711,476,000 for the assets of Sears, Roebeck and Co.

Largest Vase (page 165). The largest vase on record is one 8 ft *2,78 m* in height weighing 650 lb. *294,8 kg* thrown by Sebastino Maglio at Haeyer Potteries of Dundee, Illinois, U.S.A. (founded 1872) during August 1976.

Longest Embroidery (page 165). The length of the embroidery is 825 ft *250.25 m* as at 12 Aug. 1977.

Most Yolks (page 168). Another egg with 9 yolks was laid by a hen at Kirghizia, Russia in August 1977.

Highest Priced Turkey (page 169). For the latest price, see Turkey Most Expensive, page 36.

CHAPTER 10

Oldest "Royal" (page 174). The most senior member of the United Kingdom's royal family is H.R.H. Princess Alice, Countess of Athlone V.A., G.C.V.O., G.B.E. who celebrated her 94th birthday on 25 Feb. 1977.

Lowest Poll (page 178). Extremely low polls are in part due to out-dated electoral registers. Since the introduction of a female vote in 1918 the lowest turnout has been in the Poplar South, East London by-election in 1942 with 9.3%. The lowest *peacetime* by-election turnout was in nearby Shoreditch and Finsbury in 1958 with 24.9%. The record low for a General Election was Lambeth, Kennington with 29.7% in 1918.

The record high for by-elections for the U.K. has been 91.8% in Mid-Ulster in 1969 and G.B. 87.5% in Carmarthen in 1957. (Abraham Flint (b. 1903 d. 1971).

Mayoralty Longest (page 180). Henry A. Proesel was elected Resident (Mayor) of Lincolnwood (formerly Tessville), Illinois in Apr. 1931 and served for 46 consecutive terms till 1 May 1977.

Longest Span (page 182). The World War II participant with the longest span of combatant service is 52 years in the case of Wing Cdr. Lionel Cohen D.S.O., M.C., D.F.C., who was a trooper in the Matebele war of 1893 and won a D.F.C. in air crew aged 69 in 1944.

Youngest Soldier (page 182). The Public Record Office has a document showing the enlistment of Private Martin McCormick into the 99th Regiment of Foot at Portsmouth on 23 Mar. 1825 aged 11 years 5 months.

Suicide (page 188). The 600th Suicide from San Francisco's Golden Gate Bridge, Sharon Ungewitter, jumped on 28 May 1977. The first was on 28 Jan. 1938. Only four of those who have jumped have survived.

Greatest Robbery (page 188). The greatest robbery on record was that of the Berlin Reichsbank's reserves during April and May 1945. The largest single haul was of $400 millions worth of Westphalia bearer bonds repayable in gold. On 5 Apr. 1977 three men were arrested in Brantford, Ontario and charged with attempting to obtain credit on a batch of these.

Last Guillotining (page 190). The last person guillotined in a French prison was a 22 year old child murderer named Christian Ranucci at Baumettes prison, nr. Marseilles on 28 July 1976.

Largest Pizza Pie (page 197). The largest pizza ever baked was one measuring 26 ft 3½ in × 33 ft 2½ in *8,01 m × 10,12 m* hence 873.1 ft² *81,11 m²* in area, by Dunsmuir Secondary School, Victoria, B.C., Canada on 10 June 1977.

Largest Sundae (page 198). The largest ice cream sundae ever made is one of 7250 lb. *3 288 kg*, constructed by Mr. Edward Bartyzel and a team of 6, of Sealtest Foods, New York, U.S.A. on 30 Aug. 1976.

CHAPTER 11

Most Travelled Woman (page 209). Mrs. Ersöz's total was 163 countries by 1 July 1977.

Accordion Playing (page 214) For Accordian read Accordion

Boomerang Throwing (page 216). The longest distance thrown and returned recognised by the Boomerang Association of Australia is 88,2 m *89.8 yds* diameter (orbital path 270 m *295 yds*) by Leo Meir (Switzerland) at Darlington Point, N.S.W. on 6 Nov. 1976. Herb. A. Smith's throw of 108.4 yds *99,1 m* at Littlehampton, West Sussex on 17 June 1972 is recognised as the world's longest outside Australia.

Brick Carrying (page 216). David and Kym Barger of Lamar, Missouri, U.S.A. carried an 8 lb. 15 oz. *4,053 kg* brick for 45 miles *72,4 km* in 13 hr 7 min on 21 May 1977.

Dancing—Belly Dancing (page 218). Sabra Starr (Vikki Canale) raised her record to 100 hours at Teplitzki's Hotel, Atlantic City, New Jersey on 4–8 July 1977.

Domino Tumbling (page 219). Bob Speca recaptured his record with 50,000 in 17 min. 46.27 sec at the University of Pennsylvania, U.S.A. on 21 June 1977.

Jiving (page 219). For U.S.A. read Canada.

Drumming (page 219). The world's duration drumming record is 505 hours (21 days) by Tracy Burroughs of Westport, Connecticut, U.S.A. on 3–24 June 1977.

Fashion Show Longest (page 219). A fashion parade with 1,671 garments modelled by Lyn Snowdon, Kay Hammond, Virginia

Connor and compèred by Patrick Bollen in 48 hours on the Roseland catwalk, Sydney, Australia on 16–18 June 1977. The girls each completed 41.4 miles *66,6 km* on the catwalk.

Gold Panning (page 221). Mrs. Marie Bertles lowered the women's record to 17.8 sec on 6 Mar. 1977.

Golf Ball Balancing (page 221). Lang Martin, 16, balanced 6 golf balls vertically without adhesive at Charlotte, North Carolina on 10 July 1977.

Grape Catching (page 221). The longest recorded distance for catching a thrown grape in the mouth is 251 ft *76,5 m* by Paul Tavila at the Memorial Park, Dedham Mass., U.S.A. on 19 July 1977. The grape thrower was Mike Weir.

Hod Carrying (page 223). Colin With carried 51 4.4 lb. *2 kg* bricks up a 15 ft *4,57 m* ladder at Edmonton, London on 1 Aug. 1977.

House of Cards (page 223). A 51 storey tower 9½ ft *2,89 m* tall was achieved by Carter Cummins at Westgate Mall, Texas U.S.A. on 4 June 1977. He also achieved a 31 storey house of alternate 8 and 6 card storeys on the same day.

Message in a Bottle (page 225). For Colombus read Columbus.

Model Highest Paid (page 225). For longest read largest.

Parachuting—Oldest Woman (page 226). Mrs. Ann Howard Cassell (U.S.) 69 years 9 months at Medford, New Jersey on 23 May 1977.

Onion Peeling (page 226). The record for onion peeling is 50 lb. *22,67 kg* 31 min 21 sec by Gene Pingle of Myrtle Creek, Oregon on 14 May 1977.

Organ Marathon (page 226). The longest church organ recital ever sustained has been 90 hours by Frank Hughes at Wesley College Chapel, Dublin Ireland on 31 Oct.–4 Nov. 1975.

Pond Bailing (page 227). For baling read bailing.

Talking (After Dinner Speaking) (page 229). Nicholas Parsons of *Just A Minute* fame spoke for 428 min 3 sec (over 7 hours) at the 25th Anniversary of Action Research at Ashridge College, Hertfordshire on 9–10 July 1977.

Switchback riding (page 229). The endurance record for rides on a roller coaster is 100 hours by James Bruse, Noel Aube and John Bock at Kings Dominion, Doswell, Virginia, U.S.A. on 6–10 June 1977. They completed 1411.2 miles *2 271,1 km.*

Spitting (page 229). For Eau Claire, Michigan, read Eau Claire Wisconsin.

Circus Records (page 230). Trampolining—Marco Canestrelli performed a sextuple twisting back somersault at Sarasota, Florida, U.S.A. on 18 Dec. 1976.

Gluttony Records (page 233). Peter Dowdeswell also holds the records for Yards of Ale (2½ pts. 4 May 1975, 3 pts. 23 Jan. 1976) and Upsidedown (25 May 1975).

CHAPTER 12

Basketball—Most Accurate (page 246). Ted St. Martin has increased his consecutive free throw total to 2,036 on 25 June 1977 at Jacksonville, Florida, U.S.A.

Canoeing—Most Titles (page 252). In the World Whitewater championships, at Spittal, Austria on 24 July 1977, Albert Kerr, in the K1 slalom event, became only the third Briton to win a world canoeing title.

Cricket—Wicket Keeping (page 259). Knott 251 dismissals (232 catches, 19 stumpings) after his 88th Test on 15 Aug. 1977.

Equestrian Sports—King George V Cup (page 265). On 20 July 1977, David Broome (G.B.) riding *Philco* won the event for a record fourth time.

Football (Professional)—Transfer Fees (page 270). The highest fee paid for a British player was £500,000 reported on 3 June 1977 for Kevin Keegan by SV Hamburg. The highest fee paid by a British club was the reported £440,000 by Liverpool for Keegan's replacement, Scottish international, Kenny Dalglish of Celtic, on 10 Aug. 1977.

Gliding—Hang Gliding (page 278). Ken Messenger, of Marlborough, Wiltshire equalled the British distance record of 22 miles when he crossed the English Channel on 21 July 1977.

Golf—Most Tournament Wins (page 282). Kathy Whitworth won 79 tournaments to July 1977.

Horse Racing—Highest Price (pages 24 and 286). The Minstrel was reported to have been sold in Aug. 1977 to Edward P. Taylor for $9 million £5,300,000. The Minstrel has won a record sum for a horse trained in England or Ireland of £315,217.

Mountaineering (page 304). Philip Cooper of Matlock, Derbyshire, climbed the highest points in every county and region in Great Britain (66) and Ireland (32) in 708 days ending on 2 May 1977.

Pelota Vasca—Highest Speed (page 307). At the Newport Jai-Alai Fronton on 1 June 1977, Jose Ramon Areitio was electronically measured to hurl a ball at 174 m.p.h. *280 km/h.*

Swimming—Cross Channel Relay (page 318). A Saudi Arabian team established a two-way record on 11 Aug. 1977. They swam from Dover to France and back in 16 hr 3½ min.

Swimming (page 320). World records: Mens 100 m Breaststroke, 1:02.86, Gerald Morken (W. Ger.); Womens 400 m Freestyle, 4:08.91, Petra Thumer (E. Ger.), Jonkoping, Sweden 17 Aug. and British women's 100 m freestyle 58.24 Cheryl Brazendale 18 Aug. 1977.

Track & Field—Highland Games (page 325). Grant Thomas Anderson (b. 30 June 1945) has also thrown a 56 lb. weight 16 ft *4,87 m*, at Lauder, Borders, Scotland on 4 June 1977.

ACKNOWLEDGEMENTS

J. W. Arblaster, A.I.M.; Howard Bass; Pat Besford; James Bond; British Airways; British Museum (Natural History); British Rail; British Travel; British Waterworks Association; A. W. Bulley; Henry G. Button; Kenneth H. Chandler; Central Electricity Generating Board; Central Office of Information; Dr. A. J. C. Charig; Sq. Ldr. D. H. Clarke, D.F.C., A.F.C.; Clerk of Dail Eireann; Clive Everton; Fédération Aéronautique Internationale; Fédération Internationale de l'Automobile; Fédération Internationale des Hôpitaux; Frank L. Forster, Esq.; *Fortune*; Dr. Francis C. Fraser; Norman Graveson; General Post Office; A. Herbert, (New Zealand); Michael E. R. R. Herridge; Dr. Arthur H. Hughes (Chairman Guinness Superlatives Ltd., 1954–1966); Derek Hurst; Imperial War Museum; Institute of Strategic Studies; Sir Peter Johnson; Erich Kamper; Kline Iron and Steel Company; Mr. Michael D. Lampen; The Library of Congress, Washington D.C.; *Lloyd's Register of Shipping*; London Transport Board; The late T. L. Marks, O.B.E., T.D. (Chairman 1966–71); K. G. McWhirter, M.A., M.SC.; Meteorological Office; Metropolitan Police; Alan Mitchell, B.A., B.Ag. (For); Music Research Bureau; National Aeronautics and Space Administration; National Geographic Society; National Maritime Museum; National Physical Laboratory; Michael S. Nimmo; Mrs. Susann Palmer; Christopher Plumridge; E. T. Pugh, Editor *Manned Spacecraft*; A. J. R. Purssell (Chairman 1971–75); *The Racing Pigeon*, London; John Randall; Jean Reville; Irving Rosenwater; Jack Rollin; Royal Astronomical Society; Royal Botanic Gardens; Royal Geographic Society; Royal National Life-boat Institution; Graham Snowdon; Sports Federation of Canada; John H. Stephens; John W. R. Taylor; Lance Tingay; U.N. Statistical Office; Juhani Virola; Gerry L. Wood F.Z.S.; World Meteorological Organization; Francis Albert Young; Zoological Society of London, and various sports associations and governing bodies.

G. Howard Garrard D.S.C. (Correspondence Editor); Amanda Clark (Editor's Secretary); Moira F. Browne (Editor's Assistant); Beverley Waites (Sports Editor's Assistant); Mary Crowder, Lucie Phillippo, Peter J. Matthews and Bernadette Bidwell.

Also to Barbara Anderson, Anne Belsham, Sally V. Bennett, Christine Bethlehem, Rosemary Bevan, Suzi M. Ross-Browne, D. Richard Bowen, Signa. Wendy Cirillo, Pamela Croome, Trudy Doyle, Mlle. Béatrice Frei, Jacqueline Gould, Susan Gullen, Tessa Hegley, E. C. Henniker, David N. Hewlett, Angela Hoaen, David F. Hoy, (Managing Director), Paul Hurren, Eileen Jackson, Hilary Leavey, Diana Lloyd, Jane Mayo, G. M. Nutbrown, W. E. Nutbrown, Margaret Orr-Deas, Peter B. Page, (1954–57), John Rivers, Judith Sleath, Anne Symonds, Andrew Thomas, (Associate Editor 1964–68), Gillian Turner, Winnie Ulrich, Peter Whatley, Stephen James Clarke, (1948–1976) (Management Accountant).

Colour Film 1978 Edition supplied by NEWSELE Litho Ltd. (Director: Janice Tennant)

Back Cover: *Top left:* Tony Duffy, All-Sport Photographic *Bottom left:* The Associated Press

An asterisk against a page reference indicates that there is a further reference in the Stop Press section (pages 372–374)

TELESCOPE, earliest, largest refracting, reflecting world, G.B. 79, largest radio 79–80, solar 80

TELEVISION, earliest, first public service 106–7, first trans-Atlantic transmission, longest telecast, most durable show and B.B.C. programme, most sets, greatest audience 238, largest contracts, world, G.B., highest paid performer, largest prize, world, G.B. 107, most successful appeal, first critic, biggest sale, most prolific scriptwriter, highest advertising rates, most takes, most exposed star 108, tallest mast, (progressive records) transmitting tower G.B. 116

TEMPERATURE, progressive extremes highest, lowest, most equable, greatest ranges, longest freeze 66, lowest atmospheric 66–7, deepest permafrost, humidity and discomfort 67, highest shade, lowest screen 68, sun 71, lowest stellar 72, man made, highest, lowest 82

TEMPERATURE, bird 23, animal, highest, lowest 24

TEMPERATURE, human, highest, lowest 19, highest endured 21

TEMPERATURE, sea 59

TEMPLE, largest, 204, tallest Chinese 205

TENNIS (Lawn), 296–7, (Real or Royal), 323

TEN PIN BOWLING, 247–8

TENSILE STRENGTH, highest 78

TENT, largest world, G.B. 124

TEXT, oldest written 91, printed 91–2, largest book, publication, dictionary, smallest, longest novel most valuable book, broadsheet, manuscript 92

TEXTBOOKS, most successful writer 93*

THEATRE, earliest, oldest world, G.B. 101, largest world, largest G.B., smallest G.B., largest amphitheatre 101, longest runs 101–2 most durable leading actress, shortest runs, longest play, longest by Shakespeare, longest chorus line, most ardent threatre-goer 102*

THREE-LEGGED RACE, 326

THUG, worst 188

THUNDER-DAYS, most 68

TICK, smallest, largest 43

TIDAL POWER STATION, world's first 148

"TIDAL WAVE", highest, fastest 60

TIDDLYWINKS, 294

TIDE, greatest world, G.B., Ireland 60

TIE, oldest old school 203

TIERS, most in opera-house 99

TIGER, largest 26

TIGHTROPE WALKING, greatest walker, endurance record, longest walk, highest high wire act 230

TIGRESS, man-eating, worst 207

TIME, scale of 11, longest, shortest measure 82, most accurate measure 152

TIME CAPSULE, largest 165

TIME MEASURER, most accurate world, G.B., 152

TIN MINE, deepest Cornish 128

TITHE BARN, longest Britain 123

TITLE, highest selling 94, most titled person 234

TOAD, largest world, British, smallest world 39

TOASTMASTERS, founder, most boring speaker 213

TOBACCO, largest company 160, heaviest smokers, 162, most expensive snuff 165

TOBOGGANING, 247

TOMATO, largest plant 52

TOMB, largest 122

TONGUE, heaviest and longest 24

TOPAZ, largest 81

TORNADO, highest speed 68 worst world, U.K. 207

TORTILLA, eating record 233

TORTOISE, heaviest, longest lived, slowest 37, largest extinct 48

TOSSING THE CABER, 325

TOTE WIN, biggest 276

TOTEM POLE, tallest 121

TOUCH, sensitivity 17

TOUR DE FRANCE (Cycling), 237, 262

TOURISTS, most, highest spending 171

TOW, car longest 137

TOWER, tallest world, U.K. 116*

TOWN, largest, smallest (earliest walled), 173, highest 173–4, oldest, world, Great Britain, 173, northernmost, southernmost, most remote from sea 174

TOWN CRIER, most title wins 228

TOXIN, most deadly 77

TOY MANUFACTURER, largest 160

TOY SHOP, biggest world, G.B. 161

TRACK AND FIELD, ATHLETICS, 324–331*

TRACKING, greatest feat 32

TRACTION ENGINE, largest steam 137

TRADE UNION, oldest, largest world, G.B., longest name, smallest 196

TRAFFIC, highest density, worst jams 199, lights—first in U.K. 200

TRAIN, see Railway

TRAM, longest journey 140

TRAMPOLINING, 331, 342

TRANS-ATLANTIC CROSSING, see Atlantic Crossing

TRANSFER FEES, Association Football 270, Rugby League 274

TRANSFORMER, largest 149–50

TRANSMISSION LINE, longest, highest world, G.B. 150, highest voltages 151

TRANSMISSIONS, earliest radio broadcasts world, G.B., earliest trans-Atlantic wireless 106, television; earliest trans-Atlantic, earliest satellite 107

TRANSMITTERS, greatest number radio, earliest television 106

TRANSPORTER, largest road 136

TRAVELLED (person), most on land, woman*, disabled person 209, on horseback, passport records, in space 210

TRAVOLATOR, longest 150

TREADING WATER, 321

TREASURE FINDING, most successful 230

TREASURE TROVE, largest 195

TREATY, oldest 176

TREE, largest, most massive living thing, tallest world, all-time, Britain, Ireland, tallest in U.K., and Ireland, by species 53, tallest Christmas tree 51, 53, greatest girth world 53, Britain 51, 53, greatest oaks Britain 53, oldest living world 53–4, G.B., earliest, fastest growing, slowest growing, remotest, most expensive 54, largest rose 55

TREE-CLIMBING, fastest 230

TREE-FROG, largest, smallest 39

TREE-SITTING, duration record 230

TRENCHERMAN, greatest 233

TRIAL, longest 184, longest shortest, murder, shortest, best attended, longest divorce trial 185

TRIBES, tallest, shortest 10

TRIBUTARY, longest 64

TRIPLETS, oldest 14, heaviest, most 15, fastest birth 16

TROGGING, 253

TROPHY, largest 237

TROTTING AND PACING, 331

TSUNAMI, highest, fastest 60

TUBA, largest 97

TUBE, see Underground

TUBING, smallest 153

TUG, first power-driven vessel, most powerful 129

TUG OF WAR, 331–2

TUMBLER, greatest 283

TUNGSTEN MINE, largest 128

TUNNEL, largest, most powerful wind world, G.B. 84, longest water supply world, G.B., longest passenger railway world, G.B., mainline, G.B., sub-aqueous subway, longest road, world, G.B. largest diameter road, longest hydro-electric—world, G.B. 120, longest bridge-tunnel, longest canal world, G.B., tunnelling record 121

TUNNEL OF FIRE, longest 230

TURBINE, first ship 129, largest, reversible pump 148

TURKEY, largest, most expensive 36*, largest farm 166, record price 169*

TURTLE, fastest, largest, heaviest 37, largest extinct 48

TUSKS, longest, heaviest 30, (extinct animals) 49

TWINS, oldest, world, G.B. 14, lightest 15, heaviest 11, 15, most 15, Siamese 15, rarest 16

TWIST, duration record 219

TYPEWRITING, fastest 230–1 slowest, longest 231

TYPHOID CARRIER, most notorious 20

TYPE WRITING, record 231

TYPING, see Typewriting

TYRE LIFTING, record 231

TYRES, largest 137

U-BOAT, see Submarine

UNCONSCIOUSNESS, longest 20

UNDERGRADUATE, youngest 202

UNDERGROUND CHAMBER, largest 62

UNDERGROUND RAILWAY, most extensive, oldest, passenger records, greatest depth 140, busiest subway, tour record 140,

UNDERWATER, longest stay 21, 321, deepest escape 212

UNEMPLOYMENT, highest, lowest, U.K. 196

UNICYCLE, tallest, distance record 138

UNION, see Trade Union

UNIT OF AREA, smallest 82

UNIT OF LENGTH, earliest, shortest 82

UNIVERSE, farthest visible object, quasars, "pulsars", remotest object, age of 74

UNIVERSITY, oldest, oldest colleges G.B., greatest enrolment, largest building, youngest, most durable professor, senior wranglers, most eternal student, youngest undergraduate 202, boat race 311

UNSUPPORTED CIRCLE, biggest 231

VACUUM, highest 83

VALVE, largest 149

VASE, most expensive 161, 164, largest 341

VAT, largest blending 115, largest 124

VAULT, Bank, largest 156

V.C., see Victoria Cross

VEGETABLES, record dimensions and weights U.K. 52

VEHICLE, most massive 136, Road, see Road Vehicle

VEIN, largest human 19

VELOCIPEDE, see Bicycle

VENOM, most active (frog) 39

VERBS, most forms, most and least regular 88

VERSE, longest, shortest Bible 92–3

VERTEBRATE, shortest 40, shortest lived 41, earliest 49

VESSEL, largest fermentation 124

VIADUCT, road, longest in world 116–17, G.B. 200, rail; longest in world 117

VICTORIA CROSS, most expensive, most bars, youngest person awarded, longest lived, 234

VILLAGE, shortest name 90, oldest 173, highest 173–4 southernmost 174

VINE, largest 53

VINTAGE, oldest 79

VINEYARD, most northerly 53, largest 166

VINTNERS, oldest 161

VIOLIN, most valuable 97

VIOLINIST, underwater, most durable 97, highest paid 99

VIRUS, largest, smallest 50

VISCOSITY, lowest 83

VISION, most acute (bird) 35

VOCABULARY, richest 88

VOICE, highest, lowest 18–19, greatest range 19

VOLCANO, total number, greatest eruption, greatest explosion, highest extinct, highest dormant, highest active, northernmost, southernmost, largest crater 58

VOLLEYBALL, 332

VOTE, fewest received by Parliamentary candidate 178, largest parliamentary monetary 236

VOTING AGE, extremes 177

VOWELS, language with most, least 88

VOYAGE, longest possible 59, longest by sailing boat 210

WAIST, smallest 17

WAITING ROOM, railway, largest 140

WALKING, in space 75* on stilts 229, tightrope 230, on hands 231, track records 332, endurance 332–3, non-stop, backwards 333

WALL, sheerest mountain 63, thickest 112, longest world, G.B. 123

WALL OF DEATH, endurance feat 231

WALLPAPERING, fastest 231

WALRUS, see Pinnipeds

WAR, longest, shortest, bloodiest, bloodiest civil war, most costly, last battle in Britain, bloodiest battle modern, ancient 180, British, greatest naval battle, greatest invasions seaborne, airborne, last invasion of Great Britain, greatest evacuation, worst sieges, largest armed forces 181

WARSHIP, largest 129–30, fastest 130

WASP, smallest, smallest eggs 43

WATCH, oldest, smallest, most expensive 152*

WATER, Fresh, survival without 21, biggest consumers 197

WATERFALL, highest world, U.K., Ireland 64, greatest 64–5, 67, widest 65

WATER POLO, 333

WATER SKI-ING, oldest, 333–4

WATER SPEED RECORDS, 208, 209

WATERSPOUT, highest 67

WATER TREADING, 321

WATERWAY, (inland), longest G.B., artificial seaway, irrigation canal 118, country with greatest navigable length, longest navigable river 200

WATER WELL, deepest world, Britain greatest flow 127

WATERWHEEL, largest world, G.B., 123

WAVE, highest 60, highest and fastest seismic 60

WAVELENGTH, shortest 84

WEALTH, national 193 individual 231–3

WEATHER, records 66–8

WEB, largest 42

WEDDING CEREMONY, largest mass 213

WEED, worst 50

WEIGHT, heaviest men, women 10–11, lightest 11, greatest lifted 149, 335

WEIGHT DIFFERENTIAL, 11

WEIGHT GAIN AND LOSS, 11

WEIGHTLIFTING, 334–5

WEIGHT-MEASURE, earliest 82

WELL, deepest oil world, British 126, deepest water world, G.B. 127

WETTEST PLACE, world, U.K., Ireland annual mean 68

WHALE, largest, heaviest 24–5 greatest recorded depth 25

WHALE FACTORY SHIP, largest 131

WHEAT, largest field, record yield 166

WHELKS, eating record 233

WHIP, longest cracked 231

WHIST, 295

"WHITE" CHRISTMAS, 67

WHITE HORSE, oldest in Britain 88

WHO'S WHO, longest entry, youngest entrant, most brothers 236

WIG, largest 165

WILL, shortest, longest 186 greatest in U.K., Ireland 232

WINDIEST PLACE, 68

WINDMILL, earliest recorded*, oldest still complete, largest in Holland, England 123

WINDOW, largest 124, stained glass, oldest, largest 205

WIND-SPEED, highest surface 68

WIND-TUNNEL, largest, most powerful 84

WINE, oldest vintage, most expensive, largest bottles*, greatest auction 79, highest consumption Britain 197

WINE CELLAR, largest 115

WING AREA, greatest (bird) 34

WING BEAT, fastest, slowest (bird) 34, fastest, slowest (insect) 43

WING SPAN, longest (bird) 34, (Aeroplane) 142

WINTER, earliest severe, worst in Britain 66

WIRE, high and low 222, 230

WIRELESS, see Radio

WIRE-ROPE, longest 151

WOMEN, tallest 8–9, shortest 9, heaviest 10–11, oldest 13, 14, reproductivity 14–16, smallest waists, longest necks 17, lowest temperature 19, longest coma 20, first cosmonaut 75, greatest altitude, fastest 208, highest climb 302, longest delayed, oldest parachute drop 226*, piano playing record 226, submergence record 229, richest 232, most titles 234, leading air ace 235, greatest surplus, shortage 172, earliest, longest serving M.P.s 180 oldest, youngest George Cross 234

WOMEN'S CRICKET, 259–60

WOMEN'S HOCKEY, 285

WONDERS OF THE WORLD, seven 121

WOOD, heaviest, lightest 54

WOOD-CUTTING, world record, sawing 231

WOODEN BUILDINGS, oldest largest 111

WOODEN SHIP, heaviest, longest 131

WOOL, highest price 169

WORD, oldest English 88, longest in various languages*, longest world, longest English longest palindrome, longest anagrams 89, commonest, most meanings, most homophones, most accents 90

WORK FORCE, biggest 155

WORKING CAREER, longest 213

WORKING WEEK, longest, shortest 213

WORLD RECORD BREAKER, (Sport), youngest and oldest 238

WORM, longest, shortest 34 earthworm 44, longest ribbon 46

WORSHIP, oldest places of 204

WRANGLER, Senior order of 202

WREATH, largest 54, costliest 165

WRECK, largest, oldest ship 132

WRESTLING, 336

WRIST WATCH, earliest, most expensive 152

WRITE-OFF, biggest 155

WRITER, most prolific, most novels, most textbooks*, fastest novelist, highest paid, top-selling, highest selling title 93, least successful 93–4, most publishers' rejections, oldest authoress, youngest author, longest gestation, youngest, oldest Poet Laureate 94

WRITING, handicapped, minuscule 231

WRITING PAPER, most expensive 165

YACHT, largest ice 291, largest 337

YACHTING, Atlantic crossing 212 sport 336–7

YARD-ARM, last execution 190

YAWNING, most persistent 21

YEW, tallest hedge 51, tallest tree 53, oldest G.B. 54

YODELLING, endurance record 231

YOLKS, most 168*

YORKSHIRE PUDDING, largest 198

YO-YO, records 231

ZINC, largest mine, smelter 128

ZIQQURAT, largest 122

ZOO, largest game reserve, largest collection, oldest, oldest privately owned, most comprehensive in U.K., greatest attendances 56

Indexing by

Anna Pavord

An asterisk against a page reference indicates that there is a further reference in the Stop Press section (pages 372–374)